AN INDEX
TO BOOK REVIEWS
IN THE HUMANITIES

VOLUME 21

1980

PHILLIP THOMSON
WILLIAMSTON, MICHIGAN

This Volume of the INDEX contains data collected up to 31 December 1980.

This is an index to book reviews in humanities periodicals. Beginning with volume 12 of this Index (dated 1971), the former policy of selectively indexing reviews of books in certain subject categories only was dropped in favor of a policy of indexing all reviews in the periodicals indexed, with the one exception of children's books — the reviews of which will not be indexed.

The form of the entries used is as follows:

> Author. Title.
> Reviewer. Identifying Legend.

The author's name used is the name that appears on the title-page of the book being reviewed, as well as we are able to determine, even though this name is known to be a pseudonym. The title only is shown; subtitles are included only where they are necessary to identify a book in a series. The identifying legend consists of the periodical, each of which has a code number, and the date and page number of the periodical where the review is to be found. PMLA abbreviations are also shown (when a periodical has such an abbreviation, but such abbreviations are limited to four letters) immediately following the code number of the periodical. To learn the name of the periodical in which the review appears, it is necessary to refer the code number to the numerically-arranged list of periodicals beginning on page iii. This list also shows the volume and number of the periodical issues indexed.

Reviews are indexed as they appear and no attempt is made to hold the title until all the reviews are published. For this reason it is necessary to refer to previous and subsequent volumes of this Index to be sure that the complete roster of reviews of any title is seen. As an aid to the user, an asterisk (*) has been added immediately following any title that was also indexed in Volume 20 (1979) of this Index.

Authors with hyphenated surnames are indexed under the name before the hyphen, and the name following the hyphen is not cross-indexed. Authors with more than one surname, but where the names are not hyphenated, are indexed under the first of the names and the last name is cross-indexed. When alphabetizing surnames containing umlauts, the umlauts are ignored. Editors are always shown in the author-title entry, and they are cross-indexed (except where the editor's surname is the same as that of the author). Translators are shown only when they are necessary to identify the book being reviewed (as in the classics), and they are not cross-indexed unless the book being reviewed has no author or editor. Certain reference works and anonymous works that are known primarily by their title are indexed under that title and their editors are cross-indexed.

A list of abbreviations used is shown on page ii.

ABBREVIATIONS

```
Anon........Anonymous
Apr.........April
Aug.........August
Bk..........Book
Comp(s).....Compiler(s)
Cont........Continued
Dec.........December
Ed(s).......Editor(s) [or] Edition(s)
Fasc........Fascicule
Feb.........February
Jan.........January
Jul.........July
Jun.........June
Mar.........March
No. (or #)...Number
Nov.........November
Oct.........October
Prev........Previous volume of this Index
Pt..........Part
Rev.........Revised
Sep.........September
Ser.........Series
Supp........Supplement
Trans.......Translator(s)
Vol.........Volume
* (asterisk)....This title was also shown
                in the volume of this Index
                immediately preceding this
                one
```

The periodicals in which the reviews appear are identified in this Index by a number. To supplement this number, and to promote ready identification, PMLA abbreviations are also given following this number. Every attempt will be made to index those issues shown here as "missing" in a later volume of this Index.

The following is a list of the periodicals indexed in volume 21:

2(AfrA) – African Arts. Los Angeles.
    Nov78 thru Aug79 (vol 12 complete)
9(AlaR) – Alabama Review. University, Alabama.
    Jan79 thru Oct79 (vol 32 complete)
14 – American Archivist. Washington.
    Jan79 thru Oct79 (vol 42 complete)
18 – American Film. Washington.
    Oct78 thru Sep79 (vol 4 complete)
24 – American Journal of Philology. Baltimore.
    Spring79 thru Winter79 (vol 100 complete)
26(ALR) – American Literary Realism, 1870-1910. Arlington, Texas.
    Spring79 and Autumn79 (vol 12 complete)
27(AL) – American Literature. Durham.
    Mar79 thru Jan80 (vol 51 complete)
29 – The American Poetry Review. Philadelphia.
    Jan-Feb80 thru Nov-Dec80 (vol 9 complete)
31(ASch) – American Scholar. Washington.
    Winter79/80 thru Autumn80 (vol 49 complete)
35(AS) – American Speech. University, Alabama.
    Spring79 thru Winter79 (vol 54 complete)
37 – The Américas. Washington.
    Jan79 thru Nov-Dec79 (vol 31 complete)
38 – Anglia. Tübingen.
    Band 96 complete
39 – Apollo. London.
    Jan79 thru Dec79 (vols 109 and 110 complete)
42(AR) – Antioch Review. Yellow Springs.
    Winter79 thru Fall79 (vol 37 complete)
45 – Architectural Record. New York.
    Jan79 thru Dec79 (vols 165 and 166 complete)
46 – Architectural Review. London.
    Jan79 thru Dec79 (vols 165 and 166 complete)
47(ArL) – Archivum Linguisticum. Menston.
    Vol 10 complete
48 – Archivo Español de Arte. Madrid.
    Jan-Mar78 thru Oct-Dec78 (vol 51 complete)
49 – Ariel. Calgary.
    Jan79 thru Oct79 (vol 10 complete)

50(ArQ) – Arizona Quarterly. Tucson.
    Spring79 thru Winter79 (vol 35 complete)
52 – Arcadia. Berlin.
    Band 13 complete
53(AGP) – Archiv für Geschichte der Philosophie. Berlin.
    Band 60 complete
54 – Art Bulletin. New York.
    Mar78 thru Dec78 (vol 60 complete)
55 – Art News. New York.
    Jan79 thru Dec79 (vol 78 complete)
56 – Art Quarterly. New York.
    Winter79 and Spring79 (vol 2 no 1 and 2)
57 – Artibus Asiae. Ascona.
    Vol 40 complete
60 – Arts of Asia. Hong Kong.
    Jan-Feb79 thru Nov-Dec79 (vol 9 complete)
61 – Atlantic Monthly. Boston.
    Jan80 thru Dec80 (vols 245 and 246 complete)
62 – Artforum. New York.
    Sep78 thru Summer79 (vol 17 complete)
63 – Australasian Journal of Philosophy. Canberra.
    Mar79 thru Dec79 (vol 57 complete)
67 – AUMLA (Journal of the Australasian Universities Language and Literature Assn.) James Cook University.
    May79 and Nov79 (no 51 and 52)
69 – Africa. London.
    Vol 48 complete
71(ALS) – Australian Literary Studies. Hobart.
    May79 and Oct79 (vol 9 no 1 and 2)
72 – Archiv für das Studium der neueren Sprachen und Literaturen. Braunschweig.
    Band 216 complete
73 – Art Magazine. Toronto.
    Sep/Oct78 thru May/Jun79 (vol 10 complete) [no reviews indexed]
75 – Babel. Budapest.
    1/1978 thru 3-4/1978 (vol 24 complete)
77 – Biography. Honolulu.
    Winter78 thru Fall78 (vol 1 complete)
78(BC) – Book Collector. London.
    Spring79 thru Winter79 (vol 28 complete)
84 – The British Journal for the Philosophy of Science. Aberdeen.
    Mar79 thru Dec79 (vol 30 complete)
85(SBHC) – Studies in Browning and His Circle. Waco.
    Spring78 and Fall78 (vol 6 complete)
86(BHS) – Bulletin of Hispanic Studies. Liverpool.
    Jan79 thru Oct79 (vol 56 complete)

89(BJA) - The British Journal of Aesthetics. London.
Winter79 thru Summer79 (vol 19
no 1-3)
90 - Burlington Magazine. London.
Jan79 thru Dec79 (vol 121 complete)
95(CLAJ) - CLA Journal. Atlanta.
Sep78 thru Jun79 (vol 22 complete)
96 - Artscanada. Toronto.
Feb-Mar78 thru Dec78-Jan79 (vol
35 complete)
97(CQ) - The Cambridge Quarterly. Cambridge, England.
Vol 8 no 3
98 - Critique. Paris.
Jan78 thru Dec78 (vol 34 complete)
99 - Canadian Forum. Toronto.
Feb80 thru Dec80/Jan81 (vol 59
no 696 and 697, vol 60 no 698-705)
[Vol 60 begins with the April 80
issue.]
102(CanL) - Canadian Literature. Vancouver.
Winter78 thru Winter79 (No 79-83)
104(CASS) - Canadian-American Slavic
Studies/Revue canadienne-américaine
d'études slaves. Tempe.
Spring78 thru Winter78 (Vol 12
complete)
105 - Canadian Poetry. London, Ontario.
Fall/Winter78 and Spring/Summer79
(No 3 and 4)
106 - The Canadian Review of American
Studies. Winnipeg.
Spring79 thru Winter79 (vol 10
complete)
107(CRCL) - Canadian Review of Comparative Literature/Revue Canadienne de
Littérature Comparée. Downsview.
Winter79 thru Fall79 (vol 6 complete)
108 - Canadian Theatre Review. Downsview.
Winter79 thru Fall79 (no 21-24)
109 - The Carleton Miscellany. Northfield.
Winter79/80 thru Winter80 (vol 18
complete) [Ceased publication.]
113 - Centrum. Minneapolis.
Fall78 (vol 6 no 2)
114(ChiR) - Chicago Review. Chicago.
Summer78 thru Spring79 (vol 30
complete)
121(CJ) - Classical Journal. Tallahassee.
Oct-Nov79 thru Apr-May80 (Vol 75
complete)
122 - Classical Philology. Chicago.
Jan79 thru Oct79 (vol 74 complete)
123 - Classical Review. London.
Vol 29 complete
124 - Classical World. University Park.
Sep79 thru Apr-May80 (vol 73 complete)
125 - Clio. Ft. Wayne.
Fall78 thru Spring79 (vol 8 complete)
127 - Art Journal. New York.
Fall78 thru Summer79 (vol 38
complete)

128(CE) - College English. Champaign.
Sep78 thru Apr79 (vol 40 complete)
130 - Comparative Drama. Kalamazoo.
Spring79 thru Winter79/80 (vol
13 complete)
131(CL) - Comparative Literature. Eugene.
Winter79 thru Fall79 (vol 31 complete)
133 - Colloquia Germanica. Bern.
Band 12 complete
134(CP) - Concerning Poetry. Bellingham.
Spring78 and Fall78 (vol 11 complete)
135 - Connoisseur. London and New York.
Jan79 thru Dec79 (vols 200-202
complete)
136 - Conradiana. Lubbock.
Vol 11 complete
139 - Craft Horizons (name changed to
American Craft with Jun/Jul79 issue)
New York.
Feb79 thru Dec79/Jan80 (vol 39
complete)
140(CR) - The Critical Review. Melbourne.
No. 21
141 - Criticism. Detroit.
Winter79 thru Fall79 (vol 21 complete)
142 - Philosophy and Social Criticism.
Dordrecht.
Sep-Dec78 (vol 5 no 3/4)
145(Crit) - Critique. Atlanta.
Vol 20 complete
148 - Critical Quarterly. Manchester.
Spring79 thru Winter79 (vol 21
complete)
149(CLS) - Comparative Literature Studies.
Urbana.
Mar79 thru Dec79 (Vol 16 complete)
150(DR) - Dalhousie Review. Halifax.
Spring79 thru Winter79/80 (vol
59 complete)
151 - Dance Magazine. New York.
Jan78 thru Dec78 (vol 52 complete)
152(UDQ) - The Denver Quarterly. Denver.
Spring78 thru Winter79 (vol 13
complete)
153 - Diacritics. Baltimore.
Spring79 and Summer79 (vol 9
no 1 and 2)
154 - Dialogue. Montreal.
Mar78 thru Dec78 (vol 17 complete)
155 - The Dickensian. London.
Spring79 and Summer79 (vol 75
no 1 and 2)
157 - Drama/The Quarterly Theatre Review.
London.
Winter79 thru Autumn79 (no 131-134)
161(DUJ) - Durham University Journal.
Durham.
Dec78 and Jun79 (vol 71 complete)
165(EAL) - Early American Literature.
Amherst.
Winter79/80 thru Winter80/81
(vol 14 no 3 and vol 15 complete)

168(ECW) - Essays on Canadian Writing.
Downsview.
　　Spring78 thru Winter/Spring78/79
　　(No 10 thru 13/14)
173(ECS) - Eighteenth-Century Studies.
Philadelphia.
　　Fall78 thru Summer79 (vol 12 complete)
174(Éire) - Éire - Ireland. St. Paul.
　　Spring79 thru Winter79 (vol 14
　　complete)
175 - English. London.
　　Spring79 thru Autumn79 (vol 28
　　complete)
177(ELT) - English Literature in Transition. Tempe.
　　Vol 22 complete
178 - English Studies in Canada. Downsview.
　　Spring79 thru Winter79 (vol 5
　　complete)
179(ES) - English Studies. Amsterdam.
　　Feb79 thru Dec79 (vol 60 complete)
180(ESA) - English Studies in Africa.
Johannesburg.
　　Mar79 and Sep79 (vol 22 complete)
　　[no reviews indexed]
181 - Epoch. Ithaca.
　　Fall78 thru Spring-Summer79 (vol
　　28 complete)
182 - Erasmus. Wiesbaden.
　　Vol 31 complete
183(ESQ) - ESQ: A Journal of the American
Renaissance. Pullman.
　　Vol 25 complete
184(EIC) - Essays in Criticism. Oxford.
　　Jan79 thru Oct79 (vol 29 complete)
185 - Ethics. Chicago.
　　Oct78 thru Jul79 (vol 89 complete)
186(ETC.) - ETC. San Francisco.
　　Jun77 thru Dec77 and Mar78 thru
　　Winter78 (vol 34 no 2-4, vol 35
　　complete)
187 - Ethnomusicology. Ann Arbor.
　　Jan80 thru Sep80 (vol 24 complete)
188(ECr) - L'Esprit Créateur. Lawrence.
　　Spring78 thru Winter78 (vol 18
　　complete)
189(EA) - Etudes Anglaises. Paris.
　　Jan-Mar78 thru Jul-Dec78 (vol 31
　　complete)
190 - Euphorion. Heidelberg.
　　Band 72 complete [no reviews
　　indexed]
191(ELN) - English Language Notes.
Boulder.
　　Sep78 thru Jun79 (vol 16 complete)
192(EP) - Les Études Philosophiques.
Paris.
　　Jan-Mar79 thru Oct-Dec79
193(ELit) - Études Littéraires. Québec.
　　Apr78 thru Dec78 (vol 11 complete)
194(EC) - Études Celtiques. Paris.
　　Vol 15 fasc 2
196 - Fabula. Berlin.
　　Band 19 complete

198 - The Fiddlehead. Fredericton.
　　Winter80 thru Fall80 (No 124-127)
200 - Films in Review. New York.
　　Jan79 thru Dec79 (vol 30 complete)
203 - Folklore. London.
　　Vol 89 complete
204(FdL) - Forum der Letteren. Leiden.
　　Mar79 thru Dec79 (vol 20 complete)
205(FMLS) - Forum for Modern Language
Studies. St. Andrews.
　　Jan78 thru Oct78 (vol 14 complete)
207(FR) - French Review. Champaign.
　　Oct78 thru May79 (vol 52 complete)
208(FS) - French Studies. Cambridge.
　　Jan79 thru Oct79 (vol 33 complete)
　　and special issue Vol 33 Pt 2
209(FM) - Le Français Moderne. Paris.
　　Jan78 thru Oct78 (vol 46 complete)
215(GL) - General Linguistics. University Park.
　　Spring78 thru Winter78 (vol 18
　　complete)
219(GaR) - Georgia Review. Athens.
　　Spring79 thru Winter79 (vol 33
　　complete)
220(GL&L) - German Life and Letters.
Oxford.
　　Oct78 thru Jul80 (vols 32 and 33
　　complete)
221(GQ) - German Quarterly. Philadelphia.
　　Jan79 thru Nov79 (vol 52 complete)
222(GR) - Germanic Review. Washington.
　　Winter78 thru Fall79 (vols 53 and
　　54 complete)
224(GRM) - Germanisch-Romanische Monatsschrift. Heidelberg.
　　Band 28 complete
227(GCFI) - Giornale Critico della Filosofia Italiana. Firenze.
　　Jan-Mar78 thru Jul-Dec78 (vol 9
　　complete)
228(GSLI) - Giornale storico della letteratura italiana. Torino.
　　Vol 155 complete
231 - Harper's Magazine. New York.
　　Jan80 thru Dec80 (vols 260 and
　　261 complete)
238 - Hispania. Worcester, Mass.
　　Mar79 thru Dec79 (vol 62 complete)
240(HR) - Hispanic Review. Philadelphia.
　　Winter78 thru Autumn78 (vol 46
　　complete)
241 - Hispanófila. Chapel Hill.
　　Jan79 thru Sep79 (No 65-67)
244(HJAS) - Harvard Journal of Asiatic
Studies. Cambridge, Mass.
　　Jun78 and Dec78 (vol 38 complete)
249(HudR) - Hudson Review. New York.
　　Spring79 thru Winter79/80 (vol
　　32 complete)
255(HAB) - Humanities Association Review/
La Revue de l'Association des Humanités. Kingston.
　　Winter/Spring79 thru Fall79 (vol
　　30 complete)

256 - Humanities in Society. Los Angeles.
Winter79 thru Fall79 (vol 2
complete)
257(IRAL) - IRAL: International Review of
Applied Linguistics in Language Teaching. Heidelberg.
Feb79 thru Aug79 (vol 17 no 1-3)
258 - International Philosophical Quarterly. New York and Heverlee-Leuven.
Mar79 thru Dec79 (vol 19 complete)
259(IIJ) - Indo-Iranian Journal. Dordrecht.
Jan79 thru Oct79 (vol 21 complete)
260(IF) - Indogermanische Forschungen.
Berlin.
Band 83
261 - Indian Linguistics. Poona.
Volume 39 complete [No reviews
indexed]
262 - Inquiry. Oslo.
Spring78 thru Winter78 (vol 21
complete)
263(RIB) - Revista Interamericana de
Bibliografía/Inter-American Review of
Bibliography. Washington.
Vol 29 complete
268(IFR) - The International Fiction
Review. Fredericton.
Winter80 and Summer80 (vol 7 complete)
269(IJAL) - International Journal of American Linguistics. Chicago.
Jan78 thru Oct78 (vol 44 complete)
273(IC) - Islamic Culture. Hyderabad.
Jan76 thru Oct78 (vols 50 thru 52
complete)
276 - Italica. New York.
Spring79 thru Winter79 (vol 56
complete)
277(ITL) - ITL, a Review of Applied Linguistics. Leuven.
No 39/40 and 41/42
285(JapQ) - Japan Quarterly. Tokyo.
Jan-Mar79 thru Oct-Dec79 (vol 26
complete)
287 - Jewish Frontier. New York.
Jan78 thru Dec78 (vol 45 complete)
290(JAAC) - Journal of Aesthetics and
Art Criticism. Philadelphia.
Fall79 thru Summer80 (vol 38 complete)
292(JAF) - Journal of American Folklore.
Austin.
Jan-Mar79 thru Oct-Dec79 (vol 92
complete)
293(JASt) - Journal of Asian Studies.
Ann Arbor.
Nov78 thru Aug79 (vol 38 complete)
294 - Journal of Arabic Literature.
Leiden.
Volume 9
295(JML) - Journal of Modern Literature.
Philadelphia.
Feb79 thru Vol7no4 (vol 7 complete)
296(JCF) - Journal of Canadian Fiction.
Guelph.
No 27 and 28/29

297(JL) - Journal of Linguistics. Cambridge, England.
Mar79 and Sep79 (vol 15 complete)
300 - Journal of English Linguistics. Bellingham.
Mar79 (vol 13 complete)
301(JEGP) - Journal of English and Germanic Philology. Urbana.
Jan79 thru Oct79 (vol 78 complete)
302 - Journal of Oriental Studies. Hong
Kong.
Vol 16 complete. [Entries wholly
in Chinese are not indexed.]
303(JoHS) - Journal of Hellenic Studies.
London.
Volume 99
304(JHP) - Journal of Hispanic Philology.
Tallahassee.
Autumn79 thru Spring80 (vol 4
complete)
305(JIL) - The Journal of Irish Literature. Newark.
Jan78 thru Sep78 (vol 7 complete)
307 - Journal of Literary Semantics.
Heidelberg.
Apr79 and Oct79 (vol 8 complete)
308 - Journal of Music Theory. New Haven.
Spring78 and Fall78 (vol 22 complete)
311(JP) - Journal of Philosophy. New
York.
Jan80 thru Dec80 (vol 77 complete)
313 - Journal of Roman Studies. London.
Volume 69
316 - Journal of Symbolic Logic. Providence.
Mar79 thru Dec79 (vol 44 complete)
317 - Journal of the American Musicologi-
cal Society. Richmond.
Spring79 thru Fall79 (vol 32 complete)
318(JAOS) - Journal of the American
Oriental Society. Baltimore.
Jan-Mar78 thru Oct-Dec78 (vol 98
complete)
320(CJL) - Canadian Journal of Linguistics. Toronto.
Spring-Fall78 (vol 23 complete)
321 - The Journal of Value Inquiry. The
Hague.
Spring78 thru Winter78 (vol 12
complete)
322(JHI) - Journal of the History of Ideas.
Philadelphia.
Jan-Mar79 thru Oct-Dec79 (vol 40
complete)
325 - Journal of the Society of Archivists.
London.
Apr79 and Oct79 (vol 6 no 3 and 4)
340(KSJ) - Keats-Shelley Journal. New
York.
Volume 28
341 - Konsthistorisk Tidskrift. Stock-
holm.
Jun78 thru 1978/4 (vol 47 complete)

342 - Kant-Studien. Bonn.
Band 69 complete
343 - Kratylos. Wiesbaden.
Band 23
344 - The Kenyon Review. Gambier.
Winter80 thru Fall80 (vol 2 complete) [no reviews indexed]
349 - Language and Style. New York.
Winter78 thru Fall78 (vol 11 complete)
350 - Language. Baltimore.
Mar79 thru Dec79 (vol 55 complete)
351(LL) - Language Learning. Ann Arbor.
Jun79 and Dec79 (vol 29 complete)
353 - Linguistics. The Hague.
Jan78 thru Dec78 (no 203-214)
354 - The Library. London.
Mar79 thru Dec79 (new series
vol 1 complete)
355(LSoc) - Language in Society. London.
Apr78 thru Dec78 (vol 7 complete)
360(LP) - Lingua Posnaniensis. Poznań.
Volume 21
361 - Lingua. Amsterdam.
Jan78 thru Dec78 (vols 44-46 complete)
362 - The Listener. London.
3Jan80 thru 18and25Dec80 (vols
103 and 104 complete)
364 - London Magazine. London.
Apr/May79 thru Mar80 (vol 19 complete)
365 - Literary Research Newsletter.
Brockport.
Winter80 thru Summer80 (vol 5
no 1-3)
368 - Landfall. Christchurch.
Mar74 thru Dec78 (vols 28 thru
32 complete) (entire vol 27 is
missing)
376 - The Malahat Review. Victoria.
Jan79 thru Oct79 (No 49-52)
377 - Manuscripta. St. Louis.
Mar79 and Jul79 (vol 23 no 1 and 2)
382(MAE) - Medium Aevum. Oxford.
1979/1 and 1979/2 (vol 48 complete)
385(MQR) - Michigan Quarterly Review.
Ann Arbor.
Winter80 thru Fall80/Winter81
(vol 19 no 1 thru vol 19 no 4
and vol 20 no 1 - joint issue)
390 - Midstream. New York.
Jan79 thru Dec79 (vol 25 complete)
393(Mind) - Mind. Oxford.
Jan79 thru Oct79 (vol 88 complete)
394 - Mnemosyne. Leiden.
Volume 30 complete
395(MFS) - Modern Fiction Studies. West
Lafayette.
Spring78 thru Winter78/79 (vol 24
complete)
396(ModA) - Modern Age. Chicago.
Winter79 thru Fall79 (vol 23 complete)
397(MD) - Modern Drama. Toronto.
Mar79 thru Dec79 (vol 22 complete)

398(MPS) - Modern Poetry Studies. Buffalo.
Vol 10 no 1 [no reviews indexed]
399(MLJ) - Modern Language Journal. St.
Louis.
Jan-Feb79 thru Dec79 (vol 63 complete)
400(MLN) - MLN [Modern Language Notes].
Baltimore.
Jan79 thru Dec79 (vol 94 complete)
401(MLQ) - Modern Language Quarterly.
Seattle.
Mar79 thru Dec79 (vol 40 complete)
402(MLR) - Modern Language Review. London.
Jan79 thru Oct79 (vol 74 complete)
405(MP) - Modern Philology. Chicago.
Aug79 thru May80 (vol 77 complete)
406 - Monatshefte. Madison.
Spring79 thru Winter79 (vol 71
complete)
408 - Mosaic. Winnipeg.
Fall78 thru Summer79 (vol 12 complete)
410(M&L) - Music and Letters. London.
Jan79 thru Oct79 (vol 60 complete)
412 - Music Review. Cambridge, England.
Feb78 thru Aug-Nov78 (vol 39 complete)
414(MusQ) - Musical Quarterly. New York.
Jan78 thru Oct79 (vols 64 and
65 complete)
415 - Musical Times. London.
Jan79 thru Dec79 (vol 120 complete)
418(MR) - Massachusetts Review. Amherst.
Spring79 thru Winter79 (vol 20
complete)
424 - Names. Potsdam.
Sep77 and Dec77 and Mar78 thru
Dec78 (vol 25 no 3 and 4, vol 26
complete)
430(NS) - Die Neueren Sprachen. Frankfurt
am Main.
Feb78 thru Dec78 (vol 77 complete)
432(NEQ) - New England Quarterly. Brunswick.
Mar79 thru Dec79 (vol 52 complete)
433 - Neophilologus. Groningen.
Jan79 thru Oct79 (vol 63 complete)
439(NM) - Neuphilologische Mitteilungen.
Helsinki.
1978/1 thru 1978/4 (vol 79 complete)
441 - New York Times.
1Jan80 thru 31Dec80 [Sunday dates
refer to The New York Times Book
Review section.]
442(NY) - New Yorker.
7Jan80 thru 29Dec80 (vol 55 no 47-
53; vol 56 no 1-45) (Vol 56
begins with the 25Feb80 issue.)
445(NCF) - Nineteenth-Century Fiction.
Berkeley.
Jun78 thru Mar79 (vol 33 complete)
446(NCFS) - Nineteenth-Century French
Studies. Fredonia.
Fall-Winter78/79 (vol 7 no 1/2)
447(N&Q) - Notes and Queries. London.
Feb78 thru Dec78 (Vol 25 complete)

448 - Northwest Review. Eugene.
Vol 17 complete
449 - Noûs. Bloomington.
Mar79 thru Nov79 (vol 13 complete)
450(NRF) - La Nouvelle Revue Français.
Paris.
Jan79 thru Dec79 (vols 53 and 54
complete)
453(NYRB) - The New York Review of Books.
24Jan80 thru 18Dec80 (vol 26 no
21/22, vol 27 no 1-20)
454 - Novel. Providence.
Fall178 thru Spring79 (vol 12 complete)
460(OhR) - The Ohio Review. Athens.
No 24 and No 25
461 - The Ontario Review. Windsor.
Spring-Summer79 and Fall-
Winter79/80 (no 10 and 11)
462(OL) - Orbis Litterarum. Copenhagen.
Vol 33 complete
463 - Oriental Art. Richmond.
Spring78 thru Winter79/80 (vols
24 and 25 complete)
468 - Paideuma. Orono.
Spring79 thru Winter79 (vol 8 complete)
471 - Pantheon. Munich.
Jan/Feb/Mar79 thru Oct/Nov/Dec79
(vol 37 complete)
472 - Parnassus: Poetry in Review. New
York.
Fall/Winter79 (vol 8 no 1)
473(PR) - Partisan Review. New York.
1/1979 thru 4/1979 (vol 46 complete)
474(PIL) - Papers in Linguistics. Edmon-
ton.
Spring-Summer78 and Fall-Winter78
(vol 11 complete)
475 - Papers on French Seventeenth Century
Literature. Tübingen.
No 10 Pts 1 and 2
477 - Personalist. Los Angeles.
Jan79 thru Oct79 (vol 60 complete)
478 - The Philosophical Journal. Glasgow.
Vol 14 no 2 (ceased publication)
479(PhQ) - Philosophical Quarterly. St.
Andrews.
Jan79 thru Oct79 (vol 29 complete)
481(PQ) - Philological Quarterly. Iowa
City.
Winter78 thru Fall78 (vol 57 complete)
482(PhR) - Philosophical Review. Ithaca.
Jan79 thru Oct79 (vol 88 complete)
483 - Philosophy. London.
Jan79 thru Oct79 (vol 54 complete)
484(PPR) - Philosophy and Phenomenologi-
cal Research. Buffalo.
Sep79 thru Jun80 (vol 40 complete)
485(PE&W) - Philosophy East and West.
Honolulu.
Jan79 thru Oct79 (vol 29 complete)
486 - Philosophy of Science. East Lansing.
Mar78 thru Dec78 (vol 45 complete)

487 - Phoenix. Toronto.
Spring79 thru Winter79 (vol 33 complete)
488 - Philosophy of the Social Sciences.
Waterloo.
Mar79 thru Dec79 (vol 9 complete)
489(PJGG) - Philosophisches Jahrbuch.
Freiburg.
Band 86 complete
490 - Poetica. Amsterdam.
Band 10 complete
491 - Poetry. Chicago.
Oct79 thru Sep80 (vols 135 and
136 complete)
492 - Poetics. Amsterdam.
Apr79 thru Dec79 (vol 8 complete)
[no reviews indexed]
493 - Poetry Review. London.
Jul79 thru Mar80 (vol 69 no 1-3)
497(PolR) - Polish Review. New York.
Vol 23 complete
502(PrS) - Prairie Schooner. Lincoln.
Spring78 thru Winter78/79 (vol 52
complete)
503 - The Private Library. Pinner.
Winter77 and Spring78 thru Win-
ter78 (vol 10 no 4 and new series
vol 1 complete)
505 - Progressive Architecture. New York.
Jan78 thru Dec79 (vols 59 and 60
complete)
513 - Perspectives of New Music. Princeton.
Fall-Winter78 and Spring-Summer79
(vol 17 complete)
517(PBSA) - Papers of the Bibliographical
Society of America. New Haven.
Jan-Mar78 thru Oct-Dec78 (vol 72
complete)
518 - Philosophical Books. Leicester.
Jan79 thru Oct79 (vol 20 complete)
526 - Quarry. Kingston.
Winter79 thru Summer79 (vol 28
no 1-3)
529(QQ) - Queen's Quarterly. Kingston.
Spring79 thru Winter79/80 (vol 86
complete)
535(RHL) - Revue d'Histoire Littéraire de
la France. Paris.
Jan-Feb78 thru Nov-Dec79 (vols 78
and 79 complete)
536 - Ratio. Oxford.
Jun79 and Dec79 (vol 21 complete)
[no reviews indexed]
539 - Renaissance and Reformation/Renais-
sance et Réforme. Mississauga.
Vol 4 complete
541(RES) - Review of English Studies.
London.
Feb79 thru Nov79 (vol 30 complete)
542 - Revue Philosophique de la France
et de l'Étranger. Paris.
Jan-Mar78 thru Oct-Dec79 (vols
168 and 169 complete)
543 - Review of Metaphysics. New Haven.
Sep78 thru Jun79 (vol 32 complete)

544(RNL) - Review of National Literatures.
Jamaica, N.Y.
Volume 9 [no reviews indexed]
545(RPh) - Romance Philology. Berkeley.
Aug78 thru May79 (vol 32 complete)
546(RR) - Romanic Review. New York.
Jan79 thru Nov79 (vol 70 complete)
547(RF) - Romanische Forschungen. Frank-
furt am Main.
Band 91 complete
548(RCSF) - Rivista critica di storia
della filosofia. Firenze.
Jan-Mar79 thru Oct-Dec79 (vol 34
complete)
549(RLC) - Revue de Littérature Comparée.
Paris.
Jan-Mar77, Jan-Mar78 and Apr-Dec78
(vol 51 no 1 and vol 52 complete)
550(RusR) - Russian Review. Stanford.
Jan79 thru Oct79 (vol 38 complete)
552(REH) - Revista de estudios hispánicos.
University, Alabama.
Jan79 thru Oct79 (vol 13 complete)
553(RLiR) - Revue de Linguistique Romane.
Strasbourg.
Jan-Jun78 and Jul-Dec78 (vol 42
complete)
555 - Revue de Philologie. Paris.
Vol 52 complete
556(RLV) - Revue des Langues Vivantes/
Tijdschrift voor Levende Talen. Liège.
1978/1 thru 1978/6 (vol 44 complete)
557(RSH) - Revue des Sciences Humaines.
Lille.
Jan-Mar78 thru Oct-Dec79 (vols
43 and 44 complete) [no reviews
indexed]
558(RLJ) - Russian Language Journal. East
Lansing.
Winter79 thru Fall79 (vol 33 complete)
560 - Salmagundi. Saratoga Springs.
Winter79 thru Fall79 (No 43-46)
562(Scan) - Scandinavica. London.
Nov78 thru Nov 79 (vol 17 no 2,
vol 18 complete)
563(SS) - Scandinavian Studies. Lawrence.
Winter79 thru Autumn79 (vol 51
complete)
564 - Seminar. Toronto.
Feb79 thru Nov79 (vol 15 complete)
565 - Stand. Newcastle upon Tyne.
Vol 20 complete
566 - The Scriblerian. Philadelphia.
Autumn78 and Spring79 (vol 11
complete)
567 - Semiotica. The Hague.
Vols 23 thru 26 complete
568(SCN) - Seventeenth-Century News.
University Park.
Spring-Summer79 and Fall-Winter79
(vol 37 complete)
569(SR) - Sewanee Review.
Winter79 thru Fall79 (vol 87 complete)

570(SQ) - Shakespeare Quarterly. Washington.
Winter79 thru Autumn79 (vol 30 complete)
572 - Shaw Review. University Park.
Jan79 thru Sep79 (vol 22 complete)
573(SSF) - Studies in Short Fiction.
Newberry.
Winter78 thru Fall78 (vol 15 complete)
574(SEEJ) - Slavic and East European Journal. Tucson.
Spring79 thru Winter79 (vol 23
complete)
575(SEER) - Slavonic and East European
Review. London.
Jan79 thru Oct79 (vol 57 complete)
576 - Journal of the Society of Architectural Historians. Philadelphia.
Mar78 thru Dec78 (vol 37 complete)
577(SHR) - Southern Humanities Review.
Auburn.
Winter79 thru Fall79 (vol 13 complete)
578 - Southern Literary Journal. Chapel
Hill.
Spring80 and Fall80 (vol 12 no 2
and vol 13 no 1)
579(SAQ) - South Atlantic Quarterly. Durham.
Winter79 thru Autumn79 (vol 78
complete)
580(SCR) - The South Carolina Review.
Clemson.
Nov78 and Spring79 (vol 11 complete)
581 - Southerly. Sydney.
Mar79 thru Dec79 (vol 39 complete)
582(SFQ) - Southern Folklore Quarterly.
Gainesville.
Volume 41
583 - Southern Speech Communication Journal. Knoxville.
Fall78 thru Summer79 (vol 44 complete)
584(SWR) - Southwest Review. Dallas.
Winter79 thru Autumn79 (vol 64
complete)
585(SoQ) - The Southern Quarterly. Hat-
tiesburg.
Fall78 thru Spring-Summer79 (vol
17 complete)
586(SoRA) - Southern Review. Adelaide.
Mar78 thru Nov78 (vol 11 complete)
587(SAF) - Studies in American Fiction.
Boston.
Spring79 and Autumn79 (vol 7 complete)
588(SSL) - Studies in Scottish Literature.
Columbia.
Volumes 13 and 14
589 - Speculum. Cambridge, Mass.
Jan79 thru Oct79 (vol 54 complete)
590 - Spirit. South Orange.
Spring/Summer78 and Fall/Winter
78/79 (vol 46 complete) (issue
dated Fall/Winter77/78 missing)

591(SIR) - Studies in Romanticism. Boston.
Spring79 thru Winter79 (vol 18 complete)

593 - Symposium. Syracuse.
Spring79 thru Winter79 (vol 33 complete)

594 - Studies in the Novel. Denton.
Spring79 thru Winter79 (vol 11 complete)

595(ScS) - Scottish Studies. Edinburgh.
Volumes 22 and 23

596(SL) - Studia Linguistica. Lund.
Vols 31 and 32 complete

597(SN) - Studia Neophilologica. Uppsala.
Vol 50 complete

598(SoR) - The Southern Review. Baton Rouge.
Winter80 thru Autumn80 (vol 16 complete)

599 - Style. Fayetteville.
Winter79 thru Summer79 (vol 13 no 1-3)

600 - Simiolus. Utrecht.
Vol 10 no 1 and 2

601 - Southern Poetry Review. Charlotte.
Spring78 and Fall78 (vol 18 complete) [no reviews indexed]

602 - Sprachkunst. Vienna.
Volume 10

603 - Studies in Language. Amsterdam.
Vol 3 complete

606(TamR) - Tamarack Review. Toronto.
Spring80 (no 80) [no reviews indexed]

607 - Tempo. London.
Dec77 thru Dec78 (no 123-127)

608 - TESOL Quarterly. Washington.
Mar80 thru Dec80 (vol 14 complete)

609 - Theater. New Haven.
Fall178 thru Summer79 (vol 10 complete)

610 - Theatre Research International. London.
May78 and Oct78 thru May79 (vol 3 no 3 and vol 4 complete)

611(TN) - Theatre Notebook. London.
Vol 32 no 3 and Vol 33 complete

613 - Thought. Bronx.
Mar79 thru Dec79 (vol 54 complete)

617(TLS) - The Times Literary Supplement. London.
4Jan80 thru 19Sep80 (no 4006-4042)

627(UTQ) - University of Toronto Quarterly.
Fal178 thru Summer79 (vol 48 complete) (in Summer issue, only the "Humanities" section is indexed)

628(UWR) - University of Windsor Review.
Fall-Winter78 and Spring-Summer79 (vol 14 complete)

636(VP) - Victorian Poetry. Morgantown.
Spring/Summer78 thru Winter78 (vol 16 complete)

637(VS) - Victorian Studies. Bloomington.
Autumn77 thru Summer79 (vols 21 and 22 complete)

639(VQR) - Virginia Quarterly Review. Charlottesville.
Winter78 thru Autumn79 (vols 54 and 55 complete)

646(WWR) - Walt Whitman Review. Detroit.
Mar78 thru Dec78 (vol 24 complete)

648(WCR) - West Coast Review. Burnaby.
Jun78 thru Apr79 (vol 13 complete)

649(WAL) - Western American Literature. Logan.
Spring79 thru Winter80 (vol 14 complete)

650(WF) - Western Folklore. Berkeley.
Jan79 thru Oct79 (vol 38 complete)

651(WHR) - Western Humanities Review. Salt Lake City.
Winter79 thru Autumn79 (vol 33 complete)

654(WB) - Weimarer Beiträge. Berlin.
1/1978 thru 12/1978 (vol 24 complete)

656(WMQ) - William and Mary Quarterly. Williamsburg.
Jan79 thru Oct79 (vol 36 complete)

657(WW) - Wirkendes Wort. Düsseldorf.
Jan-Feb78 thru Nov-Dec78 (vol 28 complete)

658 - Winterthur Portfolio. Chicago.
Spring79 thru Winter79 (vol 14 complete)

659(ConL) - Contemporary Literature. Madison.
Winter80 thru Autumn80 (vol 21 complete)

660(Word) - Word. New York.
Aug78 and Dec78 (vol 29 no 2 and 3)

661(WC) - The Wordsworth Circle. Washington.
Winter79 thru Autumn79 (vol 10 complete)

676(YR) - Yale Review. New Haven.
Autumn79 thru Summer80 (vol 69 complete)

677(YES) - The Yearbook of English Studies. London.
Volume 9

678(YCGL) - Yearbook of Comparative and General Literature. Bloomington.
No 27

679 - Zeitschrift für allgemeine Wissenschaftstheorie. Wiesbaden.
Band 9 complete

680(ZDP) - Zeitschrift für deutsche Philologie. Berlin.
Band 97 complete

682(ZPSK) - Zeitschrift für Phonetik, Sprachwissenschaft und Kommunikationsforschung. Berlin.
Band 31 complete

683 - Zeitschrift für Kunstgeschichte. München.
Band 41 complete

684(ZDA) - Zeitschrift für deutsches Altertum und deutsche Literatur [Anzeiger section]. Wiesbaden.
Band 107 complete

685(ZDL) - Zeitschrift für Dialektologie
und Linguistik. Wiesbaden.
1/1979 thru 3/1979 (vol 46 complete)
686(ZGL) - Zeitschrift für germanistische
Linguistik. Berlin.
Band 7 complete
687 - Zeitschrift für Philosophische Forschung. Meisenheim/Glan.
Jan-Mar79 thru Oct-Dec79 (vol 33
complete)
688(ZSP) - Zeitschrift für slavische
Philologie. Heidelberg.
Band 40 Heft 1 and 2

Each year we are unable (for one reason
or another) to index the reviews appearing
in all of the periodicals scanned. The
following is a list of the periodicals
whose reviews were not included in this
volume of the Index. Every attempt will
be made to index these reviews in the next
volume of the Index:

1(ALH) - Acta Linguistica Hafniensia.
Copenhagen.
70(AN&Q) - American Notes and Queries.
Owingsville.
81 - Boundary 2. Binghamton.
112 - Celtica. Dublin.
171 - The Eighteenth Century: A Current
Bibliography. New York.
172(Edda) - Edda. Oslo.
202(FMod) - Filología Moderna. Madrid.
214 - Gambit. London.
279 - International Journal of Slavic
Linguistics and Poetics. Lisse.
319 - Journal of the History of Philosophy.
Claremont.
329(JJQ) - James Joyce Quarterly. Tulsa.
381 - Meanjin Quarterly. Parkville.
440 - The New Review. London.
470 - Pan Pipes. Des Moines.
480(P&R) - Philosophy and Rhetoric. University Park.
551(RenQ) - Renaissance Quarterly. New
York.
592 - Studio International. London.
662(W&L) - Women and Literature. New
Brunswick.

Aagaard-Mogensen, L. Aestetisk kultur.
S. Kjørup, 290(JAAC):Summer80-458
Aaltio, M-H. Finnish for Foreigners 1-3.
A. Grannes, 277(ITL):#39/40-132
Aalto, A. Alvar Aalto/Sketches. (G.
Schildt, ed)
L.K. Eaton, 505:Nov79-120
Aarbakke, J.H. Høyt på en vinget hest.
P.G. Silcock, 562(Scan):Nov78-178
Aarflot, A. Norsk kirke i tusen år.
T.R. Skarsten, 563(SS):Autumn79-512
Aaron, D., ed. Studies in Biography.
M. Goldstein, 569(SR):Fall79-667
Aaron, D. The Unwritten War.
A. Hook, 447(N&Q):Jun78-283
Aarts, J.M.G. and J.P. Calbert. Metaphor
and non-Metaphor.
B. Lindemann, 182:Vol131#23/24-851
Abad, G.H. A Formal Approach to Lyric
Poetry.
C. Clausen, 569(SR):Spring79-314
Abailard, P. Sic et non. (B.B. Boyer and
R. McKeon, eds)
F.E. Kelley, 589:Oct79-785
Abbad, F. and others. Classes dominantes
et société rurale en Basse-Andalousie.
J. Naylon, 86(BHS):Jan79-75
Abbey, E. Good News.
T. Walton, 441:14Dec80-10
Abbey, L. Braindances.
P. Lanthier, 99:Apr80-40
D. Precosky, 198:Summer80-156
Abbott, C.S. Marianne Moore.*
B.C. Bloomfield, 78(BC):Spring79-135
P.C. Willis, 354:Jun79-186
Abbott, H.P. The Fiction of Samuel
Beckett.
K. Klein, 38:Band96Heft1/2-268
Abbott, K. Rhino Ritz.
A. Young, 617(TLS):13Jun80-682
Abe, K. Secret Rendezvous.*
J. Updike, 442(NY):14Jan80-100
Abel, F. Le mouvement occitaniste contem-
porain.*
D.G., 355(LSoc):Aug78-289
Abélard. Du Bien suprême.
P-F. Moreau, 450(NRF):May79-128
Abélard, J. "Les Illustrations de Gaule
et Singularitez de Troye" de Jean Le-
maire de Belges.
J. Bailbé, 535(RHL):Jul-Aug78-631
M.J. Freeman, 208(FS):Vol133Pt2-614
Abelson, R. Persons.*
A. Baier, 482(PhR):Jan79-112
A.R. White, 393(Mind):Jan79-146
Abercrombie, S. Ferrocement.
P. Collins, 576:Dec78-302
Abirached, R. - see de Laclos, C.
Abler, R., ed. A Comparative Atlas of
America's Great Cities.
W.W. Goldsmith, 576:Mar78-40
Abraham, A. Mende Government and Politics
under Colonial Rule.
R. Oliver, 617(TLS):4Jan80-21
Abraham, C. Jean Racine.
H.T. Barnwell, 208(FS):Jan79-79

Abraham, C.K., J.W. Schweitzer and J. Van
Baelen - see Tristan L'Hermite
Abraham, N. L'Ecorce et le Noyau.
P. Kamuf, 153:Spring79-32
Abraham, N. and M. Torok. Cryptonymie.
P. Kamuf, 153:Spring79-32
Abraham, W. A Linguistic Approach to
Metaphor.
G.C. Lepschy, 402(MLR):Apr79-388
Abrahams, W., ed. Prize Stories 1978: The
O. Henry Awards.*
639(VQR):Autumn78-138
Abrams, L. Charting by the Stars.
R. Kiely, 441:6Jan80-10
Abrams, M.H., ed. English Romantic Poets.
M.I., 189(EA):Jul-Dec78-425
Abse, D. - see "Best of the Poetry Year 6"
Abse, J. John Ruskin.
J.S. Collis, 362:31Jul80-149
M. Lutyens, 617(TLS):25Jul80-846
Achebe, C. Le Démagogue.
H. Cronel, 450(NRF):Sep79-73
Achen, S.T. Symbols Around Us.
C.C. Brookes, 39:Dec79-538
Acheson, D. Among Friends. (D.S.
McLellan and D.C. Acheson, eds)
J. Greenfield, 441:9Mar80-11
J. Leonard, 441:11Mar80-C8
442(NY):9Jun80-156
Acker, W.R.B., ed. Some T'ang and Pre-
T'ang Texts on Chinese Painting. (Vol 2)
E.J. Laing, 318(JAOS):Apr-Jun78-176
Ackerman, B.A. Private Property and the
Constitution.*
D.P. Emond, 529(QQ):Winter79/80-724
Ackerman, B.A. Social Justice in the
Liberal State.
C. Orwin, 441:19Oct80-14
Ackerman, D. Twilight of the Tenderfoot.
D. Grumbach, 441:29Jun80-15
Ackermann, R.J. The Philosophy of Karl
Popper.*
J.H. Fetzer, 486:Sep78-491
J. Largeault, 542:Jul-Sep79-315
van Ackern, K-D. Bulat Okudžava und die
kritische Literatur über den Krieg.
G.S. Smith, 575(SEER):Jan79-151
Acquaviva, S. and M. Vitali. Felice Giani.
A.D.L., 90:Dec79-804
"Actas del coloquio internacional sobre
literatura aljamiada y morisca."
R.E. Surtz, 304(JHP):Autumn79-79
"Actas del Primer Congreso Internacional
de Estudios Galdosianos."
E. Rodgers, 86(BHS):Jul79-259
"Actes de la journée Maupertuis."
M. Martinet, 542:Apr-Jun79-232
"Actes du Colloque François Guizot (Paris
22-25 octobre 1974)."
J.P.T. Bury, 208(FS):Vol133Pt2-1009
"Actes du Colloque international 'Saint-
Simon et son temps.'"
M. Cermakian, 535(RHL):Jul-Aug78-638
"Actes du Colloque L'Amiral Coligny et son
temps (Paris, 24-28 octobre 1972)."
P. Chilton, 208(FS):Vol133Pt2-658

"Actes du Colloque Renaissance-Classicisme du Maine."
Y. Bellenger, 535(RHL):Jan-Feb78-104
"Actes du 4ème colloque de Marseille (Janvier 1974)."
R.C. Knight, 208(FS):Vol33Pt2-719
"Actes du XIIIe Congrès International de Linguistique et Philologie Romanes."
F. Helgorsky, 209(FM):Apr78-186
Acton, E. Alexander Herzen and the Role of the Intellectual Revolutionary.
H. Gifford, 617(TLS):18Jan80-53
Adachi, B. The Voices and Hands of Bunraku.
D. Currell, 157:Summer79-77
Adam de la Halle. Le Jeu de la Feuillée. (J. Dufournet, ed and trans)
K. Varty, 208(FS):Vol33Pt2-561
Adam, B. Katechetische Vaterunserauslegungen.
E. Bauer, 684(ZDA):Band107Heft1-28
Adam, J-M. and J-P. Goldenstein. Linguistique et discours littéraire.
D. Bouverot, 209(FM):Jul78-277
Adam, W. Vitruvius Scoticus.
D. Walker, 617(TLS):12Sep80-988
Adamesteanu, D. La Basilicata Antica.
E. Simon, 471:Jan/Feb/Mar79-76
Adamietz, J. Zur Komposition der Argonautica des Valerius Flaccus.
D.E. Hill, 123:Vol129No1-150
Adams, A. Beautiful Girl.*
D. Flower, 249(HudR):Summer79-295
Adams, A. Rich Rewards.
A. Tyler, 441:14Sep80-13
"Ansel Adams: Yosemite and the Range of Light."*
G. Thornton, 55:Nov79-48
Adams, C. English Speech Rhythm and the Foreign Learner.
B.L. Dubois, 608:Sep80-375
Adams, C. Lee Strasberg.
P. Bosworth, 441:16Mar80-13
Adams, D. The Restaurant at the End of the Universe.
P. Kemp, 362:18and25Dec80-866
Adams, D.J. La Femme dans les Contes et les Romans de Voltaire.
W.H. Barber, 208(FS):Vol33Pt2-740
Adams, D.R., Jr. Finance and Enterprise in Early America.
F.W. Gregory, 656(WMQ):Jan79-152
Adams, E.W. The Logic of Conditionals.*
I.F. Carlstrom and C.S. Hill, 486:Mar78-155
Adams, H. Art of the Sixties.
C. Cannon-Brookes, 39:Mar79-242
Adams, I.H. The Making of Urban Scotland.
H.G. Thorburn, 529(QQ):Spring79-164
Adams, J. Papers of John Adams.* (Vols 1 and 2) (R.J. Taylor, with M-J. Kline and G.L. Lint, eds)
H.A. Johnson, 432(NEQ):Mar79-130
Adams, J.N. The Text and Language of a Vulgar Latin Chronicle (Anonymus Valesianus II).*
V. Väänänen, 439(NM):1978/2-186

Adams, J.N. The Vulgar Latin of the Letters of Claudius Terentianus (P. Mich. VIII, 467-72).
A. Önnerfors, 123:Vol129No1-94
V. Väänänen, 439(NM):1978/2-186
Adams, J.S. Citizen Inspectors in the Soviet Union.
B.A. Ruble, 550(RusR):Jan79-112
Adams, M. García Lorca.
R.G. Sánchez, 240(HR):Autumn78-504
Adams, M.C.C. Our Masters the Rebels.
639(VQR):Summer79-89
Adams, P.G. Graces of Harmony.*
R.G. Walker, 577(SHR):Summer79-256
A.J. Weitzman, 405(MP):May80-438
Adams, P.R. Walt Kuhn, Painter.*
M.S. Young, 39:Mar79-239
Adams, R. The Girl in a Swing.
R. Kiely, 441:27Apr80-14
D. May, 362:23Oct80-546
R. Sale, 453(NYRB):29May80-39
442(NY):9Jun80-154
Adams, R. and others. Dry Lands.
C. Leakey, 46:May79-314
Adams, R.F. The Language of the Railroader.*
D.K. Barnhart, 35(AS):Summer79-138
Adams, R.M. AfterJoyce.*
D.L. Eder, 152(UDQ):Winter79-112
V. Mercier, 405(MP):Aug79-59
R.F. Peterson, 395(MFS):Winter78/79-571
Adams, R.M. Bad Mouth.*
639(VQR):Spring78-52
Adams, R.M. - see Machiavelli, N.
Adams, W.H. Atget's Gardens.*
G. Thornton, 55:Nov79-44
Adamson, A. The Inside Animal.*
D. Barbour, 150(DR):Spring79-154
Adamson, J. Lawren S. Harris.
W.N., 102(CanL):Spring79-147
Adamson, J. Queen of Shaba.
J.W. Miller, 441:26Oct80-12
Adaskin, H. A Fiddler's World.
R.W. Ingram, 102(CanL):Autumn79-124
Adcock, F. The Inner Harbour.
C. Hope, 364:Nov79-85
E. Longley, 617(TLS):18Jan80-64
Adcock, F. The Scenic Route.
A. Paterson, 368:Jun75-168
Adcock, F. and A. Thwaite - see "New Poetry 4"
Addis, J.M. Chinese Ceramics from Dateable Tombs.
M. Medley, 90:Jul79-451
W.B.R. Neave-Hill, 135:Mar79-207
Adejuyigbe, O. Boundary Problems in Western Nigeria.
A.I. Asiwaju, 69:Vol148#2-194
Adelman, C.M. Cypro-geometric Pottery.*
Y. Calvet, 555:Vol52fasc2-353
Adelman, I. and S. Robinson. Income Distribution Policy in Developing Countries.
C.W. Lindsey, 293(JASt):May79-591
Adelman, J., ed. Twentieth Century Interpretations of "King Lear."
M. Goldman, 570(SQ):Summer79-419

2

Aden, J.M. Pope's Once and Future Kings.*
  M.R. Brownell, 566:Spring79-122
  D. Griffin, 401(MLQ):Jun79-201
  R.L. Hayley, 150(DR):Spring79-194
  C.L. Horne, 67:Nov79-322
Aderman, R.M., H.L. Kleinfield and J.S.
  Banks - see Irving, W.
Ades, D. Photomontage.
  J. Arrouye, 98:Jan78-72
Adey, L. C.S. Lewis's "Great War" with
  Owen Barfield.
  R.P. Bilan, 627(UTQ):Summer79-418
Adlard, J. Owen Seaman.
  B.W. Martin, 447(N&Q):Jun78-277
  J. Stokes, 402(MLR):Oct79-926
Adler, A. Epische Spekulanten.
  W.G. van Emden, 208(FS):Vol33Pt2-522
Adler, E. Märchen der Südsee.
  H-J. Uther, 196:Band19Heft1/2-126
Adler, K. Camille Pissarro.*
  R. Pickvance, 39:Aug79-155
Adler, M. Drawing Down the Moon.
  R. Lingeman, 441:20Jan80-12
Adler, M.J. Aristotle for Everybody.
  H.L. Shapiro, 529(QQ):Autumn79-551
Adler, M.J. Some Questions about Lan-
  guage.*
  M. MacCarthy, 567:Vol123#1/2-165
Adler, T.P. Robert Anderson.
  J.R. Taylor, 157:Spring79-79
Adorno, T. Minima Moralia.
  185:Jul79-415
Adorno, T.W. Dialectique négative.
  A. Reix, 542:Jul-Sep79-339
Adorno, T.W. and others. The Positivist
  Dispute in German Sociology.
  L.J. Goldstein, 488:Sep79-347
  C. Jenks, 488:Sep79-377
Adrados, F.R. Festival, Comedy and Trag-
  edy.
  R. Seaford, 123:Vol29No1-3
Adrados, F.R. and others. Introducción a
  la Lexicografía griega.
  W.J. Slater, 123:Vol29No1-88
Aebischer, P. Des Annales carolingiennes
  à Doon de Mayence.
  W.G. van Emden, 208(FS):Vol33Pt2-519
  A. Iker-Gittleman, 545(RPh):Feb79-373
Aebischer, P. Etudes de stratigraphie
  linguistique.
  O. Gsell, 547(RF):Band91Heft3-313
Aebischer, P. Textes norrois et littéra-
  ture française du moyen âge.
  C. Minis, 224(GRM):Band28Heft1-101
Aelfric. Lives of Three English Saints.
  (rev) (G.I. Needham, ed)
  J.S. Ryan, 67:Nov79-309
Aers, D. Chaucer, Langland and the Cre-
  ative Imagination.
  V. Rothschild, 617(TLS):8Aug80-901
Aeschylus. The Oresteia.* (R. Fagles,
  trans; R. Fagles and W.B. Stanford, eds)
  K.J. Dover, 447(N&Q):Oct78-446
  E.M. Jenkinson, 161(DUJ):Jun79-268

Aeschylus. The "Oresteia" of Aeschylus.*
  (R. Lowell, trans)
  J. Coleby, 157:Summer79-81
  S.P. Edelman, 584(SWR):Spring79-200
  E. Segal, 617(TLS):25Jan80-97
  639(VQR):Autumn79-148
Aeschylus. The Oresteian Trilogy. (R.
  Rehm, ed and trans)
  R.H. Allison, 67:Nov79-302
Aeschylus. The Serpent Son.* (F. Raphael
  and K. McLeish, trans)
  J. Coleby, 157:Summer79-81
Afanasjew, A.N., comp. Erotische Märchen
  aus Russland. (A. Baar, ed and trans)
  H-J. Uther, 196:Band19Heft1/2-126
Agacinski, S. Aparté.
  J. Colette, 98:Oct78-947
  N. Viallaneix, 542:Jan-Mar78-122
Agawa, H. The Reluctant Admiral.*
  442(NY):31Mar80-123
Ageno, F.B. - see under Brambilla Ageno,
  F.
Agesthialingom, S. and S. Sakthivel. A
  Bibliography for the Study of Nilagiri
  Hill Tribes.
  P. Hockings, 350:Jun79-489
Aggeler, G. Anthony Burgess.
  C.R. La Bossière, 268(IFR):Winter80-73
  D.W. Nichol, 617(TLS):23May80-594
  E.R., 148:Winter79-92
Aghassian, M. and others. Les migrations
  africaines.
  H. Knoop, 69:Vol148#2-196
Agnew, S.T. Go Quietly ... or Else.
  J. Herbers, 441:22Jun80-14
Agosti, V. Filosofia e religione nell'at-
  tualismo gentiliano.
  E. Namer, 542:Jul-Sep79-319
Ågren, J. Étude sur quelques liaisons
  facultatives dans le français de con-
  versation radiophonique.
  D. Willems, 545(RPh):Feb79-363
Agricola, C., ed. Englische und wali-
  sische Sagen.
  G. Petschel, 196:Band19Heft1/2-130
Aguilar Piñal, F. Bibliografía funda-
  mental de la literatura española,
  siglo XVIII.
  R.M. Cox, 240(HR):Autumn78-498
Aguilera Malta, D. Seven Serpents and
  Seven Moons.
  A. Feinstein, 617(TLS):11Jan80-30
Aguinaga, C.B. - see under Blanco Aguinaga,
  C.
Ahmad, K., ed. Islam. (2nd ed)
  M.E. Yapp, 617(TLS):19Sep80-1040
Ahmed, M.A. The Nature of Islamic Politi-
  cal Theory.
  S.A. Akbarabadi, 273(IC):Oct78-276
Ahner, D. Arbeitsmarkt und Lohnstruktur.
  G. Blümle, 182:Vol131#7/8-204
Ahrens, R. Die Essays von Francis Bacon.*
  W. Zacharasiewicz, 224(GRM):Band28
  Heft1-116
Ahrweiler, G. Hegels Gesellschaftslehre.
  S. Decloux, 182:Vol131#19-641

3

Ai. Killing Floor.*
R. Albers, 114(ChiR):Spring79-119
N.J. Herrington, 584(SWR):Autumn79-402
T.R. Jahns, 460(OhR):No.25-108
S. Mayfield, 181:Winter79-219
P. Stitt, 219(GaR):Winter79-927
639(VQR):Summer79-106
Aichinger, P. Earle Birney.
R.H. Ramsey, 99:Oct80-34
Aid, F.M., M.C. Resnick and B. Saciuk, eds.
1975 Colloquium on Hispanic Linguistics.
F.H. Nuessel, Jr., 399(MLJ):Sep-Oct79-
304
Aijazuddin, F.S. Pahari Paintings and
Sikh Portraits in the Lahore Museum.*
M.C. Beach, 57:Vol40#1-84
T. Falk, 463:Autumn78-330
Aijazuddin, F.S. Sikh Portraits by Euro-
pean Artists.
D. Piper, 617(TLS):1Feb80-119
Aiken, C. The Selected Letters of Conrad
Aiken.* (J. Killorin, ed)
S. Donaldson, 569(SR):Summer79-460
J. Tharpe, 585(SoQ):Fall78-102
H.L. Weatherby, 396(ModA):Spring79-213
"Aiōn."
J. André, 555:Vol152fasc1-211
Aitchison, J. The Articulate Mammal.
S.M. Klein, 399(MLJ):Sep-Oct79-302
Aitchison, J. Linguistics. (2nd ed)
R. Coates, 297(JL):Sep79-378
Aitzetmüller, R. Belegstellenverzeichnis
der altkirchenslavischen Verbalformen.
(fasc 1-5)
F. Scholz, 343:Band23-134
Ajar, É. L'Angoisse du roi Salomon.
L. Kovacs, 450(NRF):May79-123
Ajdukiewicz, K. The Scientific World-
Perspective and Other Essays, 1931-1963.*
(J. Giedymin, ed)
S. Moser, 484(PPR):Sep79-135
D.E. Over, 479(PhQ):Jan79-77
Akbar, R. Sharh-e-Ahwāl-e-Sabuk Ash'ār-e-
Baba Fughani Shirazi.
S.A.W. Bukhari, 273(IC):Jan76-52
Ake, C. Revolutionary Pressures in Africa.
T.M. Shaw, 529(QQ):Winter79/80-723
Akerman, S. Le Mythe de Bérénice.
C. Roquin, 207(FR):May79-928
Akers, C.W. Abigail Adams.
J. Greenfield, 441:10Feb80-16
442(NY):18Feb80-131
Akhmanova, O. Linguistic Terminology.
R. Anttila, 350:Jun79-477
Akhmanova, O. and others. Linguostylis-
tics.
M.H. Short, 307:Apr79-59
Akhmanova, O. and D. Melenčuk. The Prin-
ciples of Linguistic Confrontation.
P.A. Luelsdorff, 257(IRAL):Feb79-90
Akhmatova, A. [Axmatova, A.] Stixotvor-
enija i Poemy.* (V.M. Žirmunsky, ed)
R.D.B. Thomson, 575(SEER):Jul79-436
Akhmatova, A. White Flock. (G. Thurley,
trans)
D. Graham, 565:Vol120#4-75

Akpabot, S.E. Ibibio Music in Nigerian
Culture.
G. Baumann, 69:Vol148#2-199
"Akten zur deutschen auswärtigen Politik,
1918-1945." (Ser B, Vol 11)
F.L. Carsten, 575(SEER):Oct79-618
Al, B.P.F. Normatieve Taalkunde.
M. Debrock, 277(ITL):#41/42-119
Al, B.P.F. La notion de grammaticalité en
grammaire générative-transformation-
nelle.*
L. van Kerchove, 277(ITL):#39/40-140
Aladé, R.B. The Broken Bridge.
P. Mustell, 69:Vol148#2-189
Alamanni, A. Commedia della conversione
di Santa Maria Maddalena. (P. Jodogne,
ed)
M.M., 228(GSLI):Vol155fasc491-473
Alan, R. The Beirut Pipeline.
T.J. Binyon, 617(TLS):5Sep80-948
S. Ellin, 441:2Mar80-8
Alatis, J.E. and K. Twaddell, eds.
English as a Second Language in Bilin-
gual Education.
H.B. Beardsmore, 556(RLV):1978/1-84
R.L. Light, 355(LSoc):Aug78-284
Alazraki, J. Versiones; Inversiones;
Reversiones.*
S. Boldy, 402(MLR):Apr79-482
G. Figueira, 263(RIB):Vol29No1-85
D.L. Shaw, 86(BHS):Apr79-166
W.L. Siemens, 238:Mar79-186
Alazraki, J. and I. Ivask, eds. The Final
Island.
S. Boldy, 86(BHS):Oct79-353
Alba, M.S. Montherlant et l'Espagne.
R. Smith, 149(CLS):Sep79-269
Alba, V. Peru.
J. Fisher, 86(BHS):Jan79-87
Albanese, R., Jr. Le Dynamisme de la Peur
chez Molière.*
B. Cap, 207(FR):Dec78-347
R. Guichemerre, 535(RHL):Jan-Feb78-115
M.S. Koppisch, 400(MLN):May79-913
Albanese, R., Jr. Initiation aux prob-
lèmes socioculturels de la France au
dix-septième siècle.
J. Barchilon, 207(FR):Oct78-189
Albert, K. Meister Eckharts These vom
Sein.
B. Mojsisch, 53(AGP):Band60Heft2-221
Albert, K. Zur Metaphysik Lavelles.
E. Diet, 542:Apr-Jun78-205
Albert, M.L. and L.K. Obler. The Bilin-
gual Brain.
L. Galloway, 608:Jun80-244
"Alberto Pio III, Signore di Carpi (1475-
1975)."
A.S., 228(GSLI):Vol155fasc491-474
Alberts, R.C. Benjamin West.*
L.B. Miller, 656(WMQ):Oct79-650
Albertson, S.H. Endings and Beginnings.
D. Grumbach, 441:24Aug80-16
von Albrecht, M. Römische Poesie.*
B.K. Gold, 24:Fall79-449
G. Petersmann, 52:Band13Heft3-314

Albrecht, M.C., J.H. Barnett and M. Griff, eds. The Sociology of Art and Literature.
  M.H. Bornstein, 127:Spring79-220
Albrektsen, B.H. - see under Halsaa Albrektsen, B.
Albright, D. Personality and Impersonality.*
  R. Bowen, 50(ArQ):Autumn79-271
  D.R. Schwarz, 569(SR):Fall79-cii
  295(JML):Vol17#4-603
Albuquerque, P.D. - see under de Medeiros e Albuquerque, P.
Alcock, F.B. As It Was.
  W. Lucas, 157:Spring79-85
Alcorn, J. The Nature Novel from Hardy to Lawrence.*
  K.M. Hewitt, 447(N&Q):Jun78-276
  W. Myers, 637(VS):Spring79-355
  M. Squires, 594:Spring79-118
Alcott, L.M. Work.* (S. Elbert, ed)
  N. Auerbach, 445(NCF):Mar79-475
Aldecoa, I. Cuentos. (J. Alegre Peyrón, ed)
  E.C. Torbert, 238:Mar79-196
Alderman, H. Nietzsche's Gift.*
  P. Foot, 453(NYRB):1May80-35
Alderson, J. Policing Freedom.
  A.W.B. Simpson, 617(TLS):21Mar80-337
Alderson, N.T. and H.H. Smith. A Bride Goes West.
  A. Ronald, 649(WAL):Summer79-171
Aldiss, B. Moreau's Other Island.
  G. Strawson, 617(TLS):22Aug80-930
Aldiss, B.W. Life in the West.
  E. Korn, 617(TLS):7Mar80-258
  J. Naughton, 362:6Mar80-318
Aldous, T. and B. Clouston. Landscape by Design.
  R. MacCormack, 617(TLS):23May80-588
Aldus, P.J. Mousetrap.*
  B. Corman, 539:Vol14No2-238
Aldwell, E. and C. Schachter. Harmony and Voice Leading, 1.
  W. Drabkin, 415:Jun79-485
Alegre Peyrón, J. - see Aldecoa, I.
Alegre Peyrón, J. - see Asturias, M.Á.
Alegria, C. Los perros hambrientos.
  J. Victorio, 556(RLV):1978/5-463
Alegría, F. The Chilean Spring.
  J. Burke, 441:11May80-14
Aleixandre, V. Antología poética. (L. de Luis, ed)
  R. Warner, 86(BHS):Jan79-84
Aleixandre, V. A Longing for the Light.
  H.J.F. de Aguilar, 472:Fall/Winter79-64
  J. Simon, 491:Apr80-40
Aleixandre, V. Twenty Poems.* (L. Hyde, ed)
  H.J.F. de Aguilar, 472:Fall/Winter79-64
  H.L. Boudreau, 399(MLJ):Jan-Feb79-75
  639(VQR):Winter79-25
Aleksandrov, G.M. Ja Uvožu k Otveržennym Selenijam.
  V. Bolen, 558(RLJ):Winter79-222

Alent, R.M.B. - see under Bachem Alent, R.M.
Aler, J. Symbol und Verkündigung.
  V.A. Schmitz, 52:Band13Heft1-110
Alexander, A. Billabong's Author.
  R. Stow, 617(TLS):28Mar80-374
Alexander, J.J.G. The Decorated Letter.
  J. Masheck, 62:Dec78-60
Alexander, J.J.G. Insular Manuscripts 6th to the 9th Century.
  J. Beckwith, 39:Apr79-328
  J. Backhouse, 90:Dec79-802
  78(BC):Summer79-183
Alexander, M. and S. Anand. Queen Victoria's Maharajah.
  J. Morris, 617(TLS):22Feb80-197
Alexander, P. Show Me a Hero.*
  N. Callendar, 441:31Aug80-17
Alexander, S. Marc Chagall.
  M.S. Young, 55:Jan79-30
Alexander, Y. and R.A. Kilmarx, eds. Political Terrorism and Business.
  R. Clutterbuck, 617(TLS):29Feb80-232
Alexandre, M. Journal (1951-1975).
  M. Godin, 208(FS):Vol33Pt2-904
Alexandrescu, S. Logique du personnage.
  T.G. Pavel, 567:Vol125#3/4-335
Alexandrescu, S., ed. Transformational Grammar and the Rumanian Language.
  R. Posner, 575(SEER):Apr79-270
Alexandru, T. Folcloristică, Organologie, Muzicologie. Muzica Populară Românească.
  R. Garfias, 187:Jan80-105
Alexy, R. Theorie der juristischen Argumentation.
  P. Mazurek, 687:Jan-Mar79-157
Alföldi, A. Oktavians Aufstieg zur Macht.
  A. Lintott, 313:Vol69-189
Alföldy, G. Römische Sozialgeschichte.*
  W.V. Harris, 24:Summer79-334
Alföldy, G. and others. Krisen in der Antike.
  É. Will, 555:Vol152fasc1-141
Algoud, P. L'homme et l'absolu.
  A. Reix, 542:Jul-Sep79-340
Algoud, P. Le monde spirituel de l'Asie orientale.
  M. Adam, 542:Jul-Sep79-340
Ali-Zade, E.A. Yegipyetskaya novyella.
  J.M. Landau, 294:Vol9-154
Princess Alice. For My Grandchildren.
  A. Forbes, 617(TLS):4Jan80-7
Aliger, M., Y. Moritz and B. Akhmadulina. Three Russian Poets.
  D.M. Thomas, 617(TLS):18Jan80-66
Alighieri, D. - see under Dante Alighieri
Alker, E. Profile und Gestalten der deutschen Literatur nach 1914.
  H. Seidler, 602:Vol10-257
Alkire, L.G., Jr. Periodical Title Abbreviations. (2nd ed)
  K.B. Harder, 424:Sep77-179
Alkon, P.K. Defoe and Fictional Time.*
  S. Pickering, 569(SR):Fall79-656
Allaback, S. Alexander Solzhenitsyn.
  639(VQR):Winter79-10

Allaire, S. La subordination dans le Français parlé devant les micros de la Radiodiffusion.*
 E. Rattunde, 430(NS):Apr78-177
Allan, T. Americans in Paris.
 295(JML):Vol7#4-572
Allard, G-H. and others. Aspects de la marginalité au Moyen Age.
 C. Lindahl, 292(JAF):Apr-Jun79-235
Allbeury, T. The Alpha List.
 N. Callendar, 441:9Nov80-26
Alldritt, K. Elgar on the Journey to Hanley.*
 S. Banfield, 415:Oct79-830
Alldritt, K. Eliot's Four Quartets.
 42(AR):Fall79-488
Allen, A.J. A Whaler and Trader in the Arctic.
 J.C. George, 649(WAL):Summer79-177
Allen, D., ed. Off the Wall.
 A. Saijo, 649(WAL):Spring79-85
Allen, D. - see Dorn, E.
Allen, D.F. The Coins of the Ancient Celts. (D. Nash, ed)
 J.P.C. Kent, 617(TLS):15Aug80-919
Allen, E. How Buildings Work.
 S. Gardiner, 362:18Sep80-376
Allen, E.D. and others. ¿Habla español?
 A.J. Vetrano, 238:May-Sep79-417
Allen, E.D. and R.M. Valette. Classroom Techniques: Foreign Languages and English as a Second Language.
 S.L. Shinall, 207(FR):Feb79-528
Allen, H.B. The Linguistic Atlas of the Upper Midwest. (Vol 1)
 W. Bright, 350:Sep79-742
 W.R. Van Riper, 35(AS):Fall79-222
 W. Viereck, 685(ZDL):1/1979-108
Allen, H.B. The Linguistic Atlas of the Upper Midwest. (Vol 2)
 W. Bright, 350:Sep79-742
 W.R. Van Riper, 35(AS):Fall79-222
 W. Viereck, 685(ZDL):1/1979-108
 S. Whitley, 353:Apr78-70
Allen, H.B. The Linguistic Atlas of the Upper Midwest.* (Vol 3)
 W. Bright, 350:Sep79-742
 W. Viereck, 685(ZDL):1/1979-108
 S. Whitley, 353:Apr78-70
Allen, J. Drama in Schools.
 G. Wickham, 157:Spring79-37
Allen, J. and M. Gin. Innards and Other Variety Meats.
 W. and C. Cowen, 639(VQR):Autumn79-153
Allen, J.J. Don Quixote: Hero or Fool? (Pt 2)
 R. El Saffar, 304(JHP):Spring80-237
Allen, J.J. - see de Cervantes, M.
Allen, J.M. Candles and Carnival Lights.*
 295(JML):Vol7#4-703
Allen, L. - see Newman, J.H.
Allen, M. Damn Yankee.
 J. Greenfield, 441:4May80-18
Allen, M. Falconry in Arabia.
 J. Morris, 617(TLS):1Aug80-870
Allen, M. The Necessary Blankness.*
 M. Couturier, 189(EA):Apr-Jun78-239

Allen, M.J.B. - see Ficino, M.
Allen, M.J.B. and D.G. Calder, eds and trans. Sources and Analogues of Old English Poetry.*
 J.E. Cross, 677(YES):Vol9-359
Allen, P. The Cambridge Apostles: The Early Years.
 639(VQR):Autumn79-130
Allen, R. The Assumption of Private Lives.*
 R. Miles, 102(CanL):Summer79-138
Allen, R.E. and D.J. Furley, eds. Studies in Presocratic Philosophy.* (Vol 2)
 R.K. Sprague, 122:Apr79-176
Allen, W. Side Effects.
 J. Lahr, 441:26Oct80-3
 J. Leonard, 441:19Sep80-C23
Allhoff, D-W. Rhetorische Analyse der Reden und Debatten des ersten deutschen Parlamentes von 1848/49 insbesondere auf syntaktischer und semantischer Ebene.
 H. Schmidt, 682(ZPSK):Band31Heft3-321
Allhouse, R.H. - see Prokudin-Gorskii, S.M.
Allis, F.S., Jr. Youth from Every Quarter.
 H.W. Bragdon, 432(NEQ):Dec79-581
Allison, A.F. Robert Greene 1558-1592.
 P.B., 189(EA):Jan-Mar78-110
 N. Sanders, 677(YES):Vol9-306
Allison, A.F. and V.F. Goldsmith, comps. Titles of English Books (and of foreign books printed in England).* (Vol 1)
 K.F. Pantzer, 517(PBSA):Jul-Sep78-391
Allison, A.F. and V.F. Goldsmith, comps. Titles of English Books (and of foreign books printed in England). (Vol 2)
 K.F. Pantzer, 517(PBSA):Jul-Sep78-391
 R.J. Roberts, 447(N&Q):Dec78-547
Allison, D. Poems.
 J. Symons, 617(TLS):14Mar80-301
Allison, D.B., ed. The New Nietzsche.
 E. Blondel, 542:Jan-Mar79-83
Allison, H.E. Benedict de Spinoza.*
 D.R.L., 543:Mar79-531
Allman, J. Walking Four Ways to the Wind.
 H. Carr, 617(TLS):25Apr80-477
 R. Saner, 460(OhR):No.25-113
Allott, K., ed. Writers and Their Background: Matthew Arnold.
 T. Eagleton, 447(N&Q):Jun78-267
Allshouse, R.H., ed. Photographs for the Tsar.
 442(NY):8Dec80-240
Allwood, J., L-G. Andersson and Ö. Dahl. Logic in Linguistics.*
 W. Hodges, 297(JL):Mar79-150
 R.T. Oehrle, 399(MLJ):Jan-Feb79-65
 J.E. Tiles, 518:Oct79-119
Allwood, M. The Truth of the Wind.
 G. Singh, 563(SS):Winter79-105
Allworth, E., ed. Nationality Group Survival in Multi-Ethnic States.
 V.S. Vardys, 550(RusR):Jan79-116
Alm, G. Enkel men värdig, Metodistisk kyrkoarkitektur i Sverige 1869-1910.
 T. Hall, 341:1978/2-55
Almana, M. Arabia Unified.
 M.E. Yapp, 617(TLS):19Sep80-1040

Almansi, G. and B. Merry. Eugenio Montale.
  L. Rebay, 276:Summer79-249
Almási, M. Phänomenologie des Scheins.
  J-M. Gabaude, 542:Apr-Jun78-237
Almazy, P. La photographie moyen d'information.
  J. Arrouye, 98:Jan78-72
Almeida Rodrigues, G. - see Damião de Góis
Almenas-Lipowsky, A.J. The Position of
  Indian Women in the Light of Legal
  Reform.
  R.D. Lambert, 182:Vol31#1/2-16
Almoina de Carrera, P. Diez romances hispanos en la tradición oral venezolana.
  S.G. Armistead, 545(RPh):Nov78-245
Almoina de Carrera, P. Reactivación
  novelesca de la primera visión de la
  selva americana.
  R. Chang-Rodríguez, 263(RIB):Vol29No1-88
Almon, B. Blue Sunrise.
  T. Wayman, 99:Nov80-32
Almon, B. Taking Possession.
  R.I. Scott, 648(WCR):Jun78-33
Alonso, R. Cimarron.
  D. Smith, 29:Mar/Apr80-40
Alonso Hernández, J.L. Léxico del marginalismo del Siglo de Oro.
  H. Bursch, 72:Band216Heft1-144
Alonso Hernandez, J.L. and others. Espace
  idéologique et société au XVIe siècle.
  F. Schalk, 182:Vol131#21/22-806
Alpers, A. The Life of Katherine Mansfield.
  P-L. Adams, 61:Apr80-127
  J. Atlas, 441:28Mar80-C33
  R. Davies, 362:14Aug80-212
  R. Dinnage, 617(TLS):16May80-543
  H. Kirkwood, 99:Sep80-35
  H. Moss, 441:9Mar80-1
  C. Tomalin, 453(NYRB):15May80-38
Alpert, B. - see Davie, D.
Alphant, M. Grandes "O" [et] Le ciel à
  Bezons.
  F. de Martinoir, 450(NRF):Jan79-119
Alquié, F. Le cartésianisme de Malebranche.
  G. Gori, 548(RCSF):Apr-Jun79-211
Alquié, F., ed. Malebranche et le rationalisme chrétien.
  G. Rodis-Lewis, 542:Apr-Jun79-218
Alsina, F.L. - see under López Alsina, F.
Alston, R.C. and M.C. Jannetta. Bibliography, Machine Readable Cataloguing,
  and the ESTC.
  P.J. Korshin, 173(ECS):Winter78/79-209
Altbach, P.G. and G.P. Kelly, eds. Education and Colonialism.
  P. Hackett, 293(JASt):Aug79-743
Alter, R. Gottfried Benn.*
  J.D. Barlow, 406:Spring79-84
  W. Pape, 556(RLV):1978/4-362
  U. Weisstein, 133:Band12Heft1/2-175
Alter, R. Partial Magic.
  M. Bell, 402(MLR):Jan79-145
Alter, R. Stendhal.
  A. Brookner, 617(TLS):30May80-599

Alter, S. Neglected Lives.*
  P. Lewis, 565:Vol20#3-62
  J. Mellors, 364:Jul79-86
  42(AR):Winter79-125
Alter, S. Silk and Steel.
  J. Atlas, 441:22Aug80-C22
  H. Eley, 617(TLS):25Jul80-836
  J. Mellors, 362:31Jul80-153
  J. Yohalem, 441:27Jul80-12
Althaus, F. and T. Carlyle. Two Reminiscences of Thomas Carlyle.* (J. Clubbe,
  ed)
  R.J. Dunn, 588(SSL):Vol14-293
Altholz, J.L., ed. The Mind and Art of
  Victorian England.*
  P. Brantlinger, 637(VS):Autumn78-98
  N.K. Hill, 152(UDQ):Summer78-152
  V.H. Winner, 445(NCF):Sep78-255
Althusser, L. Positions (1964-1975).
  J-M. Gabaude, 542:Jul-Sep79-341
Altick, R.D. The Shows of London.*
  C.E. Pierce, Jr., 173(ECS):Summer79-559
  J.W. Stedman, 637(VS):Summer79-470
  566:Spring79-141
  639(VQR):Autumn78-150
Altieri, C. Enlarging the Temple.
  J.D. McClatchy, 676(YR):Winter80-289
Altman, J.B. The Tudor Play of Mind.*
  W.J. Kennedy, 131(CL):Fall79-413
  639(VQR):Summer79-104
Altmann, A. Friedrich Nietzsche.
  E. Blondel, 542:Jan-Mar79-83
Altmann, H. Die Gradpartikeln im
  Deutschen.*
  R.P. Ebert, 406:Spring79-57
Altoma, S.J. Modern Arabic Literature.
  S.A.W. Bukhari, 273(IC):Jan77-76
Alvar, M. Atlas lingüístico y etnográfico
  de las Islas Canarias.
  M-R. Simoni-Aurembou, 553(RLiR):Jul-Dec78-470
Alvar, M. Niveles socio-culturales en el
  habla de Las Palmas de Gran Canaria.
  M-R. Simoni-Aurembou, 553(RLiR):Jul-Dec78-461
Álvarez, E.Z. - see under Zuleta Álvarez,
  E.
Álvarez, L.R. - see under Rojas Álvarez, L.
Alvarez, M.F. - see under Fernández
  Alvarez, M.
Amabile, G. Flower and Song.
  D. Barbour, 150(DR):Spring79-154
Amado, J. Tieta.*
  C.C. Park, 249(HudR):Winter79/80-575
Amado, J. Tieta do Agreste.*
  B.J. Chamberlain, 399(MLJ):Apr79-215
Amann, K. Adalbert Stifters "Nachsommer."
  E. Mason, 402(MLR):Jul79-754
Amato, J. Mounier and Maritain.
  M. Kelly, 208(FS):Vol33Pt2-943
Ambirajan, S. Classical Political Economy
  and British Policy in India.
  P. Harnetty, 293(JASt):May79-603

Amborn, H. Die Bedeutung der Kulturen des Niltals für die Eisenproduktion im subsaharischen Afrika.
R. Pittioni, 182:Vol31#17/18-618
Ambros, A. Damascus Arabic.
A-G. Abdul-Ghani, 350:Jun79-488
Amburger, E., M. Cieśla and A. Szikaly, eds. Wissenschaftspolitik in Mittel- und Osteuropa.
J.J. Tomiak, 575(SEER):Jan79-129
Ameln, K., C. Mahrenholz, and K.F. Müller, eds. Jahrbuch für Liturgik und Hymnologie. (Vols 1-20)
G. Hahn, 684(ZDA):Band107Heft2-66
"The American Image."
W. Morris, 441:20Jan80-13
Amery, L. The Leo Amery Diaries. (Vol 1) (J. Barnes and D. Nicholson, eds)
R.A. Butler, 362:16Oct80-509
Ames, K.L. Beyond Necessity.
J.A. Chinn, 650(WF):Jul79-200
Ames, L.B. and others. The Gesell Institute's Child from One to Six.
J. Dunn, 362:10Apr80-481
Amfitheatrof, E. The Enchanted Ground.
S. Jacoby, 441:21Dec80-12
J. Leonard, 441:8Dec80-C17
Amichai, Y. Amen.*
E. Longley, 617(TLS):18Jan80-64
639(VQR):Spring78-58
Amichai, Y. Time.*
E. Longley, 617(TLS):18Jan80-64
639(VQR):Summer79-108
Amiel, C. - see Enríquez Gómez, A.
Amiel, H-F. Journal intime. (Vol 1) (B. Gagnebin and P.M. Monnier, eds)
G. Guisan, 535(RHL):Jul-Aug79-688
Amiel, J. Hawks.
T.J. Binyon, 617(TLS):7Mar80-258
Amigues, S. Les subordonnées finales par "opōs" en attique classique.
P. Monteil, 555:Vol52fasc2-374
J.H.W. Penney, 123:Vol29No2-326
Amin, S. The Arab Nation.
E. Zureik, 529(QQ):Summer79-281
Amis, K. Collected Poems, 1944-1979.*
H. Carruth, 231:Dec80-74
J. Cassidy, 493:Dec79-60
Amis, K. Collected Short Stories.
J. Fenton, 362:23Oct80-543
Amis, K. Jake's Thing.*
376:Oct79-142
Amis, K., ed. The New Oxford Book of English Light Verse.*
E. Mendelson, 569(SR):Spring79-320
Amis, K. Russian Hide-and-Seek.
D.A.N. Jones, 362:22May80-659
B. Morrison, 617(TLS):16May80-548
Ammon, U. Probleme der Soziolinguistik.*
D. Goyvaerts, 556(RLV):1978/3-267
Ammon, U. and U. Loewer. Schwäbisch.
I. Guentherodt, 685(ZDL):3/1979-384
Amoia, A. The Italian Theatre Today.*
A. Musumeci, 397(MD):Dec79-424
Amory, M. - see Waugh, E.
Amos, A.K., Jr. Time, Space, and Value.*
M. Packert-Hall, 599:Summer79-305

Amoss, P. Coast Salish Spirit Dancing.
I. Halpern, 187:May80-287
Amprimoz, A. Against the Cold.*
G. Hamel, 198:Winter80-138
Amtmann, R. Die Bussbruderschaften in Frankreich.
F. Rapp, 182:Vol31#23/24-892
Anania, M. Riversongs.
J. Mole, 493:Mar80-65
W.H. Pritchard, 249(HudR):Summer79-252
P. Stitt, 491:Jan80-229
639(VQR):Summer79-108
Ananoff, A., with D. Wildenstein. François Boucher.
D. Posner, 54:Sep78-560
R.S. Slatkin, 90:Feb79-117
Anbeek van der Meijden, A.G.H. De schrijver tussen de coulisses.
J.J. Oversteegen, 204(FdL):Dec79-514
Ancel, A. Dialogue en vérité.
J-M. Gabaude, 542:Oct-Dec79-455
Ancelet-Hustache, J. - see Suso, H.
Anceschi, L., ed. Perche' continuamo a fare e a insegnare arte?
C. Dyke, 290(JAAC):Summer78-458
Anciferov, N.P. Duša Peterburga.
R. Pletnev, 558(RLJ):Winter79-214
And, M. Karagöz: Turkish Shadow Theatre.
W.H. Jansen, 292(JAF):Jan-Mar79-93
G. Speaight, 610:Oct78-66
Andaya, L.Y. The Kingdom of Johor, 1641-1728.
C.M. Turnbull, 302:Vol16#1and2-133
Anderegg, J. Literaturwissenschaftliche Stiltheorie.
L.W. Kahn, 406:Fall79-335
H. Seidler, 133:Band12Heft1/2-121
Andersch, A. Winterspelt.*
M. Butler, 617(TLS):18Apr80-442
P. Kemp, 362:3Apr80-450
Andersen, C.P. The Name Game.
E.B. Vest, 424:Sep78-291
Andersen, J.K. Feudalistisk fantasteri og liberalistisk virkelighed.
T. Petersen, 562(Scan):Nov79-161
Andersen, K. The Real Thing.
C. Lehmann-Haupt, 441:7Nov80-C25
Andersen, K.B. African Traditional Architecture.*
P. Oliver, 46:Feb79-123
Andersen, Ø. Die Diomedesgestalt in der Ilias.*
J.T. Hooker, 303(JoHS):Vol99-168
Andersen, R. Muckaluck.
J. Burke, 231:May80-90
M. Malone, 441:15Jun80-15
Andersen, W. American Sculpture in Process: 1930/1970.
K. Varnedoe, 54:Jun78-384
Anderson, A.J.O., F. Berdan and J. Lockhart, eds and trans. Beyond the Codices.
K. Dakin and T.D. Sullivan, 269(IJAL):Oct78-339
Anderson, A.R., R.B. Marcus and R.M. Martin, eds. The Logical Enterprise.
J.E.J. Altham, 518:Oct79-134

Appleyard, D.L. A Comparative Approach to the Amharic Lexicon.
  G. Hudson, 350:Jun79-489
Appold, M.L. The Oneness Motif in the 4th Gospel.
  S.S. Smalley, 182:Vol131#3/4-87
Apresjan, J.D. Leksičeskaja semantika.
  V. Raskin, 574(SEEJ):Spring79-114
Apuleius. Verteidigungsrede [&] Blüten-lese. (R. Helm, trans)
  J. André, 555:Vol52fasc1-198
  F. Lasserre, 182:Vol131#5/6-170
Aquila, R.E. Intentionality.
  S.F.B., 543:Dec78-349
  J.M. Hinton, 479(PhQ):Jan79-88
Aquin, H. Hamlet's Twin.*
  G. Davies, 198:Summer80-163
Åqvist, L. and F. Guenthner, eds. Tense Logic.
  P. Needham, 479(PhQ):Oct79-372
Aragno, P. Il romanzo di Silone.
  A. Traldi, 276:Summer79-245
Arājs, K. and A. Medne. Latviešu pasaku tipu rādītājs.
  V. Voigt, 196:Band19Heft3/4-309
Arakawa and M.H. Gins. The Mechanism of Meaning.
  S. Gablik, 441:20Jan80-28
Aranguren, J.L.L. Estudios literarios.
  N.G. Round, 86(BHS):Jan79-53
Araujo, N. In Search of Eden.
  A.J. Steele, 402(MLR):Jan79-209
Arbour, R. L'Ère baroque en France.
  M. Lever, 535(RHL):Jul-Aug79-646
  R. Ouellet, 193(ELit):Apr78-238
Arbuthnot, J. The History of John Bull.* (A.W. Bower and R.A. Erickson, eds)
  D.F. Bond, 405(MP):Nov79-224
Arce, H. Gary Cooper.
  J. Maslin, 441:17Feb80-13
Archambault, P. Seven French Chroniclers.
  M.R. Morgan, 208(FS):Jan79-58
"Archeologia Palestyny."
  M.C. Astour, 318(JAOS):Apr-Jun78-152
Archer, J. Kane and Abel.*
  M. Levin, 441:6Jul80-9
Archer, M. India and British Portraiture 1770-1825.
  R. Ormond, 39:Dec79-529
  D. Piper, 617(TLS):1Feb80-119
Archer, M. Indian Popular Painting in the India Office Library.
  R.C. Craven, Jr., 60:Mar-Apr79-141
  T. Falk, 463:Winter79/80-498
Archer, M. and B. Morgan. Fair as China Dishes.
  G. Wills, 39:Dec79-532
Archer, W.G. Visions of Courtly India.*
  T. Falk, 463:Spring78-92
Ardagh, J. A Tale of Five Cities.*
  442(NY):17Mar80-167
Ardelius, L. and G. Rydström, eds. Författarnas Litteraturhistoria. (Vols 1 and 2)
  K. Petherick, 563(SS):Winter79-85

Ardizzone, E. Nicholas and the Fast Moving Diesel.
  Q. Bell, 453(NYRB):18Dec80-50
Arendt, H. The Jew as Pariah.* (R.H. Feldman, ed)
  D. Donoghue, 249(HudR):Summer79-282
Arendt, H. The Life of the Mind.*
  D. Donoghue, 249(HudR):Summer79-281
  B. Elevitch, 418(MR):Summer79-369
Arens, R., ed. Genocide in Paraguay.
  639(VQR):Spring78-63
Arens, W. The Man-Eating Myth.*
  R. Needham, 617(TLS):25Jan80-75
Arensberg, A. Sister Wolf.
  E. Leffland, 441:28Dec80-9
Aretz, I., ed. América Latina en su música.
  E. Paesky, 263(RIB):Vol129No2-226
Argote de Molina, G. - see Manuel, J.
Arguedas, J.M. Deep Rivers.
  639(VQR):Autumn78-134
Argüelles, J.A. Charles Henry and the Formation of a Psychophysical Aesthetic.
  H.B. Chipp, 54:Mar78-182
Argyle, M. and M. Cook. Gaze and Mutual Gaze.
  P.C. Ellsworth, 567:Vol24#3/4-341
Arias, J. Guzmán de Alfarache.
  C.A. Longhurst, 402(MLR):Apr79-476
  T.A. Paulson, 238:May-Sep79-398
Arias, R. - see Romero de Cepeda, J.
Arieti, S. Creativity.
  D.S. Werman, 127:Spring79-224
Arieti, S. and J. Bemporad. Severe and Mild Depression.
  A. Storr, 617(TLS):4Jul80-746
Ariosto, L. Orlando Furioso.* (Vol 1) (R. Hodgens, trans)
  J.A. Molinaro, 627(UTQ):Winter78/79-172
Ariosto, L. The Satires of Ludovico Ariosto. (P.D. Wiggins, trans)
  J.A. Molinaro, 627(UTQ):Winter78/79-172
Ariotti, P.E. and R. Bronowski - see Bronowski, J.
Aristides. P. Aelii Aristidis Opera Quae Exstant Omnia. (Vol 1, fasc 2 and 3) (F.W. Lenzt and C.A. Behr, eds)
  I. Avotins, 124:Dec79/Jan80-251
Aristophanes. Wasps. (D.M. MacDowell, ed)
  J.T.M.F. Pieters, 394:Vol30fasc3-309
Aristotle. Aristote, "Anthropologie." (J-C. Fraisse, ed and trans)
  J-L. Poirier, 542:Jan-Mar79-129
Aristotle. Aristote, "Éthique a Eudème." (V. Décarie, with R. Houdé-Sauvé, eds)
  A.G-L. 543:Jun79-735
Aristotle. Aristotele, "La generazione e la corruzione." (M. Migliori, ed and trans)
  H.J.B., 543:Sep78-124
  P.M. Huby, 123:Vol129No2-321
  P. Louis, 555:Vol52fasc1-164

Aristotle. Aristotele, "Trattato sul
cosmo per Alessandro."* (G. Reale, ed
and trans)
    J. den Boeft, 394:Vol32fasc1/2-187
    J-L. Poirier, 542:Jan-Mar79-130
Aristotle. Aristotelis "Ars rhetorica."
(R. Kassel, ed)
    F. Solmsen, 122:Jan79-68
Aristotle. Aristotle's "De Motu Animal-
ium." (M.C. Nussbaum, ed and trans)
    A. Gotthelf, 311(JP):Jun80-365
Aristotle. Aristotle's "Metaphysics."*
(Bks M and N) (J. Annas, ed and trans)
    S.R.L. Clark, 393(Mind):Jan79-125
Aristotle. Aristotle's Posterior Ana-
lytics.* (J. Barnes, ed and trans)
    J.D.G. Evans, 303(JoHS):Vol99-178
Ariyoshi, S. The Doctor's Wife.
    A.E. Imamura, 285(JapQ):Jan-Mar79-119
Arizcuren, F.J.O. - see under Oroz Ariz-
curen, F.J.
Arkell, D. Looking for Laforgue.
    M. Bowie, 362:28Feb80-284
    A. Broyard, 441:23Feb80-19
    R. Shattuck, 441:11May80-11
Arland, M. Ce fut ainsi.
    J. Duvignaud, 450(NRF):Jun79-117
Arlen, M.J. Thirty Seconds.
    B. De Mott, 441:4May80-12
    C. Lehmann-Haupt, 441:25Apr80-C25
Armes, R. The Ambiguous Image.
    A. Greenspan, 207(FR):Mar79-652
Armitage, I. - see de l'Estoile, P.
Armogathe, J-R. and J-L. Marion. Index
des "Regulae ad directionem ingenii" de
René Descartes.*
    S. Auroux, 154:Jun78-396
Armstrong, D.M. Universals and Scientific
Realism.
    M.C. Bradley, 63:Dec79-350
    L. Goldstein, 479(PhQ):Oct79-360
    D.W. Hamlyn, 617(TLS):4Jan80-19
Armstrong, E.C. The Medieval French Roman
d'Alexandre: Introduction and Notes to
Branch III. (A. Foulet, ed)
    D.J.A. Ross, 208(FS):Jan79-61
Armstrong, J. The Novel of Adultery.*
    M. Ferguson, 637(VS):Winter78-280
    C.L. Walker, 395(MFS):Winter78/79-658
Armstrong, T., ed. Yermak's Campaign in
Siberia.*
    N. Andreyev, 575(SEER):Oct79-596
Armstrong, W.M. E.L. Godkin.
    H.S. Merrill, 579(SAQ):Summer79-410
Arnason, D. - see Livesay, D.
Arnaud, A. and G. Excoffon-Lafarge.
Bataille.
    J. Pfeiffer, 450(NRF):Jan79-126
Arnauld, A. and C. Lancelot. General and
Rational Grammar.* (J. Rieux and B.E.
Rollin, eds and trans)
    M. Breva-Claramonte, 567:Vol124#3/4-353
Arndt, H. Markt und Macht. (2nd ed)
    K. Brandt, 182:Vol31#9/10-273
Arndt, K.J.R. - see Sealsfield, C.

Arnesen, P.J. The Medieval Japanese
Daimyo.
    C.J. Dunn, 617(TLS):27Jun80-725
Arngart, O. The Proverbs of Alfred.
    H. Sauer, 72:Band216Heft2-407
Arnheim, M.T.W. Aristocracy in Greek
Society.
    M.F. McGregor, 487:Autumn79-258
    P.J. Rhodes, 123:Vol29No1-105
von Arnim, L.A. Gedichte von Ludwig Achim
von Arnim. (Pt 2, Vol 7) (H.E. Liedke
and A. Anger, eds)
    J.F.F., 191(ELN):Sep78(supp)-140
Arnold, B. The Song of the Nightingale.
    P. Kemp, 362:30Oct80-588
Arnold, D. The Congress in Tamilnad.
    E.F. Irschick, 293(JASt):Feb79-397
Arnold, E. In China.
    C. James, 453(NYRB):18Dec80-22
    J. Naughton, 362:18and25Dec80-865
Arnold, G. Held Fast for England.
    E. Stokes, 617(TLS):11Apr80-406
Arnold, L. Some Notes on the Paintings of
Francis Bacon.
    D. Barbour, 150(DR):Spring79-154
Arnold, M. The Complete Prose Works of
Matthew Arnold.* (Vol 11) (R.H. Super,
ed)
    A.D. Culler, 405(MP):Feb80-347
    P. Keating, 447(N&Q):Jun78-268
Arnold, M. - see "Steve Biko: Black Con-
sciousness in South Africa"
Arnold, R. and K. Hansen. Englische
Phonetik.
    W. Jassem, 682(ZPSK):Band31Heft3-298
Arnopoulos, S.M. and D. Clift. The
English Fact in Quebec.
    J.M. Cameron, 453(NYRB):17Jul80-29
Arnott, J.F., ed. Sale Catalogues of
Libraries of Eminent Persons. (Vol 12:
Actors.)
    I. Jack, 541(RES):May79-241
Arnott, P.D. An Introduction to the
French Theatre.*
    W.D. Howarth, 208(FS):Apr79-237
Arnow, H. The Dollmaker.
    D.H. Lee, 145(Crit):Vol120#2-92
Arntzen, H. and others, eds. Literatur-
wissenschaft und Geschichtsphilosophie.*
    J.J. White, 220(GL&L):Oct78-63
    W.D. Williams, 182:Vol31#7/8-229
Aronoff, M. Word Formation in Generative
Grammar.*
    J. Carrier, 350:Jun79-415
Arora, S.L. Proverbial Comparisons and
Related Expressions in Spanish.
    W. Mieder, 650(WF):Apr79-126
    G. Monteiro, 292(JAF):Jul-Sep79-344
Arpin, G.Q. The Poetry of John Berryman.*
    K.D. Finney, 219(GaR):Fall79-721
    J. Mazzaro, 141:Spring79-182
Arrian. Anabasis Alexandri Books I-IV.*
(P.A. Brunt, ed and trans)
    P. Pédech, 555:Vol52fasc2-384

Arrivé, M. Les remembrances du vieillard
idiot.
  V. Brady-Papadopoulou, 207(FR):Mar79-
  665
  P. Fresnault-Deruelle, 98:Jun-Jul78-
  652
Arrivé, M. and J-C. Chevalier. La Gram-
maire.
  J. Levitt, 660(Word):Dec78-261
Arrom, J.J. Esquema generacional de las
letras hispanoamericanas. (2nd ed)
  R. Chang-Rodríguez, 263(RIB):Vol29No1-
  89
Artaud, A. Héliogabale ou l'anarchiste
couronné.
  D. Leuwers, 450(NRF):Jul79-101
Artaud, A. Oeuvres complètes. (Vol 14)
  C. Binder, 98:Oct78-927
Artemidorus. Artemidorus Daldianus, "The
Interpretation of Dreams."* (R.J. White,
ed and trans)
  A.H.M. Kessels, 394:Vol30fasc3-318
Arthos, J. Shakespeare's Use of Dream and
Vision.*
  L.G. Black, 447(N&Q):Oct78-457
  A.D. Nuttall, 570(SQ):Summer79-421
Artiss, D. Theodor Storm.
  L.W. Tusken, 564:Nov79-321
Arvidson, K.O. Riding the Pendulum.
  A. Paterson, 368:Jun74-177
Asbell, B. The Senate Nobody Knows.
  639(VQR):Winter79-28
Ascher, A., ed. The Mensheviks in the Rus-
sian Revolution.
  R.H. McNeal, 104(CASS):Summer78-303
Aschwanden, H. Symbole des Lebens.
  A.K.H. Weinrich, 69:Vol48#4-409
Asenjo Sendano, J. Conversación sobre la
guerra.
  J.W. Díaz, 399(MLJ):Mar79-151
  R.W. Hatton, 238:May-Sep79-405
Asensio, G.R. - see under Ramallo Asensio,
G.
Ash, B. Who's Who in Science Fiction.
  T.C. Holyoke, 42(AR):Winter79-122
Ashbery, J. As We Know.
  D. Bromwich, 441:6Jan80-6
  D. Donoghue, 453(NYRB):24Jan80-36
  W. Harmon, 472:Fall/Winter79-213
Ashbery, J. Houseboat Days.*
  E. Larrissy, 617(TLS):14Mar80-301
  R. Miklitsch, 134(CP):Spring78-84
  R. Miklitsch, 659(ConL):Winter80-118
  639(VQR):Winter78-10
Ashbery, J. Rivers and Mountains.
  639(VQR):Spring79-66
Ashbery, J. Self-Portrait in a Convex
Mirror.*
  R. Miklitsch, 659(ConL):Winter80-118
Ashby, C. Lies and Dreams.
  J. Lasdun, 617(TLS):1Aug80-876
Ashby, E. Reconciling Man with the Envi-
ronment.
  R.V. Francaviglia, 42(AR):Winter79-116
Ashby, W.J. Clitic Inflection in French.
  G. Price, 208(FS):Vol133Pt2-1035

Ashkenazi, A. Modern German Nationalism.
  J. Toews, 222(GR):Spring78-77
Ashley, M. James II.
  639(VQR):Spring79-69
Ashley, M. Who's Who in Horror and
Fantasy Fiction.
  T.C. Holyoke, 42(AR):Winter79-122
Ashraf, S.V. Hayat-e-Ashraf Jahangir
Simnani.
  S.A.W. Bukhari, 273(IC):Apr78-127
Ashton, D. A Fable of Modern Art.
  J. Russell, 441:24Apr80-C26
Ashton, R. The German Idea.
  S.S. Prawer, 617(TLS):20Jun80-693
Ashton, T.S. Economic and Social Investi-
gations in Manchester, 1833-1933.
  R.N. Soffer, 637(VS):Autumn78-112
"Asian and Pacific Short Stories."
  M.L. Wagner, 318(JAOS):Jul-Sep78-292
"Asian Puppets, Wall of the World."
  J. Lowry, 463:Summer79-254
Asimov, I. Isaac Asimov's Book of Facts.
  J. Leonard, 441:1Jan80-6
Asimov, I. The Collapsing Universe.
  J. Galt, 529(QQ):Autumn79-516
Asimov, I. In Joy Still Felt.
  C. Seebohm, 441:13Apr80-16
Asiwaju, A.I. Western Yorubaland under
European Rule 1889-1945.
  P.C. Lloyd, 69:Vol48#4-418
Aspe Ansa, M.P. Constantino Ponce de la
Fuente — el hombre y su lenguaje.
  A.G. Kinder, 86(BHS):Jan79-62
van Assendelft, M.M. Sol ecce surgit
igneus.
  J.B. Hall, 123:Vol29No2-226
de Assis, J.M.M. - see under Machado de
Assis, J.M.
Assoun, P-L. Freud, la philosophie et les
philosophes.*
  J-M. Gabaude, 542:Apr-Jun78-183
Assoun, P-L. Marx et la répétition histor-
ique.
  J-M. Gabaude, 542:Apr-Jun79-262
Assunto, R. Intervengono i personaggi
(col permesso degli Autori).
  A. Corsano, 227(GCFI):Jan-Mar78-141
Aster, H. - see Layton, I.
Astier, C. Le Mythe d'Oedipe.
  H. Godin, 208(FS):Vol133Pt2-980
Astin, A.E. Cato the Censor.
  J.R. Ruebel, 124:Dec79/Jan80-242
  E.T. Salmon, 487:Winter79-367
Aston, C. A Durable Love.
  L. Duguid, 617(TLS):29Feb80-228
Astor, B. Footprints.
  E.R. Lipson, 441:7Sep80-14
Astro, R. and J.J. Benson, eds. The Fic-
tion of Bernard Malamud.*
  D.R. Mesher, 573(SSF):Fall78-465
  S. Pinsker, 395(MFS):Summer78-278
  529(QQ):Summer79-369
Åström, P. The Cuirass Tomb and other
Finds at Dendra. (Pt 1)
  O.T.P.K. Dickinson, 303(JoHS):Vol199-
  203

[continued]

Åström, P. The Cuirass Tomb and other
Finds at Dendra. (Pt 1) [continuing]
  S. Hood, 123:Vol29No2-331
  W. McLeod, 124:Dec79/Jan80-244
Åström, P., G. Hult and M.S. Olofsson.
Hala Sultan Tekke. (Vol 3)
  S. Hood, 123:Vol29No2-332
Asturias, M.Á. Leyendas de Guatemala. (J.
Alegre Peyrón, ed)
  E.C. Torbert, 238:Mar79-196
Asturias, M.A. El Señor Presidente.
  D.L. Shaw, 402(MLR):Oct79-972
Asturias, M.A. Tres de cuatro soles. (D.
Nouhaud, ed)
  L. King, 86(BHS):Jan79-88
  L. Lorenzo-Rivero, 182:Vol131#19-672
  A. McDermott, 402(MLR):Apr79-481
  H. Rogmann, 72:Band216Heft1-239
  205(FMLS):Apr78-183
Atget, E. and M. Proust. A Vision of
Paris. (A.D. Trottenberg, ed)
  H. Kramer, 441:30Nov80-66
Saint Athanasius. Athanase d'Alexandrie,
"Sur l'incarnation du Verbe." (C.
Kannengiesser, ed and trans)
  H. Savon, 555:Vol52fasc2-406
Atkin, M. Russia and Iran, 1780-1828.
  P. Avery, 617(TLS):19Sep80-1043
Atkin, R. Dieppe 1942.
  J. Grigg, 362:22May80-655
Atkins, S., with O. Schönberg and O. Boeck -
see Heine, H.
Atkinson, D., A. Dallin and G.W. Lapidus,
eds. Women in Russia.
  N.V. Riasanovsky, 550(RusR):Jan79-81
Atkinson, F. Dictionary of Literary Pseu-
donyms. (2nd ed)
  K.B. Harder, 424:Sep78-288
Atkinson, J.C. The Two Forms of Subject
Inversion in Modern French.
  F.M. Jenkins, 545(RPh):May79-436
Atkinson, R.F. Knowledge and Explanation
in History.
  639(VQR):Spring79-55
  A. Quinton, 617(TLS):4Jan80-18
Atlas, J. Delmore Schwartz.*
  C.B.C., 148:Spring79-95
  F. Day, 580(SCR):Nov78-133
  T. Kennedy, 502(PrS):Winter78/79-384
  J. Ludwig, 473(PR):4/1979-636
  J. Mazzaro, 219(GaR):Fall79-712
  639(VQR):Spring78-47
Atlas, J. - see Schwartz, D.
Attal, R. A Bibliography of the Writings
of Prof. Shelomo Dov Goitein.
  H. Zafrani, 318(JAOS):Apr-Jun78-155
Atticus. Fragments. (É. Des Places, ed
and trans)
  P. Louis, 555:Vol52fasc1-176
  A.H. Armstrong, 303(JoHS):Vol99-185
Attila, F. A Jónás-téma a világirodalom-
ban.
  G. Hellenbart, 52:Band13Heft3-304
Attridge, D. Well-Weighed Syllables.*
  H-J. Diller, 38:Band96Heft1/2-231
  E.R. Weismiller, 402(MLR):Apr79-407

Attridge, H.W. First-Century Cynicism in
the Epistles of Heraclitus.
  É. Des Places, 555:Vol52fasc1-176
Attridge, H.W. The Interpretation of
Biblical History in the Antiquitates
Judaicae of Flavius Josephus.
  É. Des Places, 555:Vol52fasc1-175
Atwood, M. Life Before Man.*
  H. Dahlie, 150(DR):Autumn79-561
  M. French, 441:3Feb80-1
  L. Harris, 442(NY):7Jul80-98
  P. Kemp, 362:13Mar80-350
  C. Lehmann-Haupt, 441:10Jan80-C21
  L. Sage, 617(TLS):14Mar80-289
  M. Taylor, 198:Winter80-111
  J. Wolcott, 453(NYRB):3Apr80-34
  61:Apr80-123
Atwood, M. Two-Headed Poems.*
  D. Barbour, 150(DR):Spring79-154
  J. David, 628(UWR):Spring-Summer79-100
  R. Gibbons, 461:Spring-Summer79-87
Atwood, W.G. The Lioness and the Little
One.
  A. Broyard, 441:19Sep80-C24
  442(NY):6Oct80-197
Aubailly, J-C. Le Monologue, le Dialogue
et la Sottie, essai sur quelques genres
dramatiques de la fin du Moyen Age et du
début du XVIe siècle.
  D. Ménager, 535(RHL):Jul-Aug79-636
Aubert, R. Two Kinds of Honey.*
  D. Barbour, 150(DR):Spring79-154
Aubin, F., ed. Études Song.* (Ser 1,
Vol 3)
  P.J. Golas, 318(JAOS):Jul-Sep78-342
Aubrun, C.V. La littérature espagnole.
  N.G. Round, 86(BHS):Oct79-329
Auburn, M.S. Sheridan's Comedies.*
  J. Milhous, 130:Spring79-91
Auchincloss, L. The Country Cousin.
  639(VQR):Spring79-56
Auchincloss, L. The House of the Prophet.
  R. Kiely, 441:30Mar80-7
  C. Lehmann-Haupt, 441:4Mar80-C10
  C. Wheeler, 617(TLS):2May80-486
  61:May80-101
"The Auchinleck Manuscript: National
Library of Scotland Advocates' MS.
19.2.1."*
  J. Fellows, 382(MAE):1979/2-308
  G.R. Keiser, 589:Apr79-332
Audel, S. - see Poulenc, F.
Audemars, P. Slay Me a Sinner.
  N. Callendar, 441:4May80-24
Auden, W.H. W.H. Auden Selected Poems.
(E. Mendelson, ed)
  E. Longley, 617(TLS):18Jan80-64
Auden, W.H. The English Auden.* (E.
Mendelson, ed)
  M. Alexander, 184(EIC):Apr79-198
  B. Hardy, 175:Summer79-185
"Audio-Visual Materials on Drama 1978."
(2nd ed)
  K. Worth, 611(TN):Vol133#3-140
Audoubert, N. Dussane ou la servante de
Molière.
  C. Saint-Léon, 207(FR):Apr79-806

von Aue, H. - see under Hartmann von Aue

Auel, J.M. The Clan of the Cave Bear.
   P. Kemp, 362:30Oct80-588
   J. Pfeiffer, 441:31Aug80-7

Auer, A. Erleben — Erfahren — Schreiben.
   M. Krumrey, 654(WB):9/1978-179

Auerbach, N. Communities of Women.*
   J. Grumman, 395(MFS):Winter78/79-665
   E. Showalter, 141:Spring79-172
   M. Vicinus, 445(NCF):Dec78-387

Augello, G. Studi Apuleiani.
   J. André, 555:Vol52fasc2-398
   K. Dowden, 123:Vol29No1-154

Augst, G. Zum Pluralsystem.
   G. Augst, 686(ZGL):Band7Heft2-220

Augst, G., A. Bauer and A. Stein. Grund-
wortschatz und Ideolekt.
   E.H. Yarrill, 182:Vol31#9/10-286

Augstein, R. Jesus Son of Man.
   J. Carmichael, 390:Apr79-56

August, E. John Stuart Mill.*
   J. Weissman, 637(VS):Winter78-275

Aujac, G. - see Dionysius of Halicarnassus

Aujac, G. - see Geminus

Auletta, K. Hard Feelings.
   B. Kuttner, 441:10Aug80-11

Aulotte, R. Montaigne: Apologie de
Raimond Sebond.
   P.J. Hendrick, 208(FS):Oct79-438

Aune, B. Kant's Theory of Morals.
   R.C.S. Walker, 617(TLS):2May80-506

Aune, B. Reason and Action.
   M. Cohen, 518:Jan79-19
   J.M. Fischer, 482(PhR):Jul79-453
   R.D. Parry, 484(PPR):Sep79-145
   J. Watling, 393(Mind):Oct79-617

Aurelius Victor, S. Livre des Césars. (P.
Dufraigne, ed and trans)
   W. den Boer, 394:Vol30fasc3-333
   R.P.H. Green, 313:Vol69-225

Aurthur, J. Socialism in the Soviet Union.
   V. Bunce, 550(RusR):Apr79-244

Austen-Leigh, J. Stephanie.
   R. Schieder, 99:Jun-Jul80-44

Austin, J.C. American Humor in France.
   R.J. Niess, 27(AL):Jan80-586

Austin, J.H. Chase, Chance and Creativity.
   639(VQR):Summer78-106

Austin, M.M. and P. Vidal-Naquet. Eco-
nomic and Social History of Ancient
Greece.*
   N.R.E. Fisher, 123:Vol29No2-264

Austin, R.G. - see Vergil

Autpertus, A. Opera. (Pt 1) (R. Weber,
ed)
   E.A. Matter, 589:Apr79-331

Auty, R. and J.L.I. Fennell - see "Oxford
Slavonic Papers"

Auty, R., J.L.I. Fennell and I.P. Foote -
see "Oxford Slavonic Papers"

Auty, R. and D. Obolensky, eds. An Introduction to Russian History.
   R. Pipes, 550(RusR):Jan79-80

Auty, R. and D. Obolensky, eds. An Introduction to Russian Language and Litera-

[continued]

[continuing]
ture.*
   P. Carden, 104(CASS):Fall78-418
   M.K. Frank, 399(MLJ):Apr79-232
   A. McMillin, 402(MLR):Jan79-253

Auty, S.G. The Comic Spirit of Eighteenth-
Century Novels.
   L. Hartley, 402(MLR):Jul79-661

Avalle-Arce, J.B. Don Quijote como forma
de vida.*
   F. Pierce, 86(BHS):Apr79-153

de Avellaneda, G.G. - see under Gómez de
Avellaneda, G.

Avellini, L. - see Dossi, C.

Avenary, H. The Ashkenazi Tradition of
Biblical Chant Between 1500 and 1900.
   I. Ross, 187:May80-290

Averoff-Tossizza, E. By Fire and Axe.
   C.M. Woodhouse, 396(ModA):Spring79-217

Averroes. Averroes' Three Short Commentaries on Aristotle's "Topics," "Rhetoric," and "Poetics." (C.E. Butterworth,
ed and trans)
   K.V. and M.T. Erickson, 583:Winter79-
   204

Avery, D. Dangerous Foreigners.
   P. Craven, 99:Feb80-38

Avery, G. The Lost Railway.
   S. Clayton, 617(TLS):28Mar80-345
   J. Mellors, 362:20Mar80-382

Avery, L.G. - see Anderson, M.

Avery, S.P. The Diaries 1871-1882.
   W. Mostyn-Owen, 617(TLS):28Mar80-348

Avicenna. Liber de philosophia prima sive
scientia divina, I-IV. (S. Van Riet, ed
and trans)
   J-F. Courtine, 192(EP):Oct-Dec79-497

"Avimāraka (Love's Enchanted World)."
(J.L. Masson and D.D. Kosambi, trans)
   W.H. Maurer, 318(JAOS):Oct-Dec78-545

Avineri, S., ed. Varieties of Marxism.
   D.X.B., 543:Sep78-125

Avotins, I. and M.M. An Index to the
"Lives of the Sophists" of Philostratos.
   R.J. Penella, 124:Feb80-313

Avril, F. Manuscript Painting at the
Court of France: The Fourteenth Century
(1310-1380).
   J. Masheck, 62:Dec78-60

Avtorkhanov, A. Zagadka smerti Stalina
(Zagovor Beriia).
   T.J. Uldricks, 550(RusR):Apr79-237

Awoonor, K. The House by the Sea.
   J. Povey, 2(AfrA):Feb79-86

Axelos, C. Die ontologischen Grundlagen
der Freiheitstheorie von Leibniz.
   A. Doz, 192(EP):Oct-Dec79-453

Axelos, K. Alienation, Praxis, and Techné
in the Thought of Karl Marx.
   J.E. Hansen, 484(PPR):Mar80-453

Axelos, K. Contribution à la logique.
   M. Adam, 542:Jan-Mar79-107
   A. Jacob, 542:Apr-Jun78-217
   R. Sasso, 192(EP):Apr-Jun79-237

Axelrad, A.M. History and Utopia.
  J.F. Beard, 591(SIR):Fall79-479
  K.S. House, 27(AL):Mar79-113
  R.C. Poulsen, 649(WAL):Spring79-84
Axelrod, C.D. Studies in Intellectual
  Breakthrough.
  S.J. Antosik, 222(GR):Fall79-169
Axelrod, S.G. Robert Lowell.*
  B. Duffey, 27(AL):Nov79-435
  R.A. Johnson, 432(NEQ):Dec79-564
  G. McFadden, 659(ConL):Spring80-297
  R. Tillinghast, 569(SR):Spring79-xxxix
  639(VQR):Summer79-105
Axinn, D. Sliding Down the Wind.
  R. De Mott, 651(WHR):Spring79-173
Axionov, V. Recherche d'un genre.
  J. Blot, 450(NRF):Aug79-144
Axline, W.A. Caribbean Integration.
  R.M. Spector, 263(RIB):Vol29No3/4-352
Axmadulina, B. Sveča. Metel'. Sny o
  Gruzii.
  Z. Dolgopolova, 558(RLJ):Winter79-236
Axmatova, A. - see under Akhmatova, A.
Axton, M. and R. Williams, eds. English
  Drama.*
  D. Cole, 405(MP):May80-453
  E.A.M. Colman, 67:Nov79-320
  R. Gill, 184(EIC):Jan79-96
  R. Soellner, 130:Summer79-168
  P. Walls, 410(M&L):Apr79-211
de Ayala, P.L. - see under López de Ayala,
  P.
Ayer, A.J. Les Grands domaines de la
  philosophie.
  J. Largeault, 154:Sep78-556
Ayer, A.J. Hume.
  C.H. Sisson, 617(TLS):9May80-531
Ayer, A.J. Part of My Life.*
  639(VQR):Spring78-48
Aylen, L. Return to Zululand.
  D. Davis, 362:5Jun80-729
Ayling, R. Continuity and Innovation in
  Sean O'Casey's Drama.*
  N. Grene, 677(YES):Vol9-344
Ayling, R. and M.J. Durkan. Sean O'Casey,
  a Bibliography.
  S. Sweeney, 305(JIL):Sep78-172
el-Ayouty, Y., ed. The Organization of
  African Unity after Ten Years.
  J. Vanderlinden, 69:Vol148#1-88
Ayres, P.J. Tourneur: "The Revenger's
  Tragedy."
  L.W. Conolly, 447(N&Q):Feb78-79
  R.A. Foakes, 677(YES):Vol9-331
Azad, M.A.K. Khutbat-i-Azad.
  K.A. Farugi, 273(IC):Jan76-49
Azaretti, E. L'evoluzione dei dialetti
  liguri esaminata attraverso la gramma-
  tica storica del Ventimigliese.
  R. Arveiller, 553(RLiR):Jan-Jun78-209
Azéma, J-P. De Munich a la Libération
  1938-1944.
  D. Johnson, 617(TLS):4Jan80-15
Azevedo, M.M. and K.K. McMahon. Lecturas
  periodísticas.
  J.E. McKinney, 238:Dec79-744
Aziz, M. - see James, H.

Aziza, C. Tertullien et le Judaïsme.
  T. Rajak, 313:Vol69-192
Aznavour, C. Yesterday When I Was Young.
  E. Cameron, 364:Dec79/Jan80-121
Azouvi, F. - see de Villers, C.

Baader, R. Wider den Zufall der Geburt.
  H-G. Funke, 547(RF):Band91Heft1/2-185
  S. Harvey, 208(FS):Vol133Pt2-726
  J. von Stackelberg, 535(RHL):Sep-Oct78-
  828
Baar, A. - see Afanasjew, A.N.
Baar, J. The Great Free Enterprise Gambit.
  M. Malone, 441:15Jun80-15
Babcock, B.A., ed. The Reversible World.
  D. Pocock, 89(BJA):Spring79-177
Babinger, F. Mehmed the Conqueror and his
  Time. (W.C. Hickman, ed)
  K.A. Nizami, 273(IC):Oct78-273
Babris, P.J. Silent Churches.
  R.S. Haugh, 550(RusR):Jul79-384
Babson, M. Dangerous to Know.
  T.J. Binyon, 617(TLS):18Jul80-823
Babson, M. Murder, Murder Little Star.
  N. Callendar, 441:30Mar80-17
Bacall, L. Lauren Bacall by Myself.*
  B. Weeks, 18:Mar79-73
Bach, C.P.E. Essay on the True Art of
  Playing Keyboard Instruments. (W.J.
  Mitchell, ed and trans)
  A.F.L.T., 412:Feb78-69
Bach, K.F. and G. Price. Romance Linguis-
  tics and the Romance Languages.
  K.J. Hollyman, 67:Nov79-348
  W. Rothwell, 208(FS):Oct79-494
  H.C. Woodbridge, 399(MLJ):Sep-Oct79-
  302
Bachelard, G. I segmenti della ragione.
  E. Namer, 542:Apr-Jun78-184
Bachem Alent, R.M. The Companion to For-
  eign Language Composition. (Vol 1)
  C. Pagnoulle, 556(RLV):1978/5-459
Bachmann, E., ed. Romantik in Böhmen.
  T. Müller, 471:Oct/Nov/Dec79-408
Bachmann, H. Joseph Maria Baernreither
  (1845-1925).
  H.J. Gordon, Jr. and N.M. Gordon,
  182:Vol131#11/12-377
Bachrach, B.S. Early Medieval Jewish
  Policy in Western Europe.
  G.I. Langmuir, 589:Jan79-104
  C. Wickham, 382(MAE):1979/1-153
Bachtin, M. Semiotica Teoria della Let-
  teratura e Marxismo. (A. Ponzio, ed)
  E. Namer, 542:Apr-Jun79-264
Bacigalupo, M. The Forméd Trace.
  A.D. Moody, 617(TLS):15Aug80-917
Bäcker, N. Probleme des inneren Lehnguts
  dargestellt an den Anglizismen der fran-
  zösischen Sportsprache.
  P. Pupier, 545(RPh):May79-483
Backstrom, P. Christian Socialism and Co-
  operation in Victorian England.
  H. McLeod, 637(VS):Winter78-245
Bacon, M.H. Valiant Friend.
  D. Grumbach, 441:29Jun80-15

Bacquet, P. L'étymologie anglaise.*
   C. Peeters, 556(RLV):1978/2-172
Bacquet, P. Les pièces historiques de
   Shakespeare. (Vol 1)
   H.W. Donner, 597(SN):Vol50#2-330
Bader, A. and L. Navratil. Zwischen Wahn
   und Wirklichkeit.
   E. Eng, 127:Spring79-222
Badgley, R.F., D.F. Caron and M.G. Powell.
   Report of the Committee on the Operation
   of the Abortion Law.
   S.R. Isbister, 529(QQ):Spring79-127
Badian, E. - see Syme, R.
Badiou, A. Le concept de modèle.
   Y. Gauthier, 98:Jan78-3
Badir, M.G. Voltaire et l'Islam.
   J.H. Brumfitt, 208(FS):Vol33Pt2-736
Baehr, R. - see Chrétien de Troyes
Baetke, W. Wörterbuch zur altnordischen
   Prosaliteratur. (2nd ed)
   N. Wagner, 684(ZDA):Band107Heft2-52
Baglow, J. Emergency Measures.
   A. Amprimoz, 102(CanL):Spring79-72
Bagnall, R.S. The Florida Ostraka (O.
   Florida).
   J.F. Gilliam, 24:Summer79-339
   J.C. Mann, 313:Vol69-223
Bagnold, E. A Matter of Gravity.
   J. Coleby, 157:Winter79-86
Baguley, D. Bibliographie de la critique
   sur Émile Zola, 1864-1970.*
   C. Becker, 535(RHL):Sep-Oct79-868
Bahm, A. Comparative Philosophy.
   S. Merrill, 125:Fall78-156
Bahm, A.J. The Specialist.
   P. Dubois, 542:Apr-Jun79-226
Bahr, D.M. Pima and Papago Ritual Oratory.
   J.H. Hill, 269(IJAL):Jan78-80
Bähr, H.W. - see Spranger, E.
Baier, W. Untersuchungen zu den Passions-
   betrachtungen in der "Vita Christi" des
   Ludolf von Sachsen.
   E. Colledge, 589:Jul79-543
de Baïf, J-A. Le Premier Livre des poèmes.
   (G. Demerson, ed)
   M. Quainton, 208(FS):Vol33Pt2-636
Baigell, M. Dictionary of American Art.
   E. Lucie-Smith, 617(TLS):21Mar80-308
Bail, M. Homesickness.
   P. Lewis, 617(TLS):19Sep80-1044
   J. Naughton, 362:4Sep80-313
Bailbé, J-M. Nerval.
   P.J. Edwards, 446(NCFS):Fall-Winter
   78/79-131
Bailbé, J-M. - see Janin, J.
Bailes, K.E. Technology and Society under
   Lenin and Stalin.
   A. Brown, 617(TLS):25Jan80-95
   P.H. Solomon, Jr., 550(RusR):Jul79-371
Bailey, A. Acts of Union.
   R. Eder, 441:26Jul80-15
   T. Flanagan, 441:1Jun80-11
   61:Jul80-84
Bailey, A. Rembrandt's House.
   K. Roberts, 90:Feb79-124
Bailey, D. Mrs. David Bailey.
   C. James, 453(NYRB):18Dec80-22

Bailey, D. The Sorry Papers.
   A.S. Brennan, 198:Summer80-139
Bailey, D.M. Catalogue of Lamps in the
   British Museum. (Vol 2)
   H. Plommer, 617(TLS):21Mar80-338
Bailey, D.R.S. - see under Shackleton
   Bailey, D.R.
Bailey, P. Old Soldiers.
   P. Lewis, 617(TLS):29Feb80-228
   J. Naughton, 362:6Mar80-318
Bailey, R.N. Viking Age Sculpture in
   Northern England.
   J. Graham-Campbell, 617(TLS):7Mar80-
   262
Bailey, R.W., L. Matejka and P. Steiner,
   eds. The Sign.
   M.C. Beardsley, 290(JAAC):Spring80-337
Bailey, T.A. The Pugnacious Presidents.
   T.E. Cronin, 441:19Oct80-7
Bailyn, B. and J.B. Hench, eds. The
   Press and the American Revolution.
   P. Marshall, 617(TLS):1Aug80-869
Bain, D. Actors and Audience.*
   K.J. Dover, 447(N&Q):Apr78-162
   O. Taplin, 303(JoHS):Vol199-187
Bain, I. - see Bewick, T.
Bainbridge, B. Another Part of the Wood.*
   P. Beer, 617(TLS):29Feb80-246
   A. Broyard, 441:5Mar80-C26
   J. O'Faolain, 441:13Apr80-14
   J. Symons, 453(NYRB):17Jul80-39
Bainbridge, B. Winter Garden.
   P. Conrad, 362:20Nov80-699
Bainbridge, B. Young Adolf.*
   J. Chernaik, 364:Apr/May79-140
   J.S. Conway, 529(QQ):Autumn79-510
   C. Sparks, 42(AR):Fall79-504
Baines, J. Mandelstam: The Later Poetry.*
   L. Dienes, 558(RLJ):Fall79-225
   A. Pyman, 161(DUJ):Dec78-144
   639(VQR):Spring78-56
Bainton, A.J.C., comp. "Comedias sueltas"
   in Cambridge University Library.
   K. and R. Reichenberger, 304(JHP):
   Autumn79-92
Bair, D. Samuel Beckett.*
   R. Cohn, 397(MD):Sep79-315
   D. Hayman, 219(GaR):Spring79-221
   J.W. Lambert, 157:Spring79-78
   R. Morton, 529(QQ):Autumn79-515
   J. Pilling, 184(EIC):Jul79-279
   295(JML):Vol7#4-660
Bairati, E. and others. La Belle Epoque.
   B.M-P. Leefmans, 55:Nov79-30
Baird, L.Y. A Bibliography of Chaucer,
   1964-1973.
   D. Mehl, 72:Band216Heft1-168
Bakcsi, G. Forradalmak, háborúk, iroda-
   lom.
   L. Dienes, 574(SEEJ):Summer79-287
Baker, D.C. and J.L. Murphy, eds. The
   Digby Plays.
   D. Bevington, 677(YES):Vol9-295
Baker, D.V., ed. Cornish Short Stories.
   A. Varley, 161(DUJ):Jun79-292
Baker, D.V. Karenza.
   D.M. Thomas, 617(TLS):1Aug80-868

17

Baker, D.V., ed. Women Writing: 3.
   J. Uglow, 617(TLS):28Mar80-368
Baker, H. Persephone's Cave.
   S. Pembroke, 617(TLS):11Jan80-43
   C.G. Starr, 385(MQR):Winter80-132
Baker, H.A., Jr. The Journey Back.
   S. Mitchell, 617(TLS):30May80-626
Baker, H.A., Jr. A Many Colored Coat of
   Dreams.
   R. Hemenway, 582(SFQ):Vol41-286
Baker, J. and E.W. Nicholson - see Kimḥi,
   D.
Baker, J.H. Ambivalent Americans.
   639(VQR):Winter78-8
Baker, J.H. and M.E. Hoffman - see "Minor
   White: Rites and Passages"
Baker, J.P. and M.C. Soroka, eds. Library
   Conservation.
   C.C. Morrow, 14:Jul79-354
Baker, K.M. Condorcet.*
   R. Grimsley, 208(FS):Vol33Pt2-783
   J. Mayer, 535(RHL):Mar-Apr78-313
Baker, M. The Doyle Diary.
   V. Powell, 39:Jan79-73
Baker, M. The Rise of the Victorian
   Actor.*
   M.R. Booth, 611(TN):Vol33#1-43
Baker, N.C. Babyselling.
   639(VQR):Winter79-27
Baker, P. Kreol.
   A. Valdman, 545(RPh):Aug78-65
Baker, P.R. Richard Morris Hunt.
   P. Goldberger, 441:30Nov80-12
Baker, R. and F. Elliston, eds. Philoso-
   phy and Sex.
   J. Trebilcot, 449:Mar79-91
Baker, R.E., ed. Teaching for Tomorrow in
   the Foreign Language Classroom.
   G.A. Olivier, Jr., 399(MJL):Apr79-225
Baker, R.K. Introduction to Library
   Research in French Literature.
   C.O. Cook, 365:Spring80-101
   S. Haig, 207(FR):Dec78-360
Baker, W. - see Eliot, G.
Bakere, J.A. The Cornish Ordinalia.
   T. Tiller, 617(TLS):1Aug80-880
Bakhtine, M. Esthétique et théorie du
   roman.
   P. Dulac, 450(NRF):Apr79-121
Bakker, B.H. - see Zola, É.
Bakunin, M. The Confession of Mikhail
   Bakunin, with the Marginal Comments of
   Tsar Nicholas I. (L.D. Orton, ed)
   H.E. Bowman, 104(CASS):Fall78-428
   A. Kelly, 575(SEER):Jan79-130
Balakian, A. The Symbolist Movement.
   (2nd ed)
   D. Festa-McCormick, 399(MLJ):Jan-Feb79-
   53
   U. Weisstein, 107(CRCL):Fall79-450
Balanchine, G. and F. Mason. Balanchine's
   Complete Stories of the Great Ballets.
   (rev)
   D. Vaughan, 151:Aug78-104
Balasubramanian, R. Advaita Vedānta.
   B. Gupta, 485(PE&W):Apr79-247

Balayé, S. Madame de Staël, lumières et
   liberté.
   A. Fairlie, 208(FS):Oct79-455
Balcer, J.M. The Athenian Regulations
   for Chalkis.
   L.R.F. Germain, 182:Vol31#11/12-370
Balcou, J. Fréron contre les philosophes.*
   J.H. Brumfitt, 208(FS):Vol33Pt2-785
   C. Lauriol, 535(RHL):May-Jun78-483
Baldassare, M. Residential Crowding in
   Urban America.
   J. Potter, 617(TLS):25Jan80-93
Baldassari, M. - see Plutarch
Baldi, P. and R.N. Werth, eds. Readings
   in Historical Phonology.
   K. Chang, 350:Sep79-739
Baldinger, K. Dictionnaire onomasiolo-
   gique de l'ancien occitan.* (fasc 1)
   Dictionnaire onomasiologique de l'ancien
   gascon.* (fasc 1)
   A. Bollée, 547(RF):Band91Heft4-449
Baldinger, K., ed. Festschrift Walther
   von Wartburg zum 80. Geburtstag.
   H.J. Wolf, 72:Band216Heft2-455
Baldridge, M.H. the loneliness of the
   poet/housewife.
   D. Barbour, 150(DR):Spring79-154
Balducci, C. A Self-Made Woman.
   A.M. Gisolfi, 276:Autumn79-305
Baldwin, B. Studies in Aulus Gellius.*
   P.K. Marshall, 122:Apr79-173
Baldwin, D.E. and C.M. The Yoruba of
   Southwestern Nigeria.
   J.D.Y. Peel, 69:Vol148#3-314
Baldwin, J. Just Above My Head.*
   J. Mellors, 362:3Jan80-30
Baldwin, M. The Gamecock.
   H. Eley, 617(TLS):9May80-537
Balibar, E. and others. Sur la dialec-
   tique.
   J-M. Gabaude, 542:Jul-Sep78-372
"Balkanistica." (Vol 3) (K.E. Naylor, ed)
   J.M. Foley, 574(SEEJ):Fall79-422
Ball, G. - see Ginsberg, A.
Ball, P.M. The Heart's Events.*
   P. Honan, 447(N&Q):Jun78-270
Ballard, E.G. Man and Technology.
   M.E. Zimmerman, 258:Sep79-368
Ballard, J.G. The Unlimited Dream Com-
   pany.*
   W. Boyd, 364:Feb80-89
Ballester, G.T. - see under Torrente
   Ballester, G.
Ballhatchet, K. Race, Sex and Class under
   the Raj.
   P. Mason, 617(TLS):8Feb80-139
Balmary, M. L'Homme aux statues.
   J. Le Hardi, 450(NRF):Jul79-118
Baloyra, E.A. and J.D. Martz. Political
   Attitudes in Venezuela.
   G. Hoskin, 263(RIB):Vol29No3/4-353
Baltaxe, C.A.M. Foundations of Distinc-
   tive Feature Theory.
   W.G. Franklin, 583:Summer79-433
   A.H. Sommerstein, 297(JL):Sep79-379

18

Baltes, M. Timaios Lokros über die Natur des Kosmos und der Seele.
D.O., 543:Dec78-350
Baltes, M. Die Weltentstehung des platonischen Timaios nach den antiken Interpreten. (Pt 1)
G.B. Kerferd, 123:Vol29No2-316
J. Whittaker, 303(JoHS):Vol99-191
Baltzell, E.D. Puritan Boston and Quaker Philadelphia.
L.A. Coser, 676(YR):Summer80-583
A. Hacker, 441:9Mar80-7
de Balzac, H. La Comédie Humaine. (Vols 1-4) (P-G. Castex, ed)
M. Milner, 535(RHL):Jan-Feb78-92
de Balzac, H. La Comédie Humaine.* (Vols 5 and 6) (P-G. Castex, with others, eds)
M. Milner, 535(RHL):Jul-Aug79-681
de Balzac, H. La Comédie Humaine. (Vol 7) (P-G. Castex, with others, eds)
D. Adamson, 208(FS):Jan79-91
de Balzac, H. La Comédie Humaine. (Vol 8) (P-G. Castex, ed)
D. Adamson, 208(FS):Apr79-210
de Balzac, H. Illusions perdues.* (J-C. Lieber, ed)
C. Smethurst, 208(FS):Vol33Pt2-811
205(FMLS):Jul78-283
de Balzac, H. Splendeurs et misères des courtisanes. (D. Oster, ed)
C. Smethurst, 208(FS):Vol33Pt2-811
Bambara, T.C. The Salt Eaters.
S. Lardner, 442(NY):5May80-169
J. Leonard, 441:4Apr80-C23
J. Wideman, 441:1Jun80-14
Bambeck, M. Göttliche Komödie und Exegese.*
J.P. Holoka, 546(RR):Nov79-409
Ban, S-W. Das Verhältnis der Ästhetik Georg Lukács' zur deutschen Klassik und zu Thomas Mann.
D.H. Miles, 221(GQ):Jan79-141
Bancquart, M-C. Images littéraires de Paris "fin-de-siècle."
E. Weber, 617(TLS):22Feb80-203
Bander, R.G. From Sentence to Paragraph.
D. Cone, 608:Dec80-516
Bandhu, V. Vedic Textuo-Linguistic Studies.
L. Rocher, 318(JAOS):Jul-Sep78-326
Bandy, W.T. - see Baudelaire, C.
Bandy, W.T. - see Poe, E.A.
Banerjee, J. India in Soviet Global Strategy.
S.K. Gupta, 550(RusR):Apr79-255
Banerji, S.C. Aspects of Ancient Indian Life from Sanskrit Sources.
L. Sternbach, 318(JAOS):Oct-Dec78-560
Bankier, J. and others, eds. The Other Voice.*
J.P. Stanley, 502(PrS):Fall78-298
Banks, A., ed. First-Person America.
S. Kauffmann, 441:28Dec80-5
Banks, C. The Darkroom.
N. Callendar, 441:20Jul80-16
Banks, G.V. Camus: "L'Étranger."*
E. Zants, 395(MFS):Winter78/79-625

Banks, L.R. Dark Quartet.
J.B., 189(EA):Jul-Dec78-426
Banks, O. The Rembrandt Panel.
N. Callendar, 441:28Sep80-20
442(NY):4Aug80-91
Banks, R. The Book of Jamaica.
D. Pinckney, 441:1Jun80-15
442(NY):19May80-158
Bannach, K. Die Lehre von der doppelten Macht Gottes bei Wilhelm von Ockham.
R. Haubst, 182:Vol131#5/6-134
Banner, L.W. Elizabeth Cady Stanton.
C. Seebohm, 441:20Jan80-16
Banning, L. The Jeffersonian Persuasion.*
639(VQR):Winter79-14
Banó, I. and L. Fülöp, eds. Egy néprajztudós műhelyéből.
A. Scheiber, 196:Band19Heft3/4-312
Bänsch, D., ed. Zur Modernität der Romantik.
A. Antler, 221(GQ):Jan79-115
C.G. Grawe, 67:May79-159
Banta, M. Failure and Success in America.*
N. Baym, 301(JEGP):Oct79-584
Bantock, G. Dragons.
D. Sealy, 617(TLS):22Feb80-214
Bar-Zohar, M. The Deadly Document.
N. Callendar, 441:20Jan80-26
Barakat, H. Lebanon in Strife.
639(VQR):Summer78-106
Barakat, R.A. The Cistercian Sign Language.
W.C. Stokoe, 567:Vol124#1/2-181
Baran, H., ed and trans. Semiotics and Structuralism.*
D.H. Hirsch, 569(SR):Fall79-628
K. Silverman, 567:Vol125#3/4-257
Baranoff, N., comp. Bibliographie des études sur Léon Chestov.*
D.M. Fiene, 399(MLJ):Apr79-213
Barasch, M. Gestures of Despair in Medieval and Early Renaissance Art.*
R. Mellinkoff, 589:Apr79-333
Barasch, M. Light and Color in the Italian Renaissance Theory of Art.
J. Goldberg, 290(JAAC):Fall79-105
Barba, V. Sade.
E. Namer, 542:Apr-Jun79-226
Barbé-Coquelin de Lisle, G. El Tratado de Arquitectura de Alonso de Vandelvira.
F. Marías, 48:Apr-Jun78-187
Barbeau, M. Le Rossignol y Chante.
J. Guilbault, 187:May80-313
Barber, C. Early Modern English.
M. Görlach, 38:Band96Heft1/2-174
Barber, J.D. The Pulse of Politics.
G. Hodgson, 441:11May80-7
Barber, R. Edward, Prince of Wales and Aquitaine.
639(VQR):Spring79-70
Barbéris, P. Chateaubriand, une réaction au monde moderne.*
G.R. Besser, 446(NCFS):Fall-Winter 78/79-127
D. Rincé, 535(RHL):Jan-Feb78-137

Barbéris, P. A la recherche d'un écriture: Chateaubriand.*
  D. Rincé, 535(RHL):Sep-Oct78-837
Barbey d'Aurevilly, J. Amaïdée. (J. Greene, A. Hirschi and J. Petit, eds)
  P. Berthier, 535(RHL):Sep-Oct78-851
Barbier, C.P., ed. Colloque Mallarmé (Glasgow, novembre 1973) en l'honneur de Austin Gill.*
  L. Forani-Wills, 207(FR):Oct78-169
Barbier, C.P. Documents Stéphane Mallarmé. (Vol 5)
  L. Forani-Wills, 207(FR):Oct78-169
Barbier, C.P., with L.A. Joseph - see Mallarmé, S.
"Herculine Barbin: Being the Recently Discovered Memoirs of a Nineteenth-Century French Hermaphrodite."
  F. Brown, 453(NYRB):9Oct80-8
Barbour, B.A. Private Recipes from Private Clubs.
  W. and C. Cowen, 639(VQR):Autumn79-156
Barbour, D. Visions of My Grandfather.
  B. Whiteman, 168(ECW):Spring78-57
Barbour, R.W. and W.H. Davis. Bats of America.
  P.A. Zahl, 31(ASch):Summer80-410
Barchilon, J. Le Conte merveilleux français de 1690 à 1790.
  R.R. Hubert, 207(FR):Oct78-162
Barclay Fox, R. Barclay Fox's Journal.* (R.L. Brett, ed)
  E.J. Hobsbawm, 453(NYRB):3Apr80-35
Bare, J.S. Phonetics and Phonology in Pāṇini.
  R. Rocher, 318(JAOS):Jul-Sep78-329
Bareham, T. George Crabbe.
  R.B. Hatch, 661(WC):Summer79-311
  S.D. Lavine, 173(ECS):Winter78/79-225
Bareiss, O. and F. Ohloff. Ingeborg Bachmann.
  R. Pichl, 602:Vol10-248
Barfoot, J. Gaining Ground.
  P. Craig, 617(TLS):18Apr80-450
Barich, B. Laughing in the Hills.
  J. Flaherty, 441:15Jun80-7
  C. Lehmann-Haupt, 441:16Jun80-C16
Barile, L. Bibliografia montaliana.
  E. Saccone, 400(MLN):Jan79-183
Barion, J. Philosophie.
  J-M. Gabaude, 542:Apr-Jun78-239
Barker, F. Solzhenitsyn.
  D. Pike, 550(RusR):Jan79-128
Barker, F.G. - see under Granville Barker, F.
Barker, G. Villa Stellar.*
  F. Grubb, 364:Oct79-82
  L. Sail, 493:Mar80-71
Barker, J. Fourth at Junction.
  N. Callendar, 441:15Jun80-17
Barker, J. Strange Contrarieties.
  J.H. Broome, 208(FS):Vol33Pt2-685
Barker, N. The Oxford University Press and the Spread of Learning 1478-1978.
  P.C. Bayley, 569(SR):Winter79-191
  W. Kellaway, 325:Apr79-161
  J.C. Olin, 613:Mar79-94

Barker, N. - see Munby, A.N.L.
Barker, S. On the Rocks.*
  A. Cluysenaar, 565:Vol20#3-68
Barkóczi, L. and A. Mócsy, eds. Die römischen Inschriften Ungarns. (Pts 1 and 2)
  J.J. Wilkes, 313:Vol69-206
Barksdale, R.K. Langston Hughes.
  R.A. Carroll, 95(CLAJ):Dec78-173
Barling, T. Goodbye Piccadilly.
  M. Laski, 362:14Aug80-216
Barling, T.J. - see Palissot de Montenoy, C.
Barloy, J.J. Man and Animal.
  42(AR):Winter79-123
Barltrop, R. Jack London.
  C. Cass, 141:Summer79-286
  639(VQR):Winter78-25
Barnabas, A.P. Population Control in India.
  G.B. Simmons, 293(JASt):Aug79-814
Barnard, C.K. Sylvia Plath.
  M. Perloff, 651(WHR):Autumn79-365
Barnard, E. English for Everybody.
  D. Bush, 31(ASch):Summer80-420
Barnard, M. Collected Poems.
  V. Trueblood, 29:Nov/Dec80-9
Barnard, R. Death in a Cold Climate.
  T.J. Binyon, 617(TLS):18Apr80-450
Barnard, R. A Talent to Deceive.
  E. Auchincloss, 441:20Jul80-14
Barner, W. and others. Lessing.
  H.B. Garland, 220(GL&L):Oct78-69
Barnes, C. - see Pasternak, B.
Barnes, C.J., ed. Studies in Twentieth-Century Russian Literature.*
  M.H. Shotton, 447(N&Q):Dec78-572
Barnes, D. Le Bois de la nuit.
  G. Quinsat, 450(NRF):May79-134
Barnes, D. Selected Works of Djuna Barnes.
  W. Boyd, 617(TLS):12Sep80-984
  A. Broyard, 441:28Jun80-19
Barnes, J. Ahead of His Age.*
  T. Fitton, 617(TLS):28Mar80-372
Barnes, J. Metroland.
  P. Bailey, 617(TLS):28Mar80-345
  J. Naughton, 362:27Mar80-419
Barnes, J. The Presocratic Philosophers.
  D.W. Hamlyn, 617(TLS):4Jan80-19
  483:Apr79-267
Barnes, J. - see Aristotle
Barnes, J. and D. Nicholson - see Amery, L.
Barnes, J., M. Schofield and R. Sorabji, eds. Articles on Aristotle.* (Vol 1)
  J. Longrigg, 123:Vol29No1-164
Barnes, J.A. The Ethics of Inquiry in Social Science.
  V. Pratt, 518:May79-72
Barnes, M. Draumkvaede.*
  P. Gronow, 187:May80-291
Barnes, T.D. The Sources of the "Historia Augusta."
  R.P.H. Green, 313:Vol69-225
  R.M. Ogilvie, 123:Vol29No2-329
Barnet, R.J. The Giants.
  639(VQR):Summer78-105

Barnet, R.J. The Lean Years.
R.O. Keohane, 453(NYRB):6Nov80-44
R. Lekachman, 441:8Jun80-13
61:Jun80-92
Barnett, A.D. China and the Major Powers in Asia.
639(VQR):Summer78-105
Barnett, C. Bonaparte.*
639(VQR):Spring79-69
Barnett, G.A. Denis Johnston.
R.H., 305(JIL):Sep78-168
Barnett, G.L. Charles Lamb.
W. Buck, 661(WC):Summer79-271
Barnett, J. Palmprint.
T.J. Binyon, 617(TLS):6Jun80-654
M. Laski, 362:14Aug80-216
Barnett, M. La Bataille Loquifer.*
W.G. van Emden, 208(FS):Vol33Pt2-521
Barney, S.A., with E. Wertheimer and D. Stevens. Word-Hoard.*
A. Crépin, 189(EA):Jul-Dec78-374
M. Görlach, 38:Band96Heft3/4-465
Barnum, P.H., ed. Dives and Pauper.
O. Arngart, 179(ES):Jun79-319
J.M. Cowen, 447(N&Q):Apr78-170
Barnwell, H.T. and others, eds. The Classical Tradition in French Literature.
I.W. Alexander, 402(MLR):Apr79-445
A.C. Keys, 67:Nov79-342
205(FMLS):Apr78-184
Maharaja of Baroda. The Palaces of India.
P. Goldberger, 441:30Nov80-68
Baroin, J. Simon de Pouille.
B. Guidot, 547(RF):Band91Heft4-458
Barolsky, P. Infinite Jest.*
C. Gould, 39:Aug79-156
G. Martin, 617(TLS):1Feb80-120
D. Rosand, 55:Nov79-27
Baron, F., ed. Joachim Camerarius (1500-1574).
F.L. Borchardt, 221(GQ):May79-401
Baron, F. Doctor Faustus.
F.L. Borchardt, 221(GQ):May79-401
Baron, N.S. Language Acquisition and Historical Change.
G. Branigan, 350:Sep79-721
Baron, W. The Camden Town Group.
R. Shone, 90:Oct79-662
F. Spalding, 617(TLS):2May80-506
Barone, M., G. Ujifusa and D. Matthews. The Almanac of American Politics 1980.
J. Herbers, 441:13Apr80-12
Baronio, J. 42nd Street Studio.
C. James, 453(NYRB):18Dec80-22
Barooshian, V.D. Brik and Mayakovsky.
H. Baran, 550(RusR):Jul79-401
C.A. Johnson, 617(TLS):8Aug80-903
H. Muchnic, 453(NYRB):29May80-36
Barr, A.P. Victorian Stage Pulpiteer.
A. Easson, 447(N&Q):Dec78-567
Barr, P. The Memsahibs.
A.J. Greenberger, 637(VS):Spring79-363
Barraclough, C. - see "The Times Atlas of World History"
Barrault, J-L. Comme je le pense.
D. Knowles, 208(FS):Vol33Pt2-928

Barreda, P. The Black Protagonist in the Cuban Novel.
I.A. Schulman, 263(RIB):Vol129No3/4-355
Barrera-Vidal, A. Parfait simple et parfait composé en castillan moderne.
R. Pellen, 553(RLiR):Jul-Dec78-463
Barrère, J-B. Claudel.
E.T. Dubois, 208(FS):Oct79-473
Barrère, J-B. Le Regard d'Orphée ou l'échange poétique.
M. Davies, 208(FS):Apr79-234
M. Eigeldinger, 535(RHL):Nov-Dec79-1065
Barret, L. Méthode de prononciation du Français.
P. Pohl, 430(NS):Apr78-185
Barret, P. and J-N. Gurgand. Les Tournois de Dieu. (Vol 1)
J.J. Smith, 207(FR):Dec78-375
Barrett, D. and B. Gray. Indian Painting.
M.C. Beach, 39:Jul79-81
Barrett, S.R. Two Villages on Stilts.
V. De Lancey, 69:Vol148#2-200
Barrett, W. The Illusion of Technique.*
E.G.B., 543:Jun79-736
F.W. Dillistone, 396(ModA):Fall79-434
R. Harper, 529(QQ):Autumn79-460
Barrio-Garay, J.L. José Gutiérrez Solana.
P. Ilie, 238:Dec79-732
Barroso, J. "Realismo mágico" y "lo real maravilloso" en "El reino de este mundo" y "El siglo de las luces."
R. Larson, 238:May-Sep79-412
Barrow, G.W.S. Robert Bruce and the Community of the Realm of Scotland. (2nd ed)
J.R.S. Phillips, 161(DUJ):Dec78-101
Barrow, I., R. South and J. Tillotson. Three Restoration Divines.* (Vol 1) (I. Simon, ed)
G. Reedy, 173(ECS):Winter78/79-234
Barrow, I., R. South and J. Tillotson. Three Restoration Divines.* (Vol 2) (I. Simon, ed)
M.C. Battestin, 402(MLR):Apr79-412
P. Danchin, 179(ES):Dec79-808
G. Reedy, 173(ECS):Winter78/79-234
Barrow, I., R. South and J. Tillotson. Three Restoration Divines.* (Vol 3) (I. Simon, ed)
P. Danchin, 179(ES):Dec79-808
G. Reedy, 173(ECS):Winter78/79-234
Barrows, W. Grassroots Politics in an African State.
J. Vanderlinden, 69:Vol148#4-413
Barrs, M., ed. Shakespeare Superscribe.
D.J. Enright, 617(TLS):18Apr80-429
Barry, W.J. Perzeption und Produktion in subphonematischen Bereich.
A.R. Tellier, 189(EA):Jan-Mar78-81
Barsacq, L. Caligari's Cabinet and Other Grand Illusions.
C. Rickey, 127:Summer79-297
Barson, J. and V. Bertrand. Intrigues.
L.D. Joiner, 399(MLJ):Nov79-387
J. Walz, 399(MLJ):Nov79-381

Barstow, S. A Brother's Tale.
   J. Mellors, 362:22May80-660.
   V. Scannell, 617(TLS):2May80-487
Bart, B.F. and R.F. Cook. The Legendary
   Sources of Flaubert's "Saint Julien."*
   P.H. Dubé, 107(CRCL):Winter79-98
   S. Haig, 207(FR):Oct78-168
   W.J.S. Kirton, 402(MLR):Jul79-702
Barth, D. Das Familienblatt – ein Phäno-
   men der Unterhaltungspresse des 19.
   Jahrhunderts.
   W. Martens, 182:Vol131#15/16-513
Barth, G. City People.
   442(NY):15Dec80-174
Barth, H. Truth and Ideology.
   T. Eagleton, 447(N&Q):Aug78-361
Barth, J. Letters.*
   P. Kemp, 362:8May80-621
   D. Lodge, 617(TLS):30May80-607
   G. Thompson, 385(MQR):Spring80-270
Barth, J.R. The Symbolic Imagination.*
   M. Baron, 175:Spring79-65
   J. Colmer, 402(MLR):Oct79-910
   J.D.P., 191(ELN):Sep78(supp)-56
Barthelme, D. The Dead Father. Guilty
   Pleasures.
   N. Schmitz, 473(PR):2/1979-306
Barthelme, D. Great Days.*
   D. Flower, 249(HudR):Summer79-296
   N. Schmitz, 473(PR):2/1979-306
   42(AR):Spring79-253
Barthes, R. Roland Barthes.* (French
   title: Roland Barthes par Roland
   Barthes.)
   A. Jefferson, 447(N&Q):Aug78-360
   A. Thiher, 395(MFS):Winter78/79-612
Barthes, R. Image-Music-Text.* (S. Heath,
   ed and trans)
   J.V. Harari, 400(MLN):May79-784
   A. Thiher, 395(MFS):Winter78/79-612
Barthes, R. Leçon.
   P. Dulac, 450(NRF):Feb79-102
Barthes, R. A Lover's Discourse.*
   R. Vine, 219(GaR):Winter79-918
Barthes, R. New Critical Essays.
   J. Sturrock, 441:24Aug80-11
   J. Updike, 442(NY):22Sep80-151
Bartlett, E. A Lifetime of Dying.
   C. Rumens, 617(TLS):22Feb80-214
Bartlett, I.H. Daniel Webster.*
   H.D. Moser, 432(NEQ):Jun79-297
Bartlett, J.R. A Word Index to Rainer
   Maria Rilke's German Lyric Poetry.*
   G. Benda, 406:Winter79-454
Bartlett, L., ed. Benchmark and Blaze.
   G. Holthaus, 649(WAL):Winter80-331
Bartlett, P.B. – see Meredith, G.
Bartley, R.H. Imperial Russia and the
   Struggle for Latin American Independence,
   1808-1828.
   R. Etcheparaborda, 263(RIB):Vol129No2-
   209
   A.J.R. Russell-Wood, 550(RusR):Jul79-
   361
Bartley, W.W. 3d – see Carroll, L.

Bartning, I. Remarques sur la syntaxe et
   la sémantique des pseudo-adjectifs
   dénominaux en français.
   M. Forsgren, 597(SN):Vol150#2-344
Bartók, B. Béla Bartók Essays.* (B.
   Suchoff, ed)
   J. Samson, 607:Dec77-39
Bartók, B. Rumanian Folk Music. (Vols
   4 and 5) Serbo-Croatian Folksongs.
   R. Stevenson, 607:Mar78-34
Bartók, B. Turkish Folk Music from Asia
   Minor.* (B. Suchoff, ed)
   L. Picken, 410(M&L):Jan79-81
   R. Stevenson, 607:Mar78-34
Bartoli, C. and P. Swenson. Basic Conver-
   sational Italian. (2nd ed)
   J. Vizmuller, 399(MLJ):Apr79-218
Bartolini, G. Iperide.
   D.M. MacDowell, 123:Vol129No2-308
Barton, I.M. and A.J. Brothers – see
   Harris, H.A.
Bartos, T., comp. Zigeunermärchen aus
   Ungarn.
   H-J. Uther, 196:Band19Heft1/2-126
Baruque, J.V. – see under Valdeón Baruque,
   J.
Barwise, J., ed. Handbook of Mathematical
   Logic.
   J. Bell, 84:Sep79-306
Barxudarov, S.G. and others – see "Slo-
   var' russkogo jazyka XI-XVII vv"
Barz, P. Götz Friedrich.
   E. Forbes, 415:May79-405
Barz, R. The Bhakti Sect of Vallabhācārya.
   C. Vaudeville, 259(IIJ):Jan79-55
Basetti-Sani, G. Louis Massignon. (A.H.
   Cutler, ed and trans)
   H. Mason, 318(JAOS):Apr-Jun78-166
Saint Basil. Basilio di Cesarea, "Il
   Battesimo." (U. Neri, ed and trans)
   É. Des Places, 555:Vol152fasc1-179
Basinger, J. Anthony Mann.
   D. Wilson, 617(TLS):18Jan80-62
Basiuk, V. Technology, World Politics and
   American Policy.
   639(VQR):Winter78-19
Basler, O. and others – see "Deutsches
   Fremdwörterbuch"
Bass, R.D. Ninety Six.
   G.C. Rogers, Jr., 579(SAQ):Autumn79-
   531
Bassan, F., P.F. Breed and D.C. Spinelli.
   An Annotated Bibliography of French
   Language and Literature.*
   D. Bellos, 208(FS):Vol33Pt2-949
Bassani, E. Gli antichi strumenti musi-
   cali dell' Africa nera.
   L. White, Jr., 2(AfrA):Feb79-84
Bassani, E. Scultura africana nei musei
   Italiani.
   V.L. Grottanelli, 2(AfrA):Feb79-82
Bassani, G. L'Odeur du foin.
   F. de Martinoir, 450(NRF):Nov79-127
"La Basse-Normandie et ses poètes à
   l'époque classique."
   J. Pineaux, 535(RHL):Sep-Oct78-819

Basseches, B. A Bibliography of Brazilian Bibliographies.
  A.E. Gropp, 263(RIB):Vol29No1-73
Bassham, B.L. The Theatrical Photographs of Napoleon Sarony.
  C.D. Johnson, 658:Winter79-417
  R. Kohn, 42(AR):Summer79-372
Bassin, E. The Old Songs of Skye.* (D. Bowman, ed)
  E.B. Lyle, 203:Vol189#1-117
Bassmann, W. Siegfried Lenz.
  G. Buehler, 182:Vol31#5/6-149
  A.R. Schmitt, 406:Winter79-471
Basso, I.D. La Princesse Julia Bonaparte Marquise de Roccagiovine et son temps.
  J.P.T. Bury, 208(FS):Vol33Pt2-834
Bastable, P.K. Logic.
  M.A.F., 543:Sep78-126
Bastaire, J. Alain-Fournier ou l'Anti-Rimbaud.
  R. Gibson, 208(FS):Oct79-478
Bataille, G. Blue of Noon.*
  G. Perez, 249(HudR):Autumn79-467
Bataille, G. Oeuvres complètes. (Vol 9)
  P. Collier, 617(TLS):11Apr80-422
Bataille, G. Story of the Eye.*
  J. O'Faolain, 364:Aug/Sep79-129
  G. Perez, 249(HudR):Autumn79-467
  639(VQR):Spring78-54
Bataillon, M. El hispanismo y los problemas de la historia de la espiritualidad española.
  A.G. Kinder, 86(BHS):Jul79-249
Batalha, G.N. - see under Nogueira Batalha, G.
Bate, W.J. Samuel Johnson.*
  P.K. Alkon, 173(ECS):Fall78-131
  J.J. Gold, 301(JEGP):Mar79-130
  R.D. Stock, 502(Prs):Spring78-109
  639(VQR):Spring78-47
Bater, J.H. The Soviet City.
  A. Nove, 617(TLS):18Jul80-803
Bates, D. The Abyssinian Difficulty.
  T. Pakenham, 617(TLS):18Apr80-434
  442(NY):21Jan80-129
Bates, E. Language and Context.*
  A.D. Grimshaw, 355(LSoc):Aug78-255
Bates, R.H. Rural Responses to Industrialization.
  A.K.H. Weinrich, 69:Vol148#3-308
Bateson, G. Mind and Nature.*
  H.L. Fairlamb, 400(MLN):Dec79-1218
  N. Mosley, 362:24Jul80-118
  S. Toulmin, 453(NYRB):3Apr80-38
Bätschmann, E., ed. Das St. Galler Weihnachtsspiel.*
  S.L. Wailes, 406:Winter79-478
Batt, K. Revolte intern.*
  J. Sandford, 220(GL&L):Oct78-91
Battaglia, L. Sociologia e morale in Eugène Dupréel.
  P.P., 227(GCFI):Jul-Dec78-577
Batten, C.L., Jr. Pleasurable Instruction.*
  W.P. Jones, 301(JEGP):Jul79-430
  566:Spring79-135

Baud-Bovy, M. and F. Lawson. Tourism and Recreation Development.
  G. Shankland, 46:Feb79-126
Baudelaire, C. Les Fleurs du Mal. (M. Milner, ed)
  A. Fairlie, 208(FS):Jul79-352
Baudelaire, C. Un mangeur d'opium. (M. Stäuble, ed)
  K.A. Knauth, 52:Band13Heft1-96
Baudelaire, C. Oeuvres complètes.* (C. Pichois, ed)
  A. Kies, 535(RHL):Mar-Apr78-319
Baudelaire, C. Edgar Allan Poe.* (W.T. Bandy, ed)
  C. Pichois, 549(RLC):Jan-Mar78-121
Baudelaire, C. Edgar Allan Poe. (C. Richard, ed)
  C. Pichois, 549(RLC):Jan-Mar78-121
Baudelaire, C. Selected Poems. (J. Richardson, ed and trans)
  P.S. Hambly, 208(FS):Jul79-354
Baudin, H. Les monstres dans la science-fiction.
  H. Godin, 208(FS):Vol33Pt2-982
Baudouin, R.S. - see Froissart, J.
Baudrillard, J. A l'ombre des majorités silencieuses ou la fin du social.
  V. Descombes, 98:Nov78-1086
Baudry, G-H. Socialisme et humanisme.
  M. Adam, 542:Jul-Sep79-342
Bauer, E. - see Haller, H.
Bauer, G., F.K. Stanzel and F. Zaic, eds. Festschrift Prof. Dr. Herbert Koziol zum siebzigsten Geburtstag.
  K. Reichl, 72:Band216Heft1-161
Bauer, N.S. William Wordsworth.
  R. Noyes, 661(WC):Summer79-249
Bauer, W. A Family Album.
  J. Mills, 198:Winter80-115
Bauer, W. The Terrible Word.*
  D. Barbour, 150(DR):Spring79-154
Bauer, Y. The Holocaust in Historical Perspective.
  T. Ziolkowski, 569(SR):Fall79-676
  639(VQR):Summer79-92
Baugh, A.C. and T. Cable. A History of the English Language. (3rd ed)
  R.A. Peters, 300:Mar79-94
  J.B. Trahern, Jr., 301(JEGP):Apr79-242
Baum, H. Lucien Goldmann.
  D. Hoeges, 430(NS):Feb78-89
Baum, R. "Dependenzgrammatik."*
  H-W. Eroms, 685(ZDL):2/1979-249
  H. Kahane, 545(RPh):Aug78-95
  N.C.W. Spence, 208(FS):Vol33Pt2-1073
Baum, W.K. Transcribing and Editing Oral History.*
  W.K. McNeil, 292(JAF):Apr-Jun79-244
Bauman, Z. Hermeneutics and Social Science.
  W.L. McBride, 529(QQ):Winter79/80-730
Baumann, G., ed and trans. Drei Jaina-Gedichte in Alt-Gujarātī.
  L.A. Schwarzschild, 259(IIJ):Jan79-70
Baumann, G. Goethe.
  H. Emmel, 406:Fall79-340

Baumann, H.H. Linguistik für den Ver-
braucher.
  H. Christ, 430(NS):Jul78-381
Baumann, M. Die Anakreonteen in englis-
chen Übersetzungen.*
  H.F. Plett, 38:Band96Heft3/4-518
  H. Zeman, 52:Band13Heft2-199
Baumanns, P. Einführung in die praktische
Philosophie.
  J-M. Gabaude, 542:Jul-Sep78-373
Baumanns, P. - see Fichte, J.G.
Baumbach, J. Chez Charlotte and Emily.
  R. Buffington, 441:13Jan80-22
Baumbach, J. The Return of Service.
  D. Evanier, 441:27Jul80-18
Baumeister, F.C. Philosophia definitiva.
  J. Ecole, 192(EP):Jul-Sep79-351
Baumeister, F.C. and J. Messerschmid.
Philosophiae definitivae pars altera.
  J. Ecole, 192(EP):Jul-Sep79-351
Baumert, N. Täglich sterben und aufer-
stehen.
  P.W. van der Horst, 394:Vol30fasc3-322
Baumgardt, D. Jenseits von Machtmoral und
Masochismus.*
  J-L. Nancy, 182:Vol31#17/18-577
Baumgartner, E. Le "Tristan en Prose."*
  E. Kennedy, 208(FS):Vol33Pt2-558
Baumgartner, H-M. and J. Rüsen, eds.
Geschichte und Theorie.
  L. Geldsetzer, 679:Band9Heft2-399
Baumgartner, W. Tarjei Vesaas.
  W. Mishler, 562(Scan):Nov78-181
Bäuml, B.J. and F.H. A Dictionary of
Gestures.
  R.L. Welsch, 582(SFQ):Vol41-255
Bausch, K-R. and H-M. Gauger, eds. "Inter-
linguistica."*
  H. Kahane, 545(RPh):Aug78-107
Bausch, R. Real Presence.
  S. Spencer, 441:7Sep80-13
Bausola, A. Natura e progetto dell'uomo.
  E. Namer, 542:Jul-Sep79-342
Bawcutt, N.W. - see Marlowe, C.
Bawcutt, N.W. - see Shakespeare, W.
Bawcutt, P. Gavin Douglas.*
  D. Fox, 447(N&Q):Feb78-74
Bax, D. Hieronymus Bosch.
  G. Martin, 617(TLS):1Feb80-120
Baxandall, M. The Limewood Sculptors of
Renaissance Germany.
  H. Zerner, 453(NYRB):18Dec80-52
Baxter, A.K., with C. Jacobs. To Be a
Woman in America, 1850-1930.
  K.A. Marling, 658:Winter79-410
Baxter, D.C. Servants of the Sword.
  J. Lough, 208(FS):Vol33Pt2-718
Baxter, J.K. The Bone Chanter.
  M. Doyle, 648(WCR):Feb79-45
Baxter, J.K. The Labyrinth.
  R. Jackaman, 368:Dec74-353
Bayard, T. Bourges Cathedral: The West
Portals.
  S. Gardner, 54:Mar78-163
Baybars, T. Narcissus in a Dry Pool.*
  J. Cotton, 493:Dec79-72

Bayer, H. Sprache als praktisches Be-
wusstsein.
  W. Neumann, 682(ZPSK):Band31Heft3-311
Bayer, J. Reading Photographs.
  J. Copeland, 290(JAAC):Spring80-349
Bayer, K. Sprecher und Situation.
  E.H. Yarrill, 182:Vol131#9/10-285
Bayerdörfer, H-P. - see Dingelstedt, F.
del Bayle, J-L.L. - see under Loubet del
Bayle, J-L.
Bayle, P. Dictionnaire historique et
critique. (A. Niderst, ed)
  P. Rétat, 535(RHL):Jan-Feb78-121
Bayles, M.D. Principles of Legislation.
  J. Narveson, 482(PhR):Oct79-656
Bayley, B.J. The Fall of Chronopolis.
  E. Korn, 617(TLS):30May80-626
Bayley, C.C. Mercenaries for the Crimea.*
  R.L. Blanco, 637(VS):Winter79-221
Bayley, J. An Essay on Hardy.*
  M. Bath, 637(VS):Spring79-348
  H. Orel, 395(MFS):Winter78/79-582
  A. Poole, 184(EIC):Apr79-191
  M. Ragussis, 445(NCF):Dec78-398
  K. Wilson, 255(HAB):Summer79-228
  G.J. Worth, 301(JEGP):Oct79-565
  295(JML):Vol7#4-720
Bayley, J. - see Tolstoy, L.N.
Bayley, P. Edmund Spenser.
  H.L. Weatherby, 569(SR):Summer79-490
Bayley, P., ed. Spenser: "The Faerie
Queene."
  H. Dubrow, 161(DUJ):Jun79-283
  H.L. Weatherby, 569(SR):Summer79-490
Baym, N. The Shape of Hawthorne's Career.*
  J. Arac, 153:Summer79-42
  L. Ziff, 447(N&Q):Jun78-279
Baym, N. Woman's Fiction.*
  B. Kuklick, 301(JEGP):Apr79-280
  J. Pappworth, 541(RES):Nov79-485
  H.N. Smith, 445(NCF):Mar79-483
Bayor, R. Neighbours in Conflict.
  E. Wright, 617(TLS):25Jan80-91
Bays, D.H. China Enters the Twentieth
Century.*
  R.J. Smith, 293(JASt):Nov78-159
Baysting, A., ed. The Young New Zealand
Poets.
  R. Jackaman, 368:Jun74-167
Bazelon, I. Knowing the Score.
  412:May78-141
Bazik, M.S. The Life and Works of Luis
Carlos López.*
  P.R. Beardsell, 86(BHS):Jan79-89
Bazin, A. Orson Welles.*
  M. Wood, 18:Oct78-75
  639(VQR):Winter79-30
"Beads: Their Use by Upper Great Lakes
Indians."
  R.K. Liu, 2(AfrA):Feb79-85
Beam, J.D. Multiple Exposure.*
  K.W. Ryavec, 550(RusR):Jan79-104
Beam, P.C. Winslow Homer's Magazine
Engravings.
  P-L. Adams, 61:Jan80-89

Bean, S.S. Symbolic and Pragmatic Semantics.
    H.E. Ullrich, 293(JASt):May79-615
Beane, W.C. Myth, Cult and Symbols of Sākta Hinduism.
    S.S. Wadley, 293(JASt):May79-597
Bear, D. Keeping Time.
    N. Callendar, 441:13Jan80-18
Beard, J., M. Glaser and B. Wolf, eds. The International Cooks' Catalog.
    W. and C. Cowen, 639(VQR):Spring78-76
Beardsell, P.R. Winds of Exile.
    J. Higgins, 86(BHS):Jan79-80
Beardslee, W.R. The Way Out Must Lead In.
    P. Watters, 639(VQR):Summer78-530
Beardsley, D. Play on the Water.
    D. Barbour, 150(DR):Spring79-154
    P. Hall, 628(UWR):Spring-Summer79-107
Beasley, J.C. English Fiction, 1660-1800.
    566:Autumn78-51
Beaton, C. Self Portrait with Friends.* (R. Buckle, ed)
    G. Naylor, 617(TLS):15Feb80-188
Beatson, P. The Eye in the Mandala.*
    K. Garebian, 395(MFS):Summer78-327
    J. Leclaire, 189(EA):Jan-Mar78-100
Beattie, A. Falling in Place.
    W. Balliett, 442(NY):9Jun80-148
    J. Burke, 231:May80-90
    J. Leonard, 441:2May80-C25
    R. Locke, 441:11May80-1
    R. Towers, 453(NYRB):15May80-32
    61:Jun80-93
Beattie, A. Secrets and Surprises.*
    D. Flower, 249(HudR):Summer79-293
    639(VQR):Spring79-56
Beattie, S. Alfred Stevens.
    D. Stillman, 576:May78-117
Beaudiquez, M. Bibliographical Services Throughout the World, 1970-1974.
    A.E. Schorr, 14:Oct79-478
Beaulieu, V-L. Don Quixote in Nightown.
    376:Oct79-142
Beaulieu, V-L. Jack Kerouac.*
    J.W. Robinson, 102(CanL):Spring79-71
Beaulieu, V-L. Monsieur Melville.
    S. Simon, 99:Feb80-35
Beaulieu, V-L. A Québécois Dream.
    M. Benazon, 99:Feb80-34
Beaumont, F. and J. Fletcher. The Dramatic Works in the Beaumont and Fletcher Canon. (Vol 3) (F. Bowers, ed)
    J. Gerritsen, 541(RES):May79-245
    M. Mincoff, 447(N&Q):Apr78-177
Beaumont, J. Comrades in Arms.
    J. Keegan, 617(TLS):25Apr80-457
Beaumont, J. The Shorter Poems of Sir John Beaumont.* (R.D. Sell, ed)
    J. Robertson, 541(RES):May79-209
Beaurline, L.A. Jonson and Elizabethan Comedy.
    J. Arnold, 568(SCN):Fall-Winter79-76
    A. Barton, 541(RES):Nov79-466
    M. Eccles, 130:Fall79-271
Beauroy, J., M. Bertrand and E.T. Gargan, eds. The Wolf and the Lamb.
    E. Marks, 207(FR):Feb79-520

Beausant, P. L'Archéologue.
    G. Quinsat, 450(NRF):Dec79-111
Beauvais, R. The Half Jew.
    N. Ascherson, 453(NYRB):12Jun80-34
de Beauvoir, S. Quand prime le spirituel.
    P. Thody, 617(TLS):4Apr80-391
Beaver, B. Death's Directives.
    C. Pollnitz, 581:Dec79-462
Bec, C., ed. L'Umanesimo civile. L'Umanesimo letterario.
    M.C., 228(GSLI):Vol155fasc492-630
Bec, C. De Pétrarque à Machiavel.
    P.P., 227(GCFI):Apr-Jun78-283
Bec, C. Le siècle des Médicis.
    M.C., 228(GSLI):Vol155fasc492-630
Becco, A. Du simple selon G.W. Leibniz.
    A. Reix, 192(EP):Jul-Sep79-352
Bechtle, T.C. and M.F. Riley. Dissertations in Philosophy Accepted at American Universities, 1861-1975.
    W.N. Clarke, 258:Mar79-125
Beck, C.T. Scream Queens.
    W.K. Everson, 200:Mar79-178
Beck, I. Das Problem des Bösen und seiner Bewältigung.
    G. Hummel, 182:Vol131#15/16-521
Beck, J. Masaccio: The Documents.
    K. Christiansen, 39:Jul79-80
Beck, L.W. The Actor and the Spectator.* (German title: Akteur und Betrachter.)
    L. Samson, 687:Apr-Jun79-325
Beck, L.W. Essays on Kant and Hume.
    L. Guillermit, 542:Apr-Jun79-244
Beck, T.D. French Legislators 1800-1834.
    J.P.T. Bury, 208(FS):Vol33Pt2-1008
Becker, G.S. The Economic Approach to Human Behavior.*
    A. Rosenberg, 488:Dec79-509
Becker, H.J. Mit geballter Faust.
    H. Zohn, 222(GR):Summer79-134
Becker, H.K. and E.O. Hjellemo. Justice in Modern Sweden.
    D. Orrick, 563(SS):Summer79-293
Becker, J.F. Marxian Political Economy.
    H. Laycock, 529(QQ):Summer79-350
Becker, L.C. Property Rights.
    G.A. Cohen, 393(Mind):Jul79-469
    G.W. Smith, 518:Jan79-21
    R. Young, 63:Jun79-194
    185:Oct78-121
Becker, L.F. Georges Simenon.
    L. Greene, 207(FR):Feb79-496
Becker, P.J. Handschriften und Frühdrucke mittelhochdeutscher Epen.
    J.L. Flood, 354:Jun79-174
    N.F. Palmer, 402(MLR):Jan79-237
Beckerman, W., ed. Slow Growth in Britain — Causes and Consequences.
    J. Hardie, 617(TLS):25Jan80-90
Beckett, J.C. The Anglo-Irish Tradition.
    L.J. McCaffrey, 637(VS):Summer79-449
Beckett, S. Company.
    J. Leonard, 441:22Dec80-C16
    J.D. O'Hara, 441:2Nov80-7
    J. Treglown, 617(TLS):27Jun80-726
Beckett, S. Six Residua.
    J.R.B., 148:Spring79-93

Beckinsale, R. and M. The English Heart-
land.
R. Blythe, 362:4Sep80-310
Beckman, B. Organising the Farmers.
R.M. Lawson, 69:Vol48#2-195
Beckman, T. Milwaukee Illustrated.
W.E. Washburn, 658:Autumn79-319
Bédarida, F., ed. La Stratégie secrète de
la Drôle de Guerre.
D. Johnson, 617(TLS):4Jan80-15
Bédarida, R. Témoignage Chrétien (1941-
1944).
C.W. Obuchowski, 207(FR):Feb79-523
Bedell, M. The Alcotts.
P-L. Adams, 61:Oct80-101
J. Hendin, 441:21Dec80-8
Bedoire, F. En arkitekt och hans verksam-
het kring sekelskiftet, Gustaf Wickmans
arbeten 1884-1916.
T. Hall, 341:1978/2-55
Bédouelle, G. Lefèvre d'Étaples et
l'intelligence des Écritures.
C. Béné, 535(RHL):May-Jun78-455
Bédouelle, G. and F. Giacone - see Lefèvre
d'Étaples, J. and others
Beecher, C.E. and H.B. Stowe. The
American Woman's Home or Principles of
Domestic Science.
D. Hayden, 576:Dec78-311
Beehler, R. Moral Life.
E.J. Bond, 483:Apr79-260
A. Quinton, 617(TLS):4Jan80-18
Beele, W. Studie van de Ieperse persoons-
namen uit de stads- en baljuwsrekeningen
1250-1400.
G.B. Droege, 424:Jun78-199
Beeler, J. Dowry.*
639(VQR):Spring79-68
Beer, C. This Fig Tree Has Thorns.
E. Caffin, 368:Jun76-124
de Beer, E.S. - see Locke, J.
Beer, F. - see Julian of Norwich
Beer, J. Coleridge's Poetic Intelligence.*
M. Baron, 175:Spring79-65
G. Cullum, 586(SoRA):Jul78-205
J.D. Gutteridge, 447(N&Q):Aug78-369
L.S. Lockridge, 661(WC):Summer79-265
639(VQR):Winter79-24
Beer, J. Wordsworth and the Human Heart.*
M. Baron, 175:Autumn79-259
J.R. Barth, 613:Dec79-456
D.P., 148:Summer79-92
Beer, J. Wordsworth in Time.*
M. Baron, 175:Autumn79-259
Beer, J.M.A. A Medieval Caesar.*
W. Rothwell, 208(FS):Vol33Pt2-554
Beer, O. Pas de Deux.
G. Strawson, 617(TLS):15Aug80-909
Beer, P. Selected Poems.
J. Bayley, 362:29May80-691
C. Rumens, 617(TLS):12Sep80-990
Beer, R., ed. Der Prinz als Papagei.
G. von Simson, 196:Band19Heft1/2-131
Beesly, P. Very Special Admiral.
P. Gretton, 617(TLS):22Aug80-937

Beeson, M. and others. Hispanic Writers
in French Journals.
D.C. Scroggins, 238:May-Sep79-407
van Beethoven, L. Two Beethoven Sketch-
books.* (G. Nottebohm, ed)
W. Drabkin, 415:Aug79-652
Beffa, B. Antonio Vinciguerra Cronico,
segretario della Serenissima e letterato.
M.P., 228(GSLI):Vol155fasc492-630
Begley, M. Rambles in Ireland and a
County-by-County Guide for Discriminat-
ing Travelers.
R.H., 305(JIL):May78-187
Béguin, A. Création et destinée. Créa-
tion et destinée II. (P. Grotzer, ed of
both)
H. Godin, 208(FS):Jan79-106
J. Starobinski, 98:Apr78-352
Béguin, A. and M. Raymond. Lettres, 1920-
1957. (G. Guisan, ed)
R. Bessède, 535(RHL):Nov-Dec78-1034
J. Starobinski, 98:Apr78-352
Béguin, A. and G. Roud. Lettres sur le
romantisme allemand.* (F. Fornerod, ed)
P.J. Whyte, 208(FS):Jul79-363
Behan, B. Time to Go.*
P. Raine, 617(TLS):8Feb80-146
Behm, M. The Eye of the Beholder.
N. Callendar, 441:10Feb80-22
Behn, M. DDR-Literatur in der Bundesre-
publik Deutschland.
H. Müssener, 406:Winter79-474
Behnen, M., ed. Quellen zur deutschen
Aussenpolitik im Zeitalter des Imperial-
ismus 1890-1911.
F. L'Huillier, 182:Vol131#5/6-180
Behr, B. Das alemannische Herzogtum bis
750.
B.S. Bachrach, 589:Jan79-107
Behre, F. Get, Come and Go.
B.M.H. Strang, 597(SN):Vol50#1-148
Behrman, C.F. Victorian Myths of the Sea.
J.R. Reed, 125:Winter79-296
Beidelman, T.O. W. Robertson Smith and
the Sociological Study of Religion.
N. Yoffee, 318(JAOS):Jul-Sep78-309
Beierwaltes, W. Identität und Differenz.
H. Meinhardt, 687:Jul-Sep79-458
Beijbom, U. Amerika, Amerika.
H.A. Barton, 563(SS):Winter79-69
Beinhauer, W. Stilistisch-phraseologis-
ches Wörterbuch: Spanisch-Deutsch.
R. Eberenz, 547(RF):Band91Heft3-298
de Beir, L. Les Bayaka de M'Nene N'toomba
Lenge-lenge.
W. MacGaffey, 69:Vol48#1-95
Beissel, H. The Salt I Taste.
A. Amprimoz, 102(CanL):Spring79-72
Beja, M. Film and Literature.
J.R.B., 148:Winter79-92
D. Wilson, 617(TLS):18Jan80-62
Bekker, H. Friedrich von Hausen.
F.H. Bäuml, 221(GQ):Mar79-274
R.T. Morewedge, 564:Nov79-319
T.P. Thornton, 301(JEGP):Jan79-85

Benchley, P. The Island.*
639(VQR):Autumn79-136

Benda, J. La fin de l'éternel.
O. de Mourgues, 208(FS):Vol33Pt2-854

Bendala Galán, M. La necrópolis romana de Carmona (Sevilla).
R.F.J. Jones, 313:Vol69-221

Bender, H. Archäologische Untersuchungen zur Ausgrabung Augst-Kurzenbettli.
D. Baatz, 182:Vol31#20-750

Bender, M.O. - see Huon de Méri

Bender, T. Community and Social Change in America.
J.A. Henretta, 656(WMQ):Apr79-292

Bender, T. Toward an Urban Vision.
D. Schuyler, 576:Oct78-218

Bendiner, E. The Fall of Fortresses.
· C. Lehmann-Haupt, 441:9May80-C27
D. Middleton, 441:25May80-6

Bendt, W. Topographische Karte von Milet (I:2000), mit erläuterndem Text.
S.C. Bakhuizen and F.L.T. van der Weiden, 394:Vol132fasc3/4-449

Benes, P. The Masks of Orthodoxy.
J. Baker, 432(NEQ):Dec79-596
C.A. Prioli, 165(EAL):Winter79/80-328

Benevolo, L. The Architecture of the Renaissance.
J.Q. Hughes, 46:Apr79-250

Benevolo, L. La casa dell'uomo.
P. Micheli, 576:Dec78-322

Benevolo, L. The History of the City.
P. Goldberger, 441:28Sep80-13

Bengtson, H. Griechische Geschichte. (5th ed)
N.G.L. Hammond, 123:Vol129No2-262

Bengtson, H. Marcus Antonius, Triumvir und Herrscher des Orients.
J. Briscoe, 123:Vol129No1-178
J. Carter, 313:Vol69-184
P. Jal, 555:Vol52fasc2-414

Bénichou, P. Le temps des prophètes.*
D.G. Charlton, 402(MLR):Oct79-941
J. Gaulmier, 535(RHL):Jul-Aug79-674

Benito Ruano, E. Estudios Santiaguistas.
T.F. Ruiz, 589:Apr79-337

Benjamin, W. The Origins of German Tragic Drama.* Gesammelte Schriften.
C. Rosen, 98:Mar78-253

Benjamin, W. Correspondance. (Vol 1)
L. Arénilla, 450(NRF):Sep79-60

Benjamin, W. and G. Scholem. Walter Benjamin-Gershom Scholem Briefwechsel 1933-1940. (G. Scholem, ed)
G. Steiner, 617(TLS):27Jun80-723

Ben Jelloun, T. Harrouda. Les amandiers sont morts de leurs blessures. La réclusion solitaire.
D.T. Analis, 98:Apr78-432

Benkovitz, M.J. Frederick Rolfe: Baron Corvo.
295(JML):Vol17#4-678

Benn, M.B. The Drama of Revolt.*
M. Jacobs, 220(GL&L):Oct78-75

Benn, S.I. and G.W. Mortimore, eds. Rationality and the Social Sciences.*
J. Kekes, 488:Mar79-105

Benner, M. and E. Tengström. On the Interpretation of Learned Neo-Latin.
B. Löfstedt, 350:Jun79-482

Bennett, B.T. - see Shelley, M.W.

Bennett, D. Queen Victoria's Children.
442(NY):13Oct80-193

Bennett, D.C. Spatial and Temporal Uses of English Prepositions.*
E.A. Nida, 353:Feb78-90
N.W. Shumaker, 35(AS):Summer79-132

Bennett, E.L., Jr. and J-P. Olivier. The Pylos Tablets Transcribed. (Pt 1)
C.J. Ruijgh, 394:Vol130fasc3-297

Bennett, E.L., Jr. and J-P. Olivier. The Pylos Tablets Transcribed. (Pt 2)
P. Monteil, 555:Vol52fasc1-138
C.J. Ruijgh, 394:Vol130fasc3-297

Bennett, G.N., D.J. Nordloh and D. Kleinman - see Howells, W.D.

Bennett, H. Insanity Runs in Our Family.
N.H. Packer, 573(SSF):Summer78-335

Bennett, I., ed. Rugs and Carpets of the World.*
M. Beattie, 463:Autumn79-361

Bennett, J. Linguistic Behaviour.*
J.E. Llewelyn, 262:Spring78-120
K. Sterelny, 63:Sep79-280

Bennett, L., ed. The Western Wind American Tune Book.
H.B.R., 412:May78-131

Bennett, P., ed. Mantel et Cor.
M.D. Legge, 208(FS):Vol33Pt2-550

Bennett, R. Ultra in the West.
M. Carver, 617(TLS):4Jan80-17
R. Lewin, 362:17Jan80-93

Bennett, W.H., ed. Letters from the Federal Farmer to the Republican.
R.S. Sliwoski, 432(NEQ):Jun79-282

Bennion, E. Antique Medical Instruments.*
G. Wills, 39:Dec79-532

de Benoist, A. Les idées à l'endroit. Vu de droite.
T. Sheehan, 453(NYRB):24Jan80-13

Benoît, J. The Princes.*
L. Leith, 102(CanL):Autumn79-120

Benot, J.M.C. - see under Capote Benot, J.M.

Bénouis, M.K. Le Dialogue philosophique dans la littérature française du seizième siècle.
T. Peach, 208(FS):Jul79-327

Benson, C.D. The History of Troy in Middle English Literature.
V. Adams, 617(TLS):25Jul80-855

Benson, J. and A. Mackenzie. Sauternes.
J. Jeffs, 617(TLS):23May80-588

Benson, J. and R.G. Neville, eds. Studies in the Yorkshire Coal Industry.
M.J. Daunton, 161(DUJ):Dec78-109

Benson, L.D. Malory's "Morte Darthur."*
D. Brewer, 677(YES):Vol9-364
M. Murrin, 405(MP):Aug79-70

Bensoussan, D. La Maladie de Rousseau.
P. Robinson, 208(FS):Vol33Pt2-759

Bergren, A.L.T. The Etymology and Usage of "Peirar" in Early Greek Poetry.
J.H.W. Penney, 123:Vol29No2-324

Bering, D. Die Intellektuellen.
B. Löfstedt, 350:Sep79-743

Berkeley, E., Jr., ed. Autographs and Manuscripts.
J.D. Knowlton, 14:Oct79-472

Berkin, C.R. and M.B. Norton, eds. Women of America.
R. Guild, 432(NEQ):Dec79-575

Berkofer, R.F., Jr. The White Man's Indian.
P.F. Boller, Jr., 584(SWR):Winter79-107

Berkowitz, L. Thesaurus Linguae Graecae Canon of Greek Authors and Works from Homer to A.D. 200.
C.R. Rubincam, 487:Autumn79-281

Berlanstein, L.R. The Barristers of Toulouse in the Eighteenth Century (1740-1793).*
J. Lough, 208(FS):Vol33Pt2-797

Berlin, B., D.E. Breedlove and P.H. Raven. Principles of Tzeltal Plant Classification.
E.P. Hamp, 269(IJAL):Apr78-162

Berlin, I. Against the Current.* (H. Hardy, ed)
J. Leonard, 441:8Feb80-C27
J. Lieberson and S. Morgenbesser, 453(NYRB):6Mar80-38 [and cont in] 20Mar80-31
S. Wolin, 441:16Mar80-1

Berlin, I. Concepts and Categories.* (H. Hardy, ed)
R. Harper, 529(QQ):Autumn79-460

Berlin, I. Personal Impressions.
M. Warnock, 362:30Oct80-583

Berlin, I. Russian Thinkers.* (H. Hardy and A. Kelly, eds)
M. Friedberg, 390:Nov79-67
E. Lampert, 575(SEER):Apr79-297
G. Woodcock, 569(SR):Summer79-480
M-B. Zeldin, 550(RusR):Jul79-364

Berlin, I. Slaves Without Masters.
L. Krieger, 473(PR):1/1979-152

Berlin, J.B. An Annotated Arthur Schnitzler Bibliography 1965-1977.
M. Swales, 402(MLR):Oct79-994

Berliner, J.S. The Innovation Decision in Soviet Industry.
B. Horowitz, 104(CASS):Summer78-308

Berliner, P.F. The Soul of Mbira.
K.A. Gourlay, 187:Jan80-128
R. Knight, 2(AfrA):Aug79-87

Berman, E., ed. Ten of the Best British Short Plays.
J. Coleby, 157:Autumn79-89

Berman, J. Joseph Conrad.*
J.J. Riley, 395(MFS):Summer78-314
295(JML):Vol7#4-676

Bernal, A.M. and M. Drain. Les Campagnes sévillanes aux XIXe-XXe siècles.
J. Naylon, 86(BHS):Jan79-75

Bernal, I. A History of Mexican Archaeology.
W. Bray, 617(TLS):4Jul80-760

Bernard, B. The Sunday Times Book of Photodiscovery.
J. Naughton, 362:18and25Dec80-865

Bernard, F.D. Anatomy of Film.
V. Carrabino, 207(FR):May79-959

Bernard, S. Rencontre avec un paysan français révolutionnaire.
H.L. Butler, 207(FR):Dec78-369

Bernardi Perini, G. Due problemi di fonetica latina.
M.A. Nyman, 215(GL):Spring78-53

Bernardo, A.S. Petrarch, Laura, and the "Triumphs."*
P.C. Viglionese, 546(RR):Mar79-198

Bernays, A. The School Book.
A. Tyler, 441:3Aug80-14

Bernen, R. Tales from the Blue Stacks.
R. Bonaccorso, 174(Éire):Summer79-133
G. O'Brien, 97(CQ):Vol18#3-260

Bernhard, T. Correction.
C.C. Park, 249(HudR):Winter79/80-582

Bernhard, T. Der Weltverbesserer. Vor dem Ruhestand. Der Stimmenimitator.
G. Steiner, 617(TLS):29Feb80-238

Bernhart, W. Ein metrisch-rhythmischer Vergleich der beiden Fassungen von Wordsworths "Prelude" unter Verwendung eines phonologisch begründeten graphischen Analyseverfahrens.
E. Standop, 224(GRM):Band28Heft3-372

Bernikow, L. Among Women.
D. Grumbach, 441:19Oct80-16

Berning, S. Sinnbildsprache.
G. Häntzschel, 224(GRM):Band28Heft1-98

Bernsen, N.O. Knowledge.
A. Reix, 542:Jul-Sep79-343

Bernstein, A.H. Tiberius Sempronius Gracchus.
A.E. Astin, 123:Vol29No1-111
E. Badian, 24:Fall79-452
S. Treggiari, 487:Summer79-178

Bernstein, B. Sinai.
R.A. Sokolov, 441:20Apr80-18

Bernstein, J. Hans Bethe, Prophet of Energy.
T. Ferris, 441:28Sep80-16

Bernstein, R.J. The Restructuring of Social and Political Theory.*
L. Harris, 258:Dec79-485

Bernstein, T.P. Up to the Mountains and Down to the Villages.
S.L. Shirk, 293(JASt):Nov78-148

Béroul. Le Roman de Tristan.* (H. Braet, trans)
C.E. Pickford, 208(FS):Jan79-64

Berque, J. L'Islam au défi.
M.E. Yapp, 617(TLS):19Sep80-1040

Le Chevalier de Berquin. Declamation des Louenges de mariage [1525]. (É.V. Telle, ed)
A. Gendre, 535(RHL):Jul-Aug78-630

de Berrêdo Carneiro, P.E. and P. Arnaud – see Comte, A.

Berridge, E. Family Matters.
  M. Johnson, 617(TLS):13Jun80-674
Berrigan, J.R. Leonardo Dati: Hiensal
  tragoedia.
  A.S., 228(GSLI):Vol155fasc490-313
Berrin, K., ed. Art of the Huichol
  Indians.
  M. Fox, 529(QQ):Autumn79-561
  A. Franz, 2(AfrA):Aug79-88
Berrone, L. - see Joyce, J.
Berry, A. The Iron Sun.
  R.N. Bracewell, 529(QQ):Spring79-138
Berry, B.M. Process of Speech.*
  S.P. Revard, 405(MP):Aug79-89
Berry, G. and G. Beard. The Lake District.
  N. Nicholson, 617(TLS):1Aug80-864
Berry, H., ed. The First Public Playhouse.
  R.V. Holdsworth, 617(TLS):28Mar80-370
Berry, J. Fractured Circles.*
  S. Brown, 493:Dec79-47
Berry, R. The Shakespearean Metaphor.
  E.M. Yearling, 541(RES):Feb79-75
Berry, T. Russian For Business.
  S. Orth, 574(SEEJ):Fall79-425
Berry, T.E. Plots and Characters in
  Major Russian Fiction. (Vol 1)
  D.E. Budgen, 575(SEER):Oct79-583
  R.E. Richardson, 558(RLJ):Winter79-212
Berry, T.E. Plots and Characters in Major
  Russian Fiction. (Vol 2)
  R.B. Anderson, 395(MFS):Winter78/79-
  605
Berry, W. Clearing.*
  J. Parini, 639(VQR):Autumn78-762
Bersani, L. Baudelaire and Freud.
  J. Culler, 131(CL):Spring79-176
Bersani, L. A Future for Astyanax.*
  G. Chaitin, 131(CL):Summer79-306
  L.D. Joiner, 188(ECr):Winter78-72
Berschin, H., J. Felixberger and H. Goebl.
  Französische Sprachgeschichte.
  K. Hunnius, 547(RF):Band91Heft3-301
Bertaux, D. Destins personnels et
  structure de classe.
  J-J. Thomas, 207(FR):Feb79-524
Bertaux, P. Friedrich Hölderlin.
  R. Gray, 617(TLS):11Jan80-45
Bertelli, L. Historia e methodos.
  P.M. Huby, 123:Vol129No2-320
Bertelli, L. and I. Lana. Lessici poli-
  tici del mondo antico. (Vol 1, fasc 1)
  F. Vian, 555:Vol52fasc2-348
Berthier, P. Barbey d'Aurevilly et
  l'imagination.
  A.S. Rosenthal, 399(MLJ):Apr79-221
Berthier, P. Stendhal et ses peintres
  italiens.*
  C.W. Thompson, 208(FS):Vol33Pt2-808
Berthoff, W. A Literature Without
  Qualities.
  A. Broyard, 441:1Mar80-19
  I. Ehrenpreis, 441:6Apr80-10
  E. Homberger, 617(TLS):30May80-622
Berthoud, J. Joseph Conrad: The Major
  Phase.*
  D. Kramer, 301(JEGP):Oct79-567
  [continued]

[continuing]
  C.R. La Bossière, 268(IFR):Winter80-60
  R.F. Peterson, 395(MFS):Winter78/79-
  571
Berti, E. Aristotele, dalla dialettica
  alla filosofia prima.*
  G.B. Kerferd, 123:Vol129No2-318
de Bertier de Sauvigny, G. Histoire de
  France.*
  A. Forrest, 208(FS):Vol33Pt2-1001
Bertière, A. Le Cardinal de Retz mémor-
  ialiste.
  Y. Coirault, 535(RHL):Sep-Oct79-851
  D.A. Watts, 208(FS):Apr79-185
Bertini, F. and others. Commedie latine
  del XII e XIII Secolo. (Vol 1)
  J.C. McKeown, 123:Vol129No1-192
Bertini, G. La quadreria Farnesiana e i
  quadri confiscati nel 1612 al feudatari
  parmensi.
  C. Gould, 39:Jan79-72
Bertman, S., ed. The Conflict of Genera-
  tions in Ancient Greece and Rome.
  N.R.E. Fisher, 123:Vol129No1-158
  M. Menu, 555:Vol52fasc2-376
Bertocchi, D. and E. Lugarini. Corso di
  lingua italiana per stranieri.
  M. Danesi, 399(MLJ):Jan-Feb79-74
Berton, K. Moscow.*
  A. Farkas, 550(RusR):Jan79-83
Bertrand-Jennings, C. L'Eros et la femme
  chez Zola.
  I. Finel-Honigman, 207(FR):Feb79-490
  F.W.J. Hemmings, 402(MLR):Oct79-943
Berzon, J.R. Neither White Nor Black.
  W.J. Scheick, 587(SAF):Autumn79-246
Besançon, A. The Soviet Syndrome.
  639(VQR):Winter79-27
Beschloss, M.R. Kennedy and Roosevelt.
  L. Silk, 441:13Aug80-C21
  R. Steel, 453(NYRB):14Aug80-37
  D. Yergin, 441:22Jun80-15
  442(NY):26May80-127
Beskow, B. Two by Two.
  P. Lewis, 617(TLS):7Mar80-278
Bessai, D. and D. Jackel, eds. Figures in
  a Ground.*
  F. Nolan, 627(UTQ):Summer79-433
Bessinger, J.B., Jr., ed. A Concordance
  to "The Anglo-Saxon Poetic Records."
  E.G. Stanley, 541(RES):Aug79-328
  J.B. Trahern, Jr., 301(JEGP):Apr79-242
Best, D. Philosophy and Human Movement.
  D. Williams, 187:May80-294
Best, G. Vom Rindernomadismus zum Fisch-
  fang.
  P. Erny, 182:Vol31#9/10-318
Best, O.F. Das verbotene Glück.
  W. Koepke, 221(GQ):May79-419
"Best of the Poetry Year 6." (D. Abse, ed)
  P. Mills, 493:Dec79-64
"Best Poems of 1976: Borestone Mountain
  Poetry Awards 1976."
  639(VQR):Summer78-100
"Best Radio Plays of 1978."
  J. Coleby, 157:Autumn79-89

31

Bester, A. Golem [100].
   G. Jonas, 441:14Sep80-12
Besterman, T. Some Eighteenth-Century
  Voltaire Editions Unknown to Bengesco.
  (4th ed)
   M.H. Waddicor, 208(FS):Apr79-195
Besterman, T., ed. Studies on Voltaire
  and the Eighteenth Century. (Vol 71)
   M.H. Waddicor, 208(FS):Apr79-193
Besterman, T., ed. Studies on Voltaire
  and the Eighteenth Century. (Vol 124)
   J.H. Brumfitt, 208(FS):Vol33Pt2-731
Besterman, T., ed. Studies on Voltaire
  and the Eighteenth Century. (Vol 127)
   M.H. Waddicor, 208(FS):Apr79-193
Besterman, T., ed. Studies on Voltaire
  and the Eighteenth Century. (Vol 129)
   M.H. Waddicor, 208(FS):Vol33Pt2-749
Besterman, T., ed. Studies on Voltaire
  and the Eighteenth Century. (Vol 137)
   M.H. Waddicor, 208(FS):Vol33Pt2-750
Besterman, T., ed. Studies on Voltaire
  and the Eighteenth Century. (Vols 140
  and 143)
   M.H. Waddicor, 208(FS):Vol33Pt2-754
Besterman, T., ed. Studies on Voltaire
  and the Eighteenth Century. (Vol 148)
   J. Balcou, 535(RHL):Mar-Apr78-310
   L.W. Lynch, 207(FR):Oct78-163
   M.H. Waddicor, 208(FS):Vol33Pt2-754
Besterman, T., ed. Studies on Voltaire
  and the Eighteenth Century.* (Vol 150)
   M. Delon, 535(RHL):May-Jun78-482
Besterman, T., ed. Studies on Voltaire
  and the Eighteenth Century.* (Vols 151-
  155)
   J.H. Brumfitt, 208(FS):Vol33Pt2-731
   M. Delon, 535(RHL):Jul-Aug78-645
Besterman, T., ed. Studies on Voltaire
  and the Eighteenth Century.* (Vol 160)
   J. Sgard, 535(RHL):Jul-Aug78-649
   M.H. Waddicor, 208(FS):Vol33Pt2-754
Besterman, T., ed. Studies on Voltaire
  and the Eighteenth Century.* (Vol 161)
   J. Balcou, 535(RHL):Jul-Aug78-650
   M.H. Waddicor, 208(FS):Vol33Pt2-751
Besterman, T., ed. Studies on Voltaire
  and the Eighteenth Century.* (Vol 163)
   J. Balcou, 535(RHL):Jul-Aug78-651
   M.H. Waddicor, 208(FS):Vol33Pt2-752
Besterman, T., ed. Studies on Voltaire
  and the Eighteenth Century. (Vol 169)
   M.H. Waddicor, 208(FS):Vol33Pt2-753
Besterman, T. Voltaire.* (3rd ed)
   J.H. Brumfitt, 208(FS):Vol33Pt2-731
Besterman, T. - see de Voltaire, F.M.A.
Besterman, T. and A. Brown, eds. Concor-
  dance to the Correspondence of Voltaire.
   J.H. Brumfitt, 208(FS):Vol33Pt2-731
Bestor, D.K. Aside from Teaching English,
  What in the World Can You Do?
   C.H. Harm, 128(CE):Oct78-206
   R.T. Lenaghan, 128(CE):Oct78-212
Betancourt, P.P. The Aeolic Style in
  Architecture.
   J.J. Coulton, 123:Vol29No1-116
   F.E. Winter, 576:Oct78-198

Betancourt, R. Venezuela.
   639(VQR):Autumn79-145
Bethell, N. The Palestine Triangle.*
   R. Wistrich, 617(TLS):23May80-591
Bethge, W. Beschreibung einer hochsprach-
  lichen Tonbandaufnahme.
   H. Ulbrich, 682(ZPSK):Band31Heft1-103
Bethge, W. Textliste zu III/50.*
   H. Ulbrich, 682(ZPSK):Band31Heft1-105
Betjeman, J. The Best of Betjeman. (J.
  Guest, ed)
   C. Hope, 364:Jun79-75
Bettelhäuser, H-J. Studien zur Substantiv-
  flexion der deutschen Gegenwartssprache.
   G. Augst, 686(ZGL):Band7Heft2-220
Bettelheim, B. Surviving and Other
  Essays.*
   T. Ziolkowski, 569(SR):Fall79-676
Bettelheim, C. The Transition to Social-
  ist Economy. Economic Calculation and
  Forms of Property.
   J.P. Scott, 488:Sep79-327
Bettinson, C. André Gide.*
   V. Conley, 395(MFS):Winter78/79-615
Beugnot, B. La Critique de notre temps et
  Anouilh.
   J. Bouchard, 207(FR):Apr79-783
Beumann, J. Sigebert von Gembloux und der
  Traktat de investitura episcoporum.
   K. Pennington, 589:Jul79-545
Beutler, G. Estudios sobre el romancero
  español en Colombia en su tradición
  escrita y oral desde la época de la
  conquista hasta la actualidad.
   F. Goodwyn, 263(RIB):Vol29No2-220
Bevan, D.G. The Art and Poetry of Charles-
  Ferdinand Ramuz.*
   D.L. Parris, 208(FS):Vol33Pt2-870
Bever, T.G., J.J. Katz and D.T. Langendoen.
  An Integrated Theory of Linguistic
  Ability.
   P.H. Matthews, 307:Oct79-128
Beveridge, J. John Grierson.
   S. Kula, 18:Oct78-78
Bevington, D. and J.L. Halio, eds. Shakes-
  peare.
   R. Berry, 529(QQ):Autumn79-470
Bewick, T. Thomas Bewick, a Memoir Writ-
  ten by Himself. (I. Bain, ed)
   K. Garlick, 447(N&Q):Jun78-259
Beyer, E. Ibsen.
   I-S. Ewbank, 157:Winter79-82
   A.P. Hinchliffe, 148:Autumn79-87
Beyer, E. and others, eds. Kvinner og
  bøker.
   J. Hareide, 562(Scan):Nov78-184
Beyer, K. and H-D. Kreuder. Lernziel:
  Kommunikation.
   K. Schröder, 430(NS):Jul78-377
Beyerle, M. "Madame Bovary" als Roman
  der Versuchung.
   R. Huss, 208(FS):Vol33Pt2-832
Bezzel, I. Erasmusdrucke des 16. Jahr-
  hunderts in bayerischen Bibliotheken.
   O. Herding, 182:Vol31#23/24-833

"Bhagavad Gita." (W. Sargeant, ed and trans)
S. Rama Rau, 442(NY):14Apr80-170
"The Bhagavad-gītā." (R.C. Zaehner, ed)
L.A. Schwarzschild, 259(IIJ):Jan79-68
Bharadwaja, S. Philosophy of Common Sense.
L.C.R., 543:Mar79-532
Bhartrihari and Bilhana. The Hermit and the Love-Thief. (B.S. Miller, trans)
639(VQR):Summer79-108
Bhat, D.N.S. Pronominalization.
R.W. Langacker, 350:Sep79-687
Bhattacharya, S. Pursuit of National Interests Through Neutralism.
C.H. Heimsath, 293(JASt):Aug79-812
Bhattacharyya, K. A Modern Understanding of Advaita Vedānta.
Sengaku Mayeda, 318(JAOS):Jul-Sep78-333
Bhojak, P.A.M. and N.J. Śāha - see "Jineśvarasūri's Gāhārayaṇakosa"
Bialer, S. Stalin's Successors.
J. Chace, 441:21Sep80-3
L. Schapiro, 453(NYRB):9Oct80-11
Białostocki, J. The Art of the Renaissance in Eastern Europe.*
T.D. Kaufmann, 54:Mar78-164
Białoszewski, M. A Memoir of the Warsaw Uprising. (M.G. Levine, ed and trans)
R. Cleary, 497(PolR):Vol23#1-93
Biard, J.D. - see Chauveau, F.
Biard, J.D. - see Quinault, P.
Biardeau, M. and C. Malamoud. Le sacrifice, dans l'Inde ancienne.
J.C. Heesterman, 259(IIJ):Jan79-47
Biaudet, J-C. and F. Nicod - see de La Harpe, F-C. and others
Bibeau, G. Introduction à la phonologie générative du français.
J. Durand and C. Lyche, 209(FM):Apr78-169
"Biblia Patristica."
A. Kemmer, 182:Vol31#13-390
Bichel, U. Problem und Begriff der Umgangssprache in der germanistischen Forschung.
D. Stellmacher, 685(ZDL):3/1979-372
Bickham, G. The Beauties of Stow (1750).
568(SCN):Fall-Winter79-83
Bickham, J.M. The Regensburg Legacy.
N. Callendar, 441:11May80-21
Bickley, R.B., Jr. Joel Chandler Harris.*
W.B. Strickland, 26(ALR):Spring79-168
Bickley, R.B., Jr. The Method of Melville's Short Fiction.*
B. Hitchcock, 577(SHR):Spring79-166
H. Kosok, 447(N&Q):Jun78-280
M.M. Sealts, Jr., 183(ESQ):Vol25#1-43
Bicknell, A.J. Victorian Village Builder.
K.N. Morgan, 576:Mar78-52
Bidart, F. The Book of the Body.*
J. Fuller, 617(TLS):18Jan80-65
Bieber, M. Ancient Copies.*
C.E. Vafopoulou-Richardson, 123:Vol129-No2-291
de Biedma, J.G. - see under Gil de Biedma, J.

Bielaire, F. Erasme et ses Colloques.
P.J. Brandwein, 149(CLS):Jun79-168
Bielfeldt, S. Die tschechische Moderne im Frühwerk Šaldas.
R.B. Pynsent, 575(SEER):Apr79-283
Bierbach, C. Sprache als "Fait social."
J. Albrecht, 343:Band23-12
Bierce, A. The Devil's Dictionary.
J.R. Gaskin, 569(SR):Summer79-455
Bierlaire, F. Les Colloques d'Erasme.
B. Beaulieu, 539:Vol4No2-229
Biers, W.R. The Archaeology of Greece.
D. Hunt, 617(TLS):22Aug80-938
Biguenet, J., ed. Foreign Fictions.
D. Kirby, 639(VQR):Spring79-358
Bijl, S.W. Erasmus in het Nederlands to 1617.
R. Padberg, 182:Vol31#9/10-257
Bikle, G.B., Jr. The New Jerusalem.*
F.W. Iklé, 302:Vol16#1and2-132
"Steve Biko: Black Consciousness in South Africa." (M. Arnold, ed)
639(VQR):Spring79-62
Bilenkin, D. The Uncertainty Principle.
E. Korn, 617(TLS):30May80-626
Biles, J.I., ed. Studies in the Literary Imagination.
G. Negley, 322(JHI):Apr-Jun79-315
Biliński, B. Il Pitagorismo di Nicolò Copernico.*
H. Wagner, 53(AGP):Band60Heft2-228
Billcliffe, R. Mackintosh Watercolours.
L. Ormond, 39:Dec79-537
R. Whelan, 55:Feb79-32
Billing, G. The Slipway.
M.K. Joseph, 368:Jun74-162
Billington, D.P. Robert Maillart's Bridges.
J.M. Richards, 617(TLS):1Feb80-122
Billington, E.T., ed. The Randolph Caldecott Treasury.
C. Cannon-Brookes, 39:Mar79-242
Billington, J.H. Fire in the Minds of Men.
M. Berman, 441:14Sep80-11
J. Leonard, 441:8Aug80-C18
P. Singer, 453(NYRB):6Nov80-51
Billington, R. A Woman's Age.*
J. Leonard, 441:29Jan80-C20
A. Tyler, 441:10Feb80-15
Billington, R.A. America's Frontier Culture.*
L. Nash, 649(WAL):Spring79-82
Bin-Nun, S.R. The Tawananna in the Hittite Kingdom.
G. Beckman, 318(JAOS):Oct-Dec78-513
Binchy, M. Victoria Line.
J. Mellors, 362:18and25Dec80-867
Binder, H. Kafka-Kommentar zu sämtlichen Erzählungen.
R. Sheppard, 220(GL&L):Oct78-83
Bindman, D. Blake as an Artist.*
A. Atkinson, 173(ECS):Winter78/79-229
I.H.C., 191(ELN):Sep78(supp)-46
Z. Leader, 184(EIC):Jan79-81
A.K. Mellor, 591(SIR):Spring79-155
B.M. Stafford, 56:Winter79-118

Bindman, D., ed. John Flaxman.
    F. Haskell, 453(NYRB):9Oct80-29
Bingham, M. Earls and Girls.
    E.S. Turner, 617(TLS):5Sep80-972
Bingham, M. The "Great Lover."*
    A.N. Athanason, 572:Sep79-151
Binney, M. and D. Pearce, eds. Railway
Architecture.
    J.M. Richards, 617(TLS):1Feb80-122
Binns, J.W., ed. The Latin Poetry of
English Poets.*
    J.P. Russo, 122:Jul79-261
"Biografie e Bibliografie degli Accademici
Lincei."
    D.E. Rhodes, 354:Sep79-291
Bioy Casares, A. L'Invention de Morel.
    A. Calame, 450(NRF):Feb79-111
Birault, H. Heidegger et l'expérience de
la pensée.
    D. Janicaud, 192(EP):Apr-Jun79-229
Bird, A. The Plays of Oscar Wilde.
    K. Beckson, 651(WHR):Winter79-73
    I. Fletcher, 637(VS):Summer79-487
Bird, C. Divining.
    R. Haynes, 617(TLS):11Apr80-420
Bird, C.G. The Role of Family in Melo-
drama (1797-1827).
    J-M. Thomasseau, 535(RHL):Jul-Aug79-
    668
Bird, J. Percy Grainger.
    D.S. Josephson, 414(MusQ):Apr78-255
Bird, O.A. Cultures in Conflict.
    H.M. Curtler, 396(ModA):Winter79-93
Birdwell, C. Amazons.
    C. Lehmann-Haupt, 441:16Sep80-C16
Birk, D.B.W. The MalakMalak Language,
Daly River (Western Arnhem Land).
    R.M.W. Dixon, 350:Mar79-260
Birke, J., B. Birke and P.M. Mitchell -
see Gottsched, J.C.
Birkenhauer, K. Kleist.
    M. Gelus, 221(GQ):Jan79-91
Lord Birkenhead. Rudyard Kipling.*
    S. Pickering, 569(SR):Winter79-165
    639(VQR):Summer79-94
Birkin, A. J.M. Barrie and the Lost Boys.*
    M.N. Cohen, 441:13Jan80-3
    V.S. Pritchett, 442(NY):31Mar80-117
    J.C. Trewin, 157:Summer79-74
Birkin, A. The Lost Boys.
    D. Wheeler, 362:6Mar80-316
Birley, A. The People of Roman Britain.
    B. Cunliffe, 617(TLS):18Apr80-447
Birnbaum, H., ed. American Contributions
to the Eighth International Congress of
Slavists. (Vol 1)
    C.E. Townsend, 574(SEEJ):Winter79-545
Birnbaum, P. An Eastern Tradition.
    F. Taliaferro, 441:12Oct80-15
Birney, E. Fall by Fury.*
    D. Barbour, 150(DR):Spring79-154
Birney, E. Ghost in the Wheels.*
    J. Ditsky, 628(UWR):Fall-Winter78-86
    D.S. West, 102(CanL):Spring79-109
Birstein, A. American Children.
    C. Lehmann-Haupt, 441:27Feb80-C25

Birtwhistle, J. Tidal Models.
    G. Lindop, 617(TLS):16May80-562
Bischof, B., J. Duft and S. Sonderegger,
eds. Das älteste deutsche Buch.
    P.F. Ganz, 402(MLR):Apr79-485
    T.W. Juntune, 301(JEGP):Jan79-83
Bishirjian, R. The Development of Polit-
ical Theory.
    T. Molnar, 396(ModA):Fall79-426
Bishop, E. Moments of Grace.
    C. Hope, 364:Mar80-75
Bishop, N., S. Hamilton and C. Bowman.
Nan, Sarah and Clare.
    D. Grumbach, 441:27Jul80-14
Bishop, T. and R. Federman, eds. Samuel
Beckett.
    F. Busi, 207(FR):Apr79-781
Bisilliat, M., O. Villas Boas and C.
Villas Boas. Xingu.
    P. Henley, 617(TLS):7Mar80-276
Bissell, C.T. Humanities in the Univer-
sity.
    J.F. Leddy, 627(UTQ):Summer79-468
Bissett, B. Plutonium Missing. Pomes
for Yoshi.
    D. Barbour, 198:Winter80-129
Bissett, B. Sailor.*
    D. Barbour, 150(DR):Spring79-154
    D. Barbour, 198:Winter80-129
Bisztray, G. Marxist Models of Literary
Realism.*
    J.H. Kavanagh, 107(CRCL):Fall79-410
    M. Silver, 125:Spring79-447
Bitov, A. Puškinskij dom.
    L. Koehler, 574(SEEJ):Summer79-291
Bittmann, I., comp. Catalogue of Giedde's
Music Collection in the Royal Library of
Copenhagen.
    P.W. Jones, 410(M&L):Jul79-335
Bizot, F. Le figuier à 5 branches.
    O. von Hinüber, 182:Vol131#11/12-332
Björkman, S. Le type "avoir besoin."
    K. Hunnius, 547(RF):Band91Heft3-305
    L. Löfstedt, 350:Jun79-482
Bjornson, B. Land of the Free. (E.L. and
E. Haugen, eds and trans)
    C. Glasrud, 587(SAF):Autumn79-249
Bjurström, P. French Drawings, Sixteenth
and Seventeenth Centuries.
    P. Reuterswärd, 341:1978/2-77
Bjurström, P. Sergel tecknar.
    S.Å. Nilsson, 341:1978/2-81
Black, G. Night Run from Java.
    M. Laski, 362:10Jan80-62
Black, J. - see Tate, N.
Black, J.K. United States Penetration of
Brazil.*
    G. MacEoin, 399(MLJ):Jan-Feb79-63
Black, L. Glendraco.
    639(VQR):Spring78-67
Black, M. Poetic Drama as Mirror of the
Will.*
    J. Milhous, 130:Fall79-269
Blackall, E.A. The Emergence of German as
a Literary Language 1700-1775. (2nd ed)
    F.A. Brown, 301(JEGP):Jul79-396

Blackburn, P., ed and trans. Proensa.*
(G. Economou, ed)
S. Fredman, 114(ChiR):Winter79-152
Blackburn, P. - see Lorca, F.G.
Blackburn, S., ed. Meaning, Reference,
and Necessity.*
G.A. Malinas, 63:Mar79-101
Blackie, J. Bradfield, 1850-1975.
V.A. McClelland, 637(VS):Autumn77-116
Blackman, M.E., ed. Ashley House (Walton-
on-Thames) Building Accounts 1602-1607.
C.W. Chalklin, 325:Oct79-233
Blackmur, R.P. Henry Adams. (V.A.
Makowsky, ed)
R.M. Adams, 617(TLS):11Jul80-771
A. Broyard, 441:10May80-21
442(NY):30Jun80-106
Blackmur, R.P. The Poems of R.P. Black-
mur.*
R. Fraser, 560:Spring-Summer79-205
639(VQR):Summer78-100
Blackstone, W.T. and R.D. Heslep, eds.
Social Justice and Preferential Treat-
ment.
R.H.S. Tur, 518:Jan79-41
Blackwood, C. Great Granny Webster.
K. Warren, 577(SHR):Fall79-365
Blackwood, C. The Stepdaughter.
G.W. Jarecke, 577(SHR):Summer79-276
Blades, J. Drum Roll.
J.H.E., 412:Aug-Nov78-287
Blaicher, G. Freie Zeit — Langeweile —
Literatur.
N. Würzbach, 490:Band10Heft4-522
Blair, D. A History of Glass in Japan.
A. Polak, 135:Nov79-201
Blair, I. The Dark Rainbow.
D.M. Day, 157:Winter79-88
Blair, J.G. The Confidence Man in Modern
Fiction.*
L.M. Whitehead, 150(DR):Winter79/80-
759
Blair, P.H. An Introduction to Anglo-
Saxon England. (2nd ed)
A.N. Doane, 529(QQ):Summer79-302
Blair, W. and H. Hill. America's Humor.*
E. Current-Garcia, 577(SHR):Spring79-
165
S. Pinsker, 219(GaR):Spring79-218
L.D. Rubin, Jr., 27(AL):Nov79-423
Blais, J. De l'Ordre et de l'Aventure.
R. Robidoux, 208(FS):Vol33Pt2-939
Blais, J. Présence d'Alain Grandbois,
avec quatorze poèmes parus de 1956 à
1969.
B-Z. Shek, 208(FS):Vol33Pt2-940
Blais, M-C. A Literary Affair.
D.W. Russell, 198:Summer80-159
Blais, M-C. Nights in the Underground.*
(French title: Les Nuits de l'Under-
ground.)
M.A. Fitzpatrick, 207(FR):May79-948
D.W. Russell, 198:Summer80-159
Blaisdell, F.W., Jr. and M.E. Kalinke -
see "Erex Saga and Ivens Saga"
Blaise, C. Lunar Attractions.*
M. Dixon, 529(QQ):Winter79/80-722

de Blaison, T. - see under Thibaut de
Blaison
Blake, N.F. The English Language in
Medieval Literature.*
A. Bliss, 447(N&Q):Aug78-353
G. Kristensson, 179(ES):Jun79-321
Blake, N.F., ed. Quattuor Sermones
Printed by William Caxton.*
D. Speed, 67:May79-84
K. Sperk, 224(GRM):Band28Heft4-493
Blake, W. William Blake's Writings. (G.E.
Bentley, Jr., ed)
G. Lindop, 148:Autumn79-86
Blake, W. Songs of Innocence and Experi-
ence. (G. Keynes, ed)
639(VQR):Spring78-58
Blakemore, C. Mechanics of the Mind.
529(QQ):Spring79-183
Blaker, M. Japanese International Nego-
tiating Style.
A. Iriye, 293(JASt):May79-589
Blakiston, G. Woburn and the Russells.
R. Stewart, 362:18Sep80-374
Blanc, A. Le Théâtre de Dancourt.
R. Guichemerre, 535(RHL):Nov-Dec79-
1048
Blanc, M. Les Paysanneries françaises.
H.L. Butler, 207(FR):Apr79-810
Blanchard, P. Margaret Fuller.
W. Randel, 27(AL):May79-282
Blanche-Benvéniste, C. Recherches en vue
d'une théorie de la grammaire française.
P. Cannings, 207(FR):Oct78-202
Blanco, I.M. - see under Matte Blanco, I.
Blanco, J.J. Se llamaba Vasconcelos.
M-C. Petit, 182:Vol131#13-416
Blanco Aguinaga, C. De Mitólogos y Novel-
istas.
M. Zimmerman, 125:Spring79-460
Blane, A., ed. The Religious World of
Russian Culture.*
F.C.M. Kitch, 575(SEER):Jul79-475
Blanke, G.H. Einführung in die semantis-
che Analyse.
K-E. Sommerfeldt, 682(ZPSK):Band31
Heft6-662
Blankfort, M. An Exceptional Man.
E. Wagner, 441:16Nov80-14
Blanshard, B. Reason and Belief.
A.J.R., 543:Sep78-127
Blanton, L.L. Elementary Composition
Practice. (Bk 1)
E. Storey, 608:Mar80-112
Blaser, W. After Mies.
R.G. Wilson, 505:Oct79-102
Blasier, C. and C. Mesa-Lago, eds. Cuba
in the World.
L.D. Langley, 263(RIB):Vol129No3/4-357
Blasing, M.K. The Art of Life.*
E.N. Harbert, 295(JML):Vol17#4-620
Blasquez, J.M. Diccionario a las Reli-
giones Prerromanas de Hispania.
C. Bémont, 194(EC):Vol15fasc2-726
Blassingame, J.W., ed. Slave Testimony.*
W.E. Perkins, 9(AlaR):Apr79-150
Blassingame, J.W. - see Douglass, F.

Blázquez, J.M. Cástulo. (Vol 1)
R.F.J. Jones, 313:Vol69-221
Blázquez, J.M. Economía de la Hispania
romana.
J.M-F. Marique, 124:Dec79/Jan80-245
Blechman, R.O. Behind the Lines.
D. Hill, 441:14Dec80-18
Bleich, D. Subjective Criticism.*
E. Goodheart, 125:Spring79-450
S. Mailloux, 290(JAAC):Winter69-211
M. Shechner, 141:Spring79-153
M. Steig, 599:Summer79-300
Bleicken, J., C. Meier and H. Strasburger.
Matthias Gelzer und die römische Gesch-
ichte.
R. Seager, 123:Vol129No1-193
Bleikasten, A. The Most Splendid Failure.*
K. McSweeney, 148:Spring79-73
Bleiler, E.F., ed. A Treasury of Victo-
rian Detective Stories.
H. Greene, 362:12Jun80-772
Blesh, R. Keaton.
D. Macdonald, 453(NYRB):9Oct80-33
Blewett, D. Defoe's Art of Fiction.
D. Fairer, 617(TLS):30May80-625
Bliesener, U. and H. Brinkmann. Pro-
gramme zur englischen Grammatik: Some
and any.
K. Macht, 430(NS):Feb78-87
Blishen, E. A Nest of Teachers.
N. Tucker, 617(TLS):21Mar80-337
K. Wright, 362:13Mar80-350
Bliss, A. - see Swift, J.
Bliss, D.P. Edward Bawden.
D. Piper, 617(TLS):1Feb80-119
Blixen, K. Les Chevaux fantômes et autres
contes.
C. Jordis, 450(NRF):May79-139
Bloch, E. Héritage de ce temps.*
A. Reix, 542:Jul-Sep78-376
Bloch, M. Memoirs of War, 1914-1915.
J. Russell, 441:3Sep80-C20
Bloch, R. and others. Recherches sur les
religions de l'Italie antique.*
J-C. Richard, 555:Vol52fasc1-205
Bloch, R.H. Medieval French Literature
and Law.*
P.F. Dembowski, 589:Jan79-112
B. Stock, 188(ECr):Fall78-96
Bloch, S., ed. Ernest Bloch.
A. Knapp, 410(M&L):Oct79-461
Bloch, S. and P. Reddaway. Psychiatric
Terror.
P.S. Appelbaum, 390:May79-74
F. Barghoorn, 550(RusR):Jan79-113
Block, A. East Side — West Side.
E. Hobsbawm, 617(TLS):27Jun80-728
Block, A. and C. Riley - see "Children's
Literature Review"
Block, H. Herblock on All Fronts.
D. Hill, 441:14Dec80-13
Block, L. Ariel.
M. Levin, 441:10Feb80-14
Block, T.H. Mayday.
P. Andrews, 441:27Jan80-15
Blocker, H.G. Philosophy of Art.
R.J. Matthews, 290(JAAC):Spring80-328

Blodgett, E.D. Sounding.*
R.B. Hatch, 102(CanL):Summer79-129
Blodgett, M. Captain Blood.
M. Levin, 441:3Aug80-12
Blodgett, R. Photographs.
G. Thornton, 55:Nov79-46
Blom, J.P., S. Nyhus and R. Sevag, eds.
Norwegian Folk Music: Harding Fiddle
Music.
F. Wilhelmsen, 187:May80-298
Blomqvist, A. The Health Care Business.
R.S. Tonks, 150(DR):Autumn79-580
Blond, G. Julie des Arques.
P.V. Conroy, Jr., 207(FR):May79-949
Blondel, J. The Government of France.
(2nd ed)
M. Anderson, 208(FS):Vol133Pt2-1011
Blondel, J. Imaginaire et Croyance.
H. Dubrow, 161(DUJ):Dec78-133
Blondel, M. Les journaux français.
E. Namenwirth, 556(RLV):1978/1-96
Blondin, A. Sur le tour de France.
P. Fournel, 450(NRF):Aug79-139
Bloodworth, D. Trapdoor.
M. Laski, 362:13Nov80-665
Bloom, E. and L., eds. Addison and Steele:
The Critical Heritage.
K. Walker, 617(TLS):25Jul80-849
Bloom, E.A. and L.D. Satire's Persuasive
Voice.
P.M. Spacks, 401(MLQ):Dec79-403
Bloom, H. The Flight to Lucifer.*
D.T. O'Hara, 659(ConL):Autumn80-649
L. Sage, 617(TLS):20Jun80-690
Bloom, H. Wallace Stevens.*
J.E. Miller, Jr., 405(MP):Nov79-249
Bloom, H. and others. Deconstruction and
Criticism.
D. Donoghue, 453(NYRB):12Jun80-37
T. Hawkes, 676(YR):Summer80-560
Bloom, L. and M. Lahey. Language Develop-
ment and Language Disorders.
C. Garvey, 350:Dec79-945
Bloom, R. Anatomies of Egotism.*
J.R. Reed, 141:Summer79-284
Bloomberg, E. Les Raisons de Pascal.
J.H. Broome, 208(FS):Jul79-344
Bloomer, K.C. and C.W. Moore, with R.J.
Yudell. Body, Memory, and Architecture.*
C. Jencks, 46:Mar79-130
M.O. Jones, 658:Summer79-204
Bloomfield, B.C. An Author Index to
Selected British "Little Magazines"
1930-1939.*
B. Bergonzi, 402(MLR):Oct79-932
L. Madden, 447(N&Q):Oct78-478
Bloomfield, B.C., ed. Middle East Studies
and Libraries.
M.E. Yapp, 617(TLS):19Sep80-1040
Bloomfield, M. and E. Haugen, eds. Lan-
guage as a Human Problem.
A.R. Tellier, 189(EA):Jan-Mar78-75
Bloor, D. Knowledge and Social Imagery.*
L. Boon, 84:Jun79-195
Blotner, J. - see Faulkner, W.

Blount, B.G. and M. Sanches, eds. Socio-
cultural Dimensions of Language Change.
   R. Burling, 350:Jun79-457
   M. Saville-Troike, 355(LSoc):Apr78-125
Blount, R., Jr. Crackers.
   P-L. Adams, 61:Oct80-101
   A. Broyard, 441:27Sep80-15
   C. Simmons, 441:28Sep80-3
Blount, T. The Correspondence of Thomas
Blount (1618-1679) A Recusant Antiquary.
(T. Bongaerts, ed)
   G. Williams, 354:Jun79-176
"The Blue Cliff Record." (T. and J.C.
Cleary, trans)
   B.M. Wilson, 485(PE&W):Apr79-249
Blum, A.F. Socrates.*
   T.G.W., 543:Mar79-534
Blum, C. Diderot.
   R. Niklaus, 208(FS):Vol33Pt2-771
Blum, D. Casals and the Art of Interpreta-
tion.
   412:Aug-Nov78-287
Blum, J. The End of the Old Order in
Rural Europe.*
   L. Daly, 377:Jul79-121
Blum, J.M. The Progressive Presidents.
   G. Hodgson, 441:11May80-7
Blum, R. Kallimachos und die Literatur-
verzeichnung bei den Griechen.*
   J. Irigoin, 555:Vol52fasc2-382
Blumberg, A.E. Logic.
   L.S. Cauman, 316:Jun79-281
Blumberg, P. Inequality in an Age of
Decline.
   L.C. Thurow, 441:26Oct80-9
Blumensath, H. and C. Uebach. Einführung
in die Literaturgeschichte der DDR.
   P. Hutchinson, 220(GL&L):Oct78-93
Blumenthal, J. The Printed Book in
America.*
   P.J. Parker, 658:Autumn79-314
Blumenthal, S. The Permanent Campaign.
   J. Fallows, 441:11May80-7
Blumenthal, U-R. The Early Councils of
Pope Paschal II 1100-1110.
   D. Bethell, 382(MAE):1979/1-109
Blumstein, A.K. Misogyny and Idealization
in the Courtly Romance.*
   W.T.H. Jackson, 222(GR):Winter79-35
Blunck, J. Mars and its Satellites.
   E.B. Vest, 424:Dec78-423
Blunt, A., ed. Baroque and Rococo Archi-
tecture and Decoration.
   G. Beard, 135:Aug79-288
Blunt, A. Borromini.*
   K. Downes, 90:Dec79-803
   G. Masson, 46:Dec79-397
Blunt, A. The Drawings of Poussin.
   G. Martin, 617(TLS):1Feb80-120
Blusch, J. Formen und Inhalt von Hesiods
individuellem Denken.
   W.J. Verdenius, 394:Vol130fasc3-302
Bly, R. This Tree Will be Here for a
Thousand Years.
   H. Carruth, 231:Jan80-77
   G.S., 109:Summer80-228
   A. Williamson, 441:9Mar80-8

Blythe, R. The View in Winter.*
   J. Updike, 442(NY):7Apr80-143
Blyton, G. and R. Capps. Speaking Out.
   T.W. Cole, 583:Winter79-207
Boaistuau, P. Histoires tragiques. (R.A.
Carr, ed)
   P.A. Chilton, 402(MLR):Apr79-453
Boardman, J. Athenian Black Figure Vases.
   T.H. Price, 122:Jan79-82
Boardman, J. Corpus Vasorum Antiquorum.
(Great Britain, fasc 14)
   C. Sourvinou-Inwood, 303(JoHS):Vol199-
   214
Boardman, J. Greek Sculpture: The Archaic
Period.
   W.R. Biers, 124:Sep79-46
   R.M. Cook, 303(JoHS):Vol199-211
   M. Robertson, 90:Aug79-527
Boardman, J. and D. Scarisbrick. The
Ralph Harari Collection of Finger Rings.
   M. Henig, 303(JoHS):Vol199-216
Boardman, J. and M-L. Vollenweider. Ash-
molean Museum, Oxford: Catalogue of the
Engraved Gems and Finger Rings. (Vol 1)
   G. Heres, 182:Vol131#15/16-563
   M. Robertson, 90:Jul79-442
Boardman, P. The Worlds of Patrick Geddes.
   C. Ward, 46:Feb79-124
Boas, H.U. Syntactic Generalizations and
Linear Order in Generative Transforma-
tional Grammar.
   J.G. Kooij, 361:Feb/Mar78-285
Boase, A. Vie de Jean de Sponde.*
   H. Lafay, 535(RHL):Nov-Dec79-1041
   M. Malley, 207(FR):Dec78-343
Boase, A. - see de Sponde, J.
Boase, R. The Origin and Meaning of
Courtly Love.*
   S.A. Barney, 191(ELN):Jun79-331
   J.C. Hirsh, 382(MAE):1979/1-124
   H.A. Kelly, 589:Apr79-338
Boase, R. The Troubadour Revival.
   G.M. Cropp, 67:Nov79-338
   J. Snow, 304(JHP):Autumn79-83
Boase, T.S.R. Giorgio Vasari.
   M. Baxandall, 617(TLS):1Feb80-111
Boberach, H. and H. Booms, eds. Aus der
Arbeit des Bundesarchivs (Schriften des
Bundesarchivs 25).
   R. Storey, 325:Oct79-241
Bobinski, G.S., J.H. Shera and B.S. Wynar,
eds. Dictionary of American Library
Biography.
   S. Vann, 77:Winter78-90
Boccaccio, G. Boccaccio in Defense of
Poetry. (J. Reedy, ed)
   L.V.R., 568(SCN):Spring-Summer79-64
Boccaccio, M. - see Mucci, P.
Bochner, J. Blaise Cendrars.*
   M. Parmentier, 627(UTQ):Summer79-427
Bociurkiw, B.R. and J.W. Strong, eds.
Religion and Atheism in the USSR and
Eastern Europe.
   T.L. Zawistowski, 497(PolR):Vol123#1-
   105

Bock, A. Japanese Film Directors.
  Hazumi Arihiro, 285(JapQ):Jan-Mar79-
  115
Bock, M. Architectura: 1893-1918.
  H. Searing, 576:Dec78-305
Bockholdt, U., R. Machold and L. Thew, eds.
  Thematischer Katalog der Benediktinerin-
  nenabtei Frauenwörth und der Pfarrkir-
  chen Indersdorf, Wasserburg am Inn und
  Bad Tölz.
  B.S. Brook, 317:Fall79-549
Bocking, D.H., ed. Pages from the Past.
  C. Armstrong, 99:Apr80-37
Bocuse, P. Paul Bocuse's French Cooking.
  W. and C. Cowen, 639(VQR):Spring78-71
Bodel, J. Das Spiel vom heiligen Nikolaus.
  (K-H. Schroeder, W. Nitsch and M. Wenzel,
  eds and trans)
  T.D. Hemming, 208(FS):Vol33Pt2-555
  A. Serper, 545(RPh):Nov78-256
Boden, M.A. Artificial Intelligence and
  Natural Man.*
  M. Atkinson, 479(PhQ):Jul79-278
  D.C. Dennett, 486:Dec78-648
  A. Reeves, 63:Mar79-106
  G. Robinson, 483:Jan79-130
Boden, M.A. Jean Piaget.
  H.E. Gruber, 441:19Oct80-15
  J. Leonard, 441:25Jan80-C24
Bodenstedt, F. Phokäisches Elektron-Geld
  von 600-326 v. Chr.*
  J.P. Guépin, 303(JoHS):Vol99-217
Bodewig, M., J. Schmitz and R. Weier, eds.
  Das Menschenbild des Nikolaus von Kues
  und der christliche Humanismus.
  J-C. Margolin, 182:Vol31#11/12-334
Bodewitz, H.W. Jaiminīya-Brāhmaṇa I, 1-65.
  K. Mylius, 259(IIJ):Apr79-142
Bodi, L. Tauwetter in Wien.
  A.E. Ratz, 564:Feb79-71
  A. Schneider, 182:Vol31#21/22-807
  E. Wangermann, 220(GL&L):Apr80-257
Bodrogligeti, A.J.E. - see "Ḥāliṣ's Story
  of Ibrāhīm"
Boeck, W., C. Fleckenstein and D. Freydank.
  Geschichte der russischen Literatur-
  sprache.
  G.F. Meier, 682(ZPSK):Band31Heft2-199
Boehme, J. De l'élection de la grâce ou
  de la volonté de Dieu envers les hommes.
  A. Reix, 542:Apr-Jun79-219
Boening, J., ed. The Reception of Class-
  ical German Literature in England, 1760-
  1860.
  D.E. Wellbery, 149(CLS):Dec79-361
den Boer, W. Private Morality in Greece
  and Rome.
  J. Henderson, 124:Apr-May80-426
den Boer, W. Progress in the Greece of
  Thucydides.
  C.W. MacLeod, 123:Vol129No2-315
Boeta, J.R. Bernardo de Gálvez.
  J.J. Te Paske, 263(RIB):Vol129No1-76
Boethius. Boethii Daci: "Quaestiones
  super libros Physicorum." (G. Sajó, ed)
  A. Zimmermann, 53(AGP):Band60Heft2-218

Boethius. Corpus Philosophorum Danicorum
  Medii Aevi. (Vol 6) (J. Pinborg, ed)
  A. Zimmermann, 53(AGP):Band60Heft1-68
Boethius. De topicis differentiis. (E.
  Stump, ed and trans)
  J.F. Boler, 482(PhR):Jul79-486
  P.A. Clarke, 518:Oct79-107
  G. Gál, 589:Jul79-614
  R.M., 543:Dec78-371
Boettcher, R., with G.L. Freedman. Gifts
  of Deceit.
  W. Goodman, 441:11May80-18
  G. Vecsey, 441:23Jun80-C16
Boettcher, W. and H. Sitta. Der andere
  Grammatikunterricht.
  W. Vesper, 686(ZGL):Band7Heft3-360
Boetticher, W. Handschriftlich überlie-
  ferte Lauten- und Gitarrentabulaturen
  des 15. bis 18. Jahrhunderts.
  I. Fenlon, 415:Jun79-489
Bogan, L. The Blue Estuaries.
  639(VQR):Summer78-102
Bogan, L. Journey Around My Room. (R.
  Limmer, ed)
  A. Broyard, 441:8Nov80-21
  F. Taliaferro, 231:Dec80-78
Bogard, T., R. Moody and W.J. Meserve.
  American Drama.
  K. Tetzeli von Rosador, 72:Band216
  Heft2-426
Bogarde, D. A Gentle Occupation.
  P-L. Adams, 61:May80-103
  R. Kiely, 441:29Jun80-14
  J. Mellors, 362:20Mar80-382
  D. Wilson, 617(TLS):21Mar80-312
  442(NY):26May80-127
Bogarde, D. Snakes and Ladders.*
  B. Weeks, 18:Jul-Aug79-64
  639(VQR):Autumn79-143
Bogdanor, V. Devolution.
  D. Murison, 595(ScS):Vol123-88
Boghardt, M. Analytische Druckforschung.*
  L.S. Thompson, 133:Band12Heft1/2-189
Bögl, H. Soziale Anschauungen bei Hein-
  rich dem Teichner.*
  R. Schnell, 680(ZDP):Band97Heft3-440
Bogumil, S. Rousseau und die Erziehung
  des Lesers.
  J.S. Spink, 208(FS):Apr79-200
Bohlin, D.D. Prints and Related Drawings
  by the Carracci Family.
  J.T. Spike, 90:Aug79-526
Böhm, R. Das Motto in der englischen Lit-
  eratur des 19. Jahrhunderts.
  E. Tetzeli von Rosador, 72:Band216
  Heft1-182
Böhm, R.G. Gaiusstudien. (Vols 13 and 14)
  W.M. Gordon, 123:Vol129No2-323
Böhme, R. Aeschylus correctus.*
  J. Diggle, 123:Vol129No2-307
  A.F. Garvie, 303(JoHS):Vol99-172
  G. Ronnet, 555:Vol152fasc1-159
Boime, A. Thomas Couture and the Eclectic
  Vision.
  J. Russell, 441:14Sep80-3

Boissard, J. A Matter of Feeling.
   A. Tyler, 441:9Mar80-10
   442(NY):11Feb80-117
Boissel, J. Gobineau, l'Orient et l'Iran.
   (Vol 1)
   M.D. Biddiss, 208(FS):Vol33Pt2-827
Boitani, P. Chaucer and Boccaccio.
   R.D.S. Jack, 402(MLR):Jul79-713
Bok, S. Lying.
   H. Rank, 128(CE):Apr79-950
Bol, L.J. Adriaen Coorte.*
   I. Bergström, 341:1978/2-80
   R. Mandle, 90:May79-326
Bolamba, A-R. Esanzo.
   J. Decock, 207(FR):Feb79-507
Bolchazy, L.J. Hospitality in Early Rome.
   K. Gries, 124:Sep79-39
   R. Saller, 24:Fall79-465
Bolckmans, A., ed. Literature and Reality,
   Creatio versus Mimesis.*
   M. Gravier, 562(Scan):May79-84
Bold, A., ed. Cambridge Book of English
   Verse 1939-1975.
   C. Guillot, 189(EA):Apr-Jun78-238
Bold, A., ed. Making Love.
   B. Morrison, 364:Apr/May79-129
Bold, A. This Fine Day.
   G. Lindop, 617(TLS):22Feb80-214
"Boletín Interamericano de Archivos."
   (Vol 4)
   C. Rodríguez, 263(RIB):Vol29No2-219
Bolinger, D. Degree Words.
   G. Lepschy, 545(RPh):May79-411
Bolinger, D. Meaning and Form.*
   M.L. Geis, 350:Sep79-684
   D. Hymes, 361:Jun78-175
   R.A. Jacobs, 300:Mar79-86
Bolívar, S. Correspondencia del Liberta-
   dor con el General Juan José Flores
   (1826-1830).
   J.L. Helguera, 263(RIB):Vol29No3/4-351
Böll, H. Fürsorgliche Belagerung.
   M. Butler, 617(TLS):7Mar80-278
Böll, H. Missing Persons.
   639(VQR):Summer78-96
Bollacher, M. Lessing.
   R.R. Heitner, 221(GQ):May79-406
   H. Reichelt, 564:Feb79-73
Bollack, J. - see Epicurus
Bollack, J., P. Judet de la Combe and H.
   Wismann. La réplique de Jocaste.*
   F.C. Kohler, 24:Fall79-428
   G. Ronnet, 555:Vol52fasc1-155
Bollack, J. and A. Laks. Epicure à Pyth-
   oclès.
   F. Lasserre, 182:Vol31#21/22-819
Bollack, J. and A. Laks, eds. Etudes sur
   l'épicurisme antique.*
   O. Bloch, 542:Jan-Mar79-137
   C.W. Chilton, 123:Vol29No1-84
Bollack, M. La raison de Lucrèce.
   M. Cariou, 542:Apr-Jun79-193
   A. Dalzell, 124:Nov79-199
   D. and P. Fowler, 123:Vol29No1-32
   C. Rosset, 98:Apr78-347

Bollée, A. Le Créole français des Sey-
   chelles.*
   A. Hull, 207(FR):Feb79-506
Bollée, A. Zur Entstehung der französis-
   chen Kreolendialekte im indischen Ozean.
   R.A. Hall, Jr., 350:Dec79-913
Boller, P.F., Jr. Freedom and Fate in
   American Thought from Edwards to Dewey.
   R.L. Davis, 584(SWR):Winter79-vi
   R.E. Spiller, 27(AL):Mar79-110
Bolloten, B. The Spanish Revolution.
   B. Knox, 453(NYRB):6Nov80-34
Bologna, C., ed. Liber monstrorum de
   diversis generibus.
   A. Knock, 382(MAE):1979/2-259
Bölöni Farkas, A. Journey in North
   America. (T. and H.B. Schoenman, eds
   and trans)
   I. Deak, 575(SEER):Apr79-293
Bolten, J. and H. Bolten-Rempt. The Hid-
   den Rembrandt.
   K. Roberts, 90:Feb79-124
Bolter, J. and P.A. Stadter. A Concor-
   dance to Arrian.
   E.N. Borza, 124:Dec79/Jan80-250
Bolton, W.F. Alcuin and "Beowulf."*
   T.D. Hill, 301(JEGP):Jul79-408
   M. Stevens, 401(MLQ):Dec79-412
Boltzmann, L. Theoretical Physics and
   Philosophical Problems. (B. McGuinness,
   ed)
   M.V. Curd, 486:Mar78-148
Bömer, F. P. Ovidius Naso, "Metamorpho-
   sen," Buch VI-IX.
   W.S. Anderson, 124:Sep79-42
   E.J. Kenney, 123:Vol29No2-223
Bomse, M.D. Practical Spanish Grammar.
   R.H. Gilmore, 399(MLJ):Mar79-157
   A.M. MacLean, 238:Dec79-744
Bonaccorso, G. Sul testo di "Madame
   Bovary."
   A. Fairlie, 208(FS):Oct79-466
Bonaccorso, G. and R.M. de Stefano - see
   Du Camp, M.
Bonachía Hernando, J.A. El concejo de
   Burgos en la Baja Edad Media (1345-1426).
   T.F. Ruiz, 589:Apr79-343
Bonanno, M.W. A Certain Slant of Light.*
   J. Kavanagh, 617(TLS):12Sep80-984
Bonavia, D. The Chinese.
   R. Elegant, 441:23Nov80-12
Boncompain, J. Auteurs et comédiens au
   XVIIIe siècle.
   T.E.D. Braun, 207(FR):Dec78-350
Bond, G., W. Johnson and S.S. Walker, eds.
   African Christianity.
   L. Mair, 617(TLS):15Aug80-918
Bondanella, P. and M. Musa - see Machia-
   velli, N.
Bondy, R. The Emissary.*
   M. Cohen, 287:Mar78-28
Bonelli, G. Aporie etiche in Epicuro.
   D. Konstan, 124:Mar80-368
Bonelli, M.L.R. and W.R. Shea - see under
   Righini Bonelli, M.L. and W.R. Shea
Bonet Correa, A. Andalucía Barroca.
   D. Angulo Íñiguez, 48:Jul-Sep78-352

Bordman, G. Jerome Kern.
R. Fuller, 617(TLS):19Sep80-1015
G. Kaufman, 362:18Sep80-375
S. Peck, 441:6Jul80-4
J.S. Wilson, 441:29Dec80-C18
Borduas, P-É. Écrits/Writings 1942-1958.
(F-M. Gagnon, ed)
J-A. Isaak, 150(DR):Autumn79-566
Borel, J. Commentaires.
J. Cruickshank, 208(FS):Jul79-371
Borenstein, I. Ancient Music.
G. Hamel, 198:Winter80-138
Borg, B., with E.L. Scott. My Life and
Game.
P-L. Adams, 61:Oct80-102
Borger, R. Assyrisch-babylonische Zeichen-
liste.
W. von Soden, 182:Vol131#20-755
Borges, J.L. The Book of Sand.
R. O'Mara, 639(VQR):Summer78-552
D.A. Wilson, 152(UDQ):Summer78-138
Borges, J.L. Sur le Cinéma. (E. Cozarin-
sky, ed)
J. Prieur, 450(NRF):Sep79-75
Borges, J.L. A Universal History of
Infamy.
639(VQR):Autumn79-136
Borghart, K.H.R. "Das Nibelungenlied."*
D.R. McLintock, 447(N&Q):Apr78-182
Borghello, G., ed. Interpretazioni di
Pasolini.
M.C., 228(GSLI):Vol155fasc492-633
Borgmeier, R. The Dying Shepherd.*
B. Rojahn-Deyk, 402(MLR):Apr79-415
Borgolte, M. Des Gesandtenaustausch der
Karolinger mit den Abbasiden und mit den
Patriarchen von Jerusalem.
R.G. Heath, 589:Apr79-344
Borie, J. - see Zola, É.
Borinski, L. and C. Uhlig. Literatur der
Renaissance.
K. Klein, 224(GRM):Band28Heft1-115
Borinsky, A. Ver/Ser visto.
J. Deredita, 400(MLN):Mar79-405
Boris, E.Z. Shakespeare's English Kings,
The People, and the Law.
C.S.L. Davies, 541(RES):Nov79-464
von Bormann, A., ed. Wissen aus Erfahrun-
gen.*
W. Ross, 52:Band13Heft1-75
Bormann, D.R. and E. Leinfellner - see
Müller, A.
Bormann, K. Parmenides.
W.J. Verdenius, 394:Vol32fasc1/2-180
Bornand, O. - see Rossetti, W.M.
Borne, D. Petits Bourgeois en révolte.
G. Klin, 207(FR):Dec78-368
Bornecque, J-H. - see Verlaine, P.
Bornemann, U. Anlehnung und Abgrenzung.
B. Becker-Cantarino, 406:Spring79-65
Börner, W. Die französische Orthographie.*
M. Govaert, 556(RLV):1978/6-550
G. Price, 208(FS):Vol133Pt2-1057
Bornheim, G.A. Dialética.
F.G. Sturm, 399(MLJ):Jan-Feb79-55
Bornheim, G.A. - see Heidegger, M.

Bornscheuer, L. Topik.
O. Pöggeler, 490:Band10Heft1-106
Bornstein, D. - see Christine de Pisan
Bornstein, D.D. An Introduction to Trans-
formational Grammar.
C. Crain, 399(MLJ):Jan-Feb79-68
Bornstein, G. The Postromantic Conscious-
ness of Ezra Pound.*
D. Pearlman, 659(ConL):Spring80-308
L. Surette, 106:Spring79-63
Bornstein, G. Transformations of Romanti-
cism in Yeats, Eliot, and Stevens.*
R. Buttel, 295(JML):Vol7#4-603
M.G. Cooke, 591(SIR):Summer79-323
D. Wagenknecht, 131(CL):Spring79-190
Borras, F.M. and R.F. Christian. Russian
Syntax. (2nd ed)
C.E. Townsend, 353:Jun78-83
Borrero, M.M. - see under Morales Borrero,
M.
Borret, M. Origène, "Contre Celse." (Vol
5)
P. Nautin, 555:Vol52fasc1-178
Borroff, M. Language and the Poet.
676(YR):Autumn79-VII
Borroff, M. - see "Pearl"
Borsa, G. La Nascita del mondo moderno
in Asia Orientale.
J.W. Sedlar, 293(JASt):Feb79-317
Borsdorff, U. and L. Niethammer, eds.
Zwischen Befreiung und Besatzung.
F. L'Huillier, 182:Vol31#9/10-307
Borsi, F. Firenze del Cinquecento.
L. Satkowski, 576:Oct78-205
Borsi, F. and others. Giovanni Antonio
Dosio.
R. Brilliant, 576:Dec78-318
von Borsig, M. Leben aus der Lotosblüte,
Nichiren Shōnin.
L. Hurvitz, 244(HJAS):Dec78-488
Borst, A., ed. Mönchtum, Episkopat und
Adel zur Gründungszeit des Klosters
Reichenau.
W. Berschin, 182:Vol31#3/4-65
Borup, M. - see Brandes, G.
Bos, D., R. Horville and B. Lecherbonnier.
La Littérature et les idées.
J. Cruickshank, 208(FS):Vol133Pt2-970
Bosanquet, R. Let's Get Through Wednesday.
M. Weigall, 362:2Oct80-445
Bosch García, C. Latinoamérica; una inter-
pretación global de la dispersión en el
siglo XIX.
E.O. Acevedo, 263(RIB):Vol129No3/4-358
Böschenstein, B. Leuchttürme.
K. Weissenberger, 133:Band12Heft1/2-
181
Boscher, W.B. and P.T. Liên. Wörterbuch
Vietnamesisch-Deutsch.
G.F. Meier, 682(ZPSK):Band31Heft6-652
de Boschère, J. Marthe et l'enragé.
Satan l'obscur.
G. Macé, 450(NRF):Jun79-113
Bosco, R.A. - see Mather, C.
Bosco, U. and G. Reggio - see Dante
Alighieri

41

Bosio, F. L'idea dell'uomo e la filosofia nel pensiero di Max Scheler.
D. Rolando, 227(GCFI):Apr-Jun78-272
Boskovits, M. Pittura fiorentina alla vigilia del Rinascimento 1370-1400.
M.S. Frinta, 54:Jun78-366
Bosley, K. Stations.
A. Stevenson, 617(TLS):23May80-586
Bosley, R. Aspects of Aristotle's Logic.*
J.D., 543:Dec78-350
Bosonnet, F. The Function of Stage Properties in Christopher Marlowe's Plays.
S. Wyler, 182:Vol31#21/22-811
Bosquet, A. Anthologie de la poésie française depuis 1950.
G.L., 450(NRF):Nov79-133
Bosshard, S.N. Zwingli-Erasmus-Cajetan.
H.J. Grimm, 182:Vol31#20-714
Bossong, G. Probleme der Übersetzung wissenschaftlicher Werke aus dem Arabischen in das Altspanische zur Z. Alfons des Weisen.
W.W. Müller, 182:Vol31#19-664
Bossuet, J-B. Discourse on Universal History. (O. Ranum, ed)
R.N. Nicolich, 207(FR):Feb79-486
Bostanzoglu, T. Eikonographon Onomastikon tēs Neoellēnikēs Glōssēs, me pinakas eikonōn apo to egkyklopaidikon lexikon Duden.
J. Werner, 682(ZPSK):Band31Heft3-331
Bostick, W.A. The Guarding of Cultural Property.
T. Walch, 14:Jan79-67
Bostock, D. Logic and Arithmetic. (Vol 2)
G. Hunter, 617(TLS):25Apr80-474
Bostock, J.K. A Handbook on Old High German Literature.* (2nd ed rev by K.C. King and D.R. McLintock)
C.D.M. Cossar, 47(ArL):Vol10#2-146
Bostok, J.M. On Sparse Brush.
C. Pollnitz, 581:Dec79-462
Boswell, J. Boswell, Laird of Anchinleck, 1778-1782. (J.W. Reed and F.A. Pottle, eds)
O.W. Ferguson, 579(SAQ):Winter79-137
Boswell, J. Christianity, Social Tolerance, and Homosexuality.
P. Robinson, 441:10Aug80-12
K. Thomas, 453(NYRB):4Dec80-26
Boswell, J. The Royal Treasure.
R.I. Burns, 589:Jul79-546
A.J. Forey, 86(BHS):Apr79-149
Bosworth, A.B. and others. Alexandre le Grand, image et réalité.*
R.W., 555:Vol52fasc1-144
Bosworth, R.J.B. Italy.
C. Seton-Watson, 617(TLS):22Feb80-217
Botha, R.P., with W.K. Winckler. The Justification of Linguistic Hypotheses.
B.L. Derwing, 297(JL):Sep79-341
Bothwell, R. Pearson.
G.W., 102(CanL):Summer79-164
Bothwell, R. and W. Kilbourn. C.D. Howe.
W.L. Gordon, 99:Mar80-31

Bott, M. and J.A. Edwards. Records Management in British Universities.
R.E. Goerler, 14:Jul79-358
Bottin, F. Le antinomie semantiche nella logica medievale.
P.V. Spade, 154:Jun78-384
Botto, E. Il neomarxismo.
L. Bertolini, 548(RCSF):Apr-Jun79-233
Bottorff, W.K. Thomas Jefferson.
E.L. Huddleston, 165(EAL):Spring80-89
Bottrall, R. Reflections on the Nile.
D. Davis, 362:28Aug80-277
A. Jenkins, 617(TLS):25Jul80-851
Botturi, F. Struttura e Soggettività.
E. Namer, 542:Jul-Sep79-320
Botz, G. Wien vom "Anschluss" zum Krieg.
Z. Zeman, 617(TLS):16May80-560
Bouamrane, C. Le problème de la liberté humaine dans la pensée musulmane (Solution mutazilite).
P. Trotignon, 542:Jul-Sep79-344
Bouchard, D.F. - see Foucault, M.
Bouchard, R. and D. Kennedy, eds. Lillooet Stories.
J. Ramsey, 292(JAF):Oct-Dec79-500
Bouché, C. Lautréamont.
M. Pierssens, 98:May78-493
Boucher, J-P. Jacques Ferron au pays des amélanchiers.
D.M. Hayne, 208(FS):Apr79-239
Bouchon, G. Mamale de Cananor, un Adversaire de l'Inde Portugaise (1507-1528).
H.K. Sherwani, 273(IC):Jul76-191
Boudard, A. Les Combattants du petit bonheur.
R.L. Léguillon, 207(FR):Dec78-376
Boudon, F. and others. Système de l'architecture urbaine.
W. Weyres, 182:Vol31#23/24-866
Bouffartigue, J. and M. Patillon - see Porphyry
Bouissac, P. Circus and Culture.
D. Coelho, 292(JAF):Jan-Mar79-82
D. Gronau, 182:Vol31#20-742
Boulanger, D. Un arbre dans Babylone.
L. Kovacs, 450(NRF):Jul79-108
Boulanger, D. La Dame de coeur. Le Gouverneur Polygame.
R. Buss, 617(TLS):29Feb80-238
Boulbet, J. Paysans de la forêt.
H. Uhlig, 182:Vol31#5/6-185
Boulby, M. Karl Philipp Moritz.
T.J. Reed, 617(TLS):4Jul80-766
Boulding, K.E. Ecodynamics.
K.E.F. Watt, 658:Winter79-427
Boullart, K.E. Gottlob Ernst Schulze.
L.C.R., 543:Mar79-535
Boulter, C.G. and K.T. Luckner. Corpus Vasorum Antiquorum.* (USA, fasc 17)
D. Buitron, 54:Sep78-552
R. Heidenreich, 182:Vol31#11/12-367
Bouniort, J. - see Carroll, L.
Bouraoui, H. Without Boundaries.
L. Welch, 150(DR):Summer79-368

42

Bouraoui, H-A. Structure intentionnelle du "Grand Meaulnes."*
J. Bastaire, 535(RHL):Jul-Aug79-707
M. Maclean, 208(FS):Vol33Pt2-879
R. Tarica, 207(FR):Oct78-171
Bourassa, A-G. Surréalisme et littérature québécoise.*
R. Ellenwood, 593:Spring79-89
Bourcier, E. Les Journaux privés en Angleterre de 1600 à 1660.*
I. Simon, 556(RLV):1978/1-82
Bourcier, G. Les Propositions Relative en Vieil-Anglais.
M. Huld, 350:Jun79-483
B. Mitchell, 382(MAE):1979/1-121
Bourdieu, P. Outline of a Theory of Practice.
185:Apr79-312
Bourdillon, M.F.C. The Shona Peoples.
P. Fry, 69:Vol148#1-92
Bourgain-Hemeryck, P. - see Chartier, A.
Bourgeade, P. Le Camp.
V. Beauvois, 450(NRF):Nov79-115
Bourgeois, B. - see Hegel, G.W.F.
Bourjaily, V. A Game Men Play.
A. Broyard, 441:19Jan80-21
L. McMurtry, 441:27Jan80-14
Bournonville, A. My Theater Life.* (P.N. McAndrew, ed and trans)
L. Kirstein, 453(NYRB):20Mar80-18
Bourriot, F. Recherches sur la nature du génos.
N.R.E. Fisher, 303(JoHS):Vol199-193
Boutang, P. Gabriel Marcel.
M. Adam, 542:Jul-Sep79-329
Bouveresse, J. Le mythe de l'intériorité.
Y. Michaud, 192(EP):Apr-Jun79-242
Bouveresse, R. Karl Popper, ou le rationalisme critique.
G. Brykman, 542:Jul-Sep79-321
Bouvier, J-C. Les Parlers provençaux de la Drôme.*
D. Evans, 208(FS):Vol33Pt2-1031
Bowen, D. The Protestant Crusade in Ireland, 1800-1870.
L.J. McCaffrey, 637(VS):Summer79-449
Bower, A.W. and R.A. Erickson - see Arbuthnot, J.
Bower, G. November ... December.
639(VQR):Spring78-66
Bowering, G. The Concrete Island.*
G. Davies, 168(ECW):Spring78-82
Bowering, G., ed. Great Canadian Sports Stories.
R. Ploude, 198:Summer80-136
Bowering, G. Protective Footwear.*
M. Cohen, 168(ECW):Fall78-51
J. Cutt, 526:Winter79-91
E. Thompson, 628(UWR):Fall-Winter78-76
Bowering, G. A Short Sad Book.
L. Surette, 102(CanL):Autumn79-84
Bowering, M. The Killing Room.* One Who Became Lost.
M. Darling, 102(CanL):Autumn79-91

Bowering, M. The Visitors Have All Returned.
J. Cook, 99:Mar80-38
376:Oct79-142
Bowers, F. - see Beaumont, F. and J. Fletcher
Bowers, F. - see Fielding, H.
Bowers, F. - see Nabokov, V.
Bowersock, G.W. Julian the Apostate.
M. Woloch, 121(CJ):Apr-May80-366
Bowie, M. Mallarmé and the Art of Being Difficult.
E. Souffrin-Le Breton, 208(FS):Oct79-468
Bowie, M. Proust, Jealousy, Knowledge.
J.M. Cocking, 208(FS):Oct79-475
Bowlby, J. Loss: Sadness and Depression.
L.J. Kaplan, 441:24Aug80-9
D.W. Harding, 617(TLS):4Jul80-747
C.M. Parkes, 362:5Jun80-728
Bowle, J. A History of Europe.
Z. Zeman, 617(TLS):7Mar80-254
Bowle, J. Man Through the Ages.
639(VQR):Winter78-9
Bowler, P.J. Fossils and Progress.
D. Ospovat, 637(VS):Winter78-266
Bowles, E.A. Musikleben im 15. Jahrhundert.
D. Fallows, 415:Aug79-654
Bowles, J. A Thousand Sundays.
J. Greenfield, 441:3Aug80-13
Bowles, P. Things Gone and Things Still Here.
376:Oct79-142
Bowman, A.K. and others. The Oxyrhynchus papyri. (Vol 45)
J.D. Thomas, 123:Vol29No2-296
Bowman, D. - see Bassin, E.
Box, E. Death in the Fifth Position.* Death Before Bedtime.* Death Likes it Hot.*
D.S., 109:Summer80-223
Boyarsky, A. A Pyramid of Time.
J.M. Kertzer, 198:Summer80-142
Boyce, M., ed. A Reader in Manichaean Middle Persian and Parthian.
W. Heston, 318(JAOS):Apr-Jun78-164
Boyd, E.F. Bloomsbury Heritage.*
C.S. Stern, 637(VS):Spring79-352
Boyd, R. Etude comparative dans le groupe Adamawa.
J. Knappert, 353:Sep78-94
Boyd-Carpenter, J. Way of Life.
J. Campbell, 362:29May80-694
Boydston, J.A. - see Dewey, J.
Boyeldieu, P. Etudes Yakoma, langue du Groupe Oubanguien (RCA).
J. Knappert, 353:Mar78-93
Boyer, B.B. and R. McKeon - see Abailard, P.
Boyer, M.V. The Texas Collection of "comedias sueltas."
S. García Castañeda, 173(ECS):Spring79-450
K. and R. Reichenberger, 304(JHP):Autumn79-92

Boyer, P. Urban Masses and Moral Order in America, 1820-1920.*
  C.E. Clark, Jr., 658:Winter79-406
  J. Potter, 617(TLS):25Jan80-93
  639(VQR):Summer79-88
Boyers, R., ed. Contemporary Poetry in America.
  V. Contoski, 114(ChiR):Autumn78-136
Boyers, R. F.R. Leavis.
  W.E. Cain, 219(GaR):Summer79-457
  639(VQR):Autumn79-127
Boyers, R. Lionel Trilling.*
  W.E. Cain, 639(VQR):Summer78-565
  R. Christiansen, 184(EIC):Oct79-380
Boyle, A. The Fourth Man.*
  R. Holmes, 231:Apr80-102
  A. Weinstein, 441:6Jan80-1
Boyle, A.J., ed. Ancient Pastoral.*
  J. Péron, 555:Vol52fasc1-153
Boyle, A.J. - see Vergil
Boyle, E. Obsession.
  376:Oct79-142
Boyle, J.A. The Mongol World Empire 1206-1370.
  C.R. Bawden, 203:Vol189#1-112
Boyle, J.M., Jr., G. Grisez and O. Tollefsen. Free Choice.*
  S.J.B., 543:Jun79-738
Boyle, K. Fifty Stories.
  V. Bourjaily, 441:28Sep80-9
Boyle, M.O. Erasmus on Language and Method in Theology.*
  J.H. Bentley, 539:Vol14No1-102
Boyle, R. James Joyce's Pauline Vision.*
  295(JML):Vol7#4-745
Boyle, T.C. Descent of Man.*
  L. Burnard, 617(TLS):20Jun80-718
  J. Mellors, 362:10Jul80-56
Bozeman, A.B. Conflict in Africa.
  T.H. Henriksen, 69:Vol148#3-304
Braccesi, L. Introduzione al de Viris Illustribus.
  R.P.H. Green, 313:Vol169-225
Brackert, H. Bauernkrieg und Literatur.*
  W. Theiss, 224(GRM):Band28Heft2-241
Brackman, A.C. A Delicate Arrangement.
  G. Himmelfarb, 441:6Jul80-7
  C. Lehmann-Haupt, 441:30Jun80-C17
Bradbrook, M.C. A History of Elizabethan Drama.
  J.C. Trewin, 157:Autumn79-83
Bradbrook, M.C. Shakespeare.*
  639(VQR):Spring79-47
Bradbury, M., ed. The Novel Today.
  529(QQ):Summer79-374
Bradbury, M. and J. McFarlane, eds. Modernism 1890-1930.
  295(JML):Vol7#4-583
Bradbury, N. Henry James: The Later Novels.
  D. Seed, 617(TLS):27Jun80-741
Bradbury, R. The Stories of Ray Bradbury.
  T.M. Disch, 441:26Oct80-14
Bradby, D. Adamov.
  K.R. Dutton, 67:May79-136
  D. Knowles, 208(FS):Vol33Pt2-925

Bradby, D. and J. McCormick. People's Theatre.
  S. Shepherd, 611(TN):Vol33#3-137
Braddy, H. The Paradox of Pancho Villa.
  W. Gard, 584(SWR):Winter79-89
  R.B. Olafson, 649(WAL):Summer79-182
Braden, G. The Classics and English Renaissance Poetry.
  D. Bush, 301(JEGP):Jan79-111
  R. Lunt, 541(RES):Aug79-350
  R.B. Rollin, 568(SCN):Spring-Summer79-5
Bradford, A.S. A Prosopography of Lacedaemonians from the Death of Alexander the Great, 323 B.C., to the Sack of Sparta by Alaric, A.D. 396.
  D.J. Geagan, 487:Spring79-70
Bradford, C.B. - see Shelley
Bradford, E. The Year of Thermopylae.
  P. Cartledge, 617(TLS):4Apr80-385
Bradford, P. Chair. (B. Prete, ed)
  G. Allen, 45:Jan79-51
Bradley, B.L. Rainer Maria Rilkes "Der Neuen Gedichte anderer Teil."*
  E.F. George, 182:Vol131#9/10-292
Bradley, I. The Optimists.
  S. Collini, 617(TLS):29Feb80-233
Bradley, I.C. The Call to Seriousness.*
  H. McLeod, 637(VS):Winter78-245
Bradley, J.D., W.G. Tremewan and A. Smith. British Tortricoid Moths: Tortricidae Olethrentinae. British Tortricoid Moths: Cochylidae and Tortricidae; Tortricinae.
  G.E.J. Nixon, 617(TLS):9May80-536
Bradley, K.R. Suetonius' Life of Nero.
  A.F. Wallace-Hadrill, 313:Vol169-224
Bradley, P. An Index to the Waverley Novels.*
  C.O. Parsons, 588(SSL):Vol13-301
Bradshaw, G. Hawk of May.
  J. Sullivan, 441:3Aug80-12
Brady, A.P. Lyricism in the Poetry of T.S. Eliot.
  H. Gardner, 402(MLR):Apr79-438
Brady, K. Father's Days.*
  J.S. Gordon, 441:27Jan80-12
Brady, P. Marcel Proust.
  H. Nitzberg, 207(FR):May79-935
Braet, H. Le Songe dans la chanson de geste au XIIe siècle.*
  G.S. Burgess, 208(FS):Vol33Pt2-523
Bragg, M. Kingdom Come.
  C. Brown, 617(TLS):4Apr80-382
  P. Kemp, 362:3Apr80-450
Bragger, J.D. and R.P. Shupp. Chère Françoise.* Le Monde français.
  T.M. Scanlan, 207(FR):Feb79-529
Brague, R. Le Restant.
  S.R., 543:Dec78-351
  A. Reix, 542:Jan-Mar79-128
Braham, A. The Architecture of the French Enlightenment.
  A. Blunt, 617(TLS):20Jun80-694
  F. Haskell, 453(NYRB):9Oct80-29
Braham, A. and H. Hager. Carlo Fontana: The Drawings at Windsor Castle.*
  T.A. Marder, 46:Oct79-206

Brahimi, D. Voyageurs français du XVIIIe
siècle en Barbarie.
  J. Lough, 208(FS):Vol33Pt2-789
  R. Mercier, 535(RHL):Sep-Oct78-829
Brahms, C. Stroganov in Company.
  J. Kavanagh, 617(TLS):19Sep80-1047
Brain, R. The Decorated Body.
  A. Hollander, 441:2Mar80-11
  M. Traherne, 617(TLS):7Mar80-276
Braine, J. Waiting for Sheila.
  442(NY):7Apr80-149
Brainerd, B. Introduction to Mathematics
of Language Study.
  G.F. Meier, 682(ZPSK):Band31Heft6-639
Braithwaite, J. Inequality, Crime and
Public Policy.
  L. Taylor, 617(TLS):29Feb80-232
Braithwaite, M. The Commodore's Barge Is
Alongside. Lusty Winter.
  B. Rasporich, 296(JCF):28/29-207
Brakel, L.F. and others. Literaturen.
  D. Carr, 318(JAOS):Oct-Dec78-540
Bräker, U. A Few Words about William
Shakespeare's Plays.
  R. Gray, 617(TLS):11Jan80-45
Brambilla Ageno, F. L'edizione critica
dei testi volgari.
  M.B. Speer, 545(RPh):Feb79-335
Brame, P. and C.M. de Hauke - see Dortu,
M.G.
Branca, G. Le Machine (1629). (L. Firpo,
ed)
  A. Corsano, 227(GCFI):Jan-Mar78-140
Branca, V. Giovanni Boccaccio.*
  M.M., 228(GSLI):Vol155fasc491-472
Branca, V., ed. Italia, Venezia e Polonia
tra illuminismo e romanticismo.
  K.Z., 228(GSLI):Vol155fasc490-314
Branca, V. and others, eds. Innovazioni
tematiche espressive e linguistiche
della letteratura italiana del Novecento.
  T. de Lauretis, 276:Summer79-241
Brancaforte, B. and C.L., eds. La primera
traducción italiana del "Lazarillo de
Tormes" por Giulio Strozzi.*
  R.C. Melzi, 240(HR):Summer78-390
Brancati, V. Bell'Antonio.
  R.S. Dombroski, 399(MLJ):Dec79-462
"Brancusi Photographer."
  C.S., 441:5Oct80-15
Brand, G. Welt, Geschichte, Mythos und
Politik.
  S.L. Hart, 484(PPR):Mar80-444
Brand, M. Peace March.
  B.J. Lifton, 441:7Dec80-39
Brand, M. and D. Walton, eds. Action
Theory.*
  S. Lee, 488:Dec79-531
  J.E. Tomberlin, 484(PPR):Jun80-576
van den Branden, L., E. Cockx-Indestege
and F. Sillis. Bio-bibliografie van
Cornelis Kiliaan.
  E. Zimmermann, 182:Vol31#1/2-1
Branden, V. Mrs. Job.*
  R. Schieder, 99:Jun-Jul80-44
Brander, M. The Victorian Gentleman.
  L. Senelick, 637(VS):Summer78-493

Brandes, D. Die Tschechen unter deut-
schen Protektorat.
  F.L. Carsten, 575(SEER):Jul79-462
Brandes, G. Breve til Foraeldrene 1859-71.
(M. Borup, ed)
  S.H. Rossel, 563(SS):Summer79-300
Brandl, H. Persönlichkeitsidealismus und
Willenskult.
  H. Borland, 562(Scan):May79-67
Brandon, J.R., W.P. Malm and D.H. Shively.
Studies in Kabuki.
  F.T. Motofuji, 293(JASt):Nov78-182
Brandon, R. The Dollar Princesses.
  E.S. Turner, 362:11Sep80-343
  442(NY):15Dec80-173
Brandt, R.B. A Theory of the Good and the
Right.
  A. Quinton, 617(TLS):4Jan80-18
Brandwajn, R. Aspects méconnus de
l'oeuvre de Molière.
  O. de Mourgues, 208(FS):Vol33Pt2-685
Branford, J. A Dictionary of South
African English.
  B. Cottle, 541(RES):Aug79-323
Branford, K.A. A Study of Jean-Jacques
Bernard's "Théâtre de l'inexprimé."*
  D. O'Connell, 207(FR):May79-938
  205(FMLS):Apr78-183
Brann, E.T.H. Paradoxes of Education in a
Republic.
  D.C., 543:Jun79-740
Branner, R. Manuscript Painting in Paris
during the Reign of St. Louis.*
  J. Backhouse, 90:Jun79-390
Brantley, R.E. Wordsworth's "Natural
Methodism."
  M. Isnard, 189(EA):Jul-Dec78-392
Brantlinger, P. The Spirit of Reform.*
  R. O'Kell, 637(VS):Summer78-504
Brasas Egido, C. Antiguo Partido Judicial
de Olmedo.
  M. Estella, 48:Jul-Sep78-354
Brasch, C. Home Ground.
  R. Jackaman, 368:Sep75-251
Braudy, L. Narrative Form in History and
Fiction.
  H. White, 599:Winter79-42
Braudy, L. The World in a Frame.*
  C. Rickey, 127:Fall78-78
Brauer, C.M. John F. Kennedy and the
Second Reconstruction.*
  A.L. Hamby, 639(VQR):Winter78-154
Brault, G.J. - see "The Song of Roland"
Brault, J. L'En dessous l'admirable.
  J.M. Weiss, 207(FR):Feb79-508
Brault-Lerch, S. Les Orfèvres de Franche-
Comté.*
  C. le Corbeiller, 90:Mar79-187
Braun, E. Deborah Kerr.
  J. Basinger, 18:Feb79-68
Braun, E. and H. Radermacher, eds. Wissen-
schaftstheoretisches Lexikon.
  H. Holz, 687:Apr-Jun79-317
Braun, R. Deus Christianorum. (2nd ed)
  J.H. Waszink, 394:Vol32fasc1/2-197

Braune, W. Althochdeutsche Grammatik.*
  (13th ed rev by H. Eggers)
  E. Erämetsä, 439(NM):1978/2-190
Braunrot, B. L'Imagination poétique chez
  Du Bartas.
  T.C. Cave, 208(FS):Vol33Pt2-641
Bräutigan, H., comp and trans. Märchen
  aus Tibet.
  H-J. Uther, 196:Band19Heft1/2-126
Brautigan, R. The Tokyo-Montana Express.
  B. Yourgrau, 441:2Nov80-13
Bray, B., J. Schlobach and J. Varloot, eds.
  La Correspondance Littéraire de Grimm et
  de Meister (1754-1813).*
  J.H. Brumfitt, 208(FS):Vol33Pt2-793
Bray, H. The Pillars of the Post.
  A. Smith, 441:27Jul80-10
Bray, R. and P. Bushnell - see Greenman, J.
  "Brayer Graveur."
  M. Sheringham, 208(FS):Oct79-488
Brazda, M.K. Zur Bedeutung des Apfels in
  der antiken Kultur.
  F. Vian, 555:Vol52fasc2-351
Breathnach, B. Ceol Rince na hÉireann, II.
  L. McCullough, 292(JAF):Apr-Jun79-241
Breatnach, P.A. Die Regensburger Schot-
  tenlegende — Libellus de fundacione
  ecclesie Consecrati Petri.
  M.L. Colker, 589:Jul79-548
Brecht, B. Bertolt Brecht Collected Plays.
  (Vol 2) (J. Willett and R. Manheim, eds)
  J. Coleby, 157:Spring79-85
Brecht, B. Diaries 1920-1922.* (H. Ram-
  thun, ed)
  M. Wood, 453(NYRB):15May80-13
Brecht, B. Poems.* (Pts 1-3) (J. Willett
  and R. Manheim, with E. Fried, eds)
  D.J. Constantine, 161(DUJ):Dec78-141
  S. Spender, 441:10Feb80-1
  M. Wood, 453(NYRB):15May80-13
Brecht, B. Die Stücke von Bertolt Brecht
  in einem Band.
  S. Mews, 221(GQ):Mar79-288
Bredin, J-D. Les Français au pouvoir?
  D. Koenig, 207(FR):Oct78-195
Brednich, R.W., ed. Die Darfelder Lieder-
  handschrift 1546-1565.
  O. Holzapfel, 196:Band19Heft3/4-313
Brednich, R.W. - see "Jahrbuch für Volks-
  liedforschung"
Bredsdorff, E. Fra Andersen til Scherfig.
  V. Greene-Gantzberg, 562(Scan):May79-
  82
Brée, G. Littérature française: Le XXe
  siècle. (Vol 2)
  K.R. Dutton, 67:Nov79-345
  L.S. Roudiez, 546(RR):May79-317
Brée, G. Narcissus Absconditus.
  J.M. Cocking, 208(FS):Apr79-232
Breed, B. White Collar Bird.
  T. Parker, 617(TLS):25Jan80-80
Breem, W. The Leopard and the Cliff.
  J. Mellors, 364:Jul79-86
Breeze, P. Back Street Runner.
  G. Strawson, 617(TLS):23May80-575
de Breffny, B. Castles of Ireland.
  E. Michels, 174(Éire):Summer79-128

Breitinger, E., ed. Black Literature.
  D. Riemenschneider, 72:Band216Heft2-
  439
Brekle, H.E. Sémantique.*
  G. Charron and C. Germain, 320(CJL):
  Spring-Fall78-198
Brekle, H.E. and D. Kastovsky, eds. Per-
  spektiven der Wortbildungsforschung.
  L. Bauer, 297(JL):Sep79-364
Bremer, D. Licht und Dunkel in der früh-
  griechischen Dichtung.*
  M. Davies, 123:Vol129No1-1
  É. Des Places, 555:Vol52fasc1-149
  P. Somville, 542:Jan-Mar79-127
Bremer, K-J. Montesquieus "Lettres per-
  sanes" und Cadalsos "Cartas Marruecas."
  R. Gutiérrez Girardot, 72:Band216Heft2-
  465
Brendon, P. Eminent Edwardians.*
  N. Annan, 453(NYRB):20Nov80-12
  P. Fussell, 441:20Apr80-13
  442(NY):28Apr80-142
Brenk, F.E. In Mist Apparelled.
  D.A. Russell, 123:Vol129No1-144
Brennan, J.M. The Open Texture of Moral
  Concepts.*
  A.S.C., 543:Dec78-352
Brennan, P. Release.
  G. Hamel, 198:Winter80-138
Brennecke, D. Tegnér in Deutschland.
  L.L. Albertsen, 224(GRM):Band28Heft4-
  488
Brenner, R.R. The Faith and Doubt of Holo-
  caust Survivors.
  J. Greenfield, 441:7Sep80-35
Brent, J. A Few Days in Weasel Creek.
  R. Bradford, 441:4May80-14
Brentano, C. Clemens Brentano Poesie.
  (R. Fertonani, ed and trans)
  J.F.F., 191(ELN):Sep78(supp)-143
Brentano, F. Aristotle and his World View.
  (R. George and R.M. Chisholm, eds and
  trans)
  J.E. Llewelyn, 479(PhQ):Oct79-355
Brentano, F. The Psychology of Aristotle.*
  (R. George, ed and trans)
  J.L. Ackrill, 123:Vol129No1-165
  J. Barnes, 518:May79-57
  E. Hartman, 482(PhR):Apr79-306
Brereton, G. French Comic Drama from the
  Sixteenth to the Eighteenth Century.
  C.J. Gossip, 402(MLR):Apr79-454
  W.D. Howarth, 208(FS):Jan79-71
  J. Lough, 161(DUJ):Dec78-134
  D.L. Rubin, 207(FR):Dec78-341
  205(FMLS):Jan78-87
Brereton, G. A Short History of French
  Literature. (2nd ed)
  W.G. Moore, 208(FS):Vol33Pt2-951
Bresc, G. and D. Lucchetti. Au Musée du
  Louvre, la sculpture française du XVIIe
  siècle.
  T. Hodgkinson, 39:Aug79-155
Breslauer, G.W. and S. Rothman. Soviet
  Politics and Society.
  C.E. Ziegler, 550(RusR):Jan79-110

Breton, A. and P. Éluard. L'Immaculée Conception/Die unbefleckte Empfängnis.
R. Cardinal, 208(FS):Apr79-228
Breton, S. Ecriture et révélation.
A. Reix, 542:Jul-Sep79-345
Breton, S. Spinoza.
J-L. Marion, 192(EP):Apr-Jun79-244
Breton, S. and others. Manifestation et révélation.
A. Reix, 192(EP):Jul-Sep79-354
de la Bretonne, R. - see under Restif de la Bretonne
Brett, B. There Ain't No Such Animal, and Other East Texas Tales.
W. Gard, 584(SWR):Autumn79-398
Brett, R.L., ed. Andrew Marvell.*
A.W., 148:Autumn79-89
Brett, R.L. - see Barclay Fox, R.
Brett, S. The Dead Side of the Mike.
T.J. Binyon, 617(TLS):25Jul80-858
Brett, V. Paul Éluard.
J.O. Fischer, 535(RHL):Mar-Apr78-335
Brett, V. Molière. (2nd ed)
J.O. Fischer, 535(RHL):Mar-Apr78-304
Brett-Evans, D. Von Hrotsvit bis Folz und Gengenbach.* (Pts 1 and 2)
B. Murdoch, 182:Vol31#11/12-353
Brettner-Messler, H., ed. Die Protokolle des österreichischen Ministerrates (1848-1867). (Section 5, Vol 1)
F.L. Carsten, 575(SEER):Oct79-598
Breuer, D. Einführung in die pragmatische Texttheorie.
Z. Szabó, 353:Jul78-93
Breuer, R. Die Kunst der Paradoxie.*
V. Conley, 395(MFS):Winter78/79-615
Breuer, R. and R. Schöwerling. Das Studium der Anglistik.
R. Borgmeier, 38:Band96Heft3/4-548
Brewer, D. Chaucer and His World.
42(AR):Winter79-123
580(SCR):Nov78-135
Brewer, D.S., ed. Chaucer: The Critical Heritage.* (Vols 1 and 2)
A.G. Rigg, 541(RES):Aug79-336
Brewer, J. and J. Styles, eds. An Ungovernable People.
L. Stone, 453(NYRB):29May80-45
Brewster, E. It's Easy to Fall on the Ice.*
D. Bessai, 102(CanL):Summer79-119
R. Gibbs, 168(ECW):Spring78-122
Brewster, E. Sometimes I Think of Moving.*
R. Gibbs, 168(ECW):Spring78-122
Breymeyer, R. and F. Häussermann - see Oetinger, F.C.
Breytenbach, B. And Death White as Words. (A.J. Coetzee, ed)
D. Graham, 565:Vol20#4-75
Y. Lovelock, 493:Dec79-57
Breytenbach, B. In Africa Even the Flies Are Happy.
D. Graham, 565:Vol20#4-75
Breytenbach, B. A Season in Paradise.
J. Leonard, 441:31Mar80-C15
P. Theroux, 441:30Mar80-8

Brezhnev, L. Peace, Détente and Soviet-American Relations.
639(VQR):Autumn79-145
"Leonid I. Brezhnev."
639(VQR):Autumn78-140
Brian, D. Tallulah, Darling.
C. Curtis, 441:29Jun80-9
Briard, J. The Bronze Age in Barbarian Europe.
N. Hammond, 617(TLS):8Feb80-147
Brichant, C. Premier Guide de France.*
P.J. Edwards, 399(MLJ):Jan-Feb79-56
Briçonnet, G. and Marguerite d'Angoulême. Correspondance (1521-1524). (Vol 1) (C. Martineau and M. Veissière, with H. Heller, eds)
K.M. Hall, 208(FS):Vol33Pt2-622
Bridenbaugh, C. Jamestown 1544-1699.
D. Grumbach, 441:2Mar80-12
442(NY):14Apr80-175
Bridge, J. Beginning Model Theory.*
M. Tiles, 518:Oct79-122
Bridgeman, H. and E. Drury, eds. Needlework.
G. Moss, 139:Apr79-12
Bridges, M.L. A Border of Beauty.*
A. Purdy, 102(CanL):Summer79-132
Bridges, R. Selected Poems. (D.E. Stanford, ed)
W.G. Holzberger, 385(MQR):Winter80-117
G.S. Lensing, 249(HudR):Summer79-308
Bridges, R. and W.B. Yeats. The Correspondence of Robert Bridges and W.B. Yeats.*
(R.J. Finneran, ed)
J. Brown, 174(Éire):Winter79-153
W.G. Holzberger, 385(MQR):Winter80-117
Brierley, D. Blood Group O.
M. Laski, 362:17Apr80-514
Brierley, D. Cold War.
M. Laski, 362:10Jan80-62
617(TLS):29Feb80-246
Briggs, A. Governing the BBC.
G. Williams, 362:10Jan80-61
Briggs, A. Iron Bridge to Crystal Palace.
E.J. Hobsbawm, 453(NYRB):3Apr80-35
Briggs, K. British Folktales. An Encyclopedia of Fairies.
W.K. McNeil, 292(JAF):Jan-Mar79-106
Briggs, K.M. The Fairies in Tradition and Literature.*
A.C. Percival, 203:Vol189#1-116
Briggs, K.M. Nine Lives.
P-L. Adams, 61:Nov80-99
Briggs, R. Early Modern France 1560-1715.
R. Mettam, 161(DUJ):Dec78-106
Briggum, S.M. and T.K. Bender. A Concordance to Conrad's "Almayer's Folly."
E.S. Davidson, 136:Vol11#3-294
Brighton, A. and L. Morris, eds. Towards Another Picture.
K. O'Shea, 89(BJA):Spring79-187
Brigstocke, H. Italian and Spanish Paintings in the National Gallery of Scotland.
C. Gould, 90:Jul79-445
E. Young, 135:Apr79-295

Bringuier, J-C. Conversations with Jean Piaget.
H.E. Gruber, 441:19Oct80-15
Brink, A. A Dry White Season.*
C. Hope, 364:Dec79/Jan80-126
M. Watkins, 441:23Mar80-15
442(NY):14Apr80-174
Brink, A. Rumours of Rain.
J. Marquand, 364:Jun79-93
Brinker, K. Konstituentenstrukturgrammatik und operationale Satzgliedanalyse.
G. Öhlschläger, 685(ZDL):2/1979-251
Brinker-Gabler, G., ed. Deutsche Dichterinnen vom 16. Jahrhundert bis zur Gegenwart.
J.E. Michaels, 221(GQ):Nov79-572
Brinkhus, G. Eine bayerische Fürstenspiegelkompilation des 15. Jahrhunderts.
J.A. Davidson, 589:Oct79-786
B. Murdoch, 182:Vol131#15/16-537
Brinkmann, R., K. Ezawa and F. Hackert, eds. Germanistik International.
L. Bodi, 67:Nov79-365
Brion, M. L'Allemagne romantique.*
B.L. Knapp, 399(MLJ):Apr79-219
Briscoe, L.E. and E. Lamadrid. Lectura y lengua.
E. Echevarría, 399(MLJ):Nov79-378
Brisebare. Le Plait de l'Evesque et de Droit. (J. Kjaer, ed)
B. Cazelles, 545(RPh):May79-490
Brisman, L. Romantic Origins.*
D. Hughes, 591(SIR):Summer79-316
D.H. Reiman, 340(KSJ):Vol28-161
M. Roberts, 541(RES):Nov79-478
L.J. Swingle, 301(JEGP):Jan79-139
Brissenden, A., ed. Shakespeare and Some Others.*
E.A.J. Honigmann, 447(N&Q):Apr78-175
E. Perkins, 67:May79-90
Brissenden, C., ed. I Love You, Baby Blue.
M. Page, 648(WCR):Oct78-55
Brisson, L. Le même et l'autre dans la structure ontologique du Timée de Platon.
G.B. Kerferd, 303(JoHS):Vol99-176
Brisson, M., ed. A Critical Edition and Study of Frere Robert (Chartreux) "Le Chastel Perilleux."
W. Rothwell, 208(FS):Jan79-67
Bristow, E.J. Vice and Vigilance.
J.A. Banks, 637(VS):Summer79-467
Bristow, E.K. - see Chekhov, A.
"The British Library General Catalogue of Printed Books to 1975." (Vol 1)
J. Roberts, 617(TLS):4Apr80-398
Brittain, J.T. Laurence Stallings.
H. Claridge, 402(MLR):Jul79-684
Brittan, G.G., Jr. Kant's Theory of Science.
R.C.S. Walker, 479(PhQ):Jul79-269
Britten, B. The Operas of Benjamin Britten.* (D. Herbert, ed)
A. Hughes, 441:16Apr80-C28
B. Northcott, 617(TLS):15Feb80-182
Britton, E. The Community of the Vill.
J.S. Beckerman, 589:Jul79-551

Brixhe, C. Le dialecte grec de Pamphylie.*
C. Dobias-Lalou, 555:Vol52fasc1-138
Broad, C.D. Kant. (C. Lewy, ed)
P. Guyer, 482(PhR):Jul79-640
J.A. Reuscher, 613:Jun79-218
L. Stevenson, 479(PhQ):Oct79-345
Broadbent, J. and R. Hodge - see Milton, J.
Broc, N. La Géographie des Philosophes.
J. Lough, 208(FS):Vol33Pt2-790
Brochier, J-J. L'Aventure des Surréalistes, 1914-1940.
E. Wayne, 188(ECr):Spring78-97
Brock, E. The River and the Train.
H. Carruth, 231:Jan80-77
C. Hope, 364:Mar80-74
E. Longley, 617(TLS):18Jan80-64
D. Smith, 29:Sep/Oct80-30
Brock, P. Polish Revolutionary Populism.
T.N. Cieplak, 497(PolR):Vol23#1-99
A. Gleason, 104(CASS):Fall78-440
Brock, P. The Slovak National Awakening.*
T. Spira, 104(CASS):Summer78-310
Brockbank, P. - see Shakespeare, W.
Brocke, B. Technologische Prognosen.
M. Perrez, 687:Apr-Jun79-322
Brockway, F. Britain's First Socialists.
J. Mapplebeck, 362:29May80-694
Broder, D.S. Changing of the Guard.
A. Wildavsky, 441:31Aug80-3
61:Oct80-100
Brodhead, R.H. Hawthorne, Melville, and the Novel.*
D.H. Hirsch, 454:Fall78-86
B. Hitchcock, 577(SHR):Spring79-166
Brodsky, J. A Part of Speech.
C. Brown, 441:7Sep80-11
C. Milosz, 453(NYRB):14Aug80-23
Brodsky, M. Detour.
D. Merkin, 473(PR):3/1979-453
639(VQR):Spring79-59
Brodwin, L.L. Elizabethan Love Tragedy, 1587-1625.
C.R. Forker, 570(SQ):Winter79-107
van den Broecke, M.P.R. Hierarchies and Rank Orders in Distinctive Features.
K. Kohler, 361:Jun78-183
van den Broek, M.A. Der Spiegel des Sünders.*
N.F. Palmer, 447(N&Q):Oct78-468
Broich, U. Gattungen des modernen englischen Romans.
I. Bünsch, 224(GRM):Band28Heft1-123
K.L. Pfeiffer, 38:Band96Heft3/4-532
Broido, V. Apostles into Terrorists.*
A. Brown, 617(TLS):25Jan80-95
D. Footman, 575(SEER):Oct79-635
Brombert, B.A. Cristina.*
S. Dijkstra, 207(FR):Oct78-190
Brombert, V. The Romantic Prison.*
(French title: La Prison romantique.)
D.I. Grossvogel, 400(MLN):May79-879
B.O. States, 249(HudR):Winter79/80-617
J-L. Steinmetz, 535(RHL):Jan-Feb79-146
Brome, V. Havelock Ellis, Philosopher of Sex.
P. Dickinson, 364:Jul79-78

Brome, V. Jung.
A. McGlashan, 364:Jul79-81
Bromell, H. I Know Your Heart, Marco
Polo.*
K.S., 109:Summer80-224
Bromhall, D. Devil Birds.
P.J.K. Burton, 617(TLS):1Aug80-870
Brommelle, N. and P. Smith, eds. Conser-
vation and Restoration of Pictorial Art.
T. Crombie, 39:May79-407
Bronowski, J. The Origins of Knowledge
and Imagination.
H. Meynell, 483:Jul79-425
Bronowski, J. The Visionary Eye. (P.E.
Ariotti and R. Bronowski, eds)
T.C. Holyoke, 42(AR):Summer79-376
C. Lord, 290(JAAC):Winter79-204
Bronson, B.H., ed. The Singing Tradition
of Child's Popular Ballads.*
F.W. Sternfeld and C.R. Wilson,
541(RES):May79-239
Bronstein, A.J., L.J. Raphael and C.J.
Stevens, eds. A Biographical Diction-
ary of the Phonetic Sciences.
J. Algeo, 300:Mar79-72
B. Davis, 35(AS):Winter79-304
R.A. Hall, Jr., 350:Mar79-250
Brontë, A. The Poems of Anne Brontë. (E.
Chitham, ed)
A. Shelston, 148:Autumn79-86
Brontë, C. Two Tales by Charlotte Brontë:
"The Secret" and "Lily Hart." (W. Holtz,
ed)
B.B. Pratt, 445(NCF):Mar79-515
636(VP):Winter78-400
Brontë, C. and another Lady. Emma.
G. Annan, 362:7Feb80-190
A.N. Wilson, 617(TLS):25Jan80-78
Brontë, E. Wuthering Heights.* (H.
Marsden and I. Jack, eds)
J. Beaty, 402(MLR):Oct79-925
Brook, G.L. The Language of Shakespeare.
M.C. Bradbrook, 349:Summer78-197
M. Görlach, 38:Band96Heft1/2-174
Brooke, N. Horrid Laughter in Jacobean
Tragedy.
G. Salgado, 617(TLS):7Mar80-262
Brookhouse, C. Wintermute.
639(VQR):Autumn78-138
Brooks, C. William Faulkner.*
C.S. Brown, 131(CL):Summer79-313
A.W. Friedman, 594:Summer79-236
P. Samway, 639(VQR):Spring79-350
295(JML):Vol7#4-694
Brooks, J. The Games Players.
P.E. Erdman, 441:3Feb80-7
Brooks, M.Z. Polish Reference Grammar.*
B.W. Mazur, 575(SEER):Oct79-579
Brooks, P. The Melodramatic Imagination.*
G. Bearse, 678(YCGL):No.27-102
J.M. Cocking, 208(FS):Vol33Pt2-990
J-P. Davoine, 535(RHL):Jul-Aug79-679
J.W. Tuttleton, 402(MLR):Jan79-149
Brooks, R.R.R. and V.S. Wakankar. Stone
Age Painting in India.
G.F. Dales, 293(JASt):Nov78-197

Brooks-Davies, D. Spenser's "Faerie
Queene."
M. Dodsworth, 175:Spring79-43
M. Evans, 541(RES):Feb79-67
J.K. Hale, 67:May79-89
T.L. Steinberg, 568(SCN):Spring-
Summer79-13
H.L. Weatherby, 569(SR):Summer79-490
Brooks-Davies, D. - see Spenser, E.
Broome, P. Henri Michaux.*
M. Blackman, 67:May79-132
205(FMLS):Apr78-184
Broome, P. - see Michaux, H.
Broome, P. and G. Chesters, eds. An
Anthology of Modern French Poetry, 1850-
1950.*
M. Bowie, 208(FS):Apr79-235
É-A. Hubert, 535(RHL):Jul-Aug79-719
Broome, P. and G. Chesters. The Apprecia-
tion of Modern French Poetry, 1850-1950.*
M. Bowie, 208(FS):Apr79-235
É-A. Hubert, 535(RHL):Jul-Aug79-719
Broos, B.P.J. Index to the Formal Sources
of Rembrandt's Art.
K. Roberts, 90:Feb79-124
Brophy, R.J. - see Jeffers, R.
Brostoff, A., ed. I Could be Mute.
42(AR):Spring79-253
Brotherston, G. The Emergence of the
Latin American Novel.*
J.M. Flint, 86(BHS):Jan79-81
M.P. Levitt, 295(JML):Vol7#4-591
J.A. Weiss, 454:Spring79-264
Brough, J. Miss Lillian Russell.
639(VQR):Spring79-59
Broughton, G. and others. Teaching
English as a Foreign Language.
L.E. Henrichsen, 399(MLJ):Nov79-376
Broughton, T.A. A Family Gathering.
639(VQR):Winter78-21
Broughton, T.A. Far From Home.
639(VQR):Autumn79-147
Broughton, T.A. Winter Journey.
J. Casey, 441:20Jan80-14
J. Leonard, 441:11Jan80-C21
61:Feb80-96
442(NY):25Feb80-134
Broumas, O. Beginning with O.*
T.A. Stumpf, 114(ChiR):Autumn78-127
J. Williams, 448:Vol17#1-107
Brouwer, D. and others. Vrouwentaal en
Mannenpraat.
R. Schenk-van Witsen, 204(FdL):Jun79-
192
Brouwer, L.E.J. Collected Works. (Vol 1)
(A. Heyting, ed)
J.R. Moschovakis, 316:Jun79-271
Browder, F.E., ed. Mathematical Develop-
ments Arising from Hilbert Problems.
C. Smoryński, 316:Mar79-116
Brower, K. The Starship and the Canoe.
P.T. Bryant, 649(WAL):Summer79-175
Brower, R.H. - see Teika, F.
Brown, A. and M. Kaser, eds. The Soviet
Union Since the Fall of Khrushchev.*
(2nd ed)
A. Yanov, 550(RusR):Apr79-238

Brown, A.F.J. Essex People 1750-1900.
D.J. Johnson, 325:Apr79-165
Brown, A.P. Carlo d'Ordonez, 1734-1786.
A. Tyson, 415:Apr79-306
Brown, B., ed. The England of Henry Taunt.
B. Jay, 637(VS):Winter78-294
Brown, C. Mandelstam.
L. Dienes, 558(RLJ):Fall79-225
Brown, C.B. Wieland and "Memoirs of Carwin." (S. Krause and S.W. Reid, eds)
639(VQR):Winter78-17
Brown, C.B. Wieland or the Transformation.
E. Emerson, 587(SAF):Autumn79-245
Brown, C.M. God As Mother.
N. Schuster, 485(PE&W):Jan79-112
Brown, C.S. A Glossary of Faulkner's
South.*
M. Grimwood, 402(MLR):Apr79-441
K.B. Harder, 424:Sep77-177
Brown, D. Creek Mary's Blood.
L.M. Silko, 441:25May80-10
442(NY):7Apr80-149
Brown, D. Soviet Russian Literature
since Stalin.*
R. Dessaix, 67:May79-168
J. Grayson, 575(SEER):Oct79-592
205(FMLS):Jul78-283
Brown, D. Tchaikovsky: The Early Years.*
E. Garden, 415:May79-402
Brown, D.M. Mother Tongue to English.
F. Dubin, 608:Mar80-95
Brown, E. Interior Views.
S. Slesin, 441:14Dec80-12
Brown, E.K. Responses and Evaluations.
(D. Staines, ed) Rhythm in the Novel.
D. Bush, 569(SR):Winter79-186
Brown, F. Theater and Revolution.
P. Brooks, 441:28Sep80-12
A. Broyard, 441:22Nov80-15
M. Wood, 453(NYRB):4Dec80-37
Brown, F.S., ed. Renaissance Studies in
Honor of Isidore Silver.
Y. Bellenger, 535(RHL):Jul-Aug79-639
A.P. Kouidis, 207(FR):May79-923
Brown, C. The New Celibacy.
D. Grumbach, 441:21Sep80-16
Brown, G.M. Fishermen with Ploughs.
D. Davis, 362:31Jan80-157
D. Sealy, 617(TLS):22Feb80-214
Brown, H. Man and the Stars.
529(QQ):Summer79-371
Brown, H. Science and the Human Comedy.*
M. Baym, 188(ECr):Winter78-69
J.V. and E.M. Brown, 154:Mar78-198
J. Mayer, 535(RHL):Mar-Jun79-523
R. Rappaport, 173(ECS):Fall78-107
J.S. Spink, 208(FS):Vol33Pt2-976
Brown, H.D. Principles of Language Learning and Teaching.
S. McKay, 608:Jun80-240
Brown, H.I. Perception, Theory and Commitment.*
C. Wright, 518:May79-87
Brown, J. Images and Ideas in Seventeenth-Century Spanish Painting.
G. Martin, 617(TLS):1Feb80-120

Brown, J. Murillo and His Drawings.*
J.F. Moffitt, 56:Winter79-115
G.M. Smith, 54:Sep78-558
Brown, J. Northern Light.
D. Barbour, 150(DR):Spring79-154
M. Darling, 102(CanL):Autumn79-91
Brown, J. Jusepe de Ribera: Prints and
Drawings.
J.F. Moffitt, 56:Winter79-115 .
Brown, J.C. Loglan 1. (3d ed)
G.L. Dillon, 350:Mar79-248
Brown, J.K. Goethe's Cyclical Narratives.*
H. Reiss, 133:Band12Heft1/2-160
Brown, J.M., ed. Scottish Society in the
Fifteenth Century.
C.M.D. Crowder, 589:Apr79-346
Brown, J.P. Jane Austen's Novels.*
A.M. Duckworth, 141:Fall79-374
Brown, K. French Country Inns and Château
Hotels.
F.W. Nachtmann, 207(FR):Mar79-662
Brown, K.D. John Burns.
N.C. Soldon, 637(VS):Summer79-472
Brown, L.M. and I.R. Christie, eds. Bibliography of British History, 1789-1851.
J. Saville, 637(VS):Winter79-203
Brown, L.W., ed. The Black Writer in
Africa and the Americas.
B. Lindfors, 678(YCGL):No.27-105
Brown, L.W., with C.L. Briggs and M.
Weigle. Hispano Folklife of New Mexico.
W. Gard, 584(SWR):Winter79-89
L. Moncus, 649(WAL):Fall79-251
B.A. Roeder, 650(WF):Apr79-131
Brown, M.H. Laying Waste.
K.T. Erikson, 441:18May80-3
Brown, M.W. American Art to 1900.*
C.T. Walters, 658:Winter79-396
Brown, N. Sexuality and Feminism in
Shelley.
L. Sage, 617(TLS):22Feb80-199
Brown, N.B. Hugo and Dostoevsky.
E. Chances, 558(RLJ):Fall79-223
R.F. Miller, 574(SEEJ):Fall79-403
Brown, P.C. Eyeshine.
G. Hamel, 198:Winter80-138
Brown, R. Tender Mercies.*
G. Johnson, 584(SWR):Summer79-300
Brown, R.D. Massachusetts.
C.M. Fennelly, 432(NEQ):Jun79-270
Brown, R.F. The Later Philosophy of Schelling.*
T.F. O'Meara, 125:Winter79-310
Brown, R.F. Schelling's Treatise on "The
Deities of Samothrace."
L.S.S., 543:Sep78-128
Brown, R.H. A Poetic for Sociology.*
E. Garver, 185:Jan79-217
J.R. Kelly, 613:Dec79-444
Brown, R.M. The Ceramics of South-East
Asia.*
J. Addis, 463:Autumn78-330
Brown, S.C., ed. Reason and Religion.*
M. Adam, 542:Jul-Sep79-346
G. Graham, 479(PhQ):Oct79-378
R.S. Laura, 63:Dec79-366

[continued]

50

[continuing]
P. Masterson, 518:May79-80
S.R. Sutherland, 393(Mind):Oct79-628
Browne, M.D. The Sun Fetcher.*
J.F. Cotter, 249(HudR):Spring79-113
Browne, V.G. and D.J. Johnson. A Guide to
the State Archives of Michigan: State
Records.
D.P. Swanson, 14:Jan79-72
Brownell, B.A. The Urban Ethos in the
South, 1920-1930.
E.C. Williamson, 9(AlaR):Jul79-234
Brownell, M.R. Alexander Pope and the
Arts of Georgian England.*
P. Caracciolo, 175:Spring79-54
J.H. Hagstrum, 173(ECS):Spring79-391
H.J. Jensen, 566:Spring79-119
R. Paulson, 301(JEGP):Jul79-431
G.S. Rousseau, 617(TLS):18Jan80-68
A.A. Tait, 90:Jul79-447
639(VQR):Spring79-48
Browning, E.B. Casa Guidi Windows. (J.
Markus, ed)
P. Drew, 541(RES):Feb79-102
G. Taplin, 85:Spring78-91
Browning, E.B. Sonnets from the Portu-
guese. (W.S. Peterson, ed)
M. Timko, 85:Spring78-95
Browning, I. Palmyra.
M. Colledge, 617(TLS):11Jan80-42
Browning, R. Sordello. (M. Peckham, ed)
J. Woolford, 85(SBHC):Fall78-82
Browning, R.M. German Poetry in the Age
of the Enlightenment.
R. Gray, 617(TLS):11Jan80-45
"Browning Institute Studies."* (Vol 4)
(W.S. Peterson, ed)
J.B. Bullen, 447(N&Q):Jun78-264
"Browning Institute Studies." (Vol 5)
(W.S. Peterson, ed)
M.B. Cramer, 85(SBHC):Fall78-69
P. Drew, 541(RES):Feb79-102
Brownlow, F.W. Two Shakespearean
Sequences.*
N.A. Brittin, 577(SHR):Summer79-249
N.L. Harvey, 125:Fall78-157
Brownlow, K. The War, the West and the
Wilderness.*
A. Slide, 200:Jun-Jul79-367
T. Sobchack, 649(WAL):Winter80-334
D. Wilson, 617(TLS):18Jan80-62
Bruccoli, M.J., ed. James Gould Cozzens.
R. Christiansen, 617(TLS):23May80-594
Bruccoli, M.J. "The Last of the Novel-
ists."*
B. Oldsey, 395(MFS):Summer78-272
Bruccoli, M.J. Scott and Ernest.*
J.E. Miller, Jr., 27(AL):Jan80-574
295(JML):Vol7#4-605
Bruccoli, M.J. - see Cozzens, J.G.
Bruccoli, M.J. - see Fitzgerald, F.S.
Bruccoli, M.J. - see O'Hara, J.
Bruccoli, M.J. and C.E.F. Clark, Jr.
First Printings of American Authors.
42(AR):Summer79-377
Bruccoli, M.J. and M.M. Duggan, with S.
Walker - see Fitzgerald, F.S.

Bruce, D.D., Jr. Violence and Culture in
the Antebellum South.
J.A.L. Lemay, 165(EAL):Fall80-198
Bruce, C. Second Front Now!
B. Montgomery, 617(TLS):15Feb80-189
Bruce, R.D. Dream Symbolism and Interpre-
tation.
D. Davis, 269(IJAL):Jan78-79
Bruch, R. Gesammelte Aufsätze. (F. Hoff-
mann and C. Hurri, eds)
K.L. Rein, 685(ZDL):3/1979-375
"Die Brücke - Edvard Munch."
J.G. Holland, 563(SS):Summer79-306
Brucker, G. The Civic World of Early
Renaissance Florence.*
W.M. Bowsky, 377:Mar79-55
J.F. D'Amico, 539:Vol14No1-97
Brückmann, P., ed. Familiar Colloquy.
J. Dale, 627(UTQ):Summer79-411
P.G. Stanwood, 102(CanL):Winter79-196
Bruckner, P. Allez jouer ailleurs.
P.H. Solomon, 207(FR):Oct78-175
Bruening, W.H. Wittgenstein.
G.L.H., 543:Mar79-535
Bruezière, M. and J. Charon. Le Français
commercial. (2nd ed) (Vol 2)
B. Braude, 207(FR):May79-964
Brugger, B. Contemporary China.
H.B. Chamberlain, 293(JASt):Aug79-766
Brugger, R.J. Beverly Tucker.
639(VQR):Winter79-7
Brugnolo, F. Il Canzoniere di Nicolò de'
Rossi.
L. Banfi, 228(GSLI):Vol155fasc491-456
Bruhn, K. - see Schubring, W.
Bruhns, H. Caesar und die römische Ober-
schicht in den Jahren 49-44 v. Chr.
E. Badian, 124:Nov79-188
Brulé, P. La piraterie crétoise hellén-
istique.
G.M. Cohen, 121(CJ):Feb-Mar80-259
Bruller, J. Rocaïdour.
P. Astier, 207(FR):Dec78-377
Brumm, U. Puritanismus und Literatur in
Amerika.
H. Helmcke, 224(GRM):Band28Heft3-375
Brümmer, E. Corpus Vasorum Antiquorum.
(Deutschland, fasc 41)
D.C. Kurtz, 303(JoHS):Vol199-214
le Brun, J. La Spiritualité de Bossuet.
A.H.T. Levi, 208(FS):Apr79-187
Brundage, A. The Making of the New Poor
Law.
U.R.Q. Henriques, 637(VS):Spring79-349
Brundage, B.C. The Fifth Sun.
K.L. Brown, 263(RIB):Vol129No2-205
Brunel, P. Le Mythe de la métamorphose.
H. Godin, 208(FS):Vol33Pt2-979
Brunelli, G.A. François Villon, Commenti
e contributi.
J. Fox, 208(FS):Vol33Pt2-582
Brunet, M. Montaña adentro y otros
cuentos.
M. Agosín, 263(RIB):Vol129No2-221
Brunhölzl, F. Geschichte der lateinischen
Literatur des Mittelalters.* (Vol 1)
D.J. Sheerin, 589:Jul79-553

Bruni, R.L. and D.W. Evans, comps. A Cata-
logue of Italian Books, 1471-1600, in
the Libraries of Exeter University,
Exeter Cathedral, and the Devon and
Exeter Institution.
  D.E. Rhodes, 78(BC):Winter79-588
Brunner, A. Kant und die Wirklichkeit des
Geistigen.
  R.B.P., 543:Mar79-536
Brunner, H. Die alten Meister.*
  P.W. Tax, 589:Jan79-115
Brunner, H., U. Müller and F.V. Spechtler -
see Walther von der Vogelweide
Bruno, G. The Ash Wednesday Supper. (E.A.
Gosselin and L.S. Lerner, eds and trans)
  J. Barnouw, 543:Jun79-742
  J.J. Kockelmans, 568(SCN):Fall-
  Winter79-83
Bruno, V.J. Form and Colour in Greek
Painting.*
  R.M. Cook, 303(JoHS):Vol99-213
Bruns, R.A. Knights of the Road.
  A. Broyard, 441:11Oct80-14
  D. Grumbach, 441:14Dec80-11
Brunskill, R. and A. Clifton-Taylor.
English Brickwork.
  G. Hines, 576:Dec78-314
Brunskill, R.W. Illustrated Handbook of
Vernacular Architecture.
  C.C. Brookes, 39:Dec79-538
Brunt, P.A. - see Arrian
Brusatti, O. Nationalismus und Ideologie
in der Musik.
  R. Hollinrake, 410(M&L):Jul79-348
Bruss, E.W. Autobiographical Acts.*
  M.A. Doody, 454:Winter79-185
Bruss, P. Conrad's Early Sea Fiction.
  C.R. La Bossière, 268(IFR):Summer80-
  157
Brustein, R. Critical Moments.
  A. Broyard, 441:14Jun80-21
  W. Goodman, 441:13Jul80-15
Brütting, R. "Écriture" and "texte."
  A. Viatte, 182:Vol131#3/4-99
van den Bruwaene, M. - see Cicero
Bryan, J. 3d and C.J.V. Murphy. The
Windsor Story.*
  A. Forbes, 617(TLS):4Jan80-7
  J. Richardson, 453(NYRB):21Feb80-23
Bryan, J.M. An Architectural History of
the South Carolina College, 1801-1855.
  P.V. Turner, 576:May78-112
Bryans, J.V. Calderón de la Barca.*
  C. Bainton, 402(MLR):Apr79-478
  T.R.A. Mason, 86(BHS):Jul79-254
  W.M. Whitby, 238:Dec79-730
Bryant, K.E. Poems to the Child-God.
  R.A. Williams, 293(JASt):May79-599
Bryant, P.T. H.L. Davis.
  J.H. Brunvand, 649(WAL):Spring79-71
Bryer, A.A.M. The Empire of Trebizond and
the Pontos.
  M. Angold, 617(TLS):4Jul80-763
Brykczynski, T. Caged.
  N. Callendar, 441:1Jun80-18
Bryson, J. - see Rossetti, D.G. and J.
Morris

Bubner, R. Hegel und Goethe.
  H. Schmitz, 489(PJGG):Band86Heft2-438
Buchan, D. The Ballad and the Folk.
  W.F.H. Nicolaisen, 588(SSL):Vol13-290
Buchan, D., ed. A Scottish Ballad Book.
  W.F.H. Nicolaisen, 588(SSL):Vol13-290
Buchan, J. The Best Short Stories. (D.
Daniell, ed)
  H. Greene, 362:24Jul80-121
  M. Trend, 617(TLS):1Aug80-882
Buchanan, D. The Treasure of Auchinleck.
  F.W. Hilles, 588(SSL):Vol13-283
Buchanan, M. The Countess of Sedgwick.
  L. Duguid, 617(TLS):16May80-558
Buchholz, E.H. Zwang zur Freiheit.
  A. Hüfner, 182:Vol31#7/8-211
Buchholz, H-G., G. Jöhrens and I. Maull.
Jagd und Fischfang.
  J.K. Anderson, 121(CJ):Feb-Mar80-271
Buchholz, H-G. and V. Karageorghis. Pre-
historic Greece and Cyprus.
  M.H. Wiencke, 54:Dec78-706
Buchholz, H-G. and J. Wiesner. Kriegs-
wesen. (Pt 1)
  W. McLeod, 124:Dec79/Jan80-244
Buchholz, O., W. Fiedler and G. Uhlisch.
Wörterbuch Albanisch-Deutsch.
  W.B. Lockwood, 297(JL):Sep79-379
Buchloh, P.G. and J.P. Becker. Der Detek-
tivroman.
  B. Schultze, 38:Band96Heft1/2-249
Büchner, G. The Complete Collected Works.
(H.J. Schmidt, ed and trans)
  R.C. Cowen, 406:Winter79-450
  W. Schumann, 399(MLJ):Mar79-145
Büchner, G. Woyzeck. Danton's Death.
  J. Coleby, 157:Summer79-81
Buchwald, A. Down the Seine and up the
Potomac with Art Buchwald.
  M.G. Hydak, 399(MLJ):Jan-Feb79-82
Buchwald, A. and A. Seems Like Yesterday.
  442(NY):13Oct80-195
Buck, D.D. Urban Change in China.
  A. Feuerwerker, 293(JASt):Feb79-345
Buck, P.S. The Woman Who Was Changed and
Other Stories.*
  V. Cunningham, 617(TLS):21Mar80-326
  T.C. Holyoke, 42(AR):Summer79-370
  639(VQR):Autumn79-140
Buck, R.J. A History of Boeotia.
  P.W. Wallace, 124:Apr-May80-427
Buck, W. Ramayana.
  I. Shetterly, 293(JASt):Feb79-387
Bucke, R.M. Richard Maurice Bucke, Medi-
cal Mystic.* (A. Lozynsky, ed)
  D. Latham, 168(ECW):Summer78-242
Buckland, G. First Photographs.
  H. Kramer, 441:30Nov80-13
Buckland, G. Fox Talbot and the Invention
of Photography.
  C. James, 453(NYRB):18Dec80-22
  H. Kramer, 441:17Aug80-6
Buckle, R. Buckle at the Ballet.
  H. Brubach, 441:23Nov80-11
Buckle, R. Diaghilev.*
  A. Croce, 442(NY):12May80-142

Buckle, R., ed. U and Non-U Revisited.*
  J.R. Gaskin, 569(SR):Summer79-455
  42(AR):Summer79-378
Buckle, R. - see Beaton, C.
Buckler, E. Whirligig.*
  L. Weir, 102(CanL):Spring79-85
Buckley, P. Ernest.
  G. Monteiro, 569(SR):Fall79-xcviii
  295(JML):Vol7#4-726
Buckley, W.F., Jr. Who's On First.
  A. Broyard, 441:6Feb80-C24
  N. Callendar, 441:17Feb80-7
Buckman, P. The Rothschild Conversion.*
  B. Garfield, 441:10Feb80-14
Buckman, R. Jogging from Memory.
  D. Thomas, 362:18and25Dec80-863
Budd, S. Varieties of Unbelief.
  H. McLeod, 637(VS):Winter78-245
Budde, A. Zur Syntax geschriebener und
  gesprochener Sprache von Grundschülern.
  E.H. Yarrill, 182:Vol131#7/8-220
Buddemeier, H. Kommunikation als Verstän-
  digungshandlung.
  D. Stellmacher, 685(ZDL):3/1979-407
Budden, J. The Operas of Verdi. (Vol 1)
  M.J.P. Matz, 414(MusQ):Jul79-451
Budden, J. The Operas of Verdi.* (Vol 2)
  D. Kimbell, 410(M&L):Jul79-323
  M.J.P. Matz, 414(MusQ):Jul79-451
Budka, M.J.E. - see Kościuszko, T.A.B.
Budurowycz, B. Slavic and East European
  Resources in Canadian Academic and
  Research Libraries.
  P.J. Wreath, 104(CASS):Summer78-284
Buechner, F. Godric.
  P-L. Adams, 61:Dec80-96
  B. De Mott, 441:23Nov80-15
Buehler, P.G. The Middle English "Genesis
  and Exodus."
  F. Diekstra, 179(ES):Oct79-661
Buenker, J.D. and N.C. Burckel. Immigra-
  tion and Ethnicity.
  F. Miller, 14:Apr79-203
de Buffon, G.L.L. Un autre Buffon. (J.
  Roger, ed)
  N. Suckling, 208(FS):Jan79-84
Bughici, D. Dictionar de Forme și Genuri
  Muzicale.
  R. Garfias, 187:Jan80-105
Bugliani, A. La presenza di D'Annunzio in
  Valle-Inclán.
  G. Güntert, 547(RF):Band91Heft4-484
Bugliani, A. Women and the Feminine
  Principle in the Works of Paul Claudel.
  E.T. Dubois, 402(MLR):Jul79-707
  H. Watson, 399(MLJ):Dec79-464
Bühler, H. and G. Mühle, eds. Sprachent-
  wicklungspsychologie.
  D. Lange, 685(ZDL):1/1979-115
Bühner, J-A. Der Gesandte und sein Weg
  im 4. Evangelium.
  J. Becker, 182:Vol131#13-392
van Buitenen, J.A.B., ed and trans. The
  Mahābhārata. (Vols 1 and 2)
  L. Rocher, 318(JAOS):Apr-Jun78-193

van Buitenen, J.A.B., ed and trans. The
  Mahābhārata. (Vol 3)
  W.G. Regier, 502(PrS):Winter78/79-392
Bujak, A. and M.B. Young. Journeys to
  Glory.
  S.L. Cuba, 497(PolR):Vol123#1-109
Bujum, S. Voprosy termi perevoda.
  S.I. Lubensky, 574(SEEJ):Spring79-142
Bukovsky, V. To Build a Castle.*
  T.D. Eisele, 396(ModA):Fall79-430
  639(VQR):Summer79-94
Bukowski, C. Love is a Dog from Hell.
  J. Freeman, 97(CQ):Vol18#3-282
Bukowski, C. Post Office.
  V. Cunningham, 617(TLS):20Jun80-706
Buksbazen, J.D. To Forget the Self.
  R.B. Zeuschner, 485(PE&W):Jan79-107
"Bulfinch's Mythology." (B. Holme, comp)
  P-L. Adams, 61:Jan80-89
Bulgakov, M. The White Guard.
  J. Coleby, 157:Summer79-81
Bulgakov, N. Neizdannyy Bulgakov: teksty
  i materialy. (E. Proffer, ed)
  J. Grayson, 575(SEER):Apr79-286
Bulgakov, S. A Bulgakov Anthology.* (N.
  Zernov and J. Pain, eds)
  P. Popov, 558(RLJ):Winter79-209
Bulhof, F., ed. Nijhoff, Van Ostaijen,
  "De Stijl."
  L. Gillet, 556(RLV):1978/2-167
  C.V. Poling, 127:Winter78/79-143
Bull, H. The Anarchial Society.
  639(VQR):Winter78-20
Bullard, P. and J. Stoia. The Hardest
  Lesson.
  M. Bayles, 231:Jul80-77
Bullaty, S. Sudek.
  C. James, 453(NYRB):18Dec80-22
  F. Neugass, 471:Oct/Nov/Dec79-409
  R. Whelan, 55:Sep79-30
"Bulletin de la Commission Royale de
  Toponymie et Dialectologie 50."
  H.J. Wolf, 547(RF):Band91Heft1/2-206
Bulliet, R. The Tomb of the Twelfth Imam.
  N. Callendar, 441:27Apr80-20
Bulliet, R.W. The Camel and the Wheel.*
  P. von Sivers, 318(JAOS):Apr-Jun78-163
Bulliet, R.W. Conversion to Islam in the
  Medieval Period.
  M. Hinds, 617(TLS):19Sep80-1043
Bullivant, K., ed. Culture and Society in
  the Weimar Republic.
  A. Bance, 402(MLR):Jul79-757
Bullock, M. Black Wings White Dead.*
  G. Hamel, 198:Winter80-138
  W. Stevenson, 102(CanL):Spring79-103
  E. Varney, 648(WCR):Jun78-26
Bullock-Davies, C. Menestrellorum multi-
  tudo.
  E.A. Bowles, 589:Apr79-349
Bulovas, A.J. El amor divino en la obra
  del Beato Alonso de Orozco.
  J.A. Jones, 86(BHS):Jan79-83
Bulpin, T.V. Southern Africa.
  529(QQ):Autumn79-558

Bumke, J. Ministerialität und Ritterdich-
tung.*
   W. Labuhn, 680(ZDP):Band97Heft3-458
Bumke, J. Studien zum Ritterbegriff im
12. und 13. Jahrhundert.* (2nd ed)
   H. Kratz, 133:Band12Heft1/2-138
Bunce, D. Travels with Dr. Leichhardt in
Australia.
   R. Stow, 617(TLS):12Sep80-999
Bunch, W.A. Jean Mairet.
   C.N. Smith, 208(FS):Vol33Pt2-672
Bundy, C. The Rise and Fall of the South
African Peasantry.
   R. Oliver, 617(TLS):4Jan80-21
Bungarten, T. Präsentische Partizipial-
konstruktionen in der deutschen Gegen-
wartssprache.
   W.M. Voge, 350:Jun79-486
Bunge, M. Treatise on Basic Philosophy.
(Vol 3, Pt 1)
   A. Reix, 542:Jul-Sep78-376
Bunnag, T. The Provincial Administration
of Siam, 1892-1915.
   C.M. Wilson, 293(JASt):Feb79-437
Bunting, B. Collected Poems.*
   C. Bedient, 569(SR):Spring79-296
   J. Freeman, 97(CQ):Vol8#3-276
   B. Howard, 472:Fall/Winter79-169
Bunting, J. Early Victorian Methodism.
(W.R. Ward, ed)
   H. McLeod, 637(VS):Winter78-245
Bunyan, J. The Pilgrim's Progress. (R.
Sharrock, ed)
   R. Wehse, 196:Band19Heft3/4-315
Burbank, J. and P. Steiner - see Mukařov-
ský, J.
Burbank, R.J. Thornton Wilder. (2nd ed)
   J.R. Taylor, 157:Spring79-79
Burbidge, P. and R. Sutton, eds. The
Wagner Companion.*
   R. Anderson, 415:Oct79-830
Burch, F.F. Sur Tristan Corbière.
   P.O. Walzer, 535(RHL):Mar-Apr78-329
Burch, N. To the Distant Observer.* (rev
by A. Michelson)
   J. Rosenbaum, 18:Jul-Aug79-66
Burchfield, J.D. Lord Kelvin and the Age
of the Earth.
   A. Thackray, 637(VS):Autumn77-125
Burchfield, R.W. - see "A Supplement to
the Oxford English Dictionary"
Burckhardt, L., ed. Werkbund.
   J. Campbell, 576:Dec78-300
Burckhardt-Seebass, C. Konfirmation in
Stadt und Landschaft Basel.
   E. Harvolk, 182:Vol31#5/6-187
Burd, V.A. - see La Touche, W.
Bureau, C. Linguistique fonctionnelle et
stylistique objective.*
   W. Geerts, 209(FM):Apr78-179
   G.D. Martin, 402(MLR):Apr79-389
Buren, D. Limites critiques. Five Texts.
Von da an. P.H. Opera. Rebondissements.
   J-F. Lyotard, 98:Nov78-1075
Buren, D., G. Celant and M. Claura. Vanaf.
Hier. Ailleurs-Elders.
   J-F. Lyotard, 98:Nov78-1075

Burger, A. Turold, poète de la fidélité.*
   H-W. Klein, 547(RF):Band91Heft3-322
   I. Short, 382(MAE):1979/1-129
Bürger, P. Der Französische Surrealismus.
   R. Cardinal, 208(FS):Apr79-228
Burgess, A. Earthly Powers.
   M. Amis, 441:7Dec80-1
   D.A.N. Jones, 362:23Oct80-544
   J. Leonard, 441:19Nov80-C33
Burgess, A. Ernest Hemingway and his
World.
   G. Monteiro, 569(SR):Fall79-xcviii
   295(JML):Vol7#4-726
Burgess, A. 1985.
   G. Negley, 322(JHI):Apr-Jun79-315
Burgess, C. Cooking With Country.
   W. and C. Cowen, 639(VQR):Autumn79-157
Burgess, G.S. Marie de France.
   C.W. Aspland, 67:May79-120
   I. Burr, 547(RF):Band91Heft1/2-164
Bürgin, H. and H-O. Mayer, eds. Die
Briefe Thomas Mann: Regesten und
Register. (Vol 1)
   A.D. Latta, 406:Fall79-346
Burgos, J. and R. Little, eds. Lectures
de Saint-John Perse.
   205(FMLS):Apr78-187
de Burgos, J.M. - see under Martínez de
Burgos, J.
Burgschmidt, E. and D. Götz. Kontrastive
Linguistik Deutsch/Englisch.*
   O.C. Grannis, 38:Band96Heft1/2-180
Buridant, C., ed. La Traduction du Pseudo-
Turpin du manuscrit Vatican Regina 624.*
   W.G. van Emden, 208(FS):Vol33Pt2-532
   B. Horiot, 553(RLiR):Jan-Jun78-213
Buridanus, J. Sophismata. (T.K. Scott,
ed and trans)
   J-F. Courtine, 192(EP):Oct-Dec79-498
Burke, A.D. Fire Watch.
   M. Bayles, 231:Jul80-77
   J. Yardley, 441:11May80-15
Burke, P., ed. The New Cambridge Modern
History. (Vol 13)
   639(VQR):Autumn79-134
Burke, P. Popular Culture in Early Modern
Europe.
   E. Weber, 322(JHI):Jul-Sep79-481
Burkert, W. Griechische Religion der
archaischen und klassischen Epoche.*
   R.C.T. Parker, 123:Vol29No1-86
Burkhard, M. Conrad Ferdinand Meyer.
   G. Reinhardt, 222(GR):Spring79-85
Burkhardt, F. - see James, W.
Burkholder, M.A. and D.S. Chandler. From
Impotence to Authority.
   J. Lynch, 86(BHS):Jul79-269
Burki, S.J. Pakistan Under Bhutto, 1971-
1977.
   H. Tinker, 617(TLS):8Feb80-139
Burks, A.W. Chance, Cause and Reason.
   H.E. Kyburg, Jr., 482(PhR):Jul79-500
   W. Newton-Smith, 518:Oct79-124
Burl, A. Rings of Stone.
   C. Thomas, 617(TLS):29Feb80-243

Burlin, R.B. Chaucerian Fiction.*
  J.B. Allen, 589:Jan79-116
  R.T. Davies, 447(N&Q):Aug78-356
  G.S. Ivy, 161(DUJ):Dec78-121
  L.W. Patterson, 627(UTQ):Spring79-263
Burmeister, K.H., ed. Vorarlberger Weis-
  tümer. (Pt 1)
  R. Ganghofer, 182:Vol31#20-764
Burn, A.R. and M. The Living Past of
  Greece.
  D. Hunt, 617(TLS):9May80-535
Burnam, T. More Misinformation.
  C. Lehmann-Haupt, 441:20Jun80-C29
Burnet, T. and G. Duckett. A Second
  Tale of a Tub, or, the History of Rob-
  ert Powel the Puppet-Show-Man.
  566:Spring79-140
Burnett, A.P. Catastrophe Survived.
  C. de Heer, 394:Vol32fasc3/4-407
Burnett, J. A Social History of Housing,
  1815-1970.
  A.S. Wohl, 637(VS):Summer79-483
Burnett, V. Towers at the Edge of a
  World.
  A. Broyard, 441:27Dec80-19
Burnham, A. New York Landmarks.
  P. Goldberger, 576:May78-113
Burnier/Rambaud. Le Roland Barthes sans
  peine.
  P. Dulac, 450(NRF):Feb79-102
Burnley, J.D. Chaucer's Language and the
  Philosophers' Tradition.
  T.A. Shippey, 617(TLS):7Mar80-272
Burns, D.H. and P. Alcócer Hinostra. Un
  Analisis Preliminar de Discurso en Que-
  chua.
  T.T. Büttner, 269(IJAL):Oct78-343
Burns, G. The Third Time Around.
  J. Lahr, 441:10Feb80-12
Burns, N.T. and C.J. Regan, eds. Concepts
  of the Hero in the Middle Ages and the
  Renaissance.
  H.H. Kalwies, 546(RR):Mar79-188
Burns, R.A. Ben Neptune.
  G. Hamel, 198:Winter80-138
Burns, T.A., with I.H. Burns. Doing the
  Wash.*
  C.C. Drake, 292(JAF):Apr-Jun79-224
  J.P. Leary, 582(SFQ):Vol41-259
  E. Oring, 650(WF):Apr79-122
Burose, H. and U. Schmidt, comps. Katalog
  der Calvörschen Bibliothek. (Vols 1-3)
  (H-O. Weber, ed)
  D. Gutzen, 52:Band13Heft3-320
Burr, B. Blue Ladies.
  M. Malone, 441:17Aug80-10
Burros, M. Pure and Simple.
  W. and C. Cowen, 639(VQR):Autumn79-154
Burroughs, W. Le métro blanc. Colloque
  de Tanger. Havre des Saints.
  J-F. Chevrier and P. Roussin, 98:May78-
  450
Burroughs, W.S. Port of Saints.
  J. Updike, 442(NY):11Aug80-82

Burroughs, W.S. and B. Gysin. The Third
  Mind.*
  N. Calas, 62:Summer79-62
  P. Lewis, 565:Vol20#4-67
Burrow, J., ed. English Verse 1300-1500.*
  A. Crépin, 189(EA):Jul-Dec78-374
Burroway, J. Raw Silk.
  S. Brett, 502(PrS):Summer78-204
Burrows, A. Honest, Abe.
  J. Lahr, 441:16Mar80-12
Burrows, E.G. Properties.
  D. Smith, 29:Mar/Apr80-40
Burrs, M. Children on the Edge of Space.
  D. Barbour, 150(DR):Spring79-154
Bursch, H. Die lateinisch-romanische Wort-
  familie von *Interpedare und seinen
  Parallelbildungen.*
  C. Schmitt, 547(RF):Band91Heft3-315
Bursk, C. Standing Watch.
  M. Heffernan, 491:Jun80-170
  C. Molesworth, 461:Fall-Winter79/80-91
  P. Stitt, 219(GaR):Fall79-699
  42(AR):Summer79-380
Burt, N. Palaces for the People.*
  R.V. Hadley, 576:Dec78-323
Burton, D.M. Shakespeare's Grammatical
  Style.*
  E.C. Davies, 349:Summer78-193
Burton, F. The Politics of Legitimacy.
  I. McAllister, 174(Éire):Fall79-144
Burton, J. The Collection of the Qur'ān.*
  H.A. Ali, 273(IC):Jul78-203
Busch, F. Rounds.
  A. Broyard, 441:9Jan80-C22
  R. Buffington, 441:13Jan80-22
  J. Mellors, 362:31Jul80-153
  F. Taliaferro, 231:Feb80-84
Busch, H., ed and trans. Verdi's "Aida."
  J. Budden, 410(M&L):Jan79-83
Busch, N. Continent's Edge.
  M. Levin, 441:16Mar80-15
Buschhausen, H. and H. Die Marienkirche
  von Apollonia in Albanien.
  S. Ćurčić, 589:Apr79-353
Buschhausen, H. and H., with E. Zimmermann.
  Die illuminierten armenischen Hand-
  schriften der Mechitharisten-Congrega-
  tion in Wien.
  S. Der Nersessian, 589:Jan79-118
Bush, C. The Dream of Reason.
  R.E. Spiller, 27(AL):Jan80-568
Bush-Brown, H. Beaux Arts to Bauhaus and
  Beyond.*
  S. Abercrombie, 576:Mar78-45
Busiri Vici, A. Andrea Locatelli e il
  paesaggio romano del settecento. Trit-
  tico paesistico romano del '700.
  P. Conisbee, 90:Sep79-588
Busk, R.H. The Folk-Songs of Italy (1887).
  A.L. Chairetakis, 187:May80-300
Busoni, F. Lo sguardo lieto. (F. d'Amico,
  ed)
  J.C.G. Waterhouse, 410(M&L):Jul79-366
Busse, J., comp. Internationales Handbuch
  aller Maler und Bildhauer des 19. Jahr-
  hunderts.*
  F-G. Pariset, 182:Vol131#15/16-553

Busse, W. Klasse Transitivität Valenz.
  J.N. Green, 208(FS):Oct79-498
Busse, W. and J-P. Dubost. Französisches
Verblexikon.
  J. Albrecht, 343:Band23-189
  F.J. Hausmann, 257(IRAL):Feb79-93
Butenschön, M. - see Nikitin, B. and L.
Butler, A.J. The Arab Conquest of Egypt
and the Last Thirty Years of the Roman
Dominion. (2nd ed) (P.M. Fraser, ed)
  R.S. Bagnall, 121(CJ):Apr-May80-347
Butler, C. After the Wake.
  A. Broyard, 441:20Dec80-23
Butler, D. and D. Kavanagh. The British
General Election of 1979.
  G. Kaufman, 362:19Jun80-804
Butler, D. and A. Ranney, eds. Referen-
dums.
  639(VQR):Summer79-92
Butler, D. and A. Sloman. British Politi-
cal Facts 1900-1979.
  G. Kaufman, 362:20Mar80-376
  S. Koss, 617(TLS):18Apr80-448
Butler, J. Power, Authority, and the
Origins of American Denominational Order.
  M.E. Lodge, 656(WMQ):Jul79-483
Butler, J. - see Wordsworth, W.
Butler, L.S. Thomas Hardy.*
  M. Bath, 637(VS):Spring79-348
  H. Orel, 395(MFS):Winter78/79-582
  A. Poole, 184(EIC):Apr79-191
  M. Ragussis, 445(NCF):Dec78-397
  T. Slade, 67:May79-104
  K. Wilson, 255(HAB):Summer79-228
Butler, L.S., ed. Thomas Hardy After
Fifty Years.*
  M. Bath, 637(VS):Spring79-348
  W.E. Harrold, 125:Spring79-471
  H. Orel, 395(MFS):Winter78/79-582
  A. Poole, 184(EIC):Apr79-191
  M. Ragussis, 445(NCF):Dec78-397
  636(VP):Winter78-399
Butler, M. The Novels of Max Frisch.
  C. Burke, 402(MLR):Apr79-504
Butler, M. Peacock Displayed.*
  S. Tumim, 617(TLS):15Feb80-187
  G. Vidal, 453(NYRB):4Dec80-10
Butler, M.D. Street and Sky.
  J. Symons, 617(TLS):23May80-586
Butler, R. Western Sculpture.
  K. Varnedoe, 54:Dec78-737
Butler, W.E. International Straits of
the World: Northeast Arctic Passage.
  T. Armstrong, 575(SEER):Oct79-626
Butlin, M. and E. Joll, comps. The Paint-
ings of J.M.W. Turner.*
  M. Schneckenburger, 471:Oct/Nov/Dec79-
409
Butor, M. Boomerang.
  L.S. Roudiez, 207(FR):Apr79-788
Butor, M. Les Compagnons de Pantagruel.
  D.G. Coleman, 208(FS):Vol33Pt2-617
Butscher, E., ed. Sylvia Plath.
  639(VQR):Spring78-48

Butt, J. The Oxford History of English
Literature.* (Vol 8: The Mid-Eighteenth
Century.) (ed and completed by G.
Carnall)
  W.H., 148:Winter79-90
  639(VQR):Autumn79-128
Butt, J. Writers and Politics in Modern
Spain.
  C.L. King, 399(MLJ):Nov79-393
Butt, W. Mobilmachung des Elfenbeinturms.
  R. Kejzlar, 562(Scan):May79-77
Butterick, G.F. A Guide to the Maximus
Poems of Charles Olson.*
  P. Breslin, 491:Jul80-219
  L.S. Dembo, 27(AL):May79-289
  C. Molesworth, 219(GaR):Summer79-438
  G. Selerie, 301(JEGP):Oct79-582
  468:Winter79-583
Butterick, G.F. - see Olson, C.
Butterworth, C.E. - see Averroes
Butts, R.E. and J. Hintikka, eds. Founda-
tional Problems in the Special Sciences.
  G.O., 543:Sep78-129
Butts, R.E. and J. Hintikka, eds. Histori-
cal and Philosophical Dimensions of
Logic, Methodology and Philosophy of
Science.
  J.J.K., 543:Sep78-130
Buus, E., ed. Consuetudines Lundenses.
  G. Constable, 589:Oct79-874
Buxton, J. The Grecian Taste.*
  K.H., 148:Summer79-91
  R. Quintana, 402(MLR):Oct79-909
Buxton, N.K. and D.M. Aldcroft, eds.
British Industry Between the Wars.
  T.C. Barker, 617(TLS):18Apr80-448
Buyssens, E. Les Catégories grammaticales
du français.*
  J. Bourguignon, 553(RLiR):Jan-Jun78-
  227
  K. Connors, 545(RPh):Nov78-241
  N.C.W. Spence, 208(FS):Vol33Pt2-1047
Byatt, A.S. The Virgin in the Garden.*
  J. Chernaik, 364:Apr/May79-140
Byerlee, D. and others. Rural-Urban
Migration in Sierra Leone.
  R.M. Lawson, 69:Vol148#3-309
Byers, M., J. Kennedy and M. McBurney.
Rural Roots.
  H. Kalman, 576:Oct78-214
Bynner, W. The Works of Witter Bynner:
Prose Pieces. (J. Kraft, ed)
  42(AR):Summer79-378
Bynon, T. Historical Linguistics.
  A. Fox, 47(ArL):Vol10#2-147
  G. Hudson, 603:Vol13#2-253
  J. Klausenburger, 399(MLJ):Jan-Feb79-
  58
  P. Rickard, 208(FS):Vol33Pt2-1065
  W.P. Schmid, 260(IF):Band83-370
  205(FMLS):Apr78-184
Bynum, D.E. The Daemon in the Wood.
  J. Fletcher, 268(IFR):Summer80-153
  J.M. Foley, 574(SEEJ):Fall79-420

Calame, C. Les choeurs de jeunes filles en Grèce archaïque.
É. Des Places, 555:Vol52fasc2-360
M.R. Lefkowitz, 124:Sep79-56
Calame, C., ed. Rito e poesia corale in Grecia.
É. Des Places, 555:Vol52fasc2-361
M.R. Lefkowitz, 124:Sep79-57
de Calan, P. Cosmas, or the Love of God.
M. Trend, 617(TLS):23May80-574
Calbert, J.P. Dimensions of Style and Meaning in the Language of Trakl and Rilke.
J. Scharnhorst, 682(ZPSK):Band31Heft4-438
Calboli, G. - see Cato
Caldarini, E. - see Du Bellay, J.
Caldarola, C., ed. Society and Politics in Alberta.
C. Armstrong, 99:Apr80-37
Calder, D.G. and M.J.B. Allen. Sources and Analogues of Old English Poetry.
A. Crépin, 189(EA):Apr-Jun78-222
T.D. Hill, 447(N&Q):Jun78-247
Calder, J. Robert Louis Stevenson. (British title: RLS: A Life Study.)
J. Bayley, 362:11Sep80-340
J. Leonard, 441:10Sep80-C25
J.A. Smith, 617(TLS):6Jun80-635
Calder, J. Women and Marriage in Victorian Fiction.*
S. Gubar, 637(VS):Autumn78-90
S. Hudson, 577(SHR):Summer79-258
Calder, N. Einstein's Universe.*
529(QQ):Winter79/80-737
639(VQR):Summer79-110
Calder, N. Nuclear Nightmares.
T. Ferris, 441:23Nov80-18
Calder-Marshall, A. The Grand Century of the Lady, 1780-1870.
L. Senelick, 637(VS):Summer78-493
Calder-Marshall, A. - see Dickens, C.
Calderón Quijano, J.A. and others. Cartografía militar y marítima de Cadiz, 1513-1878.
D. Angulo Íñiguez, 48:Jul-Sep78-347
Caldicott, H., with N. Herrington and N. Stiskin. Nuclear Madness.*
529(QQ):Winter79/80-738
Calet, H. La Belle Lurette.
G. Quinsat, 450(NRF):Sep79-47
Calhoun, F.B. Miss Minerva and William Green Hill.
E.F. Bargainnier, 578:Spring80-150
Calì, A. and others. Il Romanzo al tempo di Luigi XIII.
G. Hainsworth, 208(FS):Vol33Pt2-697
Calin, F. La Vie retrouvée.
V. Minogue, 208(FS):Vol33Pt2-912
M. Tison-Braun, 535(RHL):Jul-Aug79-718
Calin, V. Auferstehung der Allegorie.
W. Helmich, 224(GRM):Band28Heft4-489
Calin, W. Crown, Cross, and "Fleur-de-lis."
R.T. Corum, Jr., 207(FR):Feb79-483
R.G. Maber, 402(MLR):Jul79-697

Calin, W. A Poet at the Fountain.*
M-A. Bossy, 546(RR):Mar79-187
Cǎlinescu, G. and A. Rosetti. Corespondenţa lui G. Cǎlinescu cu Al. Rosetti (1935-1951). (A. Rosetti, ed)
D.J. Deletant, 575(SEER):Oct79-588
Calinescu, M. Faces of Modernity.*
V. Calin, 125:Fall78-126
295(JML):Vol7#4-622
Callaghan, B. The Hogg Poems and Drawings.*
D. Barbour, 150(DR):Spring79-154
G. Hamel, 198:Winter80-138
Callaghan, M. No Man's Meat and The Enchanted Pimp.*
L.K. MacKendrick, 198:Winter80-124
Callahan, H. Water's Edge.
C. James, 453(NYRB):18Dec80-22
H. Kramer, 441:30Nov80-13
Callen, A. Angel in the Studio.
L. Ormond, 39:Dec79-537
J.M. Richards, 617(TLS):15Feb80-178
Callen, A. Women Artists of the Arts and Crafts Movement, 1870-1914.
Q. Bell, 453(NYRB):15May80-41
Callender, J.B. Middle Egyptian.
D.W. Young, 318(JAOS):Jul-Sep78-345
Calleo, D. The German Problem Reconsidered.*
D. Barnouw, 221(GQ):Nov79-573
Callot, E. La Philosophie instituée.
J.B. Ayoub, 154:Sep78-552
J-M. Gabaude, 542:Jul-Sep79-350
Callot, E. Les trois moments de la philosophie théologique de l'histoire.
J-M. Gabaude, 542:Jul-Sep79-347
Calloud, J. Structural Analysis of Narrative.
H.A. Hatton, 355(LSoc):Aug78-267
Calloway, S. Charles Ricketts.
376:Oct79-144
Callu, F., ed. Georges Bernanos.
E.M. O'Sharkey, 208(FS):Jul79-360
Calvert, L. Francisco de Osuna and the Spirit of the Letter.*
G.A. Davies, 86(BHS):Oct79-339
J.W. Grant, 539:Vol4No2-228
Calvino, I., ed. Italian Folktales.
J. Gardner, 441:12Oct80-1
Calvino, I. Se una notte d'inverno un viaggiatore.
L.M. Picchione, 268(IFR):Winter80-75
Calvo, F. Vitruvio e Raffaello. (V. Fontana and P. Morachiello, eds)
R.J. Betts, 576:May78-128
de' Calzabigi, R. La Lulliade o i buffi italiani scacciati da Parigi. (G. Muresu, ed)
E.B., 228(GSLI):Vol155fasc491-476
de la Calzada, L.S. - see under Sáenz de la Calzada, L.
Camamis, G. Estudios sobre el cautiverio en el Siglo de Oro.*
J. Weiner, 238:Dec79-728
Camara, J.M., Jr. - see under Mattoso Camara, J., Jr.

Caputo, P. Horn of Africa.
P-L. Adams, 61:Dec80-96
P. Andrews, 441:2Nov80-12
C. Lehmann-Haupt, 441:17Nov80-C21
442(NY):17Nov80-240
Caputo, P. A Rumor of War.
639(VQR):Winter78-25
Caradec, F. Dictionnaire du français argo-
tique et populaire.*
M.G. Hydak, 207(FR):May79-940
Caradec, F. Isidore Ducasse, comte de
Lautréamont.
M. Bonnet, 535(RHL):May-Jun78-500
Caradec, F. and A. Weill. Le Café concert.
P. O'Connor, 617(TLS):11Jul80-784
Carandini, A. - see Annecchino, M. and
others
Cardauns, B. M. Terentius Varro. (Pts 1
and 2)
J. André, 555:Vol52fasc2-390
Cardauns, B. - see Varro
Carden, G. English Quantifiers, Logical
Structure and Linguistic Variation.
D.E. Elliott, 350:Mar79-215
P. Muysken, 361:Apr78-392
Cardinal, M. Une Vie pour deux.
M. Whiting, 207(FR):May79-950
Cardinal, R., ed. Sensibility and Crea-
tion.*
K.R. Aspley, 205(FMLS):Jan78-79
Cardini, R. La critica del Landino.*
D. Aguzzi-Barbagli, 276:Spring79-60
Cardona, G.R. Introduzione all'etnolin-
guistica.
M.P., 228(GSLI):Vol155fasc490-319
Cardona, R., ed. Novelistas españoles de
postguerra.* (Vol 1)
W.I. Pertaub, 86(BHS):Jan79-85
Cardozo, N. Lucky Eyes and a High Heart.
J.F. Cotter, 249(HudR):Summer79-289
Cardwell, K.H. Bernard Maybeck.*
A. Batey, 46:Jun79-362
Cardwell, R.A. - see Gil, R.
Cardwell, R.A. - see Reina, M.
Caress, J. Hank Williams.*
N. Cohen, 187:Sep80-580
Carey, J. Thackeray.*
M. Harris, 72:Band216Heft1-185
J. McMaster, 445(NCF):Sep78-259
S. Monod, 189(EA):Apr-Jun78-231
D.W. Pitre, 577(SHR):Summer79-257
A. Shelston, 148:Spring79-86
Carey, P. The Fat Man in History.*
J. Naughton, 362:16Oct80-513
Cargile, J. Paradoxes.
D.W. Hamlyn, 617(TLS):4Jan80-19
Carile, P. Céline, oggi.
L. Davis, 208(FS):Vol33Pt2-892
Carile, P. - see de Saint-Évremond, C. and
Comte d'Etelan
Carlerius, E. Duo tractatuli de musica.
R. Woodley, 410(M&L):Jul79-357
Carley, L. and R. Threlfall. Delius: a
Life in Pictures.*
J.B., 412:Feb78-63

Carlisle, C.R. Ecos del viento, silencios
del mar.
W.J. Grupp, 238:May-Sep79-406
Carlisle, O. Island in Time.
E. Auchincloss, 441:11May80-12
442(NY):12May80-162
Carlisle, O. Solzhenitsyn and the Secret
Circle.
M. Geltman, 390:Jan79-71
Carlo, A.M. - see under Millares Carlo, A.
Carlson, E.W. - see Emerson, R.W.
Carlson, M. Goethe and the Weimar Theatre.
S. Atkins, 221(GQ):May79-413
R. Gray, 617(TLS):11Jan80-45
O. Mann, 301(JEGP):Oct79-599
M. Meisel, 222(GR):Summer79-132
Carlson, P.A. Hawthorne's Functional
Settings.*
K. Carabine, 447(N&Q):Jun78-278
Carlucci, C. A Field Guide to Greek Metre.
R.D. Dawe, 121(CJ):Dec79/Jan80-183
Carlut, C., P.H. Dubé and J.R. Dugan. A
Concordance to Flaubert's "Madame
Bovary." A Concordance to Flaubert's
"L'Éducation sentimentale."
A. Fairlie, 208(FS):Oct79-467
Carlyle, J.W. I Too Am Here.* (A. and
M.M. Simpson, eds)
M.F., 191(ELN):Sep78(supp)-55
E.M. Fulton, 637(VS):Summer78-502
Carlyle, T. and J.W. The Collected Let-
ters of Thomas and Jane Welsh Carlyle.*
(Vols 5-7) (C.R. Sanders and K.J. Field-
ing, eds)
C. Moore, 588(SSL):Vol14-263
A. and M.M. Simpson, 637(VS):Spring78-
424
Carman, J.N. A Study of the Psuedo-Map
Cycle of Arthurian Romance.
L.A. Arrathoon, 546(RR):May79-299
Carmichael, M. Oyster Wine.
D. Barbour, 150(DR):Spring79-154
Carnac, N. Tournament of Shadows.
639(VQR):Autumn79-138
Carnall, G. - see Butt, J.
Carnap, R. Two Essays on Entropy. (A.
Shimony, ed)
M. Redhead, 479(PhQ):Oct79-364
Lord Carnarvon. Ermine Tales.
E.S. Turner, 362:22May80-656
Carne-Ross, D.S. Instaurations.
H. Lloyd-Jones, 617(TLS):11Apr80-419
Carneiro, P.E.D. and P. Arnaud - see under
de Berrêdo Carneiro and P. Arnaud
Carner, M. Major and Minor.
H. Cole, 362:12Jun80-767
M. Cooper, 617(TLS):11Jul80-790
Carnochan, W.B. Confinement and Flight.*
J. Stedmond, 529(QQ):Summer79-335
D.W. Tarbet, 173(ECS):Summer79-549
Caro, R. Días geniales o lúdicros. (J-P.
Etienvre, ed)
J.R. Jones, 304(JHP):Autumn79-94
Caroli, F. Pragmatische Aspekte syntaktis-
cher Variation in der gesprochenen
Sprache.
D. Karch, 133:Band12Heft4-358

Carpenter, A. - see "Archbishop King's
Sermon on Predestination"
Carpenter, D. A Couple of Comedians.*
R. Kiely, 441:6Jan80-10
Carpenter, D., ed. Stories from Alberta.
C. Ross, 102(CanL):Autumn79-86
Carpenter, H. Jesus.
C.H. Sisson, 617(TLS):9May80-531
Carpenter, J. and B. - see Herbert, Z.
Carpenter, R. Thomas Hardy.
S. Hunter, 402(MLR):Jan79-178
H. Lee, 447(N&Q):Aug78-370
Carpentier, A. Rue Saint Denis.
A.L. Amprimoz, 526:Spring79-85
Carpio, L.D. - see under de Vega Carpio, L.
Carr, D.C. - see de Villena, E.
Carr, E.H. A History of Soviet Russia.
(14 volumes)
A. Nove, 617(TLS):11Jan80-37
Carr, E.H. The Russian Revolution from
Lenin to Stalin (1917-1929).*
A. Brown, 617(TLS):25Jan80-95
Carr, J.L. A Month in the Country.
J. Lasdun, 617(TLS):2May80-510
Carr, L. Four Fabulous Faces.
D. Bodeen, 200:May79-306
Carr, L. More Fabulous Faces.
D. Bodeen, 200:Oct79-493
Carr, P. The Song of the Siren.
L. Duguid, 617(TLS):16May80-558
Carr, P. The Women in the Mirror.*
S. Purdin, 598(SoR):Spring80-516
639(VQR):Summer78-94
Carr, R. Anarchism in France.*
V. Conley, 395(MFS):Winter78/79-615
J. Flower, 208(FS):Oct79-470
A. Gruzinska, 446(NCFS):Fall-Winter
78/79-148
Carr, R. The Spanish Tragedy.*
J.W.D. Trythall, 86(BHS):Jan79-76
Carr, R.A. - see Boaistuau, P.
Carr-Gomm, R. Push on the Door.
V. Powell, 617(TLS):8Feb80-140
Carrard, P. Malraux ou le récit hybride.*
J. Dale, 208(FS):Vol33Pt2-910
J. Leeker, 547(RF):Band91Heft1/2-184
Carrasquilla, T. La Marquesa de Yolombó.
(K.L. Levy, ed)
P.G. Earle, 240(HR):Winter78-108
le Carré, J. The Honourable Schoolboy.*
639(VQR):Spring78-65
le Carré, J. Smiley's People.*
R. Kee, 362:7Feb80-191
S.S. Prawer, 617(TLS):8Feb80-131
V.S. Pritchett, 453(NYRB):7Feb80-22
M. Wood, 441:6Jan80-1
442(NY):7Jan80-87
Carré, M-R. Cyrano de Bergerac — voyages
imaginaires à la recherche de la vérité
humaine.
K. Raymer-Simon, 399(MLJ):Jan-Feb79-83
de Carrera, P.A. - see under Almoina de
Carrera, P.
Carrère d'Encausse, H. L'Empire éclaté.
H. Cronel, 450(NRF):Nov79-119

Carrier, R. The Garden of Delights.
G. Davies, 198:Summer80-163
J. Kertzer, 168(ECW):Fall78-79
K. Mezei, 648(WCR):Oct78-54
Carrier, R. The Hockey Sweater and Other
Stories.
G. Davies, 198:Summer80-163
J. Kertzer, 99:Mar80-36
Carrier, R. Il n'y a pas de pays sans
grand-père.*
P.G. Lewis, 207(FR):Apr79-789
Carrière, J. Le Choeur secondaire dans le
drame grec.
D. Bain, 123:Vol129No1-138
T.J. Sienkewicz, 24:Winter79-586
Carrington, G.W. Foreigners in Formosa,
1841-1874.
H.J. Lamley, 293(JASt):Feb79-333
Carrington, N. Carrington.
F. Spalding, 90:Jan79-47
442(NY):8Dec80-240
Carroll, E.A. The Drawings of Rosso
Fiorentino.
L.O. Larsson, 341:1978/2-76
Carroll, J. Fault Lines.
S. Ellin, 441:14Dec80-10
C. Lehmann-Haupt, 441:2Oct80-C21
Carroll, J.B. The Teaching of French as a
Foreign Language in Eight Countries.
H. Düwell, 430(NS):Dec78-613
Carroll, L. Lewis Carroll's "Symbolic
Logic."* (W.W. Bartley 3d, ed)
J.R. Kincaid, 445(NCF):Sep78-272
Carroll, L. The Letters of Lewis Carroll.*
(M.N. Cohen, with R.L. Green, eds)
A.D. Culler, 676(YR):Autumn79-108
V.S. Pritchett, 442(NY):3Mar80-123
F. Watson, 617(TLS):11Jul80-776
Carroll, L. Le Magazine du presbytère.
(J. Bouniort, ed and trans)
C. Jordis, 450(NRF):Feb79-122
Carroll, L. The Rectory Magazine.
J.R. Kincaid, 445(NCF):Sep78-272
Carroll, L. The Story of Sylvie and Bruno.
F. Huxley, 617(TLS):11Jul80-776
Carroll, P.N. The Other Samuel Johnson.
D. Hattenhauer, 432(NEQ):Jun79-275
Carroni, E. Estetica ed Epistemologia.
K. Oedingen, 342:Band69Heft4-469
Carruth, H. Brothers, I Loved You All.*
P. Ramsey, 569(SR):Fall79-686
639(VQR):Summer79-107
Carsaniga, G. Leopardi.
E.F., 228(GSLI):Vol155fasc492-633
Carson, E.J. Scenes.
D. Barbour, 150(DR):Spring79-154
Carsten, F.L. Fascist Movements in
Austria.
T.W. Mason, 575(SEER):Apr79-314
Carstens, K. Zusammenleben in Freiheit.
F. L'Huillier, 182:Vol131#21/22-790
Carswell, J. Lives and Letters.*
639(VQR):Spring79-68
Cartagena, J.E. - see under Enríquez
Cartagena, J.

Carter, A. The Bloody Chamber.*
  A. Friedman, 441:17Feb80-14
  S. Kennedy, 617(TLS):8Feb80-146
Carter, A. The Sadeian Woman.*
  J. O'Faolain, 364:Aug/Sep79-129
Carter, A.E. Charles Baudelaire.*
  F.S. Heck, 188(ECr):Summer78-87
  L.D. Joiner, 446(NCFS):Fall-Winter
  78/79-133
Carter, E. The Writings of Elliott Car-
  ter.* (E. and K. Stone, eds)
  A. Whittall, 607:Mar78-40
Carter, E.C., 2d - see Latrobe, B.H.
Carter, E.C. 2d, R. Forster and J.N.
  Moody, eds. Enterprise and Entre-
  preneurs in Nineteenth- and Twentieth-
  Century France.
  N. Hampson, 208(FS):Vol33Pt2-1010
Carter, E.C. 2d and T.E. Jeffrey - see
  Latrobe, B.H.
Carter, F.T.C. Quer durch Deutschland.
  R.B. Tilford, 220(GL&L):Oct78-60
Carter, J. A Government as Good as Its
  People.
  639(VQR):Spring78-64
Carter, M. Poems of Succession.
  S. Brown, 493:Dec79-47
Carter, P.A. The Creation of Tomorrow.
  R.H.C., 125:Winter79-307
Carter, S. The Politics of Solzhenitsyn.*
  S. Pratt, 395(MFS):Summer78-292
  J. Schillinger, 558(RLJ):Winter79-227
"Henri Cartier-Bresson: Photographer."*
  P. Keating, 617(TLS):28Mar80-344
Cartledge, P. Sparta and Laconia.
  S. Hornblower, 617(TLS):15Feb80-186
Carton, F. Introduction à la Phonétique
  du Français.*
  A. Classe, 208(FS):Apr79-243
Cartwright, J. The Horse of Darius.
  N. Callendar, 441:27Jul80-23
  M. Laski, 362:13Nov80-665
de Carvalho, M.J., Jr. - see under Joaquim
  de Carvalho, M., Jr.
de Carvalho-Neto, P. Mi tío Atahualpa.*
  R. Layera, 263(RIB):Vol29No1-90
Carver, M. War Since 1945.
  C. Wain, 362:30Oct80-586
Carver, R. Will You Please Be Quiet,
  Please?
  J. Benson, 573(SSF):Fall178-462
  W.S. Penn, 577(SHR):Fall179-362
Cary, D.S. Hollywood's Children.*
  R.L. Davis, 584(SWR):Summer79-306
Cary, P. The Poems of Patrick Cary. (V.
  Delany, ed)
  K.J. Höltgen, 541(RES):Nov79-470
Carynnyk, M. - see Plyushch, L.
Carynnyk, M. and M. Horban - see Nekipelov,
  V.
Casa, F.P. and B. Primorac - see Moreto, A.
Casado, A.H. - see under Herrero Casado, A.
del Casal, J. The Poetry. (R.J. Glickman,
  ed)
  P.R. Beardsell, 86(BHS):Jul79-270
Casares, A.B. - see under Bioy Casares, A.

Casarès, M. Résidente privilégiée.
  P. McCarthy, 617(TLS):25Jul80-830
Cascio Pratilli, G. L'Università e il
  principe.
  M.P., 228(GSLI):Vol155fasc491-475
Case, B. and S. Britt. The Illustrated
  Encyclopedia of Jazz.
  B. Pennycook, 529(QQ):Autumn79-537
Case, F.I. La Cité idéale dans "Travail"
  d'Émile Zola.*
  T.G.S. Combe, 208(FS):Vol33Pt2-840
Caselberg, J. Chart to My Country.
  K.O. Arvidson, 368:Jun74-164
Caselberg, J., ed. Maori is My Name.
  M. Orbell, 368:Jun76-171
Caserio, R. Plot, Story, and the Novel.
  R. Howard, 676(YR):Spring80-466
Casey, D.J. and R.E. Rhodes, eds. Views
  of the Irish Peasantry, 1800-1916.
  L.J. McCaffrey, 637(VS):Summer79-449
Casey, D.R. Crisis Investing.
  J. Epstein, 453(NYRB):23Oct80-10
Casey, E.S. Imagining.*
  I.H.C., 191(ELN):Sep78(supp)-19
  D.H. Hirsch, 569(SR):Fall179-628
Cashmore, E. Rastaman.
  R. Hodgkin, 362:10Jan80-60
  D. Martin, 617(TLS):25Jan80-76
Casiño, E.S. The Jama Mapun.
  M. Mednick, 293(JASt):Feb79-435
Caskey, M. Chariot of Fire.
  D. Weber, 432(NEQ):Mar79-134
  639(VQR):Winter79-15
de Casparis, J.G. Indonesian Palaeography.
  J.M. Echols, 318(JAOS):Apr-Jun78-204
Caspary, V. The Secrets of Grown-Ups.*
  C. Seebohm, 441:20Jan80-16
"Cassell's Spanish Dictionary (Spanish-
  English, English-Spanish)." (rev) (A.
  Gooch and Á. García de Paredes, eds)
  R. Wright, 86(BHS):Oct79-325
Cassidy, J. An Attitude of Mind.*
  D. Graham, 565:Vol120#2-75
Cassidy, R. Livable Cities.
  61:Aug80-83
Cassill, R.V. Labors of Love.
  J. Moynahan, 441:4May80-14
Cassinelli, C.W. and R.B. Ekvall. A
  Tibetan Principality.
  M.C. Goldstein, 259(IIJ):Jul79-207
Cassirer, E. Substance et fonction.
  G. Brykman, 542:Jul-Sep79-323
Cassius, B. Institutiones Linguae Illyri-
  cae.
  P. Herrity, 575(SEER):Apr79-268
Casson, C. and S. Lee. The Compleat
  Lemon.
  W. and C. Cowen, 639(VQR):Autumn79-153
Cassuto, U. Biblical and Oriental Stud-
  ies. (Vol 2)
  D. Pardee, 318(JAOS):Jul-Sep78-343
Castagnino, R.H. Crónicas del pasado
  teatral argentino (siglo XIX).
  G. Woodyard, 238:May-Sep79-409
Castañeda, H-N. Thinking and Doing.*
  R.M. Chisholm, 449:Sep79-385
  W. Petschen, 682(ZPSK):Band31Heft6-658

63

Castex, M-M. - see Rousseau, J-J.

Castex, P-G. - see de Balzac, H.

Castex, P-G., with others - see de Balzac, H.

Castillo, F., ed. Theologie aus der Praxis des Volkes.
J. Galot, 182:Vol131#19-654

Castillo-Feliú, G., ed. Cuentos y micro-cuentos.*
F.W. Frank, 238:May-Sep79-418

Castle, B. The Castle Diaries 1974-76.
M. Foot, 362:25Sep80-386

Castor, G. and T. Cave - see de Ronsard, P.

Castoriadis, C. Les Carrefours du labyrinthe.
M. Pierssens, 207(FR):May79-945

Castrén, P. Ordo populusque Pompeianus.*
M.G. Morgan, 122:Jul79-257

Castro, A. An Idea of History.* (S. Gilman and E.L. King, eds)
N.G. Round, 86(BHS):Jul79-239

Catach, N. L'Orthographe.
A. Greive, 547(RF):Band91Heft4-448

Catalano, G. Remembering the Rural Life.
C. Pollnitz, 581:Dec79-462
639(VQR):Summer79-109

Catalano, P. Populus Romanus Quirites.
J. Hellegouarc'h, 555:Vol52fasc1-207

Cataldi, L. Invitation to a Marxist Lesbian Party.
C. Pollnitz, 581:Dec79-462

"A Catalogue of the Icelandic Collection." [University of Leeds]
M.E. Kalinke, 563(SS):Summer79-289

Catanoy, N., ed. Modern Romanian Poetry.
W.R. Keitner, 102(CanL):Autumn79-97

Catford, J.C. Fundamental Problems in Phonetics.
P. Ladefoged, 350:Dec79-904

Cathelat, B. Les Styles de vie des Français 1978-1998.
J-P. Ponchie, 207(FR):Mar79-661

Catling, P.S. - see under Skene Catling, P.

Cato. Caton, "de l'agriculture."* (R. Goujard, ed and trans)
M. Pasquinucci, 313:Vol69-229

Cato. Marci Porci Catonis "Oratio pro Rhodiensibus." (G. Calboli, ed and trans)
E. Badian, 24:Winter79-578

Catteau, J. La Création Littéraire chez Dostoevski.
J. Frank, 574(SEEJ):Winter79-529
E. Wasiolek, 550(RusR):Oct79-505

Catullus. Catullo, Le Poesie.* (F. Della Corte, ed)
T.P. Wiseman, 313:Vol69-237

Catullus. The Poems of Catullus. (F. Raphael and K. McLeish, trans)
P. Jay, 493:Jul79-62
J. Simon, 491:Apr80-40

"Catullus." (D.F.S. Thomson, ed)
J.H. Gaisser, 124:Apr-May80-428
W.C. Scott, 121(CJ):Apr-May80-345

"Caucasian Carpets."
J. Housego, 463:Summer78-215

Causey, A. Paul Nash.
F. Spalding, 617(TLS):15Aug80-921

Causey, R.L. Unity of Science.*
F. Jackson, 63:Jun79-195

Caute, D. The Great Fear.
K. Fitzlyon, 364:Jun79-86

Cauvin, J. Les 1ers villages de Syrie-Palestine du IXe-VIIe millénaire av. J-C.
R. Pittioni, 182:Vol131#5/6-158

Cauvin, J-P. Henri Bosco et la poétique du sacré.
F.W. Saunders, 208(FS):Jul79-360

Cauvin, J-P. and M.J. Baker. Panaché littéraire.
P.J. Edwards, 207(FR):Oct78-204
T.M. Scanlan, 399(MLJ):Apr79-212

Cavaillès, J. Philosophie mathématique.
Y. Gauthier, 98:Jan78-3

Cavaliero, G. A Reading of E.M. Forster.
J.I.M. Stewart, 617(TLS):7Mar80-263

Cavaliero, G. The Rural Tradition in the English Novel 1900-1939.
G.G. Fromm, 395(MFS):Summer78-306

Cavell, S. The Claim of Reason.*
J. Hollander, 676(YR):Summer80-577
A. Kenny, 617(TLS):18Apr80-449

Cavell, S. Must We Mean What We Say?
M. Warner, 402(MLR):Jan79-122

Caven, B. The Punic Wars.
A.E. Astin, 617(TLS):1Aug80-878

Cavendish, R., ed. Mythology.
R.A. Sokolov, 441:22Jun80-16

Cavigelli, P. Die Germanisierung von Bonaduz in geschichtlicher und sprachlicher Schau.
K.L. Rein, 685(ZDL):3/1979-379

Caviness, M.H. The Early Stained Glass of Canterbury Cathedral, circa 1175-1220.
P.T-D. Chu, 590:Spring/Summer78-36
M.P. Lillich, 589:Jul79-555

Cawelti, J.G. Adventure, Mystery, and Romance.*
J.R. Christopher, 573(SSF):Spring78-209

Cawkwell, G. Philip of Macedon.
J.R. Hamilton, 67:May79-82
P.E. Harding, 487:Summer79-173
R. Higgins, 39:Feb79-167
C. Tuplin, 123:Vol29No2-268

Caws, M.A. René Char.
V.A. La Charité, 207(FR):Apr79-783

Caws, M.A. The Presence of René Char.*
L. Rice-Sayre, 577(SHR):Summer79-278

Caws, M.A., ed. Le Siècle éclaté, 1.
M. Bonnet, 535(RHL):Sep-Oct78-859

Caws, M.A. The Surrealist Voice of Robert Desnos.*
L.C. Breunig, 546(RR):May79-316
W.G.R., 502(PrS):Summer78-211
F.R. Smith, 208(FS):Vol33Pt2-905
205(FMLS):Apr78-184

Caws, M.A. and J. Griffin - see Char, R.

Cazauran, N. "L'Heptaméron" de Marguerite de Navarre.*
M-M. de la Garanderie, 535(RHL):Nov-Dec79-1037

Cazeaux, I. French Music in the Fifteenth and Sixteenth Centuries.
  J.R., 412:Feb78-61
Cazeaux, J. Critique du langage chez les Prophètes d'Israël.
  R.N. Whybray, 182:Vol31#5/6-138
Cazenave, M. Les Fusils de l'IRA.
  J. Greenlee, 207(FR):Feb79-509
Cazeneuve, J. Aimer la vie.
  E. Namer, 542:Jul-Sep78-377
Ceadel, M. Pacifism in Britain, 1914-1945.
  K.O. Morgan, 617(TLS):8Aug80-887
Céard, J. La Nature et les prodiges.
  C-G. Dubois, 535(RHL):Nov-Dec79-1035
Cèbe, J-P. - see Varro
Cecchettini, P.A. and D. Whittemore. Art America.
  M. Thistlethwaite, 658:Autumn79-311
Cecchin, G. Con Hemingway e Dos Passos sui campi di battaglia italiani della Grande Guerra.
  M. d'Amico, 617(TLS):25Jul80-857
Cech, D. Inhambane.
  P. Erny, 182:Vol31#19-699
Cecioni, G. Lingua e cultura nel pensiero di Pietro Giordani.
  M.C., 228(GSLI):Vol155fasc492-633
Celaya, G. Poesía. (Á. González, ed)
  G.R. Barrow, 86(BHS):Jul79-277
Çelebī, S. - see under Seyfī Çelebī
Céline, L-F. Lettres à des amies. (C.W. Nettelbeck, ed)
  J. Sturrock, 617(TLS):14Mar80-286
"L-F. Céline 2 (1976)." (J-P. Dauphin, ed)
  L. Davis, 208(FS):Vol33Pt2-892
Celis, R. L'oeuvre et l'imaginaire.
  J. Sivak, 542:Oct-Dec79-443
Cell, C.P. Revolution at Work.
  R. Baum, 293(JASt):Nov78-152
Celluprica, V. Il capitolo 9 del "De interpretatione" di Aristotele, Rassegna di studi 1930-1973.
  W. Kneale, 123:Vol129No1-165
Cendrars, B. Complete Postcards from the Americas.*
  M.J. King, 447(N&Q):Oct78-475
Cenker, W. The Hindu Personality in Education.
  S. Lavan, 293(JASt):Feb79-394
Censer, J.R. Prelude to Power.*
  N. Hampson, 208(FS):Vol33Pt2-802
Censer, J.R., N.S. Steinert and A.M. McCandless, eds. South Atlantic Urban Studies. (Vol 1)
  R.A. Mohl, 579(SAQ):Spring79-264
"Central Asian Carpets."
  J. Housego, 463:Summer78-215
"The Central Records of the Church of England."*
  P. Morgan, 447(N&Q):Dec78-548
de Cepeda, J.R. - see under Romero de Cepeda, J.
"Le Cercle amoureux d'Henry Legrand."
  P-L.R., 450(NRF):Dec79-130

Cerf, B. At Random.* (P.C. Wagner and A. Erskine, eds)
  295(JML):Vol7#4-573
  639(VQR):Winter78-25
Cerf, W. and H.S. Harris - see Hegel, G.W.F.
Cergoly, C.L. Il complesso dell'imperatore.
  F. Donini, 617(TLS):29Feb80-238
Cernuda, L. Ocnos. Variaciones sobre tema mexicano. (J. Gil de Biedma, ed of both)
  R. Warner, 86(BHS):Jan79-84
Cernuda, L. Selected Poems.*
  D.R. Harris, 86(BHS):Jul79-276
Cerny, C. Navajo Pictorial Weaving.
  W.K. McNeil, 292(JAF):Apr-Jun79-245
Černý, F. and L. Klosová, eds. Dějiny ceského divadla. (Vol 3)
  V.V. Kusin, 610:May78-222
Cerny, L. Erinnerung bei Dickens.*
  H-D. Gelfert, 224(GRM):Band28Heft1-120
  S. Monod, 189(EA):Jan-Mar78-90
Cerny, P.G. The Politics of Grandeur.
  M. Jobert, 617(TLS):27Jun80-729
Cerou, P. L'Amant auteur et valet, comédie. (H.G. Hall, ed)
  W.D. Howarth, 208(FS):Apr79-204
Cerri, G. Il linguaggio politico nel Prometeo di Eschilo.
  A. Lebeau, 555:Vol52fasc2-364
de Certeau, M., D. Julia and J. Revel. Une Politique de la langue.
  P. Rickard, 208(FS):Vol33Pt2-1038
de Cervantes, M. El Ingenioso Hidalgo Don Quijote de la Mancha.* (J.J. Allen, ed)
  S.H. Ackerman, 238:Dec79-727
Cervellati, P.L. and F. Fontana. Bologna.
  N. Miller, 576:May78-108
Cervellati, P.L., R. Scannavini and C. De Angelis. La Nuova Cultura delle Città.
  P.G. Raman, 576:May78-108
Cesbron, G. Edouard Estaunié, romancier de l'être.
  C. Delmas, 535(RHL):Nov-Dec79-1063
  E. Jasenas, 446(NCFS):Fall-Winter78/79-143
  R.J. Nelson, 207(FR):Feb79-491
Cesbron, G. Mais moi je vous aimais.
  D. O'Connell, 207(FR):Oct78-176
de Cespedes y Meneses, G. Varia fortuna del soldado Píndaro. (A. Pacheco, ed)
  D. McGrady, 240(HR):Spring78-264
Chadbourne, R. and H. Dahlie, eds. The New Land.
  W.J. Keith, 627(UTQ):Summer79-440
Chadwick, C. Rimbaud.*
  R. Gibson, 208(FS):Oct79-471
Chadwick, N. A Descriptive Study of the Djingili Language.
  D.T. Tyron, 67:May79-183
Chadwick, O. The Secularization of the European Mind in the Nineteenth Century.*
  M. Fichman, 125:Fall178-117
  J. McManners, 447(N&Q):Aug78-368
Chafe, W.H. Civilities and Civil Rights.
  J. Reston, Jr., 441:6Apr80-6

Chafe, W.L., ed. American Indian Languages and American Linguistics.
W. Bright, 350:Mar79-231
Chak, I. Z. Biohrafii Slova.
L.M.L. Onyshkevych, 424:Sep78-292
Chakrabarti, K.K. The Logic of Gotama.
D. Daor, 518:Oct79-106
Chalfant, F.C. Ben Jonson's London.
639(VQR):Winter79-24
Lord Chalfont, ed. Waterloo.
P-L. Adams, 61:Apr80-129
Challe, R. Journal d'un voyage fait aux Indes Orientales (1690-1691). (F. Deloffre and M. Menemencioglu, eds)
J. Rougeot, 535(RHL):Nov-Dec79-1025
Chamberlain, N. and N. The Flavor of France in Recipes and Pictures.
W. and C. Cowen, 639(VQR):Spring79-73
Chamberlin, E.R. Preserving the Past.
N. Hammond, 617(TLS):8Feb80-147
Chamberlin, J. On Our Own.
F.J. Jarrett, 529(QQ):Autumn79-547
Chamberlin, J.E. Ripe Was the Drowsy Hour.*
K. Beckson, 651(WHR):Winter79-73
V. Brombert, 249(HudR):Spring79-135
R. Dellamora, 627(UTQ):Summer79-417
I. Fletcher, 637(VS):Summer79-487
J. Wolff, 395(MFS):Winter78/79-591
Chamberlin, V.A. Galdós and Beethoven.
P.A. Bly, 238:May-Sep79-401
E. Rodgers, 402(MLR):Apr79-480
D.M. Rogers, 593:Spring79-91
Chambers, R. Traditions of Edinburgh.
J. Campbell, 617(TLS):25Jul80-840
Chambers, R.D. Sinclair Ross and Ernest Buckler.
J. Ferns, 402(MLR):Jul79-689
Chambert, C. Drömmen Verkligheten Upproret.
M. kossholm, 341:1978/2-90
Chambert-Loir, H. Mochtar Lubis.
J.M. Echols, 318(JAOS):Jul-Sep78-328
"The Chameleon."
A. Rodway, 617(TLS):11Apr80-419
Chametzsky, J. From the Ghetto.*
S. Pinsker, 395(MFS):Summer78-278
W. Sollors, 473(PR):3/1979-475
Champagne, R. Dodécaèdre ou les eaux sans terre.
J.B. Ayoub, ˙ 4:Dec78-743
Champagne, R.A. Beyond the Structuralist Myth of Écriture.
P. Newman-Gordon, 399(MLJ):Nov79-386
Champigny, R. Ontology of the Narrative.
J. Cruickshank, 208(FS):Jul79-373
C. Di Girolamo, 545(RPh):Aug78-137
Champigny, R. What Will Have Happened.
J.G. Cawelti, 141:Winter79-86
Champion, L.S. Tragic Patterns in Jacobean and Caroline Drama.
M.C. Bradbrook, 570(SQ):Summer79-435
D.B.J. Randall, 579(SAQ):Spring79-269
G.F. Sensabaugh, 301(JEGP):Apr79-253
M.L. Wine, 405(MP):May80-430

Champollion, J.F. Notices Descriptives. (Vol 2)
E. Cruz-Uribe, 318(JAOS):Jul-Sep78-314
Chamson, A. Sans Peur et les brigands aux visages noirs.
R.A. Smernoff, 207(FR):Mar79-666
Chan, L.M. Marlowe Criticism.
R. Gill, 541(RES):May79-244
Chan, W.K.K. Merchants, Mandarins, and Modern Enterprise in Late Ch'ing China.
D. Faure, 293(JASt):May79-561
Chancellor, J. Audubon.
B.W. Chambers, 658:Winter79-400
A. Frankenstein, 55:Jan79-28
Chancellor, J. Charles Darwin.
D. Ospovat, 637(VS):Winter78-266
Chand, M. The Gossamer Fly.
P-L. Adams, 61:Jun80-95
Chandler, A. - see Hayakawa, S.I.
Chandler, A.D., Jr. The Visible Hand.
R.D. Cuff, 106:Spring79-47
P. Uselding, 639(VQR):Summer78-571
T.E. Vadney, 529(QQ):Summer79-323
Chandler, B.J. The Bandit King.
J.D. Wirth, 263(RIB):Vol29No3/4-359
Chandler, D.C. Dictionary of the Napoleonic Wars.
A. Horne, 362:31Jan80-159
Chandler, D.L. The Natural Superiority of Southern Politicians.*
639(VQR):Spring78-64
Chandola, A. Folk Drumming in the Himalayas.
W. Bright, 350:Mar79-266
Chandos Herald. "La Vie du Prince Noir" by Chandos Herald.* (D.B. Tyson, ed) [shown in prev under Herald, C.]
A.H. Diverres, 208(FS):Vol33Pt2-576
Chandra, M. Studies in Early Indian Painting.
J. Williams, 293(JASt):May79-595
Chandra, M. Trade and Trade Routes in Ancient India.
L. Casson, 124:Sep79-33
Chandra, P. The Tuti-nama of the Cleveland Museum of Art and the Origins of Mughal Painting.
M.C. Beach, 57:Vol40#1-81
Chang, H.C. Chinese Literature II: Nature Poetry.*
M.L. Wagner, 293(JASt):Aug79-771
Chang, K.C., ed. Food in Chinese Culture.*
W. and C. Cowen, 639(VQR):Spring78-72
J.W. Haeger, 244(HJAS):Jun78-267
Chang, K-C. Shang Civilization.
M. Sullivan, 441:31Aug80-10
Chang-Rodríguez, R. and D.A. Yates, eds. Homage to Irving A. Leonard.
B.A. Shaw, 238:May-Sep79-409
Chang Yu-fa. Ch'ing-chi ti ko-ming t'uanti (Revolutionaries of the Late Ch'ing Period).
C-T. Hsüeh, 302:Vol16#1and2-123
Chantraine, P. Dictionnaire étymologique de la langue grecque. (Vol 3)
C.J. Ruijgh, 361:Jan78-93

Chantraine, P. Dictionnaire étymologique
de la langue grecque: histoire des mots.
(Vol 4, Pt 1)
D.M. Jones, 123:Vol29No2-324
J.W. Poultney, 24:Winter79-593
Chao, Y.R. Aspects of Chinese Sociolin-
guistics.* (A.S. Dil, ed)
W.A.C.H. Dobson, 302:Vol16#1and2-124
R. Hymes, 355(LSoc):Aug78-275
Chaplin, P. The Siesta.*
S. Kennedy, 617(TLS):1Feb80-123
Chaplin, S. The Bachelor Uncle.
J. Mellors, 362:10Jul80-56
Chapman, J. Adult English One. Adult
English Two.
G. Browning, 399(MJL):Apr79-224
Chapman, J.C. and F.J-L. Mouret - see de
Montaigne, M.
Chapman, R. The Duchess's Diary.
E.C. Riley, 617(TLS):29Feb80-238
Chapman, S.D., ed. The Devon Cloth Indus-
try in the Eighteenth Century.
W.B. Stephens, 325:Oct79-234
Chappell, F. Bloodfire.*
J. Mole, 493:Mar80-65
Char, R. Poems of René Char.* (M.A. Caws
and J. Griffin, eds and trans)
L. Rice-Sayre, 577(SHR):Summer79-278
Chardri. La Vie des Set Dormanz. (B.S.
Merrilees, ed)
P.B. Grout, 402(MLR):Oct79-935
Chariton. Chariton von Aphrodisias:
"Kallirhoe." (K. Plepelits, ed and
trans)
G. Anderson, 303(JoHS):Vol199-183
F. Lasserre, 182:Vol31#7/8-241
B.P. Reardon, 123:Vol29No1-145
Charles, A.M. A Life of George Herbert.*
A.L. De Neef, 579(SAQ):Winter79-130
D.W. Doerksen, 539:Vol4No1-117
M.E. Rickey, 405(MP):Nov79-221
Charleston, R.J. and M. Archer. The James
A. de Rothschild Collection at Waddesdon
Manor: Glass and Enamels.
E. Schrijver, 90:Feb79-126
Charleston, R.J., M. Archer and M. Mar-
cheix. The James A. de Rothschild Col-
lection at Waddesdon Manor: Glass and
Stained Glass [and] Limoges and Other
Painted Enamels.*
E. Schrijver, 90:Feb79-126
G. Wills, 39:Jan79-71
Charpin, F. L'idée de phrase grammaticale
et son expression en latin.
F. Murru, 343:Band23-170
"Le Charroi de Nîmes." (2nd ed) (D.
McMillan, ed)
D.G. Hoggan, 208(FS):Jan79-60
Charters, A. and S. I Love.*
H. Muchnic, 453(NYRB):29May80-36
Charters, S. - see Södergran, E.
Chartier, A. Les Oeuvres latines d'Alain
Chartier. (P. Bourgain-Hemeryck, ed)
W. Rothwell, 182:Vol31#13-417

Chartier, A.B. Barbey d'Aurevilly.
J.O. Lowrie, 207(FR):Dec78-353
G. Turgeon, 446(NCFS):Fall-Winter
78/79-128
"Chartres et Péguy, 1973."
S. Fraisse, 535(RHL):May-Jun78-501
Charyn, J. The Catfish Man.
W. Pritchard, 441:20Apr80-15
Charyn, J. Darlin' Bill.
B. De Mott, 441:7Dec80-11
de Chasca, E.S. John Gould Fletcher and
Imagism.*
468:Winter79-584
Chase-Riboud, B. Sally Hemings.*
E. Wright, 617(TLS):25Jan80-91
Chasins, A. Leopold Stokowski.
S. Lipman, 617(TLS):7Mar80-255
M. Steinberg, 441:20Jan80-12
Chassard, J. and V. Schenker. Also los!
M. Vandegans-Salvérius, 556(RLV):
1978/1-88
Château, J. Les grandes psychologies dans
l'antiquité.
M. Bédard, 154:Dec78-726
A. Reix, 542:Jan-Mar79-142
Château, J. and others. Les grandes
psychologies modernes.
M. Adam, 542:Apr-Jun78-207
de Chateaubriand, F.R. Chateaubriand:
Correspondance générale. (Vol 1) (B.
D'Andlau, P. Christophorov and P.
Riberette, eds)
R. Lebègue, 535(RHL):Jul-Aug78-617
de Chateaubriand, F.R. Chateaubriand:
Correspondance générale. (Vol 2) (P.
Riberette, ed)
G.D. Painter, 617(TLS):14Mar80-286
de Chateaubriand, F.R. Essai sur les
révolutions [&] Génie du christianisme.
(M. Regard, ed)
D.G. Charlton, 208(FS):Oct79-458
de Chateaubriand, F.R. Mémoires de ma
vie.* (J-M. Gautier, ed)
J-C. Berchet, 535(RHL):Jul-Aug79-671
de Chateaubriand, F.R. Vie de Rancé. (P.
Clarac, ed)
R. Lebègue, 535(RHL):Jan-Feb79-132
Chatman, S. Story and Discourse.
T.R. Austin, 290(JAAC):Winter79-207
P. Harcourt, 255(HAB):Summer79-209
H.F. Mosher, Jr., 594:Fall79-364
G. Prince, 400(MLN):May79-866
Chatterji, S.K. Kirāta-Jana-Kr̥ti.
L. Sternbach, 318(JAOS):Jul-Sep78-320
Chatterji, S.K. Selected Papers: Angla-
Nibandha Chayana. (Vol 1) Jayadeva.
E. Bender, 318(JAOS):Jul-Sep78-335
Chattopadhyay, B. Water, Cereals and Eco-
nomic Growth in South and East Asia in
the Fifties and Sixties.
N.K. Nicholson, 293(JASt):Feb79-318
Chattopadhyaya, D. Science and Society in
Ancient India.
D. Riepe, 484(PPR):Mar80-439
Chatwin, B. In Patagonia.
F.L. Phelps, 37:Mar79-56

Chatwin, B. The Viceroy of Ouidah.
  V. Glendinning, 362:27Nov80-733
  J. Leonard, 441:28Nov80-C25
  J. Thompson, 441:14Dec80-7
Chaudenson, R. Le lexique du parler
  créole de la Réunion.*
  A. Valdman, 545(RPh):Aug78-65
Chaudhuri, K.N. The Trading World of Asia
  and the English East India Company 1660-
  1760.
  C.J. Dewey, 617(TLS):25Jul80-853
de la Chaussée, F. Initiation à la phoné-
  tique historique de l'ancien français.
  E.J. Matte, 320(CJL):Spring-Fall78-160
  G. Price, 208(FS):Oct79-496
Chauveau, F. Vignettes des "Fables" de La
  Fontaine (1668). (J.D. Biard, ed)
  D. Kuizenga, 207(FR):Feb79-485
Chauveau, J-P. - see Tristan L'Hermite
Chaves, J. Mei Yao-ch'en and the Develop-
  ment of Early Sung Poetry.
  W.H. Nienhauser, Jr., 318(JAOS):
  Oct-Dec78-529
Chavette, E. Aimé de son concierge.
  P. Dulac, 450(NRF):Jul79-113
Chavkin, S. The Mind Stealers.*
  A.W. Clare, 529(QQ):Winter79/80-637
Chay, J., with C-H. Cho, eds. The Prob-
  lems and Prospects of American-East
  Asian Relations.
  R.E. Bedeski, 293(JASt):Feb79-324
de Chazal, M. L'Homme et la Connaissance.
  H. Godin, 208(FS):Vol33Pt2-906
Cheddadi, A. - see Ibn Khaldun
Chee, T.S. - see under Tham Seong Chee
Cheeseman, P. Fight for Shelton Bar.
  M. Page, 397(MD):Dec79-427
Cheever, S. Looking for Work.*
  P. Kemp, 362:21Feb80-254
  S. Kennedy, 617(TLS):22Feb80-210
  R. Kiely, 441:6Jan80-10
  61:Jan80-88
Chefresne, D. Noëlla.
  E. Marks, 207(FR):Mar79-667
Chekhov, A. Anton Chekhov's Life and
  Thought.* (S. Karlinsky and M.H. Heim,
  eds)
  J.D. Clayton, 104(CASS):Summer78-286
Chekhov, A. The Oxford Chekhov. (Vol 7)
  (R. Hingley, ed and trans)
  639(VQR):Summer79-100
Chekhov, A. Plays. (E.K. Bristow, ed
  and trans)
  T. Clyman, 574(SEEJ):Summer79-275
Chelkowski, P.J., ed. Studies in Art and
  Literature of the Near East in honor of
  Richard Ettinghausen.
  R. Hillenbrand, 463:Summer78-201
Ch'en, J. China and the West.
  R. Dawson, 617(TLS):8Feb80-151
Chen, J. The Sinkiang Story.
  J. Lipman, 293(JASt):Aug79-768
Chen Jo-hsi. The Execution of Mayor Yin
  and Other Stories from the Great Prole-
  tarian Cultural Revolution.*
  M. Goldman, 293(JASt):Feb79-371
  639(VQR):Winter79-16

Chen, Y-T. The Dragon's Village.
  O. Schell, 441:4May80-11
  J. Spence, 453(NYRB):17Apr80-20
  442(NY):12May80-161
Chénique, F. Le Yoga spirituel de saint
  François d'Assise.
  M. Adam, 542:Jul-Sep79-351
Chenique, F. - see Stéphane, H.
Chennault, A. The Education of Anna.
  R. Shaplen, 441:3Feb80-12
Chenoweth, V. The Usarufas and Their
  Music.
  S. Feld, 187:Sep80-573
Chenoweth, V. - see Vela, D.
Lord Cherbury. The Life of Edward, First
  Lord of Cherbury, Written by Himself.
  (J.M. Shuttleworth, ed)
  D.F. Bratchell, 447(N&Q):Feb78-81
  G. Guffey, 301(JEGP):Apr79-258
Chernaik, J. The Daughter.*
  E. Milton, 676(YR):Autumn79-89
Chernenko, K.U. Soviet Democracy.
  C.E. Ziegler, 550(RusR):Jan79-110
Cherniss, H. Selected Papers.* (L. Taran,
  ed)
  J.L. Ackrill, 123:Vol129No2-343
  T.V.U., 543:Jun79-775
Chernoff, J.M. African Rhythm and African
  Sensibility.
  A.P. Merriam, 187:Sep80-559
Cherry, C. On Human Communication. (3rd
  ed)
  E.P. Hamp, 269(IJAL):Oct78-352
Cherry, K. Augusta Played.*
  42(AR):Summer79-380
Chervel, A. ...et il fallut apprendre à
  écrire à tous les petits Français.*
  K. Hunnius, 72:Band216Heft2-445
Chesler, P. About Men.*
  T. McCormack, 529(QQ):Winter79/80-671
  639(VQR):Summer78-103
Chesneaux, J. Pasts and Futures, or What
  Is History For?
  C. Duncan, 658:Winter79-425
Chesneaux, J., F. Le Barbier and M-C.
  Bergère. China from the 1911 Revolu-
  tion to Liberation.
  M.B. Rankin, 293(JASt):Feb79-331
Chester, D. A Love So Wild.
  L. Duguid, 617(TLS):16May80-558
Chesterman, R.G.A. Laughter in the House.
  R. Storey, 325:Oct79-239
Chetrit, J. Syntaxe de la phrase complexe
  à subordonnée temporelle.
  G. Price, 208(FS):Vol33Pt2-1056
  M. Tsiapera and R. Shafer, 399(MLJ):
  Jan-Feb79-51
Cheuse, A. Candace and Other Stories.
  L.S. Schwartz, 441:9Nov80-15
Chevalier, J-C. and M. Gross, eds.
  Méthodes en grammaire française.*
  W.D. Donaldson, Jr., 207(FR):Dec78-366
Chevalier, J-L. - see Welch, J.
Chevalley, S., ed. Les Dossiers Molière:
  "Le Bourgeois gentilhomme."
  A. Blanc, 535(RHL):Mar-Apr78-302

Cheyne, G.J.G. Joaquín Costa, el gran
desconocido. A Bibliographical Study of
the Writings of Joaquín Costa (1846-
1911).
  R.F. Brown, 86(BHS):Apr79-156
Chi, L. - see under Li Chi
Chi Pang-yuan and others, eds. An Anthol-
ogy of Contemporary Chinese Literature:
Taiwan, 1949-1974.
  J.M. Hargett, 318(JAOS):Jul-Sep78-338
Chi, W-S., comp. Chinese-English Dic-
tionary of Contemporary Usage.*
  N.G.D. Malmqvist, 302:Vol16#1and2-116
Chiari, A. Ancora con Dante.
  M.M., 228(GSLI):Vol55fasc491-471
Chiari, J. Twentieth Century French
Thought.
  R. McLure, 208(FS):Vol33Pt2-948
Chibbett, D.G. The History of Japanese
Printing and Book Illustration.*
  B.C. Bloomfield, 354:Mar79-86
Chibnall, M. - see Orderic Vitalis
Ch'ien Chung-shu. Fortress Besieged.
  D. Hawkes, 617(TLS):27Jun80-725
  J. Spence, 453(NYRB):17Apr80-20
Chiesa, G.S. - see under Sena Chiesa, G.
Chiesa, M. and G. Tesio, eds. Il dialetto
da lingua della realtà a lingua della
poesia.
  228(GSLI):Vol55fasc491-477
Child, J. Julia Child and Company.
  W. and C. Cowen, 639(VQR):Spring79-74
Child, J., with E.S. Yntema. Julia Child
and More Company.
  J. Seaver, 441:6Jan80-10
Childers, J.W. Tales from Spanish
Picaresque Novels.*
  V.G. Agüera, 238:Mar79-172
  H. Baader, 547(RF):Band91Heft3-340
  B.W. Ife, 402(MLR):Oct79-968
"Children As Writers."
  V. Glendinning, 617(TLS):19Sep80-1021
"Children's Book Review Index." (Vols 1-3)
(G.C. Tarbert, ed)
  J. Oldfield, 677(YES):Vol9-354
"Children's Literature." (Vol 8)
  H. Eley, 617(TLS):28Mar80-354
"Children's Literature Review." (Vol 1 ed
by A. Block and C. Riley; Vol 2 ed by C.
Riley)
  J. Oldfield, 677(YES):Vol9-354
Childs, A.P. The City-Reliefs of Lycia.
  S. Pembroke, 617(TLS):11Jan80-43
Childs, D. Britain since 1945.
  K.O. Morgan, 617(TLS):29Feb80-225
Chilton, P.A. The Poetry of Jean de La
Ceppède.
  T. Allott, 402(MLR):Apr79-456
  G. Demerson, 535(RHL):Nov-Dec79-1040
  J.D. Lyons, 207(FR):May79-927
Chimombo, S. The Rainmaker.
  J. Povey, 2(AfrA):May79-92
Ching, J. Confucianism and Christianity.*
  W-T. Chan, 293(JASt):Nov78-173
  L.H. Yearley, 485(PE&W):Oct79-509
Ching-chuan, D. - see under Dzo Ching-
chuan

Chinnery, V. Oak Furniture: the British
Tradition.
  A. Wells-Cole, 617(TLS):29Feb80-244
Chiodi, P. Sartre and Marxism.*
  W. Mays, 518:Jan79-25
  R.E. Santoni, 258:Mar79-120
Chirac, M. Aix-en-Provence à travers la
litterature française.
  R. Lebègue, 535(RHL):Jul-Aug79-722
Chisholm, A. Nancy Cunard.*
  A. Ross, 364:Oct79-3
Chiss, J-L., J. Filliolet and D. Maingue-
neau. Linguistique française.* (Vol 1)
  C. Hagège, 209(FM):Oct78-361
  N.C.W. Spence, 208(FS):Vol33Pt2-1059
Chiss, J-L., J. Filliolet and D. Maingue-
neau. Linguistique française. (Vol 2)
  M.C. Jacobs, 399(MLJ):Nov79-382
Chissell, J. Brahms.
  J.B., 412:Aug-Nov78-278
Chitham, E. - see Brontë, A.
Chitnis, A.C. The Scottish Enlightenment.*
  M. Peckham, 588(SSL):Vol14-299
  M. Volpato, 548(RCSF):Apr-Jun79-221
Chitty, S. Charles Kingsley's Landscape.
  M. Banton, 637(VS):Spring78-421
Chiu, T.N. The Port of Hong Kong.
  A. Birch, 302:Vol16#1and2-130
Cho, S.Y., comp. Japanese Writings on
Communist Chinese Law, 1946-1974.
  H. Chiu, 293(JASt):May79-570
Chocheyras, J. Le Théâtre religieux en
Dauphiné du moyen âge au XVIIIe siècle
(Domaine français et provençal).
  C.N. Smith, 208(FS):Vol33Pt2-962
Cholodenko, M. Dem folgt deutscher Gesang,
Tombeau de Hölderlin.
  J.R., 450(NRF):Dec79-130
Chomsky, N. Essays on Form and Interpreta-
tion.
  A. Grosu, 297(JL):Sep79-356
  A. Grosu, 482(PhR):Jul79-457
  J.L., 543:Sep78-131
  C.F. Voegelin, 269(IJAL):Apr78-159
Chomsky, N. Reflections on Language.*
  J. Andor, 353:Jul78-71
  M. Atkinson, 307:Apr79-41
  L.P. Davies, 186(ETC.):Jun78-207
Chomsky, N. Rules and Representations.
  I. Hacking, 453(NYRB):23Oct80-47
Chorpenning, J.F. - see Enríquez Cartagena,
J.
Chotard, J-R. Séminaristes ... une espèce
disparue?
  H.P. Salomon, 207(FR):May79-941
Chothia, J. Forging a Language.
  D. Welland, 617(TLS):4Apr80-399
Chouillet, J. Diderot.
  J. Undank, 207(FR):Dec78-348
Chouillet, J. L'esthétique des Lumières.*
  D. Leduc-Fayette, 542:Apr-Jun79-227
Chouillet, J. La formation des idées
esthétiques de Diderot.*
  D. Leduc-Fayette, 542:Jan-Mar78-110
Chowder, K. Blackbird Days.
  S. Spencer, 441:7Sep80-13
  442(NY):4Aug80-90

Ciucci, G. and others. The American City.
S. Gardiner, 362:10Apr80-480
Claessens, D. Instinkt, Psyche, Geltung.
(2nd ed)
H. Ottmann, 489(PJGG):Band86Heft1-148
Claiborne, C. Craig Claiborne's Favorites
from the New York Times. (Vol 4)
W. and C. Cowen, 639(VQR):Spring79-75
Claiborne, C., with P. Franey. The New
New York Times Cookbook.
J. Seaver, 441:6Jan80-10
Claiborne, C. and P. Franey. Veal Cookery.
W. and C. Cowen, 639(VQR):Autumn79-152
Clair, C. A History of European Printing.
J.L. Flood, 684(ZDA):Band107Heft1-32
Clairmont, C.W., with S.H. Auth and V.
Gozenbach. Excavations at Salona,
Yugoslavia (1969-1972).
J.J. Wilkes, 123:Vol29No1-122
Clancy, A. Blind Pilot.
J. Moynahan, 441:7Sep80-12
Clancy, P. and S. Elder. Tip.
J. Greenfield, 441:3Aug80-13
Clante, C. and N. Frederiksen, eds.
Omkring Det forsømte forår.
M. Brøndsted, 562(Scan):Nov78-180
Clapin, S. Dictionnaire canadien-français.
R. Robidoux, 208(FS):Vol33Pt2-1064
D.F. Rogers, 320(CJL):Spring-Fall178-
186
Clarac, P. - see de Chateaubriand, F.R.
Clare, J. John Clare: The Midsummer Cush-
ion.* (A. Tibble, with R.K.R. Thornton,
eds)
P.W., 148:Summer79-91
Clare, J. Selected Poems and Prose of
John Clare. (E. Robinson and G. Summer-
field, eds)
P. Whiteley, 148:Spring79-85
Clarence-Smith, W.G. Slaves, Peasants and
Capitalists in Southern Angola 1840-1926.
R. Oliver, 617(TLS):4Jan80-21
Clarens, C. Crime Movies.
N. Roddick, 617(TLS):8Aug80-900
Clark, A. Domestic Drama.
M.T. Jones-Davies, 677(YES):Vol9-302
Clark, C. The Web of Metaphor.
J. Grieve, 67:May79-123
M.M. McGowan, 208(FS):Jul79-338
Clark, C.E., Jr. Henry Ward Beecher.
R.V. Sparks, 432(NEQ):Sep79-439
639(VQR):Summer79-97
Clark, C.E.F., Jr. Nathaniel Hawthorne.
A. Turner, 594:Winter79-484
Clark, E. The Sleeper.
N. Callendar, 441:18May80-16
Clark, E.E. and M. Edmonds. Sacagawea of
the Lewis and Clark Expedition.
442(NY):11Aug80-90
Clark, G. Michael Cardew.
C.C. Brookes, 39:Dec79-538
Clark, G. Mesolithic Prelude.
J. Bintliff, 362:18Sep80-374
Clark, H.H. Semantics and Comprehension.*
L. Zgusta, 361:Apr78-391

Clark, H.H. and E.V. Psychology and Lan-
guage.
D.A.W., 355(LSoc):Apr78-148
L.H. Waterhouse, 350:Jun79-436
Clark, J. and others, eds. Culture and
Crisis in Britain in the Thirties.
E. Homberger, 617(TLS):11Jan80-33
Clark, J.P. The Philosophical Anarchism
of William Godwin.*
D.V.E., 191(ELN):Sep78(supp)-61
G. Kelly, 340(KSJ):Vol28-148
M. Warner, 402(MLR):Oct79-921
185:Oct78-123
Clark, J.W. The Language and Style of
Anthony Trollope.*
W.M. Kendrick, 637(VS):Spring78-417
Clark, K. Feminine Beauty.
P-L. Adams, 61:Dec80-96
A. Broyard, 441:29Nov80-21
Clark, K. An Introduction to Rembrandt.*
K. Roberts, 90:Feb79-124
Clark, K. The Other Half.*
M. Ellmann, 569(SR):Spring79-332
R. Varney, 219(GaR):Spring79-233
639(VQR):Autumn78-140
Clark, M. Antonio Gramsci and the Revolu-
tion That Failed.
S. Hellman, 529(QQ):Spring79-141
Clark, M.H. The Cradle Will Fall.
442(NY):4Aug80-92
Clark, P. and P. Slack. English Towns in
Transition 1500-1700.*
K. Downes, 576:Oct78-219
Clark, P.P. The Battle of the Bourgeois.
J. Cruickshank, 208(FS):Apr79-209
Clark, R. The Japanese Company.*
Man'nari Hiroshi, 285(JapQ):Oct-Dec79-
554
Clark, R. Thrusting Into Darkness.
S.E. Lee, 581:Dec79-432
Clark, R.W. Freud.
P. Grosskurth, 617(TLS):8Aug80-889
C. Lehmann-Haupt, 441:29May80-C19
E. Rothstein, 453(NYRB):90ct80-14
M. Warnock, 362:21Aug80-246
R. Wollheim, 441:13Jul80-1
Clark, R.W. The Greatest Power on Earth.
H. Brogan, 362:11Dec80-795
Clark, R.W. The Role of the Bomber.
639(VQR):Autumn78-150
Clark, S.R.L. Aristotle's Man.*
D.R. Lachterman, 53(AGP):Band60Heft2-
209
Clark, S.R.L. The Moral Status of Ani-
mals.*
O. O'Neill, 311(JP):Jul80-440
L.W. Sumner, 154:Sep78-570
A. Townsend, 63:Mar79-85
Clark, T. Who is Sylvia?
A. Young, 617(TLS):13Jun80-682
Clark, T. The World of Damon Runyon.
639(VQR):Autumn79-142
Clark, T.D. Agrarian Kentucky.
639(VQR):Autumn78-149
Clarke, A. Liberty Lane.
F. McCluskey, 305(JIL):Sep78-165
G.B. Saul, 174(Éire):Summer79-157

Clarke, B. and J. Goddard. The Trout and
the Fly.
  C. Lehmann-Haupt, 441:28Jul80-C15
Clarke, D., ed. The Encyclopedia of How
It's Made.
  529(QQ):Summer79-370
Clarke, G. The Sundial.
  A. Cluysenaar, 565:Vol20#3-68
  P. Eckhard, 493:Jul79-69
Clarke, T. Victims of Apartheid.
  J. Coleby, 157:Winter79-86
Clasen, K.H. Der Meister der Schönen
Madonnen.
  G. Schmidt, 683:Band41Heft1-61
"Le classe ouvrière et le processus révol-
utionnaire mondial."
  J-M. Gabaude, 542:Oct-Dec79-482
Classen, P. Sprachsystem und Sprach-
funktion.
  D. Wolf, 430(NS):Oct78-481
"The Classical Tradition in French Litera-
ture: Essays presented to R.C. Knight."
  H. Peyre, 535(RHL):Nov-Dec79-1047
"The Classical World Bibliography of Greek
Drama and Poetry." "The Classical World
Bibliography of Philosophy, Religion,
and Rhetoric." "The Classical World Bib-
liography of Vergil." "The Classical
World Bibliography of Roman Drama and
Poetry and Ancient Fiction."
  J.W. Binns, 354:Sep79-286
Claudian. Claudii Claudiani "De Bello
Gildonico."* (E.M. Olechowska, ed and
trans)
  C.J. McDonough, 487:Spring79-79
Claudín, F. The Communist Movement from
Cominterm to Cominform.*
  A. Dallin, 104(CASS):Summer78-304
Claudin-Urondo, C. Lenin and the Cultural
Revolution.
  S. Fitzpatrick, 550(RusR):Jan79-100
Clausberg, K. Zeppelin.
  C.H. Gibbs-Smith, 617(TLS):13Jun80-678
Clausen, P., comp. Dansk Musik.
  R. Andrewes, 415:Apr79-309
Clavelin, M. The Natural Philosophy of
Galileo.
  W.L. Wisan, 53(AGP):Band60Heft1-71
Clavreul, J. L'Ordre médical.
  J. le Hardi, 450(NRF):Jan79-134
Clay, J. Modern Art 1890-1918.
  J. Masheck, 62:Dec78-60
Clayton, A. The Enemy is Listening.
  R. Lewin, 362:21Aug80-247
Clayton, A.J. - see "Jean Giono"
Clayton, T., ed. Cavalier Poets: Selected
Poems.
  P.W. Thomas, 541(RES):May79-213
  639(VQR):Autumn78-146
Cleary, T. and J.C. - see "The Blue Cliff
Record"
Cleaveland, A.M. No Life For A Lady.
  A. Ronald, 649(WAL):Summer79-171
Cleaveland, H.W., W. Backus and S.D.
Backus. Village and Farm Cottages.
  K.N. Morgan, 576:Mar78-52

Clemens, B. The Edge of Darkness.
  J. Coleby, 157:Winter79-86
Clément, D. and W. Thümmel. Grundzüge
einer syntax der deutschen standard-
sprache.*
  G. Starke, 682(ZPSK):Band31Heft3-327
Clément, J-M. Lexique des anciennes
règles monastiques occidentales.
  G. Constable, 589:Oct79-882
Clément, O. The Spirit of Solzhenitsyn.*
  E. Mossman, 395(MFS):Summer78-289
Clément, P-P. Jean-Jacques Rousseau.*
  B.C. Fink, 207(FR):Oct78-141
  B. Fort, 188(ECr):Summer78-84
Clement, T. and T. Plantos, eds. Poems
for Sale in the Street.
  376:Oct79-141
Clementi, M. Opere sinfoniche complete.
(P. Spada, ed)
  J.W. Hill, 317:Fall79-577
Clements, R.J. Comparative Literature as
Academic Discipline.
  J-P. Barricelli, 149(CLS):Sep79-265
  S.S. Prawer, 402(MLR):Jul79-649
Clements, R.J. and J. Gibaldi. Anatomy
of the Novella.*
  L.G. Clubb, 149(CLS):Jun79-177
  G. Mermier, 573(SSF):Summer78-336
  F. Pierce, 402(MLR):Apr79-392
  M.D. Springer, 678(YCGL):No.27-98
Clemoes, P., ed. Anglo-Saxon England.*
(Vol 6)
  G. Bourcier, 189(EA):Jul-Dec78-372
  E.G. Stanley, 72:Band216Heft1-166
Clemoes, P., ed. Anglo-Saxon England.
(Vol 7)
  E.G. Stanley, 72:Band216Heft2-404
Clemoes, P. and others, eds. Anglo-Saxon
England.* (Vols 1-3)
  K.R. Grinda, 38:Band96Heft3/4-496
Clerc, G. and others. Fouilles de Kition.
(Vol 2)
  J.G. Griffiths, 123:Vol29No2-332
Clever, G., ed. The E.J. Pratt Symposium.
  B. Belyea, 49:Jul79-118
  T. Marshall, 178:Fall79-370
Cliff, M. - see Smith, L.
Clifford, D.P. Mine Eyes Have Seen the
Glory.*
  M. Banta, 27(AL):Jan80-584
  N. Pettit, 432(NEQ):Jun79-262
Clifford, J. From Puzzles to Portraits.
  A.M. Friedson, 77:Summer78-83
Clifford, J.L. Dictionary Johnson.*
  W. Haley, 617(TLS):22Feb80-198
  L. Lipking, 31(ASch):Autumn80-560
  F.A. Pottle, 676(YR):Spring80-456
Clifford, P. To Aspen and Back.
  W. Goodman, 441:2Nov80-16
Clignet, R. The Africanization of the
Labor Market.
  M.W. De Lancey, 69:Vol148#4-412
Clive, H.P. Pierre Louÿs (1870-1925).*
  W.N. Ince, 208(FS):Apr79-218
Clive, J. The Last Liberator.
  N. Callendar, 441:27Jan80-22

Clivio, G.P. Storia linguistica e dialettologia piemontese.
E. Hirsch, 685(ZDL):1/1979-113
Cloonan, W.J. Racine's Theatre.
H.T. Barnwell, 208(FS):Jan79-79
Close, A. The Romantic Approach to "Don Quixote."*
R. El Saffar, 400(MLN):Mar79-399
T.R.H., 131(CL):Summer79-305
F. Pierce, 402(MLR):Apr79-477
R.L. Predmore, 405(MP):Nov79-257
Close, E. The Development of Modern Rumanian.*
T.G. Pavel, 353:Dec78-93
de Closets, F. La France et ses mensonges.
R.H. Simon, 207(FR):Feb79-526
Clottès, J. Inventaire des mégalithes de la France.
R. Pittioni, 182:Vol131#5/6-160
Clouard, H. and R. Leggewie, eds. Anthologie de la littérature française.* (new ed)
H. Godin, 208(FS):Vol33Pt2-950
Cloud, P. Cosmos, Earth and Man.*
R.E. Munn, 529(QQ):Autumn79-557
Cloudsley-Thompson, J. Animal Migration.
529(QQ):Summer79-368
Cloudsley-Thompson, J.L. Tooth and Claw.
J. Cherfas, 617(TLS):19Sep80-1014
Clough, C.H., ed. Cultural Aspects of the Italian Renaissance.*
B. Vickers, 402(MLR):Jan79-134
Clover, H. and M. Gibson - see Lanfranc of Bec
Clubbe, J., ed. Carlyle and His Contemporaries.*
R.J. Dingley, 447(N&Q):Jun78-260
R.J. Dunn, 588(SSL):Vol14-293
R.E. Kowalski, 637(VS):Winter78-283
Clubbe, J. - see Althaus, F. and T. Carlyle
Cluny, C.M. Inconnu passager.
B. Chambaz, 450(NRF):Feb79-96
Clurman, H. Ibsen.
A.P. Hinchliffe, 148:Autumn79-87
Cluysenaar, A. - see Singer, B.
Clymer, K.J. John Hay.
R.D. Accinelli, 106:Fall79-195
Clyne, M., ed. Australia Talks.
J. Platt, 350:Jun79-466
Cobb, G. English Cathedrals.
P. Metcalf, 617(TLS):18Jul80-818
Cobb, R. Death in Paris, 1795-1801.*
B. Rigby, 208(FS):Oct79-492
639(VQR):Autumn79-134
Cobb, R. Paris and its Provinces, 1792-1802.
D. Higgs, 208(FS):Vol33Pt2-1005
Cobb, R. Promenades.
E. Weber, 617(TLS):22Aug80-933
Cobb, R.C. Modern French History in Britain.
N. Hampson, 208(FS):Vol33Pt2-1012
Cobin, M., ed. Colorado Shakespeare Festival Annual, 1976. Colorado Shakespeare Festival Annual, 1977.
M. Mullin, 570(SQ):Summer79-446

Coburn, A. Off Duty.
S. Ellin, 441:13Jul80-15
Coburn, K. Experience into Thought.
R. Ashton, 617(TLS):2May80-508
Coburn, K. In Pursuit of Coleridge.*
C. Brooks, 661(WC):Summer79-259
R. Dunham, 648(WCR):Jun78-37
D.V.E., 191(ELN):Sep78(supp)-57
Cocharne, I. F for Ferg.
L. Burnard, 617(TLS):22Aug80-943
P. Kemp, 362:17Jul80-89
Cochrane, S.T. The Collaboration of Nečaev, Ogarev and Bakunin in 1869.*
A. Lehning, 575(SEER):Oct79-601
Cockshut, A.O.J. Man and Woman.*
N. Auerbach, 637(VS):Winter79-204
H.L. Hennedy, 594:Fall79-378
639(VQR):Autumn78-127
"The Cocktail Party Cookbook and Guide."
W. and C. Cowen, 639(VQR):Spring78-78
Cody, J.V. Horace and Callimachean Aesthetics.
J-M. André, 555:Vol52fasc1-201
Coe, B. The Birth of Photography.
M. Roskill, 637(VS):Spring79-335
Coe, L. and S. Benedict. Arts Management.
B. Bordelon, 151:Dec78-96
Coe, M.D. Lords of the Underworld.
R. Lopez, 2(AfrA):Nov78-102
Coekelberghs, D. Les peintres belges à Rome de 1700 à 1830.
P. Conisbee, 90:Sep79-589
Coelho, J.D. - see under do Prado Coelho, J.
Coelho, M.H.D. - see under da Cruz Coelho, M.H.
Coetzee, A.J. - see Breytenbach, B.
Coetzee, J.M. Waiting for the Barbarians.
J. Mellors, 362:6Nov80-623
Coffey, J.W. Political Realism in American Thought.*
639(VQR):Autumn78-132
Coffey, P. The Social Economy of France.
D.B. Goldey, 208(FS):Oct79-493
Coffin, D.R. The Villa in the Life of Renaissance Rome.
G. Martin, 617(TLS):1Feb80-120
676(YR):Autumn79-X
Coffin, T.P. The British Traditional Ballad in North America. (rev by R.D. Renwick)
W.K. McNeil, 292(JAF):Jan-Mar79-105
N.V. Rosenberg, 187:Jan80-109
Coffin, W.S., Jr. Once to Every Man.
639(VQR):Summer78-89
Coffman, V. The Alpine Coach.
L. Duguid, 617(TLS):16May80-558
Cofield, J.R. William Faulkner: The Cofield Collection. (L. Wells, ed)
J. Ditsky, 628(UWR):Spring-Summer79-103
Cogan, M. Imperialism and Religion.
G.W. Ahlström, 318(JAOS):Oct-Dec78-509
Coggeshall, R. Hymn for Drum.*
J. Agar, 580(SCR):Spring79-80

Cogny, P. "L'Éducation sentimentale" de Flaubert, le monde en creux.
J. Bem, 535(RHL):Mar-Apr78-325
Cogny, P., ed. Mélanges Pierre Lambert, consacrés à Huysmans.
F. Zayed, 535(RHL):Mar-Apr78-327
Cogswell, F. Against Perspective.*
W. Stevenson, 102(CanL):Spring79-103
Cohen, A. Carnets 1978.
L. Kovacs, 450(NRF):Jun79-119
Cohen, A. and S.G. Nooteboom, eds. Structure and Process in Speech Perception.
Z.S. Bond, 353:Dec78-89
Cohen, A.A. Acts of Theft.
J. Leonard, 441:12Feb80-C9
J. Naughton, 362:27Mar80-419
M. Shechner, 441:9Mar80-10
Cohen, D. J.B. Watson.*
S. Sutherland, 617(TLS):29Feb80-241
Cohen, E., L. Namir and I.M. Schlesinger. A New Dictionary of Sign Language.
M.R. Key, 350:Sep79-117
Cohen, G.A. Karl Marx's Theory of History.*
A. Quinton, 617(TLS):4Jan80-18
Cohen, G.M. The Seleucid Colonies.
S.M. Burstein, 124:Sep79-56
Cohen, H. La Figure dialogique dans "Jacques le fataliste."*
P. France, 208(FS):Vol33Pt2-766
F. Sturzer, 400(MLN):May79-904
Cohen, H.H. The Drunkenness of Noah.
D. Pardee, 318(JAOS):Jul-Sep78-310
Cohen, J.T. In/Sights.
J. Naughton, 362:3Jan80-29
A. Ross, 364:Oct79-7
Cohen, K. Film and Fiction.
P. Willemen, 617(TLS):30May80-624
Cohen, L. Death of a Lady's Man.*
J. David, 628(UWR):Spring-Summer79-100
P. McNally, 529(QQ):Summer79-343
S. Scobie, 526:Spring79-73
Cohen, L.J. The Probable and the Provable.
M.A.F., 543:Sep78-131
I. Levi, 84:Sep79-279
A.R. White, 479(PhQ):Jan79-89
Cohen, M. Night Flights.*
G.T. Davenport, 569(SR):Winter79-xix
L. Leith, 168(ECW):Fall78-56
W.H. New, 102(CanL):Autumn79-79
F. Timleck, 526:Spring79-91
Cohen, M. Sensible Words.*
G. Cannon, 567:Vol126#1/2-121
W. Harsh, 301(JEGP):Jul79-419
A.C. Kelly, 566:Autumn78-48
J. Shay, 173(ECS):Fall78-126
K. Sørensen, 179(ES):Feb79-87
J.L. Subbiondo, 350:Jun79-479
M. West, 568(SCN):Fall-Winter79-65
Cohen, M., T. Nagel and T. Scanlon, eds. Equality and Preferential Treatment.
R.H.S. Tur, 518:Jan79-41
Cohen, M.N., with R.L. Green - see Carroll, L.
Cohen, R., ed. New Directions in Literary History.
T. Eagleton, 349:Spring78-129

Cohen, R.S. and Y. Elkana - see Helmholtz, H.
Cohen, R.S., P.K. Feyerabend and M.W. Wartofsky, eds. Essays in Memory of Imre Lakatos.*
A. Lyon, 518:May79-89
Cohen, S. and L. Taylor. Escape Attempts.
D.I. Davies, 99:Jun-Jul80-44
Cohen, S.B., ed. Comic Relief.
J.E. Dunleavy, 587(SAF):Autumn79-252
Cohen, W.I. The Chinese Connection.
639(VQR):Winter79-7
Cohler, D.K. Gamemaker.
N. Callendar, 441:27Jul80-23
Cohn, D. Transparent Minds.
A. Banfield, 290(JAAC):Winter79-208
L. Surette, 255(HAB):Summer79-197
Coirault, Y. - see Duc de Saint-Simon
Coke, V., ed. One Hundred Years of Photographic History.
B. Jay, 637(VS):Winter78-294
D.D. Keyes, 54:Mar78-188
Coke, V. Photography in New Mexico.
G. Thornton, 55:Nov79-52
Coker, J. Listening to Jazz.
M. Harrison, 415:Mar79-223
Colaianne, A.J. "Piers Plowman."
P.M. Kean, 541(RES):Nov79-457
Colardelle-Diarrassouba, M. Le Lièvre et l'Araignée dans les contes de l'ouest africain.
R. Mercier, 549(RLC):Jan-Mar77-112
Colbert, E. Southeast Asia in International Politics, 1941-1956.
M. Leifer, 293(JASt):Nov78-207
Colby, V. Yesterday's Woman.
W. Franke, 38:Band96Heft1/2-247
Colby, W. Honorable Men.
639(VQR):Autumn78-130
Coldstream, J.N. Geometric Greece.
P. Cartledge, 303(JoHS):Vol199-201
J.V. Luce, 123:Vol29No2-286
Coldwell, J. - see Lamb, C.
Cole, B. Blood Knot.
N. Callendar, 441:31Aug80-17
Cole, B. Agnolo Gaddi.
M. Boskovits, 54:Dec78-707
Cole, D. The Work of Sir Gilbert Scott.
D. Watkin, 617(TLS):20Jun80-698
Cole, G. American Travelers in Mexico, 1821-1972.
H.C. Woodbridge, 399(MLJ):Mar79-131
Cole, H. The Changing Face of Music.*
A. Jacobs, 415:Feb79-129
Cole, J.Y. For Congress and the Nation.
R.A. McCown, 14:Oct79-469
Cole, P., ed. Studies in Modern Hebrew Syntax and Semantics.
R. Hetzron, 361:Aug78-381
Cole, P. and J.L. Morgan, eds. Syntax and Semantics.* (Vol 3: Speech Acts.)
B.G. Campbell, 215(GL):Fall78-128
Cole, W.O. and P.S. Sambhi. The Sikhs.
M. Juergensmeyer, 293(JASt):Aug79-793
Colebrook, J. Innocents of the West.
639(VQR):Summer79-92

Colegate, I. The Shooting Party.
   A. Motion, 617(TLS):12Sep80-983
   J. Naughton, 362:4Sep80-313
Coleman, A.D. Light Readings.
   R. Whelan, 55:Dec79-34
Coleman, D.C. Courtaulds. (Vol 3)
   T.C. Barker, 617(TLS):12Sep80-998
Coleman, F.M. Hobbes and America.
   S.A. Bill, 173(ECS):Winter78/79-241
Coleman, J.E. Keos.* (Vol 1)
   W.W. Phelps, 303(JoHS):Vol199-205
Coleman, K., general ed. A History of
Georgia.*
   R.F. Durden, 579(SAQ):Winter79-138
Coleman, R. - see Vergil
Coleman, R.P. and L. Rainwater, with K.A.
McClelland. Social Standing in America.
   J. Potter, 617(TLS):25Jan80-93
Coleridge, S.T. The Collected Works of
Samuel Taylor Coleridge: Essays on His
Times in The Morning Post and The Cour-
ier.* (D.V. Erdman, ed)
   J.R. Barth, 301(JEGP):Jul79-444
   J. Beer, 402(MLR):Oct79-914
   R.L. Brett, 148:Autumn79-83
   A.G. Hill, 541(RES):Feb79-98
   D.H. Reiman, 591(SIR):Spring79-141
   E.P. Thompson, 661(WC):Summer79-261
Coleridge, S.T. The Collected Works of
Samuel Taylor Coleridge: On the Constitu-
tion of the Church and State. (J.
Colmer, ed)
   J. Beer, 402(MLR):Oct79-914
Coleridge-Taylor, A. The Heritage of
Samuel Coleridge-Taylor.
   A. Burgess, 617(TLS):15Feb80-167
Coles, D. Anniversaries.*
   G. Hamel, 198:Winter80-139
Coles, G.M. The Flower of Light.
   C. Sanders, 177(ELT):Vol22#3-228
Coles, J.M. and A. Harding. The Bronze
Age in Europe.
   N. Hammond, 617(TLS):8Feb80-147
Coles, R. Walker Percy.*
   L. Leary, 27(AL):Jan80-579
Coles, R. and J.H. Women of Crisis. (Vol
2)
   J. Greenfield, 441:6Jul80-10
Colette. Letters from Colette. (R.
Phelps, ed and trans)
   D. Grumbach, 441:16Nov80-16
   J. Updike, 442(NY):29Dec80-69
Colette, J. - see Schulz, W.
Coley, W.B. - see Fielding, H.
Colinvaux, P. The Fates of Nations.
   P-L. Adams, 61:Sep80-109
   J.H. Hexter, 441:19Oct80-14
Collantes de Terán Sanchez, A. Sevilla en
la Baja Edad Media.
   T.F. Ruiz, 589:Apr79-358
Colledge, M.A.R. The Art of Palmyra.
   S.B. Downey, 54:Jun78-358
Collet, G-P. - see Mauriac, F. and J-É.
Blanche
Collet, J. Le Cinéma de François Truf-
faut.
   O. Mille, 400(MLN):Dec79-1265

Colley, I. Dos Passos and the Fiction of
Despair.*
   T. Ludington, 27(AL):Jan80-576
Colli, G. La sapienza greca. (Vol 1)
   F. Graf, 123:Vol29No2-239
   R.W., 555:Vol52fasc2-377
Colli, G. La sapienza greca. (Vol 2)
   J. Barnes, 123:Vol29No2-242
Colli, G. and M. Montinari - see Nietzsche,
F.
Collie, M. George Gissing: A Biography.*
   P. Keating, 447(N&Q):Oct78-479
   J. Wolff, 395(MFS):Winter78/79-590
Collie, M. Jules Laforgue.*
   J.A. Hiddleston, 402(MLR):Apr79-466
   205(FMLS):Jan78-87
Collie, M. George Meredith.*
   B.F. Fisher 4th, 191(ELN):Sep78-61
Collie, M. - see Laforgue, J.
Collier, A. R.D. Laing.
   P. Sedgwick, 560:Spring-Summer79-217
Collier, B. Arms and the Men.
   J. Keegan, 617(TLS):18Jan80-59
Collier, R.J. Poetry and Drama in the
York Corpus Christi Play.*
   D. Staines, 589:Oct79-789
Collin, H.S. and C.J. Schlyter, eds.
Westgöta-Lagen.
   J.E. Cathey, 563(SS):Winter79-54
Collinder, B. Sprache und Sprachen.
   W.P. Schmid, 260(IF):Band83-364
Collinet, J-P. Lectures de Molière.
   C.N. Smith, 208(FS):Vol33Pt2-684
Collins, G.R. Fantastic Architecture.
(M. Schuyt and J. Elffers, eds)
   P. Goldberger, 441:30Nov80-12
Collins, G.R. - see Martinell, C.
Collins, H.B. and others. The Far North.
   C. Cannon-Brookes, 39:Mar79-241
Collins, J.J. Primitive Religion.
   W.M. Clements, 292(JAF):Oct-Dec79-510
Collins, J.J. The Sibylline Oracles of
Egyptian Judaism.
   Z. Garber, 318(JAOS):Apr-Jun78-149
Collins, L. and D. Lapierre. The Fifth
Horseman.
   P. Andrews, 441:17Aug80-11
   A. Broyard, 441:4Sep80-C26
   A. Cockburn, 453(NYRB):6Nov80-48
   61:Oct80-98
Collins, M. Flying to the Moon and Other
Strange Places.
   D.W. Strangway, 529(QQ):Spring79-181
Collins, M. The Slasher.
   N. Callendar, 441:28Sep80-22
Collins, P. Charles Dickens: "David Cop-
perfield."
   E.M. Eigner, 402(MLR):Oct79-920
   S. Monod, 189(EA):Jul-Dec78-403
   P. Preston, 447(N&Q):Jun78-262
Collins, R. The Credential Society.
   A. Hacker, 453(NYRB):20Mar80-20
Collins, R. A Voice from Afar.
   R. Lorimer, 102(CanL):Winter78-82
Collins, W.W. Memoirs of the Life of
William Collins.
   G. Reynolds, 617(TLS):12Sep80-988

Collinson, P. Archbishop Grindal 1519-1583.
D. Cupitt, 362:21Feb80-251
C.S.L. Davies, 617(TLS):25Apr80-475

Colliot, R., ed. L'ystoire du vaillant chevalier Pierre filz du conte de Provence et de la belle Maguelonne.
T. Hunt, 402(MLR):Oct79-934

Colliva, P. Il Cardinale Albornoz, Lo Stato della Chiesa, Le "Constitutiones Aegidianae" (1353-1357), con in Appendice il testo volgare delle Costituzione di Fano dal Ms. Vat. Lat. 3939.
J.N. Hillgarth, 589:Jan79-121

"Colloque Mallarmé (Glasgow, Novembre 1973) en l'honneur de Austin Gill."
J-L. Backès, 535(RHL):Mar-Apr78-329

Colls, R. The Collier's Rant.
M. Neuman, 637(VS):Spring79-369

Colmer, J. Coleridge to Catch-22.
T. Eagleton, 541(RES):Feb79-116

Colmer, J. E.M. Forster.*
L.K. Ferres, 67:May79-113
E. Hanquart, 189(EA):Jan-Mar78-94

Colmer, J. Patrick White's "Riders in the Chariot."
A. Mitchell, 71(ALS):Oct79-248

Colmer, J. - see Coleridge, S.T.

Colombo, A. The Better Class.
J. Burke, 231:Sep80-90

Colombo, A. La società del futuro.
E. Namer, 542:Oct-Dec79-445

Colombo, J.R. Mostly Monsters.*
F. Cogswell, 102(CanL):Winter78-106

Colón, G. Die ersten romanischen und germanischen Übersetzungen des "Don Quijote."*
Z. Takacs, 182:Vol131#23/24-856

Colón, G. El léxico catalán en la Romania.*
M.W. Wheeler, 86(BHS):Jan79-79

Colonna, A. - see Sophocles

Colp, R., Jr. To Be an Invalid.*
F.B. Smith, 637(VS):Winter79-222

Colter, C. Night Studies.
S. Salmans, 617(TLS):1Aug80-882

Colver, A.W. - see Hume, D.

Colvin, C., ed. Maria Edgeworth in France and Switzerland.
J. Moynahan, 617(TLS):25Apr80-464

Colvin, H.M. A Biographical Dictionary of British Architects, 1600-1840.*
J.M. Crook, 46:May79-313

Colwin, L. Happy All the Time.*
G. Davenport, 249(HudR):Spring79-148
W. Spiegelman, 584(SWR):Spring79-190
W. Sullivan, 569(SR):Spring79-337

Combs, H.B., with M. Caidin. Kill Devil Hill.*
C.H. Gibbs-Smith, 617(TLS):4Jul80-750
D. Grumbach, 441:3Feb80-15

Combs, R. Vision of the Voyage.
D.D. Kummings, 125:Winter79-313
D.E. Stanford, 27(AL):May79-285

Comeau, R.F., F.L. Bustin, and N.J. Lamoureux. Ensemble: Grammaire.* Ensemble: Littérature.* Ensemble: Culture et société.*
W. Staaks, 207(FR):Dec78-361

Comella, A. Il materiale votivo tardo di Gravisca.
T. Dohrn, 182:Vol131#14-489

Comenius, J.A. Comenius' självbiografi. (W. Sjöstrand and S. Nordström, eds)
J.V. Polišenský, 575(SEER):Jan79-126

Comfort, A. I and That.
A.E., 148:Winter79-93

Comfort, A. Tetrarch.
G. Jonas, 441:14Sep80-38

Comini, A. The Fantastic Art of Vienna.*
C.T. Whaley, 584(SWR):Spring79-186

Comişel, E. Folclor Muzical.
R. Garfias, 187:Jan80-105

Comitas, L. The Complete Caribbeana, 1900-1975.
L.S. Thompson, 263(RIB):Vol29No2-206

Comito, T. The Idea of the Garden in the Renaissance.
H. Toliver, 401(MLQ):Jun79-196
J.J. Yoch, 219(GaR):Fall79-717

de Comminges, E. Anouilh, littérature et politique.
T.J. Kline, 207(FR):May79-939

Commins, D. What is an Editor?*
295(JML):Vol7#4-574

Commire, A. - see "Something About the Author"

Commoner, B. The Politics of Energy.*
L.C. Gould, 676(YR):Spring80-446

"Communication Yearbook I." (B.D. Ruben, ed)
R.R. Lee, 583:Fall78-103

"Communication Yearbook 2." (B.D. Ruben, ed)
R.R. Lee, 583:Summer79-423

Como, J.T., ed. C.S. Lewis at the Breakfast Table, and Other Reminiscences.*
J. Fenton, 362:14Aug80-213

Compagnon, A. La Seconde Main ou le travail de la citation.
P-L. Rey, 450(NRF):Jul79-116

Compaine, B.M., ed. Who Owns the Media?
A. Smith, 441:27Jul80-10

Compère, D. Approche de l'île chez Jules Verne.
P.M. Wetherill, 402(MLR):Oct79-944

Compton, H. A Particular Account of the European Military Adventurers of Hindustan from 1784 to 1803.
T.R. Metcalf, 293(JASt):Aug79-801

Compton, L.F. Andalusian Lyrical Poetry and Old Spanish Love Songs.
S.G. Armistead, 240(HR):Winter78-92
R. Hitchcock, 131(CL):Fall79-424

Compton, S. The World Backwards.
M. Chamot, 39:Dec79-535

Comrie, B. Aspect.*
V. Bubenik, 353:Oct78-89
S. Potter, 402(MLR):Jan79-128

Constantine, D.J. The Significance of
Locality in the Poetry of Friedrich
Hölderlin.
R. Gray, 617(TLS):11Jan80-45
Contat, M. and M. Rybalka - see Sartre,
J-P.
Conti, F. How to Recognize Art.
C.C. Brookes, 39:Dec79-538
Conti, P.G. Saggio pascoliano.
E.F., 228(GSLI):Vol155fasc491-476
Contogiorgis, G.D. La théorie des révolu-
tions chez Aristote.
A. Reix, 542:Jan-Mar79-131
Contosta, D.R. Henry Adams and the Ameri-
can Experiment.
J. Leonard, 441:4Nov80-C8
"Contributi dell'Istituto di Filologia
Moderna." (Serie Francese, Vol 8)
G. Hainsworth, 208(FS):Vol33Pt2-986
Conzen, K.N. Immigrant Milwaukee, 1836-
1860.
J. Potter, 617(TLS):25Jan80-93
Coogan, M.D. West Semitic Personal Names
in the Murašû Documents.
E.C. Smith, 424:Jun78-202
Cook, B. Private View.
C. Rumens, 617(TLS):16May80-552
Cook, C., with others. Sources in British
Political History, 1900-1951. (Vols 3
and 4)
V. Cromwell, 325:Apr79-171
Cook, D. Winter Doves.*
D. Durrant, 364:Feb80-92
Cook, D.J. Language in the Philosophy of
Hegel.
K. Hartmann, 53(AGP):Band60Heft1-101
Cook, E. The Ordinary and the Fabulous.
(2nd ed)
G. Smith, 292(JAF):Jul-Sep79-356
Cook, F.H. Hua-yen Buddhism.
T. Unno, 293(JASt):Nov78-163
Cook, H.E. Shaker Music.
H.B.R., 412:May78-131
Cook, J. The Architecture of Bruce Goff.
P.B. Jones, 46:May79-311
Cook, R-F. and L-S. Crist. Le Deuxième
Cycle de la Croisade.
M.R. Morgan, 208(FS):Jul79-324
Cook, S.J. From Tobacco Road to Route 66.*
K. King, 577(SHR):Summer79-270
Cooke, A. Six Men.
639(VQR):Winter78-28
Cooke, D. I Saw the World End.*
R. Anderson, 415:Sep79-743
Cooke, J.E. Tench Coxe and the Early
Republic.
P. Goodman, 656(WMQ):Apr79-298
F. McDonald, 579(SAQ):Summer79-413
K. Newmyer, 432(NEQ):Jun79-295
Cooke, M.G. The Romantic Will.*
J. Blondel, 189(EA):Jul-Dec78-392
H. Lindenberger, 402(MLR):Jul79-666
E.D. Mackerness, 447(N&Q):Jun78-251
639(VQR):Summer78-103
Cooke, T.D. The Old French and Chaucerian
Fabliaux.
E. Giaccherini, 382(MAE):1979/2-300

Cookson, C. Tilly Trotter.
L. Duguid, 617(TLS):16May80-558
Cooley, T. Educated Lives.*
Q. Anderson, 191(ELN):Mar79-266
E.N. Harbert, 295(JML):Vol17#4-620
Coomaraswamy, A. Coomaraswamy 1.* Cooma-
raswamy 2.* (R. Lipsey, ed of both)
H. Smith, 485(PE&W):Jul79-347
Coomaraswamy, A.K. La doctrine du sacri-
fice.
M. Adam, 542:Jul-Sep79-352
Coombs, D. Sport and the Countryside.*
J. Egerton, 90:Aug79-531
Cooney, S. - see Reznikoff, C.
Cooper, A. - see "Li Po and Tu Fu"
Cooper, B. Merleau-Ponty and Marxism.
P. Resnick, 99:Apr80-44
Cooper, D. Men at Axlir.
442(NY):17Mar80-165
Cooper, H. Pastoral.
G.S. Ivy, 161(DUJ):Dec78-125
Cooper, H.R., Jr. The Igor Tale.
G.A. Perfecky, 574(SEEJ):Fall79-395
W.F. Ryan, 402(MLR):Oct79-1006
J.S.G. Simmons, 382(MAE):1979/2-289
V.A. Tumins, 550(RusR):Jul79-407
Cooper, J. Class.
R. Coleridge, 617(TLS):11Jan80-32
Cooper, J., ed. Mackintosh: Architecture.
505:Sep79-224
Cooper, J. Supercooper.
D. Thomas, 362:18and25Dec80-863
Cooper, J.M. Reason and Human Good in
Aristotle.*
J. Dybikowski, 154:Mar78-190
Cooper, L. Desirable Residence.
K. Flint, 617(TLS):9May80-538
Cooper, M. and J. Lucas. Panzer.
639(VQR):Autumn79-132
Cooper, N. The Opulent Eye.*
J. Petrowsky, 637(VS):Winter79-207
Cooper, T. and P. Hill. Dialogue With
Photography.
42(AR):Fall79-507
Cooper, W.S. Foundations of Logico-Lin-
guistics.
D.E. Over, 479(PhQ):Jul79-275
Coox, A.D. and H. Conroy, eds. China and
Japan.
W.I. Cohen, 293(JASt):Aug79-741
Copeland, A. At Peace.*
P. Monk, 529(QQ):Autumn79-525
Copeland, J.G., R. Kite and L. Sandstedt.
Intermediate Spanish.*
H. Frey, 238:May-Sep79-418
Copeland, M.W. Charles Alexander Eastman
(Ohiyesa).
R. Gish, 649(WAL):Winter80-335
Copley, I. The Music of Charles Wood.
A. Hutchings, 410(M&L):Jul79-351
C. Palmer, 415:Aug79-653
Copley, I.A. The Music of Peter Warlock.
E. Sams, 617(TLS):11Jul80-790
Coppel, A. The Hastings Conspiracy.
P. Andrews, 441:16Nov80-14
M. Laski, 362:13Nov80-665
B. Roueché, 442(NY):24Nov80-206

Copper, B. The Werewolf.
639(VQR):Spring78-69
Coppola, E. Notes.*
M. McCreadie, 18:Sep79-70
Coppolino, S. Estetica ed ermeneutica di
Luigi Pareyson.
F.P. Ciglia, 227(GCFI):Apr-Jun78-260
Corbett, M. and R.W. Lightbown. The
Comely Frontispiece.*
D. de Chapeaurouge, 182:Vol31#15/16-
555
M. Hunter, 78(BC):Autumn79-335
Corbett, N.L. - see de Joinville, J.
Corbin, A. Les Filles de Noce.
J. Duvignaud, 450(NRF):Mar79-119
Corbin, H. L'imagination créatrice dans
le soufisme d'Ibn 'Arabî.
A. Reix, 542:Apr-Jun79-203
Corbin, H. - see "L'Archange empourpré"
Corbin, S. Die Neumen.
R. Steiner, 317:Fall79-555
Corcoran, J., ed. Ancient Logic and Its
Modern Interpretations.
R. Bosley, 393(Mind):Apr79-284
Cordes, G. Altniederdeutsches Elementar-
buch.*
W. Sanders, 684(ZDA):Band107Heft4-153
Cordier, S.S. Calculus of Power.
J.S. Thach, Jr., 550(RusR):Jul79-388
Cordner, M. - see Farquhar, G.
Cordor, S-M.H., ed. Modern West African
Short Stories from Liberia.
A. Sistrunk, 95(CLAJ):Mar79-283
Coren, A., ed. Pick of Punch.
D. Thomas, 362:18and25Dec80-863
Coren, A. Tissues for Men. The Best of
Alan Coren.
D. Thomas, 362:18and25Dec80-863
Cork, R. The Social Role of Art.
R. Calvocoressi, 617(TLS):13Jun80-677
Cork, R. Vorticism and Abstract Art in
the First Machine Age.* (Vols 1 and 2)
W.C. Lipke, 127:Fall78-74
Corley, E. The Genesis Rock.
P. Andrews, 441:27Jan80-15
Cormack, M. J.M.W. Turner, R.A., 1775-
1851.
J. Ziff, 637(VS):Autumn77-113
Corman, A. The Old Neighborhood.
C. Lehmann-Haupt, 441:26Sep80-C30
R. Miner, 441:5Oct80-15
Cormeau, C. "Wigalois" und "Diu Crône."*
F.H. Bäuml, 406:Fall79-337
D.H. Green, 402(MLR):Jul79-738
J.A. Schultz, 222(GR):Summer79-131
Cormier, F. LBJ: The Way He Was.
639(VQR):Summer78-90
Cormier, R.J., ed. Voices of Conscience.
P.E. Barrette, 207(FR):Dec78-340
D.D.R. Owen, 402(MLR):Jan79-193
Corn, A. A Call in the Midst of the
Crowd.*
J.F. Cotter, 249(HudR):Spring79-114
Corn, A. The Various Light.
C. Molesworth, 441:12Oct80-14

Cornagliotti, A., ed. La Passione di
Revello.
M. Pozzi, 228(GSLI):Vol155fasc492-601
Corne, C. Seychelles Creole Grammar.
L. Todd, 350:Dec79-916
Corneille, J-P. La linguistique struc-
turale.
D. Goyvaerts, 556(RLV):1978/6-550
C. Hagège, 209(FM):Oct78-361
Corneille, P. Le Cid. (P.H. Nurse, ed)
M-O. Sweetser, 207(FR):May79-930
Corneille, T. Camma.* (D.A. Watts, ed)
C.J. Gossip, 402(MLR):Jul79-696
M.B. Nelson, 207(FR):May79-931
Cornelisen, A. Flight from Torregreca.
P. Nichols, 617(TLS):15Aug80-913
E.S. Turner, 362:28Aug80-279
Cornelisen, A. Strangers and Pilgrims.
R. Blythe, 441:13Apr80-7
Cornet, J. A Survey of Zairian Art.
D.P. Biebuyck, 2(AfrA):Feb79-81
Cornevin, R. Histoire de l'Afrique. (Vol
3)
A.H.M. Kirk-Greene, 69:Vol48#2-191
Cornforth, J. English Interiors 1790-
1848.*
A. Sanders, 155:Spring79-46
L. Wright, 46:Jan79-4
Corngold, S., V. Lange and T. Ziolkowski.
Thomas Mann 1875-1955.
H.R. Vaget, 222(GR):Spring78-83
Corngold, S.A., M. Curschmann and T.J.
Ziolkowski, eds. Aspekte der Goethe-
zeit.*
D.G. Little, 402(MLR):Oct79-990
H. Reiss, 133:Band12Heft1/2-158
H. Seidler, 602:Vol10-254
Cornides, T. Ordinale Deontik.*
R. Hilpinen, 316:Mar79-121
Cornman, J.W. Perception, Common Sense,
and Science.*
D.H. Sanford, 486:Mar78-163
Corral, C.G-C. - see under Gutiérrez-
Cortines Corral, C.
Correa, A.B. - see under Bonet Correa, A.
Corrigan, P., H. Ramsay and D. Sayer.
Socialist Construction and Marxist
Theory.
R. North, 550(RusR):Jul79-390
Corriveau, H.G. Gilles Hénault.
B. Gill, 107(CRCL):Fall79-452
M. Parmentier, 627(UTQ):Summer79-463
Corsetti, R., ed. Lingua e politica.
R.E. Wood, 399(MLJ):Jan-Feb79-61
Corsi, M. - see Scaravelli, L.
Corsini, G. and G. Melchiori - see Joyce,
J.
Corson, J.C. Notes and Index to Sir
Herbert Grierson's Edition of The Let-
ters of Sir Walter Scott.
G. Naylor, 617(TLS):14Mar80-300
Cortázar, J. A Change of Light.
J.C. Oates, 441:9Nov80-9
Cortázar, J. Façons de perdre.
F. de Martinoir, 450(NRF):Jun79-139

Cortelazzo, M. and P. Zolli. Dizionario etimologico della lingua italiana. (Vol 1)
  H. Meier, 547(RF):Band91Heft3-289
Cortés, E.F. - see under Frutos Cortés, E.
Corti, M. An Introduction to Literary Semiotics.
  U. Margolin, 107(CRCL):Fall79-422
  G. Prince, 400(MLN):May79-866
Corti, M. Principi della communicazione letteraria.*
  R. Berteau, 209(FM):Jul78-278
Corvez, M. Aspects modernes du problème de Dieu.
  A. Reix, 542:Apr-Jun78-240
Cosentino, F.J. The Boehm Journey to Ching-te-chen, China, Birthplace of Porcelain.
  I.L. Legeza, 463:Autumn79-361
Coseriu, E. Die Sprachgeographie.
  P.A. McGraw, 685(ZDL):3/1979-354
Cosic, D. Reach to Eternity.
  J.P. Sloan, 441:3Feb80-14
Ćosić, D. A Time of Death.
  L.T.L., 502(PrS):Spring78-116
Cosman, C., J. Keefe and K. Weaver, eds. The Penguin Book of Women Poets.
  A. Cluysenaar, 565:Vol20#3-68
Cosman, M.P. Fabulous Feasts.
  P.D. La Bahn, 377:Mar79-51
de Cossart, M. The Food of Love.
  R. Crichton, 415:Mar79-219
Costa, C.D.N., ed. Seneca.
  A.J. Woodman, 313:Vol69-238
Costa, J. Le Conflit moral dans l'oeuvre romanesque de Jean-Pierre Camus (1584-1652).
  P.J. Bayley, 208(FS):Vol33Pt2-670
  J. Descrains, 535(RHL):Mar-Apr78-295
de Costa, R. The Poetry of Pablo Neruda.
  L.F. González-Cruz, 593:Winter79-367
Costello, J.R. A Generative Grammar of Old Frisian.
  P. Baldi, 350:Jun79-485
  D.R. McLintock, 541(RES):Aug79-368
Costello, P. The Heart Grown Brutal.
  M.J. and J.J. Egan, 395(MFS): Winter78/79-594
Costikyan, E.N. How to Win Votes.
  J. Herbers, 441:13Apr80-12
Cotes, P. J.P.: The Man Called Mitch.
  J.C. Trewin, 611(TN):Vol133#1-46
Cotnam, J. Bibliographie chronologique de l'oeuvre d'André Gide (1889-1973). Inventaire bibliographique et index analytique de la correspondance d'André Gide (publiée de 1897 à 1971).
  D.H. Walker, 208(FS):Vol33Pt2-854
Cotrus, O. Opera lui Mateiu Caragiale.
  V. Nemoianu, 617(TLS):25Jul80-857
Cott, J. and M. Gimbel, eds. Wonders.
  J. Romano, 441:21Dec80-6
Cott, N.F. The Bonds of Womanhood.*
  S. Armeny, 658:Summer79-203
  E.L. Steeves, 173(ECS):Summer79-556

Cott, N.F. and E.H. Pleck, eds. A Heritage of Her Own.
  D. Grumbach, 441:2Mar80-12
Cottino-Jones, M. and E.F. Tuttle, eds. Boccaccio: secoli di vita.
  M.M., 228(GSLI):Vol155fasc492-629
  G.H. McWilliam, 402(MLR):Jul79-715
Cottle, T.J. Hidden Survivors.
  J. Greenfield, 441:4May80-16
Cotton, J. The Parnasse François.
  G. Martin, 617(TLS):1Feb80-120
Cotton, N. In the Senate Amidst the Conflict and the Turmoil.
  S.E. Kennedy, 432(NEQ):Mar79-122
Cottrell, A.J., and others, eds. The Persian Gulf States.
  C. Campbell, 441:7Dec80-7
Cottrell, A.P. Goethe's "Faust."
  H.G. Haile, 301(JEGP):Apr79-299
Cottrell, P.L. Industrial Finance 1830-1914.
  S. Pollard, 617(TLS):6Jun80-652
Cottrell, R.D. Simone de Beauvoir.
  C. Radford, 208(FS):Vol33Pt2-923
Couch, S. Nauka i tekhnika v našej žizni.* Fisičeskij i naučnyj mir vokrug nas.
  M. Bayuk, 399(MLJ):Dec79-467
Coughlin, E.V. Adelardo López de Ayala.
  R.J. Quirk, 238:May-Sep79-400
  D.L. Shaw, 86(BHS):Jan79-83
Coughlin, W.J. Day of Wrath.
  J. Burke, 441:28Sep80-14
Coulson, J. and others - see "The Oxford Illustrated Dictionary"
Coulson, M. Sanskrit.
  J.W. De Jong, 259(IIJ):Jan79-64
Coulter, J.A. The Literary Microcosm.*
  R. Ferwerda, 349:Vol32fasc3/4-416
Coulton, B. Louis MacNeice in the BBC.
  D. Cleverdon, 362:19Jun80-799
  T. Paulin, 617(TLS):16May80-547
Coulton, J.J. Ancient Greek Architects at Work.*
  J.R. McCredie, 576:Oct78-198
  H. Plommer, 303(JoHS):Vol99-209
Coulton, J.J. The Architectural Development of the Greek Stoa.*
  J.R. McCredie, 576:Oct78-199
"The Country Life Book of Europe's Royal Families."
  A. Forbes, 617(TLS):4Jan80-7
Courier, P-L. Correspondance générale. (Vols 1 and 2) (G. Viollet-le-Duc, ed)
  R. Bourgeois, 535(RHL):Nov-Dec79-1060
Courlander, H. A Treasury of Afro-American Folklore.
  U. Kutter, 196:Band19Heft1/2-135
Cournot, A-A. Des institutions d'instruction publique en France. (A. Kremer-Marietti, ed)
  J-M. Besnier, 192(EP):Jul-Sep79-345
Coursen, H.R., Jr. Christian Ritual and the World of Shakespeare's Tragedies.*
  R. Battenhouse, 301(JEGP):Jan79-122
Courtenay, W.J., W.H. Hay and K.E. Yandell - see Weinberg, J.R.

Courtes, J. Introduction à la sémiotique narrative et discursiva.
  F. Willaert, 277(ITL):#41/42-128
Couser, F.T. American Autobiography.*
  A. Douglas, 165(EAL):Spring80-96
Cousin, J. Recherches sur Quintilien.
  F. Ahlheid, 394:Vol32fasc3/4-433
Cousin, J. - see Quintilian
Cousins, N. Anatomy of an Illness as Perceived by the Patient.
  617(TLS):27Jun80-736
Cousteau, J. The Ocean World. (E. Pavese, ed)
  J.P. Sterba, 441:13Jan80-12
Coustillas, P. - see Gissing, G.
Couto, F.J. Hoffnung im Unglauben.
  J. Galot, 182:Vol131#20-715
Couton, G. and Y. Giraud - see Le Père Hercule
Couturier, M. and R. Groborne. Constante parité.
  A-M. Albiach, 98:Jun-Jul78-648
Couzyn, J. House of Changes.
  D. Barbour, 150(DR):Spring79-154
  A. Cluysenaar, 565:Vol20#3-68
  C. MacMillan, 198:Summer80-151
Cowan, I.B. and D.E. Easson. Medieval Religious Houses: Scotland. (2nd ed)
  P. Fergusson, 576:Mar78-57
Coward, H. and K. Sivaraman, eds. Revelation in Indian Thought.
  A. Wayman, 485(PE&W):Jan79-110
Coward, R. and J. Ellis. Language and Materialism.*
  P. Collier, 208(FS):Vol33Pt2-999
  V.B. Leitch, 125:Winter79-311
Cowell, F.R. The Garden as Fine Art.
  G. Darley, 135:Mar79-208
Cowen, P. Rose Windows.
  A. Clifton-Taylor, 135:Nov79-200
Cowherd, R.G. Political Economists and the English Poor Laws.
  U.R.Q. Henriques, 637(VS):Spring79-349
Cowles, V. The Astors.*
  442(NY):14Jan80-103
Cowley, F.G. The Monastic Order in South Wales, 1066-1349.
  G. Constable, 589:Oct79-791
Cowley, M. And I Worked at the Writer's Trade.*
  W.M. Gibson, 27(AL):Mar79-131
Cowley, M. The Dream of the Golden Mountains.
  S. Hook, 31(ASch):Autumn80-556
  A. Kazin, 441:23Mar80-7
  C. Lehmann-Haupt, 441:26Mar80-C29
  61:Apr80-122
  442(NY):28Apr80-145
Cowley, M. The View From 80.
  A. Broyard, 441:1Oct80-C28
  D. Hall, 441:7Sep80-15
Cowper, W. The Letters and Prose Writings of William Cowper. (Vol 1) (J. King and C. Ryskamp, eds)
  P.N. Furbank, 362:3Jan80-27
Cox, C.B. Joseph Conrad.
  J.B. Batchelor, 447(N&Q):Aug78-376

Cox, D. The Henry Wood Proms.
  H. Cole, 362:28Aug80-280
Cox, H. Turning East.
  C. Davis, 529(QQ):Summer79-354
Cox, M.H. and W. Chatterton. Nelson Algren.
  H. Claridge, 402(MLR):Jul79-684
Cox, R. Caroline Durieux.
  E.H. Fine, 585(SoQ):Winter79-135
Cox-Ife, W. W.S. Gilbert.
  C. Parrott, 410(M&L):Jul79-349
Coxe, L. Passage.
  J. Fuller, 617(TLS):18Jan80-65
Coyne, J.R., Jr. Fall In and Cheer.*
  639(VQR):Spring79-62
Cozarinsky, E. - see Borges, J.L.
Cozzens, J.G. Just Representations. (M.J. Bruccoli, ed)
  F.X. Duggan, 396(ModA):Summer79-318
  639(VQR):Winter79-18
Crabtree, T. Tom Crabtree on Teenagers.
  C. Brown, 617(TLS):5Sep80-964
Crackanthorpe, D. Hubert Crackanthorpe and English Realism in the 1890s.
  J.L. Halio, 573(SSF):Fall78-471
  S. Olding, 541(RES):May79-230
  J. Wolff, 395(MFS):Winter78/79-590
Craft, R. Current Convictions.
  B. Northcott, 607:Sep78-49
Cragg, G.R. - see Wesley, J.
Cragg, K. The House of Islam. (2nd ed)
  A.A.A. Fyzee, 273(IC):Jan76-48
Cragg, K., comp. The Wisdom of the Sufis.
  S. Vahiduddin, 273(IC):Jan77-70
Craig, D., ed. Marxists on Literature.*
  C.A. Prendergast, 208(FS):Vol33Pt2-998
Craig, D. On Singing Onstage.
  E. Forbes, 415:Nov79-919
Craig, C.A. Germany 1866-1945.*
  D. Barnouw, 221(GQ):Nov79-573
  M. Kitchen, 529(QQ):Winter79/80-707
  H. Ridley, 220(GL&L):Jul80-334
"Gordon Craig on Movement and Dance." (A. Rood, ed)
  C.K. Fletcher, 611(TN):Vol133#3-140
Craig, L. and others. The Federal Presence.
  J. Jordan, 42(AR):Spring79-252
Craig, M. Classic Irish Houses of the Middle Size.*
  P.J. Quinn, 576:May78-115
Craig, W. Sweet and Lowdown.
  A. Lamb, 415:Jul79-580
Craik, E.M. The Dorian Aegean.
  G. Huxley, 617(TLS):4Apr80-385
Cramer, T., ed. Die kleineren Liederdichter des 14. und 15. Jahrhunderts.* (Vol 1)
  C. Petzsch, 72:Band216Heft1-153
Cramp, S., chief ed. Handbook of the Birds of Europe, the Middle East and North Africa: The Birds of the Western Palearctic. (Vol 2)
  C.M. Perrins, 617(TLS):9May80-536
Crampton, G.R. The Condition of Creatures.
  G. Schmitz, 38:Band96Heft3/4-511
Crane, D.E.L. - see Villiers, G.

Crane, H. Hart Crane and Yvor Winters.*
(T. Parkinson, ed)
  S. Paul, 301(JEGP):Apr79-284
  D.E. Stanford, 27(AL):May79-285
  639(VQR):Winter79-23
Crankshaw, E. Joseph Conrad. (2nd ed)
  J.B. Batchelor, 447(N&Q):Aug78-375
  J. McLauchlan, 136:Vol11#2-197
Craven, M. Again Calls the Owl.
  P-L. Adams, 61:Apr80-128
Cravens, G. Speed of Light.
  S. Isaacs, 441:3Feb80-14
Cravens, H. The Triumph of Evolution.
  F.A. Jenkins, 613:Dec79-448
Crawford, A. Thunder on the Right.
  J. Herbers, 441:10Aug80-9
  R. Sennett, 453(NYRB):25Sep80-24
Crawford, H.H. Crawford's Encyclopedia of
Comic Books.
  H. Woodell, 658:Autumn79-337
Crawford, J. The Creation of States in
International Law.
  H. Bull, 617(TLS):4Jan80-20
Crawford, J.M., ed. Studies in South-
eastern Indian Languages.*
  K.V. Teeter, 603:Vol3#2-261
Crawford, L. Las Casas, hombre de los
siglos.
  R.S. Poole, 263(RIB):Vol129No3/4-360
Crawford, T., ed. Love, Labour and Lib-
erty.
  D. Hannah, 179(ES):Jun79-341
Crawford, T. Society and the Lyric.
  D. Daiches, 617(TLS):27Jun80-735
  E. Morgan, 362:17Jul80-86
Crawford, T. The Werewolf Miracles.
  S. Scobie, 102(CanL):Winter78-89
Crawley, W.B., Jr. Bill Tuck.
  639(VQR):Summer79-96
Cray, E. Chrome Colossus.
  442(NY):15Dec80-170
Craze, M. The Life and Lyrics of Andrew
Marvell.
  S. Wintle, 617(TLS):14Mar80-300
Creaser, J.W. - see Jonson, B.
"Creative Cooking."
  529(QQ):Spring79-184
Creed, W.G. The Muse of Science and the
"Alexandria Quartet."
  G. Blake, 395(MFS):Summer78-310
Creeley, R. Hello.
  P. Ramsey, 569(SR):Fall79-686
Creeley, R. Later.
  A. Williamson, 441:9Mar80-8
Creeley, R. Was That a Real Poem and Other
Essays.
  J. Campbell, 617(TLS):30May80-620
Creeth, E. Mankynde in Shakespeare.
  L. Barkan, 405(MP):May80-420
  R. Battenhouse, 570(SQ):Summer79-433
  C. Belsey, 677(YES):Vol9-315
Cregier, D.M. Bounder from Wales.
  S. Meacham, 637(VS):Winter78-257
Creighton, D. Harold Adams Innis.
  D.J. Hall, 102(CanL):Winter79-198
Creighton, J. Joyce Carol Oates.
  R. Labrie, 150(DR):Autumn79-565

Creighton, J.V. William Faulkner's Craft
of Revision.*
  M.A. Haynes, 395(MFS):Winter78/79-637
  N. Polk, 573(SSF):Summer78-331
Cremascoli, G. - see Hugutio of Pisa
Cremin, L.A. American Education: The
National Experience 1783-1876.
  61:Nov80-98
Crenshaw, J.L. and J.T. Wallis, eds.
Essays in Old Testament Ethics.
  D. Pardee, 318(JAOS):Jul-Sep78-312
Crespo, A. - see Dante Alighieri
Crespo, E. Elementos antiguos y modernos
en la prosodia homérica.
  R. Führer, 343:Band23-181
Cresswell, K.A.C. A Bibliography of the
Architecture, Arts and Crafts of Islam
to 1st January 1960.
  Y. Crowe, 463:Autumn79-358
Creswell, T.J. Usage in Dictionaries and
Dictionaries of Usage.
  O. Thomas, 350:Sep79-754
Crews, H. A Childhood.*
  T. Graves, 577(SHR):Fall79-360
  T. Graves, 585(SoQ):Spring-Summer79-
  239
  P. Vansittart, 364:Dec79/Jan80-139
Crews, J. and A.T. Trusky - see Greasybear,
C.J.
Crichton, M. Congo.
  A. Broyard, 441:15Nov80-15
  H. Hayes, 441:7Dec80-13
Crick, B. George Orwell.
  R. Hoggart, 362:27Nov80-718
Crick, M. Exploration in Language and
Meaning.
  T.F. Hoad, 447(N&Q):Aug78-352
  J.T. Irvine, 350:Dec79-954
"Crime and Punishment in Medieval Chinese
Drama — Three Judge Pao Plays." (G.A.
Hayden, trans)
  R. Strassberg, 293(JASt):Feb79-362
Crisp, O. Studies in the Russian Economy
before 1914.
  P. O'Brien, 575(SEER):Oct79-604
Crisp, Q. How to Have a Life-Style.
  D. Grumbach, 441:3Feb80-15
Crispin, E. Fen Country.
  T.J. Binyon, 617(TLS):22Feb80-210
Crist, L.S., ed. "Saladin."
  I. Short, 545(RPh):Aug78-147
Cristesco, D. and H., comps. Bibliogra-
phie des oeuvres de Marc Aldanov.*
  D.M. Fiene, 399(MLJ):Apr79-213
Critchley, J.S. Feudalism.
  A.R. Lewis, 589:Apr79-360
Critchley, M. and R.A. Henson, eds. Music
and the Brain.
  R.G., 412:May78-138
  M. Williams, 255(HAB):Winter/Spring79-
  119
"Critique et création littéraires en
France au XVIIe siècle."
  R.D., 543:Mar79-539
  P. France, 402(MLR):Oct79-938
  V. Kapp, 547(RF):Band91Heft1/2-169
  H.T. Siepe, 182:Vol131#19-674

Crivelli, J.D. - see de Montchrestien, A.
Cro, S. A Forerunner of the Enlightenment
   in Spain.
   J.D. Browning, 173(ECS):Winter78/79-
   254
Crochet, M. Les Mythes dans l'oeuvre de
   Camus.*
   I.H. Walker, 208(FS):Jul79-366
Crocker, R.L. The Early Medieval
   Sequence.*
   A. Enrique Planchart, 317:Spring79-141
Crompton, L. - see Shaw, G.B.
Crone, A.L. Rozanov and the End of Lit-
   erature.
   C.G. Emerson, 550(RusR):Oct79-513
   G. Ivask, 574(SEEJ):Fall79-405
   H.A. Stammler, 558(RLJ):Fall79-259
Cronheim, F. Deutsch-Englische Wander-
   schaft.
   S. Hoefert, 406:Winter79-469
Cronin, A. Identity Papers.
   P. Craig, 617(TLS):21Mar80-326
Cronin, J. Gerald Griffin, 1803-1840.
   H. Pyle, 541(RES):Nov79-501
   639(VQR):Summer79-97
Cronin, T.E. The State of the Presidency.
   (2nd ed)
   G. Hodgson, 441:11May80-7
   442(NY):24Mar80-134
Crookshank, A. and the Knight of Glin.
   The Painters of Ireland c. 1660-1920.*
   C. Barrett, 135:Mar79-206
   B. Guinness, 39:May79-406
Cropp, G.M. Le Vocabulaire courtois des
   troubadours de l'époque classique.*
   J.H. Marshall, 208(FS):Vol33Pt2-1033
Croquette, B. Pascal et Montaigne.*
   E. Moles, 208(FS):Vol33Pt2-687
   V. Thweatt, 546(RR):Mar79-189
Cros, E. L'Aristocrate et le carnaval des
   gueux.
   A. Egido, 240(HR):Spring78-173
   J. Victorio, 556(RLV):1978/5-462
Crosby, D.F. God, Church, and Flag.
   R.M. Crunden, 396(ModA):Spring79-203
   639(VQR):Spring79-63
Crosby, J. Party of the Year.*
   M. Laski, 362:17Apr80-514
Cross, A.G. "By the Banks of the Thames."
   K. Fitzlyon, 617(TLS):22Aug80-929
Cross, A.G., ed. Russian Literature in
   the Age of Catherine the Great.*
   A. McMillin, 402(MLR):Apr79-507
Cross, G.B. Next Week — "East Lynne."
   R. Jackson, 611(TN):Vol132#3-142
   R.L. Lorenzen, 637(VS):Autumn78-109
   J.P. Wearing, 50(ArQ):Spring79-90
Cross, R.K. Malcolm Lowry.
   R. Chapman, 268(IFR):Summer80-160
Crossick, G., ed. The Lower Middle Class
   in Britain, 1870-1914.
   R.K. Webb, 637(VS):Spring78-403
Crotty, W.J. Decision for the Democrats.
   639(VQR):Summer79-90
Crouch, H. The Army and Politics in Indo-
   nesia.
   A. Gregory, 293(JASt):May79-634

Crouzel, H. - see Pic de la Mirandole, J.
   and P. Garcia
Crow, C., ed. Itinerary.
   F. Robinson, 649(WAL):Spring79-67
Crow, C.P. No More Monday Mornings.
   N. Callendar, 441:28Sep80-22
   442(NY):23Jun80-104
Crow, D. The Edwardian Woman.
   639(VQR):Autumn78-150
Crowder, C.M.D. Unity, Heresy and Reform
   1378-1460.*
   D. Fenlon, 382(MAE):1979/1-155
Crowell, J. and S.J. Searl, Jr. - see
   Miller, P.
Crowley, E.T., ed. New Acronyms, Initial-
   isms, and Abbreviations: 1976 Supplement.
   (5th ed)
   K.B. Harder, 424:Sep77-179
Crowley, E.T., ed. New Acronyms, Initial-
   isms, and Abbreviations 1977. New Trade
   Names 1977.
   K.B. Harder, 424:Dec78-427
Crowley, E.T., ed. New Trade Names 1976.
   K.B. Harder, 424:Sep78-294
Crowley, J.D., ed. Hawthorne: The Criti-
   cal Heritage.
   J. Arac, 153:Summer79-42
Crowson, L. The Esthetic of Jean Cocteau.
   J. Coakley, 130:Winter79/80-374
Crowther, R.L. Sun Earth.
   J. Cook, 576:Oct78-220
Croydon, M. Ivan Albright.
   A. Frankenstein, 55:Feb79-32
Crozier, B. Strategy of Survival.
   L. Raditsa, 390:Feb79-59
Cruikshank, M.L. Thomas Babington Macau-
   lay.
   636(VP):Winter78-397
Crum, M., comp. English and American
   Autographs in the Bodmeriana.
   P.J. Croft, 447(N&Q):Oct78-471
Crumley, J. The Last Good Kiss.
   J.K. Folsom, 649(WAL):Fall79-243
   639(VQR):Spring79-58
Crump, G.B. The Novels of Wright Morris.*
   M. Washington, 649(WAL):Spring79-75
Crump, R.W. - see Rossetti, C.
Crunden, R.M., ed. The Superfluous Men.*
   E.S. Shapiro, 639(VQR):Spring78-377
Crutchley, B. To be a printer.
   P. Sutcliffe, 617(TLS):5Sep80-952
da Cruz Coelho, M.H. O Mosteiro de Arouca
   do século X ao século XIII.
   C.H. Clough, 86(BHS):Jan79-85
Cruz Hernández, M. El pensamiento de
   Ramon Llull.
   J.N. Hillgarth, 589:Oct79-792
Crystal, D. Child Language, Learning and
   Linguistics.
   C. Baltaxe, 350:Jun79-492
Cua, A.S. Dimensions of Morality.
   H.B.V., 543:Jun79-743
Cuddon, J.A. A Dictionary of Literary
   Terms.
   H.A. Pausch, 107(CRCL):Fall79-454

Cudlipp, H. The Prerogative of the Harlot.
  A. Howard, 362:8May80-615
  S. Koss, 617(TLS):16May80-549
de Cuenca, L.A. - see Euphorion
Čukovskaja, L. Process Isključenija.
  S. Kryzytski, 558(RLJ):Fall79-230
Cullen, C.T. and H.A. Johnson - see
  Marshall, J.
Cullen, M.J. The Statistical Movement in
  Early Victorian Britain.
  A. Engel, 637(VS):Autumn78-101
Cullen, P. Infernal Triad.*
  J-F. Camé, 189(EA):Jul-Dec78-384
Culler, A.D. The Poetry of Tennyson.*
  J.D. Boyd, 636(VP):Autumn78-285
  E. Jordan, 184(EIC):Apr79-175
  J. Kissane, 637(VS):Autumn78-96
  J. Kolb, 405(MP):Feb80-349
Culler, J. Ferdinand de Saussure.*
  R.W. Bailey, 599:Summer79-295
  E.A. Lovatt, 208(FS):Vol33Pt2-1072
Culler, J. Structuralist Poetics.*
  S.R. Levin, 361:Dec78-383
Culver, R. Not Quite a Gentleman.
  R. Morley, 617(TLS):4Jan80-10
Cummings, A.L. The Framed Houses of
  Massachusetts Bay, 1625-1725.
  P.L. Goss, 292(JAF):Oct-Dec79-513
Cummins, J.G., ed. The Spanish Tradi-
  tional Lyric.
  S.G. Armistead, 240(HR):Summer78-387
Cummins, J.G. - see de Mena, J.
Cummins, P.W., ed. Le Regime tresutile et
  tresproufitable pour conserver et garder
  la Santé du Corps humain.*
  W. Rothwell, 208(FS):Vol33Pt2-585
Cundiff, P.A. Robert Browning.
  N.B. Crowell, 85:Spring78-85
Cunico, G. Essere come utopia.*
  E. Namer, 542:Apr-Jun78-186
  P.P., 227(GCFI):Jan-Mar78-148
Cunliffe, B. The Celtic World.
  C. Grandjouan, 124:Mar80-370
Cunningham, F. Understanding Marxism.
  529(QQ):Summer79-369
Cunningham, J.V. The Collected Essays.
  R. Fraser, 570(SQ):Summer79-437
  R.T. Smith, 577(SHR):Summer79-275
Cunningham, L. Third Parties.
  E.F. Hailey, 441:26Oct80-14
Cunningham, M.S. The Woman's Club of El
  Paso.
  W. Gard, 584(SWR):Spring79-vi
Cunningham, N., Jr. The Process of Govern-
  ment under Jefferson.
  C. McKee, 656(WMQ):Apr79-300
Cunningham, N.E., Jr., ed. Circular Let-
  ters of Congressmen to Their Constit-
  uents, 1789-1829.*
  R.P. Formisano, 656(WMQ):Jul79-486
  639(VQR):Summer79-89
Cunningham, R. Lovesongs and Others.
  G. Hamel, 198:Winter80-139
Cunningham, V. Everywhere Spoken
  Against.*
  F.W. Bradbrook, 447(N&Q):Jun78-271

Cunningham, V., ed. The Penguin Book of
  Spanish Civil War Verse.
  H. Corke, 362:11Sep80-344
  A. Terry, 617(TLS):8Aug80-895
Cunninghame Graham, R.B. Reincarnation.
  P. Rose, 441:20Jul80-8
Curl, J.S. A Celebration of Death.
  M. Craig, 617(TLS):29Feb80-244
  S. Slesin, 441:14Dec80-12
Curley, E.M. Descartes Against the Scep-
  tics.
  W. Charlton, 479(PhQ):Jul79-264
  P.A. Schouls, 518:May79-61
Curley, M.J. - see "Physiologus"
Curley, T.M. Samuel Johnson and the Age
  of Travel.*
  P-G. Boucé, 189(EA):Jul-Dec78-387
  R.P. Doig, 447(N&Q):Feb78-91
  J.D. Fleeman, 402(MLR):Apr79-418
"Current Population Reports, Series P-60
  No. 120."
  A. Hacker, 453(NYRB):20Mar80-20
Curry, R.A. Ramón de Mesonero Romanos.
  191(ELN):Sep78(supp)-194
Curtin, M. The Self-Made Men.
  P. Lewis, 617(TLS):6Jun80-636
Curtin, P. and others. African History.
  R. Oliver, 617(TLS):4Jan80-21
Curtis, A. Somerset Maugham.*
  R.A. Cordell, 395(MFS):Winter78/79-599
Curtis, B. and W. Mays, eds. Phenomen-
  ology and Education.
  M. Adams, 89(BJA):Winter79-92
  W.G. Warren, 63:Dec79-361
Curtis, J. - see d'Allainval, L.J.C.S.
Curtis, L.A. - see Defoe, D.
Curtis, R.L., ed. Le Roman de Tristan en
  prose.
  A.J. Holden, 402(MLR):Apr79-451
Curtiss, M. Other People's Letters.
  M. Ellmann, 569(SR):Spring79-332
  W. Fowlie, 579(SAQ):Winter79-123
  295(JML):Vol7#4-574
  580(SCR):Nov78-134
Curtiss, S. Genie.
  M.W. Salus, 350:Sep79-725
Cushman, K. D.H. Lawrence at Work.*
  J.H. Harris, 401(MLQ):Mar79-85
  K. Widmer, 594:Summer79-241
  295(JML):Vol7#4-758
Cuthbertson, B. Canadian Military Inde-
  pendence in the Age of the Superpowers.
  H.G. Classen, 529(QQ):Summer79-327
Cutler, A.H. - see Basetti-Sani, G.
Čyževs'kyj, D. A History of Ukrainian
  Literature (from the 11th to the End of
  the 19th Century). (G.S.N. Luckyj, ed)
  V. Swoboda, 575(SEER):Jul79-418
Czerniakow, A. The Warsaw Diary of Adam
  Czerniakow.* (R. Hilberg, S. Staron and
  J. Kermisz, eds)
  T. Ziolkowski, 569(SR):Fall79-676
  639(VQR):Summer79-94
Czerniawski, A. - see Różewicz, T.

"DEMEP: English Pronunciation 1500-1800."
  M. Görlach, 38:Band96Heft3/4-474
Daalder, J. - see Wyatt, T.
Daan, J. and H. Heikens. Dialectresisten-
tie bij kleuters en eerste-klassertjes.
  J. van den Broeck, 355(LSoc):Apr78-133
Dabney, V. Across The Years.
  P.M. Gaston, 579(SAQ):Summer79-401
  R. Mason, 639(VQR):Winter79-160
Dabydeen, C. Goatsong.
  G. Hamel, 198:Winter80-139
  R. Miles, 102(CanL):Summer79-138
Da Canal, M. - see under Martin Da Canal
Dacey, P. How I Escaped From the Laby-
rinth.*
  639(VQR):Winter78-12
Dafoe, C. The Frog Galliard.
  A. Wagner, 526:Summer79-86
Dagen, J. L'histoire de l'esprit humain
dans la pensée française de Fontenelle à
Condorcet.
  J.A. Perkins, 207(FR):Feb79-487
  C. Rosso, 535(RHL):Mar-Jun79-515
Dagognet, F. Une épistémologie de
l'espace concret.
  J. Brun, 192(EP):Apr-Jun79-247
D'Agostino, A. Marxism and the Russian
Anarchists.
  P. Avrich, 550(RusR):Jul79-368
D'Agostino, B. Tombe "principesche" dell'
orientalizzante antico da Pontecagnano.
  D. and F.R. Ridgway, 313:Vol69-212
Daguerressar, P. Jean-Jacques Rousseau ou
la fonction d'un refus.
  S. Goyard-Fabre, 542:Jul-Sep78-359
Dahl, R. My Uncle Oswald.*
  P-L. Adams, 61:May80-104
  V. Bourjaily, 441:20Apr80-15
  J. Burke, 231:May80-90
  C. Lehmann-Haupt, 441:29Apr80-C9
Dahl, S. Relativität und Absolutheit.
  J. Hardin, 221(GQ):Jan79-137
Dahl, W. Kristian Elster.*
  I. Lunden, 562(Scan):Nov79-163
Dahlén, E. Remarques syntaxiques sur cer-
tains verbes pronominaux en latin et en
langues romanes.
  J.N. Adams, 123:Vol29No2-326
Dahlheim, W. Gewalt und Herrschaft.
  J. Richardson, 313:Vol69-156
Dahlmann, H. Über Helvius Cinna.
  E.J. Kenney, 123:Vol29No2-310
Dahrendorf, R. Life Chances.
  M. Warnock, 362:17Jan80-91
Daive, J. Imaginary Who pour B.N. et 12
postes de radio.
  J-M. Le Sidaner, 98:Apr78-436
Daix, P. and J. Rosselet. Picasso: The
Cubist Years 1907-1916.*
  C. Green, 617(TLS):21Mar80-331
  J. Richardson, 453(NYRB):17Jul80-16
Daji, B. Writings and Speeches of Dr.
Bhau Daji. (T.G. Mainkar, ed)
  E. Bender, 318(JAOS):Jul-Sep78-335
Dakers, L. Making Church Music Work.
  G. Reynolds, 415:Jul79-580

Dale, A.S. Maker and Craftsman.
  376:Oct79-143
Dale, P. One Another.*
  T. Eagleton, 565:Vol20#1-74
  J. Sail, 493:Dec79-66
Dale, P.A. The Victorian Critic and the
Idea of History.*
  J. Diedrick, 125:Winter79-294
  G. Newman, 637(VS):Spring79-371
  636(VP):Winter78-396
  639(VQR):Summer78-98
Dales, R.C. - see Marius
Daleski, H.M. Joseph Conrad.*
  T.K. Bender, 191(ELN):Mar79-263
  D. Kramer, 573(SSF):Winter78-116
  S. Monod, 189(EA):Jul-Dec78-406
  295(JML):Vol7#4-676
Dalhaus, C. Richard Wagner's Music Dramas.
  O. Lee, 99:May80-36
Lord Dalhousie. The Dalhousie Journals.
(M. Whitelaw, ed)
  T. Vincent, 529(QQ):Summer79-325
d'Allainval, L.J.C.S. L'Ecole des bour-
geois, comédie. (J. Curtis, ed)
  C. Bonfils, 535(RHL):May-Jun78-475
  W.D. Howarth, 208(FS):Vol33Pt2-757
Dallas, R. Walking on the Snow.
  R. Jackaman, 368:Dec76-369
Dalla Valle, D. Barocco e Classicismo
nella letteratura francese del Seicento.
  G. Hainsworth, 208(FS):Vol33Pt2-699
Dallek, R. Franklin D. Roosevelt and
American Foreign Policy 1932-1945.*
  D.C. Watt, 617(TLS):22Feb80-213
Dällenbach, L. Le Récit spéculaire.*
  H. Charney, 207(FR):Apr79-776
Dallett, F.J., comp. Guide to the
Archives of the University of Pennsyl-
vania from 1740 to 1820.
  J.K. Reynolds, 14:Oct79-475
Dallin, A., ed. The Twenty-Fifth Congress
of the CPSU.
  M. McCauley, 575(SEER):Jan79-145
Dallinger, P., C. Bode and F. Dellian.
Hochschulrahmengesetz.
  H.P. Tschudi, 182:Vol31#20-723
d'Allonnes, O.R. - see under Revault
d'Allonnes, O.
Dalton, E. Unconscious Structure in "The
Idiot."
  G. Pirog, 594:Winter79-485
  A.C. Wright, 255(HAB):Fall79-322
Daly, J. Sir Robert Filmer and English
Political Thought.*
  R. Rudolph, 99:Sep80-35
Daly, R. God's Altar.*
  P. Caldwell, 165(EAL):Winter79/80-337
  E. Emerson, 432(NEQ):Mar79-125
  M.I. Lowance, Jr., 656(WMQ):Oct79-628
  L. Ziff, 27(AL):Mar79-111
al-Damanhūrī, A. Shaykh Damanhūrī on
the Churches of Cairo (1739). (M.
Perlmann, ed and trans)
  S. Moreh, 318(JAOS):Apr-Jun78-165
Damerau, F.J. Markov Models and Linguis-
tic Theory.
  G.F. Meier, 682(ZPSK):Band31Heft6-641

Damiani, B. and G. Allegra - see Delicado, F.

Damiani, B.M. Francisco Delicado.*
   F.A. de Armas, 241:Jan79-113
Damiani, B.M. Francisco López de Úbeda.*
   D.W. McPheeters, 240(HR):Spring78-259
Damião de Góis. Crônica do Príncipe D. João. (G. Almeida Rodrigues, ed)
   R.J. Oakley, 86(BHS):Jan79-78
d'Amico, F. - see Busoni, F.
d'Amiens, E. - see under Eustache d'Amiens
Damsteegt, T. Epigraphical Hybrid Sanskrit.
   R. Salomon, 293(JASt):May79-601
Dan, J. The Hebrew Story in the Middle Ages. The Hassidic Story.
   M. Saperstein, 322(JHI):Jan-Mar79-159
Dance, D.C. Shuckin' and Jivin'.
   T. Harris, 95(CLAJ):Dec78-182
Dance, S. The World of Earl Hines.
   C. Fox, 617(TLS):13Jun80-676
Danchin, P. The Prologues and Epilogues of the Restoration (1660-1700).
   J.J. Keenan, Jr., 568(SCN):Fall-Winter79-82
   S. Rosenfeld, 611(TN):Vol133#3-134
   J-P. Vander Motten, 179(ES):Feb79-95
Dancy, R.M. Sense and Contradiction.
   R. Kraut, 449:Nov79-527
d'Andlau, B. - see Madame de Staël and P. de Souza
D'Andlau, B., P. Christophorov and P. Riberette - see de Chateaubriand, F.R.
Danesi, M. La Lingua dei "Sermoni Sub-alpini."*
   F.J. Bosco, 399(MLJ):Mar79-149
Đặng Chấn Liêu and Bùi Ý. Tù'-điển Anh-Việt.
   Nguyễn Đình-hoà, 350:Jun79-490
Danger, P. Sensations et objets dans le roman de Flaubert.
   L. Czyba, 535(RHL):May-Jun78-499
Dangez, H. Onze letterkund 1.
   M-R. Blommaert, 556(RLV):1978/1-90
Daniele, A. - see de' Dottori, C.
Daniell, D. - see Buchan, J.
Daniell, R. Fatal Flowers.
   P-L. Adams, 61:May80-104
Daniels, B.C., ed. Town and County.
   L.W. Potts, 432(NEQ):Sep79-436
Daniels, K., M. Murnane and A. Picot, eds. Women in Australia.
   M. Pamplin, 325:Oct79-237
Daniels, S. The Salt Doll.
   K.H., 109:Summer80-223
Danilewicz-Zielińska, M. Bibliografia.
   B.W. Mazur, 575(SEER):Jan79-157
Danilov, V.P. Sovetskaia dokolkhoznaia derevnia.
   D. Atkinson, 550(RusR):Oct79-481
Daninos, P. Made in France.
   J.G. Miller, 207(FR):Dec78-378
Dann, J.C., ed. The Revolution Remembered.
   P-L. Adams, 61:Jul80-86
   J. Keegan, 441:6Jul80-3

Dannhauser, W.J. Nietzsche's View of Socrates.
   J. Philippoussis, 154:Dec78-713
d'Annunzio, G. Alcyone, a Selection. (J.R. Woodhouse, ed)
   J.G. Fucilla, 399(MLJ):Sep-Oct79-314
   C. Wagstaff, 402(MLR):Jul79-717
Danos, J.R. A Concordance to the "Roman de la Rose" of Guillaume de Lorris.
   F.W.A. George, 208(FS):Vol33Pt2-560
d'Ans, A-M. Le dit des vrais hommes.
   L. Chalon, 556(RLV):1978/3-266
Danson, L. The Harmonies of "The Merchant of Venice."*
   C. Spencer, 570(SQ):Summer79-426
   M. Williamson, 141:Winter79-76
Danson, L. Tragic Alphabet.*
   J. Drakakis, 349:Summer78-195
Dante, O.L. - see under Lazzarin Dante, O.
Dante Alighieri. Comedía. (Vol 3: Paraíso.) (A. Crespo, ed and trans)
   M.M., 228(GSLI):Vol155fasc492-628
Dante Alighieri. La Divina Commedia. (U. Bosco and G. Reggio, eds)
   P. Shaw, 617(TLS):2May80-501
Dante Alighieri. La Divina Commedia. (C.H. Grandgent, ed; rev by C.S. Singleton)
   C. Kleinhenz, 545(RPh):Aug78-128
Dante Alighieri. The Divine Comedy: Inferno. The Divine Comedy: Paradiso.* The Divine Comedy: Purgatorio. (C.S. Singleton, ed and trans of all)
   J. Ahern, 29:May/Jun80-12
   J.D. O'Hara, 639(VQR):Summer78-538
Dany, M., J. Geliot and M-L. Parizet. Le Français du secrétariat commercial.
   B. Braude, 207(FR):Mar79-677
Danziger, J., ed. Beaton.
   A. Fern, 441:21Sep80-13
   C. James, 453(NYRB):18Dec80-22
   J. Naughton, 362:18and25Dec80-865
Danzuso, D. - see Aniante, A.
d'Aragon, C. La Résistance sans héroïsme.
   C.W. Obuchowski, 207(FR):May79-943
D'Arcais, F., F. Zava Boccazzi and G. Pavanello. Gli affreschi nelle Ville Venete dal Seicento all'Ottocento.
   L. Larcher Crosato, 471:Oct/Nov/Dec79-408
Darcy, C.P. The Encouragement of the Fine Arts in Lancashire, 1760-1860.
   J. Jacob, 90:Jan79-46
D'Arcy, P. L'Argent et le pouvoir.
   M. Lageux, 154:Mar78-173
d'Ardenne, S.T.R.O., ed. The Katherine Group.
   B. Millett, 541(RES):Aug79-333
Dardis, T. Keaton.
   D. Macdonald, 453(NYRB):9Oct80-33
   E.S. Turner, 617(TLS):4Jan80-10
   M. Wood, 18:Jun79-68
D'Arezzo, R. La composizione del mondo con le sue cascioni. (A. Morino, ed)
   M.M., 228(GSLI):Vol155fasc490-312

d'Argencourt, L. and D. Druick, eds. The Other Nineteenth Century.
    529(QQ):Spring79-180
d'Argenteuil, R. The ME Prose Translation of Roger d'Argenteuil's "Bible en François." (P. Moe, ed)
    D. Speed, 67:May79-86
    E.G. Stanley, 447(N&Q):Dec78-543
Darian, S.G. The Ganges in Myth and History.
    R. Salomon, 293(JASt):Nov78-198
d'Arles, H. - see under Hilaire d'Arles
Darley, G. Selected Poems of George Darley. (A. Ridler, ed)
    J. Heath-Stubbs, 617(TLS):13Jun80-680
Darley, G. Villages of Vision.
    D. Hayden, 576:Oct78-217
Darling, C. and J. Fraser. Kain and Augustyn.
    O. Maynard, 151:Aug78-44
Darlington, B. - see Wordsworth, W.
Darlow, M. and G. Hodson. Terence Rattigan.*
    P. Bailey, 364:Nov79-79
Darnton, R. The Business of Enlightenment.*
    J.M. Roberts, 453(NYRB):7Feb80-49
Darnton, R., B. Fabian and R.M. Wiles. The Widening Circle.* (P.J. Korshin, ed)
    K.E. Carpenter, 517(PBSA):Jan-Mar78-156
    R.J. Roberts, 447(N&Q):Feb78-93
d'Arras, G. - see under Gautier d'Arras
Darroch, S.J. Ottoline.
    E. Delavenay, 189(EA):Apr-Jun78-237
Darst, D.H. Juan Boscán.
    E.L. Rivers, 399(MLJ):Sep-Oct79-312
Daruwalla, K.N. Crossing of Rivers.
    U. Parameswaran, 529(QQ):Spring79-172
Darwin, C. The Red Notebook of Charles Darwin. (S. Herbert, ed)
    R. O'Hanlon, 617(TLS):12Sep80-1000
"Darwin's Forgotten World."
    529(QQ):Spring79-183
Das, A.K. Treasures of Indian Painting from the Maharaja Sawai Man Singh II Museum, Jaipur.
    E. De Unger, 463:Winter78/79-467
Das, G.K. E.M. Forster's India.*
    R.J. Van Dellen, 395(MFS):Winter78/79-579
Das, G.K. and J. Beer, eds. E.M. Forster.
    J.R.B., 148:Winter79-93
Das Gupta, A. Indian Merchants and the Decline of Surat, c. 1700-50.
    J. Comte, 182:Vol131#21/22-791
Dassonville, M. Ronsard: Etude historique et littéraire, III.*
    G. Castor, 208(FS):Vol133Pt2-634
    F. Joukovsky, 535(RHL):May-Jun78-459
Da Tempo, A. Summa artis rithimici vulgaris dictaminis. (R. Andrews, ed)
    M. Marti, 228(GSLI):Vol155fasc490-295
Dauber, K. Rediscovering Hawthorne.*
    J. Arac, 153:Summer79-42

Dauer, A.M. and F. Kerschbaumer, eds. Jazzforschung/Jazz Research. (Vol 8)
    R. Middleton, 410(M&L):Apr79-218
Daumal, R. A Night of Serious Drinking.*
    M. Wood, 453(NYRB):17Apr80-41
Dauphin, J-P. - see "L-F. Céline 2 (1976)"
d'Aurevilly, J.B. - see under Barbey d'Aurevilly, J.
Davanture, M. La jeunesse de Maurice Barrès (1862-1888).
    M-C. Bancquart, 535(RHL):Jul-Aug78-668
Davenport, W.A. The Art of the Gawain-Poet.
    R.W.V. Elliott, 382(MAE):1979/2-312
    M. Godden, 175:Summer79-160
    D.R. Howard, 589:Jul79-561
    J. Strauss, 67:May79-87
    H.L.C. Tristram, 182:Vol131#7/8-228
    E. Wilson, 541(RES):Feb79-65
Davey, C.R., ed. Education in Hampshire and the Isle of Wight.
    R.J. Hind, 325:Oct79-237
Davey, F., ed. Tish No. 1-19.*
    D. Cooley, 105:Fall/Winter78-98
Davey, P. - see Lewis, W.
Daviau, D.G. and G.J. Buelow. The "Ariadne auf Naxos" of Hugo von Hofmannsthal and Richard Strauss.*
    P. Howe, 220(GL&L):Oct78-82
David, A. The Strumpet Muse.*
    L.W. Patterson, 627(UTQ):Spring79-263
    L.M. Sklute, 191(ELN):Jun79-325
David, A.R., ed. The Manchester Museum Mummy Project.
    N. Hammond, 617(TLS):8Feb80-147
David, C. - see Kafka, F.
David, E. - see Hobhouse, C.
David, J. and R. Martin, eds. Études de statistique linguistique.
    N.L. Corbett, 545(RPh):May79-478
    M. Hug, 209(FM):Jan78-90
David, J. and R. Martin, eds. Modèles logiques et niveaux d'analyse linguistique.
    N.C.W. Spence, 208(FS):Vol33Pt2-1070
    J. Stéfanini, 209(FM):Oct78-376
David, M-L. Du Noir pour du Bleu.
    L. Kovacs, 450(NRF):Aug79-127
David, N., ed. TV Season 1974-75; 1975-76; 1976-77.
    A.H. Marill, 200:Jan79-49
David, R. Shakespeare in the Theatre.
    R. Berry, 529(QQ):Autumn79-470
    W.L. Godshalk, 130:Winter79/80-372
    D. Marsh, 67:Nov79-316
    J.C. Trewin, 157:Spring79-80
    S. Wells, 617(TLS):28Mar80-370
Davidson, A. Antonio Gramsci.
    S. Hellman, 529(QQ):Spring79-141
Davidson, A. North Atlantic Seafood.
    M. Hodgson, 441:2Jul80-13
Davidson, A. Substance and Manner.
    P.J.P., 412:Aug-Nov78-289
Davidson, B. Special Operations Europe.
    D. Hunt, 362:31Jul80-148
Davidson, D. and G. Harman, eds. Semantics of Natural Language.
    A. Leist, 685(ZDL):1/1979-124

Davidson, E.H., C.M. Simpson and L.N. Smith - see Hawthorne, N.

Davidson, H.E. - see Saxo Grammaticus

Davidson, H.M. and P.H. Dubé, eds. A Concordance to Pascal's Pensées.
   J.H. Broome, 208(FS):Vol33Pt2-685

Davidson, J.W. The Logic of Millennial Thought.*
   B. Tucker, 173(ECS):Spring79-415

Davidson, L. Under Plum Lake.
   P. Zweig, 441:7Dec80-12

Davidson, R. Tracks.
   E.S. Turner, 362:18and25Dec80-862

Davidson, S. Real Property.
   J. Howard, 441:11May80-13
   C. Lehmann-Haupt, 441:18Jun80-C29

Davie, D. In the Stopping Train and Other Poems.*
   C. Bedient, 569(SR):Spring79-296

Davie, D. The Poet in the Imaginary Museum.* (B. Alpert, ed)
   R. von Hallberg, 114(ChiR):Summer78-108

Davie, D. Trying to Explain.
   B. Bergonzi, 617(TLS):23May80-578
   P.N. Furbank, 362:14Aug80-214

Davie, E. The Night of the Funny Hats.
   J. Mellors, 362:18and25Dec80-867
   J. Uglow, 617(TLS):18Apr80-430

Davie, M. - see Waugh, E.

Davies, A. Dictionary of British Portraiture. (Vol 1) (R. Ormond and M. Rogers, eds)
   D. Piper, 617(TLS):1Feb80-119

Davies, A.M. and W. Meid, eds. Studies in Greek, Italic, and Indo-European Linguistics Offered to Leonard R. Palmer.*
   W.P. Lehmann, 350:Sep79-694

Davies, G. Mallarmé et le rêve d'Hérodiade.
   D.J. Mossop, 208(FS):Jan79-97

Davies, G.A. A Poet at Court.
   G. Hughes, 539:Vol4No2-240

Davies, H. William Wordsworth.
   P. Beer, 362:31Jul80-150
   A. Broyard, 441:29Oct80-C27
   D. Grumbach, 441:14Dec80-11

Davies, J.B. The Psychology of Music.*
   42(AR):Fall79-488

Davies, R. Fifth Business. The Manticore. World of Wonders.
   D. Paschall, 569(SR):Winter79-180

Davies, R. A Mixture of Frailties.
   C.C. Park, 249(HudR):Winter79/80-579

Davies, R. One Half of Robertson Davies.*
   A. Mitchell, 102(CanL):Spring79-86
   D. Paschall, 569(SR):Winter79-180

Davies, R.H. Capital, State and White Labour in South Africa, 1900-1960.
   J. Lewin, 617(TLS):7Mar80-276

Davies, R.T., ed. The Corpus Christi Play of the English Middle Ages.
   T. Stemmler, 38:Band96Heft3/4-514

Davies, R.T. and B.G. Beatty, eds. Literature of the Romantic Period, 1750-
   [continued]

[continuing]
1850.*
   J. Blondel, 189(EA):Apr-Jun78-228
   E.D. Mackerness, 447(N&Q):Jun78-251

Davies, W. - see Wordsworth, W.

Davis, B. Sherman's March.
   P-L. Adams, 61:Jun80-94
   H. Mitgang, 441:25Aug80-C22
   442(NY):23Jun80-102

Davis, B.J. The Storytellers in Marguerite de Navarre's "Heptaméron."
   H. Sckommodau, 547(RF):Band91Heft1/2-207

Davis, C. Suicide Note.
   639(VQR):Spring78-66

Davis, C. Waiting for It.
   A. Broyard, 441:15Mar80-17

Davis, D. Artculture.*
   R. Whelan, 55:Nov79-42

Davis, D. Seeing the World.
   M. Schmidt, 617(TLS):4Jul80-762

Davis, D.B. The Problem of Slavery in the Age of Revolution, 1770-1823.
   L. Krieger, 473(PR):1/1979-152

Davis, D.S. Scarlet Night.
   A. Broyard, 441:5Jul80-11
   N. Callendar, 441:28Sep80-20

Davis, F. Eloquent Animals.
   R.E. Lemon, 529(QQ):Summer79-287

Davis, F-L. Primitive Revolutionaries of China.*
   J. Porter, 302:Vol16#1and2-119

Davis, F.M., Jr. Across the Rhine.
   C. James, 453(NYRB):18Dec80-22

Davis, H. - see Pope, A.

Davis, H.B. - see Luxemburg, R.

Davis, H.E., J.J. Finan and F.T. Peck. Latin American Diplomatic History.
   J.E. Fagg, 639(VQR):Winter79-188

Davis, J.G. Typhoon.
   639(VQR):Autumn79-138

Davis, M. William Blake.*
   I.H.C., 191(ELN):Sep78(supp)-46
   B.M. Stafford, 56:Winter79-118
   B. Stillians, 77:Summer78-86
   639(VQR):Winter78-25

Davis, M. The Potato Book.
   W. and C. Cowen, 639(VQR):Autumn79-154

Davis, M., ed. With Eyes Toward Zion.
   S. Adler, 390:Jun/Jul79-87

Davis, M., ed. World Jewry and the State of Israel.
   M. Brown, 390:Mar79-75

Davis, N., ed. Paston Letters and Papers of the Fifteenth Century.* (Pt 1)
   K.G. Madison, 589:Apr79-361

Davis, N., ed. Paston Letters and Papers of the Fifteenth Century.* (Pt 2)
   G.C. Britton, 447(N&Q):Aug78-358
   K.G. Madison, 589:Apr79-361

Davis, P. English Structure in Focus.
   S. Britsch, 351(LL):Jun79-209

Davis, R.B. Intellectual Life in the Colonial South, 1585-1763.*
   P. Marambaud, 656(WMQ):Jul79-469

Davis, R.B. George William Russell ("AE").
   R.M. Kain, 305(JIL):May78-177

88

Davis, S., Jr. Hollywood in a Suitcase.
  C. Kaiser, 441:12Oct80-18
Davis, S.H. Victims of the Miracle.*
  C. Henfrey, 86(BHS):Oct79-354
Davis, U. Israel.
  E. Zureik, 529(QQ):Summer79-281
Davis, W. Dojo.
  C. Blacker, 617(TLS):22Aug80-940
Davis, W.A. The Act of Interpretation.*
  R. Wellek, 402(MLR):Oct79-897
Davison, J. The Fall of a Doll's House.
  P-L. Adams, 61:May80-103
  A. Broyard, 441:9Jul80-C20
Davison, P. A Voice in the Mountain.*
  J. Parini, 639(VQR):Autumn78-762
Davison, P. - see Sissman, L.E.
d'Avost, H. Essais sur les Sonets du
  divin Petrarque. (K. Cameron and M.
  Constable, ed)
  D.G. Coleman, 208(FS):Vol33Pt2-644
Dawe, B. Sometimes Gladness.
  P. Law, 581:Jun79-192
  P. Martin, 581:Dec79-355
Dawe, G. Sheltering Places.
  T. Eagleton, 565:Vol20#3-75
  N. Jenckes, 174(Éire):Summer79-143
  J. Thibodeau, 174(Éire):Spring79-151
Dawisha, K. Soviet Foreign Policy Towards
  Egypt.
  A. Brown, 617(TLS):25Jan80-95
Daws, G. A Dream of Islands.
  E. Hoagland, 441:23Mar80-9
Dawson, C. Victorian Noon.*
  J. Diedrick, 401(MLQ):Sep79-317
  L. Poston, 594:Winter79-487
  J.H. Raleigh, 301(JEGP):Jul79-450
  A.J.S., 148:Winter79-91
Dawson, R.L. Baculard d'Arnaud.*
  V. Mylne, 208(FS):Vol33Pt2-778
Day, I. Ghost Waltz.
  C. Lehmann-Haupt, 441:4Dec80-C21
Day, P.S. Le Miroir allégorique de Louis-
  Ferdinand Céline.
  L. Davis, 208(FS):Vol33Pt2-892
Day, R.H. and I. Singh. Economic Develop-
  ment as an Adaptive Process.
  G. Blyn, 293(JASt):Aug79-817
Day-Lewis, S. C. Day-Lewis.
  B. Bergonzi, 617(TLS):21Mar80-310
  H. Corke, 362:20Mar80-373
Daymond, D. and L. Monkman, eds. Litera-
  ture in Canada.
  R.L. McDougall, 529(QQ):Winter79/80-
  714
Deagon, A. There Is No Balm in Birming-
  ham.*
  639(VQR):Winter79-25
Deák, I. The Lawful Revolution.*
  N. Stone, 617(TLS):1Aug80-871
  639(VQR):Autumn79-130
Dean, D.M. Defender of the Race.
  W.D. Boyd, 263(RIB):Vol29No3/4-362
Dean, S. Hardy's Poetic Vision in "The
  Dynasts."*
  W.E. Harrold, 125:Spring79-471
  J. Korg, 401(MLQ):Mar79-82
  M. Saunders, 395(MFS):Winter78/79-586

Deane, B. Alun Hoddinott.
  P. Griffiths, 415:Mar79-219
Deane, J.F. Stalking After Time.
  F. Kersnowski, 305(JIL):May78-179
Deane, S. Rumours.* Gradual Wars.
  R. Tracy, 109:Summer80-180
"Dear Comrade."
  A. Dynnik, 558(RLJ):Fall79-228
Deathridge, J. Wagner's "Rienzi."*
  A.E.F.D., 412:May78-129
  J.M. Knapp, 317:Spring79-158
  P.S. Machlin, 410(M&L):Apr79-204
  M. Saffle, 414(MusQ):Oct78-536
Debeauvais, M. L'Université ouverte.
  J-J. Thomas, 207(FR):Mar79-659
Debenedetti, G. Verga e il naturalismo.
  H. Grosser, 228(GSLI):Vol155fasc490-
  301
Debicki, A.P., ed. Antología de la
  poesía mexicana moderna.*
  205(FMLS):Apr78-183
Debnam, B. The Mini Page Kid's Cookbook.
  W. and C. Cowen, 639(VQR):Autumn79-157
De Bolt, J., ed. The Happening Worlds of
  John Brunner.
  K. Hume, 402(MLR):Jan79-192
De Bonnières, F. Guide de l'étudiant en
  russe.
  J.E.O. Screen, 575(SEER):Jan79-158
Debout, S. L'utopie de Charles Fourier.
  A. Reix, 542:Apr-Jun79-248
Debreczeny, P. and T. Eekman, eds.
  Chekhov's Art of Writing.
  J.W. Connolly, 399(MLJ):Sep-Oct79-319
  S.J. Rabinowitz, 574(SEEJ):Spring79-
  130
Debreuille, J-Y. Eluard ou le pouvoir du
  mot.
  E. Wayne, 207(FR):Dec78-356
Debussy, C. Debussy on Music.* (F.
  Lesure, comp; R.L. Smith, ed and trans)
  A.E.F.D., 412:Aug-Nov78-283
Décarie, V., with R. Houdé-Sauvé - see
  Aristotle
Décaudin, M., ed. Guillaume Apollinaire 9.
  Guillaume Apollinaire 10. Guillaume
  Apollinaire 11.
  G. Rees, 208(FS):Oct79-476
Décaudin, M., ed. Cendrars aujourd'hui —
  présence d'un romancier.
  S. Taylor, 402(MLR):Jul79-709
Decaux, E. Leçons de grammaire polonaise.
  R.A. Rothstein, 574(SEEJ):Winter79-
  561
De Cesare, G.B. - see Neruda, P.
"Declaration on Some Major Points in the
  Theological Doctrine of Professor Hans
  Küng."
  T. Sheehan, 453(NYRB):7Feb80-38
Decottignies, J. Prélude à "Maldoror."
  M. Bowie, 208(FS):Apr79-217
Décsy, G. Sprachherkunftsforschung.*
  (Vol 1)
  B. Rosenkranz, 343:Band23-164
Dedel, P. Johannes Brahms.
  R. Pascall, 410(M&L):Apr79-226

Dédéyan, C. La fortune de l'Arioste en France du XIXe siècle à nos jours.
  F. Claudon, 535(RHL):Jan-Feb79-150
De Domenico, E. Musset et l'Italie.
  S. Jeune, 535(RHL):Jul-Aug79-683
Dee, J. John Dee on Astronomy. (W. Shumaker, ed and trans)
  R.M. Schuler, 301(JEGP):Oct79-545
De Fanti, C., Jr. The Wages of Expectation.
  D. Aaron, 27(AL):Nov79-437
  42(AR):Spring79-254
De Felice, R. Ebrei in un paese arabo.
  S. Woolf, 617(TLS):8Feb80-153
Defoe, D. The Versatile Defoe.* (L.A. Curtis, ed)
  W.H., 148:Autumn79-90
De Francis, J. Colonialism and Language Policy in Viet Nam.
  J.K. Whitmore, 293(JASt):May79-620
De Francis, J. - see Mao Tse-tung
De Gaetano, A.L. Giambattista Gelli and the Florentine Academy.*
  M.P., 228(GSLI):Vol155fasc491-474
Deger, E. - see Du Bellay, J.
Deger-Jalkotzy, S. Fremde Zuwanderer im spätmykenischen Griechenland.*
  S. Sherratt, 303(JoHS):Vol199-200
Degering, T. Das Verhältnis von Individuum und Gesellschaft in Fontanes "Efi Briest" und Flauberts "Madame Bovary."
  F. Betz, 221(GQ):May79-423
Dégh, L. People in the Tobacco Belt.*
  B.L. Pearson, 582(SFQ):Vol141-263
Dégh, L., H. Glassie and F.J. Oinas, eds. Folklore Today.*
  U. Kutter, 196:Band19Heft3/4-316
  J.D.A. Widdowson, 203:Vol189#1-110
Degler, C.N. At Odds.
  C. Lasch, 453(NYRB):12Jun80-24
  L. Stone, 441:20Apr80-9
Degler, C.N. Place Over Time.
  D.L. Smiley, 579(SAQ):Winter79-125
De Gorog, R. and L.S. Concordancias del "Arcipreste de Talavera."
  E.M. Gerli, 304(JHP):Autumn79-87
De Gouy, L.P. The Gold Cookbook.
  W. and C. Cowen, 639(VQR):Spring79-76
Deguy, M. Jumelages suivi de Made in USA.
  S. Levy, 400(MLN):May79-888
Dei, A.D. - see under de Villa Dei, A.
Deichmann, F.W. Ravenna, Hauptstadt des spätantiken Abendlandes. (Vol 2, Pt 2)
  C. Delvoye, 182:Vol131#13-422
Deighton, L. The Battle of Britain.
  D. Hunt, 362:25Sep80-407
Deighton, L. Où Est le Garlic.
  W. and C. Cowen, 639(VQR):Spring78-71
Deighton, L. SS/GB.*
  639(VQR):Summer79-100
Deimer, G. Argumentative Dialoge.
  G. Öhlschläger, 686(ZGL):Band7Heft1-83
De Jean, J.E. Scarron's "Roman comique."
  J. Alter, 475:No.10Pt1-180
  P.V. Conroy, Jr., 207(FR):Feb79-483
  J. Lafond, 535(RHL):Sep-Oct79-850

"Dějiny Francouzské Literatury XIXe a XXe Stol." (Vol 2)
  M. Cermakian, 535(RHL):Jul-Aug78-681
Dekker, G. Coleridge and the Literature of Sensibility.*
  M. Baron, 175:Spring79-65
  D. Fairer, 541(RES):Nov79-481
  L. Goldstein, 661(WC):Summer79-256
Dekkers, R., P. Foriers, and C. Perelman, eds. L'égalité. (Vol 5)
  J-L. Gardies, 542:Oct-Dec79-482
Delacampagne, C. Figures de l'oppression.
  M. Pierssens, 98:Dec78-1151
Delafosse, L. Maurice Delafosse.*
  R. Cornevin, 69:Vol148#2-202
Delahaye, Y. La frontière et le texte.
  A. Jacob, 542:Jul-Sep78-379
Delaissé, L.M.J., J. Marrow and J. de Wit. The James A. de Rothschild Collection at Waddesdon Manor: Illuminated Manuscripts.
  L. Randall, 377:Jul79-117
Delale, A. and G. Ragache. La France de 68.
  M.G. Hydak, 399(MLJ):Apr79-218
Delamont, S. and L. Duffin, eds. The Nineteenth Century Woman.
  A. Davin, 637(VS):Summer79-477
Delany, P. D.H. Lawrence's Nightmare.*
  K.A. Herzinger, 594:Winter79-489
Delany, V. - see Cary, P.
Delatte, L., S. Govaerts and J. Denooz. Index du "Corpus Hermeticum."
  É. Des Places, 555:Vol52fasc2-385
Delattre, P. Walking on Air.
  J. Burke, 231:May80-90
  R. Miner, 441:15Jun80-14
"Sonia et Robert Delaunay."
  M. Sheringham, 208(FS):Oct79-487
De La Vega, S.L. and C.S. Parr. Avanzando.
  D.T. Gies, 238:May-Sep79-415
Delay, F. and J. Roubaud. Graal théâtre.
  B. Cerquiglini, 98:Mar78-298
Delay, J. Avant-Mémoire.
  M. Mohrt, 450(NRF):Aug79-109
Delaygues, J.C., A. Faivre and B. Teyssier. Les Auvergnats sont incroyables.
  H.L. Butler, 207(FR):Oct78-193
Delbanco, N. Stillness.
  F. Busch, 441:9Nov80-14
Delbono, F. - see Oswald von Wolkenstein
Deleon, D. The American as Anarchist.*
  639(VQR):Summer79-93
Deleuze, G. Différence et répétition.
  J-M. Salanskis, 98:Dec78-1155
Deleuze, G. Proust and Signs.
  M. Hollington, 349:Summer78-190
Deleuze, G. and F. Guattari. Anti-Oedipus.
  R. Jacoby, 529(QQ):Spring79-105
Deleuze, G. and F. Guattari. Kafka.
  R.R. Nicolai, 597(SN):Vol150#1-156
Delgado, A. The Annual Outing and Other Excursions.
  J. Burnett, 637(VS):Summer79-469
Delibes, M. Cinco horas con Mario.
  205(FMLS):Jul78-284

Delibes, M. El disputado voto del señor
Cayo.
T.A. Sackett, 399(MLJ):Nov79-392
Delicado, F. Retrato de la loçana anda-
luza. (B. Damiani and G. Allegra, eds)
S.P. Ghertman, 545(RPh):May79-468
De Lillo, D. Players.
J. Atlas, 473(PR):3/1979-482
639(VQR):Spring78-68
Della Corte, F. - see Catullus
Della Morte, P.M. - see under Militerni
della Morte, P.
Dell'Aquila, M. Primo romanticismo
italiano.
I.R., 228(GSLI):Vol155fasc490-315
Del Litto, V., ed. Stendhal et les prob-
lèmes de l'autobiographie.
F.W. Saunders, 208(FS):Vol33Pt2-806
Del Litto, V. - see Stendhal
Delmore, A. Truth is Stranger Than Public-
ity. (C.K. Wolfe, ed)
B.C. Malone, 585(SoQ):Spring-Summer79-
241
Deloffre, F. and M. Menemencioglu - see
Challe, R.
Deloffre, F. and J. Rougeot - see
Guilleragues
Deloria, E.C., ed. Dakota Texts.
J. Ramsey, 649(WAL):Fall79-231
Deloria, E.C. Speaking of Indians.
W. Bloodworth, 649(WAL):Fall79-235
Delp, P.S. The Gentle Way.
P. Dubois, 542:Jul-Sep79-352
Delpino, M.A.F. - see under Fugazzola
Delpino, M.A.
Delporte, H. L'image de la femme dans
l'art préhistorique.
R. Pittioni, 182:Vol131#23/24-873
Delsemme, P., R. Mortier and J. Detemmer-
man, eds. Regards sur les lettres fran-
çaises de Belgique.
J. Decreus, 208(FS):Vol33Pt2-988
Del Torre, M.A. Le origini moderne della
storiografia filosofica.
E. Namer, 542:Oct-Dec78-505
Délu, C. French Provincial Cuisine.
W. and C. Cowen, 639(VQR):Spring78-71
Delumeau, J. La peur en Occident (XIVe —
XVIIIe siècles).
B. Lacroix, 539:Vol4No2-227
Delzant, A. La Communication de Dieu.
A. Jacob, 542:Jul-Sep79-353
Delzell, C.F., ed. The Future of History.
N.C. Burckel, 125:Winter79-316
Dembowski, P.F., ed. La Vie de Sainte
Marie l'Egyptienne.*
W. Rothwell, 208(FS):Vol33Pt2-607
Deme, L. The Radical Left in the Hun-
garian Revolution of 1848.*
É.H. Haraszti, 104(CASS):Summer78-312
Demedts, A. De esthetica van Hugo
Verriest.
W. Gobbers, 556(RLV):1978/2-168
Demerson, G. - see de Baïf, J-A.
Demetz, H. The House on Prague Street.
N. Ascherson, 453(NYRB):12Jun80-34
442(NY):1Sep80-89

Demicheli, A.M. Rapporti di pace e di
guerra dell' Egitto romano con le popo-
lazioni dei deserti africani.
J.C. Mann, 313:Vol69-223
Deming, R.H. A Bibliography of James
Joyce Studies.* (2nd ed)
R.M. Kain, 395(MFS):Winter78/79-568
Démoris, R. Le Roman à la première per-
sonne.*
V. Mylne, 208(FS):Vol33Pt2-952
De Mott, R.J. and S.E. Marovitz, eds.
Artful Thunder.
B. Hitchcock, 577(SHR):Spring79-166
Dempsey, C. Annibale Carracci and the
Beginnings of Baroque Style.
C. Goldstein, 56:Winter79-112
D. Posner, 90:Jan79-44
N. Turner, 39:Mar79-237
Demus, O. - see Hutter, I.
Den Boeft, J. Calcidius on Demons.
A. Meredith, 123:Vol29No1-155
d'Encausse, H.C. - see under Carrère
d'Encausse, H.
Dendurent, H.O. Thomas De Quincey.
J.E. Jordan, 661(WC):Summer79-308
Denham, R.D. Northrop Frye and Critical
Method.*
F.W. Conner, 290(JAAC):Fall79-97
T. Hawkes, 676(YR):Summer80-560
M. Steig, 102(CanL):Winter79-190
Denham, R.D. - see Frye, N.
Denis, A. La Fortune littéraire et
théâtrale de Kotzebue en France pendant
la Révolution, le Consulat et l'Empire.
W.D. Howarth, 208(FS):Vol33Pt2-965
Denis, S., M. Maraval and L. Pompidou.
Dictionnaire Espagnol-Français et
Français-Espagnol.
J.J. Victorio, 556(RLV):1978/3-271
Denkler, H. Restauration and Revolution.
J. Hibberd, 182:Vol131#9/10-294
Dennerele, D. Kunst als Kommunikations-
prozess.*
J.F.F., 191(ELN):Sep78(supp)-143
Dennett, D.C. Brainstorms.
D.R. Hofstadter, 453(NYRB):29May80-32
Dennis, B. and B. Case. Houseboat.
505:Sep78-150
Dennis, G.T. - see Manuel II Palaeologus
Dennison, S. Sidehill Gouger or What's So
Deadly About Caterpillars.
C. McLay, 102(CanL):Autumn79-125
Dennon, J. The Salmon Cookbook.
W. and C. Cowen, 639(VQR):Spring79-77
Dent, E.J. Ferruccio Busoni.
A.F.L.T., 412:Feb78-69
Dent, P. Distant Lamps.
D. Davis, 362:28Aug80-277
Dentan, M. C.F. Ramuz.
R. Francillon, 535(RHL):Jul-Aug78-672
D.R. Haggis, 208(FS):Vol33Pt2-869
Denuzière, M. Louisiane.
R. Merker, 207(FR):Dec78-379
Denyer, S. African Traditional Architec-
ture.
D. Fraser, 2(AfrA):Nov78-14
[continued]

91

Denyer, S. African Traditional Architecture. [continuing]
E.L.R. Meyerowitz, 39:Jan79-73
P. Oliver, 46:Feb79-123
Déon, M. Mes Arches de Noé.
J.J. Carre, 207(FR):Apr79-790
De Osma, G. Mariano Fortuny.
S. Slesin, 441:14Dec80-29
"Department of Defense Annual Report, Fiscal Year 1981."
E. Rothschild, 453(NYRB):3Apr80-31
De Porte, M.V. Nightmares and Hobby-horses.*
D. Fairer, 447(N&Q):Dec78-560
Deprez, K. and G. Geerts. Lexical and Pronominal Standardization.
B. Panzer, 343:Band23-205
Deregibus, A. Frédéric Rauh, esperienza e moralità.
E. Namer, 542:Apr-Jun79-249
Der Hovanessian, D. and M. Margossian, eds and trans. Anthology of Armenian Poetry.
D.M. Thomas, 617(TLS):18Jan80-66
639(VQR):Autumn79-148
De Rivoyre, C. Le Voyage à l'envers.
M.E. Birkett, 207(FR):Dec78-379
Derogy, J. and H. Carmel. The Untold History of Israel.
R.L., 109:Summer80-226
Derrett, J.D.M., ed and trans. Bhāruci's Commentary on the Manusmṛti (The Manu-Śāstra-Vivarana, Books 6-12).*
J.W. De Jong, 259(IIJ):Jan79-57
L. Rocher, 318(JAOS):Apr-Jun78-194
Derrett, J.D.M. Essays in Classical and Modern Hindu Law. (Vol 2)
L. Rocher, 293(JASt):Feb79-410
Derrick, D. The Healer.
D.M. Day, 157:Winter79-88
Derrida, J. La Carte Postale.
C. Norris, 617(TLS):4Jul80-761
Derrida, J. Edmund Husserl's "Origin of Geometry."
R.M. Martin, 484(PPR):Mar80-436
Derrida, J. Of Grammatology.*
H.M. Davidson, 131(CL):Spring79-167
J.S. Hans, 400(MLN):May79-809
Derrida, J. Writing and Difference.
W.E. Cain, 569(SR):Fall79-xciii
Desai, A. Clear Light of Day.
G. Annan, 617(TLS):5Sep80-948
P. Kemp, 362:21Aug80-249
J. Leonard, 441:24Nov80-C18
A. Tyler, 441:23Nov80-1
Desai, A. Games at Twilight.*
A. Adams, 441:22Jun80-12
Desanti, D. Drieu la Rochelle ou le séducteur mystifié.
E. Weber, 617(TLS):6Jun80-631
Desanti, J.T. Les idéalités mathématiques. La philosophie silencieuse.
Y. Gauthier, 98:Jan78-3
Descalzo, J.L.M. - see under Martín Descalzo, J.L.
Des Cars, G. Le Château du Clown.
J.D. Erickson, 207(FR):Feb79-510

"Descriptive Inventory of the Archives of the State of Illinois."
M.E. Deutrich, 14:Apr79-201
Désilets, G. O que la vie est ronde.
M. Recurt, 102(CanL):Spring79-98
De Silva, M.W.S. and G.D. Wijayawardhana - see under Sugathapala De Silva, M.W. and G.D. Wijayawardhana
Désiré, A. Le Contrepoison des cinquante-deux chansons de Clément Marot.* (J. Pineaux, ed)
P.M. Smith, 402(MLR):Jan79-196
D. Stone, Jr., 207(FR):Feb79-480
Desmond, J.F., ed. A Still Moment.
M. Kreyling, 579(SAQ):Summer79-412
D.M. Scura, 577(SHR):Fall79-357
"DESMOS - Aphieröma ston I.N. Theodōrako-poulo." [title in Greek]
T. Nikolaou, 53(AGP):Band60Heft1-108
Desmouliez, A. Cicéron et son goût.*
E. De Saint-Denis, 555:Vol152fasc2-331
Des Places, É. - see Atticus
Dessain, C.S. Newman's Spiritual Themes.
A. Billioque, 189(EA):Jul-Dec78-404
Dessen, A.C. Elizabethan Drama and the Viewer's Eye.*
W.W. Wooden, 577(SHR):Summer79-248
Dessner, L.J. The Homely Web of Truth.*
S.M. Gilbert, 637(VS):Winter78-263
Destler, I.M. and others. Managing an Alliance.
A. Iriye, 293(JASt):May79-590
De Stoop, C. Drama in Barak 15.
M-C. Bergans-Libioul, 556(RLV):1978/5-464
Desvignes, M. Demain, la participation.
J. Hardré, 207(FR):Apr79-806
Detalle, A. Mythes, merveilleux et légendes dans la poésie française de 1840 à 1860.*
E. Pich, 535(RHL):May-Jun78-495
d'Étaples, J.L. and others - see under Lefèvre d'Étaples, J. and others
Detel, W. Scientia rerum natura occulta-rum.
K. Fischer, 687:Oct-Dec79-644
Dethan, G. The Young Mazarin.*
639(VQR):Spring78-47
Dethloff, U. Das Romanwerk Gustave Flau-berts.*
R. Huss, 208(FS):Vol33Pt2-832
Detienne, M. Dionysos mis à mort.*
R.C.T. Parker, 123:Vol29No1-168
Detienne, M. Dionysos Slain.
S. Pembroke, 617(TLS):11Jan80-43
C.A.P. Ruck, 124:Mar80-370
Deuchler, M. Confucian Gentlemen and Barbarian Envoys.
Y.I. Lew, 293(JASt):Feb79-382
639(VQR):Winter79-12
D'Eugenio, A. L'Insegnamento della Pronuncia Inglese agli Italiani. (Vol 1)
E. La Pergola Arezzo, 399(MLJ):Jan-Feb79-65
Deutsch, O.E. Schubert. (rev by W. Dürr and others)
E. Sams, 415:Jul79-577

"Deutsche Shakespeare-Gesellschaft West, Jahrbuch 1975." (H. Heuer, with E.T. Sehrt and R. Stamm, eds)
W. Zacharasiewicz, 677(YES):Vol9-319
"Deutsche Shakespeare-Gesellschaft West, Jahrbuch 1976." (H. Heuer, with E.T. Sehrt and R. Stamm, eds)
C. Barker, 402(MLR):Oct79-899
"Deutsches Fremdwörterbuch." (Vol 3, Pts 1 and 2) (O. Basler and others, eds)
W. Betz, 72:Band216Heft1-152
Deva, B.C. Musical Instruments of India, Their History and Development.
E.O. Henry, 187:May80-302
Deverell, W.H. Needles.*
K. Gibson, 99:Jun-Jul80-33
Devine, D.J. Does Freedom Work?
D.K. Adie, 396(ModA):Winter79-91
Devine, P.E. The Ethics of Homicide.
R.J. Regan, 258:Dec79-501
Devisse, J. Hincmar, archévêque de Reims, 845-882.*
W. Goffart, 589:Oct79-793
Devisse, J. The Image of the Black in Western Art. (Vol 2, Pt 1)
J. Russell, 441:29Jun80-7
Devisse, J. and M. Mollat. The Image of the Black in Western Art. (Vol 2, Pt 2)
J. Russell, 441:29Jun80-7
Devlin, P. Vogue Book of Fashion Photography, 1919-79.
442(NY):14Jan80-104
Devoto, G. The Languages of Italy.
H. Haller, 276:Autumn79-297
Devoto, M. - see Piston, W.
De Vries, D. Dickens's Apprentice Years.*
E. Engel, 405(MP):Aug79-102
R. Maxwell, 637(VS):Winter79-216
De Vries, H. "Materia mirable."
A. Deyermond, 545(RPh):May79-458
De Vries, P. Consenting Adults.
C. Cerf, 441:17Aug80-1
J. Leonard, 441:31Jul80-C18
442(NY):18Aug80-92
Dewald, J. The Formation of a Provincial Nobility.
R.J. Knecht, 617(TLS):6Jun80-652
Dewdney, S. Christopher Breton.
S. Atherton, 628(UWR):Spring-Summer79-111
Dewey, J. Lectures on Psychological and Political Ethics: 1898.* (D.F. Koch, ed)
J. Barnouw, 543:Jun79-745
Dewey, J. The Middle Works of John Dewey, 1899-1924. (Vols 5 and 6) (J.A. Boydston, ed)
J. Gouinlock, 484(PPR):Mar80-436
Dewhurst, J. Royal Confinements.
E.S. Turner, 362:20Nov80-694
Dewhurst, K. and N. Reeves. Friedrich Schiller.
C.G. Grawe, 67:Nov79-359
R.W. Pickford, 89(BJA):Summer79-276
Dewlen, A. Next of Kin.
639(VQR):Winter78-24

Dexter, C. Service of All the Dead.
T.J. Binyon, 617(TLS):7Mar80-258
N. Callendar, 441:10Feb80-22
Deyermond, A.D., ed. Medieval Hispanic Studies Presented to Rita Hamilton.*
S.G. Armistead, 240(HR):Winter78-89
F. Hodcroft, 86(BHS):Jan79-54
Deyermond, A.D., ed. "Mio Cid" Studies.
D. Eisenberg, 304(JHP):Winter80-169
L.P. Harvey, 86(BHS):Jul79-241
Dezső, L. and P. Hajdú, eds. Theoretical Problems of Typology and the Northern Eurasian Languages.
G.F. Meier, 682(ZPSK):Band31Heft2-210
Dhamotharan, A. Tamil Dictionaries.
J. Filliozat, 182:Vol31#19-666
d'Hondt, J. L'idéologie de la rupture.
A. Reix, 542:Oct-Dec78-512
d'Hondt, J., ed. La logique de Marx.
J-M. Gabaude, 542:Apr-Jun79-266
Dhôtel, A. Bonne Nuit Barbara.
N. Kostis, 207(FR):Apr79-791
Dhôtel, A. L'Ile de la Croix d'Or.
L. Kovacs, 450(NRF):Mar79-113
Dhôtel, A. La Vie passagère.
D. Leuwers, 450(NRF):Aug79-105
d'Hulst, R-A. Jordaens Drawings.
J.S. Held, 54:Dec78-717
Diakonoff, I.M. and V.A. Livshits. Corpus Inscriptionum Iranicarum. (Pt 2, Vol 2) (D.N. Mackenzie, ed)
C.J. Brunner, 318(JAOS):Apr-Jun78-132
Diamond, C. - see Wittgenstein, L.
Diamond, I. Sex Roles in the State House.
639(VQR):Spring78-63
Diamond, S. In Search of the Primitive.
D. Hymes, 292(JAF):Oct-Dec79-491
Diamonstein, B. Buildings Reborn.*
D.S., 109:Summer80-225
Diaz, F. Il Granducato di Toscana: I Medici.
M.P., 228(GSLI):Vol155fasc490-319
Díaz, J.S. - see under Simón Díaz, J.
Díaz Tejera, A. - see Polybius
d'Iberville-Moreau, L. Lost Montreal.
F. Toker, 576:Mar78-64
Di Cesare, M.A. and R. Mignani, eds. A Concordance to the Complete Writings of George Herbert.*
D.W. Doerksen, 539:Vol4No1-117
Di Cicco, P.G. The Circular Dark.*
R.B. Hatch, 102(CanL):Summer79-129
Di Cicco, P.G. The Tough Romance.*
D. Barbour, 150(DR):Spring79-154
Di Cicco, P.G. We Are the Light Turning.
B. Whiteman, 168(ECW):Spring78-57
Dick, P.K. Clans of the Alphane Moon.
G. Jonas, 441:11May80-22
Dickens, C. Bleak House. (A. Calder-Marshall, ed)
P. Preston, 447(N&Q):Jun78-262
Dickens, C. Bleak House. (G. Ford and S. Monod, eds)
M. Salter, 617(TLS):20Jun80-716
H.P. Sucksmith, 155:Summer79-107

van Dijk, J. Texts in the Iraq Museum.
(Vol 9)
B. Groneberg and H. Hunger, 318(JAOS):
Oct-Dec78-521
van Dijk, T.A. Text and Context.
J.F. Kess, 257(IRAL):Aug79-268
I. Pörn, 399(MLJ):Jan-Feb79-63
A-M. Simon-Vandenbergen, 179(ES):Dec79-824
van Dijk, T.A. and J.S. Petöfi, eds. Grammars and Descriptions.
W. Nöth, 307:Apr79-58
Dijkstra, B. - see Williams, W.C.
Dik, S.C. Functional Grammar.*
B. Comrie, 603:Vol3#2-267
Dil, A.S. - see Chao, Y.R.
Dilke, O.A.W. Roman Books and their Impact.*
H.L. Kessler, 24:Fall79-447
Dill, H-O. Sieben Aufsätze zur latein-amerikanischen Literatur.
C. Lucyga, 654(WB):12/1978-187
Dillard, J.L. American Talk.*
K.B. Harder, 424:Sep77-174
Dillard, J.L. Black English.
R.W. Wescott, 660(Word):Aug78-186
Dillard, J.L. Lexicon of Black English.*
R.W. Wescott, 292(JAF):Oct-Dec79-509
Dillard, J.L. Perspectives on Black English.
M.M. Bryant, 660(Word):Aug78-191
Dille, G.F., ed. La comedia llamada Serafina.
R.L. Hathaway, 304(JHP):Autumn79-88
Dillenberger, J. Benjamin West.
R. Kraemer, 54:Sep78-564
Diller, H-J. and J. Kornelius. Linguistische Probleme der Übersetzung.
C.V.J. Russ, 541(RES):Nov79-446
Dillingham, W.B. Melville's Short Fiction, 1853-1856.*
H. Golemba, 141:Summer79-285
D.L. Parker, 454:Winter79-190
E.H. Redekop, 106:Fall79-175
M.M. Sealts, Jr., 183(ESQ):Vol125#1-43
E.J. Wilcox, 573(SSF):Fall78-466
N. Wright, 580(SCR):Nov78-122
Dillon, B. A Malory Handbook.
M. Lambert, 589:Apr79-400
Dillon, G.L. Introduction to Contemporary Linguistic Semantics.*
D.A. Cruse, 297(JL):Mar79-145
D. Wilson, 350:Jun79-423
Dillon, J. The Middle Platonists 80 B.C. to A.D. 220.*
H.J. Blumenthal, 303(JoHS):Vol199-190
A. Madigan, 613:Mar79-107
G.J.P. O'Daly, 518:Jan79-12
Dilman, I. Morality and the Inner Life.
T. Irwin, 617(TLS):20Jun80-712
Dilworth, D. and J.T. Rimer - see Ōgai, M.
Di Marco V. and L. Perelman. The Middle English "Letter of Alexander to Aristotle."
H.L.C. Tristram, 182:Vol131#15/16-539
Dimbleby, G. Plants and Archaeology.
N. Hammond, 617(TLS):8Feb80-147

Dimbleby, J. The Palestinians.*
442(NY):26May80-128
Dimmitt, C. and J.A.B. van Buitenen, eds and trans. Classical Hindu Mythology.
K.E. Bryant, 293(JASt):Aug79-788
Dimock, E.C., Jr. and others. The Indian Literature.
P. Gaeffke, 318(JAOS):Oct-Dec78-548
Dinesen, I. The Angelic Avengers.*
L. Hartley, 569(SR):Winter79-169
Dinesen, I. Carnival.*
F. Gado, 573(SSF):Summer78-334
L. Hartley, 569(SR):Winter79-169
Y.L. Sandstroem, 563(SS):Winter79-78
Dinesen, I. Daguerreotypes and Other Essays.*
A. Born, 617(TLS):4Apr80-392
Dinesen, I. - see also under Blixen, K.
Dingelstedt, F. Lieder eines kosmopolitischen Nachtwächters. (H-P. Bayerdörfer, ed)
J.L. Sammons, 221(GQ):May79-422
Dinges, J. and S. Landau. Assassination on Embassy Row.
T. Hauser, 441:27Jul80-9
N. von Hoffman, 453(NYRB):25Sep80-20
C. Lehmann-Haupt, 441:10Jul80-C18
Dinkelacker, I. and W. Häring - see Wyssenherre, M.
Dinkin, R.J. Voting in Provincial America.*
D.C. Skaggs, 656(WMQ):Jan79-127
Dinser, G. Kohärenz und Struktur.*
H. Stopp, 684(ZDA):Band107Heft2-57
Diodorus Siculus. Diodore de Sicile, "Bibliothèque historique." (Bk 15)
(C. Vial, ed and trans)
N.G.L. Hammond, 123:Vol29No1-143
Diodorus Siculus. Diodore de Sicile, "Bibliothèque historique."* (Bk 17) (P. Goukowsky, ed and trans)
M. Casevitz, 555:Vol52fasc1-171
Dion, A.P. Auto-Correct-Art.
R.J. Melpignano, 399(MLJ):Nov79-383
Dionne, N-E. Le Parler populaire des Canadiens français.
R. Robidoux, 208(FS):Vol33Pt2-1064
D.F. Rogers, 320(CJL):Spring-Fall78-186
Dionysius of Halicarnassus. The Critical Essays.* (Vol 1) (S. Usher, trans)
M. McCall, 24:Summer79-318
Dionysius of Halicarnassus. Opuscules rhétoriques. (Vol 1) (G. Aujac, ed and trans)
S. Usher, 303(JoHS):Vol199-182
Di Perna, P. The Complete Travel Guide to Cuba.
639(VQR):Autumn79-151
Dippel, H. Germany and the American Revolution, 1770-1800.*
R. Howell, Jr., 182:Vol131#1/2-52
639(VQR):Autumn78-147
"Directory of Archives and Manuscript Repositories in the United States."
D. Bearman, 14:Jul79-350

Dirlik, A. Revolution and History.*
C. Furth, 293(JASt):Aug79-754
Dirlmeier, U. Untersuchungen zu Einkommensverhältnissen und Lebenshaltungskosten in Oberdeutschen Städten des Spätmittelalters.
B. Arnold, 182:Vol131#3/4-117
Dirscherl, K. Zur Typologie der poetischen Sprechweisen bei Baudelaire.
G. Chesters, 208(FS):Vol133Pt2-829
H. Stenzel, 535(RHL):Sep-Oct78-852
Dirven, R. and others. Die Leistung der Linguistik für den Englischunterricht.
D. Goyvaerts, 556(RLV):1978/6-555
"Disposition of Federal Records."
M.V. Lewellyn, 14:Jul79-357
Disraeli, B. Sybil.
M. Foot, 617(TLS):18Apr80-433
Ditsky, J. Essays on "East of Eden."
S. Cohen, 577(SHR):Summer79-273
Dittmann, J. Sprechhandlungstheorie und Tempusgrammatik.
W. Zydatiss, 257(IRAL):May79-169
Dittmar, N. A Critical Survey of Sociolinguistics.
G.D. Bills, 350:Jun79-454
R.B. Le Page, 297(JL):Mar79-168
Dittmar, N. Sociolinguistics.*
B.R. Lavandera, 355(LSoc):Dec78-421
Ditton, J. Copley's Hunch.
M. Laski, 362:14Aug80-216
Dittrich, E. Das Westzimmer: Hsi-hsiang chi.
J. Hiller, 463:Winter78/79-463
Diurni, G. L'"Expositio ad Librum Papiensem" e la scienza giuridica preirneriana.
J.A.C. Smith, 589:Oct79-796
"Divers aspects de la réforme aux XVIe et XVIIe siècles."
F.M. Higman, 208(FS):Vol133Pt2-656
Diwald, S. Arabische Philosophie und Wissenschaft in der Enzyklopädie: Kitāb Iḫwān aṣ-ṣafā'. (Pt 3)
A. Hamdani, 318(JAOS):Apr-Jun78-158
"18 millions de bonnes à tout faire."
E. Gelfand, 207(FR):May79-947
Dixon, R.M.W. A Grammar of Yidinj.
B. Comrie, 361:Oct/Nov78-281
J. Heath, 350:Sep79-706
D.T. Tryon, 67:May79-180
Dixon, R.M.W., ed. Grammatical Categories in Australian Languages.
B. Comrie, 361:May78-79
R.H. Robins, 297(JL):Mar79-141
D.T. Tyron, 67:May79-182
Dixon, S. No Relief.
W. Koon, 573(SSF):Spring78-207
T.A. Stumpf, 580(SCR):Nov78-129
Dixon, S. Work.
T.A. Stumpf, 580(SCR):Nov78-129
Djamîn, N. Le Départ de l'Enfant Prodigue.
J.M. Echols, 318(JAOS):Jul-Sep78-329
Djaout, T. Solstice barbelé.
J. Bryson, 207(FR):Oct78-177
DjeDje, J.C. American Black Spiritual and Gospel Songs from Southeast Georgia.
D. Evans, 187:Sep80-587

Djerassi, C. The Politics of Contraception.
A. Hacker, 441:10Feb80-7
Djilas, M. Tito.
D. Binder, 441:16Nov80-13
J. Leonard, 441:21Oct80-C11
442(NY):15Dec80-170
Dlugosch, I. Anton Pavlovič Čechov und das Theater des Absurden.*
Y. Elliott, 575(SEER):Jul79-433
C. Saal-Losq, 550(RusR):Jan79-127
Dmytryshyn, B. A History of Russia.*
P. Call, 104(CASS):Fall78-427
G.A. Hosking, 575(SEER):Jan79-153
Doane, A.N. Genesis A.*
S.B. Greenfield, 301(JEGP):Apr79-244
Dobai, J. Die Kunstliteratur des Klassizismus und der Romantik in England. (Vol 3)
G.C. Rump, 576:Dec78-307
Dobbs, B. and J. Dante Gabriel Rossetti.
D. Sonstroem, 637(VS):Winter79-230
Dobkin, M.H. - see Thomas, M.C.
Doblhofer, E., ed. Rutilus Claudius Namatianus. (Vol 2)
M.P. McHugh, 124:Nov79-194
Dobremez, J-F. Le Népal.
U. Schweinfurth, 182:Vol131#23/24-894
Dobrinsky, J. La Jeunesse de Somerset Maugham (1874-1903).
R.L. Calder, 189(EA):Jul-Dec78-331
L.D. Joiner, 395(MFS):Winter78/79-601
"Dobromirovo Evangelie."
F. Otten, 688(ZSP):Band40Heft2-440
Dobson, R.B. and J. Taylor. Rymes of Robyn Hood.
L. Haring, 292(JAF):Jan-Mar79-101
Dobyns, H.F. and P.L. Doughty. Peru.*
J. Higgins, 86(BHS):Jan79-90
Dobyns, S. Griffon.
639(VQR):Winter78-13
Dockstader, F.J. Great North American Indians.*
A.P. Merriam, 292(JAF):Jul-Sep79-346
Doctorow, E.L. Loon Lake.
W. Balliett, 442(NY):8Dec80-232
B. De Mott, 61:Sep80-105
D. Johnson, 453(NYRB):6Nov80-18
P. Kemp, 362:4Dec80-765
C. Lehmann-Haupt, 441:12Sep80-C21
R. Towers, 441:28Sep80-1
Dodderidge, E. The New Gulliver.
J. Mellors, 362:22May80-660
P. Rogers, 617(TLS):9May80-538
Dodds, E.R. Missing Persons.*
E. Delavenay, 189(EA):Jul-Dec78-415
P. Levi, 123:Vol29No1-132
Dodds, E.R. - see MacNeice, L.
Doderer, K., ed. Lexicon der Kinder — und Jugendliteratur. (Vol 3)
B. Alderson, 617(TLS):19Sep80-1032
Dody, S. Giving Up the Ghost.
C. Seebohm, 441:16Mar80-15
Doebele-Flügel, V. Die Lerche.
H. Rölleke, 196:Band19Heft1/2-138

Donnelly, M.C. A Short History of Observatories.
J-C. Klamt, 683:Band41Heft2-172
Donner, F.J. The Age of Surveillance.
P. Taubman, 441:11Aug80-C16
Donner, W. The Five Faces of Thailand.
J.A. Hafner, 293(JASt):May79-618
Donnert, E. Johann Georg Eisen, 1717-1779.
R.P. Bartlett, 575(SEER):Jul79-446
Donnini, C. Contributo a una cronologia del lessico spagnolo.
R. Wright, 86(BHS):Jul79-273
Donno, E. - see Madox, R.
Donno, E.S., ed. Andrew Marvell: The Critical Heritage.*
B. Worden, 541(RES):Nov79-469
Donoghue, D. The Sovereign Ghost.*
D.V.E., 191(ELN):Sep78(supp)-20
R.F. Gleckner, 661(WC):Summer79-283
Donohue, J. Theatre in the Age of Kean.
C.S. Stern, 637(VS):Autumn77-123
Donoso, J. The Boom in Spanish American Literature.*
M.P. Levitt, 295(JML):Vol7#4-575
Donoso, J. Sacred Families.
639(VQR):Spring78-68
Donovan, D.G. and A.L. Deneef, eds. Renaissance Papers 1975.
J.M. Kennedy, 402(MLR):Jan79-132
Donovan, L.G. Recherches sur le Roman de Thèbes.
A.H. Diverres, 208(FS):Vol33Pt2-526
A. Iker-Gittleman, 545(RPh):Nov78-252
Donovan, R.J. Conflict and Crisis.*
C. Kilpatrick, 639(VQR):Summer78-560
H.P. Luks, 287:Jun/Jul78-27
Donzelot, J. The Policing of Families.
C. Lasch, 453(NYRB):12Jun80-24
R. Sennett, 441:24Feb80-3
Doob, L.W. - see Pound, E.
Doody, M. The Alchemists.
J. Mellors, 362:24Apr80-546
A.N. Wilson, 617(TLS):25Apr80-470
Dor, M. Maps of Time.
A. Cluysenaar, 565:Vol20#3-68
Doran, M. Shakespeare's Dramatic Language.*
A.B. Kernan, 570(SQ):Winter79-101
Dorey, T.A. - see Livy
Dörflinger, J. Die Geographie in der "Encyclopédie."
J. Proust, 535(RHL):Sep-Oct78-831
Döring, K. Exemplum Socratis.
F. Lasserre, 182:Vol131#23/24-880
Dorion, G. Presence de Paul Bourget au Canada.*
K. Mezei, 102(CanL):Winter79-194
D'Ormesson, J. At God's Pleasure.
639(VQR):Spring78-68
Dorn, E. Hello, La Jolla.
S.S. Moorty, 649(WAL):Winter80-340
N. Wheale, 493:Dec79-43
Dorn, E. Interviews.
J. Campbell, 617(TLS):30May80-620
Dorn, E. Rules and Racial Equality.
A. Hacker, 453(NYRB):20Mar80-20

Dorn, E. Selected Poems. (D. Allen, ed)
P. Breslin, 491:Jul80-219
G. Butterick, 114(ChiR):Winter79-157
Dörner, F.C., with M-B. von Stritzky, eds. Tituli Asiae Minoris. (Vol 4, fasc 1)
J.H. Oliver, 24:Winter79-590
Doron, P. - see Kalomiti, N.
Dörrenhaus, F. Villa und Villegiatura in der Toscana.
L.O. Larsson, 341:1978/2-77
Dorschner, J. and R. Fabricio. The Winds cf December.
H. Thomas, 441:15Jun80-3
Dorsey, J., ed. On Mencken.
J. Kaplan, 441:7Sep80-1
D'Orsi, D. - see Spaventa, B.
Dortu, M.G. Toulouse-Lautrec et son oeuvre. (P. Brame and C.M. de Hauke, eds)
G.B. Murray, 54:Mar78-179
Dorul'a, J. Slováci v Dejinách Jazykových Vzt'ahov.
H. Galton, 361:Aug78-374
P. Petro, 574(SEEJ):Spring79-144
Dossi, C. Amori. (D. Isella, ed)
G. Pacchiano, 228(GSLI):Vol155fasc492-623
Dossi, C. La critica e Dossi. (L. Avellini, ed)
F. Marri, 228(GSLI):Vol155fasc492-601
Dotoli, G. Il Cerchio aperto.
R. Guichemerre, 535(RHL):Sep-Oct79-847
Dotoli, G. Jean Mairet: dalla Finzione alla Realtà.
H.T. Barnwell, 208(FS):Vol33Pt2-671
Dotoli, G. Matière et Dramaturgie dans le Théâtre de Jean Mairet.*
R. Guichemerre, 535(RHL):Sep-Oct78-820
Dotti, U. Petrarca e la scoperta della coscienza moderna.
E.B., 228(GSLI):Vol155fasc491-471
N. Mann, 617(TLS):2May80-502
de' Dottori, C. Galatea. (A. Daniele, ed)
M.M., 228(GSLI):Vol155fasc491-475
Doty, C. A Day Late.
R. Bradford, 441:4May80-14
A. Broyard, 441:16Apr80-C28
Doty, C.S. From Cultural Rebellion to Counterrevolution.
P.A. Ouston, 208(FS):Vol33Pt2-852
Doughty, C.M. Travels in Arabia Deserta.
G. Strawson, 617(TLS):12Sep80-1000
Douglas, A. The Feminization of American Culture.*
G. Stephens, 473(PR):4/1979-620
Douglas, C. The Houseman's Tale.
639(VQR):Autumn79-136
Douglas, D. Henry Handel Richardson's "Maurice Guest."
A. Mitchell, 71(ALS):Oct79-248
Douglas, G.H. H.L. Mencken.
L. Filler, 42(AR):Spring79-250
Douglas, M. and B. Isherwood. The World of Goods.*
D. Martin, 617(TLS):20Jun80-711

Douglas, N. and P. Slinger. Sexual
Secrets.
    P. Redgrove and P. Shuttle, 617(TLS):
    18Jul80-819
Douglas, W.O. The Court Years, 1939-1975.
    A.M. Dershowitz, 441:2Nov80-9
    C. Lehmann-Haupt, 441:30Sep80-C12
Douglass, F. The Frederick Douglass
Papers. (Ser 1, Vol 1) (J.W. Blassin-
game, ed)
    E. Wright, 617(TLS):25Jan80-91
Douglass, W.A., R.W. Etulain and W.A.
Jacobsen, Jr., eds. Anglo-American Con-
tributions to Basque Studies.
    L. Bloom, 238:Mar79-182
    D. Gifford, 86(BHS):Jul79-240
Douin de Lavesne. Trubert, fabliau du
XIIIe siècle.* (G. Raynaud de Lage, ed)
    W.G. van Emden, 208(FS):Vol33Pt2-567
Doulis, T. Disaster and Fiction.*
    M. Koutsoudaki, 395(MFS):Summer78-301
Doumas, C. Early Bronze Age Burial Habits
in the Cyclades.
    K. Branigan, 303(JoHS):Vol199-198
Doumet, C. Les thèmes aériens dans
l'oeuvre de Saint-John Perse.
    A. Berrie, 208(FS):Vol33Pt2-885
Dourado, A. Uma poética de romance.
    M. Silverman, 240(HR):Winter78-112
Dourado, A. Voices of the Dead.
    J. Naughton, 362:20Nov80-700
Dournon-Taurelle, G. and J. Wright. Les
guimbardes du Musée de l'Homme.
    O.K. Ledang, 187:Sep80-599
Doutreleau, L. - see Origen
Douyère, S.E. - see Flaubert, G.
Dover, K.J. Greek Homosexuality.*
    J.A.S. Evans, 529(QQ):Autumn79-493
Dow, F.D. Cromwellian Scotland, 1651-1660.
    E. Playfair, 617(TLS):22Feb80-216
Dower, J.W. Empire and Aftermath.
    R. Storry, 617(TLS):5Sep80-970
Dowling, J. Diego de Saavedra Fajardo.*
    M.Z. Hafter, 240(HR):Autumn78-496
Downes, E. Everyman's Guide to Orchestral
Music.
    A. Jacobs, 415:Apr79-310
Downes, K. Vanbrugh.
    A. Gomme, 46:Feb79-123
Downes, L.S. Palavras amigas da onça.
(2nd ed)
    J.B. Jensen, 399(MLJ):Apr79-235
    N.J. Lamb, 86(BHS):Jul79-277
Downes, P. Shadows on the Stage.
    J. Dale, 368:Dec75-352
Downie, J.A. Robert Harley and the Press.
    G.S. Holmes, 617(TLS):18Apr80-428
Downing, D. The Devil's Virtuosos.
    639(VQR):Spring78-60
Downing, D. and G. Herman. War Without
End, Peace Without Hope.
    E. Zureik, 529(QQ):Summer79-281
Downs, R.B. Books That Changed the South.
    C.B. Green, 580(SCR):Spring79-78
    J.B. Meriwether, 27(AL):Mar79-132
Doyle, A.C. Tales of Terror and Mystery.
    H. Lachtman, 573(SSF):Winter78-117

Doyle, C., ed. William Carlos Williams:
The Critical Heritage.
    S. Fender, 617(TLS):30May80-617
Doyle, M. Stonedancer.*
    A. Amprimoz, 102(CanL):Winter78-92
Doz, A. - see Hegel, G.W.F.
Drabble, M., ed. The Genius of Thomas
Hardy.*
    B. Johnson, 637(VS):Spring78-405
Drabble, M. The Ice Age.*
    639(VQR):Summer78-93
Drabble, M. The Middle Ground.
    W. Boyd, 617(TLS):11Jul80-772
    A. Broyard, 441:6Sep80-19
    D. Donoghue, 453(NYRB):20Nov80-20
    D.A.N. Jones, 362:3Jul80-24
    P. Rose, 441:7Sep80-1
    F. Taliaferro, 231:Oct80-90
    61:Nov80-96
Drabble, M. A Writer's Britain.*
    P. Beer, 362:17Jan80-94
Drachenberg, E., K-J. Maercker and C.
Schmidt. Die mittelalterliche Glasmale-
rei in den Ordenskirchen und im Anger-
museum zu Erfurt.
    M.P. Lillich, 90:Jun79-386
Drack, W., ed. Ur- und frühgeschichtliche
Archäologie der Schweiz. (Vol 6)
    R. Pittioni, 182:Vol131#20-751
Dragisic, P. From the Medley.
    D. Barbour, 150(DR):Spring79-154
Drain, M., R. Lhénaff and J.R. Vanney. Le
Bas Guadalquivir.
    J. Naylon, 86(BHS):Jan79-75
Draitser, E., ed. Forbidden Laughter.
    P-L. Adams, 61:Feb80-98
Drake, D.B. Don Quijote (1894-1970).
(Vol 2)
    H.C. Woodbridge, 399(MLJ):Sep-Oct79-
    311
Drake, F.W. China Charts the World.*
    P.A. Cohen, 318(JAOS):Oct-Dec78-535
Drake, G.C. and C.A. Forbes - see Vida,
M.G.
Drake, H.A. In Praise of Constantine.
    E.D. Hunt, 123:Vol129No1-27
Drake, S. Galileo at Work.
    M. Crosland, 529(QQ):Winter79/80-692
    639(VQR):Summer79-96
Drake, W. Sare Teasdale.*
    P-L. Adams, 61:Jan80-88
Draper, R.P. D.H. Lawrence.
    F. McCombie, 447(N&Q):Dec78-569
    H.T. Moore, 402(MLR):Jul79-683
Draper, R.P. - see Eliot, G.
Draviņš, K. and M. Ozola - see
"Evangelien und Episteln"
Dreiser, T. Theodore Dreiser: A Selection
of Uncollected Prose.* (D. Pizer, ed)
    E. Guereschi, 395(MFS):Winter78/79-633
Dreman, D. Contrarian Investment Strat-
egy.
    R. Lamb, 441:23Mar80-12
    C. Lehmann-Haupt, 441:28Jan80-C14
Drescher, S. Econocide.*
    A.J.H. Latham, 161(DUJ):Dec78-109

Dressler, W.U., ed. Current Trends in Textlinguistics.*
A-M. Simon-Vandenbergen, 179(ES):Dec79-824

Dressler, W.U. Grundfragen der Morphonologie.
M.S. Flier, 350:Jun79-413

Dressler, W.U. and F.V. Mareš, eds. Phonologica 1972.*
A. Liberman, 353:Apr78-59

Dressler, W.U. and O.E. Pfeiffer, with T. Herok, eds. Phonologica 1976.
P. Pétursson, 343:Band23-16

Drew, E. Senator.*
639(VQR):Autumn79-145

Drewe, R. A Cry in the Jungle Bar.
D. Wilson, 617(TLS):11Apr80-416

Drexler, A., ed. The Architecture of the Ecole des Beaux-Arts.*
J.P. Carlhian, 45:Mar79-47

Drey, R.E.A. Pharmacy Jars.
G. Wills, 39:Dec79-532

Dreyer, P. Martyrs and Fanatics.
D. Grumbach, 441:24Aug80-15

Driberg, T. Ruling Passions.
639(VQR):Autumn78-139

Drinan, R.F. America's Commitment to Israel.
G. Sauer, 287:Jan78-25

Drone, J. Index to Opera, Operetta and Musical Comedy Synopses in Collections and Periodicals.
R. Andrewes, 415:Apr79-310

Dronke, P. Abelard and Heloise in Medieval Testimonies.*
W. Rothwell, 208(FS):Vol33Pt2-598

Dronke, P. "Fabula."
S.P. Coy, 545(RPh):Feb79-366

Drop, W. and J.H.L. de Vries. Taalbeheersing Handboek voor taalhantering.
A. Braet and J. Vos, 204(FdL):Mar79-73

Drozdowski, B., ed. Twentieth-Century Polish Theatre.
J. Elsom, 362:17Apr80-514

Drucker, P. The Unseen Revolution.
K.J. Arrow, 473(PR):1/1979-113

Druet, P-P. Fichte.
J-M. Gabaude, 542:Jan-Mar78-113

Drummond, I. The Diamonds of Loreta.
N. Callendar, 441:17Aug80-19

Drummond, W. William Drummond of Hawthornden: Poems and Prose. (R.H. MacDonald, ed)
G. Parfitt, 447(N&Q):Oct78-455

Drury, A. Mark Coffin.*
639(VQR):Summer79-100

Drutman, I. - see Flanner, J.

Dryden, E.A. Nathaniel Hawthorne.*
J. Arac, 153:Summer79-42
K. Bales, 191(ELN):Mar79-259
H. Kerr, 573(SSF):Summer78-332

Dryden, J. The Works of John Dryden. (Vol 11) (J. Loftis, D.S. Rodes and V.A. Dearing, eds)
E.L. Saslow, 566:Spring79-126

Dryden, J. The Works of John Dryden.* (Vol 15) (E. Miner and G.R. Guffey, eds)
A. Poyet, 189(EA):Jul-Dec78-385
J.P. Vander Motten, 179(ES):Dec79-794

Dryland, G. A Multiple Texture.
L. Wilson, 368:Sep74-267

Drysdall, D.L. - see de La Taille, J.

Drysdall, D.L. - see de Rojas, F.

Dubarle, D. Logos et formalisme du langage.
J. Largeault, 542:Apr-Jun78-217

Du Bellay, J. L'Olive. (E. Caldarini, ed)
M.C. Smith, 208(FS):Vol33Pt2-627

Du Bellay, J. Die römischen Sonette. (E. Deger, ed and trans)
Y. Giraud, 535(RHL):Sep-Oct78-816

Dubie, N. The City of the Olesha Fruit.
J. Vernon, 651(WHR):Autumn79-345

Dubin, F. and M. Margol. It's Time to Talk.
T. Bofman, 608:Jun80-238

Dublin, T. Women at Work.
676(YR):Winter80-X

Dubois, C-G. Le Maniérisme.
A.M. Boase, 208(FS):Jul79-326

Du Bois, E.C. Feminism and Suffrage.
R. Rosenberg, 432(NEQ):Mar79-127
639(VQR):Winter79-14

Dubois, H. Les Foires de Chalon et la commerce dans la vallée de la Saône à la fin du moyen âge (vers 1280 — vers 1430).
T.N. Bisson, 589:Jan79-122

Dubois, J. and others. Rhétorique de la poésie.
C. Guéricolas, 553(RLiR):Jan-Jun78-234

Dubois, M-M. and others, eds. Modern Dictionary: English-French, Français-Anglais.
R.J. Melpignano, 399(MLJ):Sep-Oct79-306

Du Bois, P. Drieu la Rochelle.
E. Weber, 617(TLS):6Jun80-631

Dubois-Charlier, F. Comment S'initier a la linguistique?
P. Blumenthal, 430(NS):Oct78-471

Dubos, R. The Wooing of Earth.
J. Kastner, 441:1Jun80-7

Dubrovina, V.F., P.V. Baxturina and V.S. Golyšenko, eds. Vygoleksinskij sbornik.
H.G. Lunt, 574(SEEJ):Winter79-551

Dubus, A. Finding a Girl in America.
P-L. Adams, 61:Jul80-86
A. Broyard, 441:25Jun80-C28
J. Moynahan, 441:22Jun80-12

Duby, G. Medieval Marriage.
T.N. Bisson, 589:Apr79-364

Duby, G. Les Trois Ordres ou l'imaginaire du féodalisme.
H. Cronel, 450(NRF):May79-129
J-P. Guinle, 450(NRF):Aug79-130

Du Camp, M. Lettres inédites à Gustave Flaubert. (G. Bonaccorso and R.M. de Stefano, eds)
A. Fairlie, 208(FS):Jan79-95

Ducasse, I. - see under Comte de Lautréamont

Ducharme, R. Ines Perée et Inat-Tendu.
L. Rièse, 108:Spring79-114

Duchein, M., comp. Basic International
Bibliography of Archive Administration/
Bibliographie internationale fonda-
mentale d'archivistique.
J. Fyfe, 14:Jul79-349

Duchêne, R. - see Madame de Sévigné

Duchesneau, F. L'Empirisme de Locke.
H. Laboucheix, 189(EA):Jan-Mar78-83

Dudbridge, G. The Legend of Miao-shen.
A. Seidel, 293(JASt):Aug79-770

Dudek, L. Selected Essays and Criticism.*
Technology and Culture.
W.J. Keith, 99:Apr80-35

"Duden: Das grosse Wörterbuch der deutschen Sprache in sechs Bänden." (Vols
1-3)
R.L. Jones, 221(GQ):Nov79-527

Duff, D. - see Queen Victoria

Duffey, B. Poetry in America.*
J.E. Breslin, 219(GaR):Spring79-227
W.M. Chace, 301(JEGP):Jan79-148
A. Gelpi, 27(AL):Jan80-560
S. Lea, 432(NEQ):Sep79-426
L. Surette, 106:Spring79-63
G.M. White, 646(WWR):Sep78-130

Dufournet, J. Adam de la Halle à la
recherche de lui-même ou le Jeu drama-
tique de la Feuillée.
L.R. Muir, 208(FS):Vol33Pt2-562

Dufournet, J. Les écrivains de la IVe
croisade: Villehardouin et Clari.*
(Vol 1)
M.R. Morgan, 208(FS):Jan79-58

Dufournet, J. - see Adam de la Halle

Dufraigne, P. - see Aurelius Victor, S.

Dufrenne, M. Subversion perversion.
M. Adam, 542:Oct-Dec78-506

Dufrenoy, M-L. L'Orient romanesque en
France 1704-1789.* (Vol 3)
M.H. Waddicor, 208(FS):Vol33Pt2-788

Dufresny, C. Amusemens sérieux et
comiques.* (J. Dunkley, ed)
W.D. Howarth, 208(FS):Oct79-445
J.S. Munro, 402(MLR):Jan79-206

Duggan, J.J. A Guide to Studies on the
"Chanson de Roland."*
C.W. Aspland, 67:May79-120
T. Hunt, 402(MLR):Apr79-446
H-W. Klein, 547(RF):Band91Heft3-324
I. Short, 382(MAE):1979/1-132
205(FMLS):Apr78-185

Duggan, L. Under the Weather.
C. Pollnitz, 581:Dec79-462

Duggan, L.G. Bishop and Chapter.
P.W. Strait, 589:Oct79-799

Duhoux, Y., ed. Études minoennes I.
A. Heubeck, 343:Band23-104

Duijker, H.C.J. and M.J. Van Rijswijk.
Dictionnaire de psychologie en trois
langues. (2nd ed) (Vol 2)
J-M. Gabaude, 542:Apr-Jun78-208

Duiker, W.J. Ts'ai Yüan-p'ei.
E. Lubot, 293(JASt):May79-565

Dukes, P. October and the World.
A. Brown, 617(TLS):25Jan80-95

Dull, J.L. - see Ch'ü T'ung-tsu

Dull, J.R. The French Navy and American
Independence.
J.M.J. Rogister, 161(DUJ):Jun79-273

Düll, S. Die Götterkulte Nordmakedoniens
in römischer Zeit.
S.R.F. Price, 313:Vol69-204

"Eleanor Lansing Dulles: Chances of a Lifetime."
E. Auchincloss, 441:20Apr80-7

Dulles, J.W.F. Castello Branco.
R. Roett, 263(RIB):Vol129No3/4-363

Dumas, A. - see Hugo, V.

Duménil, G. Le concept de loi économique
dans "Le Capital."
A. Reix, 542:Apr-Jun79-265

Dumitriu, A. History of Logic.
I.A., 543:Mar79-540

Dummett, M. Elements of Intuitionism.*
N.D. Goodman, 316:Jun79-276
C. Lyas, 307:Apr79-35

Dummett, M. The Game of Tarot. Twelve
Tarot Games.
H. Maccoby, 362:28Aug80-276

Dummett, M. Truth and Other Enigmas.
C.J.F. Williams, 518:Oct79-136

Dumonceaux, P. Langue et Sensibilité en
France au XVIIe siècle.*
H.T. Barnwell, 208(FS):Vol33Pt2-703
G. Montbertrand, 546(RR):May79-305

Dumont, J-P. Under the Rainbow.
S. Leacock, 263(RIB):Vol129No1-71

Dumortier, J. and J. Defradas - see
Plutarch

Dumoulin, H. and J.C. Maraldo, eds. The
Cultural, Political and Religious Signif-
icance of Buddhism in the Modern World.
H.V. Guenther, 302:Vol16#1and2-115

Dunaway, N.M. The Metamorphoses of the
Self.
639(VQR):Summer79-106

Dunbar, C., comp. A Bibliography of
Shelley Studies: 1823-1950.*
K. Engelberg, 78(BC):Summer79-297
G.W. Matthews, 402(MLR):Jul79-668

Dunbar, M. Fundamentals of Book Collecting.
G.T. Tanselle, 517(PBSA):Apr-Jun78-265

Duncan, A. Art Nouveau and Art Deco Lighting.
G. Allen, 45:Jan79-51

Duncan, C. The Pursuit of Pleasure.
N.D. Ziff, 54:Jun78-375

Duncan, D. Ben Jonson and the Lucianic
Tradition.*
R.J. Booth, 175:Autumn79-254

Duncan, J.A. Les Romans de Paul Adam.
B.C. Swift, 208(FS):Jan79-98
205(FMLS):Jul78-284

Duncan, R. Selected Poems 1940-1971.
J.R.B., 148:Summer79-92
J. Cotton, 493:Dec79-72

Duncan, R. and M. Weston-Smith, eds. The
Encyclopedia of Ignorance.
529(QQ):Spring79-183

Duncan, R.L. Brimstone.
N. Callendar, 441:23Nov80-37

Duncan-Jones, R. The Economy of Roman Empire.
  S.I. Oost, 122:Jan79-86
Dundes, A. Analytic Essays in Folklore.
  L. Dégh, 196:Band19Heft3/4-320
Dundes, A., comp. Folklore Theses and Dissertations in the United States.*
  G.E. Lankford, 292(JAF):Jan-Mar79-102
Dundes, A. The Hero Pattern and the Life of Jesus.*
  C. Jolley, 650(WF):Jan79-56
Dundes, A. and A. Falassi. La Terra in Piazza.*
  W.H. Jansen, 582(SFQ):Vol41-264
Dundes, A. and C.R. Pagter. Urban Folklore from the Paperwork Empire.
  U. Kutter, 196:Band19Heft1/2-139
  C.L. Perdue, Jr., 582(SFQ):Vol41-268
Dundy, E. Finch, Bloody Finch.
  J. Elsom, 362:26Jun80-838
Dunham, V. and M. Hayward - see Voznesensky, A.
Dunham, V.S. In Stalin's Time.*
  K.H. Ober, 107(CRCL):Winter79-109
  R.M. Slusser, 558(RLJ):Winter79-224
  A.C. Wright, 104(CASS):Summer78-289
Dunkley, J. - see Dufresny, C.
Dunkling, L.A. First Names First.
  M. Dilkes, 35(AS):Summer79-136
  K.B. Harder, 424:Sep78-289
Dunleavy, S. The Very First Lady.
  N. von Hoffman, 441:12Oct80-14
Dunlop, I. Degas.*
  R. Pickvance, 617(TLS):21Mar80-330
  J. Russell, 441:13Jan80-25
Dunlop, R. Behind Japanese Lines.
  R.A. Sokolov, 441:24Feb80-18
Dunn, D. Barbarians.*
  J. Cassidy, 493:Dec79-60
  C. Hope, 364:Nov79-82
  E. Longley, 617(TLS):18Jan80-64
Dunn, D.J. The Catholic Church and the Soviet Government 1939-1949.
  L. Blit, 575(SEER):Apr79-308
  A. Katz, 497(PolR):Vol123#3-120
  639(VQR):Summer78-87
Dunn, D.J., ed. Religion and Modernization in the Soviet Union.
  P.J.S. Duncan, 550(RusR):Jan79-117
Dunn, J. Moon in Eclipse.
  W. St. Clair, 402(MLR):Apr79-426
Dunn, J. Western Political Theory in the Face of the Future.*
  H. Bull, 617(TLS):4Jan80-20
Dunn, M. The Drawings of Russell Clark.
  T. Bracey, 368:Sep76-268
Dunn, P.N. Fernando de Rojas.
  D. Severin, 400(MLN):Mar79-416
Dunn, S. A Circus of Needs.*
  W.H. Pritchard, 249(HudR):Summer79-252
  P. Stitt, 219(GaR):Fall79-699
  D. Wojahn, 109:Winter79/80-184
  639(VQR):Spring79-66
Dunne, J.G. Quintana and Friends.*
  P. Grosskurth, 617(TLS):8Feb80-140
Dunne, J.G. True Confessions.*
  639(VQR):Spring78-66

Dunne, L. Ringleader.
  N. Callendar, 441:13Jul80-25
Dunstan, S. Tarot Poems.
  A. Stevenson, 617(TLS):23May80-586
Dunston, A.J., ed. Essays in Roman Culture.*
  C. Moussy, 555:Vol52fasc1-213
Dunwell, S. The Run of the Mill.*
  G. Allen, 45:Jan79-51
  T.W. Leavitt, 432(NEQ):Sep79-429
Du Plaisir. Sentiments sur les lettres et sur l'histoire avec des Scrupules sur le style. (P. Hourcade, ed)
  P. France, 208(FS):Vol33Pt2-692
Dupont, J-C. Contes de Bûcherons.
  A. Coelho, 292(JAF):Jul-Sep79-360
Dupouy, P., F. Gentile and P. Grosclaude. Études sur Montesquieu (1975).
  C.P. Courtney, 208(FS):Vol33Pt2-728
Dupre, C. Gentleman's Child.
  L. Duguid, 617(TLS):16May80-558
Dupré, L. Transcendent Selfhood.*
  E.T.L., 543:Sep78-133
Dupuy, T.N. Elusive Victory.
  639(VQR):Spring79-64
Duque, B.J. - see under Jiménez Duque, B.
Durán, C. The Yellow Canary Whose Eye Is So Black.
  639(VQR):Spring78-58
Durán, M., ed. Rafael Alberti.
  H.T. Young, 240(HR):Spring78-274
Durán, M. De Valle-Inclán a León Felipe.
  G. Gullón, 240(HR):Spring78-272
Durán, M. and N. Cortés-Rivas. Graded Spanish Reader. (3rd ed)
  M.E. Beeson, 238:Mar79-195
Durán, M., G. Durán and C.E. Kany. Spoken Spanish for Students and Travelers. (3rd ed)
  E. Spinelli, 238:Mar79-193
Durán, M. and R. González Echevarría. Calderón y la crítica.*
  A.K.G. Paterson, 86(BHS):Jan79-68
Durand, P. and Y. Languirand. Brunch.
  W. and C. Cowen, 639(VQR):Autumn79-156
Durandeaux, J. Du renoncement homosexuel au double jeu de charme.
  E. Marty, 98:Apr78-425
Durant, M. and M. Harwood. On the Road with John James Audubon.
  E. Hoagland, 441:17Aug80-7
  B. Webster, 441:16Aug80-19
Duranton, H. - see Goujet, C-P.
Duras, M. India-Song.
  Y. Guers-Villate, 207(FR):Mar79-655
Duras, M. L'Eden Cinéma.
  C.J. Murphy, 207(FR):Dec78-380
Duras, M. Le Square. (W.J. Strachan, ed)
  J. Cruickshank, 208(FS):Vol33Pt2-933
Duras, M. and M. Porte. Les Lieux de Marguerite Duras.
  J.J. Michalczyk, 207(FR):Feb79-501
Dürbeck, H. Zur Charakteristik der griechischen Farbenbezeichnungen.
  M. Murtez, 343:Band23-183

d'Urfé, A. Oeuvres morales et spiritu-
elles inédites.* (Y. Le Hir, ed)
K.M. Hall, 208(FS):Oct79-441
Durling, R.J. - see Galen
Duroselle, J-B. La Décadence, 1932-1939.
D. Johnson, 617(TLS):4Jan80-15
Durozoi, G. and B. Lecherbonnier. Le
Surréalisme.
R. Cardinal, 208(FS):Apr79-228
Dürr, A. Studien über die frühen Kantaten
Johann Sebastian Bachs. (rev) Zur
Chronologie der Leipziger Vokalwerke
J.S. Bachs.
B. Lam, 410(M&L):Jul79-325
Dürr, V. and G. von Molnár, eds. Versuch
zu Goethe.*
O. Durrani, 402(MLR):Jan79-244
H. Reiss, 133:Band12Heft1/2-158
Dürr, W. and others - see Deutsch, O.E.
Durrani, O. Faust and the Bible.
M. Vos, 221(GQ):May79-409
Durrant, D. Addle.
Z. Leader, 617(TLS):28Mar80-345
J. Mellors, 362:10Apr80-482
Durrant, S., ed and trans. The Tale of
the Nisǎn Shamaness.
R-I. Heinze, 293(JASt):Feb79-374
Durrell, L. Sicilian Carousel.*
639(VQR):Winter78-30
Durrell, L. A Smile in the Mind's Eye.
M. Warnock, 362:25Sep80-411
Durrell, M. Die semantische Entwicklung
der Synonymik für "warten."
R. Ris, 685(ZDL):3/1979-381
Dürst, R. Heinrich von Kleist. (2nd ed)
M. Gelus, 221(GQ):Jan79-119
Dusinberre, W. Henry Adams.
R.M. Adams, 617(TLS):11Jul80-771
Düsing, K. Das problem der Subjektivität
in Hegels Logik.
M-J. Königson, 542:Apr-Jun79-250
Dussutour-Hammer, M. Amos Tutuola.
K. Barber, 69:Vol48#3-299
Dusza, E.L. Poets of Warsaw Aflame.
B.T. Lupack, 497(PolR):Vol23#4-95
Dutton, G. A Body of Words.
S.E. Lee, 581:Dec79-432
Dutton, G.F. Camp One.
T. Eagleton, 565:Vol20#3-75
Duțu, A. Cultura română în civilizația
europeană modernă.
D.J. Deletant, 575(SEER):Oct79-633
Duval, F.Y. and I.B. Rigby. Early Ameri-
can Gravestone Art in Photographs.
D. Tashjian, 165(EAL):Spring80-92
Duval, N., with D. Briquel and M. Hamiaux,
eds. L'onomastique latine.
K-W. Welwei, 182:Vol131#20-758
Duval, P. The Art of Glen Loates.*
W. Blunt, 39:Sep79-238
Duval, P. Recherches sur les structures
de la pensée alchimique (Gestalten) et
leurs correspondances dans "Le Conte du
Graal" de Chrétien de Troyes et
l'influence de l'Espagne mozarabe de
l'Ebre sur la pensée symbolique de
[continued]

[continuing]
l'oeuvre.
D.J. Shirt, 208(FS):Vol33Pt2-544
Duval, P. The Tangled Garden.
R.M. Alway, 529(QQ):Autumn79-550
Duval, P-M. Les Celtes.
V. Kruta, 194(EC):Vol15fasc2-721
Duval, P-M. Les Dieux de la Gaule. (new
ed)
E. Bachellery, 194(EC):Vol15fasc2-728
Duval, P-M. Die Kelten.
L. Pauli, 471:Jul/Aug/Sep79-287
Düwell, H., ed. Eine Altfranzösische Über-
setzung des Elucidarium.
W. Rothwell, 208(FS):Jul79-321
Dvivedī, R. - see Kālidāsa
Dwivedi, A.N. Indian Thought and Tradi-
tion in T.S. Eliot's Poetry.
K.S.N. Rao, 27(AL):Jan80-572
Dworkin, R. Taking Rights Seriously.*
D.D. Raphael, 393(Mind):Apr79-305
S. Sherwin, 529(QQ):Autumn79-552
Dwyer, R.A. Boethian Fictions.*
W. Rothwell, 208(FS):Vol33Pt2-596
Dwyer, T.R. Irish Neutrality and the
U.S.A.: 1939-1947.
J. Lordson, 174(Éire):Summer79-156
Dybek, S. Brass Knuckles.
R. Saner, 460(OhR):No.25-113
Dybek, S. Childhood and Other Neighbor-
hoods.
I. Gold, 441:24Feb80-14
61:Feb80-95
Dyck, J. Athen und Jerusalem.
M.L. Baeumer, 301(JEGP):Jul79-394
G. Gillespie, 406:Winter79-444
A.J. Harper, 402(MLR):Jan79-242
Dyer, C. The Carter Family Favorites Cook
Book.
W. and C. Cowen, 639(VQR):Spring78-76
Dyer, C. Population and Society in
Twentieth Century France.
205(FMLS):Jul78-284
Dyer, D. The Stories of Kleist.*
R. Cardinal, 529(QQ):Spring79-98
S. Friebert, 573(SSF):Winter78-119
M. Garland, 402(MLR):Jul79-748
M.K. Rogister, 161(DUJ):Dec78-139
J.L. Sammons, 221(GQ):Nov79-543
M.M. Tatar, 406:Summer79-204
Dyker, D. The Soviet Economy.
M.C. Kaser, 575(SEER):Jul79-467
Dymoke, J. Lady of the Garter.
L. Duguid, 617(TLS):16May80-558
Dynnik, A. Russkaja literatura do 1837
goda.
T.J. Watts, 574(SEEJ):Fall79-397
Dyson, F. Disturbing the Universe.*
C. Longuet-Higgins, 617(TLS):29Feb80-
223
Dyson, J. The Hot Arctic.
A. Broyard, 441:16Feb80-19
R. Coleridge, 617(TLS):22Feb80-217
Dziewanowski, M.K. Poland in the Twenti-
eth Century.*
L. Blit, 575(SEER):Jul79-458

Dzo Ching-chuan. Sseu-ma Ts'ien et
l'historiographie chinoise.
E.G. Pulleyblank, 293(JASt):Aug79-745

Eades, D.K. The Dharawal and Dhurga Lan-
guages of the New South Wales South
Coast.
R.M.W. Dixon, 350:Mar79-261
Eagle, D., with J. Hawkins - see "The
Oxford Illustrated Dictionary"
Eagleton, M. and D. Pierce. Attitudes to
Class in the English Novel.
L. Lerner, 617(TLS):8Feb80-134
Eagleton, T. Marxism and Literary Criti-
cism.*
C. Cook, 447(N&Q):Aug78-362
J. Duparc, 189(EA):Apr-Jun78-221
C.L. and J.B. Holm, 128(CE):Dec78-450
M. Wilding, 402(MLR):Jan79-151
Eakins, B.W. and R.G. Sex Differences in
Human Communication.
D.E. Phillips, 583:Spring79-316
Earman, J., C. Glymour and J. Stachel.
Minnesota Studies in the Philosophy of
Science. (Vol 8)
G. Nerlich, 63:Jun79-186
Easterlin, R.A. Birth and Fortune.
E.J. Dionne, 441:9Nov80-7
C. Lehmann-Haupt, 441:20Oct80-C16
Eastman, C.M. Linguistic Theory and Lan-
guage Description.
R.A. Randall, 350:Jun79-478
Eaton, C.E. The Case of the Missing Photo-
graphs.
K. Warren, 577(SHR):Fall79-364
Eaton, C.E. The Man in the Green Chair.*
M.L. Hester, 577(SHR):Fall79-363
Eaton, T., ed. Essays in Literary Seman-
tics.
M.C. Beardsley, 290(JAAC):Winter79-215
Eban, A. Abba Eban.
G. Sauer, 287:Jun/Jul78-22
Ebejer, F. Come Again in Spring.
A.N. Wilson, 617(TLS):29Feb80-246
Ebel, C. Transalpine Gaul.*
J. Richardson, 313:Vol69-156
Eberenz, R. Schiffe an den Küsten der
Pyrenäenhalbinsel.
W. Mettmann, 72:Band216Heft2-462
Eberhard, W. Studies in Hakka Folktales.
H.S. Levy, 292(JAF):Apr-Jun79-223
Eberhardt, W. Fontane und Thackeray.*
H. Oppel, 224(GRM):Band28Heft1-102
Eberhart, R. Of Poetry and Poets.*
S. Corey, 639(VQR):Autumn79-763
Ebersohn, W. Store up the Anger.
S. Ramsey, 617(TLS):19Sep80-1044
Ebrey, P.B. The Aristocratic Families of
Early Imperial China.
R.M. Somers, 293(JASt):Nov78-127
Eccleston, J. Jest a Moment/Englische
Witze.
J. Wells, 617(TLS):2May80-492
Echeruo, M.J.C. The Conditioned Imagina-
tion from Shakespeare to Conrad.
295(JML):Vol17#4-623

Echevarría, R.G. - see under González
Echevarría, R.
Eckhart, J. Master Eckhart: Parisian
Questions and Prologues. (A.A. Maurer,
ed and trans)
A.W.J. Harper, 154:Dec78-718
Eckman, F.R. Current Themes in Linguis-
tics.
H.B. Beardsmore, 556(RLV):1978/3-267
Eckmann, J. Middle Turkic Glosses of the
Rylands Interlinear Koran Translation.
R. Dankoff, 318(JAOS):Apr-Jun78-135
Eco, U. The Role of the Reader.
L. Hanlon, 290(JAAC):Spring80-336
T. Hawkes, 676(YR):Summer80-560
D.H. Hirsch, 569(SR):Fall79-628
Eco, U. A Theory of Semiotics.*
W. Godzich, 308:Spring78-117
D.H. Hirsch, 569(SR):Fall79-628
Ecole, J. - see Wolff, C.
Economou, G. - see Blackburn, P.
Edel, L. Bloomsbury.*
D.C. Betts, 584(SWR):Autumn79-406
J. Halperin, 150(DR):Summer79-367
J. L'Enfant, 598(SoR):Spring80-499
T.M. McLaughlin, 659(ConL):Autumn80-
639
S. Rudikoff, 31(ASch):Spring80-280
S. Rudikoff, 249(HudR):Winter79/80-540
Edel, L. Literary Biography.
A.M. Friedson, 77:Summer78-83
Edel, L. - see James, H.
Edel, L. - see Wilson, E.
Edel, L. and others. Telling Lives.* (M.
Pachter, ed)
G.W. Allen, 219(GaR):Fall79-726
M. Goldstein, 569(SR):Fall79-667
Edelberg, C.D. Robert Creeley's Poetry.*
P. Breslin, 491:Jul80-219
M.G. Meek, 27(AL):Jan80-581
S. Paul, 301(JEGP):Oct79-579
Edelen, G. - see Hooker, R.
Edelmann, J.C. Sämtliche Schriften in
Einzelausgaben. (Vol 9) (W. Grossmann,
ed)
T.P. Saine, 680(ZDP):Band97Heft4-629
Eden, A. Another World, 1897-1917.*
639(VQR):Spring78-62
Edens, W. and others, eds. Teaching
Shakespeare.*
V.K. Whitaker, 570(SQ):Summer79-429
Edery, M. El sentimiento filosófico de
Unamuno.
R. Wright, 86(BHS):Jul79-275
Edgell, S. Middle-Class Couples.
P. Willmot, 617(TLS):4Jul80-765
Edie, J.M. Speaking and Meaning.*
P. Ricoeur, 567:Vol25#1/2-167
Edinger, E.F. Melville's "Moby-Dick."
H. Parker, 594:Summer79-242
Edinger, W. Samuel Johnson and Poetic
Style.*
J.L. Battersby, 405(MP):Feb80-332
H.D. Weinbrot, 173(ECS):Summer79-542
Edler, E. Die Anfänge des sozialen Romans
und der sozialen Novelle in Deutschland.
H.R. Vaget, 221(GQ):Mar79-280

Eigeldinger, F. and A. Gendre. Delahaye témoin de Rimbaud.
   C. Chadwick, 535(RHL):Jul-Aug79-694
Eigeldinger, J-J., ed. Chopin vu par ses élèves.
   M. Cooper, 617(TLS):22Aug80-941
Eigeldinger, M. Jean-Jacques Rousseau.
   R. Trousson, 535(RHL):Mar-Jun79-507
"Eight Chinese Plays — from the 13th Century to the Present." (W. Dolby, trans)
   R. Strassberg, 293(JASt):Feb79-361
"Eighteenth-Century Moscow."
   A.G. Cross, 575(SEER):Apr79-289
Eigner, E.M. The Metaphysical Novel in England and America.*
   A.M.C. Brown, 155:Summer79-106
   R.A. Levine, 594:Spring79-119
   R.B. Salomon, 445(NCF):Dec78-384
Eiland, M.L. Chinese and Exotic Rugs.
   J. Housego, 617(TLS):15Aug80-921
"Eilhart von Oberge's 'Tristrant.'" (J.W. Thomas, trans)
   K. Hume, 301(JEGP):Jan79-86
   D.N. Yeandle, 382(MAE):1979/2-278
Eimer, H. Berichte über das Leben des Atiśa (Dīpaṃkaraśrījñāna).
   P. Kvaerne, 259(IIJ):Jan79-76
von Einem, H. Deutsche Malerei des Klassizismus und der Romantik: 1760-1840.
   F. Büttner, 471:Apr/May/Jun79-179
von Einem, H. Michelangelo.*
   E.H. Ramsden, 39:May79-404
Einhorn, E. Old French.*
   G. Price, 208(FS):Oct79-494
Einhorn, J.W. Spiritalis unicornis.*
   F.P. Pickering, 72:Band216Heft1-140
   R. Schenda, 196:Band19Heft3/4-324
Eisele, U. Realismus und Ideologie.
   H. Denkler, 406:Spring79-73
Eisenberg, D. "Poeta en Nueva York."*
   M. Adams, 240(HR):Winter78-106
   205(FMLS):Jan78-88
Eisenberg, D. - see Ortúñez de Calahorra, D.
Eisenberg, H. The Reinhard Action.
   N. Callendar, 441:24Feb80-31
Eisenhut, W. - see Dictys Cretensis
Eisenmeier, E. Adalbert-Stifter-Bibliographie: 2. Fortsetzung.
   B.W. Browning, 133:Band12Heft4-374
Eisenstadt, S.N. Revolution and the Transformation of Societies.
   R.P. Madsen, 293(JASt):Aug79-735
Eisenstein, E.L. The Printing Press as an Agent of Change.*
   M. Hunter, 78(BC):Autumn79-336
   R. Mitchison, 362:10Jan80-58
Eisenzweig, U. L'espace imaginaire d'un récit.*
   G. Schaeffer, 535(RHL):Jul-Aug79-687
Eisner, J. The Survivor. (I.A. Leitner, ed)
   H. Epstein, 441:7Dec80-14
Ekdahl, S. Die "Banderia Prutenorum" des Jan Długosz.
   F. Deuchler, 589:Oct79-800

Ekelöf, G. Diwan I, II, III.
   J. Grosjean, 450(NRF):May79-112
Ekmanis, R. Latvian Literature Under the Soviets, 1940-1975.
   A. Ziedonis, Jr., 550(RusR):Oct79-517
Elat, M. Qišrey kalkalāh beyn 'arṣôt hammiqrā'.
   S.A. Kaufman, 318(JAOS):Jul-Sep78-344
Elbaz, A-E. Correspondance d'Edmond Fleg pendant l'Affaire Dreyfus.
   A. Roche, 535(RHL):Jul-Aug79-701
Elbert, S. - see Alcott, L.M.
Elbourne, R. Music and Tradition in Early Industrial Lancashire 1780-1840.
   A. Burgess, 617(TLS):27Jun80-735
Elbow, P. Oppositions in Chaucer.
   C. Wilcockson, 382(MAE):1979/1-146
Elbrønd-Bek, B. and O. Ravn, eds. Omkring Fiskerne.
   E. Bredsdorff, 562(Scan):Nov78-176
Elcock, W.D. The Romance Languages.* (2nd ed) (rev by J.N. Green)
   M.R. Harris, 545(RPh):Feb79-345
   P.M. Lloyd, 240(HR):Spring78-241
   T.B.W. Reid, 208(FS):Vol33Pt2-1017
Elder, A.A. The "Hindered Hand."
   E. Blicksilver, 95(CLAJ):Jun79-424
Elderfield, J. The "Wild Beasts."
   C.R. Baldwin, 54:Mar78-187
Eley, G. Reshaping the German Right.
   F.L. Carsten, 617(TLS):2May80-484
Eley, L. Hegels Wissenschaft der Logik.
   G. Siegwart, 489(PJGG):Band86Heft1-209
Elgood, R., ed. Islamic Arms and Armour.
   S. Digby, 617(TLS):1Aug80-878
Elias, N. What Is Sociology?
   639(VQR):Spring79-64
Eliot, G. The George Eliot Letters.* (Vols 8 and 9) (G.S. Haight, ed)
   I. Adam, 49:Oct79-97
   D.P. Deneau, 268(IFR):Winter80-65
Eliot, G. The Mill on the Floss [&] Silas Marner. (R.P. Draper, ed)
   A. Easson, 148:Spring79-85
Eliot, G. The Mill on the Floss. (G.S. Haight, ed) George Eliot's "Middlemarch" Notebooks. (J.C. Pratt and V.A. Neufeldt, eds)
   B. Hardy, 617(TLS):15Aug80-907
Eliot, G. Scenes of Clerical Life.
   A. Jumeau, 189(EA):Apr-Jun78-235
Eliot, G. Some George Eliot Notebooks.* (Vol 1) (W. Baker, ed)
   W. Myers, 402(MLR):Jul79-676
   P. Swinden, 447(N&Q):Jun78-265
Elisofon, E. and W.B. Fagg. The Sculpture of Africa.
   H.M. Cole, 2(AfrA):May79-20
Elkin, P.K., ed. Australian Poems in Perspective.
   J. Colmer, 71(ALS):May79-123
Elkin, S. The Living End.*
   P. Bailey, 617(TLS):18Jan80-54
   J. Naughton, 362:14Feb80-222

Ellenberger, B. The Latin Element in the Vocabulary of the Earlier Makars Henryson and Dunbar.
P. Bawcutt, 447(N&Q):Apr78-168
Ellenburg, S. Rousseau's Political Philosophy.*
R. Grimsley, 208(FS):Vol33Pt2-762
Elliger, W. Die Darstellung der Landschaft in der griechischen Dichtung.*
F. Jouan, 555:Vol52fasc1-155
Elliott, J. Blood on the Snow.
639(VQR):Winter78-9
Elliott, J. Summer People.
W. Boyd, 617(TLS):18Apr80-430
J. Mellors, 362:10Apr80-482
Elliott, O. The World of Oz.
W. Goodman, 441:15Jun80-16
Ellis, A.T. The Birds of the Air.
P. Kemp, 362:21Aug80-249
J. Uglow, 617(TLS):15Aug80-923
Ellis, B. Rational Belief Systems.
D.W. Hamlyn, 617(TLS):4Jan80-19
Ellis, D.M. New York.
E. Wright, 617(TLS):25Jan80-91
Ellis, E.A. André Malraux et le monde de la nature.
D. Gascoigne, 208(FS):Vol33Pt2-907
A. Vandegans, 535(RHL):Jan-Feb78-151
Ellis, H.F. A.J. Wentforth, B.A.
R. Usborne, 617(TLS):11Jul80-788
Ellis, J.M. Heinrich von Kleist.
R.E. Helbling, 401(MLQ):Dec79-418
Ellis, J.M. Narration in the German Novelle.
I. Schuster, 268(IFR):Summer80-156
Ellis, J.R. Philip II and Macedonian Imperialism.*
M.M. Markle 3d, 24:Summer79-327
Ellis, M.B. Rousseau's Socratic Aemilian Myths.*
R. Grimsley, 402(MLR):Jan79-207
P.D. Jimack, 208(FS):Vol33Pt2-763
A. Rosenberg, 627(UTQ):Fall78-66
Ellis, P.B. H. Rider Haggard.*
W. Katz, 150(DR):Summer79-371
Ellis-Fermor, U. The Irish Dramatic Movement.
M. Levin, 174(Éire):Summer79-152
Ellmann, R. The Consciousness of Joyce.*
S. Brivic, 295(JML):Vol7#4-746
V. Mercier, 405(MP):Aug79-59
R. Splitter, 395(MFS):Summer78-317
Ellmann, R. Golden Codgers.
R. Fréchet, 189(EA):Jan-Mar78-71
Ellmann, R., ed. The New Oxford Book of American Verse.
R. Asselineau, 189(EA):Jan-Mar78-106
Ellul, J. The Betrayal of the West.*
J.D. Hoeveler, Jr., 396(ModA):Winter79-102
Elman, R. The Breadfruit Lotteries.
S. Ellin, 441:2Mar80-8
J. Leonard, 441:7Mar80-C25
Elon, A. Flight into Egypt.
J. Morris, 441:9Nov80-3
Elon, A. Timetable.
F. Morton, 441:7Sep80-12

Elovaara, R. The Problem of Identity in Samuel Beckett's Prose.*
R.L. Admussen, 207(FR):Mar79-649
J. Knowlson, 208(FS):Vol33Pt2-919
J-J. Mayoux, 189(EA):Jan-Mar78-96
J. Pilling, 402(MLR):Jan79-151
van Els, T. and others. Handboek voor de Toegepaste Taalkunde.
A.J. van Essen and others, 204(FdL): Mar79-61
D. Goyvaerts, 556(RLV):1978/6-555
El Saffar, R. Distance and Control in "Don Quixote."
J.A. Parr, 240(HR):Spring78-261
El Saffar, R.S. Novel to Romance.*
G. Sobejano, 240(HR):Winter78-65
Else, G.F. The Madness of Antigone.*
R.E. Doyle, 124:Dec79/Jan80-260
Elsen, A.E. In Rodin's Studio.
R.A. Sokolov, 441:18May80-15
Elsner, R. Zeichen und literarische Praxis.
A.J. Niesz, 221(GQ):Jan79-106
Elsom, J. Post-War British Theatre.*
G. Bas, 189(EA):Jul-Dec78-411
J. De Vos, 179(ES):Dec79-816
D. Jarrett, 447(N&Q):Dec78-570
Elster, J. Leibniz et la formation de l'esprit capitaliste.
R. Prévost, 192(EP):Jul-Sep79-355
Elton, G.R. Reform and Reformation.
M. Tolmie, 529(QQ):Summer79-334
Elvey, E.M., ed. The Courts of the Archdeaconry of Buckingham, 1483-1523.
R. Dunning, 325:Apr79-164
Elvin, M. The Pattern of the Chinese Past.
N. Sivin, 244(HJAS):Dec78-449
Elwell-Sutton, L.P. The Persian Metres.
J.R. Perry, 294:Vol9-157
Elwood, R.C. Roman Malinovsky.
J. Bradley, 575(SEER):Jan79-154
Elwood, R.C., ed. Reconsiderations on the Russian Revolution.
M. McCauley, 575(SEER):Apr79-304
Ely, J.H. Democracy and Distrust.
J.R. Pole, 617(TLS):12Sep80-979
T. Taylor, 441:16Mar80-11
Elytis, O. The Axion Esti.
P. Green, 453(NYRB):26Jun80-40
M. Schmidt, 362:18Sep80-377
Elytis, O. Eklogi, 1935-1977.
R. Beaton, 617(TLS):23May80-580
Elytis, O. The Sovereign Sun.
P. Green, 453(NYRB):26Jun80-40
Embery, J., with D. Demong. My Wild World.
J.W. Miller, 441:26Oct80-12
Embree, A.T., ed. Pakistan's Western Borderlands.
S.M.M. Qureshi, 293(JASt):Feb79-411
Emerson, E., ed. American Literature, 1764-1789.*
J.S. Martin, 106:Spring79-103
Emerson, R.W. Emerson's Literary Criticism. (E.W. Carlson, ed)
F.W. Conner, 290(JAAC):Summer80-471

Emerson, R.W. The Journals and Miscel-
laneous Notebooks of Ralph Waldo
Emerson.* (Vol 14) (S.S. Smith and H.
Hayford, eds)
    L.J. Budd, 579(SAQ):Winter79-139
Emerson, S. Second Sight.
    L.D. Burnard, 617(TLS):12Sep80-984
Emery, L.C. George Eliot's Creative Con-
flict.*
    K.B. Mann, 637(VS):Summer78-507
    D. Postlethwaite, 405(MP):Aug79-105
Emmel, H. - see Rupp, H.
Emmerson, G.S. Arthur Darling.
    P.M. Young, 617(TLS):11Jul80-790
Emmet, D. The Moral Prism.
    A. Quinton, 617(TLS):4Jan80-18
Emmison, F.G. Elizabethan Life.
    D.J. Johnson, 325:Apr79-165
Emonds, J.E. A Transformational Approach
to English Syntax.*
    W. Bauer, 677(YES):Vol9-357
Emons, R. Valenzen englischer Prädikats-
verben.
    A.R. Tellier, 189(EA):Jan-Mar78-81
Emrich, W. and M. Linke - see Sternheim, C.
En-han, L. - see under Lee En-han
"Enciclopedia dantesca." (Vol 5)
    M. Marti, 228(GSLI):Vol155fasc490-289
del Encina, J. Obras dramáticas. (Vol 1)
(R. Gimeno, ed)
    C. Stern, 545(RPh):Nov78-219
Enckell, P. Matériaux pour l'histoire du
vocabulaire français. (2nd Ser, fasc 12)
    R. Arveiller, 553(RLiR):Jul-Dec78-448
Ende, S.A. Keats and the Sublime.*
    K. Muir, 402(MLR):Oct79-919
Endo, S. Silence.
    C.C. Park, 249(HudR):Winter79/80-581
    J. Updike, 442(NY):14Jan80-94
Endo, S. Volcano.
    A. Thwaite, 441:1Jun80-15
Endo, S. When I Whistle.*
    A. Thwaite, 441:13Jan80-14
    J. Updike, 442(NY):14Jan80-98
Enekwe, O.O. Broken Pots.
    J. Povey, 2(AfrA):Feb79-86
Enesciana, I. La personnalité artistique
de Georges Enesco.
    P. Somville, 542:Oct-Dec79-471
van der Eng, J., J.M. Meijer and H. Schmid.
On the Theory of Descriptive Poetics.
    C.S. Losq, 550(RusR):Jul79-399
Engel, H. The Suicide Murders.
    C. Fagan, 99:Dec80/Jan81-43
Engel, J., ed. Mittel und Wege früher
Verfassungspolitik. (Vol 1)
    B. Arnold, 182:Vol31#21/22-824
Engel, M. The Glassy Sea.*
    S. Atherton, 628(UWR):Spring-Summer79-
    111
    L. Manning, 526:Winter79-89
    J.C. Oates, 461:Fall-Winter79/80-87
Engel, U. and S. Grosse, eds. Grammatik
und Deutschunterricht.
    W. Vesper, 686(ZGL):Band7Heft3-360
Engel, W.P. - see Shirley, J.

Engel-Braunschmidt, A. Deutsche Dichter
in Russland im 19. Jahrhundert.
    E. Reissner, 688(ZSP):Band40Heft1-220
Engelbert, J.A. Macedonio Fernández and
the Spanish American New Novel.
    M. Coddou, 238:Dec79-738
    A. McDermott, 402(MLR):Oct79-972
    C.R. Perricone, 552(REH):Oct79-475
Engelen, U. Die Edelsteine in der
deutschen Dichtung des 12. und 13.
Jahrhunderts.
    F.L. Borchardt, 221(GQ):May79-400
von Engelhardt, D. Hegel und die Chemie.
    R. Löw, 687:Jul-Sep79-461
    H.A.M. Snelders, 125:Winter79-309
Engelmann, H., ed. Die Inschriften von
Kyme.
    A.G. Woodhead, 303(JoHS):Vol199-219
Engels, D.W. Alexander the Great and the
Logistics of the Macedonian Army.*
    R.S. Bagnall, 121(CJ):Apr-May80-348
    A.M. Devine, 487:Autumn79-272
    S. Pembroke, 617(TLS):11Jan80-43
Engels, J. Blood Mountain.*
    R.H.W. Dillard, 134(CP):Spring78-88
Engle, G.D. This Grotesque Essence.
    G. Pound, 585(SoQ):Fall178-101
Engle, P. and H.N., eds. Writing from the
World.
    G.M., 502(PrS):Spring78-116
Englefield, F.R.H. Language. (G.A. Wells
and D.R. Oppenheimer, eds)
    P. Salmon, 402(MLR):Apr79-386
Engler, B. - see Shakespeare, W.
Engler, K. The Structure of Realism.*
    E. Rodgers, 86(BHS):Apr79-154
Engler, W., ed. Der französische Roman im
19. Jahrhundert.
    G. Hainsworth, 208(FS):Vol33Pt2-850
"English-Cheyenne Student Dictionary."
    D.G. Frantz, 269(IJAL):Jan78-77
Englund, B. Yes/No-Questions in Bulgar-
ian and Macedonian.
    V.A. Friedman, 574(SEEJ):Fall79-426
Engwall, G. Fréquence et distribution
du vocabulaire dans un choix de romans
français.
    F.M. Jenkins, 545(RPh):Nov78-238
Enninger, W. Übungen zu einem strukturell-
taxonomischen Modell der englischen Gram-
matik.*
    U. Kruppa, 430(NS):Jul78-387
Enrico, H. Now, a thousand years from now.
    S.G. Radhuber, 448:Vol17#1-120
Enright, D.J. A Faust Book.*
    C. Hope, 364:Mar80-76
    S.S. Prawer, 617(TLS):4Jan80-5
Enright, D.J., ed. The Oxford Book of
Contemporary Verse 1945-1980.
    J. Bayley, 362:29May80-691
Enright, D.J. Paradise Illustrated.*
    A. Cluysenaar, 565:Vol20#3-68
Enríquez Cartagena, J. El thesoro de
varias poesías espirituales. (J.F.
Chorpenning, ed)
    D.G. Walters, 86(BHS):Jul79-251

Enríquez Gómez, A. El siglo pitagórico y Vida de don Gregorio Guadaña. (C. Amiel, ed)
 J.V. Ricapito, 304(JHP):Spring80-272
Enser, A.G.S. A Subject Bibliography of the First World War.
 B.B., 617(TLS):4Jan80-16
Enstice, A. Thomas Hardy.
 R. Swigg, 617(TLS):1Feb80-126
Enteen, G.M. The Soviet Scholar-Bureaucrat.
 A. Brown, 617(TLS):25Jan80-95
 N.V. Riasanovsky, 550(RusR):Oct79-485
Enteen, G.M. and T. Gorn. Soviet Historians and the Study of Russian Imperialism.
 T. Emmons, 550(RusR):Oct79-486
de Enterría, M.C.G. - see under García de Enterría, M.C.
Enthoven, J-P. - see Comte, A.
Enzensberger, H.M. The Sinking of the Titanic.
 V. Trueblood, 29:Nov/Dec80-9
Epicurus. Epicure, "Lettres et maximes." (M. Conche, ed and trans)
 O. Bloch, 542:Jan-Mar79-138
Epicurus. La Pensée du plaisir. (J. Bollack, ed)
 D.N. Sedley, 123:Vol29No1-82
Epps, G. The Shad Treatment.
 W.C. Havard, 639(VQR):Winter78-161
Epstein, D. Beyond Orpheus.
 W. Webster, 290(JAAC):Summer80-480
Epstein, D.J. Sinful Tunes and Spirituals.
 639(VQR):Summer78-109
Epstein, D.M. Young Men's Gold.*
 639(VQR):Winter79-25
Epstein, F.T. Die Hof- und Zentralverwaltung im Moskauer Staat und die Bedeutung von G.K. Kotošichins zeitgenössischen Werk "Über Russland unter der Herrschaft des Zaren Aleksej Michajlovic" für die russische Verwaltungsgeschichte. (G. Specovius, ed)
 R. Bosley, 550(RusR):Jan79-84
 W. Kirchner, 182:Vol131#17/18-627
Epstein, H. Children of the Holocaust.*
 K. Hoffman, 99:May80-34
Epstein, J. Wild Oats.*
 S. Fender, 617(TLS):22Feb80-202
 P. Kemp, 362:21Feb80-254
Epstein, J.J. Francis Bacon.*
 J. Stephens, 125:Fall78-136
Epstein, L. King of the Jews.*
 E. Milton, 676(YR):Autumn79-89
 A.H. Rosenfeld, 390:Oct79-55
 T. Ziolkowski, 569(SR):Fall79-676
Erades, P.A. Points of Modern English Syntax.
 J. Bourke, 38:Band96Heft1/2-192
Erart, J. Les Poésies du trouvère Jehan Erart. (T. Newcombe, ed)
 M. Thiry-Stassin, 556(RLV):1978/1-78
Erasmus. The Collected Works of Erasmus. (Vols 23 and 24) (C.R. Thompson, ed)
 A. Levi, 617(TLS):16May80-565
 [continued]

[continuing]
 L.V.R., 568(SCN):Fall-Winter79-inside back cover
Erasmus. Declamation des Louenges de Mariage [1525]. (Le Chevalier de Berquin, trans; É.V. Telle, ed)
 J. Crow, 208(FS):Vol33Pt2-624
Erasmus. Erasmo di Rotterdam: "L'educazione del principe cristiano." (M. Isnardi Parente, ed)
 E. Namer, 542:Apr-Jun79-210
Erbse, H., ed. Scholia Graeca in Homeri "Iliadem."* (Vol 3)
 F.M. Combellack, 122:Apr79-179
de Ercilla y Zúñiga, A. La Araucana. (O. Lazzarin Dante, ed)
 M. Camurati, 263(RIB):Vol129No1-92
Erdman, D.V. - see Coleridge, S.T.
Erdmann, E. Ausgrabungen in Alt-Paphos auf Cypern. (Vol 1, Pt 1)
 A.M. Snodgrass, 303(JoHS):Vol199-206
Erdmann, P. "There" Sentences in English.*
 L.E. Breivik, 179(ES):Apr79-216
 M.M. Bryant, 660(Word):Dec80-264
"Eretria." (Vol 6)
 R. Heidenreich, 182:Vol131#23/24-874
"Erex Saga and Ivens Saga."* (F.W. Blaisdell, Jr. and M.E. Kalinke, trans)
 J.M. Stitt, 292(JAF):Oct-Dec79-494
Ergardt, J.T. Faith and Knowledge in Early Buddhism.
 D.K. Swearer, 293(JASt):Nov78-201
Erhel, C. and C. Leguay. Prisonnières.
 E.D. Gelfand, 207(FR):Apr79-811
Erickson, C. Great Harry.
 P-L. Adams, 61:Aug80-85
 C. Hibbert, 441:29Jun80-11
 G.M. Wilson, 617(TLS):12Sep80-985
Erickson, R. Sound Structure in Music.
 W. Slawson, 308:Spring78-105
"Jean Scot Erigène et l'histoire de la philosophie."
 G. Madec, 192(EP):Oct-Dec79-484
Erikson, D. Oscar Wilde.
 I. Fletcher, 637(VS):Summer79-487
Erler, A. and E. Kaufmann, eds. Handwörterbuch zur deutschen Rechtsgeschichte. (Vols 1 and 2)
 T. Bühler, 182:Vol131#21/22-783
Erlich, V., ed. Pasternak.*
 I. Masing-Delic, 550(RusR):Jul79-402
Erlich, V., ed. Twentieth-Century Russian Literary Criticism.
 E. Mossman, 395(MFS):Summer78-289
 M.H. Shotton, 447(N&Q):Dec78-572
 V. Terras, 131(CL):Winter79-95
Ermarth, M. Wilhelm Dilthey: The Critique of Historical Reason.
 J. Barnouw, 543:Jun79-746
 A.W. Novitsky, 613:Jun79-211
Ernst, D. The Evolution of Electronic Music.
 C. Bennett, 607:Jun78-31
Ernst, G. Einführungkurs Italienisch.
 W. Geerts, 556(RLV):1978/3-269
"Max Ernst."
 M. Huggler, 182:Vol131#23/24-868

109

Erskine-Hill, H. and A. Smith, eds. The
Art of Alexander Pope.*
 W.H., 148:Autumn79-89
Ervin-Tripp, S. and C. Mitchell-Kernan,
eds. Child Discourse.
 B. MacWhinney, 350:Mar79-242
Erwitt, E. Recent Developments.*
 R. Whelan, 55:Oct79-53
Escal, F. Espaces sociaux, espaces musi-
caux.
 P-L. Rey, 450(NRF):Sep79-58
Escarpit, R. Théorie générale de l'infor-
mation et de la communication.*
 K.E.M. George, 208(FS):Oct79-499
 B. Lamiroy, 277(ITL):#41/42-132
Eschbach, A. Pragmasemiotik und Theater.
 M. Nadin, 290(JAAC):Spring80-338
von Eschenbach, W. - see under Wolfram von
Eschenbach
Eschmann, J. Die Numerusmarkierung des
Substantivs im gesprochenen Französisch.
 W. Geerts, 556(RLV):1978/2-169
 K.E.M. George, 208(FS):Vol33Pt2-1052
 K. Hunnius, 72:Band216Heft1-193
Escoffier, S. and C. Longeon, eds and
trans. Le Ballet en langage forésien
(1605).
 M.M. McGowan, 208(FS):Vol33Pt2-702
Escott, P.D. After Secession.
 R.W. Johannsen, 579(SAQ):Autumn79-528
Esherick, J.W. Reform and Revolution in
China.*
 O.Y.K. Wou, 302:Vol16#1and2-125
Eshleman, C. New Poems and Translations.
 N. Wheale, 493:Dec79-43
Eshleman, C. What She Means.
 N. Wheale, 493:Dec79-43
 A. Williamson, 472:Fall/Winter79-184
Eskow, J. Smokestack Lightning.
 A. Cheuse, 441:28Dec80-8
Esmonde, J. and B. Larbey. A Touch of the
Tiny Hacketts.
 J. Coleby, 157:Winter79-86
Espantoso Foley, A. Delicado: "La Lozana
andaluza."
 F.L. Trice, 239:May-Sep79-398
 K. Whinnom, 86(BHS):Jan79-61
Esper, E.A. Analogy and Association in
Linguistics and Psychology.*
 J.S. Klein, 35(AS):Summer79-124
Espriu, S. The Bull-Hide.
 H.J.F. de Aguilar, 472:Fall/Winter79-
64
Espy, W.R. Say It My Way.
 R.A. Sokolov, 441:22Jun80-16
Esquyo, F. Le Poesie. (F. Toriello, ed)
 D.M. Atkinson, 86(BHS):Apr79-164
Essar, D.F. The Language Theory, Episte-
mology and Aesthetics of Jean Lerond
D'Alembert.*
 D.A. Coward, 208(FS):Vol33Pt2-776
 J. Pappas, 535(RHL):Mar-Jun79-518
Esselborn, K.G. Gesellschaftskritische
Literatur nach 1945.*
 H. Wagener, 406:Winter79-470

Esser, D. Untersuchungen zu den Oden-
schlüssen bei Horaz.
 R.G.M. Nisbet, 123:Vol129No1-148
Esslin, M. Artaud.
 M. Sheringham, 208(FS):Vol33Pt2-901
Essop, A. The Hajji and Other Stories.
 J. Marquand, 364:Apr/May79-137
Estang, L. La Laisse du temps.
 A. Bugliani, 207(FR):Mar79-668
Estermann, C. The Ethnology of Southwest-
ern Angola. (Vol 1) (G.D. Gibson, ed)
 A. Barnard, 69:Vol48#1-95
Estévez, A.P. - see under Pérez Estévez, A.
Estham, I. Kyrkliga textilier.
 A.M. Karlsson, 341:1978/2-70
Estleman, L.D. Motor City Blue.
 N. Callendar, 441:26Oct80-28
Étaix, R. and J. Lemarié - see Chromatius
Etchepareborda, R. Historia de las rela-
ciones internacionales argentinas.
 J.J. Finan, 263(RIB):Vol29No2-210
Etcherelli, C. Un Arbre voyageur.
 J.G. Miller, 207(FR):Apr79-792
"Ethics: Report of the Consultative Group
on Ethics."
 L.W. Sumner, 154:Sep78-575
"Ethnologia Slavica." (Vol 7)
 H. Leeming, 575(SEER):Jul79-410
Étienne, R., G. Fabre and M. Lévêque.
Fouilles de Conimbriga.* (Vol 2)
 J. Marcillet-Jaubert, 555:Vol52fasc2-
359
Étienne, R. and D. Knoepfler. Hyettos de
Béotie et la chronologie des archontes
fédéraux entre 250 et 171 avant J-C.
 O. Masson, 555:Vol52fasc2-357
Etienvre, J-P. - see Caro, R.
Ètkind, E. Materija stixa.
 B.P. Scherr, 574(SEEJ):Winter79-537
"Étrennes de septentaine."
 J. André, 555:Vol52fasc2-387
 A. Heubeck, 260(IF):Band83-380
Ettinger, E. - see Luxemburg, R.
Ettinger, S. Form und Funktion in der
Wortbildung.* Diminutiv- und Augmenta-
tivbildung.*
 E. Seebold, 685(ZDL):3/1979-367
Ettinger, S. Norm und System beim Verb.*
 K.E.M. George, 208(FS):Vol33Pt2-1053
 H. Kahane, 545(RPh):Aug78-101
Ettlinger, L.D. Antonio and Piero
Pollaiuolo.*
 G. Martin, 617(TLS):1Feb80-120
 G. Turner, 135:Jan79-67
"Études Gobiniennes, 1974-75."
 M.D. Biddiss, 208(FS):Vol33Pt2-827
"Études historiques hongroises 1975."*
 L. Péter, 575(SEER):Jul79-447
"Études proustiennes I." "Études proust-
iennes II."
 J.M. Cocking, 208(FS):Apr79-219
"Études Rabelaisiennes." (Vol 11)
 D.G. Coleman, 208(FS):Jul79-334
"Études Rabelaisiennes." (Vol 13)
 J. Chomarat, 545(RHL):May-Jun78-456
 D.G. Coleman, 208(FS):Vol33Pt2-620

Faber, B.L., ed. The Social Structure of Eastern Europe.
V.A. Tomović, 104(CASS):Summer78-318
Faber, E. The Life of Lorena Hickok, E.R.'s Friend.
C. Lehmann-Haupt, 441:5Feb80-C9
K.S. Lynn, 617(TLS):11Jul80-787
A. Schlesinger, Jr., 441:17Feb80-3
442(NY):11Feb80-118
Fabian, M.H. The Pennsylvania-German Decorated Chest.
S.T. Swank, 658:Winter79-402
Fabre, C. Dans le sillage des caravelles.
B. Muller, 207(FR):May79-948
Fabre, D. and C. Camberoque. La fête en Languedoc.
P. Gardy, 98:Apr78-399
de Fabry, A.S. Etudes autour de "La Nouvelle Héloïse."
G. May, 546(RR):Nov79-405
Facius, F., H. Booms and H. Boberach. Das Bundesarchiv und seine Bestände. (rev by G. Granier, J. Henke and K. Oldenhage)
R. Storey, 325:Apr79-171
Fackenheim, E.L. Encounters Between Judaism and Modern Philosophy.
R.J. Bernstein, 390:Dec79-62
Fackenheim, E.L. The Jewish Return into History.
L.F. Barmann, 613:Jun79-214
M.I. Urofsky, 390:Oct79-62
G. Woodcock, 529(QQ):Winter79/80-733
Fackert, J. - see von Hofmannsthal, H.
Fackler, H.V. That Tragic Queen.
S. Sweeney, 305(JIL):Sep78-173
Fadda, A.M.L. - see under Luiselli Fadda, A.M.
Fadiman, J. Mountain Warriors.
M. Hill, 69:Vol148#1-86
Fadiman, R.K. Faulkner's "Intruder in the Dust."
N. Polk, 585(SoQ):Fall78-93
Faensen, H. and V.I. Ivanov. Early Russian Architecture.
A. Senkevitch, Jr., 576:May78-123
Faessler, S. Everything in the Window.
G. Dretzsky, 198:Summer80-132
442(NY):28Jul80-100
Fagan, B. Elusive Treasure.
639(VQR):Spring78-69
Fagan, B.M. Return to Babylon.
P-L. Adams, 61:Jan80-88
Fage, J.D. A History of Africa.
R. Oliver, 617(TLS):4Jan80-21
Fagg, J.E. Latin America.
J. Fisher, 86(BHS):Jan79-86
Fagles, R. I, Vincent.
639(VQR):Autumn79-147
Fagles, R. and W.B. Stanford - see Aeschylus
Fahy, E. Some Followers of Domenico Ghirlandaio.
J. Beck, 54:Dec78-712
Fainberg, L.V. - see de Mena, J.
Fainlight, R. Sibyls and Others.
D. Davis, 362:5Jun80-729
V. Feaver, 617(TLS):23May80-586

Fairbank, W. America's Cultural Experiment in China 1942-49.
D. Bryan, 293(JASt):May79-568
Fairchilds, C.C. Poverty and Charity in Aix-en-Provence, 1640-1789.
J. Lough, 208(FS):Vol33Pt2-801
Fairfax, J. Bone Harvest Done.
J. Lasdun, 617(TLS):1Aug80-876
Fairley, P. The Conquest of Pain.
A. Broyard, 441:21Jun80-21
Fairlie, H. The Parties.
639(VQR):Autumn78-130
Faith, N. The Winemasters.
42(AR):Fall79-488
Falaschi, G. Progetto corporativo e autonomia dell'arte in Pietro Aretino.
C. Cairns, 402(MLR):Apr79-470
Falck, C. In This Dark Light.*
C. Hope, 364:Jun79-76
Falco, N. Manual for the Organization of Manuscripts.
J. Fogerty, 14:Apr79-204
Falk, J.S. Linguistics and Language. (2nd ed)
J. Hinds, 399(MLJ):Sep-Oct79-300
Falk, S. Tennessee Williams. (2nd ed)
J.R. Taylor, 157:Spring79-79
Falk, W. Vom Strukturalismus zum Potentialismus.*
J. Link, 490:Band10Heft2/3-400
Falkus, H. Wildtrack.
639(VQR):Autumn79-150
Fallaci, O. A Man.
J. Burke, 231:Nov80-98
V. Gornick, 441:23Nov80-14
Fallani, G. Dante autobiografico.
V. Cioffari, 276:Winter79-403
Fallenstein, R. and C. Hennig. Rezeption skandinavischer Literatur in Deutschland 1870-1914.
A. Jørgensen, 562(Scan):May79-72
Fallet, R. Y a-t-il un docteur dans la salle?
M.E. Birkett, 207(FR):Feb79-511
Fallis, G.V., L.H. Turk and A.M. Espinosa - see under Valdés Fallis, G., L.H. Turk and A.M. Espinosa
Fallis, R. The Irish Renaissance.*
M.J. and J.J. Egan, 395(MFS):Winter78/79-594
R.M. Kain, 305(JIL):May78-178
S. Sweeney, 305(JIL):Sep78-174
Fallon, M., ed. The Sketches of Erinensis.
B. Kiely, 617(TLS):20Jun80-688
"Familienavn i Norden."
R.E. Wood, 424:Jun78-204
Fancher, R.E. Pioneers of Psychology.
D. Murray, 529(QQ):Winter79/80-727
Fane, J. Happy Endings.
D. Durrant, 364:Jul79-89
Fane, J. Revolution Island.*
W. Boyd, 364:Feb80-89
Fanelli, M. Histoires et idées.
G.R. Danner, 207(FR):Oct78-205
J. Walz, 399(MLJ):Nov79-382
Fang-shang, L. - see under Lü Fang-shang

Fanger, D. The Creation of Nikolai Gogol.
J. Bayley, 617(TLS):22Feb80-195
Fanning, C. Finley Peter Dunne and Mr.
Dooley: The Chicago Years.
W. Blair, 27(AL):May79-284
S.E. Marovitz, 26(ALR):Spring79-158
Fant, G. and M.A.A. Tatham, eds. Auditory
Analysis and Perception of Speech.
Z.N. Džaparidze, 682(ZPSK):Band31Heft6-
622
Fantini, A.E. Language Acquisition of a
Bilingual Child.
H. Lijerón, 238:May-Sep79-414
Fantoni, B. Mike Dime.
C. Brown, 617(TLS):27Jun80-743
C. Sigal, 362:5Jun80-731
Fantuzzi, M. Meccanismi narrativi nel
romanzo barocco.
A.N. Mancini, 276:Spring79-56
Farag, F. The Opposing Virtues.
P. Holland, 408:Spring79-171
Faragher, J.M. Women and Men on the Over-
land Trail.
E. Wright, 617(TLS):25Jan80-91
Farb, P. and G. Armelagos. Consuming
Passions.
A. Broyard, 441:30Aug80-19
61:Oct80-99
Farington, J. The Diary of Joseph Faring-
ton. (Vols 1 and 2) (K. Garlick and A.
Macintyre, eds)
L. Herrmann, 90:Sep79-594
Farington, J. The Diary of Joseph Faring-
ton. (Vols 3 and 4) (K. Garlick and A.
Macintyre, eds)
E. Adams, 617(TLS):23May80-588
L. Herrmann, 90:Sep79-594
Farka, C. Die römischen Lampen vom Magda-
lensberg.
A. Leibundgut, 182:Vol31#1/2-46
Farkas, A. Murders in the Welcome Cafe.
G. Davies, 168(ECW):Spring78-82
K. Garebian, 102(CanL):Summer79-126
Farkas, A. and K. Norris, eds. Montréal:
English Poetry of the Seventies.*
D. Carpenter, 102(CanL):Spring79-101
M. Darling, 168(ECW):Summer78-280
Farkas, A.B. - see under Bölöni Farkas, A.
Farley, J. The Spontaneous Generation Con-
troversy from Descartes to Oparin.
A.F. Chalmers, 84:Mar79-93
Farley, L. Sexual Shakedown.*
C. Sigal, 362:17Jul80-84
Farley-Hills, D. Rochester's Poetry.
A.W., 148:Summer79-90
Farmer, E.L. Early Ming Government.
Pei Huang, 302:Vol16#1and2-118
Farnham, F. Madame Dacier.*
E.E. Flinders, Jr., 207(FR):Dec78-347
N. Suckling, 208(FS):Jul79-347
205(FMLS):Apr78-185
Farquhar, G. The Beaux' Stratagem.* (M.
Cordner, ed)
A. Roper, 677(YES):Vol9-338

Farquhar, G. The Beaux' Stratagem.* (C.N.
Fifer, ed)
J. Milhous, 568(SCN):Fall-Winter79-81
E. Rothstein, 130:Summer79-175
Farquhar, J.D. Creation and Imitation.
W.B. Clark, 589:Apr79-366
Farr, D. English Art 1870-1940.
D. Piper, 617(TLS):1Feb80-119
Farrar, L.L., Jr. Divide and Conquer.
639(VQR):Spring79-54
Farrell, J.G. The Singapore Grip.*
639(VQR):Autumn79-140
Farrell, J.T. The Death of Nora Ryan.*
639(VQR):Winter79-18
Farrell, J.T. James T. Farrell: Literary
Essays, 1954-1974. (J.A. Robbins, ed)
L. Waldeland, 395(MFS):Summer78-265
Farrell, R.B. Dictionary of German Syno-
nyms.* (3rd ed)
205(FMLS):Jan78-88
Faruqi, K.A. Chiragh-i-Rah-e-Guzar.
M.F. Rahman, 273(IC):Apr76-129
Faruqui, N.A. Talāsh-e-Mīr in Urdu.
M.G. Khan, 273(IC):Jul76-195
Fasholé-Luke, E. and others, eds. Chris-
tianity in Independent Africa.
R. Oliver, 617(TLS):4Jan80-21
Fass, P.S. The Damned and the Beautiful.*
M. Vipond, 106:Winter79-363
Fasske, H., H. Jentsch and S. Michalk, eds.
Sorbischer Sprachatlas. (Vol 4)
F. Hinze, 682(ZPSK):Band31Heft1-81
Fasske, H., H. Jentsch and S. Michalk, eds.
Sorbischer Sprachatlas. (Vol 5)
G. Stone, 575(SEER):Jul79-417
Fathy, H. Architecture for the Poor.
L. Prussin, 576:Mar78-55
Fatout, P. - see Twain, M.
Faucon, J-C., ed. Le Livre de l'amoureuse
aliance.
T. Hunt, 402(MLR):Oct79-934
Faulkner, P. Modernism.
295(JML):Vol7#4-584
Faulkner, P. Angus Wilson.
B. Bergonzi, 617(TLS):11Jul80-773
M. Drabble, 362:10Jul80-51
R. Kiely, 441:16Nov80-1
Faulkner, W. The Marionettes. (N. Polk,
ed)
E.T. Arnold 3d, 585(SoQ):Spring-
Summer79-244
J. Ditsky, 628(UWR):Spring-Summer79-
103
Faulkner, W. Mayday.
H. Beaver, 617(TLS):18Jul80-821
Faulkner, W. The Selected Letters of Wil-
liam Faulkner.* (J. Blotner, ed)
K. McSweeney, 148:Spring79-76
S.M. Ross, 395(MFS):Summer78-275
Faulkner, W. Uncollected Stories of
William Faulkner.* (J. Blotner, ed)
R.K. Fadiman, 578:Spring80-137
Faulseit, D. Das Fachwort in unserem
Sprachalltag.
U. Stötzer, 682(ZPSK):Band31Heft3-329
Faure, J-P. Le cas Lamarck.
A. Reix, 542:Apr-Jun79-231

Feldman, R.H. - see Arendt, H.

Feldstein, S. The Land That I Show You.
    H.L. Feingold, 390:Oct79-68

Fell, B. Saga America.
    P-L. Adams, 61:Jul80-86

Fellows, J. The Failing Distance.
    F.G. Townsend, 405(MP):Aug79-109

Fellows, O. Diderot.*
    H. Josephs, 173(ECS):Fall78-110
    J. Undank, 546(RR):Jan79-103

Fellows, O. and D.G. Carr - see "Diderot
    Studies XIX"

Fellows, O. and D. Guiragossian - see
    "Diderot Studies XVIII"

Felman, S. Le Scandale du corps parlant.
    J. Culler, 617(TLS):13Jun80-662

Felperin, H. Shakespearean Representa-
    tion.*
    W.D. Kay, 130:Summer79-178
    639(VQR):Winter79-24

Felsch, A. Arthur Rimbaud.
    S. Bogumil, 547(RF):Band91Heft3-333

Felt, W.M. The FBI Pyramid.
    D. Wise, 441:27Jan80-12

Feltenius, L. Intransitivations in Latin.
    J.N. Adams, 123:Vol29No1-171
    G. Serbat, 555:Vol52fasc2-389

"La Femme dans les civilisations des Xe-
    XIIIe siècles: Actes du colloque tenu à
    Poitiers les 23-25 septembre 1976."
    M.L. Colish, 589:Jan79-124

Fénelon, F. Correspondance. (Vols 4 and
    5) (J. Orcibal, ed)
    E.T. Dubois, 402(MLR):Jan79-206
    J. Le Brun, 535(RHL):Nov-Dec78-1030

Fénelon, F. Playing for Time.
    639(VQR):Winter78-27

Fenik, B.C., ed. Homer.*
    N.J. Richardson, 123:Vol29No2-201

Fenn, G. The Development of Syntax in a
    Group of Educationally Severely Sub-
    normal Children.*
    A.A.A., 355(LSoc):Aug78-290

Fennario, D. Nothing to Lose.*
    D. McCaughna, 526:Summer79-82
    B. Neil, 108:Winter79-141

Fennell, J., L. Müller and A. Poppe - see
    "Russia Mediaevalis"

Fennell, J. and A. Stokes. Early Russian
    Literature.
    O. Hughes, 550(RusR):Apr79-215

Fennis, J. La "Stolonomie" et son vocabu-
    laire maritime marseillais.
    A. Bollée, 547(RF):Band91Heft3-349
    W. Rothwell, 182:Vol131#3/4-91

Fenton, J. A Vacant Possession.*
    C. Hope, 364:Jun79-76

Ferencz, B.B. Less Than Slaves.*
    L. Silk, 441:3Jan80-C17
    B. Wasserstein, 617(TLS):25Jul80-839

Ferenczy, E. From the Patrician State to
    the Patricio-Plebian State.
    R.M. Ogilvie, 123:Vol29No1-109

Ferguson, C.A. and D.I. Slobin, eds.
    Studies of Child Language Development.
    T. van der Geest, 603:Vol13#2-276

Ferguson, F. Wordsworth.*
    G. Little, 541(RES):Nov79-480
    W.J.B. Owen, 191(ELN):Jun79-339

Ferguson, J. Utopias of the Classical
    World.
    G. Negley, 322(JHI):Apr-Jun79-315

Ferguson, J. and K. Chisholm, eds. Polit-
    ical and Social Life in the Great Age of
    Athens.
    S. Pembroke, 617(TLS):11Jan80-43

Ferguson, T. High Water Chants.
    G. Noonan, 296(JCF):28/29-221
    R. Willmot, 102(CanL):Autumn79-106

Fergusson, F. Trope and Allegory.*
    S. Barnet, 405(MP):Feb80-324
    M-M. Martinet, 189(EA):Jul-Dec78-380
    M. Murrin, 191(ELN):Jun79-324

Fergusson, J.P. - see Mendelson, E.M.

Ferid, M., G. Kegel and K. Zweigert, eds.
    Gutachten zum internationalen und aus-
    ländischen Privatrecht 1975.
    R. Hepting, 182:Vol131#14-474

Ferling, J.E. The Loyalist Mind.
    N.S. Cohen, 656(WMQ):Jan79-145

Ferlinghetti, L. Who Are We Now?*
    D.O.S., 502(PrS):Summer78-209

Ferlinghetti, L. and N.J. Peters. Liter-
    ary San Francisco.
    D. Grumbach, 441:21Sep80-16

Fermor, P.L. A Time of Gifts.
    M. Ellmann, 569(SR):Spring79-332

Fernández, A.L. - see under Labandeira
    Fernández, A.

Fernández, L. El anarquista desnudo.
    N. Torrents, 617(TLS):25Apr80-478

Fernández, L.G. - see under Gil Fernández,
    L.

Fernández, P.H. Estudios sobre Ramón
    Pérez de Ayala.
    C.A. Sullivan, 238:Dec79-733

Fernandez-Galiano, E. Lexico de los
    Himnos de Calimaco. (Vol 1)
    R.W., 555:Vol52fasc1-165

Fernández Alvarez, M. Charles V.*
    639(VQR):Spring78-50

Fernández Herr, E. Les origines de
    l'Espagne romantique.*
    A. Cioranescu, 549(RLC):Jan-Mar77-105

Fernando, L. "New Women" in the Late
    Victorian Novel.*
    E.A. Daniels, 637(VS):Autumn78-114

Ferniot, J. C'est ça la France.
    J-P. Ponchie, 207(FR):Oct78-194

Ferns, C.S. Aldous Huxley: Novelist.
    R. Robbins, 617(TLS):19Sep80-1013

Ferns, J. A.J.M. Smith.
    R.H. Ramsey, 99:Oct80-34

Ferns, J. The Snow Horses.
    D. Barbour, 150(DR):Spring79-154

Ferrán, J. and D.P. Testa, eds. Spanish
    Writers of 1936.
    M.T. Halsey, 546(RR):Mar79-196

Ferrante, J.M. Woman as Image in Medieval
    Literature from the Twelfth Century to
    Dante.*
    W. Calin, 131(CL):Summer79-319
    E. Webb, 648(WCR):Jun78-39

Ferrari, I.A. Apologia paradossica della
città di Lecce. (A. Laporta, ed)
M.M., 228(GSLI):Vol155fasc491-475
Ferrars, E.X. Witness Before the Fact.
N. Callendar, 441:10Feb80-22
442(NY):28Apr80-147
Ferreira, J.V. and S.S. Jha, eds. The Out-
look Tower.
W. Reed, 293(JASt):Nov78-186
Ferrell, R.H. - see Truman, H.S.
Ferrer, V. Tractatus de suppositionibus.
(J.A. Trentman, ed)
J-F. Courtine, 192(EP):Oct-Dec79-498
Ferreras, J.I. El triunfo del liberalismo
y de la novela histórica (1830-1870).*
A.H. Clarke, 86(BHS):Jan79-70
Ferres, J.H. and M. Tucker, eds. Modern
Commonwealth Literature.
W.N., 102(CanL):Winter78-132
Ferrey, B. Recollections of A.W.N. Pugin.
A. Sanders, 155:Spring79-46
Ferris, B. and J. Peiser - see Lipson, C.
Ferris, P. Dylan Thomas.*
F. Day, 580(SCR):Nov78-133
295(JML):Vol17#4-824
Ferris, T. Galaxies.
442(NY):8Dec80-243
Ferris, W. Blues from the Delta.
R. Coles, 152(UDQ):Fall78-156
Ferron, J. Escarmouches. Wild Roses.
L. Shohet, 102(CanL):Autumn79-118
Ferron, J. Quince Jam.
C. Gerson, 102(CanL):Autumn79-115
Ferry, L. and A. Renaut - see Horkheimer,
M.
Fersh, S. Asia.
S.C. Chu, 293(JASt):Aug79-738
Fertonani, R. - see Brentano, C.
Festa-McCormick, D. Honoré de Balzac.
A.R. Pugh, 268(IFR):Summer80-150
Fetherling, D. The Five Lives of Ben
Hecht.
A. Appenzell, 102(CanL):Spring79-74
Fetterley, J. The Resisting Reader.
M.J. Friedman, 27(AL):Nov79-426
J. Pappworth, 541(RES):Nov79-485
Fetzer, J.F. and C. Wheatley. Bibliogra-
phie der Buchrezensionen für deutsche
Literatur 1973-1974.
K.F. Otto, Jr., 406:Fall79-336
Feuer, K., ed. Solzhenitsyn.*
M. Futrell, 104(CASS):Summer78-291
Feuerwerker, D. L'émancipation des Juifs
en France.
E.A.L.V., 98:Oct78-996
Fey, H., ed and trans. Märchen aus
Bulgarien.
H-J. Uther, 196:Band19Heft1/2-126
Feyerabend, P. Science in a Free Society.*
J. Largeault, 542:Oct-Dec79-448
Feyerabend, P. Wider den Methodenzwang.
W. Rehder, 679:Band9Heft2-404
Fiacc, P. Nights in the Bad Place.*
F. Kiley, 174(Éire):Summer79-145
Fiacc, P. The Selected Padraic Fiacc.
E. Longley, 617(TLS):18Jan80-64

Fichte, J.G. Grundriss des Eigentümlichen
der Wissenschaftslehre. (W.G. Jacobs,
ed) Versuch einer neuen Darstellung der
Wissenschaftslehre. (P. Baumanns, ed)
L. Siep, 53(AGP):Band60Heft1-84
Ficino, M. Lessico greco-latino: Laur.
Ashb. 1439. (R. Pintaudi, ed)
A.C. Dionisotti, 123:Vol29No2-341
Ficino, M. The "Philebus" Commentary.*
(M.J.B. Allen, ed and trans)
M. Lentzen, 72:Band216Heft1-218
Fick, B.W. El libro de viajes en la
España medieval.*
A. Mutton, 402(MLR):Jul79-721
Fickert, K.J. Kafka's Doubles.
J.L. Hibberd, 268(IFR):Summer80-151
Fiebach, J. Von Craig bis Brecht.
D. Hoffmeier, 654(WB):2/1978-188
Fiedler, L. A Fiedler Reader.
D. Kirby, 639(VQR):Spring78-381
Fiedler, W. Analogiemodelle bei Aristo-
teles.
A.R. Lacey, 123:Vol29No2-319
Fieguth, R. - see Ingarden, R.
Field, A. Nabokov.*
C. Brown, 473(PR):1/1979-143
R. Forrey, 395(MFS):Winter78/79-636
M.T. Naumann, 558(RLJ):Winter79-206
295(JML):Vol17#4-779
Field, E. A Full Heart.*
J.R. Paris, 590:Spring/Summer78-40
Field, G.W. Hermann Hesse.
F. Wagner, 402(MLR):Jul79-760
Field, M. Michael Field's Cooking School.
W. and C. Cowen, 639(VQR):Spring78-76
Field, P.J.C. - see Malory, T.
Fielding, H. The History of Tom Jones:
A Foundling.* (F. Bowers, ed)
P. Miles, 354:Jun79-182
Fielding, H. The Jacobite's Journal and
Related Writings.* (W.B. Coley, ed)
C.J. Rawson, 447(N&Q):Apr78-190
Fielding, K.J. and R.L. Tarr, eds.
Carlyle Past and Present.*
R.E. Kowalski, 637(VS):Winter78-283
Fields, J. and J. Stacpoole. Victorian
Auckland.
P. Sargisson, 368:Mar74-85
Fiess, D. Siedlungsmundart — Heimatmun-
dart.
H. Tatzreiter, 685(ZDL):1/1979-90
Fifer, C.N. - see Farquhar, G.
Fika, A.M. The Kano Civil War and British
Overrule 1882-1940.
R. Oliver, 617(TLS):4Jan80-21
Filedt Kok, J.P. Lucas van Leyden:
grafiek.
P.W. Parshall, 600:Vol10#1-51
Filho, H.B. - see under Borba Filho, H.
Filip, R. Somebody Told Me I Looked Like
Everyman.
G. Hamel, 198:Winter80-139
Filliozat, P. - see "Le Mahābhāṣya de
Patañjali, avec le Pradīpa de Kaiyaṭa et
l'Uddyota de Nāgeśa: Adhyāya 1 Pāda 1
Āhnika 1-4"

Firmin, F. and J. Gazio. Etre jeune en
France.
  E. Namenwirth, 556(RLV):1978/1-96
Firpo, L. - see Branca, G.
First, R. and A. Scott. Olive Schreiner.
  N. Ascherson, 453(NYRB):18Dec80-17
  S.M. Gilbert, 441:14Dec80-8
  N. Gordimer, 617(TLS):15Aug80-918
  J. Lewin, 362:5Jun80-727
Fischer, A. Dialects in the South-West of
England.*
  M. Durrell, 685(ZDL):3/1979-402
  W. Kleiber, 182:Vol31#15/16-543
  J. Vachek, 682(ZPSK):Band31Heft3-330
Fischer, H. Théorie de l'art sociologique.
  J-F. Lyotard, 98:Nov78-1076
Fischer, H. - see "Der Stricker: Verserzäh-
lungen II"
Fischer, J. From the High Plains.
  J.O. Underwood, 649(WAL):Summer79-183
  42(AR):Winter79-124
Fischer, J.I. On Swift's Poetry.*
  F. Doherty, 541(RES):Aug79-353
  C. Fabricant, 141:Fall79-369
  J.L. Tyne, 613:Mar79-111
  K.J. Wagner, 627(UTQ):Winter78/79-182
Fischer, K. Dächer, Decken und Gewölbe
indischer Kultstätten und Nutzbauten.
  A. Gail, 182:Vol31#3/4-110
von Fischer, K. and F.A. Gallo, eds. Poly-
phonic Music of the Fourteenth Century.
(Vol 12)
  M. Bent, 317:Fall79-561
Fischer, L., K. Hickethier and K. Riha,
eds. Gebrauchsliteratur.
  K.F. Geiger, 196:Band19Heft1/2-145
Fischer, M. Kunstbibliothek Berlin: Kata-
log der Architektur- und Ornamentstich-
sammlung. (Pt 1)
  A. Blunt, 90:Jan79-45
Fischer, M.M.J. Iran.
  S. Bakhash, 453(NYRB):26Jun80-22
  442(NY):8Sep80-115
Fischer, P. Music in Paintings of the Low
Countries in the 16th and 17th Centuries.
  P. Reuterswärd, 341:1978/2-78
Fischer, W.L. Äquivalenz- und Toleranz-
strukturen in der Linguistik.
  J. Pogonowski, 360(LP):Vol21-187
Fischler, S.I. Moving Millions.
  442(NY):28Apr80-146
Fish, S. The Living Temple.*
  C. Bloch, 568(SCN):Spring-Summer79-1
  G. Hammond, 148:Autumn79-83
  V.R. Mollenkott, 301(JEGP):Apr79-255
Fishburn, K. Richard Wright's Hero.*
  E.L. Steeves, 395(MFS):Winter78/79-643
Fishel, J., ed. Parties and Elections in
an Anti-Party Age.
  639(VQR):Spring79-60
Fisher, A. The Crimean Tatars.
  E.J. Lazzerini, 550(RusR):Apr79-224
Fisher, B. Joyce Cary.
  C. Cook, 617(TLS):4Jul80-766
Fisher, B.F. 4th, ed. Poe at Work.*
  P.F. Quinn, 445(NCF):Mar79-486

Fisher, D. and R.B. Stepto, eds. Afro-
American Literature.
  C. Scruggs, 27(AL):Jan80-563
Fisher, J.R. Silver Mines and Silver
Miners in Colonial Peru, 1776-1824.
  P.T. Bradley, 86(BHS):Jan79-90
Fisher, M. Going Under.*
  A.M. Emery, 445(NCF):Sep78-239
  E.H. Redekop, 106:Fall79-175
  M.M. Sealts, Jr., 183(ESQ):Vol25#1-43
  N. Wright, 580(SCR):Nov78-122
  639(VQR):Spring78-53
Fisher, R. The Thing About Joe Sullivan.
  J. Cassidy, 493:Jul79-66
  A. Cluysenaar, 565:Vol120#3-68
  J. Freeman, 97(CQ):Vol18#3-274
Fishlow, A. and others. Rich and Poor
Nations in the World Economy.
  W. Leontief, 453(NYRB):4Dec80-45
Fishman, J.A. Bilingual Education.*
  R.W. Newman, 207(FR):Dec78-363
Fishman, J.A., R.L. Cooper and A.W. Conrad,
eds. The Spread of English.*
  A.D. Cohen, 350:Jun79-463
Fishman, R. Urban Utopias in the Twen-
tieth Century.*
  T. Boddy, 529(QQ):Spring79-134
  B. Horrigan, 576:Dec78-299
  J. Rykwert, 90:Oct79-661
Fisiak, J., ed. Papers and Studies in Con-
trastive Linguistics. (Vol 3)
  A.R. Tellier, 189(EA):Jan-Mar78-77
Fisiak, J., ed. Recent Developments in
Historical Phonology.
  P.V. Cubberley, 67:Nov79-376
Fiske, R. Beethoven's Missa Solemnis.
  W. Drabkin, 415:Jul79-579
  42(AR):Fall79-488
Fitch, B. and P.C. Hoy. Albert Camus I.
(3rd ed)
  I.H. Walker, 208(FS):Jul79-365
Fitch, B.T. Dimensions, structures, et
textualité dans la trilogie romanesque
de Beckett.*
  M.W. Blades, 207(FR):Apr79-782
  J. Fletcher, 402(MLR):Jul79-712
Fitch, B.T. "L'Étranger" d'Albert Camus.
  S.M. Bell, 208(FS):Jan79-110
Fitz Gerald, E. The Letters of Edward
Fitz Gerald. (A.M. and A.B. Terhune,
eds)
  442(NY):8Dec80-238
Fitz Gerald, F. America Revised.*
  W. Karp, 231:May80-80
Fitzgerald, F.S. Correspondence of F.
Scott Fitzgerald. (M.J. Bruccoli and
M.M. Duggan, with S. Walker, eds)
  J. Leonard, 441:18Apr80-C27
  G. Vidal, 453(NYRB):1May80-3
Fitzgerald, F.S. The Notebooks of F.
Scott Fitzgerald. (M.J. Bruccoli, ed)
  G. Vidal, 453(NYRB):1May80-12
  639(VQR):Spring79-68
Fitzgerald, J. Lacerating Heartwood.
  D. Barbour, 150(DR):Spring79-154
Fitzgerald, P. Human Voices.
  P.H. Newby, 362:2Oct80-445

Fitzgerald, P. Offshore.*
  D. Durrant, 364:Feb80-92
Fitz Gerald, R.D. Product.
  S.E. Lee, 581:Dec79-432
Fitzgerald, S. - see O'Connor, F.
Fitz Gibbon, C. Drink.*
  E.S. Turner, 617(TLS):14Mar80-295
  61:Jan80-88
Fitz Gibbon, C. The Rat Report.
  C. Brown, 617(TLS):27Jun80-743
Fitzhardinge, L.F. The Spartans.
  P. Cartledge, 617(TLS):4Apr80-385
Fitzpatrick, S., ed. Cultural Revolution
  in Russia, 1928-1931.
  J.C. Moses, 550(RusR):Jan79-99
  639(VQR):Autumn78-149
Fitzpatrick, S. Education and Social
  Mobility in the Soviet Union 1921-1934.
  A. Brown, 617(TLS):25Jan80-95
  G. Hosking, 617(TLS):15Aug80-910
Fitzsimons, C. Reflex Action.
  N. Callendar, 441:31Aug80-17
Fitz Simons, R. Edmund Kean.
  C.S. Stern, 637(VS):Autumn77-123
Fiukowski, H. and others. Einführung in
  die Sprechwissenschaft.
  E. Kurka, 682(ZPSK):Band31Heft6-630
Fjelde, R. - see Ibsen, H.
Flacelière, R. and E. Chambry - see Plu-
  tarch
Flaherty, G. Opera in the Development of
  German Critical Thought.
  C. Morey, 255(HAB):Summer79-217
  P. Weiss, 222(GR):Fall79-172
Flamain, A. and M. Nicolas, eds and trans.
  Contes de Turquie.
  O. Spies, 196:Band19Heft1/2-147
Flanagan, C.C. and J.T. American Folk-
  lore.*
  J.H. Brunvand, 650(WF):Jan79-66
Flanagan, R. Gravity.
  D. Barbour, 150(DR):Spring79-154
Flanagan, R. Once You Learn You Never For-
  get.
  G. Hamel, 198:Winter80-139
Flanner, J. Janet Flanner's World.* (I.
  Drutman, ed)
  R. Mayne, 617(TLS):22Feb80-203
  V. Thomson, 453(NYRB):24Jan80-6
Flannery, J.W. W.B. Yeats and the Idea of
  a Theatre.*
  A.N. Jeffares, 610:Oct78-68
  G-D. Zimmermann, 179(ES):Aug79-526
Flannery, M.C. Yeats and Magic.*
  R.A. Cave, 541(RES):Feb79-106
Flasche, H. Geschichte der spanischen
  Literatur.* (Vol 1)
  J.L. Laurenti, 399(MLJ):Jan-Feb79-78
  C.R. Owen, 182:Vol131#14-483
Flasche, H. and H-D. Merl, eds. Aufsätze
  zur portugiesischen Kulturgeschichte.
  (Vol 14)
  G.M. Moser, 238:Mar79-182
"Flathead Cultural and Language Materials."
  (Bk 1)
  E.P. Hamp, 269(IJAL):Oct78-352

Flaubert, G. The Letters of Gustave
  Flaubert, 1830-1857. (F. Steegmuller,
  ed and trans)
  R.M. Adams, 31(ASch):Autumn80-540
  A. Broyard, 441:20Feb80-C23
  D. Johnson, 441:17Feb80-1
  V.S. Pritchett, 453(NYRB):3Apr80-3
  J. Updike, 442(NY):25Feb80-127
Flaubert, G. Plans, Notes et Scénarios de
  "Un Coeur Simple."* (F. Fleury, ed)
  A.W. Raitt, 402(MLR):Jul79-699
  U. Schulz-Buschhaus, 547(RF):Band91
  Heft3-327
Flaubert, G. The Temptation of Saint
  Antony. (K. Mrosovsky, trans)
  D.J. Enright, 362:11Dec80-801
Flaubert, G. "Un Coeur simple." (S.E.
  Douyère, ed)
  A.W. Raitt, 402(MLR):Jul79-699
Fleck, R.F. Cottonwood Moon.
  S.S. Moorty, 649(WAL):Winter80-340
Fleckenstein, J., ed. Herrschaft und
  Stand.
  B. Arnold, 182:Vol131#23/24-889
Fleetwood, H. Fictional Lives.
  P. Bailey, 617(TLS):18Jul80-798
Fleetwood, H. The Redeemer.*
  N. Callendar, 441:7Sep80-37
Fleischer, E. Hebrew Liturgical Poetry in
  the Middle Ages.
  M. Saperstein, 322(JHI):Jan-Mar79-159
Fleischhauer, I. Philosophische Aufklä-
  rung in Russland.
  H.A. Stammler, 550(RusR):Apr79-228
Fleischman, S. Cultural and Linguistic
  Factors in Word Formation.
  N. Corbett, 320(CJL):Spring-Fall78-144
  J. Palermo, 589:Apr79-368
Fleischmann, K. Verbstellung und Relief-
  theorie.
  R. Kern, 277(ITL):#41/42-124
Fleishman, A. Fiction and the Ways of
  Knowing.
  T. Eagleton, 541(RES):Aug79-370
  R.F. Kennedy, 268(IFR):Summer80-150
  R. Saldívar, 594:Fall79-362
  639(VQR):Spring79-49
Fleishman, L., O. Ronen and D. Segal -
  see "Slavica Hierosolymitana"
Fleming, J. and H. Honour. The Penguin
  Dictionary of Decorative Arts.
  U. Middeldorf, 471:Jan/Feb/Mar79-82
Fleming, J.V. An Introduction to the Fran-
  ciscan Literature of the Middle Ages.
  I.D.L. Clark, 402(MLR):Apr79-391
  W.R. Thomson, 589:Jan79-126
Fleming, R.E. James Weldon Johnson and
  Arna Wendell Bontemps.
  M. Gray, 95(CLAJ):Jun79-425
Fleming, R.E. Willard Motley.
  M. Gray, 95(CLAJ):Jun79-425
  A. Rayson, 594:Summer79-244
Fleron, F.A., Jr., ed. Technology and
  Communist Culture.
  T. Fingar, 293(JASt):Feb79-357
Fletcher, I., ed. Decadence of the 1890s.
  P. Keating, 617(TLS):11Jan80-34

Fletcher, R.A. The Episcopate of the King-
dom of León in the Twelfth Century.
   J. Edwards, 86(BHS):Oct79-334
Fleury, F. - see Flaubert, G.
Flew, A. Sociology, Equality and Educa-
tion.
   H. Siegel, 488:Mar79-116
Flew, A.G.N. Thinking Straight.
   D.N. Walton, 154:Sep78-582
Flexner, J.T. America's Old Masters.
   J. Russell, 441:30Nov80-72
Flexner, J.T. States Dyckman.
   P-L. Adams, 61:Sep80-108
   E. Auchincloss, 441:17Aug80-12
   442(NY):25Aug80-102
Flexner, S.B. I Hear America Talking.*
   T.C. Frazer, 300:Mar79-82
   K.B. Harder, 424:Sep77-174
   O. Hatteras 3d, 269(IJAL):Oct78-350
Flobert, P. Les Verbes déponents latins
des origines à Charlemagne.*
   E. Laughton, 123:Vol29No1-90
Flood, J. The Land They Occupied.*
   D.G. Jones, 102(CanL):Winter78-77
Flores, A., ed. Aproximaciones a Horacio
Quiroga.*
   R.H. Ferguson, 263(RIB):Vol29No1-93
Flores, A. A Kafka Bibliography 1908-
1976.*
   H. Reiss, 402(MLR):Jan79-249
Flores, A., ed. The Kafka Debate.*
   H.S. Daemmrich, 395(MFS):Winter78/79-
   609
   T.C. Hanlin, 295(JML):Vol7#4-752
   I.C. Henel, 301(JEGP):Apr79-301
   J.L. Hibberd, 402(MLR):Oct79-996
Flores, A., ed. The Problem of "The Judg-
ment."*
   J.L. Hibberd, 402(MLR):Oct79-996
Flores, L. Apuntes de español.
   R.R. Young, 238:Mar79-191
Florey, K.B. Family Matters.
   S. Isaacs, 441:16Mar80-14
de Florian, J-P.C. Nouvelles. (R.
Godenne, ed)
   V. Mylne, 208(FS):Vol33Pt2-786
Floriani, P. Bembo e Castiglione.
   M. Pozzi, 228(GSLI):Vol155fasc490-299
Flory, M.A. A Book About Fans.
   W.K. McNeil, 292(JAF):Apr-Jun79-244
Flottes, P. Histoire de la poésie politi-
que et sociale en France de 1815 à 1939.
   J.O. Fischer, 535(RHL):Jan-Feb79-150
Flower, E. and M.G. Murphey. A History
of Philosophy in America.* (Vol 1)
   N.S. Fiering, 656(WMQ):Jan79-133
   D.M. Orange, 258:Sep79-366
Flower, E. and M.G. Murphey. A History
of Philosophy in America.* (Vol 2)
   D.M. Orange, 258:Sep79-366
Flower, J.E., ed. France Today.* (3rd
ed)
   205(FMLS):Apr78-186
Flower, J.E. Writers and Politics in
Modern France (1909-1961).
   P.A. Ouston, 208(FS):Vol33Pt2-944
   205(FMLS):Jan78-88

Flowers, B.S. Browning and the Modern
Tradition.*
   J.B. Bullen, 447(N&Q):Jun78-264
   R. Jackson, 402(MLR):Jul79-674
Fluck, H-R. Arbeit und Gerät im Wort-
schatz der Fischer des badischen Hanauer-
landes.
   P. Dalcher, 182:Vol131#5/6-141
Fluck, H-R. Fachsprachen.*
   J. Dückert, 682(ZPSK):Band31Heft3-290
Flückiger, J-C. Au coeur du texte.*
   E. Sellin, 207(FR):Feb79-493
   205(FMLS):Apr78-185
Flukinger, R., L. Schaaf and S. Meacham.
Paul Martin, Victorian Photographer.
   M. Roskill, 637(VS):Spring79-335
Fly, R. Shakespeare's Mediated World.*
   J.H. Summers, 570(SQ):Winter79-103
Flynn, G. Manuel Brêton de los Herreros.
   R.J. Quirk, 593:Winter79-362
Flynn, P. Francis Jeffrey.
   S. Bennett, 301(JEGP):Apr79-267
   F. Jordan, 661(WC):Summer79-314
   J.U. Peters, 651(WHR):Spring79-154
   639(VQR):Winter79-8
Flynt, C. Chasing Dad.
   S. Spencer, 441:7Sep80-13
Flynt, J.W. Dixie's Forgotten People.
   H. Brogan, 617(TLS):22Feb80-213
Flynt, W. Cracker Messiah.
   J.H. Shofner, 9(AlaR):Jan79-71
Fodor, J.D. Semantics.*
   G.L. Ioup, 350:Jun79-425
Foerst, G. Die Gravierungen der pränestin-
ischen Cisten.
   K. Schauenburg, 182:Vol131#17/18-619
Fogarty, N. Shelley in the Twentieth
Century.
   P. Magnuson, 402(MLR):Jul79-667
Fogel, R.W. and S.L. Engerman. Time on
the Cross.*
   L. Krieger, 473(PR):1/1979-152
Fokkema, D.W. and E. Kunne-Ibsch. Theor-
ies of Literature in the Twentieth Cen-
tury.*
   J. Barnouw, 149(CLS):Jun79-183
   T. Hawkes, 89(BJA):Winter79-86
   H. Servotte, 179(ES):Dec79-819
   W.G. Weststeijn, 204(FdL):Jun79-187
Fokkema, D.W., E. Kunne-Ibsch and A.J.A.
van Zoest, eds. Comparative Poetics —
Poétique comparative — Vergleichende
Poetik — In Honour of Jan Kamerbeek Jr.
   W. Ross, 52:Band13Heft3-303
Folb, E.A. Runnin' Down Some Lines.
   P-L. Adams, 61:May80-104
Folda, J. Crusader Manuscript Illumina-
tion at Saint-Jean d'Acre, 1275-1291.*
   M.P. Lillich, 54:Mar78-161
Folejewski, Z. and others, eds. Canadian
Contributions to the VIII International
Congress of Slavists (Zagreb-Ljubljana,
1978). (Pt 1)
   H.R. Cooper, Jr., 574(SEEJ):Fall79-
   415
   F.C.M. Kitch, 575(SEER):Oct79-631

120

Folejewski, Z. and others, eds. Canadian
Contributions to the VIII International
Congress of Slavists (Zagreb-Ljubljana,
1978). (Pts 2 and 3)
    R. Dunatov, 574(SEEJ):Fall79-416
Foley, A.E. - see under Espantoso Foley, A.
Foley, J. Foundations of Theoretical
Phonology.*
    R. Coates, 297(JL):Mar79-132
    D.C. Walker, 320(CJL):Spring-Fall78-
    138
    205(FMLS):Apr78-185
Foley, M. The Story of Story Magazine.
(J. Neugeboren, ed)
    W. Saroyan, 441:8Jun80-11
    442(NY):16Jun80-123
Foley, M.M. The American House.
    P-L. Adams, 61:May80-104
Foley, V. The Social Physics of Adam
Smith.
    M.L. Myers, 173(ECS):Fall78-134
Folkenflik, R. Samuel Johnson, Biographer.
    F. Brady, 676(YR):Autumn79-118
    H.W. Hamilton, 301(JEGP):Oct79-556
"Folklore and Fakelore."
    W.K. McNeil, 292(JAF):Apr-Jun79-243
Follain, J. Présent jour.
    V. Godel, 98:Nov78-1090
Follain, J. A World Rich in Anniversaries.
    R. Morgan, 181:Spring-Summer79-299
Follett, K. The Key to Rebecca.
    P. Andrews, 441:21Sep80-9
Folsom, J.K., ed. The Western.
    D.E. Wylder, 649(WAL):Winter80-322
Folsome, C.E. The Origin of Life.
    529(QQ):Winter79/80-735
Foltin, H.F. and G. Würzberg. Arbeitswelt
im Fernsehen.
    B. Tümmler, 654(WB):6/1978-178
Fondiller, H., ed. The Best of Popular
Photography.
    J. Manning, 441:11Aug80-C17
Fong, W., ed. The Great Bronze Age of
China.
    M. Sullivan, 441:31Aug80-10
Fong, W. Summer Mountains.
    A.C. Soper, 54:Sep80-568
da Fonseca, E.N. - see under Nery da
Fonseca, E.
Fontaine, J. No Bed of Roses.*
    B. Weeks, 18:Dec78/Jan79-74
Fontana, V. and P. Morachiello - see Calvo,
F.
Fontane, T. Jenny Treibel.* (U. Zimmer-
mann, ed and trans)
    G. Schulz-Behrend, 406:Fall79-345
Fontane, T. Werke, Schriften und Briefe.
(Section 4, Vol 1) (W. Keitel and H.
Nürnberger, eds)
    W. Paulsen, 222(GR):Winter79-38
Fontane, T. The Woman Taken in Adultery
[and] The Poggenpuhl Family. (G. Annan,
ed and trans)
    J. Weightman, 362:21Feb80-252

Fontanella de Weinberg, M.B. La lengua
española fuera de España.
    G. Carrillo-Herrera, 72:Band216Heft2-
    448
Fonteyn, M. The Magic of Dance.
    M. Hodgson, 441:13Jan80-13
Foot, M. Debts of Honour.
    A. Howard, 362:13Nov80-659
Foot, P. Virtues and Vices and Other
Essays in Moral Philosophy.
    J. Donnelly, 258:Dec79-493
    A. Quinton, 617(TLS):4Jan80-18
Foote, I.P. - see Saltykov-Shchedrin, M.E.
Foote, R.L. The Case of Port Hawkesbury.
    D. Frank, 99:Jun-Jul80-33
Foote, S. September, September.*
    J.N. Gretlund, 577(SHR):Fall79-361
Forbes, B. Dame Edith Evans: Ned's Girl.
    B. Weeks, 18:Nov78-72
Forbes, B. Stranger.
    J. Burke, 441:11May80-14
Forbes, B. That Despicable Race.
    J. Elsom, 362:27Nov80-731
Forbes, C. Avalanche Express.
    639(VQR):Winter78-24
Forbis, W.H. Fall of the Peacock Throne.
    F. Ajami, 441:2Mar80-6
    442(NY):24Mar80-134
Forcadel, E. Oeuvres poétiques.* (F.
Joukovsky, ed)
    F.C. Cornfield, 207(FR):Dec78-342
    A. Saunders, 402(MLR):Jan79-197
Ford, C. The Cameron Collection.
    B. Jay, 637(VS):Winter78-294
Ford, C. and R. Strong. An Early Victo-
rian Album.
    B. Jay, 637(VS):Winter78-294
"Charlotte Ford's Book of Modern Manners."
    D. Grumbach, 441:30Mar80-12
Ford, D. Pappy.
    D. Grumbach, 441:6Jan80-14
Ford, E. The Playhouse.
    G. Godwin, 441:5Oct80-14
Ford, G. and S. Monod - see Dickens, C.
Ford, G.H., ed. Victorian Fiction: A
Second Guide to Research.*
    D.J. De Laura, 191(ELN):Dec78-178
Ford, J. Paradigms and Fairy Tales.
    K.F. Geiger, 196:Band19Heft3/4-325
Ford, P.K., ed and trans. The "Mabinogi"
and Other Medieval Welsh Tales.*
    B.A. Rosenberg, 292(JAF):Oct-Dec79-496
    D. Skeels, 650(WF):Jul79-202
Ford, R.A.D. Holes in Space.
    D. Precosky, 198:Summer80-156
    376:Oct79-141
Fordyce, C.J. - see Vergil
Foreman, L. - see O'Byrne, D.
Foreman, W.C., Jr. The Music of the Close.
    J.L. Calderwood, 401(MLQ):Dec79-415
Forer, L.G. Criminals and Victims.
    L. Greenhouse, 441:6Jul80-6
    G. Hughes, 453(NYRB):20Nov80-47
    442(NY):18Aug80-92
Forest, A. L'avvento dell'anima.
    E. Namer, 542:Jul-Sep79-354

Foresti, A. Aneddoti della vita di Francesco Petrarca. (new ed) (A. Tissoni Benvenuti, ed)
E. Bigi, 228(GSLI):Vol155fasc491-445
Forestier, L., ed. "Agencer un univers nouveau."
P. Cogny, 535(RHL):Jul-Aug79-702
Forestier, L. - see "Arthur Rimbaud 3"
de Forêt, N.C. Charon's Daughter.
639(VQR):Autumn78-145
"Forging the Links."
R.D. Heyding, 529(QQ):Winter79/80-695
"Form and Substance."
G.F. Meier, 682(ZPSK):Band31Heft2-200
Formaggio, D. Arte e civiltà.
P.P., 227(GCFI):Apr-Jun78-286
Forman, M.L. Kapampangan Dictionary.
G.F. Meier, 682(ZPSK):Band31Heft2-202
Forman, M.L. Kapampangan Grammar Notes.
G.F. Meier, 682(ZPSK):Band31Heft2-203
Fornaro, M. Il lavoro negli scritti jenesi di Hegel.
E. Namer, 542:Apr-Jun79-251
Fornerod, F. - see Béguin, A. and G. Roud
Forrest, A. Society and Politics in Revolutionary Bordeaux.
W. Scott, 208(FS):Vol33Pt2-1002
Forrest-Thomson, V. Poetic Artifice.
M. Perloff, 659(ConL):Spring80-291
Forrester, W. Great-Grandmama's Weekly.
P. Keating, 617(TLS):15Aug80-908
Forschner, M. Gesetz und Freiheit.
J. Schindler, 342:Band69Heft2-218
"Forschungen zur osteuropäischen Geschichte." (Vol 23)
J. Raba, 104(CASS):Summer78-291
Forsgren, K-Å. Wortdefinition und Feldstruktur.
E. Beneš, 685(ZDL):3/1979-366
Forsgren, M. La place de l'adjectif épithète en français contemporain.
I. Burr, 547(RF):Band91Heft3-319
Förster, E. Romanstruktur und Weltanschauung im Werk L-F. Célines.
A. Thiher, 395(MFS):Winter78/79-612
Forster, E.M. Arctic Summer, and Other Fiction.
P. Conrad, 362:18and25Dec80-861
Forster, M. The Bride of Lowther Fell.
J. Mellors, 362:6Nov80-623
Forster, R. and O. Ranum, eds. Rural Society in France.
H.L. Butler, 207(FR):Oct78-193
Förster, U. Zur Aktivierung und Reaktivierung sprachlicher Kenntnisse im Fortgeschrittenenunterricht.
I-E. Rachmankulowa, 682(ZPSK):Band31-Heft1-100
Forsthoff, E. and R. Hörstel, eds. Standorte im Zeitstrom.
H. Ottmann, 489(PJGG):Band86Heft1-148
Forsyth, F. The Devil's Alternative.
A. Cockburn, 453(NYRB):6Nov80-48
I.P. Heldman, 441:24Feb80-30
M. Laski, 362:10Jan80-62
J. Leonard, 441:17Jan80-C21

Forsyth, J. A Grammar of Aspect.
D. Huntley, 320(CJL):Spring-Fall78-162
Forsyth, J. Listening to the Wind.
J. Graffy, 575(SEER):Jul79-435
R.J. Keys, 402(MLR):Apr79-510
L. Vogel, 574(SEEJ):Spring79-132
Forsythe, D.W. Taxation and Political Change in the Young Nation, 1781-1833.
P.W. Brewer, 656(WMQ):Jan79-151
"Fort Stanwix."
W.B. Robinson, 576:Mar78-48
Forti, F. Magnanimitade.
M. Marti, 228(GSLI):Vol155fasc491-443
Fortier, P.A. Une lecture de Camus.*
V. Conley, 395(MFS):Winter78/79-615
P. Henry, 207(FR):Feb79-497
Fortmüller, H-J. Clemens Brentano als Briefschreiber.
J.F.F., 191(ELN):Sep78(supp)-144
Foscolo, U. Scritti vari di critica storica e letteraria (1817-1827). (U. Limentani, with J.M.A. Lindon, eds)
G. Carsaniga, 402(MLR):Jul79-716
Foscolo, U. Studi su Dante. (Pt 1) (G. da Pozza, ed)
P. Shaw, 617(TLS):2May80-501
Fösel, K.R. Der Deus ex machina in der Komödie.
E. Sallager, 72:Band216Heft1-149
Foskett, D. Collecting Miniatures.
G. Reynolds, 39:Nov79-453
Foss, D.J. and D.T. Hakes. Psycholinguistics.
D. MacKay, 350:Jun79-491
Foster, B. and I. Short - see Thomas of Kent
Foster, D.W. Chilean Literature.
J.A. Epple, 263(RIB):Vol29No2-207
Foster, D.W. and V.R. Manual of Hispanic Bibliography.* (2nd ed)
A.J.C. Bainton, 86(BHS):Jul79-272
Foster, J. Class Struggle and the Industrial Revolution.
D. Fraser, 161(DUJ):Dec78-107
Foster, J. An Un-American Lady.
H. Brogan, 362:30Oct80-586
Foster, K. The Two Dantes and Other Studies.
C. Hardie, 382(MAE):1979/2-302
Foster, K.P. Aegean Faience of the Bronze Age.
P. Warren, 617(TLS):25Apr80-478
Foster, P. The Buddhist Influence in T.S. Eliot's "Four Quartets."
H. Servotte, 179(ES):Dec79-811
Foster, R.F. Charles Stewart Parnell.*
L.J. McCaffrey, 637(VS):Summer79-449
Foster, S. and R. Kuenzli, eds. Dada Spectrum.
D. Ades, 617(TLS):11Apr80-422
Fothergill, B. Beckford of Fonthill.
A. Dickins, 364:Oct79-90
Fothergill-Payne, L. La alegoría en los autos y farsas anteriores a Calderón.
H.E. Bergman, 405(MP):May80-411
P.N. Dunn, 593:Winter79-371

[continued]

Fraser, D. Urban Politics in Victorian England.
  E.P. Hennock, 637(VS):Winter78-288
Fraser, G.M., ed. The World of the Public School.
  639(VQR):Summer78-108
Fraser, G.S. Alexander Pope.*
  M.R. Brownell, 566:Spring79-122
  C.L. Horne, 67:Nov79-322
Fraser, J. The Chinese.
  R. Elegant, 441:23Nov80-12
  J. Leonard, 441:16Dec80-C9
Fraser, J. Violence in the Arts.
  R.G. Cox, 447(N&Q):Aug78-366
Fraser, J.T. and N. Lawrence, eds. The Study of Time II.
  J. Leslie, 486:Jun78-322
Fraser, K. New Shoes.*
  639(VQR):Autumn78-146
Fraser, P.M. - see Butler, A.J.
Fraser, R. The Language of Adam.*
  W.E. Cain, 125:Winter79-299
  M. McCanles, 301(JEGP):Jan79-109
  639(VQR):Spring78-54
Fraser, S. A Casual Affair.*
  L. Rogers, 102(CanL):Summer79-137
  S. Wood, 168(ECW):Summer78-130
Fraser, S.E., ed. 100 Great Chinese Posters.
  R. Croizier, 293(JASt):Feb79-303
Fraser, W.D. Nor'east for Louisburg.
  S.E. Read, 102(CanL):Summer79-112
Frassatti, L. Un uomo, un giornale. (Pt 1)
  J.A. Davis, 617(TLS):2May80-503
Fratangelo, A. and M. Guy de Maupassant scrittore moderno.
  E.D. Sullivan, 535(RHL):Jul-Aug79-669
Frauenrath, M. Le fils assassiné.*
  W. Rothwell, 182:Vol131#19-677
Frede, H.J., ed. Vetus Latina. (Fasc 25)
  P. Courcelle, 555:Vol52fasc1-203
Fredeman, W.E. - see Rossetti, W.M.
Fredericksen, D.L. The Aesthetic of Isolation in Film Theory.
  J. Stolnitz, 290(JAAC):Summer80-473
Frederickson, H. Baudelaire, héros et fils.
  W.T. Bandy, 207(FR):Mar79-645
  S.D. Braun, 446(NCFS):Fall-Winter78/79-134
Fredman, M. Kisses Leave No Fingerprints.
  N. Callendar, 441:17Aug80-19
Freeborn, R., G. Donchin and N.J. Anning, eds. Russian Literary Attitudes from Pushkin to Solzhenitsyn.*
  M.H. Shotton, 447(N&Q):Dec78-572
Freeborn, R., R.R. Milner-Gulland and C.A. Ward, eds. Russian and Slavic Literature.
  J. Grayson, 575(SEER):Apr79-278
Freeden, M. The New Liberalism.
  D. Spring, 637(VS):Spring79-378
Freedman, M.H. Lawyer's Ethics in an Adversary System.
  A.R., 543:Mar79-542

Freedman, R. Hermann Hesse.*
  W. Blomster, 399(MLJ):Sep-Oct79-310
  R. Gray, 617(TLS):11Jan80-45
  P. Vansittart, 364:Oct79-87
  639(VQR):Spring79-72
Freedman, W. Laurence Sterne and the Origins of the Musical Novel.
  A. Burke, 50(ArQ):Autumn79-281
  K.E. Maus, 594:Summer79-237
  D. Melnick, 569(SR):Fall79-cviii
Freeling, N. Castang's City.
  T.J. Binyon, 617(TLS):30May80-606
  M. Laski, 362:14Aug80-216
Freely, M. Mother's Helper.*
  J. Chernaik, 364:Mar80-90
Freeman, G. The Schoolgirl Ethic.
  C.S. Stern, 637(VS):Spring79-352
Freeman, J.M. Untouchable.
  H. Tinker, 617(TLS):5Sep80-970
Freeman, M.J. - see de Larivey, P.
Freeman, R.B. The Works of Charles Darwin.
  F. Burkhardt, 517(PBSA):Apr-Jun78-282
Freemantle, B. Charlie Muffin U.S.A.
  N. Callendar, 441:7Dec80-45
Freese, P., ed. Die amerikanische Short Story der Gegenwart.*
  R. Asselineau, 189(EA):Jul-Dec78-420
  A. Guttmann and D. Bargen, 72:Band216 Heft2-429
Frege, G. Logical Investigations.
  J. Largeault, 542:Apr-Jun78-219
  N. Tennant, 518:Oct79-112
Frei-Lüthy, C. Der Einfluss der griechischen Personennamen auf die Wortbildung.
  H. Schmeja, 343:Band23-115
von Freiberg, D. Opera omnia. (Vol 1) (B. Mojsisch, ed)
  H. Weidemann, 489(PJGG):Band86Heft2-425
Freiberg, M., ed. Journals of the House of Representatives of Massachusetts, 1769-1770 and 1770-1771. (Vols 46 and 47)
  J.A. Schutz, 432(NEQ):Sep79-441
Freieleben, H-C. Geschichte der Navigation.
  H. Meinhold, 182:Vol31#14-507
Freigrossen, Z. Yoman HaZichronos.
  T.N. Lewis, 287:Jun/Jul78-25
Freile Granizo, C. and others. Espejo.
  P.L. Astuto, 263(RIB):Vol29No3/4-364
Freiman, G. It Seems I Am a Jew. (M.B. Nathanson, ed and trans)
  W. Goodman, 441:13Jul80-16
Freire, P. Pedagogy in Process.
  C.S. Taylor, 42(AR):Winter79-116
Fremantle, F. and C. Trungpa - see "The Tibetan Book of the Dead"
Fremlin, C. With No Crying.
  T.J. Binyon, 617(TLS):30May80-606
  M. Laski, 362:14Aug80-216
Frénaud, A. Notre inhabileté fatale.
  D. Leuwers, 450(NRF):Aug79-119
Frénaud, A. A Round O.
  J. Freeman, 97(CQ):Vol8#3-283

Friesen, G.K. and W. Schatzberg, eds. The German Contribution to the Building of the Americas.*
  L. Dorsett, 152(UDQ):Summer78-154
Friesen, P. Bluebottle.*
  G. Hamel, 198:Winter80-139
Friman, K. Zum angloamerikanischen Einfluss auf die heutige deutsche Werbesprache.
  E. Erämetsä, 439(NM):1978/4-440
Frisby, J.P. Seeing: Illusion, Brain, and Mind.
  442(NY):24Mar80-135
von Frisch, K. Les insectes, maîtres de la terre?
  J. Bouveresse, 98:Aug-Sep78-764
Frisch, M. Man in the Holocene.
  P-L. Adams, 61:Aug80-85
  M. Hamburger, 617(TLS):12Sep80-983
  J. Leonard, 441:22May80-C25
  G. Stade, 441:22Jun80-1
Frisé, A. - see Musil, R.
Frithjof, B. On Being Free.
  R. Young, 63:Jun79-193
Fritz, G., ed. Abbildungen zur Neidhart-Überlieferung I.
  B. Murdoch, 182:Vol131#11/12-345
Fritz, G. Bedeutungswandel im Deutschen.*
  J. Wiktorowicz, 360(LP):Vol21-164
von Fritz, K. Schriften zur griechischen und römischen Verfassungsgeschichte und Verfassungstheorie.*
  G.J.D. Aalders H. Wzn., 394: Vol32fasc3/4-438
  R.W., 555:Vol152fasc2-360
Fritz, P. and D. Williams, eds. City and Society in the 18th Century.
  M.H. Waddicor, 208(FS):Apr79-191
Fritz, W.D., ed. Die Goldene Bulle Kaiser Karls IV. vom Jahre 1356.
  R. Ganghofer, 182:Vol131#14-471
Frizman, L.G., ed. Literaturno-kritičeskie raboty dekabristov.
  L.C. O'Bell, 574(SEEJ):Summer79-265
Froissart, J. Ballades et rondeaux. (R.S. Baudouin, ed)
  N.B. Smith, 589:Jul79-590
Froissart, J. Le Joli Buisson de Jonece. (A. Fourrier, ed) The Lyric Poems of Jehan Froissart. (R.R. McGregor, Jr., ed)
  A.H. Diverres, 208(FS):Vol33Pt2-574
Froissart, J. La Prison amoureuse.* (A. Fourrier, ed)
  J.C. Laidlaw, 208(FS):Vol33Pt2-573
Frolic, B.M. Mao's People.
  J. Lelyveld, 441:17Jul80-C17
  R. Witke, 441:18May80-15
Frolov, I.T. Dialectique et éthique en biologie.
  J-M. Gabaude, 542:Jul-Sep79-355
de Froment, D. and L. Lewis, eds. Art at Auction.
  F. Neugass, 471:Jul/Aug/Sep79-289

Fromkin, V. and R. Rodman. An Introduction to Language. (2nd ed)
  G. Horrocks, 297(JL):Sep79-384
  S. Whitley, 353:Mar78-65
Fromm, E. Le cœur de l'homme.
  M. Adam, 542:Jul-Sep79-356
Fromm, E. La conception de l'homme chez Marx.
  A. Reix, 542:Jan-Mar78-121
Fromm, G.G. Dorothy Richardson.*
  R.F. Peterson, 395(MFS):Winter78/79-571
Fromm, H. and others - see von Fussesbrunnen, K.
Frommelt, R. Paneuropa oder Mitteleuropa.
  J. Hiden, 575(SEER):Oct79-620
Frommer, H. New York City Baseball.
  J. Oppenheimer, 441:15Jun80-7
Frost, D.L. - see Middleton, T.
Frühwald, W. Eichendorff-Chronik.
  J.F.F., 191(ELN):Sep78(supp)-150
Frühwald, W. Das Spätwerk Clemens Brentanos (1815-1842).*
  J.F.F., 191(ELN):Sep78(supp)-145
  J. Fetzer, 133:Band12Heft4-370
  E.W. Herd, 67:May79-142
  R. Liwerski, 684(ZDA):Band107Heft3-139
  E. Stopp, 402(MLR):Jul79-750
Frutos Cortés, E. Creación poética.*
  E.A. Southworth, 402(MLR):Jul79-731
Fruttero, C. and F. Lucentini. A che punto è la notte.
  F. Donini, 617(TLS):11Jan80-30
Fry, C. Can You Find Me?*
  H. Hobson, 157:Spring79-13
Fry, G-M. Night Riders in Black Folk History.
  C.L. Perdue, Jr., 582(SFQ):Vol141-269
Fry, J., ed. Twenty-Five African Sculptures/Vingt-cinq sculptures africaines.
  529(QQ):Summer79-371
Fry, P. Spirits of Protest.
  M.F.C. Bourdillon, 69:Vol148#4-410
Fry, P.H. The Poet's Calling in the English Ode.
  P. Rogers, 617(TLS):8Aug80-891
Frye, N. Northrup Frye on Culture and Literature.* (R.D. Denham, ed)
  W.E. Cain, 580(SCR):Nov78-123
  C.P. Crowley, 628(UWR):Spring-Summer79-96
  S. Kane, 627(UTQ):Summer79-431
  W.N., 102(CanL):Winter78-132
Frye, N. The Secular Scripture.*
  C. Lindahl, 292(JAF):Jan-Mar79-80
Frye, N. Spiritus Mundi.*
  W.E. Cain, 580(SCR):Nov78-123
  D.L. Eder, 152(UDQ):Spring78-81
Frye, R.M. Milton's Imagery and the Visual Arts.*
  D.D.C. Chambers, 541(RES):Feb79-82
  M. Pointon, 90:May79-328
  D.E. Ray, 49:Jan79-97
  639(VQR):Winter79-22
Fryer, J. The Faces of Eve.*
  E. Moers, 402(MLR):Apr79-431

Frykman, E. "Unemphatic Marvels."
C. Guillot, 189(EA):Jul-Dec78-421
Fu, J.S. Mystic and Comic Aspects of the Quest.
N. Simms, 107(CRCL):Fall79-440
Fubini, M. Tre note manzoniane.
D. Conrieri, 228(GSLI):Vol55fasc489-154
Fuchs, A. Le "Faust" de Goethe.
D.B. Richards, 182:Vol31#15/16-544
Fuchs, A. Goethe-Studien.
D. Hochstätter, 657(WW):Mar-Apr78-134
Fuchs, D. The Apathetic Bookie Joint.*
H. Beaver, 617(TLS):18Apr80-431
Fuchs, M. Funktionelle Entspannung.
H. Wendt, 682(ZPSK):Band31Heft2-222
Fuchs, R.H. Dutch Painting.
C. Brown, 39:Dec79-540
Fuchs, S.M. Die Mundart des Kantons Schwyz.*
W. König, 685(ZDL):3/1979-377
Fuchs, W. Die Bilderalben für die Südreisen des Kaisers Kienlung im 18. Jahrhundert.
M. Gimm, 182:Vol31#15/16-557
de Fuenllana, M. Miguel de Fuenllana: Orphenica Lyra (Seville, 1554). (C. Jacobs, ed)
S. Bloch, 414(MusQ):Jul79-445
de Fuentes, Á.G. - see under Galmés de Fuentes, Á.
Fuentes, C. Burnt Water.
E. Connell, 441:19Oct80-9
J. Leonard, 441:3Dec80-C29
61:Nov80-96
Fuentes, C. Holy Place.
639(VQR):Autumn79-140
Fuentes, C. The Hydra Head.*
A.J. MacAdam, 37:Apr79-37
639(VQR):Autumn79-135
Fuerst, N. Ideologie und Literatur.*
G.M. Vajda, 52:Band13Heft1-108
Fuertes, L.A. To a Young Bird Artist. (G.M. Sutton, ed)
W. Gard, 584(SWR):Autumn79-399
R.A. Sokolov, 441:18May80-15
Fugard, A. Tsotsi.
J. Mellors, 362:10Apr80-482
A. Niven, 617(TLS):2May80-500
Fugazzola Delpino, M.A. Testimonianze di cultura appenninica nel Lazio.
D. and F.R. Ridgway, 313:Vol69-212
Fuhrmann, F. - see Plutarch
Fuhrmann, M., ed. Christianisme et formes littéraires de l'antiquité tardive en occident.
P. Courcelle, 555:Vol52fasc2-407
G.H. Ettlinger, 124:Nov79-189
Fuhrmans, H. - see Schelling, F.W.J.
Fujii, H. Time, Landscape and the Ideal Life.*
J-F. Camé, 189(EA):Jul-Dec78-365
Fujioka, R. Shino and Oribe Ceramics.*
P.C. Swann, 463:Spring79-117
Fukazawa, S. Études à propos des chansons de Narayama.
G. Quinsat, 450(NRF):Feb79-124

Fülberth, G. and J. Harrer. Die deutsche Sozialdemokratie 1890-1933.
A. Lasserre, 182:Vol31#23/24-890
Fulco, W. The Canaanite God Rešep.
A. Spalinger, 318(JAOS):Oct-Dec78-515
Fullenwider, H.J. Rilke and His Reviewers.
L.S. Pickle, 301(JEGP):Apr79-300
Fuller, J. Lies and Secrets.
D. Davis, 362:31Jan80-157
A. Elliot, 617(TLS):4Jan80-4
Fuller, R. The Reign of Sparrows. Souvenirs.
P. Beer, 362:21Feb80-254
J. Lucas, 617(TLS):7Mar80-259
Fullerton, D.H. The Dangerous Delusion.*
K. McRoberts, 529(QQ):Spring79-143
Fullerton, G.L. Historical Germanic Verb Morphology.
T.W. Juntune, 320(CJL):Spring-Fall78-154
O.W. Robinson, 221(GQ):Jan79-99
A.W. Stanforth, 402(MLR):Jul79-732
Fulmer, C.M. George Eliot.
W. Baker, 354:Mar79-92
Fulton, R. Selected Poems 1963-1978.
J. Campbell, 617(TLS):8Aug80-903
Fumio, K., T. Yoshihiko and Y. Osamu - see under Koizumi Fumio, Tokumaru Yoshihiko and Yamaguchi Osamu
"Fund og Forskning XXIII."
B.G. Fletcher Holt, 78(BC):Spring79-139
Funston, R. Constitutional Counter-Revolution?
K. Swinton, 106:Spring79-89
Funt, M. Are You Anybody?
J. Greenfield, 441:10Feb80-18
Furbank, P.N. E.M. Forster. (Vol 1)
M. Dodsworth, 175:Autumn79-281
E. Heine, 77:Spring78-107
A. Wilde, 295(JML):Vol7#4-707
Furbank, P.N. E.M. Forster. (Vol 2)
M. Dodsworth, 175:Autumn79-281
F.P.W. McDowell, 177(ELT):Vol22#1-73
W. Stone, 401(MLQ):Sep79-324
A. Wilde, 295(JML):Vol7#4-707
Furbank, P.N. E.M. Forster.* [U.S. one-vol ed]
F. Brady, 676(YR):Autumn79-118
J. Meyers, 639(VQR):Winter79-154
N. Miller, 42(AR):Spring79-242
J. Russell, 396(ModA):Fall79-427
A. Zwerdling, 569(SR):Spring79-xlv
Furber, H. Rival Empires of Trade in the Orient, 1600-1800. (Vol 2)
A. Das Gupta, 293(JASt):Feb79-315
Furet, F. Penser la Révolution française.
J. Duvignaud, 450(NRF):Feb79-98
J. Largeault, 542:Oct-Dec79-483
Furet, F. and J. Ozouf. Lire et écrire.
R. Chartier, 98:Oct78-973
Furlong, M. Merton.
F.D. Gray, 441:19Oct80-3
Furman, L. The Glass House.
L.S. Schwartz, 441:9Nov80-15

Furness, R. The Twentieth Century: 1890–
1945.*
    H. Hatfield, 301(JEGP):Apr79-306
Fürnkas, J. Der Ursprung des psycholo-
gischen Romans.
    B. Zimmermann, 406:Winter79-480
Furst, A. The Paris Drop.
    N. Callendar, 441:3Feb80-22
Furst, L.R. Counterparts.*
    D.J. Constantine, 161(DUJ):Jun79-288
    S.S. Prawer, 447(N&Q):Apr78-185
    A.W. Raitt, 402(MLR):Apr79-463
    M. Sonnenfeld, 446(NCFS):Fall-Winter
    78/79-144
Furth, C., ed. The Limits of Change.
    E. Rhoads, 318(JAOS):Jul-Sep78-338
Fussell, P. Abroad.
    C. Lehmann-Haupt, 441:11Sep80-C18
    J. Raban, 441:31Aug80-1
Fussell, P. The Great War and Modern
Memory.*
    A. Thomson, 179(ES):Jun79-324
von Fussesbrunnen, K. Die Kindheit Jesu.
    (H. Fromm and others, eds)
    W. Fechter, 684(ZDA):Band107Heft3-113
    I. Glier, 221(GQ):Nov79-533
Fuzulī. Leylā and Mejnūn. (S. Huri,
trans)
    J. Stewart-Robinson, 318(JAOS):
    Oct-Dec78-574

von Gabain, A. Alttürkische Grammatik.
(3rd ed)
    L.V. Clark, 318(JAOS):Jul-Sep78-319
El-Gabalawy, S., ed and trans. Three Con-
temporary Egyptian Novels.*
    V.J. Ramraj, 49:Oct79-104
Gabaude, J-M. Sur Epicure et l'épicurisme.
    O. Bloch, 542:Jan-Mar79-141
Gabbard, L.P. The Dream Structure of
Pinter's Plays.*
    D. Dervin, 397(MD):Mar79-89
Gabbay, D.M. Investigations in Modal and
Tense Logics with Application to Prob-
lems in Philosophy and Linguistics.*
    K. Fine, 316:Dec79-656
Gabel, G.U. and G.R. Dissertations in
English and American Literature: Theses
Accepted by Austrian, French, and Swiss
Universities, 1875-1970
    G. Irvin, 177(ELT):Vol22#4-295
Gaborieau, M. Minorites musulmanes dans
le royaume hindou de Nepaal.
    C.W. Troll, 273(IC):Jul78-205
Gabriel, G. Fiktion und Wahrheit.*
    G. Gebauer, 603:Vol13#1-133
Gadamer, H-G. Philosophical Hermeneu-
tics.* (D.E. Linge, ed and trans)
    R.J. Matthews, 482(PhR):Jan79-114
    A. Montefiore, 447(N&Q):Oct78-474
Gadamer, H-G. Philosophische Lehrjahre.*
(V. Klossermann, ed)
    T.J.S., 543:Dec78-354
Gadamer, H-G. Truth and Method.
    D. Misgeld, 488:Jun79-221

Gadamer, H-G. Variationen.
    A. Stern, 182:Vol131#21/22-769
Gadamer, H-G. Vérité et méthode, les
grandes lignes d'une herméneutique phil-
osophique.
    J. Lefranc, 192(EP):Jul-Sep79-357
Gadd, E.W., ed. Victorian Logs.
    R.C., 617(TLS):20Jun80-688
Gadda, C.E. La verità sospetta.
    E. Saccone, 400(MLN):Jan79-179
Gaddis, V.H. American Indian Myths and
Mysteries.
    W.K. Powers, 292(JAF):Oct-Dec79-501
Gaeng, P.A. A Study of Nominal Inflection
in Latin Inscriptions.
    V. Väänänen, 439(NM):1978/2-185
Gagarin, M. Aeschylean Drama.
    F. Jouan, 555:Vol152fasc2-362
Gagé, J. Enquêtes sur les structures
sociales et religieuses de la Rome
primitive.
    A. Hus, 555:Vol152fasc2-412
Gage, J. - see Turner, J.M.W.
Gage, R.L. - see Toynbee, A. and D. Ikeda
Gagliardi, D. - see Lucan
Gagnebin, B. and P.M. Monnier - see Amiel,
H-F.
Gagnon, F-M. - see Borduas, P-É.
Gagnon, F-M. and N. Cloutier. Premiers
Peintres de la Nouvelle-France.
    E.J. Talbot, 207(FR):Dec78-374
Gail, A. Paraśurāma, Brahmane und Krieger.
    J.W. de Jong, 259(IIJ):Oct79-296
Gaillard, Y. Buffon.
    N. Suckling, 208(FS):Jan79-84
Gaines, C. Dangler.
    W. Schott, 441:27Jul80-13
Gaines, J.R. Wit's End.*
    639(VQR):Spring78-50
Gair, W.R. - see Marston, J.
Gaiser, K. Menanders "Hydria."
    R.L. Hunter, 123:Vol129No2-209
Gaite, C.M. - see under Martín Gaite, C.
Gaither, G.H. Blacks and the Populist
Revolt.
    W.I. Hair, 9(AlaR):Jan79-73
Gajek, B. and E. Haufe. Johannes Bobrow-
ski.
    J. Glenn, 221(GQ):May79-427
    L.I. Kersten, 67:May79-158
Galán, M.B. - see under Bendala Galán, M.
Galante Garrone, A. and F. Della Peruta.
La Stampa Italiana del Risorgimento.
    J.A. Davis, 617(TLS):2May80-503
Galanti, M.E. Lectures et fantaisies.
    E. Spinelli, 399(MLJ):Nov79-378
Galbert de Bruges. Le Meurtre de Charles
le Bon. (J. Gengoux, trans)
    B. Lyon, 589:Jul79-568
Galbraith, J.K. Annals of an Abiding
Liberal.* (A.D. Williams, ed)
    G. Marshall, 617(TLS):11Apr80-405
    A. Ryan, 362:22May80-657
Galbraith, J.K. The Nature of Mass
Poverty.*
    639(VQR):Summer79-90

Galbraith, J.K. Le Temps des incertitudes.
   H. Cronel, 450(NRF):Aug79-134
Galbreath, D.L. Manuel du blason. (rev
   by L. Jéquier)
   G.J. Brault, 589:Jan79-128
Galdós, B.P. La incógnita.* (R. Gullón,
   ed)
   R.G. Sánchez, 240(HR):Spring78-269
Galdós, B.P. Realidad. (R. Gullón, ed)
   A.M. Penuel, 238:May-Sep79-400
   G.M. Scanlon, 86(BHS):Jul79-275
Galdós, B.P. Tormento. (E. Rodgers, ed)
   G.M. Scanlon, 86(BHS):Jul79-260
Gale, J. Camera Man.*
   A. Ross, 364:Aug/Sep79-4
Gale, R. John Hay.
   R.G. Androne, 26(ALR):Spring79-167
Gale, S.H. Butter's Going Up.*
   M. Anderson, 610:May78-226
   S.M. Elliott, 295(JML):Vol7#4-793
   A. Fischer, 179(ES):Aug79-529
   A. Sykes, 397(MD):Mar79-92
Galen. Galenus Latinus. (Vol 1) (R.J.
   Durling, ed)
   J. André, 555:Vol52fasc1-213
Galimberti, U. Linguaggio e civiltà.
   P.P., 227(GCFI):Apr-Jun78-282
Gall, J. Systemantics.
   D.L. Quinby, 186(ETC.):Dec77-467
Gall, U. Philosophie bei Heinrich von
   Kleist.
   R.A. Stelzmann, 406:Winter79-449
Gallagher, E.J., ed. "La Passion Nostre
   Seigneur" from MS 1131 from the Biblio-
   thèque Sainte-Geneviève.*
   L.R. Muir, 208(FS):Vol33Pt2-564
   205(FMLS):Jan78-93
Gallagher, T. Under Stars.*
   M. Heffernan, 491:Jun80-170
   T.R. Jahns, 460(OhR):No.24-96
   639(VQR):Spring79-66
Gallant, C. Blake and the Assimilation of
   Chaos.
   A.K. Mellor, 301(JEGP):Jul79-442
   639(VQR):Summer79-104
Gallant, M. From the Fifteenth District.*
   G. Dretzsky, 198:Winter80-108
   P. Grosskurth, 617(TLS):14Mar80-289
   G.D. Killam, 99:Jun-Jul80-30
   V.S. Pritchett, 453(NYRB):24Jan80-31
Gallazzi, C. and M. Vandoni. Papiri della
   Università degli Studi di Milano. (Vol
   6)
   A.K. Bowman, 123:Vol129No1-188
Galleni Luisi, L. - see Bonini, S.
Galler, D. Third Poems: 1965-78.
   D. Smith, 29:Mar/Apr80-40
Gallet-Guerne, D. Vasque de Lucène et la
   Cyropédie à la cour de Bourgogne (1470).
   W. Rothwell, 208(FS):Vol33Pt2-584
Gallie, W.B. Philosophers of Peace and
   War.
   B. Paskins, 483:Jan79-132
Galligan, E.L. - see Mencken, H.L.
Gallivan, P. and R.J. Merrett, eds. Lit-
   erature, Language and Culture.
   G.D. Killam, 178:Summer79-216

Gallop, D. - see Plato
Galloway, D. A Family Album.*
   P. Lewis, 565:Vol20#1-49
Gallup, D. - see O'Neill, E.
Galmés de Fuentes, Á. "El libro de las
   batallas."*
   R. Kontzi, 547(RF):Band91Heft4-491
Galván, R.A. and R.V. Teschner, comps. El
   diccionario del español chicano/The Dic-
   tionary of Chicano Spanish.
   D. Gerdes, 238:Mar79-191
   K.E. Sauer, 399(MLJ):Jan-Feb79-52
Galván, R.A. and R.V. Teschner, comps.
   El diccionario del español de Tejas/
   The Dictionary of the Spanish of Texas
   (Spanish-English).*
   P.B. George, 582(SFQ):Vol41-271
de Gálvez, B. Yo Solo. (E.A. Montemayor,
   trans)
   W.S. Coker, 9(AlaR):Apr79-148
Gambarara, D. and P. Ramat, eds. Dieci
   anni di linguistica italiana (1965-1975).
   G.C. Lepschy, 402(MLR):Oct79-956
   Y. Malkiel, 350:Sep79-739
   G. Ronco, 553(RLiR):Jul-Dec78-431
Gamberini, L. La vita musicale europea
   del 1800. (Vol 1)
   D. Kimbell, 410(M&L):Apr79-213
Gandini, L., ed. Ambarabá.
   A. Burgess, 617(TLS):28Mar80-360
Gann, L.H. and P. Duignan, eds. African
   Proconsuls.
   R. Oliver, 617(TLS):4Jan80-21
Gann, L.H. and P. Duignan. The Rulers of
   British Africa 1870-1914.
   R. Oliver, 617(TLS):4Jan80-21
Gann, L.H. and P. Duignan. South Africa.
   T.C. Holyoke, 42(AR):Summer79-374
Ganne, G. Comme les roses de Jéricho.
   J.N. Megay, 207(FR):May79-951
Gara, A. Prosdiagraphomena e circola-
   zione monetaria.
   E. Christiansen, 313:Vol69-204
de la Garanderie, M-M. Christianisme et
   Lettres profanes (1515-1535).*
   A. Buck, 52:Band13Heft3-317
   P. Sharratt, 208(FS):Vol33Pt2-612
de la Garanderie, M-M. Le Dialogue des
   romanciers.
   N. Cazauran, 535(RHL):Nov-Dec79-1038
Garapon, R. Les Caractères de La Bruyère.
   O. de Mourgues, 208(FS):Apr79-190
Garapon, R. Le Dernier Molière.*
   R. Guichemerre, 535(RHL):Jan-Feb79-125
Garber, F. Thoreau's Redemptive Imagina-
   tion.*
   R.E. Abrams, 149(CLS):Jun79-180
   C.C. Walcutt, 50(ArQ):Spring79-92
Garber, K., ed. Europäische Bukolik und
   Georgik.
   H.H.F. Henning, 406:Spring79-58
Garber, K. Martin Opitz — "der Vater der
   deutschen Dichtung."*
   J.L. Gellinek, 406:Spring79-66
   G. Guntermann, 680(ZDP):Band97Heft4-
   635

Garbo, N. Spy.
    N. Callendar, 441:7Sep80-37
García, C. La desordenada codicia de los
    bienes agenos.* (G. Massano, ed)
    S.H. Ackerman, 238:May-Sep79-396
    J.A. Whitenack, 402(MLR):Jul79-728
García, C.B. - see under Bosch García, C.
García, M. - see under López de Ayala, P.
García-Pelayo y Gross, R., ed. Pequeño
    Larousse ilustrado. (15th ed)
    R.V. Teschner, 399(MLJ):Nov79-375
García-Ramón, J.L. Les origines post-
    mycéniennes du groupe dialectal éolien.*
    P. Considine, 303(JoHS):Vol99-188
    P. Monteil, 555:Vol52fasc1-136
    F.M.J. Waanders, 353:Aug78-85
García-Viedma, J.M.J. - see under Junoy
    García-Viedma, J.M.
García Cisneros, F. Santos of Puerto Rico
    and the Americas.
    P. Vivó, 37:Sep79-48
García de Enterría, M.C. Catálogo de los
    pliegos poéticos españoles del siglo
    XVII en el British Museum de Londres.
    D.W. Cruickshank, 86(BHS):Jul79-251
García Hortelano, J. El grupo poético de
    los años 50 (Una antología).
    G.R. Barrow, 86(BHS):Jul79-277
García Márquez, G. In Evil Hour.*
    J. Mellors, 362:20Mar80-382
    J. Sturrock, 617(TLS):1Feb80-108
    M. Wood, 453(NYRB):24Jan80-43
García Márquez, G. Innocent Eréndira and
    Other Stories.*
    A. Graham-Yooll, 364:Nov79-91
    639(VQR):Winter79-20
García Melero, J.E. Bibliografía de la
    pintura española.
    I. Mateo and A. López Yarto, 48:Oct-
    Dec78-447
García Sarriá, F. Clarín o la herejía
    amorosa.*
    J.W. Díaz, 241:May79-126
Gardam, J. The Sidmouth Letters.
    A. Broyard, 441:19Dec80-C32
    V. Glendinning, 617(TLS):18Apr80-430
    J. Mellors, 362:10Jul80-56
Garde, P. Histoire de l'accentuation
    slave.
    F. Kortlandt, 361:Jan78-67
Garden, E. Tchaikovsky. (2nd ed)
    412:Aug-Nov78-278
"A Gardener's Dozen: 12 Broadcast Talks."
    R. Blythe, 362:4Sep80-310
Gardies, J-L. Esquisse d'une grammaire
    pure.*
    A. Jacob, 542:Apr-Jun78-219
Gardiner, D. A Soul Station in My Ear.
    D.G. Jones, 102(CanL):Winter78-77
Gardner, H. Artful Scribbles.
    P. Fuller, 617(TLS):19Sep80-1022
    M. Winn, 441:6Apr80-10
Gardner, H. The Composition of "Four
    Quartets."*
    R.G. Frean, 67:May79-106
    B. Rajan, 651(WHR):Spring79-158

Gardner, H. The Quest for Mind.
    S. Blackburn, 447(N&Q):Oct78-479
Gardner, H. - see Donne, J.
Gardner, I. That Was Then.
    V. Young, 441:21Sep80-14
Gardner, J. Freddy's Book.
    P-L. Adams, 61:Apr80-129
    C. Lehmann-Haupt, 441:12Mar80-C26
    J. Romano, 441:23Mar80-1
    R. Sale, 453(NYRB):29May80-39
Gardner, J. Golgotha.
    T.J. Binyon, 617(TLS):14Mar80-296
Gardner, J. Grendel.
    C.J. Stromme, 145(Crit):Vol20#1-83
Gardner, J. In the Suicide Mountains.
    639(VQR):Spring78-67
Gardner, J. The Life and Times of
    Chaucer.*
    639(VQR):Winter78-14
Gardner, J. Morale.
    M. Nelson, 639(VQR):Winter79-164
Gardner, J. On Moral Fiction.*
    M. Birnbaum, 396(ModA):Spring79-204
    S.G. Kellman, 395(MFS):Winter78/79-650
    R. Vine, 560:Spring-Summer79-262
Gardner, J. The Poetry of Chaucer.*
    L.W. Patterson, 627(UTQ):Spring79-263
    R.A. Shoaf, 405(MP):Feb80-317
Gardner, R.D. Horatio Alger.
    G. Scharnhorst, 26(ALR):Autumn79-356
Gardner, T. Einführung in die moderne
    englische Phonologie.
    F.W. Gester, 38:Band96Heft1/2-183
Garfias, R. Music of a Thousand Autumns.
    S. Kishibe, 318(JAOS):Apr-Jun78-185
Garfield, B. The Paladin.
    R. Lingeman, 441:30Mar80-6
Garfield, D. A Player's Place.
    J. Lahr, 441:8Jun80-12
Garfield, E.P. - see under Picón Garfield,
    E.
Garfinkel, A. and S. Hamilton, eds.
    Designs for Foreign Language Teacher
    Education.
    R. Boswell, 399(MLJ):Apr79-226
Garforth, F.W. Educative Democracy.
    M. Warnock, 617(TLS):16May80-565
Garguilo, R. La Genèse des Thibault de
    Roger Martin du Gard.
    S. Spurdle, 208(FS):Vol33Pt2-872
Garin, E. Filosofia e scienze nel Nove-
    cento.
    F. Volpi, 687:Oct-Dec79-656
Garioch, R. Collected Poems.
    J. Campbell, 617(TLS):8Aug80-903
Garlick, K. and A. Macintyre - see Faring-
    ton, J.
Garliński, J. Intercept.
    R. Lewin, 362:17Jan80-93
Garner, H. Monkey Grip.
    G. Strawson, 617(TLS):18Jan80-54
Garnet, E. A Martyrdom of Jean de
    Brebeuf.*
    D. Watmough, 102(CanL):Spring79-75

Garnett, D. Great Friends.*
  T. Fitton, 617(TLS):1Feb80-112
  J. Leonard, 441:10Apr80-C18
  V.S. Pritchett, 442(NY):18Aug80-89
  A. Ross, 364:Oct79-3
  N. Sayre, 441:27Apr80-7
Garnier, R. Two Tragedies. (C.M. Hill
  and M.G. Morrison, eds)
  G. Jondorf, 208(FS):Vol33Pt2-643
Garnsey, P.D.A. and C.R. Whittaker, eds.
  Imperialism in the Ancient World.
  A.N. Sherwin-White, 617(TLS):18Apr80-
  447
Garrett, A. A History of British Wood
  Engraving.
  S. Lambert, 135:Feb79-139
Garrett, C. Respectable Folly.*
  F.P. Bowman, 208(FS):Vol33Pt2-1003
Garrett, R. Mrs. Simpson.
  R. Coleridge, 617(TLS):25Jan80-90
Garrison, D.H. Mild Frenzy.
  J. Clack, 124:Sep79-46
  F. Lasserre, 182:Vol131#23/24-878
Garrone, A.G. and F. Della Peruta - see
  under Galante Garrone, A. and F. Della
  Peruta
Garten, H.F. Wagner the Dramatist.
  R.L.J., 412:Aug-Nov78-276
von Gartenaere, W. - see under Wernher von
  Gartenaere
Gartenberg, E. Mahler.
  M. Kennedy, 410(M&L):Jan79-90
Gärtner, H.A. Beobachtungen zu Bauelemen-
  ten in der antiken Historiographie,
  besonders bei Livius und Caesar.
  A.J.L. van Hooff, 394:Vol32fasc3/4-431
Gärtner, H.A. Cicero und Panaitios.
  A. Léonard, 555:Vol52fasc2-399
Gärtner, K. Theodor Fontane.
  F. Betz, 221(GQ):Jan79-128
Gartside, L. English for Business Studies.
  J. Kornelius, 430(NS):Oct78-473
Garvan, A.N.B. and others. The Mutual
  Assurance Company Papers: The Archi-
  tectural Surveys, 1784-1794.*
  M.B. Tinkcom, 576:May78-114
Garvey, G. Money, Financial Flows, and
  Credit in the Soviet Union.
  J.P. Farrell, 104(CASS):Fall78-438
Garvin, H.R., ed. Makers of the Twentieth
  Century Novel.
  J.V. Knapp, 395(MFS):Winter78/79-654
Garvin, H.R., ed. New Dimensions in the
  Humanities and Social Sciences.
  639(VQR):Summer78-97
Garvin, J. James Joyce's Disunited King-
  dom.*
  A. Goldman, 541(RES):Feb79-108
Garvin, P.L. Breve introducción a la
  computación lingüística.
  G.F. Meier, 682(ZPSK):Band31Heft6-642
Garvin, P.L., ed. Cognition.
  P.G. Patel, 320(CJL):Spring-Fall78-128
Gary, R. Europa.
  639(VQR):Autumn78-138

Garzetti, A. From Tiberius to the Anto-
  nines.
  P. Jal, 555:Vol52fasc1-210
Gash, J. The Grail Tree.
  N. Callendar, 441:17Aug80-19
  M. Laski, 362:10Jan80-62
Gash, J. Spend Game.
  T.J. Binyon, 617(TLS):18Jul80-823
  M. Laski, 362:13Nov80-665
Gash, N. Aristocracy and the People:
  Britain 1815-1865.*
  E.J. Hobsbawm, 453(NYRB):3Apr80-35
Gasiorowska, X. The Image of Peter the
  Great in Russian Fiction.
  H. Gifford, 617(TLS):4Jan80-17
  V.D. Mihailovich, 268(IFR):Winter80-77
Gaskell, A.P. All Part of the Game.
  G. Davenport, 249(HudR):Spring79-141
Gaskell, E. Cranford and Cousin Phillis.
  (P. Keating, ed)
  M.D. Wheeler, 161(DUJ):Dec78-136
Gaskell, P. From Writer to Reader.
  J.R. Banks, 148:Spring79-88
  D.F. Foxon, 541(RES):May79-237
  J. Stillinger, 301(JEGP):Jul79-422
Gaskill, P.H. - see Mason, E.C.
Gaskin, J.C.A. Hume's Philosophy of
  Religion.
  P.F. Brownsey, 479(PhQ):Jul79-265
  E. Sprague, 518:May79-68
Gaspar, L. Approche de la parole.
  D.L., 450(NRF):Mar79-107
Gass, F., ed. Five Canadian Plays.
  A.L. Amprimoz, 526:Summer79-79
Gass, W.H. The World within the Word.*
  T.H. Adamowski, 529(QQ):Winter79/80-
  711
  S.I. Bellman, 584(SWR):Spring79-202
  B.H. Gelfant, 569(SR):Fall79-1xxxviii
Gasset, J.O. - see under Ortega y Gasset,
  J.
Gasson, R. - see Wilde, O.
Gaston, J.C., ed. London Poets and the
  American Revolution.
  M. Kallich, 165(EAL):Spring80-95
Gaston Phébus. Livre des Oraisons, les
  Prières d'un Chasseur. (G. Tilander, ed)
  M.D. Legge, 208(FS):Vol33Pt2-577
Gatch, M.M. Preaching and Theology in
  Anglo-Saxon England.*
  A. Crépin, 189(EA):Jul-Dec78-375
  A.N. Doane, 529(QQ):Summer79-302
  J. Dutka, 539:Vol4No1-95
  T.J.A. Heffernan, 382(MAE):1979/2-266
  J.D.A. Ogilvy, 191(ELN):Mar79-235
  R.C. Payne, 405(MP):May80-404
  J.C. Pope, 589:Jan79-129
Gatenby, G., ed. Whale Sound.*
  J. Ferns, 102(CanL):Spring79-92
Gates, G.P. Air Time.
  639(VQR):Autumn78-130
Gatt-Rutter, J. Writers and Politics in
  Modern Italy.
  A. Stott, 402(MLR):Apr79-473

Gatty, J.C. Beaumarchais sous la Révolution l'Affaire des fusils de Hollande.
    J-P. de Beaumarchais, 535(RHL):Jan-Feb79-131
Gaube, H. Arabische Inschriften aus Syrien.
    L. Golvin, 182:Vol31#14-490
Gauger, H-M. Sprachbewusstsein und Sprachwissenschaft.
    E. Beneš, 685(ZDL):3/1979-356
Gauger, W. Wandlungsmotive in Rudyard Kiplings Prosawerk.
    A. Clayborough, 179(ES):Apr79-239
Gauhar, A., ed. The Challenge of Islam.
    M.E. Yapp, 617(TLS):19Sep80-1040
Gaume, M., ed. La Triomphante Entrée de très illustre Dame Magdeleine de la Rochefoucauld.
    E. Balmas, 535(RHL):Nov-Dec78-1023
Gaunt, W. The World of William Hogarth.
    C.C. Brookes, 39:Dec78-77
Gaur, A. Indian Charters on Copper Plates in the Department of Oriental Manuscripts and Printed Books.
    W.H. Maurer, 318(JAOS):Apr-Jun78-198
Gaustad, E.S. - see Holmes, O.
Gauthier, C.A. Haïti, qui es-tu?
    C. Zimra, 207(FR):Dec78-373
Gauthier, H. L'Homme intérieur dans la vision de Balzac.
    D. Adamson, 208(FS):Vol33Pt2-814
    A. Michel, 535(RHL):Jan-Feb79-140
Gauthier, P. Un commentaire historique des "Poroi" de Xénophon.
    G.L. Cawkwell, 123:Vol29No1-17
Gauthier, Y. Méthodes et concepts de la logique formelle.
    F. Wilson, 627(UTQ):Summer79-474
Gauthier-Larouche, G. Évolution de la Maison Rurale Traditionelle dans la Région de Québec.
    F. Toker, 576:Mar78-64
Gautier d'Arras. Eracle.* (G. Raynaud de Lage, ed)
    G.S. Burgess, 545(RPh):Nov78-254
Gautier, J-M. Les Émerveillements du mousse Olivier.
    N.Q. Maurer, 450(NRF):Oct79-138
Gautier, J-M. - see de Chateaubriand, F.R.
Gautier, M. - see Bereau, J.
Gautier-Vignal, L. Proust connu et inconnu.
    D.P. Wainwright, 207(FR):Oct78-170
Gauvin, J. Wortindex zur Phänomenologie des Geistes.
    W.V.E., 543:Mar79-543
Gavin, J.M. On to Berlin.*
    T.H. Etzold, 396(ModA):Summer79-325
Gavoty, B. Frederic Chopin.*
    B.J. Tepa, 497(PolR):Vol23#1-107
Gawalt, G.W. The Promise of Power.
    C.W. McCurdy, 432(NEQ):Sep79-432
Gawalt, G.W. - see Olmsted, G.
Gawlick, G. - see de Spinoza, B.
Gay, P. Freud, Jews and Other Germans.*
    P. Loewenberg, 473(PR):3/1979-461
    L.D. Nachman, 560:Spring-Summer79-166

Gay-Crosier, R. Camus.
    G.A. Bond, 207(FR):Mar79-651
    A. Espiau de La Maëstre, 535(RHL):Jul-Aug79-717
    B.G. Garnham, 208(FS):Vol33Pt2-931
Gay-Lussac, B. L'Heure.
    J.R., 450(NRF):Nov79-130
Gaya Nuño, J.A. L'opera completa di Murillo.
    E. Young, 90:Jul79-445
Gayle, A. Richard Wright.
    P-L. Adams, 61:Aug80-84
    R. Kennedy, 441:3Aug80-10
Gazdar, G., E. Klein and G.K. Pullum, comps. A Bibliography of Contemporary Linguistic Research.
    W. Bright, 350:Mar79-250
Geach, P.T. Providence and Evil.*
    P. Helm, 393(Mind):Jul79-459
Geach, P.T. The Virtues.*
    H.O. Mounce, 393(Mind):Jan79-134
Gear, M.C. and E.C. Liendo, with L.J. Prieto. Sémiologie psychanalytique.
    E.S. Bär, 567:Vol126#1/2-99
Geary, P.J. Furta Sacra.
    R.E. Reynolds, 589:Jul79-570
Geber, B.A., ed. Piaget and Knowing.
    R. Horwood, 84:Mar79-86
Gebhard, D. and others. A Guide to Architecture in San Francisco and Northern California.
    E. McCoy, 505:Feb79-100
Gebhard, D. and D. Nevins. 200 Years of American Architectural Drawing.*
    L.B. Anderson, 576:Dec78-313
Gebhard, D. and R. Winter. A Guide to Architecture in Los Angeles and Southern California.
    R. Banham, 576:Oct78-213
    E. McCoy, 505:Feb79-100
Gebhardt/Grzimek/Harth/Rumpf/Schödlbauer/Witte. Walter Benjamin — Zeitgenosse der Moderne.
    G. Hemmerich, 489(PJGG):Band86Heft1-196
Gebhardt, K. Das okzitanische Lehngut im Französischen.
    J.H. Marshall, 208(FS):Vol33Pt2-1019
Gebser, J. Verfall und Teilhabe.
    S. Decloux, 182:Vol131#19-643
Geddes, G. . . . War and Other Measures.
    R.J. Merrett, 102(CanL):Winter78-96
Gee, M. Games of Choice.*
    A. Loney, 368:Dec76-338
Gee, M. A Glorious Morning, Comrade.
    D. Norton, 368:Jun76-150
Geertman, H. More Veterum.*
    P. Llewellyn, 313:Vol69-217
Gehlen, A. Theorie der Willensfreiheit und frühe philosophische Schriften. Studien zur Anthropologie und Soziologie.
    G. Kortian, 98:Mar78-303
Gehrardt, C.I. - see Hofmann, J.E.
Gehrke, H-J. Phokion.
    G.L. Cawkwell, 123:Vol29No2-270
    L.A. Tritle, 24:Summer79-332

Geier, M. and others. Sprache als Struktur.*
  G. Kolde, 260(IF):Band83-357
Geiger, W.E. Phytonymic Derivational Systems in the Romance Languages.
  R. Penny, 86(BHS):Oct79-326
Geijer, A. A History of Textile Art.
  S.M. Newton, 617(TLS):18Jan80-52
Geist, K.L. Pictures Will Talk.
  D. Bodeen, 200:Mar79-177
  D. Jacobs, 18:Feb79-70
Geist, S. Brancusi: The Kiss.
  90:Feb79-138
Geist, S. Brancusi, the Sculpture and Drawings.
  K.J. Michaelsen, 54:Jun78-383
Geith, K-E. Carolus Magnus.*
  D.H. Green, 382(MAE):1979/2-276
  F. Shaw, 402(MLR):Oct79-984
Gekoski, R.A. Conrad.
  B. Johnson, 136:Vol11#3-291
  J. Kertzer, 49:Apr79-101
  D. Kramer, 301(JEGP):Oct79-567
Gelfand, L.E., ed. Herbert Hoover: The Great War and its Aftermath, 1914-1923.
  H. Brogan, 617(TLS):20Jun80-692
Gelhaus, H. Das Futur in ausgewählten Texten der geschriebenen deutschen Sprache der Gegenwart.*
  H. Gross, 685(ZDL):2/1979-265
Gellhorn, M. The Weather in Africa.*
  P-L. Adams, 61:Apr80-128
  V. Glendinning, 441:30Mar80-9
Gelli, G.B. Opere. (D. Maestri, ed)
  M. Chiesa, 228(GSLI):Vol155fasc492-603
Gelling, M. Signposts to the Past.
  E.B. Vest, 424:Dec78-423
Gellner, E. Spectacles and Predicaments.
  A. Giddens, 617(TLS):14Mar80-302
Gelpi, A. The Tenth Muse.
  J.T. Flanagan, 179(ES):Jun79-323
Gelwick, R. The Way of Discovery.
  S.C. Jansen, 488:Sep79-392
  H. Prosch, 185:Jan79-211
  S. Richmond, 488:Sep79-390
Geminus. Geminos, "Introduction aux Phénomènes."* (G. Aujac, ed and trans)
  P. Pédech, 555:Vol52fasc1-172
"Gemma Sena Chiesa: Gemme di Luni."
  A. Krug, 182:Vol31#13-433
Gendreau, M. Héritage et Création.
  W.H. Clamurro, 400(MLN):Mar79-418
Genet, J. Oeuvres complètes. (Vol 5)
  J. Duvignaud, 450(NRF):Sep79-44
Genet, J-P., ed. Four English Political Tracts of the Later Middle Ages.
  W.C. Jordan, 589:Oct79-801
Genette, G. Mimologiques.*
  F. Rigolot, 535(RHL):Sep-Oct78-864
Genevoix, M. Lorelei.
  J. Carleton, 207(FR):Apr79-794
Genovese, E.D. From Rebellion to Revolution.
  W.D. Jordan, 453(NYRB):17Apr80-18
Genovese, E.D. Roll, Jordan, Roll.*
  L. Krieger, 473(PR):1/1979-152

Gentile, G. Lettere a Benedetto Croce. (S. Giannantoni, ed)
  K-E. Lönne, 182:Vol131#20-705
Gentile, M. Iam rude donatus.
  E. Namer, 542:Oct-Dec79-451
Gentili, B. Lo spettacolo nel mondo antico.
  W.G. Arnott, 123:Vol29No1-140
  F. Jouan, 555:Vol52fasc2-361
Gentili, B. and G. Cerri. Le teorie del discorso storico nel pensiero greco e la storiografia romana arcaica.
  P. Pédech, 555:Vol52fasc1-167
George, F., ed. Science Fact.
  529(QQ):Winter79/80-737
George, K.E.M. Les Désignations du Tisserand dans le Domaine Gallo-Roman.*
  K.A. Goddard, 208(FS):Jul79-375
George, R. - see Brentano, F.
George, R. and R.M. Chisholm - see Brentano, F.
George, S. Dokumente seiner Wirkung. (L. Helbing and C.V. Bock, with K. Kluncker, eds)
  H. Naumann, 680(ZDP):Band97Heft2-307
George, S. Vybranyj Stefan George po ukrains'komu ta inshymy peredusim slov'yans'kymy movamy. (I. Kostec'kyj and O. Zujevs'kyj, eds) Stefan George ausgewählte Gedichte Ukrainisch und in anderen vorzüglich slawischen Sprachen. (E.G. Kostetzky and O. Zujewskyj, eds)
  M.V.D., 107(CRCL):Winter79-105
  R.S. Struc, 107(CRCL):Winter79-100
George, W.R.P. The Making of Lloyd George.
  S. Meacham, 637(VS):Winter78-257
Georgel, P. - see Hugo, L.
Georgiev, V.I. Trakite i technijat ezik.*
  G.F. Meier, 682(ZPSK):Band31Heft1-86
  W. Merlingen, 343:Band23-118
Gera, G. L'imposizione progressiva nell'antica Atene.
  F. Lasserre, 182:Vol131#21/22-823
Geraghty, T. Who Dares Wins.
  C. Wain, 362:20ct80-441
Gerhardus, D., S.M. Kledzik and G.H. Reitzig. Schlüssiges Argumentieren.
  G. Öhlschläger, 686(ZGL):Band7Heft1-83
Gérin, W. Elizabeth Gaskell.*
  M.T. Davis, 637(VS):Spring79-359
  A. Easson, 191(ELN):Sep78-58
  A. Shelston, 402(MLR):Jan79-170
Gerlach, L.R. The Men in Blue.
  442(NY):4Aug80-91
Gerlach, U.H. - see Hebbel, F. and others
Gerlach-Nielsen, M., H. Hertel and M. Nøjgaard, eds. Romanteori og romananalyse.
  J. Aarkrog, 562(Scan):Nov79-173
  M. Johns, 563(SS):Winter79-71
Gerli, M. - see Martínez de Toledo, A.
"The Germ: The Literary Magazine of the Pre-Raphaelites."
  A. Rodway, 617(TLS):6Jun80-654
Germani, G. Authoritarianism, Fascism, and National Populism.
  R.M. Perina, 263(RIB):Vol29No2-227

Germer, F. A l'heure française I.
E. Namenwirth, 556(RLV):1978/1-93

Gero, S. Byzantine Iconoclasm during the Reign of Constantine V, with Particular Attention to the Oriental Sources.
J. Rosser, 589:Oct79-803

Gero, S. Byzantine Iconoclasm during the Reign of Leo III, with Particular Attention to the Oriental Sources.
J. Rosser, 589:Oct79-804

Geroch, R. General Relativity from A to B.
W. Israel, 529(QQ):Autumn79-555

Gerould, D., ed. Twentieth-Century Polish Avant-Garde Drama.
B.H. Bennett, 577(SHR):Spring79-174
Z. Folejewski, 104(CASS):Fall78-426
R. Grol-Prokopczyk, 497(PolR):Vol123#2-80
J. Peterkiewicz, 575(SEER):Jan79-119

Gerow, E. A Glossary of Indian Figures of Speech.
A. Aklujkar, 259(IIJ):Jul79-191

Gerow, E. Indian Poetics.
A. Aklujkar, 259(IIJ):Jul79-196

Gerrard, C.F. Montherlant and Suicide.*
J. Cruickshank, 402(MLR):Oct79-949
R.G. Geen, 399(MLJ):Mar79-144

Gersch, W. Film bei Brecht.
J. Fuegi, 400(MLN):Apr79-638

Gersh, S. From Iamblichus to Eriugena.
J. Dillon, 124:Nov79-203
G.J.P. O'Daly, 123:Vol29No2-255

Gershon, K. Burn Helen.
J. Mellors, 362:28Aug80-281

Gershon, K. Coming Back From Babylon.
C. Rumens, 617(TLS):22Feb80-214

ben Gershon, L. - see under Gersonides

Gershuny, T. Soon to be a Major Motion Picture.
J. Greenfield, 441:1Jun80-18

Geršič, S. Materialien zur phonetischen Variabilität.
G. Lerchner, 682(ZPSK):Band31Heft1-84

Gerson, N.B. Trelawny's World.*
639(VQR):Winter78-28

Gerson-Kiwi, E. - see Lachmann, R.

Gersonides. [L. ben Gershon] The Wars of the Lord, Treatise Three: On God's Knowledge. (N.M. Samuelson, ed and trans)
M.W. Bloomfield, 589:Jan79-136

Gerulaitis, L.V. Printing and Publishing in Fifteenth-Century Venice.*
C.F. Bühler, 517(PBSA):Jan-Mar78-149

Gervais, C.H. The Believable Body.
G. Hamel, 198:Winter80-139

Gervais, C.H. Poems for American Daughters.*
D.G. Jones, 102(CanL):Winter78-77

Gervais, C.H., ed. The Writing Life.*
D. Cooley, 105:Fall/Winter78-98

Gervais, C.H. and J. Reaney. Baldoon.
A.P. Messenger, 102(CanL):Autumn79-95
G. Wicken, 168(ECW):Summer78-260

Gervasi, T. Arsenal of Democracy.
639(VQR):Winter79-27

"Gesamtkatalog der Wiegendrucke."* (Vol 8)
P. Needham, 617(TLS):15Aug80-922

Gesche, H. Caesar.*
J. Carter, 313:Vol69-184

Gewirth, A. Reason and Morality.*
A.S.C., 543:Dec78-356
M.B. Mahowald, 484(PPR):Mar80-446
A. Schwartz, 482(PhR):Oct79-654
H.B. Veatch, 185:Jul79-401

Geyer, D. Der russische Imperialismus.
D.S.M. Williams, 575(SEER):Oct79-634

Geymonat, M. - see Nicander

al-Ghazālī, A.Ḥ. al-Ghazali, On the Duties of Brotherhood. (M. Holland, trans)
M.A. Ashruff, 273(IC):Jan76-47

Ghee, L.T. - see under Lim Teck Ghee

Gheorghe, I. Les Images du poète et de la poésie dans l'oeuvre de Valéry.
C.M. Crow, 402(MLR):Jul79-705
R. Galand, 207(FR):Apr79-777

Ghertman, S. Petrarch and Garcilaso.*
A. Cioranescu, 549(RLC):Jan-Mar77-113

Ghiron-Bistagne, P. Recherches sur les acteurs dans la Grèce antique.*
F. Jouan, 555:Vol52fasc1-157

Ghose, Z. Hamlet, Prufrock and Language.
S. Wells, 617(TLS):30May80-625

Ghurye, C.W. The Writer and Society.
M. Jurgensen, 67:May79-154

Giacchero, M. Edictum Diocletiani et Collegarum de pretiis rerum venalium.
H.W. Pleket, 394:Vol32fasc3/4-448

Giancotti, F. Il preludio di Lucrezio e altri scritti lucreziani ed epicurei.
E. Tiffou, 487:Autumn79-276

Giannantoni, G., ed. Scuole socratiche minori e filosofia ellenistica.
R.W. Sharples, 303(JoHS):Vol199-189

Giannantoni, S. - see Gentile, G.

Giannone, R. Vonnegut.*
J.H. Justus, 27(AL):Nov79-438
R.F. Kiernan, 295(JML):Vol7#4-828

"Giant Canadian Poetry Annual 1977."
F. Cogswell, 102(CanL):Winter78-106

Gianturco, C. Claudio Monteverdi.
D.A., 410(M&L):Jan79-102

Giardina, I.C. - see Propertius

Gibbons, B. - see Shakespeare, W.

Gibbons, F. Catalogue of Italian Drawings in the Art Museum, Princeton University.
I. Ragusa, 276:Spring79-64

Gibbons, R., ed. The Poet's Work.*
42(AR):Fall79-507

Gibbons, R. Roofs, Voices, Roads.
D. Smith, 29:Mar/Apr80-40

Gibbs, R. All This Night Long.*
D. Barbour, 150(DR):Spring79-154

Gibson, C. - see Massinger, P.

Gibson, E.J. and H. Levin. The Psychology of Reading.*
A. Davies, 603:Vol3#1-114

Gibson, G.D. - see Estermann, C.

Gibson, I. The English Vice.*
L. Frank, 184(EIC):Oct79-361

Gibson, J. - see Hardy, T.

Gibson, J.R., ed. European Settlement and Development in North America.
J. Axtell, 656(WMQ):Jul79-475
Gibson, J.R. Imperial Russia in Frontier America.
S.M. Johnson, 104(CASS):Summer78-293
Gibson, M. Lanfranc of Bec.
J.W. Alexander, 589:Apr79-375
J.F. Kelly, 613:Mar79-103
Gibson, M. Signs.
D. Smith, 29:Mar/Apr80-40
Gibson, R. Catalogue of Portraits in the Collection of the Earl of Clarendon.*
K. Garlick, 447(N&Q):Dec78-546
Gibson, W.M. The Art of Mark Twain.*
R. Asselineau, 189(EA):Jul-Dec78-418
H. Cohen, 191(ELN):Mar79-261
S. Fender, 402(MLR):Jul79-677
A. Hook, 447(N&Q):Dec78-565
Gidding, J. The Old Girl.
F. Taliaferro, 441:12Oct80-15
"André Gide 5." (C. Martin, ed)
D.H. Walker, 208(FS):Vol33Pt2-857
Gide, A. and D. Bussy. Correspondance André Gide/Dorothy Bussy. (Vol 1) (J. Lambert, ed)
P. Pollard, 617(TLS):14Mar80-286
Gide, A. and H. Ghéon. Correspondance 1897-1944. (J. Tipy, ed)
K. O'Neill, 67:Nov79-296
Gide, A. and A. Mockel. Correspondance (1891-1938). (G. Vanwelkenhuyzen, ed)
D.H. Walker, 208(FS):Vol33Pt2-858
Gidel, H. La dramaturgie de Georges Feydeau.
F-J. Meissner, 547(RF):Band91Heft3-350
Gieber, R.L., ed. La Vie Saint Jehan-Baptiste.
C. Story, 382(MAE):1979/2-294
Giedymin, J. - see Ajdukiewicz, K.
Gielgud, J., with J. Miller and J. Powell. Gielgud.* (British title: An Actor and His Time.)
P-L. Adams, 61:Dec80-98
F. Rich, 441:19Oct80-11
Gierczyński, Z. Rabelais ou l'Humainisme des Lumières. Rabelais et la Religion.
J. Larmat, 535(RHL):Jul-Aug78-632
Giese, F.S. Artus Désiré.
G. Castor and S. Rawles, 208(FS):Apr79-183
Giesen, W. Heinrich Manns Roman "Empfang bei der Welt."
D. Roberts, 67:Nov79-362
Giesselmann, W. Die brumairianische Elite.
M.S. Staum, 173(ECS):Winter78/79-245
Gieysztor, A., ed. Polska dzielnicowa i zjednoczona.
P.W. Knoll, 497(PolR):Vol123#2-40
Gifford, B. Kerouac's Town.
G. Haslam, 649(WAL):Fall79-245
Gifford, B. - see Ginsberg, A. and N. Cassady
Gifford, D. James Hogg.
B. Bloedé, 189(EA):Jul-Dec78-388
F.R. Hart, 445(NCF):Dec78-391

Gifford, D. and R.J. Seidman. Notes for Joyce.
U. Schneider, 38:Band96Heft1/2-254
Gifford, H. Pasternak.*
R.L. Chapple, 104(CASS):Fall78-423
E. Mossman, 395(MFS):Summer78-289
205(FMLS):Jan78-88
Gifford, T. Hollywood Gothic.*
M. Laski, 362:17Apr80-514
Gigante, M. - see Polemon
Gigante, M. and W. Schmid - see Usener, H.K.
Giger, R. The Creative Void.
B. Oldsey, 395(MFS):Summer78-272
Gigli, S.Q. - see under Quilici Gigli, S.
Giglio, R. Per la storia di una amicizia (D'Annunzio, Hérelle, Scarfoglio, Serao).
W. De Nunzio-Schilardi, 228(GSLI):Vol155fasc491-462
Giglioli, P.P. Baroni e burocrati.
M. Clark, 617(TLS):2May80-490
Gigliotti, G. Hermann Cohen e la fondazione kantiana dell'etica.
P.P., 227(GCFI):Apr-Jun78-280
Gignac, F.T. A Grammar of the Greek Papyri of the Roman and Byzantine Periods.* (Vol 1)
R. Browning, 123:Vol29No1-92
J.F. Oates, 121(CJ):Feb-Mar80-262
Gigot, J-G. - see Monfrin, J., with L. Fossier
Gil, R. La caja de música. (R.A. Cardwell, ed)
P. McDermott, 86(BHS):Jan79-71
Gil de Biedma, J. - see Cernuda, L.
Gil Fernández, L. Campomanes, un helenista en el poder.
P.B. Goldman, 238:Dec79-730
Gilabert, J. Narciso Oller.
S.J. Canepari, 238:May-Sep79-401
Gilbert, A.D. Religion and Society in Industrial England.
H. McLeod, 637(VS):Winter78-245
Gilbert, A.J. Literary Language from Chaucer to Johnson.
B. Cottle, 617(TLS):14Mar80-300
Gilbert, C. Furniture at Temple Newsam House and Lotherton Hall, Yorkshire.*
G. Wills, 39:Feb79-164
Gilbert, C. The Life and Work of Thomas Chippendale.
S. Jervis, 135:Jan79-66
Gilbert, G. From Next Spring.
L.K. MacKendrick, 168(ECW):Fall78-235
Gilbert, G. Grounds.*
K. Fraser, 168(ECW):Summer78-284
K. Garebian, 102(CanL):Summer79-126
Gilbert, J.G. Ferber.*
G. Scharnhorst, 395(MFS):Winter78/79-645
Gilbert, K. People are Legends.
639(VQR):Autumn79-148
Gilbert, M. Winston S. Churchill. (Companion Vol 5, Pt 1)
J. Grigg, 362:20Nov80-697

Gilbert, M. Death of a Favourite Girl.
M. Laski, 362:14Aug80-216
J. Symons, 617(TLS):16May80-558
Gilbert, M. Exile and Return.
639(VQR):Spring79-54
Gilbert, M. The Holocaust.
T. Ziolkowski, 569(SR):Fall79-676
Gilbert, M. The Killing of Katie Steel-
stock.
P-L. Adams, 61:Aug80-84
A. Broyard, 441:5Jul80-11
N. Callendar, 441:23Nov80-38
442(NY):8Sep80-116
Gilbert, S.M. In the Fourth World.
J. Fuller, 617(TLS):18Jan80-65
Gilbert, S.M. and S. Gubar. The Madwoman
in the Attic.*
R. Ashton, 617(TLS):8Aug80-901
P.M. Spacks, 676(YR):Winter80-266
Gilchrist, A. Life of William Etty, RA.
G. Reynolds, 617(TLS):12Sep80-988
Gilderhus, M.T. Diplomacy and Revolution.
J.C.M. Ogelsby, 106:Fall79-223
Giles, H. and P.F. Powesland. Speech
Style and Social Evaluation.*
F. Erickson, 355(LSoc):Dec78-428
Giles, P. A Monster Unto Many.
C. Rumens, 617(TLS):19Sep80-1012
Gilhuly, G. Not Having Constructed My Arc.
D. Barbour, 150(DR):Spring79-154
Gill, A. The Early Mallarmé. (Vol 1)
J.M. Cocking, 617(TLS):6Jun80-653
Gill, B. The Dream Come True.
P. Goldberger, 441:30Nov80-70
Gill, B. McGarr at the Dublin Horse Show.
N. Callendar, 441:10Feb80-22
442(NY):24Mar80-135
Gill, B.M. Death Drop.
N. Callendar, 441:28Sep80-20
442(NY):1Sep80-92
Gill, G.J. Peasants and Government in the
Russian Revolution.
A. Brown, 617(TLS):25Jan80-95
Gill, M.L. Novena to St. Jude Thaddeus.
D. Precosky, 198:Summer80-156
Gill, S. Scientific Romances of H.G.
Wells.
J.P. Henry, 648(WCR):Jun78-35
Gillard, D. The Struggle for Asia, 1828-
1914.
F. Kazemsadeh, 550(RusR):Jan79-85
H. Seton-Watson, 575(SEER):Oct79-602
Gillatt, P. Three Quarter Face.
J. Lahr, 441:29Jun80-9
Gillel'son, M.I. Ot arzamasskogo bratstva
k pushkinskomu krugu pisatelei.
R. Gregg, 550(RusR):Jul79-394
Gillès, D. La Tache de sang.
C.W. Obuchowski, 207(FR):Mar79-668
Gillespie, D., with A. Fraser. To Be,
Or Not ... To Bop.
C. Brown, 441:3Feb80-13
C. Fox, 617(TLS):13Jun80-676
Gillespie, G. and E. Lohner, eds. Herkom-
men und Erneuerung.*
E. Schiffer, 400(MLN):Apr79-613

Gillespie, N.C. Charles Darwin and the
Problem of Creation.
J.Z. Young, 453(NYRB):7Feb80-45
Gillet, J. Le "Paradis perdu" dans la lit-
térature française de Voltaire à
Chateaubriand.*
F.J-L. Mouret, 208(FS):Vol33Pt2-977
M. Mueller, 107(CRCL):Fall79-447
Gillet, L. - see Huysmans, J-K.
Gillette, J.M. Designing with Light.
R. Ornbo, 157:Winter79-84
Gillette, W. Retreat from Reconstruction
1869-1879.
E. Genovese, 441:4May80-9
C.V. Woodward, 453(NYRB):20Nov80-49
Gilliatt, P. Splendid Lives.*
C. Petroski, 502(PrS):Fall78-299
Gilliatt, P. Three-Quarter Face.
R. Davies, 362:23Oct80-551
Gillispie, C.C. - see "Dictionary of
Scientific Biography"
Gillman, P. and L. "Collar the Lot!"
B. Wasserstein, 617(TLS):27Jun80-731
Gillon, A. Conrad and Shakespeare and
Other Essays.*
J.S. Lewis, 136:Vol11#2-193
Gillon, E.V., Jr. Early New England Grave-
stone Rubbings.
D. Tashjian, 165(EAL):Spring80-92
Gillott, J. Intimate Relations.
L. Duguid, 617(TLS):1Aug80-868
Gilman, E.B. The Curious Perspective.*
F.N. Lees, 148:Summer79-86
Gilman, R. Decadence.*
W.H. Pritchard, 31(ASch):Winter79/80-
136
639(VQR):Autumn79-127
Gilman, S. and E.L. King - see Castro, A.
Gilmore, C.C. Atlantic City Proof.
L. Duguid, 617(TLS):30May80-626
Gilmore, M.P. Il mondo dell'Umanesimo —
1453-1517.
P.P., 227(GCFI):Apr-Jun78-278
Gilmore, M.T. The Middle Way.*
R.H. Brodhead, 445(NCF):Sep78-234
T.W. Herbert, Jr., 594:Summer79-247
R.F. Lucid, 405(MP):May80-445
M.R. Stern, 587(SAF):Autumn79-243
Gilmour, D. Dispossessed.
D. Steel, 362:4Dec80-759
Gilomen, H-J. Die Grundherrschaft des
Basler Cluniazenser-Priorates St. Alban
im Mittelalter.
L.G. Duggan, 589:Apr79-376
Gilot, M. Les Journaux de Marivaux.
H.T. Mason, 208(FS):Vol33Pt2-722
Gilpin, L. The Hocus-Pocus of the Uni-
verse.*
T.A. Stumpf, 114(ChiR):Autumn78-127
639(VQR):Winter79-26
Gimeno, R. - see del Encina, J.
Gindele, H. Lateinische Scholastik und
deutsche Sprache.* (Pt 1)
N.R. Wolf, 684(ZDA):Band107Heft3-129
Gindin, J. The English Climate.
A. Wilson, 385(MQR):Summer80-427

Gingras, R.C., ed. Second Language Acquisition and Foreign Language Teaching.
 L. Beebe, 351(LL):Dec79-377
Ginsberg, A. Journals: Early Fifties, Early Sixties. (G. Ball, ed)
 P.L. Berman, 472:Fall/Winter79-283
 M. Shechner, 473(PR):1/1979-105
Ginsberg, A. Mind Breaths.
 P.L. Berman, 472:Fall/Winter79-283
 M. Shechner, 473(PR):1/1979-105
Ginsberg, A. and N. Cassady. As Ever.*
 (B. Gifford, ed)
 M. Shechner, 473(PR):1/1979-105
Ginsborg, P. Daniele Manin and the Venetian Revolution of 1848-49.
 H. Hearder, 617(TLS):7Mar80-277
Ginzburg, C. The Cheese and the Worms.
 P-L. Adams, 61:Aug80-85
 J.H. Elliott, 453(NYRB):26Jun80-38
Gioanola, E. Il Decadentismo.
 P.Z., 228(GSLI):Vol155fasc490-316
Giono, J. Angélique.
 W.D. Redfern, 617(TLS):5Sep80-950
Giono, J. Fragments d'un Paradis.
 M. Mohrt, 450(NRF):May79-114
"Jean Giono I (1974)." (A.J. Clayton, ed)
 M. Scott, 208(FS):Vol33Pt2-896
"Jean Giono 2." (A.J. Clayton, ed)
 L. Ricatte, 535(RHL):Jul-Aug79-713
Giordan, H. Paul Claudel en Italie.
 J-N. Segrestaa, 535(RHL):Jan-Feb79-147
Giorgi, G. "L'Astrée" di Honoré d'Urfé tra barocco e classicismo.
 R. Lathuillère, 535(RHL):Jan-Feb78-111
Giovannoni, J.M. and R.M. Becerra. Defining Child Abuse.
 J.S. Gordon, 441:27Jan80-12
Girard, C. and D. Lambert. Coast to Coast.
 J. Pint, 399(MLJ):Apr79-231
Girard, R. "To double business bound."*
 R.D. Cottrell, 399(MLJ):Apr79-223
 T.L. Jeffers, 385(MQR):Summer80-421
Girard, R. Violence and the Sacred.*
 B. Bassoff, 152(UDQ):Summer78-134
 T.L. Jeffers, 385(MQR):Summer80-421
Girard, R., with J.M. Oughourlian and G. Lefort. Des choses cachées depuis la fondation du monde.*
 M. Deguy, 98:Oct78-911
Giraud, Y. Bibliographie du roman épistolaire en France des origines à 1842.
 H. Coulet, 535(RHL):Jul-Aug79-662
 V. Mylne, 208(FS):Vol33Pt2-954
 E. Showalter, Jr., 207(FR):May79-932
Giraud, Y. Les Fantaisies du farceur Tabarin.*
 M. Lazard, 535(RHL):Mar-Apr78-295
Giraud, Y., ed. Antoine Godeau (1605-1672).
 H.T. Barnwell, 208(FS):Vol33Pt2-673
Giraud, Y. - see Godeau, A.
Giraudoux, J. Intermezzo. (C. Weil, ed)
 E.E. Tory, 208(FS):Vol33Pt2-873
Girodias, M. The Frog Prince.
 C. Lehmann-Haupt, 441:11Dec80-C25
 J.R. Mellow, 441:21Dec80-8

Girouard, M. Life in the English Country House.*
 G. Jackson-Stops, 46:Mar79-130
 J. Lees-Milne, 39:Aug79-153
 J. Riely, 173(ECS):Spring79-400
 529(QQ):Spring79-181
 639(VQR):Summer79-88
Girouard, M. The Victorian Country House.*
 D. Piper, 617(TLS):1Feb80-119
 R.A. Sokolov, 441:18May80-15
Giroud, F. La Comédie du pouvoir.
 P.A. Mankin, 207(FR):Dec78-373
Giry-Schneider, J. Les nominalisations en français.
 S. Fleischman, 350:Dec79-961
Gissing, G. London and the Life of Literature in Late Victorian England.* (P. Coustillas, ed)
 K. Flint, 175:Autumn79-270
Gissing, G. The Odd Women.
 J. Lucas, 617(TLS):23May80-574
Gissing, G. Our Friend the Charlatan. (P. Coustillas, ed)
 S. Monod, 189(EA):Apr-Jun78-235
Gissler, E., B. Lecherbonnier and H. Mitterand. L'Esprit et la lettre. (Vol 2)
 W. Wrage, 207(FR):May79-963
Giteau, M. The Civilization of Angkor.
 P. Chandra, 576:Mar78-56
Giteau, M. Iconographie du Cambodge postangkorien.
 H.H.E. Loofs, 259(IIJ):Jan79-72
Gitlin, T. The Whole World is Watching.
 W. Goodman, 441:31Aug80-11
 J. Leonard, 441:9Sep80-C11
 T. McCormack, 99:Dec80/Jan81-30
Gittings, R. Thomas Hardy's Later Years.*
 R. Beards, 295(JML):Vol7#4-721
 T. Slade, 67:May79-104
 S. Weintraub, 445(NCF):Mar79-523
Gittings, R. The Nature of Biography.*
 M. Goldstein, 569(SR):Fall79-667
Gittleman, S. From Shtetl to Suburbia.
 S.B. Cohen, 27(AL):May79-292
Giudici, E. - see Scève, M.
Giuliano, W. Spanish Grammar for Reading.
 J.R. Strozer, 238:Mar79-195
Given, J.P. Society and Homicide in Thirteenth-Century England.
 T.A. Green, 589:Jan79-137
Gjaerder, P. Norske drikkekar av tre.
 L. Karlsson, 341:1978/2-70
Gjerstad, E. and others. Greek Geometric and Archaic Pottery Found in Cyprus.
 J. Boardman, 123:Vol129No2-334
 R. Heidenreich, 182:Vol131#17/18-624
Glad, B. Jimmy Carter.
 J. Greenfield, 441:21Sep80-3
Glad, J. Russian Pronunciation.
 I. Pizem-Karczag, 574(SEEJ):Fall79-424
Glad, J. and D. Weissbort, eds. Russian Poetry: The Modern Period.
 M. Bayuk, 399(MLJ):Nov79-388
 V. Terras, 574(SEEJ):Fall79-407
 A.J. Wehrle, 558(RLJ):Winter79-232

Gladkov, A. Meetings with Pasternak.*
(M. Hayward, ed and trans)
F.D. Reeve, 651(WHR):Winter79-83
Gladstone, W.E. The Gladstone Diaries.
(Vols 5 and 6) (H.C.G. Matthew, ed)
W.L. Arnstein, 637(VS):Summer79-465
Glaeser, E. Fazit.
A. Kaes, 221(GQ):Jan79-87
"Glagol." (Vol 1)
C.J. Barnes, 575(SEER):Jan79-107
Glanville, B. A Book of Soccer.
H.H. Broun, 31(ASch):Spring80-274
P. Gardner, 441:27Jan80-22
Glanville, B. Never Look Back.
J. Mellors, 362:6Nov80-623
Glare, P.G.W. - see "Oxford Latin Diction-
ary"
Glaser, H. The Cultural Roots of National
Socialism (Spiesser-ideology).
G.L. Mosse, 125:Spring79-434
639(VQR):Winter79-14
Glaser, W.R. Soziales und instrumentelles
Handeln.
H. Ottmann, 489(PJGG):Band86Heft1-148
Glasgow, E. The Descendant.
N. Auerbach, 445(NCF):Mar79-475
Glasheen, A. Third Census of "Finnegans
Wake."* (2nd ed)
M.H. Begnal, 174(Éire):Summer79-139
B.P. O Hehir, 454:Fall78-78
Glass, M. Bone Love.
P. Ramsey, 569(SR):Fall79-686
Glauser, A. Le Faux Rabelais ou De
l'inauthenticité du Cinquième Livre.
K.H. Francis, 208(FS):Vol33Pt2-616
Glauser, B. The Scottish-English Linguis-
tic Border.*
W. Viereck, 182:Vol31#3/4-94
Glendinning, N. Goya and His Critics.*
I.L. McClelland, 86(BHS):Jan79-69
Glendinning, V. Elizabeth Bowen.*
W. Sullivan, 579(SAQ):Summer79-406
Glenny, M. - see Lakshin, V.
Glickman, R.J. - see del Casal, J.
Gliedman, J. and W. Roth. The Unexpected
Minority.
E. Simpson, 441:12Oct80-13
Gloag, J. Sleeping Dogs Lie.
E. Hunter, 441:20Jul80-12
P. Kemp, 362:4Dec80-765
442(NY):13Oct80-191
"Glossaire du Parler français au Canada."
D.F. Rogers, 320(CJL):Spring-Fall78-
186
Glover, D. Dancing to My Tune. Welling-
ton Harbour.
A. Paterson, 368:Mar75-82
Glover, J. Cavalli.*
H.T.E.M., 412:Aug-Nov78-273
Gloversmith, F., ed. Class, Culture and
Social Change.
W.H. Pritchard, 362:21Aug80-248
Glück, A. Schillers "Wallenstein."*
H. Reinhardt, 224(GRM):Band28Heft3-364
Gluck, F.W. and A.B. Morgan - see Hawes, S.
Glück, H. - see Medvedev, P.

Gluck, J. and S.H., eds. A Survey of
Persian Handicraft.
U. Roberts, 60:Jul-Aug79-126
Glück, L. Descending Figure.
C. Molesworth, 441:12Oct80-14
Glucksmann, A. The Master Thinkers.
(French title: Les Maîtres penseurs.)
W.J. Dannhauser, 441:28Sep80-12
J. Donzelot, 98:Jun-Jul78-572
Gnarowski, M., ed. Leonard Cohen.
L. Ricou, 178:Summer79-238
Gnarowski, M., comp. A Concise Bibliog-
raphy of English-Canadian Literature.
(rev)
R. Thacker, 649(WAL):Fall79-229
Gneuss, H. Die "Battle of Maldon" als his-
torisches und literarisches Zeugnis.*
D.G. Scragg, 72:Band216Heft2-408
Gnilka, J. Das Evangelium nach Markus.
(Vol 1)
I.H. Marshall, 182:Vol31#19-656
Gobbi, T. My Life.*
E. Forbes, 415:Dec79-1004
J. Yohalem, 441:28Dec80-9
Göbel, W. Der Kurt Wolff Verlag, 1913
bis 1930.
J.A. Kruse, 182:Vol31#13-385
Gobetz, G.E. and A. Donchenko, eds.
Anthology of Slovenian American Litera-
ture.
W.R. Keitner, 102(CanL):Autumn79-97
Gobin, P. Le Fou et ses doubles.
B. Andrès, 627(UTQ):Summer79-459
Goblot, J-J. Aux origines du socialisme
français.
J.P. Gilroy, 446(NCFS):Fall-Winter
78/79-147
Gochet, P. Quine en perspective.*
J. Largeault, 154:Dec78-736
J. Largeault, 542:Apr-Jun78-220
M. Meyer, 154:Dec78-731
Godard, H., ed. Album Giono.
W.D. Redfern, 617(TLS):5Sep80-950
Goddard, L. Philosophical Problems.
G.J. Warnock, 479(PhQ):Jan79-803
Godeau, A. De la galanterie à la sainteté.
(Y. Giraud, ed)
V. Kapp, 547(RF):Band91Heft1/2-172
Godel, V. Du même desert à la même nuit.
A. Clavel, 98:Oct78-995
J-C. Gateau, 450(NRF):Feb79-110
Godenne, R. La nouvelle française.
V. Mylne, 208(FS):Jan79-116
Godenne, R. - see de Florian, J-P.C.
Godfrey, D. Dark Must Yield.*
P. Monk, 529(QQ):Autumn79-525
W.H. New, 102(CanL):Autumn79-79
G. Sinclair, 648(WCR):Oct78-78
E. Thompson, 628(UWR):Fall-Winter78-76
F. Timleck, 526:Spring79-91
Godfrey, E. Murder Among the Well-To-Do.
S.J. Warwick, 168(ECW):Spring78-126
Godfrey, R.T. Printmaking in Britain.
C. Cannon-Brookes, 39:Mar79-241
"Gods and Heroes."
W.K. McNeil, 292(JAF):Jul-Sep79-363

Godson, R. The Kremlin and Labor.
  M.P. Sacks, 550(RusR):Apr79-246
Godwin, G. The Odd Woman.
  S.E. Lorsch, 145(Crit):Vol20#2-21
Godwin, J. - see Scarlatti, A.
Goebbels, J. Final Entries 1945. (British title: The Goebbels Diaries; The Last Days. German title: Tagebücher 1945.) (H.R. Trevor-Roper, ed of U.S. and British editions)
  H.M. Adams, 396(ModA):Winter79-100
  A.M.F., 77:Summer78-94
Goedert, G. Nietzsche critique des valeurs Chrétiennes.
  E. Blondel, 542:Jan-Mar79-83
  G.F., 543:Jun79-754
Goedicke, P. Crossing the Same River.
  D. Kirby, 617(TLS):13Jun80-680
Goedicke, P. The Dog That Was Barking Yesterday.
  H. Carruth, 231:Dec80-74
Goesch, K. - see Mauriac, F.
von Goethe, J.W. Goethe: Begegnungen und Gespräche.* (Vol 3) (R. Grumach, ed)
  R.H. Spaethling, 406:Summer79-200
von Goethe, J.W. Goethe's Roman Elegies. (D. Luke, ed and trans)
  L.R. Atkins, 301(JEGP):Jan79-93
  D. Graham, 565:Vol20#1-65
von Goethe, J.W. Die Schriften zur Naturwissenschaft. (K.L. Wolf and others, eds) (Section 1, Vol 11 ed by D. Kuhn and W. von Engelhardt; Section 2, Vol 4 ed by R. Matthaei and D. Kuhn; Section 2, Vol 9A ed by D. Kuhn)
  N.H. Smith, 182:Vol131#23/24-859
von Goethe, J.W. Torquato Tasso. (J. Prudhoe, trans)
  J. Coleby, 157:Summer79-81
Goethert-Polaschek, K. Katalog der römischen Gläser des Rheinischen Landesmuseums Trier.
  G. Faider-Feytmans, 182:Vol131#7/8-235
Goetsch, P. Bauformen des modernen englischen und amerikanischen Dramas.
  R. Imhof, 397(MD):Sep79-317
  M. Pfister, 490:Band10Heft2/3-396
  K. Tetzeli von Rosador, 72:Band216 Heft1-186
Goetz, H. The Inuit Print.
  G.P. Turner, 529(QQ):Winter79/80-716
Goffin, M. Maria Pasqua.*
  A. Bell, 617(TLS):15Feb80-162
Goffman, E. Gender Advertisements.*
  B.A. Babcock, 567:Vol24#1/2-149
van Gogh, V. The Complete Letters of Vincent van Gogh.*
  M. Mudrick, 249(HudR):Winter79/80-601
van Gogh, V. Letters of Vincent van Gogh, 1886-1890.* (V.W. van Gogh, ed)
  B. Petrie, 90:Jan79-48
Gohin, Y. - see Hugo, V.
Goichet, P. Quine en perspective.
  H.B.V., 543:Sep78-135
Going, W.T. Scanty Plot of Ground.*
  L. Poston, 637(VS):Spring78-413
de Góis, D. - see under Damião de Góis

Goist, P.D. From Main Street to State Street.*
  D.D. Anderson, 658:Autumn79-330
Golab, C. Immigrant Destinations.
  N. Lederer, 497(PolR):Vol23#4-110
Gold, A. Some of the Cat Poems.
  D. Barbour, 150(DR):Spring79-154
Gold, A. and R. Fizdale. Misia.
  P-L. Adams, 61:Mar80-101
  E. Auchincloss, 441:10Feb80-11
  A. Brookner, 617(TLS):27Jun80-730
  A. Croce, 442(NY):12May80-158
  J. Leonard, 441:18Feb80-C15
  J. Russell, 453(NYRB):6Mar80-6
Gold, H. He/She.
  A. Broyard, 441:6Jun80-C23
  L. McMurtry, 441:25May80-10
Gold, J., ed. In the Name of Language.
  G.D. Killam, 178:Summer79-216
Gold, M.J. Crossroads Marseilles 1940.
  W. Goodman, 441:5Oct80-18
Gold, V. PR as in President.
  639(VQR):Summer78-103
Goldammer, P., ed. Schriftsteller über Kleist.
  R. Heukenkamp, 654(WB):7/1978-180
Goldbarth, A. Different Fleshes.
  H. Carruth, 231:Dec80-74
  M. King, 29:Mar/Apr80-5
Goldberg, M. Carlyle and Dickens.
  A. Easson, 447(N&Q):Apr78-191
Goldberg, N.L. John Crome the Elder.
  A. Frankenstein, 55:Jan79-28
  A. Hemingway, 90:May79-327
  D. Piper, 617(TLS):1Feb80-119
  M. Rajnai, 135:Jun79-132
  G. Reynolds, 39:Jun79-489
Goldberg, S. The Inevitability of Patriarchy.
  C. Stasz, 529(QQ):Autumn79-499
Goldberger, P. The City Observed: New York.*
  F. Schulze, 55:Nov79-34
Golden, R.E. and M.C. Sullivan. Flannery O'Connor and Caroline Gordon.
  M.J. Friedman, 578:Spring80-114
Goldensohn, B. Uncarving the Block.
  E. Milton, 472:Fall/Winter79-270
Goldfarb, R.M. and C.R. Spiritualism and Nineteenth-Century Letters.*
  J.W. Crowley, 445(NCF):Mar79-503
Goldgar, B.A. Walpole and the Wits.*
  H. Erskine-Hill, 541(RES):Feb79-90
  F.P. Lock, 586(SoRA):Jul78-188
Goldhurst, R. The Midnight War.
  C.F. Smith, 550(RusR):Oct79-481
Goldin, F. - see "The Song of Roland"
Golding, W. Darkness Visible.*
  P. Bailey, 364:Mar80-94
  C.B. Cox, 148:Winter79-3
Golding, W. Rites of Passage.
  P-L. Adams, 61:Nov80-98
  A. Broyard, 441:15Oct80-C29
  D. May, 362:23Oct80-546
  G. Stade, 441:2Nov80-7
  R. Towers, 453(NYRB):18Dec80-4

Goldman, A. A Theory of Human Action.
  H-N. Castañeda, 449:May79-235
Goldman, B. - see Hopkins, C.
Goldman, D. Full-Time Restless.
  M. Levin, 441:16Mar80-14
Goldman, J. Myself as Witness.
  P-L. Adams, 61:Mar80-102
  R.B., 109:Summer80-224
  B. Garfield, 441:10Feb80-14
Goldman, W. Tinsel.*
  M. Wood, 18:Sep79-68
Goldmann, L. Lukács and Heidegger.
  J.D. Rabb, 518:May79-71
  T.J.S., 543:Sep78-136
Goldmann, N. The Jewish Paradox.
  H. Feingold, 390:Jan79-74
Goldrosen, J. The Buddy Holly Story.
  B.A. Mendheim, 187:Jan80-114
Goldschmidt, G-A. Jean-Jacques Rousseau
  ou l'esprit de solitude.
  P-F. Moreau, 542:Jul-Sep78-360
Goldschmidt, H. Um die Unsterbliche
  Geliebte.*
  B. Cooper, 410(M&L):Oct79-463
Goldschmidt, V. Anthropologie et poli-
  tique.*
  S. Goyard-Fabre, 542:Jul-Sep78-360
  J.S. Spink, 208(FS):Apr79-200
Goldschmidt, V. La doctrine d'Epicure et
  le droit.
  O. Bloch, 542:Jan-Mar79-134
Goldsen, R.K. The Show and Tell Machine.
  R.S. Tedlow, 658:Winter79-430
Goldsmith, B. Little Gloria ... Happy at
  Last.
  P-L. Adams, 61:Jul80-87
  C. Lehmann-Haupt, 441:26Jun80-C18
  E. Morris, 441:22Jun80-9
  C. Sigal, 362:20ct80-439
  442(NY):25Aug80-103
Goldsmith, D., ed. Scientists Confront
  Velikovsky.
  A.H. Bridle, 529(QQ):Spring79-136
Goldsmith, E.S. Architects of Yiddishism
  at the Beginning of the Twentieth Cen-
  tury.
  Y.H. Frank, 390:Mar79-68
  S. Rothchild, 390:Jun/Jul79-102
Goldsmith, M. Sage.
  B. Norton, 617(TLS):23May80-576
Goldstein, J. Philadelphia and the China
  Trade, 1682-1846.
  R.P. Gardella, 293(JASt):Feb79-329
  F.W. Gregory, 656(WMQ):Jan79-153
  E. Wolf 2d, 658:Summer79-200
Goldstein, L. George Chapman.
  R.P. Corballis, 677(YES):Vol9-304
Goldstein, L. Ruins and Empire.*
  J. Barnard, 175:Spring79-61
  I.H.C., 191(ELN):Sep78(supp)-39
  S. Peterfreund, 566:Autumn78-50
  E. Tomarken, 219(GaR):Summer79-448
Goldstein, R. Spartan Seasons.
  J. Oppenheimer, 441:15Jun80-7
Goldstein, T. Dawn of Modern Science.
  D. Lindberg, 441:18May80-7

Goldstene, P.N. The Collapse of Liberal
  Empire.
  639(VQR):Winter78-20
Goldstone, H.H. and M. Dalrymple. His-
  tory Preserved.
  P. Goldberger, 576:May78-113
Goldsworthy, D., C. Falk and B. Kornhauser.
  Studies in Indonesian Music. (M.
  Kartomi, ed)
  J. Becker, 187:Jan80-115
Goldthorpe, J.H., with C. Llewellyn and C.
  Payne. Social Mobility and Class Struc-
  ture in Modern Britain.
  W.G. Runciman, 617(TLS):15Feb80-159
  M. Warnock, 362:14Feb80-219
Goldwater, R. Symbolism.
  N. Lynton, 617(TLS):21Mar80-328
Golenishcheva-Kutuzova, I.V. Istorija
  ital'janskoj literatury.
  G.C. Lepschy, 402(MLR):Oct79-960
Goller, N. Tomorrow's Silence.*
  N. Callendar, 441:4May80-24
Gollin, J. The Philomel Foundation.
  N. Callendar, 441:27Apr80-18
  442(NY):28Jul80-104
Golomshtok, I. and A. Glezer. Soviet Art
  in Exile.* (M. Scammell, ed)
  J.E. Bowlt, 575(SEER):Jan79-121
Goltschnigg, D. Mystische Tradition im
  Roman Robert Musils.
  M-L. Grzegorzewski, 182:Vol31#11/12-
  356
Gom, L. The Singletree.*
  A. Amprimoz, 102(CanL):Spring79-72
Gombrich, E.H. Art History and the Social
  Sciences.
  M.H. Bornstein, 127:Spring79-220
Gombrich, E.H. The Heritage of Apelles.*
  P. Fehl, 90:Mar79-178
Gombrich, E.H. The Sense of Order.*
  D. Carrier, 311(JP):Mar80-179
  S. Durant, 46:Aug79-70
  C. Eisler, 39:Dec79-536
  J.M. Kennedy, 290(JAAC):Summer80-453
  D. Rosand, 55:Nov79-27
  L. Wieder, 139:Dec79/Jan80-58
  R. Wollheim, 90:May79-322
  529(QQ):Autumn79-558
Gombrowicz, W. Possessed.
  M. Irwin, 617(TLS):25Apr80-463
Gomes, C.M. O conto brasileiro e sua
  crítica.* (Vol 2)
  R.E. Dimmick, 263(RIB):Vol29No1-74
Gomes, S.F. Tempo de Mudar.
  P. Evans, 399(MLJ):Apr79-220
Gomes de Matos, F. Lingüística Aplicada
  ao Ensino de Inglês.
  J.B. Jensen, 399(MLJ):Mar79-133
Gómez, A.E. - see under Enríquez Gómez, A.
Gomez, I.M. - see under Mateo Gómez, I.
Gómez-Arcos, A. Ana No.
  P. Preston, 617(TLS):8Feb80-134
Gómez de Avellaneda, G. Cartas inéditas
  existentes en el Museo del Ejército.
  (J. Priego Fernández del Campo, ed)
  D.T. Gies, 86(BHS):Jan79-83

Gómez Paz, J. La luz de otras tierras.
J.D. de Carvalho, 263(RIB):Vol29No1-94
Gomme, A. - see Middleton, T. and T.
Dekker
Gomme, A., M. Jenner and B. Little.
Bristol — an Architectural History.*
M. Robertson, 617(TLS):25Jul80-848
L.W., 46:Oct79-206
Gomme, A.H., ed. D.H. Lawrence.*
P. Eggert, 140(CR):#21-72
K.M. Hewitt, 541(RES):May79-232
Gonda, I. Verfall der Kaiserreiche in
Mitteleuropa.
J. Leslie, 575(SEER):Oct79-616
Gonda, J., ed. A History of Indian Litera-
ture. (Vol 5, Pt 2, fasc 2)
G. Cardona, 259(IIJ):Apr79-117
Gonda, J. Medieval Religious Literature
in Sanskrit.
J.W. De Jong, 259(IIJ):Jan79-45
Gonda, J. Old Indian.
W. Morgenroth, 682(ZPSK):Band31Heft4-
434
de Góngora, L. Polyphemus and Galatea.*
(A.A. Parker, ed; G.F. Cunningham, trans)
T.R.H., 131(CL):Fall79-415
M. McKendrick, 402(MLR):Oct79-966
Gonick, C. Out of Work.*
T.K. Rymes, 529(QQ):Autumn79-523
Gonon, M., ed. Documents Linguistiques du
Forez (1260-1498).
J.H. Marshall, 208(FS):Vol33Pt2-1026
Gontier, F. La femme et le couple dans le
roman (1919-1939).
S. Ravis, 535(RHL):Jul-Aug79-707
Gonzales, L. Jambeaux.*
M. Malone, 441:20Jan80-15
González, A., ed. El grupo poético de
1927.
R. Warner, 86(BHS):Jan79-84
González, A. "Harsh World" and Other
Poems.
H.J.F. de Aguilar, 472:Fall/Winter79-
64
González, Á. - see Celaya, G.
González, J.G. - see under Gutiérrez
González, J.
González Echevarría, R. Alejo Carpentier.*
A. Borinsky, 400(MLN):Mar79-420
R.K. Britton, 402(MLR):Apr79-483
L. González, 395(MFS):Summer78-328
K. Müller-Bergh, 399(MLJ):Jan-Feb79-70
J.A. Weiss, 454:Spring79-264
F. Wyers, 405(MP):May80-456
González Echevarría, R. Relecturas.*
E.M. Santí, 240(HR):Summer78-400
González Ollé, F. Manual bibliográfico de
estudios españoles.*
A.J.C. Bainton, 86(BHS):Jul79-272
González Ollé, F. - see de Horozco, S.
González Torres, R. Los cuentos de Emilia
Pardo Bazán.
M. Hemingway, 86(BHS):Jul79-262
Gooch, A. and Á. García de Paredes - see
"Cassell's Spanish Dictionary (Spanish-
English, English-Spanish)"

Gooch, B.S. and D.S. Thatcher. Musical
Settings of Early and Mid-Victorian Lit-
erature.
S. Banfield, 415:Oct79-832
Gooch, J. Armies in Europe.
B. Bond, 617(TLS):16May80-560
Good, P., ed. Max Scheler im Gegenwarts-
geschehen der Philosophie.
S. Decloux, 182:Vol131#20-709
Goodard, D. Easy Money.
T.C. Holyoke, 42(AR):Winter79-120
Goodchild, P. J. Robert Oppenheimer.
H. Brogan, 362:11Dec80-795
Goodchild, R.G. Libyan Studies. (J.
Reynolds, ed)
F. Millar, 313:Vol69-237
Goode, C.T., Jr. - see Santucho, O.J.
Goode, J. George Gissing.
K. Flint, 175:Autumn79-270
J. Halperin, 401(MLQ):Sep79-322
Goodheart, E. The Failure of Criticism.*
M. Grimaud, 141:Summer79-262
Goodley, N. - see Horry, N.
Goodman, E.K. High on the Energy Bridge.
R. Bradford, 441:4May80-14
Goodman, N. Ways of Worldmaking.*
R. Rorty, 676(YR):Winter80-276
Goodrich, L.C., with C. Fang, eds. Dic-
tionary of Ming Biography, 1368-1644.
W.J. Peterson, 293(JASt):May79-558
Goodwin, B. Social Science and Utopia.
G. Beauchamp, 385(MQR):Spring80-261
R. Larry and L. Van Every, 529(QQ):
Winter79/80-729
Goodwin, G.C. Cherokees in Transition.
T. Perdue, 656(WMQ):Apr79-320
Goodwin, S. The Blood of Paradise.*
639(VQR):Autumn79-136
Goodwyn, F.L., Jr. Image Pattern and
Moral Vision in John Webster.*
R.P. Merrix, 568(SCN):Fall-Winter79-79
Goody, J. The Domestication of the Savage
Mind.
D.H. Turner, 529(QQ):Summer79-359
Goold, G.P. - see Manilius
Goonatilleka, M.H. Masks and Mask Systems
of Sri Lanka.
J.B. Donne, 617(TLS):7Mar80-276
Gooneratne, Y. Alexander Pope.*
P-G.B., 189(EA):Jan-Mar78-110
P. Dixon, 447(N&Q):Feb78-87
D. Nokes, 402(MLR):Jan78-166
Goonetilleke, D.C.R.A. Developing Coun-
tries in British Fiction.*
S. Chew, 402(MLR):Oct79-928
G.G. Fromm, 395(MFS):Summer78-305
D. Hewitt, 447(N&Q):Aug78-382
Goosse, A. La néologie française aujourd'-
hui.*
N.C.W. Spence, 208(FS):Vol33Pt2-1041
Goosse, A. Qu'est-ce qu'un belgicisme?
H.J. Wolf, 547(RF):Band91Heft1/2-198
Gopal, S. Commerce and Crafts in Gujarat
(16th and 17th Centuries).*
M.A. Nayeem, 273(IC):Jan77-75
Gopal, S. Jawaharlal Nehru. (Vol 1)
M.C. Carras, 318(JAOS):Jul-Sep78-323

Gopal, S. Jawaharlal Nehru. (Vol 2)
J. Grigg, 362:24Jan80-122
E. Stokes, 617(TLS):25Jan80-77
Gopnik, M. Linguistic Structures in Scientific Texts.
G.F. Meier, 682(ZPSK):Band31Heft2-205
Gordian, F., ed. Märchen aus Italien.
H-J. Uther, 196:Band19Heft1/2-126
Gordimer, N. Burger's Daughter.*
C. Hope, 364:Aug/Sep79-137
Gordimer, N. A Soldier's Embrace.
A. Broyard, 441:20Aug80-C20
D.A.N. Jones, 362:24Apr80-547
A.G. Mojtabai, 441:24Aug80-7
J. Thompson, 453(NYRB):23Oct80-46
F. Tuohy, 617(TLS):25Apr80-462
Gordis, R. The Biblical Text in the Making. (rev)
D. Pardee, 318(JAOS):Jul-Sep78-312
Gordon, B. I'm Dancing as Fast as I Can.*
S. Sutherland, 617(TLS):16May80-544
Gordon, C. A Richer Dust.
529(QQ):Winter79/80-738
Gordon, D.J. The Renaissance Imagination.
(S. Orgel, ed)
A. Levitan, 576:Oct78-204
Gordon, D.K. Los cuentos de Juan Rulfo.
I.A. Luraschi, 238:Mar79-189
Gordon, E.E. Tonal and Rhythm Patterns.
412:May78-140
Gordon, E.V., ed. The Battle of Maldon.
(supp by D.G. Scragg)
F.C. Robinson, 677(YES):Vol9-360
Gordon, G. Ambrose's Vision.
P. Lewis, 617(TLS):13Jun80-664
J. Naughton, 362:3Jul80-25
Gordon, G. The Illusionist.*
D. Durrant, 364:Jul79-89
Gordon, I.A. - see Mansfield, K.
Gordon, K. In the Shadow of the Peacock.
L. Duguid, 617(TLS):16May80-558
Gordon, L. Eliot's Early Years.*
M. Dodsworth, 541(RES):Feb79-113
J.E. Miller, Jr., 405(MP):Feb80-354
295(JML):Vol17#4-689
Gordon, M. Final Payments.*
J. Chernaik, 364:Aug/Sep79-140
W. Sullivan, 569(SR):Spring79-337
Gordon, R. Ruth Gordon: An Open Book.
D. Grumbach, 441:27Jul80-13
Gordon, R. Jack the Ripper.
S. Ellin, 441:28Sep80-14
Gordon, R. The Private Life of Jack the Ripper.
C. Brown, 617(TLS):22Aug80-943
Gordon, W.L. A Political Memoir.
E. Bradley, 628(UWR):Fall-Winter78-79
The Gordons. Night After the Wedding.
N. Callendar, 441:6Jan80-15
Goreau, A. Reconstructing Aphra.
P-L. Adams, 61:Sep80-107
J.R. Goulianos, 441:9Nov80-24
442(NY):25Aug80-102
Gorfunkel, A.K. Katalog Paleotipov iz Sobraniya Nauchnoĭ Biblioteki im. M. Gor'kogo Leningradskogo Universiteta.
J.S.G. Simmons, 78(BC):Spring79-140

Görgemanns, H. and H. Karpp - see Origen
Gorges, T. The Letters of Thomas Gorges.
(R.E. Moody, ed)
D.B. Quinn, 432(NEQ):Jun79-293
Gorissen, F. Das Stundenbuch der Katharina von Kleve.
B. Fischer, 182:Vol131#17/18-587
Görlach, M., ed. An East Midland Revision of the South English Legendary.*
D. Speed, 67:May79-85
E.G. Stanley, 447(N&Q):Dec78-543
Görlach, M. Einführung ins Frühneuenglische.
R.D. Eagleson, 67:Nov79-333
Gorman, P. Pythagoras.
S. Pembroke, 617(TLS):11Jan80-43
J. Scarborough, 121(CJ):Apr-May80-354
Gornick, V. The Romance of American Communism.
R. de Toledano, 396(ModA):Winter79-89
de Gorter, S. Klein.
E.S., 90:Apr79-276
Göschel, J. Strukturelle und instrumentalphonetische Untersuchungen zur gesprochenen Sprache.*
G. Lindner, 682(ZPSK):Band31Heft6-634
Gosling, J.C.B. - see Plato
Gosling, N. The Adventurous World of Paris 1900-1914.
B.M-P. Leefmans, 55:Nov79-30
Gosling, P. The Zero Trap.
N. Callendar, 441:14Sep80-22
Gosling, R. Personal Copy.
E.S. Turner, 362:18and25Dec80-862
Gosselin, E.A. and L.S. Lerner - see Bruno, G.
Goštautas, S. Buenos Aires y Arlt.*
J.M. Flint, 86(BHS):Oct79-351
J. Walker, 238:May-Sep79-410
Goswamy, B.N. Pahari Paintings of the Nala-Damayanti Theme in the Collection of Dr. Karan Singh.*
M.C. Beach, 57:Vol40#1-84
Goswamy, B.N. Painters at the Sikh Court.
B.D.H. Miller, 463:Autumn79-360
Gosztonyi, A. Der Raum.*
M. Thürkauf, 182:Vol131#5/6-129
Gotoff, H.C. Cicero's Elegant Style.
T.J. Luce, 124:Apr-May80-429
Gotro, P. Spider in the Sumac.
G. Hamel, 198:Winter80-139
Gottfried, R.S. Epidemic Disease in Fifteenth-Century England.
J. Shatzmiller, 589:Apr79-378
Gotti, E. Die gotischen Bewegungsverben.
N. Danielsen, 684(ZDA):Band107Heft2-47
Gottlieb, C. Beyond Modern Art.
A. Sondheim, 127:Winter78/79-146
Gottlieb, M. Nunca se termina de nacer.
S. Gostautas, 238:Dec79-740
Gotto, K. and others. Untersuchungen und Dokumente zur Ostpolitik und Biographie.
F. L'Huillier, 182:Vol131#1/2-56
Gottschalk, L., P.S. Pestieau and L.J. Pike, eds. Lafayette.
J. Lough, 208(FS):Vol133Pt2-798

Gottsched, J.C. Ausgewählte Werke. (Vol
6) (J. Birke, B. Birke and P.M. Mitchell,
eds)
  H. Eichner, 301(JEGP):Oct79-597
Gottwald, C., ed. Die Musikhandschriften
der Universitätsbibliothek und andere
öffentlicher Sammlungen in Freiburg i.
Br. und Umgebung.
  A.H. King, 182:Vol31#21/22-816
Gotzkowsky, B. - see Kirchhof, H.W.
Gougenheim, G. Grammaire de la langue
française du seizième siècle. (new ed)
  P. Rickard, 208(FS):Vol33Pt2-1036
Gougenot. La Comédie des Comédiens. (D.
Shaw, ed)
  W.D. Howarth, 208(FS):Vol33Pt2-674
Gough, R. The History of Myddle.
  J. Treglown, 617(TLS):18Apr80-432
Goujard, R. - see Cato
Goujet, C-P. Correspondance littéraire
du Président Bouhier.* (Vol 2) (H.
Duranton, ed)
  J. Balcou, 535(RHL):Nov-Dec78-1031
  J. Lough, 208(FS):Vol33Pt2-729
Goukowsky, P. - see Diodorus Siculus
Gould, C. The Paintings of Correggio.*
  E.J. Olszewski, 127:Winter78/79-141
Gould, C.C. Marx's Social Ontology.
  W.G., 543:Jun79-755
  D. Vandeveer, 484(PPR):Dec79-292
Gould, C.C. and M.W. Wartofsky, eds.
Women and Philosophy.*
  J.G. Vance, 577(SHR):Summer79-263
Gould, S.J. Ever Since Darwin.*
  639(VQR):Spring78-70
Gould, S.J. Ontogeny and Phylogeny.
  D.A. Chant, 529(QQ):Spring79-157
  M.J.S. Hodge, 486:Dec78-652
Gould, S.J. The Panda's Thumb.
  P-L. Adams, 61:Oct80-101
  H.J. Geiger, 441:14Sep80-7
  C. Lehmann-Haupt, 441:9Oct80-C23
  442(NY):29Sep80-151
Gould, W., ed. Lives of the Georgian Age.
  T. Atkins, 566:Spring79-135
Gouldner, A.W. The Future of Intellec-
tuals and the Rise of the New Class.*
  M. Walzer, 453(NYRB):20Mar80-37
Gouldner, A.W. The Two Marxisms.
  F. Parkin, 617(TLS):25Jul80-838
  P. Singer, 453(NYRB):25Sep80-62
Goulemot, J-M. Discours, histoire, et
révolutions.
  S. Bartolommei and A. Spini, 548(RCSF):
  Jan-Mar79-26
Gouvêa, F.D. Oliveira Lima.
  D.R. Cordeiro, 263(RIB):Vol29No3/4-361
Gowda, H.H.A. - see under Anniah Gowda,
H.H.
Gowing, L. Matisse.
  H. Hodgkin, 617(TLS):21Mar80-330
Gowing, L. - see Stokes, A.
Goy, R. Die Überlieferung der Werke Hugos
von St. Viktor.*
  V. Honemann, 684(ZDA):Band107Heft4-158

Goyard-Fabre, S. Kant et le Problème du
Droit.
  J. Kopper, 342:Band69Heft2-220
Gozzoli, M.C. Gothic Art.
  C.C. Brookes, 39:Dec79-538
Grabar, O. The Alhambra.
  L.P. Harvey, 86(BHS):Oct79-333
Grabar, O. Studies in Medieval Islamic
Art.
  O. Watson, 463:Spring79-115
Grabbe, P. Windows on the River Neva.
  J. Bayley, 453(NYRB):21Feb80-14
  J.S. Curtiss, 550(RusR):Jan79-93
  J. Ivask, 558(RLJ):Spring79-214
Grabmeyer, B. Die Mischsprache in Wil-
lirams Paraphrase des Hohen Liedes.*
  P.K. Stein, 680(ZDP):Band97Heft3-445
Grabner-Haider, A. Theorie der Theologie
als Wissenschaft.
  E. Herms, 685(ZDL):1/1979-125
Graburn, N.H.H., ed. Ethnic and Tourist
Arts.*
  J.A. Chinn, 650(WF):Jul79-200
Grace, P. Mutuwhenua.
  P. Evans, 368:Dec78-372
Grace, P. Waiariki.
  D. Norton, 368:Jun76-150
Grade, C. The Yeshiva.* (Vols 1 and 2)
  F. Kolko, 287:May78-27
Gradidge, R. Dream Houses.
  P. Goldberger, 441:30Nov80-70
Gradischnig, H. Das Bild des Dichters bei
Robert Musil.
  B. Pike, 406:Spring79-94
Graeser, A., ed. Die logischen Fragmente
des Theophrast.
  F. Lasserre, 182:Vol31#9/10-300
von Graevenitz, G. Eduard Mörike.
  D. Barnouw, 221(GQ):Nov79-546
  G. Storz, 182:Vol31#9/10-296
Graf, R. Der Konjunktiv in gesprochener
Sprache.
  K.B. Lindgren, 343:Band23-202
von Grafenberg, W. - see under Wirnt von
Grafenberg
Graff, G. Literature Against Itself.*
  J.P. Degnan, 569(SR):Fall79-646
  M. Fischer, 219(GaR):Summer79-433
  H.S. Guagliardo, 598(SoR):Spring80-523
  L. Lane, Jr., 255(HAB):Fall79-330
  G. Mead, 290(JAAC):Summer80-466
  D.T. O'Hara, 659(ConL):Autumn80-649
  J. Reichert, 594:Fall79-368
  N.A. Scott, Jr., 639(VQR):Autumn79-734
  J.P. Sisk, 31(ASch):Winter79/80-126
Graffigny, F. Voltaire et ses amis
d'après la correspondance de Mme. de
Graffigny.* (Vol 1) (E. Showalter, Jr.,
ed)
  J.H. Brumfitt, 208(FS):Vol33Pt2-744
Graham, D. The Fiction of Frank Norris.
  G.A. Love, 649(WAL):Fall79-262
  S.S. Moorty, 26(ALR):Autumn79-360
  R.A. Morace, 26(ALR):Spring79-155
  D. Pizer, 27(AL):Nov79-431
Graham, H.F. - see Possevino, A.

Graham, I. Goethe: Portrait of the Artist.*
  E. Boa, 402(MLR):Apr79-496
  D.B. Richards, 133:Band12Heft4-364
  J.L. Sammons, 680(ZDP):Band97Heft2-293
Graham, I. Heinrich von Kleist.
  M. Garland, 402(MLR):Jul79-748
  J.M. McGlathery, 301(JEGP):Jul79-398
Graham, J.W. Virginia Woolf's "The Waves."
  J.J. Wilson, 454:Fall78-93
Graham, K. J.L. Austin.*
  L.W. Forguson, 518:Oct79-117
  A. Palmer, 307:Apr79-44
Graham, P. The Vanishings.
  639(VQR):Spring79-67
Graham, R.B.C. - see under Cunninghame Graham, R.B.
Graham, V.E. and W.M. Johnson. The Paris Entries of Charles IX and Elisabeth of Austria 1571 with an Analysis of Simon Bouquet's Bref et Sommaire Recueil.
  M.M. McGowan, 208(FS):Vol33Pt2-664
  M.N. Rosenfeld, 54:Jun78-372
Graham, W.S. Collected Poems.
  E. Longley, 617(TLS):14Mar80-301
Graham, W.S. Selected Poems.
  H. Carruth, 231:Dec80-74
Graham-Campbell, J. The Viking World.
  P-L. Adams, 61:Jun80-94
  G. Jones, 453(NYRB):9Oct80-23
Graham-Campbell, J. and D. Kidd. The Vikings.
  G. Jones, 453(NYRB):9Oct80-23
Grajewski, H. Aleksander Napoleon Dybowski i jego projekt konstytucji dla Polski z 1848 roku.
  A. Uschakow, 182:Vol31#14-502
Grall, X. Le Cheval couché.
  R. Galand, 207(FR):Oct78-196
Grammaticus, S. - see under Saxo Grammaticus
de Granda, G. Estudios sobre un área dialectal hispanoamericana de población negra, las tierras bajas occidentales de Colombia.
  J-C. Dinguirard, 553(RLiR):Jul-Dec78-469
Grandgent, C.H. - see Dante Alighieri
Grandien, B. Drömmen om medeltiden, Carl Georg Brunius som byggmästare och idéförmedlare.
  T. Hall, 341:1978/2-55
Grandy, R.E. Advanced Logic for Applications.
  M. Davies, 393(Mind):Oct79-621
Granell, M. Etología y existencia.
  Z. Kouřím, 542:Jul-Sep79-357
Grange, H. Les Idées de Necker.
  J. Lough, 208(FS):Vol33Pt2-780
Granger, B. American Essay Serials from Franklin to Irving.*
  J.K. Kribbs, 656(WMQ):Oct79-643
Granger, B. Public Murders.
  N. Callendar, 441:9Mar80-17
Granger, B.H. A Motif Index for Lost Mines and Treasures Applied to Redaction
[continued]

[continuing]
of Arizona Legends, and to Lost Mine and Treasure Legends Exterior to Arizona.
  P.B. Mullen, 650(WF):Oct79-267
  E.H. Rehermann, 196:Band19Heft3/4-326
Granger, G-G. La théorie aristotélicienne de la science.
  J-L. Poirier, 542:Jan-Mar79-132
Granier, G., J. Henke and K. Oldenhage - see Facius, F., H. Booms and H. Boberach
Granier, J. Le discours du monde.
  A. Jacob, 542:Oct-Dec78-508
  G-F. Lenoble, 542:Jan-Mar79-87
  S. Valdinoci, 192(EP):Oct-Dec79-465
Granit, R. The Purposive Brain.
  H. Barlow, 84:Jun79-204
Granizo, C.F. and others - see under Freile Granizo, C. and others
Grano, P. Selected Verse of Paul Grano.
  S.E. Lee, 581:Dec79-432
Gransden, K.W. - see Vergil
Grant, D. Emerald Decision.
  M. Laski, 362:13Nov80-665
Grant, D. Tobias Smollett.*
  A. Morvan, 189(EA):Jul-Dec78-391
  205(FMLS):Jan78-89
Grant, E.J. The Manual of Heraldry. (rev)
  K.B. Harder, 424:Dec77-237
Grant, J., ed. La Passiun de Seint Edmund.
  W. Rothwell, 208(FS):Oct79-433
Grant, J.S. Robertson Davies.
  K. Garebian, 296(JCF):28/29-198
  J.M. Kertzer, 627(UTQ):Summer79-451
Grant, M. Greek and Latin Authors 800 B.C.-A.D. 1000.
  M.R. Lefkowitz, 617(TLS):8Aug80-893
Grant, M. An Historian's Review of the Gospels.
  J. Carmichael, 390:Apr79-56
Grant, M. Jesus.*
  T. Rajak, 123:Vol29No1-114
Grant, M.A. Michel Butor.
  J. Cruickshank, 208(FS):Jan79-112
Grant, M.K. The Tragic Vision of Joyce Carol Oates.*
  J.V. Creighton, 141:Winter79-91
  D.A. Dike, 301(JEGP):Jan79-150
  J.R. Giles, 50(ArQ):Autumn79-270
  C. Goodman, 587(SAF):Autumn79-247
  L.W. Wagner, 573(SSF):Fall78-459
Grant, R. The Great Canal.
  639(VQR):Autumn79-134
Grant, R.B. Théophile Gautier.*
  D.G. Burnett, 188(ECr):Spring78-94
Granville Barker, F. The Flying Dutchman.
  R. Anderson, 415:Oct79-830
Grape, A., G. Kallstenius and O. Thorell - see Snorri Sturluson
Grappe, A. and R. Guyot. Maurice Pradines ou l'épopée de la raison.
  M. Adam, 542:Apr-Jun78-187
Grass, G. The Flounder.*
  G. Perez, 249(HudR):Autumn79-478
  U. Zimmermann, 109:Summer80-210
Grass, G. In the Egg.
  Y. Lovelock, 493:Dec79-57

Grass, G. Das Treffen in Telgte.
  D.A. Myers, 268(IFR):Summer80-144
Grass, G. Le Turbot.
  L. Kovacs, 450(NRF):Sep79-70
Grassegger, H. Merkmalsredundanz und
  Sprachverständlichkeit.
  C. Lehmann, 343:Band23-19
Grassi, L. and M. Pepe. Dizionario della
  critica d'arte.
  E.H. Ramsden, 39:Nov79-453
Grathoff, R., ed. The Theory of Social
  Action.
  H.R. Wagner, 484(PPR):Sep79-136
Grattan-Guinness, I. - see Jourdain, P.
  and B. Russell
Gratzik, P. Transportpaule.
  M. Berger, 654(WB):3/1978-159
Graubner, H. Form und Wesen.
  G. Lehmann, 342:Band69Heft4-461
Graur, A. Scrieri de ieri şi de azi.
  G.F. Meier, 682(ZPSK):Band31Heft3-333
Graver, L. and R. Federman, eds. Samuel
  Beckett: The Critical Heritage.
  J. Acheson, 67:Nov79-332
Graves, J. From a Limestone Ledge.
  442(NY):29Dec80-73
Graves, R. La Déesse blanche.
  J. Roudaut, 450(NRF):Oct79-143
Graves, R.P. A.E. Housman.*
  P-L. Adams, 61:Jun80-94
  J. Atlas, 441:25May80-9
  442(NY):18Aug80-93
Graves, R.P. Lawrence of Arabia and His
  World.
  B. Morris, 152(UDQ):Fall78-155
Gray, B. The Grammatical Functions of
  Rhetoric.
  R.B. Kaplan, 350:Sep79-752
Gray, F. Rabelais et l'écriture.
  D.G. Coleman, 208(FS):Jul79-335
Gray, F.D. Lovers and Tyrants.
  K. Eldred, 152(UDQ):Spring78-99
Gray, M. and G. Gibson. Bibliography of
  Discographies. (Vol 1)
  R. Andrewes, 415:Apr79-310
Gray, R., ed. American Poetry of the Twen-
  tieth Century.
  R. Asselineau, 189(EA):Jul-Dec78-420
Gray, R. Brecht the Dramatist.*
  A. Tatlow, 161(DUJ):Dec78-142
Gray, R. Ibsen — A Dissenting View.*
  J.S. Chamberlain, 397(MD):Sep79-321
  I-S. Ewbank, 157:Winter79-82
  O. Reinert, 130:Fall79-263
  205(FMLS):Jul78-285
Gray, R. The Literature of Memory.*
  R.S. Kennedy, 395(MFS):Summer78-270
  L. Willson, 295(JML):Vol7#4-593
Gray, R.Q. The Labour Aristocracy in
  Victorian Edinburgh.
  R.I. McKibbin, 637(VS):Spring78-410
Grayeff, F. Descartes.
  J-M. Gabaude, 542:Jan-Mar78-106
Grayson, A.K. Babylonian Historical-
  Literary Texts.
  R.D. Biggs, 318(JAOS):Apr-Jun78-144

Grayson, B.L., ed. The American Image of
  Russia: 1917-1977.
  K.W. Ryavec, 550(RusR):Jan79-104
Grayson, C., ed. The World of Dante.
  P. Shaw, 617(TLS):2May80-501
Grayson, J., ed. Environments of Musical
  Sculpture You Can Build: Phase I.
  P.J.P., 412:Aug-Nov78-289
Grayson, J., ed. Sound Sculpture.
  P.J.P., 412:Aug-Nov78-289
Grayson, J.P., ed. Class, State, Ideology
  and Change.
  P. Marchak, 99:Dec80/Jan81-33
Grayson, R. The Monterant Affair.
  T.J. Binyon, 617(TLS):6Jun80-654
  M. Laski, 362:17Apr80-514
Greasybear, C.J. Greasybear Songs. (J.
  Crews and A.T. Trusky, eds)
  S.S. Moorty, 649(WAL):Winter80-341
"The Great Roll of the Pipe for the Third
  Year of the Reign of King Henry III,
  Michaelmas 1219 (Pipe Roll 63)."
  D.E. Greenway, 325:Apr79-162
Grebe, P., R. Köster and W. Müller, eds.
  Duden Bedeutungswörterbuch.
  M. Kantola, 439(NM):1978/3-314
Greeley, A.M. The Making of the Popes
  1978.*
  639(VQR):Autumn79-146
Greeley, A.M. An Ugly Little Secret.
  J.R. Kelly, 613:Jun79-208
Green, A. Tormented Master.
  A.A. Cohen, 441:13Jan80-9
Green, G. Cactus Pie.*
  L. Duguid, 617(TLS):9May80-537
Green, G. The Chains.
  J. Burke, 441:11May80-14
Green, G.F. A Skilled Hand. (C. Green
  and A.D. Maclean, eds)
  G. Ewart, 617(TLS):11Apr80-416
Green, H. Blindness.*
  G. Davenport, 249(HudR):Spring79-146
  639(VQR):Spring79-59
Green, H. En gare.
  C. Jordis, 450(NRF):Jul79-128
Green, H. Marinade Cookbook.
  W. and C. Cowen, 639(VQR):Autumn79-153
Green, J. Memories of Evil Days.* (J-P.J.
  Piriou, ed)
  J-P. Cap, 207(FR):Oct78-173
  J. Cruickshank, 208(FS):Vol33Pt2-902
Green, J. Oeuvres Complètes. (Vol 4) (J.
  Petit, ed)
  J. Onimus, 535(RHL):Mar-Apr78-337
Green, J. Winners.
  A. McCarthy, 441:13Apr80-14
Green, J.N. - see Elcock, W.D.
Green, J.R. Gnathia Pottery in the
  Akademisches Kunstmuseum Bonn.
  B.A. Sparkes, 123:Vol129No2-336
Green, M. Dreams of Adventure, Deeds of
  Empire.*
  D.A.N. Jones, 617(TLS):18Jul80-820
  F. Kermode, 362:10Apr80-478
Green, P.S., ed. The Language Laboratory
  in School.
  W.T. Littlewood, 257(IRAL):Aug79-273

Green, R.L. The Tale of Thebes.
  G. Smith, 292(JAF):Jul-Sep79-356
Green, R.L. - see under Lancelyn Green, R.
Green, W.A. British Slave Emancipation.
  P. Burroughs, 637(VS):Autumn77-111
van Greenaway, P. The Dissident.
  M. Laski, 362:14Aug80-216
Greenbaum, S., ed. Acceptability in Lan-
  guage.
  G. Sampson, 297(JL):Mar79-126
Greenberg, J. High Crimes and Misdemean-
  ors.
  I. Gold, 441:3Feb80-1
  J. Mellors, 362:10Jul80-56
Greenberg, R.M., ed-in-chief. The
  National Register of Historic Places
  1976. (S.A. Marusin, ed)
  D. Hoffmann, 576:Dec78-312
Greene, A.C. - see Horchow, R.
Greene, D.C., comp. Diaries of the Popish
  Plot.
  J.P. Anglin, 568(SCN):Spring-Summer79-
  27
Greene, D.J. - see Johnson, S.
Greene, G. Doctor Fischer of Geneva [or]
  the Bomb Party.
  P-L. Adams, 61:Jun80-94
  T.J. Binyon, 617(TLS):28Mar80-345
  M. Drabble, 362:27Mar80-415
  C. Lehmann-Haupt, 441:19May80-C18
  R. Schieder, 99:Aug80-28
  J. Symons, 441:25May80-4
  R. Towers, 453(NYRB):12Jun80-22
  442(NY):2Jun80-138
Greene, G. The Human Factor.*
  R. Jones, 639(VQR):Spring79-338
Greene, G. Ways of Escape.
  D.A.N. Jones, 362:20Oct80-444
  R. Schieder, 99:Aug80-28
Greene, H. Mind and Image.
  L. Reinold, 109:Winter79/80-170
Greene, J. Dead-man's-fall.
  D.M. Thomas, 617(TLS):25Apr80-477
Greene, J. - see Mandelstam, O.
Greene, J., A. Hirschi and J. Petit - see
  Barbey d'Aurevilly, J.
Greene, R.L., ed. The Early English
  Carols.* (2nd ed)
  R.T. Davies, 447(N&Q):Apr78-163
  S. Wenzel, 589:Jan79-140
Greene, R.L., ed. The Lyrics of the Red
  Book of Ossory.
  W. Rothwell, 208(FS):Vol33Pt2-571
Greene, S. Lost and Found.
  E. Wagner, 441:16Nov80-14
Greene, T. Transfuges, [précédé de]
  Pierres perdues.
  R. Kuhn, 207(FR):Mar79-669
Greene, T.M. The Descent from Heaven.
  G.K. Hunter, 402(MLR):Jan79-131
Greenfield, E., R. Layton and I. March.
  The Penguin Stereo Record Guide. (I.
  March, ed)
  P.J.P., 412:May78-142
Greenfield, J. Playing to Win.
  G.E. Reedy, 441:22Jun80-14

Greenfield, J. Television.*
  H.J. Boyle, 529(QQ):Winter79/80-681
  639(VQR):Spring78-69
Greenfield, P.M. and J.H. Smith. The
  Structure of Communication in Early Lan-
  guage Development.
  D. Keller-Cohen, 350:Jun79-444
Greenhalgh, M. and V. Megaw, eds. Art in
  Society.
  V. Kavolis, 290(JAAC):Fall79-83
Greenhalgh, P.A.L. The Year of the Four
  Emperors.*
  K.R. Bradley, 122:Jul79-258
Greenlee, J.W. Malraux's Heroes and His-
  tory.*
  D. Gascoigne, 208(FS):Vol33Pt2-907
Greenman, J. Diary of a Common Soldier in
  the American Revolution. (R. Bray and P.
  Bushnell, eds)
  G.A. Billias, 432(NEQ):Mar79-120
Greenway, J.L. The Golden Horns.*
  C.W. Thompson, 562(Scan):May79-59
Greer, D., ed. Hamilton Harty.*
  N. Goodwin, 415:Dec79-1003
Greer, G. The Obstacle Race.*
  M. Price, 676(YR):Summer80-588
Gregersen, K., ed. Papers from the Fourth
  Scandinavian Conference of Linguistics.
  B. Löfstedt, 350:Sep79-744
Gregg, E. Queen Anne.
  J.P. Kenyon, 617(TLS):18Apr80-427
Gregor, A.J. Sergio Panunzio.
  D. Mack Smith, 453(NYRB):1May80-30
Gregor, A.J. Young Mussolini and the
  Intellectual Origins of Fascism. Ital-
  ian Fascism and Developmental Dictator-
  ship.
  M. Blinkhorn, 617(TLS):2May80-484
  D. Mack Smith, 453(NYRB):1May80-30
Gregor, D.B. Friulan: Language and Litera-
  ture.*
  R. Stefanini, 545(RPh):May79-419
Gregor, I., ed. Reading the Victorian
  Novel.
  R. Swigg, 617(TLS):1Aug80-883
Gregor-Dellin, M. and D. Mack - see Wagner,
  C.
de Gregorio, J.V. - see under Verdú de
  Gregorio, J.
Gregson, J.M. Poetry of the First World
  War.
  G. David, 189(EA):Jul-Dec78-405
Greiner, T. Die Poetische Gleichung.
  C.E.J. Dolamore, 402(MLR):Oct79-950
Greive, A. Etymologische Untersuchungen
  zum französischen "h aspiré."
  H. Kahane, 545(RPh):Aug78-102
Greive, A. Neufranzösische Formen der
  Satzfrage im Kontext.
  E. Rattunde, 430(NS):Apr78-177
  N.C.W. Spence, 208(FS):Vol33Pt2-1053
Grendler, P.F. The Roman Inquisition and
  the Venetian Press, 1540-1605.
  C. Cairns, 78(BC):Summer79-289
  L.V. Gerulaitis, 539:Vol4No2-235
  J.R. Hale, 402(MLR):Apr79-470

Grene, N. Synge: A Critical Study of the Plays.*
  H. Kosok, 447(N&Q):Aug78-377
  T.R. Whitaker, 677(YES):Vol9-342
Grenfell, R. and R. Garnett, eds. Joyce.
  R. Fuller, 362:25Sep80-405
Grenier, R. Un air de famille.
  N.Q. Maurer, 450(NRF):May79-119
Greppi Olivetti, A. Due Saggi su R.G. Collingwood.
  E. Namer, 542:Apr-Jun78-188
Greshoff, C.J. An Introduction to the Novels of André Malraux.
  D. Gascoigne, 208(FS):Vol33Pt2-907
Greven, P. The Protestant Temperament.
  C. Lasch, 656(WMQ):Apr79-290
Grévy, N., E. Ornato and G. Guy - see Jean de Montreuil
Grévy-Pons, N. Célibat et Nature.
  W. Rothwell, 208(FS):Vol33Pt2-606
Grew, R., ed. Crises of Political Development in Europe and the United States.
  639(VQR):Autumn79-146
Grex, L. Mystery Stranger Than Fiction.
  C. Seebohm, 441:16Mar80-15
Grice, E. Rogues and Vagabonds, or The Actor's Road to Respectability.*
  S. Rosenfeld, 611(TN):Vol133#1-41
Grieder, J. Translations of French Sentimental Prose Fiction in Late Eighteenth-Century England.*
  M. Lévy, 535(RHL):May-Jun78-486
  A-M. Rousseau, 549(RLC):Jan-Mar77-106
  I. Simon, 179(ES):Dec79-806
Grier, E. The Assassination of Colour.*
  D. Barbour, 150(DR):Spring79-154
Grieve, A.I. The Art of Dante Gabriel Rossetti.* [shown in prev under subtitles]
  F.S. Boos, 637(VS):Summer78-509
Grieve, M. and W.R. Aitken - see MacDiarmid, H.
Griffin, D.H. Alexander Pope.*
  J.I. Fischer, 566:Spring79-124
  W.H., 148:Summer79-90
  P.M. Spacks, 401(MLQ):Dec79-403
Griffin, D.R. The Question of Animal Awareness.
  C.P. Haskins, 567:Vol123#3/4-381
Griffin, E. Turning.
  B.G. Harrison, 441:13Jul80-12
Griffin, K. International Inequality and National Poverty.
  H. Bull, 617(TLS):4Jan80-20
Griffin, N. Relative Identity.*
  C. McGinn, 482(PhR):Jan79-137
  H.W. Noonan, 393(Mind):Apr79-299
  G. Stahl, 542:Apr-Jun78-226
Griffin, N. - see Venegas, M. and anon.
Griffin, R. Clément Marot and the Inflections of Poetic Voice.
  K. Lloyd-Jones, 188(ECr):Spring78-92
  P.M. Smith, 208(FS):Vol33Pt2-623
Griffith, M. The Authenticity of "Prometheus Bound."
  M. Davies, 123:Vol129No1-5

[continued]

[continuing]
  A.F. Garvie, 303(JoHS):Vol199-172
  C.J. Herington, 24:Fall79-420
Griffiths, D., comp. A Catalogue of the Printed Music Published before 1850 in York Minster Library.
  R. Andrewes, 415:Apr79-309
Griffiths, P. Boulez.*
  B. Hopkins, 415:Oct79-827
Griffiths, P. A Concise History of Modern Music from Debussy to Boulez.*
  C. Bennett, 607:Sep78-46
  P. Evans, 410(M&L):Jan79-94
Griffiths, R. Fellow Travellers of the Right.
  A. Howard, 362:23Oct80-548
Griffiths, R. - see de Montherlant, H.
Griffiths, T. Contemporary Australia.
  H.S. Albinski, 529(QQ):Spring79-140
Grigg, J. 1943.
  P.N. Furbank, 362:24Apr80-539
  J. Greenfield, 441:1Jun80-16
  J. Keegan, 617(TLS):25Apr80-457
Grigson, G., ed. The Faber Book of Nonsense Verse.
  R. Boorstin, 31(ASch):Summer80-412
Grigson, G. The Fiesta.*
  F. Grubb, 364:Oct79-82
  L. Sail, 493:Dec79-66
Grigson, G. History of Him.
  D. Davis, 362:28Aug80-277
  P. Scupham, 617(TLS):12Sep80-990
Grigson, G., ed. The Oxford Book of Satirical Verse.
  B. Brophy, 362:25Sep80-403
  P. Rogers, 617(TLS):12Sep80-981
  442(NY):8Dec80-243
Grillone, A. Hygini qui dicitur De metatione castrorum.
  O.A.W. Dilke, 123:Vol29No1-156
Grimal, P. Le lyrisme à Rome.
  J.K. Newman, 24:Winter79-588
Grimal, P. Sénèque ou la conscience de l'Empire.
  M.E. Reesor, 487:Autumn79-284
Grimal, P. - see Cicero
Grimaldi, N. L'expérience de la pensée dans la philosophie de Descartes.
  N. Beyssade, 542:Apr-Jun79-219
Grimes, J.E. The Thread of Discourse.*
  R.M. Brend, 361:Aug78-377
Grimes, R.L. Symbol and Conquest.
  C.R. Farrer, 292(JAF):Apr-Jun79-232
Grimm, H. Psychologie der Sprachentwicklung.
  P. Kunsmann, 257(IRAL):Feb79-88
Grimm, J. La Fontaines Fabeln.*
  C.N. Smith, 208(FS):Vol33Pt2-682
Grimm, J. and W. Grimm's Tales for Young and Old. (R. Manheim, trans)
  255(HAB):Summer79-235
Grimm, M. Paris zündet die Lichter an, Literarische Korrespondenz.* (K. Schnelle, ed)
  J. Varloot, 535(RHL):Jul-Aug79-666

Grimm, R. and J. Hermand, eds. Deutsche Feiern.
A.J. Niesz, 221(GQ):Nov79-568
Grimm, R.H. Nietzsche's Theory of Knowledge.
C.O., 543:Jun79-758
Grimm, R.R. Paradisus coelestis, paradisus terrestris.*
P.W. Tax, 221(GQ):May79-392
Grimond, J. Memoirs.*
J. Morgan, 617(TLS):18Jan80-67
Grimsley, R. The Philosophy of Rousseau.
J.S. Spink, 208(FS):Apr79-200
Grimsted, P.K. Archives and Manuscript Depositories in the USSR: Moscow and Leningrad. (Supp 1)
W.F. Ryan, 575(SEER):Oct79-581
Grimsted, P.K., ed. Finding Aids on Microfiche: Archives and Manuscript Collections in the USSR; Moscow and Leningrad.
W.F. Ryan, 575(SEER):Oct79-581
Grinberg, M. Introduction au Zohar.
A. Reix, 542:Jul-Sep79-358
Grinda, K.R. "Arbeit" und "Mühe."*
C.T. Berkhout, 589:Oct79-807
Grinstead, D. The Earth Movers.
P. Andrews, 441:17Feb80-15
Grinstein, A. Sigmund Freud's Dreams.
E. Rothstein, 453(NYRB):9Oct80-14
Griot, J. - see Manet, J.
Grisanti, G.T. - see under Tedeschi Grisanti, G.
Grisewood, H. - see Jones, D.
Grishin, D.V. Young Dostoevsky.
S. Vladiv, 67:Nov79-368
Grob, G.N. Edward Jarvis and the Medical World of Nineteenth-Century America.
E. Dwyer, 432(NEQ):Dec79-591
Grodecki, L. and others. Die Zeit der Ottonen und Salier.
C. Delvoye, 182:Vol131#3/4-111
Groedecki, L., with C. Brisac and C. Lautier. Le vitrail roman.*
W. Sauerländer, 471:Jan/Feb/Mar79-77
Grodecki, L., with A. Prache and R. Recht. Gothic Architecture.
C.F. Barnes, Jr., 576:Dec78-316
Groden, M., comp. James Joyce's Manuscripts.
H. Kenner, 441:22Jun80-7
Groden, M. "Ulysses" in Progress.*
W. De Meritt, 174(Éire):Spring79-139
S. Helmling, 249(HudR):Spring79-156
S.A. Henke, 639(VQR):Winter79-181
V. Mercier, 405(MP):Aug79-59
Groen, B.M. A Structural Description of the Macedonian Dialect of Dihovo.*
H.G. Lunt, 343:Band23-137
C. Wukasch, 574(SEEJ):Fall79-428
Grollenberg, L. Palestine Comes First.
J. Grigg, 362:13Mar80-347
Grønbech, K. and J.R. Krueger. An Introduction to Classical (Literary) Mongolian. (2nd ed)
L.V. Clark, 318(JAOS):Apr-Jun78-141
van Groningen, B.A. - see "Euphorion"

Groom, W. As Summers Die.
C. Lehmann-Haupt, 441:6Oct80-C16
L. McMurtry, 441:9Nov80-14
Groom, W. Better Times Than These.*
639(VQR):Autumn78-136
de Groot, C. Zeitgestaltung im Drama Max Frischs.
C. Burke, 402(MLR):Apr79-504
M.E. Musgrave, 406:Winter79-477
Gros, B. Victor Hugo, Le visionnaire de Guernesey.
C. Gély, 535(RHL):Jan-Feb79-145
Gros, P. Aurea Templa.
H. Plommer, 313:Vol69-215
Grose, C. Milton's Epic Process.
R. Lejosne, 189(EA):Jul-Dec78-384
Grosrichard, A. Structure du sérail.
A. Clerval, 450(NRF):May79-132
Gross, B. Friendly Fascism.
J. Epstein, 453(NYRB):23Oct80-10
J. Greenfield, 441:3Aug80-13
Gross, B. and R., eds. The Children's Rights Movement.
M. Vipond, 106:Winter79-363
Gross, B.R., ed. Reverse Discrimination.*
R.H.S. Tur, 518:Jan79-41
Gross, J. The Books of Rachel.
M. Levin, 441:10Feb80-14
Gross, J.T. Polish Society under German Occupation.*
639(VQR):Autumn79-130
Gross, M. Grammaire transformationnelle du français: syntaxe du nom.
W.J. Ashby, 350:Sep79-741
A. Crompton, 297(JL):Sep79-369
Gross, M.L. The Psychological Society.
E.Z. Friedenberg, 529(QQ):Summer79-293
Gross, R.G-P. - see under García-Pelayo y Gross, R.
Gross, T.L. Academic Turmoil.
B. De Mott, 61:Jan80-84
J. Featherstone, 441:3Feb80-11
"Der Grosse Duden." (17th ed)
D. Herberg, 682(ZPSK):Band31Heft1-80
"Der grosse Duden." (Vol 6) (2nd ed) (M. Mangold, ed)
D. Karch, 353:Dec78-86
Grossinger, T. and A. Neiderman. Weekend.
N. Callendar, 441:26Oct80-29
Grosskurth, P. Havelock Ellis.
N. Annan, 453(NYRB):20Nov80-12
J.S. Collis, 362:26Jun80-836
J. Leonard, 441:8May80-C23
S. Marcus, 441:22Jun80-3
442(NY):16Jun80-122
Grossman, A. The Woman on the Bridge over the Chicago River.*
D. Bromwich, 472:Fall/Winter79-144
H. Carruth, 231:Jan80-77
Grossmann, W. Johann Christian Edelmann.
E. Winter, 182:Vol131#17/18-629
Grossmann, W. - see Edelmann, J.C.
Grote, A. - see Heikamp, D.
ten Grotenhuis, E. - see Okazaki, J.
Grotta, D. The Biography of J.R.R. Tolkien. (2nd ed)
D.M. Miller, 395(MFS):Winter78/79-602

Grotzer, B. Les archives Albert Béguin.
  J. Onimus, 535(RHL):Jul-Aug79-711
  J. Starobinski, 98:Apr78-352
Grotzer, P. Albert Béguin ou la passion
  des autres.*
  H. Godin, 208(FS):Jan79-106
  S.N. Lawall, 207(FR):Feb79-493
  J. Onimus, 535(RHL):Jul-Aug79-711
  J. Starobinski, 98:Apr78-352
Grotzer, P. Les écrits d'Albert Béguin.
  J. Onimus, 535(RHL):Jul-Aug79-711
Grotzer, P. Existence et destinée
  d'Albert Béguin.*
  H. Godin, 208(FS):Apr79-225
  S.N. Lawall, 207(FR):Feb79-493
  J. Onimus, 535(RHL):Jul-Aug79-711
  J. Starobinski, 98:Apr78-352
Grotzer, P. - see Béguin, A.
Groupe d'Entrevernes. Signes et parboles.
  G. Prince, 355(LSoc):Aug78-266
"Le Groupe de Coppet."
  A.B. Smith, 207(FR):Mar79-643
Groupe μ. Rhétorique de la poésie.*
  D. Bouverot, 209(FM):Apr78-157
Grout, D.J. - see Scarlatti, A.
Grow, L.M. The Prose Style of Samuel
  Taylor Coleridge.*
  R. Gravil, 402(MLR):Jan79-168
Grubb, D.M. A Practical Writing System
  and Short Dictionary of Kwakw'ala
  (Kwakiutl).
  S.R. Anderson, 350:Mar79-256
Grubb, F. - see Roberts, M.
Grugel, L.E. George Jacob Holyoake.
  B.C. Malament, 637(VS):Autumn78-106
Grumach, I. Untersuchungen zur Lebens-
  lehre des Amenope.
  M. Gilula, 318(JAOS):Oct-Dec78-503
Grumach, R. - see von Goethe, J.W.
Grumbach, D. Chamber Music.*
  D. Flower, 249(HudR):Summer79-299
  E. Milton, 676(YR):Autumn79-89
von der Grün, M. Wie war das eigentlich?
  P. Brady, 617(TLS):4Jul80-764
Grünbeck, B. Moderne deutsch-französische
  Stilistik auf der Basis des Übersetzungs-
  vergleichs. (Pt 1)
  D. Woll, 72:Band216Heft1-201
Grundtvig, S. Dansken paa Faerøerne.
  H. Brønner, 563(SS):Summer79-298
Grundy, J. Hardy and the Sister Arts.
  R. Swigg, 617(TLS):1Feb80-126
Gruner, E. Die Wahlen in den schweizer-
  ischen Nationalrat 1848-1919.
  J. Steinberg, 182:Vol31#21/22-825
Grünewald, B. Der phänomenologische
  Ursprung des Logischen.
  J.J.D., 543:Mar79-544
Grunfeld, F.V. Prophets Without Honour.*
  J.P. Stern, 617(TLS):5Sep80-968
Grüssner, K-H. Arleng Alam, die Sprache
  der Mikir.
  J. Filliozat, 182:Vol131#20-734
Gruyer, F. Les Oubliés des nuits romanes.
  L.S. Crist, 207(FR):Feb79-511

Grylls, D. Guardians and Angels.*
  D.J. Smith, 67:Nov79-325
  J.M.S. Tompkins, 541(RES):May79-246
Grzeloński, B. - see Jefferson, T. and
  T.A.B. Kościuszko
Gschwind, U., ed. Le Roman de Flamenca.*
  P. Zumthor, 589:Apr79-379
Guarini, B. Il pastor fido.* (J.H. Whit-
  field, ed)
  205(FMLS):Jan78-89
Guelfi, F.F. - see under Franchini Guelfi,
  F.
Guenther, H.V. Tibetan Buddhism in West-
  ern Perspective.
  R. Sherburne, 318(JAOS):Oct-Dec78-576
Guenther, H.V. Treasures on the Tibetan
  Middle Way. (2nd ed)
  R. Sherburne, 293(JASt):Feb79-326
Guenthner, F. and M. Guenthner-Reutter.
  Meaning and Translation.
  M. Partridge, 479(PhQ):Oct79-373
Guerard, A.J. The Triumph of the Novel.*
  J.M. Holquist, 131(CL):Spring79-185
  R.L. Patten, 155:Spring79-39
Guérard, M. Michel Guérard's Cuisine
  Gourmande.*
  W. and C. Cowen, 639(VQR):Spring79-73
Gueret, M., A. Robinet and P. Tombeur.
  Spinoza, "Ethica."
  E. Giancotti Boscherini, 227(GCFI):
  Jul-Dec78-554
Guérin, D. - see Fourier, C.
Guérin, J-Y. Le Théâtre d'Audiberti et le
  baroque.
  A. Cismaru, 207(FR):Dec78-357
  G-D. Farcy, 535(RHL):Jan-Feb79-155
  C. Toloudis, 188(ECr):Summer78-88
Guérin, P. Essai pour une philosophie
  ésotérique de l'histoire.
  M. Adam, 542:Jul-Sep79-358
Guerman, M., comp. Art of the October
  Revolution.*
  M. Chamot, 39:Dec79-535
Guerri, G.B. Galeazzo Ciano.
  D. Mack Smith, 617(TLS):2May80-483
Guerry, H., ed. A Bibliography of Philo-
  sophical Bibliographies.
  G. Paradis, 154:Dec78-745
Guery, F. Lou Salomé, génie de la vie.
  O. Marcel, 542:Apr-Jun78-177
Guest, H. Days.
  P. Lewis, 565:Vol20#1-49
Guest, J. - see Betjeman, J.
Guest, L. Children of Hachiman.
  M. Furness, 617(TLS):27Jun80-743
Guggenheim, P. Out Of This Century.*
  G. Annan, 617(TLS):14Mar80-284
  M. Levey, 362:20Mar80-372
Guglielmi, J. Le dégagement multiple.
  J. Tortel, 98:May78-526
Guibert, A.J. Bibliographie des oeuvres
  de René Descartes publiées au XVIIe
  siècle.
  K.E. Carpenter, 517(PBSA):Jan-Mar78-
  158

Guicharnaud, J. Modern French Theatre from Giraudoux to Genet. (rev)
  E. Freeman, 208(FS):Vol33Pt2-942
"Guide to the German Records." [Tanzania]
  A. Redmayne, 69:Vol48#2-192
Guido of Arezzo. Prologus in Antiphonarium. (J. Smits van Waesberghe, ed)
  C.M. Atkinson, 589:Jul79-564
Guido, G. - see Petronius
Guiette, R. Forme et senefiance.
  A.H. Diverres, 208(FS):Jul79-321
Guilbert, L. La créativité lexicale.*
  D. Godard, 355(LSoc):Apr78-135
Guillaume de Lorris and Jean de Meun. Der Rosenroman. (K.A. Ott, ed and trans)
  M. Bambeck, 72:Band216Heft1-214
Guillaume de Machaut. "La Louange des Dames" by Guillaume de Machaut. (N. Wilkins, ed)
  J. Stevens, 382(MAE):1979/1-167
Guillaume, J. - see de Nerval, G.
Guillaume, M. Le capital et son double.
  A. Jacob, 542:Apr-Jun78-211
Guillemain, B. Machiavel.*
  E. Namer, 542:Apr-Jun79-211
Guillemin, H. Précisions.
  J. Cruickshank, 208(FS):Jul79-372
Guillén, L.F. Aristoteles y la comedia media.
  W.G. Arnott, 123:Vol29No1-140
  R.L. Hunter, 303(JoHS):Vol99-187
  P. Louis, 555:Vol52fasc2-378
Guilleragues. Correspondance.* (F. Deloffre and J. Rougeot, eds)
  J-M. Pelous, 535(RHL):Sep-Oct78-823
Guillevic. Élégies. (M. O'Meara, ed and trans)
  G.D. Martin, 208(FS):Vol33Pt2-922
Guillevic, E. Du domaine.
  M. Bishop, 207(FR):Feb79-512
Guilloux, L. Carnets.
  J. Blot, 450(NRF):Jan79-109
Guindey, G. Le Drame de la pensée dialectique.
  J.P. Mayer, 208(FS):Vol33Pt2-945
Guisan, G. - see Béguin, A. and M. Raymond
Guisan, G. and D. Jakubec, eds. Jacques Rivière et ses amitiés suisses.
  H. Godin, 208(FS):Vol33Pt2-880
Guisso, R.W.L. Wu Tse-t'ien and the Politics of Legitimation in T'ang China.
  H.J. Wechsler, 293(JASt):Aug79-747
Gülich, E. and W. Raible. Linguistische Textmodelle.
  A-M. Simon-Vandenbergen, 179(ES):Dec79-824
Gullans, C. Imperfect Correspondences.
  J. Goodman, 598(SoR):Spring80-519
Gulley, B., with M.E. Reese. Breaking Cover.
  W. Goodman, 441:31Aug80-11
"Gulliver 1, 1976."
  J. Kramer, 224(GRM):Band28Heft4-494
Gullón, R. - see Galdós, B.P.
Gumbert, H.L. - see Lichtenberg, G.C.

Gumbert, J.P. Die Utrechter Kartäuser und ihre Bücher im frühen fünfzehnten Jahrhundert.
  A.I. Doyle, 354:Sep79-295
Gumbrecht, H.U. Zola im historischen Kontext.
  D. Baguley, 395(MFS):Winter78/79-623
Gumpel, L. "Concrete" Poetry from East and West Germany.*
  J. Penelope, 290(JAAC):Spring80-333
Gunn, G. The Interpretation of Otherness.*
  L.P. Simpson, 27(AL):Jan80-562
  639(VQR):Summer79-106
Gunn, T. Jack Straw's Castle.*
  L. Lee, 114(ChiR):Spring79-108
Gunn, T. Selected Poems 1950-75.
  R. Murphy, 453(NYRB):20Mar80-28
  M.L. Rosenthal, 441:20Jan80-20
  D. Smith, 29:Sep/Oct80-30
Gunther, E. A Catalogue of the Ethnological Collections in the Sheldon Jackson Museum.
  R. Lopez, 2(AfrA):Nov78-106
Günther, W. Das portugiesische Kreolisch der Ilha do Príncipe.*
  H. Schulz, 682(ZPSK):Band31Heft1-101
Gupta, A.K. North West Frontier Province Legislature and Freedom Struggle, 1932-47.
  L. Ziring, 293(JASt):Feb79-398
Guralnick, P. Lost Highway.
  R. Davies, 617(TLS):6Jun80-633
Gurdus, L.K. The Death Train.
  T. Ziolkowski, 569(SR):Fall79-676
Gurney, O.R. Middle Babylonian Legal Documents and Other Texts.
  W.H. van Soldt, 318(JAOS):Oct-Dec78-498
Gurza, E. Lectura existencialista de "La Celestina."*
  J.F. Burke, 589:Jul79-572
Gusdorf, G. Naissance de la conscience romantique au siècle des lumières.*
  B.T. Cooper, 446(NCFS):Fall-Winter 78/79-124
  D. Leduc-Fayette, 192(EP):Jul-Sep79-358
Güse, E-G. Das Frühwerk Max Beckmanns.
  D. Schubert, 683:Band41Heft3/4-342
Gustafson, J.M. Protestant and Roman Catholic Ethics.
  185:Apr79-313
Gustafson, R. Corners In the Glass.*
  D. Beardsley, 168(ECW):Spring78-55
  D.S. West, 102(CanL):Spring79-109
Gustafson, R. Soviet Poems.*
  E. Folsom, 526:Winter79-81
Gustafsson, M. Binomial Expressions in Present-Day English.
  A. Fill, 38:Band96Heft1/2-194
Gutas, D. Greek Wisdom Literature in Arabic Translation.*
  J. Glucker, 123:Vol29No1-167
"Gutenberg-Jahrbuch 1977."
  J.L. Flood, 354:Sep79-293

Guthke, K.S. Literarisches Leben im ach-tzehnten Jahrhundert in Deutschland und in der Schweiz.
G. Flaherty, 222(GR):Winter78-37
N. Oellers, 52:Band13Heft2-204
Guthmüller, H-B. Die Rezeption Mussets im Second Empire.
P.J. Whyte, 208(FS):Apr79-212
Guthrie, A.B., Jr. No Second Wind.
P-L. Adams, 61:Mar80-101
N. Callendar, 441:30Mar80-17
Guthrie, W.K.C. A History of Greek Philosophy.* (Vol 4)
K. Dorter, 154:Mar78-186
M. Schofield, 447(N&Q):Oct78-466
R.K. Sprague, 122:Apr79-174
P. Vicaire, 555:Vol52fasc1-161
Guthrie, W.K.C. A History of Greek Philosophy. (Vol 5)
I.M. Crombie, 483:Oct79-559
J.M. Osborn, 123:Vol129No2-243
F. Solmsen, 124:Feb80-315
S. Waterlow, 479(PhQ):Jul79-260
Guthrie, W.K.C. Les sophistes.
J-L. Poirier, 542:Jan-Mar79-126
de Gutiérrez, V.M. - see under Montori de Gutiérrez, V.
Gutiérrez-Cortines Corral, C. La iglesia y el colegio de San Esteban de Murcia.
F. Marías, 48:Oct-Dec78-447
Gutiérrez González, J. The New Libertar-ian Gospel.
A.T. Hennelly, 613:Mar79-101
Gutiérrez Marrone, N. El estilo de Juan Rulfo.
J. Himelblau, 238:Dec79-740
Gutknecht, C. and K-U. Panther. Genera-tive Linguistik.
G. Van der Elst, 685(ZDL):2/1979-257
Gutmann, J., ed. The Synagogue.
J.C. Greenfield, 318(JAOS):Jul-Sep78-310
Gutteridge, D. A True History of Lambton County.*
D.H. Sullivan, 648(WCR):Feb79-42
Guttmann, A. From Ritual to Record.*
B. Lowrey, 639(VQR):Winter79-170
D.L. Vanderwerken, 219(GaR):Fall79-707
Gutwirth, M. Michel de Montaigne ou le pari d'exemplarité.*
D.M. Frame, 546(RR):Jan79-102
P. Koppisch, 400(MLN):May79-886
Gutwirth, M. Madame de Staël, Novelist.
A. Fairlie, 208(FS):Oct79-455
Guy, D. Football Dreams.
C. Lehmann-Haupt, 441:23Dec80-C9
Guy, J. The Destruction of the Zulu King-dom.
K. Ingham, 617(TLS):21Mar80-336
Guy, R. Axiologie et métaphysique selon Joaquim Xirau.
H. Wagner, 53(AGP):Band60Heft1-116
Guyard, M-R. Le vocabulaire politique de Paul Éluard.*
M. Giuglio, 209(FM):Apr78-175
Guyer, P. Kant and the Claims of Taste.
E. Schaper, 290(JAAC):Winter79-198

Guyon, M. Le Principe de solitude.
J. Stéfan, 450(NRF):Apr79-116
Guyonvarc'h, C-J. - see Lagadeuc, J.
Guzzoni, U., B. Rang and L. Siep, eds. Der Idealismus und seine Gegenwart.
J-F. Courtine, 192(EP):Apr-Jun79-248
Gvozdetsky, N.A. Soviet Geographical Explorations and Discoveries.
T. Shabad, 550(RusR):Apr79-268
Gwaltney, J.L. Drylongso.
P-L. Adams, 61:Jul80-87
W. Balliett, 442(NY):6Oct80-194
M. Watkins, 441:2Sep80-C11
Gysin, F. The Grotesque in American Negro Fiction.*
M. Diedrich, 72:Band216Heft2-434
Gzowski, P. The Sacrament.
D. Grumbach, 441:14Dec80-14

Haack, S. Deviant Logic.*
M.A. Gilbert, 486:Mar78-149
Haack, S. Philosophy of Logics.
S. Read, 518:Oct79-138
C.J.F. Williams, 479(PhQ):Jul79-277
Haagensen, J. Like a Diamondback in the Trunk of a Witness's Buick.
N.J. Herrington, 584(SWR):Autumn79-402
ter Haar, C. - see von Eichendorff, J.
Haarder, A. "Beowulf."*
R.P. Tripp, Jr., 152(UDQ):Winter79-121
Haarløv, B. The Half-Open Door.*
M.A.R. Colledge, 123:Vol129No1-186
Haarmann, H. Grundzüge der Sprachtyp-ologie.*
C.V.J. Russ, 402(MLR):Jan79-127
Haas, G. Kinder- und Jugendliteratur.
E. Breitinger, 430(NS):Feb78-83
Haas, W., ed. Alphabets for English.
A. Wollmann, 38:Band96Heft3/4-492
Haas, W. Franz Alois Schumachers "Isaac."
R.M. Kully, 657(WW):May-Jun78-218
Hába, A. Neue Harmonielehre.
W. Drabkin, 415:Jun79-485
D. Puffett, 410(M&L):Jul79-332
Habel, C. and S. Kanngiesser, eds. Sprach-dynamik und Sprachstruktur.
K. Spalding, 182:Vol131#13-406
Haberly, L. An American Bookbuilder in England and Wales.
D.A. Harrop, 78(BC):Autumn79-441
Haberkamp, G., ed. Thematischer Katalog der Musikhandschriften der Fürstlich Oettingen-Wallerstein'schen Bibliothek Schloss Harburg.*
B.S. Brook, 317:Fall79-549
Habermas, J. Legitimation Crisis.
P.D. Shaw, 488:Mar79-119
Habermas, J. Raison et légitimité.
A. Reix, 542:Oct-Dec79-484
Habermas, J. Theory and Practice.
(French title: Théorie et pratique.)
R. Nelson, 154:Dec78-710
C. Roëls, 192(EP):Jul-Sep79-360
Habra, G. La mort et l'au-delà.
A. Reix, 542:Oct-Dec78-510

153

Hailey, E.F. A Woman of Independent
Means.*
  639(VQR):Autumn78-138
Hain, P., ed. Policing the Police. (Vol
2)
  B. Whitaker, 362:17Apr80-512
Haines, R.M. The Church and Politics in
Fourteenth-Century England.
  R.W. Pfaff, 589:Apr79-381
Hakim, H.E. Islam and Sufism in the Light
of Theosophy.
  S.A.W. Bukhari, 273(IC):Oct76-247
Haksar, V. Equality, Liberty and Perfec-
tionism.
  A. Ryan, 617(TLS):29Feb80-233
Hakutani, Y. and L. Fried, eds. American
Literary Naturalism.
  H. Beaver, 402(MLR):Apr79-435
Halberstam, D. The Powers That Be.*
  J. Morgan, 617(TLS):11Jan80-32
Halberstam, M. The Wanting of Levine.
  639(VQR):Autumn78-138
Halbfas, H. Aufklärung und Widerstand.
  H. Grosch, 182:Vol31#14-463
Halbritter, R. Konzeptionsformen des
modernen angloamerikanischen Kurzdramas.*
  H. Kosok, 224(GRM):Band28Heft3-373
Hale, G., ed. The Source Book for the
Disabled.
  S. Curtin, 441:6Jan80-8
Halevy, Z. Jewish Schools under Czarism
and Communism.*
  J.J. Tomiak, 575(SEER):Apr79-307
Haley, B. The Healthy Body and Victorian
Culture.*
  C. Woodring, 651(WHR):Spring79-161
  42(AR):Winter79-123
"Ḥāliṣ's Story of Ibrāhim." (A.J.E.
Bodrogligeti, ed and trans)
  W.C. Hickman, 318(JAOS):Oct-Dec78-570
Halkin, H. Letters to an American Jewish
Friend.*
  E. King, 287:Feb78-27
Hall, A. The Scorpion Signal.
  N. Callendar, 441:15Jun80-17
  M. Laski, 362:17Apr80-514
Hall, A.R. and M.B. - see Oldenburg, H.
Hall, A.R. and L. Tilling - see Newton, I.
Hall, B.F. The Chinese Maritime Customs.
  A. Birch, 302:Vol16#1and2-123
Hall, C. Lightly.*
  C. Gerson, 168(ECW):Spring78-119
  T. Vincent, 296(JCF):28/29-228
Hall, D. Kicking the Leaves.*
  J.F. Cotter, 249(HudR):Spring79-110
  J. Fuller, 617(TLS):18Jan80-65
  P. Stitt, 219(GaR):Summer79-463
Hall, D. Remembering Poets.*
  R. Jellema, 396(ModA):Fall79-437
  639(VQR):Summer78-90
Hall, H.G. - see Cerou, P.
Hall, H.G. - see de Molière, J.B.P.
Hall, J.W. and T. Takeshi, eds. Japan in
the Muromachi Age.
  M.C. Collcutt, 244(HJAS):Jun78-247
Hall, P. Great Planning Disasters.
  P. Self, 617(TLS):4Jul80-765

Hall, R. Fifty Years of Hume Scholarship.
  A. Flew, 518:May79-68
Hall, R. Lovers on the Nile.
  A. Broyard, 441:19Mar80-C25
  C. Oliver, 617(TLS):11Apr80-410
  E.S. Turner, 362:28Feb80-282
Hall, R. J.S. Manifold.*
  C. Hanna, 71(ALS):May79-129
Hall, R. Selected Poems.* Black Baga-
telles.*
  S.E. Lee, 581:Dec79-432
Hall, R.A., Jr. Antonio Fogazzaro.
  G. Carsaniga, 402(MLR):Oct79-959
  S.B. Chandler, 399(MLJ):Mar79-148
Hall, R.A., Jr. Proto-Romance Phonology.*
  S.N. Dworkin, 320(CJL):Spring-Fall78-
  136
  R. Posner, 353:Jun78-71
Hall, R.L. The King Edward Plot.
  N. Callendar, 441:23Mar80-33
Hall, T.H. The Strange Case of Edmund
Gurney. The Strange Story of Ada Good-
rich Freer.
  V. Glendinning, 617(TLS):1Aug80-867
Hallager, E. The Mycenaean Palace at
Knossos.
  S. Hood, 123:Vol29No2-283
  M.R. Popham, 303(JoHS):Vol199-202
al-Ḥallāj, M. The Ṭawāsīn.
  H. Algar, 318(JAOS):Oct-Dec78-486
Hallam, A., ed. Patterns of Evolution.
  J.Z. Young, 453(NYRB):7Feb80-45
von Hallberg, R. Charles Olson.*
  P. Breslin, 491:Jul80-219
  L.S. Dembo, 27(AL):May79-289
  S. Loevy, 114(ChiR):Winter79-163
  C. Molesworth, 219(GaR):Summer79-438
  M. Perloff, 141:Summer79-251
de la Halle, A. - see under Adam de la
Halle
Halle, L.J. Out of Chaos.
  K.W. Thompson, 639(VQR):Summer78-546
Haller, H. Der deiktische Gebrauch des
Demonstrativums im Altitalienischen.
  R. Stefanini, 545(RPh):Aug78-119
Haller, H. Übersetzungen im "gemeinen
Deutsch" (1464). (E. Bauer, ed)
  B. Murdoch, 182:Vol31#11/12-345
Haller, M. The Book Collector's Fact Book.
  G.T. Tanselle, 517(PBSA):Apr-Jun78-265
Hallett, G. A Companion to Wittgenstein's
"Philosophical Investigations."*
  A. Ellis, 393(Mind):Jul79-452
  R.E. Innis, 567:Vol125#1/2-175
Halliday, M.A.K. Language as Social
Semiotic.
  M. Garner, 67:Nov79-379
Halliday, M.A.K. Learning How to Mean.*
  J. Local and G. McGregor, 603:Vol13#1-
  91
  J.R. Martin, 320(CJL):Spring-Fall78-
  187
  E.A. Nida, 353:Feb78-86
Halliday, M.A.K. System and Function in
Language.* (G. Kress, ed)
  R. Veltman, 307:Apr79-36

Halliday, M.A.K. and R. Hasan. Cohesion in English.*
  T.F. Hoad, 447(N&Q):Aug78-352
  R. Huddleston, 361:Aug78-333
Halliday, R.J. John Stuart Mill.
  H. Laboucheix, 189(EA):Jan-Mar78-91
  J. Weissman, 637(VS):Winter78-275
Hallie, P.P. Lest Innocent Blood Be Shed.*
  N. Bliven, 442(NY):21Jan80-125
  T. Ziolkowski, 569(SR):Fall79-676
Hallig, R. Spracherlebnis und Sprachfor-schung.
  H. Kahane, 545(RPh):Aug78-94
Hallissey, R.C. The Rajput Rebellion against Aurangzeb.
  N.P. Ziegler and R. Saran, 293(JASt): Feb79-389
Hallowell, C. People of the Bayou.
  D. Grumbach, 441:6Jan80-12
  442(NY):7Jan80-86
Hallpike, C.R. The Foundations of Primitive Thought.
  E. Gellner, 617(TLS):15Aug80-911
Halls, G. The Felling of the Thawle.
  D. Durrant, 364:Dec79/Jan80-132
Hallyn, F. Formes métaphoriques dans la poésie lyrique de l'âge baroque en France.*
  G. Mathieu-Castellani, 535(RHL):May-Jun78-463
Halpenny, F.G. - see "The Dictionary of Canadian Biography"
Halperin, J., ed. Jane Austen.
  F. McCombie, 447(N&Q):Apr78-187
Halperin, J. Trollope and Politics.*
  G. Butte, 637(VS):Summer78-518
  A. Pollard, 125:Winter79-291
  R.C. Terry, 405(MP):Feb80-310
Halperin, J. and J. Kunert. Plots and Characters in the Fiction of Jane Austen, the Brontës, and George Eliot.
  T.J. Winnifrith, 402(MLR):Jul79-663
Halpern, D. Life Among Others.*
  J. Parini, 114(ChiR):Spring79-117
  P. Stitt, 219(GaR):Summer79-463
  639(VQR):Summer78-100
Halpern, P., ed. The Keyes Papers.
  B. Ranft, 617(TLS):12Sep80-1005
Halsaa Albrektsen, B. Kvinner og politisk deltakelse.
  I.N. Means, 563(SS):Winter79-68
Halsband, R. - see Montagu, M.W.
Halsband, R. and I. Grundy - see Montagu, M.W.
Halsey, A.H., A.F. Heath and J.M. Ridge. Origins and Destinations.
  J. Vaizey, 617(TLS):1Aug80-881
  M. Warnock, 362:14Feb80-219
Haltzel, M. Der Abbau der deutschen ständischen Selbstverwaltung in den Ostseeprovinzen Russlands.
  J. Hiden, 575(SEER):Oct79-608
Hamann, R. and J. Hermand. Expressionismus.*
  T. Meyer, 680(ZDP):Band97Heft2-312
Hamblen, A.A. Ruth Suckow.
  R. Gish, 649(WAL):Winter80-335

Hamburger, J. Macaulay and the Whig Tradition.*
  A. Welsh, 637(VS):Autumn77-130
Hamel, P.B. and M.U. Chiltoskey. Cherokee Plants.
  R.L. Welsch, 582(SFQ):Vol41-273
Hamel, P.M. Through Music to the Self.
  P. Griffiths, 415:Apr79-311
Hamelin, O. Sur le De Fato. (M. Conche, ed)
  J-M. Gabaude, 542:Jan-Mar79-142
  A. Reix, 542:Jul-Sep79-325
Hamer, D.A. The Politics of Electoral Pressure.
  J.B. Conacher, 637(VS):Winter79-219
  J.S. Newton, 161(DUJ):Jun79-274
Hamidulla, M. Mohammad Rasulullah (Sall-allahu alaihi wa sallam).
  S. Vahiduddin, 273(IC):Apr76-123
Hamill, D. Stomping Ground.
  S. Ellin, 441:13Jul80-15
Hamill, P. Flesh and Blood.
  639(VQR):Spring78-65
Hamill, S. Triada.
  L.L. Lee, 649(WAL):Spring79-80
Hamilton, A. The Papers of Alexander Hamilton. (Vol 25) (H.C. Syrett, ed)
  639(VQR):Spring78-50
Hamilton, A.C. Sir Philip Sidney.*
  A.K. Hieatt, 178:Fall79-355
  D.C. Kay, 447(N&Q):Oct78-460
  N. Lindheim, 539:Vol4No1-115
  C.F. Williamson, 184(EIC):Jan79-75
Hamilton, A.C. - see Spenser, E.
Hamilton, C.D. Sparta's Bitter Victories.
  S. Pembroke, 617(TLS):11Jan80-43
Hamilton, E. The Illustrious Lady.
  J. Barnard, 617(TLS):13Jun80-679
Hamilton, G.H. The Art and Architecture of Russia. (2nd ed)
  A. Senkevitch, Jr., 576:May78-123
Hamilton, H. The Three Kentucky Presidents.
  T.H. Williams, 9(AlaR):Oct79-317
Hamilton, I. The Little Magazines.
  B. Bergonzi, 402(MLR):Oct79-932
Hamilton, J. Oiseaux.
  A.L. Amprimoz, 526:Spring79-82
Hamilton, K. and A. Condemned to Life.*
  M. Neill, 178:Summer79-235
Hamilton, N. The Brothers Mann.*
  J. Meyers, 639(VQR):Autumn79-748
Hamilton, R. Epinikion.
  S.L. Radt, 394:Vol32fasc3/4-396
Hamilton, R.C. Americanismos en las obras del padre Bernabé Cobo.
  S.N. Dworkin, 545(RPh):May79-486
Hamilton, V. and M. Vernon, eds. The Development of Cognitive Processes.
  D.A. Warden, 307:Apr79-52
Hamilton, W.B. The Macmillan Book of Canadian Place Names.
  K.B. Harder, 424:Sep78-287
Hamilton-Edwards, G. In Search of Army Ancestry.
  B.D. Evans, 325:Oct79-236

Hamlin, M.C.W. Legends of le Détroit.*
  K.B. Harder, 424:Dec78-427
Hamlyn, D.W. Experience and the Growth of
Understanding.
  D.E. Cooper, 518:Jan79-26
  K.S., 543:Sep78-137
Hamm, C. Yesterdays.*
  C. Keil, 187:Sep80-576
Hamm, M.F., ed. The City in Russian His-
tory.*
  A. Senkevitch, Jr., 576:May78-123
Hammacher, A.M. Jacques Lipchitz.
  K.J. Michaelsen, 54:Jun78-383
Hammer, T.A. Die Orts- und Flurnamen des
St.-Galler Rheintals.
  G. Hilty, 182:Vol131#7/8-221
Hammial, P. Foot Falls and Notes.*
  C. Pollnitz, 581:Dec79-462
Hammond, G. The Reward Game.
  T.J. Binyon, 617(TLS):30May80-606
Hammond, J.R. Herbert George Wells.
  A.M., 125:Winter79-308
Hammond, M. Latin.
  J.N. Adams, 123:Vol129No1-170
Hammond, N. and M. Everett. Birds of
Britain and Europe.
  R. O'Hanlon, 617(TLS):9May80-536
Hammond, N. and G.R. Willey, eds. Maya
Archaeology and Ethnohistory.
  B.W. Warren, 263(RIB):Vol29No3/4-365
Hammond, N.G.L. Migrations and Invasions
in Greece and Adjacent Areas.*
  K. Branigan, 123:Vol129No1-98
Hammond, N.G.L. and G.T. Griffith. His-
tory of Macedonia. (Vol 2)
  S. Pembroke, 617(TLS):11Jan80-43
Hamon, P. Semiologia lessico leggibilità
del testo narrativo.
  D. Robey, 307:Oct79-129
Hampl, P. Woman Before an Aquarium.
  J.F. Cotter, 249(HudR):Spring79-115
  P. Ramsey, 569(SR):Fall79-686
  639(VQR):Summer79-107
Hampp, I. and P. Assion, eds. Forschungen
und Berichte zur Volkskunde in Baden-
Württemberg 1971-73.
  H. Schwendt, 685(ZDL):2/1979-266
Hampshire, S. Two Theories of Morality.*
  N.J.H. Dent, 393(Mind):Jan79-138
  H. Wagner, 53(AGP):Band60Heft3-334
Hampson, N. Danton.
  M. Anderson, 208(FS):Oct79-491
Hampton, C. Able's Will.
  J. Coleby, 157:Summer79-81
Hamsun, K. Wayfarers.
  R. Coles, 441:18May80-9
  P. Lewis, 617(TLS):18Jul80-798
  J. Mellors, 362:31Jul80-153
Hamsun, K. The Women at the Pump.
  S. Lawson, 114(ChiR):Spring79-102
Han Suyin. My House Has Two Doors.
  H.G. Porteus, 362:5Jun80-730
  O. Schell, 441:20Jul80-10
Hanagan, E. Holding On.
  P. Craig, 617(TLS):18Jul80-823
  P. Kemp, 362:19Jun80-805

Hanak, M.J. Maeterlinck's Symbolic Drama.
  J. Decreus, 208(FS):Vol33Pt2-853
Hanawalt, B.A. Crime and Conflict in
English Communities 1300-1348.
  R.B. Pugh, 617(TLS):15Feb80-184
Hand, W.D., ed. American Folk Medicine.
  W.M. Clements, 292(JAF):Jan-Mar79-86
  R.C. Poulsen, 650(WF):Jan79-64
  E. Trimmer, 203:Vol189#1-115
Handke, K. and E. Rzetelska-Feleszko.
Przewodnik po językoznawstwie polskim.
  M.Z. Brooks, 497(PolR):Vol23#2-88
Handke, P. The Left-Handed Woman.*
  L. Graver, 473(PR):3/1979-457
  S. Stern, 617(TLS):18Apr80-442
Handke, P. Nonsense and Happiness.* The
Innerworld of the Outerworld of the
Innerworld.
  K. Agena, 473(PR):1/1979-126
Handler, J.S. and F.W. Lange. Plantation
Slavery in Barbados.
  M. Craton, 529(QQ):Summer79-330
Handoo, J. Kashmiri Phonetic Reader.
  B.B. Kachru, 350:Mar79-228
Hands, R., ed. English Hawking and Hunt-
ing in "The Boke of St. Albans."*
  A. Zettersten, 179(ES):Feb79-95
Handy, R.H. A History of the Churches in
the United States and Canada.*
  W.N., 102(CanL):Spring79-147
Hanff, H. Underfoot in Show Business.
  S. Trotter, 362:4Dec80-764
Hanfmann, G.M.A. and N.H. Ramage. Sculp-
ture from Sardis.
  R. Heidenreich, 182:Vol131#20-753
  R. Higgins, 39:Feb79-167
Hanfmann, G.M.A. and J.C. Waldbaum. A Sur-
vey of Sardis and the Major Monuments
Outside the City Walls.
  M.J. Mellink, 54:Mar78-154
  W. Müller-Wiener, 182:Vol131#7/8-236
Hanham, H.J., ed. Bibliography of British
History, 1851-1914.
  J.L. Altholz, 637(VS):Autumn77-108
Hanke, H. and G. Rossow. Sozialistische
Kulturrevolution.
  T. Koch, 654(WB):6/1978-168
Hanks, D.A. The Decorative Designs of
Frank Lloyd Wright.
  J. Sergeant, 46:Oct79-204
Hanley, J. A Kingdom.
  G. Davenport, 249(HudR):Spring79-144
Hanley, J. The Welsh Sonata.
  P. Lewis, 565:Vol20#1-49
  639(VQR):Winter79-20
Hanly, C. Existentialism and Psycho-
analysis.
  S.K. Levine, 99:Oct80-31
Hanna, W.L. Lost Harbor.*
  D.B. Quinn, 617(TLS):4Apr80-396
Hannah, B. Ray.
  B. De Mott, 441:16Nov80-7
  C. Lehmann-Haupt, 441:11Nov80-C8
Hannan, J. Peeling Oranges in the Shade.
  G. Hamel, 198:Winter80-139

Hannavy, J. Masters of Victorian Photography.
  B. Jay, 637(VS):Winter78-294
Hannich-Bode, I., comp. Germanistik in Festschriften von den Anfängen (1877) bis 1973.
  W.A. Reichart, 406:Summer79-187
Hanning, R. and J. Ferrante - see Marie de France
Hanning, R.W. The Individual in Twelfth-Century Romance.*
  R.H. Bloch, 400(MLN):May79-898
  D. Bornstein, 125:Fall78-133
  R.J. Cormier, 207(FR):May79-921
  D.H. Green, 402(MLR):Oct79-979
  H.C.R. Laurie, 382(MAE):1979/1-122
  B. Nolan, 589:Jan79-142
  C.T. Swan, 377:Jul79-116
Hannon, M. My Mother Walked Out.
  N. Moser, 584(SWR):Autumn79-412
Hanrahan, B. The Peach Groves.
  S. Ramsey, 617(TLS):30May80-606
Hänsch, H. Innovationsfaktoren in der Landwirtschaft Indiens.
  P. Vosseler, 182:Vol31#19-700
Hansel, C.E.M. ESP and Parapsychology.
  G. Hough, 617(TLS):25Jul80-854
Hansen, E.C. Rural Catalonia under the Franco Régime.
  L. Flaquer, 86(BHS):Jul79-265
Hansen, J. Skinflick.*
  T.J. Binyon, 617(TLS):6Jun80-654
Hansen, K.C. and L.E. Pintupi Dictionary.
  R.M.W. Dixon, 350:Mar79-262
Hansen, T. Prosessen mot Hamsun.
  H. Naess, 563(SS):Summer79-308
Hansen, T. School in the Woods.
  J.R. Christianson, 563(SS):Spring79-203
Hansen, T.L. and E.J. Wilkins. Español a lo vivo. (4th ed)
  D.A. Klein, 399(MLJ):Jan-Feb79-49
Hansen, T.L., E.J. Wilkins and J.G. Enos. Le Français vivant. (2nd ed rev by J. Kaplow)
  J. Ludwig, 399(MLJ):Mar79-138
  N.A. Poulin, 207(FR):Apr79-785
Hanson, A.C. Manet and the Modern Tradition.*
  K. Garlick, 447(N&Q):Jun78-286
  A. de Leiris, 54:Dec78-734
  G.P. Weisberg, 127:Spring79-212
  639(VQR):Winter78-29
Hanson, R.P.C. and C. Blanc. Saint Patrick: Confession et Lettre à Coroticus.
  M. Winterbottom, 123:Vol29No2-302
Hantrais, L. Le vocabulaire de Georges Brassens.
  G. Price, 208(FS):Vol33Pt2-1044
  A. Schneider, 209(FM):Jan78-84
Häntzschel, G. Johann Heinrich Voss.
  J.K. Fugate, 406:Fall79-339
Hapgood, F. Why Males Exist.
  R.A. Sokolov, 441:27Jan80-18
  61:Feb80-96

Happ, H. Grundfragen einer Dependenz-Grammatik des Lateinischen.
  C. Guiraud, 555:Vol52fasc1-106
Haq, Z. Landlord and Peasant in Islam.
  S.A. Akbarabadi, 273(IC):Apr78-133
Haraguchi, S. The Tone Pattern of Japanese.
  M. Shibatani, 350:Dec79-928
Haraguchi, T. and others, eds and trans. The Status System and Social Organization of Satsuma.*
  C. Totman, 318(JAOS):Apr-Jun78-184
Harari, J.V., ed. Textual Strategies.
  S. Loveday, 617(TLS):4Jul80-761
Harbert, E.N. The Force So Much Closer Home.*
  C. Stark, 125:Winter79-282
  E. Waterston, 106:Fall79-205
Harbison, C. The Last Judgment in Sixteenth-Century Northern Europe.
  C. Andersson, 54:Sep78-553
Harbison, R. Deliberate Regression.
  J. Leonard, 441:14May80-C28
Harbron, J.D. Canada Without Quebec.
  K. McRoberts, 529(QQ):Spring79-143
Harcourt, J. and J. Metcalf, eds. 77: Best Canadian Stories.*
  C. Ross, 102(CanL):Autumn79-86
Harden, E.F. The Emergence of Thackeray's Serial Fiction.
  D. Hawes, 617(TLS):14Mar80-290
Hardin, H. The Great Wave of Civilization.
  K. Fraser, 168(ECW):Spring78-104
  J. Ripley, 102(CanL):Autumn79-110
Harding, F.J.W. Jean-Marie Guyau (1854-1888), Aesthetician and Sociologist.
  D.G. Charlton, 208(FS):Vol33Pt2-848
Harding, J. Lost Illusions.
  G. Rees, 208(FS):Oct79-475
Harding, R.E.M. The Piano-forte.
  C. Ehrlich, 415:May79-403
Harding, S. Can Theories Be Refuted?*
  J. Largeault, 542:Jan-Mar79-112
Hardjono, J.M. Transmigration in Indonesia.
  R.D. Hill, 302:Vol16#1and2-134
Hardouin-Fugier, E. Le Poème de l'ame par Janmot.
  F.P. Bowman, 446(NCFS):Fall-Winter 78/79-129
Hardt, M. Poetik und Semiotik.*
  D. Ingenschay, 490:Band10Heft4-507
  J.J. White, 402(MLR):Jan79-129
Hardwick, E. Sleepless Nights.*
  B. Caplan, 219(GaR):Winter79-933
  C.C. Park, 249(HudR):Winter79/80-582
Hardy, A. The Spiritual Nature of Man.
  J.R. Lucas, 617(TLS):4Apr80-397
Hardy, B. The Advantage of Lyric.*
  C. Clausen, 569(SR):Spring79-314
  P. Faulkner, 161(DUJ):Dec78-135
  K.L. Goodwin, 67:May79-110
  C. Guillot, 189(EA):Jul-Dec78-366
  A. Rodway, 447(N&Q):Feb78-96
Hardy, B. Tellers and Listeners.*
  F. McCombie, 447(N&Q):Jun78-275
  R.B. Yeazell, 637(VS):Autumn77-120

Hardy, D. Petr Tkachev.*
R.H.W. Theen, 104(CASS):Fall78-429
A. Walker, 575(SEER):Jul79-456
Hardy, F.E. The Life of Thomas Hardy 1840-
1928.
S. Hunter, 402(MLR):Jan79-175
Hardy, H. - see Berlin, I.
Hardy, H. and A. Kelly - see Berlin, I.
Hardy, R. Rivers of Darkness.*
C. Hope, 364:Dec79/Jan80-127
Hardy, T. The Collected Letters of Thomas
Hardy.* (Vol 1) (R.L. Purdy and M. Mill-
gate, eds)
T.R.M. Creighton, 541(RES):Feb79-104
S. Gatrell, 301(JEGP):Apr79-272
D. Kramer, 627(UTQ):Fall78-92
H. Orel, 405(MP):May80-447
J.K. Robinson, 637(VS):Summer79-485
R.C. Schweik, 177(ELT):Vol22#1-71
T. Slade, 67:May79-104
P. Zietlow, 445(NCF):Mar79-520
639(VQR):Winter79-7
Hardy, T. The Collected Letters of
Thomas Hardy. (Vol 2) (R.L. Purdy and
M. Millgate, eds)
C. Lock, 362:13Nov80-662
Hardy, T. The Complete Poems of Thomas
Hardy.* (J. Gibson, ed)
R.G.C., 148:Winter79-90
Hardy, T. The Personal Notebooks of
Thomas Hardy. (R.H. Taylor, ed)
R.G.C., 148:Autumn79-91
P. Keating, 617(TLS):18Jan80-69
42(AR):Summer79-378
Hardy, T. The Variorum Edition of the
Complete Poems of Thomas Hardy. (J.
Gibson, ed)
P. Keating, 617(TLS):18Jan80-69
C.H. Sisson, 441:27Apr80-11
Hardy, W.G. The Scarlet Mantle.
S.E. Read, 102(CanL):Summer79-112
S. Treggiari, 296(JCF):28/29-246
Hare, A., ed. Theatre Royal, Bath.*
B.R. Schneider, 610:May79-229
Hare, P.H. and E.H. Madden. Causing, Per-
ceiving and Believing.*
J.A. Benardete, 449:Sep79-403
Hareven, T.K. and R. Langenbach. Amos-
keag.*
T.W. Leavitt, 432(NEQ):Sep79-429
J.F. Sutherland, 14:Oct79-484
Harkabi, Y. The Palestinian Covenant and
Its Meaning.
T. Smith, 453(NYRB):12Jun80-42
Harlan, J., J. De Wet and B.L. Stemler,
eds. Origins of African Plant Domestica-
tion.
J. Alexander, 69:Vol48#4-418
Harlan, L.R. and R.W. Smock - see Washing-
ton, B.T.
Harlech, P. Feast without Fuss.
W. and C. Cowen, 639(VQR):Spring78-76
Harman, G. The Nature of Morality.*
A. Altman, 258:Jun79-237
J.M. Brown, 393(Mind):Jan79-140

Harman, N. Dunkirk.
E. Auchincloss, 441:20Jul80-15
N. Frankland, 617(TLS):8Aug80-899
J. Grigg, 362:22May80-655
Harmatta, J. and G. Komoróczy, eds. Wirt-
schaft und Gesellschaft im Alten Vorder-
asien.
J.M. Sasson, 318(JAOS):Jul-Sep78-316
Harmer, L.C. Uncertainties in French Gram-
mar. (P. Rickard and T.G.S. Combe, eds)
M. Harris, 617(TLS):9May80-534
Harmetz, A. The Making of The Wizard of
Oz.*
639(VQR):Spring78-70
Harmon, C., ed. Great Days in the Rockies.
W.N., 102(CanL):Spring79-147
Harmon, M. Select Bibliography for the
Study of Anglo-Irish Literature and Its
Backgrounds.*
E. Kennedy, 174(Éire):Summer79-158
S. Sweeney, 305(JIL):May78-185
Harmon, M.H. Psycho-Decorating.
S. Stephens, 505:Jun78-98
Harmon, W., ed. The Oxford Book of
American Light Verse.*
R. Boorstin, 31(ASch):Summer80-412
Harmon, W. Time in Ezra Pound's Work.*
D.L. Eder, 468:Spring79-165
"Iohannis Harmonii Marsi, 'De rebus
italicis deque triumpho Ludovici XII
regis Francorum tragoedia.'" (G. Tour-
noy, ed)
L.V.R., 568(SCN):Spring-Summer79-64
A.S., 228(GSLI):Vol155fasc491-473
Harms, W. and H. Freytag, eds. Ausser-
literarische Wirkungen barocker Emblem-
bücher.*
D. Sulzer, 52:Band13Heft1-84
Harms, W. and L.P. Johnson, eds. Deutsche
Literatur des späten Mittelalters.
K. Aichele, 222(GR):Spring78-80
J.M. Clifton-Everest, 67:Nov79-355
Harned, D.B. Images for Self-Recognition.
639(VQR):Spring78-52
Harney, K.R. Beating Inflation With Real
Estate.
639(VQR):Autumn79-146
Harp, R.L. - see Percy, T.
Harpaz, E. - see Constant, B.
Harper, G.M. and W.K. Hood - see Yeats,
W.B.
Harper, J.R. Krieghoff.
K. Mulhallen, 99:Aug80-32
Harper, M.S. Images of Kin.*
376:Oct79-141
Harper, M.S. and R.B. Stepto, eds. Chant
of Saints.
R. Gibbons, 385(MQR):Summer80-430
S. Mitchell, 617(TLS):30May80-626
J. Wright, 109:Winter80-215
Harré, R. and E.H. Madden. Causal Powers.*
R. Farrell, 63:Mar79-114
Harries-Jenkins, G. The Army in Victorian
Society.*
A. Tucker, 637(VS):Autumn78-100
Harrigan, S. Aransas.
M. Malone, 441:15Jun80-15

Harrington, E. and A.J. Abadie, eds. The
Maker and the Myth.
  K. McSweeney, 106:Winter79-355
  P. Samway, 613:Mar79-110
Harrington, E. and A.J. Abadie, eds. The
South and Faulkner's Yoknapatawpha.
  M. Smelstor, 585(SoQ):Fall78-104
Harrington, L. Ceramics in the Pacific
Northwest.
  J.S. Schwartz, 139:Dec79/Jan80-58
Harrington, M. Decade of Decision.
  C. Lehmann-Haupt, 441:15Apr80-C11
  61:Apr80-124
Harrington, M. The Twilight of Capital-
ism.
  K.J. Arrow, 473(PR):1/1979-113
Harrington, M. The Vast Majority.
  M. Cohen, 287:May78-25
  639(VQR):Summer78-104
Harris, C.V. Political Power in Birming-
ham, 1871-1921.
  W. Flynt, 9(AlaR):Apr79-147
Harris, E. and C. Sisson. The Common
Press.*
  D. Chambers, 503:Winter78-197
Harris, E.E. Atheism and Theism.
  T.J.J. Altizer, 125:Spring79-465
Harris, E.K. The Drum Concerto.
  H.F.C. Prynne-Jones, 590:Fall/Winter
  78/79-61
Harris, E.P. and R.E. Schade, eds. Les-
sing in heutiger Sicht.*
  U-K. Ketelsen, 680(ZDP):Band97Heft4-
  633
Harris, H., ed. Astride the Two Cultures.
  C.L. Nystrom, 186(ETC.):Jun78-202
Harris, H.A. Greek Athletics and the
Jews. (I.M. Barton and A.J. Brothers,
eds)
  T. Rajak, 123:Vol29No1-127
Harris, J. Alaska.
  M. Malone, 441:16Nov80-15
Harris, J. The Artist and the Country
House.
  M. Girouard, 617(TLS):29Feb80-243
Harris, J. A Dance on the High Wire.
  442(NY):25Feb80-135
Harris, J. and A. Lévêque. Basic Conversa-
tional French. (6th ed)
  J.H. Williston, 207(FR):May79-961
Harris, J.G. - see Mandelstam, O.
Harris, K.M. Carlyle and Emerson.
  J. Porte, 141:Winter79-82
Harris, M. Saul Bellow: Drumlin Wood-
chuck.
  J. Atlas, 441:16Nov80-3
  A. Broyard, 441:26Nov80-C17
Harris, M. Cannibals and Kings.
  K. Squadrito, 125:Spring79-478
  639(VQR):Summer78-108
Harris, M. The Evolution of French Syn-
tax.*
  K.Å. Gunnarson, 596(SL):Vol33#2-150
  R. Wright, 86(BHS):Jul79-273
Harris, M. Grace.*
  R. Miles, 102(CanL):Summer79-138

Harris, M. Short Work of It.
  W. Zinsser, 441:13Jan80-15
Harris, M. The Treasure of Sainte Foy.
  M. Anania, 441:13Jul80-14
  P. Sturgess, 617(TLS):22Aug80-943
  442(NY):30Jun80-108
Harris, R. The Language-Maker.
  T.P. Waldron, 617(TLS):11Jul80-785
Harris, R.D. Necker.
  N. Hampson, 617(TLS):7Mar80-277
Harris, W.A. Keeping the Faith.
  E. Wright, 617(TLS):25Jan80-91
Harris, W.S. Dead Towns of Alabama.*
  K.B. Harder, 424:Mar78-118
Harris, W.V. War and Imperialism in
Republican Rome 327-70 B.C.
  R. Seager, 617(TLS):11Jan80-44
Harrison, A. Making and Thinking.
  P. Lewis, 479(PhQ):Oct79-362
Harrison, A.T. Charles d'Orléans and the
Allegorical Mode.
  J. Fox, 208(FS):Vol33Pt2-578
Harrison, B. An Introduction to the
Philosophy of Language.
  D. Holdcroft, 617(TLS):4Apr80-397
Harrison, B. Separate Spheres.
  A. Davin, 637(VS):Summer79-477
Harrison, B. and P. Hollis - see Lowery, R.
Harrison, B.G. Off Center.
  A. Broyard, 441:12Jun80-C21
  L. Dickstein, 441:15Jun80-12
Harrison, C.C. The Anglomaniacs.
  N. Auerbach, 445(NCF):Mar79-475
Harrison, D., ed. Best Mounted Police
Stories.
  R. Thacker, 150(DR):Autumn79-552
Harrison, D., ed. Crossing Frontiers.
  R. Thacker, 649(WAL):Winter80-325
Harrison, D. Unnamed Country.*
  W.J. Keith, 627(UTQ):Summer79-440
  R. Kroetsch, 168(ECW):Summer78-7
  D. Staines, 529(QQ):Autumn79-479
  K.P. Stich, 296(JCF):28/29-233
Harrison, F. The Dark Angel.*
  A. McLaren, 637(VS):Spring79-372
Harrison, G. Mosquitoes, Malaria, and Man.
  A.S. West, 529(QQ):Autumn79-546
  639(VQR):Autumn79-131
Harrison, G.A. A Timeless Affair.
  676(YR):Summer80-XVII
Harrison, J. Ancient Art and Ritual.
  K. Worth, 157:Spring79-83
Harrison, J. Hume's Moral Epistemology.*
  R.J. Fogelin, 449:Nov79-523
Harrison, J. Legends of the Fall.*
  J. Mellors, 362:28Feb80-286
  V. Scannell, 617(TLS):21Mar80-326
Harrison, P., H. Potterton and J. Sheehy.
Irish Art and Architecture from Pre-
History to the Present.
  C. Barrett, 135:Mar79-206
Harrison, R., ed and trans. Gallic Salt.*
  J. Fox, 208(FS):Vol33Pt2-568
Harrison, R., G. Woolven and R. Duncan,
comps. The Warwick Guide to British
Labour Periodicals, 1790-1970.
  R. Price, 637(VS):Summer78-501

Harrison, R.B. Hölderlin and Greek Literature.*
  R. Furness, 220(GL&L):Oct78-71
  G.W. Most, 182:Vol31#1/2-31
Harrison, S. The Flowers of the Field.
  W. Schott, 441:27Jul80-13
Harrison, S.S. China, Oil and Asia.
  R.W. Hardy, 293(JASt):May79-576
Harrison, T. The School of Eloquence.
  D. Graham, 565:Vol120#4-75
  C. Hope, 364:Jun79-79
  J. Wainwright, 493:Jul79-57
Harrisson, B. Oriental Celadon: The Princessehof Collections.
  M. Medley, 463:Spring79-115
Harrisson, B. Swatow In Het Princessehof.
  S. Markbreiter, 60:Sep-Oct79-129
Harrop, D. America's Paychecks.
  J. Greenfield, 441:6Jul80-10
Harsanyi, J.C. Essays on Ethics, Social Behavior, and Scientific Explanation.
  D. Gauthier, 154:Dec78-696
Harshe, R.G. Observations on the Life and Works of Bhavabhūti.
  L. Sternbach, 318(JAOS):Jul-Sep78-322
Harsløf, O., ed. Omkring Stuk.
  A. Jensen, 562(Scan):Nov78-171
Hart, C. and D. Hayman, eds. James Joyce's "Ulysses."
  U. Schneider, 38:Band96Heft1/2-254
Hart, D.V. Compadrinazgo.
  R. Rosaldo, 293(JASt):Nov78-215
Hart, F.R. The Scottish Novel from Smollett to Spark.
  J. Clubbe, 301(JEGP):Jul79-439
  M.J. and J.J. Egan, 395(MFS): Winter78/79-594
  J. Kestner, 661(WC):Summer79-310
  A. Massie, 364:Oct79-92
  639(VQR):Autumn78-128
Hart, G.L. The Relation Between Tamil and Classical Sanskrit Literature.*
  T. Burrow, 259(IIJ):Oct79-282
Hart, G.L. 3d. The Poems of Ancient Tamil.*
  D. Shulman, 259(IJJ):Apr79-144
Hart, H., ed. Indira Gandhi's India.
  C.M. Elliott, 293(JASt):Aug79-808
Hart, J. The Climbers.*
  J.F. Cotter, 249(HudR):Spring79-116
Hart, P. Conductors: A New Generation.*
  H. Cole, 362:12Jun80-767
Hart, P.R. G.R. Derzhavin.
  L. Hecht, 399(MLJ):Nov79-395
  T.J. Watts 3d, 574(SEEJ):Winter79-525
Hart-Davis, R. The Arms of Time.*
  A. Bell, 617(TLS):25Jan80-90
Hart-Davis, R. - see Hutchinson, R.C. and M. Skinner
Hart-Davis, R. - see Lyttelton, G. and R. Hart-Davis
Hart-Davis, R. - see Plomer, W.
Hart-Davis, R. - see Wilde, O.
Hartkopf, W. Der Durchbruch zur Dialektik in Hegels Denken.
  S. Decloux, 182:Vol31#20-711

Hartl, J. Eponyme Fundstelle Knovíz.
  U. Fischer, 182:Vol31#15/16-565
Hartley, A.J. The Novels of Charles Kingsley.
  M. Banton, 637(VS):Spring78-421
  P. Brantlinger, 445(NCF):Sep78-268
  E. Brewer, 155:Summer79-110
  T.J. Winnifrith, 402(MLR):Apr79-430
Hartley, D. Lost Country Life.
  N. Bliven, 442(NY):28Jul80-97
  J. Burke, 231:Jul80-80
  C. Seebohm, 441:13Apr80-15
Hartley, L. Laurence Sterne.
  K.E. Maus, 594:Summer79-237
Hartley, M. and J. Ingilby. Life and Tradition in West Yorkshire.
  G.L. Pocius, 292(JAF):Jan-Mar79-99
Hartman, D. Maimonides.*
  B. Steinberg, 390:Dec79-59
Hartman, E. Substance, Body, and Soul.*
  J.L. Ackrill, 393(Mind):Oct79-600
  J. Annas, 123:Vol29No2-252
  J. Barnes, 518:May79-57
  T.H. Irwin, 482(PhR):Jan79-124
  M.C. Nussbaum, 311(JP):Jun80-355
  M. Schofield, 483:Jul79-427
  H.B.V., 543:Sep78-138
Hartman, G.H. Criticism in the Wilderness.
  D. Donoghue, 441:9Nov80-11
Hartman, G.H. The Fate of Reading and Other Essays.*
  J. Blondel, 189(EA):Jan-Mar78-70
  C. Norris, 349:Fall78-261
Hartman, M.S. Victorian Murderesses.*
  S. Dijkstra, 207(FR):Oct78-190
  L. Senelick, 637(VS):Summer78-493
Hartman, R. La Quête et la croisade.*
  P.F. Dembowski, 589:Jan79-145
Hartmann von Aue. Der arme Heinrich. (C. Sommer, ed)
  B. Murdoch, 182:Vol31#11/12-345
Hartmann, K. Deutsche Gartenstadtbewegung/ Kulturpolitik und Gesellschafts-Reform.
  S. Muthesius, 576:May78-120
Hartmann, K., ed. Die ontologische Option.
  K-H. Nusser, 687:Oct-Dec79-638
Hartmann, R. Allegorisches Wörterbuch zu Otfrieds von Weissenburg Evangeliendichtung.
  W. Schröder, 684(ZDA):Band107Heft3-95
Hartmann, R.T. Palace Politics.
  J. Osborne, 441:10Aug80-9
Hartmann, S. The Valiant Knights of Daguerre.* (H.W. Lawton and G. Knox, with W.H. Linton, eds)
  J. Fuller, 127:Summer79-295
  M. Roskill, 637(VS):Spring79-335
Hartmann-Werner, I. Gemüt bei Goethe.
  J.F. Hyde, Jr., 406:Spring79-71
Hartrich, E. The Fourth and Richest Reich.
  D. Schoenbrun, 441:23Mar80-13
Hartung, A.E., ed. A Manual of the Writings in Middle English 1050-1500.* (Vol 5)
  A. Hudson, 677(YES):Vol9-361

Hausmann, F.J. Einführung in die Benut-
zung der neufranzösischen Wörterbücher.
  P. Lerat, 209(FM):Jul78-267
  W. Rothwell, 208(FS):Vol33Pt2-1061
  M. Wigger, 547(RF):Band91Heft3-352
Hausmann, F.J. Linguistik und Fremdsprach-
enunterricht 1964-1975.*
  G.A. Plangg, 547(RF):Band91Heft3-307
Hausser, M. Le deux "Batouala" de René
Maran.*
  S. Faïk, 209(FM):Jan78-87
Hauswedell, E.L. and C. Voigt, eds. Buch-
kunst und Literatur in Deutschland 1750
bis 1850.
  W.J. Lillyman, 221(GQ):Jan79-94
de Hauvilla, J. Architrenius. (P.G.
Schmidt, ed)
  W. Berschin, 38:Band96Heft3/4-506
Havekamp, K. Love Comes in Buckets.
  P. Lewis, 565:Vol20#3-62
Havelock, E.A. The Greek Concept of
Justice.*
  J. Dybikowski, 487:Winter79-357
  S. Pembroke, 617(TLS):11Jan80-43
Haven, R., J. Haven and M. Adams, eds.
Samuel Taylor Coleridge. (Vol 1)
  P. Cook, 354:Mar79-89
Havens, T.R.H. Valley of Darkness.*
  G.D. Allinson, 293(JASt):Nov78-175
Haver, R. David O. Selznick's Hollywood.
  C. Lehmann-Haupt, 441:15Dec80-C16
  F. Rich, 441:21Dec80-1
Havet, J., ed. Tendances principales de
la recherche dans les sciences sociales
et humaines. (Pt 2)
  J-M. Gabaude, 542:Oct-Dec79-485
Haviaras, S. When the Tree Sings.*
  J. Mellors, 362:3Jan80-30
Haviland, J.B. Gossip, Reputation, and
Knowledge in Zinacantan.
  R.D. Abrahams, 350:Mar79-241
  V.R. Bricker, 355(LSoc):Aug78-251
Havlík, L.E. Morava v 9.-10. století.
  P.W. Knoll, 589:Oct79-808
Havoc, J. More Havoc.
  C. Curtis, 441:29Jun80-9
Hawes, S. Stephen Hawes: The Minor Poems.*
(F.W. Gluck and A.B. Morgan, eds)
  A. Crépin, 189(EA):Jan-Mar78-82
Hawke, D.F. John D.
  J. Greenfield, 441:1Jun80-16
  A. Whitman, 617(TLS):11Jul80-788
Hawke, D.F. Those Tremendous Mountains.
  442(NY):31Mar80-122
Hawkes, A.D. The Flavors of the Caribbean
and Latin America.
  W. and C. Cowen, 639(VQR):Spring79-76
Hawkes, J. The Passion Artist.*
  G. Thompson, 385(MQR):Spring80-270
  R. Towers, 453(NYRB):15May80-32
Hawkes, J. A Quest of Love.
  J. Mellors, 362:9Oct80-481
Hawkes, R. Spring That Never Freezes.
  W. Stevenson, 102(CanL):Spring79-103

Hawkes, T. Structuralism and Semiotics.*
  P. Collier, 208(FS):Vol33Pt2-999
  D. Laferrière, 567:Vol125#3/4-307
  G. Trengrove, 349:Spring78-131
  205(FMLS):Apr78-186
Hawkins, D. Cranborne Chase.
  R. Blythe, 617(TLS):2May80-485
Hawkins, D. Hardy.*
  M. Bath, 637(VS):Winter78-268
Hawkins, H. Poetic Freedom and Poetic
Truth.*
  M.C. Bradbrook, 402(MLR):Jan79-157
  M. Novy, 568(SCN):Spring-Summer79-11
Hawley, H. Gathering Fire.
  J. Flick, 102(CanL):Spring79-105
Haworth-Booth, M. E. McKnight Kauffer.
  C. Fox, 617(TLS):25Jan80-84
Hawthorne, N. The American Claimant Manu-
scripts. The Elixir of Life Manuscripts.
(E.H. Davidson, C.M. Simpson and L.N.
Smith, eds of both)
  H. Parker, 445(NCF):Mar79-489
  A. Turner, 579(SAQ):Winter79-133
Hawthorne, N. Hawthorne's Lost Notebook
1835-1841.
  L. Buell, 432(NEQ):Sep79-418
  A. Turner, 27(AL):Nov79-415
Hay, D. Annalists and Historians.
  R. Ray, 589:Jul79-577
Hay, D. The Church in Italy in the Fif-
teenth Century.*
  P. Partner, 382(MAE):1979/1-155
Hay, G. - see Voss, J.H.
Hay, J. Have.
  J. Ripley, 102(CanL):Autumn79-110
Hayakawa, S.I. Through the Communication
Barrier. (A. Chandler, ed)
  J.R. Gaskin, 569(SR):Summer79-455
Hayashi, T., ed. A Study Guide to Stein-
beck's "The Long Valley."*
  J.A. Gertzman, 573(SSF):Summer78-337
Hayden, G.A. - see "Crime and Punishment
in Medieval Chinese Drama — Three Judge
Pao Plays"
Hayden, J. The Lists of the Past.
  J.L. Abbott, 573(SSF):Spring78-206
Hayden, J.O. - see Wordsworth, W.
Hayden, R. American Journal.*
  R. Gibbons, 461:Spring-Summer79-87
Hayden, T.L. One Child.
  J. Greenfield, 441:4May80-16
Hayek, F.A. The Three Sources of Human
Values.
  E. Butler, 479(PhQ):Jul79-281
Hayer, G., ed. Daz buoch von guoter spîse.
  K. Kehr, 133:Band12Heft1/2-148
Hayes, D. Moving Inland.
  G. Hamel, 198:Winter80-139
Hayes, J. The Art of Graham Sutherland.
  S. Gardiner, 362:11Dec80-802
Hayes, J. French Cooking for People Who
Can't.
  W. and C. Cowen, 639(VQR):Autumn79-153
Hayes, J. The Hong Kong Region, 1850-1911.
  J.L. Watson, 293(JASt):Aug79-750

Hayes, J.R., ed. The Genius of Arab Civilization.*
J. Jordan, 42(AR):Spring79-251
Hayes, J.W. Roman Pottery in the Royal Ontario Museum.*
K.S. Wright, 487:Spring79-93
Hayfield, N. Cleaning House.
A. Broyard, 441:6Dec80-21
E. Leffland, 441:28Dec80-9
Haylock, J. One Hot Summer in Kyoto.
A. Hislop, 617(TLS):18Jul80-799
Hayman, D. and E. Anderson, eds. In the Wake of the "Wake."*
P. Lewis, 565:Vol120#4-67
Hayman, R. Artaud and After.*
C. Campos, 402(MLR):Apr79-469
E.T. Dubois, 610:May78-224
Hayman, R. British Theatre since 1955.
D. Wright, 157:Summer79-80
639(VQR):Autumn79-128
Hayman, R. Eugène Ionesco.
C. Burkhart, 295(JML):Vol7#4-736
Hayman, R. Leavis.*
W.E. Cain, 152(UDQ):Spring78-76
Hayman, R. Nietzsche.
J.M. Cameron, 453(NYRB):9Oct80-26
J. Leonard, 441:25Jul80-C23
442(NY):1Sep80-91
Hayman, R. Theatre and Anti-Theatre.
C. Ludlow, 364:Jul79-71
Haymes, E.R. Das mündliche Epos.
D.H. Green, 402(MLR):Jul79-734
Haymon, S.T. Death and the Pregnant Virgin.
T.J. Binyon, 617(TLS):6Jun80-654
M. Laski, 362:14Aug80-216
Hayter, W. Spooner.
D. Spring, 637(VS):Spring79-378
Hayward, M. - see Gladkov, A.
Hazan, H. The Limbo People.
R. Blythe, 617(TLS):11Jul80-778
Hazard, H.W., ed. The Art and Architecture of the Crusader States.
A. Cutler, 589:Oct79-810
Hazard, H.W., ed. A History of the Crusades. (Vol 3)
J.A. Subhan, 273(IC):Apr76-135
Hazleton, L. Where Mountains Roar.
P. Zweig, 441:14Sep80-15
442(NY):11Aug80-91
Hazlitt, H. The Inflation Crisis and How to Resolve It.
D.K. Adie, 396(ModA):Fall79-423
Hazlitt, W. The Letters of William Hazlitt.* (H.M. Sikes, with W.H. Bonner and G. Lahey, eds)
D. Bromwich, 617(TLS):1Feb80-103
D.H. Reiman, 661(WC):Summer79-298
639(VQR):Summer79-96
Hazzard, S. The Transit of Venus.
V. Cunningham, 617(TLS):4Apr80-382
G. Godwin, 441:16Mar80-7
J. Leonard, 441:26Feb80-C9
F. Taliaferro, 231:Feb80-84
R. Towers, 453(NYRB):15May80-32
61:Feb80-95

Head, J.H. Public Goods and Public Welfare.
W.V.E., 543:Mar79-545
Headington, C. Illustrated Dictionary of Musical Terms.
C. Wintle, 617(TLS):9May80-538
Healey, A., ed. Language Learner's Field Guide.
A.L. Rumsey, 269(IJAL):Jan78-73
Healy, J.F. Mining and Metallurgy in the Greek and Roman World.
M. Hassall, 313:Vol69-202
J.G. Landels, 123:Vol29No2-297
M.B. Walbank, 487:Summer79-190
Healy, J.J. Literature and the Aborigine in Australia.
B. Kiernan, 71(ALS):Oct79-251
Heaney, S. Field Work.*
A. Alvarez, 453(NYRB):6Mar80-16
C. Bedient, 472:Fall/Winter79-109
H. Bloom, 617(TLS):8Feb80-137
D. Smith, 29:Sep/Oct80-30
Heaney, S. North. Wintering Out.
R. Tracy, 109:Summer80-180
Heaney, S. Preoccupations.
J. Bayley, 362:20Nov80-691
R. Pinsky, 441:21Dec80-4
Heath, C. Lady on the Burning Deck.*
C.C. Park, 249(HudR):Winter79/80-578
Heath, J. Linguistic Diffusion in Arnhem Land.
C. Yallop, 67:May79-184
Heath, S. - see Barthes, R.
Heathcote, A.A. Vicente Espinel.*
H. Ettinghausen, 86(BHS):Jan79-63
Heatter, M. Maida Heatter's Book of Great Chocolate Desserts.
M. Sheraton, 441:30Nov80-82
Hebbel, F. and others. Briefe von und an Friedrich Hebbel. (U.H. Gerlach, ed)
A.T. Alt, 221(GQ):Nov79-551
D. Barlow, 301(JEGP):Oct79-608
Hebblethwaite, P. The New Inquisition.
D. Cupitt, 617(TLS):25Apr80-458
Hebdige, D. Subculture.
D.I. Davies, 99:Jun-Jul80-45
Hébert, F. Triptyque de la mort.
B. Thompson, 399(MLJ):Dec79-464
Hébert, R. Mobiles du discours philosophique.
F. Wilson, 627(UTQ):Summer79-474
Hecht, A. Millions of Strange Shadows.*
D. Graham, 565:Vol20#1-65
G. Hart, 134(CP):Fall78-91
639(VQR):Winter78-13
Hecht, A. The Venetian Vespers.*
D. Davie, 472:Fall/Winter79-84
R. Garfitt, 617(TLS):30May80-623
Heckscher, A. St. Paul's.
E.B. Fiske, 441:28Nov80-C25
Hedlin, E. Business Archives.
P.F. Mooney, 14:Oct79-478
Heeg, G. Die Wendung zur Geschichte.
B. Zimmermann, 406:Summer79-211
Heeney, B. A Different Kind of Gentleman.
C. Kent, 637(VS):Spring78-419

Heers, J. Parties and Political Life in
the Medieval West.
B. Lyon, 589:Jul79-580
Heffernan, C.F., ed. Le Bone Florence of
Rome.*
D. Mehl, 402(MLR):Jan79-153
Hefti, P. and C. Schmid - see Maurer, F.
and H. Rupp
Heftrich, E. Lessings Aufklärung.
R.R. Heitner, 221(GQ):May79-406
Hegel, G.W.F. The Difference Between
Fichte's and Schelling's System of Phi-
losophy. (W. Cerf and H.S. Harris, eds
and trans)
J.P. Anton, 484(PPR):Mar80-441
E.E. Harris, 125:Fall78-144
E.E. Harris, 518:Jan79-14
Hegel, G.W.F. Le droit, la morale et la
politique. (M-J. Königson, ed)
A. Reix, 542:Jan-Mar78-117
Hegel, G.W.F. Faith and Knowledge. (W.
Cerf and H.S. Harris, eds and trans)
J.P. Anton, 484(PPR):Mar80-441
E.E. Harris, 518:Jan79-14
R.L. Perkins, 125:Fall78-146
Hegel, G.W.F. Fenomenologia dello spirito.
(M. Paolinelli, trans)
E. Namer, 542:Apr-Jun79-252
Hegel, G.W.F. Hegel's Philosophy of Sub-
jective Spirit. (M.J. Petry, ed and
trans)
T.M. Knox, 125:Fall78-141
Q. Lauer, 258:Jun79-243
Hegel, G.W.F. Leçons sur Platon. (J-L.
Vieillard-Baron, ed and trans)
J. Lefranc, 192(EP):Jul-Sep79-362
Hegel, G.W.F. On the Arts. (abridged and
trans by H. Paolucci)
H.M. Schueller, 290(JAAC):Winter79-200
Hegel, G.W.F. Phenomenology of Spirit.*
(A.V. Miller, trans)
E.E. Harris, 518:Jan79-14
K. Hartmann, 53(AGP):Band60Heft3-353
A. Reix, 542:Jan-Mar78-116
639(VQR):Summer78-97
Hegel, G.W.F. Recension des oeuvres de
F.H. Jacobi. (A. Doz, ed and trans)
A. Reix, 542:Jan-Mar78-118
Hegel, G.W.F. Système de la vie éthique.*
(J. Taminiaux, ed and trans)
J. Lefranc, 192(EP):Jul-Sep79-361
Hegel, G.W.F. Textes pédagogiques. (B.
Bourgeois, ed and trans)
D. Janicaud, 192(EP):Jul-Sep79-363
"Hegel-Studien."* (Vol 10)
G. Maluschke, 53(AGP):Band60Heft2-232
Hegenberg, L. Lógica.
G.W. Jones, 316:Mar79-126
Heger, H., ed. Die deutsche Literatur.
(Vol 2, Pt 1)
D. Blamires, 402(MLR):Apr79-490
F.V. Spechtler, 680(ZDP):Band97Heft1-
146
Heger, H., ed. Spätmittelalter, Humanis-
mus, Reformation. (Vol 1)
K. Aichele, 222(GR):Spring78-81

Heger, H., ed. Spätmittelalter, Humanis-
mus, Reformation. (Vol 2)
E. Bernstein, 221(GQ):Jan79-96
Heger, K. Monem, Wort, Satz und Text.
(2nd ed)
D. Goyvaerts, 556(RLV):1978/2-171
G.F. Meier, 682(ZPSK):Band31Heft4-422
K.H. Schmidt, 685(ZDL):3/1979-358
Hehn, V. Cultivated Plants and Domesti-
cated Animals in their Migration from
Asia to Europe. (J.P. Mallory, ed)
R. Rocher, 318(JAOS):Jul-Sep78-347
Heide, C. Poems of a Very Simple Man.
D. Barbour, 150(DR):Spring79-154
Heidegger, M. Early Greek Thinking. (D.
Krell and F.A. Capuzzi, trans)
J.D.C., 543:Jun79-759
Heidegger, M. Die Frage nach dem Ding.
M. Kleinschnieder, 342:Band69Heft3-371
Heidegger, M. Gesamtausgabe. (vols un-
known) (F-W. von Herrmann, ed)
T. Sheehan, 453(NYRB):4Dec80-39
Heidegger, M. Gesamtausgabe. (Vols 1 and
2) (F-W. von Herrmann, ed)
R.A. Bast and H.P. Delfosse, 489(PJGG):
Band86Heft1-184
Heidegger, M. Gesamtausgabe. (Pt 1, Vol
5) (F-W. von Herrmann, ed)
T.J.S., 543:Mar79-546
Heidegger, M. L'être et le temps. (G.A.
Bornheim, ed)
P. Trotignon, 542:Apr-Jun78-188
Heidegger, M. Nietzsche. (Vol 1)
P. Foot, 453(NYRB):1May80-35
Heidegger, M. Questions IV.*
P. Trotignon, 542:Apr-Jun78-189
Heidegger, M. Sein und Zeit. (14th ed)
R.A. Bast and H.P. Delfosse, 489(PJGG):
Band86Heft1-184
Heidegger, M. Vier Seminare.
T.J.S., 543:Sep78-140
Heidegger, M. and E. Fink. Heraclitus
Seminar 1966-67.
M. Schofield, 617(TLS):15Feb80-186
Heidemann, I. - see Kant, I.
Heidish, M.M. Witnesses.
P-L. Adams, 61:Sep80-108
W. Schott, 441:14Sep80-12
442(NY):1Sep80-90
Heidrich, H. Allgemeinwissenschaftlicher
Wortschatz Englisch.
E. Hahn, 682(ZPSK):Band31Heft2-198
Heiduczek, W. Im Querschnitt.
I. Hiebel, 654(WB):3/1978-168
Heiduczek, W. Tod am Meer.
H.J. Geerdts, 654(WB):5/1978-143
van Heijenoort, J. With Trotsky in Exile.
639(VQR):Winter79-8
Heikal, M. The Sphinx and the Commissar.*
K. Fitzlyon, 364:Jun79-86
Heikamp, D. Il Tesoro di Lorenzo Magnif-
ico. (Vol 2) (A. Grote, ed)
H. Kiel, 471:Jan/Feb/Mar79-78
Heiké. Le Dit des Heiké. (R. Sieffert,
trans)
Tanaka Chiharu, 75:2/1978-85

Hellegouarc'h, J. La phrase dans les
"Caractères" de La Bruyère.*
   J. Marmier, 535(RHL):May-Jun78-473
Heller, C.S. On the Edge of Destruction.*
   H.L. Adelson, 390:Aug-Sep79-64
   J. Chametzky, 473(PR):2/1979-298
Heller, J. Good as Gold.*
   J. Mills, 529(QQ):Winter79/80-646
   C.C. Park, 249(HudR):Winter79/80-584
   639(VQR):Summer79-98
Heller, P. Probleme der Zivilisation.
   S.J. Antosik, 222(GR):Spring79-84
Hellman, L. Maybe.
   A. Broyard, 441:13May80-C20
   A. Duchêne, 617(TLS):18Jul80-799
   P. Kemp, 362:17Jul80-89
   R. Towers, 441:1Jun80-3
   R. White, 99:Nov80-31
   442(NY):26May80-127
Hellman, L. Three.
   B. Caplan, 219(GaR):Winter79-933
Hellman, P. Avenue of the Righteous.
   H. Epstein, 441:7Dec80-14
Hellmann, M.W. and others, comps. Biblio-
graphie zum Öffentlichen Sprachgebrauch
in der Bundesrepublik Deutschland und in
der DDR.
   N. Nail, 685(ZDL):1/1979-101
Hellström, P. Luni sul Mignone. (Vol 2,
fasc 2)
   D. Ridgway, 182:Vol31#14-491
Helm, J. Johannes Kentmann 1518-74.
   F. Grass, 182:Vol31#15/16-515
Helmholtz, H. Epistemological Writings.
(R.S. Cohen and Y. Elkana, eds)
   J.M.Z., 543:Sep78-141
Helmich, W. Die Allegorie im französis-
chen Theater des 15. und 16. Jahrhun-
derts. (Vol 1)
   L. Muir, 610:May78-216
   W. Rothwell, 208(FS):Vol33Pt2-604
Helmreich, E.C. The German Churches under
Hitler.*
   A.W. Novitsky, 613:Dec79-459
Helms, F.P. Die Auswirkungen der EG-
Erweiterung auf Aussenhandel und Pro-
duktion von Grundmetallen in Danemark,
Norwegen und Schweden.
   J. Comte, 182:Vol31#15/16-530
Helprin, M. Refiner's Fire.*
   639(VQR):Spring78-66
Helwig, D., ed. The Human Elements.
   D. Staines, 529(QQ):Autumn79-479
Helwig, D. Jennifer.*
   M. Taylor, 198:Summer80-134
Hemacandra. Yogaśāstram. (M. Jambūvijaya,
ed)
   259(IIJ):Jul79-216
Hemenway, R.E. Zora Neale Hurston.*
   R. Sale, 249(HudR):Spring79-151
   E.L. Steeves, 395(MFS):Winter78/79-643
   K.J. Williams, 579(SAQ):Autumn79-526
Hemingway, J. and C. Maricich. The Picnic
Gourmet.
   W. and C. Cowen, 639(VQR):Spring78-75
Hemmings, F.W.J. The King of Romance.*
   M. Bowie, 362:28Feb80-284

Hemmings, F.W.J. The Life and Times of
Émile Zola.*
   D. Baguley, 395(MFS):Winter78/79-623
   F.E. Humphreys 3d, 207(FR):Feb79-489
   M. Larkin, 402(MLR):Jan79-211
Hempfer, K.W. Gattungstheorie.
   N.C.W. Spence, 208(FS):Apr79-238
Henden, J. Vulnerable People.
   J.T. Hansen, 295(JML):Vol7#4-633
Henderson, B. The Expanding Room.*
   A. Archer, 526:Winter79-75
   D.G. Jones, 168(ECW):Summer78-266
Henderson, B. Paracelsus.*
   D.G. Jones, 102(CanL):Winter78-77
   D.G. Jones, 168(ECW):Summer78-266
Henderson, B., ed. The Pushcart Prize,
III.
   P. Meisel, 461:Spring-Summer79-99
Henderson, B., ed. The Pushcart Prize, V.
   D. Pinckney, 441:24Aug80-14
Henderson, H. Elegies.
   D. Graham, 565:Vol20#1-65
Henderson, I. Strickers Daniel von dem
Blühenden Tal.*
   S.C. Van D'Elden, 406:Summer79-216
Henderson, M. The Log of a Superfluous
Son.
   K. McVeigh, 368:Mar76-88
Henderson, P. Tennyson, Poet and Prophet.
   E. Jordan, 184(EIC):Apr79-175
Henderson, W.D. Why the Vietcong Fought.
   D. Duncanson, 617(TLS):27Jun80-729
Hendin, J. Vulnerable People.*
   J.T. Flanagan, 651(WHR):Spring79-169
Hendrick, G. - see Hosmer, H.
Hendricks, W.O. Grammars of Style and
Styles of Grammar.*
   D. Stein, 350:Sep79-712
Hendriks, P. The Radožda-Vevčani Dialect
of Macedonian.*
   H.G. Lunt, 343:Band23-137
Hendrix, W.S. and W. Meiden. Beginning
French. (5th ed)
   M.M. Celler, 207(FR):May79-962
Hendy, P. European Paintings in the
Isabella Stewart Gardner Museum.
   D. Robinson, 90:Feb79-129
Heneage, S. and H. Ford. Sidney Sime.
   K. Flint, 617(TLS):21Mar80-332
Heninger, S.K., Jr. The Cosmographical
Glass.*
   L. Babb, 191(ELN):Jun79-332
   L. Barkan, 570(SQ):Winter79-116
   S. Drake, 627(UTQ):Summer79-405
   A.C. Hamilton, 301(JEGP):Jan79-106
   H. Levin, 131(CL):Winter79-79
   H. Ormsby-Lennon, 405(MP):May80-432
Henissart, P. Margin of Error.
   N. Callendar, 441:18May80-16
Henke, S.A. Joyce's Moraculous Sindbook.*
   R.M. Kain, 395(MFS):Winter78/79-568
   295(JML):Vol7#4-747
Henkel, N. Studien zum Physiologus im
Mittelalter.*
   M. Schmidt, 133:Band12Heft1/2-133
   H-J. Uther, 196:Band19Heft1/2-154

van Herk, A. Judith.*
  S. Atherton, 628(UWR):Spring-Summer79-111
  B. Hjartarson, 526:Winter79-85
  P. Lewis, 565:Vol20#3-62
  L. McMullen, 296(JCF):28/29-253
Herman, S.N. Jewish Identity.
  H.L. Feingold, 390:Aug-Sep79-58
Hermann, I. Die Gedankenwelt von Georg
  Lukács.
  P. Somville, 542:Oct-Dec79-471
Hermanns, F. Die Kalkülisierung der Gram-
  matik.
  P. Erdmann, 343:Band23-8
Hermans, E. American Topics.
  A. Michiels, 556(RLV):1978/6-557
Hermerén, L. On Modality in English.
  L. Haegeman, 179(ES):Jun79-338
  N-L. Johannesson, 596(SL):Vol133#2-155
Hermet, J. Albert Camus et le Christian-
  isme.
  J. Cruickshank, 208(FS):Vol33Pt2-932
Hermey, C., ed and trans. Contemporary
  French Women Poets.
  M.C. Davies, 208(FS):Vol33Pt2-961
Hernadi, P., ed. What is Literature?
  M. Grimaud, 141:Summer79-262
  M. Hancher, 290(JAAC):Summer80-468
  639(VQR):Spring79-47
Hernández, J.L.A. - see under Alonso Her-
  nández, J.L.
Hernandez, J.L.A. and others - see under
  Alonso Hernandez, J.L. and others
Hernández, M.C. - see under Cruz Hernández,
  M.
Hernández-Chávez, E., A.D. Cohen and A.F.
  Beltramo, eds. El lenguaje de los
  chicanos.*
  D. Gifford, 86(BHS):Jul79-267
Hernández de Mendoza, C. - see Marroquín,
  J.M.
Hernando, J.A.B. - see under Bonachía
  Hernando, J.A.
Herndon, M. and N. McLeod. Music As
  Culture.
  D.P. McAllester, 187:May80-305
Hernmarck, C. The Art of the European
  Silversmith 1430-1830.
  A.S. Cocks, 39:Feb79-165
  C. Oman, 90:Jun79-383
Herodotus. Erodoto: "La battaglia di
  Salamina: Libro VIII delle Storie." (A.
  Masaracchia, ed)
  A.R. Burn, 123:Vol29No1-141
Heron, C., ed. Imperialism, Nationalism
  and Canada.
  T. Morley, 529(QQ):Spring79-110
Herr, E.F. - see under Fernández Herr, E.
Herr, M. Dispatches.
  639(VQR):Spring78-63
Herrero Casado, A. Glosario Alcarreño.
  (Vol 2)
  J.J. Luna, 48:Jan-Mar78-109
Herring, P.F. - see Joyce, J.
Herriot, J. All Things Wise and Wonderful.
  639(VQR):Winter78-30

Herrmann, E.R. and E.H. Spitz, eds. Ger-
  man Women Writers of the Twentieth Cent-
  tury.
  J.E. Michaels, 221(GQ):Nov79-572
von Herrmann, F-W. - see Heidegger, M.
Herrmann, L. British Landscape Painting
  of the Eighteenth Century.
  A.G.H. Bachrach, 54:Dec78-732
Herrmann, L. Turner.
  J. Ziff, 637(VS):Autumn77-113
Hersey, G.I. Pythagorean Palaces.*
  J. Onians, 576:May78-127
Hersey, J. Aspects of the Presidency.
  J. Greenfield, 441:1Jun80-16
Hersey, J. The Walnut Door.*
  639(VQR):Winter78-23
Herslund, M. Structure phonologique de
  l'ancien français.
  C. Lyche, 597(SN):Vol150#1-159
Hertel, H., ed. Kønsroller i litteraturen.
  H. Kress, 562(Scan):Nov78-186
Hertling, G.H. Conrad Ferdinand Meyers
  Epik.*
  M. Burkhard, 182:Vol131#15/16-546
Hertzberg, A. Being Jewish in America.*
  M.I. Urofsky, 390:Jun/Jul79-89
Hertzberg, S. Strangers Within the Gate
  City.
  C.E. Wynes, 579(SAQ):Autumn79-529
Hervier, J. Deux individus contre l'his-
  toire.
  M. Hanrez, 149(CLS):Dec79-360
Hervouet, Y., ed and trans. Le chapitre
  117 du Che-ki (Biographie de Sseu-ma
  Siang-jou).
  C.S. Goodrich, 318(JAOS):Oct-Dec78-541
Herzberg, S. Strangers Within the Gate
  City.
  E. Wright, 617(TLS):25Jan80-91
Herzberger, D.K. The Novelistic World of
  Juan Benet.*
  E.W. Nelson, 400(MLN):Mar79-422
  205(FMLS):Jan78-89
Herzog, R. Die Bibelepik der lateinischen
  Spätantike. (Vol 1)
  E. Wimmer, 196:Band19Heft1/2-156
Herzog, T. Pneumatic Structures.
  R. Graefe and J. Hennicke, 576:Oct78-222
Herzog, U. Der deutsche Roman des 17.
  Jahrhunderts.
  H. Kurzke, 684(ZDA):Band107Heft1-41
  J. Leighton, 402(MLR):Apr79-493
Hesiod. Works and Days. (M.L. West, ed)
  M. Davies, 123:Vol29No2-202
  N.J. Richardson, 303(JoHS):Vol199-169
Hess, R. Die Anfänge der modernen Lyrik
  in Portugal, 1865-1890.
  G.R. Lind, 72:Band216Heft1-224
Hess, U. Heinrich Steinhöwels "Grisel-
  dis."*
  J. Heinzle, 680(ZDP):Band97Heft1-141
  W. McConnell, 589:Apr79-384
Hesse, E. Ezra Pound.
  W. Baumann, 468:Winter79-573
Hesse, E.W. Interpretando la comedia.
  R.W. Tyler, 238:May-Sep79-397

Hesse, E.W. New Perspectives on "Comedia" Criticism.
D.H. Darst, 304(JHP):Spring80-270
Hesse, H. Hours in the Garden and Other Poems.
H. Carruth, 231:Dec80-74
J. Simon, 491:Apr80-40
Hessing, S., ed. Speculum Spinozanum 1677-1977.*
R.H. Popkin, 84:Jun79-205
Heston, L.L. and R. The Medical Casebook of Adolf Hitler.
A. Bullock, 453(NYRB):17Jul80-27
Hetmann, F., ed. Dämonengeschichten aus den Alpen.
H-J. Uther, 196:Band19Heft1/2-126
Hetmann, F., ed. Englische Märchen.
A. Ehrentreich, 224(GRM):Band28Heft2-239
H-J. Uther, 196:Band19Heft1/2-126
Hetmann, F., ed. Keltische Märchen. Irische Märchen. Nordamerikanische Märchen.
A. Ehrentreich, 224(GRM):Band28Heft2-239
Hetmann, F., ed and trans. Zaubermärchen aus Wales.
H-J. Uther, 196:Band19Heft1/2-126
Hettrich, H. Kontext und Aspekt in der altgriechischen Prosa Herodots.*
C.J. Ruijgh, 394:Vol132fasc3/4-402
Hetzron, R. Ethiopian Semitic.*
G.B. Gragg, 318(JAOS):Oct-Dec78-519
Heuer, F. and W. Keller, eds. Schillers Wallenstein.
S.L. Cocalis, 406:Summer79-202
Heuer, H., with E.T. Sehrt and R. Stamm - see "Deutsche Shakespeare-Gesellschaft West"
Heuman, F.S. The Uses of Hebraisms in Recent Bible Translations.
J. Dierickx, 179(ES):Dec79-812
Heurgon, J. - see Varro
Heward, E. Lord Mansfield.
P. Devlin, 617(TLS):13Jun80-667
Hewett, C.A. English Cathedral Carpentry.
J.T. Smith, 54:Jun78-365
Hewett, D. The Chapel Perilous.
W. Dean, 368:Jun76-162
Hewison, R. John Ruskin.*
D. Sonstroem, 637(VS):Winter78-287
R.L. Wilson, 127:Summer79-292
Hewison, R. Ruskin and Venice.*
D. Gervais, 97(CQ):Vol8#3-256
J.G. Links, 39:Apr79-326
Hewison, R. Salt Pan.
S. Ramsey, 617(TLS):28Mar80-368
Hewison, R. Under Siege.
K.C. Gaston, 577(SHR):Summer79-262
J. Gindin, 396(ModA):Spring79-206
Hewitt, D. Conrad. (3rd ed)
J. McLauchlan, 136:Vol11#2-197
Hewitt, J. The Family Circle Quick Menu Cookbook.
W. and C. Cowen, 639(VQR):Autumn79-156
Hewitt, J. Kites in Spring.
E.L. Wright, 617(TLS):25Jul80-851

Hewitt, J. The Rain Dance.
E. Longley, 617(TLS):18Jan80-64
Hewitt, J.R. André Malraux.
B. Thompson, 399(MLJ):Dec79-466
Hewitt, J.R. Marcel Proust.
R. Shattuck, 207(FR):Mar79-646
Hewitt, W.R. Through Those Living Pillars.*
C. Jennings, 546(RR):Mar79-192
Hexter, J.H. On Historians.* Reappraisals in History. (2nd ed)
Q. Skinner, 453(NYRB):24Jan80-39
Heyde, H. Flöten.
N. O'Loughlin, 415:May79-405
Heydecker, J. and J. Leeb. Der Nürnberger Prozess.
A-R. Werner, 182:Vol131#21/22-785
Heydenreich, T. Culteranismo und theologische Poetik.
F. Latorre, 182:Vol131#11/12-360
Heyen, W. Long Island Light.
D. Smith, 29:Mar/Apr80-40
V. Young, 249(HudR):Winter79/80-630
639(VQR):Autumn79-149
Heyer, J. and others. Agricultural Development in Kenya.
E.S. Clayton, 69:Vol148#3-311
Heymann, C.D. American Aristocracy.
W. Pritchard, 441:3Aug80-11
Heyting, A. - see Brouwer, L.E.J.
Heywood, C., ed. Papers on African Literature.
M. Fabre, 189(EA):Jul-Dec78-424
Heywood, T. Love's Mistress, or The Queen's Masque.* (R.C. Shady, ed)
H.A. Hargreaves, 178:Winter79-489
Hiatt, M. The Way Women Write.*
P.M. Horodowich, 125:Winter79-318
Hibbard, G.R., ed. The Elizabethan Theatre, V.*
C. Belsey, 677(YES):Vol9-300
Hibbard, G.R., ed. The Elizabethan Theatre VI.*
H.D. Janzen, 628(UWR):Fall-Winter78-88
K.M. Lea, 541(RES):Nov79-461
J.A.B. Somerset, 539:Vol4No1-107
S.P. Zitner, 627(UTQ):Summer79-408
Hibbard, G.R. - see Jonson, B.
Hibbard, H. The Metropolitan Museum of Art.
S. Gardiner, 362:11Dec80-802
J. Russell, 441:30Nov80-11
Hibberd, J. Salomon Gessner.*
G.N. Davis, 400(MLN):Apr79-615
Hibberd, J. Kafka in Context.
R. Sheppard, 220(GL&L):Oct78-85
Hibbert, C. The Days of the French Revolution.
A. Broyard, 441:12Nov80-C29
W. Goodman, 441:2Nov80-15
Hibbert, C. The Great Mutiny.
P.W. Fay, 529(QQ):Winter79/80-705
639(VQR):Spring79-54
Hick, J. God Has Many Names.
D. Cupitt, 617(TLS):8Aug80-902
Hickman, W.C. - see Babinger, F.

Hickok, L.A. Eleanor Roosevelt.
  C. Lehmann-Haupt, 441:5Feb80-C9
  A. Schlesinger, Jr., 441:17Feb80-3
Hicks, E. - see Christine de Pisan and
  others
Hicks, J. and others. The Persians.
  P. Albenda, 318(JAOS):Apr-Jun78-155
Hieatt, A.K. Chaucer, Spenser, Milton.*
  P.C. Kolin, 568(SCN):Spring-Summer79-
  12
Hieatt, C.B. and S. Butler. Pleyn Delit.
  M.E. Milham, 178:Spring79-112
Hienger, J., ed. Unterhaltungsliteratur.
  R.J. Rundell, 406:Spring79-60
Hiersche, A. Sowjetliteratur und wissen-
  schaftlich-technische Revolution.*
  P. Kessler, 654(WB):1/1978-187
Higdon, D.L. Time and English Fiction.
  W. Harmon, 594:Winter79-492
  R.F. Peterson, 395(MFS):Winter78/79-
  571
Higginbotham, J. Old Mobile Fort Louis de
  la Louisiane 1702-1711.
  W. De Ville, 9(AlaR):Jan79-69
Higginbotham, V. The Comic Spirit of
  Federico García Lorca.*
  J.W. Díaz, 241:May79-123
Higgins, A. Scenes from a Receding Past.
  P. Lewis, 565:Vol20#1-49
Higgins, D. Catlin.
  442(NY):21Apr80-145
Higgins, D.S. - see Haggard, H.R.
Higgins, G.V. Kennedy for the Defense.
  P-L. Adams, 61:Mar80-102
  E. Hunter, 441:2Mar80-8
  C. Lehmann-Haupt, 441:14Feb80-C24
  442(NY):17Mar80-168
Higgins, I., ed. Literature and the
  Plastic Arts 1880-1930.
  M. Sheringham, 208(FS):Apr79-242
Higgins, J. Solo.
  442(NY):30Jun80-108
Higgins, W.E. Xenophon the Athenian.*
  P. Cartledge, 123:Vol29No2-213
  M. MacLaren, 24:Winter79-574
  J.M. Redfield, 122:Oct79-352
  S. Usher, 303(JoHS):Vol199-175
  F.V., 543:Dec78-360
Higgs, J. and C. Milligan. The Wizard's
  Eye. (J. Vandenburgh, ed)
  R. Bender, 658:Winter79-423
Higham, C. Errol Flynn.
  L.S. Dietz, 441:20Apr80-12
  J. Wolcott, 453(NYRB):15May80-40
Highsmith, P. The Boy Who Followed Ripley.
  C. Brown, 617(TLS):25Apr80-462
Highsmith, P. Slowly, Slowly in the Wind.
  D. Durrant, 364:Jul79-89
Highwater, J. Dance.
  N.M. Stoop, 151:Aug78-48
Highwater, J. Ritual of the Wind.
  C.J. Frisbie, 187:Sep80-589
  N.M. Stoop, 151:Aug78-48
Highwater, J. The Sun, He Dies.
  W. Schott, 441:27Jul80-13

Higounet-Nadal, A. Périgueux aux XIVe et
  XVe siècles.
  D. Herlihy, 589:Jul79-582
Hijmans, B.L., Jr. and others. Apuleius
  Madaurensis: "Metamorphoses:" Book IV 1-
  27.
  K. Dowden, 123:Vol29No1-68
Hilaire d'Arles. Vie de saint Honorat.
  (M-D. Valentin, ed)
  J. André, 555:Vol52fasc1-202
Hilberg, R., S. Staron and J. Kermisz -
  see Czerniakow, A.
Hildebrand, K. Das Deutsche Reich und
  die Sowjetunion im internationalen
  System 1918-1932.
  J. Hiden, 575(SEER):Oct79-636
Hildeman, K-I. En löskekarl.
  G. Hird, 563(SS):Winter79-94
Hiley, M. Frank Sutcliffe.
  639(VQR):Winter78-30
Hilka, A., ed. Das altfranzösische
  Rolandslied nach der Oxforder Hand-
  schrift. (7th ed rev by G. Rohlfs)
  W.G. van Emden, 208(FS):Vol33Pt2-518
Hill, A. I Don't Care If I Never Come
  Back.
  C. Lehmann-Haupt, 441:4Jul80-C15
  442(NY):18Aug80-94
Hill, A.G. - see Wordsworth, W. and D.
Hill, B.W. The Growth of Parliamentary
  Parties 1689-1742.
  F.D. Dow, 566:Autumn78-41
Hill, C. Milton and the English Revolu-
  tion.*
  W.E. Cain, 152(UDQ):Fall78-150
  J. Harvey, 97(CQ):Vol18#3-265
  J.R. MacCormack, 529(QQ):Spring79-161
  P. Zagorin, 447(N&Q):Dec78-549
Hill, C. The Religion of Gerrard Win-
  stanley.
  T.W. Hayes, 568(SCN):Fall-Winter79-66
Hill, C. Ferdinand Ries.
  W. Drabkin, 415:Apr79-306
Hill, C.M. and M.G. Morrison - see Garnier,
  R.
Hill, D., L. Golvin and R. Hillenbrand.
  Islamic Architecture in North Africa.*
  J.W. Allan, 463:Summer78-216
Hill, E.C. George Bernard Shaw.
  A.H. Nethercot, 572:Jan79-50
Hill, F. The Autumn Rose.
  L. Duguid, 617(TLS):16May80-558
Hill, G. Tenebrae.*
  H. Carruth, 231:Jan80-77
  T. Eagleton, 565:Vol20#3-75
  F. Grubb, 364:Oct79-82
  D. Hall, 491:May80-102
  J.R. Lindroth, 590:Fall/Winter78/79-53
  B. Oxley, 184(EIC):Jul79-285
  D. Smith, 29:Sep/Oct80-30
  V. Young, 249(HudR):Winter79/80-621
  639(VQR):Summer79-108
Hill, J.P. and E. Caracciolo-Trejo, eds
  and trans. Baroque Poetry.*
  D.H. Pageaux and J. Voisine, 549(RLC):
  Jan-Mar77-104

Hill, J.S., ed. Imagination in Coleridge.
K. Hanley, 148:Summer79-88
W.J.B. Owen, 541(RES):Aug79-362
Hill, L.A. An Elementary Refresher Course.
(2nd ed)
M.C. Bergans-Libioul, 556(RLV):1978/4-364
Hill, L.M. Language as Aggression.
M. Bickelmann, 221(GL):Jan79-143
Hill, M.A., ed. Hannah Arendt.*
M. Levin, 99:Sep80-29
Hill, M.A. Charlotte Perkins Gilman.
M. Bell, 453(NYRB):17Apr80-10
Hill, P., ed. Password 7-12.
H.S. Madsen, 399(MLJ):Mar79-135
Hill, P. Stranger's Forest.
639(VQR):Autumn78-138
Hill, P. The Washermen.
M. Laski, 362:17Apr80-514
Hill, P. and T. Cooper, eds. Dialogue
with Photography.
C. James, 453(NYRB):18Dec80-22
Hill, R. The Spy's Wife.
T.J. Binyon, 617(TLS):18Apr80-450
M. Laski, 362:14Aug80-216
Hill, R.B. Hanta Yo.*
W. Bloodworth, 649(WAL):Fall79-238
Hill, R.J. Soviet Political Elites.*
S.W. Page, 550(RusR):Jan79-111
Hill, R.J. Soviet Politics, Political
Science and Reform.
A. Nove, 617(TLS):18Jul80-803
Hill, R.S. and M.D.W. Hodder, eds.
Archives and Manuscripts.
M. Pamplin, 325:Apr79-172
Hill, S. and I. Quigly, eds. New Stories
5.
J. Mellors, 362:18and25Dec80-867
Hill, S.P. The N-Factor and Russian
Prepositions.
V.M. Du Feu, 575(SEER):Oct79-578
Hill, W.S. - see Hooker, R.
Hiller, G.G., ed. Poems of the Eliza-
bethan Age.
H.R. Woudhuysen, 447(N&Q):Oct78-464
Hillerman, T. People of Darkness.
442(NY):29Dec80-74
Hillery, D. - see Verlaine, P.
Hilliard, N. Maori Woman.
H.W. Rhodes, 368:Mar75-76
Hilliard, N. Selected Stories.
368:Mar78-92
Hillier, B., with others. Victorian
Studio Photographs From the Collections
of Studio Bassano and Elliott and Fry,
London.
M. Roskill, 637(VS):Spring79-335
Hillier, J. Hokusai Paintings, Drawings,
and Woodcuts.
J.V. Earle, 463:Summer79-252
Hilling, J.B. The Historic Architecture
of Wales.
M. Allentuck, 576:May78-116
P. Howell, 46:Apr79-251
Hillman, J. Le mythe de la psychanalyse.
M. Perrot, 192(EP):Oct-Dec79-496

Hilmar, E. and O. Brusatti, eds. Cata-
logue of the Vienna City Library Exhibi-
tion commemorating the 150th anniversary
of Schubert's Death.
E. Sams, 415:Apr79-305
Hilscher, E. Poetische Weltbilder.*
L. Kahn, 222(GR):Summer78-135
Hilsinger, S.S. and L. Brynes - see Sarton,
M.
Hilson, J.C., M.M.B. Jones and J.R. Wat-
son, eds. Augustan Worlds.
M. Golden, 301(JEGP):Jul79-428
L.S. Horsley, 566:Spring79-131
Hiltebeitel, A. The Ritual of Battle.
J. Scheuer, 259(IIJ):Jan79-50
S. Williams, 582(SFQ):Vol41-275
Hilton, J.B. The Anathema Stone.
N. Callendar, 441:5Oct80-31
M. Laski, 362:17Apr80-514
Hilton, R. Bond Men Made Free.
D. Harrison, 161(DUJ):Dec78-102
Hilton, R. Night Letters and Selected
Drawings.
S. Gardiner, 362:19Jun80-803
Hilton, R.B. An Index to Early Music in
Selected Anthologies.
R. Andrewes, 415:Apr79-309
P.W. Jones, 410(M&L):Apr79-229
Hilzinger, K.H. Die Dramaturgie des
dokumentarischen Theaters.*
A. Hillach, 406:Spring79-92
"Himalaya."
H. Janetschek, 182:Vol131#14-508
Himmelfarb, G. On Liberty and Liberalism.
H. Laboucheix, 189(EA):Jan-Mar78-91
Himmler, H. Discours secrets.
H. Cronel, 450(NRF):Jan79-131
Himsworth, S., with P. Gwyn and J. Harvey.
Winchester College Muniments. (Vol 1)
F. Strong, 325:Apr79-168
Hinck, W., ed. Ausgewählte Gedichte
Brechts mit Interpretationen.
M. Morley, 400(MLN):Apr79-616
Hinde, T. Daymare. Sir Henry and Sons.
Mr. Nicholas.
V. Glendinning, 362:14Aug80-211
P. Lewis, 617(TLS):15Aug80-909
Hinderer, W., ed. Geschichte der politis-
chen Lyrik in Deutschland.
J.L. Sammons, 221(GQ):Nov79-570
Hindess, B. Philosophy and Methodology in
the Social Sciences.
S.W. Gaukroger, 488:Sep79-379
Hindess, B. and P.Q. Hirst. Pre-Capital-
ist Modes of Production.
J.P. Scott, 488:Sep79-327
Hindley, P., G.M. Martin and J. McNulty.
The Tangled Net.
R. Lorimer, 102(CanL):Winter78-82
Hindman, S. Text and Image in Fifteenth-
Century Illustrated Dutch Bibles.
M.B. McNamee, 589:Jul79-583
B. Nolan, 377:Mar79-56
Hindman, S. and J.D. Farquhar. Pen to
Press.
W.H. Bond, 589:Apr79-386

Hindus, M. Charles Reznikoff.
  E. Roditi, 390:Aug-Sep79-59
Hine, D. Daylight Saving.*
  639(VQR):Autumn78-144
Hine, D. and J. Parisi, eds. The Poetry
  Anthology, 1912-1977.*
  B. Duffey, 579(SAQ):Spring79-271
Hines, B. The Price of Coal.*
  J. Coleby, 157:Summer79-81
Hingley, R. Dostoyevsky.
  E. Chances, 550(RusR):Oct79-504
  R.M. Davison, 402(MLR):Jul79-765
  R. Freeborn, 575(SEER):Oct79-587
  639(VQR):Summer79-97
Hingley, R. The Russian Mind.*
  G. Struve, 558(RLJ):Fall79-238
Hingley, R. Russian Writers and Soviet
  Society 1917-1978.*
  A. Brown, 617(TLS):25Jan80-95
  A. Corn, 676(YR):Spring80-459
Hingley, R. - see Chekhov, A.
Hiniker, P.J. Revolutionary Ideology and
  Chinese Reality.
  L. Dittmer, 293(JASt):Nov78-156
Hinkle, G.H. Art as Event.
  A. Berleant, 290(JAAC):Spring80-345
Hinkle, R.C. Founding Theory of American
  Sociology 1881-1915.
  A. Giddens, 617(TLS):23May80-579
Hinks, R.P. Greek and Roman Portraits.
  J.J. Coulton, 123:Vol29No1-184
Hinnant, C.H. Thomas Hobbes.
  S. Archer, 568(SCN):Spring-Summer79-20
Hinsley, F.H., ed. British Foreign Policy
  under Sir Edward Grey.
  V. Cromwell, 161(DUJ):Dec78-112
  639(VQR):Spring78-60
Hinson, M. The Piano in Chamber Ensemble.
  P.W. Jones, 410(M&L):Jul79-335
Hinterhäuser, H. Fin de siècle.*
  L. Hönnighausen, 52:Band13Heft1-105
Hinterhäuser, H., ed. Jahrhundertende —
  Jahrhundertwende. (Pt 2)
  W. Hirdt, 547(RF):Band91Heft4-466
Hintikka, J., ed. Essays on Wittgenstein
  in Honour of G.H. von Wright.
  T.E. Burke, 518:Jan79-29
Hintikka, J. The Semantics of Questions
  and the Questions of Semantics.
  D. Harrah, 449:Mar79-95
Hinz, B. Art in the Third Reich.
  J. Russell, 441:3Apr80-C15
  J. Willett, 453(NYRB):26Jun80-9
Hinz, E.J. and J.J. Teunissen - see Miller,
  H.
Hipp, M-T. Mythes et réalités.*
  J. Campbell, 208(FS):Vol33Pt2-711
von Hippel, F. Ideologie und Wahrheit
  in der Jurisprudenz.
  F. Gilliard, 182:Vol31#14-472
Hippius, Z. Zerkala. Tretja kniga rasska-
  zov.
  I. Kirillova, 575(SEER):Apr79-284
Hirdt, W. Italienischer Bänkelsang.
  U. Schulz-Buschhaus, 547(RF):Band91
  Heft3-328

Hirsch, E.D., Jr. The Aims of Interpreta-
  tion.*
  J.M. Ellis, 131(CL):Fall79-417
Hirsch, E.D., Jr. The Philosophy of Compo-
  sition.*
  L. Behrens, 290(JAAC):Fall79-98
  G.H. Brookes, 502(PrS):Summer78-196
  J.D. Canfield, 50(ArQ):Summer79-188
  W.W. Douglas, 128(CE):Sep78-90
Hirsch, E.S. Painted Decoration on the
  Floors of Bronze Age Structures on Crete
  and the Greek Mainland.
  S. Hood, 123:Vol29No2-330
  M.L. Lang, 124:Sep79-43
Hirschberg, D. Untersuchungen zur Erzähl-
  struktur von Wolframs "Parzival."*
  P. Grundlehner, 406:Summer79-195
Hirschman, A.O. The Passions and the In-
  terests.*
  T.E. Kaiser, 173(ECS):Spring79-419
Hirst, P.Q. Durkheim, Bernard and Epis-
  temology.* Social Evolution and Soci-
  ological Categories.
  J.P. Scott, 488:Sep79-327
Hirtle, W.H. Time, Aspect, and the Verb.*
  A.R. Tellier, 189(EA):Jan-Mar78-80
Hissiger, P.F. - see Malory, T.
"Historiographia Antiqua."
  J. Briscoe, 123:Vol29No2-343
Hitchcock, B. Richard Malcolm Johnston.
  A. Rowe, 578:Fall80-126
Hitchcock, H-R. American Architectural
  Books.
  S.B. Landau, 576:Mar78-50
Hitchcock, H-R. and W. Seale. Temples of
  Democracy.*
  W.A. Coles, 576:Mar78-46
Hitchcock, H.W. Ives.*
  D. Keane, 529(QQ):Spring79-169
Hitchcock, H.W. and V. Perlis, eds. An
  Ives Celebration.
  S. Banfield, 410(M&L):Apr79-216
Hitchcock, J.T. and R.L. Jones, eds.
  Spirit Possession in the Nepal Himalayas.
  S.B. Ortner, 293(JASt):Feb79-413
Hitchcock, R. The Kharjas.
  L.F. Compton, 304(JHP):Autumn79-77
  L.P. Harvey, 86(BHS):Jul79-273
Hitchins, K. Orthodoxy and Nationality.
  D.J. Deletant, 575(SEER):Oct79-599
Hitchins, K., ed. Studies in East Euro-
  pean Social History. (Vol 1)
  B.K. Király, 575(SEER):Apr79-291
Hittle, J.M. The Service City.
  I. de Madariaga, 617(TLS):22Aug80-929
Ho Ping-ti. The Cradle of the East.*
  K.C. Chang, 318(JAOS):Jan-Mar78-85
Hoag, J.D. Islamic Architecture.
  O. Grabar, 576:May78-106
  J. Masheck, 62:Dec78-60
Hoagland, E. African Calliope.*
  T. Jacoby, 453(NYRB):17Apr80-43
  J. Updike, 442(NY):10Mar80-156
Hoang-Thi-Bich. Étude et traduction du
  Gakudōyōjin-shū.
  F.H. Cook, 318(JAOS):Apr-Jun78-183

172

Hoban, R. Riddley Walker.
V. Glendinning, 362:30ct80-589
Hobbes, T. Les éléments du droit naturel
et politique. (L. Roux, ed and trans)
J. Bernhardt, 542:Jan-Mar78-104
Hobbes, T. Thomas White's "De Mundo"
Examined.
J.B., 543:Dec78-361
Hobhouse, C. Inside Asquith's Cabinet.
(E. David, ed)
M. Bentley, 161(DUJ):Jun79-276
Hobsbaum, P. Tradition and Experiment in
English Poetry.
A. Brownjohn, 617(TLS):1Feb80-112
W.H., 148:Autumn79-90
566:Spring79-137
Hobson, H. French Theatre Since 1830.
J. Allen, 157:Spring79-82
Hobson, H. Indirect Journey.
M. Horsman, 157:Winter79-81
Hobson, M. This Place is a Madhouse.
C. Brown, 617(TLS):7Mar80-258
Hochhuth, R. A German Love Story.
G. Butler, 617(TLS):2May80-510
J. Mellors, 362:10Apr80-482
Hocker, M. Spiel als Spiegel der Wirk-
lichkeit.*
R.N. Linn, 406:Winter79-455
Hockett, C.F. The View from Language.*
W.M. Christie, Jr., 361:Dec78-388
L.M. Davis, 35(AS):Summer79-120
M. Silverstein, 269(IJAL):Jul78-235
C.F. Voegelin and M.B. Kendall,
355(LSoc):Aug78-277
Hockey, S. A Guide to Computer Applica-
tions in the Humanities.
L.D. Burnard, 617(TLS):9May80-533
Hockney, D. David Hockney by David
Hockney.* (N. Stangos, ed)
J. Siegel, 127:Fall78-66
Hocks, P. and P. Schmidt. Literarische
und politische Zeitschriften 1789-1805.
J.E. Fletcher, 67:May79-140
Hodges, D.C. Argentina 1943-1976.
205(FMLS):Apr78-186
Hodges, W. Logic.
M. Partridge, 479(PhQ):Apr79-181
T.J. Richards, 63:Dec79-364
J.E. Tiles, 518:Oct79-119
Hodgins, J. The Resurrection of Joseph
Bourne.*
E.L. Bobak, 150(DR):Autumn79-575
W.J. Keith, 198:Winter80-105
Hodgson, G. All Things to All Men.
T.E. Cronin, 441:19Oct80-7
P. Whitehead, 362:6Nov80-619
442(NY):20Oct80-207
Hodgson, M. The Hot and Spicy Cookbook.
W. and C. Cowen, 639(VQR):Spring78-75
Hodgson, M.G.S. The Venture of Islam.
R.W. Bulliet, 318(JAOS):Apr-Jun78-157
Hodgson, P. The War Illustrators.
P.J. Widdowson, 637(VS):Autumn78-92
Hødnebo, F. and H. Mageroy, eds. Norges
kongesagaer.
G. Jones, 617(TLS):8Feb80-135

Hodnett, E. Aesop in England.
D. Piper, 617(TLS):1Feb80-119
Hodnett, E. Marcus Gheeraerts the Elder
of Bruges, London, and Antwerp.
M. Huggler, 182:Vol31#13-425
Hoeveler, J.D., Jr. The New Humanism.*
F.X. Duggan, 396(ModA):Spring79-197
J.D. Margolis, 125:Fall78-120
Hof, W. Die Schwierigkeit, sich über
Hölderlin zu verständigen.
R. Nägele, 406:Summer79-203
Hofer, H. Barbey d'Aurevilly Romancier.
H. Thoma, 224(GRM):Band28Heft3-369
P.J. Yarrow, 208(FS):Vol133Pt2-821
Hofer, H. and others. Louis-Sébastien
Mercier précurseur et sa fortune, avec
des documents inédits.
C.H. Moore, 107(CRCL):Winter79-93
R. Theis, 182:Vol31#17/18-611
Hoff, A. Dutch Firearms.
H.L. Blackmore, 135:Feb79-138
Höffe, O. Lexicon der Ethik.
M. Adam, 542:Oct-Dec78-512
Höffe, O. Strategien der Humanität.
R. Bittner, 342:Band69Heft2-205
Hoffer, P.T. Klaus Mann.
H. Lehnert, 221(GQ):Jan79-134
Hoffman, A. Angel Landing.
L. McMurtry, 441:9Nov80-14
Hoffman, A. The Drowning Season.*
J. Chernaik, 364:Mar80-90
Hoffman, A. Soon to be a Major Motion
Picture.
M. Dickstein, 441:21Sep80-7
B.G. Harrison, 231:Sep80-84
N. von Hoffman, 453(NYRB):6Nov80-3
J. Leonard, 441:1Sep80-C13
Hoffman, D. Able Was I Ere I Saw Elba.
R. Asselineau, 189(EA):Jul-Dec78-422
Hoffman, D., ed. Harvard Guide to Con-
temporary American Writing.*
I. Ehrenpreis, 453(NYRB):29May80-12
D. Hall, 617(TLS):5Sep80-969
Hoffman, M.A. Egypt Before the Pharaohs.
J. Baines, 617(TLS):25Apr80-478
Hoffman, N. Spenser's Pastorals.*
J.H. Anderson, 301(JEGP):Jan79-120
J.H. Sims, 568(SCN):Spring-Summer79-16
H.L. Weatherby, 569(SR):Summer79-490
Hoffman, R. Some Musical Recollections of
Fifty Years.
J.H.E., 412:May78-134
Hoffman, W. Mittelhochdeutsche Heldendich-
tung.
J.M. Clifton-Everest, 67:Nov79-352
Hoffmann, C. Theater für junge Zuschauer.
C. Emmrich, 654(WB):3/1978-175
Hoffmann, D. Frank Lloyd Wright's Falling
Water.
J. Sergeant, 46:Oct79-204
Hoffmann, E.T.A. Selected Letters of
E.T.A. Hoffmann. (J.C. Sahlin, ed and
trans)
R. Cardinal, 529(QQ):Spring79-98
M.T. Jones, 221(GQ):Jan79-122
Hoffmann, F. Der Kitsch bei Max Frisch.
R. Gray, 617(TLS):11Jan80-45

Hoffmann, F. and J. Berlinger. Die neue
deutsche Mundartdichtung.
J. Koppensteiner, 221(GL):Jan79-146
Hoffmann, F. and C. Hurri - see Bruch, R.
Hoffmann, G. Raum, Situation, erzählte
Wirklichkeit.
E. Giddey, 182:Vol31#21/22-813
Hoffmann, H. Sexual and Asexual Pursuit.
J. Boardman, 123:Vol29No1-118
Hoffmann, L., ed. Fachsprachen und Sprach-
statistik.
H-J. Mattusch, 682(ZPSK):Band31Heft3-
305
Hoffmann, L. Kommunikationsmittel Fach-
sprache.
G. Fischer, 682(ZPSK):Band31Heft3-291
Hoffmann, P. La Femme dans la pensée des
lumières.
H. Monod-Cassidy, 173(ECS):Winter78/79-
251
J.G. Rosso, 535(RHL):Nov-Dec79-1057
J.S. Spink, 402(MLR):Oct79-940
Hoffmann, S. Primacy or World Order.
639(VQR):Summer79-90
Hoffmeister, G. Deutsche und europäische
Romantik.
J.M. McGlathery, 301(JEGP):Oct79-605
H.M.K. Riley, 221(GQ):May79-415
Hoffmeister, G. Spanien und Deutschland.*
C.E. Schweitzer, 597(SN):Vol50#1-154
Hofheinz, R., Jr. The Broken Wave.
M. Meisner, 293(JASt):Feb79-340
Hofinger, M. Lexicon Hesiodeum cum Indice
Inverso. (Vols 2-4)
M.L. West, 123:Vol29No2-305
Hofmann, J. Flor Peeters.
A. Bond, 415:Mar79-221
Hofmann, J.E. Register zu Gottfried Wil-
helm Leibniz Mathematische Schriften und
der Briefwechsel mit Mathematikern.
(C.I. Gehrardt, ed)
J. Ecole, 192(EP):Jul-Sep79-354
von Hofmannsthal, H. Sämtliche Werke.*
(Vol 14 ed by J. Fackert; Vol 28 ed by E.
Ritter)
H.D. Cohn, 222(GR):Fall78-180
Hofstadter, D. - see Sand, G.
Hofstadter, D.R. Gödel, Escher, Bach.*
M. Delbrück and S.W. Golomb, 31(ASch):
Autumn80-550
J. Lieberson, 311(JP):Jan80-45
I.G. Mattingly, 676(YR):Winter80-270
P. Miers, 400(MLN):Dec79-1214
Hogan, D. The Diamonds at the Bottom of
the Sea.*
J. O'Faolain, 441:2Nov80-13
Hogan, D. The Ikon Maker.*
R. Buffington, 441:13Jan80-22
Hogan, D. The Leaves on Grey.
V. Cunningham, 617(TLS):15Feb80-171
P. Kemp, 362:21Feb80-254
Hogan, R. and others, eds. The Macmillan
Dictionary of Irish Literature.
617(TLS):15Feb80-169
Hogan, W. The Quartzsite Trip.
R. Bradford, 441:8Jun80-14

Hogenhout, J. De geschiedenis van Torec
en Miraude.
L.M. Swennen, 196:Band19Heft3/4-328
Hogg, J., ed. Recent Research on Ben
Jonson.
J. Arnold, 568(SCN):Fall-Winter79-78
Hogg, R. Of Light.
376:Oct79-141
Hogg, R.M. English Quantifier Systems.
E.A. Moravcsik, 350:Sep79-692
Hoggart, R. An Idea and its Servant.
639(VQR):Summer79-93
Höggmayr, A. Monasteria Ordinis FF. Ere-
mitarum S. Augustini per Germaniam aeri
incisa Augustae Vindelicorum a Iohanne
Matthia Steidlin sine loco et anno
(ca. 1731).
F. Rapp, 182:Vol131#23/24-845
Hogrefe, P. Women of Action in Tudor
England.*
V.W. Beauchamp, 539:Vol14No1-100
Hogue, H. Wintu Trails. (M.M. Kardell,
ed)
J. Koenig, 649(WAL):Spring79-87
Hohenberg, J. A Crisis For the American
Press.
639(VQR):Summer79-93
Hohendahl, P.U. Der europäische Roman der
Empfindsamkeit.
H. Wetzel, 678(YCGL):No.27-100
Hohmann, T. Heinrich von Langenstein
"Unterscheidung der Geister" lateinisch
und deutsch.
J.B. Freed, 589:Jul79-587
N.F. Palmer, 402(MLR):Oct79-986
Höhn-Ochsner, W. Pflanzen in Zürcher Mun-
dart und Volksleben. Tierwelt in Zür-
cher Mundart und Volksleben.
K. Kehr, 685(ZDL):3/1979-397
Höhne, H. Canaris.
D. Hunt, 617(TLS):4Jan80-16
H. Trevor-Roper, 362:12Jun80-750
Hoisington, D.J., ed. A Castle Hill Cook-
book.
W. and C. Cowen, 639(VQR):Autumn79-156
Holas, B. Le Gagou, son portrait cultu-
rel.
M. Augé, 69:Vol148#1-94
Holbraad, C. Superpowers and Interna-
tional Conflict.
H. Bull, 617(TLS):4Jan80-20
Holbrook, D. Chance of a Lifetime.*
C. Hope, 364:Jun79-77
Holbrook, D. Sylvia Plath.*
C. Butler, 447(N&Q):Apr78-183
Hold, T. The Walled-in Garden.
S. Banfield, 415:Mar79-221
Holdcroft, D., ed. Papers in Logic and
Language.
A.J. Dale, 84:Sep79-304
J.E. Tiles, 518:Jan79-30
Holdcroft, D. Words and Deeds.
G. Bird, 479(PhQ):Jul79-272
R.M. Harnish, 311(JP):Aug80-495
J. Heal, 518:Oct79-97
O. Thomas, 350:Dec79-968

Holub, M. Notes of a Clay Pigeon.*
  D. Graham, 565:Vol120#1-65
Holz, H.H. Die abenteuerliche Rebellion.
  J-D. de Lannoy, 182:Vol131#17/18-581
"Holz Schnitt im Neuen China."
  R. Croizier, 293(JASt):Feb79-303
Holzhey, H. and W.C. Zimmerli, eds. Eso-
  terik und Exoterik der Philosophie.
  S. Decloux, 182:Vol131#7/8-193
Hölzler, H. Der Einfluss des Gesell-
  schaftsrechts auf die Konzentration in
  den USA.
  W. Feuring, 182:Vol131#1/2-18
Holzman, R. and L. Lewin. A View From
  the Bench.
  C. Lehmann-Haupt, 441:18Dec80-C23
Homann, R. - see "Pai Wen P'ien, or The
  Hundred Questions"
Homberger, E. The Art of the Real.*
  J. Stokes, 402(MLR):Oct79-930
  295(JML):Vol7#4-642
Lord Home. Border Reflections.*
  J. Morgan, 617(TLS):18Jan80-67
"Homenaje a Luis Vives."
  A.G. Kinder, 86(BHS):Jul79-274
Homer. The Iliad. (R. Fitzgerald, trans)
  M. Mueller, 107(CRCL):Fall79-428
Homer, W.I. Alfred Stieglitz and the
  American Avant-Garde.*
  H.W. Morgan, 658:Autumn79-325
Honderich, T. Three Essays on Political
  Violence.*
  H.J.N. Horsburgh, 262:Autumn78-363
  M. Martin, 488:Jun79-244
Hone, J. The Flowers of the Forest.
  M. Laski, 362:13Nov80-665
Hone, J. The Oxford Gambit.
  P. Andrews, 441:16Nov80-14
Honemann, V. Die "Epistola ad fratres de
  Monte Dei" des Wilhelm von Saint-Thierry.
  B. Murdoch, 182:Vol131#17/18-604
Honey, J.R.D. Tom Brown's Universe.
  P. Scott, 637(VS):Spring79-357
Hong, H.V. and E.H. - see Kierkegaard, S.
Honig, E. Selected Poems (1955-1976).
  H. Carruth, 231:Jan80-77
Honigmann, E.A.J. Shakespeare: Seven
  Tragedies.*
  L.S. Champion, 677(YES):Vol9-313
Honoré, A.M. Tribonian.
  A. Cameron, 313:Vol69-199
  C.G. Starr, 124:Sep79-47
Honour, H. Romanticism.*
  P. Spencer-Longhurst, 135:Sep79-69
Hood, E.M. The Story of Scottish Country
  Dancing.
  H. Cole, 362:12Jun80-767
Hood, G. Charles Bridges and William
  Dering.
  M. Thistlethwaite, 658:Winter79-401
  G. Wills, 39:Jul79-81
Hood, H. A New Athens.*
  H. Dahlie, 168(ECW):Summer78-138
  D. Salter, 150(DR):Spring79-184
Hood, H. None Genuine Without This Signa-
  ture.
  W.J. Keith, 99:Oct80-27

Hood, H. Selected Stories.*
  P. Monk, 529(QQ):Autumn79-525
Hood, H. The Swing in the Garden.
  D. Salter, 150(DR):Spring79-184
Hoog, A. Le Temps du lecteur, ou l'agent
  secret.
  H. Godin, 208(FS):Vol33Pt2-972
Hook, D.F. The "I Ching" and Mankind.
  J. Hart, 485(PE&W):Jul79-362
Hooker, C.A., ed. The Logico-algebraic
  Approach to Quantum Mechanics. (Vol 1)
  J.H. McGrath, 486:Mar78-145
Hooker, J. Landscape of the Daylight
  Moon.*
  A. Stevenson, 617(TLS):23May80-586
Hooker, J.T. The Language and Text of the
  Lesbian Poets.
  A.M. Davies, 343:Band23-112
  G.P. Edwards, 123:Vol129No2-306
Hooker, M., ed. Descartes.
  E.J. Ashworth, 529(QQ):Winter79/80-653
  D. Judovitz, 400(MLN):Dec79-1241
Hooker, R. Of the Laws of Ecclesiastical
  Polity. (Bks 1-4 ed by G. Edelen, Bk 5
  ed by W.S. Hill)
  R.M. Frye, 570(SQ):Summer79-443
  L.M. Knox, 568(SCN):Spring-Summer79-24
  F.B. Williams, Jr., 354:Dec79-384
Hooker, R. Of the Laws of Ecclesiastical
  Polity. (A.S. McGrade and B. Vickers,
  eds)
  L.G. Black, 447(N&Q):Oct78-454
  V. Mahon, 402(MLR):Jul79-653
Hookway, C. and P. Pettit, eds. Action
  and Interpretation.
  G. Harrison, 518:May79-73
  G. Marshall, 63:Dec79-359
Hoole, W.S. - see Anderson, E.C.
Hooper, W. - see Lewis, C.S.
Hoopes, J. Van Wyck Brooks.*
  639(VQR):Spring78-54
Hope, A.D. The New Cratylus.
  G. Hough, 617(TLS):22Feb80-215
Hopkins, C. The Discovery of Dura-Europos.
  (B. Goldman, ed)
  M. Colledge, 617(TLS):25Jan80-98
Hopkins, J. and D. Sugerman. No One Here
  Gets Out Alive.
  J. Maslin, 441:21Sep80-7
Hopkirk, P. Foreign Devils on the Silk
  Road.
  E. Monroe, 617(TLS):11Jul80-786
Hopp, J. Untersuchungen zur Geschichte
  der letzten Attaliden.
  R.E. Allen, 123:Vol129No1-176
Hoppenkamps, H. Information oder Manipula-
  tion?*
  E.H. Yarrill, 182:Vol131#9/10-287
Hopper, P.J., ed. Studies in Descriptive
  and Historical Linguistics.
  K.H. Schmidt, 343:Band23-160
Hopper, R.J. Trade and Industry in Classi-
  cal Greece.
  S. Pembroke, 617(TLS):11Jan80-43
Hoppin, R.H. Medieval Music.
  C. Roederer, 414(MusQ):Jul79-447

Horace. Satires and Epistles. (J. Fuchs, trans)
A.G. Robson, 399(MLJ):Jan-Feb79-85
Horak, S.M., comp. Russia, the USSR, and Eastern Europe. (R. Neiswender, ed)
I. Banac, 550(RusR):Jul79-404
Horchow, R. Elephants in Your Mailbox. (A.C. Greene, ed)
C. Lehmann-Haupt, 441:14Jul80-C16
Horecky, P.L., with D.H. Kraus, eds. East Central and Southeast Europe.
Z. Sywak, 14:Jul79-362
W. Veryha, 104(CASS):Summer78-283
M.T. Znayenko, 558(RLJ):Winter79-201
Horkheimer, M. Théorie critique. (L. Ferry and A. Renaut, eds)
A. Reix, 542:Oct-Dec79-489
Hörling, H. Heinrich Heine im Spiegel der politischen Presse Frankreichs von 1831-1841.
J.L. Sammons, 221(GQ):Jan79-123
Horn, A. Geschichte der anthropologischen Fragestellung in der englischen Ästhetik von Bacon bis Alison.
H. Osborne, 89(BJA):Winter79-81
Horn, M. The League for Social Reconstruction.
W.D. Young, 99:Dec80/Jan81-38
Horn, M., ed. The World Encyclopedia of Comics.
R. Schenda, 196:Band19Heft3/4-329
Horn, M., with R.E. Marschall, eds. The World Encyclopedia of Cartoons.
S. Heller, 441:21Dec80-19
Horn, P. Heinrich von Kleists Erzählungen.
M. Jurgensen, 67:Nov79-361
Horn, W. and E. Born. The Plan of St. Gall.
E. Le Roy Ladurie, 441:15Jun80-9
J.M. Wallace-Hadrill, 453(NYRB): 6Nov80-46
Hornby, A.S., with C. Ruse. Oxford Student's Dictionary of Current English.
J. De Smet-D'hondt, 179(ES):Dec79-831
Hornby, R. Script into Performance.
M. Craven, 108:Summer79-117
I.R. Hark, 130:Fall79-274
W.I. Oliver, 141:Summer79-283
Horne, A. A Savage War of Peace.*
F. Busi, 207(FR):May79-944
S.T. Francis, 396(ModA):Summer79-327
Horne, T.A. The Social Thought of Bernard Mandeville.
S.H. Good, 173(ECS):Spring79-413
W.A. Speck, 566:Autumn78-38
639(VQR):Summer78-98
Horney, K. The Adolescent Diaries of Karen Horney.
E. Levenson, 441:21Dec80-9
Hornsby, J. Actions.
A. Goldman, 617(TLS):11Jul80-779
Horovitz, I. The Primary English Class.
K. Garebian, 99:May80-38
Horovitz, M. Growing Up.
G. Lindop, 617(TLS):22Feb80-214
Horowitz, D. The First Frontier.*
639(VQR):Autumn79-132

Horowitz, G. Repression.*
R. Jacoby, 529(QQ):Spring79-105
Horowitz, L.K. Love and Language.
M.S. Koppisch, 207(FR):Mar79-639
O. de Mourgues, 208(FS):Vol33Pt2-710
639(VQR):Winter78-14
Horowitz, M. and C. Palmer - see Huxley, A.
de Horozco, S. Representaciones. (F. González Ollé, ed)
J. Weiner, 304(JHP):Spring80-265
de Horozco, S. El teatro de Sebastián de Horozco. (O. Mazur, ed)
D.W. McPheeters, 240(HR):Spring78-254
Horrocks, B., with E. Belfield and H. Essame. Corps Commander.
639(VQR):Autumn78-149
Horry, N. Rabelais ressuscité.* (N. Goodley, ed)
J. Céard, 535(RHL):Sep-Oct78-817
D.G. Coleman, 208(FS):Vol33Pt2-618
Hortelano, J.G. - see under García Hortelano, J.
Horton, C. - see Steinbeck, J.
Horton, J.J. Yugoslavia.
G.M. Terry, 575(SEER):Jul79-466
Horton, R.A. The Unity of "The Faerie Queene."*
H.L. Weatherby, 569(SR):Summer79-490
Horwitz, R. Buber's Way to "I and Thou."
O. Michel, 182:Vol131#20-717
Horwitz, S.L. The Find of a Lifetime.
J. Leonard, 441:31Dec80-C12
Horwood, H. Only the Gods Speak.
A.S. Brennan, 198:Summer80-139
Horwood, W. Duncton Wood.
P-L. Adams, 61:May80-104
P. Kemp, 362:4Dec80-765
Hösch, E. Die Kultur der Ostslaven.
J. Fennell, 575(SEER):Oct79-632
Hosein, C. The Killing of Nelson John.
P. Norman, 617(TLS):19Sep80-1047
Hosking, G. Beyond Socialist Realism.
S.F. Cohen, 441:4May80-1
Hoskins, J. Polish Books in English, 1945-1971.
B.W. Mazur, 575(SEER):Jan79-157
Hosmer, H. Remembrances of Concord and the Thoreaus.* (G. Hendrick, ed)
F. Day, 580(SCR):Spring79-83
Hosono, M. Nagasaki Prints and Early Copperplates.
P.C. Swann, 463:Spring79-117
Hossenfelder, M. Kants Konstitutionstheorie und die transzendentale Deduktion.*
P.G., 543:Mar79-548
W. Steinbeck, 342:Band69Heft4-465
Hostler, J. Leibniz's Moral Philosophy.*
A.W.J. Harper, 154:Mar78-201
Hotchner, A.E. Sophia.*
200:Apr79-239
Hotson, L. Shakespeare by Hilliard.*
G.P.V. Akrigg, 405(MP):May80-427
Hotz, R. - see Nikodim
Hötzer, U. - see Mörike, E.
Hough, G. Selected Essays.
S. Musgrove, 67:May79-111

Hough, J.F. The Soviet Union and Social
Science Theory.
  J.P. Shapiro, 550(RusR):Apr79-239
Hough, J.F. and M. Fainsod. How the
Soviet Union Is Governed.*
  A. Brown, 617(TLS):25Jan80-95
  R.S. Osborn, 550(RusR):Oct79-486
Hough, R. Mountbatten: Hero of Our Time.
  A. Boyle, 362:28Aug80-275
Hougron, J. L'Anti-jeu.
  C.W. Obuchowski, 207(FR):Oct78-178
Hourani, A. Europe and the Middle East.
  W. Montgomery Watt, 617(TLS):19Sep80-
  1042
Hourani, G.F., ed. Essays on Islamic
Philosophy and Science.
  M.S. Khan, 273(IC):Jul78-197
Hourcade, P. - see Du Plaisir
House, J.D. The Last of the Free
Enterprisers.
  P. Marchak, 99:Dec80/Jan81-33
Housego, J. Tribal Rugs.
  M. Beattie, 463:Winter78/79-464
Household, G. The Sending.
  M. Trend, 617(TLS):2May80-500
  442(NY):7Apr80-151
Houston, J. Spirit Wrestler.
  J. Kertzer, 198:Fall80-101
  J.P. Sloan, 441:3Feb80-14
Houzel, C. and others. Philosophie et
calcul de l'infini.
  J-M. Gabaude, 542:Apr-Jun78-228
Hovenkamp, H. Science and Religion in
America, 1800-1860.
  J. Lankford, 432(NEQ):Sep79-424
Hoveyda, F. The Fall of the Shah.
  S. Bakhash, 453(NYRB):26Jun80-22
  J. Simpson, 362:31Jan80-154
  R. Steel, 441:1Jun80-1
Hoving, T. Tutankhamun.
  639(VQR):Winter79-15
Hoving, T. Two Worlds of Andrew Wyeth.
  R. Urquhart, 432(NEQ):Jun79-273
Howard, D. Jacopo Sansovino.*
  D. Lewis, 90:Jan79-38
Howard, D.R. The Idea of the "Canterbury
Tales."*
  L.W. Patterson, 627(UTQ):Spring79-263
  D. Pearsall, 402(MLR):Jan79-154
Howard, D.S. and J. Ayers. China for the
West.*
  M. Markbreiter, 60:Jan-Feb79-130
  G. Wills, 39:Dec79-532
  90:Aug79-544
Howard, H.A. The Saga of Chief Joseph.
  F.E. Hoxie, 42(AR):Spring79-245
Howard, M. Facts of Life.*
  G. Davenport, 249(HudR):Winter79/80-
  598
Howard, M., ed. Restraints on War.
  H. Bull, 617(TLS):4Jan80-20
Howard, P. New Words for Old.*
  D.H., 355(LSoc):Aug78-290
Howard, P. Weasel Words.
  J.R. Gaskin, 569(SR):Summer79-455
Howard, P. Words Fail Me.
  D.A.N. Jones, 362:11Dec80-800

Howard, R. Misgivings.
  R.B. Shaw, 441:3Feb80-9
Howard, R. and The Duke of Buckingham.
The Country Gentleman.* (A.H. Scouten
and R.D. Hume, eds)
  H.J. Oliver, 402(MLR):Oct79-903
  R.G. Ralph, 447(N&Q):Dec78-555
Howard-Hill, T.H. British Bibliography
and Textual Criticism. (Vols 4 and 5)
  G. Naylor, 617(TLS):16May80-566
Howarth, P. Undercover.
  R. Lewin, 362:29May80-692
  A.M. Rendel, 617(TLS):8Aug80-899
Howarth, R.G. and A.W. Barker - see Lind-
say, N.
Howarth, T. Charles Rennie Mackintosh
and the Modern Movement.* (2nd ed)
  M. Holzman, 505:Sep79-218
Howarth, W.D., ed. Comic Drama.
  H.G. Hall, 208(FS):Jul79-369
Howarth, W.L. - see McPhee, J.
Howarth-Williams, M. R.D. Laing.
  P. Sedgwick, 560:Spring-Summer79-217
Howatch, S. Sins of the Fathers.
  R. Freedman, 441:29Jun80-14
Howe, G. and J. Markham. Paul Outerbridge
Jr.: Photographs. (G. Howe and G.R.
Hawkins, eds)
  H. Kramer, 441:30Nov80-64
Howe, I. William Faulkner.* (3rd ed)
  K. McSweeney, 148:Spring79-72
Howe, I. Trotsky.*
  J. Carmichael, 390:Jun/Jul79-68
  639(VQR):Spring79-72
Howe, I., comp. Twenty-Five Years of
Dissent.
  P. Steinfels, 441:13Jan80-1
Howe, J.R. Marlowe, "Tamburlaine" and
Magic.
  R.H. West, 405(MP):Nov79-204
  R.S. White, 447(N&Q):Oct78-458
Howe, M.B. The Art of the Self in D.H.
Lawrence.*
  J.W. Haegert, 573(SSF):Summer78-338
  295(JML):Vol7#4-758
Howell, M. and P. Ford. The True History
of the Elephant Man.
  A. Broyard, 441:19Jun80-C21
  P. Grosskurth, 617(TLS):28Mar80-349
Howell, W.S. Poetics, Rhetoric and Logic.*
  L. Gallet, 189(EA):Apr-Jun78-219
Howells, C.A. Love, Mystery, and Misery.
  F.G. Atkinson, 67:Nov79-324
  K. Miller, 175:Summer79-176
Howells, R. Heronsmill.
  442(NY):28Apr80-142
Howells, W.D. The Minister's Charge, or,
The Apprenticeship of Lemuel Barker.
(H.M. Munford, D.J. Nordloh and D.
Kleinman, eds)
  S.A. Dennis, 26(ALR):Spring79-161
Howells, W.D. A Modern Instance. (G.N.
Bennett, D.J. Nordloh and D. Kleinman,
eds)
  S.A. Dennis, 26(ALR):Spring79-161
  R.H. Hirst, 445(NCF):Mar79-493

Hower, E.   The New Life Hotel.
   T. Walton, 441:14Dec80-10
Howes, B.   A Private Signal.*
   B. Raffel, 385(MQR):Spring80-251
Howgego, J.L.   The Victorian and Edwardian
   City of London from Old Photographs.
   T.C. Barker, 325:Oct79-240
Howie, J. and L. Rouner, eds.   The Wisdom
   of William Ernest Hocking.
   W.G., 543:Jun79-760
Howith, H.   Multiple Choices.*
   A. Amprimoz, 102(CanL):Autumn79-99
Howland, B.   Blue in Chicago.*
   B. Lyons, 573(SSF):Fall78-463
Howse, D.   Greenwich Time.
   442(NY):9Jun80-155
Howse, R.   French Cooking Simplified with
   a Food Processor.
   W. and C. Cowen, 639(VQR):Spring78-72
Howson, C., ed.   Method and Appraisal in
   the Physical Sciences.*
   R. Laymon, 486:Jun78-318
Hoy, D.C.   The Critical Circle.*
   639(VQR):Autumn79-127
Hoyle, F.   Energy or Extinction?
   H. Inhaber, 529(QQ):Autumn79-504
Hoyle, F. and C. Wickramasinghe.   Diseases
   from Space.*
   P.B. Medawar, 453(NYRB):23Oct80-45
   J.F. Watkins, 617(TLS):25Jan80-80
Hoyningen-Huene, G.   Eye for Elegance.
   C. James, 453(NYRB):18Dec80-22
Hoyt, G.R.   The Development of Anton
   Ulrich's Narrative Prose on the Basis of
   Surviving "Octavia" Manuscripts and
   Prints.*
   K.F. Otto, Jr., 406:Summer79-196
Hrabák, J.   Literární komparatistika.
   W. Gesemann, 52:Band13Heft2-189
Hrabanus Maurus.   Liber de laudibus Sanc-
   tae Crucis.   (K. Holter, ed)
   H. Belting, 683:Band41Heft2-162
Hsiao Hung.   The Field of Life and Death
   and Tales of Hulan River.*
   J. Spence, 453(NYRB):17Apr80-20
Hsü, K-Y., ed.   Literature of the People's
   Republic of China.
   J. Spence, 453(NYRB):17Apr80-20
Hu Shi-ming and E. Seifman, eds.   Toward a
   New World Outlook.
   P.J. Seybolt, 293(JASt):Aug79-760
Huan T'an.   Hsin-lun (New Treatise) and
   Other Writings by Huan T'an 43 B.C.-28
   A.D.   (T. Pokora, trans)
   W.G. Boltz, 318(JAOS):Oct-Dec78-527
Huang, P.C.C., L.S. Bell and K.L. Walker.
   Chinese Communists and Rural Society,
   1927-1934.
   E.J. Perry, 293(JASt):Aug79-757
Hubbard, M.M.A.   Propertius.*
   K. Galinsky, 121(CJ):Oct-Nov79-78
Hubbard, W.   Complicity and Conviction.
   P. Goldberger, 441:7Sep80-9
Hubenka, L.J. - see Shaw, G.B.
Huber, C.   Wort sint der dinge zeichen.*
   H. Heinen, 589:Jul79-588

Huber, H.D.   Historische Romane in der
   ersten Hälfte des 19. Jahrhunderts.
   J.L. Sammons, 222(GR):Fall79-173
Huber, M.   Clemens Brentano, Die Chronika
   des fahrenden Schülers.*
   J.F.F., 191(ELN):Sep78(supp)-146
   G. Schaub, 133:Band12Heft1/2-165
Huber, W.   Kirche und Öffentlichkeit.
   M. Rock, 182:Vol31#15/16-524
Hubert, É-A.   Bibliographie des écrits de
   Pierre Reverdy, précédée d'une lettre de
   Pierre Reverdy.
   M. Bishop, 208(FS):Vol33Pt2-891
Huberty, M. and others.   L'Allemagne
   dynastique.   (Vol 1)
   F. Knöpp, 182:Vol31#9/10-313
Hübner, K.   Kritik der wissenschaftlichen
   Vernunft.
   L. Schäfer, 687:Oct-Dec79-641
Hübscher, A. - see Schopenhauer, A.
Huch, R.   Erinnerungen an Kreise und
   Krisen der Jahrhundertwende in München-
   Schwabing.
   H. Naumann, 680(ZDP):Band97Heft2-308
Huch, R.K.   The Radical Lord Radnor.
   D.V.E., 191(ELN):Sep78(supp)-32
Huchel, P.   Die neunte Stunde.
   D. Johnson, 617(TLS):11Apr80-422
Huddle, D.   Paper Boy.
   D. Smith, 29:Mar/Apr80-40
Huddleston, R.   An Introduction to English
   Transformational Syntax.*
   O.S. Axmanova, N.P. Gaman and L.V.
   Polubičenko, 682(ZPSK):Band31Heft4-
   413
   R. Emons, 72:Band216Heft1-164
   V. Meus, 179(ES):Feb79-92
Hudson, A., ed.   Selections from English
   Wycliffite Writings.*
   M.W. Bloomfield, 589:Jul79-588
   J. Dahmus, 377:Mar79-52
   O.S. Pickering, 72:Band216Heft1-171
   P.B. Taylor, 179(ES):Aug79-523
Hudson, C.   The Final Act.
   M. Laski, 362:17Apr80-514
Hudson, C.   The Southeastern Indians.*
   M.A. Lofaro, 292(JAF):Jan-Mar79-91
Hudson, D.   Lewis Carroll.
   J. Bump, 637(VS):Summer78-521
   J.R. Kincaid, 445(NCF):Sep78-272
Hudson, J. and E. Richards, with others.
   The Walmatjari.
   R.M.W. Dixon, 350:Mar79-258
Hudson, J.B.   Rivers of Time.
   42(AR):Summer79-380
Hudson, K.   The Dictionary of Diseased
   English.
   R.E. Allen, 447(N&Q):Aug78-351
   J.R. Gaskin, 569(SR):Summer79-455
Hudson, M.C.   Arab Politics.
   639(VQR):Winter79-28
Hudson, R.A.   Arguments for a Non-Transfor-
   mational Grammar.*
   L. Haegeman, 179(ES):Dec79-821
   J. Lenerz, 603:Vol13#2-237

Huebert, R. John Ford.
S.G. Putt, 175:Summer79-170
S.P. Zitner, 627(UTQ):Summer79-408
Huemer, F. Corpus Rubenianum Ludwig Burchard. (Pt 19, Portraits I)
E. Young, 39:Jun79-492
Huerga, Á. - see de Valdivia, D.P.
Huettich, H.G. Theater in the Planned Society.
H.K. Doswald, 221(GQ):Mar79-295
S. Hoefert, 564:May79-163
K.H. Schoeps, 301(JEGP):Apr79-307
Huff, T.E. Marabelle.
N. Johnson, 441:24Feb80-15
Huffman, F.E. and I. Proum. English-Khmer Dictionary.
P.N. Jenner, 293(JASt):Aug79-839
Hufstader, A.A. Sisters of the Quill.
639(VQR):Autumn79-142
Hufton, O.H. The Poor of Eighteenth-Century France 1750-1789.
J. Lough, 208(FS):Vol33Pt2-802
Hügel, H-O. Untersuchungsrichter, Diebsfänger, Detektive.
J.L. Sammons, 222(GR):Winter79-46
P. Ruppert, 221(GQ):May79-421
Huggins, N. Slave and Citizen.
61:Jul80-86
Huggins, N.I. Black Odyssey.
M. Diedrich, 72:Band216Heft2-437
Hughes, A. Medieval Music.
J. Stevens, 382(MAE):1979/1-168
Hughes, A. and P. Trudgill. English Accents and Dialects.
B. Robinson, 179(ES):Dec79-839
Hughes, B. Tribal Chieftains.
D. Wilson, 617(TLS):25Jul80-858
Hughes, G. Best of Neighbours.
D. Davis, 362:5Jun80-729
D.M. Thomas, 617(TLS):25Apr80-477
Hughes, G.R. and R. Bury. Eugène Ionesco.
J. Knowlson, 208(FS):Vol33Pt2-929
Hughes, G.T. Romantic German Literature.
R. Gray, 617(TLS):11Jan80-45
Hughes, L. Langston Hughes in the Hispanic World and Haiti.* (E.J. Mullen, ed)
L. King, 86(BHS):Jan79-88
Hughes, R. The Shock of the New.
B. Robertson, 362:27Nov80-727
Hughes, S. Washi.
H. Schmoller, 78(BC):Winter79-579
Hughes, T. Cave Birds.*
D. Graham, 565:Vol20#4-75
639(VQR):Summer79-109
Hughes, T. Gaudete.*
L. Lee, 114(ChiR):Spring79-108
639(VQR):Summer78-98
Hughes, T. Moortown.
J. Harvey, 362:17Apr80-510
C. Ricks, 441:20Jul80-13
P. Scupham, 617(TLS):4Jan80-6
61:Jun80-92
Hughes, T. Remains of Elmet.*
E. Longley, 617(TLS):18Jan80-64
A. Ross, 364:Aug/Sep79-8
D. Smith, 29:Sep/Oct80-30

Hughes, T. - see Plath, S.
Hugo, L. Correspondance. (P. Georgel, ed)
Y. Gohin, 535(RHL):Nov-Dec78-1032
Hugo, R. Selected Poems.
J. Vernon, 651(WHR):Autumn79-352
V. Young, 472:Fall/Winter79-227
Hugo, R. 31 Letters and 13 Dreams.*
F. Garber, 29:Jan/Feb80-16
R. Jackson, 502(PrS):Fall78-292
Hugo, R. White Center.
V. Young, 472:Fall/Winter79-227
Hugo, V. La Légend des siècles. (A. Dumas, ed)
W.J.S. Kirton, 208(FS):Vol33Pt2-819
Hugo, V. Notre-Dame de Paris (J. Seebacher, ed) [together with] Les Travailleurs de la mer. (Y. Gohin, ed)
C. Duchet and G. Rosa, 535(RHL):Sep-Oct79-824
Hugolin, L. and L. Luciano-Hugolin. L'inertie, la force d'inertie.
A. Reix, 542:Apr-Jun78-229
Hugon, P.D. The Modern Word-Finder. (rev)
K.B. Harder, 424:Dec78-427
Hugutio of Pisa. Uguccione da Pisa, "De dubio accentu, Agiographia, Expositio de symbolo Apostolorum." (G. Cremascoli, ed)
C.V. Franklin, 589:Oct79-870
Huitrón, J. Orígenes e historia del movimiento obrero en México.
S.R. Ross, 263(RIB):Vol29No1-78
Hulburt, S. The Mussel Cookbook.
W. and C. Cowen, 639(VQR):Spring78-74
Hulliung, M. Montesquieu and the Old Regime.*
T.M. Adams, 173(ECS):Winter78/79-249
Hulsker, J. The Complete van Gogh.
J. Russell, 441:30Nov80-74
Hulton, P., ed. The Work of Jacques Le Moyne de Morgues.*
J. Collins, 78(BC):Autumn79-445
M. Rogers, 90:May79-324
Hulton, P. and L. Smith. Flowers in Art from East to West.
J. Figgess, 463:Winter79/80-499
"The Humanities in American Life."
H. Kramer, 441:28Dec80-1
Humbert, M-T. A l'autre bout de moi.
M. Gourmelon-Berman, 450(NRF):Dec79-117
Hume, D. The Natural History of Religion (A.W. Colver, ed) [and] Dialogues Concerning Natural Religion.* (J.V. Price, ed)
P. Carrive, 192(EP):Jul-Sep79-364
Hume, I.N. Early English Delftware from London and Virginia.
G. Wills, 39:Jul79-81
Hume, K. The Owl and the Nightingale.*
S. Wenzel, 38:Band96Heft1/2-213
Hume, R.D. The Development of English Drama in the Late Seventeenth Century.*
B. Corman, 627(UTQ):Fall78-53
F.P. Lock, 586(SoRA):Jul78-188
H. Love, 677(YES):Vol9-335
J. Treglown, 447(N&Q):Dec78-554

Humfrey, B., ed. Recollections of the
Powys Brothers.
 442(NY):29Dec80-73
 I. Colegate, 617(TLS):1Aug80-880
Humpherys, A. Travels into the Poor Man's
Country.
 P. Brantlinger, 445(NCF):Sep78-268
 L. James, 637(VS):Spring79-375
 G. Parry, 155:Spring79-42
 636(VP):Winter78-397
Humphreys, E. The Anchor Tree.
 P. Beer, 617(TLS):1Aug80-868
 J. Mellors, 362:31Jul80-153
Humphreys, R.S. From Saladin to the Mon-
gols.
 M.S. Khan, 273(IC):Oct78-282
Humphreys, S.C. Anthropology and the
Greeks.
 W.F. Wyatt, Jr., 124:Sep79-37
Hunczak, T., ed. The Ukraine, 1917-1921.
 J.F.N. Bradley, 575(SEER):Oct79-613
Hundsnurscher, F. - see Wernher von Gar-
tenaere
Hung, G.N.T. Economic Development of
Socialist Vietnam, 1955-80.
 W.S. Turley, 293(JASt):Nov78-211
Hung, H. - see under Hsiao Hung
Hunger, H. Die hochsprachliche profane
Literatur der Byzantiner. (Vol 1)
 R. Browning, 123:Vol29No2-300
 J.F. Haldon, 182:Vol131#5/6-172
Hunger, H. Die hochsprachliche profane
Literatur der Byzantiner. (Vol 2)
 J.F. Haldon, 182:Vol131#23/24-882
Hungry Wolf, B. The Ways of My Grand-
mothers.
 E. Auchincloss, 441:17Aug80-12
Hunn, E.S. Tzeltal Folk Zoology.
 E.P. Hamp, 269(IJAL):Apr78-162
Hunnisett, R.F. Editing Records for Publi-
cation.*
 G.L. Vogt, 14:Jan79-70
Hunt, C. "Lycidas" and the Italian
Critics.*
 H. Maclean, 301(JEGP):Jul79-411
Hunt, E.H. The Hargrave Deception.
 R. Freedman, 441:29Jun80-14
Hunt, H., K. Richards and J.R. Taylor.
The Revels History of Drama in English.
 (Vol 7)
 A.P. Hinchliffe, 148:Summer79-87
Hunt, H.A.K. A Physical Interpretation of
the Universe.*
 J. Mansfield, 394:Vol32fasc3/4-411
Hunt, J.D. The Figure in the Landscape.*
 W.H. Adams, 576:Mar78-60
 I.H.C., 191(ELN):Sep78(supp)-22
 J. Pinto, 54:Sep78-562
Hunt, J.D. Andrew Marvell.*
 A.E. Berthoff, 401(MLQ):Mar79-77
 H. Toliver, 301(JEGP):Apr79-261
 42(AR):Spring79-252
Hunt, J.D. and P. Willis, eds. The Genius
of the Place.*
 J. Pinto, 54:Sep78-562
Hunt, S. South into Winter.
 P. Crisp, 368:Mar74-74

Hunt, S. Time to Ride.
 H. Cooper, 368:Mar76-91
 S. Lewis, 368:Mar76-92
Hunt, T. - see Jeffers, R.
Hunter, G.K. Dramatic Identities and
Cultural Tradition.
 A.B. Kernan, 676(YR):Autumn79-124
 L. Tennenhouse, 141:Fall79-365
Hunter, G.K. and C.J. Rawson - see "The
Yearbook of English Studies"
Hunter, H., ed. The Future of the Soviet
Economy, 1978-1985.
 V.N. Bandera, 550(RusR):Jul79-379
Hunter, I. Malcolm Muggeridge.
 R. Davies, 362:20Nov80-698
Hunter, J.F.M. Intending.
 L.H. Davis, 482(PhR):Oct79-652
Hunter, R.G. Shakespeare and the Mystery
of God's Judgments.*
 J.H. Summers, 570(SQ):Winter79-103
Hunter, S. The Master Sniper.
 M. Levin, 441:6Jul80-9
Hunter, W.B., Jr., ed. The English
Spenserians.*
 S.W. May, 405(MP):May80-419
 D.W. Pearson, 568(SCN):Spring-Summer79-
16
Hunter, W.B., Jr. and others, eds. A
Milton Encyclopedia.*
 C.A. Patrides, 541(RES):May79-215
Hunter, W.F., ed. El auto sacramental de
la Universal Redemción.*
 205(FMLS):Jan78-94
Huntford, R. Scott and Amundsen.*
 P-L. Adams, 61:Jun80-95
 G. Jones, 453(NYRB):17Jul80-33
 W. Sullivan, 441:14Aug80-C22
 442(NY):2Jun80-139
Huon de Méri. Le Torneiment Anticrist.*
 (M.O. Bender, ed)
 W. Rothwell, 208(FS):Vol33Pt2-531
Huppert, G. Les Bourgeois Gentilshommes.*
 A.L. Moote, 255(HAB):Fall79-328
Hurd, M. The Ordeal of Ivor Gurney.*
 S. Banfield, 410(M&L):Jul79-339
 J. Silkin, 493:Jul79-60
Hurford, J.R. The Linguistic Theory of
Numerals.*
 B. Sigurd, 596(SL):Vol131#2-192
Hurston, Z.N. Their Eyes Were Watching
God.
 R. Sale, 249(HudR):Spring79-153
Hurvitz, L. - see "Scripture of the Lotus
Blossom of the Fine Dharma (The Lotus
Sūtra)"
Hurwood, B.J. My Savage Muse.
 D. Grumbach, 441:3Feb80-15
Hus, A. - see Livy
Huseboe, A.R. and W. Geyer, eds. Where
the West Begins.
 J. Milton, 649(WAL):Spring79-57
 M. Westbrook, 651(WHR):Spring79-163
Huss, W. Untersuchungen zur Aussenpolitik
Ptolemaios' IV.*
 R.M. Errington, 303(JoHS):Vol199-196

"The International Geographic Encyclopedia
and Atlas."
D. Weber, 617(TLS):9May80-538
Ionesco, E. Antidotes.
B.L. Knapp, 188(ECr):Summer78-90
R.C. Lamont, 207(FR):Feb79-513
Ionesco, E. Plays. (Vol 11)
J. Coleby, 157:Autumn79-89
Ionesco, E. Proses.
D. Leuwers, 450(NRF):Apr79-108
Ippolito, D.S. The Budget and National
Politics.
639(VQR):Spring79-64
Iqbal, F.M. Hubert Aquin romancier.
J. Melançon, 627(UTQ):Summer79-460
Irele, A. - see Senghor, L.S.
Iribe, M. and B. Wilder. Pâtés for Kings
and Commoners.
W. and C. Cowen, 639(VQR):Spring78-72
Irigaray, L. Ce sexe qui n'en est pas un.
M. Marini, 98:Jun-Jul78-603
Irigaray, L. Speculum de l'autre femme.
S. Gearhart, 153:Spring79-114
Irizarry, E. La inventiva surrealista de
E.F. Granell.
G. Sobejano, 238:Dec79-735
Irmen, H-J. Thematisches Verzeichnis der
musikalischen Werke Gabriel Josef Rhein-
bergers.
J. Dalton, 182:Vol131#21/22-817
Irving, C. Axis.
M. Malone, 441:17Aug80-10
Irving, D. The War Path.
J.S. Conway, 529(QQ):Autumn79-510
639(VQR):Spring79-55
Irving, E.B. A Reading of "Beowulf."
(2nd ed)
J. De Caluwé-Dor, 556(RLV):1978/1-83
Irving, J. The World According to Garp.*
C. Mason, 502(PrS):Fall78-303
639(VQR):Winter79-16
Irving, W. Bracebridge Hall, or, The
Humorists. (H.F. Smith, ed)
J.E. Devlin, 587(SAF):Autumn79-253
Irving, W. The Complete Works of Washing-
ton Irving: Letters. (Vol 1) (R.M.
Aderman, H.L. Kleinfield and J.S. Banks,
eds)
N. Wright, 165(EAL):Winter79/80-345
Irving, W. The Complete Works of Washing-
ton Irving: Letters. (Vol 2) (R.M.
Aderman, H.L. Kleinfield and J.S. Banks,
eds)
W. Hesford, 165(EAL):Spring80-93
Irving, W. The Crayon Miscellany. (D.K.
Terrell, ed)
W.R. Kime, 649(WAL):Winter80-321
Irwin, D. John Flaxman 1755-1826.
P-L. Adams, 61:Jun80-94
Irwin, J.T. Doubling and Incest/Repeti-
tion and Revenge.*
B. Bassoff, 152(UDQ):Summer78-134
K. McSweeney, 148:Spring79-73
S. Raval, 50(ArQ):Summer79-183
N. Schmitz, 473(PR):3/1979-445

Irwin, T. Plato's Moral Theory.*
C. Chalier, 192(EP):Apr-Jun79-249
C. Gill, 303(JoHS):Vol199-176
R. Kraut, 482(PhR):Oct79-633
F. Ricken, 687:Apr-Jun79-311
M. Schofield, 123:Vol129No2-246
C.C.W. Taylor, 393(Mind):Oct79-597
Irwin, T. - see Plato
Irwin, W.R. The Game of the Impossible.*
J. Gattegno, 189(EA):Jul-Dec78-369
K. Hume, 402(MLR):Jul79-680
Isaacman, A.F., with B. Isaacman. The
Tradition of Resistance in Mozambique.
T.T. Spear, 69:Vol148#3-301
Isaacs, S. Close Relations.
P-L. Adams, 61:Oct80-102
E.F. Hailey, 441:26Oct80-14
Isager, S. and M.H. Hansen. Aspects of
Athenian Society in the Fourth Century
B.C.
H.W. Pleket, 394:Vol132fasc3/4-445
Isayev, M.I. National Languages in the
USSR.*
S.R. Crisp, 575(SEER):Oct79-629
R.E. Wood, 399(MLJ):Jan-Feb79-72
Isella, D. - see Dossi, C.
Iser, W. The Act of Reading.* (German
title: Der Akt des Lesens.)
D. Barnouw, 400(MLN):Dec79-1207
M.C. Beardsley, 569(SR):Fall79-639
D.P. Deneau, 268(IFR):Winter80-76
T. Hawkes, 676(YR):Summer80-560
W. Martin, 141:Summer79-260
D.T. O'Hara, 290(JAAC):Fall79-88
R. Saldívar, 594:Winter79-472
Iser, W. The Implied Reader.* (German
title: Der implizite Leser.)
D. Barnouw, 400(MLN):Dec79-1207
Isherwood, C. My Guru and His Disciple.
J. Atlas, 441:27Aug80-C22
P. Binding, 617(TLS):18Jul80-800
R. Blythe, 362:10Jul80-55
S. Spender, 453(NYRB):14Aug80-18
E. White, 441:1Jun80-9
"Iskandanamah, A Persian Medieval Alex-
ander-Romance." (M.S. Southgate, trans)
P. Avery, 382(MAE):1972/2-286
Isla Mingorance, E. José de Bada y
Navajas, arquitecto andaluz (1691-1755).
A. Rodríguez G. de Ceballos, 48:Apr-
Jun78-188
Iṣlāḥi, A.R.P. - see under Parwāz Iṣlāḥi,
A.R.
Islam, S. Kipling's "Law."*
D. Hewitt, 447(N&Q):Aug78-382
Ismayr, W. Das politische Theater in West-
deutschland.
J.J. White, 402(MLR):Oct79-997
Isnardi Parente, M. - see Erasmus
Israel, L. Conquering Cancer.*
M.A. Epstein, 617(TLS):11Apr80-420
Itani, F. No Other Lodgings.
D. Precosky, 198:Summer80-156
Itzin, C. Stages in the Revolution.
J. Elsom, 362:27Nov80-731
Itzkowitz, D.C. Peculiar Privilege.
P. Dunkley, 637(VS):Winter79-215

Ivaldo, M. Religione e cristianesimo in Alfred Loisy.
  E. Namer, 542:Apr-Jun79-253
  P.P., 227(GCFI):Apr-Jun78-281
Iventosch, H. Los nombres bucólicos en Sannazaro y La Pastoral española.
  J.A. Dabbs, 424:Jun78-198
Ives, A., comp. Archives in Australia.
  V.L. Russell, 14:Oct79-481
Ives, E.D. Joe Scott.
  P. Seeger, 187:Sep80-578
Ives, N. and J.T. Hill, eds. Walker Evans.
  R. Whelan, 55:Apr79-32
Izenour, G.C. Theater Design.
  R. Leacroft, 611(TN):Vol33#2-87

Jääskinen, A. The Icon of the Virgin of Tikhvin.
  U. Abel, 341:1978/2-74
Jabès, E. The Book of Questions. The Book of Questions II and III.
  M.A. Caws, 207(FR):Mar79-651
  R. Stamelman, 400(MLN):May79-869
Jabès, E. Je bâtis ma demeure, Poèmes 1943-1957. (new ed)
  G.D. Martin, 208(FS):Vol33Pt2-933
Jaccard, J-L. "Manon Lescaut."
  J. Sgard, 535(RHL):Jul-Aug79-663
Jaccottet, P. A la lumière d'hiver, [précédé de] Leçons [et de] Chants d'en bas.
  M. Bishop, 207(FR):Mar79-670
Jackaman, R. Hemispheres.
  L. Edmond, 368:Dec76-322
Jackman, S. Sandcatcher.
  442(NY):28Jul80-104
Jackman, S.W. - Sturgis, W.
Jackson, B. Killing Time.
  K. Warren, 577(SHR):Fall79-366
Jackson, C.C. Radnage.
  R. Dunning, 325:Oct79-233
Jackson, D., with others - see Washington, G.
Jackson, F. Perception.*
  J.W.R. Cox, 393(Mind):Jan79-142
  P. Fitzgerald, 258:Mar79-103
Jackson, J.R.D. Poetry of the Romantic Period.
  D. Bromwich, 617(TLS):4Jul80-753
Jackson, K.D. and L.W. Pye, eds. Political Power and Communications in Indonesia.
  D.S. Lev, 293(JASt):Aug79-842
Jackson, L.E.B. Elli.
  D. Rabinowitz, 441:29Jun80-12
  442(NY):19May80-162
Jackson, M. Latitudes of Exile.
  A. Paterson, 368:Dec76-358
Jackson, R. Bomber!
  D. Middleton, 441:25May80-6
Jackson, R.L. The Black Image in Latin American Literature.*
  J.A. Weiss, 454:Spring79-264
  205(FMLS):Jan78-90
Jackson, R.L. Dostoevsky's Quest for Form. (2nd ed)
  S. Linnér, 574(SEEJ):Summer79-269

Jackson, W. The Probable and the Marvelous.
  L. Goldstein, 661(WC):Summer79-256
  S. Peterfreund, 566:Spring79-137
  J. Wittreich, 401(MLQ):Sep79-312
  639(VQR):Spring79-48
Jackson, W.A., P.S. Ferguson and K.F. Pantzer - see Pollard, A.W. and G.R. Redgrave
Jacob, J.R. Robert Boyle and the English Revolution.
  R.F.S. Borkat, 566:Spring79-139
  T.W. Hayes, 568(SCN):Spring-Summer79-22
Jacobowski, L. Auftakt zur Literatur des 20. Jahrhunderts.* (F.B. Stern, ed)
  T.P. Freeman, 222(GR):Winter79-41
Jacobs, C. The Dissimulating Harmony.
  R. González Echevarría, 400(MLN):Dec79-1257
Jacobs, C. - see de Fuenllana, M.
Jacobs, H.E. and C.D. Johnson. An Annotated Bibliography of Shakespearean Burlesques, Parodies, and Travesties.*
  S. Wells, 677(YES):Vol9-324
Jacobs, J. New York a la Carte.
  W. and C. Cowen, 639(VQR):Spring79-75
Jacobs, J. The Question of Separatism.
  E.Z. Friedenberg, 453(NYRB):20Nov80-35
  W. Goodman, 441:5Oct80-16
  J. Leonard, 441:5Sep80-C21
  442(NY):13Oct80-192
Jacobs, L., ed. Jewish Mystical Testimonies.
  B.W. Holtz, 390:Aug-Sep79-57
Jacobs, R.A. and P.S. Rosenbaum. Transformationelle grammatik der englischen sprache.
  G. Graustein, 682(ZPSK):Band31Heft4-416
Jacobs, W.G. - see Fichte, J.G.
Jacobsen, B. Transformational-Generative Grammar.
  J. Aissen, 350:Sep79-679
  V. Meus, 179(ES):Feb79-92
Jacobsen, R. Twenty Poems.
  639(VQR):Winter79-26
Jacobson, D. The Confessions of Josef Baisz.*
  D. Flower, 249(HudR):Summer79-303
Jacobson, G.C. Money in Congressional Elections.
  J. Herbers, 441:13Apr80-12
Jacobson, H. Ovid's "Heroides."*
  P.F. Hovingh, 394:Vol32fascl/2-196
Jacobson, N. Pride and Solace.
  B. Kuklick, 256:Spring79-177
Jacobson, S. Factors Influencing the Placement of English Adverbs in Relation to Auxiliaries.*
  J. Buysschaert, 179(ES):Jun79-332
Jacobson, S. On the Use, Meaning, and Syntax of English Preverbal Adverbs.
  J. Buysschaert, 179(ES):Dec79-836
  D. James, 320(CJL):Spring-Fall78-148

Jacobson, S.A. A Grammatical Sketch of Siberian Yupik Eskimo.
B. Comrie, 350:Sep79-751

Jacobus, M. Tradition and Experiment in Wordsworth's "Lyrical Ballads" (1798).*
R. Gravil, 72:Band216Heft1-180
M. Isnard, 189(EA):Jul-Dec78-395

Jacoebée, W.P. La Persuasion de la charité.*
S. Jüttner, 547(RF):Band91Heft4-474
H.T. Mason, 208(FS):Vol133Pt2-722

Jaconelli, J. Enacting a Bill of Rights.
H.W.R. Wade, 617(TLS):13Jun80-666

Jacquart, E.C. Le Théâtre de dérision.*
D. Knowles, 208(FS):Vol133Pt2-920

Jacquemont, V. Letters from India.
H. Tinker, 617(TLS):12Sep80-1000

Jacques de Cambrai. Les Poésies du trouvère Jacques de Cambrai. (J-C. Rivière, ed)
N.B. Smith, 589:Jul79-590

Jacques, G. Paysages et structures dans "La Comédie Humaine."
D. Adamson, 208(FS):Vol133Pt2-814
L. Frappier-Mazur, 207(FR):Apr79-772
N. Mozet, 535(RHL):Sep-Oct78-841

Jacquet, C. La pensée religieuse de Jean-Jacques Rousseau.
D. Leduc-Fayette, 542:Jul-Sep78-363
W. Ritzel, 53(AGP):Band60Heft1-74

Jacquot, J. and E. Konigson. Les Fêtes de la Renaissance. (Vol 3)
C. Eisler, 576:Dec78-319

Jaeger, C.S. Medieval Humanism in Gottfried von Strassburg's "Tristan und Isolde."
W.T.H. Jackson, 221(GQ):Nov79-534

Jaffa, H.V. How to Think About the American Revolution.
G. Anastaplo, 396(ModA):Summer79-314

Jaffé, D. The Stormy Petrel and the Whale.
R. Mason, 447(N&Q):Jun78-281

Jaffé, J.B. John Trumbull.*
L.B. Miller, 656(WMQ):Oct79-650

Jaffé, M. Rubens and Italy.*
E. Waterhouse, 54:Sep78-555

Jaffe, N.C. The Poet Swift.*
K.J. Wagner, 627(UTQ):Winter78/79-182

Jaffin, D. Space of.
P. Ramsey, 569(SR):Fall79-686

Jäger, G., A. Martino and F. Sengle, eds. Internationales Archiv für Sozialgeschichte der deutschen Literatur.* (Vol 1)
H. Jaumann, 224(GRM):Band28Heft2-233

Jahn, G., ed. Sprachhorizonte.
B. Jecklin, 657(WW):May-Jun78-218

Jahn, K. - see Rypka, J.

Jahoda, M. Freud and the Dilemmas of Psychology.
529(QQ):Spring79-182

"Jahrbuch für Volkskunde und Kulturgeschichte." (Vol 19, 1976)
H. Groschopp, 654(WB):9/1978-186

"Jahrbuch für Volksliedforschung." (Vols 21-23) (R.W. Brednich, ed)
D. Christensen, 187:May80-299

Jain, B.B. The Poetry of George Crabbe.
A.J. Sambrook, 402(MLR):Jan79-167

Jain, J. The Vasudevahiṇḍi.
C.M. Mayrhofer, 259(IIJ):Oct79-275

Jakobson, R. Six Lectures on Sound and Meaning.
W.G. Franklin, 583:Summer79-433

Jakopin, F., ed. Slovansko jezikoslovje: Nahtigalov zbornik.
H. Leeming, 575(SEER):Oct79-576

Jakovsky, A. Naïve Painting.
C.C. Brookes, 39:Dec79-538

Jambūvijaya, M. - see Hemacandra

James, A. The Death and Letters of Alice James. (R.B. Yeazell, ed)
D. Johnson, 441:14Dec80-1

James, C. At the Pillars of Hercules.*
P. Dickinson, 364:Jun79-90

James, C. First Reactions.
T.R. Edwards, 441:9Nov80-11
442(NY):15Dec80-170

James, C. Unreliable Memoirs.
R. Davies, 362:24Apr80-545
R. Stow, 617(TLS):25Apr80-469

James, D. Arab Painting.
Y. Crowe, 463:Winter78/79-467

James, H. Henry James: Letters.* (Vol 2) (L. Edel, ed)
D. May, 362:20Mar80-379
A.N. Wilson, 617(TLS):4Apr80-380

James, H. Henry James: Letters. (Vol 3) (L. Edel, ed)
D. Johnson, 441:14Dec80-1

James, H. The Tales of Henry James.* (Vol 2) (M. Aziz, ed)
W.M. Gibson, 27(AL):Jan80-565

James, J.A. - see de Saint-Gelais, O.

James, L., ed. English Popular Literature, 1819-1851.*
A. Howkins, 637(VS):Autumn77-126

James, P.D. Innocent Blood.
P. Bailey, 617(TLS):21Mar80-312
M. Howard, 441:27Apr80-312
M. Laski, 362:17Apr80-514
C. Lehmann-Haupt, 441:7May80-C27
J. Symons, 453(NYRB):17Jul80-39
61:Jun80-93
442(NY):23Jun80-101

James, R.R. The British Revolution, 1880-1939.
639(VQR):Summer78-87

James, R.R. - see under Rhodes James, R.

James, S. Another Beginning.
M. Johnson, 617(TLS):9May80-537
J. Mellors, 362:24Apr80-546

James, W. 'Kwanim Pa.
L. Mair, 617(TLS):11Apr80-410

James, W. Pragmatism.* (F. Burkhardt, ed)
P.H. Nidditch, 354:Sep79-288

James, W. The Will to Believe and Other Essays in Popular Philosophy.
483:Oct79-570

Jameson, F. Marxism and Form. The Prison-
House of Language.
  C. Norris, 349:Winter78-59
Jameson, S. Speaking of Stendhal.
  C.R. Anderson, 219(GaR):Summer79-459
Jancar, B.W. Women under Communism.
  639(VQR):Autumn79-143
Janecek, G., ed. Andrey Bely.
  P.R. Hart, 574(SEEJ):Fall79-406
  J.L. Rice, 550(RusR):Oct79-515
Janeway, E. Powers of the Weak.
  V. Gornick, 441:20Jul80-10
  L.A. Schreiber, 441:7Aug80-C18
  61:Aug80-84
  442(NY):28Jul80-102
Janhunen, J., ed. Altaica.
  L.V. Clark, 318(JAOS):Apr-Jun78-142
Janicaud, D. Hegel et le destin de la
Grèce.
  M. Detienne, 98:Nov78-1043
Janik, A. and S. Toulmin. Wittgenstein's
Vienna.
  D. La Capra, 153:Summer79-65
Janik, A.S. and S. Toulmin. Wittgenstein,
Vienne et la modernité.
  J. Largeault, 542:Jul-Sep79-326
Janik, D. Magische Wirklichkeitsauffas-
sung im hispanoamerikanischen Roman des
20. Jahrhunderts.
  J. Hösle, 52:Band13Heft3-326
Janin, J. La fin d'un monde et du Neveu
de Rameau. (J-M. Bailbé, ed)
  L. Le Guillou, 535(RHL):Sep-Oct79-865
Janini, J. and R. Gonzálvez. Manuscritos
litúrgicos de la Catedral de Toledo.
  I. Mateo Gómez, 48:Apr-Jun78-190
Janke, R. Architectural Models.
  T. Crosby, 46:Jun79-362
Jankélévitch, V. and B. Berlowitz. Quel-
que part dans l'inachevé.
  F. de Martinoir, 450(NRF):Dec79-119
Jankola, B. Girl of the Golden West.
  D. Barbour, 150(DR):Spring79-154
Jankowski, F. Histaryčnaja hramatyka
belaruskaj movy. (Vol 2)
  P. Wexler, 574(SEEJ):Summer79-308
Janota, J. - see "Der Stricker: Verserzäh-
lungen II"
Janowitz, P. Rites of Strangers.
  M. Heffernan, 491:Jun80-170
Jansen, F., ed. Studies on Fronting.
  B. Comrie, 350:Dec79-958
Jansen, G.H. Militant Islam.
  F. Ajami, 441:2Mar80-6
  442(NY):17Mar80-167
Jansen, P. Arnold Gehlen.*
  H. Ottmann, 489(PJGG):Band86Heft1-148
Jansen, P. and J. Varloot. L'Année 1768 à
travers la presse traitée par ordinateur.
(Vol 1)
  M. Lever, 535(RHL):Jul-Aug78-657
Janssen, E.M. Jacob Burckhardt und die
Griechen.
  K. Christ, 182:Vol131#23/24-891
Janssens, U. Matthieu Maty and the
Journal britannique, 1750-1755.*
  A-M. Rousseau, 549(RLC):Jan-Mar77-117

Jansson, S.B. Medeltidens rimkrönikor.
  H. Kuhn, 563(SS):Spring79-185
Jantz, H. The Form of "Faust."
  S. Atkins, 301(JEGP):Apr79-295
  R. Gray, 617(TLS):11Jan80-45
  H. Henel, 221(GQ):Nov79-540
Jantzen, J. Parmenides zum Verhältnis von
Sprache und Wirklichkeit.*
  A.P.D. Mourelatos, 24:Summer79-342
Janz, C.P. Friedrich Nietzsche.
  R. Gray, 617(TLS):11Jan80-45
Japrisot, S. One Deadly Summer.
  N. Callendar, 441:10Aug80-34
  J. Mellors, 362:28Aug80-281
Jarka, H. - see Soyfer, J.
Jarman, A.O.H. and G.R. Hughes, eds. A
Guide to Welsh Literature.* (Vol 1)
  P.K. Ford, 589:Oct79-812
Jarman, D. The Music of Alban Berg.*
  D. Puffett, 415:Dec79-1000
  A. Whittall, 410(M&L):Jul79-328
Jarman, J. Black Case. (Vols 1 and 2)
  A. Lange, 114(ChiR):Summer78-125
Jarocinski, S. Debussy.*
  A.W., 412:Aug-Nov78-284
Jarrell, R. Kipling, Auden and Co.
  D. Davie, 441:3Aug80-10
  C. Lehmann-Haupt, 441:30Jul80-C19
  R. Towers, 453(NYRB):25Sep80-53
Jarrett, D. The English Landscape Garden.
  J.J. Yoch, 219(GaR):Fall79-717
Jarvie, I.C. Window on Hong Kong.
  C. Haye, 302:Vol16#1and2-130
Jarvis, A.C., R. Lebredo and F. Mena.
¡Continuemos!
  E. Echevarría, 399(MLJ):Nov79-379
Jäschke, K-U. Wilhelm der Eroberer.
  B.W. Scholz, 589:Jan79-153
Jasen, D.A. - see Wodehouse, P.G.
Jasenas, E. Le poétique: Desbordes-
Valmore et Nerval.*
  M. Bertrand, 535(RHL):May-Jun78-489
Jashemski, W.F. The Gardens of Pompeii,
Herculaneum and the Villas Destroyed by
Vesuvius.
  R.A. Sokolov, 441:24Feb80-16
  J.B. Ward-Perkins, 617(TLS):20Jun80-
  700
Jasienica, P. Jagiellonian Poland.
  B.J. Tepa, 497(PolR):Vol123#4-87
Jasinski, B.W. - see Madame de Staël
Jasinski, R. A travers le XIXe siècle.
  E. Morot-Sir, 207(FR):Mar79-644
Jaspers, K. Notizen zu Martin Heidegger.
(H. Saner, ed)
  T.J.S., 543:Mar79-550
Jaspers, K. Raison et existence.
  M. Adam, 542:Jul-Sep79-327
Jauss, H.R. Alterität und Modernität der
mittelalterlichen Literatur.
  B. Guidot, 547(RF):Band91Heft1/2-149
  B. Murdoch, 182:Vol131#14-485
Jauss, H.R. Ästhetische Erfahrung und lit-
erarische Hermeneutik.* (Vol 1)
  K. Weinberg, 149(CLS):Dec79-358

Javitch, D. Poetry and Courtliness in Renaissance England.*
L.G. Black, 541(RES):Aug79-352
J. Stevens, 131(CL):Fall79-422
639(VQR):Autumn78-127
Jaworski, R. Vorposten oder Minderheit?
F.L. Carsten, 575(SEER):Jul79-461
Jay, D. Change and Fortune.
J. Morgan, 617(TLS):5Sep80-952
R.R. James, 362:12Jun80-761
Jay, E. The Religion of the Heart.*
O. Chadwick, 617(TLS):15Feb80-187
Jay, M. L'imagination dialectique.
A. Jacob, 192(EP):Jul-Sep79-365
Jayadeva. Love Song of the Dark Lord: Jayadeva's "Gitagovinda." (B.S. Miller, ed and trans)
J.W. de Jong, 259(IIJ):Oct79-288
D. Nelson, 293(JASt):Nov78-196
Jaynes, J. The Origin of Consciousness in the Breakdown of the Bicameral Mind.*
J.E. Morriss, 186(ETC.):Sep78-314
J. Weissman, 219(GaR):Spring79-118
Jean de Meun. Li Abregemenz noble honme Vegesce Flave René des establissemenz apartenanz a chevalerie. (L. Löfstedt, ed)
J.M.A. Beer, 589:Jul79-593
Jean de Montreuil. Opera. (Vol 2) (N. Grévy, E. Ornato and G. Guy, eds)
N. Mann, 208(FS):Vol33Pt2-580
Jean, M. Autobiographie du surréalisme.
J.H. Matthews, 593:Summer79-186
Jean-Richard, P. L'oeuvre gravé de François Boucher dans la Collection Edmond de Rothschild.
J.G. von Hohenzollern, 471: Jan/Feb/Mar79-80
Jeane, D.G. and D.C. Purcell, eds. The Architectural Legacy of the Lower Chattahoochee Valley in Alabama and Georgia.
H.C. Bailey, 9(AlaR):Oct79-316
J.O. McKee, 585(SoQ):Spring-Summer79-243
Jędrzejewicz, W. Kronika życia Józefa Piłsudskiego, 1867-1935.
T. Swiętochowski, 497(PolR):Vol23#4-97
Jefferies, R. Nature Near London.
D.W. Snow, 617(TLS):12Sep80-999
Jeffers, L. Africa Where I Baked My Bread.
O. Dodson, 95(CLAJ):Sep78-66
Jeffers, R. Bridges of the South Wind, Poems 1917-1922. (W. Everson, ed)
R.I. Scott, 648(WCR):Jun78-27
Jeffers, R. Dear Judas and Other Poems.* (R.J. Brophy, ed) The Double Axe and Other Poems.* (W. Everson and B. Hotchkiss, eds)
W.G.R., 502(PrS):Summer78-210
R.I. Scott, 106:Fall79-231
Jeffers, R. In This Wild Water.* (J.H. Shebl, ed)
R.I. Scott, 106:Fall79-231
Jeffers, R. The Women at Point Sur and Other Poems.* (T. Hunt, ed)
W.G.R., 502(PrS):Summer78-210
[continued]

[continuing]
R.I. Scott, 106:Fall79-231
R.I. Scott, 648(WCR):Jun78-27
Jefferson, T. and T.A.B. Kościuszko. Jefferson/Kościuszko Correspondence. (B. Grzeloński, ed)
I. Nagurski, 497(PolR):Vol23#4-74
Jeffery, B., ed. Chanson Verse of the Early Renaissance.* (Vol 2)
G. Dottin, 535(RHL):Jul-Aug79-638
N. Wilkins, 208(FS):Vol33Pt2-649
205(FMLS):Jan78-87
Jēgers, B. - see Reiters, J.
Jehasse, J. Guez de Balzac et le génie romain.
R. Zuber, 535(RHL):Jul-Aug79-652
Jehasse, J. La Renaissance de la critique.*
D. Ménager, 535(RHL):Sep-Oct78-814
Jehlen, M. Class and Character in Faulkner's South.*
G.O. Carey, 573(SSF):Summer78-342
Jelavich, C. and B. The Establishment of the Balkan National States, 1804-1920.
S. Fischer-Galati, 104(CASS):Fall78-446
639(VQR):Spring78-60
Jencks, C. and others. Who Gets Ahead?*
A. Hacker, 453(NYRB):20Mar80-20
Jencks, C.A. The Language of Post-Modern Architecture.*
G. Shane, 62:Apr79-63
S. Stevens, 505:Jan78-120
Jenkins, A. Stephen Potter.
D.J. Enright, 362:19Oct80-480
Jenkins, J. Blind Spot.
L. Harrop, 565:Vol120#4-16
C. Pollnitz, 581:Dec79-462
Jenkins, L. The English Existential.
J.E. Breivik, 179(ES):Apr79-216
G. Milsark, 603:Vol3#1-99
J. Monaghan, 38:Band96Heft3/4-483
Jenkins, M. Bevanism.
K.O. Morgan, 617(TLS):11Jan80-31
Jenkins, N. and B. Churgin. Thematic Catalogue of the Works of Giovanni Battista Sammartini: Orchestral and Vocal Music.*
S.J.H.K., 412:Aug-Nov78-274
Jenkins, R. Tony Benn.
D.A.N. Jones, 362:18Sep80-372
Jenkins, R. Fergus Lamont.*
J.P. Sloan, 441:3Feb80-14
Jenkins, R. A Would-Be Saint.
442(NY):15Sep80-189
Jenkyns, R. The Victorians and Ancient Greece.
D. Donoghue, 441:28Sep80-11
D.A.N. Jones, 362:7Aug80-184
J. Leonard, 441:29Aug80-C17
Jenner, P.N., L.C. Thompson and S. Starosta, eds. Austroasiatic Studies.* (Pt 2)
G.F. Meier, 682(ZPSK):Band31Heft6-636
Jennings, C.B. L'Eros et la femme chez Zola.
D.W. Levy, 446(NCFS):Fall-Winter78/79-138

Jennings, E. After the Ark.
   A. Cluysenaar, 565:Vol20#3-68
Jennings, E. Moments of Grace.
   D. Davis, 362:31Jan80-157
   J. Symons, 617(TLS):1Feb80-112
Jennings, E. Selected Poems.
   J. Symons, 617(TLS):1Feb80-112
Jennings, G. Aztec.
   G. Jonas, 441:14Dec80-11
Jensen, A.R. Bias in Mental Testing.
   S.J. Gould, 453(NYRB):1May80-38
   D. Hawkins, 441:6Jul80-6
   S. Sutherland, 617(TLS):9May80-529
Jensen, F. The Old Provençal Noun and
   Adjective Declension.*
   J.H. Marshall, 208(FS):Vol33Pt2-1030
Jensen, H.J. The Muses' Concord.*
   E.D. Mackerness, 402(MLR):Apr79-395
Jensen, K.B. Russian Futurism, Urbanism
   and Elena Guro.*
   J. Graffy, 575(SEER):Oct79-589
Jensen, L. Bad Boats.*
   639(VQR):Spring78-56
Jeoffroy-Faggianelli, P. and L.R. Plazol-
   les. Techniques de l'expression et de
   la communication.*
   K.E.M. George, 208(FS):Vol33Pt2-1045
Jeon, S-W. Science and Technology in
   Korea.
   D. Gregory-Smith, 485(PE&W):Apr79-221
Jéquier, L. - see Galbreath, D.L.
Jeremias, J. The Prayers of Jesus.
   J.M. McDermott, 613:Jun79-203
Jerome, J. The Sweet Spot in Time.
   C. Lehmann-Haupt, 441:25Nov80-C11
   M. Watkins, 441:21Dec80-10
Jessen, K. Theodor Fontane und Skandina-
   vien.
   S-A. Jørgensen, 462(OL):Vol33#1-91
Jessup, E. Ernest Oppenheimer.
   R. West, 617(TLS):28Mar80-346
Jessup, R. Man of Many Talents.
   A.G. Dyson, 325:Apr79-161
"Le Jeu au XVIIIe siècle."*
   M. Delon, 535(RHL):Mar-Apr78-307
Jiménez, R.L. Guillermo Cabrera Infante y
   "Tres tristes tigres."
   J. Sánchez-Boudy, 238:Mar79-188
Jiménez Duque, B. La espiritualidad
   romano-visigoda y muzarabe.
   R. Collins, 86(BHS):Apr79-149
Jindel, R. Culture of a Sacred Town.
   J.M. Freeman, 293(JASt):Nov78-203
"Jineśvarasūri's Gāhārayaṇakosa." (P.A.M.
   Bhojak and N.J. Śāha, eds)
   L. Sternbach, 318(JAOS):Oct-Dec78-551
Jo-hsi, C. - see under Chen Jo-hsi
Joan, P. and A. Chesman. Guide to Women's
   Publishing.
   M.F., 502(PrS):Summer78-211
Joaquim de Carvalho, M., Jr. Contre Marx
   philosophe.
   A. Reix, 542:Apr-Jun79-264
Jochum, K.P.S. W.B. Yeats.*
   R.H., 305(JIL):May78-187

Jöckel, W. Heinrich Manns "Henri Quatre"
   als Gegenbild zum nationalsozialistis-
   chen Deutschland.
   E.C. Furthman-Durden, 400(MLN):Apr79-
   618
Jockwig, F. Der Weg der Laien auf das
   Landeskonzil der Russischen Orthodoxen
   Kirche Moskau 1917/18.
   G. May, 182:Vol131#9/10-265
Jodłowski, S. Die Grundlagen der polnis-
   chen Syntax.
   H. Zgółkowa, 360(LP):Vol21-179
Jodogne, O., ed and trans. Maître Pierre
   Pathelin.
   A. Hindley, 208(FS):Vol133Pt2-565
Jodogne, P. Jean Lemaire de Belges,
   écrivain franco-bourguignon.
   M. Quainton, 208(FS):Apr79-179
Jodogne, P. - see Alamanni, A.
Johannesson, N-L. The English Modal Auxil-
   iaries.*
   R. Wigzell, 596(SL):Vol31#2-194
Johansson, B. The Adapter Adapted.
   R.D. Hume, 568(SCN):Fall-Winter79-81
Johansson, S. Papers in Contrastive Lin-
   guistics and Language Testing.
   P. Robberecht, 179(ES):Jun79-335
Johansson, S. Studies of Error Gravity.
   J. Walz, 608:Mar80-98
John of Garland. The "Parisiana Poetria"
   of John of Garland. (T. Lawler, ed and
   trans)
   A.K. Bate, 208(FS):Jul79-323
   C.B. Faulhaber, 545(RPh):May79-444
Johne, K-P. Kaiserbiographie und Senats-
   aristokratie.
   R.P.H. Green, 313:Vol69-225
Johnes, C. Crawford — The Last Years.
   D. Bodeen, 200:Oct79-493
Johns, B. and J.S. Clancy - see Spector, H.
Johns, D. The Beatrice Mystery.
   M. Booth, 617(TLS):13Jun80-674
Johnson, A.H. Modes of Value.
   A.C. Michalos, 627(UTQ):Summer79-473
Johnson, A.W. The Thames and Hudson
   Manual of Bookbinding.*
   F. Broomhead, 503:Summer78-95
Johnson, B. Defigurations du langage
   poétique.
   J. Culler, 617(TLS):4Jul80-761
Johnson, C. Japan's Public Policy Com-
   panies.
   E.J. Lincoln, 293(JASt):May79-584
Johnson, D.G. The Medieval Chinese Oli-
   garchy.
   R.M. Somers, 293(JASt):Nov78-127
Johnson, D.L. The Architecture of Walter
   Burley Griffin.*
   P. Drew, 576:Mar78-44
Johnson, E. Charles Dickens.* (rev)
   A. Easson, 155:Spring79-37
Johnson, F.A. Defence by Ministry.
   P. Ziegler, 617(TLS):8Aug80-899
Johnson, H. In the Absence of Power.
   A. Wildavsky, 441:27Apr80-12
Johnson, J. Bad Connections.
   J. Chernaik, 364:Mar80-90

Johnson, J.H.S. and B.S. Smith, comps. Inclosure in Gloucestershire.
W.B. Stephens, 325:Apr79-173
Johnson, L.P., H-H. Steinhoff and R.A. Wisbey, eds. Studien zur frühmittelhochdeutschen Literatur.*
L. Jillings, 182:Vol31#13-410
Johnson, M.P. Toward a Patriarchal Republic.*
639(VQR):Summer78-87
Johnson, M.S. Locke on Freedom.
W. von Leyden, 518:May79-66
Johnson, P. The Civilization of Ancient Egypt.
42(AR):Spring79-252
Johnson, P. Enemies of Society.
639(VQR):Winter78-17
Johnson, P. Ireland.
S. Jacobson, 362:11Dec80-799
Johnson, P. The Recovery of Freedom.
A. Ryan, 362:7Aug80-182
Johnson, P. Writings.
D.A. Mann and J. Merkel, 290(JAAC): Spring80-343
J.M. Richards, 617(TLS):1Feb80-122
F. Schulze, 55:Nov79-34
Johnson, P. and E. Money. The Nasmyth Family of Painters.
T. Crombie, 39:Jan79-72
Johnson, R. The Early Sculpture of Picasso, 1901-1914.
C.R. Baldwin, 54:Mar78-187
Johnson R., Jr., E.S. Neumann and G.T. Trail, eds. Molière and the Commonwealth of Letters.*
J-P. Collinet, 535(RHL):Mar-Apr78-298
205(FMLS):Jan78-92
Johnson, R.C. and others, eds. Commons Debates, 1628. (Vols 1-3)
C. Roberts, 656(WMQ):Apr79-308
Johnson, R.E. Peasant and Proletarian.
L. Schapiro, 617(TLS):11Apr80-418
Johnson, R.H. and J.A. Blair. Logical Self-Defense.
A.G. Michalos, 154:Sep78-584
Johnson, R.K. Francis Ford Coppola.
M. Yacowar, 106:Winter79-379
Johnson, R.W. How Long Will South Africa Survive?*
P.F. Wilmot, 69:Vol148#4-415
Johnson, S. A Dictionary of the English Language.
W. Balliett, 442(NY):14Jul80-92
Johnson, S. The Doomsday Deposit.
N. Callendar, 441:27Apr80-20
G. Strawson, 617(TLS):11Apr80-408
Johnson, S. Later Roman Britain.
B. Cunliffe, 617(TLS):18Apr80-447
Johnson, S. The Works of Samuel Johnson.* (Vol 10: Political Writings.) (D.J. Greene, ed)
J.T. Boulton, 541(RES):May79-223
Johnson, U.E. American Prints and Printmakers.
A. Fern, 441:14Dec80-31
Johnson, W., with C. Evans and C.E. Sears - see Stevenson, A.E.

Johnson, W.C. Milton Criticism.*
A.C. Labriola, 568(SCN):Spring-Summer79-10
B. Sherry, 67:May79-93
Johnson, W.R. Darkness Visible.*
N. Horsfall, 313:Vol69-231
Johnson, W.S. Sex and Marriage in Victorian Poetry.
M. Montabrut, 179(ES):Jun79-330
Johnston, C. Poems and Journeys. Rivers and Fireworks.
K. Fitz Lyon, 617(TLS):19Sep80-1019
Johnston, D.F. Copyright Handbook.
H.B. Cox, 14:Jan79-69
Johnston, G. Taking a Grip.
P. Lanthier, 99:Apr80-40
Johnston, J. The Old Jest.*
A. Broyard, 441:9Feb80-19
S. Isaacs, 441:16Mar80-14
J. Mellors, 364:Dec79/Jan80-128
442(NY):12May80-161
Johnston, M. The Cuisine of the Sun.
W. and C. Cowen, 639(VQR):Autumn79-152
Johnston, R.C. The Versification of Jordan Fantosme.
K. Varty, 208(FS):Vol33Pt2-534
Johnston, R.H. Tradition versus Revolution.
N.E. Saul, 104(CASS):Fall78-434
Johnston, T.F. Eskimo Music by Region.
M.M. Lutz, 187:Sep80-590
Johnstone, H.W., Jr. Validity and Rhetoric in Philosophical Argument.
N. Melchert, 484(PPR):Mar80-451
Johnstone, K.I. The Armley Schulze Organ.
P. Williams, 415:Feb79-131
Johnstone, P. The Sea-Craft of Prehistory. (S. McGrail, ed)
P-L. Adams, 61:Nov80-99
Johnstone, R.M., Jr. Jefferson and the Presidency.
J. Pancake, 656(WMQ):Apr79-302
639(VQR):Summer79-89
Johnstone, T.M. Ḥarsūsi Lexicon and English-Ḥarsūsi Word-List.
R.G. Schuh, 350:Sep79-747
Johnstone, W. Points In Time.
S. Gardiner, 362:16Oct80-511
Joiner, E.G., G.A. Perla and S.L. Shinall. First-Year French.*
M. Debrock, 277(ITL):#39/40-145
de Joinville, J. La Vie de Saint Louis. (N.L. Corbett, ed)
G.T. Diller, 207(FR):Mar79-635
Jokinen, U. Les relatifs en moyen français.
P. Clifford, 297(JL):Sep79-381
P. Wunderli, 182:Vol31#1/2-21
Jolliffe, J. Raymond Asquith.
M. Egremont, 617(TLS):15Aug80-912
S. Koss, 362:17Jul80-83
Jolly, A. A World Like Our Own.
P. Marnham, 231:Oct80-86
Joly, A. and J. Stéfanini, eds. La Grammaire générale des modistes aux idéologues.
S. Auroux, 154:Jun78-393

Joly, J. Le désir de l'utopie.
  D. Gronau, 182:Vol131#20-742
Joly, J. Les fêtes théâtrales de Méta-
stase à la cour de Vienne (1731-67).
  D. Gronau, 182:Vol131#17/18-613
  N. Suckling, 208(FS):Oct79-449
Joly, R., ed. Corpus Hippocraticum.
  C. Mugler, 555:Vol52fasc2-372
Jonas, F. Die Institutionenlehre Arnold
Gehlens.
  H. Ottmann, 489(PJGG):Band86Heft1-148
Jonas, I.B. Thomas Mann and Italy.
  R. Gray, 617(TLS):11Jan80-45
Jonen, G.A. Allegorie und späthöfische
Dichtung in Frankreich.
  W. Rothwell, 208(FS):Vol33Pt2-577
Jones, A. Women Who Kill.
  P-L. Adams, 61:Nov80-98
  B.G. Harrison, 441:26Oct80-7
Jones, B. Cup Full of River.
  C. Pollnitz, 581:Dec79-462
Jones, B. The Island Normal.
  G. Lindop, 617(TLS):16May80-562
Jones, B. The Russia Complex.
  H. Hanak, 575(SEER):Oct79-625
Jones, C.P. The Roman World of Dio
Chrysostom.
  K.R. Bradley, 121(CJ):Feb-Mar80-274
  R. Seager, 617(TLS):11Jan80-44
Jones, C.W. Saint Nicholas of Myra, Bari,
and Manhattan.*
  J. Wortley, 589:Oct79-817
Jones, D. Dai Greatcoat. (R. Hague, ed)
  D. Davie, 617(TLS):22Aug80-935
Jones, D. The Dime Novel Western.
  G. Topping, 649(WAL):Fall79-242
Jones, D. The Dying Gaul and Other
Writings.* (H. Grisewood, ed)
  C. Cannon-Brookes, 39:Mar79-242
  D.S. Carne-Ross, 453(NYRB):9Oct80-41
Jones, D. Introducing David Jones. (J.
Matthias, ed)
  D.S. Carne-Ross, 453(NYRB):9Oct80-41
  D. Davie, 617(TLS):22Aug80-935
Jones, D.C. Elkhorn Tavern.
  M. Malone, 441:16Nov80-15
Jones, D.G. Under the Thunder the Flowers
Light Up the Earth.*
  E. Mandel, 529(QQ):Spring79-170
  S.G. Mullins, 628(UWR):Fall-Winter78-
  71
  G. Woodcock, 168(ECW):Summer78-276
Jones, D.R., ed. Soviet Armed Forces
Review Annual.* (Vol 1)
  J.N. Westwood, 575(SEER):Jan79-146
Jones, E. Flux.
  R.B. Hatch, 102(CanL):Summer79-129
Jones, E. The Origins of Shakespeare.*
  E.A.J. Honigmann, 447(N&Q):Apr78-172
Jones, F.J. Ungaretti.
  E.F., 228(GSLI):Vol155fasc492-633
Jones, H. To the Webster-Ashburton
Treaty.*
  639(VQR):Summer78-88

Jones, H.G. Hispanic Manuscripts and
Printed Books in the Barberini Collec-
tion.
  R.G. Black, 304(JHP):Winter80-167
"Howard Mumford Jones: An Autobiography."
  R.J. Porter, 31(ASch):Summer80-417
Jones, J. Radical Cousins.
  A.J. Lawson, 67:May79-103
Jones, J. A Tree May Fall.
  J. Mellors, 362:9Oct80-481
Jones, J. Whistle.*
  J. Mills, 529(QQ):Winter79/80-646
Jones, J.M., Jr. "La Nouvelle Héloïse."
  J-L. Lecercle, 535(RHL):Mar-Jun79-508
  J.H. Stewart, 207(FR):Apr79-771
Jones, J.W. and E.F., eds. The Commentary
on the First Six Books of the "Aeneid"
of Vergil Commonly Attributed to
Bernardus Silvestris.
  T. Silverstein, 589:Jan79-154
Jones, L.E. The "Cort d'Amor."
  W.J. Beck, 207(FR):Mar79-634
  A.R. Press, 402(MLR):Oct79-936
Jones, L.Y. Great Expectations.
  E.J. Dionne, 441:9Nov80-7
  C. Lehmann-Haupt, 441:20Oct80-C16
Jones, M., ed. New Essays on Tolstoy.
  R. Freeborn, 575(SEER):Jul79-428
  D. Matual, 399(MLJ):Sep-Oct79-319
  B. Sorokin, 574(SEEJ):Summer79-271
Jones, M. Passage Through Gehenna.
  J.E. Brown, 577(SHR):Fall79-356
Jones, M. A Short Time to Live.
  J. Mellors, 362:9Oct80-481
Jones, M. and A.R. Thomas. The Welsh Lan-
guage.
  S.R. Anderson, 350:Jun79-434
  G.M. Awbery, 297(JL):Sep79-352
  G. Price, 402(MLR):Apr79-402
Jones, M.H. Le Théâtre national en France
de 1800 à 1830.
  W.D. Howarth, 208(FS):Vol33Pt2-967
Jones, M.O. The Hand Made Object and its
Maker.
  B. Herman and D. Orr, 582(SFQ):Vol41-
  279
Jones, M.P. and others, eds. The Individ-
ual and Society.
  P.H. Hare, 484(PPR):Dec79-293
Jones, M.V. Dostoyevsky.*
  R. Neuhäuser, 575(SEER):Jul79-429
  205(FMLS):Jan78-90
Jones, M.W. George Cruikshank.
  A. Burton, 155:Summer79-114
Jones, P. Philosophy and the Novel.*
  J. Cruickshank, 208(FS):Vol33Pt2-991
Jones, P.E. The Butchers of London.
  E.M. Veale, 325:Apr79-160
Jones, R. Living in the 25th Hour.
  639(VQR):Winter79-18
Jones, R.E. David Wynne.
  P. Griffiths, 415:Sep79-743
Jones, R.V. Most Secret War.
  W.A.B. Douglas, 529(QQ):Spring79-159
Jones, S. Oregon Folklore.
  J.S. Griffith, 292(JAF):Jul-Sep79-345
Jones, S. - see O'Brien, F.

Jones, T.   Chaucer's Knight.
    J.A. Burrow, 617(TLS):15Feb80-163
    J. Mann, 362:31Jan80-157
Jones, T.   Ghana's First Republic 1960-
    1966.
    C. Clapham, 69:Vol148#3-303
Jones, T.B. and B.D. Nicol.   Neo-Classical
    Dramatic Criticism 1560-1770.*
    W.D. Howarth, 208(FS):Vol33Pt2-964
Jones, W.E. and J. Laver, eds.   Phonetics
    in Linguistics.*
    D. Gibbon, 260(IF):Band83-374
Jones, W.J.   A Lexicon of French Borrow-
    ings in the German Vocabulary (1575-
    1648).
    J.R. Wilkie, 402(MLR):Jan79-229
Jong, E.   At the Edge of the Body.*
    639(VQR):Summer79-107
Jong, E.   Fanny.
    A. Broyard, 441:28Aug80-C17
    A. Friedman, 441:17Aug80-1
    C. James, 453(NYRB):6Nov80-25
    P. Kemp, 362:30Oct80-588
    442(NY):13Oct80-191
de Jong, J.W.   A Brief History of Buddhist
    Studies in Europe and America.
    E. Bender, 318(JAOS):Jul-Sep78-350
de Jonge, A.   Fire and Water.*
    R. Wortman, 441:29Jun80-11
de Jonge, P.   Philological and Historical
    Commentary on Ammianus Marcellinus
    XVII.*
    R. Browning, 123:Vol29No2-235
    R.J. Penella, 124:Sep79-55
Jonson, B.   Bartholmew Fair.*   (G.R.
    Hibbard, ed)
    F.D. Hoeniger, 178:Fall79-364
    R.V. Holdsworth, 541(RES):Aug79-344
    E.M. Waith, 677(YES):Vol9-328
Jonson, B.   The Staple of News.*   (D.R.
    Kifer, ed)
    L.W. Conolly, 447(N&Q):Feb78-79
    A.B. Kernan, 677(YES):Vol9-329
Jonson, B.   Volpone, or The Fox.*   (J.W.
    Creaser, ed)
    D. Fuller, 541(RES):Aug79-343
Jonsson, B.R., S. Solheim and E. Danielson,
    with others, eds.   The Types of the
    Scandinavian Medieval Ballad.
    A. Gardner-Medwin and D.M. Mennie,
    562(Scan):May79-61
    J. Harris, 589:Oct79-819
Jonsson, I., ed.   Vad händer med svenska
    språket?
    N. Hasselmo, 563(SS):Winter79-58
Jordan, D.A.   The Northern Expedition.*
    A.J. Nathan, 318(JAOS):Jul-Sep78-289
Jordan, D.P.   The King's Trial.*
    C. Lucas, 617(TLS):13Jun80-679
Jordan, G.   Home Below Hell's Canyon.
    A. Ronald, 649(WAL):Summer79-171
Jordan, J.   Things That I Do in the Dark.
    639(VQR):Winter78-10
Jordan, N.   The Past.
    J. Mellors, 362:6Nov80-623

Jordan, R.   Nocturne.
    R. Howat, 415:Jun79-487
    A. Walker, 410(M&L):Jul79-361
Jordan, T.G.   Texas Log Buildings.*
    H.W. Marshall, 650(WF):Jan79-60
    A. Nichols, 576:Dec78-312
Jorden, E.H. and H.I. Chaplin.   Reading
    Japanese.
    P.T. Sato, 318(JAOS):Jul-Sep78-306
Jørgensen, A., ed.   Henrich Steffens — en
    mosaik.
    N. Ingwersen, 562(Scan):May79-65
    H. Moenkemeyer, 563(SS):Winter79-74
Jørgensen, B.H.   Maskinen, det heroiske og
    det gotiske — om Johs. V. Jensen, Sophus
    Claussen og århundredeskifet.
    N. Ingwersen, 562(Scan):Nov78-173
Jorgensen, J.   The Graying of America.
    S. Jacoby, 441:26Oct80-15
Jørgensen, S-A.   Johann Georg Hamann.
    J.E. Fletcher, 67:May79-139
Joseph, J.   The Thinking Heart.*
    J. Cassidy, 493:Dec79-60
    A. Cluysenaar, 565:Vol120#3-68
Joseph, M.K.   Inscription on a Paper Dart.
    R. Jackaman, 368:Dec74-353
Josephs, A. and J. Caballero - see Lorca,
    F.G.
Josephs, R.   Early Disorder.
    A. Broyard, 441:9May80-C25
Joset, J. - see under López de Ayala, P.
Joshi, H. and V.   Surplus Labour and the
    City.
    R. Vanneman, 293(JASt):Feb79-402
Joshi, S.D. and J.A.F. Roodbergen - see
    "Patañjali's Vyākaraṇa-Mahābhāṣya:
    Kārakāhnika (P. 1.4.23-1.4.55)"
Josipovici, G.   The Echo Chamber.
    P. Lewis, 617(TLS):21Mar80-312
    J. Naughton, 362:27Mar80-419
Jossel, L. and G. Peterzell.   The Gour-
    met's Toolbox.
    W. and C. Cowen, 639(VQR):Spring78-78
Jouad, H. and B. Lortat-Jacob.   La Saison
    des fêtes dans une vallée du Haut-Atlas.
    J. Duvignaud, 450(NRF):Jul79-124
    P.D. Schuyler, 187:Sep80-563
Jouanny, R.A. - see Zola, É.
Jouhandeau, M.   Nunc dimittis.
    A. Serre, 450(NRF):Apr79-106
Joukovsky, F.   Paysages de la Renaissance.
    P. Sharratt, 208(FS):Vol33Pt2-660
Joukovsky, F. - see Forcadel, E.
Jounel, P.   Le Culte des saints dans les
    basiliques du Latran et du Vatican au
    douzième siècle.
    P.J. Geary, 589:Jan79-158
Jourdain, P. and B. Russell.   Dear Russell
    — Dear Jourdain.   (I. Grattan-Guinness,
    ed)
    G.T. Kneebone, 316:Jun79-277
    R.M. Sainsbury, 393(Mind):Oct79-604
"The Journey to the West."*   (Vol 1)   (A.C.
    Yu, ed and trans)
    F. Wakeman, Jr., 453(NYRB):29May80-28

"The Journey to the West." (Vol 2) (A.C. Yu, ed and trans)
F. Wakeman, Jr., 453(NYRB):29May80-28
639(VQR):Spring79-60
Jousse, M. L'Anthropologie du geste.
H. Godin, 208(FS):Vol33Pt2-984
Joutard, P., ed. Les Camisards.
J. Lough, 208(FS):Vol33Pt2-796
Jovicevich, A. Jean-François de La Harpe, adepte et renégat des lumières.
W.H. Barber, 208(FS):Jul79-349
Joy, E.T. English Furniture 1800-1851.*
N. Goodison, 90:Apr79-269
Joyce, J. James Joyce in Padua.* (L. Berrone, ed and trans)
S. Helmling, 249(HudR):Spring79-155
Joyce, J. Joyce's Notes and Early Drafts for "Ulysses."* (P.F. Herring, ed)
P. Gaskell, 617(TLS):7Mar80-274
S.A. Henke, 639(VQR):Winter79-181
R.M. Kain, 395(MFS):Winter78/79-568
M. Schwartzman, 301(JEGP):Jan79-144
Joyce, J. Scritti Italiani. (G. Corsini and G. Melchiori, eds)
P.N. Furbank, 617(TLS):25Jan80-84
Joynt, C.B. and P.F. Corbett. Theory and Reality in World Politics.
H. Bull, 617(TLS):4Jan80-20
Judd, D. Prince Philip.
A. Howard, 362:11Dec80-798
Judd, J., ed. Van Cortlandt Family Papers. (Vols 1-3)
A.P. Kenney, 656(WMQ):Oct79-648
Judkins, W. Fluctuant Representation in Synthetic Cubism.
C.R. Baldwin, 54:Mar78-187
Judson, H.F. The Search for Solutions.
S.J. Gould, 441:18May80-7
442(NY):19May80-163
Judson, J.R. and C. van de Velde. Book Illustrations and Title-Pages.
J.S. Held, 39:Sep79-234
Judy, S.N. The ABCs of Literacy.
J. Burke, 231:Mar80-93
Juergens, T. Gesellschaftskritische Aspekte in Joseph Roths Romanen.
J. Koppensteiner, 406:Summer79-208
Juerrs, F. Zum Erkenntnisproblem bei den frühgriechischen Denkern.
C. Mugler, 555:Vol52fasc1-150
Juhász, G. Hungarian Foreign Policy 1919-1945.
A. Sked, 617(TLS):22Aug80-939
Juhász, J. Probleme der Interferenz.
G.F. Meier, 682(ZPSK):Band31Heft6-643
Juhos, B. Selected Papers on Epistemology and Physics. (G. Frey, ed)
E.M.M., 543:Mar79-552
Juin, H. - see Comte de Lautréamont
Julian of Norwich. Julian of Norwich's Revelations of Divine Love. (F. Beer, ed)
D. Speed, 67:May79-87
E.G. Stanley, 447(N&Q):Dec78-543
Juliet, C. Journal I.
P. Dulac, 450(NRF):May79-116
E. Hagbarth, 98:Oct78-999

Juliet, C. Journal II.
P. Dulac, 450(NRF):May79-116
Jullian, P. The Orientalists.
B.D.H. Miller, 463:Winter78/79-464
Jullian, P. The Symbolists. (2nd ed)
529(QQ):Spring79-181
Jullian, P. and J. Phillips. The Other Woman.
639(VQR):Winter78-25
Jullien de Pommerol, M-H. Sources de l'histoire des universités françaises au Moyen-Age: Université d'Orléans.
F.L. Cheyette, 589:Oct79-821
Jung, U. Die Rezeption der Kunst Richard Wagners in Italien.
E. Koppen, 52:Band13Heft1-103
Jünger, E. Le Coeur aventureux.
G. Quinsat, 450(NRF):Apr79-149
Jungraithmayr, H. and W.J.G. Möhlig. Einführung in die Hausa-Sprache.*
A.H.M. Kirk-Greene, 69:Vol148#3-298
Junker, B., P. Gilg and R. Reich, eds. Geschichte und politische Wissenschaft.
J. Steinberg, 182:Vol31#21/22-826
Junkins, D. Crossing by Ferry.
R. De Mott, 651(WHR):Spring79-177
P. Ramsey, 569(SR):Fall79-686
Junoy García-Viedma, J.M. La "fe racional" y el "saber metafísico" en la filosofía crítica de Kant.
F. Duque Pajuelo, 342:Band69Heft2-216
Jupé, W. Die "List" im Tristanroman Gottfrieds von Strassburg.
T. Ehlert, 680(ZDP):Band97Heft3-453
D.H. Green, 402(MLR):Jan79-235
C.S. Jaeger, 406:Spring79-62
Jurgela, C. Lithuania.
A. Katz, 497(PolR):Vol123#3-122
Jurgensen, M., ed. Frisch.*
H.F. Pfanner, 406:Spring79-91
G.F. Probst, 133:Band12Heft4-382
M.E. Stewart, 402(MLR):Apr79-505
Justice, D. Selected Poems.
C. Molesworth, 441:9Mar80-8
A. Young, 617(TLS):30May80-620
V. Young, 472:Fall/Winter79-227
Jute, A. Reverse Negative.*
M. Laski, 362:17Apr80-514
Juul, A. On Concord of Number in Modern English.
A.R. Tellier, 189(EA):Jan-Mar78-77
H. Ulherr, 38:Band96Heft1/2-187

Kabat, G.C. Ideology and Imagination.
V. Babenko, 550(RusR):Jul79-396
D. Matual, 268(IFR):Winter80-64
V. Terras, 574(SEEJ):Winter79-528
G. Woodcock, 569(SR):Summer79-480
Kabronsky, V., ed. Nepodc enzurnaja russkaja častuška.
J.S. Elliott, 399(MLJ):Nov79-397
Kac, M.B. Corepresentation of Grammatical Structure.
R. Hudson, 350:Sep79-670
G. Mallinson, 67:Nov79-382

Kachru, B.B., ed. Dimensions of Bilingualism.
R.B. Kaplan, 350:Jun79-493
Kaczyński, T. Gespräche mit Witold Lutosławski.
N. Osborne, 410(M&L):Apr79-218
Kádár, Z. Survivals of Greek Zoological Illuminations in Byzantine Manuscripts.*
H. Buchthal, 90:Sep79-593
Kaden, K. Die wichtigsten Transkriptionssysteme für die chinesische Sprache.
G. Richter, 682(ZPSK):Band31Heft6-660
Kadir, D. Juan Carlos Onetti.
L.E. Ben-Ur, 238:Mar79-190
J.M. Lipski, 395(MFS):Winter78/79-663
Kadish, D.Y. Practices of the New Novel in Claude Simon's "L'Herbe" and "La Route des Flandres."
F.S. Heck, 268(IFR):Summer80-154
Kael, P. When the Lights Go Down.
R. Adler, 453(NYRB):14Aug80-26
M. Wood, 441:6Apr80-3
Kaeppler, A.L. "Artificial Curiosities."
G.R. Ellis, 2(AfrA):Nov78-102
Kaes, A. Expressionismus in Amerika.*
U. Weisstein, 131(CL):Winter79-82
Kaes, A. Kino-Debatte.
A. Haag, 221(GQ):Mar79-287
M. Morley, 67:May79-165
Kaes, R. and others. Désir de former et formation du savoir.
L. Millet, 192(EP):Jul-Sep79-366
Kafka, F. Letters to Friends, Family and Editors.* (R. and C. Winston, trans)
C.A.M. Noble, 529(QQ):Winter79/80-664
Kafka, F. Oeuvres complètes.* (Vol 1) (A. Vialatte, trans; C. David, ed)
I.C. Henel, 406:Winter79-456
A. Nivelle, 556(RLV):1978/1-78
Kaftal, G. Iconography of the Saints in the Painting of North East Italy.
F. Russell, 39:Jun79-490
Kagan-Kans, E. Hamlet and Don Quixote.*
M. Ledkovsky, 550(RusR):Apr79-258
Kaganoff, B.C. A Dictionary of Jewish Names and their History.
E.C. Smith, 424:Jun78-205
Kahan, G. Jacques Callot.
J. Steer, 610:Oct78-67
Kahl, D. Die Funktionen des Rollenspiels in den Dramen Anouilhs.
W.D. Howarth, 208(FS):Vol33Pt2-927
E. Rattunde, 430(NS):Oct78-489
Kahl-Pantis, B. Bauformen des bürgerlichen Trauerspiels.
R.R. Heitner, 221(GQ):Jan79-111
Kahn, C.H. The Art and Thought of Heraclitus.
M. Schofield, 617(TLS):15Feb80-186
Kahn, E.J., Jr. Far-Flung and Footloose.
W. Goodman, 441:13Jul80-15
R.F. Shepard, 441:19Jun80-C22
Kahn, H. and T. Pepper. The Japanese Challenge.*
T. Najita, 453(NYRB):21Feb80-33

Kahn, S.J. Mark Twain's Mysterious Stranger.*
R.B. Hauck, 395(MFS):Winter78/79-632
Kahr, M.M. Dutch Painting in the Seventeenth Century.
C. Brown, 39:Dec79-540
Kahr, M.M. Velázquez.*
J.F. Moffitt, 127:Spring79-213
Kahrmann, C., G. Reiss and M. Schluchter. Erzähltextanalyse.
R.F. Spiess, 556(RLV):1978/6-553
Kaimio, M. Characterization of Sound in Early Greek Literature.*
E.K. Borthwick, 303(JoHS):Vol99-186
S. Wiersma, 394:Vol132fasc3/4-382
Kainz, H.P. Hegel's Phenomenology.* (Pt 1)
O. Blanchette, 142:Sep-Dec78-389
J.L.M., 543:Sep78-142
Kaiser, G. Textauslegung und gesellschaftliche Selbstdeutung. (2nd ed)
E.R. Haymes, 221(GQ):Mar79-273
Kaiser, G. Wandrer und Idylle.
D. Barnouw, 406:Winter79-478
R. Böschenstein-Schäfer, 133:Band12-Heft1/2-162
D.G. Little, 402(MLR):Jul79-746
Kaiser, G.E., ed. Fiction, Form, Experience.*
L.E.O. Hartmann, 207(FR):Dec78-354
Kaiser, H. Studien zum deutschen Roman nach 1848.
N.A. Kaiser, 221(GQ):Jan79-129
Kakar, H.S. The Persistent Self.
S. Graver, 637(VS):Summer79-482
Kakar, S. The Inner World.
M.K. Kerr, 293(JASt):Aug79-795
Kalb, M. and T. Koppel. In the National Interest.
639(VQR):Summer78-93
Kaldor, M. The Disintegrating West.
639(VQR):Autumn79-144
Kālidāsa. Kālidāsa Granthāvalī. (R. Dvivedī, ed)
L. Rocher, 318(JAOS):Jul-Sep78-326
Kallen, L. C.B. Greenfield: The Tanglewood Murder.
N. Callendar, 441:19Oct80-41
R.F. Shepard, 441:12Aug80-C8
Kallmeyer, W. and others. Lektürekolleg zur Textlinguistik. (Vol 1)
K-E. Sommerfeldt, 682(ZPSK):Band31 Heft3-323
Kalman, R., ed. A Collection of Canadian Plays. (Vol 5)
T. Stephenson, 108:Summer79-114
Kalomiti, N. The War of Truth. (P. Doron, ed)
S.D. Breslauer, 589:Apr79-391
Kalstone, D. Five Temperaments.*
V. Bell, 569(SR):Spring79-308
C. Doyle, 529(QQ):Summer79-314
Kalvoda, J. Czechoslovakia's Role in Soviet Strategy.
J. Hajda, 550(RusR):Apr79-250
Z. Zeman, 575(SEER):Jul79-464

194

Kamenetzky, I., ed. Nationalism and Human Rights.*
  D.S.M. Williams, 575(SEER):Apr79-313
Kameneva, T.N. and A.A. Guseva. Ukrainskie knigi kirillovskoĭ pechati XVI-XVIII vv. Katalog izdaniĭ, khranyashchikhsya v Gosudarstvennoĭ biblioteke SSSR imeni V.I. Lenina. (Vol 1)
  354:Jun79-194
Kamerbeek, J.C. The Plays of Sophocles: Commentaries. (Pt 3)
  G.M. Kirkwood, 124:Feb80-316
  C. Segal, 487:Autumn79-269
Kaminsky, S.M. Coop.
  A. Broyard, 441:22Feb80-C26
  J. Maslin, 441:17Feb80-13
Kaminsky, S.M. Never Cross a Vampire.
  N. Callendar, 441:7Dec80-45
Kamm, L. The Object in Zola's Rougon-Macquart.
  J.D. Erickson, 399(MLJ):Mar79-141
Kamman, M. The Making of a Cook.
  W. and C. Cowen, 639(VQR):Spring78-71
Kammen, M., ed. The Past Before Us.
  G. Himmelfarb, 441:17Aug80-3
Kammen, M. A Season of Youth.*
  C.E. Clark, Jr., 109:Summer80-217
  J.K. Nelson, 579(SAQ):Autumn79-521
Kamp, R. Axiomatische Sprachtheorie.
  P. Janssen, 679:Band9Heft1-185
Kampits, P. - see Wiplinger, F.
Kan, A.S. Geschichte der skandinavischen Länder.
  S. Oakley, 562(Scan):Nov79-156
Kane, G. and E.T. Donaldson - see Langland, W.
Kanes, M. Balzac's Comedy of Words.*
  D. Adamson, 208(FS):Vol33Pt2-814
  G. Holoch, 546(RR):Mar79-189
Kanin, G. Moviola.*
  D. Wilson, 617(TLS):22Feb80-210
Kanin, G. Smash.
  N. Johnson, 441:23Nov80-14
Kaniuk, Y. Adam Resurrected.
  J. Kessler, 109:Summer80-198
Kannegiesser, H. Knowledge and Science.
  G. Priest, 479(PhQ):Oct79-366
Kannengiesser, C. - see Saint Athanasius
Kannenstine, L.F. The Art of Djuna Barnes.*
  M.J. Hoffman, 395(MFS):Summer78-267
Kanner, I.Z., ed. Jüdische Märchen.
  H-J. Uther, 196:Band19Heft1/2-126
Kanngiesser, S. Aspekte der synchronen und diachronen Linguistik.
  K. Reichl, 38:Band96Heft1/2-159
Kant, I. Träume eines Geistersehers, erläutert durch Träume der Metaphysik. (R. Malter, ed) Kritik der reinen Vernunft. (I. Heidemann, ed) Kritik der praktischen Vernunft. (J. Kopper, ed)
  J. Kopper, 342:Band69Heft1-118
Kant, I. Was ist Aufklärung? (2nd ed) (J. Zehbe, ed)
  J. Kopper, 342:Band69Heft2-223

Kantor, M. and R.S. White, eds and trans. The Vita of Constantine and the Vita of Methodius.
  W.S. Kucharek and T.J. Drobena, 574(SEEJ):Spring79-126
  A. Marianski, 575(SEER):Jan79-150
Kanzog, K. - see von Kleist, H.
Kapelle, W.E. The Norman Conquest of the North.
  D.J.A. Matthew, 617(TLS):15Aug80-920
Kaplan, C., ed. Salt and Bitter and Good.
  639(VQR):Winter78-13
Kaplan, E.K. Michelet's Poetic Vision.*
  B.F. Bart, 593:Summer79-189
  F.P. Bowman, 125:Winter79-315
  L. Orr, 207(FR):Dec78-352
  J.S.P., 191(ELN):Sep78(supp)-110
Kaplan, F. Dickens and Mesmerism.*
  M. Steig, 445(NCF):Mar79-505
Kaplan, F. La Vérité et ses figures.
  M. Adam, 542:Oct-Dec78-513
  J.B. Ayoub, 154:Sep78-554
  J. Lefranc, 192(EP):Oct-Dec79-494
Kaplan, F.L. Winter into Spring.
  639(VQR):Autumn78-147
Kaplan, F.M., J.M. Sobin and S. Andors. Encyclopedia of China Today.
  42(AR):Summer79-380
Kaplan, J. O My America!
  A. Adams, 441:13Jan80-14
  A. Broyard, 441:12Jan80-17
  442(NY):18Feb80-131
Kaplan, J. Walt Whitman.
  C. Lehmann-Haupt, 441:5Nov80-C30
  H. Vendler, 441:9Nov80-1
  61:Nov80-96
Kaplow, J. - see Hansen, T.L., E.J. Wilkins and J.G. Enos
Kapouya, E. and K. Tompkins - see Kropotkin, P.A.
Kappler, A. Der literarische Vergleich.
  U. Weisstein, 52:Band13Heft1-72
Karageorghis, V. Two Cypriote Sanctuaries of the End of the Cypro-Archaic Period.
  V. Wilson, 303(JoHS):Vol99-206
Karan, P.P. The Changing Face of Tibet.
  M.C. Goldstein, 293(JASt):Nov78-144
  E. Sperling, 318(JAOS):Jul-Sep78-317
Karch, D. Mannheim: Umgangssprache.
  I. Guentherodt, 685(ZDL):1/1979-97
Kardell, M.M. - see Hogue, H.
Karénine, V. Graffitis pour les murs de demain.
  F.J. Greene, 207(FR):Feb79-514
Karger, I. Heinrich Heine.
  J.L.S., 191(ELN):Sep78(supp)-160
Kargon, R.H. Science in Victorian Manchester.
  R.N. Soffer, 637(VS):Autumn78-112
Karker, A., ed. Jon Praest. Presbyter Johannes' Brev til Emanuel Komnenos.
  M.C. Seymour, 382(MAE):1979/1-150
Karl, F.R. Joseph Conrad.*
  P. Conrad, 31(ASch):Spring80-271
  M. Lebowitz, 639(VQR):Summer79-558
  W.H. Pritchard, 249(HudR):Winter79/80-585

Karlinger, F. Märchen aus Portugal.
H-J. Uther, 196:Band19Heft1/2-126
Karlinsky, S. - see Nabokov, V. and E.
Wilson
Karlinsky, S. and A. Appel, Jr., eds.
The Bitter Air of Exile.
L. Dienes, 574(SEEJ):Winter79-536
Karlinsky, S. and M.H. Heim - see Chekhov,
A.
Karlstrom, P. Louis Michel Eilshemius.
A. Frankenstein, 55:Mar79-30
Karnes, T.L. Tropical Enterprise.
K.V. Finney, 263(RIB):Vol29No3/4-366
Karpen, U., ed. Verfassungsrechtliche
Fragen des Hochschulzuganges.
P. Malanczuk, 182:Vol131#20-724
Karslake, B. 1940: The Last Act.
B. Bond, 617(TLS):4Jan80-16
Kartomi, M. - see Goldsworthy, D., C. Falk
and B. Kornhauser
Kartschoke, D. Altdeutsche Bibeldichtung.
E. Wimmer, 196:Band19Heft1/2-159
Kartschoke, D. Bibeldichtung.
G. Vollmann-Profe and B.K. Vollmann,
224(GRM):Band28Heft4-477
E. Wimmer, 196:Band19Heft1/2-158
Karttunen, F. and J. Lockhart. Nahuatl in
the Middle Years.
U. Canger, 350:Mar79-233
Kasack, W. Die Akademie der Wissenschaf-
ten der UdSSR. (3rd ed)
M. McCauley, 575(SEER):Jul79-476
Kasack, W. Lexikon der russischen Litera-
tur ab 1917.
W. Gesemann, 52:Band13Heft3-327
B. Lewis and M. Ulman, 575(SEER):
Jul79-440
E. Reissner, 688(ZSP):Band40Heft1-223
Kaschewski, R. and P. Tsering. Das Leben
der Himmelsfee 'Gro-ba bzaṅ-mo.
F.A. Bischoff, 318(JAOS):Jul-Sep78-318
Kasdorff, H. Ludwig Klages im Widerstreit
der Meinungen.
H. Schmitz, 489(PJGG):Band86Heft2-439
Kaser, M. Über Verbotsgesetze und verbots-
widrige Geschäfte im römischen Recht.
J. Crook, 313:Vol69-201
Kasetsiri, C. The Rise of Ayudhya.
F. Reynolds, 293(JASt):Nov78-216
Kasfir, N. The Shrinking Political Arena.
M.M. Kenig, 69:Vol48#4-417
Kasher, A., ed. Language in Focus.*
D.C. Ferris, 307:Apr79-48
Al-Kasimi, A.M. Linguistics and Bilingual
Dictionaries.*
C. Smith, 402(MLR):Jul79-648
Kasparek, J.L. Molière's "Tartuffe" and
the Traditions of Roman Satire.
N. Aronson, 399(MLJ):Dec79-466
Kass, J.M. Robert Altman.
T. Curran, 200:Apr79-239
Kassel, R. - see Aristotle
Kassier, T.L. The Truth Disguised.*
L. Close, 402(MLR):Jul79-729
Kassler, J.C. The Science of Music in
Britain, 1714-1830.
617(TLS):9May80-533

Kastor, F.S. Giles and Phineas Fletcher.
P.J. Klemp, 568(SCN):Spring-Summer79-
18
Kastrup, A. and N.W. Olsson, eds. Part-
ners in Progress.
M. Schiff, 563(SS):Winter79-67
Kathrithamby-Wells, J. The British West
Sumatran Presidency, 1760-1785.
Akira Oki, 302:Vol16#1and2-133
Katsenelinboigen, A. Studies in Soviet
Economic Planning.
P. Desai, 550(RusR):Jul79-377
Katsh, A.I. The Biblical Heritage of
American Democracy.*
E.M. Meyers, 318(JAOS):Jul-Sep78-345
Katsouris, A.G. Linguistic and Stylistic
Characterization.
E. Fantham, 487:Spring79-82
F.H. Sandbach, 303(JoHS):Vol99-181
Katsouris, A.G. Tragic Patterns in
Menander.*
R.L. Hunter, 303(JoHS):Vol99-180
Katz, E. The International Film Encyclo-
paedia.
G. Millar, 362:17Jul80-87
Katz, E. and G. Wedell. Broadcasting in
the Third World.
J.A. Lent, 293(JASt):Feb79-322
Katz, J.J. Propositional Structure and
Illocutionary Force.*
J.R. Cameron, 518:Oct79-142
G. Gazdar, 307:Oct79-122
D. Wilson, 393(Mind):Jul79-461
Katz, R. Days of Wrath.
F. Lewis, 441:18May80-12
C. Moorehead, 617(TLS):11Jul80-777
Katz, S. Plastics.
G. Darley, 46:Jul79-66
Katz, S.T. Jewish Ideas and Concepts.
H.J. Fields, 529(QQ):Summer79-357
Katz, S.T., ed. Mysticism and Philosophi-
cal Analysis.
T. McPherson, 483:Apr79-255
Katzman, D.M. Seven Days a Week.
S.J. Kleinberg, 658:Winter79-407
A.F. Scott, 579(SAQ):Summer79-410
639(VQR):Spring79-72
Kau, E. Den ewaldske tekst mellem himmel
og jord.
R.B. Møller, 562(Scan):Nov79-160
Kauffmann, S. Albums of Early Life.
C. Lehmann-Haupt, 441:10Oct80-C33
P. Zweig, 441:16Nov80-9
Kauffmann, S. Before My Eyes.
R. Asahina, 441:6Jul80-4
Kaufman, H. Red Tape.
H. Rank, 128(CE):Apr79-950
Kaufmann, A. Introduction à la Théorie
des sous-ensembles flous. (2nd ed) (Vol
1)
H. Sinaceur, 98:May78-512
Kaufmann, E. and H. Erwartung und Angebot.
H. Gumtau, 406:Spring79-100
Kaufmann, F. Der Fehler im Französischun-
terricht.*
K.E.M. George, 208(FS):Vol33Pt2-1058

Kaufmann, F. The Infinite in Mathematics.
J. Benardete, 543:Jun79-761
Kaufmann-Heinimann, A. Augst und das
Gebiet der Colonia Augusta Raurica.
S. Boucher, 182:Vol31#1/2-49
Kavan, A. Asylum Piece.
P-L. Adams, 61:Aug80-85
J.C. Oates, 441:1Jun80-14
Kavan, A. Sleep Has His House.
J.C. Oates, 441:1Jun80-14
442(NY):5May80-173
Kavanagh, D. Duffy.
M. Laski, 362:13Nov80-665
P. Lewis, 617(TLS):4Jul80-749
Kavanagh, J.F. and J.E. Cutting, eds. The
Role of Speech in Language.
N.V. Smith, 215(GL):Spring78-28
W.S-Y. Wang, 350:Dec79-941
Kavanagh, P. Sacred Keeper.
J. McNamara, 617(TLS):13Jun80-681
Kavanagh, P.J. Life Before Death.*
C. Hope, 364:Nov79-86
E. Longley, 617(TLS):18Jan80-64
Kawamura, L.S. and K. Scott, eds. Bud-
dhist Thought and Asian Civilization.
F.E. Reynolds, 302:Vol16#1and2-114
Kawin, B.F. Faulkner and Film.
M.A. Haynes, 395(MFS):Winter78/79-637
Kawin, B.F. Mindscreen.
J.A. Gomez, 141:Summer79-282
P. Harcourt, 255(HAB):Summer79-209
J. Monaco, 18:Apr79-72
J.M. Purcell, 290(JAAC):Spring80-347
Kay, D., ed. "A Provision of Human
Nature."*
T. Stumpf, 577(SHR):Summer79-253
Kaye, M.M. The Far Pavilions.
J. Mellors, 364:Jul79-86
Kaye, P.J., ed. National Playwrights
Directory.
M. Walker, 610:Feb79-149
Kayne, R.S. French Syntax.*
M. Ronat, 353:Apr78-81
Kazantzakis, N. Serpent and Lily.
P. Mackridge, 617(TLS):4Jul80-749
Kazin, A. New York Jew.*
M. Birnbaum, 396(ModA):Summer79-329
M. Ellmann, 569(SR):Spring79-332
M. Krupnick, 560:Spring-Summer79-197
639(VQR):Autumn78-142
Kazmer, D.R. and V. Russian Economic
History.
O. Crisp, 575(SEER):Jan79-147
Keach, W. Elizabethan Erotic Narratives.*
A.R. Bowers, 502(PrS):Summer78-200
R.T. Eriksen, 179(ES):Apr79-231
R. Gill, 541(RES):Feb79-79
R.S. White, 447(N&Q):Oct78-463
Kealey, G.S. Toronto Workers Respond to
Industrial Capitalism 1867-1892.
P. Craven, 99:Dec80/Jan81-23
Kealey, L., ed. A Not Unreasonable Claim.
M. Kinnear, 99:Aug80-35
Kearney, C. The Writings of Brendan Behan.
M.J. and J.J. Egan, 395(MFS):
Winter78/79-594
S. Poger, 174(Éire):Spring79-149

Keat, R. and J. Urry. Social Theory as
Science.
I.C. Jarvie, 84:Mar79-100
T.S. Torrance, 518:May79-75
Keating, D. In Dark Places.
D. Barbour, 150(DR):Spring79-154
Keating, H.R.F. The Murder of the Mahara-
jah.
T.J. Binyon, 617(TLS):18Apr80-450
M. Laski, 362:20Mar80-381
Keating, M. and D. Bleiman. Labour and
Scottish Nationalism.
C. Harvie, 617(TLS):28Mar80-373
Keating, P., ed. Into Unknown England
1866-1913.
J. Lucas, 402(MLR):Apr79-434
Keating, P. - see Gaskell, E.
Keats, J. The Poems of John Keats. (J.
Stillinger, ed)
T.L. Ashton, 301(JEGP):Jul79-447
M. Dodsworth, 175:Summer79-199
K. Hanley, 148:Summer79-88
S.M. Sperry, 661(WC):Summer79-305
529(QQ):Autumn79-556
Kedrov, B. La classification des sciences.
(Vol 1)
J-M. Gabaude, 542:Apr-Jun79-267
Kee, R. Ireland.
S. Jacobson, 362:11Dec80-799
Keeble, J. Yellowfish.
E. White, 441:10Feb80-15
442(NY):28Apr80-142
Keech, S. Ciphered.
N. Callendar, 441:20Apr80-25
J. Leonard, 441:7Mar80-C25
Keegan, J., ed. World Armies.
B. Bond, 617(TLS):29Feb80-245
Keeler, M.F., M.J. Cole and W.B. Bidwell,
eds. Commons Debates, 1628. (Vol 4)
C. Roberts, 656(WMQ):Apr79-306
Keenan, B. The Dewey Experiment in China.
L.A. Schneider, 293(JASt):Feb79-336
Keenan, E.L., ed. Formal Semantics of
Natural Language.*
R.D. Eagleson, 67:May79-176
J.A. Edmondson, 361:Aug78-355
D. Holdcroft, 84:Dec79-411
L. Humberstone, 63:Jun79-171
Keenan, J.G. and J.C. Shelton, eds and
trans. The Tebtunis Papyri.* (Vol 4)
D.J. Crawford, 303(JoHS):Vol99-221
Keene, D. Surviving.
D. Davis, 362:28Aug80-277
J. Symons, 617(TLS):23May80-586
Keene, D. World Within Walls.
R.W. Leutner, 244(HJAS):Jun78-225
E. Miner, 131(CL):Spring79-194
Keene, T. and B. Haynes. Spyship.
N. Callendar, 441:25May80-13
Keenleyside, T.A. The Common Touch.*
M. Northey, 168(ECW):Summer78-135
Keep, J.L.H. The Debate on Soviet Power.
A. Brown, 617(TLS):25Jan80-95
Keep, J.L.H. The Russian Revolution.*
R. Stites, 104(CASS):Fall78-435

197

Keesing, N. Hails and Farewells and Other Poems.
  S.E. Lee, 581:Dec79-432
Kehren, L. Tamerlan.
  J. Richard, 182:Vol31#20-765
Keil, C. Tiv Song.
  K.A. Gourlay, 187:Jan80-119
Kein, P.K. Der ältere Beatus-Kodex Vitr. 14-1 der Biblioteca Nacional zu Madrid.
  A. Rodríguez G. de Ceballos, 48:Apr-Jun78-91
Keitel, W. and H. Nürnberger - see Fontane, T.
Kekes, J. A Justification of Rationality.*
  W.J. Edgar, 321:Spring78-75
  M. Hollis, 488:Mar79-115
  S.L. Nathanson, 258:Jun79-227
Kelder, D.M. Aspects of "Official" Painting and Philosophic Art 1789-1799.
  B. Sandström, 341:1978/2-82
Kelen, S.K. The Gods Ash Their Cigarettes.
  C. Pollnitz, 581:Dec79-462
Kelham, R. A Dictionary of the Norman or Old French Language [and] The Laws of William the Conqueror.
  M. Jones, 325:Oct79-235
Kell, R. Humours.
  L. Sail, 493:Dec79-66
Keller, E. Kritische Intelligenz.*
  M.H., 191(ELN):Sep78(supp)-135
Keller, G.D. The Significance and Impact of Gregorio Marañón.*
  C.A. Longhurst, 86(BHS):Oct79-347
Keller, G.D., N.A. Sebastiani and F. Jiménez. Spanish Here and Now.
  J.T. Medina, 238:Mar79-194
Keller, H.H. A German Word Family Dictionary.
  E.S. Firchow, 221(GQ):Nov79-529
  W. Fleischhauer, 301(JEGP):Oct79-591
Keller, K. The Only Kangaroo Among the Beauty.
  W. Martin, 165(EAL):Fall80-194
Keller, L. Palingène — Ronsard — Du Bartas.
  T.C. Cave, 208(FS):Vol33Pt2-641
Keller, R.E. Das Oratorium von San Giovanni Decollato in Rom.
  M. Huggler, 182:Vol31#19-682
  L.O. Larsson, 341:1978/2-76
  L.W. Partridge, 54:Mar78-171
Keller, W. Goethes dichterische Bildlichkeit.
  D. Hochstätter, 657(WW):Mar-Apr78-134
Kelley, C.F. Meister Eckhart on Divine Knowledge.
  R. Kieckhefer, 589:Jan79-160
Kelley, D., ed. Baudelaire: Salon de 1846.*
  J. Newton, 402(MLR):Apr79-465
de Kelley, E.N. La poesía metafísica de Quevedo.
  J. Victorio, 556(RLV):1978/5-463
Kelley, J.H. Yaqui Women.
  P. Wild, 50(ArQ):Summer79-191

Kelley, P. and R. Hudson, comps. The Brownings' Correspondence: A Checklist.
  E.C. McAleer, 636(VP):Autumn78-290
Kelling, G.W. Language.
  M.M. Bryant, 660(Word):Dec78-269
Kelling, H-W. The Idolatry of Poetic Genius in German Goethe Criticism.
  D. Hochstätter, 657(WW):Mar-Apr78-134
Kellner, P. and Lord Crowther-Hunt. The Civil Servants.
  J. Grigg, 362:5Jun80-725
  E. Roll, 617(TLS):18Jul80-817
Kellnhauser, J.T. White Silk and Cobras.
  G. Hamel, 198:Winter80-139
Kelly, A.A. Liam O'Flaherty the Storyteller.
  G. O'Brien, 402(MLR):Apr79-443
  J.W. Weaver, 305(JIL):May78-182
Kelly, D. Chrétien de Troyes.
  C.W. Aspland, 67:May79-120
  T. Hunt, 402(MLR):Apr79-446
  D.J. Shirt, 208(FS):Vol33Pt2-537
  E.P. Wisotzka, 207(FR):Mar79-634
  205(FMLS):Apr78-187
Kelly, D. Medieval Imagination.
  L.W. Patterson, 400(MLN):Dec79-1237
  A.R. Press, 208(FS):Oct79-432
Kelly, G. The English Jacobin Novel, 1780-1805.*
  P. Faulkner, 402(MLR):Apr79-416
  M.E. Novak, 445(NCF):Sep78-248
  K. Williamson, 447(N&Q):Jun78-255
Kelly, G. - see Wollstonecraft, M.
Kelly, G.A. Hegel's Retreat from Eleusis.
  J.P.S., 543:Dec78-363
  P.G. Stillman, 125:Spring79-455
Kelly, G.P. From Vietnam to America.
  E.J. Keyes, 293(JASt):May79-624
Kelly, H.A. The Matrimonial Trials of Henry VIII.
  M.J. Havran, 377:Mar79-58
  M.M. Sheehan, 539:Vol4No1-105
Kelly, J.B. Arabia, the Gulf and the West.
  R. Graham, 453(NYRB):23Oct80-26
  P.A. Iseman, 441:14Sep80-14
  D.C. Watt, 617(TLS):18Jul80-803
  442(NY):15Sep80-190
Kelly, J.R. Pedro Prado.
  M.A. Salgado, 241:Sep79-99
Kelly, L. The Kemble Era.
  P-L. Adams, 61:Jun80-94
  W. Goodman, 441:11May80-16
  J. Treglown, 617(TLS):25Apr80-464
Kelly, L. Lermontov.
  D. Rayfield, 575(SEER):Jan79-108
Kelly, P. Irish Family Names.
  K.B. Harder, 424:Dec77-237
Kelly, T. A History of Argos to 500 B.C.*
  P. Cartledge, 123:Vol29No1-103
  R.W., 555:Vol52fasc2-352
Kelly, T.E. Le Haut Livre du Graal: Perlesvaus.
  D.D.R. Owen, 208(FS):Vol33Pt2-557
  T. Scully, 546(RR):Mar79-185
Kelner, J. and J. Munves. The Kent State Coverup.
  W. Goodman, 441:11May80-16

Kemelman, H. Thursday the Rabbi Walked Out.
M.J. King, 42(AR):Winter79-110
Kemp, E.F. Manuscript Solicitation for Libraries, Special Collections, Museums, and Archives.
D.H. Hoober, 14:Oct79-470
van der Kemp, G. Versailles.*
B. Scott, 39:Jun79-490
Kemp, P., ed. West Coast Works.
M. Darling, 102(CanL):Autumn79-91
Kempe-Oettinger, C. Rudolf Kempe.
E. Forbes, 415:Aug79-653
Kemper, A. Presentation Drawings by American Architects.
L.B. Anderson, 576:Dec78-313
Kempson, R.M. Presupposition and the Delimitation of Semantics.*
J.L. Subbiondo, 320(CJL):Spring-Fall78-170
Kempson, R.M. Semantic Theory.*
T. Baldwin, 479(PhQ):Jan79-90
C.H. Brown, 355(LSoc):Aug78-260
J.L., 543:Sep78-143
Kench, A.B. Two Plays for Students of English.
A. Michiels, 556(RLV):1978/2-174
Kendall, R.T. Calvin and English Calvinism to 1649.
P. Collinson, 617(TLS):16May80-561
Kendig, F. and R. Hutton. Life-Spans.
R.A. Sokolov, 441:22Jun80-15
Kendle, J. John Bracken.
A. Mills, 99:Apr80-40
Keneally, T. Confederates.*
J. Burke, 441:5Oct80-3
442(NY):20Oct80-207
Keneally, T. Passenger.*
C.C. Park, 249(HudR):Winter79/80-573
Kenez, P. Civil War in South Russia, 1919-1920.
G. Brinkley, 550(RusR):Jan79-95
A. Brown, 617(TLS):25Jan80-95
Kenin, R. Return to Albion.*
639(VQR):Autumn79-130
Kenji Miyazawa. Spring and Asura.
W.E. Naff, 318(JAOS):Jul-Sep78-300
Kennan, G.F. The Decline of Bismarck's European Order.*
P-L. Adams, 61:Feb80-97
J. Joll, 453(NYRB):24Jan80-33
A.J.P. Taylor, 617(TLS):18Jan80-55
442(NY):21Jan80-130
Kennard, J.E. Victims of Convention.
N. Auerbach, 637(VS):Winter79-204
M. Vicinus, 445(NCF):Dec78-387
Kennedy, A. Meaning and Signs in Fiction.
T. Hawkes, 617(TLS):22Feb80-215
Kennedy, A.J. and K. Varty - see Christine de Pisan
Kennedy, A.K. Six Dramatists in Search of a Language.*
R.A. Cave, 447(N&Q):Aug78-381
Kennedy, G.A. Classical Rhetoric and its Christian and Secular Tradition from Ancient to Modern Times.
F.L. Moreland, 124:Mar80-372

Kennedy, L. The Death of the Tirpitz.
P-L. Adams, 61:Oct80-102
Kennedy, L. The Shrouding.
D.M.R. Bentley, 102(CanL):Winter78-90
Kennedy, L., ed. Wicked Beyond Belief.
T. Mangold, 362:10Jul80-52
Kennedy, R.S. Dreams in the Mirror.
P-L. Adams, 61:Apr80-128
A. Broyard, 441:18Jan80-C22
J. Kaplan, 441:13Jan80-7
W.H. Pritchard, 31(ASch):Autumn80-567
H. Vendler, 453(NYRB):7Feb80-10
Kennedy, S.E. If All We Did Was to Weep at Home.
V. Sapiro, 617(TLS):27Jun80-736
Kennedy, T. Durango.
J. Vernon, 651(WHR):Autumn79-340
Kennedy, W.J. Rhetorical Norms in Renaissance Literature.
T.O. Sloane, 141:Spring79-164
Kennelly, B. Islandman.
F. Kersnowski, 305(JIL):May78-179
Kenner, H. Joyce's Voices.*
S. Helmling, 249(HudR):Spring79-157
G. Thurley, 67:Nov79-328
295(JML):Vol7#4-748
639(VQR):Spring79-49
Kennick, W.E., ed. Art and Philosophy.
J.E. Bachrach, 290(JAAC):Fall79-87
Kenny, A. Aquinas.
C.H. Sisson, 617(TLS):9May80-531
Kenny, A. The Aristotelian Ethics.
S.R.L. Clark, 479(PhQ):Oct79-356
T.H. Irwin, 311(JP):Jun80-338
G.R. Lambert, 487:Winter79-374
Kenny, A. Aristotle's Theory of the Will.
D.W. Hamlyn, 617(TLS):4Jan80-19
T.H. Irwin, 311(JP):Jun80-338
Kenny, A. Freewill and Responsibility.
A. Quinton, 617(TLS):4Jan80-18
483:Apr79-268
Kenny, A. The God of the Philosophers.
S. Clark, 617(TLS):25Jan80-82
Kenstowicz, M.J. and C.W. Kisseberth. Topics in Phonological Theory.*
M.L. Clayton, 350:Jun79-408
Kent, C. Brains and Numbers.
T.R. Tholfsen, 637(VS):Spring79-354
Kent, D. The Rise of the Medici: Faction in Florence, 1426-1434.
W.L. Gundersheimer, 589:Oct79-822
Kent, J.P.C. Roman Coins.
J. Beckwith, 39:Apr79-328
Kent, V. A Thousand Days in the Attic.
L. Early, 168(ECW):Summer78-109
Kenyon, J. From Room to Room.
S. Baker, 385(MQR):Spring80-279
H. Carruth, 231:Jan80-77
639(VQR):Winter79-26
Kenyon, J.P. Revolution Principles.
C.A. Edie, 656(WMQ):Apr79-308
A. McInnes, 566:Autumn78-46
639(VQR):Spring78-61
Kenyon, K. The Bible and Recent Archaeology.
N. Hammond, 617(TLS):8Feb80-147

Kenyon, R.A. Existential Structures.
    P. Dubois, 542:Jul-Sep79-359
Ker, I. and T. Gornall - see Newman, J.H.
Ker, I.T. - see Newman, J.H.
Ker, N.R. Medieval Manuscripts in British
    Libraries.* (Vol 2)
    F.C. de Vries, 541(RES):Aug79-331
Kerber, L.K. Women of the Republic.
    P. Maier, 441:28Dec80-6
Kerensky, O. The New British Drama.
    M. Anderson, 610:May78-226
Kerényi, C. Dionysos.*
    J-J. Wunenburger, 192(EP):Jul-Sep79-
    366
Kermode, F. The Genesis of Secrecy.*
    M.C. Bradbrook, 598(SoR):Spring80-528
    U.K. Goldsmith, 149(CLS):Dec79-363
    P. Honan, 113:Fall78-133
    C.H. Sisson, 617(TLS):11Jan80-33
    639(VQR):Autumn79-129
Kermode, F. - see Stern, J.P.
Kern, J.B. Dramatic Satire in the Age of
    Walpole, 1720-1750.*
    F.P. Lock, 586(SoRA):Jul78-188
Kern, J.P. Ludwig Tieck: Dichter einer
    Krise.*
    W.J.L., 191(ELN):Sep78(supp)-187
    J. Trainer, 402(MLR):Jan79-247
Kern, K.R. - see Södergran, E.
Kern, P.C. and H. Zutt. Geschichte des
    deutschen Flexionssystems.
    E. Beneš, 685(ZDL):2/1979-267
    H. Penzl, 406:Winter79-433
Kernan, A.B. The Playwright as Magician.
    S.A. Adams, 150(DR):Winter79/80-755
    M. Dodsworth, 617(TLS):20Jun80-696
Kernan, A.B., ed. Two Renaissance Myth-
    Makers.*
    J.K. Gardiner and S.C. Hulse, 405(MP):
    Nov79-207
    L. Gent, 175:Summer79-164
Kerner, M. Johannes von Salisbury und die
    logische Struktur seines Policraticus.
    W. Ullmann, 182:Vol31#1/2-6
Kerr, J.A., Jr. Miguéis — to the Seventh
    Decade.
    M.A. Duarte, 399(MLJ):Jan-Feb79-87
    E. de Lima, 238:Dec79-735
    G.M. Moser, 552(REH):Oct79-473
    D. Woll, 547(RF):Band91Heft4-499
Kerr, W. The Secret of Stalingrad.
    639(VQR):Autumn78-147
Kerrigan, A. and M. Nozick - see de
    Unamuno, M.
Kershaw, V. Rosa.
    J. Naughton, 362:11Dec80-804
Kershaw, V. The Snow Man.*
    I. Colegate, 617(TLS):11Jan80-46
Kerslake, J. National Portrait Gallery:
    Early Georgian Portraits.*
    D.T. Siebert, 566:Autumn78-49
    R. Wark, 173(ECS):Fall78-119
    P. Ziegler, 39:Jan79-70
Kerssen, L. Das Interesse am Mittelalter
    im deutschen Nationaldenkmal.
    A. Farkas, 54:Mar78-183

Kessell, J.L. Kiva, Cross, and Crown.
    W. Gard, 584(SWR):Summer79-298
    R.H. Lister, 37:Sep79-47
Kesselmann, H. Die Idyllen Salomon Gess-
    ners im Beziehungsfeld von Ästhetik und
    Geschichte im 18. Jahrhundert.
    B. Burk, 224(GRM):Band28Heft2-252
Kessels, A., comp. Stellenregister zu E.
    Bruhn "Anhang."
    G.M. Kirkwood, 124:Mar80-366
Kessler, C.S. Islam and Politics in a
    Malay State.
    R.E. Downs, 293(JASt):May79-627
Kessler, E. Coleridge's Metaphors of
    Being.
    R. Ashton, 617(TLS):2May80-508
Kessler, E. Petrarca und die Geschichte.*
    E. Loos, 547(RF):Band91Heft1/2-188
Kessler, H.L. The Illustrated Bibles from
    Tours.
    R.H. Rough, 377:Mar79-53
Kessler-Harris, A. - see Yezierska, A.
Kesteloot, L. Black Writers in French.
    D. Parmée, 208(FS):Apr79-238
Kestner, J. The Spatiality of the Novel.
    J. Fletcher, 268(IFR):Summer80-153
    R. Saldívar, 594:Winter79-472
Keswick, M. The Chinese Garden.
    H. Acton, 46:Jun79-361
    J. Rawson, 463:Winter79/80-499
Ketelsen, U-K. Die Naturpoesie der nord-
    deutschen Frühaufklärung.*
    W. Harms, 684(ZDA):Band107Heft3-136
    J.A. McCarthy, 133:Band12Heft1/2-154
Ketelsen, U-K. Völkisch-nationale und
    nationalsozialistische Literatur in
    Deutschland 1890-1945.
    E. Schwarz, 221(GQ):Jan79-133
Ketner, K.L. and J.E. Cook - see Peirce,
    C.S.
Kettemann, R. Bukolik und Georgik.
    C. Fantazzi, 124:Sep79-48
    J. Perret, 555:Vol52fasc2-402
Ketterer, D. Frankenstein's Creation.
    R. Tetreault, 150(DR):Winter79/80-765
Kettner, J.H. The Development of American
    Citizenship, 1608-1870.
    P.K. Conkin, 656(WMQ):Oct79-618
Keuls, E.C. Plato and Greek Painting.
    M. Robertson, 123:Vol129No2-317
Keutsch, M. Praxis der englischen Aus-
    sprache.* (W. Keutsch, ed and trans)
    W. Enninger, 430(NS):Apr78-187
Kevelson, R. The Inverted Pyramid.
    Inlaws/Outlaws.
    B. Gray, 567:Vol125#3/4-319
Kevles, D.J. The Physicists.*
    R.J. Noer, 109:Winter79/80-168
Key, M.R. Male/Female Language.*
    M.B. Kendall, 269(IJAL):Jul78-253
    D.E. Phillips, 583:Spring79-316
Key, M.R. Nonverbal Communication.*
    M.M. Bryant, 660(Word):Aug78-196
    B. Lynch, 355(LSoc):Aug78-254
Keyes, R. The Height of Your Life.
    J. Leonard, 441:14Apr80-C17
Keynes, G. - see Blake, W.

King, C. Beggars and Choosers.
    S. Isaacs, 441:16Mar80-14
    C. Lehmann-Haupt, 441:27Feb80-C25
King, E.H. James Beattie.*
    I. Ross, 178:Winter79-495
King, F. Indirect Method.
    J. Mellors, 362:18and25Dec80-867
King, J. Tragedy in the Victorian Novel.*
    D. Kramer, 295(JML):Vol7#4-606
    J. Paterson, 301(JEGP):Jul79-453
    M. Saunders, 395(MFS):Winter78/79-586
King, J. and C. Ryskamp - see Cowper, W.
King, J.M. - see Tsvetaeva, M.
King, K.C. and D.R. McLintock - see
    Bostock, J.K.
King, L.L. Of Outlaws, Con Men, Whores,
    Politicians, and Other Artists.
    R. Lingeman, 441:20Apr80-12
King, L.S. The Philosophy of Medicine.
    J. Sena, 566:Spring79-138
King, M., ed. Te Ao Hurihuri.
    B. Mitcalfe, 368:Jun76-174
King, N. and R. de Luppé - see Sismondi,
    G.C.L.
King, P.R. Nine Contemporary Poets.
    A. Brownjohn, 617(TLS):1Feb80-112
King, R. Botanical Illustration.
    C.C. Brookes, 39:Dec79-538
King, R.H. A Southern Renaissance.
    H.N. Smith, 441:1Jun80-12
King, R.R. and J.F. Brown. Eastern
    Europe's Uncertain Future.
    G. Schöpflin, 575(SEER):Jan79-156
King, S. Firestarter.
    C. Lehmann-Haupt, 441:8Sep80-C15
King, S. The Shining.
    C. Lehmann-Haupt, 441:24Jun80-C9
King, U. Towards a New Mysticism.
    A.O. Dyson, 617(TLS):18Jul80-800
"Archbishop King's Sermon on Predestina-
    tion."* (A. Carpenter, ed)
    S. Blackburn, 447(N&Q):Feb78-91
King-Hele, D. Doctor of Revolution.
    G. Cullum, 67:May79-95
    D.M. Hassler, 661(WC):Summer79-309
Kingman, R. A Pictorial Life of Jack
    London.
    D. Grumbach, 441:2Mar80-14
Kingsland, R. A Saint Among Savages.
    P. Henley, 617(TLS):16May80-564
Kingsley, C. The Heroes.
    H. Lloyd-Jones, 617(TLS):18Jul80-797
Kingston, M.H. China Men.
    P-L. Adams, 61:Sep80-107
    M. Gordon, 441:15Jun80-1
    J. Leonard, 441:3Jun80-C9
    F. Taliaferro, 231:Aug80-76
    F. Wakeman, Jr., 453(NYRB):14Aug80-42
Kington, M. Let's Parler Franglais Again.
    D. Thomas, 362:18and25Dec80-863
Kinkead, E. Squirrel Book.
    442(NY):24Nov80-209
Kinnaird, J. William Hazlitt.
    D. Bromwich, 617(TLS):1Feb80-103
    J.A. Houck, 661(WC):Summer79-303

Kinnard, D. President Eisenhower and
    Strategy Management.
    639(VQR):Spring78-64
Kinnell, G. The Book of Nightmares.*
    A. Cluysenaar, 565:Vol20#3-68
Kinnell, G. Mortal Acts, Mortal Words.
    H. Bloom, 441:22Jun80-13
Kinnell, G. - see Villon, F.
Kinney, A.F. Faulkner's Narrative Poetics.
    J.E. Bassett, 141:Fall79-387
    C. Collins, 27(AL):May79-287
    J.V. Hagopian, 295(JML):Vol7#4-695
    K. McSweeney, 106:Winter79-355
Kinsbury, M., C. Cowles and S. Clark.
    Northwest Traditions.
    376:Oct79-144
Kinsella, T. Poems 1956-1973. Pepper-
    canister Poems 1972-1978.
    M.L. Rosenthal, 441:24Feb80-28
Kinsella, T. Song of the Night. The Mes-
    senger.
    D. O'Hara, 174(Éire):Spring79-131
Kinsella, T. - see "The Tain"
Kinsella, W.P. Scars.*
    P. Monk, 529(QQ):Autumn79-525
Kinsella, W.P. Shoeless Joe Jackson Comes
    to Iowa.
    P. O'Flaherty, 99:Nov80-32
Kipa, A.A. Gerhart Hauptmann in Russia:
    1889-1917.
    E. Kostka, 222(GR):Spring78-87
Kipling, G. The Triumph of Honour.
    J. Grundy, 541(RES):May79-211
    H. Smith, 301(JEGP):Jan79-114
Király, B.K. Ferenc Deák.*
    L. Péter, 575(SEER):Jul79-449
Király, B.K. and G. Barany, eds. East
    Central European Perceptions of Early
    America.
    M.J.E. Copson-Niećko, 497(PolR):Vol23
    #4-112
Király, B.K. and P. Jónás, eds. The Hun-
    garian Revolution of 1956 in Retrospect.
    639(VQR):Winter79-12
Kirby, F.E. Music in the Classic Period.
    N. Zaslaw, 415:Dec79-1001
Kirby, J.T. Media-Made Dixie.*
    E.F. Bargainnier, 580(SCR):Nov78-125
    D. Paterson, 585(SoQ):Fall78-92
Kirchhof, H.W. Militaris disciplina.* (B.
    Gotzkowsky, ed)
    H. Kolb, 72:Band216Heft2-336
Kirchner, W. Studies in Russian-American
    Commerce, 1820-1860.*
    O. Crisp, 575(SEER):Apr79-294
Kirk, G. and N.H. Wessell, eds. The
    Soviet Threat.
    R.M. Slusser, 550(RusR):Oct79-498
Kirk, G.S. Homer and the Oral Tradition.*
    F.M. Combellack, 131(CL):Spring79-196
Kirk, G.S. The Nature of Greek Myths.*
    J.A.S. Evans, 529(QQ):Autumn79-493
Kirk, R. Decadence and Renewal in the
    Higher Learning.
    R.B. Hovey, 396(ModA):Fall79-417

Kirk, R.   The Secret Common-Wealth and A Short Treatise of Charms and Spels.   (S. Sanderson, ed)
  W. Scheps, 588(SSL):Vol13-295
Kirkham, E.B.   The Building of "Uncle Tom's Cabin."*
  W.D. Fields, 405(MP):Nov79-239
  J.P. Roppolo, 579(SAQ):Winter79-132
  580(SCR):Nov78-134
Kirkpatrick, B.J.   A Bibliography of Edmund Blunden.*
  C.B.C., 148:Autumn79-92
Kirkpatrick, R.   Dante's Paradiso and the Limitations of Modern Criticism.
  G. Bolognese, 67:Nov79-350
  639(VQR):Summer79-105
Kirkpatrick, S.   Larra.
  D.T. Gies, 86(BHS):Oct79-340
Kirkup, J. - see "Modern Japanese Poetry"
Kirkwood, J.   Hit Me with a Rainbow.
  J. Burke, 231:May80-90
Kirsch, D.   La Bruyère ou le style cruel.
  P. France, 402(MLR):Oct79-940
  M. Gutwirth, 399(MLJ):Sep-Oct79-307
  M.S. Koppisch, 188(ECr):Winter78-68
  O. de Mourgues, 208(FS):Apr79-190
  G. Pestureau, 207(FR):Apr79-768
Kirsch, F.P.   Probleme der Romanstruktur bei Victor Hugo.
  P.J. Whyte, 208(FS):Oct79-462
Kirsch, R. - see Trumbo, D.
Kirsch, W.   Die Motetten des Andreas de Silva.
  D. Crawford, 317:Spring79-150
Kirschbaum, J.M.   Slovak Language and Literature.
  R.B. Pynsent, 575(SEER):Jul79-474
Kirschenbaum, H.   On Becoming Carl Rogers.*
  B. Thompson, 42(AR):Summer79-375
Kirschner, J.   Die Bezeichnungen für Franz und Krone im Altenglischen.
  J.M. Bately, 38:Band96Heft3/4-467
Kirshenblatt-Gimblett, B.   Speech Play.
  W. Samarin, 355(LSoc):Dec78-447
Kirshner, J.   Pursuing Honor while Avoiding Sin.
  W.M. Bowsky, 589:Jul79-594
Kirsten, W.   Der Bleibaum.
  U. Heukenkamp, 654(WB):1/1978-131
Kirwan, C.   Logic and Argument.
  T.J. Richards, 63:Dec79-364
Kisch, G.   Das Fischereirecht im Deutschordensgebiet.   Die Kulmer Handfeste.
  W.E. Butler, 575(SEER):Oct79-634
Kishkan, T.   Ikons of the Hunt.
  D. Barbour, 150(DR):Spring79-154
  C. MacMillan, 198:Summer80-151
Kishlansky, M.A.   The Rise of the New Model Army.
  K. Sharpe, 617(TLS):23May80-593
Kissinger, H.   The White House Years.*
  M. Mayer, 31(ASch):Summer80-404
Kitch, F.C.M.   The Literary Style of Epifanij Premudryj: Pletenije sloves.
  P. Hunt, 550(RusR):Jan79-122
  G.A. Perfecky, 574(SEEJ):Summer79-263
  R.W.F. Pope, 575(SEER):Jul79-420

Kitchel, D.   The Truth About the Panama Canal.
  T.C. Holyoke, 42(AR):Winter79-115
Kitchen, M.   The Coming of Austrian Fascism.
  F.L. Carsten, 617(TLS):1Aug80-871
Kitchen, P.   Four Days.
  J. Casey, 441:5Oct80-14
Kitchen, P.   Gerard Manley Hopkins.*
  42(AR):Summer79-379
  639(VQR):Summer79-96
Kitson, M.   Claude Lorrain: Liber Veritatis.
  D. Howard, 90:Jan79-42
Kitson, V.   Life, Death and Some Words About Them.
  C. Pollnitz, 581:Dec79-462
Kittay, J.S.   From Telling to Talking.
  J-J. Thomas, 546(RR):May79-303
Kittler, F.A.   Der Traum und die Rede.
  W.D. Williams, 402(MLR):Apr79-500
  W. Wittkowski, 406:Winter79-453
Kittredge, W.   The Van Gogh Field and Other Stories.
  A. Arthur, 649(WAL):Fall79-255
Kitzinger, E.   Byzantine Art in the Making.*
  A. Cutler, 56:Spring79-218
  P. Reutersward, 341:1978/2-72
Kjaer, J. - see Brisebare
Klaerr, R. and Y. Vernière - see Plutarch
Klainer, J. and A.S.   The Judas Gene.
  N. Callendar, 441:10Aug80-34
Klaits, J.   Printed Propaganda under Louis XIV.*
  J. Chupeau, 535(RHL):Nov-Dec78-1028
Klakowicz, B.   La Necropoli anulare di Orvieto.*   (Vols 1 and 2)
  D. and F.R. Ridgway, 313:Vol69-212
Klarmann, A.D. - see Werfel, F.
Klasne, W.   Street Cops.
  N. Callendar, 441:27Jul80-23
Klassen, J-M.   L'Etoile.
  A.L. Amprimoz, 526:Spring79-82
Klassen, J.M.   The Nobility and the Making of the Hussite Revolution.
  J.B. Henneman, 589:Jul79-595
Klaus, H.G. - see Williams, R.
Klausenburger, J.   Historische französische Phonologie aus generativer Sicht.
  J.N. Green, 208(FS):Oct79-498
Klauser, T., ed.   Reallexikon für Antike und Christentum.   (Pts 72-74)
  J. André, 555:Vol52fasc1-211
Klébaner, D.   Poétique de la dérive.
  G. Quinsat, 450(NRF):Mar79-108
Klein, A.   Meister Eckhart, la dottrina mistica della giustificazione.
  E. Namer, 542:Apr-Jun79-205
Klein, C.   Aline.*
  C. Fox, 617(TLS):23May80-592
  C. Sigal, 362:22May80-658
Klein, E. and D. Landey.   Dazzle.
  N. Johnson, 441:24Feb80-15

Klein, H., ed. The First World War in Fiction.*

  W. French, 395(MFS):Winter78/79-662

  H. Kurzke, 52:Band13Heft2-219

  A. Thomson, 179(ES):Jun79-324

Klein, H.G. Making It Perfectly Clear.

  M.F. Nolan, 441:5Oct80-12

Klein, H.G. Tempus, Aspekt, Aktionsart.

  W. Oesterreicher, 685(ZDL):1/1979-118

  T.B.W. Reid, 208(FS):Vol33Pt2-1046

Klein, H.S. The Middle Passage.

  M. Craton, 529(QQ):Summer79-330

  V.B. Platt, 656(WMQ):Jul79-472

Klein, J. Woody Guthrie.

  C. Lehmann-Haupt, 441:13Nov80-C24

  M.L. Settle, 441:7Dec80-3

Klein, J. Plato's Trilogy.

  W.B.A., 543:Mar79-553

  L. Brown, 123:Vol29No2-315

  D.R. Lachterman, 449:Mar79-106

  M.A. Stewart, 479(PhQ):Apr79-170

Klein, J.R. Le Vocabulaire des moeurs de la "Vie parisienne" sous le Second Empire.

  R. Arveiller, 209(FM):Jul78-272

  E. Woods, 208(FS):Vol33Pt2-1040

Klein, K.W. The Partisan Voice.

  W.D. Paden, Jr., 545(RPh):Nov78-193

Klein, P-J. Theater für den Zuschauer — Theater mit dem Zuschauer.

  T.M. Scheerer, 430(NS):Oct78-473

Klein, R. Constantius II. und die christliche Kirche.

  J. Chandler, 123:Vol29No2-328

Klein, R. Form and Meaning.

  F.D. Martin, 290(JAAC):Summer80-479

  J. Russell, 441:13Jan80-25

  F. Yates, 453(NYRB):21Feb80-29

Klein, T. Studien zur Wechselbeziehung zwischen altsächsischem und althochdeutschem Schreibwesen und ihrer sprach- und kulturgeschichtlichen Bedeutung.

  M. Durrell, 402(MLR):Jul79-733

Kleiner, F.S. and S.P. Noe. The Early Cistophoric Coinage.

  C. Rodewald, 123:Vol29No2-339

Kleinfield, S. The Hidden Minority.

  S. Curtin, 441:6Jan80-8

Kleinhenz, C., ed. Medieval Manuscripts and Textual Criticism.*

  M.B. Speer, 545(RPh):Feb79-335

Kleinman, A. and others, eds. Medicine in Chinese Cultures.*

  J.L. McCreery, 293(JASt):May79-572

Kleinschmidt, E., ed. Das Windschiff aus Schlaraffenland.

  S.N. Werbow, 301(JEGP):Jul79-384

Kleinzahler, A. The Sausage Master of Minsk.

  M. Darling, 102(CanL):Autumn79-91

von Kleist, H. The Marquise of O and other Stories. (D. Luke and N. Reeves, trans)

  M.K. Rogister, 161(DUJ):Dec78-139

von Kleist, H. Prinz Friedrich von Homburg. (K. Kanzog, ed)

  M. Garland, 402(MLR):Oct79-992

von Kleist, H. Word into Flesh.

  J.L. Sammons, 680(ZDP):Band97Heft2-293

Klépinine, T., comp. Bibliographie des oeuvres de Nicolas Berdiaev.

  D.M. Fiene, 399(MLJ):Apr79-213

de Klerk, W. The Puritans in Africa.

  I. Hexham, 69:Vol48#1-91

Klessmann, E. Caroline

  M.H., 191(ELN):Sep78(supp)-186

Klibbe, L.H. José María de Pereda.*

  G. Gullón, 240(HR):Winter78-101

Klinck, C.F., general ed. Literary History of Canada: Canadian Literature in English.* (2nd ed)

  J. Ferns, 402(MLR):Jan79-186

  D. Staines, 569(SR):Winter79-175

Klinck, C.F. Robert Service.*

  L. Ricou, 178:Summer79-238

Kline, M. Mathematics.

  W. Barrett, 441:5Oct80-9

  E. Nagel, 453(NYRB):6Nov80-6

  442(NY):3Nov80-203

Klineman, G. and others. The Cult that Died.

  J. Klein, 441:16Nov80-11

Kling, B. Partner in Empire.

  A.T. Embree, 318(JAOS):Jul-Sep78-327

Klinghoffer, A.J. The Soviet Union and International Oil Politics.

  M.I. Goldman, 550(RusR):Jan79-120

  639(VQR):Winter78-17

Klinkowitz, J. The Life of Fiction.*

  H.A. and I. Deer, 454:Spring79-277

  295(JML):Vol17#4-634

  639(VQR):Spring78-56

Klinkowitz, J. - see Motley, W.

Kloe, D.R. A Dictionary of Onomatopoeic Sounds, Tones and Noises in English and Spanish.*

  J.J. Bergen, 238:May-Sep79-414

Kloefkorn, B. Stocker.

  C. Stubblefield, 502(PrS):Winter78/79-386

Klossermann, V. - see Gadamer, H-G.

Kloten, N. and others. Der EDV-Markt in der Bundesrepublik Deutschland.

  G.K. Englert, 182:Vol131#9/10-276

Klotman, P.R. and others, eds. Humanities Through the Black Experience.

  A. Sistrunk, 95(CLAJ):Sep78-64

Klotz, G., W. Schröder and P. Weber, eds. Literatur im Epochenumbruch.

  P.H. Meyer, 173(ECS):Spring79-405

Klotz, V. Dramaturgie des Publikums.

  H. Schramm, 654(WB):3/1978-183

Kluckhohn, P. and R. Samuel - see Novalis

Klucsarits, R. and F.G. Kürbisch, eds. Arbeiterinnen kämpfen um ihr Recht.

  A. Lasserre, 182:Vol131#1/2-55

Knaack, J. Achim von Arnim — Nicht nur Poet.

  J.F.F., 191(ELN):Sep78(supp)-139

  H.F. Weiss, 222(GR):Spring78-85

Knabe, B. Die Struktur der russischen Posadgemeinden und der Katalog der Beschwerden und Forderungen der Kaufmann-

[continued]

[continuing]
schaft (1762-1767).*
 D.L. Ransel, 550(RusR):Jul79-360
Knafla, L.A. Law and Politics in Jacobean
 England.*
 D. Ligou, 182:Vol31#13-441
 E.G. Moore, 161(DUJ):Dec78-120
Knapp, B. French Novelists Speak Out.
 A. Otten, 42(AR):Winter79-119
Knapp, B.L. Fernand Crommelynck.
 R.A. Champagne, 399(MLJ):Mar79-139
Knapp, B.L. Dream and Image.*
 W. Provost, 219(GaR):Spring79-210
 N.D. Savage, 188(ECr):Summer78-82
Knapp, B.L. Maurice Maeterlinck.*
 C. Berg, 556(RLV):1978/2-169
Knapp, B.L. Anaïs Nin.
 S. Spencer, 295(JML):Vol7#4-782
Knapp, F.P. Similitudo. (Vol 1, Pt 1)
 H-J. Behr, 684(ZDA):Band107Heft1-16
 E. Könsgen, 680(ZDP):Band97Heft3-449
Knapp, M. and H. One Potato, Two Potato...
 G.A. Fine, 292(JAF):Jan-Mar79-87
 S.A. Grider, 650(WF):Jan79-62
Knapp, P.A. The Style of John Wyclif's
 English Sermons.
 J.H. Fisher, 589:Jan79-161
 A. Hudson, 447(N&Q):Aug78-359
Knapton, A. Mythe et Psychologie chez
 Marie de France dans "Guigemar."*
 W. Rothwell, 208(FS):Vol33Pt2-551
Knecht, R.J. The Fronde.
 D.A. Watts, 208(FS):Vol33Pt2-718
Knei-Paz, B. The Social and Political
 Thought of Trotsky.
 J. Carmichael, 390:Jun/Jul79-68
 A.G. Meyer, 550(RusR):Jul79-370
Kneller, G.F. Science as a Human Endeavor.
 S. Bernstein, 42(AR):Winter79-118
Knigge, A. Die Lyrik Vl. Solov'evs und
 ihre Nachwirkung bei A. Belyj und A.
 Blok.*
 E. Reissner, 688(ZSP):Band40Heft1-221
Knight, D. Zoological Illustration.
 D.R. Dewar, 503:Summer78-97
Knight, F. Cambridge Music.
 J. Joubert, 617(TLS):25Jul80-830
Knight, J.E. The Hunter's Game Cookbook.
 W. and C. Cowen, 639(VQR):Spring79-77
Knight, M. - see Strauss, R. and S. Zweig
Knight, R.C. and H.T. Barnwell - see
 Racine, J.
Knight, R.J.B., ed. Guide to the Manu-
 scripts in the National Maritime Museum.
 (Vol 1)
 C.R. Schultz, 14:Jan79-73
 D. Woodward, 325:Apr79-169
Knights, B. The Idea of the Clerisy in
 the Nineteenth Century.
 B.W. Martin, 541(RES):Nov79-483
 639(VQR):Summer79-105
Knobloch, S. Prediger des Barock.
 W. Welzig, 602:Vol10-293
Knodel, A.J. - see Perse, S-J.

Knoepflmacher, U.C. and G.B. Tennyson, eds.
 Nature and the Victorian Imagination.*
 R.D. Altick, 639(VQR):Autumn78-748
 E.R. August, 636(VP):Winter78-385
 D.J. De Laura, 637(VS):Winter79-193
 C. Harland, 529(QQ):Summer79-337
 J.R. Reed, 141:Winter79-90
 B. Richards, 541(RES):May79-228
 C.G. Worth, 155:Spring79-44
Knoll, R.E., ed. Conversations with
 Wright Morris.
 L. Waldeland, 395(MFS):Summer78-265
Knopf, J. Friedrich Dürrenmatt.
 T.R. Nadar, 406:Spring79-85
Knopp, J.Z. The Trial of Judaism in Con-
 temporary Jewish Writing.
 E. Rothstein, 390:Jun/Jul79-99
Knoppers, J.V.T. Dutch Trade with Russia
 from the Time of Peter I to Alexander I.
 (Vol 1)
 R. Unger, 104(CASS):Spring78-185
Knorringa, R. Fonction phatique et tradi-
 tion orale.
 E.M. Wallner, 182:Vol31#5/6-189
Knowles, A.V., ed. Tolstoy: The Critical
 Heritage.
 J.M. Holquist, 594:Fall79-372
Knowles, J.H., ed. Doing Better and Feel-
 ing Worse.
 639(VQR):Winter78-20
Knowles, R. - see Shakespeare, W.
Knowles, R.S. The Greatest Gamblers.
 W. Gard, 584(SWR):Autumn79-398
Knowlson, J. Universal Language Schemes
 in England and France, 1600-1800.*
 R. Posner, 208(FS):Vol33Pt2-1067
Knowlson, J. and F. Leakey - see Rimbaud,
 A.
Knox, B. Word and Action.
 P. Green, 453(NYRB):20Mar80-39
 H. Lloyd-Jones, 617(TLS):16May80-551
Knox, R., ed. The Work of E.H. Shepard.*
 Q. Bell, 453(NYRB):18Dec80-50
Knutson, H.C. Molière.*
 S.F.R., 131(CL):Winter79-89
 P.A. Wadsworth, 188(ECr):Summer78-83
Kobal, J. The Art of the Great Hollywood
 Portrait Photographers 1925-1940.
 A. Hollander, 441:9Nov80-13
 C. James, 453(NYRB):18Dec80-22
Kobal, J. Rita Hayworth.
 J. Basinger, 18:Feb79-68
 H. Weinberg, 200:Feb79-117
Kocan, P. The Other Side of the Fence.
 A. Paterson, 368:Dec76-358
Koch, C.J. The Year of Living Dangerously.
 639(VQR):Summer79-102
Koch, D.F. - see Dewey, J.
Koch, F.C. The Volga Germans in Russia
 and the Americas, from 1763 to the
 Present.*
 A.R. Schmitt, 221(GQ):Mar79-278
Koch, G. Die mythologischen Sarkophage.
 (Pt 6)
 G.M.A. Hanfmann, 54:Jun78-354

Koch, H. and H. Hanke, eds. Die geistige
Kultur der sozialistischen Gesellschaft.
  W. Schubert, 654(WB):6/1978-173
Koch, H.W. Medieval Warfare.
  C.C. Bayley, 529(QQ):Autumn79-531
Koch, K. The Burning Mystery of Anna in
1951.
  D. Donoghue, 453(NYRB):14Aug80-49
Koch, K. The Duplicators.
  639(VQR):Spring79-67
Kochan, L. The Jew and his History.
  J. Shatzmiller, 287:Apr78-26
Kochan, L., ed. The Jews in Soviet
Russia since 1917. (3rd ed)
  R.S. Wistrich, 575(SEER):Oct79-636
Kochan, M. Catherine the Great.
  639(VQR):Summer78-90
Kodjak, A. Alexander Solzhenitsyn.
  J.B. Dunlop, 550(RusR):Apr79-263
  M. Nicholson, 575(SEER):Oct79-590
Koefoed, G.A.T. and J. van Marle, eds.
Aspecten van taalverandering.
  H. van der Hulst, 204(FdL):Jun79-177
Koepsel, W. Die Rezeption der Hegelschen
Ästhetik im 20. Jahrhundert.
  S. Decloux, 182:Vol31#17/18-583
  F.D. Wagner, 53(AGP):Band60Heft3-356
Koertge, R. The Boogeyman.
  M. Levin, 441:16Mar80-14
Koestler, A. Janus.
  639(VQR):Autumn78-127
Kogan, D. Wladimir Bechtejeff, 1878-1971.
  J. Hahl, 471:Apr/May/Jun79-180
Kohák, E. Národ v nás.
  Z. Kouřím, 542:Jul-Sep79-359
Kohanski, A.S. Philosophy and Technology.
  J-M. Gabaude, 542:Jul-Sep79-360
Kohl, N. - see Wilde, O.
Kohl, S. Realismus.*
  M. Swales, 402(MLR):Apr79-400
Kohl, W. Die Redetrias von der sizilis-
chen Expedition (Thukydides 6, 9-23).
  C.W. MacLeod, 123:Vol29No1-142
Kohl-Larsen, L., ed. Der Hasenschelm.
  R. Schott, 196:Band19Heft1/2-160
Kohlberg, E. - see al-Sulami, A.A.R.
Köhler, C., A. Herzog and W. Kursitza.
Deutsche Verbale Wendungen für Ausländer.
  I-E. Rachmankulova, 682(ZPSK):Band31-
  Heft2-216
Köhler, H. Paul Valéry: Dichtung und
Erkenntnis.*
  H. Mehnert, 72:Band216Heft1-236
Köhler, K-H. ". . . tausendmal leben!"
  W. Drabkin, 415:Apr79-305
Kohli, M., ed. Soziologie des Lebens-
laufs.
  R. Levy, 182:Vol131#15/16-532
Kohli, S. Family Planning in India.
  G.B. Simmons, 293(JASt):Aug79-814
Kohls, S. Business Russian.
  S. Orth, 574(SEEJ):Fall79-425
Kohlschmidt, H. and W. - see Storm, T.,
E. Mörike and M. Mörike
Kohn-Etiemble, J. 226 Lettres inédites de
Jean Paulhan.
  A. Anglès, 535(RHL):Sep-Oct78-809

Kohr, L. The Overdeveloped Nations.
  M. Gabbert, 529(QQ):Summer79-348
Koike, I. and others, eds. The Teaching
of English in Japan.
  R. Linde, 285(JapQ):Apr-Jun79-270
Koizumi Fumio, Tokumaru Yoshihiko and
Yamaguchi Osamu, eds. Asian Musics in
an Asian Perspective.
  P. Ackermann, 187:Sep80-571
Kok, J.P.F. - see under Filedt Kok, J.P.
Kolakowski, L. Husserl and the Search for
Certitude.*
  B. Grünewald, 53(AGP):Band60Heft3-325
Kolakowski, L. Main Currents of Marxism.*
  S. Hook, 31(ASch):Spring80-250
  S. Lukes, 453(NYRB):29May80-40
  G.H.R. Parkinson, 483:Oct79-555
  J.L. Wiser, 613:Dec79-440
Kolatkar, A. Jejuri.
  T. Eagleton, 565:Vol20#3-75
Kolb, A. East Asia.
  R.D. Hill, 302:Vol16#1and2-117
Kolb, P. - see Proust, M.
Kolb, P. - see Proust, M. and J. Rivière
Kolenda, K. - see Ryle, G.
Kolendo, J. Le colonat en Afrique sous le
Haut-Empire.*
  J. Percival, 313:Vol69-196
van der Kolk, H. - see Linck, W.
Kolker, R.P. A Cinema of Loneliness.
  N. Roddick, 617(TLS):30May80-624
Kollek, T., with A. Kollek. For Jerusalem.
  G. Sauer, 287:Aug/Sep78-26
Koller, W. Redensarten.
  E.H. Yarrill, 182:Vol131#9/10-282
Kolleritsch, O., ed. 50 Jahre Wozzeck von
Alban Berg.
  M. Carner, 415:Aug79-654
Kolmaš, J. The Iconography of the Derge
Kanjur and Tanjur.
  H. Eimer, 259(IIJ):Jul79-210
Kolnai, A. Ethics, Value and Reality.*
  A.C. Varga, 613:Dec79-439
Kolneder, W. Anton Webern.
  B. Hopkins, 607:Dec78-37
Kolodin, I. In Quest of Music.
  J. Yohalem, 441:28Dec80-9
Komorowski, M. Das Spanienbild Voltaires.
  A. Billaz, 535(RHL):Jul-Aug78-655
  W. Floeck, 547(RF):Band91Heft1/2-174
König, E. Form und Funktion.
  P. Erdmann, 257(IRAL):May79-182
König, R. and G. Winkler - see Pliny
König, W. dtv-Atlas zur deutschen Sprache.
  M.H. Folsom, 221(GQ):Jan79-102
König, W. Vinko Globokar.
  N. O'Loughlin, 415:Jan79-38
Königson, M-J. - see Hegel, G.W.F.
Konrád, G. The City Builder.
  G. Steiner, 617(TLS):20Jun80-690
Konrád, G. and I. Szelényi. The Intel-
lectuals on the Road to Class Power.
  M. Walzer, 453(NYRB):20Mar80-37
Konstantinović, Z., ed. "Expressionismus"
im europäischen Zwischenfeld.
  A. Arnold, 107(CRCL):Winter79-106

"Kontinent 2."* (V.E. Maximov, ed)
  D.L. Burgin, 574(SEEJ):Spring79-136
Kontzi, R. Aljamiado Texte.
  J.R. Craddock, 318(JAOS):Oct-Dec78-493
Kontzi, R., ed. Zur Entstehung der roman-
  ischen Sprachen.
  J. Göschel, 685(ZDL):3/1979-359
Konvitz, M.R. Judaism and the American
  Idea.
  J.J. Diamond, 390:Aug-Sep79-65
Konwicki, T. The Anthropos-Specter-Beast.
  C.W. Mignon, 502(PrS):Winter78/79-392
  B.J. Tepa, 497(PolR):Vol123#2-84
Kooijman, J., ed. Trouvères Lorrains.
  N. Wilkins, 208(FS):Vol33Pt2-590
Kooser, T. Sure Signs.
  C. Molesworth, 441:12Oct80-14
Köpeczi, B. - see Rákóczi, F. 2d
Köpeczi, B., E. Bene and I. Kovács, eds.
  Les Lumières en Hongrie, en Europe
  Centrale, et en Europe Orientale.
  I. Johnston, 678(YCGL):No.27-106
Kopelev, L. The Education of a True
  Believer.
  H. McLean, 441:31Aug80-5
Kopelev, L. I stovoril sebe kumira.
  P. Kenez, 550(RusR):Jul79-374
Kopelev, L. Vera v slovo.
  R. Sheldon, 550(RusR):Jul79-382
Köpf, G. Humanität und Vernunft.
  D. Roberts, 67:Nov79-362
Köpke, W. Erfolglosigkeit.*
  M.H., 191(ELN):Sep78(supp)-174
Kopp, A. L'architecture de la période
  stalinienne.
  Y. Perret-Gentil, 550(RusR):Jul79-407
Kopp, K. Yarbrough Mountain.*
  R.J. Stout, 584(SWR):Spring79-194
Koppe, F. Sprache und Bedürfnis.
  P. Müller, 687:Jan-Mar79-154
Köppen, E. Heeresbericht.
  A. Kaes, 221(GQ):Jan79-87
Kopper, J. - see Kant, I.
Korczak, J. Ghetto Diary.
  T. Ziolkowski, 569(SR):Fall79-676
Korda, M. Charmed Lives.*
  G. Mikes, 617(TLS):25Apr80-471
  E.S. Turner, 362:24Apr80-537
Koren, E. The Diary of Elisabeth Koren,
  1853-1855. (D.T. Nelson, ed and trans)
  E.L. Haugen, 563(SS):Summer79-285
Koren, E. "Well, There's Your Problem."
  D. Hill, 441:14Dec80-18
Korey, M.E. The Books of Isaac Norris
  (1701-1766) at Dickinson College.*
  N. Barker, 78(BC):Summer79-285
  M.A. McCorison, 517(PBSA):Jan-Mar78-
  151
Korhammer, M. Die monastischen Cantica im
  Mittelalter und ihre altenglischen Inter-
  linearversionen.
  E.G. Stanley, 447(N&Q):Jun78-246
  C. Waddell, 589:Jan79-162
Korhonen, J. Studien zu Dependenz, Valenz
  und Satzmodell. (Pt 1)
  G. Geil, 72:Band216Heft1-158
  H. Jackson, 297(JL):Sep79-347

Koritz, L.S. Scarron satirique.
  F. Bar, 535(RHL):Sep-Oct79-848
  H.G. Hall, 402(MLR):Jan79-201
  R.P. Thomas, 207(FR):Feb79-484
Korman, K. Swan Dive.
  N. Callendar, 441:7Sep80-37
Körner, S. Experience and Conduct.*
  M. Brand, 449:Mar79-100
Körner, S., ed. Philosophy of Logic.*
  J.E. Tiles, 518:Jan79-30
Koropeckyj, I.S., ed. The Ukraine within
  the U.S.S.R.
  C. Beaucourt, 575(SEER):Apr79-312
Kors, A.C. D'Holbach's Coterie.*
  G. Jourdain, 535(RHL):Mar-Jun79-521
Korshin, P.J. From Concord to Dissent.
  H. Castrop, 72:Band216Heft2-412
Korshin, P.J. - see Darnton, R., B.
  Fabian and R.M. Wiles
Kortlandt, F.H.H. Slavic Accentuation.
  V.V. Kolesov, 353:Feb78-76
Korzeniewski, D. Hirtengedichte aus
  spätrömischer und karolingischer Zeit.
  A.B.E. Hood, 123:Vol29No1-151
Koschlig, M. Das Ingenium Grimmelshausens
  und das "Kollektiv."*
  B.L. Spahr, 222(GR):Spring79-78
Koschmann, J.V., ed. Authority and the
  Individual in Japan.*
  Tsurumi Yoshiyuki, 285(JapQ):Apr-Jun79-
  266
Koschmieder, E. Phonationslehre des Pol-
  nischen.*
  F. Knowles, 575(SEER):Apr79-271
Koschmieder, E. Das Russische.
  M.I. Levin, 558(RLJ):Winter79-191
Kościuszko, T.A.B. Kościuszko Letters in
  the American Revolution. (M.J.E. Budka,
  ed)
  I. Nagurski, 497(PolR):Vol123#4-74
Kosík, K. Dialectics of the Concrete.*
  W. Gay, 142:Sep-Dec78-417
Kosinski, J. Passion Play.*
  V. Cunningham, 617(TLS):25Apr80-470
Kosinski, J. Blind Date.*
  L.T. Lemon, 502(PrS):Fall78-305
  B.J. Tepa, 497(PolR):Vol123#3-104
Kossack, E.K. Irrande stjärna.
  G.C. Schoolfield, 563(SS):Summer79-302
Kostec'kyj, I. and O. Zujevs'kyj - see
  George, S.
Kostelanetz, R., ed. Esthetics Contempor-
  ary.*
  E.M.K. Rudat, 399(MLJ):Apr79-204
Kostelanetz, R. - see Stein, G.
Kostetzky, E.G. and O. Zujewskyj - see
  George, S.
Kostić, L. Okupacija.
  E.C. Hawkesworth, 575(SEER):Apr79-281
Kostis, N. The Exorcism of Sex and Death
  in Julien Green's Novels.*
  J. Cruickshank, 208(FS):Jul79-362
Kotin, A.A. The Narrative Imagination.
  J.C. Nash, 207(FR):May79-925
  A. Saunders, 402(MLR):Oct79-937
Kotlowitz, R. The Boardwalk.
  639(VQR):Winter78-23

Kreiser, B.R. Miracles, Convulsions, and Ecclesiastical Politics in Early Eighteenth-Century Paris.
C. Fairchilds, 173(ECS):Spring79-426
Kreiter, J.A. Le Problème du Paraître dans l'oeuvre de Mme. de Lafayette.*
J. Campbell, 208(FS):Vol33Pt2-690
205(FMLS):Apr78-187
Krementz, J. The Writer's Image.
H. Kramer, 441:30Nov80-68
Kremer-Marietti, A. - see Cournot, A-A.
Kremer-Marietti, A. - see Nietzsche, F.
Kremnitz, G. Versuche zur Kodifizierung des Okzitanischen seit dem 19. Jahrhundert und ihre Annahme durch die Sprecher.
N.B. Smith, 545(RPh):Nov78-181
Kren, G.M. and L.H. Rappoport, eds. Varieties of Psychohistory.
R. Muccigrosso, 125:Fall78-154
Krenov, J. The Fine Art of Cabinetmaking.
G.E.D. Brady, 139:Feb79-18
Kress, G., ed. Halliday.
D. Goyvaerts, 556(RLV):1978/6-554
Kress, G. - see Halliday, M.A.K.
Kretzer, H. Calvinismus und französische Monarchie im 17. Jahrhundert.
J. Lough, 208(FS):Vol33Pt2-714
Kretzulesco-Quaranta, E. Les Jardins du Songe.
C. Dédéyan, 535(RHL):Jan-Feb79-119
Kreutzer, H.J. Der Mythos vom Volksbuch.
W. Scherf, 196:Band19Heft3/4-332
Kreuzer, H., ed. Jahrhundertende — Jahrhundertwende. (Pt 1)
W. Hirdt, 547(RF):Band91Heft4-466
Kreuzer, H. Veränderungen des Literaturbegriffs.
P. Hutchinson, 220(GL&L):Oct78-62
Kreyling, M. Eudora Welty's Achievement of Order.
H. Eley, 617(TLS):30May80-610
R.P. Warren, 441:2Mar80-1
Kribbs, J.K., ed. An Annotated Bibliography of American Literature Periodicals, 1741-1850.
B.F. Fisher 4th, 365:Summer80-149
Krieger, L. Ranke.*
J.A. Moses, 125:Spring79-432
Krieger, M. Theory of Criticism.*
N. Friedman, 149(CLS):Jun79-165
639(VQR):Winter78-13
Krikorian, M.K. Armenians in the Service of the Ottoman Empire, 1860-1908.
M.E. Yapp, 575(SEER):Apr79-299
Krishna, V., ed. The Alliterative "Morte Arthure."*
O. Arngart, 179(ES):Jun79-319
B. Lindström, 597(SN):Vol50#2-326
Krishnan, B. Aspects of Structure, Technique and Quest in Aldous Huxley's Major Novels.
R.J. Van Dellen, 395(MFS):Winter78/79-579
Krispyn, E. Anti-Nazi Writers in Exile.
T.S. Hansen, 221(GQ):Jan79-135

Krissdottir, M. John Cowper Powys and the Magical Quest.
P. Lewis, 617(TLS):1Aug80-880
Kristeller, P.O. Renaissance Thought and Its Sources. (M. Mooney, ed)
C.B. Schmitt, 617(TLS):25Jul80-856
Kristensson, G. Studies on the Early 14th-Century Population of Lindsey (Lincolnshire).*
B.L. Collins, 424:Mar78-121
Kristensson, G. - see Mirk, J.
Kristol, A.M. Color.*
G. Ernst, 547(RF):Band91Heft3-309
Kriwonossow, A. Der Aufstieg des P.L.
K. Kasper, 654(WB):4/1978-148
Kroeber, K. Romantic Landscape Vision.
D.G. Williams, 405(MP):Aug79-99
Kroeber, K. and W. Walling, eds. Images of Romanticism.*
W.J.T. Mitchell, 141:Fall79-376
W.J.B. Owen, 541(RES):Aug79-362
R.L. Wilson, 290(JAAC):Winter79-219
Kroetsch, R. The Crow Journals.
S. Solecki, 99:Sep80-35
Kroetsch, R. The Ledger.
J. Cook, 99:Mar80-38
Kroetz, F.X. Farmyard and Four Plays.
J. Coleby, 157:Winter79-86
Kroll, J. Chapters in a Mythology.*
C. Holdsworth, 577(SHR):Summer79-274
Kromer, M. Polska, czyli o położeniu, ludności, obyczajach, urzędach i sprawach publicznych Królestwa Polskiego księgi dwie.
S. Dąbrowski, 497(PolR):Vol23#3-117
Krömer, W., ed. Die französische Novelle.
W-D. Lange, 430(NS):Oct78-475
Krömer, W. Die französische Novelle im 19. Jahrhundert.
R. Klesczewski, 535(RHL):Jul-Aug78-660
Krömer, W. Die italienische Commedia dell'arte.
W. Hinck, 52:Band13Heft2-197
W. Theile, 547(RF):Band91Heft3-337
Kron, F. Schriftsteller und Schriftstellerverbände.
B. Elling, 406:Spring79-79
Kronborg, B., T. Nilsson and A.A. Svalestuen, eds. Nordic Population Mobility.
J.R. Christianson, 563(SS):Summer79-291
Kronenberger, L. Oscar Wilde.*
I. Fletcher, 637(VS):Summer79-487
Krooks, D.A. The Semantic Derivation of the Modal Verb in the Old High German Williram.
J.B. Voyles, 685(ZDL):3/1979-368
Kropholler, J., ed. Die deutsche Rechtsprechung auf dem Gebiete des Internationalen Privatrechts im Jahre 1975.
R. Hepting, 182:Vol31#14-474
Kropholler, J. Internationales Einheitsrecht.*
R. Ganghofer, 182:Vol31#20-729
Kropotkin, P.A. The Essential Kropotkin. (E. Kapouya and K. Tompkins, eds)
J. Joll, 575(SEER):Jul79-476

Krotkov, Y. The Nobel Prize.
   C. Brown, 441:13Jul80-1
   J. Mellors, 362:28Aug80-281
Kroy, M. The Conscience.
   I.L. Humberstone, 449:Sep79-397
Krueger, J.R. The Kalmyk-Mongolian Vocabu-
   lary in Stralenberg's Geography of 1730.
   N. Poppe, 318(JAOS):Apr-Jun78-187
Krueger, J.R. - see Pozdneyev, A.M.
Krüger, S. - see von Megenberg, K.
Krummacher, F. Mendelssohn — der Kom-
   ponist.
   D. Seaton, 317:Summer79-356
Krummacher, H-H. Der junge Gryphius und
   die Tradition.*
   W. Kühlmann, 684(ZDA):Band107Heft2-88
   A. Menhennet, 597(SN):Vol150#1-155
   W. Welzig, 602:Vol10-294
Krummel, D.W. English Music Printing 1553-
   1700.
   P. Brett, 317:Spring79-155
Krupp, E.C., ed. In Search of Ancient
   Astronomies.
   J.D. North, 617(TLS):16May80-563
Krusche, D. Reclams Filmführer. (3rd ed)
   A. Haag, 406:Summer79-191
Kruta, V. Les Celtes.
   E. Bachellery, 194(EC):Vol15fasc2-729
Kryński, M.J. and R.A. Maguire - see
   Różewicz, T.
Kubach, H.E. and A. Verbeek. Romanische
   Baukunst an Rhein und Maas.
   W. Sanderson, 576:Dec78-315
Kubler, G. The Religious Architecture of
   New Mexico in the Colonial Period and
   Since the American Occupation.
   T.P. Miller, 576:Dec78-310
Kucala, M. and others. Encyklopedia
   wiedzy o języku polskim.
   M.Z. Brooks, 574(SEEJ):Winter79-559
Kuchenbuch, L. Bäuerliche Gesellschaft
   und Klosterherrschaft im 9. Jahrhundert.
   Y. Morimoto, 182:Vol31#19-694
Kugler, H. Handwerk und Meistergesang.*
   J. Rettelbach, 680(ZDP):Band97Heft3-
   465
   W. Röll, 133:Band12Heft1/2-149
Kuhfuss, W. Mässigung und Politik.*
   R. Derathé, 535(RHL):Jul-Aug78-639
Kuhlmann, S. Knave, Fool, and Genius.
   A. Easson, 447(N&Q):Dec78-566
Kuhlwein, W., ed. Linguistics in Great
   Britain.
   G.F. Meier, 682(ZPSK):Band31Heft1-88
Kühn, A. Zeit zum Aufstehn.
   K. Pezold, 654(WB):6/1978-137
Kuhn, D. - see von Goethe, J.W.
Kuhn, D. and W. von Engelhardt - see von
   Goethe, J.W.
Kuhn, H. Das letzte Indogermanisch.
   B. Schlerath, 343:Band23-44
Kühn, P. Deutsche Wörterbucher.
   M.H. Folsom, 221(GQ):Nov79-527
   B.J. Koekkoek, 301(JEGP):Jul79-374
Kuhn, R. The Demon of Noontide.*
   J.M. Cocking, 208(FS):Vol133Pt2-993

Kuhn, T.S. The Essential Tension.
   H. Frankel, 486:Dec78-649
   D.H., 355(LSoc):Aug78-291
   639(VQR):Winter79-24
Kühnel, J. - see Wolfram von Eschenbach
Kuhnigk, W. Nordwestsemitische Studien
   zum Hoseabuch.
   D. Pardee, 318(JAOS):Jul-Sep78-343
Kuić, R. Naše narodno pesništvo u
   Nizozemskoj.
   N.R. Pribic, 574(SEEJ):Fall79-419
Kuizenga, D. Narrative Strategies in "La
   Princesse de Clèves."*
   J. Campbell, 208(FS):Vol33Pt2-690
   V. Mylne, 535(RHL):Sep-Oct78-826
Kuklick, B. The Rise of American Phil-
   osophy.*
   A.C. Danto, 473(PR):4/1979-643
Kulp-Hill, K. Rosalía de Castro.*
   C. De Coster, 238:Mar79-174
Kulshrestha, J.P. Graham Greene the Novel-
   ist.
   R.S., 148:Autumn79-92
Kumar, A. Surapati.
   Soepomo Poedjosoedarmo, 293(JASt):
   May79-632
Kumar, S.K. Subterfuges.
   U. Parameswaran, 529(QQ):Spring79-172
Kumin, M. The Retrieval System.*
   R. De Mott, 651(WHR):Spring79-176
   R. Jackson, 134(CP):Fall78-99
   639(VQR):Autumn78-144
Kundera, M. The Book of Laughter and For-
   getting. (French title: Le Livre du
   rire et de l'oubli.)
   V. Beauvois, 450(NRF):Jul79-125
   J. Leonard, 441:6Nov80-C23
   J. Updike, 441:30Nov80-7
Kundera, M. Laughable Loves.* (French
   title: Risible amours.) The Farewell
   Party.
   P. Lewis, 565:Vol20#4-67
Küng, H. Kirche — Gehalten in der
   Wahrheit?
   T. Sheehan, 453(NYRB):7Feb80-38
Küng, H. Signposts for the Future.*
   T. Molnar, 396(ModA):Spring79-199
Küng, H. Vingt propositions d'Etre
   chrétien.
   A. Jacob, 542:Jul-Sep79-361
K'ung Shang-jen. The Peach Blossom Fan
   (Ts'o-hua-shan).* (Chen Shih-hsiang and
   H. Acton, with C. Birch, trans)
   L.Y. Chiu, 302:Vol16#1and2-117
Kuniholm, B.R. The Origins of the Cold
   War in the Near East.
   C.M. Woodhouse, 617(TLS):23May80-592
Kunisch, H. Rainer Maria Rilke. (2nd ed)
   F. Seewald, 224(GRM):Band28Heft1-104
Kunitz, S. A Kind of Order, a Kind of
   Folly.
   R.J. Smith, 461:Fall-Winter79/80-103
Kunitz, S. The Poems of Stanley Kunitz,
   1928-1978.*
   S. Moss, 617(TLS):30May80-621
   G. Orr, 29:Jul/Aug80-36

                              [continued]

[continuing]
R.J. Smith, 461:Fall-Winter79/80-103
P. Stitt, 491:Sep80-347
Kunstmann, H. Tschechische Erzählkunst im
20. Jahrhundert.
W. Schamschula, 688(ZSP):Band40Heft1-
214
Kunze, R. The Lovely Years.
R. Ellis, 493:Dec79-51
Kunze, S., ed. Richard Wagner.
J. Deathridge, 410(M&L):Jan79-96
Künzle, P. Heinrich Seuses Horologium
Sapientiae.*
N.F. Palmer, 402(MLR):Jul79-742
Kuo, I. The Key to Chinese Cooking.
W. and C. Cowen, 639(VQR):Spring78-72
Kuper, H. Sobhuza II.
D. Brokensha, 2(AfrA):Aug79-86
Kuper, J., ed. The Anthropologists' Cook-
book.
W. and C. Cowen, 639(VQR):Spring79-76
Kupfermann, J. The MsTaken Body.
D.J. Enright, 362:10Jan80-59
Küppers, J. Die Fabeln Avians.
J. Henderson, 123:Vol29No2-312
Kuprin, A. The Duel.
H. Gamburg, 558(RLJ):Winter79-204
Kurath, H., with others. Handbook of the
Linguistic Geography of New England.
(2nd ed)
R.K. O'Cain, 35(AS):Winter79-243
Kurath, H., with others, eds. Linguistic
Atlas of New England.
R.K. O'Cain, 35(AS):Winter79-243
Kurelek, W. The Passion of Christ.
529(QQ):Summer79-372
Kurilecz, M. A Remarkable Half-Dozen.
S. Plann, 399(MLJ):Apr79-221
Kurland, M. and S.W. Barton. The Last
President.
N. Callendar, 441:31Aug80-17
Kurland, P.B. Watergate and the Constitu-
tion.
T.D. Eisele, 396(ModA):Spring79-191
Kurtén, B. Dance of the Tiger.
P-L. Adams, 61:Nov80-99
R.A. Sokolov, 441:26Oct80-15
442(NY):3Nov80-202
Kuryłowicz, J. Studies in Semitic Grammar
and Metrics.
S. Levin, 215(GL):Summer78-109
Kurzke, H. Thomas-Mann-Forschung 1969-
1976.*
W. Schmidt-Dengler, 602:Vol10-250
Kurzman, D. Miracle of November.
L. Collins, 441:24Feb80-12
B. Knox, 453(NYRB):6Nov80-34
R.F. Shepard, 441:7Apr80-C18
Kushner, H.I. and A.H. Sherrill. John
Milton Hay.
R.D. Accinelli, 106:Fall79-195
Kuspit, D.B. Clement Greenberg, Art
Critic.
S. Gablik, 441:17Feb80-20
Kutscher, E.Y. Studies in Galilean
Aramaic.
Z. Zevit, 318(JAOS):Oct-Dec78-512

Kuttenkeuler, W., ed. Heinrich Heine.*
J.L.S., 191(ELN):Sep78(supp)-160
Kuttner, R. Revolt of the Haves.
A. Hacker, 441:19Oct80-7
Kutzbach, K.A., ed. Paul Ernst und Georg
Lukács.*
G.M. Vajda, 52:Band13Heft1-108
Kuusi, M., K. Bosley and M. Branch, eds
and trans. Finnish Folk Poetry: Epic.*
W.G. Jones, 402(MLR):Oct79-1004
V. Newall, 575(SEER):Jan79-105
P. Rogers, 255(HAB):Summer79-224
Kuzma, G. Adirondacks.
M. Heffernan, 491:Jun80-170
Kuzma, G. Village Journal.*
P. Ramsey, 569(SR):Fall79-686
Kuzmin, M.L. Sobraniye stikhov. (Vol 3)
(J.E. Malmstad and V. Markov, eds)
J.T. Baer, 558(RLJ):Spring79-232
R.D.B. Thomson, 575(SEER):Jan79-111
Kuźmiński, E. Het prefix sq in oost-
slavische werkwoorden.
H. Leeming, 575(SEER):Jan79-103
Kuznets, P.W. Economic Growth and Struc-
ture in the Republic of Korea.
R.F. Spencer, 293(JASt):Aug79-787
Kyle, D. Green River High.*
M. Laski, 362:10Jan80-62
Kyle, E. A Summer Scandal.
L.D., 617(TLS):11Jan80-46
Kynaston, D. King Labour.
B.C. Malament, 637(VS):Autumn78-106
Kyōkai, comp. Miraculous Stories from the
Japanese Buddhist Tradition. (K.M.
Nakamura, ed and trans)
Z. Shirakawa, 244(HJAS):Jun78-271
Kyvig, D.E. Repealing National Prohibi-
tion.
A. Sinclair, 617(TLS):29Feb80-230
Kyvig, D.E. and M.A. Marty. Your Family
History.
L.B. Nauen, 14:Oct79-480

Laage, K.E. - see Storm, T. and E. Schmidt
Laage, K.E. and V. Hand, eds. Schriften
der Theodor-Storm-Gesellschaft. (No.
25 and 26)
A.O. Bönig, 67:May79-146
Labandeira Fernández, A. - see Rodríguez
de Lena, P.
Labarbe, J. Fouilles de Thorikos I.
R.E. Wycherley, 303(JHS):Vol99-203
Labarrière, P-J. Dieu aujourd'hui.
M. Adam, 542:Jul-Sep79-362
Labé, L. Sonnets. (P. Sharratt, ed)
G. Jondorf, 208(FS):Apr79-181
La Beau, D., ed. Children's Authors and
Illustrators.
J. Oldfield, 677(YES):Vol9-354
La Belle, J. The Echoing Wood of Theodore
Roethke.*
R. Reichertz, 134(CP):Spring78-94
Laberge, A. Bitter Bread.
L. Leith, 102(CanL):Autumn˜9-120
Laberthonnière, L. Dogme et théologie.
A. Forest, 542:Apr-Jun78-190

La Bossière, C.R. Joseph Conrad and the Science of Unknowing.
W.W. Bonney, 268(IFR):Summer80-142

Labov, W. Language in the Inner City. Sociolinguistic Patterns.
R.I. McDavid, Jr., 35(AS):Winter79-291

Labriola, A.C. and M. Lieb - see "Milton Studies"

de Labriolle, J. Claudel and the English-Speaking World. (R. Little, ed and trans)
J-M. Gliksohn, 549(RLC):Jan-Mar77-122

Labroisse, G., ed. Zur Literatur und Literaturwissenschaft der DDR.
G. Opie, 182:Vol131#19-678

Labruna, L. Il console "sovversivo."
J. Carter, 313:Vol69-184

Laburthe-Tolra, P. Mínlaaba.
F. Quinn, 69:Vol148#4-406

Lacan, J. Écrits.* (A. Sheridan, ed and trans)
N.H. Bruss, 418(MR):Summer79-337
S. Gearhart, 153:Spring79-114
205(FMLS):Apr78-187

Lacan, J. The Four Fundamental Concepts of Psycho-Analysis.* (J-A. Miller, ed)
N.H. Bruss, 418(MR):Summer79-337

Lacant, J. Marivaux en Allemagne.* (Vol 1)
P. Grappin, 549(RLC):Jan-Mar77-115

Lach, D.F. Asia in the Making of Europe. (Vols 1 and 2)
D.E. Mungello, 322(JHI):Oct-Dec79-649

Lach, D.F. Asia in the Making of Europe. (Vol 2, Bks 2 and 3)
J. Needham and Lu Gwei-Djen, 293(JASt):Feb79-313

Lachance, A. La Justice criminelle du roi au Canada au XVIIIe siècle.
J.A. Dickinson, 656(WMQ):Apr79-312

La Charité, R.C., ed. O un Amy!*
B.C. Bowen, 207(FR):Oct78-156
J.G. Cornell, 67:Nov79-339
M. Dassonville, 546(RR):Jan79-94
P. Henry, 399(MLJ):Jan-Feb79-48
S.J. Holyoake, 402(MLR):Jul79-694

La Charité, V.A. Henri Michaux.
P. Broome, 402(MLR):Jul79-711
J.D. Erickson, 188(ECr):Spring78-98
R.R. Hubert, 207(FR):Oct78-172

Lachmann, R. Gesänge der Juden auf der Insel Djerba. (E. Gerson-Kiwi, ed)
J. Spector, 187:Jan80-565

de Laclos, C. Les Liaisons dangereuses. (R. Abirached, ed)
205(FMLS):Jan78-90

Lacouture, J. François Mauriac.
P. Thody, 617(TLS):30May80-600

Lacy, N.J., ed. 26 Chansons d'Amour de la Renaissance.
C.N. Smith, 208(FS):Vol33Pt2-651

Lade, J., ed. Building a Library.
A. Burgess, 617(TLS):29Feb80-227

Ladner, M.D. O.C. Seltzer, Painter of the Old West.
W. Gard, 584(SWR):Autumn79-398

Ladner, P., ed. Iter Helveticum. (Pts 1 and 2)
R.W. Pfaff, 589:Apr79-392

Ladurie, E.L. - see under Le Roy Ladurie, E.

Lafay, H. - see de Vermeil, A.

Lafay, H. - see Voiture, V.

Marquis de Lafayette. Lafayette in the Age of the American Revolution. (Vol 1) (S.J. Idzerda and others, eds)
B.A. Chernow, 656(WMQ):Jul79-484

Marquis de Lafayette. Lafayette in the Age of the American Revolution. (Vol 2) (S.J. Idzerda, ed)
676(YR):Summer80-VII

La Feber, W. The Panama Canal.*
R.W. Leopold, 578(SAQ):Winter79-122

Laferrière, D. Five Russian Poems.
R.E. Matlaw, 558(RLJ):Spring79-223

Lafeuilie, G. Cinq Hymnes de Ronsard.
B.L.O. Richter, 539:Vol4No2-232

Laffineur, R. Les vases en métal précieux à l'époque mycénienne.
R. Higgins, 303(JoHS):Vol99-216

Laflèche, G. Mallarmé.*
S. Faïk, 209(FM):Jan78-87

Laflèche, G. Petit manuel des études littéraires.
H.M. Block, 107(CRCL):Winter79-82
G. Breton, 193(ELit):Apr78-239
R.A. Champagne, 207(FR):Feb79-479

Lafond, G. Les cloches d'autres mondes.
M. Recurt, 102(CanL):Spring79-98

Lafond, J. La Rochefoucauld.
M.S. Koppisch, 207(FR):Apr79-767
P. Sellier, 535(RHL):Nov-Dec79-1044

de La Fontaine, G. Hubert Aquin et le Québec.
J. Melançon, 627(UTQ):Summer79-460

de La Fontaine, J. Some Tales.* (C.H. Sisson, trans) Selected Fables.* (J. Michie, trans)
D.M. Thomas, 617(TLS):18Jan80-66

Laforgue, J. Les Complaintes.* (M. Collie, ed)
J.A. Hiddleston, 402(MLR):Apr79-466
205(FMLS):Apr78-187

Laforgue, J. Moralités légendaires. (P. Pia, ed) La parodie.
D. Grojnowski, 98:Jan78-63

Laframboise, Y. and others. Neuville. Calixa-Lavallée.
H. Kalman, 576:Oct78-214

Lagadeuc, J. Le "Catholicon" de Jehan Lagadeuc. (C-J. Guyonvarc'h, ed)
R. Arveiller, 209(FM):Jul78-265

de Lage, G.R. - see under Raynaud de Lage, G.

Lageat, R. Robert des Halles.
R. Cobb, 617(TLS):11Jul80-784

Lagemann, E.C. A Generation of Women.
E. Wright, 617(TLS):21Mar80-320

Lagerkvist, P. Antecknat. (E. Lagerkvist, ed)
I. Scobbie, 563(SS):Winter79-97

Lance, D. An Archive Approach to Oral
History.
  E.R. Cregeen, 595(ScS):Vo123-87
  R.E. Schnare, 14:Jul79-359
Lancelyn Green, R. Heroes of Greece and
Troy.
  H. Lloyd-Jones, 617(TLS):18Jul80-797
Land, A.C., L.G. Carr and E.C. Papenfuse,
eds. Law, Society and Politics in
Early Maryland.*
  D.L. Ammerman, 656(WMQ):Apr79-294
de Landa, D. Relación de las Cosas de
Yucatán.
  N. Hammond, 617(TLS):8Feb80-147
Landa, E.T. - see Terralla Landa, E.
Landauer, G. For Socialism.
  M. Cohen, 287:Dec78-23
Landberg, H., ed. Energy: The Next Twenty
Years.
  P.K. Verleger, Jr., 231:Apr80-110
Landeira, R. Ramiro de Maeztu.
  A. Hoyle, 86(BHS):Jul79-275
Landels, J.G. Engineering in the Ancient
World.
  T.N. Ballin, 124:Sep79-31
  M. Hassall, 313:Vo169-202
Lander, P.S. In the Shadow of the Factory.
  G. London, 563(SS):Spring79-179
Landerman, P. Vocabulario Quechua del
Pastaza.
  T.T. Büttner, 269(IJAL):Oct78-343
Landfester, M. Handlungsverlauf und Komik
in den frühen Komödien des Aristophanes.
  G. Ronnet, 555:Vo152fasc2-371
Landmann, G.P. Stefan George und sein
Kreis.* (2nd ed)
  U.K. Goldsmith, 301(JEGP):Jan79-95
Landmann, G.P. Vorträge über Stefan
George.
  H. Naumann, 680(ZDP):Band97Heft2-308
Landon, H.C.R. Haydn: Chronicle and
Works.* (Vol 3)
  G. Wheelock, 414(MusQ):Jan78-106
Landon, H.C.R. Haydn: The Early Years.
  H. Cole, 362:11Dec80-797
Landry, H., ed. New Essays on Shake-
speare's Sonnets.*
  K. Duncan-Jones, 447(N&Q):Apr78-173
  J. Fuzier, 189(EA):Apr-Jun78-223
  M-M. Martinet, 189(EA):Jul-Dec78-379
  K. Muir, 402(MLR):Jan79-163
Landseer, T., ed. Life and Letters of
William Bewick (Artist).
  G. Reynolds, 617(TLS):12Sep80-988
von Landskron, S. Die Hymelstrass.
  B. Murdoch, 182:Vo131#21/22-803
Landwehr, J. Studies in Dutch Books with
Coloured Plates Published 1662-1875.*
  J.A. Welu, 54:Sep78-557
Landwehr, J. Text und Fiktion.
  G. Michel, 682(ZPSK):Band31Heft1-94
Landwehr, J., M. Mitzschke and R. Paulus.
Praxis der Informationsermittlung.
  R. Atkinson, 221(GQ):Nov79-565
Lane, B.M. and L.J. Rupp, eds and trans.
Nazi Ideology before 1933.
  639(VQR):Autumn78-148

Lane, C. Christian Religion in the Soviet
Union.
  E. Dunn, 550(RusR):Oct79-493
Lane, G. A Concordance to the Poems of
Dylan Thomas.
  W. Davies, 447(N&Q):Apr78-184
  C.J. Rawson, 402(MLR):Jul79-689
Lane, G., ed. Sylvia Plath.*
  D.L. Eder, 659(ConL):Spring80-301
  639(VQR):Autumn79-127
Lane, H. The Wild Boy of Aveyron.
  M. Garner, 67:May79-185
  R. Robyn, 608:Mar80-101
Lane, M. The Magic Years of Beatrix
Potter.
  V. Powell, 39:Aug79-156
Lane, P. Poems New and Selected.*
  D. Barbour, 150(DR):Spring79-154
Lane, P. Prince Philip.
  A. Howard, 362:11Dec80-798
Lane, P. and L. Uher. No Longer Two
People.
  J. Cook, 99:Mar80-38
  M.B. Oliver, 198:Summer80-147
  376:Oct79-141
Lane, R. Images from the Floating World.
  J. Hillier, 90:Jun79-393
Lane, R. Shunga Books of the Ukiyo-e
School.
  J. Hillier, 463:Spring78-91
Lanes, S.G. The Art of Maurice Sendak.
  H. Kramer, 441:9Nov80-47
Lanfranc of Bec. The Letters of Lanfranc
Archbishop of Canterbury. (H. Clover
and M. Gibson, eds)
  F. Barlow, 617(TLS):21Mar80-336
Lang, C.L. - see Rupp, H.
Lang, D. A Backward Look.*
  639(VQR):Autumn79-144
Lang, D. Orchids of Britain.
  R. O'Hanlon, 617(TLS):25Jul80-850
Lang, D.M. The Bulgarians from Pagan
Times to the Ottoman Conquest.
  J. Scarborough, 121(CJ):Apr-May80-352
Lang, E. Semantik der koordinativen Verk-
nüpfung.
  L. Zgusta, 474(PIL):Spring-Summer78-
  267
von Lang, J., with C. Sibyll. The Secre-
tary.* (German title: Der Sekretär.)
  639(VQR):Autumn79-141
Lang, M. The Athenian Agora.* (Vol 21:
Graffiti and Dipinti.)
  D.M. Lewis, 123:Vo129No1-125
Langacker, R.W. An Overview of Uto-
Aztecan Grammar.
  W.R. Miller, 350:Sep79-708
"Langages de Flaubert."
  J. Bem, 535(RHL):Sep-Oct78-849
Langbaum, R. The Mysteries of Identity.*
  G.G. Fromm, 395(MFS):Summer78-305
  J.R. Kincaid, 639(VQR):Autumn78-742
  J.D.P., 191(ELN):Sep78(supp)-40
  W.D. Shaw, 579(SAQ):Winter79-128
  295(JML):Vo17#4-585
  529(QQ):Summer79-373

Lange, B. Literarische Form und politische Tendenz bei George Orwell.
A. Zwerdling, 125:Winter79-312
Lange, F.C. Historia da Música nas Irmandades de Vila Rica. (Vol 1, Pt 1)
R. Stevenson, 37:Sep79-45
Lange, R.A. The Phonology of Eighth-Century Japanese.
P.T. Sato, 318(JAOS):Oct-Dec78-533
Lange, T. Idyllische und exotische Sehnsucht.
B. Burk, 224(GRM):Band28Heft2-251
Lange, W-D., ed. Französische Literaturkritik der Gegenwart in Einzeldarstellungen.
J. Siess, 535(RHL):May-Jun78-512
Lange-Seidl, A. Approaches to Theories for Nonverbal Signs.
M.R. Key, 350:Dec79-969
Langer, L.L. The Age of Atrocity.
T. Ziolkowski, 569(SR):Fall79-676
639(VQR):Spring79-47
Langguth, A.J. Hidden Terrors.
639(VQR):Spring79-64
Langland, J. Any Body's Song.
W. Pritchard, 441:6Jul80-8
Langland, W. Piers Plowman: the B Version.* (G. Kane and E.T. Donaldson, eds) [shown in prev under title]
T. Lawler, 405(MP):Aug79-606
Langland, W. The Vision of Piers the Plowman: A Complete Edition of the B-Text.* (A.V.C. Schmidt, ed) Piers Plowman: An Edition of the C-Text.* (D. Pearsall, ed)
N. Jacobs, 175:Summer79-151
T. Turville-Petre, 541(RES):Nov79-454
Langlois, W.G. - see "André Malraux 3"
Langlotz, E. Studien zur nordostgriechischen Kunst.*
J.G. Pedley, 54:Mar78-155
Lanham, R.A. The Motives of Eloquence.*
P. Alpers, 599:Spring79-230
H. Hawkins, 402(MLR):Jan79-139
W.J. Kennedy, 131(CL):Winter79-85
Lanher, J. Les Contes de Fraimbois. (new ed)
B. Guidot, 547(RF):Band91Heft4-462
Lanher, J. - see Monfrin, J., with L. Fossier
Lanly, A. Morphologie historique des verbes français.*
R. Arveiller, 209(FM):Jul78-284
Lanman, C. Biographical Annals of the Civil Government of the United States During its First Century.
K.B. Harder, 424:Sep78-294
Lannestock, G. Vilhelm Moberg i Amerika.
R. Wright, 563(SS):Winter79-99
Lansard, J. La Création littéraire chez Drieu la Rochelle à travers son oeuvre théâtrale.
E. Weber, 617(TLS):6Jun80-631
Lansdowne, J.F. Birds of the West Coast. (Vol 2)
P-L. Adams, 61:Dec80-96

Lansing, R.H. From Image to Idea.
M.M., 228(GSLI):Vol155fasc492-628
M.U. Sowell, 589:Jan79-164
Lanza, D. and others. L'ideologia della città.
E. Namer, 542:Jan-Mar78-87
Lao Tzu and Wang Pi. A Translation of Lao Tzu's "Tao Te Ching" and Wang Pi's Commentary. (P.J. Lin, trans)
W-T. Chan, 485(PE&W):Jul79-357
Lapham, L.H. Fortune's Child.
W. Goodman, 441:10Feb80-7
C. Lehmann-Haupt, 441:11Feb80-C15
61:Apr80-126
Lapidus, G.W. Women in Soviet Society.
A. Brown, 617(TLS):25Jan80-95
B.A. Engle, 550(RusR):Apr79-245
Lapiner, A. Pre-Columbian Art of South America.*
J. Jones, 54:Mar78-190
Laporta, A. - see Ferrari, I.A.
Laporte, R. Suite.* Souvenir de Reims. Carnets.
P. Dulac, 450(NRF):Aug79-117
Lapp, C. Honey.*
G. Davies, 168(ECW):Spring78-82
Lapp, J.C. The Brazen Tower.
F. Gray, 207(FR):Mar79-636
Laqueur, T.W. Religion and Respectability.*
D.V.E., 191(ELN):Sep78(supp)-33
H. McLeod, 637(VS):Winter78-245
Laqueur, W., ed. Fascism.
A. Graham-Yooll, 364:Aug/Sep79-143
Laqueur, W. Guerrilla.*
J. Talbott, 639(VQR):Spring78-351
Laqueur, W. The Missing Years.
N. Ascherson, 453(NYRB):12Jun80-34
A. Brumberg, 617(TLS):4Jul80-749
C. Lehmann-Haupt, 441:11Apr80-C25
J. Naughton, 362:6Mar80-318
442(NY):31Mar80-122
Laqueur, W. Terrorism.
P. Dennis, 529(QQ):Spring79-178
"L'Archange empourpré." (H. Corbin, trans)
J. Brun, 192(EP):Apr-Jun79-236
Lardner, R., Jr. The Lardners.*
R. Forrey, 395(MFS):Winter78/79-636
de Larivey, P. Les Esprits. (M.J. Freeman, ed)
H.G. Hall, 208(FS):Jul79-339
de Larivey, P. Les Esprits. (D. Stone, Jr., ed)
N. Aronson, 399(MLJ):Apr79-217
H.G. Hall, 208(FS):Jul79-339
Larkin, E. The Historical Dimensions of Irish Catholicism. The Roman Catholic Church and the Creation of the Modern Irish State, 1876-1886.
L.J. McCaffrey, 637(VS):Summer79-449
Larkin, E. The Roman Catholic Church in Ireland and the Fall of Parnell 1888-1891.
F.S.L. Lyons, 617(TLS):15Feb80-164

215

Larkin, M. Man and Society in Nineteenth-Century Realism.
  J.M. Holquist, 445(NCF):Dec78-378
  A. Shelston, 148:Autumn79-86
  P.M. Wetherill, 402(MLR):Apr79-399
Laroch, P. Petits-Maîtres et roués.
  R. Runte, 150(DR):Spring79-193
de Laroche, R. and F. Bellair. Marie Dubas.
  P. O'Connor, 617(TLS):11Jul80-784
Larochette, J. Le Langage et la réalité.* (Vol 1)
  T.T. Büttner and A. Tovar, 685(ZDL): 1/1979-79
  N.C.W. Spence, 208(FS):Vol33Pt2-1069
La Rosa, L.J. and B. Tanenbaum. The Random Factor.
  M. Laski, 362:10Jan80-62
de Larrabeiti, M. The Bunce.
  M. Laski, 362:17Apr80-514
Larsen, E. Wit as a Weapon.
  H. Maccoby, 362:24Apr80-549
  F. Spiegl, 617(TLS):5Sep80-972
Larsen, R.W. Bundy.
  T. Thompson, 441:24Aug80-12
Larson, B.A. Prologue to Revolution.
  W.A. Linsley, 583:Spring79-309
Larson, C. and others. Assessing Functional Communication.
  M.D. Hazen, 583:Spring79-318
Larson, C.R. American Indian Fiction.
  L. Evers, 50(ArQ):Autumn79-287
  W. Ude, 649(WAL):Spring79-74
  639(VQR):Autumn79-129
Larson, R. Fantasy and Imagination in the Mexican Narrative.
  D.J. Parle, 238:Mar79-189
Larson, T.A. History of Wyoming.
  G. Holthaus, 649(WAL):Winter80-344
Larson, T.B. Soviet-American Rivalry.
  R.R. Pope, 550(RusR):Apr79-249
Larue, G.A. Ancient Myth and Modern Man.
  B. Allen, 292(JAF):Apr-Jun79-239
Laruelle, F. Au-delà du principe de pouvoir.
  J-M. Gabaude, 542:Jul-Sep79-364
Laruelle, F. and others. Le déclin de l'écriture.
  J-M. Gabaude, 542:Jul-Sep79-364
Lascault, G. Un îlot tempéré. Figurées, défigurées.
  G. Raillard, 98:Apr78-428
Lascault, G. Voyage d'automne et d'hiver.
  A. Clerval, 450(NRF):Aug79-121
Lasch, C. The Culture of Narcissism.*
  J. Doane and D.L. Hodges, 560:Fall79-185
  F. Ferré, 219(GaR):Winter79-961
  M. Fischer, 560:Fall79-166
  L.D. Nachman, 560:Fall79-173
  G. Strawson, 617(TLS):4Jul80-759
Lasch, C. Haven in a Heartless World.*
  D. Gorham, 529(QQ):Spring79-152
Lash, J.P. Helen and Teacher.
  B. Bettelheim, 442(NY):4Aug80-85
  A. Broyard, 441:24May80-21
                    [continued]

[continuing]
  J. Featherstone, 441:8Jun80-1
  61:Jul80-84
Lash, J.P. Roosevelt and Churchill, 1939-1941.*
  C. Kilpatrick, 639(VQR):Winter78-171
Lasker, D.J. Jewish Philosophical Polemics against Christianity in the Middle Ages.
  M.W. Bloomfield, 589:Jan79-167
Laski, M. Everyday Ecstasy.
  P. Beer, 362:29May80-695
  M. Warnock, 617(TLS):6Jun80-632
Lasky, M.J. Utopias and Revolution.*
  G. Negley, 322(JHI):Apr-Jun79-315
Laslett, P. Family Life and Illicit Love in Earlier Generations.
  J.A. Sharpe, 161(DUJ):Dec78-105
Laslett, P., K. Oosterveen and R.M. Smith, eds. Bastardy and its Comparative History.
  R. Mitchison, 362:24Jul80-117
Lass, R. English Phonology and Phonological Theory.*
  W.F. Koopman, 433:Jan79-148
Lass, R. and J.M. Anderson. Old English Phonology.*
  J. Algeo, 215(GL):Winter78-236
  W.F. Koopman, 433:Jan79-148
  A. Ward, 382(MAE):1979/2-272
  H. Weinstock, 179(ES):Jun79-313
Lassaletta, M.C. Aportaciones al estudio del lenguaje coloquial galdosiano.
  J. Geary, 545(RPh):May79-432
Lasserre, F. and N. Livadaras, eds. Etymologicum Magnum genuinum.* (Vol 1)
  R.W., 555:Vol152fasc1-190
Lassner, J. The Shaping of Abbasid Rule.
  E. Bosworth, 617(TLS):19Sep80-1042
Lasso de la Vega, J.S. De Safo a Platón.
  P. Louis, 555:Vol152fasc2-377
Latacz, J. Kampfparänese, Kampfdarstellung und Kampfwirklichkeit in der Ilias, bei Kallinos und Tyrtaios.
  M.L. West, 123:Vol129No1-135
de La Taille, J. Les Corrivaus (Comédie). (D.L. Drysdall, ed)
  C.N. Smith, 208(FS):Vol33Pt2-640
Lath, M. A Study of Dattilam.
  E. te Nijenhuis, 187:Sep80-568
Latham, E.C., ed. Thirteen Colonial Americana. United Statesiana.
  E. Wolf 2d, 432(NEQ):Dec79-594
Latham, R. - see Pepys, S.
La Touche, R. John Ruskin and Rose La Touche. (V.A. Burd, ed)
  H. Corke, 362:21Feb80-252
  D. Johnson, 453(NYRB):15May80-11
  M. Lutyens, 617(TLS):15Feb80-178
Latrobe, B.H. The Papers of Benjamin Henry Latrobe: The Microtext Edition. (E.C. Carter 2d and T.E. Jeffrey, eds)
  W.J. Bell, Jr., 656(WMQ):Jan79-134
  F. Toker, 576:Mar78-42

Latrobe, B.H. The Virginia Journals of Benjamin Henry Latrobe 1795-98. (E.C. Carter 2d, ed)
  F. Atkinson, 46:Apr79-252
  W.J. Bell, Jr., 656(WMQ):Jan79-134
  R.A. Rutland, 639(VQR):Winter79-176
  F.H. Sommer 3d, 658:Spring79-93
Latsis, S.J., ed. Method and Appraisal in Economics.*
  J. Agassi, 488:Sep79-316
  G.C. Archibald, 488:Sep79-304
  D.W. Hands, 488:Sep79-293
Latt, D.J. and S.H. Monk. John Dryden.
  D.W. Hopkins, 447(N&Q):Dec78-557
  R.D. Hume, 402(MLR):Jul79-658
  A. Poyet, 189(EA):Jul-Dec78-386
  J.P. Vander Motten, 179(ES):Dec79-794
Lattimore, R. - see "The Four Gospels and the Revelation"
Lau, J.S.M. and T.A. Ross, ed. Chinese Stories from Taiwan: 1960-1970.
  J. Spence, 453(NYRB):17Apr80-20
Laubin, R. and G. The Indian Tipi.
  W.K. McNeil, 292(JAF):Apr-Jun79-244
Laudan, L. Progress and its Problems.*
  R.E. Butts, 488:Dec79-475
  D.L. Hull, 488:Dec79-457
  I.C. Jarvie, 488:Dec79-484
  A. Lugg, 488:Dec79-466
Lauer, Q. Essays in Hegelian Dialectic.*
  E.E. Harris, 518:Jan79-17
Lauer, Q. A Reading of Hegel's "Phenomenology of Spirit."*
  O. Blanchette, 142:Sep-Dec78-389
Lauerbach, G. Form und Funktion englischer Konditionalsätze mit "if."
  R.H. Lawson, 182:Vol131#21/22-800
Lauf, D.I. Tibetan Sacred Art.*
  B.N. Goswamy, 318(JAOS):Jul-Sep78-332
  J. Lowry, 463:Winter79/80-498
Laufer, R. and others. Le langage, le théâtre, la parole et l'image.
  H. Godin, 208(FS):Vol133Pt2-996
Laufs, J. Der Friedensgedanke bei Augustinus.
  A. Kemmer, 182:Vol131#17/18-592
Laughlin, J. Selected Poems.
  P. Laurans, 491:Feb80-297
Laughlin, R. The Great Tzotzil Dictionary of San Lorenzo Zinacantán.
  U. Köhler, 269(IJAL):Apr78-156
Laumonier, A. Exploration archéologique de Délos faite par l'École française d'Athènes. (fasc 31)
  P.J. Callaghan, 303(JoHS):Vol199-215
Laumonier, P. - see de Ronsard, P.
Laura, A. and G. Lepschy. The Italian Language Today.
  G. Carsaniga, 402(MLR):Jan79-216
Laurence, D.H., with L.B. Garcia. Shaw: An Exhibit.*
  F.P.W. McDowell, 295(JML):Vol7#4-809
Laurence, J.C. Race Propaganda and South Africa.
  K. Heard, 150(DR):Winter79/80-770
Laurence, S. Names of Thunder.
  D. Barbour, 150(DR):Spring79-154

Laurenson, D., ed. The Sociology of Literature.
  R. Best, 89(BJA):Summer79-275
Laurenti, H., ed. Paul Valéry 2 — Recherches sur "La Jeune Parque."
  W.N. Ince, 402(MLR):Oct79-946
de Lauretis, T. La sintassi del desiderio.*
  R.S. Dombroski, 400(MLN):Jan79-176
Laurin, C. La Politique québécoise du développement culturel.
  A.B. Chartier, 207(FR):Apr79-813
Lauritzen, P. Venice.
  L.M. Ferrari, 276:Autumn79-303
  J.G. Links, 39:Mar79-240
Lauritzen, P. and A. Zielcke. Palaces of Venice.
  J.G. Links, 39:Mar79-240
Lausberg, H. Handbuch der literarischen Rhetorik. (5th ed) Elemente der literarischen Rhetorik. (2nd ed)
  P. Missac, 98:Nov78-1017
Lauterbach, A. Many Times, But Then.
  J. Fuller, 617(TLS):18Jan80-65
Lautman, A. Essai sur l'unité des mathématiques.
  Y. Gauthier, 98:Jan78-3
  A. Reix, 542:Apr-Jun78-230
Comte de Lautréamont. Les Chants de Maldoror suivi de Lettres, Poésies I et II. (D. Oster, ed)
  M.N. Evans, 207(FR):Oct78-169
  205(FMLS):Jan78-88
Comte de Lautréamont. Isidore Ducasse, Comte de Lautréamont: Oeuvres complètes; Les Chants de Maldoror, Lettres, Poésies I et II. (H. Juin, ed)
  S.I. Lockerbie, 208(FS):Apr79-214
Comte de Lautréamont. Oeuvres complètes: Chants de Maldoror.
  M. Pierssens, 98:May78-493
Lauvergant-Gagnière, C. and H. Duranton - see Abbe d'Olivet
Lauvergnat-Gagnière, C. and H. Duranton - see Thoulier, P-J.
de Lavesne, D. - see under Douin de Lavesne
Laveyssière, M-T. - see Freud, S.
Lavin, I. Bernini and the Unity of Visual Arts.
  J. Russell, 441:30Nov80-11
Lavin, I. and J. Plummer, eds. Studies in Late Mediaeval and Renaissance Painting in honor of Millard Meiss.
  C. Reynolds, 135:Jun79-133
Lavin, M. Tales from Bective Bridge.
  R.F. Peterson, 174(Éire):Summer79-135
Lavoisier, B. Mon Corps, ton corps, leur corps.
  T.M. Scanlan, 207(FR):Apr79-812
Law, C. and R. Glen. Critical Choice.
  H. Inhaber, 529(QQ):Autumn79-504
Law, T.S. and T. Bewick - see MacDiarmid, H.
Lawder, D. Trolling.*
  639(VQR):Winter78-13

Leaska, M.A. - see Woolf, V.

Leathard, A. The Fight for Family Planning.
 N. Roberts, 617(TLS):5Sep80-966

Leather, E. The Duveen Letter.
 N. Callendar, 441:7Dec80-44

Leather, E. The Mozart Score.
 N. Callendar, 441:11May80-21

Leavis, F.R. The Living Principle.
 G.W. Most, 153:Summer79-53

Leavis, F.R. Thought, Words and Creativity.*
 W.E. Cain, 454:Spring79-269

Lebeaux, R. Young Man Thoreau.*
 F. Day, 580(SCR):Spring79-83
 M. Meyer, 639(VQR):Autumn78-754
 H.D. Peck, 651(WHR):Winter79-85

Lebègue, R. Études sur le théâtre français.
 W.D. Howarth, 208(FS):Jul79-368
 J. Morel, 535(RHL):Jan-Feb79-116

Lebègue, R. - see de Peiresc, N.

Lebek, W.D. Lucans Pharsalia.
 M. Griffin, 123:Vol29No1-44

Le Berre, Y. - see Inisan, L.

Lebeuf, J-P. Études kotoko.
 N. Barley, 69:Vol48#4-408

Lebeuf, J-P. and A. Les arts des Sao.
 M. Berns, 2(AfrA):Nov78-103
 P. Guerre, 98:May78-528

Leblanc, A. Une Fille pour l'hiver.
 P. Carrard, 207(FR):Apr79-795

Le Boutillier, J. Harvard Hates America.*
 G.A. Panichas, 396(ModA):Summer79-300

Lebow, R.N. White Britain and Black Ireland.
 L.J. McCaffrey, 637(VS):Summer79-449

Léca, D. La Rupture de 1940.
 D. Johnson, 617(TLS):4Jan80-15

Lecherbonnier, B., H. Mitterand, and D. Rincé. L'Esprit et la lettre. (Vol 1)
 W. Wrage, 207(FR):May79-963

Le Clerc, P.O. Voltaire and Crébillon père.
 J.H. Brumfitt, 208(FS):Jan79-83

Lecointre, S. and J. le Galliot - see Diderot, D.

Le Comte, E. Milton and Sex.*
 M. Halliday, 184(EIC):Jul79-269
 J.P. Rosenblatt, 613:Dec79-452

Leconte de Lisle, C.M. Oeuvres. (Vol 3) (E. Pich, ed)
 A. Fairlie, 208(FS):Jan79-94

von Le Coq, A.A. and others, eds. Sprachwissenschaftliche Ergebnisse der deutschen Turfan-Forschung.
 L.V. Clark, 318(JAOS):Jul-Sep78-318

"Lectures de Saint-John Perse."
 M. Autrand, 535(RHL):May-Jun78-507

Le Cunff, M. Sur le vif.*
 P. Siegel, 207(FR):Mar79-678

Ledbetter, S. - see Marenzio, L.

Ledda, G. Le Langage de la faux (Padre Padrone II).
 H. Cronel, 450(NRF):Dec79-127

Ledeen, M. The First Duce.
 J. Meyers, 639(VQR):Winter78-176

Ledent, R. Comprendre la sémantique.
 G. Charron and C. Germain, 320(CJL): Spring-Fall78-200

Lederer, L., ed. Take Back the Night.
 C. See, 441:28Dec80-4

Ledésert, D.M. and R.P.L. - see Mansion, J.E.

Ledrut, R. La Révolution cachée.
 J. Duvignaud, 450(NRF):Dec79-121

Leduc-Fayette, D. Jean-Jacques Rousseau et le mythe de l'antiquité.
 S. Goyard-Fabre, 542:Jul-Sep78-364
 J.S. Spink, 208(FS):Apr79-200

Lee, A.J. The Origins of the Popular Press in England, 1855-1914.
 E.M. Palmegiano, 637(VS):Spring78-420

Lee, B. The Novels of Henry James.
 V. Jones, 541(RES):Aug79-366
 H. Lee, 175:Spring79-83

Lee, B. Theory and Personality.
 D. Trotter, 617(TLS):22Feb80-204

Lee, C. and others. Prospettive sui Fabliaux.*
 W. Rothwell, 208(FS):Vol33Pt2-569

Lee, D. The Gods.
 D. Cooley, 99:Mar80-34
 M.F. Dixon, 198:Fall80-90

Lee, D. - see Wittgenstein, L.

Lee En-han. China's Quest for Railway Autonomy, 1904-1911.
 C.K. Leung, 302:Vol16#1and2-126
 J.K. Ocko, 293(JASt):Feb79-334

Lee, G. Pieces for a Glass Piano.
 42(AR):Winter79-126

Lee, G.E. Monteith Bowls.
 G. Wills, 39:Dec79-532

Lee, G.E., with R.A. Lee. British Silver Monteith Bowls.
 A. Grimwade, 135:Feb79-138

Lee, H. The Novels of Virginia Woolf.
 D. Hewitt, 184(EIC):Jan79-88
 F. Pellan, 395(MFS):Summer78-321
 S. Rudikoff, 249(HudR):Winter79/80-540

Lee, H.Y. The Politics of the Chinese Cultural Revolution.
 S. Rosen, 293(JASt):Aug79-764

Lee, J. The Modernization of Irish Society, 1848-1918.
 L.J. McCaffrey, 637(VS):Summer79-449

Lee, J. My Life with Nye.
 A. Howard, 362:13Nov80-659

Lee, L. Signs of Spring.
 C. Lehmann-Haupt, 441:1Feb80-C23
 C. Seebohm, 441:17Feb80-16

Lee, L. and J. Charlton. The Hand Book.
 E. Auchincloss, 441:20Jul80-14

Lee, L.L. and S.B. Virginia Sorensen.
 R. Gish, 649(WAL):Winter80-335

Lee, L.L. and M. Lewis, eds. Women, Women Writers, and the West.
 H.C. Thompson, 649(WAL):Fall79-252

Lee, M. Studies in Goethe's Lyric Cycles.
 S. Atkins, 221(GQ):Nov79-539

Lee, P.H. Songs of Flying Dragons.
 D.R. McCann, 318(JAOS):Apr-Jun78-186

Lee, R.W. Names on Trees.*
  R.W. Hanning, 141:Winter79-71
  I. Ragusa, 276:Spring79-64
Lee, V., ed. Language Development.
  R. Sussex, 67:Nov79-375
Leech, G. Semantics.*
  M. Dascal and M. Adler, 567:Vol26#1/2-
  151
Leech-Anspach, G. Evgenij Zamjatin.
  L. Scheffler, 688(ZSP):Band40Heft2-408
Leeming, H. Rola języka polskiego w roz-
  woju leksyki rosyjskiej do roku 1696.*
  S.C. Gardiner, 575(SEER):Jan79-104
Lees-Milne, A. and R. Verey, eds. The
  Englishwoman's Garden.
  R. Blythe, 362:13Mar80-348
Lees-Milne, J. Harold Nicolson. (Vol 1)
  R. Trevelyan, 362:20Nov80-696
Leeson, R. Fluency and Language Teaching.*
  V. Meus, 179(ES):Dec79-827
Lefeuvre, A. Merleau-Ponty au delà de la
  phénoménologie.
  S. Auroux, 154:Jun78-394
  F. Tricaud, 542:Apr-Jun78-195
Lefevere, A. Literary Knowledge.
  H. Pausch, 107(CRCL):Winter79-84
Lefèvre, C. Sur l'evolution d'Aristote en
  psychologie.*
  P. Louis, 555:Vol52fasc2-379
Lefèvre, E. Der Thyestes des Lucius
  Varius Rufus.
  R.J. Tarrant, 123:Vol29No1-149
Lefèvre, R. - see Rivière, J.
Lefèvre, W. Naturtheorie und Produktions-
  weise.
  S. Decloux, 182:Vol31#5/6-130
Lefèvre d'Étaples, J. and others. Épîtres
  et Évangiles pour les cinquante et deux
  dimenches de l'an. (G. Bédouelle and F.
  Giacone, eds)
  J. Pineaux, 535(RHL):May-Jun78-454
Leffland, E. Last Courtesies.
  J. Romano, 441:5Oct80-3
Lefkowitz, M.R. The Victory Ode.*
  A. Köhnken, 24:Summer79-307
Lefkowitz, M.R. and M.B. Fant. Women in
  Greece and Rome.
  A.J. Marshall, 529(QQ):Autumn79-528
Lefrançois, A. Rémanences.
  M.A. Fitzpatrick, 207(FR):Mar79-671
Lefrançois, M. La Chasse au paysan.
  H.L. Butler, 207(FR):Dec78-369
Lefrère, J. Le Visage de Lautréamont.*
  T.M. Scheerer, 72:Band216Heft1-227
Le Galliot, J. Description génerative et
  transformationnelle de la langue fran-
  çaise.*
  N.C.W. Spence, 208(FS):Vol33Pt2-1049
Legaré, C. La Structure Sémantique.
  T.G. Pavel, 107(CRCL):Winter79-90
Legault, G.A. La structure performative
  du langage juridique.*
  E. Ortigues, 154:Sep78-528
Legge, S. Affectionate Cousins.
  H. Corke, 362:24Apr80-542
  J.I.M. Stewart, 617(TLS):25Apr80-456

Leggett, B.J. The Poetic Art of A.E.
  Housman.
  639(VQR):Winter79-22
Legman, G. No Laughing Matter.
  U. Kutter, 196:Band19Heft1/2-161
Le Goff, J. Tempo della Chiesa e tempo
  del mercante.*
  P.P., 227(GCFI):Jan-Mar78-145
Le Goffic, P. and N. Combe-MacBride. Les
  Constructions fondamentales du français.*
  N.C.W. Spence, 208(FS):Vol33Pt2-1048
Legouis, P. Aspects du XVIIe siècle.*
  F. Rau, 38:Band96Heft1/2-237
Le Guern, M. - see Pascal, B.
Le Guillou, L. - see de Lamennais, F.
Le Guin, U.K. The Beginning Place.
  J. Updike, 442(NY):23Jun80-94
Le Guin, U.K. Malafrena.
  L. Duguid, 617(TLS):11Apr80-416
Le Guin, U.K., ed. Nebula Award Stories
  Eleven.
  T.C. Holyoke, 42(AR):Winter79-122
Legum, S.E. and others. The Speech of
  Young Black Children in Los Angeles.
  A. Cartier, 353:Sep78-91
Le Hir, Y. Les Drames bibliques de 1541 à
  1600.
  P. Rickard, 208(FS):Jul79-331
Le Hir, Y. - see d'Urfé, A.
Lehmann, D. Untersuchungen zur Bezeich-
  nung der Sprechaktreferenz im Englischen.
  R. Coppieters, 179(ES):Dec79-837
Lehmann, G. Selected Poems.
  S.E. Lee, 581:Dec79-432
Lehmann, J. Rupert Brooke.
  A. Motion, 617(TLS):12Sep80-1006
Lehmann, J. Virginia Woolf and Her World.*
  A. Bell, 569(SR):Spring79-325
Lehmann, L. Mably und Rousseau.
  W. Bahner, 535(RHL):Jul-Aug78-656
Lehmann, R. A Sea-Grape Tree.
  R. Taylor, 109:Winter79/80-177
  639(VQR):Winter78-24
Lehmann, R.P.M. and W.P. An Introduction
  to Old Irish.
  R.T. Meyer, 589:Apr79-393
Lehmann, U. Popularisierung und Ironie im
  Werk Heinrich Heines.
  J.L.S., 191(ELN):Sep78(supp)-161
Lehmann, W.P., ed. Language and Linguis-
  tics in the People's Republic of China.
  Teng Shou-hsin, 318(JAOS):Jul-Sep78-
  294
Lehmberg, P. In the Strong Woods.
  442(NY):7Apr80-150
Lehrer, A. Semantic Fields and Lexical
  Structure.*
  H.G. Schogt, 320(CJL):Spring-Fall78-
  180
Lehrman, E.H. A "Handbook" to the Russian
  Text of "Crime and Punishment."*
  J.L. Laychuk, 104(CASS):Fall78-421
Leiber, J. Structuralism.*
  E. Matthews, 518:May79-77
Leibholz, G. and others, eds. Menschen-
  würde und freiheitliche Rechtsordnung.
  D. Lasok, 182:Vol131#11/12-338

Leibniz, G.W. Discourse on the Natural
Theology of the Chinese. (H. Rosemont,
Jr. and D.J. Cook, eds and trans)
A.S.C., 543:Dec78-364
Leif, I.P. An International Sourcebook
of Paper History.*
J.S.G. Simmons, 354:Jun79-173
Leigh, D. The Frontiers of Secrecy.
J. Michael, 362:28Aug80-280
Leigh, J. The Ludi Victor.
N. Callendar, 441:7Dec80-44
Leigh, R.A. - see Rousseau, J-J.
Leiland-Longuet, I. La langue parlée.
E. Rattunde, 430(NS):Apr78-183
Leiman, S.Z., ed. The Canon and Masorah
of the Hebrew Bible.
D. Pardee, 318(JAOS):Jul-Sep78-312
Leiner, W., ed. Etudes littéraires fran-
çaises. (Vol 1)
M-O. Sweetser, 475:No.10Pt1-182
Leinfellner, E. and others, eds. Wittgen-
stein and his Impact on Contemporary
Thought.
483:Apr79-269
Leipold, L. Die Auftraggeber und Gönner
Konrads von Würzburg.*
H. Wenzel, 680(ZDP):Band97Heft1-140
Leiss, W., ed. Ecology Versus Politics in
Canada.
F.K. Hare, 99:Dec80/Jan81-36
Leitao, L. Goan Tales.
W.R. Keitner, 102(CanL):Autumn79-97
Leith, J.A., ed. Facets of Education in
the Eighteenth Century.
D.F. Bradshaw, 208(FS):Oct79-446
T.E.D. Braun, 207(FR):Mar79-640
Leitner, G. Denominale Verbalisierung.
A.R. Tellier, 189(EA):Jan-Mar78-81
Leitner, I. Fragments of Isabella.*
I.A. Leitner, ed)
T. Ziolkowski, 569(SR):Fall79-676
Leitner, I.A. - see Eisner, J.
Lejeune, P. Exercices d'ambiguïté.
D. Moutote, 535(RHL):Jan-Feb78-145
Lejeune, P. Le Pacte autobiographique.*
L.D. Kritzman, 207(FR):Dec78-339
Lekachman, R. Economists at Bay.
K.J. Arrow, 473(PR):1/1979-113
Lelyveld, D. Aligarh's First Generation.
G. Minault, 293(JASt):Aug79-804
Lem, S. Return from the Stars.
J. Updike, 442(NY):8Sep80-106
Lem, S. Tales of Pirx the Pilot.
G. Jonas, 441:17Feb80-7
Lemaire, M. Le Dandysme de Baudelaire à
Mallarmé.
R.L. Mitchell, 207(FR):Apr79-773
M. Parmentier, 627(UTQ):Summer79-421
Lemarié, J. and R. Étaix, eds. Spici-
legium ad Chromatii Aquileiensis opera.
P. Courcelle, 555:Vol52fasc2-404
Le May, C.H.L. The Victorian Constitution.
G. Marshall, 617(TLS):18Jan80-67
Lembourn, H.J. Diary of a Lover of
Marilyn Monroe.*
J.R. Haspiel, 200:Aug-Sep79-428

Lemercier, J-L-N. Pinto, ou La Journée
d'une conspiration. (N. Perry, ed)
W.D. Howarth, 208(FS):Vol33Pt2-805
J-M. Thomasseau, 535(RHL):Jul-Aug79-
670
Lemmon, E.J. An Introduction to Modal
Logic. (K. Sederberg, ed)
R.A. Bull, 316:Dec79-653
Lemon, A. Apartheid.
C. Murray, 69:Vol148#4-414
Lemos, R.M. Hobbes and Locke.
G.B.H., 543:Mar79-554
Lemos, R.M. Rousseau's Political Philos-
ophy.*
H. Beran, 63:Sep79-285
de Lena, P.R. - see under Rodríguez de
Lena, P.
Lenardon, R.J. The Saga of Themistocles.
N.M. Kopff, 121(CJ):Apr-May80-364
Lencek, R.L. and T.F. Magner, eds. The
Dilemma of the Melting Pot.
C. Wukasch, 399(MLJ):Apr79-228
Lenders, W. Semantische und argumentative
Textdeskription.
G. Öhlschläger, 686(ZGL):Band7Heft1-83
Lendle, O. Schildkröten.
F. Lasserre, 182:Vol131#14-495
Lenin, V.I. V.I. Lénine, "Textes philoso-
phiques." (S. Pelta and F. Seve, eds
and trans)
J-M. Gabaude, 542:Jul-Sep79-328
Lenk, K. and F. Neumann, eds. Theorie und
Soziologie der politischen Parteien.
E. Gruner, 182:Vol31#7/8-212
Lenneberg, E.H., ed. Neue Perspektiven in
der Erforschung der Sprache.
S. Ettinger, 430(NS):Jul78-381
Lennie, C. Landseer.
L. Brake, 637(VS):Spring78-412
de Leno, A. Regulae de Contrapunto. (A.
Seay, ed)
M. Fowler, 308:Spring78-115
Lenôtre, G. Lenôtre's Desserts and Pas-
tries.
W. and C. Cowen, 639(VQR):Spring79-74
Lensing, L.A. Narrative Structure and the
Reader in Wilhelm Raabe's "Im alten
Eisen."
J.L. Sammons, 221(GQ):Jan79-98
Lentfoehr, T. Words and Silence.
J. Martin, 27(AL):Jan80-583
Lenz, H. Die neubabylonischen ḫarrânu-
Geschäftsunternehmen.
R.H. Sack, 318(JAOS):Jul-Sep78-313
Lenz, R., ed. Leichenpredigten als Quelle
historischer Wissenschaften.
R. Hildebrandt, 685(ZDL):2/1979-264
Lenz, S. Heimatmuseum.
G.P. Butler, 220(GL&L):Jan80-172
Lenzt, F.W. and C.A. Behr - see Aristides
Leo, G.F. Critica e scienza nel giovane
Kant (1747-1769).
L. Guillermit, 542:Apr-Jun79-243
Léon, P., H. Schogt, and E. Burstynsky,
eds. La Phonologie. (Vol 1)
B. Tranel, 207(FR):Dec78-364

221

Léon, P.R. and H. Mitterand. L'analyse du discours.
N.L. Corbett, 545(RPh):May79-416
"León Medieval: Doce estudios."
J.N. Hillgarth, 589:Oct79-884
Léon-Dufour, X., ed. Les miracles de Jésus.
A. Compagnon, 98:Mar78-291
León-Portilla, M. Los manifiestos en náhuatl de Emiliano Zapata.
R.A. Hayes, 263(RIB):Vol29No2-212
Leonard, D. Sex and Generation.
J. Morgan, 617(TLS):11Jul80-778
Leonard, H. Home Before Night.
R. Eder, 441:1Jun80-11
C. Lehmann-Haupt, 441:23Apr80-C28
442(NY):28Jul80-102
Leonard, J.W., ed-in-chief. Woman's Who's Who of America.
K.B. Harder, 424:Sep77-179
Leonard, L.B. Meaning in Child Language.
K.T. Kernan, 350:Mar79-245
Leonard, M. Slobodskaya.
E. Forbes, 415:Oct79-835
Leonardo da Vinci. The Notebooks of Leonardo da Vinci. (E. MacCurdy, ed and trans)
C. Gould, 39:May79-407
42(AR):Fall79-505
Leone, M. L'industria nella letteratura italiana contemporanea.
Z.L. Vella, 276:Summer79-247
Leong, S-T. Sino-Soviet Diplomatic Relations, 1917-1926.*
R. Quested, 302:Vol16#1and2-128
Leonhard, W. Eurocommunism.
W. Laqueur, 441:23Mar80-13
Leoni, F.A. Concordanze Belliane.*
W. Hirdt, 72:Band216Heft1-222
Leopold, J.A. Alfred Hugenberg.
639(VQR):Summer78-90
Lepage, Y.G. - see du Pont, A.
Leparulo, W.E. L'Italia nell'opera di Albert Camus.*
K. Anderson and I.H. Walker, 208(FS): Vol33Pt2-930
Lepenies, W. Melancholie und Gesellschaft. (2nd ed)
H. Ottmann, 489(PJGG):Band86Heft1-148
Lepper, G.M., comp. A Bibliographical Introduction to Seventy-Five Modern American Authors.
P. McLaren-Turner, 78(BC):Autumn79-449
Lepschy, A.L. and G. The Italian Language Today.*
O. Ragusa, 276:Autumn79-294
R.E. Wood, 399(MLJ):Sep-Oct79-316
Lepsius, C.R. Denkmäler aus Aegypten und Aethiopien-Text. (Vol 1)
E. Cruz-Uribe, 318(JAOS):Jul-Sep78-314
Leranbaum, M. Alexander Pope's "Opus Magnum" 1729-1744.*
M.R. Brownell, 191(ELN):Jun79-334
S.D. Lavine, 405(MP):May80-435
J. McLaverty, 447(N&Q):Dec78-559
G. Midgley, 541(RES):Feb79-88
H-J. Müllenbrock, 72:Band216Heft1-177

Lercangée, F., comp. Periodicals Relating to American Literature in Belgian Libraries.
J. De Smet-D'hondt, 179(ES):Dec79-836
Le Rider, P. Le Chevalier dans le "Conte du Graal" de Chrétien de Troyes.
L.J. Friedman, 589:Oct79-826
Léridon, H. Human Fertility.
L.P. Chow, 529(QQ):Summer79-361
Lerner, L. Love and Marriage.
P. Beer, 617(TLS):11Jan80-34
Lerner, L. The Man I Killed.
D. Davis, 362:28Aug80-277
Lerner, R. and M. Gunther. Epidemic 9.
P. Andrews, 441:27Jan80-15
Lernoux, P. Cry of the People.
A.J. Langguth, 441:27Jul80-9
Leroux, G. Le Roi Mystère.
C. Canivet, 98:Apr78-431
Leroy, M. Les grand courants de la linguistique moderne. (2nd ed)
G.F. Meier, 682(ZPSK):Band31Heft2-206
Le Roy Ladurie, E. Carnival in Romans.* (French title: Le Carnaval de Romans; British title: Carnival.)
J. Duvignaud, 450(NRF):Apr79-128
D. Luscombe, 362:12Jun80-762
Le Roy Ladurie, E. Montaillou.*
H. Cooper, 382(MAE):1979/1-151
P. Niles, 109:Summer80-201
E. Weber, 322(JHI):Jul-Sep79-481
Lervik, Å.H. Menneske og miljø i Cora Sandels diktning.
A. van Marken, 562(Scan):Nov79-168
J. Sjåvik, 563(SS):Winter79-81
Leselbaum, C. Epistolario de Rufino Jose Cuervo y Raymond Foulché-Delbosc.
J. Weiner, 552(REH):May79-319
Lesko, L.H. The Ancient Egyptian Book of Two Ways.
R. Griehammer, 318(JAOS):Oct-Dec78-501
Lesky, A. Vom Eros der Hellenen.*
P. Louis, 555:Vol52fascl-161
Leslau, W. Concise Amharic Dictionary.*
T.L. Kane, 318(JAOS):Apr-Jun78-159
Leslau, W. English-Amharic Context Dictionary.
J. Fellman, 361:Dec78-395
Lesley, C. Remembered Laughter.
A.K. Loss, 295(JML):Vol7#4-679
Leslie, A. Clare Sheridan.
639(VQR):Winter78-27
Leslie, C., ed. Asian Medical Systems.*
S. Dwyer-Shick, 292(JAF):Oct-Dec79-497
Leslie, C., G. Payn and S. Morley. Noel Coward and His Friends.
A. Forbes, 617(TLS):4Jan80-7
Leslie, C.R. Autobiographical Recollections of Charles Robert Leslie. (T. Taylor, ed)
G. Reynolds, 617(TLS):12Sep80-988
Leslie, J. Value and Existence.
D.W. Hamlyn, 617(TLS):4Jan80-19
Leslie, P. The Liberation of the Riviera.
P. Hallie, 441:29Jul80-13

Lesser, S.O. The Whispered Meanings. (R.
   Sprich and R.W. Noland, eds)
   T.H. Adamowski, 529(QQ):Winter79/80-
   711
   J.V. Knapp, 395(MFS):Winter78/79-654
Lessing, D. The Marriages Between Zones
   Three, Four and Five.
   E. Korn, 617(TLS):9May80-520
   J. Leonard, 441:27Mar80-C19
   M. Thorpe, 99:Oct80-32
   R. Towers, 441:30Mar80-1
Lessing, D. Shikasta.*
   M. Thorpe, 99:Oct80-32
Lessing, D. Stories.
   W.D. Blackmon, 152(UDQ):Fall78-157
   639(VQR):Autumn78-136
"Lessing Yearbook, 10." (R.E. Schade and
   J. Glenn, eds)
   M. Hadley, 564:Nov79-315
Lessmann, J. Italienische Majolika.
   J.V.G. Mallet, 39:Dec79-530
"L'Estampe aujourd'hui, 1973-1978."
   M. Sheringham, 208(FS):Oct79-488
Lester, M. Anthony Merry "Redivivus."
   P.P. Hill, 656(WMQ):Jul79-493
Lester, R.C. Rāmānuja on the Yoga.
   K.L.S. Rao, 485(PE&W):Jul79-361
Lestocquoy, J. Deux siècles de l'histoire
   de la tapisserie (1300-1500).
   M. Huggler, 182:Vol131#15/16-559
de l'Estoile, P. Fragment des "Recueils"
   de Pierre de L'Estoile. (I. Armitage,
   ed)
   E.M. Duval, 207(FR):Oct78-157
   I.W.F. Maclean, 208(FS):Vol33Pt2-655
   J. Pineaux, 535(RHL):Jul-Aug79-645
Lesure, F. Musique et musiciens français
   du XVIe siècle.
   I.D. McFarlane, 208(FS):Vol33Pt2-667
Lesure, F. - see Debussy, C.
Leszl, W. Aristotle's Conception of Ontol-
   ogy.*
   A. Edel, 53(AGP):Band60Heft1-61
Leszl, W. Il "De ideis" di Aristotele e
   la teoria platonica delle idee.*
   N. Gulley, 303(JoHS):Vol199-177
   C.J. Rowe, 123:Vol29No1-77
L'Etang, H. Fit to Lead?
   R. Lewin, 362:27Mar80-416
"Letteratura, storia, coscienza di classe."
   G.T., 228(GSLI):Vol155fasc491-477
Leuchtmann, H. Orlando di Lasso.
   W. Boetticher, 410(M&L):Jan79-76
   I. Fenlon, 415:Jan79-37
Leuchtmann, H., ed. Terminorum musicae
   index septem linguis redactus: Polyglot
   Dictionary of Musical Terms.*
   I. Bent, 415:Jun79-488
Leumann, M. Lateinische Laut- und Formen-
   lehre.*
   V. Pisani, 343:Band23-124
Leutze, J.R. Bargaining for Supremacy.
   639(VQR):Summer78-88
Levant, V. Capital and Labour: Partners?
   T. Morley, 529(QQ):Spring79-110

Levchenko, S.P., L.H. Skrypnyk and N.P.
   Dziatkivs'ka. Slovnyk Vlasnykh Imen
   Liudei. (L.H. Skrypnyk, ed)
   L.M.L. Onyshkevych, 424:Jun78-203
Levchev, L. The Left-Handed One.*
   W.R. Keitner, 102(CanL):Autumn79-97
Level, B. Le Poète et l'Oiseau.
   H. Godin, 208(FS):Vol33Pt2-959
Levelt, W.J.M. Formal Grammars in Lin-
   guistics and Psycholinguistics.*
   J.F. Kess, 215(GL):Winter78-228
Leven, J. Creator.
   J. Burke, 231:May80-90
   P. Lewis, 617(TLS):30May80-606
   R. Sale, 441:27Apr80-15
Levenson, C. The Journey Back and Other
   Poems.*
   D. Barbour, 150(DR):Spring79-154
Levenson, S. Maud Gonne.
   B.K. Scott, 305(JIL):May78-183
Lever, J., ed. Catalogue of the Drawings
   Collection of the Royal Institute of
   British Architects. (Vol O-R)
   D. Stillman, 576:May78-117
Levernier, J. and H. Cohen, comps. The
   Indians and Their Captives.
   W.K. McNeil, 292(JAF):Jul-Sep79-362
Le Verte, L.E. - see Nostradamus, M.
Levertov, D. Freeing the Dust. Collected
   Earlier Poems 1940-1960.
   B. Costello, 472:Fall/Winter79-198
Levertov, D. Life in the Forest.*
   P. Breslin, 491:Jul80-219
   B. Costello, 472:Fall/Winter79-198
   W.H. Pritchard, 249(HudR):Summer79-263
Levet, J-P. Le vrai et le faux dans la
   pensée grecque archaïque. (Vol 1)
   É. Des Places, 555:Vol52fascl-148
Levey, M. The Case of Walter Pater.*
   R. Calvocoressi, 135:Jan79-65
   R.M. Seiler, 49:Apr79-95
   R.L. Wilson, 127:Summer79-292
   639(VQR):Winter79-10
Levey, M. The World of Ottoman Art.
   H. Crane, 576:Mar78-56
Levi, A. Pagan Virtue and the Humanism of
   the Northern Renaissance.
   M.M. Phillips, 208(FS):Vol33Pt2-657
Levi, A. Un' Idea dell' Italia.
   P. McCarthy, 617(TLS):22Feb80-217
Levi, D. Festos e la civiltà minoica.
   K. Branigan, 123:Vol29No2-285
Levi, J.N. The Syntax and Semantics of
   Complex Nominals.
   F.J. Newmeyer, 350:Jun79-396
Levi, P. Five Ages.
   L. Sail, 493:Mar80-71
Levi, P. The Hill of Kronos.
   E.S. Turner, 362:28Aug80-279
Levi, P., ed. Pope.
   566:Spring79-134
Lévi-Strauss, C. Myth and Meaning.
   W.N., 102(CanL):Spring79-148
Lévi-Strauss, C. The Origin of Table
   Manners.*
   G. Davenport, 249(HudR):Autumn79-423
   639(VQR):Summer79-110

Lévi-Strauss, C. Structural Anthropology.*
(Vol 2)
   R. D'Amico, 484(PPR):Sep79-142
Levick, B. Tiberius the Politician.*
   J.P. Adams, 24:Fall79-460
Levillain, H. Le rituel poétique de Saint-
John Perse.
   C.E.J. Dolamore, 208(FS):Vol33Pt2-888
Levin, D. Cotton Mather.*
   N. Fiering, 639(VQR):Summer79-531
   C. Hansen, 165(EAL):Winter79/80-343
   R. Middlekauff, 27(AL):Nov79-419
Levin, G. Edward Hopper: the Complete
Prints. Edward Hopper as Illustrator.
   C. Fox, 617(TLS):30May80-611
Levin, G. Richardson the Novelist.
   E.B. Brophy, 651(WHR):Spring79-155
Levin, J.F. and P.D. Haikalis, with A.
Forostenko. Reading Modern Russian.
   M.I. Levin, 558(RLJ):Spring79-205
Levin, M. The Harvest.
   J. Greenfield, 287:Jun/Jul78-23
Levin, M.E. Metaphysics and the Mind-
Body Problem.
   C. McGinn, 617(TLS):27Jun80-738
Levin, M.I. Russian Declension and Con-
jugation.
   A.K. Donchenko, 574(SEEJ):Summer79-
304
   O. Frink, 399(MLJ):Sep-Oct79-317
Levin, N. While Messiah Tarried.*
   M.W. Kiel, 390:Mar79-63
   H.J. Tobias, 550(RusR):Jan79-107
Levin, S.R. The Semantics of Metaphor.*
   F. Edeline, 567:Vol125#3/4-379
   D.H. Hirsch, 569(SR):Fall79-628
Lévinas, E. Du sacré au saint.
   A. Reix, 542:Jul-Sep79-366
Lévinas, E., X. Tilliette and P. Ricoeur.
Jean Wahl et Gabriel Marcel.
   S. Plourde, 154:Mar78-180
Levine, A. The Politics of Autonomy.*
   H. Beran, 63:Sep79-285
   J. Kopper, 342:Band69Heft1-116
   B.M., 543:Mar79-556
Levine, D. The Art of David Levine.
   A. Frankenstein, 55:Jan79-28
Levine, D. Family Formation in an Age of
Nascent Capitalism.
   J. Thirsk, 656(WMQ):Jul79-478
Levine, F. Solomon and Sheba.
   F. Taliaferro, 441:12Oct80-15
Levine, J.M. Dr. Woodward's Shield.*
   E.J. Kenney, 123:Vol29No1-193
   E. Tomarken, 219(GaR):Summer79-448
Levine, L.G. Juan Goytisolo.
   H.R. Romero, 238:May-Sep79-404
Levine, M.G. - see Białoszewski, M.
Levine, M.H. - see Ibn Falaquera, S.T.B.
Levine, N. Canada Made Me.
   V. Glendinning, 617(TLS):14Mar80-289
Levine, N. Thin Ice.
   V. Glendinning, 617(TLS):14Mar80-289
   J. Mellors, 362:28Feb80-286

Levine, P. Ashes.*
   J. Fuller, 617(TLS):18Jan80-65
   C. Molesworth, 461:Fall-Winter79/80-91
   V. Young, 249(HudR):Winter79/80-632
Levine, P. The Names of the Lost.*
   S. Lea, 114(ChiR):Summer78-116
Levine, P. Seven Years from Somewhere.*
   H. Carruth, 231:Jan80-77
   J. Fuller, 617(TLS):18Jan80-65
   C. Molesworth, 461:Fall-Winter79/80-91
   V. Young, 249(HudR):Winter79/80-632
Levine, R.A., ed. The Victorian Experi-
ence: The Novelists.*
   R.B. Yeazell, 637(VS):Autumn77-120
Levine, R.M. Pernambuco in the Brazilian
Federation, 1889-1937.
   J.E. Hahner, 263(RIB):Vol29No3/4-367
Levine, S. and H. Lyons, with others, eds.
The Decade of Women.
   D. Grumbach, 441:30Mar80-14
Levinsohn, S.H. The Inga Language.
   W.F.H. Adelaar, 361:Aug78-390
Levitine, G. The Dawn of Bohemianism.
   A. Brookner, 90:May79-331
Levitt, I. and C. Smout. The State of the
Scottish Working Class in 1843.
   C. Harvie, 617(TLS):20Jun80-715
Levitzion, N., ed. Conversion to Islam.
   M.E. Yapp, 617(TLS):19Sep80-1040
Levno, A.W. Rencontres culturelles.
   B. Petit, 207(FR):Mar79-679
Levowitz-Treu, M. L'Amour et la Mort chez
Stendhal, Métamorphoses d'un apprentis-
sage affectif.
   J.T. Booker, 399(MLJ):Apr79-215
   G. May, 546(RR):Nov79-406
Lévy, B-H. Barbarism with a Human Face.*
(French title: La barbarie à visage
humain.)
   A. Jacob, 542:Jul-Sep79-366
   T. Sheehan, 453(NYRB):24Jan80-13
Lévy, B-H. Le testament de Dieu.
   T. Sheehan, 453(NYRB):24Jan80-13
Levy, B.M. Cotton Mather.
   K. Keller, 165(EAL):Spring80-86
Lévy, E. Athènes devant la défaite de
404.*
   G.J.D. Aalders, 394:Vol32fasc1/2-201
Levy, J. Cesar Chavez.
   N.C., 502(PrS):Spring78-116
Levy, K.L. - see Carrasquilla, T.
Levy, P. Moore.*
   J. Atlas, 441:19Aug80-C9
   S. Hampshire, 617(TLS):18Jan80-53
   J. Sturrock, 441:1Jun80-13
   442(NY):2Jun80-139
Lévy, R. Schwartzenmurtz, ou l'esprit de
parti.
   D.B. Brautman, 207(FR):Feb79-515
Levy, T. Le Désir de punir.
   J-P. Guinle, 450(NRF):Sep79-54
Lévy-Stringer, J. Les Marginaux.
   D.T. Stephens, 207(FR):Feb79-525
Lewalski, B.K. Protestant Poetics and the
Seventeenth-Century Religious Lyric.
   J. Stachniewski, 617(TLS):7Mar80-272
                  [continued]

Lim Teck Ghee. Peasants and Their Agricultural Economy in Colonial Malaya, 1874–1941.
  A.J. Stockwell, 293(JASt):May79-630
Lima, J.D. - see under da Silva Lima, J.
Limentani, A. - see Martin Da Canal
Limentani, U., with J.M.A. Lindon - see Foscolo, U.
Limmer, R. - see Bogan, L.
Linage Conde, A. El monacato en España e Hispanoamérica.
  D.W. Lomax, 86(BHS):Jul79-243
Linck, W. Erbauungsschriften. (H. van der Kolk, ed)
  I.T. Piirainen, 182:Vol31#20-736
Linck-Kesting, G. Ein Kapitel chinesischer Grenzgeschichte.
  B. Wiethoff, 182:Vol31#20-766
Lincoln, W.B. Nicholas I.
  R. Wortman, 550(RusR):Apr79-226
Lindahl, L. Position and Change.*
  R.F. Atkinson, 479(PhQ):Apr79-183
Lindberg, G. Studies in Hermogenes and Eustathios.
  R. Browning, 123:Vol29No1-145
  F. Vian, 555:Vol52fasc2-350
Lindberg, J.D. - see Weise, C.
Lindbergh, A.M. War Within and Without.
  N. Balakian, 441:2Aug80-19
  J.P. Lash, 441:20Apr80-7
Lindblom, C.E. Politics and Markets.
  A. Kemp, 396(ModA):Winter79-85
Linde, R. Untersuchungen zur ökonomischen Theorie der Produktqualität.
  K. Mellerowicz, 182:Vol31#15/16-534
Lindekens, R. Essai de sémiotique visuelle.
  J. Arrouye, 98:Jan78-72
Lindeman, F.O. Einführung in die Laryngaltheorie.
  G.F. Meier, 682(ZPSK):Band31Heft4-424
Lindenberg, D. and P-A. Meyer. Lucien Herr, le socialisme et son destin.
  A. Reix, 542:Jul-Sep79-367
Lindenberger, H. Historical Drama.*
  W.D. Howarth, 208(FS):Vol33Pt2-967
  M. Jacobs, 220(GL&L):Oct78-61
  D.R.C. Marsh, 677(YES):Vol9-296
Linder, B.R. How to Trace Your Family History.
  L.B. Nauen, 14:Oct79-480
Linder, C., ed. Oral Communication Testing.
  N.A. Poulin, 207(FR):Feb79-532
Lindfors, B. Black African Literature in English.
  R. Priebe, 365:Summer80-133
Lindholm, D., comp. Altindische Sagen.
  H-J. Uther, 196:Band19Heft1/2-126
Lindkvist, K-G. AT versus ON, IN, BY.
  B. Mitchell, 541(RES):May79-244
Lindkvist, K-G. A Comprehensive Study of Conceptions of Locality in which English Prepositions Occur.
  205(FMLS):Jan78-91
Lindner, B. Jean Paul.*
  J. Link, 490:Band10Heft4-526

Lindner, H. Didaktische Gattungsstruktur und narratives Spiel.
  C.N. Smith, 208(FS):Vol33Pt2-682
Lindow, J., eds and trans. Swedish Legends and Folktales.
  M.E. Johns, 563(SS):Spring79-196
  R. Wright, 301(JEGP):Oct79-589
Lindsay, J. William Morris.
  P. Meier, 189(EA):Jan-Mar78-92
Lindsay, J. The Troubadours and Their World of the Twelfth and Thirteenth Centuries.
  T.G. Bergin, 589:Jan79-169
Lindsay, M. History of Scottish Literature.
  S. McCarthy, 588(SSL):Vol14-280
Lindsay, N. Letters of Norman Lindsay. (R.G. Howarth and A.W. Barker, eds)
  B. Elliott, 71(ALS):Oct79-253
Lindsay, T.S. Plant Names.
  K.B. Harder, 424:Dec77-237
Lindsey, R. The Falcon and the Snowman.*
  P. Whitehead, 362:27Mar80-416
Lindstrom, T.S. A Concise History of Russian Literature: From 1900 to the Present. (Vol 2)
  H. Gamburg, 558(RLJ):Fall79-241
Linedecker, C.L. The Man Who Killed Boys.
  T. Powers, 441:30Mar80-11
Linet, B. Ladd.*
  D. Wilson, 617(TLS):2May80-492
Linfert, A. Kunstzentren hellenistischer Zeit.*
  C.E. Vafopoulou-Richardson, 123:Vol29No1-121
Ling, T.O. - see Suksamran, S.
Linge, D.E. - see Gadamer, H-G.
Lingeman, R. Small Town America.
  E. Connell, 441:6Jul80-1
  J. Leonard, 441:13Jun80-C27
Lings, M. The Quranic Art of Calligraphy and Illumination.
  J.W. Allan, 463:Spring79-115
Lings, M. What Is Sufism?*
  M.A. Ashruff, 273(IC):Oct76-237
Link, A. - see Wilson, W.
Link, F.H. Dramaturgie der Zeit.
  W. Schmitz, 72:Band216Heft2-398
Link, F.M., ed. English Drama, 1660-1800.
  H. Love, 677(YES):Vol9-334
  C. Price, 447(N&Q):Feb78-82
  P. Sorrentino, 568(SCN):Fall-Winter79-83
Link, H. Rezeptionsforschung.*
  M. Zutshi, 402(MLR):Jan79-130
Linke, K., W. Haas and S. Neitzel. Die Fragmente des Grammatikers Dionysios Thrax, Die Fragmente der Grammatiker Tyrannion und Diokles, Apions "Glōssai Homērikai."
  E. Duke, 123:Vol29No2-257
  W.J. Slater, 24:Fall79-430
Linke, N. and G. Kneip. Robert Schumann.
  E. Sams, 415:May79-402

Linklater, A. An Unhusbanded Life.
S. Jacobson, 362:31Jan80-155
D. Mitchell, 617(TLS):22Feb80-200
Lins, U. Die Ōmoto-Bewegung und der radi-
kale Nationalismus in Japan.
H.B. Earhart, 293(JASt):May79-583
Linsky, L. Names and Descriptions.*
P.T. Geach, 518:Oct79-140
C.J.F. Williams, 483:Jan79-128
Linssen, J. Yellow Pages.
M. Levin, 441:10Feb80-27
Linstrum, D. West Yorkshire.
M. Stancliffe, 46:Dec79-398
Linstrum, D. The Wyatt Family.
D. Stillman, 576:May78-117
"L'Introduction de la psychanalyse aux
États-Unis."
H. Cronel, 450(NRF):Apr79-138
Lion-Goldschmidt, D. Ming Porcelain.
M. Medley, 463:Summer79-252
W.B.R. Neave-Hill, 135:May79-67
Lipka, B. Die Kurzwörter in der heutigen
russischen Standardsprache.
C.E. Townsend, 558(RLJ):Winter79-194
Lipman, J. and T. Armstrong, eds. Ameri-
can Folk Painters of Three Centuries.
J. Russell, 441:8May80-C23
Lipman, J. and R. Marshall. Art about
Art.*
G. Hermerén, 290(JAAC):Fall79-101
Lipman, M., with F.S. Oscanyan and T.
Smith. Suki.
M.C. Beardsley, 290(JAAC):Fall79-106
Lipman, S. Music After Modernism.*
S. Blum, 99:Mar80-32
A.C. Schuldt, 31(ASch):Winter79/80-139
Lippius, J. Synopsis of New Music.
R. Woodley, 410(M&L):Jul79-357
Lippman, E.A. A Humanistic Philosophy of
Music.*
B. Bujic, 89(BJA):Summer79-284
P.J.P., 412:Aug-Nov78-289
Lippman, F., ed. Studien zur italienisch-
deutschen Musikgeschichte. (Vols 10 and
11)
F.W. Sternfeld, 410(M&L):Jan79-92
Lipset, D. Gregory Bateson.
R.A. Sokolov, 441:22Jun80-15
442(NY):18Aug80-92
Lipsey, R. Coomaraswamy 3.*
H. Smith, 485(PE&W):Jul79-347
Lipsey, R. - see Coomaraswamy, A.
Lipson, C., comp. American Folklore
Films and Videotapes. (B. Ferris and
J. Peiser, eds)
D.W. Patterson, 582(SFQ):Vol41-280
Lipson, D.A. Freemasonry in Federalist
Connecticut, 1789-1835.*
G. Weaver, 656(WMQ):Jul79-497
639(VQR):Spring79-55
Lipton, E. Picasso Criticism, 1901-1939.
C.R. Baldwin, 54:Mar78-187
Liska, G. Career of Empire.
639(VQR):Summer79-92
Liska, G. Quest for Equilibrium — America
and the Balance of Power on Land and Sea.
639(VQR):Summer78-105

de Lisle, C.M.L. - see under Leconte de
Lisle, C.M.
de Lisle, G.B-C. - see under Barbé-
Coquelin de Lisle, G.
Lisle, L. Portrait of an Artist.
J. Hobhouse, 441:11May80-13
List, D. Pathways into the Brain.
P. Crisp, 368:Jun74-170
Lister-Kaye, J. The Seeing Eye.
K. Mellanby, 617(TLS):19Sep80-1014
Liszt, F. The Letters of Franz Liszt to
Olga von Meyendorff 1871-1886. (E.N.
Waters, ed)
A. Fitz Lyon, 617(TLS):21Mar80-338
"Literaturnye vzgljady i tvorčestvo slav-
janofilov 1830-1850 gody."
L. Koehler, 574(SEEJ):Fall79-402
Littell, K.M. Jeremias Gotthelf's "Die
Käserei in der Vehfreude."
R. Kieser, 222(GR):Spring78-84
Littell, R. The Debriefing.*
M. Laski, 362:10Jan80-62
"Littératures de langue française hors de
France."
R.J. Sherrington, 208(FS):Vol33Pt2-987
Little, R. Guillaume Apollinaire.*
C. Abastado, 535(RHL):Sep-Oct78-859
Little, R. Saint-John Perse.*
K.R. Dutton, 67:May79-134
Little, R. Saint-John Perse, A Bibliogra-
phy for Students of his Poetry. (Supp
No. 1)
M. Autrand, 535(RHL):May-Jun78-508
K.R. Dutton, 67:May79-136
E.R. Jackson, 207(FR):Dec78-355
Little, R. - see de Labriolle, J.
Little, R. - see Perse, S-J.
Littleton, T., ed. A Time to Hear and
Answer.
J.S. Martin, 106:Spring79-103
Litto, G. South American Folk Pottery.
F.L. Phelps, 37:Sep79-46
"Lityeratura Vostoka v novoye vryemya."
J.M. Landau, 294:Vol9-152
Litz, A.W., ed. Major American Short
Stories.
G. Bas, 189(EA):Jan-Mar78-108
Liu, J.J.Y. Chinese Theories of Litera-
ture.*
C.H. Wang, 293(JASt):May79-529
Liu Ts'un-Yan. Selected Papers from the
Hall of Harmonious Wind.
A.P. Cohen, 318(JAOS):Jul-Sep78-308
Liu, W-C. and I.Y. Lo, eds. Sunflower
Splendor.
B. Upton, 318(JAOS):Oct-Dec78-523
Liu Wu-chi. Su Man-shu.
L.Y. Chiu, 302:Vol16#1and2-124
Lively, P. Judgement Day.
J. Naughton, 362:20Nov80-700
Lively, P. Nothing Missing But the
Samovar.*
D. Durrant, 364:Jul79-89
Liver, R. Die Nachwirkung der antiken
Sakralsprache im christlichen Gebet des
lateinischen und italienischen Mittel-
[continued]

Löffler, A. and J-C. Rojahn, eds. Englische Lyrik.
H. Foltinek, 224(GRM):Band28Heft1-113
Löffler, H. and W. Besch. Alemannisch.
I. Guentherodt, 685(ZDL):3/1979-384
Löfgren, O. and O. Traini. Catalogue of the Arabic Manuscripts in the Biblioteca Ambrosiana. (Vol 1)
R.S. Cooper, 318(JAOS):Oct-Dec78-489
Löfstedt, B., ed. Ars Laureshamensis.
J.J. Contreni, 589:Oct79-834
Löfstedt, B. - see Sedulius Scottus
Löfstedt, L. - see Jean de Meun
Loftis, J. Sheridan and the Drama of Georgian England.*
L.W. Conolly, 447(N&Q):Feb78-94
D.V.E., 191(ELN):Sep78(supp)-40
Loftis, J. and others. The Revels History of Drama in English.* (Vol 5)
F.P. Lock, 586(SoRA):Jul78-188
H. Love, 677(YES):Vol9-334
C. Price, 447(N&Q):Feb78-82
Loftis, J., D.S. Rodes and V.A. Dearing - see Dryden, J.
Loftus, E.F. Eyewitness Testimony.
J. Greenfield, 441:9Mar80-11
Logan, J. Movie Stars, Real People and Me. 639(VQR):Spring79-70
Løgstrup, K.E. Kants Kritik af erkendelsen og refleksionen.
T. Nilstun, 342:Band69Heft1-111
Lohmeier, D., ed. Arte et Marte.
E. Lunding, 301(JEGP):Jul79-389
Loman, B., ed. Språk och samhälle 3.
C. Henriksen, 563(SS):Summer79-315
Lomax, D.W. The Reconquest of Spain.
B.F. Reilly, 589:Apr79-395
K. Whinnom, 86(BHS):Oct79-332
Lombard, A. La langue roumaine.
F. Dimitrescu, 545(RPh):Aug78-133
G. Mallinson, 361:Oct/Nov78-276
Lombard, C.M. Thomas Holley Chivers.
R.S. Moore, 578:Fall80-131
Lombard, C.M. Xavier de Maistre.*
M. Gutwirth, 207(FR):Mar79-642
191(ELN):Sep78(supp)-107
Lombardo, D. Some Like It Hot.
W. and C. Cowen, 639(VQR):Autumn79-154
London, J. Jack London: No Mentor But Myself. (D.L. Walker, ed)
S. Noto, 649(WAL):Fall79-258
London, J. Jack London on the Road. (R.W. Etulain, ed)
G. Beauchamp, 26(ALR):Autumn79-353
Londyn, E. Maurice Blanchot romancier.*
G. Idt, 535(RHL):Sep-Oct79-885
C. Rigolot, 207(FR):Mar79-650
L.S. Roudiez, 546(RR):Mar79-195
de Lone, R.H. Small Futures.*
A. Hacker, 453(NYRB):20Mar80-20
Long, C.R. The Ayia Triadha Sarcophagus.
H. Tzavella-Evjen, 121(CJ):Feb-Mar80-269
Long, F.B. Howard Philips Lovecraft.
S.A. Black, 106:Fall79-243
Long, J. The German-Russians.
W.A. Kohls, 550(RusR):Oct79-520

Long, M. The Unnatural Scene.*
E.A.J. Honigmann, 677(YES):Vol9-312
Longacre, R.E. An Anatomy of Speech Notions.
R.M. Brend, 361:May78-91
Longeon, C. Documents d'archives sur Étienne Dolet.
J. Bailbé, 535(RHL):Nov-Dec79-1039
Longeon, C. Une Province française à la Renaissance.
I.D. McFarlane, 208(FS):Vol33Pt2-661
Longeon, C. - see Papon, L.
Lord Longford. Nixon.
H. Brogan, 362:9Oct80-477
Longford, E. A Pilgrimage of Passion.*
J. Atlas, 441:27Jun80-C27
F. Taliaferro, 231:Apr80-114
J. Wain, 441:20Jul80-9
442(NY):28Jul80-101
Longford, E. - see Antrim, L.
Longhurst, C.A. Pío Baroja: "El mundo es ansí."
F. Ibarra, 238:Mar79-176
H. Probyn, 402(MLR):Jan79-227
E. Rodgers, 86(BHS):Oct79-344
Longhurst, H. The Best of Henry Longhurst on Golf and Life. (M. Wilson and K. Bowden, eds)
P. Dickinson, 364:Oct79-73
Longley, E. - see Simmons, J.
Longley, M. The Echo Gate.
D. Davis, 362:31Jan80-157
J. Mole, 617(TLS):8Feb80-138
Longmate, N. The Hungry Mills.
I. Sellers, 637(VS):Summer79-475
Longoria, F.A. El arte narrativo de Max Aub.
J. Caviglia, 238:Mar79-179
Longrigg, R. The English Squire and His Sport.
639(VQR):Winter78-28
Longum, L., ed. Drama-analyser fra Holberg til Hoem.
C. Leland, 562(Scan):May79-81
Longwill, J. A Man's Jacket.
D. Graham, 565:Vol20#2-75
Lönnroth, L. Njáls Saga.*
P. Foote, 562(Scan):May79-49
R. Frank, 589:Jan79-170
Loohuis, W.J.M. Analyse von "Kabale und Liebe" und "Hermann und Dorothea."
A.J. Camigliano, 406:Fall79-341
Looney, R.F. Old Philadelphia in Early Photographs 1839-1914.
G.B. Tatum, 576:Dec78-309
Loos, E. Sugerencias para el Investigador de Campo Sobre la Negacion [together with] Weber, R. and N. Thiesen der Weber. Negacion en Quechua.
T.T. Büttner, 269(IJAL):Oct78-344
Lope, H-J. Die "Cartas Marruecas" von José Cadalso.
R. Gutiérrez Girardot, 72:Band216Heft2-466
Lopez, B.H. Giving Birth to Thunder, Sleeping with His Daughter.
D.H. Hymes, 651(WHR):Winter79-91

Lopez, B.H. Of Wolves and Men.*
M.E. Ackerman, 649(WAL):Fall79-236
López, S.S. - see under Sebastián López, S.
López Alsina, F. Introducción al fenómeno urbano medieval gallego, a través de tres ejemplos: Mondoñedo, Vivero y Ribadeo.
P. Freedman, 589:Apr79-396
López de Ayala, P. Libro rimado del Palacio. (J. Joset, ed) Libro de poemas o Rimado de Palacio. (M. García, ed)
E.W. Naylor, 304(JHP):Autumn79-80
López Morales, H. Estudios sobre el español de Cuba.
S. Pieczara, 360(LP):Vol21-167
Lora, G. A History of the Bolivian Labour Movement 1848-1971. (L. Whitehead, ed)
J. Fisher, 86(BHS):Jan79-87
Lorca, F.G. Lorca/Blackburn. (P. Blackburn, ed and trans)
S. Fredman, 114(ChiR):Winter79-152
Lorca, F.G. Poema del cante jondo. Romancero gitano. (A. Josephs and J. Caballero, eds)
E.F. Stanton, 238:Mar79-176
Lorch, F.W. The Trouble Begins at Eight.
S. Fender, 402(MLR):Jul79-677
Lord, G.D. Heroic Mockery.*
J. Fletcher, 268(IFR):Summer80-153
Lorde, A. The Black Unicorn.
R.B. Stepto, 472:Fall/Winter79-312
Loreau, M. Jean Dubuffet.
M. Sheringham, 208(FS):Jan79-103
Lorenz, B. Thessalische Grabgedichte vom 6. bis zum 4. Jahrhundert v. Chr.*
A.G. Woodhead, 303(JoHS):Vol199-219
Lorenz, K. Behind the Mirror.
P. Jensen, 109:Summer80-212
Lorenz, K. The Year of the Greylag Goose.*
A. Manning, 362:3Jan80-28
Lorenz, T. Guys Like Us.
C. Lehmann-Haupt, 441:23Dec80-C9
Lorenzen, K., ed. Theorie und Praxis des Englischunterrichts.
K. Macht, 430(NS):Oct78-487
Lorenzo-Rivero, L. Larra.
H.F. Grant, 86(BHS):Jul79-257
T. Guerra Gloss, 238:Mar79-174
J. Stevenson, 67:May79-137
de Lorris, G. and Jean de Meun - see under Guillaume de Lorris and Jean de Meun
Lortie, J.D. La Poésie nationaliste au Canada français (1606-1867).
D.M. Hayne, 208(FS):Vol33Pt2-989
Lortz, R. The Valdepeñas.
A. Broyard, 441:31Jan80-C19
442(NY):17Mar80-166
Lossky, B. and N. Bibliographie des oeuvres de Nicolas Lossky.
J.M. Curtis, 574(SEEJ):Fall79-412
D.M. Fiene, 399(MLJ):Apr79-213
Lotman, J. The Structure of the Artistic Text.
M.K. Frank, 399(MLJ):Sep-Oct79-318
A. Shukman, 575(SEER):Jan79-115
Lotman, J.M. Analiz poetičeskogo teksta.
W. Rewar, 567:Vol125#3/4-273

Lotter, F. Die Konzeption des Wendenkreuzzugs.
J.A. Brundage, 589:Jan79-172
Lottinville, S. The Rhetoric of History.*
W.B. Gatewood, Jr., 599:Winter79-37
Lottman, H.R. Albert Camus.*
F. Brown, 31(ASch):Winter79/80-132
P-L. Rey, 450(NRF):Feb79-105
639(VQR):Summer79-98
Loubère, L.A. The Red and the White.
42(AR):Fall79-488
Loubet del Bayle, J-L. Introduction aux méthodes des sciences sociales.
J-M. Gabaude, 542:Oct-Dec79-491
Loudoun, J.H. James Scott and William Scott, Bookbinders.
A. Hobson, 617(TLS):15Aug80-922
Lougee, C.C. "Le Paradis des Femmes."*
J. Lough, 208(FS):Vol33Pt2-709
Lough, J. Writer and Public in France.*
R.J. Ellrich, 401(MLQ):Sep79-307
F. Schalk, 547(RF):Band91Heft1/2-145
N. Suckling, 208(FS):Apr79-232
E. Weber, 322(JHI):Jul-Sep79-481
Loughmiller, C. and L., eds. Big Thicket Legacy.*
L. Montell, 650(WF):Apr79-129
Louis, J.C. and H.Z. Yazijian. The Cola Wars.
N. von Hoffman, 441:16Nov80-12
Louis-Combet, C. Marinus et Marina.
L. Kovacs, 450(NRF):Dec79-115
Louis-Jensen, J. Kongesagastudier.*
F.W. Blaisdell, 589:Oct79-828
Louis-Philippe. Diary of My Travels in America. (S. Becker, trans)
T. Bridges, 37:May79-46
Love, E.G. Set-up.
N. Callendar, 441:7Dec80-45
Love, G.A. Don Berry.
R. Gish, 649(WAL):Winter80-335
Love, J.O. Virginia Woolf.*
A. Bell, 569(SR):Spring79-325
D. Doner, 395(MFS):Winter78/79-575
D.F. Gillespie, 141:Winter79-78
J. Gindin, 594:Spring79-82
S. Rudikoff, 249(HudR):Winter79/80-540
M. Spilka, 454:Winter79-170
295(JML):Vol17#4-843
639(VQR):Autumn78-128
Lovell, J. British Trade Unions, 1875-1933.
B.C. Malament, 637(VS):Autumn78-106
Lovell, M. The Spy Game.
N. Callendar, 441:7Dec80-45
Lovesey, P. Waxwork.
639(VQR):Autumn78-136
Lovett, G. The Duke of Rivas.
D.L. Stixrude, 399(MLJ):Jan-Feb79-72
191(ELN):Sep78(supp)-194
Lovett, R.W. and E.C. Bishop, comps. Manuscripts in the Baker Library. (4th ed)
D.L. Vogt, 14:Oct79-476
Loving, J. Walt Whitman's Champion.*
A. Lozynsky, 646(WWR):Jun78-89
Loving, J.M. - see Whitman, G.W.

Ludwig, O. Romane und Romanstudien. (W.J. Lillyman, ed)
  B. Leuschner, 221(GQ):Nov79-550
Luecke, J-M. Measuring Old English Rhythm.
  R.W.V. Elliott, 67:May79-307
Luellsdorff, P.A., ed. Linguistic Perspectives on Black English.
  R.W. Fasold, 355(LSoc):Dec78-438
Luellsdorff, P.A. A Segmental Phonology of Black English.
  R.W. Fasold, 355(LSoc):Dec78-438
Luft, H. Der Konflikt zwischen Geist und Sinnlichkeit in Thomas Manns "Tod in Venedig."*
  E.L. Marson, 67:May79-150
Lugton, R.C. American Topics.*
  S. Plann, 399(MLJ):Apr79-214
de Luis, L. - see Aleixandre, V.
Luiselli Fadda, A.M., ed. Nuove omelie anglosassoni della rinascenza Benedettina.
  P.S. Baker, 589:Jul79-598
  T. Leinbaugh, 541(RES):Aug79-325
Luisi, F. La musica vocale nel rinascimento.
  D.A., 410(M&L):Jan79-97
Luisi, L.G. - see under Galleni Luisi, L.
Luján, M. and F. Hensey, eds. Current Studies in Romance Linguistics.
  V.E. Hanzeli, 399(MLJ):Sep-Oct79-299
Lukács, G. The Young Hegel.
  E. Tavor, 473(PR):1/1979-148
Lukacs, J. The Last European War.
  S. Dąbrowski, 497(PolR):Vol23#1-101
Lukas, R.C. The Strange Allies.
  M. Bundy, 497(PolR):Vol23#4-102
  E. Chmielewski, 550(RusR):Jan79-108
Lukashevich, S. N.F. Fedorov (1828-1903).*
  T.D. Zakydalsky, 574(SEEJ):Summer79-273
Luke, D. - see von Goethe, J.W.
Luker, N. Alexander Kuprin.
  A. Dynnik, 574(SEEJ):Summer79-276
Lumiansky, R.M. and D. Mills, eds. The Chester Mystery Cycle.*
  W. Habicht, 38:Band96Heft1/2-214
"Les Lumières en Hongrie, en Europe Centrale et en Europe Orientale."*
  G.F. Cushing, 575(SEER):Oct79-597
Lumley, E.K. Forgotten Mandate.
  A. Redmayne, 69:Vol148#1-87
Lundberg, F. Cracks in the Constitution.
  W. Goodman, 441:15Jun80-15
Lunde, D.T. and J. Morgan. The Die Song.
  T. Powers, 441:30Mar80-11
Lundell, T. Lars Ahlin.*
  I. Scobbie, 562(Scan):Nov79-172
Lundén, R. Dreiser Looks at Scandinavia.*
  E. Guereschi, 395(MFS):Winter78/79-633
Lundquist, J. Chester Himes.
  M. Fabre, 189(EA):Apr-Jun78-240
Lundquist, J. Kurt Vonnegut.
  R.F. Kiernan, 295(JML):Vol7#4-828
Lunt, H.N., ed. Language and Language Teaching.
  C.L. Drage, 575(SEER):Jan79-148

Luongo, C.P. America's Best! 100.
  B. Roueché, 442(NY):20Oct80-205
Lupi, S., ed. Dizionario critico della letteratura tedesca.*
  H.O. Burger, 224(GRM):Band28Heft1-95
  H. Seidler, 602:Vol10-261
Luppov, S.P. and others, eds. Knigopechatanie i Knizhnȳe Sobraniya v Rossii do Seredinȳ XIX Veka.
  J.S.G. Simmons, 78(BC):Winter79-587
Luria, A.R. The Making of Mind.
  O.L. Zangwill, 617(TLS):25Apr80-461
Lurie, A. Only Children.*
  J. Chernaik, 364:Aug/Sep79-140
  E. Milton, 676(YR):Autumn79-89
  639(VQR):Autumn79-136
Lüschen, G. and G.P. Stone - see Schmalenbach, H.
Lussato, B. Introduction critique aux théories d'organisation.
  A. Reix, 542:Apr-Jun78-211
Lusser-Mertelsmann, G. Max Frisch.
  M.E. Stewart, 402(MLR):Jul79-760
Lüssy, H. Umlautprobleme im Schweizerdeutschen.
  W. König, 685(ZDL):1/1979-93
Lutaud, O. Des Révolutions d'Angleterre à la Revolution française.
  M. Baridon, 189(EA):Apr-Jun78-227
Lutaud, O. Winstanley.*
  A. Woolrych, 189(EA):Apr-Jun78-224
Lütkehaus, L. Hebbel.
  H. Reinhardt, 680(ZDP):Band97Heft2-299
Lütolf, M. and others, eds. Analecta hymnica medii aevi: Register.
  W. Salmen, 182:Vol131#21/22-818
Lütterfelds, W. Kants Dialektik der Erfahrung.
  W. Stegmaier, 687:Apr-Jun79-314
Luttrell, A., ed. Hal Millieri.
  F.K.B. Toker, 589:Apr79-398
Luttrell, C. The Creation of the First Arthurian Romance.
  C.E. Pickford, 208(FS):Vol33Pt2-539
Luttwak, E.N. The Grand Strategy of the Roman Empire from the First Century A.D. to the Third.*
  A.R. Birley, 123:Vol29No1-181
  J.C. Mann, 313:Vol69-175
Lutyens, M. Edwin Lutyens.
  J. Grigg, 362:16Oct80-510
Lutz, L. Dimensionen der Textbeurteilung und ihre Beziehung zu objektiven Textmerkmalen.
  C. Good, 307:Apr79-56
Lutz, L. and others, eds. Lexikon des Mittelalters. (Vol 1, Pt 1)
  D.H. Green, 402(MLR):Apr79-389
Lutz, M.M. The Effects of Acculturation on Eskimo Music of Cumberland Peninsula.
  N. Beaudry, 187:Sep80-592
Lutzeier, P. Modelltheorie für linguisten.
  R. Murawski, 360(LP):Vol21-185
Lux, T. Sunday.
  D. Kalstone, 441:4May80-15

Luxemburg, R. Comrade and Lover. (E. Ettinger, ed and trans)
  N. Ascherson, 453(NYRB):6Mar80-14
Luxemburg, R. The National Question. (H.B. Davis, ed)
  I. Nagurski, 497(PolR):Vol123#3-124
Luxemburg, N. - see Skrjabina, E.
de Luzán, I. La poética o reglas de la poesía en general, y de sus principales especies. (R.P. Sebold, ed)
  E.V. Coughlin, 238:May-Sep79-399
  P. Deacon, 86(BHS):Jul79-255
  J. Dowling, 240(HR):Autumn78-500
Lyall, G. The Secret Servant.
  P. Andrews, 441:16Nov80-14
  T.J. Binyon, 617(TLS):20Jun80-706
  A. Broyard, 441:26Sep80-C31
  M. Laski, 362:14Aug80-216
  442(NY):17Nov80-240
Lyell, W.A., Jr. Lu Hsün's Vision of Reality.*
  Lin Yü-sheng, 293(JASt):Feb79-365
Lyman, J., ed. Perspectives on Plays.
  D. Jarrett, 447(N&Q):Dec78-570
Lyman, S.M. and M.B. Scott. The Drama of Social Reality.*
  J.B. Fort, 189(EA):Jan-Mar78-71
Lynch, D. Yeats.
  G.M. Harper, 598(SoR):Spring80-492
Lyne, R.O.A.M. - see Vergil
Lyngstad, S. Jonas Lie.*
  H. Brønner, 563(SS):Spring79-192
  I. Hauge, 562(Scan):Nov78-167
  S.F.D. Hughes, 395(MFS):Summer78-300
Lynton, N. The Story of Modern Art.
  S. Bayley, 362:7Aug80-182
  J. Russell, 441:30Nov80-74
Lyon, B. Henri Pirenne.
  J.A. Brundage, 589:Jan79-174
Lyons, A. Castles Burning.
  N. Callendar, 441:3Feb80-22
Lyons, B. Henry Roth.
  S. Pinsker, 395(MFS):Summer78-278
Lyons, B., E.G. Joiner and S.L. Shinall. Départs.
  N.A. Poulin, 207(FR):Feb79-533
  E. Spinelli, 399(MLJ):Mar79-144
Lyons, D.B. Lute, Vihuela, Guitar to 1800.
  I. Fenlon, 415:Jun79-489
Lyons, F.S.L. Culture and Anarchy in Ireland, 1890-1939.
  O. MacDonagh, 617(TLS):28Mar80-371
Lyons, F.S.L. Charles Stewart Parnell.*
  L.J. McCaffrey, 637(VS):Summer79-449
Lyons, J. Einführung in die moderne Linguistik.
  G.F. Meier, 682(ZPSK):Band31Heft6-644
Lyons, J. Semantics.*
  Ö. Dahl, 350:Mar79-199
  P. Schmitter, 567:Vol125#1/2-139
  G.W. Turner, 67:Nov79-373
  T.P. Waldron, 402(MLR):Jan79-117
  S. Weisler, 399(MLJ):Nov79-389
Lyons, J.O. The Invention of the Self.
  W.H. Epstein, 566:Spring79-140
  R.A. Lanham, 301(JEGP):Apr79-264

Lyons, M. France under the Directory.
  C.H. Church, 208(FS):Vol33Pt2-1006
Lyotard, J-F. Economie libidinale.
  M.E. Blanchard, 153:Summer79-17
Lys, D. L'Ecclésiaste ou Que vaut la vie?
  J. Brun, 192(EP):Apr-Jun79-255
Lysaght, C.E. Brendan Bracken.*
  T. Fitton, 617(TLS):11Jan80-38
Lysaght, T.A. Material towards the Compilation of a Concise Old Church Slavonic-English Dictionary.
  M. Winokur, 574(SEEJ):Winter79-553
Lysias. Lisias, "Contra Eratóstenes."*
  (L. Rojas Álvarez, ed and trans)
  R.W., 555:Vol52fasc2-375
Lytle, E.G. A Grammar of Subordinate Structures in English.*
  E. König, 38:Band96Heft1/2-188
Lyttelton, G. and R. Hart-Davis. The Lyttelton Hart-Davis Letters.* (Vol 2) (R. Hart-Davis, ed)
  A. Bell, 617(TLS):22Feb80-199

"MLA Handbook for Writers of Research Papers, Theses and Dissertations."
  P-G.B., 189(EA):Jul-Dec78-425
Ma, Y.W. and J.S.M. Lau, eds. Traditional Chinese Stories.
  K.J. De Woskin, 293(JASt):Aug79-773
  M. Mudrick, 249(HudR):Spring79-123
Maas, J. Gambart.
  L. Ormond, 637(VS):Winter78-270
Maas, P. and A. Ghiselli. Metrica Greca.
  L.P.E. Parker, 123:Vol29No2-260
Mabbott, T. - see Poe, E.A.
Mabbott, T.O., with E.D. Kewer and M.C. Mabbott - see Poe, E.A.
Mabey, R. The Common Ground.
  R. Blythe, 362:4Sep80-310
McAleer, J. Rex Stout.
  R.W. Daniel, 579(SAQ):Winter79-135
McAllister, B. More Little Boxes.
  D. Thomas, 362:18and25Dec80-863
McAlpine, M.E. The Genre of "Troilus and Criseyde."
  S.A. Barney, 589:Jul79-599
  A.C. Spearing, 541(RES):Nov79-458
MacAndrew, E. The Gothic Tradition in Fiction.
  A.N. Wilson, 617(TLS):14Mar80-290
McAndrew, J. Venetian Architecture of the Early Renaissance.
  P. Goldberger, 441:30Nov80-68
McAndrew, J. Antonio Visentini.
  D. Stillman, 576:May78-117
MacAndrew, M-C. and J.H. Moore - see Zaleski, E.
McAndrew, P.N. - see Bournonville, A.
Macary, J., ed. Essays on the Age of Enlightenment in Honor of Ira O. Wade.*
  H. Cohen, 207(FR):Feb79-488
  M. Delon, 535(RHL):Mar-Jun79-513
  N.M. O'Connor, 188(ECr):Summer78-86
McAughtry, S. Blind Spot.
  K.C. O'Brien, 617(TLS):15Feb80-170

McAughtry, S. The Sinking of the Kenbane Head.
   W. Fennell, 174(Éire):Summer79-155
Macaulay, R.K.S. Language, Social Class and Education — a Glasgow Study.
   M.W.S. De Silva, 297(JL):Mar79-199
   J.B. Pride, 350:Sep79-731
McAuley, A. Economic Welfare in the Soviet Union.
   M.G. Field, 550(RusR):Oct79-495
McAuley, J. A Map of Australian Verse.
   R.V. Johnson, 447(N&Q):Oct78-476
McAuley, J. Nothing Ever Happens in Point-Claire.*
   G. Davies, 168(ECW):Spring78-82
   K. Garebian, 102(CanL):Summer79-126
McBain, E. Calypso.*
   376:Oct79-142
McBain, E. Ghosts.
   N. Callendar, 441:27Jul80-23
MacBeth, G. Buying a Heart.
   J.F. Cotter, 249(HudR):Spring79-118
   T. Eagleton, 565:Vol20#1-74
   C. Hope, 364:Jun79-77
MacBeth, G. Poems of Love and Death.
   J. Mole, 617(TLS):1Aug80-876
McBratney, S. Lagan Valley Details.
   K. Flint, 617(TLS):19Sep80-1044
McBride, R. The Sceptical Vision of Molière.*
   M. Gutwirth, 207(FR):Feb79-486
   W.D. Howarth, 402(MLR):Jan79-203
   L. Romero, 141:Summer79-269
   E. Sabiston, 108:Fall79-128
   C.N. Smith, 208(FS):Oct79-444
McBride, W.L. The Philosophy of Marx.
   185:Oct78-123
McBrien, R.P. Catholicism.
   R.B. Kaiser, 441:13Jul80-12
McCabe, J. Charlie Chaplin.*
   S. Feldman, 529(QQ):Summer79-320
MacCaffrey, I.G. Spenser's Allegory.*
   J. Mills, 648(WCR):Oct78-65
   H.L. Weatherby, 569(SR):Summer79-490
Maccagnolo, E. Rerum universitas.
   J. Jolivet, 542:Jan-Mar78-90
McCaig, D. The Butte Polka.
   P-L. Adams, 61:Oct80-101
   442(NY):13Oct80-191
MacCaig, N. The Equal Skies.
   D. Davis, 362:5Jun80-729
McCall, A. The Medieval Underworld.
   442(NY):19May80-161
McCall, D. Beecher.
   M. Malone, 441:20Jan80-15
McCallum, G.P. More Idiom Drills.
   R. Past, 399(MLJ):Mar79-137
McCann, J.J. The Theater of Arthur Adamov.*
   D. Knowles, 208(FS):Vol33Pt2-926
McCann, P., ed. Popular Education and Socialization in the Nineteenth Century.
   J.N. Burstyn, 637(VS):Spring79-360
McCarney, J. The Real World of Ideology.
   K. Minogue, 617(TLS):18Jul80-801

McCarren, V.P. A Critical Concordance to Catullus.*
   J. André, 555:Vol52fasc2-390
McCarry, C., with others. Double Eagle.*
   M. Harris, 617(TLS):13Jun80-678
McCarter, P.K., Jr. The Antiquity of the Greek Alphabet and the Early Phoenician Scripts.
   W.C. West 3d, 318(JAOS):Jul-Sep78-346
McCarthy, C. Suttree.*
   S. Salmans, 617(TLS):2May80-500
   W. Sullivan, 569(SR):Spring79-337
   639(VQR):Summer79-102
McCarthy, D. The Fate of O'Loughlin.
   S. Chew, 617(TLS):15Aug80-923
McCarthy, E.J. America Revisited.
   R.B. Fowler, 432(NEQ):Mar79-112
   639(VQR):Winter79-29
McCarthy, E.J. The Ultimate Tyranny.
   D. Grumbach, 441:25May80-11
McCarthy, J. Fantasy and Reality.
   W. Paulsen, 400(MLN):Apr79-619
McCarthy, M. Ideas and the Novel.
   J. Leonard, 441:18Nov80-C12
   G. Vidal, 453(NYRB):4Dec80-10
McCarthy, M. On the Contrary.
   A. Ryan, 362:14Feb80-220
MacCarthy, P. The Teaching of Pronunciation.
   A.R. James, 608:Jun80-246
McCarthy, T. The Critical Theory of Jurgen Habermas.
   S.L. Kline, 583:Summer79-427
McCarthy, T. The First Convention.
   R. Bonaccorso, 174(Éire):Spring79-146
McCauley, A. Economic Welfare in the Soviet Union.
   A. Brown, 617(TLS):25Jan80-95
McCawley, J.D. Adverbs, Vowels, and Other Objects of Wonder.
   639(VQR):Autumn79-129
McCawley, J.D. Grammar and Meaning.
   M.M. Bryant, 660(Word):Aug78-195
Macchia, G. Il Silenzio di Molière.
   B. Baritaud, 535(RHL):Mar-Apr78-296
Macciocchi, M-A. De la France.
   J-P. Ponchie, 207(FR):May79-946
McClain, E.G. The Pythagorean Plato.
   S. Levarie, 414(MusQ):Jul78-402
   S.U., 543:Jun79-762
McClane, A.J. The Encyclopedia of Fish Cookery.
   W. and C. Cowen, 639(VQR):Spring78-74
McClellan, K. Whatever Happened to Shakespeare?
   P. Traci, 141:Spring79-166
McClellan, W. Revolutionary Exiles.
   P. Pomper, 550(RusR):Oct79-476
McClelland, D. Le Vocabulaire de Marie de France.
   R. Harden, 627(UTQ):Summer79-420
McClung, N. Baraka.
   G. Hamel, 198:Winter80-139
McClung, W.A. The Country House in English Renaissance Poetry.*
   A.M. Duckworth, 191(ELN):Mar79-251
                              [continued]

McClung, W.A. The Country House in English Renaissance Poetry. [continuing]
   D. Evett, 405(MP):Feb80-327
   W.A. McQueen, 577(SHR):Summer79-251
McClure, J. The Blood of an Englishman.
   T.J. Binyon, 617(TLS):25Jul80-858
   M. Laski, 362:13Nov80-665
McClure, J. Spike Island.
   P-L. Adams, 61:Oct80-101
   P.D. James, 441:24Aug80-12
   C.H. Rolph, 617(TLS):18Apr80-436
   B. Whitaker, 362:17Apr80-512
McCoard, R.W. The English Perfect.
   M. Celce-Murcia, 399(MLJ):Jan-Feb79-67
McConkey, J. The Tree House Confessions.*
   A. Duchêne, 617(TLS):28Mar80-368
   C.C. Park, 249(HudR):Winter79/80-583
McConnell, F.D. Four Postwar American Novelists.*
   W.F. Hall, 255(HAB):Summer79-231
   J.T. Hansen, 295(JML):Vol7#4-607
   639(VQR):Spring79-48
McCord, N., ed. Essays in Tyneside Labour History.
   A.J. Heesom, 161(DUJ):Jun79-274
MacCormac, E.R. Metaphor and Myth in Science and Religion.*
   J.C.A. Gaskin, 518:May79-82
McCormack, A.R. Reformers, Rebels and Revolutionaries.
   L.T.C., 102(CanL):Winter78-131
McCormack, G. Chang Tso-lin in Northeast China, 1911-1928.
   G.R. Falconeri, 293(JASt):May79-563
McCormack, W.J. Sheridan Le Fanu and Victorian Ireland.
   R. Foster, 617(TLS):2May80-491
   V. Glendinning, 362:20Mar80-380
McCormick, E.H. Omai, Pacific Envoy.
   T.M. Curley, 173(ESC):Spring79-429
McCormick, E.H. Alexander Turnbull.
   R. Grover, 368:Dec74-349
McCormick, J. Fiction as Knowledge.
   J.M. Lennon, 395(MFS):Summer78-325
McCormick, J. Last Seen Alive.
   N. Callendar, 441:6Jan80-15
McCowen, A. Double Bill.
   J. Houseman, 441:9Nov80-12
   C. Lehmann-Haupt, 441:19Dec80-C33
McCoy, D.R. The National Archives.
   W. Robertson, 14:Apr79-206
McCoy, E. Case Study Houses, 1945-1962. (2nd ed)
   T.S. Hines, 505:Oct79-98
McCracken, K. Reflections.*
   G. Hamel, 198:Winter80-139
   W. Stevenson, 102(CanL):Spring79-103
McCracken, U.E. - see Zeri, F.
McCrum, R. In the Secret State.
   T.J. Binyon, 617(TLS):22Feb80-202
   N. Callendar, 441:1Jun80-18
   M. Laski, 362:17Apr80-514
McCullagh, J. Alan Crawley and Contemporary Verse.
   D. McCarthy, 168(ECW):Summer78-211
McCullin, D. Homecoming.
   J. Naughton, 362:3Jan80-29

McCullough, J.B. Hamlin Garland.
   R.E. Bolick, Jr., 26(ALR):Spring79-165
McCully, M. Els Quatre Gats.
   C. Green, 617(TLS):1Feb80-121
MacCurdy, E. - see Leonardo da Vinci
MacCurdy, R.R. - see de Rojas Zorrilla, F.
McCusker, J.J. Money and Exchange in Europe and America, 1660-1775.*
   G.L. Main, 432(NEQ):Mar79-137
McCutchan, J.D. Mier Expedition Diary. (J.M. Nance, ed)
   W. Gard, 584(SWR):Spring79-vi
McDavid, R.I., Jr. and A.R. Duckert, eds. Lexicography in English.
   M.M. Bryant, 660(Word):Dec78-270
McDermott, A. - see Salcedo-Bastardo, J.L.
MacDiarmid, H. The Complete Poems of Hugh MacDiarmid.* (M. Grieve and W.R. Aitken, eds)
   A. Bold, 493:Dec79-53
MacDiarmid, H. The Socialist Poems of Hugh MacDiarmid. (T.S. Law and T. Bewick, eds)
   T. Eagleton, 565:Vol20#1-74
MacDonagh, O. Early Victorian Government, 1830-1870.
   J.B. Conacher, 637(VS):Winter79-219
MacDonald, A.A., P.A. O'Flaherty and G.M. Storey, eds. A Festschrift for Edgar Ronald Seary.
   F. Cogswell, 178:Fall79-372
Macdonald, A.M., ed. Chambers Twentieth Century Dictionary. (new ed)
   H. Ulherr, 38:Band96Heft1/2-198
McDonald, A.P., ed. East Texas History.
   W. Gard, 584(SWR):Winter79-89
Macdonald, C. (W)holes.
   V. Young, 441:2Mar80-16
MacDonald, D. Detroit 1985.
   R.A. Sokolov, 441:24Feb80-18
McDonald, F. Alexander Hamilton.*
   M. Beloff, 617(TLS):4Jul80-750
MacDonald, G. Training and Careers for Professional Musicians.
   A. Frank, 415:Jun79-490
Mcdonald, G. Who Took Toby Rinaldi?
   M. Levin, 441:3Aug80-12
Macdonald, G.F., ed. Perception and Identity.
   J.J.C. Smart, 617(TLS):11Jul80-779
Macdonald, H. Skryabin.*
   C. Palmer, 415:Sep79-744
McDonald, J. Petra.
   T.C. Holyoke, 42(AR):Spring79-242
MacDonald, M., comp. Dmitri Shostakovich.
   G. Norris, 415:Mar79-223
MacDonald, M. The Symphonies of Havergal Brian. (Vol 1)
   H. Cole, 415:Apr79-308
MacDonald, M. The Symphonies of Havergal Brian. (Vol 2)
   T. Bray, 410(M&L):Jul79-350
   H. Cole, 415:Apr79-308
McDonald, R. 1915.
   J. Burke, 441:11May80-14
   C. Wallace-Crabbe, 617(TLS):11Jan80-30
   442(NY):17Mar80-165

MacDonald, R.H. - see Drummond, W.
MacDonald, W.L. The Pantheon.*
    J. Russell, 121(CJ):Oct-Nov79-79
    F.K. Yegul, 576:May78-121
McDonnell, M. The Registers of St. Paul's
    School, 1509-1748.
    F. Strong, 325:Oct79-239
McDonough, J.L. Shiloh — in Hell Before
    Night.
    639(VQR):Spring78-61
McDougall, I. Foreign Correspondent.
    L. Heren, 362:25Sep80-410
McDougall, W.A. France's Rhineland Diplo-
    macy, 1914-1924.
    639(VQR):Autumn79-134
MacDowell, D.M. The Law in Classical
    Athens. (H.H. Scullard, ed)
    R.S. Stroud, 121(CJ):Oct-Nov79-69
MacDowell, D.M. - see Aristophanes
McDowell, E. To Keep Our Honor Clean.
    W. Schott, 441:27Jul80-13
    R.F. Shepard, 441:26Dec80-C30
McDowell, F.P.W., ed. E.M. Forster.*
    M.C., 395(MFS):Winter78/79-603
McDowell, J. - see Plato
McDowell, M. Cold Moon Over Babylon.
    N. Callendar, 441:23Mar80-33
Macedo, H. Do Significado Oculto da
    Menina e Moça.
    R.C. Willis, 86(BHS):Apr79-165
McEwan, I. The Cement Garden.*
    J.R.B., 148:Spring79-94
    P. Lewis, 565:Vol20#3-62
    42(AR):Winter79-125
    639(VQR):Spring79-56
McEwan, I. In Between the Sheets.*
    P. Lewis, 565:Vol20#3-62
    V.S. Pritchett, 453(NYRB):24Jan80-31
MacEwen, G. Mermaids and Ikons.
    M. Micros, 168(ECW):Fall78-72
McFadden, D. The Great Canadian Sonnet.
    B. Bailey, 102(CanL):Spring79-78
McFadden, D. I Don't Know.
    D. Barbour, 198:Winter80-129
McFadden, D. A New Romance.
    D. Barbour, 198:Winter80-129
    J. Cook, 99:Mar80-38
McFadden, D. On the Road Again.*
    D. Barbour, 150(DR):Spring79-154
    D. Barbour, 198:Winter80-129
    J. Bell, 526:Spring79-76
    S.G. Mullins, 628(UWR):Fall-Winter78-
    71
    R. Thacker, 649(WAL):Fall79-229
McFadden, D. The Saladmaker.
    A. Amprimoz, 102(CanL):Autumn79-99
    G. Davies, 168(ECW):Spring78-82
McFadden, G. Dryden the Public Writer,
    1660-1685.*
    W. Frost, 566:Spring79-120
    P. Harth, 301(JEGP):Jan79-128
    J. Sloman, 49:Oct79-99
    K. Williamson, 541(RES):May79-218
McFadzean, R. The Life and Work of Alex-
    ander Thomson.
    J.M. Richards, 617(TLS):1Feb80-122

McFarland, D.T. Flannery O'Connor.*
    E. Baldeshwiler, 573(SSF):Summer78-340
    M.J. Friedman, 578:Spring80-114
McFarland, P. Sojourners.*
    J. Atlas, 441:5Jan80-19
Macfarlane, A. and others, eds. Records
    of an English Village: Earls Colne, 1400-
    1750.
    G.E. Aylmer, 617(TLS):12Sep80-1000
Macfarlane, A., with S. Harrison and C.
    Jardine. Reconstructing Historical
    Communities.
    P. Earle, 325:Oct79-231
McFarlane, J.W. - see Ibsen, H.
McFee, O. Sandbars.*
    L. Rogers, 102(CanL):Spring79-83
McGahern, J. Getting Through.
    A. Broyard, 441:12Jul80-15
    J. Moynahan, 441:13Jul80-14
McGahern, J. The Pornographer.*
    D. Durrant, 364:Feb80-92
    P. Graig, 617(TLS):11Jan80-46
    J. Thompson, 453(NYRB):1May80-20
McGee, B. The Shanty-Horses.
    R. Miles, 102(CanL):Summer79-138
McGee, T.G. and Y.M. Yeung. Hawkers in
    Southeast Asian Cities.
    A.G. Dewey, 293(JASt):Feb79-421
McGhee, E. The Last Caesar.
    N. Callendar, 441:13Jul80-25
McGhee, H. Spanish Picture Drills and
    Dialogs.
    H. Villarreal, 399(MLJ):Nov79-380
McGinniss, J. Going to Extremes.
    A. Broyard, 441:13Sep80-19
    P. Theroux, 441:14Sep80-1
McGinniss, L.R. and H. Mitchell. Cata-
    logue of the Earl of Crawford's
    "Speculum Romanae Magnificentiae" now
    in the Avery Architectural Library.
    R. Brilliant, 576:Dec78-318
McGinty, P. Interpretation and Dionysos.
    H. Hansen, 124:Feb80-317
McGonagall, W. The World's Worst Poet.
    S. Commager, 61:Dec80-56
McGovern, E.M. Neil Simon.
    J. Lahr, 617(TLS):2May80-492
McGowan, R.A. Italian Baroque Solo Son-
    atas for the Recorder and the Flute.
    R. Andrewes, 415:Apr79-309
    N. McGegan, 410(M&L):Apr79-210
McGrade, A.S. and B. Vickers - see Hooker,
    R.
McGrady, D. - see de Tamariz, C.
McGrail, S. - see Johnstone, P.
McGrath, J.W. Dyes from Lichens and
    Plants.
    S. Andreae, 96:Oct-Nov78-69
McGrath, M. and N. Children's Spaces.
    505:Feb79-104
McGregor, L., M. Tate and K. Robinson.
    Learning Through Drama.
    C. Barker, 610:Oct78-71
McGregor, M. Early Celtic Art in North
    Britain.
    V. Kruta, 194(EC):Vol15fasc2-722
McGregor, R.R., Jr. - see Froissart, J.

MacGréil, M. Prejudice and Tolerance in
Ireland.
 P.F. Power, 174(Éire):Fall79-146
McGuinness, B. - see Boltzmann, L.
McGuinness, B. - see Waismann, F.
McGushin, P. C. Sallustius Crispus,
"Bellum Catilinae."*
 G.M. Paul, 487:Spring79-77
Machado de Assis, J.M. The Devil's Church
and Other Stories.*
 639(VQR):Spring78-66
Machamer, P.K. and R.G. Turnbull, eds.
Motion and Time, Space and Matter.
 E. Sylla, 482(PhR):Jan79-122
Machan, T.R. The Pseudo-Science of B.F.
Skinner.
 L. Briskman, 488:Mar79-81
de Machaut, G. - see under Guillaume de
Machaut
Macherel, C. and J. Le Querrec. Léry,
village normand, un croquis ethnologique.
 H.L. Butler, 207(FR):Apr79-810
Macherey, P. Hegel ou Spinoza.
 A. Reix, 542:Apr-Jun79-255
Machery, P. A Theory of Literary Produc-
tion.
 S. Zelnick, 290(JAAC):Winter79-213
Machiavelli, N. The Portable Machiavelli.
(P. Bondanella and M. Musa, eds and
trans)
 F. Rosengarten, 276:Autumn79-299
Machiavelli, N. The Prince. (R.M. Adams,
ed)
 A. Verna, 399(MLJ):Sep-Oct79-313
Machin, G.I.T. Politics and the Churches
in Great Britain, 1832-1868.
 S. Meacham, 637(VS):Winter79-209
McHugh, H. Dangers.*
 T.A. Stumpf, 114(ChiR):Autumn78-127
McHugh, P. Prostitution and Victorian
Social Reform.
 R.T. Shannon, 617(TLS):25Jul80-852
McHugh, R. The Sigla of "Finnegans Wake."*
 S.A. Henke, 639(VQR):Spring79-371
 B.P. O Hehir, 454:Fall78-78
McInerny, R. Second Vespers.
 N. Callendar, 441:7Dec80-44
McInerny, R. The Seventh Station.
 639(VQR):Summer78-93
MacInnes, C. Out of the Way.
 D.A.N. Jones, 617(TLS):8Feb80-132
 C. Sigal, 362:27Mar80-417
McInnes, E. German Social Drama 1840-1900.
 L. Löb, 402(MLR):Apr79-499
MacInnes, H. The Hidden Target.
 A. Broyard, 441:26Sep80-C31
Macintosh, D. Chinese Blue and White
Porcelain.*
 W.B.R. Neave-Hill, 463:Winter78/79-463
MacIntyre, A. Against the Self-Images of
the Age.
 R.B.P., 543:Mar79-558
Macintyre, L. Cruel In the Shadow.
 L. Duguid, 617(TLS):16May80-558
Macintyre, M. The Spirit of Asia.
 H.G. Porteus, 362:5Jun80-730

Mack, J.E. A Prince of Our Disorder.
 A.G. Marquis, 77:Fall78-82
Mack, S. Patterns of Time in Vergil.
 J. Glenn, 24:Winter79-585
 K. Morsley, 67:Nov79-305
 M.C.J. Putnam, 124:Sep79-41
MacKay, A. Spain in the Middle Ages.
 A. Pagden, 382(MAE):1979/2-327
McKay, D. Lependu.*
 D. Barbour, 150(DR):Spring79-154
MacKay, D.M. Science, Chance and Provi-
dence.
 A. Flew, 84:Jun79-183
 H. Meynell, 483:Jul79-425
McKay, D.P. and R. Crawford. William
Billings of Boston.
 H.B.R., 412:May78-131
Mackay, R., B. Barkman and R.R. Jordan,
eds. Reading in a Second Language.
 E. Schaefer, 608:Dec80-519
Mackay, R. and A. Mountford. English for
Specific Purposes.
 K. Drobnic, 351(LL):Jun79-205
McKay, S. and L. Rosenthal. Writing for a
Specific Purpose.
 M.K. Morray, 608:Dec80-515
McKean, H.F. The "Lost" Treasures of
Louis Comfort Tiffany.
 P-L. Adams, 61:Nov80-99
McKechnie, S. British Silhouette Artists
and their Work 1760-1860.
 D. Piper, 617(TLS):1Feb80-119
McKenna, F. The Railway Workers: 1840-
1970.
 J. Mapplebeck, 362:4Dec80-762
McKenna, W. Charles Lamb and the Theater.
 W. Buck, 661(WC):Summer79-271
Mackenzie, B.D. Behaviourism and the
Limits of Scientific Method.*
 A.W. MacKenzie, 482(PhR):Jan79-145
 D.C. Phillips, 84:Mar79-85
Mackenzie, D.N. - see Diakonoff, I.M. and
V.A. Livshits
MacKenzie, J. A Victorian Courtship.*
 R. Coleridge, 617(TLS):25Jan80-90
Mackenzie, M. Communities of Honor and
Love in Henry James.*
 M. Jacobson, 481(PQ):Winter78-140
Mackenzie, N. and J. Dickens.*
 C.B.C., 148:Autumn79-91
 D. Parker, 401(MLQ):Sep79-319
MacKenzie, N. and J. The Fabians.*
(British title: The First Fabians.)
 R. Barker, 637(VS):Winter79-226
McKenzie, R.H., ed. The Rising South.*
(Vol 2)
 K. King, 577(SHR):Summer79-270
McKeon, M. Politics and Poetry in Restora-
tion England.*
 A. Poyet, 189(EA):Jan-Mar78-85
McKeon, P.R. Hincmar of Laon and Carolin-
gian Politics.
 H.E. Hallam, 67:Nov79-334
McKeown, T. The Role of Medicine.
 P.B. Medawar, 453(NYRB):15May80-6
MacKerras, C., ed. China.
 P.J. Seybolt, 293(JASt):Feb79-349

Mackey, L. Kierkegaard.
G.J. Stack, 321:Summer78-157
Mackey, P.E. - see Mickle, I.
Mackey, W. and V.N. Beebe. Bilingual
Schools for a Bicultural Community.
A. Brito, Jr., 238:May-Sep79-415
Mackey, W.F. and others. The Bilingual
Education Movement.*
C.R. Hancock, 608:Mar80-111
Mackey, W.F. and T. Andersson, eds. Bilin-
gualism in Early Childhood.*
G.J. Brault, 399(MLJ):Dec79-460
Mackie, G. Lynton Lamb: Illustrator.
J. Lewis, 503:Winter78-193
Mackie, J.L. Ethics: Inventing Right and
Wrong.*
F. Feldman, 482(PhR):Jan79-134
D. Mitchell, 63:Mar79-94
Mackie, J.L. Hume's Moral Theory.
S.W. Blackburn, 617(TLS):22Aug80-942
Mackie, J.L. Problems from Locke.*
P. Dubois, 542:Apr-Jun79-222
L. Krüger, 53(AGP):Band60Heft3-340
McKie, R. Bitter Bread.
C. Hanna, 581:Jun79-224
McKilligan, K.M. Édouard Dujardin.*
P.M. Wetherill, 402(MLR):Oct79-945
E. Zants, 395(MFS):Winter78/79-625
McKillop, A.B. A Disciplined Intelligence.
L. Armour, 99:Jun-Jul80-36
McKinnon, A. - see Ostenfeld, I.
MacKinnon, K. Language, Education and
Social Processes in a Gaelic Community.
N.C. Dorian, 355(LSoc):Apr78-137
McKirahan, R.D. Plato and Socrates.
J.W. Binns, 354:Sep79-286
McKitterick, D. - see Morison, S. and D.B.
Updike
McKitterick, D.J. The Library of Sir
Thomas Knyvett of Ashwellthorpe c.
1539-1618.
G. Williams, 354:Sep79-287
McKnight, G. The Scandal of Syrie Maugham.
G. Annan, 362:8May80-617
V. Glendinning, 617(TLS):25Apr80-459
McKnight, S.A., ed. Eric Voegelin's
Search for Order in History.
M. Montgomery, 396(ModA):Summer79-233
McLaren, A. Birth Control in Nineteenth-
Century England.
J.A. Banks, 637(VS):Summer79-467
McLaughlin, B. Second-Language Acquisi-
tion in Childhood.
S. Peck, 608:Dec80-524
McLaughlin, C.C. and C.E. Beveridge - see
Olmsted, F.L.
McLaurin, M.A. The Knights of Labor in
the South.
M.E. Reed, 9(AlaR):Jul79-235
MacLaverty, B. Lamb.
J. Naughton, 362:3Jul80-25
J. O'Faolain, 441:2Nov80-13
C. Rumens, 617(TLS):13Jun80-664
MacLaverty, B. Secrets.*
K.C. O'Brien, 617(TLS):15Feb80-170
MacLean, A. Athabasca.
S. Ellin, 441:28Sep80-14

McLean, A. Lil.*
R. Miles, 102(CanL):Summer79-138
Maclean, A.D., ed. Winter's Tales 26.
J. Mellors, 362:18and25Dec80-867
McLean, A.M., ed. Shakespeare in the
Classroom.
V.K. Whitaker, 570(SQ):Summer79-429
Maclean, C. Island on the Edge of the
World.
442(NY):13Oct80-194
Maclean, F. Tito.
J. Leonard, 441:21Oct80-C11
McLean, H. Nikolai Leskov.*
R.B. Anderson, 395(MFS):Winter78/79-
605
T. Eekman, 141:Summer79-276
M. Ehre, 550(RusR):Oct79-508
W. Keenan, 575(SEER):Apr79-280
S. Monas, 405(MP):Nov79-242
Maclean, I. Woman Triumphant.*
E.J. Kearns, 402(MLR):Jan79-199
L. Romero, 141:Summer79-269
Maclean, J. Deadfall.
376:Oct79-142
McLean, M. and M. Orbell. Traditional
Songs of the Maori.
K.A. Gourlay, 187:Jan80-123
McLeave, H. No Face in the Mirror.
N. Callendar, 441:26Oct80-29
McLeish, J.A.B. A Canadian for All
Seasons.
G.W., 102(CanL):Autumn79-148
Macleish, K. The Theatre of Aristophanes.
O. Taplin, 617(TLS):22Aug80-938
MacLeish, R. The First Book of Eppe.
R. Bradford, 441:8Jun80-14
McLellan, D. Marxism After Marx.
C. Lehmann-Haupt, 441:24Mar80-C13
P. Singer, 453(NYRB):25Sep80-62
McLellan, D.S. and D.C. Acheson - see
Acheson, D.
MacLennan, H. The Other Side of Hugh
MacLennan. (E. Cameron, ed)
E.L. Bobak, 150(DR):Spring79-190
M. Peterman, 627(UTQ):Summer79-445
MacLennan, H. Voices in Time.
G. Woodcock, 99:Dec80/Jan81-22
MacLeod, C. Horatio Alger, Farewell.
L.C. Thurow, 441:26Oct80-9
McLeod, C. The Family Vault.
T.J. Binyon, 617(TLS):6Jun80-654
McLeod, J. Cleaning the Bones.*
B. Whiteman, 168(ECW):Spring78-57
McLeod, W.H. The Evolution of the Sikh
Community.*
B.G. Gokhale, 318(JAOS):Oct-Dec78-565
McLuhan, M. D'Oeil à Oreille.
R. Lorimer, 102(CanL):Winter78-82
McLuhan, M., K. Hutchon and E. McLuhan.
City as Classroom.
E. Wachtel, 186(ETC.):Jun78-195
Maclure, M., ed. Marlowe: The Critical
Heritage 1588-1896.*
J.P., 148:Winter79-89
McMahon, T. McKay's Bees.*
L. Duguid, 617(TLS):1Feb80-123

McMahon, W.E. Hans Reichenbach's Philos-
ophy of Grammar.*
    S. Soames, 350:Sep79-690
    L. Zgusta, 361:Apr78-389
McManners, J. Reflections at the Death-
Bed of Voltaire.
    J.H. Brumfitt, 208(FS):Vol33Pt2-745
McMaster, J., ed. Jane Austen's Achieve-
ment.*
    M. Butler, 447(N&Q):Dec78-562
    J.E.J., 191(ELN):Sep78(supp)-44
    A. Kennedy, 178:Spring79-122
    A. Wright, 402(MLR):Apr79-423
McMaster, J. Trollope's Palliser Novels.
    C. Diehl, 594:Winter79-494
McMillan, D. - see "Le Charroi de Nîmes"
McMillin, A.B. Die Literatur der Weiss-
russen.*
    205(FMLS):Jan78-91
McMinn, R.M.H. and R.T. Hutchings. A
Colour Atlas of Human Anatomy.
    529(QQ):Summer79-369
McMullen, L., ed. The Lampman Symposium.*
    M.J. Edwards, 102(CanL):Winter78-99
    T. Marshall, 178:Fall79-370
McMullen, M. Welcome to the Grave.
    T.J. Binyon, 617(TLS):6Jun80-654
MacMullen, R. Roman Government's Response
to Crisis, A.D. 235-337.*
    G.P. Burton, 123:Vol29No2-279
    J.C. Mann, 313:Vol69-190
McMullin, E. Newton on Matter and Activ-
ity.
    R.E. Schofield, 173(ECS):Spring79-432
McMurtry, J. The Structure of Marx's
World View.
    R. Hudelson, 482(PhR):Jul79-481
McMurtry, J. Victorian Life and Victorian
Fiction.
    42(AR):Spring79-254
NcNamara, E. In Transit.
    R.J. Merrett, 102(CanL):Winter78-96
McNamara, E. Screens.*
    D. McCarthy, 168(ECW):Fall78-60
McNamara, E. The Search for Sarah Grace.*
    D. McCarthy, 168(ECW):Fall78-60
    G. Noonan, 628(UWR):Fall-Winter78-90
MacNamara, M. The Apocrypha in the Irish
Church.
    P-Y. Lambert, 194(EC):Vol15fasc2-738
Macnaughton, W.R. Mark Twain's Last
Years as a Writer.*
    H. Hill, 26(ALR):Autumn79-343
    P.D. Morrow, 649(WAL):Winter80-337
MacNeice, L. The Collected Poems. (E.R.
Dodds, ed)
    T. Paulin, 493:Mar80-52
McNeil, G., with S. Vance. Cruel and
Unusual.
    R. Marlin, 529(QQ):Spring79-150
McNeil, J. How Does Your Garden Grow?
    W. Dean, 368:Jun76-162
McNeil, J. Spy Game.
    N. Callendar, 441:26Oct80-28
McNeill, W.H. The Human Condition.
    J.H. Hexter, 441:19Oct80-14

McNeir, W.F. and F. Provost. Edmund
Spenser.*
    R.M. Cummings, 402(MLR):Jan79-162
McNeish, J. The Glass Zoo.
    H.W. Rhodes, 368:Sep76-208
McNickle, D. The Surrounded.
    W. Ude, 649(WAL):Fall79-264
McNulty, F. The Burning Bed.
    442(NY):3Nov80-203
Maconie, R. The Works of Karlheinz Stock-
hausen.
    P.J.P., 412:Feb78-64
McPhee, J. The John McPhee Reader.* (W.L.
Howarth, ed) Coming into the Country.
    G. Core, 639(VQR):Autumn78-733
MacPhee, R. Maggie.
    B. Whiteman, 99:Nov80-34
MacPherson, I. Each For All.
    J.G. Craig, 99:Nov80-34
Macpherson, I., ed. Juan Manuel Studies.
    R. Ayerbe-Chaux, 402(MLR):Apr79-474
    D. Eisenberg, 304(JHP):Winter80-169
    D.W. Lomax, 86(BHS):Jan79-57
MacPherson, M. Protégé.
    N. Callendar, 441:12Oct80-34
McPherson, S. The Year of Our Birth.*
    P. Stitt, 219(GaR):Summer79-463
    D. Wojahn, 109:Winter79/80-184
McQueen, H. The Black Swan of Trespass.
    C. Wallace-Crabbe, 617(TLS):8Aug80-898
Macqueen, J.G. The Hittites and their
Contemporaries in Asia Minor.
    J. Scarborough, 121(CJ):Apr-May80-353
Macrí, O. La obra poética de Jorge Guil-
lén.*
    C.B. Morris, 402(MLR):Oct79-969
McRobbie, K. First Ghost to Canada.
    J. Cook, 99:Mar80-38
    D. Precosky, 198:Winter80-133
MacSeáin, P. Ceolta Theilinn.
    P-Y. Lambert, 194:Vol15fasc2-740
MacSweeney, B. Black Torch.
    J. Freeman, 97(CQ):Vol8#3-282
MacVane, J. On the Air in World War II.
    R.F. Shepard, 441:7May80-C26
McVay, G. Esenin.*
    T.J. Binyon, 402(MLR):Apr79-508
McVey, F.J. and R.B. Jewell. Uncle Will
of Wildwood.
    R.G. Alvey, 582(SFQ):Vol41-282
Macvey, J.W. Interstellar Travel.
    R.N. Bracewell, 529(QQ):Spring79-138
McWhinney, E. Quebec and the Constitution
1960-78.
    D. Smiley, 99:Feb80-31
McWilliam, C. and C. Wilson. The Build-
ings of Scotland: Lothian except Edin-
burgh.*
    R. Calvocoressi, 46:Apr79-251
McWilliams, D. The Narratives of Michel
Butor.*
    R.A. Champagne, 399(MLJ):Mar79-139
McWilliams, T.S. Hannis Taylor.
    A.J. Going, 9(AlaR):Jul79-230
McWilliams-Tullberg, R. Women at Cam-
bridge.
    S. Rothblatt, 637(VS):Spring78-422

Maddison, F., M. Pelling and C. Webster, eds. Linacre Studies.
G. Whitteridge, 382(MAE):1979/1-160
Maddow, B. and R. Sobieszek. Nude Photographs 1850-1980. (C. Sullivan, ed)
H. Kramer, 441:30Nov80-13
Maddox, D. Structure and Sacring.
B.N. Sargent-Baur, 589:Oct79-831
B. Schmolke-Hasselmann, 547(RF):Band91 Heft1/2-168
Maddox, J.H., Jr. Joyce's "Ulysses" and the Assault Upon Character.*
S.A. Henke, 639(VQR):Winter79-181
M.P. Levitt, 295(JML):Vol7#4-748
M. Magalaner, 301(JEGP):Jan79-146
Madeja, S.S., ed. The Arts, Cognition, and Basic Skills.
A.J. Cohen, 255(HAB):Winter/Spring79-114
M. Sagoff, 290(JAAC):Fall79-81
Madison, J. The Papers of James Madison. (Vol 11) (R. Rutland and C.F. Hobson, eds)
639(VQR):Summer78-92
Madison, J. Papers of James Madison. (Vol 12) (R. Rutland and C.F. Hobson, eds)
E. Wright, 617(TLS):25Jan80-91
Madox, R. An Elizabethan in 1582. (E. Donno, ed)
E. Bourcier, 189(EA):Jul-Dec78-376
Madsen, A. Hearts and Minds.
B. Erlich, 502(PrS):Summer78-197
A. van den Hoven, 628(UWR):Fall-Winter 78-94
Madsen, D. Black Plume.
J. Symons, 441:12Oct80-15
Madsen, H.S. and D.J. Bowen. Adaptation in Language Teaching.*
C.J. Cook, 351(LL):Dec79-387
de Maegd-Soëp, C. The Emancipation of Women in Russian Literature and Society.
N.G.O. Pereira, 550(RusR):Apr79-227
Maestri, D. - see Gelli, G.B.
Maezumi, H.T. and B.T. Glassman, eds. On Zen Practice.
R.B. Zeuschner, 485(PE&W):Jan79-107
Magee, B., ed. Men of Ideas.*
D. Locke, 364:Jul79-83
Magee, W. No Man's Land.
E. Longley, 617(TLS):18Jan80-64
Magis, C.H. La poesía hermética de Octavio Paz.
E. Williamson, 402(MLR):Oct79-974
Magliola, R.R. Phenomenology and Literature.*
D.H. Hirsch, 569(SR):Fall79-628
W.W. Holdheim, 153:Summer79-30
D.G. Marshall, 481(PQ):Spring78-273
W.E. Steinkraus, 484(PPR):Dec79-295
Magné, B. Crise de la littérature française sous Louis XIV.
T. Allott, 402(MLR):Jan79-202
H.T. Barnwell, 208(FS):Vol133Pt2-705
M.S. Koppisch, 400(MLN):May79-917
A. Niderst, 535(RHL):Nov-Dec78-1025

Magner, T.F., ed. Slavic Linguistics and Language Teaching.
F. Knowles, 575(SEER):Oct79-628
Magno, P. Marco Pacuvio. Teucro.
J. André, 555:Vol52fasc2-395
Magnus, B. Nietzsche's Existential Imperative.
H.J. Birx, 484(PPR):Jun80-603
J.D.W., 543:Mar79-560
Magnusson, K. Die Gliederung der Konjunktivs in Grammatiken der deutschen Sprache.
S-G. Andersson, 597(SN):Vol150#2-331
Magnússon, S.A. Northern Sphinx.*
S.F.D. Hughes, 563(SS):Winter79-49
H. Pálsson, 562(Scan):May79-60
de Magny, O. Les Souspirs. (D. Wilkin, ed)
E.T. Dubois, 182:Vol131#15/16-549
Magocsi, P.R. The Shaping of a National Identity.
S.L. Guthier, 550(RusR):Jan79-105
Magris, C. Der unauffindbare Sinn.
W. Schmidt-Dengler, 602:Vol10-252
Maguire, D.C. The Moral Choice.
F.W. Dillistone, 396(ModA):Spring79-221
Maguire, R.A. and J.E. Malmstad - see Bely, A.
"Le Mahābhāṣya de Patañjali, avec le Pradīpa de Kaiyaṭa et l'Uddyota de Nāgeśa: Adhyāya 1 Pāda 1 Āhnika 1-4." (P. Filliozat, trans)
R. Rocher, 318(JAOS):Apr-Jun78-200
Mahapatra, J. A Rain of Rites.
U. Parameswaran, 529(QQ):Spring79-172
Maharg, J. A Call to Authenticity.
J.M. Flint, 86(BHS):Oct79-352
H.E. Lewald, 238:Mar79-186
Maher, J.T. The Twilight of Splendor.*
R.G. Wilson, 576:Mar78-49
Mahon, D. Lives. The Snow Party.
R. Tracy, 109:Summer80-180
Mahon, D. Poems 1962-1978.
B. Morrison, 617(TLS):15Feb80-168
Mahoney, E.P., ed. Philosophy and Humanism.*
C. Cairns, 402(MLR):Jan79-138
Mahoney, J.L. The Logic of Passion.
W.J. Bate, 340(KSJ):Vol28-156
J. Engell, 613:Dec79-451
Mahood, M.M. The Colonial Encounter.*
G.G. Fromm, 395(MFS):Summer78-306
J. Olney, 569(SR):Winter79-vi
Maier, F. Intelligenz als Handlung.
R.L. Fetz, 687:Oct-Dec79-653
Maier, P. The Old Revolutionaries.
E. Foner, 441:12Oct80-12
J. Leonard, 441:3Oct80-C33
Mailer, N. The Executioner's Song.*
D. Lodge, 617(TLS):11Jan80-27
61:Jan80-87
442(NY):14Jan80-102
Mailer, N. Marilyn.
C.E. Rollyson, Jr., 77:Fall78-49

Mailer, N. Of Women and Their Elegance.
  A. Broyard, 441:21Nov80-C28
  L. McMurtry, 441:7Dec80-11
Mailer, N. - see Miller, H.
Maillet, A. Les Cordes-de-bois.
  R. Sutherland, 102(CanL):Spring79-76
Maillet, A. Don L'Orignal.
  G. Davies, 198:Winter80-135
Maillet, A. Gapi.
  L. Rièse, 108:Winter79-142
Maillet, A. Pélagie-la-Charrette.
  A. Prevos, 296(JCF):28/29-204
  H.R. Runte, 150(DR):Winter79/80-764
Maillet, M. Des bébés-éprouvettes à la
  biologie du futur.
  J. Duvignaud, 450(NRF):Oct79-141
Mails, T.E. Mystic Warriors of the Plains.
  R. Laubin, 649(WAL):Spring79-60
Maimonides, M. Ethical Writings of
  Maimonides. (R.L. Weiss, with C.E.
  Butterworth, eds)
  A.D. Corré, 318(JAOS):Jul-Sep78-314
Maingon, C. L'Univers artistique de J-K.
  Huysmans.
  J. Lethève, 535(RHL):Sep-Oct79-874
Maingueneau, D. Initiation aux méthodes
  d'analyse du discours.
  E. Rattunde, 430(NS):Jul78-377
Maini, D.S. Henry James — "The Portrait
  of a Lady."
  R.A., 189(EA):Jul-Dec78-427
Mainkar, T.G. - see Daji, B.
Mairet, G. - see Rousseau, J-J.
Maisani-Léonard, M. André Gide ou
  l'ironie de l'écriture.*
  J-P. Cap, 207(FR):Oct78-170
Maisel, C. Witnessing.
  G. Burns, 584(SWR):Summer79-304
Maissin, J. Un manuscrit français du
  XVIIIe siècle. (R.H. Régnier, ed)
  L. Sternbach, 318(JAOS):Jul-Sep78-322
Maistrov, L.E. Probability Theory.
  J. Largeault, 542:Jan-Mar79-115
Major, J-L. Anne Hébert et le miracle de
  la parole.*
  N.D. Savage, 207(FR):Dec78-359
Major, J-L. La Nuit incendiée.
  C. Bayard, 627(UTQ):Summer79-465
Major, R. Rêver l'autre.
  M. Nacht, 98:Apr78-369
Makarova, N. A Dance Autobiography. (G.
  Smakov, ed)
  G. Annan, 617(TLS):4Apr80-386
  M. Hodgson, 441:13Jan80-13
Makhtoumkouli Firaqui. Poèmes de Turk-
  menie. (L. Bazin and P. Boratav, trans)
  I. Başgöz, 318(JAOS):Jul-Sep78-319
Makin, P. Provence and Pound.*
  B.D. Kimpel and T.C.D. Eaves, 27(AL):
  Nov79-434
  S.Y. McDougal, 659(ConL):Spring80-311
Makinson, R.L. Greene and Greene: Archi-
  tecture as a Fine Art.
  E. McCoy, 576:Oct78-212
Makinson, R.L. Greene and Greene: Furni-
  ture and Related Designs.
  P.L. Molten, 46:Oct79-205

Makkai, A., ed. Toward a Theory of Con-
  text in Linguistics and Literature.
  H. Thun, 343:Band23-34
Makowsky, V.A. - see Blackmur, R.P.
Maksimov, D. Poèzija i proza Al. Bloka.
  G. Pirog, 574(SEEJ):Summer79-279
  E. Reissner, 688(ZSP):Band40Heft2-418
Maksimov, V.I. Suffiksal'noe slovoobrazo-
  vanie imen suščestvitel'nych v russkom
  jazyke.
  H. Spitzbardt, 682(ZPSK):Band31Heft6-
  664
Malalgoda, K. Buddhism in Sinhalese
  Society, 1750-1900.*
  B.L. Smith, 318(JAOS):Oct-Dec78-564
Malamud, B. Dubin's Lives.*
  G.W. Allen, 219(GaR):Fall79-730
  L. Edel, 31(ASch):Winter79/80-130
  D. Flower, 249(HudR):Summer79-304
  S. Pinsker, 461:Fall-Winter79/80-108
  L.M. Rosenberg, 584(SWR):Autumn79-vi
  529(QQ):Summer79-369
Malbin, M.J. Unelected Representatives.
  J. Herbers, 441:14Sep80-9
Malcolm, J. Diana and Nikon.
  A. Broyard, 441:12Apr80-21
  C. James, 453(NYRB):18Dec80-22
  H. Kramer, 441:4May80-13
Malcolm, N. Memory and Mind.*
  R. Brandt, 482(PhR):Jan79-105
  D. Odegard, 154:Sep78-566
  E. Slater, 447(N&Q):Jun78-285
Malcolm, N. Thought and Knowledge.
  D. Odegard, 154:Sep78-566
Mâle, É. Religious Art in France: The
  Twelfth Century.
  J. Seznec, 208(FS):Jul79-319
Maleady, A. - see "Index to Record and
  Tape Reviews"
Malécot, A. Introduction à la phonétique
  française.*
  A.W. Grundstrom, 207(FR):Oct78-198
  A.E. Sharp, 297(JL):Mar79-121
Malet, N. Dieu selon Calvin.
  E. Naert, 192(EP):Jul-Sep79-369
Maley, A. and A. Duff. Drama Techniques
  in Language Learning.
  E.W. Stevick, 399(MLJ):Apr79-201
Malherbe, J-F. La philosophie de Karl
  Popper et le positivisme logique.
  J. Largeault, 542:Apr-Jun78-197
Malik, S.C., ed. Dissent, Protest and
  Reform in Indian Civilization.
  R. Saran, 293(JASt):Feb79-408
Malik, Y.K., ed. Politics and the Novel
  in India.
  U.S. Nilsson, 293(JASt):May79-607
Maling, A. The Koberg Link.*
  T.J. Binyon, 617(TLS):18Apr80-450
Maling, A. The Rheingold Route.
  639(VQR):Summer79-102
Malins, E. and P. Bowe. Irish Gardens and
  Demesnes from 1830.
  R.I. Ross, 617(TLS):25Jul80-850
Maltis, E. The Solitary Explorer.
  F.D. Gray, 441:19Oct80-3

Manuel II Palaeologus. The Letters. (G.T. Dennis, ed and trans)
   D.M. Nicol, 303(JoHS):Vol99-223
Manuel, F.E. and F.P. Utopian Thought in the Western World.*
   G. Beauchamp, 385(MQR):Spring80-261
   R. Brown, 617(TLS):6Jun80-651
   H. Levin, 453(NYRB):6Mar80-47
Manuel, J. Don Juan Manuel, "El Conde Lucanor." (G. Argote de Molina, ed)
   I. Macpherson, 86(BHS):Oct79-336
Manvell, R., ed. The Penguin Film Review 1946-1949.
   J.R. Taylor, 18:Nov78-74
Manz, G., ed. Lebensweise und Lebensniveau im Sozialismus.
   J. Marten, 654(WB):8/1978-183
Manzalaoui, M.A., ed. "Secretum secretorum."* (Vol 1)
   D. Bornstein, 589:Apr79-402
Manzoni, A. Scritti filosofici. (R. Quadrelli, ed)
   A.D.B., 228(GSLI):Vol155fasc491-476
Mao, N.K. and Liu Ts'un-yan. Li Yü.
   P. Li, 293(JASt):May79-578
Mao Tse-tung. Annotated Quotations from Chairman Mao.* (J. De Francis, comp)
   M.E. van den Berg, 353:Mar78-91
Marabini Moevs, M.T. Gabriele D'Annunzio e le estetiche della fine del secolo.
   E.F., 228(GSLI):Vol155fasc490-318
Maraldo, J.C. Der hermeneutische Zirkel.
   M.H., 191(ELN):Sep78(supp)-186
Maraniss, J.E. On Calderón.
   R. El Saffar, 238:Dec79-728
Marc-Lipiansky, M. La Naissance du monde proustien dans Jean Santeuil.
   J.M. Cocking, 208(FS):Apr79-219
Marcêchal-Trudel, M. Chateaubriand, Byron et Venise.
   J.R. Loy, 149(CLS):Jun79-176
March, A. Selected Poems.* (A. Terry, ed and trans)
   R. Archer, 382(MAE):1979/2-322
   P. Russell-Gebbett, 86(BHS):Jan79-80
   205(FMLS):Jan78-91
March, I. - see Greenfield, E., R. Layton and I. March
Marchak, P. In Whose Interests.
   B. Cooper, 99:Jun-Jul80-38
Marchal, G.P. Die frommen Schweden in Schwyz.
   B. Arnold, 182:Vol131#11/12-380
Marchand, F., ed. Manuel de linguistique appliquée. (Vol 1)
   F.M. Jenkins, 207(FR):Oct78-199
Marchand, L.A. - see Lord Byron
Marchiano, G. La Parola e la Forma.
   H. Bredin, 89(BJA):Spring79-178
Marcial de Onís, C. El surrealismo y cuatro poetas de la generación del 27.
   T. Bremer, 72:Band216Heft1-233
Marcialis, M.T. Fontenelle, un filosofo mondano.
   A.J. Bingham, 547(RF):Band91Heft4-482

Marco, G., A. Garfield and S. Ferris. Information on Music. (Vol 2)
   R. Andrewes, 415:Apr79-310
Marco, J. Literatura popular en España en los siglos XVIII y XIX.
   G.E. Mazzeo, 238:Mar79-175
Marcovich, M. - see Heraclitus
Marcucci, S. Intelletto e "intellettualismo" nell'estetica di Kant.
   M. Boncompagni, 227(GCFI):Jul-Dec78-558
   L. Guillermit, 542:Apr-Jun79-240
   K. Oedingen, 342:Band69Heft1-117
Marcucci, S. Kant e le scienze.
   L. Guillermit, 542:Apr-Jun79-243
   K. Oedingen, 342:Band69Heft3-370
Marcus, G., ed. Stranded.
   L. Gonzales, 441:10Feb80-13
Marcus, G.J. Heart of Oak.*
   P-G. Boucé, 189(EA):Jan-Mar78-89
Marcus, H.G. The Life and Times of Menelik II, Ethiopia, 1844-1913.
   W.A. Shack, 69:Vol148#2-190
Marcus, L.S. The American Store Window.
   G. Allen, 45:Jan79-51
   J.M. Neil, 658:Winter79-432
Marcus, M. Diagnostic Teaching of the Language Arts.
   R. Alexander, 257(IRAL):Aug79-265
Marcus, S., ed. Semiotica folclorului.
   T.G. Pavel, 567:Vol125#3/4-335
Marei, S.A. The World Food Crisis (1976)
   S.M. Alam, 273(IC):Apr77-159
Marek, G.R. and M. Gordon-Smith. Chopin.²
   N. Temperley, 415:Oct79-831
   42(AR):Fall79-488
Maremaa, T. Studio.
   D.M. Fine, 649(WAL):Spring79-89
Marenzio, L. Madrigali a quattro, cinque e sei voci. (Vol 1) (S. Ledbetter, ed)
   I. Fenlon, 414(MusQ):Oct79-605
Marfurt, B. Textsorte witz.
   G. von Wilpert, 67:May79-162
   E.H. Yarrill, 182:Vol31#5/6-144
de Margerie, D. L'Arbre de Jessé.
   A. Clerval, 450(NRF):Oct79-139
Margitić, M.R. Essai sur la mythologie du "Cid."
   G. Defaux, 207(FR):Mar79-638
   P. Hampshire, 208(FS):Vol33Pt2-676
   A. Niderst, 535(RHL):Sep-Oct78-821
Margolin, A. Ukraine and Policy of the Entente.
   S.L. Guthier, 550(RusR):Jul79-369
Margolin, J-C. Neuf Années de Bibliographie Érasmienne (1962-1970).
   E.J. Devereux, 539:Vol4No1-122
   R.W. Truman, 402(MLR):Apr79-393
Margolis, J. Persons and Minds.
   J.C. Gosling, 479(PhQ):Oct79-367
   H. Kornblith, 482(PhR):Jan79-109
   D. Locke, 483:Jul79-421
   C. Mortensen, 63:Sep79-288
   M.A. Simon, 484(PPR):Sep79-144
Margolis, J., ed. Philosophy Looks at the Arts.
   G. Iseminger, 290(JAAC):Summer80-463

Margolis, J.D. Joseph Wood Krutch.
  D. Grumbach, 441:16Nov80-18
Margolius, I. Cubism and Architecture and
  the Applied Arts.
  D. Sharp, 617(TLS):16May80-546
Marichal, C. Spain (1834-1844).
  A. Gil Novales, 86(BHS):Oct79-341
Marie de France. The "Lais" of Marie de
  France.* (R. Hanning and J. Ferrante,
  eds and trans)
  M. Mudrick, 249(HudR):Autumn79-431
  109:Summer80-223
Princess Marie Louise. My Memoirs of Six
  Reigns.
  A. Forbes, 617(TLS):4Jan80-7
Marie, C.P. La réalité humaine chez Jean
  Giraudoux.
  H. Godin, 208(FS):Vol33Pt2-875
Marín, D. Poesía paisajística española
  1940-1970.
  H.T. Young, 593:Winter79-369
Mariner, S. Estudis estructurals de
  català.
  M.W. Wheeler, 86(BHS):Jan79-86
Marini, M. Territoires du féminin avec
  Marguerite Duras.
  C.J. Murphy, 207(FR):Feb79-498
Marino, A. Kritik der literarischen Be-
  griff.* (French title: La Critique des
  idées littéraires.)
  Etiemble, 450(NRF):Jan79-113
  A.P. Foulkes, 307:Oct79-130
Marino, G.B. L'Adone. (G. Pozzi, ed)
  L'Adone. (M. Pieri, ed)
  U. Limentani, 402(MLR):Apr79-472
Marion, D. La Chasse à l'orchidée.
  E. Marks, 207(FR):Dec78-381
Marion, J.F. Famous and Curious Ceme-
  teries.*
  T.J. Schlereth, 658:Spring79-105
Marion, J-L. L'idole et la distance.
  D. Janicaud, 192(EP):Apr-Jun79-250
Marius. Marius: "On the Elements." (R.C.
  Dales, ed and trans)
  J. Beaumont, 382(MAE):1979/1-115
Marker, F.J. Kjeld Abell.*
  D. Thomas, 562(Scan):Nov78-177
  D. Thomas, 610:Oct78-70
Markey, T.L. Germanic Dialect Grouping
  and the Position of Ingvaeonic.*
  A. Bammesberger, 38:Band96Heft3/4-457
  J. Koivulehto, 439(NM):1978/3-307
  H. Penzl, 685(ZDL):1/1979-85
Markey, T.L. A North Sea Germanic Reader.*
  A. Crépin, 189(EA):Apr-Jun78-221
  M. Durrell, 402(MLR):Jan79-228
Markey, T.L. - see Rask, R.K.
Markey, T.L. and others. Germanic and Its
  Dialects. (Vol 3)
  E.H. Antonsen, 301(JEGP):Jul79-375
Markham, E.A. Love Poems.
  S. Brown, 493:Dec79-47
Markham, J. Nina.
  J. Coleby, 157:Winter79-86
Marki, I. The Trial of the Poet.*
  R. Asselineau, 189(EA):Jul-Dec78-419
  R. Asselineau, 191(ELN):Sep78-63

Markova, A.K. Psichologija usvoenija
  jazyka kak sredstva občšenija.
  B. Kraft, 682(ZPSK):Band31Heft6-625
Marks, G.A. and C.B. Johnson. Harrap's
  English-French Dictionary of Slang and
  Colloquialisms.
  E. Woods, 208(FS):Vol33Pt2-1062
Marks, H. I Can Jump Oceans.
  J. Croft, 71(ALS):May79-125
Marks, R. and A. Payne, eds. British
  Heraldry from its Origins to c. 1800.
  P. Summers, 503:Winter78-196
Marks, S.A. Large Mammals and a Brave
  People.
  A. Barnard, 69:Vol148#2-201
Markson, D. Malcolm Lowry's Volcano.
  W.M. Hagen, 594:Spring79-121
  K. Raine, 598(SoR):Spring80-478
  T.D. Tosswill, 648(WCR):Feb79-44
Markus, J. Uncle.
  S. Salmans, 617(TLS):25Jan80-78
  42(AR):Winter79-124
Markus, J. - see Browning, E.B.
Markus, M. Tempus und Aspekt.
  H.L. Kufner, 133:Band12Heft4-360
Marlatt, D. The Story, She Said.
  W.H. New, 102(CanL):Autumn79-79
Marlatt, D. Zócalo.
  E.P. Levy, 102(CanL):Autumn79-89
Marley, B. Springtime in the Rockies.
  J. Cotton, 493:Dec79-72
Marlitt, E. Im Hause des Kommerzienrates.
  P.J. Brewster, 406:Winter79-452
Marlowe, C. The Jew of Malta. (N.W.
  Bawcutt, ed)
  A. Blake, 67:Nov79-317
  R. Gill, 541(RES):Aug79-340
Marlowe, D. The Rich Boy from Chicago.
  J. Naughton, 362:14Feb80-222
de Marly, D. Worth.
  M. Furness, 617(TLS):12Sep80-998
Marmontel, J-F. Correspondance.* (J. Ren-
  wick, ed)
  O.R. Taylor, 402(MLR):Apr79-461
Marnham, P. Fantastic Invasion.
  J. Lelyveld, 441:30Mar80-8
  J. Leonard, 441:22Feb80-C25
  E.S. Turner, 362:12Jun80-764
Marnham, P. Lourdes.
  G. Annan, 362:11Sep80-341
  P. Hebblethwaite, 617(TLS):12Sep80-986
Marolleau, J. La symbolique chinoise.
  A. Reix, 542:Jul-Sep79-368
Marot, J. Le Voyage de Gênes. (G. Triso-
  lini, ed)
  J.C. Laidlaw, 208(FS):Jul79-332
  C. Thiry, 556(RLV):1978/1-77
Marot, J. Le Voyage de Venise.* (G.
  Trisolini, ed)
  L. Brind-Amour, 539:Vol4No1-121
  E.M. Rutson, 208(FS):Oct79-436
Marquand, D. Ramsay MacDonald.
  E. Delavenay, 189(EA):Jul-Dec78-413
Márquez, G.G. - see under García Márquez,
  G.

Martin, J.H., ed. The Coming Flood.
N.S. Baer, 14:Jan79-68
Martin, J.R. and G. Feigenbaum. Van Dyck
as Religious Artist.
G. Martin, 617(TLS):1Feb80-120
Martin, J.S. E.M. Forster.*
J. Colmer, 402(MLR):Jul79-682
E. Hanquart, 189(EA):Jan-Mar78-94
R. Mason, 447(N&Q):Aug78-380
J. Sheriff, 178:Fall79-366
Martin, K. Die ottonischen Wandbilder der
St. Georgskirche Reichenau-Oberzell.
(2nd ed)
W. Berschin, 182:Vol131#3/4-65
Martin, M.A. - see under Andres Martin, M.
Martin, M.M. and P. O'Meara, eds. Africa.
M. Posnansky, 2(AfrA):May79-23
Martin, R. The French Contribution to
Modern Linguistics.
N.C.W. Spence, 208(FS):Vol33Pt2-1074
P. Wunderli, 224(GRM):Band28Heft2-238
Martin, R. Historical Explanation.*
C.B. McCullagh, 63:Jun79-192
W.H. Walsh, 393(Mind):Oct79-607
Martin, R. Inférence, autonymie et para-
phrase.
J. Bourguignon, 553(RLiR):Jul-Dec78-
429
J. Rey-Debove, 209(FM):Oct78-370
Martin, R. - see Palladius
Martin, R. and H. Metzger. La religion
grecque.*
É. Des Places, 555:Vol52fasc1-145
Martin, R.A. - see Miller, A.
Martin, R.B. Tennyson.
J. Atlas, 441:14Dec80-1
J. Bayley, 453(NYRB):18Dec80-42
A. Broyard, 441:13Dec80-25
H. Tennyson, 362:23Oct80-549
442(NY):17Nov80-240
Martin, R.B. The Triumph of Wit.*
D. Petzold, 38:Band96Heft3/4-525
Martin, R.M. Semiotics and Linguistic
Structure.
S. Haack, 518:Oct79-127
Martin, R.K. The Homosexual Tradition in
American Poetry.
R. Boyer, 617(TLS):30May80-603
Martín, R.T. - see under Torres Martín, R.
Martin, S.E. A Reference Grammar of
Japanese.*
N. Akatsuka, 293(JASt):Aug79-778
Martin, V. Alexandra.*
S. Salmans, 617(TLS):8Feb80-146
Martín Descalzo, J.L. Lobos, Perros y
Corderos.
J. Schraibman, 399(MLJ):Sep-Oct79-311
Martín Gaite, C. El cuarto de atrás.
J.W. Kronik, 399(MLJ):Nov79-394
Martindale, A. The Triumphs of Caesar by
Andrea Mantegna in the Collection of HM
the Queen at Hampton Court.
D.A.N. Jones, 362:24Jan80-125
E. Waterhouse, 617(TLS):21Mar80-314
Martineau, C. and M. Veissière, with H.
Heller - see Briçonnet, G. and Marguer-
ite d'Angoulême

Martinell, C. Gaudí.* (G.R. Collins, ed)
T. Benton, 46:Feb79-124
Martines, L. Power and Imagination.*
J. Larner, 617(TLS):25Jul80-856
Martinet, A. Studies in Functional Syntax.
H. Weinrich, 343:Band23-23
Martinet, A. and H. Walter. Dictionnaire
de la prononciation française dans son
usage réel.*
B. Müller, 353:Jul78-88
Martínez, H.S. - see under Salvador Mar-
tínez, H.
Martinez, O. Panama Canal.
T.C. Holyoke, 42(AR):Winter79-115
Martínez de Burgos, J. The Cancionero de
Martínez de Burgos. (D.S. Severin, ed)
C. Stern, 545(RPh):Jul78-493
Martínez de Toledo, A. Arcipreste de
Talavera o Corbacho. (M. Gerli, ed)
T.A. Perry, 304(JHP):Winter80-175
Martino, A. Daniel Casper von Lohenstein.*
(Vol 1)
H.K. Krausse, 564:Sep79-227
M.M. Metzger, 221(GQ):May79-403
P. Skrine, 220(GL&L):Oct78-67
Martino, V. Saint-Simon tra scienza e
utopia.
E. Namer, 542:Apr-Jun79-255
Martins, H., ed. The Brazilian Novel.
A. Coutinho, 263(RIB):Vol29No2-223
N.P. Parsons, 238:Dec79-739
Martyn, J.R.C. - see Owen, J.
Martz, L.L. Poet of Exile.
R.M. Adams, 453(NYRB):26Jun80-46
Martz, L.L. and A. Williams, eds. The
Author in his Work.*
W.W. Robson, 541(RES):May79-234
Marusin, S.A. - see Greenberg, R.M.
Marwick, A. Class.
J. Simpson, 362:31Jul80-149
Marx, A. Bibliographical Studies and
Notes on Rare Books and Manuscripts in
the Library of The Jewish Theological
Seminary of America. (M.H. Schmelzer,
ed)
A. Schischa, 354:Jun79-187
Marx, B. L'économie capitaliste.
J-M. Gabaude, 542:Oct-Dec79-491
Marx, B. Bartolomeo Pagello: Epistolae
Familiares (1464-1525).
H. Harth, 547(RF):Band91Heft1/2-192
Marx, J. Charles Bonnet contre les
Lumières, 1738-1850.*
J. Mayer, 535(RHL):Mar-Jun79-522
N. Suckling, 208(FS):Jan79-86
Marx, W. Introduction to Aristotle's
Theory of Being as Being.
J. Owens, 124:Nov79-190
Marx, W. Schelling.*
W.G. Jacobs, 489(PJGG):Band86Heft2-435
Marzahl, P. Town in the Empire.
M.A. Burkholder, 263(RIB):Vol29No2-213
Masaracchia, A. - see Herodotus
Maschino, M.T. Sauve qui peut.
P.A. Mankin, 207(FR):Mar79-660

Masciandaro, F. La problematica del tempo nella "Commedia."
S. Noakes, 276:Winter79-407

Masefield, J. Letters of John Masefield to Florence Lamont. (C. and L. Lamont, eds)
J. Bayley, 362:7Feb80-186
T.J. Binyon, 617(TLS):15Feb80-166

Masica, C.P. Defining a Linguistic Area: South Asia.*
R. Rocher, 318(JAOS):Jul-Sep78-348
L.A. Schwarzschild, 259(IIJ):Jan79-68
F.C. Southworth, 293(JASt):Feb79-385

Maslix, S.A. Russkoe izrazcovoe iskusstvo XV-XIX vekov.
G. Lenhoff, 574(SEEJ):Fall79-396

Mason, E.C. Hölderlin and Goethe. (P.H. Gaskill, ed)
W.H. Bruford, 220(GL&L):Oct78-73

Mason, H., ed. Studies on Voltaire and the Eighteenth Century. (Vols 170 and 171)
M.H. Waddicor, 208(FS):Vol33Pt2-754

Mason, H. Summer Light.
J. Casey, 441:5Oct80-14

Mason, P. A Shaft of Sunlight.*
639(VQR):Spring79-69

Mason, P. Skinner's Horse.
442(NY):24Mar80-133

Mason, S. Daniel Defoe and the Status of Women.
S.O. Taylor, 173(ECS):Summer79-555

Mason, T. Association Football and English Society 1863-1915.
P. Smith, 617(TLS):4Apr80-379

Massa, A. and S. Donaldson. American Literature, Nineteenth and Early Twentieth Centuries.
L.B. Holland, 676(YR):Winter80-279

Massa, G. Introduzione alla storia culturale dell'Uruguay.
F.O. Assunção, 263(RIB):Vol29No3/4-368

Massano, G. - see García, C.

Masser, A. Bibel- und Legendenepik des deutschen Mittelalters.*
J.M. Clifton-Everest, 67:Nov79-352
D.H. Green, 402(MLR):Jan79-230

Massie, A. The Last Peacock.
W. Boyd, 617(TLS):9May80-537
J. Mellors, 362:24Apr80-546

Massie, R.K. Peter the Great.
P-L. Adams, 61:Nov80-98
K. Fitzlyon, 441:2Nov80-14
J. Leonard, 441:7Oct80-C8
442(NY):24Nov80-208

Massie, S. Land of the Firebird.
J. Leonard, 441:8Oct80-C25
F. Maclean, 441:2Nov80-14

Massinger, P. The Plays and Poems of Philip Massinger.* (P. Edwards and C. Gibson, eds)
F. Bowers, 677(YES):Vol9-279
P. Davison, 354:Jun79-177
M. Mincoff, 447(N&Q):Apr78-177

Massinger, P. The Selected Plays of Philip Massinger.* (C. Gibson, ed)
L.A.C. Dobrez, 67:Nov79-318
G. Taylor, 541(RES):Aug79-348
J.C. Trewin, 157:Winter79-79

Massoli, M. - see de Mendoza, Í.

Masson, B. - see de Musset, A.

Masson, D. Monothéisme coranique et monothéisme biblique.
A. Reix, 542:Apr-Jun79-194

Masson, J.L. and D.D. Kosambi - see "Avimāraka (Love's Enchanted World)"

Masson, J.L. and M.V. Patwardhan. Aesthetic Rapture.
K. Bhattacharya, 318(JAOS):Apr-Jun78-192

Masson, O. Carian Inscriptions from North Saqqâra and Buhen.
R. Schmitt, 343:Band23-98

Mast, G. Film/Cinema/Movie.*
P. Harcourt, 255(HAB):Summer79-209

Mast, G. and M. Cohen, eds. Film Theory and Criticism. (2nd ed)
J. Buchsbaum, 290(JAAC):Summer80-475

Masters, B. Camus.
J. Cruickshank, 208(FS):Apr79-227

Masters, H.W. Edgar Lee Masters.
109:Summer80-225

Mastny, V. Russia's Road to the Cold War.*
A. Brown, 617(TLS):25Jan80-95
639(VQR):Autumn79-134

Matejka, L. Crossroads of a Sound and Meaning.
J. Vachek, 343:Band23-1

Matejka, L., ed. Sound, Sign and Meaning.*
N.J. Brown, 575(SEER):Jul79-411
H. Galton, 361:Feb/Mar78-283
P.L. Garvin, 355(LSoc):Apr78-141
R. Ködderitzsch, 260(IF):Band83-351

Matejka, L. and others, eds. Readings in Soviet Semiotics.
A. Shukman, 575(SEER):Jan79-115
E.M. Thompson, 574(SEEJ):Summer79-296

Matejka, L. and I.R. Titunik, eds. Semiotics of Art.*
E. Volek, 125:Spring79-439

Mateo Gómez, I. Temas profanos en la escultura gótica española.
J.M. Pita Andrade, 48:Jul-Sep78-348

Mather, B. The Pagoda Tree.
442(NY):31Mar80-122

Mather, C. Paterna. (R.A. Bosco, ed)
K. Silverman, 165(EAL):Spring80-80

Mather, F.L., ed. Who's Who of the Colored Race.
K.B. Harder, 424:Dec77-237

Mather, J.Y. and H.H. Speitel, eds. The Linguistic Atlas of Scotland: Scots Section.* (Vol 2)
R.K.S. Macaulay, 350:Mar79-224

Mathews, D.G. Religion in the Old South.*
G. Harland, 255(HAB):Summer79-216

Mathews, R. Canadian Literature.
E.D. Blodgett, 168(ECW):Fall78-261
D. Staines, 529(QQ):Autumn79-479

Mathey, F. American Realism.
A. Frankenstein, 55:Mar79-29
F. Spalding, 135:Mar79-207
M.S. Young, 39:Sep79-238
90:May79-339
Mathias, P. The Transformation of England.
B. Supple, 617(TLS):15Feb80-184
Mathias, R. Snipe's Castle.
E.L. Wright, 617(TLS):25Jul80-851
Mathieu, B. Orpheus in Brooklyn.
M.J. Hoffman, 395(MFS):Summer78-267
Mathieu, V. Introduzione a Leibniz.
A. Corsano, 227(GCFI):Apr-Jun78-258
Mathieu-Castellani, G. Les thèmes amour-
eux dans la poésie française 1570-1600.
O. de Mourgues, 208(FS):Vol33Pt2-653
Matisoff, J.A. The Grammar of Lahu.
F.K. Lehman, 318(JAOS):Jul-Sep78-296
Matisoff, S. The Legend of Semimaru,
Blind Musician of Japan.
W.M. Kelsey, 293(JASt):Nov78-186
Matoré, G. and I. Mecz. Musique et struc-
ture romanesque dans la "Recherche du
Temps perdu."
J.M. Cocking, 208(FS):Apr79-219
de Matos, F.G. - see under Gomes de Matos,
F.
Matson, K. Short Lives.
J. Updike, 442(NY):11Aug80-88
Matson, W.I. Sentience.*
R. Kirk, 393(Mind):Jan79-144
Matsubara, H. Samurai.
R. Koenig, 441:17Feb80-17
442(NY):18Feb80-131
Matte Blanco, I. The Unconscious As
Infinite Sets.
J. Gach, 400(MLN):Dec79-1228
Matthaei, R. and D. Kuhn - see von Goethe,
J.W.
Matthew, C. The Long-Haired Boy.
J. Burke, 441:11May80-14
A.N. Wilson, 617(TLS):7Mar80-278
Matthew, H.C.G. - see Gladstone, W.E.
Matthews, D. Brahms Piano Music.
F. Sams, 415:Feb79-130
Matthews, D. Michael Tippett.
H. Cole, 362:24Jan80-126
W. Mellers, 617(TLS):13Jun80-676
Matthews, F.H. Quest for an American Soci-
ology.*
G.M. Ostrander, 106:Spring79-55
J. Posner, 488:Sep79-395
Matthews, J. Collecting Rare Books for
Pleasure and Profit.
G.T. Tanselle, 517(PBSA):Apr-Jun78-265
Matthews, J.H. The Imagery of Surrealism.*
A. Otten, 42(AR):Winter79-119
Matthews, J.H. The Inner Dream.
B.L. Knapp, 593:Spring79-83
Matthews, J.H. Frank O'Connor.
J.W. Weaver, 305(JIL):May78-182
Matthews, M. Privilege in the Soviet
Union.
C.E. Ziegler, 550(RusR):Apr79-243
Matthews, M. and T.A. Jones. Soviet
Sociology, 1964-75.
E. Gellner, 575(SEER):Jul79-473

Matthews, R. The Beginning of Wisdom.
376:Oct79-141
Matthews, T.S. Jacks or Better.
M. Ellmann, 569(SR):Spring79-332
Matthews, W. Rising and Falling.*
M. Bell, 491:Jun80-164
Matthey, F. The Evolution of Keats's
Structural Imagery.*
R.P. Lessenich, 597(SN):Vol50#1-150
Matthias, J. Crossing.*
J. Fuller, 617(TLS):18Jan80-65
Matthias, J. - see Jones, D.
Matthias, J. and G.P. Pahlson, eds and
trans. Contemporary Swedish Poetry.
R. Fulton, 617(TLS):12Sep80-1006
Matthiessen, F.O. and R. Cheney. Rat and
The Devil.* (L. Hyde, ed)
F.C. Stern, 577(SHR):Spring79-157
Matthiessen, P. The Snow Leopard.*
T.J. Lyon, 649(WAL):Spring79-62
Mattoso Camara, J., Jr. Dicionário de
linguística e gramática. (7th ed)
J.R. Kelly, 238:Mar79-192
Matuz, J. - see Seyfī Çelebī
Matz, F. Die dionysischen Sarkophage.
(Pt 4)
G.M.A. Hanfmann, 54:Mar78-157
Maugendre, L-A. Alphonse de Châteaubriant,
1877-1951.
J. Cruickshank, 208(FS):Vol33Pt2-869
R. Galand, 207(FR):Mar79-658
Mauger, G. and J. Charon. Le Français
commercial. (2nd ed) (Vol 1)
B. Braude, 207(FR):May79-964
Maugham, R. The Corridor.
J. Naughton, 362:11Dec80-804
Maula, E. Studies in Eudoxus' Homocentric
Spheres.
F. Lasserre, 182:Vol131#7/8-243
Mauner, G. Manet, Peintre-Philosophe.
B. Farwell, 54:Jun78-379
G.P. Weisberg, 127:Spring79-212
de Maupassant, G. Contes et nouvelles.
P. Dulac, 450(NRF):Nov79-109
Maurer, A.A. - see Eckhart, J.
Maurer, D.W., with Q. Pearl. Kentucky
Moonshine.
L. Pederson, 35(AS):Spring79-52
Maurer, F. and C. Minis, eds. Altgerman-
istische Beiträge.
D.R. McLintock, 447(N&Q):Jun78-285
Maurer, F. and H. Rupp, eds. Deutsche
Wortgeschichte. (3rd ed) (Vol 3 comp by
P. Hefti and C. Schmid)
K. Matzel, 343:Band23-198
Maurer, H., ed. Die Abtei Reichenau.
W. Berschin, 182:Vol131#3/4-65
Maurer, H. Not Working.
A. Broyard, 441:26Jan80-19
Mauriac, F. Lacordaire. (K. Goesch, ed)
R.J. North, 208(FS):Vol33Pt2-877
Mauriac, F. Oeuvres romanesques et théâ-
trales complètes. (Vol 1) (J. Petit, ed)
J. Flower, 208(FS):Jul79-357
Mauriac, F. and J-É. Blanche. Correspon-
dance entre François Mauriac et Jacques-
[continued]

[continuing]
Émile Blanche (1916-1942). (G-P. Collet, ed)
  A. Séailles, 535(RHL):Jul-Aug79-708
"François Mauriac témoin de son temps."
  P. Thody, 617(TLS):30May80-600
du Maurier, D. The Rebecca Notebook and Other Memories.
  D. Grumbach, 441:21Sep80-15
Maurin, M. Henri de Régnier.
  B.C. Swift, 402(MLR):Jul79-704
Maurois, A. Catalogue de l'exposition organisée à la Bibliothèque nationale à l'occasion du dixième anniversaire de la mort d'André Maurois.
  H. Godin, 208(FS):Jul79-359
Mauron, M. Le Vieux de la Montagne.
  M.E. Birkett, 207(FR):Mar79-672
Maurus, H. - see under Hrabanus Maurus
Mauzi, R. and S. Menant, with J. Ehrard. Littérature française: Le XVIIIe siècle.* (Vol 2)
  É. Guitton, 535(RHL):Jan-Feb79-126
  F. Schalk, 547(RF):Band91Heft4-479
Mawdsley, E. The Russian Revolution and the Baltic Fleet.
  J.N. Westwood, 575(SEER):Oct79-610
Max, S. Dialogues et Situations. (2nd ed)
  R.J. Melpignano, 399(MLJ):Nov79-387
Maximov, V.E. - see "Kontinent 2"
Maxwell, J.C. - see Ure, P.
Maxwell, N. What's Wrong With Science?
  T.A. Goudge, 488:Jun79-241
Maxwell, W. Over by the River, and Other Stories.*
  E. Thompson, 628(UWR):Fall-Winter78-76
Maxwell, W. So Long, See You Tomorrow.*
  R. Towers, 441:13Jan80-11
May, B.D. El dilema de la nostalgia en la poesía de Alberti.
  G.G. Maccurdy, 399(MLJ):Nov79-394
May, C.E., ed. Short Story Theories.
  J.H. Harkey, 573(SSF):Fall78-464
May, D. A Revenger's Comedy.*
  D. Durrant, 364:Dec79/Jan80-132
May, E.J. Wiener Volkskomödie und Vormärz.
  P. Branscombe, 402(MLR):Oct79-993
May, G. Stendhal and the Age of Napoleon.*
  D. Clark, 400(MLN):May79-895
  F. Meltzer, 405(MP):Feb80-341
  H. Redman, Jr., 207(FR):May79-932
  E.J.T., 191(ELN):Sep78(supp)-127
  P. Wahl, 446(NCFS):Fall-Winter78/79-125
May, J.R. The Pruning Word.*
  J. Cunningham, 577(SHR):Spring79-171
  M.J. Friedman, 578:Spring80-114
May, K.M. Out of the Maelstrom.
  J.V. Knapp, 395(MFS):Winter78/79-654
May, R. Sex and Fantasy.
  J. Adelson, 441:9Mar80-3
  J. Dunn, 617(TLS):4Jul80-755
May, W. Superstitions.
  639(VQR):Spring79-65

Mayer, D. and K. Richards, eds. Western Popular Theatre.
  D. Jarrett, 447(N&Q):Dec78-570
  G. Speaight, 611(TN):Vol133#3-137
  M. Willey, 189(EA):Jul-Dec78-369
Mayer, M. The Fate of the Dollar.
  N. von Hoffman, 453(NYRB):3Apr80-16
  C. Lehmann-Haupt, 441:25Feb80-C17
  L. Silk, 441:24Feb80-9
  61:Apr80-122
  442(NY):12May80-163
Mayer, M. Trigger Points.*
  T.J. Binyon, 617(TLS):18Apr80-450
Mayer, S. Golem.*
  J.L. Hibberd, 220(GL&L):Oct78-62
Mayerson, E.W. If Birds Are Free.
  A. Cheuse, 441:28Dec80-8
Mayerson, E.W. Sanjo.*
  E. Durwood, 617(TLS):27Jun80-743
Mayerthaler, W. Einführung in die generative Phonologie.
  D. Evans, 208(FS):Oct79-495
Mayes, F. After Such Pleasures.
  H. Carruth, 231:Dec80-74
Mayes, H.R. Alger.
  G. Scharnhorst, 26(ALR):Autumn79-355
Maynard, J. Browning's Youth.*
  T.J. Collins, 637(VS):Spring78-408
Maynard, J. and B. Miles. William S. Burroughs.
  J.L.W. West 3d, 517(PBSA):Oct-Dec78-569
"Maynard et son temps."
  A. Mansau, 535(RHL):Jul-Aug79-648
Mayne, S. Diasporas.*
  K. Sherman, 102(CanL):Spring79-96
Mayne, S., ed. Irving Layton.
  P.K. Smith, 105:Spring/Summer79-125
Mayoff, S. With My Own Free Hand.
  G. Hamel, 198:Winter80-139
Mayr, R. The Concept of Love in Sidney and Spenser.
  J. Moore, 568(SCN):Spring-Summer79-15
Mayrhofer, M. Iranisches Personennamenbuch.* (Vol 1)
  M.S. Beeler, 350:Jun79-487
Mazaleyrat, J. Éléments de métrique française.
  J. Fox, 208(FS):Vol33Pt2-958
  R. Lathuillère, 535(RHL):Jan-Feb78-155
Mazlish, B. and E. Diamond. Jimmy Carter.
  C.V. Woodward, 453(NYRB):3Apr80-9
  61:Feb80-95
Mazrui, A.A. The African Condition.
  T. Hodgkin, 617(TLS):5Sep80-970
  C.C. O'Brien, 362:1May80-577
Mazur, G. Nightfire.*
  J.F. Cotter, 249(HudR):Spring79-111
Mazur, O. El teatro de Sebastián de Horozco.
  N. Griffin, 86(BHS):Apr79-151
Mazur, O. - see de Horozco, S.
Mazza, M. - see Utčenko, S.L.
Mazzocco, R. Trader.
  D. Donoghue, 453(NYRB):14Aug80-49
  V. Young, 441:2Mar80-16

Meacham, S. A Life Apart.
F.M. Leventhal, 637(VS):Autumn78-94
Mead, M. The Midday Muse.
D. Sealy, 617(TLS):22Feb80-214
Mead, M. and R. Metraux. Aspects of the
Present.
D. Grumbach, 441:27Jul80-13
Meade, M. Madame Blavatsky.
P. Zweig, 441:5Oct80-11
Meagher, R.E. An Introduction to Augus-
tine.
G.H. Ettlinger, 613:Dec79-427
Meakin, D. Man and Work.*
M. Green, 161(DUJ):Dec78-147
J. Lucas, 402(MLR):Apr79-434
Méchoulan, H. Mateo López Bravo, un
socialista español del siglo XVII.
A. Guy, 192(EP):Jul-Sep79-371
Mecklenberg, N., ed. Literarische Wertung.
D.A. Myers, 67:Nov79-364
H. Seidler, 133:Band12Heft1/2-125
Medawar, P.B. Advice to a Young Scien-
tist.*
S.J. Gould, 453(NYRB):24Jan80-47
J. Naughton, 617(TLS):4Apr80-392
442(NY):21Jan80-131
de Medeiros e Albuquerque, P. Uma idéia
do Doutor Watson.
K. Krabbenhoft, 399(MLJ):Jan-Feb79-57
"Mediaeval Scandinavia 9."
R.W. McTurk, 562(Scan):Nov79-152
Medley, M. The Chinese Potter.*
G. Wills, 39:Dec79-532
J. Wirgin, 463:Spring78-90
Medley, M. Illustrated Catalogue of
Celadon Wares.
G.S.M. Gompertz, 463:Summer78-214
Medley, M. Illustrated Catalogue of Ming
and Ch'ing Monochrome in the Percival
David Foundation of Chinese Art.*
C.F. Shangraw, 318(JAOS):Jul-Sep78-307
Medlin, V.D. and S.L. Parsons - see
Nabokov, V.D.
Medved, H. and R. Dreyfuss. The Fifty
Worst Films of All Time.
W.K. Everson, 200:Jan79-50
B. Fantoni, 362:14Feb80-223
Medvedev, P. Die formale Methode in der
Literaturwissenschaft. (H. Glück, ed
and trans)
C. Hyart, 556(RLV):1978/1-76
Medvedev, P.N. and M.M. Bakhtin. The
Formal Method in Literary Scholarship.*
P. Carden, 574(SEEJ):Fall79-411
L. Gossman, 131(CL):Fall79-403
D.H. Hirsch, 569(SR):Fall79-628
Medvedev, R. On Soviet Dissent. (G.
Saunders, ed)
S. Monas, 441:16Nov80-13
L. Schapiro, 453(NYRB):17Apr80-15
Medvedev, R., ed. The Samizdat Register.
R. Sheldon, 550(RusR):Jul79-382
Medvedev, R.A. The October Revolution.*
A. Ryan, 362:10Jan80-60
L. Schapiro, 453(NYRB):17Apr80-15
R. Wistrich, 617(TLS):11Apr80-418

Medvedev, R.A. On Stalin and Stalinism.
L. Schapiro, 453(NYRB):17Apr80-15
R. Wistrich, 617(TLS):11Apr80-418
Medvedev, R.A. Problems in the Literary
Biography of Mikhail Sholokhov.*
M. Futrell, 104(CASS):Fall78-424
R.L. White, 295(JML):Vol7#4-814
205(FMLS):Jan78-91
Medvedev, R.A. and Z.A. Khrushchev.*
B.M. Cohen, 584(SWR):Winter79-104
Medvedev, Z.A. Soviet Science.*
A. Brown, 617(TLS):25Jan80-95
A. Vucinich, 550(RusR):Jul79-375
Medwall, H. The Plays of Henry Medwall.
(A.H. Nelson, ed)
P. Neuss, 617(TLS):5Sep80-973
Mee, C.L., Jr. The End of Order.
A.J.P. Taylor, 453(NYRB):18Dec80-12
Meek, R.L. Smith, Marx, and After.
D.P. O'Brien, 161(DUJ):Dec78-99
Meer, F. Race and Suicide in South Africa.
M. Marwick, 69:Vol48#3-307
Meerson-Aksenov, M. and B. Shragin, eds.
The Political, Social and Religious
Thought of Russian "Samizdat."*
D. Pospielovsky, 550(RusR):Jul79-380
Meersseman, G.G., with G.P. Pacini. Ordo
fraternitatis.
L.K. Little, 589:Jul79-602
Megas, G.A. Folktales of Greece.
W.K. McNeil, 292(JAF):Jan-Mar79-106
Megaw, J.V.S. Art of the European Iron
Age.
V. Kruta, 194(EC):Vol15fasc2-725
von Megenberg, K. Werke, Ökonomik. (S.
Krüger, ed)
G. Steer, 684(ZDA):Band107Heft4-181
di Meglio, I. Antireligiosität und Krypto-
theologie bei Albert Camus.
E. Diet, 542:Apr-Jun78-205
Mehl, A. Tacitus über Kaiser Claudius.
D.C.A. Shotter, 122:Jul79-259
Mehlman, J. Cataract.
P. France, 617(TLS):25Apr80-472
Mehlman, J. Revolution and Repetition.*
D. Langston, 131(CL):Summer79-291
D.S. Petrey, 153:Summer79-2
B. Rigby, 208(FS):Oct79-465
Mehnert, H. Melancholie und Inspiration.
G. Butters, 547(RF):Band91Heft1/2-181
J. Schulze, 72:Band216Heft2-470
Mehrotra, R.R. Sociology of Secret Lan-
guage.
W. Bright, 350:Jun79-496
S.S. Wadley, 355(LSoc):Dec78-446
Mehta, G. Karma Cola.*
D. Murphy, 617(TLS):18Apr80-435
V. Neumark, 362:10Apr80-482
Mehta, V. Mamaji.
J. Grigg, 362:8May80-618
E. Stokes, 617(TLS):4Jul80-752
Mehta, V. The Photographs of Chachaji.
W. Goodman, 441:7Dec80-20
Meid, W. Die Romanze von Froech und Finda-
bair, Táin Bó Froich.
E. Bachellery, 194(EC):Vol15fasc2-732

Mertens, D. and T. Verweyen - see Zincgref, J.W.

Mertens, J., ed. Ordona, V.
  A. Hus, 555:Vol52fasc1-212

Mertens, V. Gregorius Eremita.
  B. Murdoch, 182:Vol31#20-739

Mertin, R-G. Ariano Suassuna: Romance d'A Pedra do Reino.
  G.R. Lind, 547(RF):Band91Heft3-345

Merton, T. and R. Lax. A Catch of Anti-Letters.
  B. Elson, 529(QQ):Autumn79-513

Mervaud, M. - see Ogarev, N.P.

Merwin, W.S. The Compass Flower.*
  W. Marling, 50(ArQ):Autumn79-277
  V.B. Sherry, Jr., 659(ConL):Winter80-159
  T. Steele, 598(SoR):Spring80-483

Merwin, W.S. Feathers from the Hill.
  T. Steele, 598(SoR):Spring80-483

Merwin, W.S. Houses and Travellers.*
  W. Marling, 50(ArQ):Autumn79-277

Merwin, W.S. Selected Translations 1968-1978.
  D.M. Thomas, 617(TLS):18Jan80-66

Merwin, W.S. and J.M. Masson - see "Sanskrit Love Poetry"

Meryman, R. Mank.
  D. Jacobs, 18:Feb79-70

de Mesa, J. and T. Gisbert. Holguín y la pintura virreinal en Bolivia.
  M.C. García Sáiz, 48:Jul-Sep78-350

Meschonnic, H. Le Signe et le poème.
  F. Van Rutten, 107(CRCL):Winter79-86

Messiaen, O. Conférence de Notre-Dame.
  P. Griffiths, 415:Jul79-580

Messner, D. Dictionnaire chronologique des langues ibéroromanes. (Vol 4)
  W.J. Ashby, 350:Dec79-961
  W. Mettmann, 547(RF):Band91Heft3-348

Messner, D. Einführung in die Geschichte des französischen Wortschatzes.
  H. Thun, 343:Band23-130

Metcalf, J. General Ludd.
  C. Fagan, 99:Dec80/Jan81-39

Metcalf, J. Girl in Gingham.*
  F. Timleck, 526:Spring79-91
  376:Oct79-143

Metcalf, J. and C. Blaise, eds. 78: Best Canadian Stories.*
  L. Horne, 461:Spring-Summer79-95

Metcalf, M.F. Russia, England and Swedish Party Politics, 1762-1766.
  I.R. Christie, 575(SEER):Jan79-128

Metcalf, P. James Knowles.
  D. Watkin, 617(TLS):1Feb80-106

Metcalf, T.R. Land, Landlords, and the British Raj.
  K. Ballhatchet, 617(TLS):18Apr80-448

Meter, H. Apollinaire und der Futurismus.
  H-J. Lope, 547(RF):Band91Heft3-336
  E. Reichel, 72:Band216Heft1-231

Méthivier, H. La France de Louis XIV.
  J. Lough, 208(FS):Vol33Pt2-715

Metlitzki, D. The Matter of Araby in Medieval England.*
  S.G. Armistead, 240(HR):Spring78-235
  P.R. Hyams, 447(N&Q):Jun78-250
  K. Olsson, 405(MP):Feb80-320
  J.M. Steadman, 131(CL):Spring79-202
  T.A. Van, 577(SHR):Summer79-247

Metner, N. Muza i Moda.
  V. Pereléšin, 558(RLJ):Fall79-245

"Metodologičeskie problemy analiza jazyka."
  K. Krüger, 682(ZPSK):Band31Heft6-627

Mettinger, T.N.D. King and Messiah.
  S.B. Parker, 318(JAOS):Oct-Dec78-508

Mettler, H. Entfremdung und Revolution.
  M.C. Ives, 402(MLR):Oct79-991

Metz, C. Essais sur la signification au cinéma. Langage et cinéma. Le signifiant imaginaire.
  L. Audibert, 98:Apr78-374

Metzeltin, M. Einführung in die hispanistische Sprachwissenschaft.
  W. Oesterreicher, 685(ZDL):1/1979-118

Metzer, J. Some Economic Aspects of Railroad Development in Tsarist Russia.
  W.M. Pintner, 550(RusR):Oct79-478

Metzing, D.W. Formen kommunikationswissenschaftlicher Argumentationsanalyse.*
  G. Öhlschläger, 686(ZGL):Band7Heft1-83

Metzner, J. Persönlichkeitszerstörung und Weltuntergang.*
  D. Bronsen, 406:Summer79-192
  J. Mahr, 52:Band13Heft3-306

Metzner, J.K. Man and Environment in Eastern Timor.
  J.A. Hafner, 293(JASt):Feb79-431

Meuche, H., ed. Flugblätter der Reformation und des Bauernkrieges.
  W.L. Strauss, 54:Jun78-372

Meulenbelt, A. The Shame Is Over.
  G. Clifford, 617(TLS):25Jul80-858

de Meun, J. - see under Jean de Meun

Mewshaw, M. Life for Death.
  T. Buckley, 441:24Aug80-13

Meyer, C. Facing Reality.
  T. Powers, 441:26Oct80-11

Meyer, D. Victoria Ocampo.*
  D.A. Yates, 263(RIB):Vol29No3/4-369

Meyer, H. Voltaire on War and Peace.
  W.H. Barber, 208(FS):Vol33Pt2-747
  R. Favre, 535(RHL):Jul-Aug78-653

Meyer, H. Die Zahlenallegorese im Mittelalter.*
  W. Schröder, 684(ZDA):Band107Heft3-95

Meyer, H. - see Mörike, E.

Meyer, J. Paul Steegemann Verlag.
  R. Sheppard, 220(GL&L):Oct78-87

Meyer, J.A. The Cristero Rebellion.*
  R. Miller, 86(BHS):Jan79-88

Meyer, K.E. The Art Museum.*
  S. Hochfield, 55:Summer79-37

Meyer, L. Mexico and the United States in the Oil Controversy, 1917-1942.
  639(VQR):Summer78-87

Meyer, S.E. America's Great Illustrators.
  G. Weales, 219(GaR):Summer79-454

Meyer-Hermann, R., ed. Sprechen-Handeln-
Interaktion.
  K. Spalding, 182:Vol31#19-669
Meyerowitz, J. St. Louis and the Arch.
  A. Fern, 441:21Sep80-13
Meyers, J. The Enemy.
  G. Grigson, 362:3Jul80-23
Meyers, J. Homosexuality and Literature,
1890-1930.*
  L. Crompton, 637(VS):Winter79-211
  E. Slater, 447(N&Q):Apr78-181
  J. Stokes, 402(MLR):Apr79-397
  C.L. Walker, 395(MFS):Winter78/79-658
  639(VQR):Spring78-54
Meyers, J. Katherine Mansfield.*
  J. Atlas, 441:28Mar80-C33
  H. Moss, 441:9Mar80-1
Meyers, J. Married to Genius.
  C.L. Walker, 395(MFS):Winter78/79-658
  295(JML):Vol7#4-579
Meyers, J. and V. George Orwell.
  R.F. Giles, 365:Spring80-104
  A.M., 125:Winter79-308
Meylan, H. D'Erasme à Théodore de Bèze.
  J.M. De Bujanda, 539:Vol4No1-104
Meys, W.J. Compound Adjectives in English
and the Ideal Speaker-Listener.
  K. Kuiper, 603:Vol3#1-119
Miazgowski, B. The Bitter Sea.
  S. Pinsker, 136:Vol11#1-108
Micha, A. De la chanson de geste au roman.
  W.G. van Emden, 208(FS):Vol33Pt2-525
Micha, R. Hélion.
  G. Auclair, 450(NRF):Oct79-160
Michael, F. Mao and the Perpetual Revo-
lution.
  J. Glassman, 293(JASt):Feb79-353
Michael, I. - see "The Poem of the Cid"
Michaelides, S. The Music of Ancient
Greece.
  J.G. Landels, 123:Vol29No1-131
  M.O. Lee, 487:Winter79-362
  J. Solomon, 121(CJ):Apr-May80-356
Michaelis, M. Mussolini and the Jews.*
  W. Shapiro, 390:Nov79-69
  S. Woolf, 617(TLS):8Feb80-153
Michaels, L. and C. Ricks, eds. The
State of the Language.*
  P-L. Adams, 61:Feb80-97
  J. Russell, 441:6Jan80-7
  R. Scruton, 617(TLS):22Feb80-211
  J. Wain, 326:21Feb80-226
Michaels-Tonks, J. D.H. Lawrence.
  E. Kreutzer, 52:Band13Heft2-217
Michalczyk, J.J. André Malraux's "Espoir."
  R. Tarica, 207(FR):May79-958
Michals, D. Homage to Cavafy.
  A. Ross, 364:Oct79-5
Michalson, G.E., Jr. The Historical
Dimensions of a Rational Faith.
  J.S. Morgan, 342:Band69Heft4-469
Michanowsky, G. The Once and Future Star.
  A.C. Lupack, 497(PoiR):Vol23#4-115
Michaud, G., ed. Négritude.
  H. Cronel, 450(NRF):Jul79-121

Michaud, J-P. Fouilles de Delphes.
(Vol 2)
  R.A. Tomlinson, 303(JoHS):Vol199-204
Michaud, Y. Violence et politique.
  H. Cronel, 450(NRF):Feb79-107
  P. Lantz, 192(EP):Jul-Sep79-372
Michaux, H. Au Pays de la Magie.* (P.
Broome, ed)
  M. Blackman, 67:May79-132
  205(FMLS):Apr78-184
Michel, A. Le Mariage et l'amour dans
l'oeuvre romanesque d'Honoré de Balzac.
  D. Adamson, 208(FS):Vol33Pt2-814
  J. Guichardet, 535(RHL):Sep-Oct78-842
Michel, H. Le Procès de Riom.
  D. Johnson, 617(TLS):4Jan80-15
Michel, J. "L'Aventure janséniste" dans
l'oeuvre de Henry de Montherlant.
  A. Blanc, 535(RHL):Sep-Oct79-881
Michel, P. "Formosa deformitas."*
  V. Honemann, 684(ZDA):Band107Heft3-105
  M.E. Kalinke, 406:Spring79-63
Michel, W. and H. Teske - see Quantz, J.J.
Michelat, G. and M. Simon. Classe,
religion et comportement politique.
  R.H. Simon, 207(FR):Apr79-809
Michelet, J. Journal. (Vols 3 and 4) (C.
Digeon, ed)
  S. Michaud, 535(RHL):May-Jun78-491
Michelet, J. The People. (J.P. McKay,
trans)
  D.G. Charlton, 208(FS):Jul79-352
Michell, G., ed. Architecture of the
Islamic World.
  J. Carswell, 39:Jul79-75
  J. Masheck, 62:Dec78-60
Michell, G. The Hindu Temple.
  T.S. Maxwell, 463:Winter79/80-498
Michelsen, P. Zeit und Bildung.
  O.F. Best, 133:Band12Heft1/2-190
Michelson, A. - see Burch, N.
Michelson, H. Almost a Famous Person.
  J. Greenfield, 441:13Jan80-18
Michener, J.A. Chesapeake.
  639(VQR):Spring79-58
Michener, J.A. The Covenant.
  J.F. Burns, 441:23Nov80-3
  J. Leonard, 441:14Nov80-C29
"The James A. Michener Collection: Twenti-
eth Century American Painting."
  M.S. Young, 39:Sep79-238
Mickel, E.J., Jr. and J.A. Nelson, eds.
The Old French Crusade Cycle. (Vol 1)
  M.W. Epro, 207(FR):Apr79-766
  N. Wilkins, 382(MAE):1979/2-295
Mickelsen, W.C. Hugo Riemann's Theory of
Harmony.
  L. Rowell, 308:Fall78-316
Mickelsen, W.C. - see Riemann, H.
Mickelson, A.Z. Thomas Hardy's Women and
Men.*
  D. Edwards, 637(VS):Summer78-511
Mickle, I. A Gentleman of Much Promise.
(P.E. Mackey, ed)
  D.J. Ratcliffe, 161(DUJ):Dec78-111
Mićunović, V. Moskovske Godine 1956/58.
  S. Clissold, 575(SEER):Jan79-141

Micunovic, V. Moscow Diary.
  D. Binder, 441:17Feb80-9
  D. Wilson, 617(TLS):25Apr80-460
Midbøe, H. Peer Gynt — teatret og tiden.
  (Vol 2)
  H. Bien, 562(Scan):Nov78-169
Middlemas, K. Politics in Industrial
  Society.
  P. Addison, 617(TLS):2May80-504
Middleton, C. Carminalenia.
  D. Davis, 362:5Jun80-729
  E. Larrissy, 617(TLS):16May80-562
Middleton, D. Duel of the Giants.*
  A.Z. Rubinstein, 550(RusR):Jul79-389
  639(VQR):Spring79-63
Middleton, O.E. Selected Stories.
  R. Corballis, 368:Sep76-273
Middleton, R. and D. Watkin. Neoclassical
  and 19th Century Architecture.
  P. Goldberger, 441:30Nov80-70
Middleton, S. In a Strange Land.
  A. Brownjohn, 617(TLS):4Jan80-9
  J. Mellors, 362:3Jan80-30
Middleton, S. The Other Side.
  P. Kemp, 362:4Dec80-765
Middleton, T. The Second Maiden's Trag-
  edy.* (A. Lancashire, ed)
  C. Spencer, 130:Winter79/80-366
  S.J. Steen, 568(SCN):Fall-Winter79-79
  J.C. Trewin, 157:Winter79-79
Middleton, T. The Selected Plays of
  Thomas Middleton.* (D.L. Frost, ed)
  G. Taylor, 541(RES):Aug79-348
  J.C. Trewin, 157:Winter79-79
Middleton, T. and T. Dekker. The Roaring
  Girl.* (A. Gomme, ed)
  L.W. Conolly, 447(N&Q):Feb78-79
  P.A. Mulholland, 677(YES):Vol9-326
Middleton, T. and W. Rowley. A Fair
  Quarrel.* (G.R. Price, ed)
  L.W. Conolly, 447(N&Q):Feb78-79
Midgley, M. Beast and Man.*
  S. Clark, 617(TLS):25Apr80-474
  529(QQ):Winter79/80-736
Midler, B. A View from a Broad.
  C. Curtis, 441:29Jun80-9
Mieder, W., comp. International Bibliogra-
  phy of Explanatory Essays on Individual
  Proverbs and Proverbial Expressions.
  Proverbs in Literature.
  D.L. Eugenio, 650(WF):Oct79-269
Mieder, W. Das Sprichwort in der deut-
  schen Prosaliteratur des neunzehnten
  Jahrhunderts.*
  R.D. Hacken, 406:Spring79-77
Mieder, W. - see Taylor, A.
Mierau, F. Erfindung und Korrektur.*
  C. Hasche, 654(WB):6/1978-182
  J-U. Peters, 490:Band10Heft1-125
Miers, S. Britain and the Ending of the
  Slave Trade.
  W.J. Reader, 637(VS):Autumn78-103
Mieth, D. Dichtung, Glaube und Moral.
  K. Ruh, 684(ZDA):Band107Heft3-117
Mieth, D. Epik und Ethik.*
  C. Koelb, 406:Spring79-91
  H. Kurzke, 684(ZDA):Band107Heft3-145

Miething, C. Marivaux' Theater — Identi-
  tätsprobleme in der Komödie.
  W.D. Howarth, 208(FS):Vol33Pt2-727
Migdal, J.S. Palestinian Society and
  Politics.
  R. Wistrich, 617(TLS):23May80-591
Migliori, M. - see Aristotle
Mignani, R., ed. Un canzoniere italiano
  inedito del secolo XIV (Beinecke Phil-
  lipps 8826).*
  G. Costa, 545(RPh):Aug78-140
Mignani, R., M.A. Di Cesare and G.F. Jones,
  eds. A Concordance to Juan Ruiz, "Libro
  de buen amor."*
  B. Dutton, 589:Jan79-177
  D.G. Pattison, 382(MAE):1979/2-325
  C. Smith, 402(MLR):Oct79-963
Mignucci, M. L'argomentazione dimostra-
  tiva in Aristotle: commento agli Ana-
  litici Secondi, I.
  J.D.G. Evans, 303(JoHS):Vol199-178
Miguel, N.S. - see under Salvador Miguel,
  N.
Mihailovich, V.D., ed. Contemporary Yugo-
  slav Poetry.
  E.C. Hawkesworth, 575(SEER):Apr79-288
Mihailovich, V.D., ed. White Stones and
  Fir Trees.
  J.B. Moore, 573(SSF):Spring78-210
Mikes, G. English Humour for Beginners.
  D. Thomas, 362:18and25Dec80-863
Mikhail, E.H. Contemporary British Drama,
  1950-1976.
  P. Brigg, 178:Summer79-231
  C.A. Carpenter, 397(MD):Jun79-210
Mikhail, E.H. English Drama, 1900-1950.*
  C.A. Carpenter, 397(MD):Jun79-210
Mikhail, E.H., ed. J.M. Synge: Interviews
  and Recollections.
  P. Brigg, 178:Summer79-231
Mikhail, E.H. Oscar Wilde: An Annotated
  Bibliography of Criticism.
  K. Beckson, 365:Summer80-138
Mikhail, E.H., ed. Oscar Wilde: Inter-
  views and Recollections.
  T.D. White, 617(TLS):18Apr80-444
Mikhail, E.H., ed. W.B. Yeats: Interviews
  and Recollections.* (Vol 1)
  P. Brigg, 178:Summer79-231
  N. Grene, 447(N&Q):Aug78-379
  E. Kennedy, 174(Éire):Summer79-150
  S. Sweeney, 305(JIL):May78-185
  G-D. Zimmermann, 179(ES):Aug79-526
Mikhail, E.H., ed. W.B. Yeats: Interviews
  and Recollections.* (Vol 2)
  P. Brigg, 178:Summer79-231
  N. Grene, 447(N&Q):Aug78-379
  E. Kennedy, 174(Éire):Summer79-150
  R.G. Yeed, 305(JIL):May78-186
  G-D. Zimmermann, 179(ES):Aug79-526
Mikhailovsky, N.K. A Cruel Talent.
  E. Chances, 558(RLJ):Fall79-251
  S. Ketchian, 574(SEEJ):Summer79-268
Mikola, T. Die alten Postpositionen des
  Nenzischen (Juraksamojedischen).
  B. Schulze, 682(ZPSK):Band31Heft1-102

Mikulášek, M., ed. Literatura, Umění a
 Revoluce.
  J. Graffy, 575(SEER):Jan79-151
Mikulashek, M. Pobednyi smekh Opyt zhan-
 rovosravnitel'nogo analiza dramaturgii
 V.V. Maiakovskogo.
  A.H. Law, 550(RusR):Apr79-261
Mikus, J.A. Slovakia and the Slovaks.
  F.L. Carsten, 575(SEER):Jan79-152
Mileck, J. Hermann Hesse: Biography and
 Bibliography.*
  M.C., 395(MFS):Winter78/79-629
  T.C. Hanlin, 295(JML):Vol7#4-729
  K.W. Jonas, 301(JEGP):Jan79-96
  R. Koester, 406:Winter79-462
  J.D. Simons, 141:Winter79-84
  F. Wagner, 402(MLR):Jul79-758
Mileck, J. Herman Hesse: Life and Art.
  M. Boulby, 301(JEGP):Apr79-304
  H.S. Daemmrich, 395(MFS):Winter78/79-
  609
  I.D. Halpert, 222(GR):Winter79-40
  T.C. Hanlin, 295(JML):Vol7#4-730
Milenky, E.S. Argentina's Foreign Poli-
 cies.
  C.J. Moneta, 263(RIB):Vol29No2-218
Miles, J. Coming to Terms.
  D. Davie, 472:Fall/Winter79-84
  R.B. Shaw, 441:3Feb80-9
Miles, R. The Problem of "Measure for
 Measure."*
  A.D. Nuttall, 677(YES):Vol9-307
  A.H. Scouten, 405(MP):Nov79-214
Milgate, W. - see Donne, J.
Milhous, J. Thomas Betterton and the
 Management of Lincoln's Inn Fields 1695-
 1708.
  P. Holland, 617(TLS):27Jun80-742
Milhous, J. and R.D. Hume - see Polwhele,
 E.
Miliband, R. Marxism and Politics.
  H. Laycock, 529(QQ):Summer79-350
Militerni della Morte, P. Studi su Cice-
 rone oratore.
  J. Cousin, 555:Vol52fasc2-399
  E. Olechowska, 487:Spring79-89
  M. Winterbottom, 123:Vol29No1-152
Miljan, T. The Reluctant Europeans.
  S. Groennings, 563(SS):Winter79-64
Mill, J.S. The Collected Works of John
 Stuart Mill. (Vol 11: Essays on Philoso-
 phy and the Classics.) (J.W. Robson and
 F.E. Sparshott, eds)
  K. Britton, 483:Oct79-561
  C.R. Sanders, 579(SAQ):Spring79-271
Millar, F. The Emperor in the Roman World
 (31 BC - AD 337).*
  R.S. Bagnall, 121(CJ):Dec79/Jan80-181
Millar, G. Road to Resistance.*
  C. Kaiser, 441:12Oct80-16
  442(NY):13Oct80-192
Millar, J. Private Sector.*
  T.J. Binyon, 617(TLS):30May80-606
Millar, M. The Murder of Miranda.
  T.J. Binyon, 617(TLS):22Feb80-210

Millares Carlo, A. Bibliografía de Andrés
 Bello.
  H.C. Woodbridge, 399(MLJ):Mar79-153
Miller, A. The Theater Essays of Arthur
 Miller.* (R.A. Martin, ed)
  R. Asahina, 609:Fall78-99
  L. Moss, 397(MD):Jun79-201
Miller, B.S. - see Jayadeva
Miller, C. and K. Swift. Words and Women.
  P.M. Spacks, 402(MLR):Apr79-444
Miller, D. Appearance and Event.
  368:Mar78-93
Miller, D.M. John Milton: Poetry.
  A.K. Nardo, 568(SCN):Fall-Winter79-70
Miller, D.T. and M. Nowak. The Fifties.
  D.L. Zins, 584(SWR):Winter79-96
Miller, D.W. Church, State and Nation in
 Ireland, 1898-1921.
  L.J. McCaffrey, 637(VS):Summer79-449
Miller, D.W. Queen's Rebels.
  I. McAllister, 174(Éire):Fall79-144
Miller, E.H. Melville.*
  N. Schmitz, 473(PR):3/1979-445
Miller, E.H. - see Whitman, W.
Miller, G.A. and P.N. Johnson-Laird. Lan-
 guage and Perception.*
  H.W. Buckingham, Jr., 215(GL):Winter78-
  201
  J. Pellowe, 161(DUJ):Dec78-118
Miller, H. Genius and Lust.* (N. Mailer,
 ed)
  J. Ditsky, 577(SHR):Summer79-275
Miller, H. Gliding Into the Everglades.
 Mother, China, and the World Beyond.
  J.O. Brown, 448:Vol7#1-117
Miller, H. The World of Lawrence. (E.J.
 Hinz and J.J. Teunissen, eds)
  A. Lelchuk, 441:23Nov80-22
Miller, J. The Body in Question.*
  529(QQ):Summer79-368
Miller, J-A. - see Lacan, J.
Miller, J.C. Building Poe Biography.*
  P.F. Quinn, 445(NCF):Mar79-486
Miller, J.C. Kings and Kinsmen.
  B. Heintze, 69:Vol48#1-85
Miller, J.C. The Wolf by the Ears.*
  R. Reid, 529(QQ):Summer79-332
  T. Wendel, 432(NEQ):Mar79-132
Miller, J.C. - see Whitman, S.H. and J.H.
 Ingram
Miller, J.E., Jr. The American Quest for
 a Supreme Fiction.*
  G. Burns, 584(SWR):Autumn79-408
  J.D. McClatchy, 676(YR):Winter80-289
Miller, J.E., Jr. T.S. Eliot's Personal
 Waste Land.*
  295(JML):Vol7#4-690
Miller, J.G. Theatre and Revolution in
 France since 1968.*
  D. Bradby, 610:May78-225
  C. Campos, 402(MLR):Oct79-953
  D. De Kerckhove, 397(MD):Mar79-94
  205(FMLS):Apr78-188
Miller, K. Cockburn's Millenium.
  P. Morere, 189(EA):Jul-Dec78-397
Miller, L. The Noble Drama of W.B. Yeats.*
  M.J. Sidnell, 397(MD):Dec79-422

Minhinnick, R. Native Ground.
    P. Lewis, 617(TLS):25Apr80-477
Minière, C. Vita nova.
    L. Edson, 207(FR):Dec78-382
Minihan, J. The Nationalization of Cul-
ture.
    D. Rubinstein, 637(VS):Summer78-506
Mink, L.O. A "Finnegans Wake" Gazetteer.
    B. Benstock, 594:Winter79-496
Minor, W.S. Creativity in Henry Nelson
Wieman.
    J.H., 543:Sep78-146
Minta, S. Love Poetry in Sixteenth-
Century France.
    G. Castor, 402(MLR):Jul79-693
    G.J. Halligan, 67:May79-125
    M.M. McGowan, 208(FS):Jul79-330
Mintz, A. George Eliot and the Novel of
Vocation.*
    E. Alexander, 529(QQ):Winter79/80-657
    J.P. Brown, 454:Spring79-260
    D. Carroll, 445(NCF):Dec78-393
    S. Graver, 637(VS):Summer79-482
    L.K. Hughes, 141:Spring79-167
Minyard, J.D. Mode and Value in the "De
rerum natura."
    E. Tiffou, 487:Autumn79-276
Miquelon, D. Dugard of Rouen.
    J.F. Bosher, 656(WMQ):Oct79-642
Mira, M. and others, eds and trans.
Quince cuentistas brasileños de hoy.
    T.J. Peavler, 399(MLJ):Apr79-224
"The Miraculous Journey of Mahomet; Miraj
Namet."* (M-R. Séguy, ed)
    R. O'Brien, 60:May-Jun79-131
Miralles, E. - see de Pereda, J.M.
Miranda, G. Listeners at the Breathing
Place.*
    M. Heffernan, 491:Jun80-170
    W.H. Pritchard, 249(HudR):Summer79-252
de la Mirandole, J.P. and P. Garcia - see
under Pic de la Mirandole, J. and P. Gar-
cia
Mirikitani, L.T. Kapampangan Syntax.
    G.F. Meier, 682(ZPSK):Band31Heft4-426
Mirk, J. John Mirk's "Instructions for
Parish Priests.* (G. Kristensson, ed)
    K. Bitterling, 38:Band96Heft1/2-225
    A. Crépin, 189(EA):Jan-Mar78-82
    B. Lindström, 597(SN):Vol50#1-146
Mirković, M. and S. Dušanić. Inscriptions
de la Mésie Supérieure. (Vol 1)
    J.J. Wilkes, 313:Vol69-206
Miron, G. The Agonized Life.
    R. Mathews, 99:Nov80-35
"El Misal de Santa Eulalia."
    I. Mateo Gómez, 48:Jan-Mar78-106
Misch, R.J. Quick Guide to the Wines of
All the Americas.
    W. and C. Cowen, 639(VQR):Spring78-78
Mischel, T., ed. The Self.*
    İ. Dilman, 393(Mind):Oct79-610
    M.S., 543:Sep78-147
Mischke, R. Launcelots allegorische Reise.
    O. Arngart, 179(ES):Jun79-319

"Misère et gueuserie au temps de la Renais-
sance."*
    E.D. Mackerness, 402(MLR):Jan79-141
Mishan, E.J. Pornography, Psychedelics
and Technology.
    W. Goodman, 441:7Dec80-16
Mishler, W. Political Patricipation in
Canada.
    R.J. Drummond, 99:May80-38
Misiri, G.S. Govorim po-russki.*
    S. Wobst, 574(SEEJ):Summer79-297
Miskimin, A.S. The Renaissance Chaucer.*
    G. Schmidt, 38:Band96Heft1/2-215
Miskimin, H.A. The Economy of Later
Renaissance Europe, 1460-1600.
    I.A.A. Thompson, 86(BHS):Jul79-245
Misra, B.B. The Bureaucracy in India.
    M. Israel, 293(JASt):Nov78-192
"Missions et démarches de la critique:
Mélanges offerts au Professeur J.A.
Vier."
    G. Hainsworth, 208(FS):Jan79-114
Mitcalfe, B. Maori Poetry.
    M. Orbell, 368:Mar75-86
Mitcalfe, B. Migrant.
    E. Caffin, 368:Jun76-124
Mitchell, B. The Education of an Editor.
    D. Grumbach, 441:3Feb80-15
    C. Lehmann-Haupt, 441:29Feb80-C27
Mitchell, B. James Joyce and the German
Novel 1922-1933.*
    J. Aubert, 189(EA):Jan-Mar78-95
    E. Schlant, 222(GR):Winter78-39
    H. Steinecke, 52:Band13Heft3-329
Mitchell, D. The Jesuits.
    P. Hebblethwaite, 617(TLS):5Sep80-971
Mitchell, D. and J. Evans, comp. Benjamin
Britten.
    K. Spence, 415:Apr79-309
    A. Whittall, 410(M&L):Oct79-454
Mitchell, E. The Human Cage.
    D. Davis, 362:31Jan80-157
    J. Symons, 617(TLS):23May80-586
Mitchell, E.V., ed. The Pleasures of Walk-
ing.
    R.A. Sokolov, 441:24Feb80-16
Mitchell, F., with C.J. Frisbie and D.P.
McAllester. Navajo Blessingway Singer.
    B. Toelken, 650(WF):Oct79-272
Mitchell, G. The Whispering Knights.
    P. Craig, 617(TLS):8Aug80-892
Mitchell, J. The Walter Scott Operas.*
    J. Ehrstine, 130:Summer79-164
    J. Lucas, 405(MP):Nov79-254
    M. Peckham, 588(SSL):Vol14-277
    U. Weisstein, 131(CL):Summer79-311
Mitchell, J.G. The Hunt.
    C. Lehmann-Haupt, 441:28Oct80-C8
Mitchell, K. The Con Man.
    A.S. Brennan, 198:Fall80-97
    R.H. Ramsey, 99:May80-37
Mitchell, K. Everybody Gets Something
Here.
    P. Stevens, 649(WAL):Fall79-257

Mitchell, K. and Humprey and the Dump-
trucks. Cruel Tears.
K. Fraser, 168(ECW):Spring78-104
M. Lefebvre, 526:Summer79-88
J. Ripley, 102(CanL):Autumn79-110
Mitchell, L. Traveling Light.
M. Malone, 441:17Aug80-10
Mitchell, M. Margaret Mitchell's "Gone
With the Wind" Letters, 1936-1949. (R.
Harwell, ed)
N.C. Carpenter, 580(SCR):Nov78-131
Mitchell, M.V. L'Art du portrait dans les
"Satyres" de Mathurin Régnier.
J.D. Biard, 208(FS):Jan79-75
Mitchell, P.M. Vilhelm Grønbech.
N.L. Jensen, 562(Scan):Nov79-165
J.E. Rasmussen, 563(SS):Spring79-191
Mitchell, P.M. and K.H. Ober, eds and
trans. The Royal Guest and other Clas-
sical Danish Narrative.*
F. Gado, 573(SSF):Summer78-334
Mitchell, R. Less Than Words Can Say.
P-L. Adams, 61:Jan80-89
D. Bush, 31(ASch):Summer80-420
Mitchell, R.D. Commercialism and
Frontier.*
S. Hilliard, 656(WMQ):Oct79-634
Mitchell, R.L. The Poetic Voice of
Charles Cros.*
C. Chadwick, 535(RHL):Nov-Dec79-1062
Mitchell, T.F. Principles of Firthian Lin-
guistics.
A.S. Kaye, 545(RPh):Nov78-233
E.W. Roberts, 353:Mar78-73
Mitchell, W.J. - see Bach, C.P.E.
Mitchell, W.J.T. Blake's Composite Art.*
H. Adams, 401(MLQ):Jun79-204
M. Eaves, 661(WC):Summer79-275
E. Kreizman, 400(MLN):Dec79-1250
P. Malekin, 541(RES):Aug79-358
B.M. Stafford, 56:Winter79-118
D. Wagenknecht, 591(SIR):Spring79-158
B. Wilkie, 301(JEGP):Jan79-137
Mitchell, Y. Colette.
R.D. Cottrell, 395(MFS):Winter78/79-
620
Mitford, J. A Fine Old Conflict.
639(VQR):Spring78-47
Mitrofanova, O.D. Jazyk naučno-techničes-
koj literatury.
H-J. Mattusch, 682(ZPSK):Band31Heft1-
84
"Mitteilungen aus der Deutschen Biblio-
thek." (No. 9 and 10)
U. Groenke, 52:Band13Heft1-111
Mitten, D.G. Museum of Art, Rhode Island
School of Design.
E. Richardson, 54:Jun78-355
Mitter, P. Much Maligned Monsters.*
C.R. Jones, 293(JASt):Feb79-391
Mittermann, H. Untersuchungen zum histor-
ischen Präsens und Perfekt in frühen
mittelenglischen Romanzen.
R. Zimmermann, 38:Band96Heft3/4-471
Mitton, J. and S. The Prentice-Hall
Concise Book of Astronomy.
529(QQ):Summer79-371

Miyazawa, K. - see under Kenji Miyazawa
Miyoshi, M. As We Saw Them.
W.G. Beasley, 617(TLS):11Apr80-410
Mizrahi, R. Adieu Eldorado.
B.B. Casey, 207(FR):Apr79-797
Mlynar, Z. Nightfrost in Prague.
D. Binder, 441:13Apr80-12
Mo, T. The Monkey King.
P. Lewis, 565:Vol20#3-62
Mócsy, A. Pannonia and Upper Moesia.
W. Schindler, 121(CJ):Feb-Mar80-260
Modal, B., ed. Nordens svale.
Å.H. Lervik, 562(Scan):Nov78-182
"Modèles logiques et niveaux d'analyse
linguistique."
J. Bourguignon, 553(RLiR):Jan-Jun78-
205
"Modern Japanese Poetry." (J. Kirkup,
trans)
Y. Lovelock, 493:Dec79-57
"Modern Linguistics and Language Teaching."
G. Wazel, 682(ZPSK):Band31Heft2-220
Modiano, P. Livret de famille.
J. Carleton, 207(FR):Mar79-673
Modiano, P. Missing Person.
J. Naughton, 362:4Sep80-313
B. Wright, 617(TLS):5Sep80-951
Modica, M. L'estetica di Galvano della
Volpe.
E. Watkins, 290(JAAC):Spring80-325
Moe, P. - see d'Argenteuil, R.
Moelleken, W.W., G. Agler-Beck and R.E.
Lewis, eds. Die Kleindichtung des
Strickers. (Vol 4)
S.L. Wailes, 133:Band12Heft1/2-144
Moeller, W.O. The Wool Trade of Ancient
Pompeii.
R.P. Duncan-Jones, 123:Vol29No1-190
Moering, R. Die offene Romanform von
Arnims "Gräfin Dolores."
H.M.K. Riley, 221(GQ):May79-416
Moers, E. Literary Women.*
G. Bowles, 637(VS):Summer78-523
Moers, E. Harriet Beecher Stowe and Amer-
ican Literature.
E.B. Kirkham, 26(ALR):Spring79-170
Moessner, L. Morphonologie.
J. Kilbury, 257(IRAL):May79-179
Moevs, M.T.M. - see under Marabini Moevs,
M.T.
Moews, D. Keaton.
D. Macdonald, 453(NYRB):9Oct80-33
Moffat, R. The Matabele Journals of
Robert Moffat. (J.P.R. Wallis, ed)
A. Kuper, 69:Vol48#2-202
Mog, P. Ratio und Gefühlskultur.*
J. Mahr, 52:Band13Heft2-202
Moggach, D. A Quiet Drink.
J. Naughton, 362:29May80-697
C. Rumens, 617(TLS):23May80-575
Moggridge, D. - see Keynes, J.M.
Moglen, H. Charlotte Brontë: The Self
Conceived.*
S.M. Gilbert, 637(VS):Winter78-263
Mohamed, E.W. My Life in Pictures.
W.K. McNeil, 292(JAF):Apr-Jun79-244

Mohen, J-P. L'Age du Bronze dans la région de Paris.
L. Pauli, 471:Apr/May/Jun79-176
Mohr, W. and W. Haug. Zweimal "Muspilli."*
J.M. Clifton-Everest, 67:Nov79-352
E.S. Dick, 589:Jan79-178
H. Finger, 133:Band12Heft1/2-129
H. Martin, 406:Winter79-437
Mohrmann, C. Études sur le latin des chrétiens. (Vol 4)
M. Winterbottom, 123:Vol29No1-172
Möhrmann, R. Die andere Frau.*
R-E.B. Joeres, 400(MLN):Apr79-623
Moilanen, M. Statische lokative Präpositionen im heutigen Deutsch.
R.H. Lawson, 182:Vol131#23/24-857
Moinot, P. Le Guetteur d'ombre.
A. Clerval, 450(NRF):Nov79-114
Mojsisch, B. Die Theorie des Intellekts bei Dietrich von Freiberg.
H. Weidemann, 489(PJGG):Band86Heft2-425
Mojsisch, B. - see von Freiberg, D.
Mojtabai, A.G. Mundome.
C.B. Olson, 145(Crit):Vol20#2-71
Mojtabai, A.G. A Stopping Place.*
61:Jan80-87
Molas, P.R. - see under Ramírez Molas, P.
Moldenhauer, H. and R. Anton von Webern.*
P. Griffiths, 415:Mar79-211
Mole, J. From the House Opposite.*
E. Longley, 617(TLS):18Jan80-64
Molesworth, C. The Fierce Embrace.
D. Hall, 460(OhR):No.25-104
J.D. McClatchy, 676(YR):Winter80-289
Molesworth, R. An Account of Denmark, as it was in the Year 1692. (Danish title: En beskrivelse af Danmark som det var i året 1692.)
P. Ries, 562(Scan):Nov79-157
de Molière, J.B.P. Les Femmes Savantes. (H.G. Hall, ed)
P.H. Nurse, 208(FS):Jan79-77
de Molière, J.B.P. The Learned Ladies. (R. Wilbur, trans)
J. Coleby, 157:Autumn79-89
G.W. Ireland, 529(QQ):Autumn79-543
"Molière."
R. Laubreaux, 535(RHL):Jan-Feb79-122
de Molina, G.A. - see under Argote de Molina, G.
Mollenhoff, C.R. The President Who Failed.
A. Wildavsky, 441:27Apr80-12
C.V. Woodward, 453(NYRB):3Apr80-9
Mollica, A. and A. Convertini. L'Italia racconta.
A.G. Dente, 399(MLJ):Nov79-391
G.P. Orwen, 276:Autumn79-311
Moloney, B. Italo Svevo.*
T. Wlassics, 546(RR):Mar79-199
Moloney, B. Italo Svevo and the European Novel.
G. Carsaniga, 402(MLR):Jul79-718
Moltke, E. Runerne i Danmark og deres oprindelse.*
N. Wagner, 684(ZDA):Band107Heft2-51

Moltmann, G., ed. Deutsche Amerikaauswanderung im 19. Jahrhundert.
R.D., 179(ES):Feb79-94
Mombello, G. Les avatars de "Talentum."*
J. Chomarat, 535(RHL):Jan-Feb79-117
D. Woll, 72:Band216Heft2-389
Momigliano, A. Essays in Ancient and Modern Historiography.
639(VQR):Summer78-97
Mommsen, K. Hofmannsthal und Fontane.
F. Betz, 221(GQ):Nov79-553
Monaco, J. American Film Now.*
L. Braudy, 18:Jun79-71
Monaco, J., ed. Celebrity. Media Culture.
M. Dickstein, 18:Nov78-70
Monaco, J. How to Read a Film.*
P. Levinson, 186(ETC.):Winter78-445
Monaghan, D. Jane Austen.
Z. Leader, 617(TLS):25Jul80-855
Monawwar, M.E. Les Étapes Mystiques du shaykh Abu Sa'id.
H. Algar, 318(JAOS):Oct-Dec78-486
Moncel, C. Baudelaire, les poisons et l'Inconnu.
G. Chesters, 208(FS):Vol33Pt2-829
Moncel, C. Exposé de poétique.
P. Broome, 208(FS):Vol33Pt2-959
P. Somville, 542:Oct-Dec79-473
Mondolfo, R. and L. Tarán - see Heraclitus
Monegal, E.R. - see under Rodríguez Monegal, E.
Monegal, E.R., with T. Colchie - see under Rodríguez Monegal, E., with T. Colchie
Money, J. Experience and Identity.
E.A. Reitan, 173(ECS):Fall78-137
Money, J. Love and Love Sickness.
J. Adelson, 441:10Aug80-13
Monfrin, J., with L. Fossier, general eds. Documents linguistiques de la France.* (série française) (Vol 1 ed by J-G. Gigot; Vol 2 ed by J. Lanher)
W. Rothwell, 208(FS):Vol33Pt2-1024
Monga, L. Le Genre pastoral au XVIe siècle.
M. Quainton, 208(FS):Vol33Pt2-635
Monge, J. Le hasard et la logique.
J-M. Gabaude, 542:Oct-Dec79-452
Monge, J. Métaphysique du hasard.
M. Adam, 542:Jul-Sep79-369
J-M. Gabaude, 542:Oct-Dec79-452
Mongis, H. Heidegger et la Critique de la Notion de Valeur, la Destruction de la Fondation métaphysique.*
M. Haar, 192(EP):Apr-Jun79-252
Mongrédien, G. Recueil des textes et des documents du XVIIe siècle relatifs à La Fontaine.
J.D. Biard, 208(FS):Jan79-76
Monheim, F. 20 Jahre Indianerkolonisation in Ostbolivien.
F. Tichy, 182:Vol131#17/18-633
Monk, J.D. Mathematical Logic.
J.B. Remmel, 316:Jun79-283
Monna, M.C. The Gathas of Zarathustra.
H. Humbach, 182:Vol131#17/18-607

Monnerot, J. Inquisitions.
H. Godin, 208(FS):Vol33Pt2-973
Monnerot, J. Intelligence de la politique.
A. Jacob, 192(EP):Jul-Sep79-373
Monnet, F-M. Le Défi québécois.
E.J. Talbot, 207(FR):Oct78-197
Monnet, J. Memoirs.*
639(VQR):Spring79-70
Monnier, G. and B. Rose. Drawing.
J. Nash, 617(TLS):21Mar80-332
Monnier, P. Ferdinand furieux.
J. Sturrock, 617(TLS)14Mar80-286
Monsarrat, N. Darken Ship.
T.J. Binyon, 617(TLS):12Sep80-984
Monson, K. Alban Berg.*
M. Taylor, 617(TLS):22Aug80-941
Montagu, J. The World of Baroque and
Classical Musical Instruments.
L.J. Carroll, 415:Nov79-917
Montagu, M.W. Court Eclogs Written in the
Year 1716: Alexander Pope's Autograph
Manuscript of Poems by Lady Mary Wortley
Montagu.* (R. Halsband, ed)
P. Brückmann, 627(UTQ):Winter78/79-180
I. Grundy, 447(N&Q):Feb78-85
S.S. Kenny, 191(ELN):Mar79-255
Montagu, M.W. Essays and Poems [and] "Sim-
plicity," a Comedy.* (R. Halsband and I.
Grundy, eds)
P-G. Boucé, 189(EA):Jul-Dec78-390
G. Midgley, 447(N&Q):Feb78-89
D. Wykes, 472:Fall/Winter79-192
205(FMLS):Jan78-92
Montague, J. The Book of Irish Verse.
J.E. Emma, 152(UDQ):Winter79-118
Montague, J. The Great Cloak.*
C.W. Barrow, 174(Éire):Summer79-141
T. Eagleton, 565:Vol20#1-74
J.D. Engle, 305(JIL):Sep78-159
P. Mariani, 472:Fall/Winter79-249
R. Tracy, 109:Summer80-180
T. Wharton, 175:Summer79-190
Montague, J. The Rough Field.
R. Tracy, 109:Summer80-180
Montague, J. A Slow Dance.*
P. Mariani, 472:Fall/Winter79-249
R. Tracy, 109:Summer80-180
de Montaigne, M. Essais. (J.C. Chapman
and F.J-L. Mouret, eds)
M.M. McGowan, 208(FS):Jan79-70
205(FMLS):Jul78-286
Montaldo, J. Les Finances du P.C.F.
J-P. Ponchie, 207(FR):Dec78-371
Montale, E. The Storm and Other Poems.*
J. Simon, 491:Apr80-40
639(VQR):Spring79-65
de Montchrestien, A. La Reine d'Escosse.*
(J.D. Crivelli, ed)
J. Bailbé, 535(RHL):Mar-Apr78-294
Montefiore, A. Neutrality and Impartial-
ity.
P. Mew, 262:Summer78-237
de Montenoy, C.P. - see under Palissot de
Montenoy, C.
de Montera, P. and G. Tosi. D'Annunzio,
Montesquiou, Matilde Serao.
J-L. Meunier, 535(RHL):Jan-Feb79-148

de Montesquiou-Fezensac, B. and D. Gaborit-
Chopin. Le trésor de Saint-Denis.
(Vols 2 and 3)
C. Hohler, 90:Jul79-452
Montessori, M.M., Jr. Education for Human
Development.
P. Koopman, 529(QQ):Winter79/80-702
Monteverdi, C. The Letters of Claudio
Monteverdi. (D. Stevens, ed and trans)
H. Cole, 362:6Nov80-622
Montgomery, R.L. The Reader's Eye.
D. Robey, 617(TLS):22Feb80-218
de Montherlant, H. Port-Royal. (R.
Griffiths, ed)
A. Blanc, 535(RHL):Sep-Oct79-880
J-P. Cap, 207(FR):Dec78-356
205(FMLS):Jul78-286
Monti, A. Lettere a Luisotta. (L.
Sturani Monti, ed)
G. Tesio, 228(GSLI):Vol155fasc491-465
Monti, L.S. - see under Sturani Monti, L.
Montiel, I. Ossián en España.
191(ELN):Sep78(supp)-190
Montori de Gutiérrez, V. Ideas estéticas
y poesía de Fernando de Herrera.
M.G. Randel, 238:May-Sep79-396
de Montreuil, J. - see under Jean de
Montreuil
de Montreux, N. La Sophonisbe, Tragédie,
(D. Stone, Jr., ed)
R. Griffiths, 402(MLR):Jan79-198
G. Jondorf, 208(FS):Vol33Pt2-648
Moodie, T.D. The Rise of Afrikanerdom.
I. Hexham, 69:Vol148#1-91
Moody, E.A. and others - see Ockham,
William of
Moody, K. Growing Up On Television.
J. Greenfield, 441:7Sep80-15
Moody, R.E. - see Gorges, T.
Mooney, M. - see Kristeller, P.O.
Mooney, M. and F. Stuber, eds. Small Com-
forts for Hard Times.
639(VQR):Summer78-104
Mooney, M.M. The Ministry of Culture.
H. Kramer, 441:28Dec80-1
de Moor, W. Fifty Topics.
W. Smets, 556(RLV):1978/1-88
Moorcock, M. The Great Rock 'n' Roll
Swindle.
C. Brown, 617(TLS):20Jun80-706
Moorcroft, W. and G. Trebeck. Travels in
the Himalayan Provinces of Hindustan and
the Panjab from 1819 to 1825. (H.H.
Wilson, ed)
H. Tinker, 617(TLS):12Sep80-1000
Moore, B. The Mangan Inheritance.*
D. Cohen, 99:Mar80-34
K. McSweeney, 529(QQ):Winter79/80-742
J. Mellors, 364:Dec79/Jan80-128
J. Mills, 198:Summer80-123
J.C. Oates, 461:Fall-Winter79/80-87
Moore, B., Jr. Injustice.*
R.F. Hopwood, 529(QQ):Autumn79-533
639(VQR):Spring79-64
Moore, B.T. The Money Doubler.
A. Sistrunk, 95(CLAJ):Mar79-284

Moore, D. Idols of the Market Place.
C. Pollnitz, 581:Dec79-462
Moore, D.C. The Politics of Deference.*
G.B.A.M. Finlayson, 637(VS):Winter79-206
Moore, D.L. Ada, Countess of Lovelace.
L.A. Marchand, 340(KSJ):Vol28-145
Moore, F.C.T. The Psychological Basis of Morality.
E. Butler, 479(PhQ):Jul79-281
J. Skorupski, 483:Oct79-565
Moore, G., ed. The Penguin Book of American Verse.
R. Asselineau, 189(EA):Jan-Mar78-106
Moore, H. and G. Levine. With Henry Moore.
C. Cannon-Brookes, 39:Mar79-242
Moore, J. Gurdjieff and Mansfield.
R. Davies, 362:14Aug80-212
R. Dinnage, 453(NYRB):23Oct80-20
Moore, J.H. The Faustball Tunnel.
639(VQR):Winter79-14
Moore, J.N., ed. The Arab-Israeli Conflict.
639(VQR):Winter78-21
Moore, J.N., ed. Music and Friends.*
R. Anderson, 415:Sep79-744
Moore, M.B. and D. von Bothmer. Corpus Vasorum Antiquorum. (USA, fasc 16)
C. Sourvinou-Inwood, 303(JoHS):Vol199-214
Moore, R.I. The Origins of European Dissent.*
A. Murray, 161(DUJ):Dec78-100
Moore, S. The Afro-Black Connection.
J. Povey, 2(AfrA):Aug79-89
Moore, S. Marx on the Choice between Socialism and Communism.
P. Singer, 453(NYRB):25Sep80-62
Moore, T. Good-bye Momma.
T. Vincent, 296(JCF):28/29-228
Moore, T.D.R. Galapagos.
P-L. Adams, 61:Oct80-103
S.J. Gould, 453(NYRB):20Nov80-23
Moore, V. The Madisons.*
639(VQR):Autumn79-142
Moorehead, A. Darwin and the Beagle.
J.Z. Young, 453(NYRB):7Feb80-45
Moorehead, C. Fortune's Hostages.
P. Johnson, 617(TLS):18Jan80-52
Moorhead, J.H. American Apocalypse.*
639(VQR):Autumn78-148
Moorman, C. Editing the Middle English Manuscript.*
E.T. Donaldson, 405(MP):Aug79-84
R.L. Hoffman, 191(ELN):Jun79-328
Moorman, C., ed. The Works of the Gawain-Poet.*
B. Nolan, 405(MP):May80-406
R.A. Waldron, 382(MAE):1979/1-140
Moorman, M. George Macaulay Trevelyan.
R. Mitchison, 362:24Apr80-538
J.H. Plumb, 617(TLS):2May80-485
Moormann, K. Subjektivismus und bürgerliche Gesellschaft.*
M. Kaiser, 133:Band12Heft1/2-172

von Moos, S. Turm und Bollwerk.*
C. Thoenes, 54:Mar78-169
Moraes, D. Indira Gandhi. (British title: Mrs. Gandhi.)
J. Grigg, 362:4Sep80-309
C. Sterling, 441:28Dec80-6
"Morale pratique et vie quotidienne dans la littérature française du moyen âge."
T. Hunt, 402(MLR):Oct79-934
Morales, H.L. - see under López Morales, H.
Morales Borrero, M. La geometría mística del alma en la literatura española del Siglo de Oro.
C. Algar, 402(MLR):Jan79-225
Morales Lezcano, V. El colonialismo hispanofrancés en Marruecos (1898-1927).
J-L. Marfany, 86(BHS):Jul79-276
Moraud, Y. Masques et Jeux dans le théâtre comique en France entre 1685 et 1730.
J. Emelina, 535(RHL):Nov-Dec79-1050
Moravia, A. Time of Desecration.
P-L. Adams, 61:Aug80-84
R.M. Adams, 453(NYRB):14Aug80-47
R. Alter, 441:1Jun80-1
J. Burke, 231:Sep80-90
A. Duchêne, 617(TLS):13Jun80-664
J. Leonard, 441:20May80-C11
J. Naughton, 362:3Jul80-25
442(NY):16Jun80-121
Moravia, S. Il Pensiero degli Idéologues.
E.M. McAllester, 208(FS):Vol133Pt2-969
Morawski, S. Inquiries into the Fundamentals of Aesthetics.*
D.H. Hirsch, 569(SR):Fall79-628
Mordden, E. The Splendid Art of Opera.
J. Yohalem, 441:28Dec80-10
More, T. The Complete Works of St. Thomas More.* (Vol 2) (R.S. Sylvester, ed)
A. Gransden, 402(MLR):Jan79-160
"More Bad News."
P. Whitehead, 362:8May80-619
Moreau, G. The Restless Journey of James Agee.*
V.A. Kramer, 395(MFS):Summer78-281
R.R. Schramm, 577(SHR):Spring79-168
Moreau, J. De la connaissance selon saint Thomas d'Aquin.
M. Adam, 542:Jan-Mar78-89
J. Trouillard, 542:Jan-Mar78-73
Moreau, J. Plotin ou la gloire de la philosophie antique.
A. Forest, 192(EP):Jul-Sep79-337
Moreau, M-L. "C'est."*
L. Chalon, 556(RLV):1978/4-360
Moreto, A. El lindo don Diego. (F.P. Casa and B. Primorac, eds)
K.C. Gregg, 238:Mar79-172
Moretti, M.S. - see under Streiff Moretti, M.
Morey, A. David Knowles: A Memoir.
A. Johnson, 362:17Jan80-92
Morf, G. The Polish Shades and Ghosts of Joseph Conrad.
W.S. Dowden, 136:Vol11#1-105
Morfaux, L-M. and P. Henriot. Philosophie.
E. Namer, 542:Oct-Dec79-455

Morford, M.P.O. and R.J. Lenardon. Classical Mythology.* (2nd ed)
V.A. Rudowski, 580(SCR):Spring79-75
Morgan, C. Heirlooms.
I. Gold, 441:21Sep80-15
Morgan, D. Merchants of Grain.*
B. Cooper, 99:Jun-Jul80-38
Morgan, E., ed. Scottish Satirical Verse.
G. Ewart, 617(TLS):19Sep80-1019
Morgan, E.S. The Meaning of Independence.
G.L. Lint, 432(NEQ):Sep79-431
Morgan, F. Death Mother.
H. Carruth, 231:Jan80-77
R.B. Shaw, 441:3Feb80-9
Morgan, K. Ovid's Art of Imitation.*
R.J. Tarrant, 487:Spring79-92
Morgan, K. and J. Portrait of a Progressive.
V. Bogdanor, 617(TLS):1Aug80-866
J. Grigg, 362:19Jun80-801
Morgan, M.J. Molyneux's Question.
G. Pitcher, 482(PhR):Apr79-304
G.J. Stack, 484(PPR):Dec79-301
R.S. Woolhouse, 483:Jan79-136
Morgan, P. The Spring Collection.
E. Longley, 617(TLS):18Jan80-64
Morgan, R. Trunk and Thicket.
G. Burns, 584(SWR):Summer79-304
Morgan, S. In the Meantime.
Z. Leader, 617(TLS):25Jul80-855
Morgan, T. Maugham.
G. Annan, 362:8May80-617
M. Drabble, 441:9Mar80-1
V. Glendinning, 617(TLS):25Apr80-459
C. Lehmann-Haupt, 441:6Mar80-C21
442(NY):7Apr80-150
Morgenstern, O. L'illusion statistique.
J. Largeault, 542:Jan-Mar79-116
Mori, H. Japanese Portrait Sculpture.
P.C. Swann, 463:Spring79-117
Morice, G.P., ed. David Hume.*
D. McQueen, 393(Mind):Jul79-450
Mörike, E. Werke und Briefe. (Vol 5 ed by H. Meyer; Vol 8, Pt 1 ed by U. Hötzer)
N.H. Smith, 182:Vol31#13-419
Morillon, P. Sentire, sensus, sententia.
G. Serbat, 555:Vol52fasc2-387
Morino, A. - see D'Arezzo, R.
Morison, S. and D.B. Updike. Stanley Morison and D.B. Updike: Selected Correspondence. (D. McKitterick, ed)
J. Dreyfus, 617(TLS):Jul80-922
Morison, S.E. The Great Explorers.*
U. Lamb, 579(SAQ):Spring79-261
Morkovkin, V.V. Opyt ideografičeskogo opisanija leksiki.
S.I. Lubensky, 574(SEEJ):Spring79-141
Morley, F. Literary Britain.
W. Haley, 617(TLS):9May80-525
Morley, H. The Diary of "Helena Morley."
S. Tapscott, 219(GaR):Winter79-941
Morley, P. Morley Callaghan.
J.M. Kertzer, 627(UTQ):Summer79-451
Morley, P. Robertson Davies.*
K. Garebian, 296(JCF):28/29-198
E. Mullaly, 178:Winter79-502

Morley, P. - see Seton, E.T.
Morley, P.A. The Comedians.*
D. McCarthy, 168(ECW):Fall78-274
A.R. Young, 178:Summer79-242
Morley, R. Robert Morley's Book of Worries.*
M. Traherne, 617(TLS):11Jan80-34
Morley, S. Oscar Wilde.
I. Fletcher, 637(VS):Summer79-487
Mornin, E. Outpourings of an Art-Loving Friar.
W.J.L., 191(ELN):Sep78(supp)-188
Morot-Sir, É., H. Harper and D. McMillan 3d, eds. Samuel Beckett.*
J. Fox, 208(FS):Vol33Pt2-917
B. Rojtman, 535(RHL):Sep-Oct78-863
Morrall, J.B. Aristotle.
S.R.L. Clark, 518:Jan79-10
"Morrice Dancers at Revesby."
W.K. McNeil, 292(JAF):Jan-Mar79-107
Morrieson, R.H. Predicament.
R.A. Copland, 368:Sep75-260
Morris, B. Victorian Table Glass and Ornaments.
A. Polak, 135:Jul79-208
Morris, B. and R. Gill - see Tourneur, C.
Morris, C.B. The Dream-House.
205(FMLS):Apr78-188
Morris, C.R. The Cost of Good Intentions.
C. Lehmann-Haupt, 441:24Jul80-C18
S.R. Weisman, 441:27Jul80-1
Morris, D. Animal Days.*
W. Goodman, 441:10Aug80-15
C. Lehmann-Haupt, 441:18Jul80-C24
Morris, E. The Rise of Theodore Roosevelt.*
E. Wright, 617(TLS):25Jan80-91
Morris, J. Destinations.
A. Broyard, 441:17May80-21
V. Glendinning, 617(TLS):5Sep80-948
J. Raban, 441:27Apr80-1
E.S. Turner, 362:28Aug80-279
Morris, J. Farewell the Trumpets.
639(VQR):Summer79-87
Morris, J., ed. The Oxford Book of Oxford.*
639(VQR):Winter79-29
Morris, J. Time and Timelessness in Virginia Woolf.
F. Pellan, 395(MFS):Summer78-321
Morris, M. Shadow Boxing.
S. Brown, 493:Dec79-47
Morris, P.S. Sartre's Concept of a Person.
P. Trotignon, 542:Apr-Jun78-199
Morris, R. Cathedrals and Abbeys of England and Wales.
J.M. Richards, 617(TLS):1Feb80-122
Morris, R. Uncertain Greatness.
639(VQR):Spring78-62
Morris, R.J. Cholera, 1832.
R.M. Gutchen, 637(VS):Spring78-411
Morris, R.J.B. Parliament and the Public Libraries.
S. Bennett, 637(VS):Winter79-228

Morris, R.K. and M.W. Fox, eds. On the
Fifth Day.*
185:Jul79-416
Morris, W. Earthly Delights, Unearthly
Adornments.
R.D. Harper, 649(WAL):Fall79-247
L.B. Holland, 676(YR):Winter80-279
Morris, W. Plains Song.*
P-L. Adams, 61:Feb80-98
Morrison, B. The Movement.
J. Bayley, 362:29May80-691
S. Hynes, 617(TLS):20Jun80-699
Morrison, D.R. Education and Politics in
Africa.
A. Redmayne, 69:Vol148#1-88
Morrison, J. and C.F. Zabusky. American
Mosaic.
N. Glazer, 441:23Nov80-7
Morrison, R.H. The Secret Greenness.
S.E. Lee, 581:Dec79-432
Morrison, T. The Bluest Eye.*
E. Durwood, 617(TLS):8Feb80-146
J. Naughton, 362:14Feb80-222
Morrison, T. Sula.
J. Naughton, 362:20Nov80-700
Morrison, V. The Season of Comfort.
J. Cassidy, 493:Dec79-60
Morrissette, B. Intertextual Assemblage
in Robbe-Grillet.
E. Kafalenos, 268(IFR):Winter80-59
Morrissey, L.J. Gulliver's Progress.
W.B. Carnochan, 566:Spring79-134
P. Harth, 173(ECS):Spring79-403
J. Mezciems, 541(RES):Nov79-474
Morrissey, S. The Trees of Unknowing.
G. Hamel, 198:Winter80-139
Morrow, B. and B. Lafourcade. A Bibliog-
raphy of the Writings of Wyndham Lewis.
T. Materer, 468:Fall79-353
Morrow, J. The Confessions of Proinsias
O'Toole. Northern Myths.
R. Brown, 617(TLS):15Feb80-170
Morrow, P.D., ed. Growing Up in North
Dakota.
C.A. Glasrud, 649(WAL):Fall79-241
Morse, R. The Mountains of Canada.
529(QQ):Summer79-367
Morsey, R. and K. Repgen, eds. Adenauer-
Studien I.
F. L'Huillier, 182:Vol31#1/2-56
Mort, V.K. Grimasy žizni.
B. Sorokin, 574(SEEJ):Winter79-539
della Morte, P.M. - see under Militerni
della Morte, P.
Mortier, R. La poétique des ruines en
France.
U. Lange, 547(RF):Band91Heft1/2-177
Mortier, R. and H. Hasquin, eds. Brux-
elles au XVIIIe siècle.
R. Mercier, 535(RHL):Nov-Dec79-1059
Mortier, R. and H. Hasquin, eds. Les pré-
occupations économiques et sociales des
philosophes, littérateurs et artistes au
XVIIIe siècle. (Vol 3)
M. Delon, 535(RHL):Jul-Aug78-641

Mortimer, A., ed. Petrarch's "Canzoniere"
in the English Renaissance.
M-M. Martinet, 189(EA):Jan-Mar78-82
M.S-L. Wulf, 179(ES):Aug79-524
Morton, M., ed and trans. Russian Plays
for Young Audiences.
J. Doolittle, 108:Spring79-111
von Morungen, H. Lieder. (H. Tervooren,
ed and trans)
G. Schweikle, 684(ZDA):Band107Heft4-
173
"Hervé Morvan: Bouquet d'affiches."
M. Sheringham, 208(FS):Oct79-489
Möschel, W. Pressekonzentration und Wett-
bewerbsgesetz.
H. Kohl, 182:Vol131#17/18-600
Moschovakis, Y.N. Elementary Induction on
Abstract Structures.
W. Richter, 316:Mar79-124
Moscovici, S. Society Against Nature.
A.R. Sandstrom, 125:Spring79-477
Moser, H. Karl Simrock.*
D.K. Watkins, 406:Summer79-219
Moser, H., H. Rupp and H. Steger, eds.
Deutsche Sprache.
B.J. Koekkoek, 221(GQ):May79-391
Moser, H. and H. Tervooren, eds. Des Min-
nesangs Frühling.*
G. Schweikle, 684(ZDA):Band107Heft4-
161
Moses, J.B. and W. Cross. Presidential
Courage.
L.K. Altman, 441:6Jul80-11
Moses, J.C. The Politics of Female Labor
in the Soviet Union.
M.P. Sacks, 550(RusR):Oct79-490
Moses, L.W. The Political Role of Mongol
Buddhism.
D.L. Overmyer, 293(JASt):Feb79-328
Mosher, H.F. Where the Rivers Flow North.
D. Flower, 249(HudR):Summer79-298
Moshier, W.F. The Films of Jennifer Jones.
D. McClelland, 200:Dec79-622
Moskal'skaja, O.I. Problemy sistemnogo
opisanija sintaksisa (na materiale
nemeckogo jazyka).
W. Gladrow, 682(ZPSK):Band31Heft3-295
Moskowitz, G. Caring and Sharing in the
Foreign Language Class.
C.T. Hartl, 399(MLJ):Apr79-228
W.F. Smith, 238:Dec79-742
Mosley, D. The Duchess of Windsor.
E.S. Turner, 362:3Jul80-23
Mosley, L. Blood Relations.
J. Leonard, 441:25Mar80-C9
C. Seebohm, 441:13Apr80-15
E.S. Turner, 362:31Jul80-147
Mosley, L. Dulles.*
639(VQR):Autumn78-140
Mosley, N. The Imago Bird.
C. Brown, 617(TLS):19Sep80-1012
J. Naughton, 362:16Oct80-513
Moss, H. Notes from the Castle.
R.B. Shaw, 441:3Feb80-9
A. Young, 617(TLS):30May80-620
Moss, H., ed. The Poet's Story.*
H.V. Callison, 573(SSF):Summer78-333

Moss, J. Sex and Violence in the Canadian Novel.*
P. Denham, 178:Winter79-496
D. Staines, 168(ECW):Spring78-97
Moss, K. Encounter in St. Ives.
D.M. Thomas, 617(TLS):1Aug80-868
Moss, S. Skull of Adam.*
H. Carr, 617(TLS):25Apr80-477
J. Mole, 493:Mar80-65
Mösser, A. Das Problem der Bewegung bei Paul Klee.
C. Chambert, 341:1978/2-89
Mossner, E.C. and I.S. Ross - see Smith, A.
Mossop, D.J., G.E. Rodmell and D.B. Wilson, eds. Studies in the French Eighteenth Century presented to John Lough.
J.H. Brumfitt, 208(FS):Oct79-447
Møster, M.E. Orda og menneskelivet.
H. Naess, 563(SS):Spring79-194
"Motifs et figures."
A-M. Rousseau, 549(RLC):Jan-Mar77-100
Motion, A. The Pleasure Steamers.*
D. Graham, 565:Vol20#2-75
Motley, W. The Diaries of Willard Motley. (J. Klinkowitz, ed)
A. Rayson, 594:Summer79-244
Motmans, R., with G. Adé. A l'heure française II.
E. Namenwirth, 556(RLV):1978/1-94
de la Motte, D. Harmonielehre.
M. Bresnick, 308:Fall78-319
Mottram, E. William Burroughs.*
R. Willett, 402(MLR):Jul79-690
Mouchard, C. Perdre.
J.R., 450(NRF):Nov79-131
Mouloud, N. L'Analyse et le Sens.*
P.J. Fitzpatrick, 393(Mind):Jan79-132
A. Virieux-Reymond, 542:Jul-Sep79-369
Mounin, G. Dictionnaire de la linguistique.
J. Pleciński, 360(LP):Vol21-168
N.C.W. Spence, 208(FS):Vol33Pt2-1064
Mounin, G. Sémiologies des textes littéraires.
D. Sherzer, 207(FR):Feb79-479
"Mountbatten: Eighty Years in Pictures."*
A. Forbes, 617(TLS):4Jan80-7
Mountcastle, W.W. Religion in Planetary Perspective.
K. Yandell, 613:Dec79-429
Mouret, F.J-L. Les traducteurs anglais de Pétrarque 1754-1798.*
S. Siegrist, 52:Band13Heft3-323
de Mourgues, O. Two French Moralists.
H.T. Barnwell, 208(FS):Apr79-188
M. Guggenheim, 188(ECr):Winter78-73
Mousnier, R.E. The Institutions of France under the Absolute Monarchy 1598-1789.
R. Darnton, 453(NYRB):3Apr80-28
Mowat, B.A. The Dramaturgy of Shakespeare's Romances.*
C. Gesner, 405(MP):Nov79-215
Mowat, F. And No Birds Sang.
C. Lehmann-Haupt, 441:19Feb80-C9
T. Morgan, 441:24Feb80-12
442(NY):17Mar80-166

Moya Pons, F. Manual de Historia Dominicana.
H.E. Davis, 37:Sep79-45
Moyes, P. Angel Death.
M. Laski, 362:13Nov80-665
Moyles, L. Alleluia Chorus.
J. Vernon, 651(WHR):Autumn79-342
639(VQR):Autumn79-149
Moyles, R.G., ed. English-Canadian Literature to 1900.
J. Ferns, 677(YES):Vol9-356
Moynihan, D.P. Counting Our Blessings.
L.H. Lapham, 441:10Aug80-7
Moynihan, D.P., with S. Weaver. A Dangerous Place.*
E. Wright, 617(TLS):25Jan80-91
Moynihan, E.B. Paradise as a Garden in Persia and Mughal India.
F. Watson, 617(TLS):25Jul80-850
Możejko, E. Der sozialistische Realismus.*
H. Stephan, 574(SEEJ):Summer79-289
Mozley, A.V., ed. American Photography.
J.C. Sloane, 127:Fall78-82
Mrázková, D. and V. Remeš, eds. The Russian War: 1941-1945.*
639(VQR):Winter78-30
Mucci, P. Paper and Leather Conservation. (M. Boccaccio, ed)
P. Aronsson, 14:Jul79-353
Muckle, J.V. Nikolai Leskov and the "Spirit of Protestantism."
T. Eekman, 399(MLJ):Nov79-396
D.W. Treadgold, 550(RusR):Oct79-509
Mudgan, J. Flexionsmorphologie und Psycholinguistik.
G. Augst, 686(ZGL):Band7Heft2-220
Mudie, I. Selected Poems.
S.E. Lee, 581:Dec79-432
Mudrick, M. Books Are Not Life, But Then What Is?*
D.J. Enright, 617(TLS):11Jan80-29
Mueller, R.R. Festival and Fiction in Heinrich Wittenwiler's "Ring."*
S.L. Wailes, 589:Jan79-181
Mueller, T.H. New Testament Greek.
F.T. Gignac, 124:Sep79-34
H.H. Keller, 350:Dec79-959
J.E. Rexine, 399(MLJ):Apr79-222
Muellner, L.C. The Meaning of Homeric "enchomai" Through its Formulas.*
N. Postlethwaite, 303(JoHS):Vol99-168
Muhly, J.D. Copper and Tin.
D.C. Snell, 318(JAOS):Apr-Jun78-150
Muir, F. and S. Brett. Frank Muir Goes Into. Frank Muir on Children.
D. Thomas, 362:18and25Dec80-863
Muir, H. The Belles Lettres of Alexandra Bonaparte.
M. Furness, 617(TLS):18Apr80-432
Muir, K., ed. Shakespeare Survey 30.*
J.W. Velz, 130:Fall79-276
Muir, K., ed. Shakespeare Survey 31.
J.C. Trewin, 157:Spring79-80
Muir, K. Shakespeare's Comic Sequence. Shakespeare's Tragic Sequence.
S. Wells, 617(TLS):15Feb80-185

Muir, K. The Sources of Shakespeare's
Plays.* (rev)
    K. Tetzeli von Rosador, 72:Band216-
    Heft2-410
Muir, K. and P. Edwards, eds. Aspects of
"Othello."* Aspects of "Macbeth."*
    E.A.J. Honigmann, 447(N&Q):Apr78-174
Muir, R. The English Village.
    R. Blythe, 362:4Sep80-310
    M. Mason, 617(TLS):22Aug80-933
    442(NY):23Jun80-101
"Mujeres en América Latina."
    B. Freitag, 182:Vol131#21/22-796
Mujica, F. History of the Skyscraper.
    M.R. Corbett, 576:Oct78-224
Mujtaba-ī, F., ed. Indo-Iranian Studies.
    S.A. Khundmiri, 273(IC):Oct77-276
Mukařovský, J. Structure, Sign, and Func-
tion.* (J. Burbank and P. Steiner, eds
and trans)
    D.C. Freeman, 290(JAAC):Fall79-95
    D.H. Hirsch, 569(SR):Fall79-628
    J.A. Radway, 577(SHR):Summer79-267
    J.P. Riquelme, 125:Spring79-443
Mukařovský, J. The Word and Verbal Art.*
(J. Burbank and P. Steiner, eds and
trans)
    E.W. Bruss, 131(CL):Spring79-170
    D.C. Freeman, 290(JAAC):Fall79-95
    D.H. Hirsch, 569(SR):Fall79-628
    205(FMLS):Jul78-287
Mukherjee, S.B. The Age Distribution of
the Indian Population.
    D. Bhattacharya, 293(JASt):May79-614
Mukhia, H. Historians and Historiography
during the Reign of Akbar.
    H.K. Sherwani, 273(IC):Apr77-151
Mulder, J.M. Woodrow Wilson.
    639(VQR):Spring79-70
Mulder, N. Mysticism and Everyday Life in
Contemporary Java.
    J.A. Boon, 293(JASt):Feb79-428
Muldoon, P., ed. The Scrake of Dawn.
    P. Craig, 617(TLS):28Mar80-373
Mulgan, R.G. Aristotle's Political Theory.
    C. Chalier, 192(EP):Jul-Sep79-374
    S.R.L. Clark, 518:Jan79-10
Mulisch, H. Two Women.
    J. Naughton, 362:11Dec80-804
Mullen, E.J. - see Hughes, L.
Müllenbrock, H-J. Popes Gesellschafts-
lehre in "An Essay on Man."
    M. Brunkhorst, 72:Band216Heft1-178
Müllenhoff, K. Sagen, Märchen und Lieder
aus Schleswig, Holstein und Lauenburg
(1845). (new ed by O. Mensing)
    E.H. Rehermann, 196:Band19Heft1/2-165
von Müller, A. Gloria Bona Fama Bonorum.
    B.G. Kohl, 589:Jul79-638
Müller, A. Adam Müller's Twelve Lectures
on Rhetoric. (D.R. Bormann and E. Leinfellner, eds and trans)
    R.D. Brooks, 583:Fall78-106
Müller, B. Das Französische der Gegenwart.*
    E. Rattunde, 430(NS):Apr78-179

Muller, C. Principes et méthodes de
statistique lexicale.
    É. Brunet, 209(FM):Jan78-80
Müller, H-C. Bernhard Schott.
    P.W. Jones, 410(M&L):Jul79-337
Müller, H-J. and W. Roll, eds. Fragen des
älteren Jiddisch.
    B. Murdoch, 684(ZDA):Band107Heft4-186
Muller, H.R.A. Javanese Terracottas.
    S. Markbreiter, 60:Sep-Oct79-134
Müller, K-D. Autobiographie und Roman.*
    K. Goodman, 406:Spring79-96
Müller, L., ed. Handbuch zur Nestorchro-
nik. (Vols 1-3)
    T. Cizevska, 574(SEEJ):Summer79-262
    J. Fennell, 575(SEER):Jan79-123
    D. Huntley, 104(CASS):Fall78-419
Müller, P. Sternwarten — Architektur und
Geschichte der Astronomischen Observa-
torien.
    J-C. Klamt, 683:Band41Heft2-172
Müller, U., ed. Politische Lyrik des
deutschen Mittelalters.
    M.G. Scholz, 680(ZDP):Band97Heft1-138
Müller, W. Etre-au-monde.
    E. Diet, 542:Apr-Jun78-205
    B. Grünewald, 53(AGP):Band60Heft2-242
Muller, W.D. The Kept Men?
    J. Lovell, 161(DUJ):Jun79-277
    N.C. Soldon, 637(VS):Summer79-472
Müller-Seidel, W. Theodor Fontane.*
    D. Barnouw, 222(GR):Summer78-132
    S-A. Jørgensen, 462(OL):Vol133#1-87
    H.H.H. Remak, 406:Spring79-74
Mulon, M. Archives Nationales: L'Onomas-
tique Française.
    F.M. Hamlin, 424:Dec78-424
    G. Tuaillon, 553(RLiR):Jul-Dec78-439
Mulot, J.P. Les Reliques d'un désabusé,
suite et fin.
    L. Hewitt, 207(FR):Oct78-180
Mumford, L. My Works and Days.*
    D. Schuyler, 432(NEQ):Dec79-579
Munari, F., ed. Mathei Vindocinensis
Opera. (Vol 1)
    B. Harbert, 382(MAE):1979/2-274
Munby, A.N.L. Essays and Papers.* (N.
Barker, ed)
    I. Jack, 541(RES):May79-241
Munby, A.N.L. and L. Coral, eds. British
Book Sale Catalogues 1676-1800.*
    I. Jack, 541(RES):May79-241
    D. McKitterick, 78(BC):Winter79-497
    566:Autumn78-51
"Edvard Munch: 1863-1944."
    J.G. Holland, 563(SS):Summer79-306
Münch, M-M. La "Symbolique" de Friedrich
Creuzer.
    A. Denis, 535(RHL):Jul-Aug79-676
    R. Theis, 182:Vol131#17/18-615
Mundle, C.W.K. Perception.
    P. Fitzgerald, 486:Mar78-165
Munford, H.M., D.J. Nordloh and D. Klein-
man - see Howells, W.D.
Mungello, D.E. Leibniz and Confucianism.
    L.B. McCullough, 485(PE&W):Apr79-241
                                    [continued]

[continuing]
E. Naert, 542:Apr-Jun79-223
J.D. Young, 302:Vol16#1and2-111
Mungo, R. Cosmic Profit.
J. Stickney, 441:13Apr80-13
Munhall, E. Jean-Baptiste Greuze, 1725-
1805.
H.N. Opperman, 173(ECS):Spring79-409
A. Schnapper, 54:Jun78-374
Munier, R., comp. Aujourd'hui Rimbaud.
M. Davies, 208(FS):Vol33Pt2-843
Munier, R. Le contour, l'éclat.
P. Somville, 542:Oct-Dec79-474
Munier, R., ed and trans. Haïku.
A. Clavel, 98:Nov78-1088
Munier, R. L'Ombre.
J.R., 450(NRF):Nov79-130
Muñoz Valle, I. Así nació el hombre
occidental. La verdad sobre Tacito.
A. Reix, 542:Jul-Sep79-370
Muñoz Valle, I. Investigaciones sobre el
estilo formular épico y sobre la lingua
de Homero.
P. Monteil, 555:Vol52fasc1-148
A. Reix, 542:Jul-Sep79-370
Munro, A. The Beggar Maid.*
T.R. Edwards, 453(NYRB):6Mar80-43
J.C. Oates, 461:Fall-Winter79/80-87
Munro, D.J. The Concept of Man in Contem-
porary China.
J.C. Hsiung, 293(JASt):Nov78-158
Munro, E. Originals.*
M. Price, 676(YR):Summer80-588
Munroe, J.A. Colonial Delaware.
J.A. Neuenschwander, 656(WMQ):Oct79-
636
Münster, R. and R. Machold, eds. Thema-
tischer Katalog der Musikhandschriften
der ehemahligen Klosterkirchen Weyarn,
Tegernsee und Benediktbeuern.
B.S. Brook, 317:Fall79-549
Munteano, B. Solitude et Contradiction de
Jean-Jacques Rousseau.*
P. Burgelin, 535(RHL):Sep-Oct78-836
Munz, P. The Shapes of Time.
D.R. Kelley, 256:Spring79-167
C.B. McCullagh, 63:Mar79-97
de Muralt, A. La connaissance intuitive
du néant et l'évidence du "je pense."
A. Reix, 542:Jan-Mar78-94
Muraro, M. I Disegni di Vittore Carpaccio.
G. Robertson, 90:Jul79-448
Murasaki Shikibu. The Tale of Genji.*
(E.G. Seidensticker, trans)
Masao Miyoshi, 293(JASt):Feb79-299
M. Mudrick, 249(HudR):Summer79-269
Muray, P. Jubila.
M. Bishop, 207(FR):Oct78-181
Murck, C.F. Artists and Traditions.
A.D. Clapp, 293(JASt):Nov78-169
Murdoch, B. Hans Folz and the Adam-
Legends.*
D. Blamires, 402(MLR):Jan79-240
J.L. Flood, 447(N&Q):Feb78-76
Murdoch, I. Un enfant du verbe.
C. Jordis, 450(NRF):Sep79-63

Murdoch, I. The Fire and the Sun.*
W. Charlton, 393(Mind):Jul79-447
I.M. Crombie, 123:Vol29No1-76
M.A. McCloskey, 63:Jun79-189
Murdoch, I. Henry and Cato.*
S. Epstein, 152(UDQ):Summer78-150
Murdoch, I. Nuns and Soldiers.
R. Dinnage, 617(TLS):5Sep80-951
V. Glendinning, 362:4Sep80-308
Murdoch, I. The Sea, the Sea.*
639(VQR):Spring79-58
Mure, G.R.G. Idealist Epilogue.
P. Dubois, 542:Jul-Sep79-371
483:Jan79-138
Muresu, G. - see de' Calzabigi, R.
Murethach [Muridac]. In Donati artem
maiorem. (L. Holtz, ed)
J.J. Contreni, 589:Oct79-834
Murfin, R.C. Swinburne, Hardy, Lawrence
and the Burden of Belief.
W.E. Cragg, 268(IFR):Winter80-72
K. Wilson, 255(HAB):Summer79-228
Müri, W. Griechische Studien. (E.
Vischer, ed)
F. Lasserre, 182:Vol131#11/12-372
Muridac - see under Murethach
Murie, M.E. Two in the Far North.
B.K. Morton, 649(WAL):Summer79-178
Murphy, C. - see Rogers, S.A.B.
Murphy, D. Wheels Within Wheels.*
D. Grumbach, 441:27Apr80-16
Murphy, E.A. The Logic of Medicine.
D.A. Albert and M.D. Resnik, 486:Sep78-
488
Murphy, J.J., ed. Medieval Eloquence.
G. Kennedy, 583:Winter79-201
S. Knight, 67:Nov79-311
Murphy, J.J. Rhetoric in the Middle Ages.*
W. von Koppenfels, 38:Band96Heft1/2-
201
Murphy, R. Selected Poems.
J. Cassidy, 493:Dec79-60
C. Hope, 364:Nov79-85
E. Longley, 617(TLS):18Jan80-64
Murphy, W.F. The Vicar of Christ.*
639(VQR):Autumn79-135
Murphy, W.M. Prodigal Father.*
R.J. Finneran, 651(WHR):Winter79-80
B. Guinness, 39:Jun79-486
639(VQR):Autumn78-142
Murray, C. - see Philips, W.
Murray, K.M.E. Caught in the Web of
Words.*
C.L. Barnhart, 35(AS):Spring79-45
R.I. McDavid, Jr., 405(MP):May80-397
S. Pickering, Jr., 639(VQR):Spring78-
338
Murray, L. The Peasant Mandarin.
M. Duwell, 71(ALS):Oct79-259
D.A. Myers, 268(IFR):Winter80-69
Murray, L.A. Ethnic Radio.
S.E. Lee, 581:Dec79-432
Murray, M., ed. Heidegger and Modern
Philosophy.
L. Snyder, 484(PPR):Sep79-147
Murray, M. Modern Critical Theory.*
S. Decloux, 182:Vol131#3/4-80

269

Murray, O. Early Greece.
P. Cartledge, 617(TLS):13Jun80-675
Murray, P. The Dulwich Picture Gallery.
S. Gardiner, 362:11Dec80-802
Murray, R. Selected Poems.
D. Smith, 29:Sep/Oct80-30
Murrell, J. Memoir.
42(AR):Fall79-505
Murrin, M. The Allegorical Epic.
L. Jardine, 617(TLS):5Sep80-973
Murtaugh, D.M. "Piers Plowman" and the
Image of God.
R.J. Heffernan, 301(JEGP):Jul79-409
P.M. Kean, 541(RES):Nov79-457
Musa, M. Advent at the Gates.*
J.T. Chiampi, 545(RPh):Nov78-230
Musgrave, B. and Z. Menell. Change and
Choice.
V. Glendinning, 617(TLS):6Jun80-634
Musgrave, S. Becky Swan's Book.*
P. Brennan, 102(CanL):Autumn79-113
Musgrave, S. A Man to Marry, A Man to
Bury.*
C. MacMillan, 198:Summer80-151
P. Monk, 150(DR):Autumn79-570
Musil, R. Tagebücher.* (A. Frisé, ed)
G. Müller, 680(ZDP):Band97Heft2-310
Muslehuddin, M. Islamic Jurisprudence and
the Rule of Necessity and Need.
R. Kemal, 273(IC):Oct76-246
"Muslim Communities in non-Muslim States."
"The Muslim World and the Future Eco-
nomic Order."
M.E. Yapp, 617(TLS):19Sep80-1040
de Musset, A. Lorenzaccio. (B. Masson,
ed)
W.D. Howarth, 208(FS):Apr79-211
Mutschler, F-H. Erzählstil und Propaganda
in Caesars Kommentarien.
M. Rambaud, 555:Vol52fasc2-401
Muybridge, E. Muybridge's Complete Human
and Animal Locomotion.*
G. Thornton, 55:Nov79-48
Muysken, P. Syntactic Developments in the
Verb Phrases of Ecuadorian Quechua.
D. Weber, 350:Dec79-939
Mùzzioli, F. La critica e Saba.
E. Favretti, 228(GSLI):Vol155fasc490-
307
Myatt, F. Peninsular General.
A. Brett-James, 617(TLS):12Sep80-1005
Mydans, S. The Vermilion Bridge.
R.F. Shepard, 441:15Jul80-C20
J. Yohalem, 441:27Jul80-12
Myers, M. Izzy Manheim's Reunion.
H. Kreisel, 168(ECW):Summer78-147
J. Wasserman, 102(CanL):Autumn79-108
Myrdal, J. The Silk Road.
H.G. Porteus, 362:5Jun80-730

"The N-Town Plays."*
R. Beadle, 382(MAE):1979/2-319
G.C. Britton, 447(N&Q):Oct78-447
M. Stevens, 589:Jul79-605

Nablow, R.A. A Study of Voltaire's
Lighter Verse.
S. Menant, 535(RHL):Jan-Feb78-127
O.R. Taylor, 208(FS):Vol33Pt2-741
Nabokov, V. Lectures on Literature. (F.
Bowers, ed)
R.M. Adams, 453(NYRB):18Dec80-61
E. Hardwick, 441:19Oct80-1
C. Lehmann-Haupt, 441:300ct80-C23
Nabokov, V. and E. Wilson. The Nabokov-
Wilson Letters 1940-1971.* (S. Karlin-
sky, ed)
G. Struve, 617(TLS):2May80-509
639(VQR):Autumn79-140
Nabokov, V.D. V.D. Nabokov and the Rus-
sian Provisional Government, 1917. (V.D.
Medlin and S.L. Parsons, eds)
R. Johnston, 104(CASS):Summer78-300
Nadeau, M. The History of Surrealism.
M.A. Menlowe, 89(BJA):Winter79-84
Nadvi, M.S.M.A. Hayat-e-Suleman.
Q.S.K. Hussaini, 273(IC):Apr76-134
Nadvi, S.A.H.A. Islamic Concept of
Prophethood.
S. Vahiduddin, 273(IC):Jul78-197
Nadwi, S.S. Mohammad the Ideal Prophet.
R. Kemal, 273(IC):Oct78-278
Naef, W.J. The Collection of Alfred
Stieglitz.*
K. Hoffman, 127:Summer79-293
Naess, A. Kommunikation und Argumentation.
G. Öhlschläger, 686(ZGL):Band7Heft1-83
Naevestad, M. The Colors of Rage and Love.
42(AR):Fall79-505
no Nagako, F. The Emperor Horikawa Diary
(Sanuki no Suke nikki). (J. Brewster,
trans)
M. Tahara, 293(JASt):Feb79-377
Nagel, B. Kafka und Goethe.
W. Pelters, 406:Winter79-458
J. Strohschänk, 400(MLN):Apr79-625
Nagel, B. Staufische Klassik.*
C.S. Jaeger, 406:Winter79-439
W. McConnell, 400(MLN):Apr79-639
Nagel, E. Teleology Revisited, and Other
Essays in the Philosophy and History of
Science.
P. Suppes, 311(JP):Dec80-820
Nagel, T. Mortal Questions.*
D.W. Hamlyn, 617(TLS):4Jan80-19
483:Oct79-570
Nagel, T. Rechtleitung und Kalifat
Versuch über eine Grundfrage der islam-
ischen Geschichte.
S. Vahiduddin, 273(IC):Jan77-73
Nägele, R. Heinrich Böll.*
H.J. Bernhard, 654(WB):6/1978-188
Nägele, R. Literatur und Utopie.
M. Brown, 301(JEGP):Oct79-602
Nagibin, J. Berendeev les.
M. Sendich, 558(RLJ):Winter79-239
Nagibin, J. Carskosel'skoe Utro.
M. Sendich, 558(RLJ):Spring79-243
Nagler, A.M. The Medieval Religious
Stage.*
W.A. Armstrong, 611(TN):Vol132#3-140
M.M. McGowan, 576:Dec78-317

Nagy, G. The Best of the Achaeans.
M.L. West, 617(TLS):8Aug80-893
Nahumck, N.C. Introduction to Dance Literacy.
A. Kaeppler, 187:May80-308
Naipaul, S. Black and White.
N. Mosley, 362:20Nov80-693
Naipaul, V.S. A Bend in the River.*
C. Hope, 364:Dec79/Jan80-124
E. Milton, 676(YR):Autumn79-89
C.C. Park, 249(HudR):Winter79/80-580
Naipaul, V.S. India.
H.H. Anniah Gowda, 49:Jan79-98
Naipaul, V.S. The Return of Eva Perón.
P. Conrad, 362:26Jun80-835
J. Didion, 453(NYRB):12Jun80-20
K. Garebian, 99:Nov80-33
J. Kramer, 441:13Apr80-1
J. Leonard, 441:13Mar80-C21
442(NY):19May80-158
Nair, S.B. - see Sternbach, L.
Nakagawa, Y. Nakagawa's "Tenno Yūgao."
(J. Ingalls, ed and trans)
W.E. Naff, 318(JAOS):Jul-Sep78-301
Nakamura, K.M. - see Kyōkai
Nakayama, S. and N. Sivin, eds. Chinese Science.
D. Gregory-Smith, 485(PE&W):Apr79-221
Nakayama, S., D.L. Swain and Y. Eri, eds. Science and Society in Modern Japan.
D. Gregory-Smith, 485(PE&W):Apr79-221
Nalbantian, S. The Symbol of the Soul from Hölderlin to Yeats.*
W.K., 191(ELN):Sep78(supp)-170
M.M. Tatar, 406:Fall79-343
Nance, J.M. - see McCutchan, J.D.
Nancy, J-L. La remarque spéculative. Le discours de la syncope. (Vol 1)
D. Kambouchner, 98:Jan78-41
Nanda, B.R. Gokhale.
K.W. Jones, 293(JASt):Nov78-190
Nanda, B.R., ed. Indian Foreign Policy: The Nehru Years.
R.G.C. Thomas, 293(JASt):Aug79-810
Nanda, B.R., ed. Indian Women.
K.H. Gould, 293(JASt):Nov78-205
Naogeorg, T. Sämtliche Werke. (Vol 1)
(H-G. Roloff, ed)
K. Aichele, 222(GR):Winter79-43
Naoshirō, T. - see under Tsuji Naoshirō
Napier, M. Blind Chance.
M. Laski, 362:13Nov80-665
Narain, I., K.C. Pande and M.L. Sharma. The Rural Elite in an Indian State.
R. Sisson, 293(JASt):May79-609
Naranjo, C. Mi guerrilla.
S. Baciu, 263(RIB):Vol29No1-96
de Nardis, L. - see Mallarmé, S.
Naremore, J. The Magic World of Orson Welles.*
S. Lawson, 18:Feb79-72
Narkiss, B., with M.E. Stone, eds. Armenian Art Treasures of Jerusalem.*
G. Fowden, 617(TLS):5Sep80-974

Narmour, E. Beyond Schenkerism.*
A.J. Cohen, 255(HAB):Winter/Spring79-114
A. Keiler, 513:Fall-Winter78-161
J. La Rue, 317:Fall79-586
H. Martin, 513:Fall-Winter78-196
A. Whittall, 410(M&L):Jan79-86
Nash, D. - see Allen, D.F.
Nash, G.B. The Urban Crucible.
J.R. Pole, 617(TLS):11Apr80-403
Nash, H., ed. The Energy Controversy.
B. De Mott, 61:Nov80-94
Nash, J.C., ed. Maurice Scève: Concordance de la "Délie."
D. Wilson, 208(FS):Jan79-69
Nash, N.R. The Last Magic.
639(VQR):Winter79-16
Nash, S. "Les Contemplations" of Victor Hugo.*
F.P. Bowman, 400(MLN):May79-912
B. Leuilliot, 535(RHL):Jul-Aug79-684
L.M. Porter, 188(ECr):Winter78-70
Nason, R. A Modern Dunciad.
J. Vernon, 651(WHR):Autumn79-350
Nasr, S.H. Ideals and Realities of Islam. (2nd ed)
A.A.A. Fyzee, 273(IC):Apr76-128
Nasr, S.H., with W.C. Chittick. An Annotated Bibliography of Islamic Science. (Vol 1)
M.Z. Chagtai, 273(IC):Jul77-222
Nassor, M.H., comp. Guide to the Microfilms of Regional and District Books.
A. Redmayne, 69:Vol48#2-192
Nathan, H. Dan Emmett and the Rise of Early Negro Minstrelsy.
W.K. McNeil, 292(JAF):Oct-Dec79-514
Nathan, L. The Transport of Love.
S. Pollock, 318(JAOS):Oct-Dec78-562
Nathan, N.M.L. Evidence and Assurance.
L.J. Cohen, 617(TLS):14Mar80-302
Nathanson, M.B. - see Freiman, G.
"National Gallery Technical Bulletin." (Vol 2)
H. Lank, 90:Nov79-733
"The National Museum of Cuba."
J.A. Findlay, 263(RIB):Vol29No3/4-370
Nations, O.L. The Strange Case of Inspector Loophole.
G. Davies, 168(ECW):Spring78-82
K. Garebian, 102(CanL):Summer79-126
Nattiez, J.J. Fondements d'une sémiologie de la musique.*
W. Godzich, 308:Spring78-117
Nauman, S., Jr. Dictionary of Asian Philosophies.
J.B. Chethimattam, 613:Dec79-431
A. Reix, 542:Jul-Sep79-358
Naumann, G. Le Français Pratique.
E. Rattunde, 430(NS):Apr78-183
Naumann, M.T. Blue Evenings in Berlin.
D.B. Johnson, 574(SEEJ):Summer79-282
Naumann, U. Predigende Poesie.
M.H., 191(ELN):Sep78(supp)-175
Naumann, W. Die Dramen Shakespeares.
G. Gillespie, 131(CL):Summer79-302

Nautin, P. and L. Doutreleau - see Didymus of Alexandria

Navarria, A. Federico De Roberto.
J-P. de Nola, 549(RLC):Jan-Mar77-118

Navarro, V. Social Security and Medicine in the USSR.
N.M. Frieden, 550(RusR):Jan79-118

Navasky, V.S. Naming Names.
D. Aaron, 453(NYRB):4Dec80-6
C. Lehmann-Haupt, 441:16Oct80-C29
R. Sennett, 441:19Oct80-1

Navickas, J.L. Consciousness and Reality.*
O. Blanchette, 142:Sep-Dec78-389

Nayak, A. La méditation dans le bhâgavata-purâna.
A. Reix, 542:Jul-Sep79-358

Nayar, B.R. American Geopolitics and India.
S.P. Cohen, 293(JASt):May79-611

Nayar, B.R. Violence and Crime in India.
S.J. Moore, 293(JASt):Feb79-406

Naylor, K.E. - see "Balkanistica"

Nebelova, S.L. Mifologija Drevneindijskogo epoca.
L. Sternbach, 318(JAOS):Jul-Sep78-323

de Nebrija, A. Reglas de orthografía en la lengua castellana. (A. Quilis, ed)
Y. Malkiel, 263(RIB):Vol29No1-103

Nédoncelle, M. Sensation séparatrice et dynamisme temporel des consciences.
M. Adam, 542:Jul-Sep79-371

Nee, V. and J. Peck, eds. China's Uninterrupted Revolution.
R. Witke, 293(JASt):Nov78-145

Needham, G.I. - see Aelfric

Needham, J., with Ho Ping-yü and Lu Gwei-djen. Science and Civilization in China. (Vol 5, Pt 3)
L.C. Goodrich, 318(JAOS):Oct-Dec78-536

Needham, P., ed. William Morris and the Art of the Book.*
M. Steig, 637(VS):Autumn77-106

Neevel, W.G., Jr. Yāmuna's Vedānta Pāñcarātra.
R.C. Lester, 293(JASt):Aug79-792

Negley, G. Utopian Literature.
A.M., 125:Winter79-308

Negoiţă, C.V. and D.A. Ralescu. Applications of Fuzzy Sets to Systems Analysis.
J.A. Goguen, 316:Jun79-284

Negoiţescu, I. and R. Stanca. Un roman epistolar.
V. Nemoianu, 574(SEEJ):Summer79-315

Nehama, J. Dictionnaire du judéo-espagnol.
D. Lida, 400(MLN):Mar79-424

Nehls, D. Semantik und Syntax des englischen Verbs. (Pt 1)
B. Kettemann, 257(IRAL):May79-176

Nehring, K. Matthias Corvinus, Kaiser Friedrich III. und das Reich.
T. von Bogyay, 182:Vol131#3/4-117

Neighbour, O. The Consort and Keyboard Music of William Byrd.*
I. Fenlon, 415:Aug79-652

Neihardt, J.G. Patterns and Coincidences.*
M. Ellmann, 569(SR):Spring79-332

Neill, W.T. Archaeology and a Science of Man.
M. Tamplin, 529(QQ):Winter79/80-731

Neinstein, R. The Ghost Country.
G. Haslam, 649(WAL):Fall79-245

Neiswender, R. - see Horak, S.M.

Nekipelov, V. Institute of Fools. (M. Carynnyk and M. Horban, eds and trans)
S. Bloch, 617(TLS):15Aug80-910
A. Clare, 362:26Jun80-837
H. Fireside, 441:16Mar80-11
P. Reddaway, 453(NYRB):20Mar80-8

Nekrich, A.M. The Punished Peoples.
L. Tillett, 550(RusR):Jan79-102

Nell, O. Acting on Principle.*
T.E. Hill, Jr., 185:Apr79-306

Nelsen, H.W. The Chinese Military System.
J.D. Pollack, 293(JASt):Feb79-355

Nelsen, R.W. and D.A. Nock, eds. Reading, Writing and Riches.
R.M. Pike, 529(QQ):Winter79/80-701

Nelson, A.H. - see Medwall, H.

Nelson, A.K., ed. The Records of Federal Officials.
F.H. Mackaman, 14:Oct79-474

Nelson, C.A., ed. A Critical Edition of "Wit's Triumvirate, or The Philosopher."*
A. Haaker, 402(MLR):Oct79-900

Nelson, D.A., ed. El Libro de Alixandre.
J.F. Burke, 304(JHP):Winter80-171

Nelson, D.T. - see Koren, E.

Nelson, G. Charity's Child.
L. Duguid, 617(TLS):16May80-558

Nelson, K. The Tennis Player and Other Stories.*
639(VQR):Autumn78-136

Nelson, S. Blood Poems.
G. Hamel, 198:Winter80-139

Nelson, S. The Last Year of the War.*
639(VQR):Summer79-102

Nelson, W. The Siege of Buckingham Palace.
N. Callendar, 441:1Jun80-20

Nelson, W.H. and T. Prittie. The Economic War Against the Jews.*
G. Sauer, 287:Feb78-26

Nemec, D. Bright Lights, Dark Rooms.
N. Callendar, 441:20Jul80-16

Nemedi, L. Die Geschichte der deutschen Literatur im 18. Jahrhundert.
A. Klingenberg, 654(WB):1/1978-183

Nemerov, H. The Collected Poems of Howard Nemerov.*
J. Ditsky, 628(UWR):Fall-Winter78-86
B. Quinn, 580(SCR):Nov78-126
B. Raffel, 385(MQR):Spring80-251
K. Whitehill, 639(VQR):Spring78-368

Nemerov, H. Figures of Thought.*
E. Proffitt, 134(CP):Fall78-97

Nemoianu, V. Micro-Harmony.
T.G. Pavel, 107(CRCL):Fall79-446

Nenci, G. and G. Vallet, eds. Bibliografia topografica della colonizzazione greca in Italia e nelle Isole Tirreniche. (Vol 1)
J. Boardman, 123:Vol29No2-327

Nenner, H. By Colour of Law.
G.H. Jones, 173(ECS):Spring79-448

Nentwich, M. Der "schottische Shaw."
  K. Tetzeli von Rosador, 72:Band216
  Heft2-416
Nepaulsingh, C.I. - see Imperial, M.F.
Nepos. Cornelii Nepotis vitae cum frag-
  mentis. (P.K. Marshall, ed)
  M. Winterbottom, 123:Vol29No1-55
Neri, U. - see Saint Basil
Nerlich, M. Kritik der Abenteuer-Ideolo-
  gie.
  M. Kesting, 547(RF):Band91Heft1/2-157
Neruda, P. Libro de las preguntas.
  O. Hahn, 263(RIB):Vol29No1-97
Neruda, P. Memoirs.
  A. Graham-Yooll, 364:Jul79-94
  R. Varney, 639(VQR):Winter78-180
Neruda, P. Odi elementari. (G.B. De
  Cesare, ed)
  G. Bellini, 263(RIB):Vol29No1-99
de Nerval, G. Pandora. (J. Guillaume, ed)
  M. Delcroix, 535(RHL):Jan-Feb78-140
de Nerval, G. Pandora, Les Amours de
  Vienne. (J. Senelier, with others, eds)
  M. Delcroix, 556(RLV):1978/3-266
Nery da Fonseca, E. - see Freyre, G.
Nesbitt, C. A Little Love and Good Com-
  pany.
  639(VQR):Winter78-28
Nestori, A. Repertorio topografico delle
  pitture delle catacombe romane.
  P. Llewellyn, 313:Vol69-237
Nestroy, J. Johann Nestroy-Briefe. (W.
  Obermaier, ed)
  J.A. Kruse, 182:Vol131#1/2-38
  H. Zohn, 222(GR):Summer79-136
Netboy, A. Salmon.
  A. Wheeler, 617(TLS):9May80-536
Nettel, R. Havergal Brian and His Music.
  J.H.E., 412:Feb78-64
Nettelbeck, C.W. - see Céline, L-F.
Nettels, E. James and Conrad.*
  C.J. Rawson, 402(MLR):Oct79-928
Nettl, B., ed. Eight Urban Musical
  Cultures.
  R. Kauffman, 187:Sep80-596
Nettleford, R.M. Caribbean Cultural Iden-
  tity.
  H. Raymont, 263(RIB):Vol29No2-202
Netzer, D. The Subsidized Muse.
  B. Bordelon, 151:Dec78-96
Neu, J. Emotion, Thought and Therapy.
  D.R.L., 543:Jun79-763
  W. Lyons, 479(PhQ):Apr79-179
  I. Thalberg, 482(PhR):Jan79-151
Neubauer, J. Symbolismus und symbolische
  Logik.
  G. Gillespie, 400(MLN):Dec79-1231
  R. Immerwahr, 564:Nov79-314
Neubecker, A.J. Altgriechische Musik.
  M.O. Lee, 487:Winter79-362
Neuberg, V.E. Popular Literature.
  L. James, 447(N&Q):Aug78-384
Neubert, B. Der Aussenseiter im deutschen
  Roman nach 1945.
  H.P. Braendlin, 406:Summer79-214
Neugeboren, J. - see Foley, M.

Neuhäuser, R., ed. The Romantic Age in
  Russian Literature.
  R.S. Struc, 107(CRCL):Fall79-448
Neumann, F. Musikalische Syntax und Form
  im Liederzyklus "Die schöne Müllerin"
  von Franz Schubert.
  J. Reed, 410(M&L):Apr79-223
Neumann, F. Ornamentation in Baroque and
  Post-Baroque Music, with Special Empha-
  sis on J.S. Bach.*
  L. Lindgren, 414(MusQ):Oct79-597
Neumann, G. Ideenparadiese.
  M.H., 191(ELN):Sep78(supp)-135
Neumeister, E. De Poetis Germanicis.
  G. Dünnhaupt, 597(SN):Vol150#2-338
Neumeister-Taroni, B. Theodor Fontane.
  F. Betz, 406:Spring79-97
Neuner, G. and others, eds. Allgemein-
  bildung, Lehrplanwerk, Unterricht.
  K. Schröder, 430(NS):Feb78-93
Neureiter, F. Geschichte der kaschu-
  bischen Literatur.
  G. Stone, 402(MLR):Apr79-511
Neusch, M. and B. Chenu. Au pays de la
  théologie.
  J-M. Gabaude, 542:Oct-Dec79-455
Neuss, P. All Girls Together.*
  I. Colegate, 617(TLS):11Jan80-46
Nevelson, L. Dawns and Dusks.
  P.K. Connor, 658:Autumn79-326
New, A. A Guide to the Cathedrals of
  Britain.
  P. Metcalf, 617(TLS):18Jul80-818
New, W.H. Malcolm Lowry.
  W.M. Hagen, 594:Spring79-121
"New Poetry 4." (F. Adcock and A. Thwaite,
  eds)
  N. Lowry, 493:Dec79-70
"New Provinces."
  W.J. Keith, 105:Spring/Summer79-120
"The 'New' World Encyclopedia of Cooking."
  W. and C. Cowen, 639(VQR):Spring79-76
Newby, E. The Big Red Train Ride.*
  639(VQR):Autumn79-143
Newby, P.H. Warrior Pharaohs.
  E.S. Turner, 362:25Sep80-410
Newcomb, W.W., Jr., with M.S. Carnahan.
  German Artist on the Texas Frontier.
  W. Gard, 584(SWR):Winter79-89
Newcombe, T. - see Erart, J.
Newcombe, T.H. - see Thibaut de Blaison
Newhall, N. Ansel Adams: The Eloquent
  Light.
  C. James, 453(NYRB):18Dec80-22
  H. Kramer, 441:30Nov80-66
Newhall, N. - see Strand, P.
Newlin, D. Schoenberg Remembered.
  R. Craft, 453(NYRB):18Dec80-34
  J. Peyser, 441:21Sep80-12
Newlove, J. The Fat Man.*
  R. Skelton, 102(CanL):Winter78-101
Newman, A. Artists.
  C.S., 441:28Dec80-5
Newman, A. The Great British.
  J. Naughton, 362:3Jan80-29

Newman, A.S. Une Poésie des Discours.*
   G. Idt, 535(RHL):Sep-Oct79-886
   V. Minogue, 208(FS):Vol33Pt2-912
Newman, D. Subscribe Now!
   B. Bordelon, 151:Dec78-97
Newman, E. Sunday Punch.*
   639(VQR):Autumn79-138
Newman, H. An Illustrated Dictionary of
   Glass.*
   H.K. Littleton, 139:Feb79-18
   G. Wills, 39:Dec79-532
Newman, J.H. The Idea of a University
   Defined and Illustrated.* (I.T. Ker, ed)
   D.J. De Laura, 402(MLR):Apr79-427
Newman, J.H. The Letters and Diaries of
   John Henry Newman. (Vol 1) (I. Ker and
   T. Gornall, eds)
   A.M. Allchin, 362:22May80-646
   V.F. Blehl, 613:Mar79-104
   A.G. Hill, 541(RES):Aug79-360
Newman, J.H. The Letters and Diaries of
   John Henry Newman. (Vols 2 and 3) (I.
   Ker and T. Gornall, eds)
   A.M. Allchin, 362:22May80-646
Newman, J.H. The Letters and Diaries of
   John Henry Newman. (Vol 4) (I. Ker and
   T. Gornall, eds)
   A.M. Allchin, 362:22May80-646
   M. Trevor, 617(TLS):1Aug80-866
Newman, J.H. John Henry Newman and the
   Abbé Jager. (L. Allen, ed)
   A.R. Vidler, 208(FS):Vol33Pt2-850
Newman, J.H. The Theological Papers of
   John Henry Newman on Biblical Inspira-
   tion and on Infallibility.* (J.D.
   Holmes, ed)
   M. Trevor, 617(TLS):1Aug80-866
Newman, L.M. Gordon Craig Archives.*
   B. Erbe, 610:May78-229
Newman, L.M. German Language and Litera-
   ture. (2nd ed)
   R. Gray, 617(TLS):11Jan80-45
Newman, O. Community of Interest.
   C. Seebohm, 441:20Jan80-16
Newsom, R. Dickens on the Romantic Side
   of Familiar Things.*
   R. Maxwell, 637(VS):Winter79-216
   B.B. Pratt, 445(NCF):Sep78-262
Newsom, S. and J.C. Picturesque Califor-
   nia Homes.
   E.A-R., 46:Aug79-69
Newsome, D. On the Edge of Paradise.
   J. Bayley, 362:3Jul80-21
   A. Bell, 617(TLS):5Sep80-953
Newton, D.A. Think Like a Man, Act Like
   a Lady, Work Like a Dog.
   639(VQR):Autumn79-151
Newton, H. Sleepless Nights.
   C. James, 453(NYRB):18Dec80-22
Newton, I. The Correspondence of Isaac
   Newton. (Vols 5-7) (A.R. Hall and L.
   Tilling, eds)
   R.S. Westfall, 84:Jun79-173
Newton, P.A. The County of Oxford.
   J. Sumption, 617(TLS):21Mar80-335

Newton-De Molina, D., ed. The Literary
   Criticism of T.S. Eliot.*
   M. Dodsworth, 541(RES):May79-247
   R.M. Ludwig, 295(JML):Vol7#4-690
Newton-Smith, W.H. The Structure of Time.
   R.G. Swinburne, 617(TLS):16May80-564
Neyt, F. La grande statuaire Hemba du
   Zaire.
   D.P. Biebuyck, 2(AfrA):Nov78-19
Nguyễn Đăng Liêm. Cases, Clauses and
   Sentences in Vietnamese.
   Nguyễn Đình-Hoà, 350:Sep79-749
Nguyễn Kim Thản. Động-từ trong tiếng Việt.
   Nguyễn Đình-Hoà, 350:Dec79-964
Nguyễn Văn Tu. Từ và vốn từ tiếng Việt
   hiện-đại.
   Nguyễn Đình-Hoà, 350:Dec79-965
Nhỉm, Đ.C. and J. Donaldson. Păp san
   khhăm pak Tãy-Keo-Eng.
   H.T. Châu, 682(ZPSK):Band31Heft1-83
Niall, B. Martin Boyd.
   A. Lawson, 71(ALS):Oct79-257
"Das Nibelungenlied, nach der Handschrift
   C."* (U. Hennig, ed)
   M.S. Batts, 133:Band12Heft1/2-140
   J.M. Clifton-Everest, 67:Nov79-352
   W. Schröder, 684(ZDA):Band107Heft3-110
Nicander. Eutecnii Paraphrasis in Nican-
   dri Alexipharmaca.* (M. Geymonat, ed)
   R. Browning, 123:Vol29No1-147
Nichol, B.P. Journal.* Craft Dinner.*
   Translating Translating Apollinaire.
   B. Henderson, 99:Feb80-36
Nicholas, H.G. The Nature of American
   Politics.
   M. Beloff, 617(TLS):29Feb80-230
Nicholl, C. The Chemical Theatre.
   D.J. Enright, 362:20Nov80-698
Nicholls, D. From Dessalines to Duvalier.
   N. Stone, 617(TLS):15Feb80-161
Nicholls, J.C. - see Riccoboni, M-J.
Nichols, C.H. - see Bontemps, A. and L.
   Hughes
Nichols, F.D. The Architecture of
   Georgia.
   S. Wilson, Jr., 576:Oct78-210
Nichols, F.D. and R.E. Griswold. Thomas
   Jefferson: Landscape Architect.
   J.F. Davis, 658:Spring79-97
Nichols, G.C. Miguel Hernández.
   J. Crispin, 399(MLJ):Apr79-234
Nichols, N. Murrey.
   42(AR):Summer79-379
Nichols, R. Ravel.*
   J.B., 412:Aug-Nov78-278
   C. Bennett, 607:Sep78-48
Nichols, R.L. and T.G. Stavrou, eds.
   Russian Orthodoxy under the Old Regime.
   N.V. Riasanovsky, 550(RusR):Apr79-223
Nicholson, D.E.T. - see Rogier, P.
Nicholson, N. The Shadow of Black Combe.
   A. Cluysenaar, 565:Vol120#3-68
   A.Y., 148:Spring79-94
Nicholson, S.T. Abortion and the Roman
   Catholic Church.
   G. Meilaender, 613:Jun79-206
   J. Teichman, 479(PhQ):Oct79-376

Nickau, K. Untersuchungen zur textkritis-
chen Methode des Zenodotos von Ephesos.
  W.L. Slater, 123:Vol29No1-20
  F. Vian, 555:Vol52fasc1-145
Nicolai, H. Zeittafel zu Goethes Leben
und Werk.
  I.H. Solbrig, 406:Winter79-447
Nicolaisen, W.F.H. Scottish Place-Names.*
  J.M. Dodgson, 203:Vol89#1-114
  K.B. Harder, 292(JAF):Jul-Sep79-357
Nicolaou, K. The Historical Topography of
Kition.*
  O. Masson, 555:Vol52fasc1-139
Nicole, C. The Secret Memoirs of Lord
Byron.
  639(VQR):Spring79-59
Nicole, C. Sunset.
  639(VQR):Autumn78-136
Nicolet, C. Rome et la conquête du monde
méditerranéen 264-27 avant J-C. (Vol 1)
  J.W. Rich, 123:Vol29No2-272
Nicoll, A. The Garrick Stage.
  R. Savage, 617(TLS):2May80-494
Nicoll, J. Dante Gabriel Rossetti.
  D. Sonstroem, 637(VS):Autumn77-131
Nicols, J. Vespasian and the Partes Flavi-
anae.
  F. Lasserre, 182:Vol131#9/10-301
Nicolson, B. The International Caravag-
gesque Movement.
  R.E. Spear, 90:May79-317
Nicolson, H. Harold Nicolson: Diaries and
Letters 1930-1964. (S. Olson, ed)
  R.R. James, 362:9Oct80-475
Nicolson, N. and J. Trautmann - see Woolf,
V.
Nicosia, S. Tradizione testuale diretta e
indiretta dei poeti di Lesbo.*
  A.M. Bowie, 123:Vol29No1-136
Nida, E. Componential Analysis of Mean-
ing.
  A. Lehrer, 603:Vol3#2-283
Niderst, A. Madeleine de Scudéry, Paul
Pellisson et leur monde.
  M. Cuénin, 535(RHL):Jul-Aug78-634
Niderst, A. Les Tragédies de Racine.
  M. Delcroix, 535(RHL):Jul-Aug79-659
Niderst, A. - see Bayle, P.
Niderst, A.L. La Princesse de Clèves de
Madame de Lafayette.
  S.W. Tiefenbrun, 475:No.10Pt1-187
Niebaum, H. Zur synchronischen und his-
torischen Phonologie des Westfälischen.
  G. Lerchner, 682(ZPSK):Band31Heft6-632
Nieddu, A.M. George Herbert Mead.
  T.J.S., 543:Jun79-765
Nielsen, G.R. In Search of a Home.
  H. Dalic, 575(SEER):Jul79-453
Nielsen, J.E. Den samtidige engelske
litteratur og Danmark, 1800-1840.
  P.M. Mitchell, 562(Scan):May79-63
  K.H. Ober, 301(JEGP):Apr79-286
Nielsen, V.L. Familiar as a Sparrow.
  M. Swenson, 649(WAL):Fall79-240
Niemeijer, J.W. Cornelis Troost, 1696-
1750.
  P. Eikemeier, 471:Apr/May/Jun79-177

Niemeyer, G. - see Voegelin, E.
Niemeyer, H.G. Studien zur statuarischen
Darstellung der römischen Kaiser.
  A.R. Neumann, 182:Vol131#5/6-161
Nienhauser, W.H. and others. Liu Tsung-
yüan.
  L.Y. Chiu, 302:Vol16#1and2-124
Nieraad, J. "bildgesegnet und bildver-
flucht."
  E. Marold, 343:Band23-40
Nies, F. Gattungspoetik und Publikums-
struktur.
  B. Bray, 535(RHL):Jan-Feb78-116
Nies, F., ed. Genres mineurs.
  J. Proust, 547(RF):Band91Heft3-325
Niethammer, L., U. Borsdorf and P. Brandt,
eds. Arbeiterinitiative 1945.
  A. Lasserre, 182:Vol131#5/6-182
Nietzsche, F. Ecrits posthumes, 1870-
1873.* (G. Colli and M. Montinari, eds)
Le nihilisme européen. (A. Kremer-
Marietti, ed and trans) La naissance de
la tragédie. (G. Colli and M. Monti-
nari, eds)
  E. Blondel, 542:Jan-Mar79-83
Niggl, G. Geschichte der deutschen Auto-
biographie im 18. Jahrhundert.
  J. Jacobs, 680(ZDP):Band97Heft4-625
  C.C. Zorach, 406:Winter79-481
Nihalani, P., R.K. Tongue and P. Hosali.
Indian and British English.
  V.D. Singh, 608:Jun80-233
Nijinsky, R. Nijinsky [and] The Last
Years of Nijinsky.
  S. Trotter, 362:10Apr80-481
Nikitin, B. and L. Die Nikitin-Kinder.
  (M. Butenschön, ed and trans)
  J-D. de Lannoy, 182:Vol131#19-650
Nikodim. Johannes XXIII. — ein unbequemer
Optimist. (R. Hotz, ed)
  E.W. Gritsch, 182:Vol131#23/24-848
Nikula, H. Verbvalenz.
  I. Persson, 597(SN):Vol50#1-123
Nilsen, D.L.F. and A.P. Language Play.
  L.F. Dean, 35(AS):Fall79-232
  C.F. McCreary, 399(MLJ):Mar79-136
  G. Morain, 399(MLJ):Sep-Oct79-301
Nilsen, D.L.F. and A.P. Pronunciation
Contrasts in English.
  O. Akhmanova, 353:Jun78-69
Nilsen, D.L.F. and A.P. Semantic Theory.
  J. Andor, 353:Jan78-63
Nilsson, N.Å., ed. Boris Pasternak.*
  W.F. Kolonosky, 574(SEEJ):Summer79-
  284
  B.H. Monter, 104(CASS):Summer78-288
Nilsson, S.Å. Hillefanten.
  G. Söderström, 341:1978/2-87
Nimmo, D. Political Communication and
Public Opinion in America.
  S.P. Gwin, 583:Spring79-314
Nin, A. Les Cités intérieures.
  C. Jordis, 450(NRF):Mar79-132
Nin, A. The Diary of Anaïs Nin. (Vol 7)
  (G. Stuhlmann, ed)
  K. Pollitt, 441:13Jul80-7
  J. Wolcott, 453(NYRB):26Jun80-21

Nin, A. Linotte.
639(VQR):Winter79-10

"The Ninth Level."
S.G. Widdifield, 2(AfrA):Feb79-85

Nisbet, R. History of the Idea of Progress.
J.M. Cameron, 453(NYRB):17Apr80-36
C. Lehmann-Haupt, 441:21Apr80-C17
F.E. Manuel, 441:16Mar80-1
61:Feb80-97
442(NY):12May80-162

Nisbet, R.G.M. and M. Hubbard. A Commentary on Horace "Odes" Book II.
R. Seager, 617(TLS):11Jan80-44

Nishikawa, K. Bugaku Masks.
P.C. Swann, 463:Spring79-117

Nitzsche, J.C. Tolkien's Art.
J. Batchelor, 617(TLS):18Jan80-69

Niven, A. D.H. Lawrence: The Novels.*
D. Bartholomeusz, 67:May79-116
P. Eggert, 140(CR):#21-72
K.M. Hewitt, 541(RES):May79-232
K. Wilson, 255(HAB):Summer79-228
295(JML):Vol7#4-759

Niven, A.C. A Brief History of Russia to 1689. Napoleon and Alexander I.
J. Cracraft, 550(RusR):Jul79-360

Nixon, R. The Real War.
F. Lewis, 441:25May80-7
R. Steel, 453(NYRB):26Jun80-18

Nkwi, P.N. Traditional Government and Social Change.
J-P. Warnier, 69:Vol48#3-305

Noble, A.G. and A.K. Dutt, eds. Indian Urbanization and Planning.
H. Spodek, 293(JASt):Aug79-815

Noble, C. Haywire Rainbow.
D. Barbour, 150(DR):Spring79-154
P. Hall, 628(UWR):Spring-Summer79-107

Noble, D.R. - see Tucker, G.

Noble, D.R. and J.L. Thomas, eds. The Rising South.* (Vol 1)
K. King, 577(SHR):Summer79-270

Noble, J. and J. Lacasa. Spanish - A Basic Course. (2nd ed)
R. Lamiroy, 277(ITL):#39/40-152

Noble, J. and W. The Private Me.
C. Seebohm, 441:13Apr80-15

Noble, P.S. - see Nompar V of Caumont

Noble, V. Nicknames Past and Present.
E.C. Smith, 424:Sep78-293

Noble, Y., ed. Twentieth Century Interpretations of "The Beggar's Opera."
J. Michon, 189(EA):Jan-Mar78-88

Noblitt, J.S. Nouveau Point de vue.
B. Ebling 2d, 207(FR):Apr79-786

Nochlin, L. Gustave Courbet.
G.P. Weisberg, 54:Jun78-376

Noël, B. Le 19 octobre 1977.
F. de Martinoir, 450(NRF):Oct79-135

Noel, G. The Anatomy of the Catholic Church.
P. Hebblethwaite, 617(TLS):21Mar80-309

Noer, D. The Modernist Muslim Movement in Indonesia, 1900-1942.
A.J.W. Huisman, 318(JAOS):Apr-Jun78-168

Nogueira Batalha, G. Glossário do dialecto macaense.
H. Kröll, 72:Band216Heft1-191

Nohlen, K. and W. Radt. Altertümer von Pergamon. (Vol 12)
M. Vickers, 123:Vol129No1-183

Nohrnberg, J. The Analogy of "The Faerie Queene."*
W. Blissett, 627(UTQ):Fall78-76
M. Dodsworth, 175:Spring79-43
A.C. Hamilton, 191(ELN):Mar79-238
J.E. Hankins, 405(MP):Nov79-200
H.L. Weatherby, 569(SR):Summer79-490

Nøjgaard, M. Elevation et expansion.
M. Delcroix, 556(RLV):1978/4-365

Nolan, B. The Gothic Visionary Perspective.*
R.K. Emmerson, 405(MP):May80-409

Nolan, C.J., Jr. Aaron Burr and the American Literary Imagination.
W.L. Hedges, 165(EAL):Winter80/81-283

Nolan, D., ed. Dante Commentaries.
J.C. Barnes, 402(MLR):Oct79-958
L.V. Ryan, 276:Winter79-405

Nolte, W.H. Rock and Hawk.
F.I. Carpenter, 27(AL):Mar79-125
J.A. Herndon, 649(WAL):Fall79-250
R.I. Scott, 106:Fall79-231

Nomani, M. Meaning and Message of the Traditions. (Vol 1)
S.A.W. Bukhari, 273(IC):Apr77-157

Nompar V of Caumont. Le Voyage d'Oultremer en Jherusalem de Nompar, Seigneur de Caumont.* (P.S. Noble, ed)
G.A. Usher, 208(FS):Vol133Pt2-581

Nonnus. Nonnos de Panopolis, "Les Dionysiaques."* (Vol 1 ed and trans by F. Vian, Vol 2 ed and trans by P. Chuvin)
G. Chrétien, 555:Vol152fasc1-181

Norbeck, E. Changing Japan. (2nd ed)
M.D. Zamora and J.H. Hicks, 302:Vol16-#1and2-106

Nordhoff, J.J. Eastwind/Westwind.
N. Callendar, 441:9Mar80-17

Nordin, S. Interpretation and Method.*
M. Wheeler, 89(BJA):Summer79-283

Nordström, F. The Auxerre Reliefs.
P. Kurmann, 683:Band41Heft2-165

Nori, C. French Photography From Its Origins to the Present.
G. Thornton, 55:Nov79-44

Norihiko, U. - see under Učida Norihiko

Norman, A.F. - see Libanius

Norman, D. Fitzempress' Law.
H. Eley, 617(TLS):29Feb80-246

Norman, E.R. Church and Society in England, 1770-1970.
H. McLeod, 637(VS):Winter78-245

Norman, F. The Dead Butler Caper.
639(VQR):Autumn79-140

Norman, F. Too Many Crooks Spoil the Caper.
N. Callendar, 441:23Nov80-37

Norman, J. A Concise Manchu-English Lexicon.
B. Comrie, 350:Sep79-750

Norris, C.C. William Empson and the Philosophy of Literary Criticism.*
  W.E. Cain, 639(VQR):Summer79-540
  J. Colmer, 67:May79-109
  G. Mead, 89(BJA):Spring79-181
  A.D. Nuttall, 479(PhQ):Oct79-380
  J.M. Purcell, 569(SR):Fall79-xcii
Norris, G. Rakhmaninov.
  J.B., 412:Aug-Nov78-278
Norris, G. Stanford, the Cambridge Jubilee and Tchaikovsky.
  J. Joubert, 617(TLS):25Jul80-830
Norris, K. Report on the Second Half of the Twentieth Century.
  G. Davies, 168(ECW):Spring78-82
Norris, K. and T. Konyves. Proverbsi.
  G. Davies, 168(ECW):Spring78-82
Norris, L. Water Voices.
  E.L. Wright, 617(TLS):25Jul80-851
Norris, M. The Decentered Universe of "Finnegans Wake."*
  S.A. Henke, 639(VQR):Spring79-371
  B.P. O Hehir, 454:Fall78-78
  295(JML):Vol7#4-749
Norris, M. Monumental Brasses — The Craft.*
  C. Oman, 90:Aug79-527
  J.T. Rosenthal, 589:Jul79-603
Norrman, M. I livets hand.
  H.H. Borland, 563(SS):Spring79-200
Norrman, R. Techniques of Ambiguity in the Fiction of Henry James.
  R. Gard, 447(N&Q):Aug78-375
  M. Hirst, 184(EIC):Oct79-369
  C. Wegelin, 395(MFS):Summer78-261
Norstedt, J.A. Thomas MacDonagh.
  F.S.L. Lyons, 617(TLS):16May80-557
North, H.F., ed. Interpretations of Plato.
  Q. Lauer, 124:Nov79-196
  J.R., 543:Dec78-365
North, S. 209 Thriller Road.
  N. Callendar, 441:14Sep80-22
"North-South, A Program for Survival."
  W. Leontief, 453(NYRB):4Dec80-45
Northey, M. The Haunted Wilderness.*
  M.V. Dimić, 107(CRCL):Spring79-222
  J. Ferns, 402(MLR):Jan79-185
Norton, B.A. Edwin Whitefield — Nineteenth-Century North American Scenery.
  W.E. Washburn, 658:Autumn79-319
Norton, D.L. Personal Destinies.*
  T.R. Machan, 321:Autumn78-204
Norton, F.J. A Descriptive Catalogue of Printing in Spain and Portugal 1501-1520.
  P. Needham, 617(TLS):4Apr80-398
  K. Whinnom, 86(BHS):Jul79-246
Norton, M.B. Liberty's Daughters.
  L. Stone, 441:20Apr80-9
Norton, P. Dissension in the House of Commons 1974-1979.
  G. Kaufman, 362:10Jul80-53
Norton, T. Thomas Norton's "Ordinal of Alchemy."* (J. Reidy, ed)
  A. Crépin, 189(EA):Jan-Mar78-82
Norton-Smith, J. Bodleian Library MS Fairfax 16.
  T.A. Shippey, 617(TLS):7Mar80-272

Norton-Smith, J. and I. Pravda, eds. The Quare of Jelusy.*
  N.F. Blake, 402(MLR):Jan79-158
  D. Speed, 67:May79-84
Norton-Taylor, D. God's Man.
  61:Apr80-125
Nostradamus, M. The Prophecies and Enigmas of Nostradamus. (L.E. Le Vert, ed and trans)
  F. Yates, 617(TLS):14Mar80-285
"Not! the Nine O'Clock News."
  M. Warnock, 362:27Nov80-729
Nöth, W. Dynamik semiotischer Systeme.
  E. Burgschmidt, 343:Band23-206
Nottebohm, G. - see van Beethoven, L.
Nouhaud, D. - see Asturias, M.A.
Nourissier, F. Le Musée de l'homme.
  M. Mohrt, 450(NRF):Apr79-118
Nourrit, C. and B. Pruitt, eds. Musique traditionnelle de l'Afrique Noire. (Vols 1-4 and 11)
  A.P. Merriam, 187:May80-309
Nouvel, A. Les Noms de la roche et de la montagne dans les termes occitans et les noms de lieux du Massif Central (Aveyron, Cantal, Gard, Lozère, Hérault).
  J-P. Chambon, 553(RLiR):Jul-Dec78-456
Nova, C. Incandescence.*
  E. Korn, 617(TLS):25Apr80-470
  G. Perez, 249(HudR):Autumn79-470
Novak, B. Nature and Culture.
  A. Broyard, 441:7Jun80-17
  B. Rose, 441:27Apr80-9
  J. Russell, 453(NYRB):29May80-22
  442(NY):30Jun80-107
Novak, D. The Wheel of Servitude.
  639(VQR):Autumn78-147
Novak, M.E., ed. English Literature in the Age of Disguise.*
  R.L. Brett, 541(RES):Feb79-94
  C.J. Horne, 67:May79-99
  P.M. Spacks, 173(ECS):Summer79-545
Novak, M.E. and D.S. Rodes - see Southerne, T.
Novak, S.J. The Rights of Youth.
  D.C. Humphrey, 656(WMQ):Jan79-149
Novak, W. High Culture.
  D. Grumbach, 441:30Mar80-13
Novalis. Schriften. (Vol 1) (3rd ed) (P. Kluckhohn and R. Samuel, with others, eds)
  R. Immerwahr, 564:Sep79-232
  E. Stopp, 402(MLR):Jan79-246
Nove, A. Political Economy and Soviet Socialism.
  A. Brown, 617(TLS):25Jan80-95
Novitz, D. Pictures and Their Use in Communication.*
  M. Stchedroff, 518:May79-96
Nowak, S. Understanding and Prediction.
  T. Benton, 393(Mind):Jan79-129
Nowlan, A. and W. Learning. Frankenstein.
  M. Page, 648(WCR):Oct78-55
Noyer-Weidner, A., ed. Baudelaire.*
  G. Chesters, 208(FS):Vol33Pt2-829
  H. Felten, 547(RF):Band91Heft1/2-204
[continued]

Noyer-Weidner, A., ed. Baudelaire. [continuing]
    M. Lehtonen, 439(NM):1978/2-187
    H. Stenzel, 535(RHL):Jul-Aug79-690
Nozick, R. Anarchy, State, and Utopia.*
    P. O'Neil, 477:Oct79-429
Nugent, R. Paul Eluard.
    M.M. Callander, 208(FS):Vol33Pt2-897
"Number One Northern, Poetry From Saskatchewan."
    D. Carpenter, 102(CanL):Spring79-101
Nuño, J.A.G. - see under Gaya Nuño, J.A.
Nurmi, R. A Plain and Easy Introduction to the Harpsichord.
    H. Schott, 415:Feb79-131
Nurse, G.T. and T. Jenkins. Health and the Hunter-Gatherer.
    A. Stevens, 69:Vol48#4-411
Nurse, P.H. - see Corneille, P.
Nussbaum, M.C. - see Aristotle
Nusser, P., ed. Didaktik der Trivialliteratur.
    K.F. Geiger, 196:Band19Heft1/2-166
Nuttall, A.D. Dostoevsky's "Crime and Punishment."
    T. Pachmuss, 550(RusR):Oct79-507
Nuttall, G.F. New College, London, and Its Library.
    J.M.P., 568(SCN):Spring-Summer79-36
Nuttall, J. Performance Art.
    M. Coveney, 617(TLS):15Feb80-188
Nye, R. Faust.
    J. Naughton, 362:16Oct80-513

Oakes, P. From Middle England.
    D.A.N. Jones, 362:19Jun80-802
    V. Scannell, 617(TLS):27Jun80-731
Oakley, B. Walking Through Tigerland.
    G. Davenport, 249(HudR):Spring79-139
Oakley, W. Sucking the Breath of Texts, Wooing the Sky.
    D. Wyrcoff, 526:Winter79-95
Oakman, R.L. Computer Methods for Literary Research.
    T.K. Bender, 365:Summer80-147
    L.D. Burnard, 617(TLS):9May80-533
Oates, J. Babylon.
    N. Hammond, 617(TLS):8Feb80-147
Oates, J.C. All the Good People I've Left Behind.
    376:Oct79-143
Oates, J.C. Bellefleur.
    J. Gardner, 441:20Jul80-1
    J. Leonard, 441:21Jul80-C15
    F. Taliaferro, 231:Oct80-90
Oates, J.C. Night-Side.*
    639(VQR):Spring78-67
Oates, J.C. Son of the Morning.*
    G. Johnson, 584(SWR):Winter79-93
Oates, J.C. Unholy Loves.*
    A. Duchêne, 617(TLS):12Sep80-983
    J. Mellors, 362:28Aug80-281
Oates, J.C. Women Whose Lives are Food, Men Whose Lives are Money.*
    A. Cluysenaar, 565:Vol120#3-68
[continued]

[continuing]
    J. Mole, 493:Mar80-65
    639(VQR):Autumn78-145
Oates, J.C. Wonderland.
    S. Pinsker, 145(Crit):Vol20#2-59
Oates, S. Our Fiery Trial.
    E. Wright, 617(TLS):25Jan80-91
O'Barr, W.M. and J.F., eds. Language and Politics.
    B.H. Jernudd, 350:Mar79-265
Obelkevich, J. Religion and Rural Society.
    H. McLeod, 637(VS):Winter78-245
Obenauer, H-G. Études de syntaxe interrogative du français.
    P. Blumenthal, 547(RF):Band91Heft1/2-195
    J. Gérard, 209(FM):Apr78-165
    N.C.W. Spence, 208(FS):Vol33Pt2-1053
Ober, K.H. Meïr Goldschmidt.*
    L. Marx, 563(SS):Spring79-188
Ober, W.B. Boswell's Clap and Other Essays.
    R. Whittemore, 109:Winter79/80-165
Oberg, A. Modern American Lyric.*
    V. Bell, 569(SR):Spring79-308
    J. Mazzaro, 141:Spring79-182
Oberg, C.H. A Pagan Prophet.
    636(VP):Winter78-398
Oberhammer, G., ed. Offenbarung, geistige Realität des Menschen. (Vol 2)
    L. Sternbach, 318(JAOS):Jul-Sep78-322
Oberling, P. The Qashqa'i Nomads of Fars.
    R. Akbar, 273(IC):Jul77-223
Obermaier, W. - see Nestroy, J.
Obermann, J. and D. Cardone. Dialoghi sulla solitudine.
    E. Namer, 542:Jul-Sep79-372
Obolensky, C. The Russian Empire, 1855-1914.
    J. Bayley, 453(NYRB):21Feb80-14
    K. Fitz Lyon, 617(TLS):11Apr80-417
    J. Simpson, 362:24Apr80-543
Obolensky, D., ed. The Penguin Book of Russian Verse.
    V. Perelešin, 558(RLJ):Spring79-216
Obregón, M. Argonauts to Astronauts.
    P-L. Adams, 61:Jul80-87
O'Brian, P. The Fortune of War.
    T.J. Binyon, 617(TLS):15Feb80-171
O'Brian, P. The Surgeon's Mate.
    T.J. Binyon, 617(TLS):1Aug80-882
O'Brien, F. A Flann O'Brien Reader.* (S. Jones, ed)
    S. Poger, 174(Éire):Summer79-131
O'Brien, T. Going After Cacciato.*
    W. Boyd, 364:Aug/Sep79-124
    639(VQR):Summer78-92
O'Brien, T. Squaw Valley.
    R. Feld, 472:Fall/Winter79-150
Ó Broin, L. Revolutionary Underground.
    L.J. McCaffrey, 637(VS):Summer79-449
"Obscenity: Report of the Committee on Obscenity and Film Censorship."
    J. Vaizey, 362:21Feb80-250
O'Byrne, D. Selected Poems of Arnold Bax. (L. Foreman, ed)
    M. Trend, 617(TLS):15Feb80-167

Ó Canainn, T. Traditional Music in Ireland.
L.E. McCullough, 174(Éire):Fall79-154
H. Shields, 187:Sep80-594
Ó Cathasaigh, T. The Heroic Biography of Cormac Mac Airt.
P.K. Ford, 589:Oct79-836
Ocholla-Ayayo, A.B.C. Traditional Ideology and Ethics among the Southern Luo.
T.O. Beidelman, 69:Vol48#1-93
Ochrymowycz, O.R. Aspects of Oral Style in the "Romances Juglarescos" of the Carolingian Cycle.
J.J. Duggan, 240(HR):Spring78-248
Ockham, William of. Guillaume d'Occam, "Commentaire sur le livre des prédicables de Porphyre." (R. Galibois, trans)
S.F.B., 543:Dec78-359
Ockham, William of. Guillelmi de Ockham: Scriptum in Librum Primum Sententiarum. (G.I. Etzkorn, ed)
M.M. Adams, 482(PhR):Jan79-117
Ockham, William of. Guillemus de Ockham, "Opera philosophica 2." (E.A. Moody and others, eds)
A.B.W., 543:Jun79-766
O'Connell, K.G. The Theodotionic Revision of the Book of Exodus.
D. Pardee, 318(JAOS):Jul-Sep78-312
O'Connell, M. Mirror and Veil.*
M. Evans, 541(RES):Feb79-67
T.L. Steinberg, 568(SCN):Spring-Summer79-14
H.L. Weatherby, 569(SR):Summer79-490
O'Connell, R.J. Art and the Christian Intelligence in St. Augustine.*
E.L.F., 543:Mar79-561
F.J. Kovach, 290(JAAC):Winter79-195
O'Connor, E. Spirit Man.
S. Ramsey, 617(TLS):30May80-606
O'Connor, F. The Habit of Being.* (S. Fitzgerald, ed)
R.H. Brodhead, 676(YR):Spring80-451
D. Bromwich, 362:14Feb80-220
G. Core, 569(SR):Summer79-1xxviii
M.J. Friedman, 578:Spring80-114
N. Miller, 42(AR):Summer79-373
F.E. Moorer and R. Macksey, 400(MLN):Dec79-1272
C. Shloss, 418(MR):Summer79-387
529(QQ):Autumn79-556
O'Connor, F.V. and E.V. Thaw, eds. Jackson Pollock.*
R. Calvocoressi, 617(TLS):7Mar80-275
O'Connor, J.E. and M.A. Jackson, eds. American History/American Film.
W. Hughes, 18:May79-74
O'Connor, J.R. Balzac's Soluble Fish.
C. Smethurst, 208(FS):Vol33Pt2-813
O'Connor, P. The Happy Elephants.
P. Craig, 617(TLS):5Sep80-950
O'Connor, P.W. Gregorio and María Martínez Sierra.*
W. Newberry, 238:Mar79-177
O'Connor, U. Three Noh Plays.
D. Couling, 617(TLS):19Sep80-1016

OCork, S. Sports Freak.
N. Callendar, 441:27Apr80-18
O'Day, A. The English Face of Irish Nationalism.
L.J. McCaffrey, 637(VS):Summer79-449
O'Day, R. The English Clergy.
I. Roots, 617(TLS):25Apr80-476
Oddy, D.J. and D.S. Miller, eds. The Making of the Modern British Diet.
A.S. Wohl, 637(VS):Autumn77-128
O'Dell, F.A. Socialisation through Children's Literature.
A. Brown, 617(TLS):25Jan80-95
G. Hosking, 617(TLS):28Mar80-374
O'Dell-Franke, I. Kupferstiche und Radierungen aus der Werkstatt des Virgil Solis.*
T. Falk, 471:Jan/Feb/Mar79-79
K. Mayer-Haunton, 617(TLS):16May80-566
K. Pilz, 182:Vol131#13-427
Oden, T.C. - see Kierkegaard, S.
Odenkirchen, C.J. The Life of St. Alexius, in the Old French Version of the Hildesheim Manuscript.
H.F. Williams, 207(FR):May79-921
O'Donnell, W.H. - see Yeats, W.B.
Odoul, P. Le Drame intime d'Alfred de Musset.
M. Bossis, 535(RHL):Jul-Aug79-684
O'Driscoll, R. and L. Reynolds, eds. Yeats and the Theatre.
G. Melchiori, 677(YES):Vol9-341
Odrowąż-Pieniążek, J., ed. Blok-Notes Muzeum Literatury im. Adama Mickiewicza.
J.T. Baer, 497(PolR):Vol23#4-89
Oellers, N., ed. Schiller — Zeitgenosse aller Epochen.* (Pts 1 and 2)
C.G. Grawe, 67:May79-143
Oellers, N. and F. Stock - see Schiller, F.
Oelmüller, W., ed. Transzendentalphilosophische Normenbegründung.
B. Haller, 687:Jan-Mar79-160
Oenslager, D.M. The Theatre of Donald Oenslager.*
676(YR):Winter80-XIII
Oetinger, F.C. Die Lehrtafel der Prinzessin Antonia. (R. Breymeyer and F. Häussermann, eds)
F.W. Kantzenbach, 182:Vol131#21/22-779
Oetke, C. Die aus dem Chinesischen übersetzten tibetischen Versionen des Suvaṃaprabhāsasūtra.
H.V. Guenther, 318(JAOS):Oct-Dec78-577
J.W. de Jong, 259(IIJ):Oct79-300
Oettinger, N. Die Militärischen Eide der Hethiter.
G. Wilhelm, 343:Band23-95
O'Faolain, J. No Country For Young Men.
P. Craig, 617(TLS):13Jun80-674
J. Naughton, 362:29May80-697
O'Faolain, S. And Again?*
P. Lewis, 617(TLS):15Feb80-170
O'Faolain, S. Collected Stories. (Vol 1)
J. Mellors, 362:18and25Dec80-867

Opie, I. and P. A Nursery Companion.
  A. Laski, 362:25Sep80-409
Oppel, H., ed. Das englische Drama der
  Gegenwart.*
  E. Zillekens, 447(N&Q):Aug78-383
Oppelt, W. Über die "Unehrlichkeit" des
  Scharfrichters.
  L. Carlen, 182:Vol131#1/2-20
Oppen, G. Collected Poems.
  J. Freeman, 97(CQ):Vol8#3-277
Oppen, G. Primitive.
  J. Taggart, 114(ChiR):Winter79-148
  N. Wheale, 493:Dec79-43
  A. Young, 617(TLS):13Jun80-682
Oppenheimer, J.R. Robert Oppenheimer:
  Letters and Recollections. (A.K. Smith
  and C. Weiner, eds)
  R.W. Clark, 441:11May80-9
  D. Joravsky, 453(NYRB):17Jul80-7
  J. Leonard, 441:12May80-C16
  D. Newth, 362:25Sep80-406
Oppler, E. Fauvism Reexamined.
  C.R. Baldwin, 54:Mar78-187
"Opuscula Romana." (Vols 8 and 9)
  A.R. Neumann, 182:Vol131#11/12-367
O'Rahilly, C., ed and trans. Táin Bó
  Cúailnge: Recension I.*
  M.C. Ward, 382(MAE):1979/1-107
Orbach, S. Fat is a Feminist Issue.
  J. Howard, 441:16Mar80-12
Orcibal, J. - see Fénelon, F.
Orde, L. and B. Michaels. The Night They
  Stole Manhattan.
  N. Callendar, 441:27Apr80-18
Orderic Vitalis. The Ecclesiastical His-
  tory of Orderic Vitalis. (Vol 6) (M.
  Chibnall, ed and trans)
  F. Barlow, 382(MAE):1979/1-118
"Les Ordres mendiants et la ville en
  Italie centrale (v. 1220-v. 1350)."
  L.K. Little, 589:Oct79-840
O'Reilly, J. The Girl I Left Behind.
  J. Leonard, 441:29Sep80-C16
  A. McCarthy, 441:12Oct80-13
Orel, H. The Final Years of Thomas Hardy,
  1912-1928.*
  J. Halperin, 395(MFS):Summer78-303
  S. Hunter, 402(MLR):Jan79-175
  B. Johnson, 637(VS):Spring78-405
  H. Lee, 447(N&Q):Aug78-370
Orel, H., ed. Irish History and Culture.
  J.W. Weaver, 177(ELT):Vol22#1-69
de Orella y Unzue, J.L. Respuestas católi-
  cas a las Centurias de Magdeburgo (1559-
  1588).
  J.A. Jones, 86(BHS):Jul79-250
Orenstein, A. Willard van Orman Quine.
  G. Priest, 479(PhQ):Apr79-173
Orenstein, G.F. The Theater of the Mar-
  velous.*
  L. Luria-Sukenick, 651(WHR):Winter79-
  89
Orga, A. Beethoven.
  W. Drabkin, 415:Apr79-305
Organ, P. Waiting for Summer.
  K. Hewitt, 617(TLS):13Jun80-674
Orgel, S. - see Gordon, D.J.

Orgill, D. and J. Gribbin. The Sixth
  Winter.
  P. Andrews, 441:27Jan80-15
  442(NY):11Feb80-117
Origen. Origène, "Homélies sur la Genèse,"
  Introduction. (L. Doutreleau, ed and
  trans)
  P. Nautin, 555:Vol52fasc2-384
Origen. Origenes, Vier Bücher von den
  Prinzipien. (H. Görgemanns and H.
  Karpp, eds and trans)
  C. Andresen, 53(AGP):Band60Heft2-213
"Original Parish Registers, Second Supple-
  ment."
  R. Dunning, 325:Apr79-173
Orizet, J. En soi le chaos. Solaire
  Apocalypse, [précédé de] Homme année
  zéro.
  T. Greene, 207(FR):Oct78-182
Orjuela, H.H. - see Silva, J.A.
Orlandis, J. Historia de España: La
  España Visigótica.
  J.N. Hillgarth, 589:Jul79-605
Orledge, R. Gabriel Fauré.
  R.L. Smith, 617(TLS):22Aug80-941
Orlev, U. The Lead Soldiers.*
  N. Ascherson, 453(NYRB):12Jun80-34
  L. Epstein, 441:23Mar80-14
  442(NY):7Apr80-149
Orlinsky, H.M. Essays in Biblical Cul-
  ture and Bible Translation.
  D. Pardee, 318(JAOS):Jul-Sep78-343
Orlović-Schwarzwald, M. Zum Gastarbeiter-
  deutsch jugoslawischer Arbeiter im Rhein-
  Main-Gebiet.
  B. Panzer, 343:Band23-203
Ormond, J., E. Humphreys and J. Tripp.
  Penguin Modern Poets 27.
  E. Longley, 617(TLS):18Jan80-64
Ormond, R. and M. Rogers - see Davies, A.
Ormond, R. and M. Rogers - see Kilmurray,
  E.
Ormsby, F., ed. Poets from the North of
  Ireland.
  R. Garfitt, 617(TLS):15Feb80-169
Ormsby, F. A Store of Candles.*
  F. Kersnowski, 305(JIL):May78-179
Ornato, M. Dictionnaire des charges,
  emplois et métiers relevant des institu-
  tions monarchiques en France aux XIVe et
  XVe siècles.
  J.C. Laidlaw, 208(FS):Vol33Pt2-609
Oroz Arizcuren, F.J., ed and trans. La
  lírica religiosa en la literatura proven-
  zal antigua.*
  A. Fontana, 72:Band216Heft1-205
Orr, C.M. and M.J. Preston, eds. Urban
  Folklore from Colorado: Typescript Broad-
  sides.
  J.H. Brunvand, 292(JAF):Jul-Sep79-361
Orr, G. The Red House.
  C. Molesworth, 441:12Oct80-14
Orr, J. Tragic Realism and Modern
  Society.*
  G. Green, 219(GaR):Winter79-954
  J.M. Holquist, 445(NCF):Dec78-377
                              [continued]

[continuing]
S.G. Kellman, 395(MFS):Winter78/79-650
K. Widmer, 594:Spring79-99
Orr, L. A Catalogue Checklist of English
Prose Fiction, 1750-1800.
J.C. Beasley, 365:Summer80-140
Orr, L. Jules Michelet.*
R. Anchor, 131(CL):Spring79-183
D.G. Charlton, 402(MLR):Jan79-210
R. Huss, 208(FS):Vol133Pt2-810
M.T. Shapiro, 400(MLN):May79-877
Országh, L. A Comprehensive English-
Hungarian Dictionary. (5th ed) A Com-
prehensive Hungarian-English Dictionary.
(5th ed)
G. Radó, 75:2/1978-84
Ortali, R. - see Malleville, C.
Ortega y Gasset, J. Phenomenology and Art.
M.S. Quinn, 290(JAAC):Winter79-203
Orth, W. Königlicher Machtanspruch und
städtische Freiheit.
S.M. Burstein, 487:Spring79-86
Ortiz, S.J. A Good Journey.
G. Hobson, 649(WAL):Spring79-87
Ortner, S.B. Sherpas Through Their
Rituals.
A.E. Manzardo, 293(JASt):Aug79-828
Orton, D. Made of Gold.
G. Battiscombe, 617(TLS):15Feb80-166
Orton, L.D. - see Bakunin, M.
Ortúñez de Calahorra, D. Espejo de prín-
cipes y cavalleros: El Cavallero del
Febo.* (D. Eisenberg, ed)
J.E. Keller, 240(HR):Summer78-392
Ortutay, G., ed. Magyar Néprajzi Lexikon.
(Vol 1)
R. Patai, 292(JAF):Jul-Sep79-352
Ory, P. Les Collaborateurs, 1940-1945.
C.W. Obuchowski, 207(FR):May79-942
Osato, S. Distant Dances.
J. Dunning, 441:27May80-C9
M. Hodgson, 441:25May80-8
Osborn, J.J., Jr. The Associates.*
639(VQR):Summer79-102
Osborn, S.C. and R.L. Phillips, Jr. Rich-
ard Harding Davis.
J.R. McElrath, Jr., 26(ALR):Autumn79-
352
Osborne, C. W.H. Auden.*
R. Ellmann, 453(NYRB):23Oct80-35
J. Fuller, 617(TLS):7Mar80-253
R. Hoggart, 362:6Mar80-314
Osborne, C. The Complete Operas of Mozart.
S. Sadie, 415:Apr79-307
Osborne, C. Wagner and His World.
639(VQR):Spring78-48
Osborne, C. and K. Thomson, eds. Klem-
perer Stories.
H. Cole, 362:12Jun80-767
Osborne, H. Abstraction and Artifice in
Twentieth Century Art.
C. Green, 617(TLS):1Feb80-121
Osborne, R. 50 Golden Years of Oscar.
R.B., 200:May79-305
Osgood, C. The Chinese.
W. Eberhard, 318(JAOS):Jul-Sep78-302

Osheim, D.J. An Italian Lordship.
P.J. Jones, 589:Apr79-410
D. Waley, 382(MAE):1979/1-152
Osipov, V. Tri otnosheniia k rodine.
A. Yanov, 550(RusR):Jul79-383
Osley, A.S. Scribes and Sources.
B. Barker-Benfield, 617(TLS):16May80-
566
Osmond, N. - see Rimbaud, A.
Ossorguine-Bakounine, T.A., comp. L'Émi-
gration russe en Europe: Catalogue
collectif des périodiques en langue
russe, 1855-1940.*
D.M. Fiene, 399(MLJ):Apr79-213
Ossowski, S. The Foundations of Aes-
thetics.
H. Khatchadourian, 290(JAAC):Winter79-
193
Ostenfeld, I. Søren Kierkegaard's Psy-
chology. (A. McKinnon, ed and trans)
529(QQ):Winter79/80-740
Oster, D. - see de Balzac, H.
Oster, D. - see Comte de Lautréamont
Ostrander, F. The Hunchback and the Swan.*
639(VQR):Summer78-102
Ostroumov, N.G. Die Wogulen (Mansi).
R-P. Ritter, 343:Band23-208
O'Sullivan, V., ed. An Anthology of
Twentieth Century New Zealand Poetry.
(2nd ed)
J. Ower, 569(SR):Winter79-xiv
O'Sullivan, V. The Boy, the Bridge, the
River.
C. Hankin, 368:Dec78-368
O'Sullivan, V. Butcher and Co.
368:Mar78-92
O'Sullivan, V., ed. New Zealand Short
Stories: Third Series.
D. Norton, 368:Jun76-150
Oswald von Wolkenstein. Lieder, Hand-
schrift A, Codex Vindobonensis 2777.*
(F. Delbono, ed)
A. Robertshaw, 402(MLR):Jul79-741
Otaka, Y. and H. Fukui. Apocalypse Anglo-
Normande, Cambridge Trinity College
Ms. R.16.2.
F. Gégou, 553(RLiR):Jan-Jun78-213
Ott, D.H. Palestine in Perspective.
D. Steel, 362:4Dec80-759
Ott, K.A. - see Guillaume de Lorris and
Jean de Meun
Ott, W., ed. Materialien zu Metrik und
Stilistik. (Vols 9-11)
F. Lasserre, 182:Vol31#23/24-885
Otto, W.F. Dionysos. Les dieux de la
Grèce.
M. Detienne, 98:Nov78-1043
Ó Tuathaigh, G. Ireland Before the Famine,
1798-1848.
L.J. McCaffrey, 637(VS):Summer79-449
Otway, T. The Orphan.* (A.M. Taylor, ed)
L.W. Conolly, 447(N&Q):Feb78-79
Oughton, F. Grinling Gibbons and the
English Woodcarving Tradition.
D. Esterley, 617(TLS):21Mar80-335
Oulton, B. Pocket Crumbs.
G. Hamel, 198:Winter80-139

[continuing]
B. Hayes, 31(ASch):Summer80-423
61:Feb80-95
442(NY):21Jan80-129
Pagis, D. Change and Tradition in Secular
Poetry.
M. Saperstein, 322(JHI):Jan-Mar79-159
Pagnol, M. Le Temps des amours.
M.G. Hydak, 207(FR):Oct78-183
Pagosse, R. - see de Voltaire, F.M.A.
Pahlavi, A. Faces in a Mirror.
R. Steel, 441:1Jun80-1
Pai Panandiker, V.A. Governmental Systems
and Development.
M.F. Katzenstein, 293(JASt):Feb79-400
"Pai Wen P'ien, or The Hundred Questions."
(R. Homann, trans)
J.S. Major, 318(JAOS):Jul-Sep78-341
Paine, R.B. A Thematic Analysis of Fran-
çois Mauriac's "Génitrix," "Le Désert
de l'amour" and "Le Noeud de vipères."*
R.J. North, 208(FS):Vol33Pt2-877
Paine, R.T. and A. Soper. The Art and
Architecture of Japan.* (rev by D.B.
Waterhouse and B. Kobayashi)
D.F. McCallum, 318(JAOS):Jul-Sep78-304
Painter, K.S. The Mildenhall Treasure.
M.A.R. Colledge, 123:Vol29No1-185
Painter, K.S. The Water Newton Early
Christian Silver.
M.A.R. Colledge, 123:Vol29No1-186
Painter, N.I. The Narrative of Hosea
Hudson.*
T.A. Johnson, 441:10Jan80-C21
"The Painterly Print."
A. Fern, 441:14Dec80-12
Paisse, J-M. L'essence du platonisme.
A. Reix, 542:Apr-Jun79-195
Palacios Martín, B. La coronación de los
reyes de Aragón, 1204-1410.
T.N. Bisson, 589:Jan79-182
Paladini, V. and P. Fedeli. Panegyrici
Latini.
M. Winterbottom, 123:Vol29No2-234
"La paléographie grecque et byzantine."
É. Des Places, 555:Vol52fasc2-386
"Paleontologia linguistica."
J. André, 555:Vol52fasc2-386
Paley, M.D. William Blake.*
Z. Leader, 184(EIC):Jan79-81
A.K. Mellor, 591(SIR):Spring79-155
B.M. Stafford, 56:Winter79-118
W. Vaughan, 90:Jun79-394
Paley, W.S. As It Happened.*
E. Diamond, 18:Jul-Aug79-62
Palij, M. The Anarchism of Nestor Makhno,
1918-1921.*
P. Avrich, 104(CASS):Fall78-437
Palisca, C.V., ed. Hucbald, Guido, and
John on Music.
D. Fallows, 415:May79-401
Palissot de Montenoy, C. Les Philosophes.
(T.J. Barling, ed)
W.D. Howarth, 208(FS):Vol33Pt2-779
Palladini, F. Discussioni seicentesche su
Samuel Pufendorf.
K-E. Lönne, 182:Vol31#20-712

Palladius. Palladius, "Traité d'agricul-
ture."* (Vol 1) (R. Martin, ed and
trans)
M. Pasquinucci, 313:Vol69-229
G. Serbat, 555:Vol52fasc1-198
Pallier, D. Recherches sur l'imprimerie à
Paris pendant la Ligue (1585-1594).
E. Benson, 207(FR):Mar79-657
Palliot, P. La Vraye et parfaite Science
des Armoiries.
T.R. Davies, 617(TLS):9May80-534
Palliser, D.M. Tudor York.
V. Pearl, 617(TLS):23May80-573
Palm, D. Ortnamnen i Göteborgs och
Bohuslän. (Vol 12, Pt 2)
G.F. Jensen, 301(JEGP):Oct79-587
Palm, L. La construction "li filz le rei"
et les constructions concurrentes avec
"a" ed "de" étudiées dans les oeuvres
littéraires de la seconde moitié du XIIe
siècle et du premier quart du XIIIe
siècle.
H. Nordahl, 597(SN):Vol150#2-339
G. Price, 208(FS):Vol33Pt2-1027
Palmer, A. The Kaiser.
F. Russell, 396(ModA):Winter79-98
Palmer, C. Herbert Howells.*
H. Ottaway, 415:Jan79-39
Palmer, F. Grammatik und Grammatiktheorie.
K-E. Sommerfeldt, 682(ZPSK):Band31
Heft3-326
Palmer, F.R. Semantics.*
C. Ruhl, 35(AS):Spring79-56
H.G. Schogt, 320(CJL):Spring-Fall78-
184
Palmer, I. The Indonesian Economy Since
1965.
R.C. Rice, 293(JASt):Aug79-844
Palmer, K. Oral Folk-Tales of Wessex.
M.F. Higgins, 582(SFQ):Vol141-283
Palmer, L.R. Descriptive and Comparative
Linguistics.
W.P. Schmid, 260(IF):Band83-367
Palmer, R. A Ballad History of England
from 1588 to the Present Day.
H. Myers, 415:Nov79-919
376:Oct79-144
Palumbo, E.M. The Literary Use of For-
mulas in "Guthlac II" and Their Relation
to Felix's "Vita Sancti Guthlaci."
K.E. Dubs, 382(MAE):1979/2-269
D.K. Fry, 589:Jul79-608
Panagl, O. and H.D. Pohl, eds. Etymologie
I and II.
N. Oettinger, 343:Band23-57
Panandiker, V.A.P. - see under Pai Panan-
diker, V.A.
Panati, C. Breakthroughs.
C. Lehamnn-Haupt, 441:28Mar80-C32
Panazza, G. and C. Boselli. Progetti per
una cattedrale.
J. Varriano, 54:Mar78-177
Panchenko, A.M. Russkaia stikhotvornaia
kul'tura XVII veka.
O. Hughes, 550(RusR):Apr79-215
Pandey, R.R. Man and the Universe.
D.C. Mathur, 484(PPR):Jun80-595

Pane, R. Il Rinascimento nell' Italia
meridionale.
H-W. Kruft, 90:Apr79-264
Pang, E-S. Bahia in the First Brazilian
Republic.
R. Seckinger, 263(RIB):Vol29No3/4-371
Pang-yuan, C. and others - see under Chi
Pang-yuan and others
Panhans-Bühler, U. Eklektizismus und
Originalität im Werk des Petrus Christus.
L. Campbell, 90:Dec79-802
Panichas, G.A. The Burden of Vision.
E. Chances, 558(RLJ):Spring79-225
Panikkar, K.M. An Autobiography.
S. Lewandowski, 293(JASt):Feb79-396
Panikkar, R. The Vedic Experience.
R.L. Brubaker, 293(JASt):Feb79-388
J.B. Chethimattam, 613:Dec79-432
A. Creel, 485(PE&W):Jan79-103
Panitch, A. In Shturemdike Yoren.
H. Seidman, 287:Oct78-25
Panov, V., with G. Feifer. To Dance.*
J. Anderson, 151:Jul78-64
Panskaya, L., with D.D. Leslie. Introduc-
tion to Palladii's Chinese Literature of
the Muslims.
E. Widmer, 293(JASt):Feb79-373
Pantham, T. Political Parties and Demo-
cratic Consensus.
H. Erdman, 293(JASt):Nov78-189
"The Panton Book of Idioms for Polyglots."
A. Urbancic, 399(MLJ):Mar79-147
Panzer, B. Strukturen des Russischen.
R-D. Keil, 688(ZSP):Band40Heft2-427
Paoli, R. Borges, percorsi di signifi-
cato.*
D.L. Shaw, 86(BHS):Apr79-166
Paolucci, H. - see Hegel, G.W.F.
Papadopoulo, A. Islam and Muslim Art.*
(French title: L'Islam et l'art musul-
man.)
O. Grabar, 441:2Mar80-7
Papadopoulo, A. Islamische Kunst.
L. Golvin, 182:Vol131#19-684
Papalia, A. and J.A. Mendoza. Lengua y
cultura, Primera etapa. Lengua y cul-
tura, Segunda etapa. Aventuras con la
lengua y la cultura.
R.H. Gilmore, 399(MLJ):Jan-Feb79-81
Papazoglu, F. The Central Balkan Tribes
in Pre-Roman Times.
R.A. Tomlinson, 123:Vol29No2-274
Pape, G. Border Crossings.*
J.F. Cotter, 249(HudR):Spring79-112
Pape, W. Wilhelm Busch.
G. Selk, 196:Band19Heft3/4-335
Papenfuss, D. and J. Söring, eds. Rezep-
tion der deutschen Gegenwartsliteratur
im Ausland.
R. Leroy, 556(RLV):1978/1-80
Paper, H.H., ed. Jewish Language.
Y. Malkiel, 350:Sep79-746
Paper, H.H., ed. Language and Texts.
F.E. Horowitz, 660(Word):Dec78-274
Papert, S. Mindstorms.
T. Ferris, 441:23Nov80-16

Papon, L. Pastorelle. (C. Longeon, ed)
I.D. McFarlane, 208(FS):Vol33Pt2-645
J. Sacré, 535(RHL):Jul-Aug79-647
Pappas, G.S. and M. Swain, eds. Essays on
Knowledge and Justification.
R.A. Fumerton, 687:Oct-Dec79-647
J. Largeault, 542:Jan-Mar79-117
Paprella, M.M., ed. Biochemical Mechan-
isms in Hearing and Deafness.
M.D. Sass, 660(Word):Dec78-281
Paquet, L. Les Cyniques grecs.
M-O. Goulet-Cazé, 555:Vol152fasc1-112
J-L. Poirier, 542:Apr-Jun79-196
Paquet, M. Saturne et Jupiter.
P. Somville, 542:Oct-Dec79-474
"Les Paradoxes du romancier: les 'Égare-
ments' de Crébillon."
V. Mylne, 208(FS):Vol33Pt2-758
Paraíso de Leal, I. Juan Ramón Jiménez.
R.A. Cardwell, 86(BHS):Oct79-345
Parajón, M. Eugenio Florit y su poesía.*
S. Davis-Lett, 238:May-Sep79-412
Parent, A. Les Métiers du Livre à Paris
au XVIe siècle (1535-1560).
E. Armstrong, 208(FS):Jul79-329
Parente, F. - see Reimarus, H.S.
Parente, M.I. - see under Isnardi Parente,
M.
Pareyson, L. Schellingiana rariora.
C. Cesa, 548(RCSF):Apr-Jun79-224
T.F.O., 543:Mar79-563
Parfit, M. Last Stand At Rosebud Creek.
G. Lichtenstein, 441:5Oct80-13
Parfitt, G. Ben Jonson.*
R.V. Holdsworth, 541(RES):May79-206
Parfitt, G. - see Tourneur, C.
Pargeter, S., comp. A Catalogue of the
Library at Tatton Park.
R. Andrewes, 415:Apr79-309
Parini, J. The Love Run.
R. Bradford, 441:8Jun80-14
Paris, S.G. Propositional Logical Think-
ing and Comprehension of Language
Connectives.
G. Carden, 353:Jan78-69
Park, R., ed. Lamb as Critic.
J. Uglow, 617(TLS):11Jul80-789
Parker, A.A. - see de Góngora, L.
Parker, G. The Dutch Revolt.
G.C. Schoolfield, 568(SCN):Spring-
Summer79-31
Parker, G.T. The Writing on the Wall.
B. De Mott, 61:Jan80-84
J. Featherstone, 441:3Feb80-11
Parker, J. The World for a Market-Place.
J.G. Garratt, 78(BC):Autumn79-446
Parker, J.H. Juan Pérez de Montalván.
C. Iranzo, 241:Sep79-102
Parker, P.R. Brazil and the Quiet Inter-
vention, 1964.
J.M. Young, 263(RIB):Vol29No3/4-372
Parker, R. Coleridge's Meditative Art.*
G. Cullum, 586(SoRA):Jul78-205
Parker, R.B. Looking for Rachel Wallace.
N. Callendar, 441:20Apr80-25
Parker-Rhodes, A.F. Inferential Semantics.
G. Sampson, 307:Oct79-118

Parkes, M.B. and A.G. Watson, eds. Medieval Scribes, Manuscripts and Libraries.
P.J. Croft, 541(RES):Nov79-449

Parkes, M.P., comp. The Medieval Manuscripts of Keble College Oxford.
78(BC):Summer79-185

Parkin, A. The Dramatic Imagination of W.B. Yeats.
J. Ronsley, 408:Spring79-177

Parkin, F. Marxism and Class Theory.
M. Mann, 617(TLS):4Apr80-387

Parkinson, C.W. Parkinson: The Law.*
A. Smith, 441:4May80-12

Parkinson, G., with C. Collier and J. Preston. Guide to Coal Mining Collections in the United States.
R.M. Kesner, 14:Oct79-472

Parkinson, G.H.R. George Lukács.*
A. Manser, 393(Mind):Jul79-455
J.D. Rabb, 518:May79-71
M. Silver, 125:Spring79-447

Parkinson, T. - see Crane, H.

Parmann, Ø. Harald Dal.
J. Stare, 341:1978/2-90

Parmet, H.S. Jack.
R. Sherrill, 441:27Jul80-11
R. Steel, 453(NYRB):14Aug80-37
442(NY):15Sep80-190

Parming, T. and E. Järvesoo, eds. A Case Study of a Soviet Republic: The Estonian SSR.*
D. Kirby, 575(SEER):Oct79-624

Parnis, A. The Proofreader.
P. Mackridge, 617(TLS):8Aug80-892

Parnwell, E.C. Oxford Picture Dictionary of American English.*
E.G. Cotton, 399(MLJ):Mar79-134

Parodi, S., ed. Inventario delle carte leopoldiane.
M.P., 228(GSLI):Vol155fasc492-631

Paroli, T. Sull'elemento formulare nella poesia germanica antica.
S. Deligiorgis, 589:Jul79-609

Parret, H., ed. History of Linguistic Thought and Contemporary Linguistics.*
R. Rocher, 318(JAOS):Apr-Jun78-201

Parrinder, G. Jesus in the Qur'ān.
J. Subhan, 273(IC):Apr77-155

Parrinder, G., ed and trans. The Wisdom of the Forest.
R.M. Smith, 318(JAOS):Jul-Sep78-332

Parrinder, P. H.G. Wells.
G. Blake, 395(MFS):Summer78-310

Parrish, S. - see Wordsworth, W.

Parrish, T., ed. The Simon and Schuster Encyclopedia of World War II.
639(VQR):Spring79-52

Parrott, C. The Bad Bohemian.
C.A.M. Noble, 529(QQ):Winter79/80-664

Parry, J.H. and P. Sherlock. Historia de las Antillas.
L. Pérez, 263(RIB):Vol29No1-79

Parry, T. and M. Morgan, eds. Llyfryddiaeth Llenyddiaeth Gymraeg.
E. Bachellery, 194(EC):Vol15fasc2-736

Parsons, D. The Directory of Tunes and Musical Themes.
H.B.R., 412:Aug-Nov78-291

Parsons, E.B. Wilsonian Diplomacy.
R. Gregory, 579(SAQ):Spring79-267

Parsons, I. - see Rosenberg, I.

Partee, B.H., ed. Montague Grammar.*
J. Higginbotham, 311(JP):May80-278

Parthasarathy, R. Rough Passage.
T. Eagleton, 565:Vol20#3-75
U. Parameswaran, 529(QQ):Spring79-172

Parthasarathy, R., ed. Ten Twentieth Century Indian Poets.*
U. Parameswaran, 529(QQ):Spring79-173

Partlow, R.B., Jr. - see "Dickens Studies Annual"

Partner, N.F. Serious Entertainments.
J.W. Alexander, 125:Fall78-131
M. Chibnall, 382(MAE):1979/2-274
R.W. Hanning, 589:Jul79-610

Partner, P. Renaissance Rome 1500-1559.*
A. Chastel, 576:Oct78-202

Partridge, A.C. A Substantive Grammar of Shakespeare's Nondramatic Texts.*
H.J. Neuhaus, 570(SQ):Summer79-445

Partridge, E. A Dictionary of Catch Phrases.*
J. Sutherland, 447(N&Q):Aug78-349

Parwāz Iṣlāḥi, A.R. Makhdoom 'Ali Mahā'imī.
S.A.W. Bukhari, 273(IC):Oct77-273

Pascal, B. Pensées. (M. Le Guern, ed)
M. Adam, 542:Jan-Mar78-109
J.H. Broome, 208(FS):Vol33Pt2-685

Pascal, B. Pensées. (P. Sellier, ed)
D. Descotes, 535(RHL):Jul-Aug79-655

Pascal, R. The Dual Voice.*
M. Swales, 402(MLR):Jan79-146
205(FMLS):Jan78-93

Pasco, A.H. The Color-Keys to "A la recherche du temps perdu."*
A. Finch, 208(FS):Vol33Pt2-861

Pasek, J.C. Memoirs of the Polish Baroque.* (C.S. Leach, ed and trans)
H. Leeming, 575(SEER):Jan79-125
D. Stone, 104(CASS):Fall78-439

Pasi, C. Théophile Gautier o il Fantastico volontario.
G. Hainsworth, 208(FS):Vol33Pt2-824

Pasley, M., ed. Nietzsche.
J.M. Grandin, 301(JEGP):Jul79-402
Q. Lauer, 613:Jun79-217

Pasquier, E. Lettres Familières. (D. Thickett, ed)
J. Crow, 208(FS):Jul79-336

von Passavant, R. Zeitdarstellung und Zeitkritik in Gottfried Kellers "Martin Salander."
H. Böschenstein, 133:Band12Heft4-374

Passmore, J. Science and its Critics.
M. Ruse, 529(QQ):Summer79-358

Pastan, L. The Five Stages of Grief.*
P. Stitt, 219(GaR):Winter79-927

Pastan, L. Selected Poems.
J. Fuller, 617(TLS):18Jan80-65

Pasternak, B. Collected Short Prose.
(C. Barnes, ed)
B.P. Scherr, 574(SEEJ):Spring79-134
"Patañjali's Vyākaraṇa-Mahābhāṣya: Kāra-
kāhnika (P. 1.4.23-1.4.55)."* (S.D.
Joshi and J.A.F. Roodbergen, eds and
trans)
R. Rocher, 318(JAOS):Jul-Sep78-330
Pateman, T. Language, Truth and Politics.
K. Graham, 488:Sep79-382
T. Kochman, 355(LSoc):Apr78-111
Paterculus, M.V. - see under Velleius
Paterculus, M.
Paterson, A. Birds Flying.
K. Smithyman, 364:Mar74-79
Paterson, A. Terra Nova.
A. Stevenson, 617(TLS):23May80-586
Paterson, L.M. Troubadours and Eloquence.
P. Cherchi, 405(MP):Aug79-74
C.B. Faulhaber, 545(RPh):Nov78-247
Patlagean, E. Pauvreté économique et
pauvreté sociale à Byzance 4e-7e siècles.
P. Garnsey, 313:Vol69-198
Patočka, J. Le monde naturel comme prob-
lème philosophique.
L. Giroux, 154:Dec78-728
Paton, A. Towards the Mountain.
T. Pakenham, 441:14Dec80-8
Patout, P. Alfonso Reyes et la France.
A. Blasi, 263(RIB):Vol29No3/4-373
Patrides, C.A., ed. Approaches to Mar-
vell.*
W.H., 148:Spring79-92
B. Worden, 541(RES):Nov79-469
Patrides, C.A. - see Herbert, G.
Patrides, C.A. - see Milton, J.
Patruno, N. Language in Giovanni Verga's
Early Novels.
R.A. Hall, Jr., 399(MLJ):Jan-Feb79-60
Patten, B. Grave Gossip.
E. Longley, 617(TLS):18Jan80-64
Patterson, A.M. Marvell and the Civic
Crown.*
S. El-Gabalawy, 49:Jan79-95
H. Toliver, 301(JEGP):Apr79-261
Patterson, C. Evolution.
529(QQ):Winter79/80-735
Patterson, F. Photography for the Joy of
It.
529(QQ):Summer79-371
Patterson, G.J. The Greeks of Vancouver.
R.T. Teske, 292(JAF):Apr-Jun79-227
Patterson, G.J. The Romanians of Saskatch-
ewan.
S. Beck, 292(JAF):Oct-Dec79-486
Patterson, R.N. The Lasko Tangent.*
T.J. Binyon, 617(TLS):5Sep80-948
Patterson, S.R. and L.S. Thompson. Medi-
cal Terms from Greek and Latin.
M.H. Charlton, 399(MLJ):Apr79-222
Patterson, W. and H. Urrutibéheity. The
Lexical Structure of Spanish.
B.R. Lavandera, 545(RPh):Nov78-237
Pattison, R. The Child Figure in English
Literature.*
A. Lincoln, 155:Spring79-43
636(VP):Winter78-396

Patzlaff, R. Otfrid von Weissenburg und
die mittelalterliche versus-Tradition.
G. Cubbin, 220(GL&L):Oct78-66
Pauck, W. and M. Paul Tillich.* (Vol 1)
C.H. Voss, 390:Apr79-70
Paufler, H-D. Lateinamerikanisches
Spanisch.
D. Gifford, 86(BHS):Jul79-266
Pauker, G.J., F.H. Golay and C.H. Enloe.
Diversity and Development in Southeast
Asia.
D.S. Paauw, 293(JASt):Feb79-424
Paul of Venice. Logica Magna. (Pt 2,
fasc 6) (F. del Punta, ed; M.M. Adams,
trans)
E.J. Ashworth, 479(PhQ):Jan79-74
G. Gál, 589:Jul79-614
D.P. Henry, 382(MAE):1979/2-329
G. Nuchelmans, 518:Oct79-110
Paul, B. The Fourth Wall.
N. Callendar, 441:6Jan80-14
Paul, B. Liars and Tyrants and People Who
Turn Blue.
N. Callendar, 441:27Jul80-23
Paul, F., ed. Henrik Ibsen.
D. Thomas, 402(MLR):Oct79-1003
D. Thomas, 562(Scan):May79-69
Paul, J. Jean Paul Sämtliche Werke. (Sec-
tion 2, Vol 2) (N. Miller and W. Schmidt-
Biggemann, eds)
M.H., 191(ELN):Sep78(supp)-175
Paul, S. Olson's Push.*
P. Breslin, 491:Jul80-219
G.F. Butterick, 432(NEQ):Mar79-117
L.S. Dembo, 27(AL):May79-289
C. Molesworth, 219(GaR):Summer79-438
M. Perloff, 141:Summer79-251
Paulhan, J. Les Fleurs de Tarbes ou La
Terreur dans les Lettres. (J-C. Zylber-
stein, ed)
J.M. Cocking, 208(FS):Jan79-101
Pauli, E. Classical Cooking the Modern
Way.
W. and C. Cowen, 639(VQR):Autumn79-152
Paulian, C. Le Kukuya.
J. Knappert, 353:Jan78-93
Paulin, B. Du Couteau a la Plume.
J.M. Patrick, 568(SCN):Spring-Summer79-
24
Paulin, T. Thomas Hardy.*
M. Bath, 637(VS):Winter78-268
Paulin, T. The Strange Museum.
J. Bayley, 617(TLS):4Apr80-384
D. Davis, 362:5Jun80-729
Pauls, J. "Les Fleurs bleues" von Raymond
Queneau.
C. Sanders, 208(FS):Apr79-226
Paulsen, W. Eichendorff und sein Tauge-
nichts.*
J.F.F., 191(ELN):Sep78(supp)-152
J. Purver, 402(MLR):Jul79-753
L. Radner, 406:Spring79-72
Paulsen, W. Johann Elias Schlegel und die
Komödie.
G. Hillen, 221(GQ):Jan79-110
P.M. Mitchell, 301(JEGP):Apr79-294

Paulsen, W. Christoph Martin Wieland.*
  W. Leppmann, 222(GR):Winter78-35
Paulsen, W. - see Schirokauer, A.
Paulson, R. and A. Stein, eds. ELH Essays
  for Earl R. Wasserman.
  A. Morvan, 189(EA):Jul-Dec78-363
Paulus, H. Die französische Zeitungs-
  annonce.
  O. Reboul, 209(FM):Apr78-181
Pausanias. Graeciae descriptio. (M.H.
  Rocha-Pereira, ed)
  P. Levi, 123:Vol29No1-21
Pautrat, P. and J. Salouadji. Fête comme
  nous.
  L.A. Dahlin, 207(FR):Oct78-184
Pavel, T. Inflexions de voix.*
  W. Krysinski, 567:Vol23#3/4-359
Pavel, T.G. La syntaxe narrative des
  tragédies de Corneille.*
  W. Krysinski, 567:Vol23#3/4-359
  G. Price, 208(FS):Vol33Pt2-677
  S.W. Tiefenbrun, 207(FR):Mar79-637
Pavese, E. - see Cousteau, J.
Pavis, P. Problèmes de sémiologie théâ-
  trale.*
  M. Nadin, 290(JAAC):Spring80-338
Pavlík, J. Intonacija povestvovatel'nogo
  predloženija v russkom jazyke. (Vol 1,
  Pts 1 and 2)
  D. Ward, 575(SEER):Apr79-273
Pavlu, A. C'est un jour comme jadis les
  dimanches.
  D.B. Parsell, 207(FR):Dec78-382
Pavone, M.A. Paolo de Majo.
  A.F.B., 90:Apr79-265
Pawelczynska, A. Values and Violence in
  Auschwitz.
  T. Ziolkowski, 569(SR):Fall79-676
Payen, J-C. La Rose et l'Utopie.
  R.H. Bloch, 400(MLN):May79-901
  J.V. Fleming, 589:Jul79-617
  S. Goyard-Fabre, 542:Jul-Sep78-365
  J. Zezula, 188(ECr):Fall78-98
Payen, J.C., ed and trans. Tristan et
  Yseut.
  J.H. Marshall, 208(FS):Vol33Pt2-535
  G.A. Savage, 545(RPh):Aug78-122
Payne, A.J. Louisa May Alcott.
  M.B. Stern, 365:Summer80-135
Payne, C. and others. American Ballet
  Theatre.
  O. Maynard, 151:Aug78-46
Payne, P.L. Colvilles and the Scottish
  Steel Industry.
  T.C. Barker, 617(TLS):11Jan80-35
Payne, R. A Rage for China.
  639(VQR):Summer78-104
Payne, R. - see Rozanov, V.
Payzant, G. Glenn Gould.*
  R. Dodson, 529(QQ):Summer79-341
  P. Helmer, 627(UTQ):Summer79-477
  G. Logan, 255(HAB):Winter/Spring79-124
Paz, J.G. - see under Gómez Paz, J.
Paz, O. Marcel Duchamp: Appearance Strip-
  ped Bare.*
  R. Boyers, 617(TLS):18Jan80-57
                              [continued]

[continuing]
  D. Carrier, 290(JAAC):Fall79-104
  R. Krauss, 473(PR):4/1979-615
  J. Robinson, 62:Feb79-59
Peacock, C. Richard Parkes Bonington.
  M. Pointon, 617(TLS):21Mar80-333
Peacock, J.L. Muslim Puritans.
  C.S. Kessler, 293(JASt):Aug79-841
Peacocke, C. Holistic Explanation.
  S. Stich, 617(TLS):27Jun80-737
Peake, C.H. James Joyce.*
  W. De Meritt, 174(Éire):Spring79-139
  A. Goldman, 541(RES):Feb79-108
  S.A. Henke, 639(VQR):Winter79-181
  J.C. Sherwood, 648(WCR):Jun78-33
  R. Splitter, 395(MFS):Summer78-317
Peale, C.G. La Anatomía de "El Diablo
  Cojuelo."
  N.C. Davis, 400(MLN):Mar79-426
Pearce, C. The Manningham Mills Strike,
  Bradford, December, 1890-April, 1891.
  R.I. McKibbin, 637(VS):Spring78-410
Pearl, L. Descartes.
  F. Hodgson, 207(FR):Feb79-482
"Pearl." (M. Borroff, trans)
  D. Fox, 447(N&Q):Feb78-74
Pearsall, D. Old English and Middle
  English Poetry.*
  S.B. Greenfield, 405(MP):Nov79-188
Pearsall, D. - see Langland, W.
Pearson, A. Freewheeling Through Gossamer
  Dragstrips.*
  R.J. Merrett, 102(CanL):Winter78-96
Pearson, B. Fretful Sleepers and Other
  Essays.
  A. Wells, 368:Sep74-263
Pearson, B. - see Finlayson, R.
Pearson, D.M. The Americanization of Carl
  Aaron Swensson.
  B.J. Nordstrom, 563(SS):Spring79-205
Pearson, H. The Man Whistler.
  639(VQR):Summer79-96
Pearson, J. The Sitwells.*
  C. Lahey-Dolega, 219(GaR):Winter79-923
  N. Miller, 42(AR):Summer79-371
Pearson, J. and J. No Time But Place.
  N. Perrin, 441:31Aug80-8
Pearson, J.D. and A. Walsh, comps. Index
  Islamicus. (4th Supp, Pt 2)
  S.A.W. Bukhari, 273(IC):Apr76-131
Pearson, P.D. Alvar Aalto and the Inter-
  national Style.*
  M. Treib, 505:May79-138
Pearson, R. The Russian Moderates and the
  Crisis of Tsarism, 1914-1917.
  N. Stone, 575(SEER):Jan79-132
Pearson, S.A., Jr. Arthur Koestler.
  639(VQR):Winter79-28
Peary, D., ed. Close-Ups.
  M. Buckley, 200:Aug-Sep79-430
"Peasant Paintings from Huhsien County."
  R. Croizier, 293(JASt):Feb79-303
Pebworth, T-L. Owen Felltham.
  J. Robertson, 402(MLR):Apr79-411
Pecere, O. - see Petronius

Peck, H.D. A World by Itself.*
  K.S. House, 445(NCF):Sep78-231
  M. Roth, 405(MP):Feb80-345
Peck, J. The Broken Blockhouse Wall.*
  J. Fuller, 617(TLS):18Jan80-65
  R. Gibbons, 461:Spring-Summer79-87
Peckham, H.H., ed. Sources of American
Independence.
  W.L. Joyce, 432(NEQ):Dec79-577
  H.H. Wehmann, 14:Oct79-488
Peckham, M. Explanation and Power.
  J.M. Cameron, 453(NYRB):17Apr80-36
Peckham, M. Romanticism and Behavior.*
  M.G. Cooke, 661(WC):Summer79-286
  S. Raval, 50(ArQ):Spring79-94
Peckham, M. - see Browning, R.
Peek, W. Griechische Vers-Inschriften aus
Thessalien.
  B. Helly, 555:Vol52fasc1-121
Peers, F.W. The Public Eye.
  T. McCormack, 99:Dec80/Jan81-30
Peeters, K.C. Miscellanea.
  E.H. Rehermann, 196:Band19Heft1/2-168
Péguy, C. De Jean Coste. (A. Roche, ed)
  J. Bastaire, 535(RHL):Jan-Feb79-155
  N. Wilson, 208(FS):Vol33Pt2-867
"Péguy mis à jour."
  A. Roche, 535(RHL):Jul-Aug78-670
Pehnt, W. Expressionist Architecture.
  R.H. Bletter, 576:May78-131
Pei, M. Weasel Words.
  J.R. Gaskin, 569(SR):Summer79-455
  N. Miller, 42(AR):Winter79-117
Pei, M. and S. Ramondino, with L. Torbet.
Dictionary of Foreign Terms.
  E. Cross, 660(Word):Aug78-198
Peirce, C.S. Charles Sanders Peirce: Con-
tributions to "The Nation." (Pt 1) (K.L.
Ketner and J.E. Cook, eds)
  K. Oehler, 567:Vol125#1/2-161
de Peiresc, N. Lettres à Malherbe (1606-
1628).* (R. Lebègue, ed)
  P.J. Bayley, 208(FS):Vol33Pt2-669
Pelan, M.M., ed. Floire et Blancheflor:
Seconde Version.
  W. Rothwell, 208(FS):Vol33Pt2-556
Pellegrini, G.B. Saggi sul Ladino Dolomi-
tico e sul Friulano.
  R. Stefanini, 545(RPh):May79-419
Pelletier, A-M. Fonctions poétiques.
  P. Somville, 542:Oct-Dec79-475
Pelta, S. and F. Seve - see Lenin, V.I.
Pemberton, J.E. Politics and Public Lib-
raries in England and Wales, 1850-1970.
  S. Bennett, 637(VS):Winter79-228
Pemble, J. The Raj, the Indian Mutiny,
and the Kingdom of Oudh, 1801-1859.
  A.J. Greenberger, 637(VS):Spring79-363
Pena, W., with W. Caudill and J. Cocke.
Problem Seeking.
  P.G. Rowe, 505:Feb79-102
Penn, I. Worlds in a Small Room.
  J. Naughton, 362:18and25Dec80-865
Penner, N. The Canadian Left.
  T. Morley, 529(QQ):Spring79-110
Penny, N. Piranesi.*
  C.C. Brookes, 39:Dec79-538

Penny, R. Estudio estructural del habla
de Tudanca.
  J.G. Cummins, 86(BHS):Oct79-327
Penoyre, J. and J. Houses in the Land-
scape.
  A. Clifton-Taylor, 46:Jun79-362
Pensel, F., comp. Verzeichnis der alt-
deutschen Handschriften in der Stadt-
bibliothek Dessau.
  C. Petzsch, 72:Band216Heft1-156
Pentikäinen, J. and T. Juurikka, eds.
Folk Narrative Research.
  R. Kvideland, 196:Band19Heft1/2-148
Pentzopoulou-Valalas, T. Le concept de
l'evidence chez sceptiques grecs.
  J. Brun, 192(EP):Apr-Jun79-254
Penzel, F. Theatre Lighting before Elec-
tricity.*
  R. Ornbo, 157:Winter79-84
Pépin, J. Dante et la tradition de
l'allégorie.
  E.C. Ronquist, 481(PQ):Winter78-137
Pepitone, L. and W. Stadiem. Marilyn
Monroe Confidential.
  J.R. Haspiel, 200:Aug-Sep79-428
Pepper, A. Straight Life.
  W. Balliett, 442(NY):7Jan80-83
Pepper, S. Civil War in China.
  D.G. Gillin, 293(JASt):Feb79-343
Pepys, S. The Illustrated Pepys.* (R.
Latham, ed)
  L. Hartley, 569(SR):Summer79-lxiv
  639(VQR):Winter79-8
Perarnau, J. L'"Alia Informatio Beguin-
orum" d'Arnau de Vilanova.
  R.E. Lerner, 589:Oct79-842
Percival, J. Modern Ballet.
  J. Kavanagh, 617(TLS):13Jun80-676
Percival, J. The Roman Villa.*
  A.D. Small, 313:Vol69-210
  J. Ward-Perkins, 576:Oct78-200
Percy, T. Thomas Percy's "Life of Dr.
Oliver Goldsmith." (R.L. Harp, ed)
  O.W. Ferguson, 402(MLR):Apr79-420
Percy, W. The Second Coming.
  W. Balliett, 442(NY):1Sep80-86
  A. Broyard, 441:3Jul80-C20
  B. De Mott, 61:Jul80-81
  J. Romano, 441:29Jun80-1
  R. Towers, 453(NYRB):14Aug80-39
Le Père Hercule. Lettres à Philandre
(1637-1638). (G. Couton and Y. Giraud,
eds)
  H.T. Barnwell, 208(FS):Vol33Pt2-675
de Pereda, J.M. Sotileza. (E. Miralles,
ed)
  A.H. Clarke, 86(BHS):Apr79-156
Pereira, J., ed. Hindu Theology.
  J.B. Chethimattam, 613:Dec79-432
Pereira, S. The Marriage of the Portu-
guese.
  G. Burns, 584(SWR):Summer79-304
  R. Feld, 472:Fall/Winter79-150
Perella, N.J. Midday in Literature.
  L. Nelson, Jr., 676(YR):Autumn79-128

Perelman, C., ed. Etudes de logique juridique. (Vol 7)
    J-L. Gardies, 542:Oct-Dec79-494
Perelman, C. L'Empire rhétorique, rhétorique et argumentation.
    H. Méchoulan, 192(EP):Apr-Jun79-256
Perelman, C. and P. Foriers, eds. Les motivations des décisions de justice.
    J-L. Gardies, 542:Oct-Dec79-493
Pérez, A.C.I. - see under Ibáñez Pérez, A.C.
Pérez Estévez, A. El concepto de materia al comienzo de la escuela franciscana de Paris.
    J. Jolivet, 542:Apr-Jun79-206
Pérez Ramírez, D. Escuela conquense de escultura renacentista.
    M. Estella, 48:Oct-Dec78-448
"The Perfect Generosity of Prince Vessantara." (M. Cone and R.F. Gombrich, trans)
    J.R. Carter, 293(JASt):Feb79-420
    J.W. de Jong, 259(IIJ):Oct79-297
"La Perfezione oggi."
    E. Namer, 542:Jul-Sep79-372
Perini, G.B. - see under Bernardi Perini, G.
Perkins, C.A., with N. Dickey. Border Patrol. (C.L. Sonnichsen, ed)
    W. Gard, 584(SWR):Winter79-89
    R.B. Olafson, 649(WAL):Summer79-182
Perkins, D. A History of Modern Poetry.* (Vol 1)
    B.F. Fisher 4th, 177(ELT):Vol22#4-293
Perkoff, S.Z. Love Is the Silence.
    R.J. Stout, 584(SWR):Spring79-194
Perle, G. The Operas of Alban Berg. (Vol 1)
    R. Craft, 453(NYRB):20Nov80-37
Perle, G. Serial Composition and Atonality. (4th ed)
    J. Dunsby, 410(M&L):Jul79-363
    P.P. Nash, 607:Dec78-35
Perle, G. Twelve-Tone Tonality.
    J. Dunsby, 410(M&L):Jul79-363
    M.M. MacLean, 414(MusQ):Jan79-117
    P.P. Nash, 607:Dec78-35
Perlin, G.C. The Tory Syndrome.
    J.L. Granatstein, 99:Jun-Jul80-36
Perlis, V. Two Men for Modern Music.
    P. Griffiths, 415:Jul79-579
Perlmann, M. - see al-Damanhūrī, A.
Perlmutter, A. The Military and Politics in Modern Times.
    639(VQR):Winter78-19
Perloff, M. Frank O'Hara.*
    P. Mariani, 152(UDQ):Spring78-91
    H. Vendler, 453(NYRB):7Feb80-10
Pérol, J. Morale provisoire.
    A. Bosquet, 450(NRF):Jan79-107
Perosa, A. and J. Sparrow, eds. Renaissance Latin Verse.
    R.W. Carrubba, 121(CJ):Apr-May80-369
Perosa, S. Henry James and the Experimental Novel.
    T. Cooley, 27(AL):Nov79-430
                [continued]

[continuing]
    M.D. Springer, 301(JEGP):Jul79-456
    295(JML):Vol7#4-738
    639(VQR):Spring79-48
Pérouse, G-A. Nouvelles françaises du XVIe siècle.*
    J. Céard, 535(RHL):Nov-Dec79-1031
Perrie, M. The Agrarian Policy of the Russian Socialist-Revolutionary Party from its Origins through the Revolution of 1905-1907.*
    D.T. La Belle, 104(CASS):Summer78-298
Perrin, N. Second Person Rural.
    R. Blount, Jr., 441:26Oct80-13
Perrone-Moisès, L. "Les Chants de Maldoror" de Lautréamont.
    M. Bonnet, 535(RHL):May-Jun78-501
Perry, A. Callander Square.
    N. Callendar, 441:23Mar80-33
Perry, E. Blue Pages.*
    M. Wood, 18:Sep79-68
Perry, G. Paula Modersohn-Becker.
    W. Feaver, 617(TLS):21Mar80-330
    M. Stevens, 441:13Jan80-13
Perry, J. James A. Herne.
    D. Pizer, 27(AL):Mar79-126
Perry, L.B. Juárez and Díaz.*
    I.E. Cadenhead, 263(RIB):Vol29No3/4-375
Perry, N. Sir Everard Fawkener.*
    J.H. Brumfitt, 208(FS):Vol33Pt2-743
    O.R. Taylor, 535(RHL):Sep-Oct79-857
Perry, N. - see Lemercier, J-L-N.
Perry, R. Denizens.
    W. Pritchard, 441:6Jul80-8
Perry, R. Grand Slam.
    N. Callendar, 441:12Oct80-34
Perry, R. Program for a Puppet.
    N. Callendar, 441:30Mar80-17
Perse, S-J. Anabasis. (R. Little, trans)
    G.D. Martin, 208(FS):Vol33Pt2-882
Perse, S-J. Evil.* (R. Little, ed)
    K.R. Dutton, 67:May79-134
Perse, S-J. Oeuvres complètes.
    J-P. Richard, 98:May78-439
Perse, S-J. St.-John Perse: Letters.* (A.J. Knodel, ed and trans)
    J. Weightman, 453(NYRB):21Feb80-16
Perse, S-J. Song for an Equinox.
    J. Lindroth, 590:Spring/Summer78-34
    J.M. Schneider, 207(FR):Apr79-780
    639(VQR):Winter78-10
"The Persian Carpet."
    J. Housego, 463:Summer78-215
Persichetti, V. Twentieth Century Harmony.
    A.W., 412:Aug-Nov78-284
Persky, S. Wrestling the Angel.
    K. Fraser, 168(ECW):Summer78-284
Pesce, D. Saggio su Epicuro.*
    A. Renault, 192(EP):Jan-Mar79-107
Peschel, E.R. Flux and Reflux.
    W. Albert, 207(FR):Apr79-775
    C.A. Hackett, 208(FS):Jul79-355
    V.A. La Charité, 446(NCFS):Fall-Winter78/79-136
    205(FMLS):Apr78-188

Peskett, W. Survivors.
  P. Scupham, 617(TLS):4Jul80-762
Peskin, A. Garfield.
  H.W. Morgan, 579(SAQ):Summer79-403
  639(VQR):Autumn78-142
Pessoa, F. Lirika.
  V. Perelešin, 558(RLJ):Winter79-217
Peters, A.K. Jean Cocteau and André Gide.
  C.S. Brosman, 546(RR):May79-314
Peters, C. How Washington Really Works.
  J. Leonard, 441:9Jun80-C14
Peters, E. Monk's-hood.
  M. Laski, 362:13Nov80-665
Peters, F.G. Robert Musil.*
  S.J. Erickson, 221(GQ):Nov79-556
  C.A.M. Noble, 529(QQ):Winter79/80-664
  B. Pike, 594:Winter79-497
  N. Rendleman, 222(GR):Spring79-81
Peters, H. - see Donne, J.
Peters, H.B., ed. Folk Songs Out of
  Wisconsin.*
  J.P. Leary, 292(JAF):Oct-Dec79-503
Peters, H.F. Zarathustra's Sister.
  H. McDonald, 396(ModA):Winter79-96
Peters, J., ed. Book Collecting.*
  W.H. Bond, 517(PBSA):Apr-Jun78-281
Peters, R.M., Jr. The Massachusetts
  Constitution of 1780.
  W.P. Adams, 656(WMQ):Apr79-315
  J.H. Kettner, 432(NEQ):Jun79-288
Peters, U. - see Ulrich von Lichtenstein
Petersen, K. Georg Kaiser.*
  L.R. Shaw, 133:Band12Heft1/2-176
Petersmann, H. Petrons urbane Prosa.*
  P.A. George, 123:Vol29No2-233
  B. Löfstedt, 343:Band23-126
Peterson, B. The Peripheral Spy.*
  N. Callendar, 441:20Apr80-25
Peterson, H.F. Diplomat of the Americas.
  J. Allison, 77:Winter78-91
Peterson, J.T. The Ecology of Social
  Boundaries.
  K.L. Hutterer, 293(JASt):Aug79-845
Peterson, M.D. Adams and Jefferson.
  639(VQR):Winter79-12
Peterson, R.T. A Field Guide to the Birds.
  (4th ed)
  K. Emerson, 441:26Oct80-12
Peterson, W.S. Victorian Heretic.*
  D.F. Howard, 637(VS):Winter78-271
Peterson, W.S. - see Browning, E.B.
Peterson, W.S. - see "Browning Institute
  Studies"
Petit, J., ed. Sur "Le Chevalier Des
  Touches."
  A. Demaitre, 207(FR):May79-934
Petit, J. - see Green, J.
Petit, J. - see Mauriac, F.
Petit, P. Pax Romana.
  K.R. Bradley, 121(CJ):Oct-Nov79-67
Petrie, G. Seahorse.
  P. Lewis, 617(TLS):8Aug80-892
Petrie, P. Light from the Furnace Rising.
  J.F. Cotter, 249(HudR):Spring79-111
  P. Ramsey, 569(SR):Fall79-686

Petrone, G. Morale e antimorale nelle
  commedie di Plauto.
  E. Segal, 24:Winter79-576
  M.M. Willcock, 123:Vol29No1-147
Petronius. Petronio Arbitro, "Dal Satyr-
  icon: Il Bellum civile." (G. Guido, ed
  and trans)
  R.R. Bolgar, 313:Vol69-234
Petronius. Petronio: La Novella della
  Matrona di Efeso. (O. Pecere, ed)
  R.R. Bolgar, 313:Vol69-234
Petrounias, E. Funktion und Thematik der
  Bilder bei Aischylos.
  A.F. Garvie, 123:Vol29No1-8
Petry, M.J. - see Hegel, G.W.F.
Petschow, H. - see San Nicolò, M.
Petsopoulos, Y. Kilims.
  J. Housego, 617(TLS):15Aug80-921
Pettenati, S., ed. I vetri dorati graf-
  fiti e i vetri dipinti.
  R. Pinkham, 39:Nov79-452
Petti, A.G. English Literary Hands from
  Chaucer to Dryden.*
  E. Bourcier, 189(EA):Jul-Dec78-370
  J.H. Fisher, 589:Jan79-183
  566:Autumn78-49
Pettigrew, J. Robber Noblemen.
  S. Saberwal, 293(JASt):Feb79-403
Pettinato, G. Ebla.
  A. Kuhrt, 617(TLS):4Jul80-760
Pettit, P. The Concept of Structuralism.*
  E. Matthews, 518:May79-77
Pettit, P. Judging Justice.
  J.E.J. Altham, 617(TLS):12Sep80-1002
Pétursson, E.G. Miðaldaaevintýri þýdd úr
  ensku.*
  E.G. Fichtner, 563(SS):Winter79-48
Pétursson, M. Drög að hljóðkerfisfraeði.
  A. Liberman, 563(SS):Spring79-183
Petzoldt, L., ed. Historische Sagen.
  (Vol 2)
  E.H. Rehermann, 196:Band19Heft3/4-336
Peukert, H. Wissenschaftstheorie — Hand-
  lungstheorie — Fundamentale Theologie.
  A. Gethmann-Siefert, 679:Band9Heft1-
  188
Peukert, W. Der atlantische Sklavenhandel
  von Dahomey 1740-97.
  P. Erny, 182:Vol131#9/10-316
Pevear, R. Night Talk and Other Poems.*
  J. Palen, 590:Spring/Summer78-38
Pevsner, N. A History of Building Types.*
  D. Stillman, 637(VS):Summer78-512
Peyre, H. French Literary Imagination and
  Dostoevsky and Other Essays.*
  J.M. Cocking, 208(FS):Vol33Pt2-974
Peyre, H. Rimbaud vu par Verlaine.*
  N. Wing, 546(RR):Jan79-108
Peyre, H. What Is Romanticism?
  M.G. Cooke, 591(SIR):Summer79-323
Peyre, H. and J. Seronde, eds. Nine
  Classic French Plays. (2nd ed)
  R.C. Knight, 208(FS):Jul79-342
Peyrón, J.A. - see under Alegre Peyrón, J.
Peyser, J. Boulez.
  B. Hopkins, 607:Dec77-43
  A.W., 412:Aug-Nov78-284

Peytard, J. Recherches sur la préfixation en français contemporain.
J. Pinchon, 209(FM):Apr78-160

Pfaff, R.W. Montague Rhodes James.
N. Annan, 362:24Jul80-118
R. Birley, 617(TLS):27Jun80-740

Pfeffer, J.A. Grunddeutsch.
E. Bauer, 685(ZDL):1/1979-86

Pfeiffer, K.L. Sprachtheorie, Wissenschaftstheorie und das Problem der Textinterpretation.
D. Harth, 72:Band216Heft2-386
L. Martens, 107(CRCL):Fall79-405

Pfeiffer, R. History of Classical Scholarship from 1300 to 1850.*
J. Willis, 394:Vol32fasc3/4-451

Pfister, H.F. Facing the Light.
J. Fuller, 127:Summer79-296

Pfohl, R. Racine's "Iphigénie."
R.C. Knight, 208(FS):Jan79-82

Pfuhl, E. and H. Möbius. Die ostgriechischen Grabreliefs. (Vol 1)
R.M. Cook, 303(JoHS):Vol99-212

Phébus, G. - see under Gaston Phébus

Pheifer, J.D., ed. Old English Glosses in the Épinal-Erfurt Glossary.
J. Giffhorn, 38:Band96Heft1/2-204

Phelps, D. And Now We'll Play a Man's Game.
T.R. Madden, 502(PrS):Spring78-111

Phelps, R. - see Colette

Phidd, R.W. and G.B. Doern. The Politics and Management of Canadian Economic Policy.
L. Salter, 529(QQ):Autumn79-521

Philbrick, C. Nobody Laughs, Nobody Cries.
639(VQR):Spring78-58

Philip, G.D.E. The Rise and Fall of the Peruvian Military Radicals 1968-1976.
W. Little, 86(BHS):Jul79-278

Philip, M. Lectures de Lautréamont.
M. Pierssens, 98:May78-493

Philippart, G. Les Légendiers latin et autres manuscrits hagiographiques.
J.M. McCulloh, 589:Oct79-845

Philippi, D.L., ed and trans. Songs of Gods, Songs of Humans.
P. Rogers, 255(HAB):Summer79-224
Tamura Suzuko, 285(JapQ):Jul-Sep79-411

Philips, D. Crime and Authority in Victorian England.
W.R. Miller, 637(VS):Summer79-486

Philips, W. St. Stephen's-Green or The Generous Lovers. (C. Murray, ed)
T. Barnard, 617(TLS):5Sep80-973

Phillipps, K.C. The Language of Thackeray.
J. Bailey, 155:Summer79-113
P. Ingham, 541(RES):Nov79-488
J.P. Rawlins, 445(NCF):Mar79-517

Phillips, A. Alejandro Sawa.
R.A. Cardwell, 86(BHS):Jan79-72
A.P. Debicki, 240(HR):Autumn78-502

Phillips, D. No, Not I.
P. Craig, 617(TLS):7Mar80-278

Phillips, D. Wittgenstein and Scientific Knowledge.
D. Rubinstein, 488:Sep79-341

Phillips, D.C. Holistic Thought in Social Science.*
W.P. Baumgarth, 258:Mar79-122

Phillips, D.Z. Religion Without Explanation.*
P. Dubois, 542:Jul-Sep79-374
J. Skorupski, 393(Mind):Jan79-152

Phillips, G.D. The Diehards.*
639(VQR):Autumn79-131

Phillips, J. Give Your Child Music.
P. Standford, 415:Dec79-1002

Phillips, J.A. Black Tickets.*
T.R. Edwards, 453(NYRB):6Mar80-43

Phillips, J.W. Washington State Place Names.
K.B. Harder, 424:Dec77-241

Phillips, M. Francesco Guicciardini.*
J.E. Law, 539:Vol4No2-242
L. Martines, 125:Spring79-429

Phillips, N.R. The Quest for Excellence.
W.G. Warren, 63:Dec79-361

Phillips, P. The Prehistory of Europe.
D. Harding, 617(TLS):4Jul80-760

Phillips, P. Regional Disparities.*
T.K. Rymes, 529(QQ):Autumn79-523

Phillips, P.T., ed. The View from the Pulpit.*
E. Alexander, 529(QQ):Winter79/80-657
J.M. Cameron, 627(UTQ):Summer79-414

Phillips, R. The Pregnant Man.*
J.F. Cotter, 249(HudR):Spring79-118
A. Williamson, 491:Mar80-348
639(VQR):Winter79-26

Phillips, R. - see Schwartz, D.

Phillips, S. Resisting Arrest.
N. Callendar, 441:17Aug80-19

Phillips, W.D., Jr. Enrique IV and the Crisis of Fifteenth-Century Castile, 1425-1480.
K. Kennelly, 589:Jul79-619

Phillipson, D.W. The Prehistory of Eastern Zambia.
P.S. Garlake, 69:Vol148#4-420

Phillipson, J.S. Thomas Wolfe.
J.L. Idol, Jr., 580(SCR):Nov78-128

Phillpotts, B. Fairy Paintings.
C. Cannon-Brookes, 39:Mar79-242

"Philosophes ibériques et ibéro-américains en exil."
E. Namer, 542:Apr-Jun78-200

"Philosophia." (Vols 5 and 6) [title in Greek]
H. Wagner, 53(AGP):Band60Heft2-242

"Philosophie et pluralisme."
J.B. Ayoub, 154:Sep78-548

Philonexus. Die Fragmente des Grammatikers Philoxenos.* (C. Theodoridis, ed)
M.D. Macleod, 303(JoHS):Vol99-182

Philp, R. and M. Whitney. Danseur.
I. Garland, 648(WCR):Oct78-75
J. Percival, 151:Aug78-44

Philpott, T.L. The Slum and the Ghetto.
B.M. Stave, 579(SAQ):Spring79-263

Photius. Bibliothèque. (Vol 8) (R. Henry, ed)
  M. Marcovich, 124:Dec79/Jan80-252
  N.G. Wilson, 123:Vol29No2-217
"The Physics of Music."
  D.B. McLay, 255(HAB):Winter/Spring79-121
"Physiologus." (M.J. Curley, trans)
  R.A. Sokolov, 441:18May80-15
Pia, P. - see Laforgue, J.
Piaget, J. and N. Chomsky. Language and Learning. (M. Piattelli-Palmarini, ed)
  H.E. Gruber, 441:19Oct80-15
  I. Hacking, 453(NYRB):23Oct80-47
Pialat, M. Passe ton bac d'abord.
  J. Prieur, 450(NRF):Oct79-149
Pianet, J. and others. Cours audiovisuel de français 6.
  E. Namenwirth, 556(RLV):1978/1-95
Piattelli-Palmarini, M. - see Piaget, J. and N. Chomsky
Pic de la Mirandole, J. and P. Garcia. Une controverse sur Origène à la Renaissance. (H. Crouzel, ed and trans)
  G. de Durand, 539:Vol4No1-120
Picard, R. Nouveau Corpus Racinianum.
  D.M. Hayne, 627(UTQ):Winter78/79-179
  R.C. Knight, 402(MLR):Jan79-205
  J.C. Lapp, 546(RR):May79-307
  J. Morel, 535(RHL):May-Jun78-466
  R.W. Tobin, 188(ECr):Spring78-93
Picard, R. De Racine au Parthénon.
  J.C. Lapp, 546(RR):May79-307
  R.W. Tobin, 188(ECr):Spring78-93
  J. Truchet, 535(RHL):May-Jun78-468
"Picasso: Oeuvres reçues en paiement des droits de succession."
  J. Richardson, 453(NYRB):17Jul80-16
Pich, E. - see Leconte de Lisle, C.M.
Pichaske, D. A Generation in Motion.
  C. Brown, 617(TLS):16May80-552
Pichois, C. Littérature et progrès.
  H. Godin, 208(FS):Apr79-241
Pichois, C. Le Romantisme II.
  J.M. Cocking, 208(FS):Oct79-459
Pichois, C. - see Baudelaire, C.
Picht, G. and C. Eisenbart, eds. Frieden und Völkerrecht.
  M. Rock, 182:Vol131#7/8-194
Pickar, G.B. The Dramatic Works of Max Frisch.
  M. Jurgensen, 67:May79-155
Pickard, R. The Oscar Movies.
  M. Buckley, 200:May79-305
Pickard, R. Who Played Who in the Movies, an A-Z.
  R. Usborne, 617(TLS):4Jan80-10
Picken, L. Folk Musical Instruments of Turkey.
  B.C. Wade, 318(JAOS):Apr-Jun78-169
Pickens, R.T. The Welsh Knight.*
  T. Hunt, 402(MLR):Apr79-448
  N.J. Lacy, 207(FR):Oct78-155
  205(FMLS):Jul78-287
Pickering, D.S., ed. The South English Nativity of Mary and Christ edited from
  [continued]

[continuing]
  MS. BM. Stowe 949.*
  D. Speed, 67:May79-83
Pickering, F.P. Augustinus oder Boethius? (Pt 2)
  S.M. Johnson, 406:Spring79-61
Pickering, S., Jr. The Moral Tradition in English Fiction, 1785-1850.*
  M. Ferguson, 637(VS):Winter78-280
  K.J. Fielding, 402(MLR):Apr79-421
Pickerodt-Uthleb, E. Die Jenaer Liederhandschrift.*
  G. Objartel, 680(ZDP):Band97Heft3-463
Pickford, C.E. - see "The Song of Songs"
Pickthall, M. and M.A.H. Eliasi, eds and trans. A New Dimension Added to the Study of Holy Qur'ān through Roman Script.
  G.D. Rasheed, 273(IC):Jul78-208
Picoche, J. Le Vocabulaire psychologique dans les "Chroniques" de Froissart.*
  J. Chaurand, 209(FM):Jul78-282
  A.H. Diverres, 208(FS):Oct79-435
Picoche, J-L. Un romántico español: Enrique Gil y Carrasco (1815-1846).
  A.D. Inglis, 86(BHS):Oct79-342
  J.H.R. Polt, 238:Dec79-731
Picon, G. The Birth of Modern Painting.*
  C.C. Brookes, 39:Dec79-538
Picon, G. Jean-Auguste-Dominique Ingres.
  J. Russell, 441:30Nov80-74
Picon, M., with J.B. Grillo. Molly!
  D. Grumbach, 441:2Mar80-15
Picón Garfield, E. Cortázar por Cortázar.
  S. Daydí-Tolson, 238:Dec79-737
Picone, G. L'eloquenza di Plinio.
  M. Winterbottom, 123:Vol29No1-67
Pieltain, P. "Le Cimetière marin" de Paul Valéry.
  D. Moutote, 535(RHL):Mar-Apr78-333
Piepmeier, R. Aporien des Lebensbegriffs seit Oetinger.
  J-L. Nancy, 182:Vol131#14-454
Pierce, F. Amadís de Gaula.*
  F.W. de Kurlat, 86(BHS):Jul79-247
  C. Smith, 382(MAE):1979/2-321
Piercy, M. The Twelve-Spoked Wheel Flashing.*
  639(VQR):Autumn78-144
Piercy, M. Vida.
  E. Langer, 441:24Feb80-1
  J. Leonard, 441:15Jan80-C10
  J. Uglow, 617(TLS):7Mar80-258
  61:Feb80-96
Pieri, A. Lucrezio in Macrobio.
  B.C. Barker-Benfield, 123:Vol29No2-310
Pieri, M. Per Marino.
  U. Limentani, 402(MLR):Apr79-472
Pieri, M. - see Marino, G.P.
Pierre, C. Histoire du Concert Spirituel 1725-1790.
  J.R., 412:Aug-Nov78-292
Pierre, C. Tourne ma toupie [suivi de] Oeil.
  C. Dodge, 207(FR):Oct78-185

Pierre, J.W. La Persuasion de la Charité, Thèmes, formes et structures dans les Journaux et Oeuvres diverses de Marivaux.
C. Bonfils, 535(RHL):Sep-Oct78-827
Pierrot, J. L'imaginaire décadent (1880-1900).
O. Marcel, 542:Oct-Dec79-477
"Piers Plowman" - see under Langland, W.
Pieters, J. Nederlands. Nederlands 4.
W. Smets, 556(RLV):1978/1-89
Pieyre de Mandiargues, A. Arcimboldo the Marvelous.
A. Frankenstein, 55:Jan79-28
Pieyre de Mandiargues, A. L'Ivre Oeil [together with] Croiseur noir [and] Passage de l'Égyptienne.
É. Boissonnas, 450(NRF):Oct79-130
Piggott, P. The Innocent Diversion.
P. Conrad, 617(TLS):7Mar80-274
Piggott, P. Rachmaninov.
G. Norris, 415:Mar79-218
Piggott, S. Antiquity Depicted.
N. Hammond, 617(TLS):8Feb80-147
Piggott, S. Ruins in a Landscape.
L.R. Laing, 161(DUJ):Jun79-266
Pignatti, T. Veronese, l'opera completa.* (Vol 2)
L. Larcher Crosato, 471:Jan/Feb/Mar79-79
Pih, I. Le Père Gabriel de Magalhães.
C.R. Boxer, 617(TLS):6Jun80-652
Piirainen, I.T. - see Helle, D. and others
Pike, D. History of Vietnamese Communism, 1925-1976.
A. Woodside, 293(JASt):May79-621
Pike, K.L. and E.G. Grammatical Analysis.
R.M. Brend, 361:May78-91
P.H. Fries, 350:Dec79-907
Pike, L. Beethoven, Sibelius and the "Profound Logic."
W. Drabkin, 410(M&L):Oct79-451
R. Pascal, 415:Mar79-219
R.A. Sharpe, 89(BJA):Summer79-282
Pikhaus, D. Levensbeschouwing en milieu in de Latijnse metrische inscripties.
G. Alföldy, 182:Vol131#14-496
Pilch, H. Altenglische Grammatik.
L-G. Hallander, 597(SN):Vol150#1-135
E. Kolb, 38:Band96Heft3/4-459
Pilch, H. Altenglischer Lehrgang.
L-G. Hallander, 597(SN):Vol150#1-135
Pildas, A. and L. Smith. Movie Palaces.
S. Slesin, 441:14Dec80-12
Pilhes, R-V. The Provocateur.
639(VQR):Spring78-66
Pilkington, A.E. Bergson and His Influence.*
G. Brée, 535(RHL):Sep-Oct79-876
Pilkington, J. - see Young, S.
Pilkington, W.T. and D. Graham, eds. Western Movies.
R.L. Davis, 584(SWR):Autumn79-416
Pilling, J. Samuel Beckett.*
J-J. Mayoux, 402(MLR):Jan79-190
Pillu, P. - see Vallès, J.
Piltz, E. Kamelaukion et mitra.
A. Cutler, 341:1978/2-73

Pimlott, B. Labour and the Left in the 1930s.
R.W. Lyman, 161(DUJ):Jun79-278
Piñal, F.A. - see under Aguilar Piñal, F.
Pinborg, J. Logik und Semantik im Mittelalter.
S.F.B., 543:Dec78-367
G.F. Meier, 682(ZPSK):Band31Heft6-655
Pinborg, J. - see Boethius
Pinchin, J.L. Alexandria Still.*
M.B. Raizis, 295(JML):Vol7#4-608
Pinchuk, I. Scientific and Technical Translation.
G. Radó, 75:3-4/1978-175
Pincus-Witten, R. Postminimalism.
D.B. Kuspit, 127:Summer79-298
Pineaux, J. - see Désiré, A.
Ping-ti, H. - see under Ho Ping-ti
Pinget, R. The Libera Me Domine.*
G. Perez, 249(HudR):Autumn79-472
639(VQR):Summer79-98
Pinget, R. Passacaglia.*
G. Perez, 249(HudR):Autumn79-472
639(VQR):Summer79-102
Pinion, F.B. A Commentary on the Poems of Thomas Hardy.*
M. Bath, 637(VS):Winter78-268
J. Dusinberre, 447(N&Q):Aug78-372
Pinion, F.B. Thomas Hardy.*
J. Dusinberre, 447(N&Q):Aug78-372
D. Edwards, 637(VS):Summer78-511
J. Halperin, 395(MFS):Summer78-303
636(VP):Winter78-399
Pinion, F.B. A Hardy Companion. (2nd ed)
S. Hunter, 402(MLR):Jan79-175
Pinkerton, S., ed. Studies in K'ekchi.*
R. Freeze, 269(IJAL):Oct78-350
Pinsky, R. An Explanation of America.*
J. Fuller, 617(TLS):18Jan80-65
D. Kalstone, 441:4May80-15
W.H. Pritchard, 491:Aug80-295
V. Rutsala, 460(OhR):No.24-102
Pinsky, R. The Situation of Poetry.*
P. Breslin, 405(MP):Aug79-113
V. Contoski, 502(PrS):Fall78-296
S. Estess, 152(UDQ):Summer78-143
R. von Hallberg, 114(ChiR):Summer78-108
W.H. Pritchard, 491:Aug80-295
Pintacuda, M. La musica nella tragedia greca.
M.O. Lee, 487:Winter79-363
Pintaudi, R. - see Ficino, M.
Pinter, H. No Man's Land.
C. Jordis, 450(NRF):Nov79-125
Pinter, H. The Proust Screenplay.*
J. Coleby, 157:Winter79-86
R.D. Frye, 207(FR):Mar79-654
R. Shattuck, 473(PR):4/1979-611
295(JML):Vol17#4-799
Pinzer, M. The Maimie Papers.* (R. Rosen and S. Davidson, eds)
M.S. Littleford, 577(SHR):Summer79-264
S. Salmans, 617(TLS):8Feb80-154
Pipes, R. Struve.
L. Schapiro, 617(TLS):20Jun80-687

Pippidi, D.M. Scythica minora.
J.G.F. Hind, 303(JoHS):Vol199-197
Pippidi, D.M. and I.I. Russu, eds. In-
scriptiones Daciae et Scythiae Minoris
antiquae. (1st Ser, Vols 1-3)
J.J. Wilkes, 313:Vol69-206
Piriou, J-P.J. - see Green, J.
Pirsig, R.M. Zen and the Art of Motor-
cycle Maintenance.* (French title:
Traité du Zen et de l'entretien des
motocyclettes.)
C. Rosset, 98:Dec78-1174
Pirumova, N.M. Zemskoe liberal'noe
dvizhenie.
G.M. Hamburg, 550(RusR):Apr79-230
de Pisan, C. - see under Christine de
Pisan
Pisani, V. Manuale storico della lingua
greca. (2nd ed)
C.J. Ruijgh, 394:Vol30fasc3-300
Pisar, S. Of Blood and Hope.
N. Ascherson, 453(NYRB):12Jun80-34
D. Rabinowitz, 441:29Jun80-12
R.F. Shepard, 441:9Jul80-C19
Piscator, E. The Political Theatre.
N. Shrimpton, 617(TLS):25Jul80-830
Pisi, G. Fedro traduttore di Esopo.
J. Henderson, 123:Vol29No2-311
Piston, W. Harmony. (rev by M. Devoto)
W. Drabkin, 415:Jun79-485
Pitcher, G. Berkeley.*
H.M. Bracken, 84:Sep79-297
R. Cummins, 482(PhR):Apr79-299
E.S., 543:Sep78-148
Pitcher, H. Chekhov's Leading Lady.
P. Miles, 617(TLS):25Apr80-476
Pitcher, H. When Miss Emmie Was in
Russia.*
N.M. Frieden, 550(RusR):Jan79-94
Pitkäranta, R. Studien zum Latein des
Victor Vitensis.
B. Löfstedt, 124:Sep79-49
"Pittura del seicento e del settecento,
ricerche in Umbria I."
F. Russell, 39:Nov79-453
Piva, F. Sulla genesi di "Manon Lescaut."
J. Sgard, 535(RHL):Jul-Aug79-664
Pivčević, E., ed. Phenomenology and Phil-
osophical Understanding.*
C. Smith, 208(FS):Vol33Pt2-946
Piven, F.F. and R.A. Cloward. Poor
People's Movements.*
T. Copp, 529(QQ):Spring79-177
Pizarro, A. Shadowinnower.
H.J.F. de Aguilar, 472:Fall/Winter79-
64
Pizer, D. The Novels of Theodore Dreiser.*
H. Beaver, 402(MLR):Apr79-435
E. Gureschi, 395(MFS):Winter78/79-633
Pizer, D. - see Dreiser, T.
Pizzamiglio, G. - see Seriman, Z.
Pizzorusso, A. Prospettive seconde.
N. Suckling, 208(FS):Jan79-118
Pizzorusso, A. Sedici Commenti a Baude-
laire.
A. Kies, 535(RHL):Sep-Oct78-855

Place, J.A. The Non-Western Films of John
Ford.
W.K. Everson, 18:May79-70
Plaisant, M., ed. L'Excentricité en
Grande-Bretagne au 18e siècle.
I. Jack, 189(EA):Jan-Mar78-87
Plaks, A.H., ed. Chinese Narrative.
Y.W. Ma, 293(JASt):Nov78-165
D.S. Willis, 399(MLJ):Apr79-230
639(VQR):Summer78-96
"Plan for Restoration and Adaptive Use of
the Frank Lloyd Wright Home and Studio."
J.M. Richards, 617(TLS):1Feb80-122
Plante, D. The Family.*
W. Sullivan, 569(SR):Spring79-337
Plantinga, L. Clementi.*
L.M. Griffel, 414(MusQ):Oct78-540
Plantos, T. The Universe Ends at Sher-
bourne and Queen. This Tavern Has No
Symmetry.
D. Precosky, 198:Summer80-156
Plater, W.M. The Grim Phoenix.*
C. Baxter, 141:Spring79-179
S. Brivic, 295(JML):Vol7#4-800
J.H. Justus, 27(AL):Jan80-582
J. Klinkowitz, 301(JEGP):Jul79-466
R. Pearce, 587(SAF):Spring79-110
K. Tololyan, 594:Summer79-224
S. Weisenburger, 401(MLQ):Mar79-88
Plath, S. Johnny Panic and the Bible of
Dreams.* (T. Hughes, ed)
C. Bere, 577(SHR):Fall79-358
Plato. Gorgias. (T. Irwin, ed and trans)
M.M. Mackenzie, 617(TLS):20Jun80-713
Plato. Phaedo.* (D. Gallop, ed and trans)
W.J. Verdenius, 394:Vol32fasc1/2-183
Plato. Philebus.* (J.C.B. Gosling, ed
and trans)
W.J. Verdenius, 394:Vol32fasc1/2-183
Plato. Plato's "Republic." (G.M.A. Grube,
trans)
R. Hogan, 154:Dec78-720
Plato. Protagoras.* (C.C.W. Taylor, ed
and trans)
W.J. Verdenius, 394:Vol32fasc1/2-183
Plato. Theaetetus.* (J. McDowell, ed and
trans)
W.J. Verdenius, 394:Vol32fasc1/2-183
"Platon et Aristote à la Renaissance."
J. Bernhardt, 542:Jan-Mar78-97
Platonov, A. Chevengur.* Collected
Works.*
R.L. Chapple, 574(SEEJ):Fall79-409
Platt, C. The English Medieval Town.*
J.M.W. Bean, 589:Apr79-413
Platt, D.C.M., ed. Business Imperialism
1840-1930.
J. Fisher, 86(BHS):Jan79-87
Platt, J.T. and H.K. The Social Signifi-
cance of Speech.*
W.J. Samarin, 320(CJL):Spring-Fall78-
197
Plattel, M.G. Utopian and Critical Think-
ing.
G. Negley, 322(JHI):Apr-Jun79-315
Platter, W.M. The Grim Phoenix.
639(VQR):Spring79-48

du Pont, A. Le Roman de Mahomet de Alex-
andre du Pont (1258). (Y.G. Lepage, ed)
N. Daniel, 382(MAE):1979/1-134
Ponzio, A. - see Bachtin, M.
Pool, J. and S. Who Financed Hitler?*
J.S. Conway, 529(QQ):Autumn79-510
Poole, A. Gissing in Context.
C.J. Francis, 637(VS):Winter78-279
Poole, R. The Unknown Virginia Woolf.*
A. Bell, 569(SR):Spring79-325
M. Church, 268(IFR):Summer80-141
J. Edge, 67:Nov79-327
J. Gindin, 594:Spring79-82
H. Harper, 579(SAQ):Summer79-404
T.M. McLaughlin, 659(ConL):Autumn80-
639
S. Rudikoff, 249(HudR):Winter79/80-540
M. Spilka, 454:Winter79-176
A.A. West, 49:Apr79-97
295(JML):Vol7#4-844
639(VQR):Winter79-23
Poortvliet, R. He Was One of Us.
529(QQ):Summer79-372
Popa, V. Collected Poems, 1943-1976.*
T. Eagleton, 565:Vol20#3-75
J. Simon, 491:Apr80-40
Popa, V. Homage to the Lame Wolf.
J. Simon, 491:Apr80-40
Pope, A. Pope: Poetical Works. (H. Davis,
ed)
P.W., 148:Spring79-92
566:Spring79-135
Pope, N. Dickens and Charity.*
A.S. Watts, 155:Summer79-111
J. Wilt, 141:Summer79-273
Pope-Hennessy, J. Luca della Robbia.
H.W. Janson, 453(NYRB):17Apr80-39
J. Russell, 441:30Nov80-11
Popham, H. and R., eds. A Thirst for the
Sea.
A. Bailey, 617(TLS):29Feb80-232
Popkess, B. The Nuclear Survival Handbook.
C. Wain, 362:30Oct80-586
Popkin, D. and M., eds. Modern French Lit-
erature.*
J. Cruickshank, 208(FS):Vol33Pt2-935
Popkin, L.B. The Theatre of Rafael
Alberti.*
G. Alvarez-Altman, 238:Mar79-178
Popovič, A. Teória umeleckého prekladu.
O. Čepan, 107(CRCL):Fall79-426
G. Radó, 75:3-4/1978-177
Popp, D. Asbjørnsen's Linguistic Re-
form.* (Vol 1)
M. Barnes, 447(N&Q):Oct78-472
Popper, K. Unended Quest.*
P. Haratonik, 186(ETC.):Jun78-199
Popper, K.R. and J.C. Eccles. The Self
and Its Brain.*
L.J. Cohen, 393(Mind):Apr79-301
R. Macklin, 484(PPR):Dec79-290
K.T. Maslin, 479(PhQ):Oct79-370
G. Vesey, 483:Apr79-249
Popperwell, R.G., ed. Expression, Communi-
cation and Experience in Literature and
Language.
G. Rees, 208(FS):Oct79-482

Popperwell, R.G. and T. Støverud, eds.
Norsk Litteraturantologi.
H. Schmidt, 682(ZPSK):Band31Heft3-322
"Popular Music Periodicals Index." (1976)
R. Andrewes, 415:Apr79-310
Porat, S. Filing Systems as an Adminis-
trative Service. [in Hebrew]
S.J. Pomrenze, 14:Oct79-481
Porges, I. Edgar Rice Burroughs.
J.Z.G., 395(MFS):Summer78-287
Porkert, M. The Theoretical Foundations
of Chinese Medicine.
D. Gregory-Smith, 485(PE&W):Apr79-221
Pörn, I. Action Theory and Social Science.
T. Horgan, 482(PhR):Apr79-308
J. Williamson, 479(PhQ):Jul79-282
Porphyry. De l'Abstinence. (Bk 1) (J.
Bouffartigue and M. Patillon, eds)
A.H. Armstrong, 303(JoHS):Vol199-185
A. Meredith, 123:Vol29No1-25
"La Porporina."
J. Gaulmier, 535(RHL):Jul-Aug78-659
Port, M.H., ed. The Houses of Parliament.*
H. Hobhouse, 637(VS):Winter78-282
Porte, J. Representative Man.*
N. Baym, 301(JEGP):Jul79-462
P.F. Gura, 432(NEQ):Sep79-407
P.F. Gura, 639(VQR):Summer79-546
W. Harding, 27(AL):May79-280
Porten, B., with J.C. Greenfield, eds and
trans. Jews of Elephantine and Arameans
of Syrene.
J.D. Whitehead, 318(JAOS):Jul-Sep78-
310
Porter, A. Music of Three Seasons: 1974-
1977.*
R.L. Davis, 584(SWR):Spring79-198
W. Dean, 415:Dec79-1004
42(AR):Fall79-488
Porter, A.J. and A.J. Dvosin - see Rahv, P.
Porter, A.N. The Origins of the South
African War.
P. Clarke, 617(TLS):5Sep80-954
Porter, B. The Refugee Question in Mid-
Victorian Politics.
M.B. Carter, 617(TLS):22Feb80-200
Porter, C. Alexandra Kollontai.
K. Fitz Lyon, 617(TLS):29Feb80-226
Porter, D. Emerson and Literary Change.*
P.F. Gura, 432(NEQ):Sep79-407
D.H. Hirsch, 569(SR):Summer79-1x
S.W. Liebman, 27(AL):Nov79-428
S. Paul, 141:Spring79-175
Porter, E. Antarctica.*
529(QQ):Summer79-368
Porter, E. and M. Harwood. Moments of
Discovery.
639(VQR):Winter78-30
Porter, E. and P. Levi. The Greek World.
H. Kramer, 441:30Nov80-64
Porter, F. - see Williams, W. and J.
Porter, J. Hapkas Girl.
S. Chew, 617(TLS):15Aug80-923
Porter, L.M. The Renaissance of the Lyric
in French Romanticism.
D. Festa-McCormick, 593:Winter79-358

Porter, P. The Cost of Seriousness.*
D. Graham, 565:Vol20#1-65
Porter, R. The Making of Geology.*
C.J. Schneer, 173(ECS):Fall78-139
Porter, T. How Architects Visualize.
C. Amery, 617(TLS):21Mar80-332
Pörtl, K. Das lyrische Werk des Damián
Cornejo (1629-1707). (Pt 1)
H. Janner, 72:Band216Heft2-463
M. Knapp, 182:Vol131#20-743
Portman, J. and J. Barnett. The Archi-
tect as Developer.
M. Lapidus, 576:Dec78-303
Pòrtulas, J. Lectura de Píndar.
M.M. Willcock, 303(JoHS):Vol99-173
Posèq, A.W.G. Format in Painting.
M. Hester, 290(JAAC):Spring80-351
Posner, D. The Sandpipers.
639(VQR):Summer78-100
Possevino, A. The Moscovia of Antonio
Possevino, S.J. (H.F. Graham, ed and
trans)
R.O. Crummey, 550(RusR):Jan79-83
J.N. Moody, 497(PolR):Vol23#4-85
van der Post, L. The Lost World of the
Kalahari.
W.K. McNeil, 292(JAF):Jul-Sep79-363
Post-Adams, R. Uwe Johnson.
E. Friedrichsmeyer, 133:Band12Heft1/2-
188
Postal, P.M. On Raising.
J.R. Hurford, 297(JL):Mar79-111
Poster, M. Critical Theory of the Family.
G. Meilaender, 613:Jun79-205
Poston, C.H. - see Wollstonecraft, M.
Potapova, Z.M. Russko-ital'janskie litera-
turnye svjazi.
W. Potthoff, 688(ZSP):Band40Heft2-419
Potok, A. Ordinary Daylight.
A. Broyard, 441:18Apr80-C26
A. Roiphe, 441:11May80-12
Potter, J.M. Thai Peasant Social Struc-
ture.*
B.L. Foster, 318(JAOS):Jul-Sep78-339
Potter, K.H., ed. Indian Metaphysics and
Epistemology.*
J.B. Chethimattam, 613:Dec79-432
D.D. Daye, 485(PE&W):Apr79-245
A. Malhotra, 484(PPR):Dec79-303
Potter, R. The English Morality Play.
C. Gauvin, 189(EA):Jan-Mar78-75
S.J. Kahrl, 191(ELN):Mar79-235
Potter, R.R. Making Sense.
H. Kirschbaum, 186(ETC.):Dec77-466
Potterton, H. Pageant and Panorama.
J.G. Links, 39:Nov79-452
Potthoff, W., ed. Dubrovniker Dramatiker
des 17. Jahrhunderts.*
E.D. Goy, 575(SEER):Jul79-422
Pottier, B., ed. Sémantique et logique.
R. Martin, 209(FM):Oct78-375
Potts, M., P. Diggory and J. Peel. Abor-
tion.
S.R. Isbister, 529(QQ):Spring79-127
Potts, W., ed. Portraits of the Artist in
Exile.*
376:Oct79-143

Pou, S., ed and trans. Rāmakerti (XVIe-
XVIIe siècles).
K. Rosenberg, 182:Vol131#17/18-608
de Pougy, L. My Blue Notebooks.*
(French title: Mes cahiers bleus.)
D. Grumbach, 441:6Jan80-12
Poulat, É. Catholicisme, democratie et
socialisme.
W.R. Ward, 161(DUJ):Dec78-113
Poulenc, F. My Friends and Myself. (S.
Audel, ed)
R. Orledge, 410(M&L):Jul79-345
Poulet, G. Entre moi et moi.*
J.M. Cocking, 208(FS):Oct79-483
J. Onimus, 535(RHL):Sep-Oct79-887
Poulet, G. Proustian Space.*
J.M. Cocking, 208(FS):Oct79-483
Poulin, J. The Jimmy Trilogy.
L. Leith, 99:Jun-Jul80-34
Poulsen, H. Gallionsfigurer og ornamenter
på danske skibe og i danske samlinger.
W. Cederlöf, 341:1978/2-69
Poulter, S. Family Law and Litigation in
Basotho Society.
C. Murray, 69:Vol148#1-89
Pound, E. Ezra Pound and Music.* (R.M.
Schafer, ed)
H. Kenner, 414(MusQ):Jul79-440
Pound, E. "Ezra Pound Speaking."* (L.W.
Doob, ed)
W. Harmon, 569(SR):Spring79-xxxiv
Pound, O.S. and P. Grover. Wyndham Lewis.*
T. Materer, 468:Fall79-353
Pounds, N.J.G. An Historical Geography of
Europe 1500-1840.
E. Le Roy Ladurie, 617(TLS):25Jul80-
829
"Pourquoi la mathématique?"
J. Largeault, 542:Apr-Jun78-231
Powell, A. Faces in My Time.
J. Bayley, 362:20Mar80-371
A. Bell, 617(TLS):28Mar80-347
Powell, A. Infants of the Spring.*
639(VQR):Spring78-47
Powell, A. Messengers of Day.*
639(VQR):Winter79-10
Powell, A.S. Voprosy istorii, Author
Index, 1945-1975. Voprosy istorii,
Subject Index, 1945-1974.
W. Zalewski, 550(RusR):Jul79-405
Powell, C. Rehearsal for Dancers.*
E. Folsom, 526:Winter79-81
G. Hamel, 198:Winter80-139
Powell, D.E. Antireligious Propaganda in
the Soviet Union.
H.L. Hull, 550(RusR):Oct79-492
Powell, L.N. New Masters.
E. Genovese, 441:4May80-9
Powell, N. Carpenters of Light.
A. Brownjohn, 617(TLS):1Feb80-112
H. Lomas, 364:Mar80-78
Powell, W.S. John Pory, 1572-1636.*
D.B. Quinn, 656(WMQ):Jan79-139
Powers, R. The Newscasters.*
639(VQR):Winter78-17
Powers, T. The Man Who Kept the Secrets.*
R.W. Apple, Jr., 362:3Apr80-446

Pownall, D. Another Country.
  C. Hope, 364:Jun79-79
Pownall, D. Between Ribble and Lune.
  R. Blythe, 362:4Sep80-310
  N. Nicholson, 617(TLS):1Aug80-864
Powys, J.C. After My Fashion.
  V. Cunningham, 617(TLS):27Jun80-726
  C. Lock, 362:7Aug80-185
Powys, J.C. Morwyn.
  C. Jordis, 450(NRF):Apr79-147
Pozdneyev, A.M. Mongolia and the Mongols.
  (Vol 2) (J.R. Krueger, ed)
  H. Serruys, 318(JAOS):Oct-Dec78-578
da Pozza, G. - see Foscolo, U.
Pozzi, G. - see Marino, G.B.
Prache, A. Saint-Remi de Reims.
  N. Coldstream, 90:Jun79-390
  S. Gardner, 589:Oct79-847
do Prado Coelho, J. Ao Contrário de
  Penélope.
  N.J. Lamb, 86(BHS):Apr79-163
do Prado Coelho, J. A Letra e o Leitor.
  (2nd ed)
  P. Bacarisse, 86(BHS):Jul79-263
Praël-Himmer, H. Der Augsburger Gold-
  schmied Johann Andreas Thelot.
  G. Schiedlausky, 471:Apr/May/Jun79-178
Prance, C.A. The Laughing Philosopher.
  H. Forster, 447(N&Q):Oct78-477
Prasad, B. The Poetry of Thomas Hardy.
  T. Paulin, 637(VS):Autumn78-102
Prasad, P.C. Foreign Trade and Commerce
  in Ancient India.
  L. Casson, 124:Sep79-33
Prasad, S.N. A Survey of the Work Done on
  the Military History of India.
  D.C. Ellinwood, 293(JASt):Aug79-799
Pratilli, G.C. - see under Cascio Pratilli,
  G.
Prätorius, S. Seefarer Trost und Krancken
  Trost. (P. Boon, ed)
  B. Murdoch, 182:Vol31#7/8-217
  N.F. Palmer, 447(N&Q):Oct78-468
Pratt, B. Rompre le silence.
  J. Robinson, 535(RHL):Jul-Aug78-665
Pratt, J.C. and V.A. Neufeldt - see Eliot,
  G.
Pratt, L.H. James Baldwin.
  R.E. Fleming, 594:Summer79-249
Pratt, M.L. Toward a Speech Act Theory of
  Literary Discourse.*
  R. Carter, 307:Apr79-45
  W.O. Hendricks, 350:Jun79-475
  D.H. Hirsch, 569(SR):Fall79-628
Pratt, V. The Philosophy of the Social
  Sciences.
  D.W. Hamlyn, 617(TLS):4Jan80-19
Pratte, A. Les Batailles économiques du
  général de Gaulle.
  J. Hardré, 207(FR):Apr79-806
Prauss, G. Kant und das Problem der Dinge
  an sich.*
  L. Gäbe, 53(AGP):Band60Heft3-347
Prawer, S.S. Karl Marx and World Litera-
  ture.*
  F.J. Beharriell, 301(JEGP):Oct79-607
  L.H. Legters, 152(UDQ):Spring78-86

Praz, M. La casa della vita.
  F. Donini, 617(TLS):2May80-489
Prebish, C.S., ed. Buddhism.
  R.J. Miller, 293(JASt):May79-593
Prebish, C.S. Buddhist Monastic Disci-
  pline.
  H. Bechert, 318(JAOS):Apr-Jun78-203
  D.K. Swearer, 293(JASt):Feb79-419
Preiser, W.F.E., ed. Facility Programming.
  P.G. Rowe, 505:Feb79-102
Prematilleke, L., K. Indrapala and J.E.
  van Lohuizen-de Leeuw, eds. Senerat
  Paranavitana Commemoration Volume.
  H.L. Seneviratne, 293(JASt):Aug79-832
"Premio Città di Monselice per una tradu-
  zione letteraria." (No. 6)
  M.M., 228(GSLI):Vol155fasc491-478
Prender, R. A Lady's Experiences in the
  Wild West in 1883.
  A. Ronald, 649(WAL):Summer79-171
Prendergast, C. Balzac.
  D. Adamson, 208(FS):Jan79-92
  D.P. Scales, 67:Nov79-344
  205(FMLS):Jul78-287
Prenshaw, P.W., ed. Eudora Welty.
  R.P. Warren, 441:2Mar80-1
Preobrazhensky, E.A. The Crisis of Soviet
  Industrialization.
  A. Nove, 617(TLS):18Jul80-803
Prescott, A.L. French Poets and the
  English Renaissance.
  V. Skretkowicz, 150(DR):Autumn79-572
  H. Smith, 301(JEGP):Jan79-116
  F.M. Weinberg, 207(FR):May79-924
  639(VQR):Autumn78-128
"Présence du monstre — mythe et réalité."
  L. Davis, 208(FS):Vol33Pt2-981
Presley, J. A Saga of Wealth.
  W. Gard, 584(SWR):Spring79-vi
Pressler, C. Gustav Kraus, 1804-52.
  G. Bergsträsser, 182:Vol131#3/4-116
Pressly, N.L. The Fuseli Circle at Rome.
  F. Haskell, 453(NYRB):9Oct80-29
Preston, M.J. A Concordance to the Middle
  English Shorter Poems.*
  N.E. Enkvist, 597(SN):Vol150#2-325
  D. Gray, 382(MAE):1979/2-306
Preston, M.J., M.G. Smith and P.S. Smith.
  An Interim Checklist of Chapbooks Con-
  taining Traditional Play Texts.
  J. Forrest, 582(SFQ):Vol141-285
Preston, R.A. The Defence of the Unde-
  fended Border.
  N.F. Dreisziger, 106:Winter79-341
  G.A. Rawlyk, 529(QQ):Spring79-148
Preston, T.R. Not in Timon's Manner.*
  B. Gassman, 405(MP):Aug79-92
Prestwich, M. The Three Edwards.
  J.R. Maddicott, 617(TLS):4Jul80-763
Prete, B. - see Bradford, P.
Pretzel, U. - see Lexer, M.
.Preus, A. Science and Philosophy in
  Aristotle's Biological Works.
  I. Mueller, 53(AGP):Band60Heft1-65
  R.K. Sprague, 122:Jan79-84
Previn, D. Bog-Trotter.
  C. Brown, 617(TLS):27Jun80-728

Prévost, J.   La Création chez Stendhal.
    F.W. Saunders, 208(FS):Vol133Pt2-806
Preziosi, D.   The Semiotics of the Built
    Environment.
    J.P. Bonta, 290(JAAC):Spring80-340
Price, A.   The Hour of the Donkey.
    M. Laski, 362:14Aug80-216
Price, G. and D.A. Wells - see "The Year's
    Work in Modern Language Studies"
Price, G.R. - see Middleton, T. and W.
    Rowley
Price, J.   Executive Style.
    S. Slesin, 441:14Dec80-12
Price, J.V. - see Hume, D.
Price, M.J. and B.L. Trell.   Coins and
    Their Cities.
    W.R. Biers, 124:Dec79/Jan80-261
Price, R.   Ladies' Man.*
    42(AR):Winter79-125
Price, T.H.   Kourotrophos.
    R. Higgins, 303(JoHS):Vol99-213
Prickett, S.   Romanticism and Religion.*
    G. Cullum, 586(SoRA):Jul78-205
    J. Gibert, 189(EA):Apr-Jun78-229
    E.D. Mackerness, 447(N&Q):Jun78-251
Priego Fernández del Campo, J. - see
    Gómez de Avellaneda, G.
Priessnitz, H., ed.   Das englische Hör-
    spiel.
    H. Groene, 72:Band216Heft2-422
Prince, C.E.   The Federalists and the
    Origins of the U.S. Civil Service.
    J.E. Cooke, 656(WMQ):Jan79-128
Prince, F.T.   Collected Poems.*
    R. Lattimore, 249(HudR):Autumn79-441
    376:Oct79-141
    639(VQR):Autumn79-147
Prince, F.T.   Drypoints of the Hasidim.
    D. Graham, 565:Vol20#4-75
Prini, P.   Il paradosso di Icaro.
    A. Erbetta, 227(GCFI):Jan-Mar78-135
Prini, P.   Storia dell'esistenzialismo.
    (2nd ed)
    R. Prévost, 192(EP):Jul-Sep79-375
Prior, A.N. and K. Fine.   Worlds, Times
    and Selves.*
    R.A. Bull, 316:Dec79-654
Pritchard, A.   Catholic Loyalism in
    Elizabethan England.*
    C.S.L. Davies, 617(TLS):22Feb80-216
Pritchard, J.B.   Recovering Sarepta.
    N. Hammond, 617(TLS):8Feb80-147
Pritchard, W.H.   Lives of the Modern Poets.
    R. Ellmann, 441:4Apr80-11
    J. Leonard, 441:24Apr80-C23
    61:May80-102
Pritchard, W.H.   Seeing through Every-
    thing.*
    A.W. Litz, 569(SR):Fall79-660
Pritchett, V.S.   The Gentle Barbarian.*
    R. Mathewson, 473(PR):1/1979-133
    S. Pratt, 395(MFS):Summer78-292
Pritchett, V.S.   The Myth Makers.*
    W. Bedford, 364:Aug/Sep79-133
    J.I.M. Stewart, 617(TLS):18Jan80-69
    639(VQR):Autumn79-127

Pritchett, V.S.   On the Edge of the Cliff.*
    V. Glendinning, 617(TLS):29Feb80-228
    J. Mellors, 362:28Feb80-286
    R. Towers, 453(NYRB):7Feb80-25
Pritchett, V.S.   The Tale Bearers.
    J. Bayley, 453(NYRB):12Jun80-32
    A. Broyard, 441:25Apr80-C26
    R. Locke, 441:29Jun80-3
    442(NY):9Jun80-155
Pritikin, N., with P.M. McGrady, Jr.   The
    Pritikin Program for Diet and Exercise.
    J. Epstein, 453(NYRB):21Feb80-7
"Private Life of the Queen 1897."
    A. Forbes, 617(TLS):4Jan80-7
Privitera, G.A.   La rete di Afrodite.*
    J. Péron, 555:Vol52fasc1-152
"Problemy kartografirovanija v jazykozna-
    nii i etnografii."
    M-A. Borodina and I. Vildé-Lot,
    553(RLiR):Jan-Jun78-216
Probyn, C.T., ed.   The Art of Jonathan
    Swift.
    M. Johnson, 566:Autumn78-37
    C.J. Rawson, 541(RES):Feb79-86
Probyn, C.T., ed.   Jonathan Swift.
    P.M. Spacks, 401(MLQ):Dec79-403
    566:Spring79-133
Procházka, V., ed.   Dějiny ceského divadla.
    (Vol 2)
    V.V. Kusin, 610:May78-222
Prochnik, L.   Endings.
    D. Grumbach, 441:27Apr80-16
    C. Lehmann-Haupt, 441:13Feb80-C23
Procter, P. and others.   Longman Diction-
    ary of Contemporary English.
    B. Cottle, 541(RES):Feb79-195
    J.R. Gaskin, 569(SR):Summer79-455
"The Professional Chef's Knife."
    W. and C. Cowen, 639(VQR):Spring79-78
Profeti, M.G.   Per una bibliografia di J.
    Pérez de Montalbán.
    V. Dixon, 86(BHS):Jan79-66
Proffer, E., ed.   Tsvetaeva.
    J. Bayley, 453(NYRB):23Oct80-3
    H. Muchnic, 441:12Oct80-7
Proffer, E. - see Bulgakov, N.
Prokofiev, S.   Prokofiev by Prokofiev.*
    (D.H. Appel, ed)
    R. Craft, 453(NYRB):24Jan80-9
Prokop, D.   Soziologie des Films.
    W. Doise, 182:Vol131#15/16-537
Prokudin-Gorskii, S.M.   Photographs for
    the Tsar.   (R.H. Allhouse, ed)
    C. James, 453(NYRB):18Dec80-22
    J. Naughton, 362:18and25Dec80-865
Prolingheuer, H.   Der Fall Karl Barth.
    J.K.S. Reid, 182:Vol131#21/22-777
Pronzini, B., ed.   The Edgar Winners.
    N. Callendar, 441:2Mar80-21
Pronzini, B.   Labyrinth.
    N. Callendar, 441:25May80-13
Propertius.   Elegies I-IV.*   (L. Richard-
    son, Jr., ed)
    W.A. Camps, 123:Vol129No1-37
Propertius.   Sex. Properti "Elegiarum"
    Liber II.*   (I.C. Giardina, ed)
    W.A. Camps, 123:Vol129No1-39

Prosdocimi, A.L., ed. Lingue e dialetti dell'Italia antica.
E. Pulgram, 121(CJ):Apr-May80-350
Prosser, M.H. The Cultural Dialogue.
W.W. Neher, 583:Summer79-432
Prosser, M.H., ed. U.S.I.A. Intercultural Communication Course: 1977 Proceedings.
W.W. Neher, 583:Summer79-432
Prost, A. Les Anciens Combattants et la société française (1914-1939).
C.W. Obuchowski, 207(FR):Feb79-522
Prost, A. Vocabulaire des proclamations électorales de 1881, 1885 et 1889.
M. Hug, 209(FM):Jan78-91
Prou, S. Les Femmes de la pluie.
A-M. O'Healy, 207(FR):Apr79-798
Proust, M. Correspondance de Marcel Proust. (Vol 5) (P. Kolb, ed)
A. Finch, 617(TLS):14Mar80-288
Proust, M. and J. Rivière. Correspondance Marcel Proust-Jacques Rivière (1914-1922). (P. Kolb, ed)
H. Bonnet, 535(RHL):Jul-Aug79-705
Proxmire, W. The Fleecing of America.
W. Goodman, 441:15Jun80-15
Pruche, B. Existant et acte d'être.* (Vol 1)
M. Adam, 542:Jul-Sep79-375
Pruitt, I. Old Madam Yin.
O. Lattimore, 617(TLS):25Jan80-77
Pruner, F. L'Esotérisme de Saint-John Perse (dans "Anabase").
C.E.J. Dolamore, 402(MLR):Oct79-950
E.R. Jackson, 207(FR):Dec78-355
M. Sacotte, 535(RHL):May-Jun78-505
205(FMLS):Apr78-189
Pryke, K.G. Nova Scotia and Confederation 1867-74.
J.M. Beck, 150(DR):Winter79/80-769
Prynne, J.H. Down where changed.
A. Stevenson, 617(TLS):23May80-586
Prezełęcki, M. and R. Wójcicki, eds. Twenty-five Years of Logical Methodology in Poland.*
S. Leeds, 484(PPR):Mar80-447
W.H. Newton-Smith, 479(PhQ):Apr79-172
Psyhogeos, M. Learn to Read and Write Greek. Conversation in Greek. Mini-Course in Modern Greek.
J.E. Rexine, 399(MLJ):Jan-Feb79-59
Pucci, P. Hesiod and the Language of Poetry.*
T. Van Nortwick, 121(CJ):Dec79/Jan80-179
Pudney, J. Lewis Carroll and his World.
J. Bump, 637(VS):Summer78-521
J.R. Kincaid, 445(NCF):Sep78-272
Puech, J-B. La Bibliothèque d'un amateur.
P-L. Rey, 450(NRF):Apr79-114
Pugh, G.E. The Biological Origins of Human Values.
E. Butler, 479(PhQ):Jul79-281
Pugh, S. What a Place to Grow Flowers.
A. Stevenson, 617(TLS):23May80-586
Puig, M. The Buenos Aires Affair.
M. Wood, 453(NYRB):24Jan80-43

Puig, M. Kiss of the Spider Woman.*
C.C. Park, 249(HudR):Winter79/80-576
M. Wood, 453(NYRB):24Jan80-43
Pulgram, E. Latin-Romance Phonology.*
H. Lausberg, 72:Band216Heft1-189
P.M. Lloyd, 350:Sep79-698
W. Rothwell, 208(FS):Vol33Pt2-1020
Puliatti, P. - see Tassoni, A.
Pulte, W. - see Feeling, D.
Punch, M. Policing the Inner City.
N. Freeling, 617(TLS):21Mar80-337
del Punta, F. - see Paul of Venice
Punzo, F.R. Walter Scott in Italia.
R. Asselineau, 189(EA):Jan-Mar78-90
Puppo, M. La critica letteraria del Novecento.
M.C., 228(GSLI):Vol155fasc492-634
Purcell, H. Mao Tse-tung.
639(VQR):Summer78-108
Purdy, A. Being Alive.*
D. Barbour, 150(DR):Spring79-154
Purdy, J. Narrow Rooms.*
S. Fender, 617(TLS):14Mar80-296
J. Naughton, 362:6Mar80-318
Purdy, R.L. and M. Millgate - see Hardy, T.
Purdy, S.B. The Hole in the Fabric.*
M. Banta, 445(NCF):Sep78-243
R.H.C., 125:Winter79-307
K. Marotta, 191(ELN):Sep78-65
C. Wegelin, 395(MFS):Summer78-261
Purekevich, R. Dr. Med. Gottfried Benn.
R. Alter, 67:May79-147
Puşcariu, S. Limba română. (2nd ed)
A. Roceric, 545(RPh):Nov78-235
Pusey, N.M. American Higher Education, 1945-1970.
C.D. Murphy, 396(ModA):Winter79-104
639(VQR):Winter79-28
Pushkarev, S.G. Krest'ianskaia pozemel'-no-peredel'naia obshchina v Rossii.*
J.R. Fisher, 104(CASS):Summer78-295
Pushkin, A. Eugene Onegin.* (C. Johnston, trans)
K. Fitz Lyon, 617(TLS):19Sep80-1019
W.H. Pritchard, 249(HudR):Summer79-264
639(VQR):Summer79-109
Putnam, G.F. Russian Alternatives to Marxism.*
B.G. Rosenthal, 550(RusR):Jan79-90
M.S. Shatz, 104(CASS):Fall78-431
Putnam, H. Mathematics, Matter and Method. Mind, Language and Reality.
H. Lehman, 486:Mar78-151
Putnam, H. Meaning and the Moral Sciences.*
K. Bach, 484(PPR):Sep79-137
M.U. Coyne, 258:Dec79-497
J.L. Koethe, 482(PhR):Jul79-460
J.L., 543:Sep78-150
B. Mayo, 518:Jan79-34
L. Stevenson, 479(PhQ):Apr79-176
Putrament, J. Akropolis.
D. Scholze, 654(WB):8/1978-144
Pye, M. and L. Myles. The Movie Brats.*
D. Wilson, 617(TLS):18Jan80-62
639(VQR):Summer79-110

Pyke, L. Prisoner.*
  D. Barbour, 150(DR):Spring79-154
  C. MacMillan, 198:Summer80-151
  L. Saunders, 526:Winter79-78
Pyke, M. Long Life.
  R. Blythe, 617(TLS):11Jul80-778
Pym, B. A Few Green Leaves.
  P. Kemp, 362:17Jul80-89
  A.N. Wilson, 617(TLS):18Jul80-799
Pyman, A. The Life of Aleksandr Blok.*
  (Vol 1)
  H. Gifford, 617(TLS):14Mar80-283
Pyman, A. The Life of Aleksandr Blok.
  (Vol 2)
  H. Gifford, 617(TLS):14Mar80-283
  S. Hackel, 362:17Apr80-512
Pynchon, T. Gravity's Rainbow.* (French
  title: Rainbow.)
  P-Y. Petillon, 98:Dec78-1107
Pynsent, R. Czech Prose and Verse.
  A. French, 67:Nov79-370

Qadir, M.A. Studies in Islamic Socio-
  Economic Thought.
  M. Naimuddin, 273(IC):Jul77-223
Qazi, M.A., comp. Bilal in Hadith.
  H.A. Ali, 273(IC):Oct76-249
Quack, J. Bemerkungen zum Sprachverständ-
  nis von Karl Kraus.
  J.D. Barlow, 406:Fall79-348
Quadrelli, R. - see Manzoni, A.
Qualter, T.H. Graham Wallas and the
  Great Society.
  S. Collini, 617(TLS):25Jul80-837
Quandt, W.B. Decade of Decisions.
  G.R. Kieval, 390:Mar79-59
  B. Rubin, 287:Oct78-23
Quantz, J.J. Solfeggi. (W. Michel and H.
  Teske, eds)
  N. O'Loughlin, 415:May79-401
Quarta, C., and others. Thomas Morus et
  Winstanley.
  E. Namer, 542:Jan-Mar78-100
Quasem, M.A. The Ethics of al-Ghazzali.
  R. Kemal, 273(IC):Jul76-196
Queller, D.E. The Fourth Crusade: The
  Conquest of Constantinople, 1201-1204.
  J. Folda, 589:Jul79-620
Queneau, R. Exercises in Style.
  D.J. Enright, 362:6Mar80-317
Queneau, R. Les Oeuvres complètes de
  Sally Mara.
  P-L. Rey, 450(NRF):Nov79-112
Quennell, P., ed. Affairs of the Mind.
  C. Seebohm, 441:16Mar80-15
Quennell, P., ed. Genius in the Drawing-
  Room.
  G. Annan, 362:12Jun80-765
  A. Brookner, 617(TLS):4Jul80-754
Quennell, P., ed. Nabokov.*
  C. Lehmann-Haupt, 441:4Jun80-C29
Quennell, P. The Wanton Chase.
  P-L. Adams, 61:Nov80-99
  M. Amory, 617(TLS):13Jun80-668
  A. Broyard, 441:24Oct80-C30
                              [continued]

[continuing]
  V. Glendinning, 362:29May80-696
  W. Pritchard, 441:21Dec80-9
  F. Taliaferro, 231:Dec80-78
Quentin, A. Naturkenntnisse und Naturan-
  schauungen bei Wilhelm von Auvergne.
  A. Zimmermann, 53(AGP):Band60Heft2-216
Quereillahc, J-L. Rouge est ma terre.
  M. Whiting, 207(FR):Mar79-674
de Quevedo, F. La vida del buscón llamado
  don Pablos.* (B.W. Ife, ed)
  J.A. Jones, 86(BHS):Jul79-253
"Qui a peur de la philosophie?"
  J-L. Poirier, 542:Oct-Dec78-508
Quignard, P. Carus.
  R. Buss, 617(TLS):25Apr80-478
Quijano, J.A.C. and others - see under
  Calderón Quijano, J.A. and others
Quilici Gigli, S. Blera.
  D. and F.R. Ridgway, 313:Vol69-212
Quilis, A. - see de Nebrija, A.
Quillard, P. and C. Van Lerberghe. Deux
  pièces symbolistes.* (J. Whistle, ed)
  J-L. Debauve, 535(RHL):Jul-Aug79-699
  D. Knowles, 208(FS):Vol133Pt2-849
Quillen, R. The Bell Witch.
  R. Feld, 472:Fall/Winter79-150
Quillet, J. La philosophie politique du
  Songe du vergier (1378).
  J. Jolivet, 542:Apr-Jun79-207
  M. Lemoine, 192(EP):Jul-Sep79-376
Quinault, P. La Comédie sans comédie.
  (J.D. Biard, ed)
  C.N. Smith, 208(FS):Jan79-78
Quine, W.V. Méthodes de Logique.* Les
  Mille et une Nuits.
  V. Descombes, 98:May78-467
Quine, W.V. Philosophie de la logique.
  J. Largeault, 192(EP):Jul-Sep79-377
Quine, W.V. The Roots of Reference.*
  C. Peacocke, 262:Spring78-105
Quiney, A. John Loughborough Pearson.
  J.M. Richards, 617(TLS):1Feb80-122
Quinn, D.B. North America From Earliest
  Discovery to First Settlements.
  J.T. Juricek, 656(WMQ):Jul79-474
  639(VQR):Winter78-8
Quinn, D.B., with A.M. Quinn and S. Hil-
  lier, eds. New American World.
  C. Bridenbaugh, 617(TLS):2May80-507
Quinnell, A.J. Man on Fire.
  A. Broyard, 441:15Nov80-15
Quintana, R. Two Augustans.
  J.M. Hill, 566:Spring79-130
  C.J. Rawson, 541(RES):May79-219
Quintilian. Quintilien, "Institution
  Oratoire." (Vol 1, Bk 1) (J. Cousin, ed
  and trans)
  F. Ahlheid, 394:Vol132fasc3/4-433
Quintilian. Quintilien, "Institution
  Oratoire." (Vol 2, Bks 2 and 3; Vol 3,
  Bks 4 and 5) (J. Cousin, ed)
  F.R.D. Goodyear, 123:Vol29No1-66
Quirk, R. The Linguist and the English
  Language.*
  S. Johnson, 353:Nov78-95
  G.R. Trengrove, 349:Summer78-191

Quondam, A., ed. Le corti farnesiane di Parma e Piacenza 1545-1622. (Vol 2)
E.B., 228(GSLI):Vol155fasc492-631
Quoniam, T. Bonheur et salut.
J-M. Gabaude, 542:Oct-Dec79-457
Quoniam, T. Introduction à une lecture de "L'Esprit des lois."
R. Mercier, 535(RHL):Jul-Aug79-665
M.H. Waddicor, 208(FS):Vol33Pt2-728

Raabe, H. Plurima Mortis Imago.
R.E.H. Westendorp Boerma, 394: Vol32fasc1/2-192
Raban, J. Arabia.*
T. Jacoby, 453(NYRB):17Apr80-43
J. Updike, 442(NY):10Mar80-150
Rabelais, F. Pantagrueline Prognostication pour l'an 1533. (M.A. Screech, with others, eds)
D. Shaw, 208(FS):Vol33Pt2-615
Rabikauskas, P., ed. Relationes status dioecesium in magno ducatu Lituaniae. (Vol 2)
H. Duchhardt, 182:Vol131#15/16-568
Rabinowitch, A. The Bolsheviks Come to Power.
R.V. Daniels, 104(CASS):Summer78-301
Rabinowitz, H.N. Race Relations in the Urban South: 1865-1890.
M.T. Carleton, 9(AlaR):Jul79-238
Rabkin, E.S. The Fantastic in Literature.*
J. Lucas, 637(VS):Spring79-373
J. Mezciems, 402(MLR):Jul79-679
W. Provost, 219(GaR):Spring79-210
Rabkin, E.S., ed. Fantastic Worlds.*
J. Fletcher, 268(IFR):Summer80-153
Raboteau, A.J. Slave Religion.
J.B. Boles, 656(WMQ):Jul79-495
Racevskis, K. Voltaire and the French Academy.
J.H. Brumfitt, 208(FS):Vol33Pt2-746
É. Lizé, 535(RHL):Mar-Jun79-501
"Racial Discrimination and Repression in Southern Rhodesia."
C. Murray, 69:Vol148#4-414
Racine, J. Andromaque.* (R.C. Knight and H.T. Barnwell, eds)
M-O. Sweetser, 207(FR):Feb79-487
205(FMLS):Apr78-189
Racine, J.E. Poèmes posthumes.
M. Recurt, 102(CanL):Spring79-98
Rackham, B. Catalogue of Italian Maiolica.
J.V.C. Mallet, 39:May79-402
Rackin, P. Shakespeare's Tragedies.
D.A. Richardson, 130:Winter79/80-379
Raczymow, H. Contes d'exil et d'oubli.
F. de Martinoir, 450(NRF):Aug79-123
Radandt, F. From Baroque to Storm and Stress: 1720-1775.*
M.K. Flavell, 402(MLR):Apr79-495
205(FMLS):Jan78-93
Radcliffe, P. Beethoven's String Quartets.
W. Drabkin, 415:Apr79-305
Radcliffe, P. Mendelssohn.
A.F.L.T., 412:Aug-Nov78-280

Raddatz, F.J. Heine.
J.L.S., 191(ELN):Sep78(supp)-163
J.L. Sammons, 222(GR):Spring78-76
Rademacher, G. Technik und industrielle Arbeitswelt in der deutschen Lyrik des 19. und 20. Jahrhunderts.
M.D. Silberman, 406:Spring79-78
Radford, A. Italian Syntax.*
M. Nespor, 350:Sep79-703
Radhuber, S. Flying over Greenland.
W. Marling, 584(SWR):Winter79-100
Radice, W. Strivings.
P. Scupham, 617(TLS):4Jul80-762
Radner, D. Malebranche.
J.M. Humber, 484(PPR):Dec79-299
R.A.W., 543:Mar79-564
Radnoti, M. Forced March.
D.M. Thomas, 617(TLS):18Jan80-66
Radt, S. Tragicorum Graecorum Fragmenta. (Vol 4)
J. Irigoin, 555:Vol52fasc2-365
Radványi, J. Delusion and Reality.
C. Johnson, 550(RusR):Apr79-247
Radzinowicz, M.A. Toward "Samson Agonistes."
W.E. Cain, 400(MLN):Dec79-1245
D. Norford, 401(MLQ):Sep79-292
B. Rajan, 301(JEGP):Oct79-552
Raffael, M. Bistro Style Cookery.
W. and C. Cowen, 639(VQR):Spring79-75
Raffeiner, H. Sklaven und Freigelassene.
H.W. Pleket, 123:Vol29Nol-175
von Raffler-Engel, W. and B. Hoffer, eds. Aspects of Nonverbal Communication.
M.R. Key, 350:Sep79-732
von Raffler-Engel, W. and Y. Lebrun, eds. Baby Talk and Infant Speech.
B.T. Tervoort, 361:Dec78-394
Rafroidi, P. and T. Brown, eds. The Irish Short Story.
R. Brown, 617(TLS):4Jul80-766
Ragazzini, G. Giovanni Faldella viaggiatore e giornalista.
G.T., 228(GSLI):Vol155fasc490-316
Raghavan, V. "Ṛtu" in Sanskrit Literature.
L. Sternbach, 318(JAOS):Apr-Jun78-195
Ragland, M.E. Rabelais and Panurge.*
D.G. Coleman, 208(FS):Vol33Pt2-617
Ragussis, M. The Subterfuge of Art.
G. Bornstein, 661(WC):Summer79-288
R.F. Gleckner, 401(MLQ):Jun79-207
P.J. Manning, 141:Summer79-271
Rahner, K. Foundations of Christian Faith.*
J.C. McLelland, 529(QQ):Summer79-355
Rahv, P. Essays on Literature and Politics: 1932-1972.* (A.J. Porter and A.J. Dvosin, eds)
G. Core, 569(SR):Fall79-lxxviii
42(AR):Spring79-253
Rahv, P. Images and Ideas in American Culture.*
G. Core, 569(SR):Fall79-lxxviii
Railton, S. Fenimore Cooper.*
J.F. Beard, 591(SIR):Fall79-479
E.A. Dryden, 301(JEGP):Jul79-461
H.D. Peck, 27(AL):Nov79-427

Randi, J. Flim-Flam!
  T. Ferris, 441:23Nov80-16
Randier, J. Marine Navigation Instruments.
  B. Greenhill, 617(TLS):19Sep80-1047
Randolph, V. Pissing in the Snow and
Other Ozark Folktales.*
  K. Periman, 292(JAF):Jan-Mar79-98
Rangel, C. The Latin Americans.
  L. Raditsa, 390:Aug-Sep79-39
Rangell, L. The Mind of Watergate.
  J. Greenfield, 441:6Apr80-11
Ranger, R. Arms and Politics 1958-1978.
  H. Bull, 617(TLS):4Jan80-20
Ranke, K. and others, eds. Enzyklopädie
des Märchens.* (Vol 1, Pts 1-3)
  H. Rölleke, 52:Band13Heft2-191
Ranke, K. and others, eds. Enzyklopädie
des Märchens.* (Vol 1, Pts 4 and 5)
  H. Rölleke, 52:Band13Heft2-191
  M. Zender, 196:Band19Heft1/2-143
Rankin, H.D. Archilochus of Paros.*
  J.M. Bell, 487:Autumn79-261
  D.E. Gerber, 24:Winter79-568
  M.L. West, 123:Vol29No1-137
Rankin, P. By the Wreckmaster's Cottage.*
  S. Donaldson, 134(CP):Fall78-96
Ranum, O. - see Bossuet, J-B.
Ranung, B. and C.A. Peterson, eds. Antro-
pologiska Studier.
  S.A. Wild, 187:Sep80-595
Raphael, F. Oxbridge Blues.
  J. Mellors, 362:18and25Dec80-867
Rapoport, J. Winter Flowers.
  D. Precosky, 198:Summer80-156
  376:Oct79-141
Rapoport, P. Opus est.
  R. Layton, 415:Oct79-827
Rapp, G., Jr. and S.E. Aschenbrenner.
Excavations at Nichoria in Southwest
Greece. (Vol 1)
  T.W. Jacobsen, 124:Sep79-52
Rarisch, I. Industrialisierung und Lit-
eratur.
  J. Bidwell, 517(PBSA):Jan-Mar78-154
Rashley, R.E. Rock Painter.
  E. Folsom, 526:Winter79-81
  G. Hamel, 198:Winter80-139
Rask, R.K. A Grammar of the Icelandic or
Old Norse Tongue.* (new ed) (T.L.
Markey, ed)
  E.A. Ebbinghaus, 215(GL):Winter78-227
  R. Rocher, 318(JAOS):Jul-Sep78-331
Raskin, V. A Concise History of Linguis-
tic Semantics.
  H. Jachnow, 353:Feb78-82
Raskin, V. and D. Segal - see "Slavica
Hierosolymitana"
Rasor, E.L. Reform in the Royal Navy.
  N.D. Lankford, 637(VS):Summer78-517
"François-Vincent Raspail, 1794-1878."
  B. Rigby, 208(FS):Oct79-461
Rasputin, V. Leb und vergiss nicht.
  B. Hiller, 654(WB):9/1978-133
Rassadin, S.B. Dramaturg Puškin.
  M.G. Pomar, 574(SEEJ):Spring79-127

Rassem, M. and H. Sedlmayr. Über Sprache
und Kunst. (2nd ed)
  M. Faust, 343:Band23-166
Rath, F.L., Jr. and M.R. O'Connell, eds.
Interpretation.
  R.H. Tryon, 14:Jul79-352
Rath, F.L., Jr. and M.R. O'Connell - see
Reese, R.S.
Rathbone, J. The Euro-Killers.
  N. Callendar, 441:18May80-16
  M. Laski, 362:10Jan80-62
Rathbone, J. A Last Resort.
  J. Naughton, 362:29May80-697
  J. Uglow, 617(TLS):20Jun80-718
Ratnachandraji. An Illustrated Ardha-
Magadhi Dictionary.
  259(IIJ):Jul79-213
Rau, W., ed. Bhartr̥haris Vākyapadīya.
  L. Schmithausen, 343:Band23-179
Rau, W. The Meaning of "Pur" in Vedic
Literature.
  K. Mylius, 682(ZPSK):Band31Heft3-309
Raucher, H. Maynard's House.
  S. Ellin, 441:28Sep80-14
Rauh, F. L'esperienza morale.
  P.P., 227(GCFI):Jul-Dec78-575
Ravalli, M.H. - see under Heimbürger
Ravalli, M.
Raven, S. An Inch of Fortune.
  D.A.N. Jones, 617(TLS):22Aug80-930
  P. Kemp, 362:21Aug80-249
Raven, S. The Roses of Picardie.
  J. Naughton, 362:14Feb80-222
  R. Usborne, 617(TLS):1Feb80-108
van Ravenswaay, C. The Arts and Architec-
ture of German Settlements in Missouri.*
  B.L. Herman, 576:Oct78-211
Ravitz, A.C. Alfred Henry Lewis.
  R. Gish, 649(WAL):Winter80-335
Raw, B.C. The Art and Background of Old
English Poetry.
  A.N. Doane, 529(QQ):Summer79-302
  S.B. Greenfield, 589:Apr79-417
  D.G. Scragg, 541(RES):Feb79-64
Rawcliffe, C. The Staffords.
  A.C. Reeves, 589:Apr79-420
Rawick, G.P., J. Hillegas and K. Lawrence,
eds. The American Slave. (Supp, Ser 1,
Vol 1)
  C.L. Mohr, 9(AlaR):Apr79-152
Rawlins, R. The Guinness Book of Auto-
graphs.
  F. Strong, 325:Oct79-240
Rawls, W., Jr. Cold Storage.
  P. Hamill, 441:24Feb80-13
  61:Apr80-124
Rawson, B. The Politics of Friendship.
  J.D. Leach, 123:Vol29No2-328
  T.N. Mitchell, 124:Nov79-200
Rawson, C.J. Henry Fielding and the
Augustan Ideal under Stress.
  B. Rojahn-Deyk, 38:Band96Heft3/4-522
Rawson, J. Animals in Art.
  A. Frankenstein, 55:Jan79-28
Ray, D. The Tramp's Cup.*
  C. Molesworth, 461:Fall-Winter79/80-91

Redondo, A., ed. L'Humanisme dans les lettres espagnoles.
   F.A. de Armas, 304(JHP):Winter80-178
Redwood, J. European Science in the Seventeenth Century.
   C.O. Cook, 568(SCN):Spring-Summer79-23
Ree, J. - see Sartre, J-P.
Rée, J., M. Ayers and A. Westoby. Philosophy and Its Past.
   M. Mandelbaum, 482(PhR):Jul79-488
Reed, B. The Verdict.
   S. Ellin, 441:13Jul80-15
Reed, E. Sexism and Science.
   C. Stasz, 529(QQ):Autumn79-499
Reed, H.O. and J.T. Leach. Scoring for Percussion and the Instruments of the Percussion Section.
   J. Blades, 415:Oct79-835
Reed, I. Shrovetide in Old New Orleans.
   M. Boccia, 502(PrS):Fall78-303
   C.W. Scruggs, 50(ArQ):Autumn79-275
   639(VQR):Summer78-97
Reed, J. From Private Vice to Public Virtue.
   A. McLaren, 529(QQ):Spring79-155
   639(VQR):Autumn78-149
Reed, J. Schubert.
   R. Pascall, 415:Jun79-486
Reed, J.D. Free Fall.
   N. Callendar, 441:13Jan80-18
   442(NY):21Jan80-128
Reed, J.R. Victorian Conventions.*
   V. Cunningham, 637(VS):Autumn77-117
Reed, J.W. and F.A. Pottle - see Boswell, J.
Reed, T.J. Thomas Mann.*
   E. Schiffer, 400(MLN):Apr79-632
Reedy, J. - see Boccaccio, G.
Reel, A.F. The Networks.
   R. Sklar, 441:20Jan80-12
"Le Réel et l'imaginaire dans l'oeuvre de Henri Bosco."*
   J. Onimus, 535(RHL):Jul-Aug78-675
   F.W. Saunders, 208(FS):Vol3Pt2-890
Rees, J. Shakespeare and the Story.
   H. Hawkins, 541(RES):Feb79-77
   E.A. Horsman, 67:May79-91
   J. Robertson, 161(DUJ):Jun79-285
   K. Tetzeli von Rosador, 72:Band216-Heft1-174
Rees, M. French Authors on Spain, 1800-1850, a Checklist.
   J. Alberich, 86(BHS):Oct79-340
Rees, T. Theatre Lighting in the Age of Gas.
   R. Ornbo, 157:Winter79-84
Reese, P.J. Moments of Inertia.
   G. Hamel, 198:Winter80-139
Reese, R.S. Care and Conservation of Collections. (F.L. Rath, Jr. and M.R. O'Connell, eds)
   R.H. Tryon, 14:Jul79-352
Reese, T.F. The Architecture of Ventura Rodríguez.*
   Y. Bottineau, 576:May78-120
Reesink, P. Contes et récits maghrébins.
   J. Monego, 207(FR):Dec78-384

Reeve, C. and A.B. James Connolly and the United States.
   S. Cronin, 174(Éire):Fall79-150
Reeves, R. Popo.
   F. Taliaferro, 441:12Oct80-15
"Referati na makedonskite slavisti za VIII megunaroden slavistički kongres vo Zagreb-L'ubl'ana."
   V.A. Friedman, 574(SEEJ):Winter79-562
Reff, T. The Notebooks of Edgar Degas.
   C.W. Millard, 54:Sep78-565
   C. Rylander-Ryl, 341:1978/2-83
Régaldo, M. Un milieu intellectuel.
   J. Gaulmier, 535(RHL):Jan-Feb78-135
Regard, M. - see de Chateaubriand, F.R.
Reger, E. Union der festen Hand.
   A. Kaes, 221(GQ):Jan79-87
Reginina, K.V., G.P. Tjurina and L.I. Širokova. Ustojčivye slovosočetanija russkogo jazyka.
   R.L. Pearce, 574(SEEJ):Summer79-299
Régnier, R.H. - see Maissin, J.
Regosin, R.L. The Matter of My Book.*
   [shown in prev under Regonsi, R.L.]
   C.H. Foster, 639(VQR):Spring79-375
   P. Henry, 399(MLJ):Jan-Feb79-86
   M.B. McKinley, 400(MLN):May79-891
Regueiro, H. The Limits of Imagination.*
   R. Buttel, 295(JML):Vol7#4-603
Rehermann, E.H. Das Predigtexempel bei protestantischen Theologen des 16. und 17. Jahrhunderts.
   W. Welzig, 602:Vol10-294
   H. Wolf, 196:Band19Heft3/4-337
Rehfeldt, P. New Directions for Clarinet.
   N. O'Loughlin, 415:Feb79-131
Rehm, R. - see Aeschylus
Reibetanz, J. The "Lear" World.*
   S. Clark, 539:Vol14No2-239
   G. Durrant, 178:Fall79-360
   M. Goldman, 570(SQ):Summer79-419
   R.Y. Turner, 405(MP):May80-424
Reich, B. Quest for Peace.
   B. Rubin, 287:Oct78-23
Reichert, H.W. Friedrich Nietzsche's Impact on Modern German Literature.*
   H.S. Daemmrich, 395(MFS):Winter78/79-609
Reichert, J. Making Sense of Literature.*
   G. Graff, 405(MP):May80-459
   S.F.R., 131(CL):Spring79-174
   S. Raval, 50(ArQ):Winter79-393
   639(VQR):Summer79-104
Reid, A. Weathering.
   J.F. Cotter, 249(HudR):Spring79-120
   D. Smith, 29:Sep/Oct80-30
   639(VQR):Spring79-65
Reid, C. Arcadia.*
   C. Hope, 364:Mar80-77
   E. Longley, 617(TLS):18Jan80-64
Reid, F. The Staging Handbook.
   R. Stacey, 157:Winter79-85
Reid, I. The Short Story.*
   P. Freese, 72:Band216Heft2-432
Reid, I. Undercover Agent.
   C. Pollnitz, 581:Dec79-462

Remnek, R.B. Soviet Scholars and Soviet
  Foreign Policy.
    R.H. Donaldson, 550(RusR):Apr79-253
Rempel, S.N. Images of Glass.
    G. Hamel, 198:Winter80-140
Remy, P-J. Les Enfants du parc.
    A.H. Pasco, 207(FR):Mar79-674
Remy, P-J. Orient-Express.
    M. Gourmelon-Berman, 450(NRF):Sep79-51
Renault, M. The Praise Singer.*
    P. Vansittart, 364:Apr/May79-143
    639(VQR):Spring79-58
Rendell, R. The Lake of Darkness.
    N. Callendar, 441:9Nov80-26
    M. Laski, 362:14Aug80-216
Rendell, R. Means of Evil.
    N. Callendar, 441:24Feb80-30
Renfrew, C. Problems in European Prehis-
  tory.
    N. Hammond, 617(TLS):8Feb80-147
Renner, R.G. Ästhetische Theorie bei
  Georg Lukács.
    Z. Takacs, 182:Vol131#7/8-231
Renou, L. L'Inde fondamentale.
    G. Barrière, 450(NRF):Jun79-136
Renouard, M. Art roman en Bretagne.
    R. Galand, 207(FR):Oct78-196
Renouard, M. Guide de Bretagne.
    R. Galand, 207(FR):Oct78-196
Rense, P., ed. Architectural Digest
  Celebrity Homes.
    S. Stephens, 505:Jun78-98
Rensi, E. L'azzardo della riflessione.
    E. Namer, 542:Jan-Mar78-126
Renwick, J. - see Marmontel, J-F.
Renwick, R.D. - see Coffin, T.P.
Renzi, L. Introduzione alla filologia
  romanza.*
    M.P., 228(GSLI):Vol155fasc491-470
Repici, L. La logica di Teofrasto.
    P.M. Huby, 393(Mind):Jul79-448
    M. Kneale, 123:Vol29No1-166
    R.W. Sharples, 303(JoHS):Vol199-179
"Report of the Department of Antiquities,
  Cyprus, 1977."
    J. Boardman, 123:Vol29No1-183
Rescher, N. Dialectics.* Plausible Rea-
  soning.*
    A.S.C., 543:Dec78-368
Rescher, N. Methodological Pragmatism.*
    B. Altshuler, 482(PhR):Jul79-490
    A.S.C., 543:Dec78-368
    P. Dubois, 542:Jul-Sep79-376
    R. Haack, 393(Mind):Apr79-292
    M. Thompson, 486:Sep78-493
Rescher, N. Peirce's Philosophy of
  Science.
    R. Haack, 483:Oct79-566
    V.G. Potter, 613:Jun79-215
    S.B.R., 543:Mar79-565
Rescher, N. and R. Brandom. The Logic of
  Inconsistency.
    N. Tennant, 617(TLS):22Aug80-942
Resnick, M.C. Phonological Variants and
  Dialect Identification in Latin American
  Spanish.
    W.U. Dressler, 353:Apr78-91

Resta, G. - see Marrasii, J.
Restif de la Bretonne. La Découverte aus-
  trale par un Homme-volant, ou le Dédale
  français.
    D. Fletcher, 208(FS):Vol33Pt2-781
Rétat, L. Religion et Imagination reli-
  gieuse.
    F.S. Heck, 546(RR):Jan79-110
Rettig, R.A. Cancer Crusade.
    639(VQR):Winter79-30
Rettig, W. Sprachsystem und Sprachnorm in
  der deutschen Substantivflexion.
    G. Augst, 686(ZGL):Band7Heft2-220
Reumaux, P. L'Homme à la main posée.
  Repérages du vif.
    A. Dhôtel, 450(NRF):May79-121
Reus, G. Oktoberrevolution und Sowjet-
  russland auf dem deutschen Theater.
    R. Jost, 130:Winter79/80-377
Revault d'Allonnes, O. La Création artis-
  tique et les promesses de la liberté.
    H. Godin, 208(FS):Jan79-117
Revel, J-F. The Totalitarian Temptation.*
    639(VQR):Winter78-20
Reveley, E. Skin Deep and Other Stories.
    L. Duguid, 617(TLS):11Jul80-773
    J. Mellors, 362:10Jul80-56
Reverdy, M. L'Oeuvre pour piano d'Olivier
  Messiaen.
    P. Griffiths, 415:Jul79-580
Reverdy, P. La Liberté des mers, Sable
  mouvant et autres poèmes.
    M. Bishop, 207(FR):May79-953
Rex, W.E. Pascal's "Provincial Letters."*
    M. Vamos, 207(FR):May79-930
Rexroth, K. The Morning Star.
    D. Kirby, 617(TLS):30May80-620
Rey, A. Construcción y sentido de Tiempo
  de silencio.
    R. Fiddian, 86(BHS):Oct79-350
Rey, P-L. Le Moindre Mal.
    V. Carrabino, 207(FR):Oct78-186
Reynolds, J. William Callow.
    G. Reynolds, 617(TLS):21Mar80-333
Reynolds, J. - see Goodchild, R.G.
Reynolds, L.D. - see Seneca
Reynolds, M.S. Hemingway's First War.*
    D.R. Noble, 577(SHR):Spring79-169
Reynolds, N. Repertory in Review.
    D. Hering, 151:Mar78-103
Reynolds, R. Les Devisants de "L'Heptamé-
  ron."
    H.G. Collins, 207(FR):May79-926
Reynolds, R.E. The Ordinals of Christ
  from Their Origins to the Twelfth Cen-
  tury.
    R.W. Pfaff, 589:Jul79-622
Rezeau, P. Un patois de Vendée.
    A. Valdman, 320(CJL):Spring-Fall78-158
Reznikoff, C. The Complete Poems of
  Charles Reznikoff.* (Vol 1) By the Well
  of Living and Seeing.* Testimony.*
  (Vol 1) (S. Cooney, ed of all) Holo-
  caust.* First, There Is the Need.
    E. Roditi, 390:Aug-Sep79-59

Reznikoff, C. The Manner Music.*
　J. Freeman, 97(CQ):Vol8#3-283
　E. Roditi, 390:Aug-Sep79-59
Rheims, M. The Glorious Obsession.
　R. Eder, 441:9Apr80-C25
Rhoden, H. High Stakes.
　R. Sherrill, 441:7Sep80-7
Rhodes, E.L. Henslowe's Rose.*
　K. Sturgess, 610:May78-216
Rhodes, R. The Last Safari.
　C. Lehmann-Haupt, 441:24Jan80-C18
　M. Malone, 441:9Mar80-11
　61:Apr80-124
Rhodes James, R. Chindit.
　R. Trevelyan, 362:9Oct80-478
Rhys, J. Quai des Grands-Augustins.
　C. Jordis, 450(NRF):Jun79-141
Rhys, J. Smile Please.*
　A. Broyard, 441:28May80-C21
　V.S. Pritchett, 453(NYRB):14Aug80-8
　P. Rose, 676(YR):Summer80-596
　D. Trilling, 441:25May80-1
　J. Updike, 442(NY):11Aug80-82
　61:Jun80-92
Riasanovsky, N.V., G. Struve and T. Eekman,
　eds. California Slavic Studies.* (Vol
　9)
　E.C. Barksdale, 104(CASS):Summer78-285
Ribard, J. - see Chrétien de Troyes
Ribbans, G. Pérez Galdós: "Fortunata y
　Jacinta."
　S. Bacarisse, 402(MLR):Apr79-479
　R.M. Fedorchek, 238:Dec79-732
　J. Whiston, 86(BHS):Jul79-261
Ribbat, E. Ludwig Tieck.
　W. Koepke, 221(GQ):May79-417
Ribeiro, J.U. Sergeant Getúlio.
　J. Bumpus, 473(PR):4/1979-634
　A. Feinstein, 617(TLS):13Jun80-674
　P. Kemp, 362:13Mar80-350
Riberette, P. - see de Chateaubriand, F.R.
Ricapito, J.V. - see "Lazarillo de Tormes"
Ricci, J. El Grongo.
　J.D. Danielson, 238:Dec79-741
　L. Leal, 263(RIB):Vol29No1-100
Riccoboni, M-J. Mme Riccoboni's Letters
　to David Hume, David Garrick and Sir
　Robert Liston (1764-1783). (J.C.
　Nicholls, ed)
　M. Servien, 535(RHL):May-Jun78-485
Rice, A. The Feast of All Saints.
　R. Koenig, 441:17Feb80-17
Rice, A.H. Mrs. Wiggs of the Cabbage
　Patch.
　E.F. Bargainnier, 578:Spring80-150
Rice, B.R. Progressive Cities.
　639(VQR):Autumn78-148
Rice, E. Eastern Definitions.
　J.B. Chethimattam, 613:Dec79-431
Rice, G.W. - see Saunders, J.J.
Rice, H.C., Jr. Thomas Jefferson's Paris.*
　J. Lough, 208(FS):Vol33Pt2-799
Rice, W. and B. Wolf, eds. Where to Eat
　in America.
　W. and C. Cowen, 639(VQR):Spring78-78
Rice-Davies, M., with S. Flack. Mandy.
　E.S. Turner, 362:18and25Dec80-862

Rich, A. The Dream of a Common Language.*
　B.L. Estrin, 560:Spring-Summer79-224
　K. Whitehill, 639(VQR):Summer79-563
Rich, A. Of Woman Born.*
　L.E. Casari, 502(PrS):Summer78-206
Rich, J.W. Declaring War in the Roman
　Republic in the Period of Transmarine
　Expansion.*
　J. Richardson, 313:Vol69-156
Richard, C. - see Baudelaire, C.
Richard, J-P. Microlectures.
　P. Dulac, 450(NRF):Jun79-128
Richard, M. La Pensée contemporaine.
　E. Benson, 207(FR):Apr79-808
Richards, A., ed. The Penguin Book of
　Welsh Short Stories.
　A. Varley, 161(DUJ):Jun79-292
Richards, D.A. Dancers at Night.*
　P. Monk, 529(QQ):Autumn79-525
　W.H. New, 102(CanL):Autumn79-79
　D. Prosser, 526:Spring79-93
Richards, D.G. Georg Büchner and the
　Birth of the Modern Drama.*
　R. Cardinal, 529(QQ):Spring79-98
　S.E. Cernyak, 406:Fall79-342
　L.F. Helbig, 301(JEGP):Jul79-401
　P.K. Jansen, 405(MP):May80-450
Richards, D.J. and C.R.S. Cockrell, eds
　and trans. Russian Views of Pushkin.*
　205(FMLS):Jan78-94
Richards, I.A. Complementarities.* (J.P.
　Russo, ed)
　G. Good, 131(CL):Summer79-309
Richards, J. Consul of God.
　J. McLure, 617(TLS):15Aug80-920
Richards, J. and L. Pratt. Prairie
　Capitalism.
　C. Armstrong, 99:Apr80-37
Richards, J.F. Mughal Administration in
　Golconda.
　M.N. Pearson, 318(JAOS):Jul-Sep78-324
Richards, J.M. 800 Years of Finnish Archi-
　tecture.*
　J. Vepsäläinen, 46:May79-311
Richards, J.M. Memoirs of an Unjust Fella.
　N. Silver, 362:3Apr80-447
Richards, P. The Medieval Leper and His
　Northern Heirs.
　D. Fox, 447(N&Q):Feb78-76
Richards, T.J. The Language of Reason.
　R. Pargetter, 63:Sep79-283
　J.E. Tiles, 518:Oct79-119
Richardson, D.A., ed. Spenser: Classical,
　Medieval, Renaissance, and Modern 1977.
　C.D. Eckhardt, 568(SCN):Fall-Winter79-
　71
Richardson, E. The Presidency of Dwight D.
　Eisenhower.
　E. Wright, 617(TLS):25Jan80-91
Richardson, J. Gustave Doré.
　C. Fox, 617(TLS):21Mar80-318
Richardson, J. Thomas Hardy.*
　W. Bies, 177(ELT):Vol122#1-67
　T. Paulin, 637(VS):Autumn78-102
Richardson, J. Keats and His Circle.
　P. Beer, 362:31Jul80-150

Richardson, J. Memoir of a Gambler.*
  A. de Jonge, 617(TLS):20Jun80-688
  442(NY):11Feb80-119
Richardson, J. Reservations.
  639(VQR):Winter78-12
Richardson, J. - see Baudelaire, C.
Richardson, K. Poetry and the Colonized
  Mind: Tish.*
  D. Cooley, 105:Fall/Winter78-98
Richardson, L., Jr. - see Propertius
Richardson, M., ed. Catalogue of the Draw-
  ings Collection of the Royal Institute
  of British Architects. (Vol S)
  D. Stillman, 576:May78-117
Richardson, M. Fits and Starts.*
  A.B., 617(TLS):4Jan80-5
Richardson, R.D., Jr. Myth and Literature
  in the American Renaissance.*
  L. Buell, 432(NEQ):Dec79-569
  R.E. Spiller, 27(AL):May79-281
Richartz, H. Literaturkritik als Gesell-
  schaftskritik.
  D. Heald, 220(GL&L):Oct78-79
Richert, H-G. Wege und Formen der Passion-
  alüberlieferung.
  B. Murdoch, 182:Vol131#7/8-225
  W.M. Resler, 589:Oct79-850
  P.W. Tax, 564:Nov79-323
Richir, M. Au-delà du renversement coper-
  nicien.
  H. Riefstahl, 182:Vol131#1/2-9
Richir, M. - see Schelling, F.W.J.
Richler, M. The Apprenticeship of Duddy
  Kravitz. St. Urbain's Horseman.
  S. Beckoff, 109:Summer80-206
Richler, M. Joshua Then and Now.
  D. Cohen, 99:Aug80-277
  T.R. Edwards, 441:22Jun80-11
  C. Lehmann-Haupt, 441:27May80-C9
  J. Mellors, 362:9Oct80-481
  J. Wolcott, 453(NYRB):17Jul80-35
  61:Jul80-84
Richner, T. Interpreting Mozart's Piano
  Sonatas.
  A.H. King, 415:May79-403
Richter, A. Der Ziegelbrenner.
  M.L. Baumann, 221(GQ):Nov79-557
Richter, E. Kleinere Schriften zur allge-
  meinen und romanischen Sprachwissen-
  schaft. (Y. Malkiel, ed)
  H. Kahane, 350:Sep79-701
Richter, H., ed. Schriftsteller und liter-
  arisches Erbe.
  H. Haase and R. Dau, 654(WB):2/1978-
  180
Richter, M. La crise du Logos et la
  quête du Mythe.*
  H-J. Lope, 547(RF):Band91Heft1/2-179
  205(FMLS):Jan78-93
Richter, M., ed. Political Theory and
  Political Education.
  S. Collini, 617(TLS):2May80-505
Richter, W. Caesar als Darsteller seiner
  Taten.*
  R.M. Ogilvie, 123:Vol129No1-51
Richter, W. Textstudien zu Lukrez.
  P.H. Schrijvers, 394:Vol32fasc1/2-189

von Richthofen, E. Tradicionalismo épico-
  novelesco.
  C. Stern, 545(RPh):May79-454
Rickard, P. A History of the French Lan-
  guage. (2nd ed)
  D.A. Dinneen, 399(MLJ):Nov79-380
Rickard, P. and T.G.S. Combe - see Harmer,
  L.C.
Rickards, M. This is Ephemera.
  W.K. McNeil, 292(JAF):Apr-Jun79-244
Ricken, F. Der Lustbegriff in der Niko-
  machischen Ethik des Aristoteles.*
  P. Louis, 555:Vol52fasc1-163
Rickett, A.A., ed. Chinese Approaches to
  Literature from Confucius to Liang Ch'i-
  ch'ao.
  C.H. Wang, 293(JASt):May79-529
Rickett, A.A. - see "Wang kuo-wei's 'Jen-
  chien Tz'u-hua'"
Ricklefs, M.C. Modern Javanese Historical
  Tradition.
  D.E. Weatherbee, 293(JASt):Feb79-427
Rickword, E. Literature in Society. (A.
  Young, ed)
  E. Homberger, 617(TLS):18Jan80-69
Ricoeur, P. The Rule of Metaphor.*
  (French title: La métaphore vive.)
  P. Lamarque, 479(PhQ):Apr79-188
  P. Missac, 98:Nov78-1017
Riddell, J. Criss-Cross.
  E.P. Levy, 102(CanL):Autumn79-89
  L.K. MacKendrick, 168(ECW):Fall78-235
Riddell, J.H. A Hole in the Head.
  L.K. MacKendrick, 168(ECW):Fall78-235
de Ridder-Symoens, H., D. Illmer and C.M.
  Ridderikhoff. Premier livre des procura-
  teurs de la Nation germanique de
  l'ancienne Université d'Orléans, 1444-
  1546. (Pt 2, section 1)
  F.L. Cheyette, 589:Oct79-821
Riddleberger, P.W. 1866, The Critical
  Year Revisited.
  E. Wright, 617(TLS):25Jan80-91
Ridgeway, J. Who Owns the Earth.
  R. Lekachman, 441:8Jun80-13
Ridgway, B.S. The Archaic Style in Greek
  Sculpture.*
  R.M. Cook, 303(JoHS):Vol99-211
Ridgway, D. and F.R., eds. Italy before
  the Romans.
  N. Hammond, 617(TLS):8Feb80-147
Ridler, A. - see Darley, G.
Ridley, J. Napoleon III and Eugénie.
  P-L. Adams, 61:Sep80-109
  J.P.T. Bury, 617(TLS):1Feb80-107
  A.J.P. Taylor, 453(NYRB):25Sep80-22
Ridpath, I. Messages from the Stars.
  T.C. Holyoke, 42(AR):Spring79-246
Ridruejo, D. Sombras y bultos.
  J.W. Díaz, 399(MLJ):Jan-Feb79-70
Riedel, N. Uwe Johnson.*
  U.K. Faulhaber, 222(GR):Winter79-43
Riedel, W., ed. Moderne Erzähler der
  Welt — Kanada.*
  U. Williams, 102(CanL):Autumn79-101
Rieff, P. Freud. (3rd ed)
  529(QQ):Winter79/80-736

313

Rieger, D. Gattungen und Gattungsbezeich-
nungen der Trobadorlyrik.
  F. Goldin, 589:Apr79-421
  J.H. Marshall, 208(FS):Vol33Pt2-515
Riemann, H. History of Music Theory. (Bk
3) (W.C. Mickelsen, ed and trans)
  L. Rowell, 308:Fall78-316
Ries, W. Friedrich Nietzsche.
  W.J.D., 543:Jun79-768
Ries, W. Transzendenz als Terror.*
  I.C. Henel, 406:Summer79-207
Rieuneau, M. Guerre et révolution dans le
roman français de 1919 à 1939.
  J. Cruickshank, 208(FS):Vol33Pt2-956
Rieux, J. and B.E. Rollin - see Arnauld,
A. and C. Lancelot
Riffaterre, M. Semiotics of Poetry.
  R.A. Champagne, 399(MLJ):Apr79-229
  D.H. Hirsch, 569(SR):Fall79-628
  R. Kuhn, 400(MLN):Dec79-1199
Rifkin, J., with T. Howard. Entropy.
  C.W. Pursell, Jr., 441:26Oct80-9
Rifkind, C. Main Street.
  D.A. Mann, 658:Autumn79-320
Rifkind, C. and C. Levine. Mansions,
Mills, and Main Streets.
  J. Zukowsky, 576:Oct78-209
Riganti, E. - see Varro
Rigby, T.H. Lenin's Government: Sovnarkom
1917-1922.
  A. Brown, 617(TLS):25Jan80-95
Rigg, A.G., ed. Editing Medieval Texts.
  P.S. Baker, 589:Jul79-624
  O.S. Pickering, 72:Band216Heft2-379
Righini Bonelli, M.L. and W.R. Shea, eds.
Reason, Experiment and Mysticism in the
Scientific Revolution.
  E. McMullin, 486:Jun78-329
Riginos, A.S. Platonica.*
  D.N. Sedley, 123:Vol29No1-75
Rigney, B.H. Madness and Sexual Politics
in the Feminist Novel.*
  E. Showalter, 141:Spring79-172
Rigobello, A. and others. L'unità del
sapere.
  P.P., 227(GCFI):Apr-Jun78-284
Rigolot, F. Les langages de Rabelais.
  F. Charpentier, 535(RHL):Jul-Aug79-633
Rigolot, F. Poétique et onomastique.*
  E. Morris, 400(MLN):May79-860
Rijksbaron, A. Temporal and Causal Con-
junctions in Ancient Greek.*
  J.H.W. Penney, 123:Vol29No2-325
Rijlaarsdam, J.C. Platon über die Sprache.
  F. Lasserre, 182:Vol131#20-761
Riley, C. - see "Children's Literature
Review"
Riley, H.M.K. Idee und Gestaltung.
  J.F.F., 191(ELN):Sep78(supp)-140
Rilinger, R. Der Einfluss des Wahlleiters
bei den römischen Konsulwahlen.
  J. Carter, 313:Vol69-184
Rilke, R.M. Duino Elegies.* (D. Young,
trans) Duino Elegies [and] The Sonnets
to Orpheus.* (A. Poulin, Jr., trans)
  J. Gleason, 472:Fall/Winter79-130

Rimanelli, G. and K.J. Atchity, eds.
Italian Literature.*
  N. Mann, 447(N&Q):Apr78-189
Rimbaud, A. Bottom.
  A. Guyaux, 98:Aug-Sep78-867
Rimbaud, A. Drunked Boat. (S. Beckett,
trans; J. Knowlson and F. Leakey, eds)
  G. Schaeffer, 535(RHL):Jul-Aug79-694
Rimbaud, A. Les Illuminations.* (N.
Osmond, ed)
  C.A. Hackett, 535(RHL):Jul-Aug79-693
  205(FMLS):Jan78-93
"Arthur Rimbaud 3." (L. Forestier, ed)
  M. Davies, 208(FS):Vol33Pt2-843
Rimer, J.T. Modern Japanese Fiction and
its Traditions.
  Sakurai Emiko, 285(JapQ):Jan-Mar79-
117
  I. Schuster, 268(IFR):Winter80-67
Rimmon, S. The Concept of Ambiguity.*
  M. Hirst, 184(EIC):Oct79-369
  A.R. Tintner, 395(MFS):Winter78/79-630
  A.R. Tintner, 594:Spring79-106
  P.M. Weinstein, 445(NCF):Mar79-498
  W.F. Wright, 405(MP):Feb80-353
  R.B. Yeazell, 401(MLQ):Dec79-420
Rimsky-Korsakov, N.A. My Musical Life.
(C. van Vechten, ed)
  A.F.L.T., 412:Feb78-69
Rincé, D. La Littérature française du
XIXe siècle.
  A. Fairlie, 208(FS):Oct79-453
Rincé, D. La Poésie française du XIXe
siècle.
  S.F. Daniel, 207(FR):Apr79-771
  A. Fairlie, 208(FS):Oct79-453
Ring, K. Life at Death.
  T. Ferris, 441:28Sep80-16
Rinner, F. Die komparatistischen Arbeiten
in der Germanisch-Romanischen Monats-
schrift.
  J. Hösle, 52:Band13Heft3-302
Rintchen, B., G. Rincinsambuu and P.
Xorloo. Mongolische Epen I-IV. (N.
Poppe, trans)
  W. Eberhard, 318(JAOS):Apr-Jun78-131
von Rintelen, F-J. Philosophie des
lebendigen Geistes in der Krise der
Gegenwart.*
  F. Mordstein, 687:Jan-Mar79-152
  R. Panikkar, 258:Jun79-242
  W. Schwarz, 484(PPR):Sep79-150
Rio, M. L'homme existe-t-il?
  M. Adam, 542:Jul-Sep79-376
Riordan, J. Sport in Soviet Society.
  J.J. Tomiak, 575(SEER):Jul79-472
Ripalda, J.M. The Divided Nation.
  H.S. Harris, 125:Spring79-458
Ripley, J. "Julius Caesar" on Stage in
England and America 1599-1973.
  G. Salgado, 617(TLS):27Jun80-742
Ripoll, R., with S. Luneau - see Zola, É.
de Riquer, M. Los Trovadores — Historia
leteraria y textos.
  P. Cherchi, 405(MP):Nov79-192

Rischer, C. Literarische Rezeption und Kulturelles Selbstverständnis in der deutschen Literatur der "Ritterrenaissance" des 15. Jahrhunderts.
  H.A. Hilgers, 684(ZDA):Band107Heft2-75
Risco, A. El Demiurgo y so mundo.*
  J. Alberich, 86(BHS):Apr79-159
  D. Dougherty, 238:Mar79-178
Riseboro, B. The Story of Western Architecture.
  J.M. Richards, 617(TLS):1Feb80-122
Risenhoover, M. and R.T. Blackburn. Artists as Professors.
  L. Finkelstein, 127:Winter78/79-148
Rist, A. - see Theocritus
Ritchie, J. The First Hundred Years.
  639(VQR):Winter79-14
Ritchie, R.C. The Duke's Province.
  L.H. Leder, 656(WMQ):Oct79-633
Ritsos, Y. The Fourth Dimension.*
  P. Green, 453(NYRB):26Jun80-40
Ritsos, Y. Ritsos in Parentheses.
  P. Green, 453(NYRB):26Jun80-40
  V. Young, 249(HudR):Winter79/80-625
Ritsos, Y. Scripture of the Blind.
  P. Green, 453(NYRB):26Jun80-40
  D.M. Thomas, 617(TLS):18Jan80-66
  V. Young, 249(HudR):Winter79/80-626
Ritter, A., ed. Deutschlands literarisches Amerikabild.
  W. Schumann, 399(MLJ):Sep-Oct79-309
  R.F. Spiess, 556(RLV):1978/6-551
Ritter, E. - see von Hofmannsthal, H.
Ritter, J. and K. Gründer, eds. Historisches Wörterbuch der Philosophie.* (Vol 4)
  J. Bernhardt, 542:Oct-Dec79-457
Ritter, J-F. Friedrich von Spee 1591-1635.
  F. Gaede, 564:Sep79-225
Ritter, K.W. and J.R. Andrews. The American Ideology.
  W.A. Linsley, 583:Spring79-309
Ritzel, W. Immanuel Kant.*
  L. Guillermit, 542:Apr-Jun79-245
de Rivers, G.S. - see under Sabat de Rivers, G.
Rivers, W.M. and M.S. Temperly. A Practical Guide to the Teaching of English as a Second or Foreign Language.*
  C.F. McCreary, 399(MLJ):Mar79-135
  J.G. Zuck, 608:Mar80-103
Riverso, E. Riferimento e struttura.
  P. Foulkes, 393(Mind):Apr79-296
Rivet, A.L.F. and C. Smith. The Place-Names of Roman Britain.
  R. Conquest, 362:1May80-584
  S.S. Frere, 617(TLS):11Jan80-42
Rivet, J. Les Beaux Moments.
  E. Wayne, 207(FR):Apr79-799
Rivière, F. Fabriques.
  D.M. Church, 207(FR):Dec78-385
Rivière, J. Rimbaud — Dossier 1905-25. (R. Lefèvre, ed)
  J. Birkett, 402(MLR):Apr79-467
  H.T. Naughton, 399(MLJ):Jan-Feb79-84

Rivière, J-C., ed. Pastourelles. (Vols 1-3)
  N. Wilkins, 208(FS):Vol33Pt2-590
Rivière, J-C. - see Jacques de Cambrai
Rizvi, S.A.A. and V.J.A. Flynn. Faṭḥpur Sikrī.
  Z.A. Desai, 273(IC):Jan78-57
Rizza, C. Barocco francese e cultura italiana.
  H.T. Barnwell, 208(FS):Jan79-72
Roazen, P. Erik H. Erikson.
  H.I. Kushner, 106:Spring79-95
Robach, I-B. Etude sociolinguistique de la segmentation syntaxique du français parlé.*
  G. Lemhagen, 597(SN):Vol150#2-305
Robb, P. and D. Taylor, eds. Rule, Protest, Identity.
  F.F. Conlon, 293(JASt):Feb79-409
Robbe-Grillet, A. Topology of a Phantom City.
  P. Lewis, 565:Vol120#1-49
Robbe-Grillet, A. Un régicide [et] Souvenirs du triangle d'or.
  P. Dulac, 450(NRF):Jan79-122
Robbins, J.A., ed. American Literary Manuscripts.* (2nd ed)
  R.A., 189(EA):Jul-Dec78-427
Robbins, J.A. - see Farrell, J.T.
Robbins, R.H., ed. Chaucer at Albany.*
  D. Pearsall, 161(DUJ):Dec78-123
Robbins, T. Still Life With Woodpecker.
  R.V. Cassill, 441:28Sep80-15
Robbins, W. The Arnoldian Principle of Flexibility.
  M. Ross, 150(DR):Autumn79-577
Robe, S.L. Azuela and the Mexican Underdogs.
  T. Murad, 263(RIB):Vol29No2-224
Robe, S.L., ed. Hispanic Folktales from New Mexico.
  F. Richie, 573(SSF):Fall78-469
Robe, S.L. Index of Mexican Folktales.
  E. Ettlinger, 203:Vol189#1-119
Robert, M. The Old and the New.*
  E.C. Riley, 402(MLR):Jan79-226
Robert, M. Seul, comme Franz Kafka.
  H. Raczymow, 450(NRF):May79-126
Robert, P-E. Marcel Proust: Lecteur des Anglo-Saxons.*
  A. Finch, 208(FS):Vol33Pt2-861
Roberts, A.D. A History of the Bemba.
  M. Wilson, 69:Vol148#4-420
Roberts, D. Paternalism in Early Victorian England.
  E.J. Hobsbawm, 453(NYRB):3Apr80-35
Roberts, D.D. The Syndicalist Tradition and Italian Fascism.
  M. Blinkhorn, 617(TLS):8Feb80-153
Roberts, F.C., comp. Obituaries from The Times, 1971-1975.
  A. Bell, 617(TLS):9May80-522
Roberts, G. Temas existencialistas en la novela española de postguerra.*
  M. Montes Huidobro, 593:Winter79-364

Roberts, G.W., ed. Bertrand Russell Memorial Volume.
D.W. Hamlyn, 617(TLS):4Jan80-19
G. Stock, 518:Oct79-113
Roberts, G.W. and S.A. Sinclair. Women in Jamaica.
N.L. Gonzalez, 263(RIB):Vol29No3/4-376
Roberts, J.M. The French Revolution.
D. Higgs, 529(QQ):Winter79/80-704
Roberts, J.M. The Hutchinson History of the World.
529(QQ):Spring79-180
Roberts, J.M. The Strayed Sheep of Charun.
E. Korn, 617(TLS):30May80-626
Roberts, J.R. John Donne.
C.A. Patrides, 568(SCN):Fall-Winter79-73
Roberts, J.R. George Herbert.
D.W. Doerksen, 539:Vol4No1-117
C.A. Patrides, 568(SCN):Fall-Winter79-73
G. Williams, 354:Dec79-387
Roberts, M. Facets of Modern Ceylon History through the Letters of Jeronis Pieris.
P. Peebles, 293(JASt):Nov78-204
Roberts, M. Selected Poems and Prose. (F. Grubb, ed)
H.G. Porteus, 362:4Dec80-764
Roberts, N. The Companion Guide to Normandy.
S. Pakenham, 617(TLS):12Sep80-986
Roberts, P. The Psychology of Tragic Drama.
G. Bas, 189(EA):Apr-Jun78-218
Roberts, R. Jack Dempsey.
A. Whitman, 617(TLS):28Mar80-346
Roberts, S.E., ed and trans. Four Faces of Rozanov.
G. Ivask, 574(SEEJ):Fall79-405
Roberts-Jones, P. Beyond Time and Place.
J. Masheck, 62:Dec78-60
Robertshaw, A. Oswald von Wolkenstein.*
D. Blamires, 402(MLR):Jul79-741
Robertson, A. The No Baloney Sandwich Book.
W. and C. Cowen, 639(VQR):Autumn79-154
Robertson, D. Sir Charles Eastlake and The Victorian Art World.
L. Herrmann, 90:Apr79-266
B.M-P. Leefmans, 55:May79-36
M. Pointon, 637(VS):Spring79-345
Robertson, E.G. and J. Cast Iron Decoration.*
M. Gayle, 576:Oct78-223
G. Wills, 39:Dec79-532
Robertson, I., ed. The Blue Guide to Spain: The Mainland. (4th ed)
D. Mitchell, 617(TLS):9May80-535
Robertson, J.O. American Myth, American Reality.
R. Asahina, 441:9Nov80-18
Robichez, J. Sur Saint-John Perse.
M. Autrand, 535(RHL):May-Jun78-508
A. Berrie, 208(FS):Vol33Pt2-885
R. Little, 402(MLR):Oct79-951

Robichez, J. Le Théâtre de Giraudoux.*
D. Knowles, 208(FS):Vol33Pt2-876
Robidoux, R. Le Traité du Narcisse d'André Gide.
J. Cotnam, 627(UTQ):Summer79-425
Robinet, I. Les commentaires du Tao tö king jusqu'au VIIe siècle.
A. Reix, 542:Jan-Mar78-88
Robinet, I. Méditation taoïste.
A. Reix, 542:Oct-Dec79-459
Robinson, B.W. Persian Paintings in the India Office Library.*
N.M. Titley, 463:Summer79-251
Robinson, B.W. Persian Paintings in the John Rylands Library.
S. Digby, 617(TLS):19Sep80-1042
Robinson, C.A., ed. J. Evetts Haley and the Passing of the Old West.
W. Gard, 584(SWR):Winter79-89
Robinson, D. Chiefs and Clerics.
M. Last, 69:Vol148#1-87
Robinson, D. The Eldorado Network.
M. Laski, 362:17Apr80-514
Robinson, D. Buster Keaton.
D. Macdonald, 453(NYRB):9Oct80-33
Robinson, D. Stanley Spencer.
F. Spalding, 135:Sep79-68
Robinson, D.R. The Bell Rings at Four.
W. Gard, 584(SWR):Spring79-vi
Robinson, E. and G. Summerfield - see Clare, J.
Robinson, F.G. and M.G. Wallace Stegner.*
C.A. Glasrud, 587(SAF):Spring79-114
Robinson, F.W. Gabriel Metsu (1629-1667).
C. Brown, 90:Oct79-656
Robinson, G.J. Tito's Maverick Media.
D. Wilson, 575(SEER):Jan79-144
Robinson, H. Somerville and Ross.
J.S. Collis, 362:4Dec80-763
V. Powell, 617(TLS):6Jun80-653
Robinson, H.L. Canada's Crippled Dollar.
P. Phillips, 99:Nov80-30
Robinson, H.L. Rising Prices.*
T.K. Rymes, 529(QQ):Autumn79-523
Robinson, I. The New Grammarians' Funeral.*
P.H. Matthews, 215(GL):Winter78-222
Robinson, I. The Survival of English.*
N. Jacobs, 439(NM):1978/3-317
Robinson, J. Duty and Hypocrisy in Hegel's "Phenomenology of Mind."*
E.S. Dalrymple, 482(PhR):Apr79-311
H.S. Harris, 125:Winter79-278
L.S.S., 543:Sep78-150
Robinson, J. In Extremity.*
T.K. Bender, 637(VS):Winter79-224
J. Bump, 301(JEGP):Apr79-269
M. Dodsworth, 175:Summer79-180
N.H. MacKenzie, 541(RES):May79-226
J. Pick, 636(VP):Winter78-390
Robinson, J.M. The Wyatts.
M. Girouard, 362:31Jan80-156
J. Summerson, 617(TLS):25Jan80-79
Robinson, P. Solti.*
E. Forbes, 415:Dec79-1003
Robinson, R. Contemporary Portugal.
R. Burriss, 617(TLS):4Jul80-764

Robinson, W.B.   American Forts.
J. Maass, 658:Summer79-198
Robinson, W.H.   Phillis Wheatley in the Black American Beginnings.
R. Hemenway, 582(SFQ):Vol41-286
Robinson, W.P.   Language Management in Education.
P.G. Peterson, 67:Nov79-383
Robson, J.M. and M. Laine, eds.   James and John Stuart Mill.
J. Weissman, 637(VS):Winter78-275
Robson, J.W. and F.E. Sparshott - see Mill, J.S.
Roca-Pons, J.   Introduction to Catalan Literature.
J.J. Gilabert, 238:Mar79-183
A.G. Hauf, 86(BHS):Jul79-264
J.M. Sobré, 240(HR):Autumn78-506
Rocamora, J.E.   Nationalism in Search of Ideology.
R.W. Liddle, 293(JASt):May79-635
Rocha-Pereira, M.H. - see Pausanias
Rochat, G.   Italo Balbo, aviatore e ministro dell' aeronautica, 1926-1933.
D. Mack Smith, 617(TLS):2May80-483
Roche, A. - see Péguy, C.
Roche, A.V.   Alphonse Daudet.*
G.E. Hare, 208(FS):Vol133Pt2-831
M. Sachs, 446(NCFS):Fall-Winter78/79-140
Roche, T.P., Jr., with C.P. O'Donnell, Jr. - see Spenser, E.
Lord Rochester.   The Letters of John Wilmot, Earl of Rochester.   (J. Treglown, ed)
H. Corke, 362:4Dec80-761
Rochet, B.L.   The Formation and the Evolution of the French Nasal Vowels.
G. Price, 208(FS):Vol133Pt2-1029
M. Ruhlen, 545(RPh):Feb79-321
Röcke, W.   Feudale Anarchie und Landesherrschaft.
F.H. Bäuml, 589:Oct79-854
Rodefer, S.   The Bell Clerk's Tears Keep Flowing.
R. Feld, 472:Fall/Winter79-150
Rodgers, B.F., Jr.   Philip Roth.
D. Monaghan, 268(IFR):Winter80-62
Rodgers, E.   Pérez Galdós: "Miau."
E.A. Southworth, 402(MLR):Oct79-968
Rodgers, E. - see Galdós, B.P.
Rodingen, H.   Aussage und Anweisung.
E. Blondel, 542:Jan-Mar79-83
Rodoreda, M.   Semblava de seda i altres contes.
J-L. Marfany, 86(BHS):Jul79-278
Rodoreda, M.   The Time of the Doves.
442(NY):6Oct80-195
Rodrigues, G.A. - see under Almeida Rodrigues, G.
Rodríguez, I.   La metáfora en la estructura poética de Jorge Guillén y Federico García Lorca.
G.E. McSpadden, 238:Mar79-180
Rodríguez, P.S. - see under Sainz Rodríguez, P.

Rodríguez-Puértolas, J.   Literatura, historia, alienación.*
A. Deyermond, 86(BHS):Jan79-56
Rodríguez de Lena, P.   El Passo Honroso de Suero de Quiñones.*   (A. Labandeira Fernández, ed)
A. Mutton, 402(MLR):Oct79-964
P. Waley, 86(BHS):Jul79-244
Rodríguez Monegal, E.   Jorge Luis Borges.*
376:Oct79-143
Rodríguez Monegal, E., with T. Colchie, eds.   The Borzoi Anthology of Latin American Literature.*
R. González Echevarría, 400(MLN): Mar79-394
Roebuck, P.   Families, Estates and Fortunes.
F.M.L. Thompson, 617(TLS):5Sep80-967
Roeder, A.   Die Gebärde im Drama des Mittelalters.*
R. Bergmann, 684(ZDA):Band107Heft4-177
Roelker, J.R.   Mathu of Kenya.
A.H.M. Kirk-Greene, 69:Vol48#3-303
Roemer, K.M.   The Obsolete Necessity.*
G. Negley, 322(JHI):Apr-Jun79-315
Roethel, H.K. and J.K. Benjamin.   Kandinsky.*
W. Vaughan, 617(TLS):21Mar80-328
de Roever, W.P., Jr.   Recursive Program Schemes: Semantics and Proof Theory.
P. Lauer, 316:Dec79-658
Rogel, C.   The Slovenes and Yugoslavism 1890-1914.*
R. Kindersley, 617(TLS):4Jan80-22
C.J. Slovak, 104(CASS):Summer78-314
Roger, J. - see de Buffon, G.L.L.
Rogers, B.   The Domestication of Women.
L. Mair, 617(TLS):12Sep80-1001
Rogers, D.   Somewhere There's Music.
639(VQR):Spring78-68
Rogers, D.   Tirso de Molina: "El burlador de Sevilla."
M. Wilson, 402(MLR):Jul79-727
Rogers, D.M., ed.   Benito Pérez Galdós.
M. Nimetz, 593:Spring79-93
Rogers, H.C.   Walking the Tightrope.
J. Greenfield, 441:9Mar80-12
Rogers, P., ed.   The Context of English Literature.
W.H., 148:Spring79-92
Rogers, P., ed.   The Eighteenth Century.
566:Spring79-129
Rogers, P.   Henry Fielding.
J. Sutherland, 617(TLS):1Feb80-126
Rogers, P.   An Introduction to Pope.*
J. McLaverty, 447(N&Q):Dec78-559
Rogers, P., P.P. and F.A. Lapuente.   Diccionario de seudónimos literarios españoles, con algunas iniciales.
R.F. Brown, 86(BHS):Oct79-329
B.G. Carter, 238:Mar79-184
W.W. Moseley, 399(MLJ):Jan-Feb79-50
Rogers, R.   Metaphor.
T. Binkley, 290(JAAC):Summer80-470
L. Waldoff, 301(JEGP):Jul79-414

317

Rogers, S.A.B. Four Acres and a Donkey.
(C. Murphy, ed)
C. Rumens, 617(TLS):18Apr80-436
Rogers, T. At the Shores.
A. Broyard, 441:1Nov80-23
E. Connell, 441:23Nov80-15
J. Rubins, 453(NYRB):18Dec80-63
Rogier, P. The Poems of the Troubadour
Peire Rogier.* (D.E.T. Nicholson, ed)
L.T. Topsfield, 382(MAE):1979/1-120
Rogin, G. Preparations for the Ascent.
A. Broyard, 441:14Mar80-C22
J. Burke, 231:May80-90
M. Richler, 441:30Mar80-6
Rognoni, L. The Second Vienna School.*
C. Bennett, 607:Mar78-38
Röhl, M. Le Roman russe de Eugène-
Melchior de Vogüé.
J-L. Backès, 535(RHL):Jul-Aug79-700
M. Cadot, 52:Band13Heft3-325
Rohlfs, G. Grammatica storica dei
dialetti italogreci (Calabria, Salento).
(new ed)
J. Kramer, 343:Band23-185
Rohlfs, G. Nuovo dizionario dialettale
della Calabria (con repertorio italo-
calabro).* (new ed)
F. Mosino, 553(RLiR):Jul-Dec78-435
Rohlfs, G. Supplemento ai vocabolari
siciliani.*
F. Mosino, 553(RLiR):Jul-Dec78-437
Rohlfs, G. - see Hilka, A.
Rohmer, É. L'Organisation de l'espace
dans le "Faust" de Murnau.
J. Prieur, 450(NRF):Apr79-157
Rohmer, E. Six Moral Tales.
R. Mayne, 617(TLS):18Apr80-442
G. Millar, 362:17Jul80-87
Rohmer, E. and C. Chabrol. Hitchcock.
H. Weinberg, 200:Oct79-493
Röhn, H. Untersuchungen zur Zeitgestal-
tung und Komposition der Íslendinga-
sögur.*
L.G. Collings, 182:Vol131#11/12-349
E.G. Fichtner, 563(SS):Winter79-47
J. Harris, 382(MAE):1979/2-332
Rohrbaugh, J.B. Women.
P. Redgrove and P. Shuttle, 617(TLS):
18Jul80-819
Rohrberger, M.H. The Art of Katherine
Mansfield.
T.K. Meier, 573(SSF):Winter78-117
Rohrer, C. and N. Ruwet, eds. Actes du
Colloque Franco-Allemand de Grammaire
Transformationnelle. (Vol 1)
J. Härmä, 439(NM):1978/2-188
M-T. Vinet, 209(FM):Jul78-279
Rohrer, C. and N. Ruwet, eds. Actes du
Colloque Franco-Allemand de Grammaire
Transformationnelle. (Vol 2)
M-T. Vinet, 209(FM):Jul78-279
Röhrich, L., ed. Probleme der Sagenfor-
schung.
E. Ettlinger, 203:Vol189#1-118
Röhrich, L. Sage und Märchen.*
H-W. Nörtersheuser, 196:Band19Heft3/4-
339

Röhrich, L. Der Witz.
G. von Wilpert, 67:May79-162
Röhrich, L. and W. Mieder. Sprichwort.
R.D. Hacken, 406:Winter79-436
M. Hain, 196:Band19Heft1/2-169
B.A. Woods, 292(JAF):Apr-Jun79-242
Rohrlach, P.P., comp. Historisches Orts-
lexikon für Brandenburg. (Pt 5)
H.K. Schulze, 182:Vol131#15/16-571
Rohs, P. Transzendentale Logik.
S. Decloux, 182:Vol131#19-644
Rojahn, J-C., ed. Einführung in das
Studium der englischen Literatur.
R. Borgmeier, 38:Band96Heft3/4-548
Rojas, C. En Valle de los Caídos.
R. Kirsner, 399(MLJ):Sep-Oct79-313
de Rojas, F. "La Celestine" in the French
translation of 1578 by Jacques de Lavar-
din.* (D.L. Drysdall, ed)
G. Hainsworth, 208(FS):Vol33Pt2-665
Rojas Álvarez, L. - see Lysias
de Rojas Zorrilla, F. Numancia cercada y
Numancia destruida. (R.R. MacCurdy, ed)
E.T. Aylward, 238:Mar79-173
Rojtman, B. Forme et signification dans
le théâtre de Beckett.*
E. Morot-Sir, 207(FR):Mar79-648
M. Sheringham, 208(FS):Vol33Pt2-915
P. Vernois, 535(RHL):Sep-Oct79-884
Roland, A., ed. Psychoanalysis, Creativ-
ity and Literature.*
J.C. McLaren, 613:Dec79-449
M.M. Schwartz, 141:Spring79-157
Roland, C.P. The Improbable Era.*
T.B. Stroup, 577(SHR):Fall79-367
Roli, R. Pittura Bolognese, 1650-1800.
D. Miller, 90:Aug79-518
Röling, B.V.A. and C.F. Rüter, eds. The
Tokyo Judgment.
A-R. Werner, 182:Vol131#14-478
Roller, D.C. and R.W. Twyman, eds. The
Encyclopedia of Southern History.
R.A. Sokolov, 441:18May80-15
Rollin, B.E. Natural and Conventional
Meaning.*
T.G. Pavel, 353:Dec78-95
Rollin, R.B. and J.M. Patrick, eds.
"Trust to Good Verses."
D. Bush, 568(SCN):Spring-Summer79-7
H.B. Norland, 502(PrS):Fall78-295
P.W. Thomas, 541(RES):May79-213
Rollins, P.A. The Cowboy. (rev)
W. Gard, 584(SWR):Spring79-vi
Roloff, H-G. - see Naogeorg, T.
Rolph, C.H. London Particulars.
A. Calder-Marshall, 617(TLS):20Jun80-
717
"Jules Romains."
J.D. Biard, 208(FS):Jan79-103
Romani, M.A., ed. Le corti farnesiane di
Parma e Piacenza 1545-1622. (Vol 1)
E.B., 228(GSLI):Vol155fasc492-631
"Romanian Folk Arts."
Y.R. Lockwood, 292(JAF):Jul-Sep79-359

Romano, J. Dickens and Reality.*
  R.H. Dabney, 445(NCF):Mar79-513
  R. Gilmour, 155:Spring79-38
  L.K. Hughes, 141:Spring79-167
  R. Maxwell, 637(VS):Winter79-216
  R. O'Kell, 529(QQ):Winter79/80-712
  R.L. Patten, 454:Spring79-254
Romano, S. Giuseppe Volpi.
  D. Mack Smith, 617(TLS):2May80-483
Romanowski, S. L'illusion chez Descartes.
  J-M. Beyssade, 192(EP):Oct-Dec79-481
  E.D. James, 208(FS):Jul79-341
"Il Romanzo al tempo di Luigi XIII."
  P.R. Berk, 207(FR):May79-929
Romberg, B. Carl Jonas Love Almqvist.*
  B. Steene, 562(Scan):Nov78-165
Rombout, A-F. La pureté dans le théâtre
  de Jean Anouilh.
  B. Beugnot, 535(RHL):Jul-Aug78-677
Romeo, L. Ecce Homo!
  E. Korn, 617(TLS):9May80-534
Romero de Cepeda, J. La historia de
  Rosián de Castilla. (R. Arias, ed)
  M.L. Cozad, 304(JHP):Spring80-266
Romeyer-Dherbey, G. Maine de Biran.*
  D. Janicaud, 542:Jan-Mar78-116
Romhild, L.P. Tradition og Fantasi.
  G. Albeck, 562(Scan):May79-73
Romhild, L.P. - see Rubow, P.V.
Romig, W. Michigan Place Names.
  R.L. Baker, 292(JAF):Jul-Sep79-350
de Romilly, J. The Rise and Fall of
  States according to Greek Authors.
  G.J.D. Aalders H. Wzn., 394:
    Vol32fasc3/4-440
  C.W. Macleod, 303(JoHS):Vol199-193
Romo, R. and R. Paredes. New Directions
  in Chicano Scholarship.
  R.G. Lint, 649(WAL):Spring79-79
Romportl, M. Studies in Phonetics.
  M. Nidecki, 360(LP):Vol21-172
Ronan, C. The Shorter Science and Civili-
  zation in China. (Vol 1)
  D. Gregory-Smith, 485(PE&W):Jul79-364
Rønning, H., ed. Linjer i norsk prosa.
  W. Baumgartner, 563(SS):Autumn79-513
de Ronsard, P. Discours des misères de ce
  temps. (M. Smith, ed)
  P.J. Ford, 208(FS):Oct79-437
de Ronsard, P. Oeuvres complètes. (Vol
  20) (P. Laumonier, ed; rev by I. Silver
  and R. Lebègue)
  G. Castor, 208(FS):Vol33Pt2-633
de Ronsard, P. Poems of Pierre de Ronsard.
  (N. Kilmer, ed and trans)
  J. Simon, 491:Apr80-40
de Ronsard, P. Ronsard II.* (G. Castor
  and T. Cave, eds)
  F.C. Cornfield, 207(FR):Dec78-341
  P. Sharratt, 402(MLR):Apr79-455
de Ronsard, P. Selected Poems. (C.M.
  Scollen, ed)
  M. Quainton, 208(FS):Vol33Pt2-631
Ronsley, J., ed. Myth and Reality in
  Irish Literature.*
  B. John, 408:Spring79-181

Roobol, W.H. Tsereteli — A Democrat in
  the Russian Revolution.
  W.E. Mosse, 575(SEER):Jan79-135
Rood, A. - see "Gordon Craig on Movement
  and Dance"
Rook, C. The Hooligan Nights.
  P. Keating, 617(TLS):29Feb80-224
Rooke, L. Cry Evil.
  R.M. Brown, 99:Aug80-36
Rooke, L. The Love Parlour.* The Broad
  Back of the Angel.*
  C. Blaise, 102(CanL):Summer79-118
Roos, P., ed. Exil.
  J. Rosellini, 406:Summer79-213
Roosevelt, J., with S. Toperoff. A Family
  Matter.
  P. Andrews, 441:20Jul80-12
Rooth, A.B., ed. The Alaska Expedition
  1966.
  W.H. Jansen, 582(SFQ):Vol141-289
Rooth, A.B. The Importance of Storytell-
  ing.
  W.H. Jansen, 292(JAF):Jan-Mar79-96
Roper, D. Reviewing before the "Edin-
  burgh," 1788-1802.
  J. Clive, 31(ASch):Summer80-414
  K.S., 148:Summer79-91
Rorabaugh, W.J. The Alcoholic Republic.
  A. Sinclair, 617(TLS):30May80-602
Roriczer, M. and H. Schmuttermayer.
  Gothic Design Techniques. (L.R. Shelby,
  ed and trans)
  C.F. Barnes, Jr., 54:Jun78-363
  E.G. Carlson, 589:Jan79-190
Rorty, A.O., ed. The Identities of Per-
  sons.*
  P. Smale, 154:Mar78-183
  B. Smart, 393(Mind):Jan79-147
Rosa, K.R. and L. Rosa-Wolff. Psychosomat-
  ische Selbstregulation.
  H. Wendt, 682(ZPSK):Band31Heft2-223
de Rosa, R.T. - see under Tullio de Rosa,
  R.
del Rosal, F. Médico de Córdoba. (B.B.
  Thompson, ed)
  E. Geisler, 196:Band19Heft3/4-343
del Rosal, F. La razón de algunos re-
  franes. (B.B. Thompson, ed)
  J. Gibbs, 402(MLR):Jul79-723
  J.R. Jones, 240(HR):Autumn78-495
  J.M. Ruano de la Haza, 86(BHS):Apr79-
    152
Rosbottom, R.C. Marivaux's Novels.
  V. Mylne, 208(FS):Vol33Pt2-725
Rosbottom, R.C., ed. Studies in Eigh-
  teenth Century Culture.* (Vol 5)
  M. Delon, 535(RHL):Mar-Jun79-511
  D. Irwin, 402(MLR):Jan79-143
Rosbottom, R.C., ed. Studies in Eigh-
  teenth-Century Culture. (Vol 6)
  M. Delon, 535(RHL):Mar-Jun79-511
  A. Scott-Prelorentzos, 107(CRCL):
    Fall79-443
Rösch, E., ed. Goethes Roman "Die Wahlver-
  wandtschaften."
  H. Reiss, 402(MLR):Oct79-987

319

Rose, A. and E. Souchon. New Orleans Jazz.
  M. Harrison, 415:Dec79-1005
Rose, P. Woman of Letters.*
  A. Bell, 569(SR):Spring79-325
  M. Church, 268(IFR):Summer80-141
  G. Davenport, 579(SAQ):Summer79-405
  J. Gindin, 594:Spring79-82
  S. Rudikoff, 249(HudR):Winter79/80-540
  E. Showalter, 301(JEGP):Jul79-459
  M. Spilka, 454:Winter79-172
  295(JML):Vol7#4-844
Rosemont, H., Jr. and D.J. Cook - see
  Leibniz, G.W.
Rosen, C. The Classical Style. (rev)
  R.L.J., 412:Feb78-67
Rosen, C. Sonata Forms.
  J. Kerman, 453(NYRB):23Oct80-50
  E. Rothstein, 441:21Dec80-6
Rosen, G. Zen in the Art of J.D. Salinger.
  G. Haslam, 649(WAL):Fall79-245
Rosén, H.B. Contemporary Hebrew.
  J. Fellman, 361:Aug78-389
Rosen, R. Prints.
  R. Whelan, 55:Mar79-29
Rosen, R. and S. Davidson - see Pinzer, M.
Rosen, R.D. Psychobabble.*
  E.Z. Friedenberg, 529(QQ):Summer79-293
Rosen, S. G.W.F. Hegel.
  K. Hartmann, 53(AGP):Band60Heft1-105
Rosen, S. Ned and Jack.
  K. Garebian, 99:May80-38
Rosenau, H. Boullée and Visionary Archi-
  tecture, including Boullée's "Architec-
  ture, Essay on Art."
  J-M. Pérouse de Montclos, 576:Dec78-
  320
Rosenberg, A. Microeconomic Laws.*
  D.M. Hausman, 449:Mar79-118
Rosenberg, D. and B. The Music Makers.*
  N. Goodwin, 415:Oct79-833
Rosenberg, H. Art on the Edge.
  N. Robinson, 39:Jul79-82
Rosenberg, H. Barnett Newman.*
  R. Whelan, 55:Oct79-53
Rosenberg, H. Saul Steinberg.
  M. Fox, 529(QQ):Spring79-185
Rosenberg, H.L. Atomic Soldiers.
  T. Ferris, 441:28Sep80-18
Rosenberg, I. The Collected Works of
  Isaac Rosenberg.* (I. Parsons, ed)
  M. Dodsworth, 175:Summer79-199
  D. Jacobson, 31(ASch):Autumn80-564
  A. Ross, 364:Aug/Sep79-7
  376:Oct79-142
Rosenberg, J.F. Linguistic Representation.
  R.M. Burian, 486:Jun78-325
Rosenberg, K. Die epischen chan-Dichtun-
  gen in der Literatur Thailands.
  P.J. Bee, 182:Vol131#3/4-100
Rosenberg, M. The Masks of "Macbeth."*
  C.J. Carlisle, 570(SQ):Winter79-99
  A.C. Sprague, 611(TN):Vol133#3-138
  J.L. Styan, 130:Summer79-171
  G.J. Williams, 301(JEGP):Oct79-550
Rosenberg, N.V., ed. Folklore and Oral
  History.
  B. Allen, 650(WF):Jan79-58

Rosenberg, P. Chardin, 1699-1779.
  F. Haskell, 453(NYRB):9Oct80-29
  G. Martin, 617(TLS):1Feb80-120
Rosenberg, R. Literaturverhältnisse im
  deutschen Vormärz.
  R. Dau, 654(WB):1/1978-175
Rosenberg, S., ed. Sentence Production.
  205(FMLS):Apr78-189
Rosenblatt, J. Sylvia Plath.
  D.L. Eder, 659(ConL):Spring80-301
Rosenblatt, J. Top Soil.*
  A. Amprimoz, 102(CanL):Autumn79-99
Rosenblatt, L.M. The Reader, the Text,
  the Poem.
  M.C. Beardsley, 569(SR):Fall79-639
  T. Hawkes, 676(YR):Summer80-560
  S. McKay, 608:Sep80-379
  J. Reichert, 290(JAAC):Fall79-91
Rosenboom, D., ed. Biofeedback and the
  Arts.
  P.J.P., 412:Aug-Nov78-289
Rosenfeld, A.H. A Double Dying.
  S. Jacoby, 441:21Dec80-11
Rosenfeld, A.H. and I. Greenberg, eds.
  Confronting the Holocaust.
  T. Ziolkowski, 569(SR):Fall79-676
Rosenfeld, M.N. - see "Sebastiano Serlio
  on Domestic Architecture"
Rosengarten, Y. Trois aspects de la
  pensée religieuse sumérienne.*
  J.S. Cooper, 318(JAOS):Apr-Jun78-147
Rosengren, P. Presencia y ausencia de los
  pronombres personales sujetos en español
  moderno.*
  O.T. Myers, 545(RPh):May79-428
Rosenshield, G. "Crime and Punishment."
  M.B. Thompson, 558(RLJ):Spring79-227
  E. Wasiolek, 550(RusR):Jul79-398
Rosenstock, W. Kants geniale Kritik der
  reinen Vernunft — ein Mythos.
  W. Steinbeck, 342:Band69Heft3-372
Rosenstrauch-Königsberg, E. Freimaurerei
  im Josephinischen Wien.
  F. Lösel, 220(GL&L):Oct78-70
Rosenthal, D.H. Modern Catalan Poetry.
  H.J.F. de Aguilar, 472:Fall/Winter79-
  64
Rosenthal, F. The Classical Heritage in
  Islam.*
  J. Dillon, 318(JAOS):Oct-Dec78-483
Rosenthal, H. and J. Warrack. The Concise
  Oxford Dictionary of Opera. (2nd ed)
  A. Jacobs, 415:Oct79-826
Rosenthal, M.L. Sailing into the Unknown.*
  C. Molesworth, 219(GaR):Spring79-230
  T. Weiss, 617(TLS):1Feb80-124
  295(JML):Vol7#4-609
Rosetti, A. - see Călinescu, G. and A.
  Rosetti
Rosidi, A. Voyage de Noces.
  J.M. Echols, 318(JAOS):Jul-Sep78-329
Rosnow, R.L. and G.A. Fine. Rumor and
  Gossip.
  S. Yerkovich, 292(JAF):Apr-Jun79-237
Rosow, E. Born To Lose.
  639(VQR):Autumn79-151

Ross, A., ed. The Cricketer's Companion.
G. Moorhouse, 364:Oct79-75
Ross, A. Death Valley.
D. Davis, 362:28Aug80-277
Ross, D.P. The Canadian Fact Book on
Income Distribution.
M.E. Cohen, 99:Nov80-34
Ross, M. Banners of the King.
N. Hampson, 208(FS):Vol33Pt2-1007
Ross, M. Beyond Metabolism.
M. Treib, 45:Jul79-194
Ross, M.S. The Literary Politicians.*
W.F. Hall, 255(HAB):Summer79-231
M. Kirby, 109:Winter79/80-181
295(JML):Vol7#4-627
639(VQR):Summer78-96
Ross, N.W. Buddhism.
J. Leonard, 441:26Dec80-C30
Ross, R. Adam Kok's Griquas.
A. Kuper, 69:Vol148#3-300
Ross, R.J. Beleaguered Tower.
R.A. Stelzmann, 613:Dec79-430
Ross, V. Goodbye Summer.
P. O'Flaherty, 99:Nov80-32
Rossabi, M. China and Inner Asia.
L.B. Fields, 293(JASt):Nov78-143
Rosset, C. Le Réel — Traité de l'idiotie.
R. Munier, 450(NRF):Apr79-124
Rossetti, C. The Complete Poems of Chris-
tina Rossetti. (Variorum Edition, Vol 1)
(R.W. Crump, ed)
G. Grigson, 617(TLS):11Apr80-409
Rossetti, D.G. and J. Morris. Dante
Gabriel Rossetti and Jane Morris: Their
Correspondence.* (J. Bryson, ed)
F.S. Boos, 405(MP):Nov79-172
D. Sonstroem, 637(VS):Autumn77-131
Rossetti, W.M. The Diary of W.M. Rossetti
1870-1873.* (O. Bornand, ed)
M. Berg, 541(RES):Feb79-116
Rossetti, W.M. The P.R.B. Journal.* (W.E.
Fredeman, ed)
F.S. Boos, 405(MP):Nov79-172
D. Sonstroem, 637(VS):Autumn77-131
Rossi, L. Situazione dell'estetica in
Italia.
F.P. Ciglia, 227(GCFI):Apr-Jun78-264
Rossi, L.E. and others - see Fraenkel, E.
Rossi, M. Huon de Bordeaux et l'évolu-
tion du genre épique au XIIIe siècle.*
A. Iker-Gittleman, 545(RPh):Aug78-145
Rossi-Landi, F. Linguistics and Economics.
J. Průcha, 353:Apr78-80
Rössler, G. Zur Problematik der Struktur
des Nordwestnormannischen Vokalismus.
M.S. La Du, 545(RPh):Aug78-115
Rössler, M. Die Liedpredigt.
W. Welzig, 602:Vol10-293
Rossman, C. and A.W. Friedman, eds. Mario
Vargas Llosa.
M.P. Levitt, 295(JML):Vol7#4-763
J.M. Lipski, 395(MFS):Winter78/79-663
Rossman, V.R. Perspectives of Irony in
Medieval French Literature.*
T. Hunt, 402(MLR):Jan79-194
W. Rothwell, 208(FS):Vol33Pt2-597

Rossman, V.R. François Villon.*
J. Fox, 208(FS):Vol33Pt2-582
Rossner, J. Attachments.*
639(VQR):Winter78-21
Rossner, J. Emmeline.
C. Lehmann-Haupt, 441:25Sep80-C25
J. Moynahan, 441:14Sep80-13
Rosso, F. Catalogo critico dell'archivo
Alessandro Antonelli. (Vol 1)
S. Kostof, 54:Jun78-382
Rostand, E. Cyrano de Bergerac. (C.
Fry, trans)
T. Gallacher, 610:May78-228
Rostow, E.V. The Ideal in Law.
V.K., 543:Sep78-152
Rostow, W.W. Getting from Here to There.
639(VQR):Autumn78-134
Roszak, T. Person/Planet.*
L. Haworth, 529(QQ):Winter79/80-698
Rotella, G.L. E.E. Cummings.
L.N. Dendinger, 365:Winter80-51
Rotenstreich, N. Theory and Practice.
T.L.S. Sprigge, 483:Apr79-263
Roth, A., ed. The New Architecture: 1930-
1940.
W.C. Miller, 505:Mar78-116
Roth, C. and G. Wigoder, eds. The New
Standard Jewish Encyclopedia. (5th ed
rev by G. Wigoder)
L. Gold, 287:Feb78-29
Roth, G. Winterreise.
P-L. Adams, 61:Mar80-102
J. Updike, 442(NY):21Apr80-130
Roth, H. Der Lehrer und seine Wissen-
schaft.
R. Thomassen, 277(ITL):#39/40-154
Roth, H-D. Institutioneller Agrarkredit
und traditionelle Schuldverhältnisse.
F. Kuhnen, 182:Vol131#20-730
Roth, K-H. "Deutsch."
B.J. Koekkoek, 221(GQ):May79-390
Roth, P. The Ghost Writer.*
B. Quart, 364:Mar80-87
Roth, P. The Professor of Desire.*
R. Alter, 473(PR):3/1979-478
B. Forer, 152(UDQ):Summer78-149
Rothblatt, S. Tradition and Change in
English Liberal Education.
D. Spring, 637(VS):Spring79-378
Rothe, K. Selbstsein und bürgerliche
Gesellschaft.*
J-M. Gabaude, 542:Jan-Mar78-119
Rothe, W. Der Expressionismus.
J.M. Ritchie, 402(MLR):Oct79-995
Rothenberg, A. The Emerging Goddess.
A. Mann, 150(DR):Winter79/80-748
Rothenberg, J. Günter Grass.*
G.P. Knapp, 182:Vol131#5/6-151
K.H. Schoeps, 406:Spring79-87
Rothenberg, J. Gottfried Keller.*
L.B. Jennings, 406:Fall79-344
Rothenstein, J., ed. Stanley Spencer.
T. Hyman, 364:Dec79/Jan80-142
Rothlach, R. Der Wandel der Wanjamwesi-
Gesellschaft in Vorkolonialer Zeit und
die Ideen Nyereres über die Tradition-
[continued]

321

Rowse, A.L. The Byrons and the Tre-
vanions.*
639(VQR):Autumn79-131
Rowse, A.L. The Casebooks of Simon For-
man.
R.E. Alton, 447(N&Q):Oct78-456
Rowse, A.L. A Man of the Thirties.
I. Ogg, 617(TLS):15Feb80-183
P. Vansittart, 364:Dec79/Jan80-139
Rowse, A.L. - see Shakespeare, W.
Roy, C. La Traversée du Pont des Arts.
F. de Martinoir, 450(NRF):Jul79-106
Roy, G. Fragiles lumières de la terre.
A. Mitcham, 150(DR):Spring79-180
Roy, G. Garden in the Wind.*
C. Gerson, 102(CanL):Autumn79-115
Roy, G-R. Contribution à l'analyse du syn-
tagme verbal.
N.C.W. Spence, 208(FS):Vol33Pt2-1050
R. Martin, 209(FM):Jan78-81
Roy, G.R. - see "Studies in Scottish Lit-
erature"
Roy, J. Julio Cortázar ante su sociedad.
M.A. Salgado, 241:Jan79-114
Roy, J-P. Bachelard, ou le concept contre
l'image.*
M. Benoît, 193(ELit):Apr78-231
G. Cesbron, 535(RHL):Sep-Oct79-878
M. Herz, 207(FR):Apr79-779
E.M. McAllester, 402(MLR):Oct79-948
Roy, R.N. George Bernard Shaw's Histori-
cal Plays.
F.P.W. McDowell, 295(JML):Vol7#4-809
Royce, K. The Third Arm.
N. Callendar, 441:8Jun80-31
M. Laski, 362:17Apr80-514
Royce, S. A Frontier Lady.
A. Ronald, 649(WAL):Summer79-171
Royle, T. Precipitous City.
J. Campbell, 617(TLS):25Jul80-840
Royster, C. A Revolutionary People at War.
P. Mackesy, 617(TLS):20Jun80-692
Rozanov, V. The Apocalypse of Our Time
and Other Writings. (R. Payne, ed)
A.L. Crone, 574(SEEJ):Spring79-129
Rozanov, V.V. Four Faces of Rozanov.
P.J.S. Duncan, 550(RusR):Jul79-367
Rozanov, V.V. Religija i Kul'tura.
J. Ivask, 558(RLJ):Fall79-261
Różewicz, T. The Survivor and Other
Poems.* (M.J. Kryński and R.A. Maguire,
eds and trans) Selected Poems.* (A.
Czerniawski, ed and trans)
G. Gömöri, 575(SEER):Apr79-287
Rožkova, G.I. and others. Učebnik russ-
kogo jazyka dlja lic, govorjaščich na
nemeckom jazyke.
D. Bock, 682(ZPSK):Band31Heft2-197
Rozman, G. Urban Networks in Russia 1750-
1800 and Premodern Periodization.*
J.T. Alexander, 104(CASS):Spring78-184
Ruano, E.B. - see under Benito Ruano, E.
Ruark, G. Reeds.*
R. De Mott, 651(WHR):Spring79-183
Ruben, B.D. - see "Communication Yearbook"
Rubens, B. Spring Sonata.*
D. Durrant, 364:Feb80-92

Rubenstein, R. The Novelistic Vision of
Doris Lessing.*
V. Tiger, 659(ConL):Spring80-286
Rubin, B. Paved With Good Intentions.
D. Pipes, 441:2Nov80-15
Rubin, J.H. Eighteenth-Century French
Life-Drawing.*
P. Conisbee, 90:Apr79-265
D. Irwin, 161(DUJ):Dec78-91
Rubin, L.D., Jr. Virginia: A History.
639(VQR):Spring78-60
Rubin, L.D., Jr. The Wary Fugitives.*
J.E. Brown, 577(SHR):Fall79-354
L. MacKethan, 639(VQR):Summer79-551
W. Thorp, 27(AL):Nov79-416
Rubin, W., ed. Pablo Picasso: A Retro-
spective.
S. Gardiner, 362:11Dec80-802
J. Richardson, 453(NYRB):17Jul80-16
Rubinstein, A. My Many Years.
H. Cole, 362:17Jul80-86
D. Henahan, 441:27Jan80-7
Rubinstein, A.Z., ed. Soviet and Chinese
Influence in the Third World.*
T.W. Robinson, 550(RusR):Apr79-251
Rubinstein, H.L. Captain Luckless.
M.R. Dickson, 588(SSL):Vol14-301
Rubinstein, J. Soviet Dissidents.
L. Schapiro, 453(NYRB):18Dec80-41
Rubow, P.V. De Franske. (L.P. Romhild,
ed)
G. Albeck, 562(Scan):May79-73
Rubrecht, W.H. Durrells Alexandria Quar-
tet.
K. Versluys, 179(ES):Aug79-516
Rücker, H. and K.O. Seidel, eds. "Sagen
mit Sinne."
D.H. Green, 402(MLR):Apr79-484
Rudd, N. Lines of Enquiry.*
K. Galinsky, 121(CJ):Oct-Nov79-76
Rudden, B. and D. Wyatt, eds. Basic
Community Laws.
M. Cremona, 617(TLS):22Aug80-932
Ruddick, W. - see Lockhart, J.G.
Rudé, G. Protest and Punishment.
639(VQR):Autumn79-132
von Rüden, M. "Wlanc" und Derivate im Alt-
und Mittelenglischen.
E.G. Stanley, 382(MAE):1979/2-271
Rüdiger, H. and W. Hirdt. Studien über
Petrarca, Boccaccio und Ariost in der
deutschen Literatur.*
J. Hösle, 52:Band13Heft1-87
Rudofsky, B. The Prodigious Builders.*
D. Hoffmann, 576:May78-105
Rudrum, A. - see Vaughan, H.
Rudy, S. - see Uspensky, B.
Rueff, J. Oeuvres complètes. (Vol 1)
A. Reix, 542:Oct-Dec79-494
Ruff, H.J. How to Prosper During the Com-
ing Bad Years.
J. Epstein, 453(NYRB):21Feb80-7
Ruffner, J.A. Eponyms Dictionaries Index.
D.H., 355(LSoc):Apr78-149
K.B. Harder, 424:Sep78-294
Ruffo-Fiore, S. Donne's Petrarchism.
M. Cocco, 149(CLS):Jun79-167

323

Rufinus. The Epigrams of Rufinus.* (D.
Page, ed)
R.C. McCail, 123:Vol29No2-211
Ruggeri, U. Francesco Capella: Dipinti
e Disegni.
J.B. Shaw, 39:Nov79-450
Ruggiers, P.G., ed. Versions of Medieval
Comedy.
J.M. Ferrante, 651(WHR):Winter79-87
Rugh, T.F. and E.R. Silva, eds. History
as a Tool in Critical Interpretation.
D. Carrier, 290(JAAC):Fall79-86
Ruh, K. and others - see Stammler, W. and
K. Langosch
Ruhe, E. De Amasio ad Amasiam.*
A.K. Bate, 208(FS):Vol33Pt2-595
T. Janson, 545(RPh):May79-440
Ruhlen, M. A Guide to the Languages of
the World.*
H.A. Gleason, Jr., 320(CJL):
Spring-Fall78-165
J. Knappert, 353:Dec78-91
Rühling, A. Negativität bei Albert Camus.
E. Diet, 542:Apr-Jun78-205
Ruiz, M.E. Cuento de niño.
R.D. Souza, 263(RIB):Vol29No1-103
Ruíz, R.E. The Great Rebellion.
K.E. Meyer, 441:16Nov80-12
Ruiz-Fornells, E. Las Concordancias de
"El Ingenioso Hidalgo Don Quijote de la
Mancha." (Vol 1)
R. Pellen, 553(RLiR):Jul-Dec78-465
Rukeyser, M. The Collected Poems of
Muriel Rukeyser.*
W.H. Pritchard, 249(HudR):Summer79-261
639(VQR):Autumn79-147
Rukeyser, M. The Gates.
639(VQR):Winter78-12
Ruland, R. America in Modern European
Literature.*
C. Wegelin, 131(CL):Winter79-87
Rule, A. The Stranger Beside Me.
T. Thompson, 441:24Aug80-12
Rumaker, M. A Day and a Night at the
Baths.
A. Young, 617(TLS):13Jun80-682
Runciman, S. The Byzantine Theocracy.
P. Charanis, 589:Jan79-184
Runciman, S. Mistra: Byzantine Capital of
the Peloponnese.
S. Raven, 362:20Mar80-374
Rundle, B. Grammar in Philosophy.
P. Geach, 617(TLS):7Mar80-268
Runnalls, G.A., ed. Le Cycle des Mystères
des Premiers Martyrs du manuscrit 1131
de la Bibliothèque Sainte-Geneviève.*
A. Serper, 545(RPh):Nov78-256
Runnalls, G.A., ed. "Le Mystère de la
Passion Nostre Seigneur" du manuscrit
1131 de la Bibliothèque Sainte-Gene-
viève.*
D. Maddox, 545(RPh):Nov78-206
van Runset, U. Ironie und Philosophie bei
Voltaire unter besonderer Berücksichti-
gung der "Dialogues et entretiens phil-
osophiques."
J.H. Brumfitt, 208(FS):Vol33Pt2-742

Runte, H.R., H. Niedzielski and W.L.
Hendrickson, eds. Jean Misrahi Memorial
Volume: Studies in Medieval Literature.
R.T. Pickens, 188(ECr):Fall78-95
K.V. Sinclair, 67:May79-121
Runte, R. - see "Studies in Eighteenth-
Century Culture"
"Ruodlieb: Faksimile-Ausgabe des Codex
Latinus Monacensis 19486 der Bayerischen
Staatsbibliothek München und der Frag-
mente von St. Florian." (Vol 1)
G. Silagi, 224(GRM):Band28Heft3-361
Rupp, H., ed. Deutsches Literatur-Lexikon.
(new ed) (Vol 5 rev by H. Emmel and
others; Vol 6 rev by C.L. Lang)
P.M. Mitchell, 301(JEGP):Apr79-290
H. Weber, 182:Vol131#1/2-35
Rupp, L.J. Mobilizing Women for War.
639(VQR):Autumn78-148
Ruppelt, H. Wettbewerbspolitik und wirt-
schaftliche Konzentration.
J. Comte, 182:Vol131#20-731
Ruprecht, H-G. Theaterpublikum und Text-
auffassung.*
B. Boudgoust, 52:Band13Heft2-206
Ruse, M. The Darwinian Revolution.
J.Z. Young, 453(NYRB):7Feb80-45
Rush, F. The Best Kept Secret.
S. Jacoby, 441:26Oct80-15
Rushforth, P.S. Kindergarten.*
C. Lehmann-Haupt, 441:8Jul80-C18
B. Yourgrau, 441:17Aug80-10
442(NY):11Aug80-89
Rushmer, R.F. Humanizing Health Care.
S. Bernstein, 42(AR):Summer79-364
Rusinow, D. The Yugoslav Experiment, 1948-
1974.
639(VQR):Spring79-54
Ruskin, J. Ruskin's Venice.* (A.
Whittick, ed)
E. Forssman, 576:Mar78-63
Rüss, G., ed. Dokumente zur Kunst-,
Literatur- und Kulturpolitik der SED
1971-1974.
A. Stephan, 406:Spring79-81
Russell, C. Parliaments and English
Politics, 1621-1629.
J.H. Hexter, 453(NYRB):18Dec80-58
Russell, D. The Tamarisk Tree 2.
S. Sutherland, 617(TLS):4Apr80-392
M. Warnock, 362:27Mar80-418
Russell, D.W., ed. "La Vie de Saint
Laurent."*
E. Baumgartner, 545(RPh):May79-489
W. Rothwell, 208(FS):Vol33Pt2-530
Russell, F., ed. Art Nouveau Architecture.
A. Saint, 617(TLS):21Mar80-316
Russell, G.W. Selections from Contribu-
tions to the Irish Homestead by G.W.
Russell — A.E.* (Vol 1) (H. Summerfield,
ed)
S. Sweeney, 305(JIL):Sep78-170
Russell, G.W. Selections from Contribu-
tions to the Irish Homestead by G.W.
Russell — A.E.* (Vol 2) (H. Summerfield,
ed)
R.G. Yeed, 305(JIL):Sep78-171

Russell, J. Francis Bacon.
  D. Piper, 617(TLS):1Feb80-119
Russell, J. Style in Modern British Fiction.*
  295(JML):Vol7#4-635
Russell, J.B. The Devil.* (Vol 1)
  F.W. Dillistone, 396(ModA):Spring79-201
  M. Lebowitz, 598(SoR):Spring80-509
Russell, M. Death Fuse.
  T.J. Binyon, 617(TLS):18Apr80-450
"Russia Mediaevalis." (Vol 3) (J. Fennell, L. Müller and A. Poppe, eds)
  G. Lenhoff, 574(SEEJ):Spring79-125
Russo, J.P. - see Richards, I.A.
Rustomji, N. Bhutan.
  L.E. Rose, 293(JASt):Aug79-831
Rutherford, A. The Literature of War.*
  T. Mallon, 659(ConL):Autumn80-646
Rutherford, P. The Making of the Canadian Media.
  R. Lorimer, 102(CanL):Winter78-82
  B. Trotter, 529(QQ):Spring79-149
Rutherford, W. Hitler's Propaganda Machine.
  J.S. Conway, 529(QQ):Autumn79-510
Ruthven, K.K. Critical Assumptions.
  T. Hawkes, 617(TLS):22Feb80-215
Ruthven, K.K. Myth.*
  M. Bell, 402(MLR):Jan79-131
Rutland, E.D. The Cranberry Tree.
  G. Hamel, 198:Winter80-140
Rutland, R. and C.F. Hobson - see Madison, J.
Rutland, R.A. The Democrats.
  442(NY):11Feb80-118
Rutledge, J. The Dialogue of the Dead in Eighteenth-Century Germany.
  H. Schelle, 52:Band13Heft1-91
Rutsala, V. Paragraphs.*
  V. Contoski, 114(ChiR):Autumn78-137
  D. Graham, 565:Vol120#2-75
van Rutten, P-M. Le Langage poétique de Saint-John Perse.*
  R. Little, 208(FS):Vol33Pt2-883
Rutter, J.B. and S.H. The Transition to Mycenaean.
  O.T.P.K. Dickinson, 303(JoHS):Vol199-199
Ruttkowski, W.V. Typen und Schichten.
  J-D. de Lannoy, 182:Vol131#19-651
Ruttmann, I. Das Alexanderlied des Pfaffen Lamprecht (Strassburger Alexander).
  L. Jillings, 182:Vol131#21/22-802
Ruusuvuori, A., with J. Pallasmaa, eds. Alvar Aalto 1898-1976.
  S. Abercrombie, 45:Aug79-148
Ryals, C.D. Browning's Later Poetry, 1871-1889.*
  P. Brantlinger, 637(VS):Spring79-367
Ryan, A., ed. The Idea of Freedom.
  J. Lieberson and S. Morgenbesser, 453(NYRB):20Mar80-31
Ryan, D.P., ed. A Salute to Courage.
  G.A. Billias, 432(NEQ):Sep79-416

Ryan, M-L. Rituel et poésie.
  D.L. Racine, 207(FR):May79-938
Ryan, P. and L. Pesek. Solar System.
  529(QQ):Summer79-371
Ryan, R.M. Keats.*
  W.H. Evert, 301(JEGP):Oct79-561
  K. Muir, 402(MLR):Jul79-671
  N. Talbot, 67:May79-101
Ryavec, K.W., ed. Soviet Society and the Communist Party.
  A. Brown, 617(TLS):25Jan80-95
  J.G. Vaillant, 550(RusR):Oct79-488
Rychner, J. - see Eustache d'Amiens
Rychner, J. and A. Henry - see Villon, F.
Rydings, H.A. A Hong Kong Union Catalogue.
  A. Birch, 302:Vol16#1and2-131
Ryga, G. Ploughmen of the Glacier.*
  L. Manning, 526:Summer79-90
  B. Neil, 108:Winter79-141
Ryle, G., ed. Contemporary Aspects of Philosophy.*
  P. Dubois, 542:Apr-Jun78-201
  J.E. Tiles, 518:Jan79-30
Ryle, G. La notion d'esprit.
  J. Largeault, 542:Jul-Sep79-376
Ryle, G. On Thinking. (K. Kolenda, ed)
  G. Harman, 617(TLS):20Jun80-701
Ryn, C.G. Democracy and the Ethical Life.*
  R.D.N., 543:Sep78-154
Ryōkan. One Robe, One Bowl.* (J. Stevens, ed and trans)
  B.M. Wilson, 485(PE&W):Jan79-105
"Ryōkan: Zen Monk-Poet of Japan." (B. Watson, trans)
  L.M. Zolbrod, 293(JASt):Aug79-783
  639(VQR):Autumn78-145
Rypka, J. History of Iranian Literature. (K. Jahn, ed)
  B. Utas, 259(IIJ):Jan79-41
Rzhevsky, L.D. Solzhenitsyn.*
  D.L. Burgin, 651(WHR):Spring79-149
  W. Krasnow, 550(RusR):Oct79-518

Saab, A.P. The Origins of the Crimean Alliance.*
  M.S. Anderson, 575(SEER):Jul79-451
Sabat de Rivers, G. El Sueño de Sor Juana Inés de la Cruz.
  R. Echavarren, 238:May-Sep79-413
Sabin, M. English Romanticism and the French Tradition.*
  M.G. Cooke, 591(SIR):Summer79-323
Sabol, A.J., ed. Four Hundred Songs and Dances from the Stuart Masque.
  S. Orgel, 141:Fall79-362
Saccaro, A.P. Französischer Humanismus des 14. und 15. Jahrhunderts.
  N. Mann, 208(FS):Vol33Pt2-605
Saccio, P. Shakespeare's English Kings.*
  S.G., 502(PrS):Spring78-115
  M. Manheim, 125:Fall78-138
Saccone, E. Il poeta travestito.
  R.S. Dombroski, 400(MLN):Jan79-178
Sachar, A.L. A Host at Last.*
  D.G. Dalin, 390:Jun/Jul79-96

Sachs, H. Toscanini.*
D. Cairns, 415:Jul79-579
Sachs, M. Le Sabbat.
G. Quinsat, 450(NRF):Aug79-113
Sachs, R. British and American Business
in Keywords.
K. Schröder, 430(NS):Dec78-621
Sachs, V. La Contre-Bible de Melville.*
R.H. Brodhead, 445(NCF):Sep78-235
Sackheim, E., comp. The Blues Line.
E.O. Henry, 582(SFQ):Vol41-294
Sacré, J. Un Sang maniériste.
T.C. Cave, 402(MLR):Apr79-457
L.K. Donaldson-Evans, 207(FR):Feb79-
481
el-Sadat, A. In Search of Identity.
M. Cohen, 287:Aug/Sep78-24
639(VQR):Autumn78-139
Sa'di Sherazi, M. "Morals Pointed and
Tales Adorned," The Bustan of Sadi.
(G.M. Wickens, trans)
Q.S.K. Hussaini, 273(IC):Jul76-191
Sadie, S., ed. The New Grove Dictionary
of Music and Musicians.
H.C. Schonberg, 441:21Dec80-7
Sadler, A.L. The Maker of Modern Japan.
Miki Seiichirō, 285(JapQ):Jan-Mar79-
113
Sadock, J.M. Toward a Linguistic Theory
of Speech Acts.*
R.M. Harnish, 361:Feb/Mar78-288
Sadoff, I. Palm Reading in Winter.*
639(VQR):Summer78-100
Sadoul, G. French Film.
E.B. Turk, 207(FR):Feb79-498
Sáenz de la Calzada, L. "La Barraca."
G. Gullón, 240(HR):Summer78-393
Sáez, E. and J. Trenchs Odena, eds. Diplo-
matario del Cardenal Gil de Albornoz,
Cancillería pontificia (1351-1353).
J.N. Hillgarth, 589:Jan79-121
Safire, W. Safire's Political Dictionary.*
J.R. Gaskin, 569(SR):Summer79-455
639(VQR):Spring79-60
Safran, N. Israel — The Embattled Ally.
G.R. Kieval, 390:Mar79-59
B. Rubin, 287:Oct78-23
Sagan, C. Broca's Brain.*
639(VQR):Autumn79-150
Sagan, C. Cosmos.
442(NY):24Nov80-210
Sagan, C. The Dragons of Eden.
M. Vozick, 186(ETC.):Jun78-209
Sagan, C. and others. Murmurs of Earth.
639(VQR):Summer79-92
Sagan, F. Silken Eyes.
639(VQR):Spring78-65
Sagan, F. The Unmade Bed.
639(VQR):Autumn79-138
Sagar, K. The Life of D.H. Lawrence.*
(British title: D.H. Lawrence.)
J. Atlas, 441:10Jun80-C9
D. Grumbach, 441:29Jun80-15
V.S. Pritchett, 453(NYRB):29May80-3
Sagarra, E. A Social History of Germany
1648-1914.
R. Pascal, 402(MLR):Jan79-242

Sage, L., ed. Peacock: The Satirical
Novels.
A. Rodway, 447(N&Q):Jun78-257
Sagola, M.J. The Naked Bishop.
N. Callendar, 441:27Jul80-23
Sahlin, J.C. - see Hoffmann, E.T.A.
Sahlins, M. Age de pierre, âge d'abon-
dance.
R. Guidieri, 98:Apr78-405
Sahlins, M. The Use and Abuse of Biology.
G.S. Stent, 473(PR):4/1979-623
Sahni, J. Classic Indian Cooking.
M. Sheraton, 441:30Nov80-12
Said, E.W. Beginnings.*
G.L. Bruns, 481(PQ):Spring78-255
D. Halliburton, 405(MP):Aug79-117
P. Sabor, 529(QQ):Summer79-339
Said, E.W. Orientalism.*
W.E. Cain, 580(SCR):Spring79-70
F. Malti-Douglas, 639(VQR):Autumn79-
724
R. Patai, 390:Nov79-62
Said, E.W. The Question of Palestine.
N. Bethell, 441:20Jan80-7
J. Grigg, 362:13Mar80-347
C. Lehmann-Haupt, 441:4Jan80-C20
R. Rudolph, 99:Jun-Jul80-41
T. Smith, 453(NYRB):12Jun80-42
R. Wistrich, 617(TLS):23May80-591
as-Said, L. The Recited Koran.
S.A. Akbarabadi, 273(IC):Apr77-153
Saïd, S. La faute tragique.
J.M. Redfield, 122:Oct79-351
Saigyō. Mirror for the Moon. (W. La
Fleur, trans)
B. Almon, 649(WAL):Fall79-253
J.T. Rimer, 293(JASt):Aug79-781
Saikal, A. The Rise and Fall of the Shah.
S. Bakhash, 453(NYRB):26Jun80-22
J. Leonard, 441:28Apr80-C15
R. Steel, 441:1Jun80-1
Sainsbury, R.M. Russell.
D.W. Hamlyn, 617(TLS):4Jan80-19
A.R. White, 518:Oct79-115
Saint, A. Richard Norman Shaw.*
D. Stillman, 637(VS):Summer78-512
Saint, B. Testament of the Compass.
J. Cotton, 493:Dec79-72
St. Armand, B.L. The Roots of Horror in
the Fiction of H.P. Lovecraft.
S.A. Black, 106:Fall79-243
St. Clair, W. Trelawny.
A.G. Fredman, 340(KSJ):Vol28-152
T. Philbrick, 661(WC):Summer79-296
J.A. Wittreich, Jr., 161(DUJ):Jun79-
267
St. James, I. The Money Stones.
N. Callendar, 441:26Oct80-28
St. John, D. The Shore.
C. Molesworth, 441:12Oct80-14
St. Martin, H., ed. Roots and Wings.*
R. Warner, 86(BHS):Jul79-262
de Saint Phalle, T. Le métronome.
A. Jenkins, 617(TLS):2May80-500
Saint-Bris, A. La Folle de Chantereine.
M.A. O'Neil, 207(FR):Apr79-800

de Saint-Évremond, C. Sir Politick Would-be. (R. Finch and E. Joliat, eds)
  Q.M. Hope, 399(MLJ):Apr79-212
  D.C. Potts, 208(FS):Oct79-443
de Saint-Évremond, C. and Comte d'Etelan.
La Comédie des Académistes [et] Les Académiciens.* (P. Carile, ed)
  H.T. Barnwell, 208(FS):Vol33Pt2-680
  C. Chantalat, 535(RHL):Jul-Aug79-649
de Saint-Gelais, O. Le Séjour d'honneur.
(J.A. James, ed)
  A. Saunders, 402(MLR):Jan79-195
Saint-Martin, F. Samuel Beckett et l'univers de la fiction.*
  H. Charney, 207(FR):Dec78-357
Saint-Réal. Don Carlos; La Conjuration des Espagnols contre le République de Venise. (A. Mansau, ed)
  E.M. Tilton, 207(FR):Oct78-162
  D.A. Watts, 208(FS):Vol33Pt2-694
Duc de Saint-Simon. Grimoires de Saint-Simon. (Y. Coirault, ed)
  H. Himelfarb, 535(RHL):Jan-Feb78-122
Sainty, J.C., comp. Office-holders in Modern Britain. (Vol 6)
  F. Strong, 325:Apr79-170
Sainty, J.C. and D. Dewar, comps. Divisions in the House of Lords: an Analytical List 1685 to 1857.
  C. Jones, 325:Apr79-167
Sainz Rodríguez, P. Menéndez Pelayo, ese desconocido.
  C. Stern, 545(RPh):May79-494
Saitz, R.L. and F.B. Stieglitz. Challenge.
  B. Soden, 608:Sep80-373
Saiyidain, K.G. Islam, the Religion of Peace.
  H.A. Ali, 273(IC):Jan77-69
Sajó, C. - see Boethius
Sak, L. Czechoslovak National Bibliography.
  S.Z. Pech, 104(CASS):Summer78-316
Sakalis, D.T. Ioniko Lektiko ston Platona.
  G.M. Messing, 124:Sep79-53
Sakamoto, N. The People's Republic of China Cookbook.
  W. and C. Cowen, 639(VQR):Spring78-72
Sakharov, A.D. Alarm and Hope.* (E. Yankelevich and A. Friendly, Jr., eds)
  J.P. Shapiro, 550(RusR):Oct79-501
Sakmyster, T.L. Hungary, the Great Powers, and the Danubian Crisis 1936-39.
  A. Sked, 617(TLS):22Aug80-939
Sakthivel, S. Phonology of Toda with Vocabulary.
  P. Hockings, 350:Jun79-489
Sala, M. Phonétique et phonologie du judéo-espagnol de Bucarest. Le judéo-espagnol.
  K.A. Goddard, 86(BHS):Oct79-328
Sala-Molins, L. - see Eymerich, N. and F. Peña
de Salas, X. Goya.
  G. Martin, 617(TLS):1Feb80-120
Salcedo-Bastardo, J.L. Bolívar. (A. McDermott, ed and trans)
  J.S. Cummins, 86(BHS):Jan79-89

Sale, K. Human Scale.
  L. Winner, 441:15Jun80-13
Sale, R. Fairy Tales and After.*
  J. Fletcher, 268(IFR):Winter80-63
  R. McGillis, 49:Oct79-101
  S. Pickering, 569(SR):Spring79-xliv
  W. Provost, 219(GaR):Spring79-210
  V. Young, 249(HudR):Summer79-314
Sale, R. On Not Being Good Enough.*
  D.J. Enright, 617(TLS):11Jan80-29
  D. Flower, 249(HudR):Winter79/80-594
Sale, W. Existentialism and Euripides.*
  P.G. Mason, 303(JoHS):Vol99-174
  G. Ronnet, 555:Vol52fasc2-368
Saliba, J.A. "Homo Religiosus" in Mircea Eliade.
  M.H. Levine, 613:Dec79-424
Salinger, W. Folly River.
  H. Carruth, 231:Dec80-74
  W. Pritchard, 441:6Jul80-8
Salins, P.D. The Ecology of Housing Destruction.
  W. Goodman, 441:10Aug80-15
Salisbury, H.E. Black Night, White Snow.*
  R.P. Browder, 50(ArQ):Summer79-186
  A. Kerrigan, 396(ModA):Summer79-322
  W.E. Mosse, 575(SEER):Oct79-609
Salisbury, H.E. Russia in Revolution, 1900-1930.
  P. Kenez, 550(RusR):Oct79-480
  639(VQR):Spring79-52
Salisbury, H.E. Without Fear or Favor.
  M. Kempton, 453(NYRB):25Sep80-30
  C. Lehmann-Haupt, 441:15May80-C25
  T. Morgan, 441:18May80-12
  442(NY):23Jun80-103
Salles, D. O Ficcionista Xavier Marques.
  M.G. Macnicoll, 399(MLJ):Apr79-216
Sallese, N.F. and O.F. de la Vega. Repaso.
(2nd ed)
  A. Snaidas, 238:Dec79-745
Salmen, W. Musikleben im 16. Jahrhundert.
  R.D. Leppert, 317:Summer79-339
Salmen, W., ed. Orgel und Orgelspiel im 16. Jahrhundert.
  P. Williams, 410(M&L):Jul79-347
Salmon, V. The Study of Language in 17th Century England.
  R.H. Robins, 617(TLS):7Mar80-252
Salter, J. Solo Faces.*
  V. Scannell, 617(TLS):15Feb80-171
Saltykov-Shchedrin, M.E. The History of a Town.
  E. Morgan, 617(TLS):23May80-572
  V.S. Pritchett, 453(NYRB):25Sep80-29
Saltykov-Shchedrin, M.E. Selected Satirical Writings.* (I.P. Foote, ed)
  H. Gamburg, 558(RLJ):Spring79-230
  D.C. Offord, 402(MLR):Jan79-254
Saltzer, W.G. Theorien und Ansätze in der griechischen Astronomie.
  F. Lasserre, 182:Vol131#11/12-374
Salu, M., ed. Essays on "Troilus and Criseyde."
  T.A. Shippey, 617(TLS):4Jul80-753

Salutin, R. and Theatre Passe Muraille.
1837: William Lyon Mackenzie and the
Canadian Revolution.*
    S. Wood, 102(CanL):Summer79-111
Salvador Martínez, H. El "Poema de
Almería" y la épica románica.
    W. Mettmann, 547(RF):Band91Heft3-348
    C. Stern, 545(RPh):Feb79-383
Salvador Miguel, N. La poesía cancioneril.
    N. Rivera Gloeckner, 238:Dec79-727
    J. Snow, 589:Oct79-855
    K. Whinnom, 402(MLR):Jan79-222
Salwak, D. Kingsley Amis.
    M.C., 395(MFS):Winter78/79-603
Samaan, S.H. and A.J. Fears and Worries
of Nigerian Igbo Secondary School Stu-
dents.
    J. Byng-Hall, 69:Vol48#4-408
Samaras, L. Photo-Transformations.
    P. Wollheim, 648(WCR):Jun78-29
Sammet, D. Die Substantivbildung mit
Suffixen bei Chrestien de Troyes.
    H. Kahane, 545(RPh):Aug78-104
Sammons, J.L. Heinrich Heine.
    D.J. Enright, 617(TLS):28Mar80-343
    H. Levin, 441:27Jan80-9
    442(NY):7Apr80-151
Sammons, J.L. Literary Sociology and Prac-
tical Criticism.*
    T. Eagleton, 402(MLR):Jul79-651
    S.G. Kellman, 395(MFS):Winter78/79-650
    H. Levin, 131(CL):Fall79-420
    J. Orr, 125:Winter79-303
Samoilovich, V.P. Narodnoe arkhitekturnoe
tvorchestvo.
    M.F. Hamm, 550(RusR):Oct79-519
Samora, J., J. Bernal and A. Pena. Gun-
powder Justice.
    W. Gard, 584(SWR):Summer79-298
Sampson, E.W. Nikolay Gumilëv.
    S. Driver, 558(RLJ):Spring79-219
Sampson, G. Making Sense.
    T.P. Waldron, 617(TLS):11Jul80-785
Samson, J. Music in Transition.*
    C. Bennett, 607:Mar78-38
Samson, L. Naturteleologie und Freiheit
bei Arnold Gehlen.
    H. Ottmann, 489(PJGG):Band86Heft1-148
Samuel, R., ed. Miners, Quarrymen, and
Saltworkers.
    M. Neuman, 637(VS):Spring79-369
Samuels, E. Bernard Berenson.*
    A. Brookner, 617(TLS):18Jan80-51
    M. Friedlaender, 432(NEQ):Dec79-560
Samuels, P. and H. - see Remington, F.
Samuelson, N.M. - see Gersonides
Samuelson, R.E. and J.L. Kitchen. Archi-
tecture: Columbus.
    R. Rubenfeld, 576:Oct78-210
de San Antonio, J.F. The Philippine Chron-
icles of Fray San Antonio. (D.P.
Picornell, trans)
    M.S. McLennan, 293(JASt):May79-637
Sanborn, R. Mohammed Wong Spouts!
    42(AR):Fall79-505

Sanborn, T.Y. Mannsrolle og kvinnesyn hjå
Agnar Mykle.
    L. Longum, 562(Scan):May79-79
    J. Sjåvik, 563(SS):Winter79-83
Sanchez, A.C.D. - see under Collantes de
Terán Sanchez, A.
Sanchez, L.D. Jean-Michel Frank/Adolphe
Chanaux.
    S. Slesin, 441:14Dec80-29
Sánchez de Zavala, V., ed. Estudios de
gramática generativa.*
    J. Schroten, 361:Oct/Nov78-263
Sánchez Trigueros, A. Francisco Villaes-
pesa y su primera obra poética (1897-
1900).
    E.A. Southworth, 402(MLR):Jul79-731
Sanchis, F.E. American Architecture:
Westchester County, New York.
    J. Zukowsky, 576:Oct78-209
de Sanctis, G. La Guerra Sociale. (L.
Polverini, ed)
    J-C. Dumont, 555:Vol52fasc1-207
Sand, G. Mauprat. Lettres d'un voyageur.
Légendes rustiques.
    H. Politis, 98:Nov78-1057
Sand, G. My Life.* (D. Hofstadter, ed
and trans)
    639(VQR):Autumn79-142
Sandahl-Forgue, S. Le Gītagovinda.
    J.W. de Jong, 259(IIJ):Oct79-291
Sandars, N.K. The Sea Peoples.
    S. Hood, 303(JoHS):Vol99-200
Sandbach, F.H. The Comic Theatre of
Greece and Rome.*
    N.V. Dunbar, 123:Vol29No1-139
Sandberg, N.C. Ethnic Identity and Assimi-
lation.
    J. Gorecki, 497(PolR):Vol23#4-109
Sandburg, C. Breathing Tokens.* (M. Sand-
burg, ed)
    639(VQR):Summer78-100
Sandburg, H. A Great and Glorious
Romance.*
    639(VQR):Summer78-90
Sande, T.A. Industrial Archaeology.
    T. Phelan, 576:May78-114
Sandell, R. Linguistic Style and Persua-
sion.*
    H. Giles, 355(LSoc):Aug78-242
Sanders, A. The Victorian Historical
Novel 1840-1880.
    A. Gibson, 175:Autumn79-266
    A. Shelston, 148:Autumn79-86
Sanders, C.R. Carlyle's Friendships and
Other Studies.
    R.L. Tarr, 637(VS):Winter79-210
Sanders, C.R. and K.J. Fielding - see
Carlyle, T. and J.W.
Sanders, D.G. The Brasspounder.
    R.V. Francaviglia, 42(AR):Summer79-375
Sanders, E. Fame and Love in New York.
    J. Leonard, 441:17Dec80-C33
Sanders, L. The Tenth Commandment.
    S. Ellin, 441:28Sep80-14

328

Sarkisyanz, E. A Modern History of Trans-
caucasian Armenia.
  R.G. Suny, 550(RusR):Oct79-483
Sarlemijn, A. Hegel's Dialectic.
  C.B., 125:Fall78-149
Sarma, K.V., ed. Līlāvatī of Bhāskarācā-
rya with Kriyākramakorī of Śaṅkara and
Nārāyaṇa.
  L. Sternbach, 318(JAOS):Jul-Sep78-321
Sarmiento, D.F. Facundo.
  C. Tatum, 552(REH):Oct79-474
Sarna, L. Letters of State.*
  D. Barbour, 150(DR):Spring79-154
Sarolli, G.R. Prolegomena alla "Divina
Commedia."
  C. Kleinhenz, 545(RPh):Aug78-128
Sarraute, N. "Fools Say."*
  W. Skakoon, 628(UWR):Fall-Winter78-82
Sarraute, N. L'Usage de la parole.
  J. Sturrock, 617(TLS):4Apr80-391
Sarri, F. Socrate e la genesi storica
dell'idea occidentale di anima.*
  P.M. Huby, 123:Vol29No1-163
  P. Louis, 555:Vol152fasc1-160
  E. Namer, 542:Jan-Mar78-85
Sarriá, F.G. - see under García Sarriá, F.
Sarris, A. Politics and Cinema.*
  M. Dickstein, 18:Mar79-70
Sartain, E.M. Jalal-al-Din al-Suyuti.
  S.A.W. Bukhari, 273(IC):Jul76-193
Sarti, S. Panorama della filosofia ispano-
americana contemporanea.
  Z. Kouřím, 542:Jul-Sep79-379
Sarton, M. A Reckoning.
  V. Cunningham, 617(TLS):8Feb80-134
Sarton, M. Recovering.
  S. Jacoby, 441:21Dec80-12
Sarton, M. Selected Poems of May Sarton.
(S.S. Hilsinger and L. Brynes, eds)
  J.F. Cotter, 249(HudR):Spring79-121
Sartre, J-P. Critique of Dialectical
Reason.* (J. Ree, ed)
  W. Desan, 125:Winter79-287
Sartre, J-P. The Writings of Jean-Paul
Sartre. (M. Contat and M. Rybalka, eds)
  G. Gillan, 484(PPR):Dec79-305
Sarwani, A.K. Tārīkh-i Ser Sāhī.
  M.A. Nayeem, 273(IC):Apr78-129
Sasaki, S. Sur le thème de Nonchaloir
dans la poésie de Charles d'Orléans.
  J. Fox, 208(FS):Vol33Pt2-578
  A. Iker-Gittleman, 545(RPh):May79-492
Sasso, G. Il "celebrato sogno" di
Machiavelli.
  A. Corsano, 227(GCFI):Jan-Mar78-137
Sasso, R. Georges Bataille, le système du
non-savoir.
  P-F. Moreau, 450(NRF):Apr79-127
  A. Reix, 542:Jul-Sep79-379
  A. Stoekl, 400(MLN):Dec79-1261
Sassoon, C. Chinese Porcelain Marks from
Kenya.
  J. da Silva, 463:Summer79-251
Satie, E. Ecrits.* (O. Volta, ed)
  H. Politis, 98:Jan78-37

Swami Satprakashananda. The Goal and the
Way.
  B. Gupta, 485(PE&W):Apr79-247
Satterfield, A. The Lewis and Clark Trail.
  R. Robinson, 649(WAL):Summer79-179
Sauder, G. Empfindsamkeit.* (Vol 1)
  D. Brüggemann, 182:Vol131#20-746
Sauer, E.F. Amerikanische philosophie von
den Puritanern bis zu Herbert Marcuse.
  A.B.W., 543:Dec78-370
Sauer, H., ed. Theodulfi Capitula in
England.
  M.R. Godden, 382(MAE):1979/2-262
Sauer, W., ed. The Metrical Life of
Christ.
  J.C. Hirsh, 382(MAE):1979/1-148
  D. Speed, 67:May79-85
  E.G. Stanley, 447(N&Q):Dec78-543
Saugnieux, J. Les jansénistes et le re-
nouveau de la prédication dans l'Espagne
de la 2e moitié du XVIIIe siècle.
  D.A. Brading, 182:Vol131#15/16-527
Saugstad, P. A Theory of Communication
and Use of Language.
  F. Hiorth, 603:Vol13#2-289
Saul, G.B. Adam Unregenerate.*
  J.D. Conway, 174(Éire):Summer79-148
  F. Kersnowski, 305(JIL):May78-179
Saul, N.E. Sailors in Revolt.*
  J.N. Westwood, 575(SEER):Apr79-306
Saunders, G. - see Medvedev, R.
Saunders, J.J. Muslims and Mongols. (G.W.
Rice, ed)
  R.P. Mottahedeh, 589:Apr79-425
Saunders, R.J. and J.J. Warford. Village
Water Supply.
  I. Carruthers, 69:Vol148#3-313
de Saussure, F. Trudy po jazykoznaniju.
  M. Pétursson, 343:Band23-172
de Sauvigny, G.D. - see under de Bertier
de Sauvigny, G.
Savage, E. Toward the End.
  J. Casey, 441:5Oct80-14
von Savigny, E. Argumentation in der
Literaturwissenschaft.*
  P. Somville, 542:Oct-Dec79-478
Saville-Troike, M., ed. Linguistics and
Anthropology.
  M. Crick, 355(LSoc):Dec78-433
  F.C. Huxley, 351(LL):Dec79-391
Savio, F. Cinecittà anni trenta.
  M. D'Amico, 617(TLS):15Feb80-188
Savitt, T.L. Medicine and Slavery.
  E. Wright, 617(TLS):25Jan80-91
  639(VQR):Spring79-55
Savitzkaya, E. Mongolie, plaine sale.
  A. Clavel, 98:Mar78-343
"Savoir, faire, espérer."
  A. Reix, 542:Jan-Mar78-128
Savona, J.L. Le Juif dans le Roman Amér-
icain Contemporain.
  R.A., 189(EA):Jan-Mar78-111
Savoret, A. Visage du druidisme.
  M. Adam, 542:Apr-Jun78-214
Sawa, A. Iluminaciones en la sombra.
  (I.M. Zavala, ed)
  R.A. Cardwell, 86(BHS):Jan79-72

Sawashima, M. and F.S. Cooper, eds.
Dynamic Aspects of Speech Production.
  I. Lehiste, 350:Dec79-957
Sawicki, S.J. Soviet Land and Housing
Law.*
  I. Lapenna, 575(SEER):Apr79-310
Sawyer, P.H. and I.N. Wood, eds. Early
Medieval Kingship.
  T.F.X. Noble, 589:Jan79-185
Saxo Grammaticus. The History of the
Danes. (Vol 1) (H.E. Davidson, ed; P.
Fisher, trans)
  G. Jones, 617(TLS):25Jan80-83
Saxon, A.H. The Life and Art of Andrew
Ducrow and The Romantic Age of the
English Circus.
  A.D. Hippisley Coxe, 611(TN):Vol33#2-
  93
  J.W. Stedman, 637(VS):Summer79-470
Saxton, M. Louisa May.*
  R. Conway, 502(PrS):Winter78/79-383
Sayer, G.R. Hong Kong, 1862-1919. (D.M.E.
Evans, ed)
  A. Birch, 302:Vol16#1and2-129
Saygun, A.A. Béla Bartók's Folk Music
Research in Turkey.* (L. Vikár, ed)
  L. Picken, 410(M&L):Jan79-81
Sayre, K.M. Cybernetics and the Philoso-
phy of Mind.*
  M.E. Levin, 486:Dec78-653
  A. Reeves, 63:Mar79-106
  Y. Wilks, 84:Jun79-191
Sayre, R. Solitude in Society.*
  P. Brooks, 131(CL):Spring79-180
  L.S. Roudiez, 546(RR):Nov79-399
  E. Zants, 395(MFS):Winter78/79-626
Sayre, R.F. Thoreau and the American
Indians.*
  M. Meyer, 639(VQR):Autumn78-754
Scaglione, A., ed. Ariosto 1974 in
America.*
  R. Andrews, 402(MLR):Jan79-219
  C.P. Brand, 276:Spring79-65
  J.A. Molinaro, 627(UTQ):Winter78/79-
  172
Scalapino, L. The Woman Who Could Read
the Minds of Dogs.
  V. Contoski, 152(UDQ):Fall178-154
Scally, R.J. The Origins of the Lloyd
George Coalition.
  S. Meacham, 637(VS):Winter78-257
Scammell, M. - see Golomshtok, I. and A.
Glezer
Scammell, W. Yes and No.
  D. Davis, 362:5Jun80-729
  G. Lindop, 617(TLS):22Feb80-214
Scannell, V. New and Collected Poems
1950-1980.
  S. Curtis, 617(TLS):1Aug80-876
  D. Davis, 362:28Aug80-277
Scaravelli, L. Giudizio e sillogismo in
Kant e in Hegel. (M. Corsi, ed)
  S. Marcucci, 548(RCSF):Jan-Mar79-112
Scarbrough, G. New and Selected Poems.*
  639(VQR):Winter78-10

Scardigli, P. and T. Gervasi. Avviamento
all'etimologia inglese e tedesca.
  K. Faiss, 182:Vol31#13-412
Scarf, M. Unfinished Business.
  M. Pines, 441:24Aug80-9
Scarlatti, A. The Operas of Alessandro
Scarlatti.* (Vol 1: Eraclea, ed by D.J.
Grout; Vol 2: Marco Attilio Regolo, ed
by J. Godwin; Vol 3: Griselda, ed by D.J.
Grout)
  O. Jander, 317:Summer79-352
Scarpat, G. Il pensiero religioso di
Seneca e l'ambiente ebraico e cristiano.
  A.L. Motto, 124:Dec79/Jan80-257
von Scarpatetti, B.M., ed. Die Hand-
schriften der Bibliotheken von Aarau,
Appenzell und Basel.
  O. Mazal, 182:Vol31#11/12-321
Scarpetta, G. Brecht ou le soldat mort.
  J. Guérin, 450(NRF):Aug79-137
Scève, M. Microcosme.* (E. Giudici, ed)
  M. Françon, 535(RHL):Mar-Apr78-292
  B. Ormerod, 208(FS):Vol33Pt2-626
Schaaf, L. Der Miles Gloriosus des
Plautus und sein griechisches Original.
  M.M. Willcock, 123:Vol29No1-30
Schab, F.G. Woodner Collection I. Wood-
ner Collection II.
  R. Harprath, 471:Apr/May/Jun79-177
Schabert, T., ed. Aufbruch zur Moderne.
  J. Lough, 208(FS):Vol33Pt2-705
Schachermeyr, F. Die ägäische Frühzeit.
(Vol 2)
  J. Rutter, 124:Sep79-32
Schade, R.E. and J. Glenn - see "Lessing
Yearbook, 10"
Schädlich, H.J. Approximation.
  R. Eder, 441:27Jan80-14
  J. Updike, 442(NY):21Apr80-136
Schädlich, H.J. Tentative d'approche.
  P. Dulac, 450(NRF):Dec79-125
Schaeffer, S.F. The Queen of Egypt.
  I. Gold, 441:24Feb80-15
Schaeffer, S.F. Time in Its Flight.*
  639(VQR):Winter79-16
Schäfer, E. Deutscher Horaz.*
  U. Herzog, 684(ZDA):Band107Heft1-36
Schafer, E.H. Pacing the Void.
  M. Dalby, 293(JASt):May79-554
Schäfer, G. "König der Könige" — "Lied
der Lieder."
  W. Betz, 72:Band216Heft1-147
Schafer, R.M. The Tuning of the World.
  O. Laske, 414(MusQ):Jul78-394
Schafer, R.M. - see Pound, E.
Schäferdiek, K. Die Kirche des früheren
Mittelalters. (Vol 1)
  R.A. Markus, 589:Oct79-857
Schaff, A. Che cosa significa essere marx-
ista.
  E. Namer, 542:Apr-Jun79-269
Schaff, A. History and Truth.
  G.B. Blumenshine, 125:Fall178-152
Schäffer, B. Introduction to Composition.
  M. Finnissy, 607:Mar78-43
Schaffner, V. Algonquin Cat.
  P-L. Adams, 61:Dec80-98

Schakel, P.J., ed. The Longing for a Form.
G. Blake, 395(MFS):Summer78-310
639(VQR):Spring78-54
Schakel, P.J. The Poetry of Jonathan
Swift.*
C. Fabricant, 141:Fall79-369
D. Griffin, 301(JEGP):Oct79-554
P.M. Spacks, 401(MLQ):Dec79-403
639(VQR):Autumn79-129
Schaller, G.B. Stones of Silence.
P-L. Adams, 61:Apr80-129
J. Bernstein, 441:23Mar80-9
C. Lehmann-Haupt, 441:18Mar80-C11
R. Trevelyan, 362:26Jun80-839
442(NY):19May80-162
Schaller, M. The U.S. Crusade in China,
1938-1945.*
639(VQR):Summer79-88
Schama, S. Two Rothschilds and the Land
of Israel.
B. Wasserstein, 390:Mar79-71
Schandler, H.Y. The Unmaking of a Presi-
dent.
639(VQR):Winter78-21
Schaper, E. Studies in Kant's Aesthetics.
N.T. Potter, Jr., 290(JAAC):Summer80-
465
Schapiro, L. Turgenev.*
639(VQR):Autumn79-141
Schapiro, M. Late Antique, Early Chris-
tian and Mediaeval Art.
J. Breckenridge, 441:24Feb80-11
Schapiro, M. Modern Art: 19th and 20th
Centuries.*
A. Corn, 249(HudR):Autumn79-461
S. Hunter, 55:Apr79-31
Schapiro, M. Romanesque Art.*
O.K. Werckmeister, 56:Spring79-211
Schapiro, M. Words and Pictures.
H. Damisch, 98:Mar78-274
Schapka, U. Die persischen Vogelnamen.
J.A.C. Greppin, 318(JAOS):Jul-Sep78-
308
Schapp, K. Die Endphase der Weimarer
Republik im Freistaat Oldenburg, 1928-
1933.
F.L. Carsten, 575(SEER):Jul79-460
Schaps, D.M. Economic Rights of Women in
Ancient Greece.
S. Pembroke, 617(TLS):11Jan80-43
Scharfe, H. Grammatical Literature.
R. Rocher, 343:Band23-81
Schary, D. Heyday.
P. Bosworth, 441:17Feb80-12
C. Lehmann-Haupt, 441:16Jan80-C24
Schatt, S. Kurt Vonnegut, Jr.
R.F. Kiernan, 295(JML):Vol7#4-829
Schaup, S. - see "The Tain"
Schaya, L. L'homme et l'absolu selon la
Kabbale.
M. Adam, 542:Jul-Sep79-380
Scheader, C. They Found a Way.
C.A. Miller, 95(CLAJ):Mar79-289
Schechner, R. Essays on Performance
Theory, 1970-1976.
C. Rosen, 560:Spring-Summer79-253

Scheck, F.R., ed. Chinesische Malerei
seit der Kulturrevolution.
R. Croizier, 293(JASt):Feb79-303
Scheerer, T.M. Textanalytische Studien
zur "écriture automatique."
R. Cardinal, 208(FS):Apr79-228
Schefe, P. Statistische syntaktische
Analyse von Fachsprachen mit Hilfe
elektronischer Rechenanlagen am Beispiel
der medizinischen, betriebswirtschaft-
lichen und literaturwissenschaftlichen
Frachsprache im Deutschen.
T. Bungarten, 680(ZDP):Band97Heft1-150
Scheffer, J. The Progressive in English.*
E.A. Nida, 353:Feb78-89
Scheffler, I. Beyond the Letter.
J. Lear, 617(TLS):7Mar80-268
Scheffler, I. Science and Subjectivity.
J. Largeault, 542:Jan-Mar79-119
Scheffler, W. Goldschmiede an Main und
Neckar.
G. Schiedlausky, 471:Jan/Feb/Mar79-81
Scheflin, A.W. and E.M. Opton, Jr. The
Mind Manipulators.
A.W. Clare, 529(QQ):Winter79/80-637
Scheible, H. Arthur Schnitzler und die
Aufklärung.
R.K. Angress, 406:Fall79-347
Scheick, W.J., ed. Critical Essays on
Jonathan Edwards.
D. Weber, 165(EAL):Winter80/81-281
Scheick, W.J. The Half-Blood.
H. Beaver, 617(TLS):30May80-619
Scheick, W.J. The Slender Human Word.
P.F. Gura, 432(NEQ):Sep79-407
Scheick, W.J. The Writings of Jonathan
Edwards.
E. Emerson, 165(EAL):Winter79/80-342
Scheid, J.R. "Enfant terrible" of Con-
temporary East German Drama.
H.K. Doswald, 221(GQ):Mar79-295
Scheler, M. Logik I.
J. Sivak, 542:Jul-Sep79-330
Schell, O. In The People's Republic.
639(VQR):Winter78-17
Schellhase, K.C. Tacitus in Renaissance
Political Thought.*
A. Momigliano, 122:Jan79-72
Schelling, F.W.J. Briefe und Dokumente.*
(H. Fuhrmans, ed)
J. Jantzen, 53(AGP):Band60Heft1-95
Schelling, F.W.J. Recherches sur la lib-
erté humaine.* (M. Richir, ed and trans)
A. Reix, 542:Jan-Mar78-121
Schenda, R. Die Lesestoffe der Kleinen
Leute.
H. Denkler, 406:Spring79-95
J. Hösle, 52:Band13Heft2-210
G. Rupp, 490:Band10Heft1-119
Schenk, D. Studien zur anakreontischen
Ode in der russischen Literatur des
Klassizismus und der Empfindsamkeit.
H. Zeman, 52:Band13Heft2-199
Schenker, H. Free Composition (Der Freie
Satz).
C. Wintle, 617(TLS):19Sep80-1046

Schlesinger, I.M. Production and Comprehension of Utterances.
  P.A. Hornby, 350:Jun79-440
Schlesinger, I.M. and L. Namir, eds. Sign Language of the Deaf.
  S.D. Fischer, 350:Dec79-948
  W. Washabaugh, 297(JL):Mar79-192
Schlesinger, K. Berliner Traum.
  B. Leistner, 654(WB):4/1978-159
Schlesinger, R. History of the Communist Party of USSR.*
  J. Zorach, 550(RusR):Jan79-98
Schlieben-Lange, B. Okzitanische und katalanische Verbprobleme.*
  G.F. Meier, 682(ZPSK):Band31Heft6-647
Schloss, E. Ancient Chinese Ceramic Sculpture.
  E. Capon, 463:Spring78-86
Schlossman, S.L. Love and the American Delinquent.
  M. Vipond, 106:Winter79-363
Schlumberger, J. Die Epitome de Caesaribus.
  R.P.H. Green, 313:Vol169-225
Schlumbohm, C. Jocus und Amor.*
  J.H. Marshall, 208(FS):Vol33Pt2-593
Schlumbohm, D. Die Welt als Konstruktion.*
  T. Bremer, 72:Band216Heft2-477
Schlumbohm, J. Freiheit.
  T. Schippan, 682(ZPSK):Band31Heft4-440
Schmähl, W. Alterssicherung und Einkommensverteilung.
  R. Hauser, 182:Vol131#9/10-280
Schmalenbach, H. On Society and Experience. (G. Lüschen and G.P. Stone, eds and trans)
  J. Ferrandino, 484(PPR):Jun80-602
Schmalstieg, W.R. Studies in Old Prussian.*
  O. Szemerényi, 215(GL):Summer78-105
Schmeling, G.L. and J.H. Stuckey. A Bibliography of Petronius.*
  M.S. Smith, 123:Vol29No1-153
Schmeling, M. Das Spiel im Spiel.
  G. Gillespie, 602:Vol10-241
Schmelzer, M.H. - see Marx, A.
Schmertz, H. and L. Woods. Takeover.
  P. Andrews, 441:17Feb80-15
Schmid, A-F. Une philosophie de savant.
  J. Largeault, 542:Jul-Sep79-331
Schmid, W. George Moore: "The Untilled Field."
  H. Papajewski, 224(GRM):Band28Heft1-126
  K. Versluys, 179(ES):Aug79-516
Schmidgall, G. Literature as Opera.*
  J. Lucas, 405(MP):Nov79-254
  J.H. Raleigh, 130:Spring79-94
  639(VQR):Spring78-52
Schmidt, A. The Egghead Republic.
  J.R.B., 148:Autumn79-93
Schmidt, A. Evening Edged in Gold.
  D.J. Enright, 362:18Sep80-377
  S.S. Prawer, 617(TLS):5Sep80-949
Schmidt, A.V.C. - see Langland, W.

Schmidt, B. Spanien im Urteil spanischer Autoren.
  U. Schulz-Buschhaus, 52:Band13Heft1-88
von Schmidt, E. and J. Rooney. Baby, Let Me Follow You Down.
  N.V. Rosenberg, 187:Sep80-582
Schmidt, G. Henri de Régnier als Erzähler.*
  P.J. Whyte, 208(FS):Oct79-472
Schmidt, G. Stammbildung und Flexion der indogermanischen Personalpronomina.
  E. Seebold, 343:Band23-63
Schmidt, G. and G. Wolandt, eds. Die Aktualität der transzendental Philosophie.
  W.V.E., 543:Mar79-566
Schmidt, H. Heinrich von Kleist.
  M. Gelus, 221(GQ):Jan79-121
Schmidt, H.C. The Roots of "lo mexicano."
  M. Stabb, 263(RIB):Vol129No3/4-377
Schmidt, H.J. - see Büchner, G.
Schmidt, L., ed. George Grant in Process.*
  D. Duffy, 627(UTQ):Summer79-467
Schmidt, M. A Change of Affairs.
  T. Eagleton, 565:Vol120#3-75
  P. Eckhard, 493:Jul79-69
  C. Hope, 364:Jun79-78
Schmidt, M. The Colonist.
  J. Mellors, 362:24Apr80-546
  D. Wilson, 617(TLS):2May80-486
Schmidt, M. - see Sisson, C.H.
Schmidt, M., A.D. Trendall and A. Cambitoglou. Eine Gruppe apulischer Grabvasen in Basel.
  H. Gabelmann, 182:Vol131#5/6-167
  B.A. Sparkes, 123:Vol129No2-335
Schmidt, P.G. - see de Hauvilla, J.
Schmidt, S.J., ed. "Schön."
  B. Sorg, 556(RLV):1978/4-361
Schmidt, T. Alexander II. (1061-1073) und die römische Reformgruppe seiner Zeit.*
  U-R. Blumenthal, 589:Jan79-187
de Schmidt, W. Psychologie und Transzendentalphilosophie.
  G. Edel, 53(AGP):Band60Heft2-236
Schmidt-Biggemann, W. Maschine und Teufel.*
  M.H., 191(ELN):Sep78(supp)-176
Schmidt-Glintzer, H. Das "Hung-ming chi" und die Aufnahme des Buddhismus in China.
  J.W. de Jong, 259(IIJ):Oct79-304
Schmitt, C. Die Sprachlandschaften der Galloromania.
  B. Foster, 208(FS):Vol33Pt2-1018
Schmitt, F.A. Stoff- und Motivgeschichte der deutschen Literatur. (3rd ed)
  R. Grimm, 406:Summer79-189
  R. Schenda, 196:Band19Heft1/2-170
Schmitt, G. The Concept of Being in Hegel and Heidegger.*
  C.O. Schrag, 125:Winter79-281
Schmitt, J-C. Mort d'une hérésie.
  R.E. Lerner, 589:Oct79-842
Schmitt, J-C. Le saint lévrier.
  B. Stock, 617(TLS):11Apr80-410

Schmitt, R., ed. Etymologie.
K.H. Schmidt, 685(ZDL):3/1979-351
C. Schmitt, 547(RF):Band91Heft1/2-200
J. Tischler, 343:Band23-177
Schmitz, A-M. In Search of Steinbeck.
S. Noto, 649(WAL):Spring79-83
Schmitz, H.W. Ethnographie der Kommunikation.
T.L., 355(LSoc):Dec78-451
Schmitz, W. Die Dichtungen des Hartwig von dem Hage.
S.L. Wailes, 406:Winter79-438
Schnackenburg, R. Christ — Present and Coming.
J.M. McDermott, 613:Jun79-203
Schnackenburg, R. The Gospel According to St. John. (Vol 2)
H.F.D. Sparks, 617(TLS):5Sep80-971
Schneeberger, P-F. The Baur Collection of Chinese Jades and Other Hardstones.*
J.H. Goldsmith, 463:Spring79-116
Schneewind, J.B. Sidgwick's Ethics and Victorian Moral Philosophy.*
J. Skorupski, 479(PhQ):Apr79-158
Schneider, C. Information und Absicht bei Thukydides.*
J.C. Kamerbeek, 394:Vol30fasc3-312
Schneider, D.J. The Crystal Cage.
M.E. Grenander, 27(AL):Mar79-122
D. Mogen, 26(ALR):Autumn79-350
A.R. Tintner, 594:Spring79-106
295(JML):Vol7#4-739
Schneider, H. Die Entstehung der römischen Militärdiktatur.
A. Lintott, 313:Vol69-189
Schneider, J. - see Thomas of Sutton
Schneider, K., comp. Die deutschen Handschriften der Bayerischen Staatsbibliothek München, Cgm 501-690.
A. Schönherr, 182:Vol131#3/4-76
E. Simon, 589:Jul79-626
Schneider, L.A. Ku Chieh-kang and China's New History.
A. Dirlik, 318(JAOS):Jul-Sep78-340
Schneider, M. Ernest Theodore Amadeus Hoffmann.
P-L. Rey, 450(NRF):Jun79-132
Schneider, M. Subversive Ästhetik.*
P. Zima, 224(GRM):Band28Heft1-112
Schneider, N. The Woman Who Lived in a Prologue.
R. Brown, 441:20Jan80-14
A. Broyard, 441:2Feb80-19
Schneider, P. Lenz.
B. Bayen, 450(NRF):Sep79-65
Schneider, R. Annette von Droste-Hülshoff.
L.D. Wells, 221(GQ):Jan79-125
Schneider, U. Der moralische Charakter.
J.W. Smeed, 402(MLR):Apr79-493
Schneider, U., comp. Persepolis and Ancient Iran.
M.C. Root, 576:Oct78-201
Schneider-Pachaly, B. - see Friedrich, H.
Schneiderman, J. Sergei Zubatov and Revolutionary Marxism.*
J. Keep, 104(CASS):Summer78-297
A. Walker, 575(SEER):Jul79-457

Schnell, R., ed. Kunst und Kultur im deutschen Faschismus.
C. Fullgraf, 182:Vol131#23/24-865
B. Zimmermann, 221(GQ):May79-436
Schnelle, K. - see Grimm, M.
Schnitzler, A. The Little Comedy and Other Stories.
P.F. Dvorak, 399(MLJ):Mar79-146
Schnitzler, A. and O. Brahm. Der Briefwechsel Arthur Schnitzler — Otto Brahm.* (O. Seidlin, ed)
J. Hibberd, 182:Vol131#17/18-617
Schoder, R.V. Das antike Griechenland aus der Luft.
S. Steingräber, 471:Jan/Feb/Mar79-76
Schoell, K. Das komische Theater des französischen Mittelalters.
L.R. Muir, 208(FS):Vol133Pt2-600
Schoenbaum, S. William Shakespeare: A Documentary Life.* William Shakespeare: A Compact Documentary Life.*
D. Bevington, 405(MP):Nov79-217
Schoenberg, A. Theory of Harmony.
P.P. Nash, 607:Dec78-35
D. Puffett, 410(M&L):Apr79-220
Schoenberg, E. Old Tales and Talking.*
J.V. Hagopian, 295(JML):Vol17#4-695
S.M. Ross, 395(MFS):Summer78-275
Schoenbrun, D. Soldiers of the Night.
P-L. Adams, 61:Aug80-84
P. Hallie, 441:29Jun80-13
J. Leonard, 441:5Jun80-C21
R. Paxton, 453(NYRB):14Aug80-16
442(NY):16Jun80-122
Schoenman, T. and H.B. - see Bölöni Farkas, A.
Schoeps, K.H. Bertolt Brecht.
S. Mews, 221(GQ):Mar79-288
Schofield, C. Mesrine.
R. Cobb, 617(TLS):9May80-515
Schofield, M. An Essay on Anaxagoras.
J. Barnes, 617(TLS):20Jun80-713
Schofield, M., M. Burnyeat and J. Barnes, eds. Doubt and Dogmatism.
A.A. Long, 617(TLS):27Jun80-739
Schofield, V. Bhutto.
A. Howard, 362:3Jan80-30
H. Tinker, 617(TLS):8Feb80-139
Schogt, H.G. Sémantique synchronique.*
J. Stéfanini, 209(FM):Oct78-380
Scholefield, A. Berlin Blind.
T.J. Binyon, 617(TLS):5Sep80-948
J. Burke, 441:28Sep80-14
M. Laski, 362:13Nov80-665
Scholem, G. Walter Benjamin — die Geschichte einer Freundschaft.
G. Hemmerich, 489(PJGG):Band86Heft1-196
Scholem, G. Fidélité et Utopie.
H. Raczymow, 450(NRF):Mar79-117
Scholem, G. From Berlin to Jerusalem.
A. Momigliano, 453(NYRB):18Dec80-37
Scholem, G. - see Benjamin, W. and G. Scholem
Scholem, G.G. Sabbatai Sevi.* Kabbalah.
J.C. Greenfield, 318(JAOS):Oct-Dec78-487

Schultz, R.J. Federalism and the Regulatory Process.
L. Salter and D. Slaco, 99:Jun-Jul80-42

Schulz, A.M. Niccolò di Giovanni Fiorention and Venetian Sculpture of the Early Renaissance.
G. Martin, 617(TLS):1Feb80-120

Schulz, B. Sanatorium under the Sign of the Hourglass.*
P. Lewis, 565:Vol20#4-67
42(AR):Spring79-254

Schulz, E.G. Rehbergs Opposition gegen Kants Ethik.*
J.S. Morgan, 342:Band69Heft1-114

Schulz, G-M. Negativität in der Dichtung Paul Celans.*
D. Robinson, 220(GQ):May79-428
A. Vieregg, 564:Feb79-75

Schulz, R. and others. Lesen, Lachen, Lernen.
R.F. Ambacher, 399(MLJ):Sep-Oct79-310

Schulz, W. Le Dieu de la métaphysique moderne. (J. Colette, ed and trans)
A. Reix, 542:Jul-Sep79-382

Schulz, W. Lambert Doomer.
C. Brown, 90:May79-325

Schulz, W. Philosophie in der veränderten Welt.
C. Roëls, 192(EP):Oct-Dec79-483

Schulz-Buschhaus, U. Formen und Ideologien des Kriminalromans.
R.F. Schönhaar, 224(GRM):Band28Heft1-106

Schulz-Buschhaus, U. Literarische Erziehung — wozu?
M. Gsteiger, 52:Band13Heft3-301

Schulze, W. Zahl, Proportion, Analogie.
G. von Bredow, 182:Vol131#14-458

Schulze-Witzenrath, E. Die Originalität der Louise Labé.*
G. Jondorf, 208(FS):Apr79-181

Schumacher, H. Narziss an der Quelle.
J.M. McGlathery, 301(JEGP):Oct79-603
M. Tatar, 564:Feb79-70

Schuman, S. Cyril Tourneur.*
J.C. Trewin, 157:Winter79-79

Schumann, M. Talleyrand.
N. Hampson, 208(FS):Vol133Pt2-1009

Schünemann, P. Gottfried Benn.
M. Bickelmann, 221(GL):Jan79-143

Schuon, F. L'ésotérisme comme principe et comme voie.
M. Adam, 542:Oct-Dec79-460

Schuon, F. De l'unité transcendante des religions. (new ed)
A. Jacob, 542:Jul-Sep79-383

Schurhammer, G. Francis Xavier. (Vol 3)
C.R. Boxer, 617(TLS):12Sep80-985

Schürmann, R. Meister Eckhart.
J.D.C., 543:Jun79-769

Schurr, S., ed. Energy in America's Future.
P.K. Verleger, Jr., 231:Apr80-110

Schuster, F. and C. Wolseley. Vases of the Sea.
C.F. Shangraw, 318(JAOS):Jul-Sep78-307

Schuster, G. Private Work and Public Causes.
D.A.N. Jones, 617(TLS):20Jun80-717

Schuster, I. China und Japan in der deutschen Literatur 1890-1925.*
J.M. Ritchie, 402(MLR):Apr79-501

Schuster, P-K. Theodor Fontane: "Effi Briest."
C.G. Grawe, 67:May79-144

Schuth, H.W. Mike Nichols.
M. Yacowar, 106:Winter79-379

Schütt, H. Fremdsprachenbegabung und Fremdsprachenenleistung.
J. Kornelius, 430(NS):Feb78-95

Schutte, A.J. Pier Paolo Vergerio.
L.V.R., 568(SCN):Spring-Summer79-61

Schütz, E. Kritik der literarischen Reportage.
K. Bohnen, 406:Fall79-350

Schutz, N.W., Jr. Kinesiology.
D.L. Kelley, 567:Vol124#1/2-177

Schütze, F. Sprache soziologisch gesehen. (Vol 2)
B. Bjorklund, 361:Aug78-379

Schützeichel, H. Wesen und Gegenstand der kirchlichen Lehrautorität nach Thomas Stapleton.
M. Löhrer, 182:Vol131#3/4-89

Schützeichel, R., ed. Das Mittelrheinische Passionsspiel der St. Galler Handschrift 919.
E. Simon, 589:Jul79-627

Schuurmans, N.J. Verbindingen met specifiek enclitische pronomina in het Westbrabants.
J.B. Berns, 685(ZDL):1/1979-106

Schuyler, J. The Morning of the Poem.
P. Breslin, 441:2Nov80-12
D. Donoghue, 453(NYRB):14Aug80-49

Schuyler, J. What's for Dinner?*
D. Flower, 249(HudR):Summer79-299

Schuyt, M. and J. Elffers - see Collins, G.R.

Schwabe, C.W. Unmentionable Cuisine.
M.F.K. Fisher, 453(NYRB):18Dec80-40
R.A. Sokolov, 441:23Mar80-18
F. Taliaferro, 231:Jun80-83

Schwamm, E. Adjacent Lives.
W. Sullivan, 569(SR):Spring79-337
639(VQR):Spring79-58

Schwan, G. Leszek Kolakowski.
W. Becker, 489(PJGG):Band86Heft1-214

Schwank, K. Bildstruktur und Romanstruktur bei Virginia Woolf.
R.W. Weber, 224(GRM):Band28Heft1-125

Schwartz, D. In Dreams Begin Responsibilities and Other Stories.* (J. Atlas, ed)
T. Hall, 268(IFR):Winter80-70

Schwartz, D. Last and Lost Poems of Delmore Schwartz.* (R. Phillips, ed)
J. Mazzaro, 219(GaR):Fall79-712

Schwartz, G. - see "Rembrandt: All the Etchings, Reproduced in True Size"

Schwartz, L.S. Rough Strife.
J. Atlas, 441:23Jul80-C20
K. Pollitt, 441:15Jun80-14

Schwartz, M. Soviet Perceptions of the
United States.
  A. Brown, 617(TLS):25Jan80-95
  P. Hollander, 550(RusR):Oct79-499
Schwartz, R.B. Boswell's Johnson.
  R.H. Bell, 401(MLQ):Mar79-80
  F. Brady, 579(SAQ):Autumn79-522
  R. Halsband, 301(JEGP):Apr79-265
Schwarz, A. From Büchner to Beckett.
  E. Brater, 130:Winter79/80-365
Schwarz, D.R. Disraeli's Fiction.
  M. Foot, 617(TLS):18Apr80-433
Schwarz, E. Keine Zeit für Eichendorff.
  H. Lehnert, 221(GQ):Nov79-567
Schwarz, H. Johann Nestroy im Bild. (J.
  Hüttner and O.G. Schindler, eds)
  J.A. Kruse, 182:Vol31#1/2-38
  H. Zohn, 222(GR):Summer79-135
Schwarz, L.W. Wolfson of Harvard.*
  J. Goldin, 31(ASch):Summer80-391
Schwarz-Liebermann von Wahlendorf, H.A.
  Les dimensions du droit.
  J-L. Gardies, 542:Oct-Dec79-495
Schweigler, P. Einrichtung und technische
  Ausstattung von Bibliotheken.
  F. Gröbli, 182:Vol31#11/12-325
Schweikle, G. Die mittelhochdeutsche
  Minnelyrik I.
  F.B. Brévart, 221(GQ):May79-399
Schweitzer, R. Autonomie und Autokratie.
  S. Jungar, 550(RusR):Oct79-478
  D. Kirby, 575(SEER):Jul79-452
Schwemmer, O. Theorie der rationalen
  Erklärung.
  K-H. Nusser, 489(PJGG):Band86Heft1-192
Schwendowius, B. and W. Dömling, eds.
  Johann Sebastian Bach.
  S. Daw, 415:Nov79-916
Schweninger, L. James T. Rapier and Recon-
  struction.
  D.H. Donald, 9(AlaR):Jul79-228
Schwerdtfeger, I.C. Fremdsprache:
  mangelhaft.
  F.J. Zapp, 430(NS):Oct78-471
Schwineköper, B. Königtum und Städte bis
  zum Ende des Investiturstreits.
  L.G. Duggan, 589:Jan79-189
Schwob, A. Oswald von Wolkenstein.
  G.F. Jones, 589:Apr79-426
  B. Murdoch, 182:Vol31#5/6-154
Sciascia, L. Dalle parti degli infedeli.
  Nero su nero. La Sicilia come metafora.
  P. McCarthy, 617(TLS):2May80-490
Sciascia, L. L'Affaire Moro.
  P. Pachet, 450(NRF):Mar79-122
"Science et métaphysique."
  M. Adam, 542:Oct-Dec79-460
"The Scientific Examination of Early
  Netherlandish Painting."
  S.R. Jones, 90:Sep79-594
Scobey, J., ed. Cooking with Michael
  Field.
  W. and C. Cowen, 639(VQR):Autumn79-157
Scollen, C.M. - see de Ronsard, P.
Scoones, S. Les Noms de quelques Offi-
  ciers féodaux des Origines à la Fin du
  [continued]

[continuing]
XIIe siècle.*
  N.L. Corbett, 545(RPh):Aug78-135
  W. Rothwell, 208(FS):Vol133Pt2-608
Scorrano, L. Modi e esempi di dantismo
  novecentesco.
  A. Pipa, 276:Winter79-413
Scorza, M. La tumba del relámpago.
  E. Echevarría, 268(IFR):Winter80-69
"Jean Scot Erigène et l'histoire de la
  philosophie."
  J. Jolivet, 542:Apr-Jun79-208
Scott, A. Selected Poems 1943-1974.
  N. MacCaig, 588(SSL):Vol13-286
Scott, C. A Learner's First Dictionary.
  E.G. Cotton, 399(MLJ):Mar79-134
Scott, D.A., H.M. Hamadani and A.A. Mir-
  hosseyni. The Birds of Iran (Paran-
  degān Irān).
  J.A.C. Greppin, 318(JAOS):Apr-Jun78-
  171
Scott, D.H.T. Sonnet Theory and Practice
  in Nineteenth-Century France.*
  H.L. Davis, 207(FR):May79-933
  R. Killick, 402(MLR):Apr79-464
Scott, D.M. From Office to Profession.
  R.L. Ferm, 656(WMQ):Apr79-305
  P.A. Treckel, 432(NEQ):Jun79-279
Scott, F.R. Essays on the Constitution.
  L. Weir, 102(CanL):Summer79-114
Scott, F.R. - see "The Poems of French
  Canada"
Scott, J. The Two Faces of Robert Just.
  N. Callendar, 441:7Sep80-37
Scott, J.A. Dante magnanimo.
  C.J. Ryan, 402(MLR):Oct79-957
Scott, J.W. Madame de Lafayette.
  K.R. Dutton, 67:May79-136
  G. Hainsworth, 208(FS):Vol33Pt2-689
Scott, M. John Marston's Plays.
  F.N. Lees, 148:Summer78-86
Scott, N. Wherever We Step the Land is
  Mined.
  P. Kemp, 362:13Mar80-350
  F. Tuohy, 617(TLS):22Feb80-210
Scott, P.J.M. Reality and Comic Confi-
  dence in Charles Dickens.
  R.J. Dunn, 594:Fall79-374
Scott, T. The Complete Book of Stuffed-
  work.
  N. Minkowitz, 139:Apr79-12
Scott, T.K. - see Buridanus, J.
Scott, W. Prefaces to the Waverley Novels.
  (M.A. Weinstein, ed)
  K.S., 148:Summer79-90
"Scottish Short Stories 1980."
  J. Campbell, 617(TLS):22Aug80-943
Scottus, S. - see under Sedulius Scottus
Scouten, A.H. and R.D. Hume - see Howard,
  R. and The Duke of Buckingham
Scragg, D.G. - see Gordon, E.V.
Screech, M.A. Rabelais.
  R.M. Adams, 617(TLS):25Apr80-472
  D.P. Walker, 453(NYRB):12Jun80-44
  T. Zeldin, 362:3Apr80-450
Screech, M.A., with others - see Rabelais,
  F.

"Scripture of the Lotus Blossom of the Fine Dharma (The Lotus Sūtra)." (L. Hurvitz, trans)
  A. Rawlinson, 259(IIJ):Oct79-284
Scruton, R. The Aesthetics of Architecture.
  A. Savile, 617(TLS):8Feb80-148
Scruton, R. The Meaning of Conservatism.
  P. Whitehead, 362:9Oct80-476
de Scudéry, M. Choix de Conversations de Mlle de Scudéry. (P.J. Wolfe, ed)
  E.T. Dubois, 402(MLR):Oct79-939
Ščukin, A.N. Russkij jazyk v dialogax.
  S. Wobst, 574(SEEJ):Summer79-297
Scullard, H.H. - see MacDowell, D.M.
Scully, D. Men Who Control Women's Health.
  S. Kitzinger, 617(TLS):1Aug80-879
"Sculptures Romanes et Gothiques du Nord de la France."
  J. Beckwith, 39:Apr79-328
Scupham, P. Natura.
  L. Sail, 493:Mar80-71
Scupham, P. Summer Palaces.
  C. Butler, 617(TLS):13Jun80-680
  D. Davis, 362:5Jun80-729
Seaborne, M. and R. Lowe. The English School. (Vol 2)
  D. Stillman, 637(VS):Summer78-512
Seabrook, J. Mother and Son.*
  R. Coleridge, 617(TLS):25Jan80-90
  A. Sillitoe, 441:20Apr80-13
Seager, R. Pompey.
  G.W. Bowersock, 31(ASch):Spring80-276
Sealey, R. A History of Greek City States, ca. 700-338 B.C.*
  P.J. Rhodes, 123:Vol129No1-100
Sealsfield, C. Sämtliche Werke. (Vols 4-17) (K.J.R. Arndt, ed)
  M. Nirenberg, 221(GQ):Jan79-81
Searle, J.R. Expression and Meaning.
  J. Lear, 617(TLS):7Mar80-268
Searles, H. L'effort pour rendre l'autre fou.
  F. Roustang, 98:Jun-Jul78-587
Sears, D.T.P. Aunty High Over the Barley Mow.*
  C. McLay, 102(CanL):Autumn79-125
Sears, H.D. The Sex Radicals.
  639(VQR):Spring78-61
Seary, E.R., with S.M.P. Lynch. Family Names of the Island of Newfoundland.
  E.C. Smith, 424:Mar78-123
Seay, A., ed. Quaestiones et Solutiones.* Quatuor Tractatuli Italici de Contrapuncto.
  M. Fowler, 308:Spring78-115
Seay, A. - see de Leno, A.
Sebastián López, S. Arte y Humanismo. Mensaje del Arte Medieval.
  A.R.G. de Ceballos, 48:Jul-Sep78-351
Sebeok, T.A., ed. Current Trends in Linguistics.* (Vol 11)
  G.F. Meier, 682(ZPSK):Band31Heft4-418
Sebeok, T.A., ed. Current Trends in Linguistics. (Vol 12)
  W.A. Koch and others, 353:May78-53

Sebeok, T.A., ed. Current Trends in Linguistics.* (Vol 13)
  N.E. Collinge, 350:Mar79-207
Sebeok, T.A., ed. How Animals Communicate.
  R.E. Lemon, 529(QQ):Summer79-287
  P.H. Salus, 350:Sep79-736
Sebeok, T.A., ed. Native Languages of the Americas.*
  K. Heger, 72:Band216Heft2-375
Sebeok, T.A., ed. A Perfusion of Signs.
  M. Shapiro, 350:Mar79-265
  W. Steiner, 567:Vol125#1/2-123
Sebeok, T.A., ed. Sight, Sound, and Sense.
  M. Shapiro, 350:Jun79-495
Sebeok, T.A. and D.J. Umiker-Sebeok, eds. Speaking of Apes.
  M. Gardner, 453(NYRB):20Mar80-3
Sébire, V. La Maison des sables.
  L. Kovacs, 450(NRF):Nov79-118
Sebold, R.P. Novela y autobiografía en la "Vida" de Torres Villarroel.
  J. Urrutia, 240(HR):Spring78-267
Sebold, R.P. - see de Luzán, I.
de Séchelles, H. Théorie de l'ambition.
  P-F. Moreau, 450(NRF):Sep79-53
"Second Maharashtra by 2005."
  G.S. Kulkarni, 293(JASt):Aug79-820
Secrest, M. Being Bernard Berenson.*
  A. Brookner, 617(TLS):18Jan80-51
Sederberg, A. The Power Players.
  P. Andrews, 441:17Feb80-15
Sederberg, K. - see Lemmon, E.J.
Sedgemore, B. The Secret Constitution.
  J. Grigg, 362:5Jun80-725
  W. Waldegrave, 617(TLS):18Jul80-816
Sédir, G. Pas.
  J.E. Preckshot, 207(FR):Oct78-187
Sedulius Scottus. In Donati artem maiorem. In Donati artem minorem. (B. Löfstedt, ed of both)
  J.J. Contreni, 589:Oct79-834
Seduro, V. Dostoevsky in Russian and World Theatre.*
  G.D. Fitzgerald, 574(SEEJ):Spring79-128
  A. Guedroïtz, 550(RusR):Jan79-125
Seebacher, J. - see Hugo, V.
Seeger, C. Studies in Musicology 1935-1975.*
  C. Longuet-Higgins, 410(M&L):Jul79-354
Seelye, J. Prophetic Waters.*
  W.H. Herendeen, 627(UTQ):Fall78-87
  639(VQR):Winter78-14
Seemann, K-D. Die altrussische Wallfahrtsliteratur.*
  A. Poppe, 575(SEER):Apr79-274
Seféris, G. Poems.
  P. Green, 453(NYRB):26Jun80-40
Segal, E. Man, Woman and Child.
  A. Broyard, 441:23May80-C28
  M. Levin, 441:8Jun80-14
Segal, P. The Man Who Walked in His Head.
  C. Seebohm, 441:17Feb80-16
Segal, R. Leon Trotsky.*
  L. Schapiro, 453(NYRB):17Apr80-15

Segebrecht, W. Das Gelegenheitsgedicht.
  J. Leighton, 402(MLR):Jul79-744
  F. Voit, 67:May79-164
Segel, H.B., ed. Polish Romantic Drama.*
  B.H. Bennett, 577(SHR):Spring79-174
  Z. Folejewski, 104(CASS):Fall78-425
  639(VQR):Summer78-97
Segers, R.T. The Evaluation of Literary
  Texts.
  T. Eaton, 307:Oct79-109
  W.N. Whisner, 290(JAAC):Fall79-93
Seghers, A. Steinzeit. Wiederbegegnung.
  F. Wagner, 654(WB):7/1978-136
Segre, C. Semiotica filologica.
  D. Robey, 617(TLS):2May80-502
Seguin, J-P. La Langue Française au
  XVIIIe siècle.*
  P. Larthomas, 209(FM):Apr78-191
Séguinot, A., ed. L'Accent d'insistance/
  Emphatic Stress.*
  A.W. Grundstrom, 207(FR):Dec78-365
  B. Saint-Jacques, 102(CanL):Spring79-
  105
Séguy, M-R. - see "The Miraculous Journey
  of Mahomet; Miraj Namet"
Seidel, F. Sunrise.
  D. Donoghue, 453(NYRB):14Aug80-49
  V. Young, 441:21Sep80-14
Seidel, G.J. Activity and Ground.*
  M.H., 191(ELN):Sep78(supp)-183
Seidel, M. Epic Geography.*
  A. Goldman, 541(RES):Feb79-108
  V. Mahon, 402(MLR):Jan79-188
Seidel, M. Satiric Inheritance.
  676(YR):Spring80-VI
Seiden, M.I. William Butler Yeats.
  R. Fréchet, 189(EA):Jan-Mar78-102
Seidenbaum, A. Los Angeles 200.
  P. Goldberger, 441:30Nov80-70
Seidensticker, E.G. Genji Days.
  M. Mudrick, 249(HudR):Summer79-269
  639(VQR):Winter79-7
Seidlin, O. Der Theaterkritiker Otto
  Brahm.
  R.V. Gross, 221(GQ):Nov79-555
Seidlin, O. - see Schnitzler, A. and O.
  Brahm
Seidman, R.J. Bucks County Idyll.
  N. Callendar, 441:10Aug80-34
Seif, K.P. Die Claudiusbücher in den
  Annalen des Tacitus.
  E. Keitel, 24:Summer79-326
Seifert, A. Logik zwischen Scholastik und
  Humanismus.
  P.V. Spade, 589:Jul79-628
Seifert, J. The Plague Column.
  A. Ross, 364:Aug/Sep79-8
  D.M. Thomas, 617(TLS):18Jan80-66
Seigel, J. Marx's Fate.
  L. Dupré, 125:Winter79-285
  G.A. Panichas, 396(ModA):Spring79-184
Seiler, A. Kurzgefasste Grammatik der
  sorben-wendischen Sprache nach dem
  Budissiner Dialekte.
  G. Stone, 575(SEER):Oct79-628
Seiler, B. Retaining Wall.
  R. Feld, 472:Fall/Winter79-150

Seiler, H. Cahuilla Grammar.*
  R.A. Jacobs, 343:Band23-209
Seiler, H. Sprache und Sprachen.*
  R. Ködderitzsch, 260(IF):Band83-361
  R.H. Robins, 297(JL):Sep79-375
Sekka, K. A Flight of Butterflies.
  P-L. Adams, 61:Jan80-89
Sekler, E. and W. Curtis, with others. Le
  Corbusier at Work.
  J.M. Richards, 617(TLS):1Feb80-122
  J.P. Snyder, 658:Autumn79-328
Sekora, J. Luxury.*
  E.A. Bloom, 579(SAQ):Summer79-408
  M. Irwin, 541(RES):Nov79-476
  J. Stedmond, 529(QQ):Summer79-335
  566:Autumn78-47
Selassie, H. - see under Haile Selassie
Selcher, W.A. Brazil's Multilateral
  Relations.
  C.N. Ronning, 263(RIB):Vol29No1-84
Self, D. and R. Speakman, eds. Act One,
  Act Two, Act Three.
  J. Coleby, 157:Summer79-81
Seliger, M. The Marxist Conception of
  Ideology.*
  R.M. Mills, 613:Mar79-108
Sell, R.D. Trespassing Ghost.
  A. Motion, 541(RES):Nov79-497
Sell, R.D. - see Beaumont, J.
Sellers, C.C. Mr. Peale's Museum.
  J. Kastner, 441:2Mar80-11
Sellers, M. Leonardo and Others.
  T.J. Binyon, 617(TLS):30May80-606
Sellier, P. - see Pascal, B.
Sellin, D. The First Pose.
  E. Johns, 127:Fall78-72
Sellin, P.R. and S.B. Baxter. Anglo-Dutch
  Cross Currents in the Seventeenth and
  Eighteenth Centuries.
  E. Bourcier, 189(EA):Jul-Dec78-386
  J. Platt, 447(N&Q):Dec78-553
Selz, J. Turner.
  J. Ziff, 637(VS):Autumn77-113
"Semasia." (Vol 1) (R. Anderson, U.
  Goebel and J. McNab, eds)
  D. Evans, 208(FS):Vol133Pt2-1028
Sembner, H. Heinrich von Kleists Nachruhm.
  G. Jordan, 221(GQ):Jan79-118
Semi, F. - see Pliny
Sempé. The Musicians.
  D. Hill, 441:14Dec80-13
Sena, M. La paideia cosmica di Emanuele
  Kant.
  F. Pfurtscheller, 342:Band69Heft4-467
Sena Chiesa, G. Gemme di Luni.
  J. Boardman, 123:Vol29No2-339
  M. Henig, 313:Vol69-218
Sendano, J.A. - see under Asenjo Sendano,
  J.
Seneca. Agamemnon.* (R.J. Tarrant, ed)
  F. Delarue, 555:Vol52fasc2-392
Seneca. L. Annaei Senecae "Dialogorum"
  libri duodecim. (L.D. Reynolds, ed)
  D.R. Shackleton Bailey, 122:Jan79-76
  M. Winterbottom, 123:Vol29No1-63
Senelier, J., with others - see de Nerval,
  G.

Madame de Sévigné. Correspondance. (Vol
3) (R. Duchêne, ed)
   H.T. Barnwell, 208(FS):Jul79-345
Sexauer, W.D. Frühneuhochdeutsche Schrif-
ten in Kartäuserbibliotheken.
   E. Bauer, 182:Vol31#11/12-327
Sexton, A. Anne Sexton: A Self-Portrait
in Letters.* (L.G. Sexton and L. Ames,
eds)
   R. Johnson, 472:Fall/Winter79-92
Sexton, A. Words for Dr. Y.* (L.G.
Sexton, ed)
   C. Bedient, 569(SR):Spring79-296
   R. Johnson, 472:Fall/Winter79-92
   C. Molesworth, 461:Fall-Winter79/80-91
   639(VQR):Winter79-25
Sexton, M. Illusions of Power.
   C. Kiernan, 617(TLS):28Mar80-373
Seybolt, P.J., ed. The Rustication of
Urban Youth in China.
   S.L. Shirk, 293(JASt):Nov78-148
Seyfī Çelebī. L'ouvrage de Seyfī Çelebī.
(J. Matuz, ed and trans)
   J. Stewart-Robinson, 318(JAOS):
    Oct-Dec78-572
Seymour, G. The Harrison Affair.
   N. Callendar, 441:9Mar80-17
   442(NY):7Apr80-152
Seymour, G. Red Fox.
   M. Laski, 362:10Jan80-62
Seymour, J. On My Own Terms.
   R. Coleridge, 617(TLS):6Jun80-632
Seymour, T.V. Dylan Thomas' New York.
   295(JML):Vol7#4-824
Sgard, J., M. Gilot and F. Weil, eds. Dic-
tionnaire des Journalistes (1600-1789).*
   P. Jansen, 535(RHL):Jan-Feb78-133
Shabtai, S.H. Five Minutes to Midnight.
   P.S. Guptara, 617(TLS):18Jul80-823
Shackleton Bailey, D.R. Two Studies in
Roman Nomenclature.*
   F. Hinard, 555:Vol52fasc2-400
   T.P. Wiseman, 123:Vol29No1-180
Shackleton Bailey, D.R. - see Cicero
Shadbolt, D. The Art of Emily Carr.
   R. Cook, 99:Jun-Jul80-32
   L.J. Milrod, 150(DR):Winter79/80-750
Shadoian, J. Dreams and Dead Ends.*
   D. Golden, 106:Spring79-71
   639(VQR):Spring78-70
Shady, R.C. - see Heywood, T.
Shafaat, A. The Gospel According to Islam.
   M.E. Yapp, 617(TLS):19Sep80-1040
Shafarevich, I. The Socialist Phenomenon.
   S. Monas, 441:16Nov80-13
Shaha, R. Nepali Politics. (2nd ed)
   L.D. Hayes, 293(JASt):Aug79-826
Shahar, D. His Majesty's Agent.
   S. Ellin, 441:14Dec80-10
Shakely, L. Guilty Bystander.
   639(VQR):Autumn78-144
Shakespeare, W. The Annotated Shake-
speare.* (A.L. Rowse, ed)
   J.A. Roberts, 570(SQ):Winter79-124

Shakespeare, W. As You Like It. (R.
Knowles, ed)
   G.B. Evans, 301(JEGP):Jan79-124
   S. Wells, 541(RES):Feb79-73
Shakespeare, W. Coriolanus. (P. Brock-
bank, ed)
   G.R. Hibbard, 677(YES):Vol9-309
   T.H. Howard-Hill, 570(SQ):Summer79-423
Shakespeare, W. Othello. (B. Engler, ed)
   P. Gebhardt, 72:Band216Heft2-354
Shakespeare, W. Romeo and Juliet. (B.
Gibbons, ed)
   S. Wells, 617(TLS):20Jun80-710
Shakespeare, W. Shakespeare's Sonnets.*
(S. Booth, ed)
   J. Fuzier, 189(EA):Jul-Dec78-377
   C.T. Neely, 405(MP):Nov79-210
Shakespeare, W. Shakespeare's Sonnets.*
(S.C. Campbell, ed)
   K. Duncan-Jones, 617(TLS):9May80-518
Shakespeare, W. The Two Noble Kinsmen.*
(N.W. Bawcutt, ed)
   R.F. Hill, 161(DUJ):Jun79-284
Shalamov, V. Kolyma Tales.
   J. Bayley, 441:4May80-1
   I. Howe, 453(NYRB):14Aug80-36
   V.S. Pritchett, 442(NY):3Nov80-198
Shale, R., comp. Academy Awards.
   M. Buckley, 200:Aug-Sep79-431
Shanes, E. Turner's Picturesque Views in
England and Wales 1825-1838.
   D. Piper, 617(TLS):1Feb80-119
Shang-jen, K. - see under K'ung Shang-jen
Shange, N. for colored girls who have
considered suicide/when the rainbow is
enuf.*
   D. Graham, 565:Vol20#4-75
Shannon, D. Felony File.
   T.J. Binyon, 617(TLS):1Aug80-868
   N. Callendar, 441:9Mar80-17
Shannon, J.R. Organ Literature of the
Seventeenth Century.
   J. Dalton, 410(M&L):Jul79-334
Shanor, D.R. The Soviet Triangle.
   J. Chace, 441:21Sep80-3
Shapcott, T.W. Selected Poems.
   S.E. Lee, 581:Dec79-432
Shapiro, A.L. Problemy sotsial'no-
ekonimicheskoi istorii Rusi XIX-XVI vv.
   P. Bushkovitch, 550(RusR):Oct79-474
Shapiro, D. John Ashbery.
   G. Burns, 584(SWR):Autumn79-408
   J.D. McClatchy, 676(YR):Winter80-289
Shapiro, H. Lauds and Nightsongs.
   H. Carruth, 231:Jan80-77
   639(VQR):Autumn79-149
Shapiro, H.D. Appalachia on Our Mind.*
   J.W. Williamson, 585(SoQ):Spring-
    Summer79-230
Shapiro, K. Collected Poems: 1940-1978.*
   639(VQR):Winter79-24
Shapiro, M. Children of the Revels.*
   K. Duncan-Jones, 447(N&Q):Apr78-180
   639(VQR):Winter78-14
Sharlet, R. The New Soviet Constitution
of 1977.
   D.D. Barry, 550(RusR):Jan79-115

Sharma, P.G. and S. Kumar, eds. Indian Bilingualism.
M.L. Apte, 350:Dec79-924
Sharp, C. The Rising in the North.
D.M. Loades, 161(DUJ):Dec78-103
Sharp, D., ed. The Rationalists.
L. Brett, 46:Jun79-361
Sharp, R.F. A Dictionary of English Authors, Biographical and Bibliographical.
L.A. Carlson, 568(SCN):Spring-Summer79-38
Sharpe, H.J. Jonathan Wade.
305(JIL):Sep78-169
Sharpe, K. Sir Robert Cotton.
J.P. Kenyon, 617(TLS):16May80-561
Sharpe, T. Ancestral Vices.
J. Mellors, 362:6Nov80-623
Sharpless, F.P. The Literary Criticism of John Stuart Mill.
H. Laboucheix, 189(EA):Jan-Mar78-91
Sharpless, R.E. Gaitán of Colombia.
W.R. Wright, 263(RIB):Vol129No1-83
Sharratt, P. - see Labé, L.
Sharrer, H.L. A Critical Bibliography of Hispanic Arthurian Material.* (Vol 1)
S.M. Bryant, 238:Dec79-726
R.B. Tate, 86(BHS):Oct79-335
Sharrer, H.L. The Legendary History of Britain in Lope García de Salazar's "Libro de las bienandanzas e fortunas."
H.F. Williams, 304(JHP):Winter80-176
Sharrock, R., ed. Bunyan, "The Pilgrim's Progress:" A Casebook.
V. Newey, 402(MLR):Jul79-656
Sharrock, R., ed. English Short Stories of Today. (4th Ser)
A. Varley, 161(DUJ):Jun79-292
Sharrock, R. - see Bunyan, J.
Sharwood Smith, J.E. On Teaching Classics.
G.R. Lambert, 121(CJ):Feb-Mar80-267
El-Shater, S. The Novels of Mary Shelley.
C.E.R., 191(ELN):Sep78(supp)-69
Shattuck, R. The Forbidden Experiment.
H.E. Bruber, 441:27Jul80-7
R. Darnton, 453(NYRB):15May80-3
D.J. Enright, 362:14Aug80-216
J. Leonard, 441:22Apr80-C10
Shaumyan, S.K. Applicational Grammar as a Semantic Theory of Natural Language.*
D.H., 355(LSoc):Apr78-149
H.J. Neuhaus, 343:Band23-167
Shaw, D. - see Gougenot
Shaw, D.L. Borges, Ficciones.*
205(FMLS):Jan78-94
Shaw, G.B. The Great Composers. (L. Crompton, ed)
R. Anderson, 415:Feb79-129
Shaw, G.B. The Portable Bernard Shaw. (S. Weintraub, ed)
F.P.W. McDowell, 295(JML):Vol17#4-809
Shaw, G.B. Practical Politics. (L.J. Hubenka, ed)
T. Eagleton, 402(MLR):Jan79-183
Shaw, G.B. An Unsocial Socialist.
J. Lucas, 617(TLS):23May80-574

Shaw, I. Short Stories: Five Decades.*
42(AR):Winter79-126
Shaw, I. and R. Searle. Paris! Paris!
M.G. Hydak, 399(MLJ):Mar79-137
Shaw, J.M., ed. Childhood in Poetry.* (2nd supp)
J. Oldfield, 677(YES):Vol9-354
Shaw, T. Nigeria.
M. Posnansky, 2(AfrA):Feb79-13
Shaw, W. Tun Razak.
M.L. Rogers, 293(JASt):Nov78-213
Shaw, W.D. Tennyson's Style.*
G. Joseph, 637(VS):Autumn77-109
Shaw, W.H. Marx's Theory of History.*
A. Gilbert, 482(PhR):Jul79-476
A.W. Novitsky, 613:Jun79-211
Shawcross, W. Sideshow.*
L. Lipson, 676(YR):Winter80-263
Shay, R.P., Jr. British Rearmament in the Thirties.
F. Coghlan, 161(DUJ):Jun79-280
639(VQR):Winter78-8
Shcharansky, A., with L. Ben-Josef. Next Year in Jerusalem.
M. Nesvisky, 441:17Feb80-9
Shead, H. The Anatomy of the Piano.
C. Ehrlich, 415:Feb79-131
Sheard, W.S. and J.T. Paoletti, eds. Collaboration in Italian Renaissance Art.
G. Martin, 617(TLS):1Feb80-120
Shebl, J.H. - see Jeffers, R.
Sheed, W. The Good Word and Other Words.*
P. Dickinson, 364:Jun79-90
Sheed, W. Transatlantic Blues.*
639(VQR):Summer78-93
Sheeran, P.F. The Novels of Liam O'Flaherty.*
J.W. Weaver, 305(JIL):May78-182
Sheick, W.J. The Slender Human Word.
J. Porte, 141:Winter79-82
Sheils, W.J., ed. Archbishop Grindal's Visitation, 1575, Comperta et Detecta Book.
J.E. Sayers, 325:Apr79-164
Sheils, W.J., comp. The Reformation in the North to 1558.
W.B. Stephens, 325:Apr79-173
Shek, B-Z. Social Realism in the French-Canadian Novel.*
C. Gerson, 102(CanL):Autumn79-115
Shelby, L.R. - see Roriczer, M. and H. Schmuttermayer
Sheldon, S. Rage of Angels.
M. Levin, 441:3Aug80-12
Shelgren, O.W., Jr., C. Lattin and R.W. Frasch. Cobblestone Landmarks of New York State.
J.R. Garrison, 658:Winter79-405
Shell, M. The Economy of Literature.*
W.E. Cain, 599:Summer79-303
Shelley, M.W. The Letters of Mary Wollstonecraft Shelley. (Vol 1) (B.T. Bennett, ed)
R. Holmes, 441:18May80-14
A.N. Wilson, 617(TLS):12Sep80-996

Shelley, P.B. Percy Bysshe Shelley:
Selected Poems. (T. Webb, ed)
M. Butler, 175:Spring79-78
S. Curran, 340(KSJ):Vol28-139
C.E.R., 191(ELN):Sep78(supp)-72
Shelley, P.B. Shelley's Poetry and Prose.*
(D.H. Reiman and S.B. Powers, eds)
C.E.R., 191(ELN):Sep78(supp)-72
Shellim, M. India and the Daniells.
N.C. Chaudhuri, 617(TLS):21Mar80-329
Shelnutt, E. The Love Child.
M.F. Greene, 219(GaR):Winter79-951
Shelton, J-A. Seneca's Hercules Furens.*
J.G. Fitch, 487:Spring79-90
Shelton, R. The Bus to Veracruz.*
D. Smith, 29:Mar/Apr80-40
A. Williamson, 491:Mar80-348
639(VQR):Summer79-106
Shendge, M.J. The Civilized Demons.
W. Rau, 259(IIJ):Oct79-281
Shenkman, R. and K. Reiger. One-Night
Stands With American History.
J. Greenfield, 441:13Jan80-16
Shepard, L. The Broadside Ballad.
W.K. McNeil, 292(JAF):Oct-Dec79-515
Shepard, L.A. American Art at Amherst.
D. Flower, 432(NEQ):Mar79-139
Shepherd, J. and others. Whose Music?*
D. Osmond-Smith, 89(BJA):Spring79-189
Shepherd, W.G. Evidences.
G. Lindop, 617(TLS):16May80-562
Sheppard, E.A. Henry James and "The Turn
of the Screw."*
H. Bonheim, 38:Band96Heft1/2-251
Sheppard, R., ed. Dada.
D. Ades, 617(TLS):11Apr80-422
Sheppard, S. The Four Hundred.*
M. Laski, 362:10Jan80-62
Sher, G.S. Praxis.
I. Banac, 550(RusR):Jul79-391
A. Ferguson, 575(SEER):Jul79-465
Sherazi, M.S. - see under Sa'di Sherazi, M.
Sherburne, J. Death's Pale Horse.
N. Callendar, 441:27Apr80-18
Sheridan, A. - see Lacan, J.
Sheridan, M. The Fifth Season.
J.F. Cotter, 249(HudR):Spring79-113
Sheringham, M. André Breton.
K.R. Dutton, 67:May79-136
Sherman, C. Diderot and the Art of Dia-
logue.*
P. France, 208(FS):Vol33Pt2-766
F. Sturzer, 400(MLN):May79-904
Sherman, J. The Drama of Denishawn Dance.
B. Dunne, 42(AR):Fall79-501
Sherratt, A., ed. The Cambridge Encyclo-
pedia of Archaeology.
S. Piggott, 617(TLS):15Aug80-919
Sherry, N., ed. Joseph Conrad: A Commemor-
ation.*
J.B. Batchelor, 447(N&Q):Dec78-566
Sherry, N. Conrad and his World.
M.C. Michael, 136:Vol11#1-107
Sherwani, H.K. and P.M. Joshi, eds. His-
tory of Medieval Deccan (1295-1724).*
(Vol 2)
M.A. Nayeem, 273(IC):Jan76-53

Sherwin, J.J. How the Dead Count.
R. De Mott, 651(WHR):Spring79-174
E. Milton, 472:Fall/Winter79-270
Sherwin, P.S. Precious Bane.*
M. Brown, 591(SIR):Summer79-311
R. Wendorf, 405(MP):May80-440
639(VQR):Winter78-16
Sherwin-White, S. Ancient Cos.
S. Pembroke, 617(TLS):11Jan80-43
Sherwood, R. Modern Housing Prototypes.
R.A.M. Stern, 45:Jun79-208
Sherzer, D. Structure de la Trilogie de
Beckett.*
H. Charney, 207(FR):Dec78-357
Shewan, R. Oscar Wilde.*
K. Beckson, 651(WHR):Winter79-73
I. Fletcher, 637(VS):Summer79-487
Shi-ming, H. and E. Seifman - see under Hu
Shi-ming and E. Seifman
Shields, C. The Box Garden.*
P. Morley, 102(CanL):Spring79-80
Shih, C-W. The Golden Age of Chinese
Drama.*
R.J. Lynn, 318(JAOS):Oct-Dec78-538
Shih T'ao. Philosophy of Painting. (E.J.
Coleman, trans)
P.K.K. Tong, 290(JAAC):Fall79-102
Shikes, R.E. and P. Harper. Pissarro.
P-L. Adams, 61:Aug80-85
A. Broyard, 441:11Jul80-C26
S. Gardiner, 362:11Dec80-802
J. Russell, 441:20Jul80-7
442(NY):25Aug80-103
Shikibu, M. - see under Murasaki Shikibu
Shimony, A. - see Carnap, R.
Shingarev, A.I. Kak eto bylo.
W.G. Rosenberg, 550(RusR):Jan79-91
Shippey, T.A. "Beowulf."*
J. Turville-Petre, 382(MAE):1979/2-334
Shiraishi, K. Seasons of Sacred Lust.
M. Tane, 42(AR):Summer79-370
Shirendev, B. and M. Sanjdorj, eds. His-
tory of the Mongolian People's Republic.*
(Vol 3)
P. Hyer, 318(JAOS):Jul-Sep78-320
Shirer, W.L. Gandhi.
J. Cameron, 441:20Jan80-10
J. Leonard, 441:7Jan80-C16
Shirley, J. The Gentleman of Venice.
(W.P. Engel, ed)
C.R. Forker, 677(YES):Vol9-332
Shirley, R. Bread of Heaven.
D.M. Day, 157:Winter79-88
Shneiderman, S.L. The River Remembers.
M. Friedberg, 390:May79-72
Shneidman, E. Voices of Death.
C. Lehmann-Haupt, 441:13Feb80-C23
Shoesmith, D.J. and T.J. Smiley. Multiple-
Conclusion Logic.
R.R. Rockingham Gill, 518:Oct79-129
Shone, R. The Century of Change.*
R. Alley, 46:Feb79-124
Shook, R.L. The Entrepreneurs.
J. Stickney, 441:13Apr80-13
Shopsin, W.C. and M.G. Broderick. The
Villard Houses.
P. Goldberger, 441:30Nov80-12

Shore, J. Eye Level.*
D. Smith, 29:Mar/Apr80-40
Shorris, E. Under the Fifth Sun.
J. Charyn, 441:5Oct80-14
Short, A. The Crescent and the Cross.
L. Duguid, 617(TLS):16May80-558
Shostakovich, D. Testimony.* (S. Vol-
kov, ed)
R. Craft, 453(NYRB):24Jan80-9
G. Steiner, 442(NY):24Mar80-129
Shoumatoff, A. The Capital of Hope.
W. Goodman, 441:2Nov80-15
Shoumatoff, A. The Rivers Amazon.
P. Henley, 617(TLS):16May80-564
Shoup, L.H. The Carter Presidency and
Beyond.
A. Wildavsky, 441:27Apr80-12
Showalter, E. A Literature of Their Own.*
V. Colby, 405(MP):Feb80-357
S. Gubar, 637(VS):Autumn78-90
R.P. Hoople, 106:Winter79-325
S. Hudson, 577(SHR):Summer79-258
L. Lerner, 89(BJA):Winter79-88
295(JML):Vol7#4-636
Showalter, E., Jr. - see Graffigny, F.
Shragin, B. and A. Todd, eds. Landmarks.
D. Rogers, 590:Fall/Winter78/79-60
Shukman, A. Literature and Semiotics.
K. Silverman, 567:Vol25#3/4-257
G.S. Smith, 575(SEER):Jan79-117
Shukshin, V. Snowball Berry Red and Other
Stories.
D. Nemec-Ignashev, 558(RLJ):Fall79-252
Shumaker, W. - see Dee, J.
Shuttle, P. The Mirror of the Giant.
A. Motion, 617(TLS):1Feb80-108
Shuttleworth, J.M. - see Lord Cherbury
Sibley, J.R. and P.A. Gunter, eds.
Process Philosophy.
A.H. Johnson, 484(PPR):Jun80-594
Sicard, C. Roger Martin du Gard, Les
années d'apprentissage littéraire (1881-
1910).
A. Daspre, 535(RHL):Jan-Feb78-142
Sicha, J. A Metaphysics of Elementary
Mathematics.
R.S. Edelstein, 316:Dec79-657
Sicherman, B. and C.H. Green, with others,
eds. Notable American Women: The Modern
Period.
G. Wills, 441:21Dec80-3
Siddal, E. Poems and Drawings of Eliza-
beth Siddal. (R.C. Lewis and M.S. Las-
ner, eds)
D. Latham, 627(UTQ):Summer79-415
Siddiqui, M.N. Contemporary Literature
on Islamic Economics.
M. Naimuddin, 273(IC):Jul78-208
Sideras, A. Rufus von Ephesos über die
Nieren- und Blasenleiden.
G.E.R. Lloyd, 123:Vol29No1-191
Sidney, P. The Countess of Pembroke's
Arcadia.* (M. Evans, ed)
K. Duncan-Jones, 447(N&Q):Oct78-461
Siebenborn, E. Die Lehre von der Sprach-
richtigkeit und ihren Kriterien.
F. Lasserre, 182:Vol31#7/8-246

Sieber, H. Language and Society in "La
Vida de Lazarillo de Tormes."
R. Moore, 268(IFR):Summer80-152
J.V. Ricapito, 594:Winter79-499
Sieber, H. The Picaresque.*
P-G. Boucé, 189(EA):Apr-Jun78-220
Siebers, G. Zeitalter im Rausch.
E. Baruffol, 182:Vol31#7/8-202
Sieburth, R. Instigations.*
W. Harmon, 569(SR):Spring79-xxxiv
H.N. Schneidau, 27(AL):Nov79-435
Sieck, A. Kleists Penthesilea.*
D. Brüggemann, 680(ZDP):Band97Heft2-
296
Siedschlag, E. Zur Form von Martials
Epigrammen.
J.P. Sullivan, 487:Autumn79-285
Sieff, C. and J-L. La photographie.
J. Arrouye, 98:Jan78-72
Siefken, H. Kafka, Ungeduld und Lässig-
keit.*
J. Born, 72:Band216Heft1-157
Siegel, M.B. Images of American Dance.
L. Pisk, 157:Summer79-80
Siegel, M.R. Pynchon.*
S. Brivic, 295(JML):Vol7#4-800
K. Tololyan, 594:Summer79-224
Siegfried, C.H. Chaos and Contest.
W.J. Gavin, 258:Sep79-373
Siegman, A.W. and S. Feldstein, eds. Non-
verbal Behavior and Communication.
M.R. Key, 350:Sep79-732
Siegmeister, E., ed. The Music Lover's
Handbook.
C. Wintle, 617(TLS):9May80-538
Siepe, H.T. Der Leser des Surrealismus.
Y. Belaval, 182:Vol31#1/2-42
Sieveking, A. The Cave Artists.
N. Hammond, 617(TLS):8Feb80-147
Sigal, C. Zone of the Interior.
P. Sedgwick, 560:Spring-Summer79-217
Siggins, M. Bassett.
T. McCormack, 99:Dec80/Jan81-30
Signoret, S. Nostalgia Isn't What It Used
To Be.*
B. Weeks, 18:Oct78-76
Sih, P.K.T., ed. Nationalist China during
the Sino-Japanese War, 1937-1945.
R.H. Yang, 396(ModA):Winter79-108
Sihanouk, N. War and Hope.
M. Field, 453(NYRB):23Oct80-17
H. Kamm, 441:13Jul80-3
442(NY):1Sep80-91
Sijpesteijn, P.J. and K.A. Worp. Fünfund-
dreissig Wiener Papyri.
R. Coles, 123:Vol29No1-189
Sikelianos, A. Selected Poems.
P. Green, 453(NYRB):26Jun80-40
Sikes, H.M., with W.H. Bonner and G. Lahey -
see Hazlitt, W.
Silber, J. Household Words.
S. Isaacs, 441:3Feb80-14
442(NY):24Mar80-132
Silby, J., A. Bogue and W. Flanigan, eds.
The History of American Electoral Behav-
ior.
J.A. Laponce, 106:Winter79-335

345

Silin, V.L. Leksičeskij ėllips v german-
skich jazykach.
  G. Frohne, 682(ZPSK):Band31Heft6-623
Silk, L. and M. The American Establish-
ment.
  J. Fallows, 441:14Sep80-9
  J. Leonard, 441:15Sep80-C21
  442(NY):6Oct80-196
Silkin, J. Flower Poems. Into Praising.
  J. Cassidy, 493:Jul79-66
Silkin, J. Out of Battle.
  A. Thomson, 179(ES):Jun79-324
Silkin, J., ed. The Penguin Book of First
World War Poetry.
  A. Ross, 364:Aug/Sep79-7
Silkin, J. The Psalms and Their Spoils.
  J. Campbell, 617(TLS):4Jul80-762
Sillitoe, A. The Storyteller.*
  A. Brownjohn, 617(TLS):4Jan80-9
  M. Cantwell, 441:28Sep80-9
  442(NY):22Sep80-157
Sillitoe, A. The Widower's Son.*
  639(VQR):Summer78-94
Silman, R. Boundaries.*
  F. Tuohy, 617(TLS):21Mar80-326
Silva, E. Dell'arte de' giardini inglesi.
  (G. Venturi, ed)
  E.B., 228(GSLI):Vol155fasc490-314
Silva, J.A. Intimidades. (H.H. Orjuela,
  ed)
  B. Gicovate, 238:May-Sep79-411
de Silva, K.M., ed. Sri Lanka.
  T. Fernando, 293(JASt):Feb79-417
da Silva Lima, J. O Folclore em Sergipe.
  (Vol 1)
  S.G. Armistead and J.H. Silverman,
  240(HR):Autumn78-509
Silver, A. and E. Ward, eds. Film Noir.
  L. Halliwell, 617(TLS):8Aug80-900
Silver, I. and R. Lebègue - see de Ronsard,
  P.
Silver, P.W. Ortega as Phenomenologist.
  N.R. Orringer, 546(RR):Nov79-407
Silverberg, R. Lord Valentine's Castle.
  J. Sullivan, 441:3Aug80-12
Silverstein, J. Burma.
  J.F. Guyot, 293(JASt):Nov78-208
Silvestroni, S. Enrico Pea.
  E.F., 228(GSLI):Vol155fasc490-318
Simco, N.D. and G.G. James. Elementary
Logic.
  R. Butrick, 316:Mar79-125
Šimečka, M. Le Rétablissement de l'ordre.
  L.K., 450(NRF):Dec79-133
Simenon, G. Maigret at the Coroner's.
  A. Broyard, 441:12Dec80-C33
  442(NY):15Dec80-174
Simenon, G. Maigret's Pipe.*
  639(VQR):Spring79-59
Simenon, G. Maigret's Rival.
  442(NY):19May80-164
Simenon, G. The Nightclub.*
  442(NY):7Jan80-85
Simenon, G. The White Horse Inn.
  442(NY):28Jul80-100
Simeon, R., ed. Must Canada Fail?
  K. McRoberts, 529(QQ):Spring79-143

Simic, C. Charon's Cosmology.*
  R. Jackson, 659(ConL):Winter80-136
Simic, C. Classic Ballroom Dances.
  C. Molesworth, 441:12Oct80-14
Simmonds, J.D. - see "Milton Studies"
Simmons, C. Wrinkles.*
  P. Bailey, 617(TLS):25Jan80-78
  D. Flower, 249(HudR):Summer79-306
  J. Mellors, 362:20Mar80-382
  N. Miller, 42(AR):Spring79-243
Simmons, J. The Selected James Simmons.*
  (E. Longley, ed)
  T. Eagleton, 565:Vol20#1-74
Simmons, J. A Selective Guide to England.
  A. Clifton-Taylor, 46:Jul79-66
Simmons, J.L. Shakespeare's Pagan World.
  I. Schabert, 38:Band96Heft3/4-515
Simmons, M.E. Folklore Bibliography for
  1973.* Folklore Bibliography for 1974.*
  J.H. Brunvand, 650(WF):Jan79-66
Simmons, M.E. Santiago F. Puglia.*
  M.J. Doudoroff, 238:Mar79-185
Simmons, P. My Secret Cookbook.
  W. and C. Cowen, 639(VQR):Autumn79-156
Simmonds, R.C. The American Colonies from
Settlement to Independence.
  J.M. Bumsted, 656(WMQ):Apr79-310
Simon, A. Le Théâtre à bout de souffle?
  J. Guérin, 450(NRF):Apr79-141
Simon, B. Mind and Madness in Ancient
Greece.*
  B. Knox, 124:Nov79-187
Simon, C. Triptych.
  P. Lewis, 565:Vol20#1-49
Simon, E. Neidhart von Reuental.
  D. Blamires, 402(MLR):Jul79-737
Simon, G., ed. Bibliographie zur Soziolin-
guistik.
  W. König, 685(ZDL):2/1979-260
Simon, H.A. Models of Discovery, and
Other Topics in the Methods of Science.*
  L.J. Cohen, 84:Sep79-293
Simon, H.A. Models of Thought.
  D. Michie, 617(TLS):22Aug80-942
Simon, I. - see Barrow, I., R. South and
J. Tillotson
Simon, J. Paradigms Lost.
  A. Burgess, 441:20Jul80-3
  J. Leonard, 441:4Aug80-C22
Simon, J. Wahrheit als Freiheit.
  S.R., 543:Mar79-568
Simon, J.F. Independent Journey.
  A.M. Dershowitz, 441:2Nov80-9
Simon, R., ed. Henri de Boulainviller:
Oeuvres philosophiques.
  J.S. Spink, 208(FS):Vol33Pt2-721
Simon, R.L. Peking Duck.*
  M. Laski, 362:17Apr80-514
Simon, T. Jupiter's Travels.
  R.A. Sokolov, 441:20Apr80-16
Simon-Schaefer, B-O. Die Romane Henry de
Montherlants.
  D. Parmée, 208(FS):Vol33Pt2-898
Simón Díaz, J. Dominicos de los siglos
XVI y XVII.
  J.A. Jones, 86(BHS):Jul79-274

Simone, R. and U. Vignuzzi, eds. Problemi della ricostruzione in linguistica.
P.J. Regier, 350:Mar79-251

Simonelli, M. Materiali per un'edizione critica del "Convivio" di Dante.
C. Kleinhenz, 545(RPh):Aug78-128

Simonetta, B. The Coins of the Cappadocian Kings.
C. Rodewald, 123:Vol29No2-340

Simonis, F. Nachsurrealistische Lyrik im zeitgenössischen Frankreich.
R. Cardinal, 208(FS):Vol33Pt2-936
T.M. Scheerer, 430(NS):Feb78-87

Simonsuuri, K. Homer's Original Genius.
W.C. Scott, 124:Mar80-364
P.W., 148:Autumn79-89

Simple, P. The Stretchford Chronicles.
D.A.N. Jones, 362:20Nov80-695

Simpson, A. and M.M. - see Carlyle, J.W.

Simpson, D. Dark Companions.
A.H.M. Kirk-Greene, 69:Vol48#2-191

Simpson, D. C.F.A. Voysey.
J. Heseltine, 617(TLS):5Sep80-974

Simpson, G.G. Splendid Isolation.
D. Snow, 617(TLS):1Aug80-870
R.A. Sokolov, 441:23Mar80-16

Simpson, L. Caviare at the Funeral.
P. Breslin, 441:2Nov80-12

Simpson, L. A Revolution in Taste.
V. Bell, 569(SR):Spring79-308

Simpson, L. Studies of Dylan Thomas, Allen Ginsberg, Sylvia Plath and Robert Lowell.
T. Paulin, 617(TLS):4Jan80-3

Simpson, M.A. and T.H. Lloyd, eds. Middle Class Housing in Britain.
N. Kunze, 637(VS):Summer78-515

Simpson, M.R. The Novels of Hermann Broch.
E.W. Herd, 67:May79-156

Sinany, H., comp. Bibliographie des oeuvres de Alexis Remizov.
R.S. Bialy, 574(SEEJ):Winter79-531
D.M. Fiene, 399(MLJ):Apr79-213

Sinclair, A., ed. The Facts in the Case of E.A. Poe.*
J. Symons, 441:12Oct80-15

Sinclair, A. Jack.*
R. Forrey, 395(MFS):Winter78/79-636

Sinclair, A. John Ford.*
W.K. Everson, 18:May79-70

Sinclair, A. Valle-Inclán's "Ruedo Ibérico."*
J. Alberich, 86(BHS):Apr79-159

Sinclair, C. Hearts of Gold.*
J. Mellors, 362:28Feb80-286

Sinclair, J.L. In Time of Harvest.
W. Gard, 584(SWR):Spring79-vi

Sinclair, J.M. and R.M. Coulthard. Toward an Analysis of Discourse.*
D. Götz, 430(NS):Jul78-379
J. Hinds, 603:Vol13#1-129

Sinclair, K. Walter Nash.
S. Newman, 368:Sep77-283

Sinclair, K.V. Prières en ancien français.
G.M. Cropp, 67:Nov79-334

Sinclair-Stevenson, C. Blood Royal.*
C. Seebohm, 441:20Jan80-18

Singelenberg, P. and M. Bock. H.P. Berlage, bouwmeester: 1856-1934.
H. Searing, 576:Dec78-305

Singer, B. The Petting Zoo.
M. Malone, 441:20Jan80-15

Singer, B. Selected Poems. (A. Cluysenaar, ed)
D. Graham, 565:Vol20#1-65

Singer, I. Mozart and Beethoven.
C. Ford, 89(BJA):Spring79-185

Singer, I.B. La Corne du bélier.
P. Giniewski, 450(NRF):Dec79-123

Singer, I.B. La Couronne de plumes.
P. Giniewski, 450(NRF):Jan79-136

Singer, I.B. The Family Moskat.
P. Binding, 617(TLS):11Apr80-408

Singer, I.B. Old Love.*
P. Binding, 617(TLS):11Apr80-408
J. Mellors, 362:10Jul80-56

Singer, I.B. Reaches of Heaven.
442(NY):10Nov80-221

Singer, I.B. Shosha.*
J. Greenfield, 390:Jan79-45

Singer, I.B. A Young Man in Search of Love.
639(VQR):Winter79-16

Singer, P. Animal Liberation.*
C. Mouchard, 98:Aug-Sep78-817
A. Townsend, 63:Mar79-85

Singer, P. Marx.
C.H. Sisson, 617(TLS):9May80-531

Singer, P. Practical Ethics.
H.L.A. Hart, 453(NYRB):15May80-25

Singh, H., ed. Perspectives on Guru Nanak.*
B.G. Gokhale, 318(JAOS):Oct-Dec78-565

Singh, V.P. Caste, Class and Democracy.
E. Friedlander, 293(JASt):Feb79-405

Singleton, C.S. - see Dante Alighieri

Singleton, F. Twentieth-Century Yugoslavia.
T.A. Meininger, 104(CASS):Summer78-315

Sinicyn, E.P. Ban'Gu - istorik drevnego Kitaja.
T. Pokora, 318(JAOS):Oct-Dec78-451

Sinyavsky, A. - see under Tertz, A.

Siotis, D. and J. Chioles, eds. Twenty Contemporary Greek Poets.
P. Green, 453(NYRB):26Jun80-40

Sipala, P.M. Scienza e Storia nella Letteratura verista.
J-P. de Nola, 549(RLC):Jan-Mar77-107

Sirica, J.J. To Set the Record Straight.*
C. Wheeler, 617(TLS):11Apr80-405

Sirisena, W.M. Sri Lanka and South-East Asia.
C.F. Keyes, 293(JASt):Aug79-837

Sismondi, G.C.L. Epistolario. (Vol 5) (N. King and R. de Luppé, eds)
É. Harpaz, 535(RHL):Mar-Apr78-314

Sissman, L.E. Hello, Darkness.* (P. Davison, ed) Innocent Bystander.
X.J. Kennedy, 472:Fall/Winter79-48

Sisson, C.H. Anchises.
C. Bedient, 569(SR):Spring79-296

Sisson, C.H. The Avoidance of Literature.*
(M. Schmidt, ed)
J. Pilling, 148:Winter79-86
Sisson, C.H. Exactions.
D. Davis, 362:5Jun80-729
J. Mole, 617(TLS):18Jul80-822
Sitta, H. and H.J. Tymister, eds. Lin-
guistik und Unterricht.
M.H. Folsom, 221(GQ):Jan79-101
Sivachev, N.V. and N.N. Yakovlev. Russia
and the United States.*
639(VQR):Autumn79-144
Sivin, N., ed. Science and Technology in
East Asia.
S.J. Bennett, 485(PE&W):Oct79-512
Sizer, S.S. Gospel Hymns and Social
Religion.
J. Potter, 617(TLS):25Jan80-93
639(VQR):Autumn79-151
Sizova, I.A. Stanovlenie germanskogo
glagol'nogo slovoobrazovanija.
B. Comrie, 350:Dec79-959
Sjöberg, S. En furstlig svindel.
L.B. Sather, 563(SS):Summer79-295
Sjöstrand, W. and S. Nordström - see
Comenius, J.A.
Sjövall, B. Det problematiska jaget.
J.F. Battail, 542:Jan-Mar78-114
Skachkov, P.E. Ocherki istorii russkogo
kitaevedenia.
N. Chou, 293(JASt):Aug79-775
Skarga, B. Kłopoty intelektu.
I. Dąmbska, 542:Apr-Jun78-201
Skármeta, A., ed. Joven narrativa chilena
después del golpe.*
205(FMLS):Jan78-90
Sked, A. The Survival of the Habsburg
Empire.
N. Stone, 617(TLS):1Aug80-871
Skelley, A.R. The Victorian Army at Home.
A. Tucker, 637(VS):Autumn78-100
Skellings, E. Heart Attacks. Face Value.
Showing My Age.
D.L. Kaufmann, 418(MR):Spring79-164
Skelton, R. Callsigns.
D. Barbour, 150(DR):Spring79-154
Skelton, R. Landmarks.
A. Stevenson, 617(TLS):23May80-586
Skelton, R. The Poet's Calling.*
C. Guillot, 189(EA):Jan-Mar78-97
Skene Catling, P. Jazz Jazz Jazz.
V. Scannell, 617(TLS):29Feb80-246
Skiklai, L. Zur Geschichte der Marxismus
und der Kunst.
P. Somville, 542:Oct-Dec79-471
Skilling, H.G. Czechoslovakia's Inter-
rupted Revolution.
H. Hanak, 575(SEER):Jan79-137
Skinner, G.W. and A.T. Kirsch, eds.
Change and Persistence in Thai Society.
F.E. Reynolds, 318(JAOS):Oct-Dec78-567
Skinner, Q. The Foundations of Modern
Political Thought.* (Vols 1 and 2)
D.R. Kelley, 322(JHI):Oct-Dec79-663
B. Kuklick, 256:Spring79-177

Skoczylas-Stawska, H. Fonetyka w gwarach
dawnej ziemi wieluńskiej.
A. Timberlake, 350:Mar79-254
Skorupski, J. Symbol and Theory.*
M.H. Levine, 613:Dec79-424
Skousen, R. Substantive Evidence in
Phonology.*
E.W. Roberts, 353:Jan78-77
Skrine, P. The Baroque Literature and
Culture in Seventeenth-Century Europe.
E. Lunding, 301(JEGP):Jul79-385
Skrjabina, E. After Leningrad. (N. Luxen-
burg, ed and trans)
J.S. Roucek, 550(RusR):Jul79-375
Skrypnyk, L.H. - see Levchenko, S.P., L.H.
Skrypnyk and N.P. Dziatkivs'ka
Skrzynecki, P. The Aviary.
C. Pollnitz, 581:Dec79-462
Skulsky, H. Spirits Finely Touched.*
K. Muir, 677(YES):Vol9-311
R. Soellner, 405(MP):Aug79-86
J.H. Summers, 570(SQ):Winter79-103
Skupinska-Løvset, I. The Ustinov Collec-
tion: The Palestinian Pottery.
T.L. Thompson, 318(JAOS):Jul-Sep78-344
Škvorecký, J. All the Bright Young Men
and Women.
A. French, 586(SoRA):Mar78-94
Sky, A. and M. Stone. Unbuilt America.*
P. Blake, 576:Mar78-41
Skyrme, R. Rubén Darío and the Pythago-
rean Tradition.*
A. Cioranescu, 549(RLC):Jan-Mar77-120
H. Rogmann, 52:Band13Heft1-101
Slabbert, F.V. and D. Welsh - see under
van Zyl Slabbert, F. and D. Welsh
Slack, A. and others. French for Communi-
cation: One and Two.
E.A. Fong, 399(MLJ):Sep-Oct79-308
Sladek, A. Wortfelder in Verbänden.*
(Pts 1 and 2)
S. Ettinger, 685(ZDL):2/1979-262
Slaski, J., ed. Barocco fra Italia e
Polonia.*
K.Z., 228(GSLI):Vol155fasc490-314
Slater, M. Humour in the Works of Proust.
J-Y. Tadié, 617(TLS):7Mar80-271
Slater, P. Wealth Addiction.
R. Lamb, 441:23Mar80-12
C. Lehmann-Haupt, 441:14Mar80-C23
61:May80-102
Slater, S. and A. Solomita. Exits.
C. Lehmann-Haupt, 441:18Jan80-C21
"Slavica Hierosolymitana." (Vol 1) (L.
Fleishman, O. Ronen and D. Segal, eds)
H. Gamburg, 574(SEEJ):Winter79-542
B. Lewis and M. Ulman, 67:May79-74
G.Y. Shevelov, 550(RusR):Apr79-266
"Slavica Hierosolymitana." (Vol 2) (V.
Raskin and D. Segal, eds)
G.Y. Shevelov, 550(RusR):Apr79-266
Slavíčková, E. Retrográdní morfematický
slovník češtiny s připojenými invent-
árními slovníky českých morfémů kořeno-
vých, prefixálních a sufixálních.
D. Armstrong, 353:Mar78-86

348

Slavitt, D. Rounding the Horn.
  W.H. Pritchard, 249(HudR):Summer79-256
  P. Ramsey, 569(SR):Fall79-686
  P. Stitt, 491:Jan80-229
  639(VQR):Autumn79-148
Slive, S. Frans Hals.
  B.P.J. Broos, 600:Vol10#2-115
Sloan, B. The Best Friend You'll Ever
  Have.
  P-L. Adams, 61:May80-103
Sloan, S. The Model Architect.
  C.W. Moore, 576:Mar78-50
Sloane, D.E.E. Mark Twain as a Literary
  Comedian.*
  M.J. Fertig, 26(ALR):Autumn79-346
Slobodin, R. W.H.R. Rivers.
  639(VQR):Spring79-69
Sloman, A. The Computer Revolution in
  Philosophy.
  D.M. MacKay, 84:Sep79-302
Slonimsky, N., ed. Baker's Biographical
  Dictionary of Musicians. (6th ed)
  L. Salter, 415:Oct79-825
Slotkin, R. and J.K. Folsom, eds. So
  Dreadfull a Judgment.*
  M.J. Westerkamp, 432(NEQ):Dec79-588
Slotta, R. Romanische Architektur im
  lothringischen Département Meurthe-et-
  Moselle.
  H.E. Kubach, 683:Band41Heft3/4-323
Slotznick, M. Industrial Stuff.
  D. Smith, 29:Mar/Apr80-40
"Slovar' russkogo jazyka XI-XVII vv."
  (Vols 1, 2 and 5) (S.G. Barxudarov and
  others, eds)
  E. Klenin, 574(SEEJ):Winter79-549
"Slovar' russkogo jazyka XI-XVII vv."
  (Vols 3 and 4) (S.G. Barxudarov and
  others, eds)
  E. Klenin, 574(SEEJ):Winter79-549
  H.G. Lunt, 350:Dec79-920
Smaby, R.M. Paraphrase Grammars.
  G.F. Meier, 682(ZPSK):Band31Heft6-648
Smakov, G. - see Makarova, N.
Small, I., ed. The Aesthetes.
  J.L. Guthrie, 290(JAAC):Spring80-329
  P. Keating, 617(TLS):11Jan80-34
Smallwood, E.M. The Jews under Roman
  Rule.*
  T. Rajak, 313:Vol69-192
Smart, A. The Dawn of Italian Painting
  1250-1400.*
  G. Turner, 135:Feb79-139
Smart, E. The Assumption of the Rogues
  and Rascals.
  J. Mallinson, 168(ECW):Fall78-134
  M.B. Oliver, 198:Summer80-127
Smart, E. A Bonus.
  J. Mallinson, 168(ECW):Fall78-134
Smetana, C.L. - see Capgrave, J.
Smidt, D. The Seized Collections of the
  Papua New Guinea Museum.
  A.L. Kaeppler, 2(AfrA):Aug79-87
Smidt, K. The Importance of Recognition.
  C. Pagnoulle, 556(RLV):1978/5-458
Smiley, J. Barn Blind.
  M. Malone, 441:17Aug80-10

Smith, A., ed. The Art of Emily Brontë.*
  T.J. Winnifrith, 677(YES):Vol9-366
Smith, A., ed. The Art of Malcolm Lowry.
  R. Chapman, 268(IFR):Winter80-64
  H. Dahlie, 49:Jul79-114
  W.M. Hagen, 594:Spring79-121
  J.A. Wainwright, 150(DR):Winter79/80-
  761
Smith, A. The Correspondence of Adam
  Smith. (E.C. Mossner and I.S. Ross, eds)
  A. Reix, 542:Apr-Jun79-235
  M.A. Stewart, 479(PhQ):Jul79-267
Smith, A. The Geopolitics of Information.
  R. Manning, 441:7Dec80-15
Smith, A. Goodbye Gutenberg.
  S. Jacobson, 362:28Aug80-278
Smith, A. An Inquiry into Nature and
  Causes of the Wealth of Nations. (R.H.
  Campbell, A.S. Kinner and V.B. Todd, eds)
  A. Reix, 542:Apr-Jun79-235
Smith, A., ed. Lawrence and Women.*
  K.M. Hewitt, 541(RES):May79-232
Smith, A. Porphyry's Place in the Neopla-
  tonic Tradition.*
  L.G. Westerink, 394:Vol32fasc3/4-418
Smith, A.B. Théophile Gautier and the
  Fantastic.*
  R. Chambers, 208(FS):Vol33Pt2-826
  R. Merker, 207(FR):Oct78-167
  205(FMLS):Apr78-190
Smith, A.J.M. The Classic Shade.*
  R. Daniells, 102(CanL):Winter78-74
  S.G. Mullins, 628(UWR):Fall-Winter78-
  71
Smith, A.K. and C. Weiner - see Oppen-
  heimer, J.R.
Smith, B.H. On the Margins of Discourse.
  M.C. Beardsley, 569(SR):Fall79-639
  T. Hawkes, 676(YR):Summer80-560
  M. Pratt, 290(JAAC):Winter79-205
  L. Surette, 255(HAB):Summer79-197
Smith, B.L., ed. Hinduism.*
  W.D. O'Flaherty, 318(JAOS):Jul-Sep78-
  325
Smith, B.L., ed. Religion and Social Con-
  flict in South Asia.*
  R.M. Smith, 318(JAOS):Jul-Sep78-333
Smith, C. Fifty Years with Mountbatten.
  A. Boyle, 362:28Aug80-275
Smith, C.D. The Early Career of Lord
  North, the Prime Minister.
  J. Cannon, 617(TLS):22Feb80-216
Smith, C.N. - see de la Taille, J.
Smith, C.V.M. The Problem of Life.
  A. Quick, 84:Jun79-199
Smith, D. Cumberland Station.*
  B. Galvin, 134(CP):Spring78-90
Smith, D. Glitter and Ash.
  A. Broyard, 441:21Mar80-C24
  M. Levin, 441:6Jul80-9
Smith, D. Goshawk, Antelope.
  H. Vendler, 442(NY):30Jun80-96
Smith, D. The Hard Rain.
  R. Freedman, 441:26Oct80-22

Smith, E. The Irish Journals of Elizabeth Smith 1840-1850. (D. Thomson and M. McGusty, eds)
P. Beer, 362:24Apr80-541
J. Johnston, 617(TLS):16May80-557

Smith, E.B. Francis Preston Blair.
K.S. Lynn, 441:27Apr80-12

Smith, G. The Casino of Pius IV.*
L.W. Partridge, 54:Jun78-369

Smith, G.B. The Soviet Procuracy and the Supervision of Administration.
J.N. Hazard, 550(RusR):Oct79-489

Smith, G.E.K. A Pictorial History of Architecture in America.*
C. Robinson, 576:Mar78-40
S. Woodbridge, 505:Sep78-142

Smith, H. Forgotten Truth.
K. Siegel, 482(PhR):Apr79-314

Smith, H.F. - see Irving, W.

Smith, H.N. Democracy and the Novel.*
N. Baym, 301(JEGP):Apr79-282
E.H. Davidson, 27(AL):May79-277
L.B. Holland, 676(YR):Winter80-279
R.S. Levine, 432(NEQ):Jun79-268
J.H. McIntosh, 165(EAL):Winter79/80-340
T. Martin, 141:Fall79-381
A. Turner, 579(SAQ):Autumn79-530

Smith, H.R.W. Funerary Symbolism in Apulian Vase-Painting.
B.A. Sparkes, 123:Vol29No2-336

Smith, I.C. In the Middle.*
D. Graham, 565:Vol20#1-65

Smith, J. The Arts Betrayed.
A. Fitzlyon, 364:Apr/May79-133
R.D. Stock, 396(ModA):Summer79-333

Smith, J. In Flight.
J. Naughton, 362:11Dec80-804

Smith, J. Shakespearian and Other Essays.*
R. Fraser, 570(SQ):Summer79-437

Smith, J.A. John Buchan and His World.
442(NY):7Jan80-86

Smith, J.A.C. Medieval Law Teachers and Writers, Civilian and Canonist.
P. Weimar, 589:Jul79-560

Smith, J.B. Munch.
J.P. Hodin, 90:Oct79-661

Smith, J.C. Legal Obligation.*
M. Hanen, 154:Jun78-371

Smith, J.C.S. Jacoby's First Case.
E. Hunter, 441:20Jul80-12

Smith, J.E. Purpose and Thought.
W.J. Gavin, 258:Dec79-473
R.J. Roth, 613:Dec79-438
483:Jan79-139

Smith, J.E.S. - see under Sharwood Smith, J.E.

Smith, K. Tristan Crazy.
D. Graham, 565:Vol20#2-75
L. Sail, 493:Mar80-71

Smith, K.N. The Watcher.
N. Callendar, 441:20Apr80-25

Smith, L. The Winner Names the Age. (M. Cliff, ed)
R. Gladney, 585(SoQ):Winter79-139

Smith, M. The Delphinium Girl.
J. Casey, 441:25May80-11
442(NY):21Apr80-142

Smith, M. An Early Mystic of Baghdad.
S. Vahiduddin, 273(IC):Jul78-202

Smith, M. Hope and History.
J.M. Cameron, 453(NYRB):17Apr80-36

Smith, M. Jesus the Magician.
D. Fraikin, 529(QQ):Winter79/80-691

Smith, M. Prudentius' "Psychomachia."*
G. Costa, 545(RPh):Aug78-138

Smith, M. The Way of the Mystics.
J.A. Subhan, 273(IC):Oct76-243

Smith, M. - see de Ronsard, P.

Smith, M.C. Nightwing.
639:Spring78-65

Smith, M.E. "Love Kindling Fire."
H.A. Hargreaves, 178:Winter79-489

Smith, M.H. The Writs of Assistance Case.
G.W. Gawalt, 656(WMQ):Apr79-313
R.B. Morris, 432(NEQ):Jun79-290

Smith, N.A., with H.M. Adams and D. Pepys Whiteley, comps. Catalogue of the Pepys Library at Magdalene College Cambridge. (Vol 1)
D. McKitterick, 78(BC):Winter79-489

Smith, N.B. Figures of Repetition in the Old Provençal Lyric.*
J.H. Marshall, 208(FS):Vol33Pt2-516

Smith, O.L. Scholia graeca in Aeschylum quae extant omnia. (Pt 1)
J. Vaio, 123:Vol29No2-307

Smith, O.L., ed. Scholia metrica anonyma in Euripidis Hecubam, Orestem, Phoenissas.
G.P. Ancher, 555:Vol52fasc2-367
C. Collard, 303(JoHS):Vol199-175

Smith, P. Vicente Blasco Ibáñez.
A.H. Clarke, 86(BHS):Jan79-75

Smith, P. Houses of the Welsh Countryside.
D. Upton, 576:May78-116

Smith, P. Le récit populaire au Rwanda.
N. Barley, 69:Vol48#1-96

Smith, P. The Shaping of America. (Vol 3)
E. Foner, 441:27Apr18-13

Smith, P.C., ed. Les Enchantemenz de Bretaigne.*
M.T. Bruckner, 207(FR):Mar79-635
B. Woledge, 402(MLR):Apr79-450

Smith, R. Le Meurtrier et la vision tragique.*
A. Vandegans, 535(RHL):Jan-Feb78-152

Smith, R.E.F. Peasant Farming in Muscovy.*
639(VQR):Winter78-9

Smith, R.G. The Message Measurement Inventory.
R. Hopper, 583:Fall78-108

Smith, R.J. Ancestor Worship in Contemporary Japan.
H.B. Earhart, 318(JAOS):Jul-Sep78-293

Smith, R.J. Kurusu.*
E. Norbeck, 293(JASt):Feb79-380

Smith, R.L. - see Debussy, C.

Smith, S. The Holiday.*
M.S., 148:Autumn79-92

Smith, S.   Over the Frontier.
   V. Glendinning, 617(TLS):18Jan80-54
Smith, S.   Selected Poems.
   A. Cluysenaar, 565:Vol20#3-68
Smith, S.B.   Meaning and Negation.*
   G. Harman, 353:Mar78-89
Smith, S.S. and H. Hayford - see Emerson,
   R.W.
Smith, T.   The French Stake in Algeria,
   1945-1962.
   639(VQR):Summer79-87
Smith, W.   Cry Wolf.
   639(VQR):Winter78-24
Smith, W.   Hungry as the Sea.
   N. Callendar, 441:24Feb80-30
Smith, W.D.   The German Colonial Empire.
   639(VQR):Summer79-88
Smith, W.D.   The Hippocratic Tradition.
   J. Scarborough, 124:Mar80-366
Smith, W.D.   Shakespeare's Playhouse
   Practice.*
   B. Beckerman, 677(YES):Vol9-320
Smith, W.I.   Archives in New Zealand.
   M. Pamplin, 325:Oct79-242
Smith, W.J.   Army Brat.
   P. Zweig, 441:16Nov80-9
   453(NYRB):20Nov80-51
Smith, W.J.   The Behavior of Communicating.
   J. Sherzer, 355(LSoc):Dec78-435
Smith, Z.N. and P. Zekman.   The Mirage.
   442(NY):21Apr80-148
Smither, E.   Here Come the Clouds.
   E. Caffin, 368:Jun76-124
Smither, H.E.   A History of the Oratorio.
   (Vol 1)
   W. Dean, 410(M&L):Jul79-341
   M.H. Frank, 568(SCN):Spring-Summer79-
   37
   S. Hansell, 317:Summer79-343
   E.T. Harris, 414(MusQ):Jul78-397
Smither, H.E.   A History of the Oratorio.
   (Vol 2)
   H.E. Baker, 414(MusQ):Jan79-128
   W. Dean, 410(M&L):Jul79-341
   M.H. Frank, 568(SCN):Spring-Summer79-
   37
   S. Hansell, 317:Summer79-343
Smither, R.B.N. and D.J. Penn.   Imperial
   War Museum Film Cataloging Rules.
   J.W. Lange, 14:Jan79-71
Smithson, R.   The Writings of Robert Smith-
   son.   (N. Holt, ed)
   D. Carrier, 290(JAAC):Spring80-330
Smithyman, K.   The Seal in the Dolphin
   Pool.
   P. Crisp, 368:Dec74-363
Smits van Waesberghe, J., ed.   De numero
   tonorum litterae episcopi A. ad coepis-
   copum E. missae ac Commentum super tonos
   episcopi E. (ad 1000).
   C.M. Atkinson, 589:Jul79-564
Smits van Waesberghe, J. - see Guido of
   Arezzo
Smits van Waesberghe, J. - see Heinrich of
   Augsburg
Smoodin, R.   Ursus Major.
   B. Yourgrau, 441:11May80-15

Smoot, J.J.   The Poets and Time.
   R. Allen, 399(MLJ):Sep-Oct79-312
Smullyan, R.   The Chess Mysteries of
   Sherlock Holmes.
   P. Jay, 617(TLS):29Feb80-224
Smullyan, R.M.   This Book Needs No Title.
   D. Hofstadter, 441:10Aug80-12
Smullyan, R.M.   What is the Name of this
   Book?
   G. Boolos, 482(PhR):Jul79-496
"Smyslovoe vosprijatie rečevogo soob-
   ščenija (v uslovijach massovoj kommuni-
   kacii)."
   K. Meng, 682(ZPSK):Band31Heft2-215
Smyth, A.P.   Scandinavian Kings in the
   British Isles, 850-880.
   H.R. Loyn, 562(Scan):Nov79-153
   J.L. Nelson, 325:Oct79-230
Snape, C.   The Churching.*
   I. Colegate, 617(TLS):11Jan80-46
Snell, B., ed.   Frühgriechische Lyriker.
   (Pt 3) (Z. Franyó, trans)
   J. Péron, 555:Vol52fasc1-152
Snell, B. and H. Erbse, eds.   Lexicon des
   frühgriechischen Epos.*   (Pt 8)
   P. Monteil, 555:Vol52fasc2-348
Snellgrove, D. and T. Skorupski.   The Cul-
   tural Hertiage of Ladakh.   (Vol 1)
   J. Lowry, 463:Summer78-217
Snetsinger, J.   Truman, the Jewish Vote
   and the Creation of Israel.
   H.P. Luks, 287:Jun/Jul78-27
Snodgrass, W.D.   The Führer Bunker.*   In
   Radical Pursuit.
   R. Asselineau, 189(EA):Jul-Dec78-423
Snodgrass, W.D.   Six Troubadour Songs.*
   639(VQR):Spring78-58
Snodgrass, W.D.   Traditional Hungarian
   Songs.
   J. Cotton, 503:Winter78-194
Snorri Sturluson.   Snorre Sturlasson,
   "Edda," II.   (A. Grape, G. Kallstenius
   and O. Thorell, eds)
   J. Lindow, 589:Jul79-632
Snow, C.E. and C.A. Ferguson, eds.   Talk-
   ing to Children.
   C.B. Farwell, 350:Jun79-449
Snow, C.P.   A Coat of Varnish.*
   R. Davies, 453(NYRB):21Feb80-31
   61:Jan80-87
Snow, C.P.   The Realists.
   W. Bedford, 364:Aug/Sep79-133
   I. Robinson, 396(ModA):Summer79-320
Snow, C.P.   Trollope.*
   W.M. Kendrick, 637(VS):Spring78-417
Snow, R.J.   The 1613 Print of Juan
   Esquivel Barahona.
   I. Fenlon, 415:Nov79-917
Lord Snowdon.   Personal View.
   J. Naughton, 362:3Jan80-29
Snyder, E. and A. Valdman, eds.   Identité
   culturelle et francophonie dans les
   Amériques.   (Vol 1)
   A. Hull, 207(FR):Oct78-200
Snyder, G.   He Who Hunted Birds in His
   Father's Village.
   J. Campbell, 617(TLS):30May80-620

351

Soames, M. Clementine Churchill.*
  A. Bell, 617(TLS):4Jan80-15
  R. Dinnage, 453(NYRB):6Mar80-36
Sobejano, G. and others. Juan Goytisolo.
  J.S. Bernstein, 240(HR):Spring78-275
Sobel, R. The Last Bull Market.
  A. Tobias, 441:15Jun80-12
Sobel, R. and D. Francis. Chaplin.
  S. Feldman, 529(QQ):Summer79-320
Soboul, A. and G. Lemarchand. Le Siècle
  des Lumières. (Vol 1)
  T.M. Scanlan, 207(FR):Feb79-521
Sobrino, E.O. Léxico di Valerio Máximo,
  A-D.
  J. André, 555:Vol52fascl-202
Sobrino, J., J.B. Silman and F. Vergara.
  Repaso de español. (2nd ed)
  R.W. Hatton, 238:Mar79-197
"Société des Peintres-Graveurs Français."
  (56e Exposition)
  M. Sheringham, 208(FS):Oct79-488
Söderberg, R. French Book Illustration
  1880-1905.
  G. Svensson, 341:1978/2-83
Södergran, E. We Women. (S. Charters,
  ed and trans) Edith Södergran: Feind-
  liche Sterne. (K.R. Kern, ed and trans)
  G.C. Schoolfield, 563(SS):Summer79-319
Söderskog, I. Joyce Cary's "Hard Concep-
  tual Labour."
  J.J. Riley, 395(MFS):Summer78-314
Sodmann, T., ed. Reynke de vos.
  J.L. Flood, 684(ZDA):Band107Heft3-133
Soffer, R.N. Ethics and Society in
  England.
  P. Clarke, 617(TLS):20Jun80-711
  T.W. Heyck, 637(VS):Summer79-466
Sokoloff, M. The Targum to Job from
  Qumran Cave XI.
  S. Segert, 318(JAOS):Apr-Jun78-145
Sokolov, G. Antique Art on the Northern
  Black Sea Coast.
  J.G.F. Hind, 303(JoHS):Vol199-207
Sokolov, R. Wayward Reporter.
  C. Lehmann-Haupt, 441:21Nov80-C27
  W. Sheed, 441:2Nov80-11
Sokolowski, R. Presence and Absence.
  P. Dubois, 542:Oct-Dec79-462
  J.G. Hart, 258:Sep79-371
  M. Shapiro, 350:Sep79-755
Sol, H.B., ed. La Vie du Pape Saint
  Grégoire.
  A.H. Diverres, 402(MLR):Jul79-692
  D. Evans, 447(N&Q):Oct78-467
  R.C. Roach, 399(MLJ):Jan-Feb79-55
Solberg, C.E. Oil and Nationalism in
  Argentina.
  L. Randall, 263(RIB):Vol129No3/4-378
Solbrig, I.H. and J.W. Storck, eds. Rilke
  heute.
  B.M. Broerman, 221(GQ):Jan79-131
Soldevila, L. - see Zanné, J.
Solin, H. Epigraphische Untersuchungen in
  Rom und Umgebung.*
  J. Reynolds, 123:Vol129No1-188

Söll, L. Gesprochenes und geschriebenes
  Französisch.*
  K.E.M. George, 208(FS):Vol33Pt2-1045
Sollertinsky, D. and L. Pages From the
  Life of Dmitri Shostakovich.
  H.C. Schonberg, 441:21Sep80-12
Solmssen, A.R.G. A Princess in Berlin.
  C. Lehmann-Haupt, 441:3Nov80-C18
  T. Walton, 441:14Dec80-10
Sologub, F. Bad Dreams.
  M.G. Barker, 574(SEEJ):Summer79-277
Solomon, J. and J. Ancient Roman Feasts
  and Recipes.
  W. and C. Cowen, 639(VQR):Spring78-74
Solomon, J. and O., comps. Cracklin Bread
  and Asfidity.
  A.H. Walle, 292(JAF):Oct-Dec79-507
Solomon, L. The Conserver Solution.
  G.W. Brandie, 529(QQ):Winter79/80-699
Solomon, M. Beethoven.
  B. Cooper, 410(M&L):Oct79-464
  W. Drabkin, 415:Apr79-304
  E. Rothstein, 414(MusQ):Jul78-389
Solomon, P.H. The Life after Birth.*
  R. Chambers, 208(FS):Vol33Pt2-914
Solomon, P.H., Jr. Soviet Criminologists
  and Criminal Policy.
  V.C. Chrypinski, 550(RusR):Apr79-241
  639(VQR):Autumn78-134
Solomon, R.C. History and Human Nature.*
  P-L. Adams, 61:Feb80-98
Solomon, R.H., with T.W. Huey. A Revolu-
  tion is Not a Dinner Party.
  R. Witke, 293(JASt):Nov78-145
Solomon, S.G. The Soviet Agrarian Debate.
  J.R. Millar, 550(RusR):Apr79-232
Solotaroff, T., with S. Ravenal, eds. The
  Best American Short Stories 1978.*
  L. Horne, 461:Spring-Summer79-95
  42(AR):Winter79-125
  639(VQR):Spring79-60
Solzhenitsyn, A.I. The Gulag Archipelago,
  1918-1956. (Vol 3)
  M. Geltman, 390:Jan79-71
  J.G. Pilon, 396(ModA):Spring79-189
Solzhenitsyn, A.I. The Mortal Danger.
  A. Broyard, 441:21Aug80-C17
  P. Windsor, 362:11Sep80-342
Solzhenitsyn, A.I. The Oak and the Calf.
  J. Bayley, 453(NYRB):26Jun80-3
  S.F. Cohen, 441:4May80-1
  A.H., 617(TLS):11Jul80-777
  J. Leonard, 441:6May80-C11
  M. Muggeridge, 362:3Jul80-19
  G. Steiner, 442(NY):25Aug80-94
Solzhenitsyn, A.I. A World Split Apart.
  639(VQR):Spring79-65
Soman, A. The Massacre of St. Bartholomew.
  C.D. Bettinson, 208(FS):Vol33Pt2-668
Somerset, A. The Life and Times of Wil-
  liam IV.
  R. Stewart, 362:13Nov80-664
Somerville, K.E.M. and G.W. Hartwig. Know-
  ing the Unknown.
  J.M. Borgatti, 2(AfrA):May79-91

Somerville, R. Pope Alexander III and the Council of Tours (1163).
   T. Reuter, 589:Oct79-861
"Something About the Author." (Vols 9-11) (A. Commire, ed)
   J. Oldfield, 677(YES):Vol9-354
Sommer, C. - see Hartmann von Aue
Sommer, F. Handbuch der lateinischen Laut- und Formenlehre. (Vol 1) (4th ed)
   C. Watkins, 124:Sep79-38
Sommer, M. Die Selbsterhaltung der Vernunft.
   W. Stegmaier, 687:Jul-Sep79-473
Sommer, R. The Other Side of Games.
   R. Miles, 102(CanL):Summer79-138
Sommer, S. Nearing's Grace.
   P. Kemp, 362:21Aug80-249
   S. Salmans, 617(TLS):22Aug80-930
Sommerstein, A.H. Modern Phonology.
   E.W. Roberts, 297(JL):Mar79-159
   205(FMLS):Apr78-190
Sommerstein, A.H. The Sound Pattern of Ancient Greek.
   G. Nagy, 122:Jul79-266
Sommerville, C.J. Popular Religion in Restoration England.
   G.E. Pruett, 566:Autumn78-49
Song, Y-Y. Bertolt Brecht und die chinesische Philosophie.
   S.L. Gilman, 221(GQ):May79-426
"The Song of Roland." (G.J. Brault, ed)
   E.S. Sklar, 141:Spring79-162
"The Song of Roland." (F. Goldin, trans)
   R. Harrison, 589:Oct79-806
   639(VQR):Spring79-67
"The Song of Songs." (C.E. Pickford, ed)
   W. Rothwell, 208(FS):Jan79-65
Sonnichsen, C.L. From Hopalong to Hud.
   J.H. Maguire, 27(AL):Nov79-424
   T. Pilkington, 649(WAL):Fall79-259
Sonnichsen, C.L. - see Perkins, C.A., with N. Dickey
Sontag, S. I, etcetera.*
   D. Durrant, 364:Jul79-89
   42(AR):Winter79-125
Sontag, S. Illness as Metaphor.*
   M.C. Darnell, 569(SR):Summer79-lxvi
   639(VQR):Autumn78-127
Sontag, S. On Photography.*
   H. Green, 658:Summer79-209
   C.J. Leonard, 186(ETC.):Winter78-442
   N.J. Peterson, 125:Winter79-318
   P. Wollheim, 648(WCR):Oct78-77
   639(VQR):Spring78-69
Sontag, S. Under the Sign of Saturn.
   D. Bromwich, 441:23Nov80-11
   K. Kermode, 453(NYRB):6Nov80-42
   J. Leonard, 441:13Oct80-C22
Soons, A. - see Terralla Landa, E.
Sophocles. Oedipus the King. (S. Berg and D. Clay, trans)
   G. Gellie, 67:May79-81
Sophocles. Sophoclis, "Fabulae."* (Vol 1) (A. Colonna, ed)
   J.C. Kamerbeek, 394:Vol32fasc1/2-181
   G.L. Koniaris, 24:Summer79-311
   R.W., 555:Vol52fasc1-160

Sorabji, R. Necessity, Cause and Blame.
   G.E.M. Anscombe, 617(TLS):20Jun80-701
Soreil, A. Loisirs de plume et dits rimés.
   P. Somville, 542:Oct-Dec79-479
Sörensen, D. James Joyce's Aesthetic Theory.
   R.M. Kain, 395(MFS):Winter78/79-568
   K.D. Parks, 305(JIL):Sep78-167
Sørensen, M. Saga og samfund.
   T.M. Andersson, 301(JEGP):Jan79-100
Sorg, B. Thomas Bernhard.
   M. Bickelmann, 221(GL):Jan79-143
   B. Hannemann, 406:Fall79-352
Sorokin, B. Tolstoy in Prerevolutionary Russian Criticism.
   H. Gifford, 617(TLS):11Apr80-418
Sorrentino, G. Aberration of Starlight.
   G. Davenport, 441:10Aug80-15
   J. Rubins, 453(NYRB):18Dec80-63
   61:Aug80-83
Sorrentino, G. Mulligan Stew.*
   Z. Leader, 617(TLS):2May80-486
   J. Mellors, 362:22May80-660
Sōseki, N. Sanshirō. (J. Rubin, trans)
   C.S. Seigle, 293(JASt):May79-586
   639(VQR):Summer78-94
Sosna, M. In Search of the Silent South.*
   B. Clayton, 579(SAQ):Winter79-124
Sőtér, I. and I. Neupokoyeva, eds. European Romanticism.
   A. McMillin, 575(SEER):Oct79-582
Soto, G. The Elements of San Joaquin.
   J. Bradley, 649(WAL):Spring79-73
   P. Cooley, 472:Fall/Winter79-297
Soto, G. The Tale of Sunlight.
   P. Cooley, 472:Fall/Winter79-297
   A. Williamson, 491:Mar80-348
Soto, M.M. - see under Méndez y Soto, M.
Soucy, J-Y. Creatures of the Chase.
   B. Godard, 198:Summer80-161
Soucy, R. Fascist Intellectual.
   E. Weber, 617(TLS):6Jun80-631
Soulié-Lapeyre, P. Le Vague et l'Aigu dans la Perception Verlainienne.
   D. Hillery, 208(FS):Vol33Pt2-841
Sourian, E. Madame de Staël et Henri Heine.*
   P.J. Whyte, 208(FS):Apr79-208
Sourvinou-Linwood, C. Theseus as Son and Stepson.
   S. Pembroke, 617(TLS):11Jan80-43
Souster, R. - see Campbell, W.
Southam, B. Lovers and Other People.
   T. Beyer, 368:Jun74-174
Southam, B.C., ed. Jane Austen: "Northanger Abbey" and "Persuasion."
   F.W. Bradbrook, 447(N&Q):Jun78-257
Southam, B.C., ed. T.S. Eliot: "Prufrock," "Gerontion," "Ash Wednesday" and Other Shorter Poems.
   H. Gardner, 402(MLR):Apr79-438
Southerland, E. Let the Lion Eat Straw.*
   P. Craig, 617(TLS):16May80-558

Southerne, T. Oroonoko.* (M.E. Novak and D.S. Rodes, eds)
  L.W. Conolly, 447(N&Q):Feb78-79
  M. Kelsall, 402(MLR):Oct79-906
Southgate, M.S. - see "Iskandanamah, A Persian Medieval Alexander-Romance"
Southworth, M-J. Etude comparée de quatre romans médiévaux.*
  S. Olson, 546(RR):May79-301
Southworth, S. and M. Ornamental Ironwork.
  G. Allen, 45:Jan79-51
Souza, M. The Emperor of the Amazon.
  W. Hjortsberg, 441:19Oct80-9
  J. Leonard, 441:23Sep80-C11
  442(NY):29Sep80-151
Sowell, T. Classical Economics Reconsidered.
  E. Allen, 161(DUJ):Dec78-98
Sowell, T. Knowledge and Decisions.
  M.F. Plattner, 441:23Mar80-12
"Sowjetunion 1976/77."
  M. McCauley, 575(SEER):Jan79-155
Soyfer, J. The Legacy of Jura Soyfer 1912-1939.* (H. Jarka, ed and trans)
  F. Achberger, 406:Winter79-459
Soyinka, W. Myth, Literature and the African World.*
  O. Owomoyela, 292(JAF):Jan-Mar79-84
Spacagna, A. Entre le oui et le non.
  D.C. Spinelli, 399(MLJ):Mar79-143
Spackman, W.M. A Presence With Secrets.
  P-L. Adams, 61:Nov80-99
  F. Busch, 441:9Nov80-14
  J. Leonard, 441:31Oct80-C25
  442(NY):8Dec80-234
Spacks, B. Imagining a Unicorn.*
  J.F. Cotter, 249(HudR):Spring79-117
Spacks, P.M. Imagining a Self.*
  M.A. Doody, 454:Winter79-185
  R.J. Merrett, 627(UTQ):Winter78/79-186
  K. Stewart, 191(ELN):Jun79-336
Spada, P. The Complete Symphonic Works of Muzio Clementi.
  J.W. Hill, 317:Fall79-577
Spada, P. - see Clementi, M.
Spadaccini, N. and A.N. Zahareas, eds. La vida y hechos de Estebanillo González hombre de buen humor.
  R. Bjornson, 304(JHP):Autumn79-97
Spaemann, R. Zur Kritik der politischen Utopie.*
  C.G., 543:Jun79-770
Spafford, F. Snowmelt.
  P. Brennan, 102(CanL):Autumn79-113
  G. Hamel, 198:Winter80-140
Spahn, P. Mittelschicht und Polisbildung.
  S. Van de Maele, 487:Summer79-186
Spalding, F. Roger Fry.
  Q. Bell, 617(TLS):21Mar80-307
  H. Kramer, 441:5Oct80-1
Spalding, F. Magnificent Dreams.*
  L. Ormond, 39:Dec79-537
Spanien, A. and Y. Imaeda, eds. Choix de documents tibétains conservés à la Bibliothèque Nationale.
  M. Aris, 617(TLS):11Jul80-786

Spark, M. Territorial Rights.*
  C.C. Park, 249(HudR):Winter79/80-578
Sparn, W. Wiederkehr der Metaphysik.
  S. Decloux, 182:Vol31#13-395
Sparnaay, H. Hartmann von Aue.
  V. Mertens, 684(ZDA):Band107Heft1-22
Spate, V. Orphism.
  T. Hilton, 617(TLS):21Mar80-315
Spater, G. and I. Parsons. A Marriage of True Minds.*
  A. Bell, 569(SR):Spring79-325
  D. Doner, 395(MFS):Winter78/79-575
  J. Giltrow, 648(WCR):Oct78-57
  F.P.W. McDowell, 77:Summer78-89
  S. Rudikoff, 249(HudR):Winter79/80-540
  295(JML):Vol17#4-844
  639(VQR):Summer78-92
Spatharakis, I. The Portrait in Byzantine Illuminated Manuscripts.*
  J.D. Breckenridge, 54:Jun78-360
Spatz, L. Aristophanes.
  P. Arnott, 130:Winter79/80-371
  K.J. Reckford, 124:Sep79-45
Spaventa, B. Lezioni di antropologia. (D. D'Orsi, ed)
  A. Savorelli, 548(RCSF):Jan-Mar79-108
Speaight, R. François Mauriac.
  R.J. North, 208(FS):Vol133Pt2-877
Speaight, R. Shakespeare.*
  C.H. Shattuck, 570(SQ):Winter79-96
Spear, R. Silks.
  W. Pritchard, 441:6Jul80-8
Spearing, A.C. Chaucer: "Troilus and Criseyde."*
  G. Clifford, 677(YES):Vol9-363
Spearing, A.C. Medieval Dream-Poetry.*
  P. Bawcutt, 161(DUJ):Dec78-127
  R.T. Davies, 402(MLR):Apr79-405
  E.T. Donaldson, 589:Jan79-191
  D. Mehl, 38:Band96Heft3/4-507
Specht, R. - see Suarez, F.
Speck, F. Naskapi.
  W.K. McNeil, 292(JAF):Jul-Sep79-363
Speck, W.A. Stability and Strife.
  K. Kramnick, 656(WMQ):Jan79-143
  P.W.J. Riley, 566:Autumn78-46
Specovius, G. - see Epstein, F.T.
Spector, H. Bastard in the Ragged Suit. (B. Johns and J.S. Clancy, eds)
  E. Roditi, 390:Aug-Sep79-59
Spence, C.H. Gathered In.
  A. Mitchell, 67:May79-115
Spence, J.D. The Death of Woman Wang.*
  639(VQR):Spring79-52
Spence, J.T. and R.L. Helmreich. Masculinity and Femininity.
  T. McCormack, 529(QQ):Winter79/80-671
Spence, K., with H. Cole. Living Music.
  A. Jacobs, 415:Oct79-833
Spencer, D.S. Louis Kossuth and Young America.
  J.I. Gow, 104(CASS):Fall78-443
  D.M. Pletcher, 579(SAQ):Winter79-126
Spencer, D.S.C. and others. Employment, Efficiency and Income in the Rice Processing Industry of Sierra Leone.
  R.M. Lawson, 69:Vol148#3-309

Spencer, S. Collage of Dreams.*
  M. Andersen, 106:Fall79-255
  R.D. Cottrell, 395(MFS):Winter78/79-
  620
Spencer, S. Endless Love.*
  P. Bailey, 617(TLS):11Apr80-408
  T.R. Edwards, 453(NYRB):6Mar80-43
Spender, S. The Thirties and After.*
  S. Corey, 219(GaR):Spring79-236
  A. Dickins, 364:Jun79-80
  A.W. Litz, 569(SR):Fall79-660
  J. Tasker, 396(ModA):Fall79-432
  42(AR):Winter79-124
  639(VQR):Spring79-68
Spender, S. World within World.
  C. Guillot, 189(EA):Jul-Dec78-414
Spengemann, W.C. The Adventurous Muse.*
  H. Hill, 405(MP):Nov79-238
  R. Mason, 447(N&Q):Jun78-282
  D. Stineback, 587(SAF):Spring79-116
Spenser, E. The Faerie Queene.* (T.P.
  Roche, Jr., with C.P. O'Donnell, Jr.,
  eds)
  J. Buxton, 541(RES):Nov79-460
  M. Dodsworth, 175:Spring79-43
  H.L. Weatherby, 569(SR):Summer79-490
Spenser, E. "The Faerie Queene," a Selec-
  tion. (D. Brooks-Davies, ed)
  R.G. Ralph, 447(N&Q):Oct78-459
Spenser, E. Spenser: "The Faerie Queene."*
  (A.C. Hamilton, ed)
  M. Dodsworth, 175:Spring79-43
  J.K. Hale, 67:Nov79-313
  J.J.M. Tobin, 184(EIC):Jul79-264
  H.L. Weatherby, 569(SR):Summer79-490
Spera, F. Il principio dell'anti-lettera-
  tura.
  G.T., 228(GSLI):Vol155fasc490-315
Speranza, F., ed. Rusticae Rei Scriptores.
  (Vol 1)
  M. Pasquinucci, 313:Vol69-229
Sperber, D. Rethinking Symbolism.*
  G.I. Wurtzel, 186(ETC.):Jun77-231
Sperber, M. Individuum und Gemeinschaft.
  A. Allemann-Tschopp, 182:Vol131#19-653
Sperlbaum, M. Proben deutscher Umgangs-
  sprache.
  D. Stellmacher, 685(ZDL):3/1979-374
Spero, R. The Duping of the American
  Voters.
  G.E. Reedy, 441:22Jun80-14
Speroni, C. and C.E. Kany. Spoken Italian
  for Students and Travelers.
  A. Papalia, 399(MLJ):Mar79-147
Spicker, S.F. and H.T. Engelhardt, eds.
  Philosophical Medical Ethics.
  B. Cohen, 393(Mind):Jul79-473
Spielmann, K.F. Analyzing Soviet Strate-
  gic Arms Decisions.
  D. Caldwell, 550(RusR):Oct79-497
Spiers, A.G.E. The Proto-Indo-European
  Labiovelars.
  K. McCune, 574(SEEJ):Winter79-552
Spiers, E.M. The Army and Society, 1815-
  1914. Haldane.
  B. Bond, 617(TLS):22Aug80-937

Spilka, M., ed. Towards a Poetics of Fic-
  tion.*
  A.S., 148:Spring79-94
Spillner, B. Linguistik und Literatur-
  wissenschaft.*
  E.W.B. Hess-Lüttich, 680(ZDP):Band97-
  Heft3-468
Spillner, B. Symmetrisches und asymmet-
  risches Prinzip in der Syntax Marcel
  Prousts.
  Y. Louria, 599:Spring79-233
Spingarn, L.P. The Dark Playground.
  S.S. Moorty, 649(WAL):Winter80-340
Spini, G., comp. Architettura e politica
  da Cosimo I a Ferdinando I.
  L. Satkowski, 576:Oct78-205
Spini, G. and others. Italia e America
  dal settecento all' eta' dell' imperial-
  ismo. Italia e America dalla grande
  guerra a oggi.
  J-M. Bonnet, 189(EA):Jul-Dec78-421
Spinner, H. Pluralismus als Erkenntnis-
  modell.
  A. Schramm, 84:Mar79-90
de Spinoza, B. Theologisch-Politischer
  Traktat. (G. Gawlick, ed)
  H.P. Rickman, 53(AGP):Band60Heft1-116
Spires, R.C. La novela española de pos-
  guerra.
  C.L. King, 399(MLJ):Dec79-461
"Spirit of Canada."
  J. Ferns, 102(CanL):Spring79-92
Spitz, H-J. Die Metaphorik des geistigen
  Schriftsinns.
  W. Schröder, 684(ZDA):Band107Heft3-95
Spivak, B. Jefferson's English Crisis.
  J.J. Hecht, 432(NEQ):Dec79-566
de Sponde, J. Oeuvres littéraires. (A.
  Boase, ed)
  T.C. Cave, 208(FS):Oct79-439
  E.T. Dubois, 182:Vol131#15/16-551
Sprague, E. Metaphysical Thinking.
  E. Matthews, 479(PhQ):Jan79-84
Sprague, R.K. Plato's Philosopher-King.*
  P.M. Huby, 123:Vol129No1-162
  P.K., 543:Sep78-155
  J.M. Osborn, 393(Mind):Jan79-124
  M.A. Stewart, 479(PhQ):Apr79-170
  G.J. de Vries, 394:Vol132fasc1/2-185
Spranger, E. Gesammelte Schriften. (Vol
  7) (H.W. Bähr, ed)
  A. Closs, 402(MLR):Jul79-756
Spreer, F. Zur Wissenschaftstheorie der
  Wirtschaftsplanung.
  G.E. Braun, 679:Band9Heft2-423
Sprengel, P. Innerlichkeit.
  W. Koepke, 133:Band12Heft4-369
Sprich, R. and R.W. Noland - see Lesser,
  S.O.
Springer, M.A., ed. What Manner of Woman.
  R.P. Hoople, 106:Winter79-325
Springer, M.D. A Rhetoric of Literary
  Character.
  M. Jacobson, 301(JEGP):Oct79-569
  R.E. Long, 27(AL):Mar79-124
  D. Mogen, 26(ALR):Autumn79-350
                                        [continued]

Springer, M.D. A Rhetoric of Literary
Character. [continuing]
A.R. Tintner, 594:Spring79-106
639(VQR):Spring79-49
Springhall, J. Youth, Empire and Society.
A.J. Greenberger, 637(VS):Winter78-278
Sprockhoff, J.F. Saṃnyāsa.
J.W. de Jong, 259(IIJ):Oct79-292
Spuhler, F. Islamic Carpets and Textiles
in the Keir Collection.
D. King, 463:Winter78/79-466
U. Roberts, 60:Nov-Dec79-123
Spyker, J.H. Little Lives.*
S. Salmans, 617(TLS):25Apr80-469
Squier, C.L. Sir John Suckling.
J.L. Selzer, 568(SCN):Fall-Winter79-75
Squire, G. Dress and Society 1560-1970.
V.H. Winner, 639(VQR):Spring78-373
Srzednicki, J.T.J. Elements of Social and
Political Philosophy.
L. Holborow, 63:Mar79-112
Staar, R.F., ed. Yearbook on Interna-
tional Communist Affairs 1976.
I. Avakumovic, 104(CASS):Summer78-306
Stacey, T. The Pandemonium.
P. Craig, 617(TLS):8Feb80-146
Stachowiak, H. Denken und Erkennen im
kybernetischen Modell. Rationalismus
im Ursprung. Allgemeine Modelltheorie.
K. Wuchterl, 489(PJGG):Band86Heft2-409
Stack, E.M. Le Pont Neuf. (3rd ed)
G.R. Danner, 207(FR):May79-965
Stack, G.J. Sartre's Philosophy of Social
Existence.
R.E. Santoni, 258:Mar79-117
von Stackelberg, J. Literarische Rezep-
tionsformen.
P-E. Knabe, 430(NS):Oct78-477
Stackell, L. Den svenska västkustens
havsbadort.
T. Hall, 341:1978/2-55
Stacy, R.H. Defamiliarization in Language
and Literature.*
V.G. Brougher, 574(SEEJ):Spring79-135
M.K. Launer, 558(RLJ):Winter79-200
E. Wasiolek, 131(CL):Winter79-93
Staehelin, M. Die Messen Heinrich Isaacs.
R. Strohm, 410(M&L):Oct79-458
Madame de Staël. Des Circonstances actu-
elles qui peuvent terminer la Révolu-
tion et des principes qui doivent fonder
la République en France. (L. Omacini,
ed)
A. Fairlie, 208(FS):Oct79-455
Madame de Staël. Correspondance générale.*
(Vol 4, Pt 1) (B.W. Jasinski, ed)
J. Gaulmier, 535(RHL):May-Jun78-487
Madame de Staël and P. de Souza. Corres-
pondance. (B. d'Andlau, ed)
A. Brookner, 617(TLS):14Mar80-287
Stafford, D. Britain and European Resist-
ance 1940-1945.
M.R.D. Foot, 617(TLS):28Mar80-372
R. Lewin, 362:29May80-692
Stafford, J. Collected Stories of Jean
Stafford.
61:Jul80-86

Stafford, W. Stories That Could Be True.*
F. Garber, 29:Jan/Feb80-16
Stage, S. Female Complaints.*
676(YR):Spring80-XIII
Stahl, G. Estructura y Conocimiento
Cientifico.
J. Largeault, 542:Jul-Sep79-384
Staines, D., ed. The Canadian Imagina-
tion.*
S.H. Uphaus, 106:Fall79-209
Staines, D. - see Brown, E.K.
Staley, T.F. Dorothy Richardson.*
R. Jackson, 402(MLR):Jan79-184
Stalhammar, M.M. Imagery in Golding's
"The Spire."
J.J. Riley, 395(MFS):Summer78-314
Stallworthy, J. A Familiar Tree.*
J.F. Cotter, 249(HudR):Spring79-109
D. Graham, 565:Vol120#4-75
H. Marten, 659(ConL):Winter80-146
P. Scupham, 617(TLS):4Jul80-762
639(VQR):Spring79-65
Stallworthy, J., ed. Love Poetry.
L.M. Findlay, 447(N&Q):Oct78-453
Stambolian, G. Twentieth Century French
Fiction, Essays for Germaine Brée.
M. Spencer, 546(RR):Mar79-194
Stambolian, G. and E. Marks, eds. Homo-
sexualities and French Literature.
P. Collier, 364:Mar80-82
Stamelman, R.H. The Drama of Self in
Guillaume Apollinaire's "Alcools."*
A. Fongaro, 535(RHL):Jan-Feb79-153
Stamer, U. Ebene Minne bei Walther von
der Vogelweide.
D.H. Green, 402(MLR):Apr79-488
Stamm, R. The Mirror-Technique in Senecan
and Pre-Shakespearean Tragedy.*
H.W. Gabler, 224(GRM):Band28Heft1-118
Stammerjohann, H. and H. Janssen, eds.
Handbuch der Linguistik.*
R. Anttila, 350:Jun79-477
Stammler, W. and K. Langosch. Die deut-
sche Literatur des Mittelalters: Verfas-
serlexikon. (2nd ed) (Vol 1, fasc 1 and
2) (K. Ruh and others, eds)
N.F. Palmer, 402(MLR):Apr79-486
E.A. Philippson, 301(JEGP):Jul79-380
Stammler, W. and K. Langosch. Die deut-
sche Literatur des Mittelalters: Verfas-
serlexikon. (2nd ed) (Vol 1, fasc 3 and
4) (K. Ruh and others, eds)
E.A. Philippson, 301(JEGP):Jul79-380
Stampp, K.M. The Imperiled Union.
C.V. Woodward, 453(NYRB):25Sep80-60
Stanford, D. Inside the Forties.
M. Remy, 189(EA):Jul-Dec78-416
Stanford, D. The Traveller Hears the
Strange Machine.
V. Feaver, 617(TLS):8Aug80-903
Stanford, D.E. In the Classic Mode.*
W.G. Holzberger, 385(MQR):Winter80-117
G.S. Lensing, 249(HudR):Summer79-308
Stanford, D.E. - see Bridges, R.
Stanford, W.B. Enemies of Poetry.
C. Macleod, 617(TLS):18Jul80-796

Stang, R. Edvard Munch.
J.P. Hodin, 90:Oct79-661
J.G. Holland, 563(SS):Summer79-306
R. Whelan, 55:Nov79-40
Stang, S.J. Ford Madox Ford.
G. Blake, 395(MFS):Summer78-310
Stange, A. Kritisches Verzeichnis der
deutschen Tafelbilder vor Dürer. (Vol 3)
(N. Lieb, ed)
G. Goldberg, 471:Apr/May/Jun79-176
Stange, M. Reinmars Lyrik.
E.S. Dick, 406:Winter79-443
Stangos, N. - see Hockney, D.
Stankiewicz, W.J. Aspects of Political
Theory.
J-L. Gardies, 542:Oct-Dec79-496
Stanley, M. The Technological Conscience.
C. Pax, 258:Sep79-369
Stannard, D.E. Shrinking History.
J. Greenfield, 441:6Jul80-10
J. Leonard, 441:26May80-C16
Stannard, U. Mrs. Man.
E.C. Smith, 424:Dec77-239
Stans, M.H. The Terrors of Justice.*
639(VQR):Autumn79-146
Stansky, P. and W. Abrahams. Orwell: The
Transformation.*
E. Homberger, 617(TLS):11Jan80-33
I. Howe, 441:20Apr80-1
C. Lehmann-Haupt, 441:1May80-C32
V.S. Pritchett, 453(NYRB):1May80-3
P. Vansittart, 364:Feb80-86
61:Apr80-126
Stanton, R.J. and G. Vidal - see Vidal, G.
Stanton, S.S., ed. Tennessee Williams.
J.H. Clark, 397(MD):Jun79-208
Stanwood, B. The Glow.*
E. Korn, 617(TLS):1Feb80-108
Stapleton, L. Marianne Moore.
T. Martin, 295(JML):Vol7#4-776
W. Sutton, 27(AL):Nov79-432
639(VQR):Spring79-49
Stark, R. Aristotelesstudien. (2nd ed)
(P. Steinmetz, ed)
W.J. Verdenius, 394:Vol30fasc3-315
Starks, R. Industry in Decline.*
T.K. Rymes, 529(QQ):Autumn79-523
Starr, C.G. The Economic and Social
Growth of Early Greece 800-500 B.C.*
P. Cartledge, 487:Winter79-354
Starr, C.G. Political Intelligence in
Classical Greece.
S.I. Oost, 122:Jan79-88
Starr, K. Land's End.
H. Lachtman, 649(WAL):Winter80-345
Starr, R.F. - see "Yearbook on Interna-
tional Communist Affairs, 1978"
Starr, S.F. Melnikov.
M. Bliznakov, 550(RusR):Apr79-260
J. Bowlt, 575(SEER):Oct79-594
C. Cooke, 46:May79-315
Startt, J.D. Journalism's Unofficial
Ambassador.
S. Koss, 617(TLS):25Jul80-832
Stassinopoulos, A. Maria Callas.
A. Quinton, 362:16Oct80-512
Stäuble, M. - see Baudelaire, C.

Stavan, H.A. Le Lyrisme dans la poésie
française de 1760 à 1820.*
F.J-L. Mouret, 208(FS):Vol33Pt2-787
Staveley, A.L. Memories of Gurdjieff.
G. Hough, 617(TLS):13Jun80-665
Stavis, B. The Politics of Agriculture
Mechanization in China.
A. Donnithorne, 293(JASt):Aug79-758
Stead, C. Divine Substance.
P. Sherry, 483:Jan79-134
Stead, C. A Christina Stead Reader.*
(J.B. Read, ed)
D. Cole, 219(GaR):Winter79-946
Stead, C.K. Quesada.
R. Jackaman, 368:Jun75-164
Steadman, J.M. Epic and Tragic Structure
in "Paradise Lost."*
E. Miner, 131(CL):Winter79-92
S.P. Revard, 405(MP):Aug79-89
Steadman, J.M. Nature into Myth.
D.B-D., 148:Winter79-89
Steadman, R. Sigmund Freud.*
D. Hill, 441:14Dec80-13
Stearns, P.N. Lives of Labor.
F.M. Leventhal, 637(VS):Autumn78-94
Stebbins, C.E., ed. A Critical Edition of
the 13th and 14th Centuries Old French
Poem Versions of the "Vie de Saint
Alexis."
W.G. van Emden, 208(FS):Vol33Pt2-570
Stebbins, S. Studien zur Tradition und
Rezeption der Bildlichkeit in der
"Eneide" Heinrichs von Veldeke.*
D.H. Green, 402(MLR):Jul79-735
Steblin-Kamenskij, M.I. The Saga Mind.
R.P. Tripp, Jr., 152(UDQ):Winter79-121
Stecenko, A.N. Istoričeskij sintaksis
russkogo jazyka.
G. Rappaport, 574(SEEJ):Winter79-555
von Stechow, A., ed. Beiträge zur genera-
tiven Grammatik.
P. Suchsland, 353:Jun78-76
Steefel, L.D., Jr. The Position of
Duchamp's "Glass" in the Development of
His Art.
D. Carrier, 290(JAAC):Fall79-104
Steegmuller, F. - see Flaubert, C.
Steel, D. A House Divided.
D. Marquand, 362:26Jun80-818
Steel, D.I.A. A Lincolnshire Village.
M. Mason, 617(TLS):22Aug80-933
Steel, R. Walter Lippmann and the Ameri-
can Century.
J.P. Lash, 441:24Aug80-1
J. Leonard, 441:22Aug80-C21
A. Lewis, 453(NYRB):9Oct80-3
442(NY):22Sep80-157
Steele, E.J. Somatic Selection and Adap-
tive Evolution.
J.Z. Young, 453(NYRB):7Feb80-45
Steele, J. Captain Mayne Reid.
M.T. Marsden, 649(WAL):Spring79-78
Steele, R. Thomas Wolfe.
R.S. Kennedy, 395(MFS):Summer78-270
Steele, T. Uncertainties and Rest.
R. Lattimore, 249(HudR):Autumn79-446

Steele, W.M. and T. Ichimata - see Whitney, C.A.N.

di Stefano, G. Essais sur le moyen français.*
N. Mann, 208(FS):Vol33Pt2-1034

de Stéfano de Taucer, L. El "Caballero Zifar."
V. Masson de Gómez, 545(RPh):Nov78-212

Steffen, R. The Horse Soldier 1776-1943. (Vol 3)
J. Taylor, 649(WAL):Spring79-64

Stegemann, H. Studien zu Alfred Döblins Bildlichkeit "Die Ermordung einer Butterblume und andere Erzählungen."
A. Obermayer, 564:Nov79-313

Steger, H., ed. Probleme der Namenforschung im deutschsprachigen Raum.
W.F.H. Nicolaisen, 424:Jun78-196

Stegmaier, W. Substanz.
J. Möller, 489(PJGG):Band86Heft2-430

Stegmüller, W. Collected Papers on Epistemology, Philosophy of Science and History of Philosophy.
P.T. Sagal, 484(PPR):Sep79-140
R.H. Stoothoff, 84:Jun79-202
N. Tennant, 479(PhQ):Jul79-270

Stegmüller, W. Personnelle und Statistische Wahrscheinlichkeit.
B.C. van Fraassen, 486:Mar78-158

Stegner, W. Recapitulation.*
H. Lachtman, 649(WAL):Fall79-261
G. Perez, 249(HudR):Autumn79-474

Steig, M. Dickens and Phiz.
G. Reynolds, 39:Jul79-82
J. Wilt, 141:Summer79-273

Stein, A. The Art of Presence.*
S.P. Revard, 405(MP):Aug79-89

Stein, A.M. The Cheating Butcher.
N. Callendar, 441:20Jul80-16

Stein, B. The View from Sunset Boulevard.*
L. McMurtry, 18:Apr79-66
N. Weyl, 390:Oct79-63

Stein, B., with H. Stein. Moneypower.
C. Lehmann-Haupt, 441:8Jan80-C11

Stein, D.L. City Boys.*
J.M. Kertzer, 198:Summer80-142
P. Monk, 529(QQ):Autumn79-525

Stein, G. L'autobiographie de tout le monde. Lectures en Amérique. Picasso. L'histoire géographique de l'Amérique.
J. Roubaud, 98:Dec78-1095

Stein, G. The Yale Gertrude Stein. (R. Kostelanetz, ed)
H. Kenner, 441:21Dec80-5

Stein, G. and A.B. Toklas. Dear Sammy.* (S.M. Steward, ed)
M.J. Hoffman, 395(MFS):Summer78-267

Stein, J.J. Making Medical Choices.
S. Bernstein, 42(AR):Summer79-364

Stein, L. Beyond Death and Exile.
B. Knox, 453(NYRB):6Nov80-34

Stein, L. San Diego County Place-Names.
R.N. Rennick, 424:Sep78-295

Stein, P. Legal Evolution.
D.D. Raphael, 617(TLS):22Aug80-932

Stein, R.G. Architecture and Energy.
J. Cook, 576:Oct78-220

Stein, S. The Resort.
M. Levin, 441:16Mar80-15

Stein, W. Das kirchliche Amt bei Luther.
G. May, 182:Vol131#14-466

Steinbeck, J. The Acts of King Arthur and His Noble Knights.* (C. Horton, ed)
T.L. Wright, 577(SHR):Spring79-173

Steinbeck, J. The Wayward Bus. East of Eden.
R. Sale, 453(NYRB):20Mar80-10

Steinberg, J. Why Switzerland?
P.A. Bromhead, 161(DUJ):Dec78-114

Steinberg, M.S. Sabers and Brown Shirts.
639(VQR):Summer78-87

Steinberg, S.H. Reformer in the Marketplace.
J. Potter, 617(TLS):25Jan80-93

Steinbrunner, C. and N. Michaels. The Films of Sherlock Holmes.
W.K. Everson, 200:Feb79-116

Steinecke, H. Romantheorie und Romankritik in Deutschland.* (Vol 2)
J.L. Sammons, 52:Band13Heft2-209

Steiner, G. After Babel.* (French title: Après Babel.)
J. Largeault, 542:Oct-Dec79-479
A.K. Lojkine, 67:May79-174

Steiner, G. Anno Domini.
61:Nov80-98

Steiner, G. Extraterritorial.
H. Godin, 208(FS):Vol33Pt2-997

Steiner, G. Martin Heidegger.*
C. Butler, 569(SR):Fall79-651
R. Harper, 529(QQ):Autumn79-460
T.J.S., 543:Jun79-772

Steiner, G. On Difficulty and Other Essays.*
C. Butler, 569(SR):Fall79-651
P.C. Hogan, 149(CLS):Sep79-272
R. King, 639(VQR):Summer79-568
M. Shapiro, 350:Sep79-754
D.H. Stewart, 651(WHR):Autumn79-356
D. Trickett, 584(SWR):Summer79-vi

Steiner, R.C. The Case for Fricative-Laterals in Proto-Semitic.
R.G. Schuh, 350:Mar79-256

Steiner, W. Exact Resemblance to Exact Resemblance.
R. Bridgman, 599:Spring79-226
M.J. Hoffman, 301(JEGP):Oct79-574

Steinfatt, T.M. Human Communication. Readings in Human Communication.
J. Aitchison, 297(JL):Mar79-197

Steinhagen, H. Wirklichkeit und Handeln im barocken Drama.
A.J. Niesz, 221(GQ):Jan79-106
R.E. Schade, 133:Band12Heft4-362

Steinhart, E.I. Conflict and Collaboration.
639(VQR):Summer78-89

Steinitz, P. Bach's Passions.
R. Bullivant, 415:Nov79-915

Steinkellner, E. Verse-index of Dharmakīrti's Works (Tibetan Version).
L.W.J. van der Kuijp, 485(PE&W):Jan79-106

Steinmetz, H. Suspensive Interpretation.*
  P. Beicken, 133:Band12Heft4-377
  E.L. Marson, 67:May79-152
Steinmetz, P. - see Stark, R.
Steinmetz-Schünemann, H. Die Bedeutung
  der Zeit in den Romanen von Marguerite
  Duras.
  W. Wehle, 52:Band13Heft3-332
Steinwachs, G. Mythologie des Surrealis-
  mus oder die Rückverwandlung von Kultur
  in Natur.
  R. Cardinal, 208(FS):Apr79-228
Stelzig, E.L. All Shades of Conscious-
  ness.*
  M. Isnard, 189(EA):Jul-Dec78-394
Stenbock-Fermor, E. The Architecture of
  "Anna Karenina."*
  R.L. Jackson, 550(RusR):Oct79-510
Stendahl, B.K. Søren Kierkegaard.
  E. Sprinchorn, 563(SS):Winter79-76
Stender, G.F. Godharda Fridricha Stendera
  Pasakas.
  A. Gāters, 343:Band23-197
Stendhal. Le Corrège. (V. Del Litto, ed)
  E.J.T., 191(ELN):Sep78(supp)-125
Stenström, T. Romantikern Eyvind Johnson.
  G. Orton, 562(Scan):Nov79-170
  M. Setterwall, 563(SS):Summer79-317
Stenz, A.M. Edward Albee.
  T. Otten, 130:Winter79/80-381
Stephan, J.J. The Russian Fascists.*
  J. Petrila, 550(RusR):Jan79-96
  R.S. Wistrich, 575(SEER):Oct79-614
  639(VQR):Winter79-12
Stephan, P. Paul Verlaine and the Deca-
  dence — 1882-1890.
  J.W. Brown, 546(RR):Mar79-193
Stéphane, H. Introduction à l'ésotérisme
  chrétien. (F. Chenique, ed)
  A. Reix, 542:Oct-Dec79-462
Stephen, L. Selected Writings in British
  Intellectual History.* (N. Annan, ed)
  S. Koss, 617(TLS):7Mar80-272
Stephen, L. Sir Leslie Stephen's "Mauso-
  leum Book."
  L. Hartley, 569(SR):Fall79-civ
  S. Rudikoff, 249(HudR):Winter79/80-540
Stephens, A., H.L. Rogers and B. Coghlan,
  eds. Festschrift for Ralph Farrell.
  J.M. Ritchie, 67:May79-163
Stephens, R.O., ed. Ernest Hemingway.*
  B. Oldsey, 395(MFS):Summer78-272
Stepto, R.B. From Behind the Veil.
  S. Mitchell, 617(TLS):30May80-626
  J. Wright, 109:Winter80-215
Stern, D. An Urban Affair.
  N. Johnson, 441:23Nov80-14
  C. Lehmann-Haupt, 441:14Oct80-C20
Stern, F.B. - see Jacobowski, L.
Stern, G. Lucky Life.*
  639(VQR):Summer78-102
Stern, J.P. History and Allegory in
  Thomas Mann's "Doktor Faustus."
  J. Crick, 220(GL&L):Oct78-89
Stern, J.P. Hitler.
  H. Ridley, 220(GL&L):Oct78-88

Stern, J.P. Friedrich Nietzsche.* (F.
  Kermode, ed)
  P. Foot, 453(NYRB):1May80-35
Stern, P.M. Lawyers on Trial.
  S. Brill, 441:5Oct80-12
Stern, R. Packages.
  R.P. Brickner, 441:7Sep80-13
  A. Broyard, 441:12Sep80-C21
Stern, S.M., A. Hourani and V. Brown, eds.
  Islamic Pholosophy and the Classical Tra-
  dition.
  M.S. Khan, 273(IC):Jul76-189
Sternbach, L. Indian Riddles.
  P. Bandyopadhyay, 318(JAOS):Apr-Jun78-
  189
Sternbach, L. Mahā-subhāṣita-saṁgraha.*
  (Vol 2) (S.B. Nair, ed)
  P. Bandyopadhyay, 318(JAOS):Oct-Dec78-
  546
Sternbach, L. Mahā-subhāṣita-saṁgraha.
  (Vol 3)
  J.W. De Jong, 259(IIJ):Jan79-62
Sternbach, L. The Mānava Dharmaśāstra
  I-III and the Bhaviṣya Purāṇa.
  P. Bandyopadhyay, 318(JAOS):Apr-Jun78-
  188
Sternberg, C. The Journey.
  A.M.F., 77:Fall78-89
Sternberg, J. mai 86.
  A. Thiher, 207(FR):May79-954
Sternberg, M. Expositional Modes and
  Temporal Ordering in Fiction.
  D.G. Marshall, 445(NCF):Dec78-373
  A. Moore, 131(CL):Fall79-426
  S. Pickering, 569(SR):Fall79-656
  P. Sabor, 529(QQ):Summer79-339
  R. Saldívar, 594:Winter79-472
Sternberger, D. Über den Tod. Drei Wur-
  zeln der Politik.
  P. Pachet, 182:Vol31#21/22-772
Sternburg, J., ed. The Writer on Her Work.
  D. Grumbach, 441:16Nov80-16
Sternfeld, R. and H. Zyskind. Plato's
  "Meno."
  G.A., 543:Jun79-773
  J. Sisson, 479(PhQ):Jul79-262
Sternheim, C. Gesamtwerk.* (Vol 10, Pts
  1 and 2) (W. Emrich and M. Linke, eds)
  W. Paulsen, 222(GR):Winter79-37
Stettler, M. and M. Lemberg. Artes
  Minores — Dank an Werner Abegg.
  C.C.M. Thurman, 54:Dec78-711
Stevens, D.A. Monteverdi.
  D.A., 410(M&L):Jul79-346
  J. Roche, 415:Jan79-37
Stevens, D. - see Monteverdi, C.
Stevens, H. Souvenirs and Prophecies.
  P.D. Morrow, 577(SHR):Summer79-273
Stevens, J. - see Ryōkan
Stevens, P., comp. Modern English-
  Canadian Poetry.
  W.H.N., 102(CanL):Summer79-164
Stevenson, A. Enough of Green.*
  H. Merten, 659(ConL):Winter80-146

Stevenson, A.E. The Papers of Adlai E. Stevenson.* (Vols 1-8) (W. Johnson, with C. Evans and C.E. Sears, eds)
N. Bliven, 442(NY):28Apr80-139
Stevenson, R. - see Ziehn, B.
Stevenson, W. The Ghosts of Africa.
S. Ellin, 441:14Dec80-10
Steward, S.M. - see Stein, G. and A.B. Toklas
Stewart, A.F. Skopas of Paros.
O. Palagia, 303(JoHS):Vol99-212
C.E. Vafopoulou-Richardson, 123:Vol129 No1-117
Stewart, A.G. Unequal Lovers.
G. Martin, 617(TLS):1Feb80-120
Stewart, A.H. Graphic Representation of Models in Linguistic Theory.*
N.S. Baron, 567:Vol24#1/2-157
Stewart, D. T.E. Lawrence.
A.G. Marquis, 77:Fall78-82
Stewart, D. A Man of Sydney.
J. Croft, 71(ALS):May79-125
Stewart, E.P. Letters of a Woman Homesteader.
A. Ronald, 649(WAL):Summer79-171
Stewart, H. Looking At Indian Art of the Northwest Coast.
376:Oct79-144
Stewart, J.H. The Novels of Mme. Riccoboni.*
M.R. Morris, 207(FR):Oct78-165
V. Mylne, 208(FS):Vol33Pt2-765
R. Niklaus, 535(RHL):Sep-Oct78-832
Stewart, J.I.M. Our England is a Garden.*
L. Duguid, 617(TLS):18Jan80-54
Stewart, M. Life and Labour.
R.R. James, 362:27Nov80-728
Stewart, R. The Mind of Norman Bethune.
L.T.C., 102(CanL):Winter78-132
Stewart, R. The Nightmare Candidate.
N. Callendar, 441:12Oct80-34
Stewart, W. Strike!
E. Bradley, 628(UWR):Fall-Winter78-79
Stich, A. Sabina — Němcová — Havlíček.
R.B. Pynsent, 575(SEER):Jul79-424
Stickney, D. Openings and Closings.
J. Greenfield, 441:10Feb80-16
Stickney, J. Self-Made.
D. Boyles, 441:14Sep80-18
Stieglitz, A. Georgia O'Keeffe.*
S. Hochfield, 55:Nov79-38
Stieler, K. Die Dichtkunst des Spaten 1685. (H. Zeman, ed)
K. Hanson, 301(JEGP):Oct79-592
Stilling, R. Love and Death in Renaissance Tragedy.*
C.R. Forker, 570(SQ):Winter79-107
Stillinger, E. The Antiquers.
A. Broyard, 441:10Dec80-C29
Stillinger, J. - see Keats, J.
Stillman, N.A. The Jews of Arab Lands.
R.A. Sokolov, 441:20Apr80-18
Stillwell, R., W.L. MacDonald and M.H. McAllister, eds. The Princeton Encyclopedia of Classical Sites.*
P. MacKendrick, 122:Jan79-78

Stimpson, K. Class Notes.*
E. Fifer, 268(IFR):Winter80-71
Stimson, H.M. Fifty-five T'ang Poems.* T'ang Poetic Vocabulary.*
E.H. Schafer, 318(JAOS):Jul-Sep78-297
Stipčević, A. The Illyrians.
J.J. Wilkes, 123:Vol129No1-174
Stirnimann, H. Existenzgrundlagen und traditionelles Handwerk der Pangwa von S.W. Tansania.
A. Redmayne, 69:Vol148#2-201
Stites, R. The Women's Liberation Movement in Russia.
B.E. Clements, 550(RusR):Jan79-89
M.K. Frank, 399(MLJ):Nov79-389
Stiverson, G.A. Poverty in a Land of Plenty.
J.T. Lemon, 656(WMQ):Jan79-125
Stobaugh, R. and D. Yergin, eds. Energy Future.*
L.C. Gould, 676(YR):Spring80-446
P.K. Verleger, Jr., 231:Apr80-110
Stöcklein, P. Literatur als Vergnügen und Erkenntnis.
J. Strelka, 222(GR):Winter78-37
Stockwell, R.P. Foundations of Syntactic Theory.*
G. Gazdar, 297(JL):Mar79-197
Stockwell, R.P., D.E. Elliott and M.C. Bean. Workbook in Syntactic Theory and Analysis.
G. Gazdar, 297(JL):Mar79-197
Stoddard, R. Stage Scenery, Machinery, and Lighting.
M. Warre, 611(TN):Vol132#3-139
Stoehr, C.E. Bonanza Victorian.
D.M. Carlson, 576:Mar78-48
Stoehr, T. Hawthorne's Mad Scientists.
L. Buell, 432(NEQ):Jun79-284
D.B. Kesterson, 27(AL):Mar79-119
Stoehr, T. Nay-Saying in Concord.
L. Buell, 27(AL):Jan80-570
A. Kermode, 617(TLS):2May80-508
L.N. Neufeldt, 432(NEQ):Sep79-434
Stoessl, F. C. Valerius Catullus.
D.O. Ross, Jr., 487:Autumn79-278
T.P. Wiseman, 313:Vol69-161
Stoever, W.K.B. "A Faire and Easie Way to Heaven."
B. Tipson, 656(WMQ):Jul79-480
B. Tucker, 432(NEQ):Jun79-277
Stoff, M.B. Oil, War, and American Security.
D. Yergin, 441:3Aug80-7
Stoffel, H.P. Studien zur Geschichte der russischen Skisportterminologie.
H. Leeming, 575(SEER):Oct79-630
Stokes, A. The Critical Writings of Adrian Stokes.* (L. Gowing, ed)
D. Craven, 127:Winter78/79-142
Stolleis, K. Die Gewänder der Lauinger Fürstengruft.*
E. Nienholdt, 683:Band41Heft3/4-334
Stoller, R. Recherches sur l'identité sexuelle.
H. Cronel, 450(NRF):Jun79-133

Stolpe, S. Den svenska romantiken.
    M. Mattsson, 563(SS):Winter79-91
Stoltzfus, B. Gide and Hemingway.
    C.S. Taylor, 42(AR):Summer79-372
Stone, D. Polish Politics and National
    Reform, 1775-1788.*
    D.L. Ransel, 104(CASS):Summer78-310
Stone, D., Jr. French Humanist Tragedy.
    G. Jondorf, 208(FS):Vol33Pt2-654
Stone, D., Jr. - see de Larivey, P.
Stone, D., Jr. - see de Montreux, N.
Stone, E. and K. - see Carter, E.
Stone, G.W. and G.M. Kahrl. David Garrick.
    N. Shrimpton, 617(TLS):19Sep80-1016
Stone, G.W., Jr. and P. Highfill, Jr. In
    Search of Restoration and Eighteenth-
    Century Theatrical Biography.*
    J. Hamard, 189(EA):Jan-Mar78-86
Stone, H. Dickens and the Invisible World.
    P. Keating, 617(TLS):18Apr80-444
Stone, I. The Origin.
    C. Lehmann-Haupt, 441:7Aug80-C18
    W. Schott, 441:14Sep80-12
Stone, I.F. Underground To Palestine.
    639(VQR):Summer79-93
Stone, J. The Mystery of B. Traven.*
    D.O. Chankin, 395(MFS):Summer78-282
Stone, L. Family and Fortune.
    H. Buszello, 182:Vol31#11/12-382
Stone, L. The Family, Sex and Marriage in
    England 1500-1800.
    P-G. Boucé, 189(EA):Jul-Dec78-370
Stone, L.W., W. Rothwell and T.B.W. Reid,
    eds. Anglo-Norman Dictionary.* (Vol 1)
    B. Merrilees, 589:Jan79-193
    G. Price, 402(MLR):Jul79-691
Stone, N. Hitler.
    A. Bullock, 453(NYRB):17Jul80-27
    J. Grigg, 362:21Aug80-245
    J. Joll, 617(TLS):12Sep80-982
Stone, R.H. Bolesław Leśmian.*
    S. Sandler, 497(PolR):Vol23#2-53
Stone, S.C.S. Spies.
    N. Callendar, 441:12Oct80-34
Stone, V.J., ed. Civil Liberties and
    Civil Rights.
    639(VQR):Spring78-64
Stoneley, J. Cauldron of Hell.
    639(VQR):Summer78-88
Stonum, G.L. Faulkner's Career.
    J.E. Bassett, 141:Fall79-387
    D. Wyatt, 639(VQR):Autumn79-757
Stopp, H. Schreibsprachwandel.
    N.R. Wolf, 684(ZDA):Band107Heft1-13
Storey, R. and L. Madden. Primary Sources
    for Victorian Studies.
    T.C. Barker, 325:Oct79-236
Storey, R.F. Pierrot.*
    J.R.B., 148:Summer79-93
    N. Ritter, 149(CLS):Dec79-355
Storm, T., E. Mörike and M. Mörike. Theo-
    dor Storms Briefwechsel mit Eduard und
    Margarethe Mörike. (H. and W. Kohl-
    schmidt, eds)
    C.A. Bernd, 301(JEGP):Oct79-609
    J. Hibberd, 182:Vol31#15/16-549

Storm, T. and E. Schmidt. Theodor Storm-
    Erich Schmidt Briefwechsel.* (Vol 2)
    (K.E. Laage, ed)
    A.O. Bönig, 67:May79-146
Storr, A. The Art of Psychotherapy.
    R. Dinnage, 617(TLS):9May80-530
    H. Gardner, 441:5Oct80-9
Stössel, H-A. Der letzte Gesang der
    "Odyssee."*
    A.H.M. Kessels, 394:Vol132fasc1/2-177
Stott, K.W., Jr. Exploring with Martin
    and Osa Johnson.
    J. Povey, 2(AfrA):Feb79-83
Stourzh, G. Kleine Geschichte des Öster-
    reichischen Staatsvertrags.
    E. Barker, 575(SEER):Jan79-140
Stout, R.J. Swallowing Dust.
    N. Moser, 584(SWR):Autumn79-412
Stove, D.C. Probability and Hume's Induc-
    tive Scepticism.
    J. Largeault, 542:Apr-Jun79-237
Stover, J.F. Iron Road to the West.
    K.L. Bryant, Jr., 658:Winter79-416
    639(VQR):Spring79-55
Stow, R. The Girl Green as Elderflower.
    V. Cunningham, 617(TLS):16May80-548
    J. Mellors, 362:22May80-660
    442(NY):1Sep80-88
Stow, R. Visitants.
    F. Tuohy, 617(TLS):4Jan80-9
Stowell, M.B. Early American Almanacs.*
    J.B. Hench, 517(PBSA):Jul-Sep78-394
    J. Seelye, 27(AL):Mar79-112
Strachan, W.J. - see Duras, M.
Strachey, B. Remarkable Relations.
    N. Annan, 617(TLS):19Sep80-1011
    E.S. Turner, 362:11Sep80-343
Strachey, L. Biographical and Literary
    Essays.
    P. Mauries, 98:Oct78-940
Strand, M. The Late Hour.*
    C. Bedient, 569(SR):Spring79-296
    R. De Mott, 651(WHR):Spring79-179
    R. Jackson, 659(ConL):Winter80-136
    H. Luke, 502(PrS):Fall78-305
    P. Stitt, 219(GaR):Summer79-463
Strand, M. The Monument.*
    C. Bedient, 569(SR):Spring79-296
    R. Jackson, 659(ConL):Winter80-136
Strand, P. Time in New England. (N. New-
    hall, ed)
    C. James, 453(NYRB):18Dec80-22
    H. Kramer, 441:30Nov80-66
Strandberg, V.H. The Poetic Vision of
    Robert Penn Warren.*
    J. Guimond, 191(ELN):Jun79-349
    639(VQR):Winter78-13
Strasberg, S. Bittersweet.
    J. Lahr, 441:8Jun80-12
Strassburg, R. Ernest Bloch.
    A. Knapp, 410(M&L):Oct79-461
Strassels, P.N., with R. Wool. All You
    Need to Know About the IRS.
    R. Lamb, 441:23Mar80-12
    C. Lehmann-Haupt, 441:7Feb80-C21
Strasser, S. Jenseits von Sein und Zeit.
    W. Krewani, 687:Jul-Sep79-464

Strathern, P. The Adventures of Spiro.
  J. Mellors, 362:3Jan80-30
Straub, P. Shadow Land.
  C. Lehmann-Haupt, 441:24Oct80-C31
Straus, M.A., R.J. Gelles and S.K. Stein-
  metz. Behind Closed Doors.
  J. Greenfield, 441:6Apr80-11
Straus, T. Les Trois Coups.*
  J. Cross, 399(MLJ):Mar79-141
Strausfeld, M., ed. Materialien zur
  lateinamerikanischen Literatur.
  A. Dessau, 654(WB):12/1978-184
Strauss, B. La Dédicace.
  B. Bayen, 450(NRF):Jul79-130
Strauss, B. Devotion.
  J. Crick, 617(TLS):2May80-510
Strauss, G. Luther's House of Learning.
  J. Whaley, 617(TLS):21Mar80-336
Strauss, R. and S. Zweig. A Confidential
  Matter.* (M. Knight, ed and trans)
  P. Loewenberg, 473(PR):3/1979-461
Strauss, W.L. The Complete Drawings of
  Albrecht Dürer.
  C.I. Minott, 54:Dec78-713
Stravinskaya, K.I. O I.F. Stravinskom y
  ego Blizkikh.
  R. Craft, 453(NYRB):24Jan80-9
Stravinsky, L. and R. Craft. Conversa-
  tions with Igor Stravinsky.
  A. Burgess, 617(TLS):29Feb80-227
Stravinsky, V. and R. Craft. Stravinsky
  in Pictures and Documents.*
  R.S. Clark, 249(HudR):Winter79/80-567
  P. Griffiths, 415:Oct79-827
Strazzullo, F. La Real Cappella del
  Tesoro di S. Gennaro.
  F. Brauen, 90:Dec79-804
Strazzullo, F. - see Vanvitelli, L.
Strecker, B. Das Problem der Stimulie-
  rung und Prüfung im Leistungsbereich
  "Sprechfertigkeit der englischen Umgangs-
  sprache."
  K. Macht, 430(NS):Apr78-185
Strecker, G., ed. Jesus Christus in
  Historie und Theologie.
  F.F. Bruce, 182:Vol31#14-460
Street, P. Arthur Bryant.
  T. Fitton, 617(TLS):18Jan80-62
Streiff Moretti, M. Le Rousseau de Gérard
  de Nerval.
  G. Schaeffer, 535(RHL):Mar-Jun79-509
Strelka, J.P., ed. Literary Criticism and
  Psychology.
  J.V. Knapp, 395(MFS):Winter78/79-654
  G.F. Probst, 678(YCGL):No.27-94
Strelka, J.P., R.F. Bell and E. Dobson,
  eds. Protest — Form — Tradition.
  R. Gray, 617(TLS):11Jan80-45
  D. Pike, 149(CLS):Dec79-365
Stremlau, J.J. The International Politics
  of the Nigerian Civil War, 1967-1970.
  639(VQR):Autumn78-132
Streuvels, S. The Long Road.
  205(FMLS):Jan78-94

Strevens, P. New Orientations in the
  Teaching of English.
  M. Celce-Murcia, 350:Dec79-967
  B.B. Kachru, 608:Jun80-242
  M. Martin, 399(MLJ):Apr79-226
  V. Meus, 179(ES):Dec79-827
Strick, I. Scot Free.
  639(VQR):Summer79-104
"Der Stricker: Verserzählungen II." (H.
  Fischer, ed; 2nd ed rev by J. Janota)
  S.L. Wailes, 133:Band12Heft1/2-143
Striedter, J. Dichtung und Geschichte
  bei Puškin.
  M.G. Pomar, 574(SEEJ):Summer79-266
Strindberg, A. Sleepwalking Nights.
  J.E. Bellquist, 563(SS):Spring79-198
Stringer, G.A., ed. New Essays on Donne.
  D.L. Russell, 568(SCN):Fall-Winter79-
  73
Strobel, G.W. Die Partei Rosa Luxemburgs,
  Lenin und die SPD.
  H. Hirsch, 182:Vol31#7/8-251
Strobel, M. Muslim Women in Mombasa 1890-
  1975.
  L. Mair, 617(TLS):7Mar80-276
Strommer, D.W., ed. "Time's Distrac-
  tions."
  J. Creaser, 541(RES):Nov79-472
Strong, D. Roman Art. (J.M.C. Toynbee,
  ed)
  R. Brilliant, 54:Mar78-159
Strong, K. Ox Against the Storm.
  J.K. Fisher, 293(JASt):Nov78-178
Stroop, J. The Stroop Report.
  R.A. Sokolov, 441:27Jan80-16
Strosetzki, C. Konversation.
  F. Londeix, 475:No.10Pt1-189
Stroud, B. Hume.*
  A. Flew, 393(Mind):Apr79-286
  185:Oct78-125
de Stroumillo, E. The Tastes of Travel.
  D. Mitchell, 617(TLS):9May80-535
Stroup, E.W. Hungary in Early 1848.*
  L. Deme, 104(CASS):Fall78-441
Strouse, J. Alice James.
  P-L. Adams, 61:Dec80-98
  D. Johnson, 441:14Dec80-1
  J. Leonard, 441:10Nov80-C19
Strunk, K. Lachmanns Regel für das Latein-
  ische.*
  A.M. Davies, 123:Vol129No2-259
Struve, T. Die Entwicklung der organolo-
  gischen Staatsauffassung im Mittelalter.
  W. Liebeschütz, 182:Vol31#15/16-571
Stuard, S.M., ed. Women in Medieval Soci-
  ety.*
  D.W. Rollason, 161(DUJ):Jun79-270
Stuart, D. Nabokov.*
  E. Pifer, 401(MLQ):Jun79-210
  639(VQR):Winter79-24
Stuart, S. New Phoenix Wings.
  L.C. Knights, 617(TLS):15Feb80-163
Stubblebine, J.H. Duccio di Buoninsegna
  and His School.
  J. Pope-Hennessy, 453(NYRB):20Nov80-45
Stuckenschmidt, H.H. Arnold Schoenberg.*
  E.S., 412:May78-135

Studdert-Kennedy, G. Evidence and Explanation in Social Science.
I.C. Jarvie, 84:Mar79-100
"Studi Americani." (Vols 19 and 20)
R. Asselineau, 189(EA):Jan-Mar78-109
"Studi collodiani."
P.Z., 228(GSLI):Vol155fasc490-315
"Studi di Letteratura Spagnola."
L. Schwartz Lerner, 545(RPh):May79-448
"Studi di storia antica, offerti dagli allievi a Eugenio Manni."
F. Lasserre, 182:Vol131#23/24-884
"Studi Secenteschi." (Vol 16)
D.C., 228(GSLI):Vol155fasc492-632
"Studi sul Boccaccio." (Vol 9)
M.M., 228(GSLI):Vol155fasc490-313
"Studies in Eighteenth-Century Culture." (Vol 7) (R. Runte, ed)
P. Rogers, 541(RES):Aug79-355
"Studies in Scottish Literature." (Vol 13) (G.R. Roy, ed)
A.H. MacLaine, 541(RES):Nov79-498
Stühler, H.J. Soziale Schichtung und gesellschaftlicher Wandel bei den Ajjer-Twareg in Südostalgerien.
P. Erny, 182:Vol131#9/10-318
Stuhlmann, G. - see Nin, A.
Stump, E. - see Boethius
Sturani Monti, L. - see Monti, A.
Sturgeon, M.C. Corinth. (Vol 9, Pt 2)
R.M. Cook, 123:Vol29No2-337
Sturges, H. 2d, L. Cregg and H.L. Herbst. Une Fois pour toutes.
B. Ebling 2d, 207(FR):May79-966
Sturgis, W. The Journal of William Sturgis. (S.W. Jackman, ed)
W.N., 102(CanL):Spring79-148
Sturluson, S. - see under Snorri Sturluson
Sturm, W. Religionsunterricht gestern, heute, morgen.
H. Grosch, 182:Vol131#14-463
Sturrock, J., ed. Structuralism and Since.
A. Montefiore, 617(TLS):5Sep80-959
Stursberg, P. Lester Pearson and the Dream of Unity.
102(CanL):Autumn79-148
Stüssi, A. Erinnerung an die Zukunft.*
H. Müssener, 406:Summer79-209
Stutley, M. and J. Harper's Dictionary of Hinduism.
J.B. Chethimattam, 613:Dec79-431
Styan, J.L. The Shakespeare Revolution.*
J.H. Astington, 627(UTQ):Fall78-80
P. Thomson, 611(TN):Vol132#3-138
Styron, W. Sophie's Choice.*
P.W. Leon, 639(VQR):Autumn79-740
E. Milton, 676(YR):Autumn79-89
A.H. Rosenfeld, 390:Dec79-43
Suarès, A. Caprices, poèmes inédits. (Y-A. Favre, ed)
F. Busi, 207(FR):Feb79-492
Suarez, F. Über die Individualität und das Individuationsprinzip.* (R. Specht, ed and trans)
A. Zimmermann, 53(AGP):Band60Heft2-226

Subba Reddy, D.V. Glimpses of Health and Medicine in Mauryan Empire.
L. Sternbach, 318(JAOS):Oct-Dec78-558
Subbanna, N.R. Kālidāsa Citations in Works on Poetics, Dramaturgy, Commentaries, etc.
L. Sternbach, 318(JAOS):Oct-Dec78-555
Subiotto, A. Bertolt Brecht's Adaptations for the Berliner Ensemble.*
J.K. Lyon, 131(CL):Spring79-192
Subrenat, J., ed. "Le Roman d'Auberon."*
H. Heger, 545(RPh):May79-475
Such, P. Dolphin's Wake.*
A.S. Brennan, 198:Winter80-120
Such, P. Fallout. (rev)
A.S. Brennan, 198:Winter80-120
R. Miles, 168(ECW):Fall78-65
Suchoff, B. - see Bartók, B.
Suckle, E. and thats all.
K. Garebian, 102(CanL):Summer79-126
Sucksmith, H.P. - see Dickens, C.
Sudermann, D.P. The Minnelieder of Albrecht von Johansdorf.*
O. Sayce, 402(MLR):Jan79-237
Suelflow, A.R., ed. Archives and History.
W.B. Miller, 14:Apr79-202
as-Sufi, 'A.Q. The Way of Muhammad.
H. Algar, 318(JAOS):Oct-Dec78-490
Sugar, P.F. Southeastern Europe Under Ottoman Rule, 1354-1804.
A.C. Hess, 104(CASS):Fall78-444
Sugathapala De Silva, M.W. and G.D. Wijayawardhana. Essentials of Sanskrit Grammar. Popular Sanskrit Texts.
K.R. Norman, 361:Feb/Mar78-309
Sugg, R.S., Jr. Motherteacher.
K.J. Blair, 432(NEQ):Sep79-414
Sugg, R.S., Jr. A Painter's Psalm.
C.M. Saunders, 585(SoQ):Winter79-142
Sugimoto, M. and D.L. Swain. Science and Culture in Traditional Japan A.D. 600-1854.
Umeda Toshirō, 285(JapQ):Jul-Sep79-403
Suh, D-S. and C-J. Lee, eds. Political Leadership in Korea.
V. Chandra, 293(JASt):Feb79-384
al-Suhrawardī, A.N. A Sufi Rule for Novices (Kitāb Ādāb al-Murīdīn). (M. Milson, ed and trans)
H. Algar, 318(JAOS):Oct-Dec78-486
Suitner, F. Petrarca e la tradizione stilnovistica.
G. Capovilla, 228(GSLI):Vol155fasc491-448
Suits, B. The Grasshopper.
J.F.M. Hunter, 627(UTQ):Summer79-471
Sukhlalji, P. Indian Philosophy.
T.W. Trexler, 318(JAOS):Jul-Sep78-333
Suknaski, A. The Ghosts Call You Poor.*
D. Brown, 526:Winter79-71
Suksamran, S. Political Buddhism in Southeast Asia. (T.O. Ling, ed)
S.J. Tambiah, 293(JASt):Nov78-210
al-Sulami, A.A.R. Jawāmi 'Ādāb al-Sufiyya and 'Uyūb al-Nafs wa-Mudāwātuha. (E. Kohlberg, ed)
S.A. Akbarabadi, 273(IC):Oct77-278

Suleiman, E.N. Elites in French Society.*
A.L. Moote, 255(HAB):Fall79-328
Sullerot, E. Women on Love.
F. Giroud, 441:20Jan80-24
Sullivan, B. Thresholds of Peace.
M. Howard, 617(TLS):7Mar80-254
Sullivan, C. - see Maddow, B. and R.
Sobieszek
Sullivan, H.W. Juan del Encina.*
C. Stern, 240(HR):Winter78-96
Sullivan, H.W. Tirso de Molina and the
Drama of the Counter Reformation.*
R. ter Horst, 400(MLN):Mar79-428
J.M. Sobré, 399(MLJ):Jan-Feb79-70
205(FMLS):Jan78-94
Sullivan, J. Elegant Nightmares.
639(VQR):Winter79-23
Sullivan, M. The Arts of China. (rev)
M. Somerville, 39:Feb79-167
Sullivan, M. The Meeting of Eastern and
Western Art from the Sixteenth Century
to the Present Day.
B.D.H. Miller, 463:Spring78-92
Sullivan, M. Symbols of Eternity.
E.H. Gombrich, 617(TLS):5Sep80-947
R.A. Sokolov, 441:18May80-15
Sullivan, N., ed. The Treasury of Ameri-
can Poetry.*
639(VQR):Autumn78-145
Sullivan, R.J. Morality and the Good Life.
C.J. Rowe, 303(JoHS):Vol99-179
Sullivan, T.D. Compendio de gramática
náhuatl.*
C.E. Dibble, 263(RIB):Vol29No1-105
Sullivan, W. Black Holes.*
T. Ferris, 441:6Jan80-8
Sulloway, F.J. Freud, Biologist of the
Mind.*
P. Brooks, 441:10Feb80-9
Sultan, S. "Ulysses," "The Waste Land,"
and Modernism.*
S. Benstock, 149(CLS):Jun79-175
Summerer, S. Wirkliche Sittlichkeit und
ästhetische Illusion.*
K. Düsing, 53(AGP):Band60Heft1-87
Summerfield, E. Ingeborg Bachmann.
A. Holschuh, 406:Spring79-88
Summerfield, H. An Introductory Guide to
"The Anathemata" and the "Sleeping Lord"
Sequence of David Jones.
D.B., 148:Autumn79-93
J. Hooker, 617(TLS):12Sep80-982
Summerfield, H. That Myriad-Minded Man.*
R. Fréchet, 189(EA):Jan-Mar78-101
Summerfield, H. - see Russell, G.W.
Summers, A. Conspiracy.
A. Hacker, 453(NYRB):17Jul80-12
C. Lehmann-Haupt, 441:22Jul80-C9
T. Powers, 441:29Jun80-12
Summers, M. The Galanty Show.
D.J. Enright, 362:10Jul80-54
A.N. Wilson, 617(TLS):25Jul80-831
Summerson, J. The Architecture of Victo-
rian London.
D. Stillman, 637(VS):Summer78-512
Summerson, J. Georgian London. (3rd ed)
42(AR):Winter79-123

Sumption, J. Pilgrimage.*
L.K. Little, 589:Jan79-194
Sundkler, B. Zulu Zion and Some Swazi
Zionists.
H. Kuper, 69:Vol48#3-306
Suñer, M., ed. Contemporary Studies in
Romance Linguistics.
V.E. Hanzeli, 399(MLJ):Sep-Oct79-299
Suñol, J. Siempre hay un nuevo día.
S. Baciu, 263(RIB):Vol29No3/4-379
Super, R.H. - see Arnold, M.
Suppan, W. and A. Mauerhofer, eds. His-
torische Volksmusikforschung: Kongress-
Bericht Seggau 1977.
D. Christensen, 187:May80-312
Suppe, F., ed. The Structure of Scien-
tific Theories.* (2nd ed)
M.H. Otero, 484(PPR):Sep79-148
"A Supplement to the Oxford English Dic-
tionary." (Vol 1) (R.W. Burchfield, ed)
H.H. Meier, 179(ES):Oct79-648
"A Supplement to the Oxford English Dic-
tionary."* (Vol 2) (R.W. Burchfield, ed)
D.H., 355(LSoc):Apr78-147
H.H. Meier, 179(ES):Oct79-648
Suri, P. Social Conditions in 18th Cen-
tury Northern India.
R. Shyam, 273(IC):Jul78-204
Susnik, B. Dispersión Tupí-Guaraní Pre-
histórica. Estudios Guayakí: Sistema
Fonético y Temático. Estudios Guayakí:
Vocabulario Ače. Lengua Maskoy.
H.E. Manelis Klein, 269(IJAL):Oct78-
345
Suso, H. Oeuvres complètes. (J. Ancelet-
Hustache, ed and trans)
A. Reix, 192(EP):Oct-Dec79-488
A. Reix, 542:Jan-Mar78-95
Sussman, L.A. The Elder Seneca.
M. Winterbottom, 123:Vol29No2-231
Suszynski, O.C. The Hagiographic-Thauma-
turgic Art of Gonzalo de Berceo; "Vida
de Santo Domingo de Silos."
C.B. Faulhaber, 238:May-Sep79-395
Sutcliffe, P.H. The Oxford University
Press.*
P.C. Bayley, 569(SR):Winter79-191
K.I.D. Maslen, 67:May79-114
639(VQR):Autumn78-148
Sutherland, F. Within the Wound.*
A. Amprimoz, 102(CanL):Winter78-92
Sutherland, J., ed. Restoration Trage-
dies.*
J. Barnard, 447(N&Q):Feb78-83
Sutherland, J.A. Victorian Novelists and
Publishers.*
D. Hewitt, 447(N&Q):Jun78-273
W.J. McCormack, 637(VS):Winter78-267
D. Roll-Hansen, 179(ES):Apr79-235
A. Shelston, 148:Spring79-86
Sutherland, M. The Fledgling.
K. Cochrane, 368:Mar76-86
Sutherland, R. The New Hero.*
P. Monk, 255(HAB):Summer79-232
W. Pache, 107(CRCL):Spring79-219
D. Staines, 529(QQ):Autumn79-479

Sutherland, S.R. Atheism and the Rejection of God.*
  R.W. Hepburn, 393(Mind):Apr79-312
  205(FMLS):Jul78-288
Sutherland, Z. The Best in Children's Books.
  C. Channell, 617(TLS):19Sep80-1035
Sutton, G.M. - see Fuertes, L.A.
Sutton, H. Travelers.
  D. Boyles, 441:14Sep80-18
Sutton, P.C. Pieter de Hooch.
  J. Russell, 441:30Nov80-72
Suvin, D. Metamorphoses of Science Fiction.
  W. Prouty, 268(IFR):Summer80-156
  T. Shippey, 617(TLS):9May80-519
Suvin, D. Pour une Poétique de la Science-Fiction.
  G. Good, 102(CanL):Autumn79-102
Suvin, D. and R.M. Philmus, eds. H.G. Wells and Modern Science Fiction.*
  S. Monod, 189(EA):Jul-Dec78-407
Suwala, H. Naissance d'une doctrine.
  C. Becker, 535(RHL):Sep-Oct79-866
Suyin, H. - see under Han Suyin
Svedlund, G. The Aramaic Portions of the Pesiqta de Rab Kahana.
  J.C. Greenfield, 318(JAOS):Oct-Dec78-511
Svensson, L., A.M. Wieselgren and Å. Hansson, eds. Nordiska studier i filologi och lingvistik.
  K. Petersson, 562(Scan):Nov78-188
Swaan, W. The Late Middle Ages.*
  W.S. Stoddard, 589:Apr79-428
Swahn, S. Ryktets förvandlingar.
  R.H. Sanders, 563(SS):Summer79-314
Swaim, L. The Killing.
  N. Callendar, 441:28Sep80-20
Swales, M. The German Bildungsroman from Wieland to Hesse.*
  G. Marahrens, 564:Sep79-229
  C.O. Sjögren, 301(JEGP):Jul79-406
  M.M. Tatar, 221(GQ):May79-408
  W. Witte, 220(GL&L):Oct79-87
Swales, M. The German Novelle.*
  J.M. Ellis, 400(MLN):Apr79-633
  I. Hobson, 395(MFS):Summer78-292
  D.G. Little, 402(MLR):Apr79-497
  M.K. Rogister, 161(DUJ):Dec78-139
  205(FMLS):Apr78-190
Swan, G. On the Edge of the Desert.
  D. Evanier, 441:27Jul80-18
Swan, J. A Door to the Forest.*
  R. Lattimore, 249(HudR):Autumn79-450
Swan, O. A Concise Grammar of Polish.
  R.A. Rothstein, 574(SEEJ):Summer79-310
Swanberg, W.A. Whitney Father, Whitney Heiress.
  J.K. Galbraith, 441:27Jul80-10
  E. Nemy, 441:19Jul80-15
  442(NY):23Jun80-103
Swann, B. Living Time.
  D. Smith, 29:Mar/Apr80-40
Swanson, G. Swanson on Swanson.
  J. Maslin, 441:9Nov80-12

Swanton, M. - see "Beowulf"
Swarthout, G. Skeletons.
  M. Laski, 362:10Jan80-62
Swearingen, J.E. Reflexivity in "Tristram Shandy."*
  A.H. Cash, 405(MP):Feb80-339
  D.H. Hirsch, 569(SR):Fall79-628
  M. New, 173(ECS):Winter78/79-215
  639(VQR):Spring78-56
Swede, G. A Snowman Headless. TellTale Feathers.
  G. Hamel, 198:Winter80-140
Sweeney, G.M. Melville's Use of Classical Mythology.*
  R.H. Brodhead, 445(NCF):Sep78-234
Sweeney, M. Without Shores.
  J. Cotton, 493:Dec79-72
Sweeney, P.L.A. The Ramayana and the Malay Shadow-play.
  B.A. van Nooten, 318(JAOS):Oct-Dec78-566
Sweetser, M-O. La dramaturgie de Corneille.
  H.R. Allentuch, 207(FR):Dec78-346
  C.B. Kerr, 546(RR):Nov79-402
  C. Miething, 547(RF):Band91Heft4-472
  A. Soare, 475:No.10Pt1-192
  P.J. Yarrow, 402(MLR):Jul79-695
Swenson, M. New and Selected Things Taking Place.*
  J. Fuller, 617(TLS):18Jan80-65
  W.H. Pritchard, 249(HudR):Summer79-261
  D. Smith, 491:Feb80-291
Swieżawski, S. Dzieje filozofii europejskiej XV wieku.
  G. Kalinowski, 192(EP):Apr-Jun79-257
Swift, E. Splendora.*
  639(VQR):Winter79-18
Swift, E.M. Vermont Place-Names.
  E. Green, 424:Mar78-116
  W.K. McNeil, 292(JAF):Apr-Jun79-243
Swift, J. A Dialogue in Hybernian Stile between A and B [and] Irish Eloquence.* (A. Bliss, ed)
  G. Leblanc, 189(EA):Jul-Dec78-389
Swift, J. Voyages de Gulliver. (J. Pons, trans)
  P. Danchin, 189(EA):Jul-Dec78-387
Swinburne, R. The Coherence of Theism.
  J.I.C., 543:Sep78-156
  I.M. Crombie, 479(PhQ):Apr79-185
  P. Helm, 518:May79-49
  R. Hepburn, 483:Jan79-125
  P. van Inwagen, 482(PhR):Oct79-668
  C. Lyas, 393(Mind):Jul79-456
  T. Penelhum, 311(JP):Aug80-502
  R. Young, 63:Mar79-100
Swinburne, R. The Existence of God.
  S. Clark, 617(TLS):25Jan80-82
Swindell, L. The Last Hero.
  A. Broyard, 441:22Feb80-C26
  J. Maslin, 441:17Feb80-13
Swinden, P., ed. Shelley, Shorter Poems and Lyrics: A Casebook.
  J. Buxton, 447(N&Q):Jun78-253
  P. Magnuson, 402(MLR):Jul79-667

Swinnerton, F. Reflections from a Village.
42(AR):Fall79-507
Swortzell, L. Here Come the Clowns.
N. Grace, 157:Winter79-83
Syberberg, H-J. Hitler, ein Film aus
Deutschland.
S. Sontag, 453(NYRB):21Feb80-36
Sychta, B. Słownik gwar kaszubskich na
tle kultury ludowej.
G. Stone, 575(SEER):Jul79-403
Sydnor, C.W., Jr. Soldiers of Destruc-
tion.
639(VQR):Spring78-61
Sykes, A. Tariff Reform in British
Politics 1903-1913.
P. Clarke, 617(TLS):15Feb80-164
Sykes, C. Evelyn Waugh.*
W.W. Robson, 473(PR):1/1979-138
Sykes, C.S. Country House Camera.
O. Lancaster, 617(TLS):13Jun80-668
Sykes, C.S. The Golden Age of the Country
House.
442(NY):4Aug80-91
Sykes, J.B. - see "The Concise Oxford Dic-
tionary of Current English"
Sykes, S.W., ed. Karl Barth: Studies of
His Theological Methods.
J. Macquarrie, 617(TLS):4Jul80-767
"Sylloge Nummorum Graecorum." (Pt 4;
Sicily, Vol 2)
B.L. Trell, 124:Dec79/Jan80-259
Sylvester, R.S. - see More, T.
Symcox, G. The Crisis of French Sea
Power 1688-1697.
J. Lough, 208(FS):Vol33Pt2-720
Syme, R. History in Ovid.
R. Seager, 617(TLS):11Jan80-44
Syme, R. Roman Papers. (E. Badian, ed)
G.W. Bowersock, 453(NYRB):6Mar80-8
Symonds, J. C.F.A. Voysey.
D. Stillman, 576:May78-117
Symons, D. The Evolution of Human Sexual-
ity.
C. Geertz, 453(NYRB):24Jan80-3
Symons, J. Sweet Adelaide.
T.J. Binyon, 617(TLS):9May80-520
M. Malone, 441:16Nov80-15
Symons, J. The Tell-Tale Heart.*
J.C. Miller, 27(AL):Mar79-115
Symons, J. The Thirties.
C.G., 189(EA):Jan-Mar78-111
Synnott, M.G. The Half-Opened Door.
H.P. Segal, 432(NEQ):Dec79-573
Synodinou, K. On the Concept of Slavery
in Euripides.
C. Collard, 123:Vol29No1-137
"Syntaktische und semantischen Studien
zur Koordination."
H. Esau, 603:Vol3#1-109
Sypher, W. The Ethic of Time.*
R.J. Quinones, 570(SQ):Winter79-114
M. Shapiro, 191(ELN):Mar79-249
Syrett, H.C. - see Hamilton, A.
Syrkin, M. Gleanings.
M. Hindus, 390:Aug-Sep79-66
"Systèmes de pensée en Afrique noire."
N. Barley, 69:Vol48#2-199

Sytchov, Y. Micromilieu et personnalité.
J-M. Gabaude, 542:Oct-Dec79-498
Szabolcsi, M., L. Illés and F. József, eds.
"Wir stürmen in die Revolution."
G.F. Cushing, 575(SEER):Jan79-120
Szarkowski, J. Looking at Photographs.
J.C. Sloane, 127:Fall78-82
Szasz, T. Schizophrenia.
M.E. Grenander, 84:Jun79-177
G.R. Lowe, 529(QQ):Autumn79-485
Szasz, T. The Theology of Medicine. Psy-
chiatric Slavery. The Myth of Psycho-
therapy.
G.R. Lowe, 529(QQ):Autumn79-485
Szeftel, M. The Russian Constitution of
April 23, 1906.
J. Keep, 575(SEER):Apr79-302
Széplaki, J. Hungarians in the United
States and Canada.
T. Kabdebo, 575(SEER):Apr79-317
Szertics, S. L'Héritage espagnol de José-
María de Heredia.
D.M. Di Orio, 207(FR):Apr79-774
Szidat, J. Historischer Kommentar zu
Ammianus Marcellinus Buch XX-XXI. (Pt 1)
R. Browning, 123:Vol29No2-237
Szigeti, J. Denis Diderot. (2nd ed)
A. Reix, 542:Jan-Mar78-111
Szigeti, J. Szigeti on the Violin.
M. Parikian, 415:Dec79-1003
Szirtes, G. The Slant Door.*
C. Hope, 364:Mar80-77
E. Longley, 617(TLS):18Jan80-64
Szöllösy, I.A. Arthur Honegger.
J.S.W., 412:Aug-Nov78-295
Szwed, J.F. and R.D. Abrahams, with others.
Afro-American Folk Culture.
J. Hasse, 187:Sep80-585

Ṭabāṭabā'ī, S.M.H. Shi'ite Islam.
A.A.A. Fyzee, 273(IC):Apr76-132
42(AR):Fall79-507
Tachau, M.K.B. Federal Courts in the
Early Republic: Kentucky, 1789-1816.
J.V. Orth, 656(WMQ):Jul79-488
Tack, R. Untersuchungen zum Philosophie —
und Wissenschaftsbegriff bei Pierre
Gassendi (1592-1655).
O. Bloch, 542:Apr-Jun79-223
Tadgell, C. Ange-Jacques Gabriel.
K. Downes, 46:Aug79-69
Taëni, R. Rolf Hochhuth.
A.D. White, 402(MLR):Oct79-999
Tafel, C.E. Beiträge zur französischen
Etymologie.
G. Price, 208(FS):Vol33Pt2-1023
Tafel, E. Apprentice to Genius.
F. Gutheim, 45:Dec79-187
Tafla, B., ed. A Chronicle of Emperor
Yohannes IV (1872-89).
J. Leroy, 182:Vol31#3/4-121
Taft, M., comp. A Regional Discography
of Newfoundland and Labrador, 1904-
1972.
C.W. Joyner, 582(SFQ):Vol141-297

Tafuri, M. Theories and History of Architecture.
R. Scruton, 617(TLS):25Jul80-847
Tafuri, M. and F. Dal Co. Modern Architecture.
P. Goldberger, 441:30Nov80-70
Taggert, G. Le français parlé contemporain.
E. Rattunde, 430(NS):Apr78-181
Taguchi, K.Y. An Annotated Catalogue of Ainu Material.
H. Aoki, 318(JAOS):Jul-Sep78-300
Taiana, F. Amor purus und die Minne.
L. Seppänen, 439(NM):1978/4-438
"Taidehistoriallisia tutkimuksia — Konsthistoriska studier." (Vols 1-3)
R. Strandberg, 341:1978/2-65
de la Taille, J. Alexandre.* (C.N. Smith, ed)
D. Ménager, 535(RHL):Sep-Oct78-816
"The Tain." (German title: Der Rinderraub.) (T. Kinsella, trans; German version trans by S. Schaup)
H.P. Neureuter, 52:Band13Heft2-195
Taiwo, O. Culture and the Nigerian Novel.
K. Barber, 69:Vol48#2-198
Takeda, T. Kanō Eitoku.
P.C. Swann, 463:Spring79-117
Talamo, G. Il Messaggero e sua città. (Vol 1)
J.A. Davis, 617(TLS):2May80-503
Talbert, R.J.A. Timoleon and the Revival of Greek Sicily 344-317 B.C.
S.I. Oost, 122:Jan79-85
Talbot, D. and B. Zheutlin. Creative Differences.
P. McGilligan, 18:Apr79-70
Talbot, M. Vivaldi.*
D.A., 410(M&L):Jul79-336
N. Kenyon, 415:Mar79-218
Talbott, J. The War Without a Name.
N. Wahl, 441:7Dec80-14
Talese, G. Thy Neighbor's Wife.
A. Broyard, 441:30Apr80-C27
A. Cockburn, 453(NYRB):29May80-6
R. Coles, 441:4May80-3
B. De Mott, 61:May80-98
V. Glendinning, 617(TLS):4Jul80-755
C. Sigal, 362:17Jul80-84
Tallanderius, P. Lectura.
R. Woodley, 410(M&L):Jul79-357
de Tamariz, C. Novelas en verso. (D. McGrady, ed)
A. Cioranescu, 549(RLC):Jan-Mar77-114
G. Sobejano, 240(HR):Spring78-256
Taminiaux, J. - see Hegel, G.W.F.
Tamke, S.S. Make a Joyful Noise Unto the Lord.
636(VP):Winter78-397
Tammelo, I. Modern Logic in the Service of Law.
L. Reisinger, 182:Vol131#21/22-776
Tamuly, A. Julien Green: à la recherche du réel.
J. Cruickshank, 208(FS):Vol33Pt2-902
T'an, H. - see under Huan T'an

Tan, H.G. La Matière de Don Juan et les genres littéraires.*
M. Franzbach, 196:Band19Heft1/2-171
H.G. Hall, 402(MLR):Jan79-142
C.N. Smith, 208(FS):Vol33Pt2-978
205(FMLS):Jan78-94
Tangermann, S. Gemeinsame Agrarpreispolitik und nationale Wirtschaftspolitik in der EWG.
R. Horber, 182:Vol131#13-401
Tannahill, R. Sex in History.
P. Grosskurth, 617(TLS):6Jun80-634
Tannen, J. How to Identify and Collect American First Editions.
G.T. Tanselle, 517(PBSA):Apr-Jun78-265
Tanner, H. and R. Wiltshire Village.
C.C. Brookes, 39:Dec79-538
Tanner, N.P., ed. Heresy Trials in the Diocese of Norwich, 1428-31.
R.E. Lerner, 589:Apr79-429
Tanner, T. Adultery in the Novel.
J. Bayley, 362:8May80-616
D. Lodge, 617(TLS):5Sep80-955
Tanzi, H.J. El poder político y la independencia argentina.
W.J. Fleming, 263(RIB):Vol29No2-214
T'ao, S. - see under Shih T'ao
Tapié, V.L. Barroco y Clasicismo.
A. Rodríguez G. de Ceballos, 48:Apr-Jun78-188
Tapié, V-L. France in the Age of Louis XIII and Richelieu. (D.M. Lockie, ed and trans)
J. Lough, 208(FS):Jul79-340
Taplin, K. The English Path.
R. Blythe, 617(TLS):25Jan80-80
Taplin, O. Greek Tragedy in Action.
M. Cropp, 487:Winter79-360
P. Walcot, 617(TLS):8Feb80-152
K. Worth, 157:Spring79-83
Taplin, O. The Stagecraft of Aeschylus.*
D. Bain, 303(JoHS):Vol199-171
J. Diggle, 123:Vol29No2-206
D. Sider, 24:Winter79-570
Tapscott, B.L. Elementary Applied Symbolic Logic.
M.L. Schagrin, 316:Jun79-281
Taran, L. - see Cherniss, H.
Taranovsky, K. Essays on Mandelstam.*
B.H. Monter, 104(CASS):Summer78-288
Tarbert, G.C. - see "Children's Book Review Index"
Tardieu, M. Trois mythes gnostiques.
G. Dorival, 542:Apr-Jun79-197
Targan, B. Kingdoms.
A. Broyard, 441:24Dec80-C15
Targan, B. Surviving Adverse Seasons.
D. Evanier, 441:27Jul80-18
Tarkka, P. Putkinotkon Tausta.
V. Zuck, 563(SS):Winter79-103
Tarnawski, W. Conrad.
I.P. Pulc, 136:Vol11#1-101
Tarnower, H. and S.S. Baker. The Complete Scarsdale Medical Diet.
J. Epstein, 453(NYRB):21Feb80-7
Tarpley, F.A., ed. Labeled for Life.
C.H. Neuffer, 424:Mar78-124

Tarr, R.L. Thomas Carlyle.*
K.J. Fielding, 402(MLR):Apr79-425
Tarr, Y.Y. The Tomato Book.
W. and C. Cowen, 639(VQR):Spring78-75
Tarrant, R.J. - see Seneca
Tarrête, J. Le Montmorencien.
R. Pittioni, 182:Vol131#7/8-240
Tarrow, S. Between Center and Periphery.
V. Wright, 208(FS):Vol33Pt2-1013
639(VQR):Winter78-19
Tarschys, D. The Soviet Political Agenda.
A. Brown, 617(TLS):25Jan80-95
Tarvainen, K. Dependenssikielioppi.
H. Nikula, 439(NM):1978/4-442
Taseer, S. Bhutto.
A. Howard, 362:3Jan80-30
Tashjian, D. William Carlos Williams and
the American Scene, 1920-1940.
L.S. Dembo, 27(AL):Jan80-577
S. Paul, 301(JEGP):Oct79-579
Tashjian, D. and A. Memorials for Chil-
dren of Change.
C.A. Prioli, 165(EAL):Winter79/80-328
Tassoni, A. Scritti inediti. (P.
Puliatti, ed)
D. Conrieri, 228(GSLI):Vol155fasc492-
609
Tatar, M.M. Spellbound.*
M. Gelus, 221(GQ):Nov79-569
S.L. Gilman, 591(SIR):Fall79-489
M. Hays, 222(GR):Fall79-171
J.M. McGlathery, 301(JEGP):Jul79-405
K. Schuchard, 594:Fall79-376
M. Steig, 445(NCF):Mar79-505
Tatarkiewicz, W. Analysis of Happiness.*
E.R., 543:Mar79-569
Tate, A. Collected Poems 1919-1976.*
S. Lang, 114(ChiR):Summer78-128
B. Raffel, 385(MQR):Spring80-251
639(VQR):Spring78-56
Tate, A. Memoirs and Opinions: 1926-1974.
T. Hubert, 577(SHR):Fall79-354
Tate, J. Riven Doggeries.
W.H. Pritchard, 491:Aug80-295
Tate, N. The History of King Lear. (J.
Black, ed)
L.W. Conolly, 447(N&Q):Feb78-79
M. Kelsall, 677(YES):Vol9-337
Tatlow, A. The Mask of Evil.*
J.M. Ritchie, 402(MLR):Jan79-250
J. Willett, 617(TLS):4Apr80-399
Tauber, G. The Hudson River Tourway.
J. Zukowsky, 576:Oct78-209
de Taucer, L.D. - see under de Stéfano de
Taucer, L.
Tausk, P. Photography in the Twentieth
Century.
C. James, 453(NYRB):18Dec80-22
Taussig, M.T. The Devil and Commodity
Fetishism in South America.
E.J. Hobsbawm, 453(NYRB):18Dec80-3
Tavernier-Courbin, J. Ernest Hemingway.
R. Asselineau, 106:Fall79-251
Taviani, H. and others. Voyage, quête,
pèlerinage dans la littérature et la
civilisation médiévales.
D.H. Green, 402(MLR):Jan79-232

Tawil, R.H. My Home, My Prison.
L. Hazleton, 441:20Jan80-7
T. Smith, 453(NYRB):12Jun80-42
Taylor, A. Parabolas.
C. Pollnitz, 581:Dec79-462
Taylor, A. Selected Writings on Proverbs.*
(W. Mieder, ed)
B. Alver, 196:Band19Heft1/2-172
Taylor, A. and I. Reid, eds. Number Two
Friendly Street.
C. Pollnitz, 581:Dec79-462
Taylor, A.J.P. Politicians, Socialism and
Historians.
J.P. Kenyon, 362:20Nov80-692
Taylor, A.J.P. Revolutions and Revolution-
aries.
J. Greenfield, 441:7Sep80-14
Taylor, A.M. - see Otway, T.
Taylor, C. Roads and Tracks of Britain.
N. Hammond, 617(TLS):8Feb80-147
Taylor, C.C.W. - see Plato
Taylor, C.D. Show of Force.
N. Callendar, 441:11May80-21
Taylor, C.T. The Values.
M. Adam, 542:Oct-Dec79-463
Taylor, D. Languages of the West Indies.
U. Corne, 350:Mar79-235
Taylor, D. Music Now.
P. Standford, 415:Dec79-1002
Taylor, D.S. Thomas Chatterton's Art.*
L. Waldoff, 301(JEGP):Jul79-436
Taylor, G.R. The Natural History of the
Mind.
M. Pines, 441:13Jan80-12
Taylor, H. James McNeill Whistler.*
M.E. Hayward, 658:Winter79-420
Taylor, H.M. Anglo-Saxon Architecture.
(Vol 3)
C.H. Lawrence, 46:May79-315
Taylor, H.M., ed. English and Japanese in
Contrast.
N.N. Hildebrandt, 608:Mar80-108
Taylor, I., comp. The Edwardian Lady.
P. Beer, 362:23Oct80-548
Taylor, J. The Architectural Medal.
L.W., 46:Feb79-126
Taylor, J. Asking for It.
C. Lehmann-Haupt, 441:27Nov80-C19
Taylor, J.C. The Fine Arts in America.
E. Lucie-Smith, 617(TLS):21Mar80-308
Taylor, J.M. Eva Perón.
442(NY):31Mar80-124
Taylor, J.R. Hitch.
K. Turan, 18:Dec78/Jan79-72
Taylor, M.F. O.P. McMains and the Maxwell
Land Grant Conflict.
W. Gard, 584(SWR):Autumn79-398
Taylor, M.G. Health Insurance and Can-
adian Public Policy.
S. Wolfe, 529(QQ):Winter79/80-696
Taylor, M.J. Martin du Gard: Jean Barois.
S. Spurdle, 208(FS):Vol33Pt2-872
Taylor, P. Beating the Terrorists?
K. Kyle, 362:27Nov80-730
Taylor, R. The Drama of W.B. Yeats.*
R. Tsukimura, 52:Band13Heft2-211
G-D. Zimmermann, 179(ES):Aug79-526

Taylor, R. Good and Evil.
J.O. Bennett, 321:Winter78-313
Taylor, R. The Politics of the Soviet
Cinema 1917-1929.
A. Brown, 617(TLS):25Jan80-95
Taylor, R. Richard Wagner.*
G. Abraham, 410(M&L):Oct79-453
R. Anderson, 415:May79-400
42(AR):Fall79-488
Taylor, R.H. - see Hardy, T.
Taylor, R.J., with M-J. Kline and G.L.
Lint - see Adams, J.
Taylor, T. - see Leslie, C.R.
Taylor, T.F. Thematic Catalog of the
Works of Jeremiah Clarke.*
P.F.W., 412:Aug-Nov78-274
Taylor, W.B. Drinking, Homicide, and
Rebellion in Colonial Mexican Villages.
D.B. Cooper, 263(RIB):Vol29No2-215
Taylor, W.D. Sherwood Anderson.
E. Baldeshwiler, 573(SSF):Summer78-340
639(VQR):Summer78-92
Tazbir, J. Bracia Polscy na wygnaniu.
S. Dąbrowski, 497(PolR):Vol23#3-114
Tazieff, H. Nyiragongo.
R.A. Sokolov, 441:27Jan80-16
Tchernia, A., P. Pomey and A. Hesnard.
L'épave romaine de la Madrague de Giens
(Var).
G. Alföldy, 182:Vol131#13-435
"Il Teatro al tempo di Luigi XIII."
H.G. Hall, 208(FS):Vol33Pt2-698
Tedeschi Grisanti, G. I "Trofei di
Mario."*
E. Simon, 471:Jan/Feb/Mar79-77
Tedesco, N. L'isola impareggiabile.
E.F., 228(GSLI):Vol155fasc491-477
Tedlock, D. - see "Finding the Center"
Tedlock, D. and B., eds. Teachings from
the American Earth.
D.L. Whelchel, 292(JAF):Jan-Mar79-90
Teichman, J. The Meaning of Illegitimacy.
G.E.M. Anscombe, 479(PhQ):Oct79-375
Teichner, W. Rekonstruktion oder Reproduk-
tion des Grundes.*
J. Schmucker-Hartmann, 342:Band69Heft3-
368
Teika, F. Fujiwara Teika's "Hundred-
Poem Sequence of the Shōji Era," 1200.
(R.H. Brower, ed and trans)
R.E. Morrell, 293(JASt):Aug79-779
Teixeira, H.G. As Tábuas do Painel de
um Auto (Antônio Serrão de Crasto).
R.C. Willis, 86(BHS):Apr79-166
Tejada, J.L. Rafael Alberti, entre la
tradición y la vanguardia.*
G. Connell, 86(BHS):Apr79-161
Tejera, A.D. - see under Díaz Tejera, A.
"Television and Human Behavior."
J. Swerdlow, 18:Dec78/Jan79-70
Telle, É.V. - see Le Chevalier de Berquin
Telle, É.V. - see Erasmus
Telles, L.F. Seminário dos Ratos.
J.S. Vincent, 399(MLJ):Jan-Feb79-58
Temple, E. Anglo-Saxon Manuscripts 900-
1066.*
78(BC):Summer79-183

Temporini, H. and W. Haase, eds. Aufstieg
und Niedergang der Römischen Welt. (Sec-
tion 2, Vol 9, Pt 1)
T.R.S. Broughton, 318(JAOS):Apr-Jun78-
153
"Le temps et les philosophies."
M. Adam, 542:Oct-Dec79-464
Tenenbaum, E.B. The Problematic Self.*
R.D. Cottrell, 395(MFS):Winter78/79-
620
H. Godin, 402(MLR):Jul79-652
J. Halpern, 400(MLN):May79-910
M.G. Rose, 446(NCFS):Fall-Winter78/79-
146
B. Thompson, 399(MLJ):Jan-Feb79-81
Tenèze, M-L. Le Conte Populaire Français.
R. Labelle, 292(JAF):Jan-Mar79-94
Tennant, E. Alice Fell.
J. Naughton, 362:20Nov80-700
Tennant, E. Wild Nights.*
D. Durrant, 364:Dec79/Jan80-132
Tennant, N. Natural Logic.
D.E. Over, 518:Oct79-132
Tennant, P.E. Théophile Gautier.*
D.G. Burnett, 188(ECr):Spring78-94
Tente, L. Die Polemik um den Ersten
Discours von Rousseau in Frankreich und
Deutschland.
U. Schulz-Buschhaus, 72:Band216Heft2-
468
Tentler, L.W. Wage-Earning Women.
V. Sapiro, 617(TLS):27Jun80-736
Tentler, T.N. Sin and Confession on the
Eve of the Reformation.*
M.O. Boyle, 539:Vol4No2-245
Teodorsson, S-T. The Phonemic System of
the Attic Dialect 400-340 B.C.*
W.F. Wyatt, Jr., 122:Jul79-264
Teodorsson, S-T. The Phonology of Ptole-
maic Koine.
J. Irigoin, 555:Vol52fasc2-381
A.H. Sommerstein, 123:Vol29No1-169
Terdiman, R. The Dialectics of Isolation.*
J. Cruickshank, 208(FS):Vol33Pt2-955
H.T. Mason, 447(N&Q):Oct78-473
Terhune, A.M. and A.B. - see Fitz Gerald,
E.
Terkel, S. American Dreams.
J. Leonard, 441:24Sep80-C29
R. Sherrill, 441:14Sep80-1
61:Nov80-96
442(NY):13Oct80-191
Terman, D. Free Flight.
N. Callendar, 441:9Nov80-26
"Terminologická studie 5."
W. Seibicke, 685(ZDL):2/1979-263
Terrace, H.S. Nim.
D.J. Enright, 362:12Jun80-763
M. Gardner, 453(NYRB):20Mar80-3
V. Reynolds, 617(TLS):1Aug80-865
Terralla Landa, E. Lima por dentro y
fuera. (A. Soons, ed)
J. Higgins, 86(BHS):Oct79-350
Terrasse, J. Rhétorique de l'essai lit-
téraire.
S.E. Melzer, 207(FR):Apr79-765
F. Roy, 193(ELit):Apr78-235

Terrell, C.F., ed. Louis Zukofsky: Man and Poet.
  M. Heller, 441:27Jul80-19
Terrell, D.K. - see Irving, W.
Terrenal, Q.C. Causa Sui and the Object of Intuition in Spinoza.
  H.P. Rickman, 53(AGP):Band60Heft3-337
Terrill, R. Mao.
  S. Karnow, 441:25May80-6
Terrill, T.E. and J. Hirsch, eds. Such As Us.
  M.C. Brown, 585(SoQ):Fall78-95
  R.L. Watson, Jr., 579(SAQ):Spring79-272
Terris, V. Tracking.
  639(VQR):Winter78-12
Terry, A. - see March, A.
Terry, A. and J. Rafel. Introducción a la lengua y literatura catalanas.
  J.M. Sobré, 240(HR):Autumn78-506
Terry, R.C. Anthony Trollope.*
  C. Herbert, 637(VS):Summer79-479
  M. Laine, 627(UTQ):Summer79-413
Terry, W. The King's Ballet Master.
  L. Kirstein, 453(NYRB):20Mar80-18
Terson, P. Rattling the Railings.
  J. Coleby, 157:Summer79-81
Tertz, A. [A. Sinyavsky] A Voice from the Chorus.*
  V. Terras, 473(PR):4/1979-630
Tervooren, H. - see von Morungen, H.
Tervooren, H. and U. Müller, eds. Die Jenaer Liederhandschrift.
  B. Murdoch, 182:Vol31#11/12-344
Tervoort, B.T.M. Developmental Features of Visual Communication.*
  S.D. Fischer, 567:Vol125#3/4-359
  D.F. Moores, 603:Vol3#2-294
Tessier, T. La poésie lyrique de Thomas Moore (1779-1852).*
  C. Lloyd, 447(N&Q):Dec78-564
Testud, P. Rétif de la Bretonne et la création littéraire.
  V. Mylne, 402(MLR):Apr79-462
  V. Mylne, 535(RHL):Mar-Jun79-524
  C.A. Porter, 207(FR):Mar79-641
Tetel, M. Marguerite de Navarre's "Heptameron."
  J. McClelland, 539:Vol4No2-226
Tetel, M. Montaigne.*
  M.M. McGowan, 208(FS):Vol33Pt2-638
Thaddeus, J. - see Marshall, L.
Thalberg, I. Perception, Emotion and Action.*
  J.W.R. Cox, 518:Jan79-36
  M.A. McCloskey, 483:Apr79-264
Tham Seong Chee. Malays and Modernization.
  C.H. Enloe, 293(JASt):May79-629
Thàn, N.K. - see under Nguyẽn Kim Thàn
Tharpe, J., ed. Tennessee Williams.*
  J.H. Clark, 397(MD):Jun79-203
Thayer, N. Stepping.
  S. Isaacs, 441:3Feb80-14
Théau, J. La philosophie française dans la première moitié du XXe siècle.
  M. Adam, 542:Jul-Sep79-333

Thelander, M. Grepp och begrepp i språksociologin.*
  K. Braunmüller, 685(ZDL):1/1979-117
Thelin, N.B. Towards a Theory of Aspect, Tense and Actionality in Slavic.
  B. Comrie, 350:Dec79-962
Thelwell, M. The Harder They Come.
  D. Pinckney, 441:1Jun80-15
  M. Watkins, 441:25Aug80-C22
Theocritus. The Poems of Theocritus. (A. Rist, ed and trans)
  G. Lawall, 487:Spring79-84
  C. Segal, 627(UTQ):Summer79-394
Theodoret of Cyrrhus. Théodoret de Cyr, "Histoire des moines de Syrie." (Vol 1) (P. Canivet and A. Leroy-Molinghen, eds and trans)
  É. Des Places, 555:Vol52fasc1-180
Theodoridis, C. - see Philoxenus
Theophrastus. De Causis Plantarum.* (Vol 1, Bks 1 and 2) (B. Einarson and G.K.K. Link, trans)
  P. Louis, 555:Vol52fasc2-380
"Theoretische Probleme der Sprachwissenschaft."*
  T. Schippan, 682(ZPSK):Band31Heft3-315
Theroux, P. California and Other States of Grace.
  E. Goodman, 441:20Jul80-11
  442(NY):30Jun80-105
Theroux, P. The Consul's File.*
  Cheng Lok Chua, 573(SSF):Fall78-470
  639(VQR):Winter78-24
Theroux, P. The Old Patagonian Express.*
  T. Jacoby, 453(NYRB):17Apr80-43
Theroux, P. Picture Palace.*
  639(VQR):Winter79-18
Theroux, P. World's End.
  A. Broyard, 441:12Sep80-C21
  B. De Mott, 441:24Aug80-7
  P. Kemp, 362:30Oct80-588
Thesiger, W. The Last Nomad.
  A. Horne, 441:20Apr80-11
Theuerkauff, C. and others. Kataloge des Museums für Kunst und Gewerbe Hamburg IV.
  T. Müller, 471:Jan/Feb/Mar79-80
Thévenon, P. L'Artefact.
  V. Carrabino, 207(FR):Mar79-676
Thibaud, P. La logique de Charles Sanders Peirce.*
  G. Stahl, 542:Apr-Jun78-236
Thibaut de Blaison. Les Poésies de Thibaut de Blaison. (T.H. Newcombe, ed)
  P. Rickard, 382(MAE):1979/1-128
  N.B. Smith, 589:Jul79-590
Thickett, D. - see Pasquier, E.
Thiébaux, M. The Stag of Love.*
  M.D. Legge, 208(FS):Vol33Pt2-592
Thiel, C., ed. Frege und die moderne Grundlagenforschung.
  E. Fries, 53(AGP):Band60Heft3-358
  M. Schirn, 316:Mar79-119
Thiele, W., ed. Racine.
  C.N. Smith, 208(FS):Vol33Pt2-693
Thiele, W., ed. Vetus Latina. (Fasc 11, Pt 1)
  P. Courcelle, 555:Vol52fasc1-204

Thiele, W., ed. Vetus Latina. (Fasc 11,
pt 1, section 2)
  P. Courcelle, 555:Vol52fasc2-412
Thielemans, M-R. Inventaire des archives
du baron de Stassart. (Vol 1)
  R. de Smedt, 535(RHL):May-Jun78-493
Thielicke, H. Der evangelische Glaube.
(Vols 2 and 3)
  J. Galot, 182:Vol31#20-720
Thieltges, G. Bürgerlicher Klassizismus
und romantisches Theater.*
  W.D. Howarth, 208(FS):Vol33Pt2-820
  E. Knecht, 535(RHL):Mar-Apr78-324
Thiering, C. Die Tradition des französis-
chen Verschwörerdramas.
  W.D. Howarth, 208(FS):Vol33Pt2-963
Thies, W.J. When Governments Collide.
  R. Asahina, 441:9Nov80-16
Thiry, C. La Plainte funèbre.
  N.B. Smith, 589:Oct79-862
Thiry-Stassin, M. and M. Tyssens, eds.
Narcisse.*
  A.H. Diverres, 208(FS):Vol33Pt2-536
"This Is My Best."*
  J. Ferns, 102(CanL):Spring79-92
Thisse, A. Rimbaud devant Dieu.
  M. Davies, 208(FS):Vol33Pt2-843
Thody, P. Roland Barthes.*
  D. Bellos, 402(MLR):Oct79-955
  A. Jefferson, 447(N&Q):Aug78-360
Thody, P. Dog Days in Babel.*
  J.R.B., 148:Summer79-93
Tholfsen, T. Working Class Radicalism in
Mid-Victorian England.
  T.W. Laqueur, 637(VS):Winter79-229
Thom, A. and A.S. Megalithic Remains in
Britain and Brittany.
  N. Hammond, 617(TLS):8Feb80-147
Thom, R. Structural Stability and Morpho-
genesis.* (French title: Stabilité
structurelle et morphogénèse.)
  Y. Gauthier, 98:Jan78-3
Thoma, W., ed. Stilistik.
  E.W.B. Hess-Lüttich, 680(ZDP):Band97-
  Heft3-474
Thomas of Kent. The Anglo-Norman Alexan-
der (Le Roman de toute Chevalerie) by
Thomas of Kent. (B. Foster and I. Short,
eds)
  B. Merrilees, 589:Oct79-863
  W. Rothwell, 208(FS):Apr79-178
  J. Weiss, 382(MAE):1979/2-291
Thomas of Sutton. Contra Quodlibet Iohan-
nis Duns Scoti. (J. Schneider, ed)
  S.P. Marrone, 589:Jul79-634
Thomas, A. Latakia.
  R.M. Brown, 99:Jun-Jul80-38
  B. Godard, 198:Summer80-121
Thomas, A. Time in a Frame.*
  M. Roskill, 637(VS):Spring79-335
Thomas, C. Love and Work Enough.
  P. Monk, 255(HAB):Summer79-232
Thomas, C. Wolfsbane.
  639(VQR):Summer79-102
Thomas, D. A Child's Christmas in Wales.
(E. Ardizzone, illustrator)
  Q. Bell, 453(NYRB):18Dec80-50

Thomas, D. The Marquis de Sade.*
  J.H. McMahon, 207(FR):Dec78-351
Thomas, D. and J. Davenport. The Death of
the King's Canary.
  639(VQR):Winter78-23
Thomas, D.D. Chrau Grammar.
  R. Gaudes, 682(ZPSK):Band31Heft1-78
Thomas, D.M. Birthstone.
  A. Motion, 617(TLS):14Mar80-296
Thomas, D.O. The Honest Mind.*
  P. Dubois, 542:Apr-Jun79-239
  E. Sprague, 482(PhR):Jan79-131
Thomas, E. The Collected Poems of Edward
Thomas.* (R.G. Thomas, ed)
  R. Gaskell, 184(EIC):Oct79-375
  S. Hynes, 491:Mar80-342
  S. Smith, 148:Winter79-86
Thomas, E. A Grammatical Description of
the Engenni Language.
  L.M. Hyman, 350:Sep79-748
Thomas, E.M. The Confederate Nation: 1861-
1865.
  639(VQR):Autumn79-132
Thomas, G.S. Gardens of the National
Trust.
  J. Lees-Milne, 39:Aug79-153
Thomas, H. A History of the World.*
(British title: An Unfinished History
of the World.)
  N. Bliven, 442(NY):17Mar80-161
  J. Sumption, 617(TLS):18Jan80-56
  C.V. Woodward, 441:20Jan80-11
Thomas, H. Les Tours de Notre Dame.
  A. Thiher, 207(FR):Dec78-386
Thomas, J. Universal Pronouncing Diction-
ary of Biography and Mythology.
  K.B. Harder, 424:Dec77-237
Thomas, J.W. - see Wirnt von Grafenberg
Thomas, L. The Lives of a Cell.
  J. Cairns, 617(TLS):1Aug80-870
Thomas, L. The Medusa and the Snail.*
  J. Cairns, 617(TLS):1Aug80-870
  639(VQR):Autumn79-150
Thomas, L-V. Civilisation et divagations.
  J. Duvignaud, 450(NRF):Nov79-123
Thomas, M. Louis-Ferdinand Céline.*
  P. Brooks, 441:11May80-11
Thomas, M. The Golden Age.
  M. Schulze, 55:Nov79-33
Thomas, M.C. The Making of a Feminist.
(M.H. Dobkin, ed)
  H. Vendler, 441:24Feb80-24
Thomas, M.M. Green Monday.
  C. Lehmann-Haupt, 441:16Jul80-C21
  L. Silk, 441:10Aug80-14
Thomas, P. Karl Marx and the Anarchists.
  P. Singer, 453(NYRB):25Sep80-62
Thomas, R. The Eighth Dwarf.*
  M. Laski, 362:10Jan80-62
Thomas, R.G.C. The Defence of India.
  R.W. Jones, 293(JASt):Aug79-813
Thomas, R.S. Frequencies.*
  D. Graham, 565:Vol20#1-65
  L. Sail, 493:Mar80-71
Thomas, S.N. The Formal Mechanics of
Mind.
  C.S. Hill, 482(PhR):Oct79-648

Thomas, W. The Philosophical Radicals.
  J.F.C. Harrison, 617(TLS):23May80-593
Thomas, W.I. and F. Znaniecki. Chłop
  polski w Europie i Ameryce.
  K. Symmons-Symonolewicz, 497(PolR):
  Vol23#2-76
Thomasson, H. The Pursuit of the Present.
  G. Hough, 617(TLS):13Jun80-665
Thompson, B.B. - see del Rosal, F.
Thompson, C.P. The Poet and the Mystic.
  M.L. Salstad, 161(DUJ):Dec78-128
  M. Wilson, 402(MLR):Jul79-724
Thompson, C.R. - see Erasmus
Thompson, D. Dante's Epic Journeys.*
  E.C. Ronquist, 481(PQ):Winter78-137
Thompson, D.F. John Stuart Mill and Repre-
  sentative Government.*
  J. Weissman, 637(VS):Winter78-275
Thompson, E.K., ed. Houses of the West.
  R. Bender, 658:Winter79-422
Thompson, E.M. Witold Gombrowicz.
  P. Petro, 268(IFR):Winter80-67
Thompson, E.P. and D. Smith, eds. Protest
  and Survive.
  C. Wain, 362:30Oct80-586
Thompson, E.T. Local History Collections.
  P.N. Cronenwett, 14:Jul79-359
Thompson, J. The Gasoline Wars.
  D. Evanier, 441:27Jul80-18
Thompson, J. Stilt Jack.* At the Edge of
  the Chopping There Are No Secrets.
  C. Levenson, 529(QQ):Winter79/80-718
  T. Marshall, 168(ECW):Fall78-204
Thompson, J.D. and G. Goldin. The Hospi-
  tal.*
  G.L. Schless, 54:Jun78-359
Thompson, J.H. The Harvests of War.
  E.L. Bobak, 150(DR):Summer79-373
Thompson, J.R. Leigh Hunt.
  T. Fenner, 340(KSJ):Vol28-159
Thompson, K. Shotgun and Other Stories.
  J. Mills, 198:Winter80-115
Thompson, K.W. Interpreters and Critics
  of the Cold War.
  639(VQR):Winter79-26
Thompson, M. Rubbish Theory.
  A. Wildavsky, 617(TLS):27Jun80-736
Thompson, R.F. African Art in Motion.
  D.W. Ames, 187:Sep80-561
Thompson, R.F. Black Gods and Kings.*
  F. Willett, 2(AfrA):Nov78-11
Thompson, S.O. American Book Design and
  William Morris.*
  D. Chambers, 503:Winter78-190
Thomsen, C.W. Das Groteske und die eng-
  lische Literatur.
  R. Imhof, 447(N&Q):Aug78-364
Thomson, B. Lot's Wife and the Venus of
  Milo.*
  C.J. Barnes, 575(SEER):Apr79-285
  E.K. Beaujour, 574(SEEJ):Summer79-293
  R. Dessaix, 67:May79-171
  V. Terras, 550(RusR):Jan79-123
  E. Wasiolek, 131(CL):Summer79-315
  A.F. Zweers, 104(CASS):Fall78-422
Thomson, D. and M. McGusty - see Smith, E.
Thomson, D.F.S. - see "Catullus"

Thomson, G.M. The First Churchill.
  442(NY):25Feb80-134
Thomson, G.M. The Prime Ministers.
  P. Johnson, 362:11Dec80-796
Thomson, J.J. Acts and Other Events.
  J. Hornsby, 483:Apr79-253
  S.P. Schwartz, 482(PhR):Jan79-100
Thomson, K. The Masonic Thread in Mozart.*
  R.L.J., 412:May78-128
Thomson, P. George Sand and the Victo-
  rians.*
  B.F. Bart, 445(NCF):Sep78-258
  N. Rogers, 637(VS):Autumn78-105
  V. Shaw, 402(MLR):Oct79-912
Thomson, R., ed. The Life of Gundulf
  Bishop of Rochester.
  M. Chibnall, 382(MAE):1979/2-258
Thong, H.S., ed and trans. The Heritage
  of Vietnamese Poetry.
  639(VQR):Summer79-109
Thoran, B., ed. Das Münchner Osterspiel
  (Cgm 147 der Bayerischen Staatsbiblio-
  thek München).
  W.F. Michael, 133:Band12Heft1/2-147
Thornberry, R.S. André Malraux et
  l'Espagne.*
  D. Boak, 67:May79-118
  V. Conley, 395(MFS):Winter78/79-615
  D. Gascoigne, 402(MLR):Jul79-708
  J.J. Michalczyk, 207(FR):Oct78-174
Thorndike, J.J., Jr. The Magnificent
  Builders and Their Dream Houses.
  D. Szatmary, 658:Winter79-424
Thorne, R. Covent Garden Market.
  C. Amery, 617(TLS):20Jun80-698
Thornton, A. The Living Universe.
  N. Horsfall, 313:Vol69-231
  W. Pötscher, 394:Vol132fasc3/4-428
  M.C.J. Putnam, 124:Sep79-40
  G.B. Townend, 123:Vol129No1-35
Thornton, A.G. Weltgeschichte und Heilsge-
  schichte in Albrechts von Scharfenberg
  Jüngerem Titurel.
  H.B. Willson, 402(MLR):Jul79-739
Thornton, J.M. 3d. Politics and Power in
  a Slave Society.
  R.F. Durden, 579(SAQ):Summer79-411
Thornton, P. Seventeenth-Century Inter-
  ior Decoration in England, France and
  Holland.
  G. Beard, 46:May79-311
  A. Blunt, 90:Oct79-657
  B. Boucher, 617(TLS):21Mar80-334
  J. Parker, 39:Jul79-77
"The Thornton Manuscript."* (2nd ed)
  E.G. Stanley, 447(N&Q):Apr78-165
Thorp, N.H., with N.M. Clark. Pardner of
  the Wind.*
  W.K. McNeil, 292(JAF):Oct-Dec79-515
Thorpe, D.R. The Uncrowned Prime Min-
  isters.
  P. Johnson, 362:11Dec80-796
Thorpe, W.H. Purpose in a World of Chance.
  H. Meynell, 483:Jul79-425
  V. Pratt, 84:Sep79-309

Thoulier, P-J. Correspondance littéraire du Président Bouhier. (Vols 3 and 4) (C. Lauvergnat-Gagnière and H. Duranton, eds)
P. Alayrangues, 535(RHL):Nov-Dec78-1032
Threlfall, R. A Catalogue of the Compositions of Frederick Delius.*
C. MacDonald, 607:Jun78-30
Threlfall, R. and L. Carley. Delius.
C. MacDonald, 607:Jun78-30
Thrower, N.J.W., ed. The Compleat Plattmaker.
S.L. Macey, 173(ECS):Summer79-527
Thülemeyer, H.G. and A. Wolf, eds. Copia manuscripti Aureae Bullae Caroli IV.
R. Folz, 182:Vol31#13-388
Thurley, G. The Dickens Myth.*
R.L. Patten, 454:Spring79-254
Thurley, G. The Psychology of Hardy's Novels.*
D. Edwards, 637(VS):Summer78-511
Thurman, H. With Head and Heart.
D. Grumbach, 441:6Jan80-12
Thurow, G.E. Abraham Lincoln and American Political Religion.
S.J. Tonsor, 396(ModA):Winter79-87
Thurow, L.C. The Zero-Sum Society.
E. Cowan, 441:1Jul80-C9
J.K. Galbraith, 453(NYRB):12Jun80-3
M.F. Plattner, 441:8Jun80-13
61:Aug80-83
Thursby, G.R. Hindu-Muslim Relations in British India.*
M. Yanuck, 293(JASt):Aug79-806
Thurston, R. Believed Dangerous.
A. Paterson, 368:Dec76-93
Thynn, A. Pillars of the Establishment.
J. Naughton, 362:20Nov80-700
Tibbetts, A. and C. What's Happening to American English?
639(VQR):Summer79-104
Tibble, A., with R.K.R. Thornton - see Clare, J.
"The Tibetan Book of the Dead." (F. Fremantle and C. Trungpa, trans)
R.A.F. Thurman, 318(JAOS):Apr-Jun78-139
Tich, M. and R. Findlater. Little Tich.
M. Norgate, 157:Autumn79-84
Tichane, R. Those Celadon Blues.
S.G. Valenstein, 463:Autumn79-359
Tichi, C. New World, New Earth.*
R.B. Davis, 27(AL):Jan80-567
D. Leverenz, 141:Fall79-379
Tieder, I. Michelet et Luther.*
H. Bluhm, 406:Spring79-64
J. Gaulmier, 535(RHL):Sep-Oct78-848
Tiefenbach, H. Althochdeutsche Aratorglossen.
H. Martin, 406:Winter79-438
Tiefenbrun, S.W. A Structural Stylistic Analysis of "La Princesse de Clèves."*
J. Campbell, 208(FS):Vol33Pt2-690
Tieffenthaler, J. The Mid-Gangetic Region in the 18th Century.
S.M. Alam, 273(IC):Jul77-221

Tiemann, B. Fabel und Emblem.
C.N. Smith, 208(FS):Vol33Pt2-630
Tierney, F.M., ed. The Crawford Symposium.
M.G. Parks, 150(DR):Winter79/80-752
Tietze, G.O.A. Einführung in die Wortbildung des heutigen Englisch.
L. Lipka, 38:Band96Heft3/4-487
Tiffin, C., ed. South Pacific Images.
K.D. Gelder, 67:May79-172
A. Mitchell, 71(ALS):Oct79-248
G. McGregor, 49:Apr79-94
Tiffou, E. Essai sur la pensée morale de Salluste à la lumière de ses prologues.*
G.M. Paul, 627(UTQ):Summer79-398
Tiger, L. Optimism.*
F.R. Hayes, 150(DR):Winter79/80-767
Tigerstedt, E.N. Interpreting Plato.
M.F. Burnyeat, 123:Vol29No1-161
Tighe, M.A. and E.E. Lang. Art America.*
M. Thistlethwaite, 658:Autumn79-311
Tikhmenev, P.A. A History of the Russian-American Company.
A.G. Mazour, 550(RusR):Apr79-225
639(VQR):Spring79-55
Tikkanen, H. Snobs' Island.
P. Kemp, 362:3Apr80-450
P. Lewis, 617(TLS):18Apr80-442
Tikkanen, H. A Winter's Day.
P-L. Adams, 61:Jun80-95
Tilander, G. - see Gaston Phébus
Tilkov, D. and T. Bojadžiev. B"garska fonetika.
E. Scatton, 574(SEEJ):Spring79-145
Tilkovszki, L. Pal Teleki (1879-1941).
L. Péter, 575(SEER):Jan79-133
Till, G. Air Power and the Royal Navy 1914-1945.
C. Lloyd, 617(TLS):15Feb80-189
Tiller, T. That Singing Mesh.*
C. Hope, 364:Nov79-84
E. Longley, 617(TLS):18Jan80-64
376:Oct79-142
Tillotson, G. A View of Victorian Literature.*
E. Alexander, 529(QQ):Winter79/80-657
R.D. Altick, 301(JEGP):Jan79-142
J.H. Buckley, 651(WHR):Spring79-167
A.D. Culler, 579(SAQ):Spring79-266
639(VQR):Autumn78-128
Tilton, J.W. Cosmic Satire in the Contemporary Novel.
S.G. Kellman, 395(MFS):Winter78/79-650
"A Time for Reason."
J.R. Seldon, 529(QQ):Autumn79-519
"The Times Atlas of World History."* (G. Barraclough, ed)
T. Hodgkin, 617(TLS):29Feb80-245
Timina, S.I., ed. Russkaja sovetskaja proza.
G. Rosenshield, 574(SEEJ):Fall79-409
Timmons, S., ed. Preservation and Conservation.
R.B. Rettig, 576:May78-110
Timpanaro, S. Contributi di filologia e di storia della lingua latina.
E.J. Kenney, 313:Vol69-238

Timpanaro, S. La filologia di Giacomo
Leopardi. (rev)
N.G. Wilson, 123:Vol29No1-192
Tindall, G. The Intruder.*
D. Durrant, 364:Dec79/Jan80-132
Tinker, H. The Ordeal of Love.
E. Stokes, 617(TLS):13Jun80-659
Tinker, H. Separate and Unequal.
B. La Brack, 293(JASt):Feb79-400
Tinker, J. The Television Barons.
R. Hoggart, 362:13Nov80-660
Tinkle, L. An American Original.*
H.L. Alsmeyer, Jr., 649(WAL):Fall79-
265
V.E. Lynch, 27(AL):Mar79-130
J.R. Milton, 651(WHR):Autumn79-370
Tinnefeld, F. Die frühbyzantinische
Gesellschaft.
B. Croke, 589:Jan79-194
Tippett, M. Emily Carr.
R. Cook, 99:Jun-Jul80-32
L.J. Milrod, 150(DR):Winter79/80-750
Tipton, L., ed. Locke on Human Understand-
ing.
S. Blackburn, 447(N&Q):Dec78-558
Tipy, J. - see Gide, A. and H. Ghéon
Tirro, F. Jazz.*
J. Dapogny, 414(MusQ):Jul78-407
Tischler, J. Hethitisches etymologisches
Glossar.* (Pt 1)
P.J. Regier, 350:Mar79-252
J.J.S. Weitenberg, 343:Band23-86
Tischler, J. Kleinasiatische Hydronymie.
A. Heubeck, 343:Band23-109
Tison-Braun, M. Tristan Tzara: Inventeur
de l'homme nouveau.*
M.A. Caws, 207(FR):Feb79-495
Tissier, A., ed. La Farce en France de
1450 à 1550.
A. Hindley, 208(FS):Vol33Pt2-602
A. Serper, 545(RPh):Nov78-256
Tissier, A. "Les Fausses Confidences" de
Marivaux.
M. Gilot, 535(RHL):May-Jun78-475
Tissoni Benvenuti, A. - see Foresti, A.
Titley, N.M. Miniatures from Persian
Manuscripts in the British Library and
the British Museum.*
B.W. Robinson, 39:May79-407
S.C. Welch, 463:Autumn78-330
Titone, R. Dallo strutturalismo alla
interdisciplinarità.
R.J. Di Pietro, 399(MLJ):Jan-Feb79-85
Tittler, R. Nicholas Bacon.*
J. Stephens, 125:Fall78-136
Tiusanen, T. Dürrenmatt.*
D.G. Daviau, 221(GQ):May79-429
E.S. Dick, 400(MLN):Apr79-635
S.G. Donald, 402(MLR):Jul79-761
B. Hannemann, 406:Winter79-475
A. Smith, 108:Fall79-131
"Tiziano nelle Gallerie Fiorentine."
E. Waterhouse, 39:Jul79-80
Tjoa, H.G. George Henry Lewes.
D. Carroll, 445(NCF):Dec78-393
636(VP):Winter78-398

"Tlumačal'ny slounik belaruskaj movy."
(Vol 1)
P. Wexler, 574(SEEJ):Winter79-557
Tobias, A. Getting By on $100,000 a Year.
W. Goodman, 441:31Aug80-18
Tobias, D. and M. Merris. The Golden
Lemon.
W. and C. Cowen, 639(VQR):Autumn79-153
Tobin, P.D. Time and the Novel.
H.O. Brown, 141:Fall79-384
J. Frank, 31(ASch):Autumn80-529
W. Harmon, 594:Fall79-369
S. Pickering, 569(SR):Fall79-656
L. Surette, 255(HAB):Summer79-197
Tobin, P.M.O., ed. Les Lais anonymes des
XIIe et XIIIe siècles.*
W. Rothwell, 208(FS):Vol33Pt2-553
Tod, I. and M. Wheeler. Utopia.
G. Beauchamp, 385(MQR):Spring80-261
G. Darley, 46:Oct79-205
Todd, J. Women's Friendship in Literature.
A. Brookner, 617(TLS):20Jun80-716
Todd, J.M. - see Wollstonecraft, M.
Todd, L. Pidgins and Creoles.
K-H. Böttcher, 430(NS):Apr78-181
Todd, R. Iris Murdoch.
P. Lewis, 617(TLS):11Apr80-419
Todd, R.B. Alexander of Aphrodisias on
Stoic Physics.*
D.O., 543:Dec78-372
Todd, W.M. 3d, ed. Literature and Society
in Imperial Russia, 1800-1914.
V. Terras, 550(RusR):Apr79-256
G. Woodcock, 569(SR):Summer79-480
Todorov, T. The Poetics of Prose.
P. Brady, 579(SAQ):Winter79-137
J.D. Erickson, 188(ECr):Summer78-91
205(FMLS):Apr78-190
Todorov, T. Théories du symbole.*
M.H., 191(ELN):Sep78(supp)-137
Todorov, T. and O. Ducrot. Enzyklopä-
disches Wörterbuch der Sprachwissen-
schaften.*
R. Ködderitzsch, 343:Band23-162
Toffler, A. The Third Wave.
A. Broyard, 441:22Mar80-19
L. Winner, 441:30Mar80-3
Toglia, M.P. and W.F. Battig, with others.
Handbook of Semantic Word Norms.
G. Keppel, 399(MLJ):Sep-Oct79-299
Togliatti, P. Sur Gramsci.
E. Namer, 542:Jul-Sep79-333
Tokayer, M. and M. Swartz. The Fugu
Plan.*
Miyazawa Masanori, 285(JapQ):Oct-Dec
79-556
Toland, J. Hitler.
J.S. Conway, 529(QQ):Autumn79-510
Toland, J. No Man's Land.
A.J.P. Taylor, 453(NYRB):18Dec80-12
R.M. Watt, 441:12Oct80-12
de Toledo, A.M. - see under Martínez de
Toledo, A.
Tolkien, J.R.R. The Silmarillion.* (C.
Tolkien, ed)
639(VQR):Winter78-23

Tolkien, J.R.R. Unfinished Tales. (C. Tolkien, ed)
  F. Buechner, 441:16Nov80-15
  B. Sibley, 362:20ct80-443
de Tollenaere, F. and R.L. Jones, with others. Word-Indices and Word-Lists to the Gothic Bible and Minor Fragments.*
  E.A. Ebbinghaus, 215(GL):Fall78-176
Tolman, B. and R. Page. The Country Dance Book.
  W.K. McNeil, 292(JAF):Jan-Mar79-107
Tolmie, M. The Triumph of the Saints.*
  K.W. Shipps, 656(WMQ):Jan79-141
  P. Wende, 182:Vol131#15/16-574
de Tolnay, C. Disegni di Michelangelo nelle collezioni italiani.
  P. Joannides, 54:Mar78-174
Tolstoy, L. The Fruits of Enlightenment.
  J. Coleby, 157:Spring79-85
Tolstoy, L.N. The Portable Tolstoy. (J. Bayley, ed)
  G. Woodcock, 569(SR):Summer79-480
Tolstoy, L.N. Tolstoy's Letters.* (R.F. Christian, ed and trans)
  T.G.S. Cain, 529(QQ):Summer79-273
  R. Freeborn, 575(SEER):Jul79-425
  J.M. Holquist, 594:Fall79-372
  A.V. Knowles, 402(MLR):Jul79-767
  G.A. Panichas, 396(ModA):Fall79-411
  G. Woodcock, 569(SR):Summer79-480
  205(FMLS):Jul78-288
Tolstoy, N. The Secret Betrayal.
  M. Elliott, 550(RusR):Apr79-235
Tolstoy, N. Victims of Yalta.
  G.F.G. Stanley, 529(QQ):Winter79/80-709
Tolton, C.D.E. André Gide and the Art of Autobiography.
  C.D. Bettinson, 208(FS):Vol33Pt2-859
  D. Moutote, 535(RHL):Sep-Oct78-860
Tomalin, C. Shelley and His World.
  P. Beer, 362:31Jul80-150
  A.N. Wilson, 617(TLS):12Sep80-996
Tomaszewski, W. Na szkockiej ziemi.
  J.J. Tomiak, 575(SEER):Jan79-155
Tomkins, C. Off the Wall.
  A. Broyard, 441:31May80-21
  P. Deitz, 441:25May80-9
Tomlinson, C., ed. The Oxford Book of Verse in English Translation.
  M. Schmidt, 362:27Nov80-732
Tomlinson, C. Selected Poems 1951-1974.*
  V. Cunningham, 175:Spring79-88
  M. Kirkham, 529(QQ):Summer79-345
Tomlinson, C. The Shaft.*
  C. Bedient, 569(SR):Spring79-296
  V. Cunningham, 175:Spring79-88
Tomlinson, R.A. Greek Sanctuaries.*
  D.W. Rupp, 576:Oct78-201
Tomlinson, T.B. The English Middle-Class Novel.*
  R.B. Yeazell, 637(VS):Autumn77-120
Tonelli, G. Heinrich Heines politische Philosophie (1830-1845).*
  S. Prawer, 220(GL&L):Oct78-77

Tontsch, U. Der "Klassiker" Fontane.
  F. Betz, 406:Summer79-220
  D.C.G. Lorenz, 221(GQ):Jan79-127
Tooker, D. and R. Hofheins. Fiction!
  J. Harris, 395(MFS):Summer78-286
Toole, J.K. A Confederacy of Dunces.
  P-L. Adams, 61:Jul80-86
  R. Brown, 617(TLS):18Jul80-821
  A. Friedman, 441:22Jun80-7
Toomer, J. The Wayward and the Seeking. (D.T. Turner, ed)
  A. Walker, 441:13Jul80-11
Topitsch, E. Die Voraussetzungen der Transzendentalphilosophie.
  E. Niebel, 342:Band69Heft1-110
Topol, A. A Woman of Valor.
  N. Callendar, 441:3Feb80-22
Toporov, V.N. Prusskij jazyk.
  S.F. Kolbuszewski, 360(LP):Vol121-153
Toppani, I. Carducci e il mondo latino.
  E.F., 228(GSLI):Vol155fasc490-315
Topping, A. The Splendors of Tibet.
  R.F. Shepard, 441:7Nov80-C24
Topsfield, L.T. Troubadours and Love.*
  G.M. Cropp, 67:Nov79-336
Topsøe-Jensen, H., comp. H.C. Andersens Dagbøger 1825-1875: Personregister.
  P.M. Mitchell, 301(JEGP):Jan79-102
Toraldo di Francia, G. L'indagine del mondo fisico.
  W.R. Shea, 486:Jun78-330
Torbert, P.M. The Ch'ing Imperial Household Department.
  B.S. Bartlett, 293(JASt):Nov78-161
  W-F. Loh, 244(HJAS):Dec78-492
Torgov, M. The Abramsky Variations.
  C. McLay, 102(CanL):Autumn79-125
Toriello, F. - see Esquyo, F.
de Torquemada, J. Monarquía indiana. (Vol 3) (3rd ed)
  E. del Hoyo, 263(RIB):Vol29No1-81
Torrance, C. Citrinas.
  J. Freeman, 97(CQ):Vol8#3-280
Torrance, R.M. The Comic Hero.
  E.L. Galligan, 579(SAQ):Spring79-262
  K. Muir, 569(SR):Fall79-671
  639(VQR):Spring79-47
"La Torre 1913-1914."
  E. Saccone, 400(MLN):Jan79-171
Torrell, J-P. Théorie de la prophétie et philosophie de la connaissance aux environs de 1230.
  M.W. Bloomfield, 589:Oct79-865
Torrente Ballester, G. Fragmentos de apocalipsis.
  S.J. Summerhill, 399(MLJ):Jan-Feb79-76
Torres, R.G. - see under González Torres, R.
Torres Martín, R. Blas de Ledesma y el bodegón español.
  J. Hernández Díaz, 48:Oct-Dec78-449
Torriti, P. La Pinacoteca Nazionale di Siena: i dipinti dal XII al XV secolo.
  J. Pope-Hennessy, 39:Apr79-325
Tort, P. and P. Désalmand. Sciences humaines et philosophie en Afrique.
  D. Merllié, 542:Oct-Dec79-496

Tully, A. William Penn's Legacy.
T.H. Wendel, 656(WMQ):Apr79-295
Tulsidas. Le Rāmāyan de Tulsī-dās. (C.
Vaudeville, ed and trans)
W. Dwyer, 259(IIJ):Apr79-143
T'ung-tsu, C. - see under Ch'ü T'ung-tsu
Tunnard, C. A World with a View.*
P.T. Newby, 89(BJA):Summer79-278
639(VQR):Winter79-30
von Tunzelmann, G.N. Steam Power and
British Industrialization to 1860.
J.R. Harris, 637(VS):Summer79-481
Tuomela, R. Human Action and Its Explana-
tion.
M. Brand, 482(PhR):Jul79-464
Tuomi, R. Studien zur Textform der Briefe
Ciceros.
A.J. Kleywegt, 394:Vol32fasc3/4-425
Türk, H.J., ed. Autorität.
M. Vidal, 182:Vol31#7/8-204
Turk, L.H., A.M. Espinosa and C.A. Solé,
Jr. Foundation Course in Spanish. (4th
ed)
S.L. Fischer, 238:Mar79-199
"Turkish Carpets."
J. Housego, 463:Summer78-215
Turkle, S. Psychoanalytic Politics.*
G. Strawson, 617(TLS):1Feb80-118
Turlot, F. Idéalisme, dialectique et
personnalisme.
M. Adam, 542:Jul-Sep79-335
L. Braun, 53(AGP):Band60Heft2-239
Turnbull, C.M. A History of Singapore,
1819-1975.
S.S. Bedlington, 293(JASt):Feb79-433
Turnell, M. The Rise of the French Novel.*
109:Summer80-224
Turner, A.T., ed. Fifty Contemporary
Poets.*
R. De Mott, 651(WHR):Spring79-186
M.A. Tapp, 114(ChiR):Spring79-123
295(JML):Vol7#4-643
Turner, C.J.G. Pechorin.
J.J. Rinkus, 574(SEEJ):Winter79-527
H. Schulak, 550(RusR):Jul79-395
Turner, D.T. - see Toomer, J.
Turner, E.G. The Typology of the Early
Codex.*
B.C. Barker-Benfield, 123:Vol29No2-294
R. Renehan, 24:Fall79-446
T.C. Skeat, 303(JoHS):Vol99-222
Turner, E.S. Dear Old Blighty.
R. Blythe, 362:7Feb80-187
A. Marwick, 617(TLS):28Mar80-372
Turner, F. Beyond Geography.
R.A. Sokolov, 441:20Apr80-16
61:Jun80-93
Turner, G. Transit of Cassidy.
G. Muirden, 581:Jun79-227
Turner, J. Lloyd George's Secretariat.
J. Grigg, 362:10Apr80-479
K.O. Morgan, 617(TLS):18Apr80-443
Turner, J. The Politics of Landscape.
M. Price, 676(YR):Autumn79-103

Turner, J.M.W. Collected Correspondence of
J.M.W. Turner. (J. Gage, ed)
G. Reynolds, 617(TLS):6Jun80-641
442(NY):18Aug80-95
Turner, P. Tennyson.*
K. McSweeney, 402(MLR):Jul79-673
S. Shatto, 447(N&Q):Jun78-263
Turville-Petre, G. and J.S. Martin, eds.
Iceland and the Mediaeval World.
P. Hallberg, 562(Scan):Nov79-149
Turville-Petre, T. The Alliterative
Revival.*
T.H.B., 502(PrS):Spring78-117
E.B. Irving, Jr., 191(ELN):Jun79-322
B. Lindström, 597(SN):Vol150#2-327
Tuska, J. The Detective in Hollywood.*
C. Steinbrunner, 18:Oct78-72
639(VQR):Summer78-106
Tussman, J. Government and the Mind.*
W.N. Denman, 583:Winter79-206
G. Dworkin, 449:Nov79-517
Tuthill, W. Interiors and Interior
Details.
J. Quinan, 576:Mar78-53
Tuttle, E.F. Studies in the Derivational
Suffix "-āculum."*
M.R. Harris, 240(HR):Spring78-244
Tuttleton, J.W. Thomas Wentworth Higgin-
son.
A.M. Wells, 26(ALR):Autumn79-358
Tuţescu, M. Le groupe nominal et la
nominalisation en français moderne.
L.R. Waugh, 545(RPh):Nov78-226
Tuve, R. Allegorical Imagery.
G.S. Ivy, 161(DUJ):Dec78-125
Tuwhare, H. Something Nothing.
P. Crisp, 368:Mar75-74
Twain, M. Mark Twain Speaks for Himself.
(P. Fatout, ed)
D.E.E. Sloane, 26(ALR):Autumn79-348
42(AR):Spring79-252
Tweedale, M.M. Abailard on Universals.*
J. Jolivet, 542:Jan-Mar78-92
Twitchett, D. and J.K. Fairbank, eds. The
Cambridge History of China. (Vol 10,
Pt 1)
R.R.C. de Crespigny, 67:Nov79-371
Twombly, R.C. Frank Lloyd Wright.
J. Sergeant, 46:Oct79-204
Tyacke, S. London Map-Sellers 1660-1720.
R. Lister, 503:Winter79-190
M. Treadwell, 354:Dec79-389
Tydeman, W. The Theatre in the Middle
Ages.
W. Temple, 157:Summer79-75
Tyler, A. Morgan's Passing.
J. Leonard, 441:17Mar80-C17
A.G. Mojtabai, 441:23Mar80-14
J. Naughton, 362:16Oct80-513
J. Updike, 442(NY):23Jun80-97
J. Wolcott, 453(NYRB):3Apr80-34
61:May80-102
Tyler, W.T. The Man Who Lost the War.
S. Ellin, 441:2Mar80-8
C. Lehmann-Haupt, 441:21Feb80-C18

Van Tassel, D.D., ed. Aging, Death, and the Completion of Being.
  R. Puccetti, 150(DR):Summer79-365
Vanvitelli, L. Le Lettere di Luigi Vanvitelli della Biblioteca Palatina di Caserta. (Vol 3) (F. Strazzullo, ed)
  J. Pinto, 90:Apr79-264
Vanwelkenhuyzen, G. - see Gide, A. and A. Mockel
Vanwijingaerden, F., ed. Handbook on the International Exchange of Publications. (4th ed)
  A.E. Schorr, 14:Oct79-478
Vardy, S.B. Modern Hungarian Historiography.
  J.M. Bak, 104(CASS):Summer78-313
Vardys, V.S. and R.J. Misiunas, eds. The Baltic States in Peace and War, 1917-1945.
  T.U. Raun, 550(RusR):Oct79-484
Varga, A.C. On Being Human.
  R.F. Harvanek, 613:Dec79-437
Varga, A.K. Les constantes du poème.
  G.R. Lind, 72:Band216Heft2-394
Vargas Llosa, M. Captain Pantoja and the Special Service.*
  J. Bumpus, 473(PR):4/1979-634
  J. Lyons, 364:Nov79-95
  M. Wood, 453(NYRB):24Jan80-43
Vargas Llosa, M. The Cubs and Other Stories.*
  M. Wood, 453(NYRB):24Jan80-43
Värilä, A. The Swedenborgian Background of William James' Philosophy.
  P. Dubois, 542:Apr-Jun79-261
Varney, C. Carleton Varney Decorates from A to Z.
  S. Stephens, 505:Jun78-98
Varro. M. Terentius Varro, "Antiquitates Rerum Divinarum." (B. Cardauns, ed)
  N. Horsfall, 123:Vol29No1-46
Varro. Varron, "Économie rurale." (Bk 1) (J. Heurgon, ed and trans)
  M. Pasquinucci, 313:Vol69-229
Varro. Varron, "Satires Ménippées." (Vol 4) (J-P. Cèbe, ed and trans)
  R. Astbury, 123:Vol29No2-313
Varro. Varrone, "De Lingua Latina," Libro VI. (E. Riganti, ed and trans)
  E. Laughton, 123:Vol29No2-228
Vartic, I. Radu Stanca.
  V. Nemoianu, 574(SEEJ):Summer79-315
Vasari, G. Artists of the Renaissance.
  E.H. Ramsden, 39:May79-404
"Il Vasari: Storiografo e artista."
  L. Satkowski, 576:Oct78-205
Vasco, G.M. Diderot and Goethe.
  N. Suckling, 208(FS):Oct79-452
Vasil'eva, E.K. The Young People of Leningrad.*
  J.J. Tomiak, 575(SEER):Jan79-142
Vāsudevāśrama. Yatidharmaprakāśa. (P. Olivelle, ed and trans)
  J.W. de Jong, 259(IIJ):Oct79-294

Vatnikova-Prizel, Z. O Russkoj Memuarnoj Literature.
  B. Plaskacz, 558(RLJ):Winter79-235
  L. Turkevich, 558(RLJ):Spring79-235
Vattimo, G., ed. Estetica moderna.
  H. Bredin, 89(BJA):Winter79-81
Vaudeville, C. Kabīr. (Vol 1)
  W. Dwyer, 259(IIJ):Jan79-56
Vaudeville, C. - see Tulsidas
Vaughan, A. Born to Please.
  N. Shrimpton, 617(TLS):19Sep80-1016
Vaughan, A.T. - see Wood, W.
Vaughan, H. The Complete Poems.* (A. Rudrum, ed)
  L.A. Mann, 178:Spring79-114
Vaughan, R. Fastnet, One Man's Voyage.
  J.A. Fishman, 441:9Aug80-17
Vaughan, W. German Romantic Painting. German Romanticism and English Art.
  J. Russell, 441:30Nov80-72
Vaughn, J.W., ed and trans. The Megara (Moschus IV).*
  D.A. Campbell, 487:Winter79-376
  F. Vian, 555:Vol52fasc2-383
Vavra, R. Such is the Real Nature of Horses.
  J. Naughton, 362:3Jan80-29
Vázquez-Ayora, G. Introducción a la Traductología.
  G. Radó, 75:3-4/1978-179
van Vechten, C. - see Rimsky-Korsakov, N.A.
Vedenina, L.G. Punktuacija francuzskogo jazyka.
  E. Jung, 209(FM):Apr78-173
de la Vega, J.S.L. - see under Lasso de la Vega, J.S.
de Vega Carpio, L. El amor enamorado. (J.B. Wooldridge, ed)
  V.G. Williamsen, 304(JHP):Autumn79-91
Veilhan, J-C. Les Règles de l'interprétation musicale à l'époque baroque.*
  S. Wollenberg, 410(M&L):Apr79-209
Veillette, J. and G. White. Early Indian Village Churches.
  H. Sonthoff, 102(CanL):Autumn79-93
Veit, W., ed. Captain James Cook.*
  F.G. Ryder, 678(YCGL):No.27-102
Vela, D. Information on the Marimba. (V. Chenoweth, ed and trans)
  H. Yurchenco, 187:Jan80-125
Velan, Y. Soft Goulag.
  J. Devaud, 207(FR):Feb79-519
van de Velde, R.G. Introduction à la méthodologie structurale de la linguistique.
  C. Hagège, 209(FM):Oct78-361
Veldman, I.M. Maarten van Heemskerck and Dutch Humanism in the Sixteenth Century.*
  E.A. Saunders, 600:Vol10#1-54
Véliz, C. The Centralist Tradition of Latin America.
  J. Lynch, 617(TLS):4Jul80-763
Velleius Paterculus, M. The Tiberian Narrative (2.94-131).* (A.J. Woodman, ed)
  B.M. Levick, 123:Vol29No1-60
  G.V. Sumner, 122:Jan79-64

Vellilamthadam, T. Tomorrow's Society.
  A.S. Rosenbaum, 484(PPR):Dec79-300
Vendler, H. Part of Nature, Part of Us.
  J. Bayley, 617(TLS):22Aug80-927
  A. Broyard, 441:29Mar80-21
  D. Donoghue, 441:23Mar80-11
  I. Ehrenpreis, 453(NYRB):29May80-12
Venegas, M. and anon. Two Jesuit Ahab
  Dramas. (N. Griffin, ed)
  205(FMLS):Jan78-95
Venema, A. and others. Amsterdamse
  School: 1910-1930.
  H. Searing, 576:Dec78-305
Venesoen, C., ed. Racine: Mythes et
  Réalités.
  H.T. Barnwell, 208(FS):Jan79-79
Venturi, G. - see Silva, E.
Venturi, L. Cézanne.
  T. Reff, 55:Summer79-37
Venzlaff, H. Der marokkanische Drogen-
  händler und seine Ware.
  O. Jastrow, 182:Vol31#19-701
Verardo, P., ed. Il Conservatorio di
  Musica Benedetto Marcello di Venezia.
  D.A., 410(M&L):Jul79-338
Vercors. Les Chevaux du temps.
  J. Hollenbeck, 207(FR):Oct78-188
Vercoutter, J. and others. The Image of
  the Black in Western Art. (Vol 1)
  J. Russell, 441:29Jun80-7
Vercruysse, J. Les Éditions encadrées des
  Oeuvres de Voltaire de 1775.
  W.H. Barber, 208(FS):Apr79-196
  M-L. Chastang, 535(RHL):Mar-Jun79-503
  O.R. Taylor, 402(MLR):Jan79-207
Vercruysse, J., M. Mat-Hasquin and A. Rou-
  zet, eds. Voltaire.
  M-L. Chastang, 535(RHL):Mar-Jun79-506
  S.S.B. Taylor, 208(FS):Apr79-197
Verdier, P., M.S. Dimand and K.C. Buhler.
  Enamels, Rugs and Silver in the Frick
  Collection.*
  H. Osborne, 89(BJA):Winter79-88
  639(VQR):Summer78-108
Verdieva, Z.N. Semantičeskij analiz pril-
  agatel'nych, oboznačajuščich ponjatie
  material'nogo sostojanija.
  G.F. Meier, 682(ZPSK):Band31Heft4-431
Verdú de Gregorio, J. La luz y la oscuri-
  dad en el teatro de Buero Vallejo.
  M.T. Halsey, 240(HR):Summer78-397
Ver Eecke, J., ed and trans. Le Dasavat-
  thuppakaraṇa.
  O. von Hinüber, 182:Vol31#9/10-270
Ver Eecke, W. Negativity and Subjectiv-
  ity.*
  C.B., 125:Fall78-151
  A. Dondeyne, 258:Jun79-240
  P. Somville, 542:Jul-Sep79-335
Vergé, R. Roger Vergé's Cuisine of the
  South of France.
  M. Sheraton, 441:30Nov80-86
Vergil. Aeneid.* (Bk 8) (K.W. Gransden,
  ed)
  N. Horsfall, 313:Vol69-231
  C. Moussy, 555:Vol152fasc1-194

Vergil. Ciris: a Poem attributed to
  Vergil. (R.O.A.M. Lyne, ed)
  D.O. Ross, Jr., 124:Dec79/Jan80-255
  R.F. Thomas, 487:Summer79-180
Vergil. Eclogues.* (R. Coleman, ed)
  J.P. Elder, 24:Winter79-580
  E.M. Jenkinson, 161(DUJ):Dec78-94
Vergil. The "Eclogues" of Virgil.* (A.J.
  Boyle, ed and trans)
  W. Nethercut, 24:Fall79-441
Vergil. P. Vergili Maronis "Aeneidos"
  Liber Sextus.* (R.G. Austin, ed)
  N. Horsfall, 313:Vol69-231
  E.A. McDermott, 24:Fall79-444
  R.D. Williams, 123:Vol29No1-33
Vergil. P. Vergili Maronis, "Aeneidos,"
  Libri vii-viii. (C.J. Fordyce, ed)
  N. Horsfall, 123:Vol29No2-219
Ver'ickaja, L.A. Russkaja orfoèpija.
  F.E. Vejsalov, 682(ZPSK):Band31Heft4-
  442
Verlaine, P. Femmes/Hombres: Women/Men.
  (A. Elliot, trans)
  J.R.B., 148:Winter79-93
  D.M. Thomas, 617(TLS):18Jan80-66
Verlaine, P. Lettres inédites à divers
  correspondants.* (G. Zayed, ed)
  J-H. Bornecque, 535(RHL):Sep-Oct78-857
Verlaine, P. Romances sans Paroles.* (D.
  Hillery, ed)
  J-H. Bornecque, 535(RHL):Sep-Oct78-856
Verlaine, P. Sagesse, Amour, Bonheur.
  (J-H. Bornecque, ed)
  C. Chadwick, 208(FS):Vol33Pt2-842
Verlet-Réauborg, N. Les Orfèvres du
  Ressort de la Monnaie de Bourges.
  C. le Corbeiller, 39:Jan79-72
Verleun, J.A. The Stone Horse.
  F. Schunck, 72:Band216Heft2-414
Verlinden, C. L'Esclavage dans l'Europe
  médiévale. (Vol 2)
  D. Herlihy, 589:Jul79-637
Vermaseren, M.J. Cybele and Attis.
  J.D. Mikalson, 124:Sep79-36
Vermeij, G.J. Biogeography and Adaptation.
  P.A. Larkin, 529(QQ):Autumn79-549
de Vermeil, A. Poésies. (H. Lafay, ed)
  E. Balmas, 535(RHL):Sep-Oct78-817
  C.N. Smith, 208(FS):Vol33Pt2-648
Vermeule, E. Aspects of Death in Early
  Greek Art and Poetry.*
  J. Boardman, 617(TLS):25Jan80-97
Vermeule, E.T. Götterkult.*
  M.H. Jameson, 122:Jul79-250
Vernant, J-P. Myth and Society in Ancient
  Greece.
  J. Gould, 617(TLS):22Aug80-938
Vernant, J-P. Religion grecque, religions
  antiques.*
  J-M. Gabaude, 542:Apr-Jun79-200
Vernay, H. Essai sur l'organisation de
  l'espace par divers systèmes linguis-
  tiques.
  N.C.W. Spence, 208(FS):Vol33Pt2-1075
Verne, J. Jules Verne I: "Le Tour du
  Monde." (F. Raymond, ed)
  H. Godin, 208(FS):Vol33Pt2-835

Vernes, P-M. La ville, la fête, la démocratie.
D. Leduc-Fayette, 542:Jul-Sep78-370
Vernet, J. La cultura hispanoárabe en oriente y occidente.
J.N. Hillgarth, 589:Oct79-873
Vernière, P. Montesquieu et "L'Esprit des lois" ou la raison impure.*
C. Rosso, 535(RHL):Nov-Dec79-1054
Vernière, P. - see Diderot, D.
Vernois, P., ed. L'onirisme et l'insolite dans le théâtre français contemporain.
H. Béhar, 535(RHL):May-Jun78-511
Vernon, J. Poetry and the Body.
D. Hall, 460(OhR):No.25-104
Verret, M. Le Temps des études.
D.F. Bradshaw, 208(FS):Vol33Pt2-1015
Versins, P. Encyclopédie de l'Utopie, des Voyages Extraordinaires, et de la Science Fiction.
G. Negley, 322(JHI):Apr-Jun79-315
"Vertalen vertolkt — verhalen over vertalen."
G. Cammarert, 75:1/1978-39
Vértes, E. Morphonematische Untersuchung der ostjakischen Vokalharmonie.
A. Plöger, 343:Band23-156
Verweyen, H. Recht und Sittlichkeit in J.G. Fichtes Gesellschaftslehre.*
R. Schottky, 53(AGP):Band60Heft1-90
Vesey, G., ed. Communication and Understanding.
D.W. Hamlyn, 483:Jul79-430
C. Lyas, 518:Jan79-38
Vesey, G., ed. Impressions of Empiricism.*
G.A.J. Rogers, 393(Mind):Apr79-289
Vesey, G. Personal Identity.
J. Ford, 154:Jun78-379
Vestergaard, T. Prepositional Phrases and Prepositional Verbs.
B. Jacobsen, 179(ES):Feb79-69
Vesterman, W. The Stylistic Life of Samuel Johnson.
R.G. Walker, 577(SHR):Summer79-255
Vető, M. Le fondement selon Schelling.
T.F.O., 543:Mar79-570
Vetterling-Braggin, M., F.A. Elliston and J. English, eds. Feminism and Philosophy.
S. Haack, 483:Apr79-242
J.L. Thompson, 63:Jun79-196
Veyrenc, M-T. Genèse d'un style.*
A. Goulet, 535(RHL):Jul-Aug79-703
Vial, A. Mallarmé.
Y-A. Favre, 535(RHL):Jul-Aug79-696
Vial, C. - see Diodorus Siculus
Viallaneix, N. Ecoute, Kierkegaard.
G. Steiner, 617(TLS):25Jan80-81
Viallaneix, N. Kierkegaard et la parole de Dieu.
M. Adam, 542:Apr-Jun79-261
Viallaneix, P. Le premier Camus suivi de "Écrits de jeunesse" d'Albert Camus.
I.H. Walker, 208(FS):Jan79-109
Vian, F. - see Nonnus

Viazzi, A. Alfredo Viazzi's Italian Cooking.
W. and C. Cowen, 639(VQR):Autumn79-152
Vici, A.B. - see under Busiri Vici, A.
Vicinus, M., ed. Broadsides of the Industrial North.
A. Howkins, 637(VS):Autumn77-126
Vicinus, M., ed. A Widening Sphere.*
M.M. Hall, 639(VQR):Spring79-364
B. Welter, 637(VS):Winter79-213
Vickers, B., ed. Shakespeare: The Critical Heritage.* (Vol 4)
G. Bullough, 677(YES):Vol9-322
G. Midgley, 447(N&Q):Apr78-175
L. Walker, 639(VQR):Winter78-185
Vickers, B., ed. Shakespeare: The Critical Heritage.* (Vol 5)
D. Hamer, 541(RES):Aug79-338
A.B. Kernan, 676(YR):Autumn79-124
Vickers, H. Gladys, Duchess of Marlborough.
R. Eder, 441:7Jul80-C14
442(NY):8Sep80-114
Vickers, M. Greek Vases.
R. Higgins, 39:Aug79-156
Victor, J.M. Charles de Bovelles, 1479-1553.
J. Fitzmaurice, 568(SCN):Spring-Summer79-61
Victor, S.A. - see under Aurelius Victor, S.
Queen Victoria. Queen Victoria's Highland Journals. (D. Duff, ed)
R. Fulford, 617(TLS):12Sep80-1001
"Victorian Life in Photographs."
B. Jay, 637(VS):Winter78-294
Vida, M.G. The Christiad. (G.C. Drake and C.A. Forbes, eds and trans)
L.V.R., 568(SCN):Spring-Summer79-63
Vida, M.G. The "De Arte Poetica" of Marco Girolamo Vida.* (R.G. Williams, ed and trans)
G. Costa, 545(RPh):Aug78-141
Vidal, G. Kalki.*
639(VQR):Summer78-93
Vidal, G. Matters of Fact and Fiction.
295(JML):Vol7#4-628
Vidal, G. Views From a Window. (R.J. Stanton and G. Vidal, eds)
S. Jacoby, 441:21Dec80-12
Vidal, M. Les "Contes moraux" d'Éric Rohmer.
J. Prieur, 450(NRF):Apr79-157
Viderman, S. Le Céleste et le Sublunaire.
F. de Gruson, 98:Jun-Jul78-649
Vido, B. Vocabolario in dialetto delle località dell'isola linguistica croata nel Molise. Grammatica del dialetto ikavo-štokavo delle località dell'isola linguistica croata nel Molise.
B. Franolic, 361:Apr78-394
Vidyasagara, I. Marriage of Hindu Widows.
I. Shetterly, 318(JAOS):Jul-Sep78-349
Vieillard-Baron, J-L. Le temps: Platon, Hegel, Heidegger.
J-M. Gabaude, 542:Oct-Dec79-468
Vieillard-Baron, J.L. - see Hegel, G.W.F.

Viellard, F. Bibliotheca Bodmeriana, Catalogues II, Manuscrits français du Moyen Age.*
D.J. Shirt, 208(FS):Vol33Pt2-587

Viennot, O. Temples de l'Inde centrale et occidentale.
K. Fischer, 259(IIJ):Jan79-74
J.C. Harle, 90:Mar79-183
J. Williams, 57:Vol40#1-75

Vier, J. Littérature à l'emporte-pièce. (8th Ser)
C. Pichois, 535(RHL):Mar-Apr78-338

Vier, J. Le Théâtre de Jean Anouilh.
M. Autrand, 535(RHL):Jul-Aug78-676

Viereck, W. Lexikalische und Grammatische Ergebnisse des Lowman-Survey von Mittel- und Südengland.
D. Nehls, 257(IRAL):Aug79-266
R. Suomala, 35(AS):Summer79-128

Viereck, W. Regionale und soziale Erscheinungsformen des britischen und amerikanischen Englisch.
G.H. Blanke, 430(NS):Apr78-189

Vieregg, A. Die Lyrik Peter Huchels.
J.D. Barlow, 406:Spring79-99

Viering, J. Schwärmerische Erwartung bei Wieland, im trivialen Geheimnisroman und bei Jean Paul.
M.H., 191(ELN):Sep78(supp)-176

Vigano, L. Nomi e titoli di YHWH alla luce del semitico del Nordouest.
R.E. Murphy, 318(JAOS):Jul-Sep78-315

Vignaux, G. L'argumentation.
R. Bautier, 209(FM):Oct78-382

Vigneau, R. Bucolique [suivi de] Élégiaque.
J. Bens, 450(NRF):Jun79-110

Viidikas, V. Condition Red.
T. Reeves, 368:Dec76-371

Viidikas, V. Knäbel.
C. Pollnitz, 581:Dec79-462

Vikár, L. - see Saygun, A.A.

de Villa Dei, A. Carmen de musica cum glossis.
R. Woodley, 410(M&L):Jul79-357

de Villavicencio, L.N. La creatividad en el estilo de Leopoldo Alas, "Clarín."
J.W. Díaz, 241:Jan79-116

de Villena, E. Tratado de la consolación. (D.C. Carr, ed)
A. Mutton, 402(MLR):Jul79-722
C.I. Nepaulsingh, 304(JHP):Spring80-263

de Villers, C. Le magnétiseur amoureux. (F. Azouvi, ed)
J. Brun, 192(EP):Jan-Mar79-109

Villiers, G. The Rehearsal.* (D.E.L. Crane, ed)
J. Kinsley, 447(N&Q):Dec78-554
A.P., 189(EA):Jul-Dec78-425

de Villiers, J.G. and P.A. Language Acquisition.
R.I. Scott, 529(QQ):Autumn79-540

Villon, F. Le "Lais" Villon et les Poèmes variés. (J. Rychner and A. Henry, eds)
P. Ménard, 535(RHL):Sep-Oct78-813

Villon, F. The Poems of François Villon.* (G. Kinnell, ed and trans)
G.W. Ireland, 529(QQ):Summer79-347

Villon, F. Le "Testament" Villon. (J. Rychner and A. Henry, eds)
J. Fox, 208(FS):Jan79-68

Vilsen, L. Joanna of de Triomf van de democratie.
M-C. Bergans-Libioul, 556(RLV):1978/6-556

Vincent, B. A Dictionary of Biography, Past and Present.
K.B. Harder, 424:Dec78-427
S. Hillman, 77:Summer78-93

Vincent, D., ed. Testaments of Radicalism.
D. Englander and L. Marlow, 637(VS):Summer78-524

Vincent, J.S. João Guimarães Rosa.
F.P. Ellison, 593:Winter79-373

Vincent, L.M. The Dancer's Book of Health.
D. Howard, 151:Dec78-96

de Vincenz, A. - see Weinreich, U.

Vincenz, S. Tematy żydowskie.
A. Hertz, 497(PolR):Vol23#4-79

da Vinci, L. - see under Leonardo da Vinci

Vine, R.A. John Barth.*
Z. Bowen, 295(JML):Vol7#4-657

Viner, J. Religious Thought and Economic Society. (J. Melitz and D. Winch, eds)
J.P.D., 543:Jun79-776

Vinge, J.D. The Snow Queen.
J. Sullivan, 441:3Aug80-12

Vinge, L. The Five Senses.*
G. Hainsworth, 208(FS):Vol33Pt2-995
M. Hugues, 549(RLC):Jan-Mar77-102
C. Stern, 545(RPh):Nov78-242

Vintilă-Rădulescu, I. Le créole français.*
R.A. Hall, Jr., 353:Apr78-92

Viollet-le-Duc, G. - see Courier, P-L.

Viorst, M. Fire in the Streets.
J.A. Lukas, 441:13Jan80-1
442(NY):31Mar80-124

Vipper, I.B. La Poésie de la Pléiade.
E. Oudiette, 535(RHL):Mar-Apr78-291

Virelet, P. and P. Rosanvallon. Pour une nouvelle culture politique.
J. Donzelot, 98:Jun-Jul78-572

Virgil - see under Vergil

Virgo, S. Deathwatch on Skidegate Narrows and Other Poems.
J. Cook, 99:Mar80-38
M.B. Oliver, 198:Summer80-147

Virilio, P. Vitesse et politique.
G. Sebbag, 98:Jun-Jul78-630

Virtanen, R. L'Imagerie scientifique de Paul Valéry.
C.M. Crow, 208(FS):Vol33Pt2-866

Visage, B. Chercher le monstre.
G. Quinsat, 450(NRF):Jan79-127

Vischer, E. - see Müri, W.

Visser, F.T. An Historical Syntax of the English Language. (Vol 3, 2nd half)
T. Kisbye, 597(SN):Vol150#1-141

Vitalis, O. - see under Orderic Vitalis

Vorpahl, B.M. Frederic Remington and the West.
W. Gard, 584(SWR):Winter79-89
M.S. Young, 39:Sep79-238
Vos, R. Lucas van Leyden.
P.W. Parshall, 600:Vol10#1-51
Voss, J.H. Johann Heinrich Voss, Briefe an Goeckingk: 1775-1786. (G. Hay, ed)
G. Häntzschel, 224(GRM):Band28Heft1-97
Voyles, J.B. The Phonology of Old High German.*
E.H. Antonsen, 301(JEGP):Jul79-377
Voznesensky, A. Nostalgia for the Present.* (V. Dunham and M. Hayward, eds)
R. Lattimore, 249(HudR):Autumn79-452
J. Simon, 491:Apr80-40
Voznjak, M. Geschichte der ukrainischen Literatur. (Vol 2, Pt 1)
A.B. McMillin, 688(ZSP):Band40Heft1-225
Vrancea, I. Intre Aristarc şi bietul Ioanide.
V. Nemoianu, 574(SEEJ):Summer79-313
Vree, D. On Synthesizing Marxism and Christianity.
G.A. Panichas, 396(ModA):Spring79-184
Vreeland, D. and C. Hemphill. Allure.
C. James, 453(NYRB):18Dec80-22
Vretska, K. C. Sallustius Crispus, "De Coniuratione Catilinae."
F. Hinard, 555:Vol152fasc2-396
Vrettos, T. Birds of Winter.
R. Freedman, 441:26Oct80-22
442(NY):25Aug80-102
de Vriendt, S., J. Dierickx and M. Wilmet. Grammaire générative et psychomécanique du langage.
A.R. Tellier, 189(EA):Jan-Mar78-78
de Vries, A.B., M. Tóth-Ubbens and W. Froentjes. Rembrandt in the Mauritshuis.
K. Roberts, 90:Feb79-124
Vrtačič, L. Der jugoslawische Marxismus.
A. Pfabigan, 182:Vol131#3/4-81
Vryonis, S., Jr. The Decline of Medieval Hellenism in Asia Minor and the Process of Islamization from the Eleventh through the Fifteenth Century.
J.V.A. Fine, Jr., 318(JAOS):Oct-Dec78-491
Vuarnet, J-N. Le philosophe-artiste.
A. Clavel, 98:Jan78-91
Vucinich, A. Social Thought in Tsarist Russia.
E. Gellner, 488:Mar79-121

Waage, F.O. Thomas Dekker's Pamphlets, 1603-1609, and Jacobean Popular Literature.
A.M. Mirenda, 568(SCN):Spring-Summer79-25
Waaijman, K. De mystiek van ik en jij.
P. Somville, 542:Jul-Sep79-336
Wacher, J. The Coming of Rome.
N. Hammond, 617(TLS):8Feb80-147
Wachinger, B. Sängerkrieg.
K. Bertau, 224(GRM):Band28Heft2-225

Wacholder, B.Z. Essays on Jewish Chronology and Chronography.
J. Vanderkam, 318(JAOS):Oct-Dec78-517
Wacholder, B.Z. Eupolemus, a Study in Judaeo-Greek Literature.
L.J. Weinberger, 318(JAOS):Apr-Jun78-150
Wachtel, N. The Vision of the Vanquished.
D. Gifford, 86(BHS):Jul79-268
Wachtel, P.L. Psychoanalysis and Behavior Therapy.
R.E. Fancher, 529(QQ):Spring79-175
de Wachter, R. and G. Schuy. Succes in spelling 3 and 4.
M-R. Blommaert, 556(RLV):1978/1-92
de Wachter, R., G. Schuy and R. Suetens. Vaardig in taal 3.
M-R. Blommaert, 556(RLV):1978/1-91
Wächtler, K. Geographie und Stratifikation der englischen Sprache.
B. Kettemann, 297(JL):Sep79-383
Wackenheim, C. La théologie catholique.
M. Adam, 542:Oct-Dec79-469
Wäckerlin-Swiagenin, K. Der "Schüpfheimer Codex."
J.M. Riddle, 589:Jan79-197
Waddicor, M.H. Montesquieu: "Lettres persanes."*
205(FMLS):Oct78-398
Waddington, M. Mister Never.*
C. MacMillan, 198:Summer80-151
Wade, B. Tanned.
M. Page, 648(WCR):Oct78-55
Wade, G. Traditions of the Classical Guitar.
H. Cole, 362:12Jun80-767
Wade, H.W.R. Constitutional Fundamentals.
D. Pannick, 362:31Jul80-151
Wade, I.O. The Structure and Form of the French Enlightenment.*
H.C. Payne, 173(ECS):Spring79-422
R. Shackleton, 161(DUJ):Jun79-287
Wade, K.E. Alternative Photographic Processes.
E. Moty, 139:Feb79-18
Wadsworth, P.A. Molière and the Italian Theatrical Tradition.*
A. Eustis, 207(FR):Oct78-161
M. Gutwirth, 188(ECr):Winter78-67
W.D. Howarth, 402(MLR):Jan79-203
van Waesberghe, J.S. - see under Smits van Waesberghe, J.
Wagener, H., ed. Gegenwartsliteratur und Drittes Reich.
U-K. Ketelsen, 221(GQ):May79-433
H. Ridley, 402(MLR):Apr79-506
Wagenknecht, E. Eve and Henry James.
M.E. Grenander, 27(AL):Mar79-123
M. Jacobson, 301(JEGP):Oct79-569
A.R. Tintner, 594:Spring79-106
Wager, W. Blue Moon.
N. Callendar, 441:20Jul80-16
Wagner, A. Heralds and Ancestors.
P. Summers, 503:Winter78-196

Wagner, A. and R. Plant, eds. Canada's Lost Plays.
R. Stuart, 526:Summer79-75
M. Tait, 627(UTQ):Summer79-438
Wagner, C. Cosima Wagner's Diaries.* (Vol 1) (M. Gregor-Dellin and D. Mack, eds)
R. Anderson, 415:May79-399
Wagner, C. and R. Strauss. Cosima Wagner — Richard Strauss: ein Briefwechsel. (F. Trenner, ed)
M. Kennedy, 410(M&L):Apr79-224
Wagner, E., ed and trans. Legende und Geschichte.
U. Braukämper, 182:Vol131#1/2-60
Wagner, E. My America!
I. Gold, 441:21Sep80-15
Wagner, G. La justice dans l'Ancien Testament et le Coran aux niveaux des mariages et des échanges de biens.
H. Räisänen, 182:Vol131#21/22-782
Wagner, L.W. Denise Levertov.
639(VQR):Autumn79-128
Wagner, P.C. and A. Erskine - see Cerf, B.
Wagner, R. The Diary of Richard Wagner, 1865-1882. (J. Bergfeld, ed)
H. Cole, 362:12Jun80-767
Wagner, W. Die Bundespräsidentenwahl 1959.
F. L'Huillier, 182:Vol131#1/2-56
Wagner, W.F., Jr., ed. A Treasury of Contemporary Houses.
R. Bender, 658:Winter79-422
Wagner-Rieger, R. and W. Krause, eds. Historismus und Schlossbau.
S. Muthesius, 576:Mar78-60
Wagoner, D. The Hanging Garden.
N. Callendar, 441:19Oct80-41
C. Lehmann-Haupt, 441:24Jun80-C9
Wagoner, D. Who Shall be the Sun?*
H. Carr, 617(TLS):25Apr80-477
J.F. Cotter, 249(HudR):Spring79-118
P. Stitt, 219(GaR):Fall79-699
Wah, F. Pictograms from the Interior of B.C.
S. Scobie, 102(CanL):Winter78-89
Wahl, A. L'option et l'émigration des Alsaciens-Lorrains (1871-72).
H. Kloss, 182:Vol131#7/8-254
Wahl, W.B. Poetic Drama Interviews.
M.J. Sidnell, 677(YES):Vol9-348
von Wahlendorf, H.A.S-L. - see under Schwarz-Liebermann von Wahlendorf, H.A.
Wahrig, G., ed. dtv-Wörterbuch der deutschen Sprache.
M.H. Folsom, 221(GQ):Jan79-104
Waiblinger, F.P. Senecas Naturales Quaestiones.
H.M. Hine, 123:Vol129No1-64
Wain, J. The Pardoner's Tale.*
G. Perez, 249(HudR):Autumn79-471
Wain, J. Professing Poetry.
C. Clausen, 569(SR):Spring79-314
Wain, J., ed. Edmund Wilson.
G. Core, 579(SAQ):Autumn79-520
Waine, A.E. Martin Walser.
G.A. Fetz, 130:Winter79/80-368

Wainwright, G. Doxology — The Praise of God in Worship, Doctrine and Life.
N. Smart, 617(TLS):5Sep80-971
Wainwright, J. The Eye of the Beholder.
N. Callendar, 441:19Oct80-41
Wainwright, J. Heart's Desire.*
T. Eagleton, 565:Vol20#1-74
Wainwright, J. The Venus Fly-Trap.
N. Callendar, 441:11May80-20
Waismann, F. Philosophical Papers.* (B. McGuinness, ed)
G. Stock, 479(PhQ):Jan79-78
M. Tiles, 518:Jan79-40
Wakefield, D. Home Free.
639(VQR):Summer78-94
Wakefield, T. Forties' Child.
V. Cunningham, 617(TLS):18Jul80-816
D.A.N. Jones, 362:19Jun80-802
Wakefield, W.L. Heresy, Crusade and Inquisition in Southern France, 1100-1250.
P. Biller, 208(FS):Jan79-57
Wakeman, F., Jr. and C. Grant, eds. Conflict and Control in Late Imperial China.
C.O. Hucker, 318(JAOS):Apr-Jun78-181
Walbank, F.W. A Historical Commentary on Polybius. (Vol 3)
R. Seager, 617(TLS):11Jan80-44
Walbank, M.B. Athenian Proxenies of the Fifth Century B.C.
D.M. Lewis, 487:Autumn79-267
Walcott, D. The Star-Apple Kingdom.*
H. Carruth, 231:Jan80-77
D. Davis, 362:5Jun80-729
V. Feaver, 617(TLS):8Aug80-903
S. Heaney, 472:Fall/Winter79-5
R. Lattimore, 249(HudR):Autumn79-442
P. Stitt, 491:Jan80-229
639(VQR):Autumn79-146
Wald, A.M. James T. Farrell: The Revolutionary Socialist Years.*
T. Ludington, 125:Spring79-475
W. Sutton, 27(AL):Jan80-558
Walden, R., ed. The Open Hand.
T. Benton, 46:May79-314
W.J.R. Curtis, 576:Dec78-295
Walder, A.G. Chang Ch'un-ch'iao and Shanghai's January Revolution.
P.H. Chang, 293(JASt):Aug79-762
Waldman, M.R. Toward a Theory of Historical Narrative.
M.E. Yapp, 617(TLS):19Sep80-1040
Waldner, G.K. and K. Mitterhauser. The Professional Chef's Book of Buffets.
W. and C. Cowen, 639(VQR):Autumn79-156
Waldron, R.H. - see Whitman, M.M.
Walhout, D. Festival of Aesthetics.
R. Ginsberg, 290(JAAC):Summer80-461
Walker, A. Good Night, Willie Lee, I'll See You in the Morning.
A. Williamson, 491:Mar80-348
Walker, A. Rudolph Valentino.
J. Raeburn, 77:Fall78-85
Walker, C.R. William Blake in the Art of his Time.
B.M. Stafford, 56:Winter79-118
Walker, D.L. - see London, J.

Walker, D.M., ed. The Oxford Companion to
Law.
G. Marshall, 617(TLS):9May80-523
D. Pannick, 362:1May80-581
Walker, G. Soviet Book Publishing Policy.
A. Kemp-Welch, 575(SEER):Oct79-627
D.H. Kraus, 574(SEEJ):Fall79-413
W. Zalewski, 550(RusR):Oct79-503
205(FMLS):Oct78-398
Walker, G.F. Three Plays.
T. Beaupre, 108:Spring79-115
Walker, G.J. Spanish Politics and Impe-
rial Trade 1700-1789.
J.S. Cummins, 617(TLS):7Mar80-277
Walker, L. The Green Wheelbarrow.*
L. Harrop, 565:Vol20#4-16
Walker, R.C.S. Kant.
D.W. Hamlyn, 617(TLS):4Jan80-19
L. Stevenson, 479(PhQ):Oct79-345
Walker, R.G. Infernal Paradise.
R.H. Costa, 651(WHR):Autumn79-363
639(VQR):Autumn79-129
Walker, R.M. Tradition and Technique in
"El Libro del Cavallero Zifar."*
V. Masson de Gómez, 545(RPh):Nov78-212
Walker, T. Burning the Ivy.
C. Hope, 364:Mar80-74
L. Sail, 493:Dec79-66
Walker, W.S. Plots and Characters in the
Fiction of James Fenimore Cooper.
J.F. Beard, 591(SIR):Fall79-479
Wallace, A.F.C. Rockdale.*
G.H. Gates, 9(AlaR):Jul79-237
Wallace, D.R. The Dark Range.
S. Kremp, 649(WAL):Fall79-256
Wallace, I. The Second Lady.
N. von Hoffman, 441:12Oct80-14
Wallace, J.D. Virtues and Vices.
D.A., 543:Jun79-777
N.J.H. Dent, 483:Oct79-568
A. Quinton, 617(TLS):4Jan80-18
Wallace, R.A. The Genesis Factor.
F.R. Hayes, 150(DR):Autumn79-578
Wallace-Hadrill, J.M. Early Medieval His-
tory.
W. Rothwell, 208(FS):Vol33Pt2-610
Wallach, B.P. Lucretius and the Diatribe
against the Fear of Death, De rerum
natura III 830-1094.
P.H. Schrijvers, 394:Vol32fasc3/4-426
Wallach, L. Diplomatic Studies in Latin
and Greek Documents from the Carolingian
Age.
J.J. Contreni, 124:Dec79/Jan80-247
Wallechinsky, D., A. Wallace and I.
Wallace. The Book of Predictions.
C. Lehmann-Haupt, 441:25Dec80-47
Waller, G.F. Dreaming America.*
R. Labrie, 150(DR):Autumn79-564
Waller, G.F. The Strong Necessity of Time.
L.G. Black, 447(N&Q):Oct78-457
Waller, G.F. - see Wroth, L.
Waller, L. The Brave and the Free.*
639(VQR):Autumn79-138
Waller, M. and A. Calabrese. Fats Waller.
B. Branklin 5th, 77:Fall78-87

Wallerstein, I. The Modern World-System.*
A. McDonald, Jr., 293(JASt):May79-535
Wallis, J.P.R. - see Moffat, R.
Wallmann, P. Münzpropaganda in den Anfän-
gen des Zweiten Triumvirats (43/42 v.
Chr.).*
M.H. Crawford, 123:Vol129No1-179
Wallraff, G. Zeugen der Anklage.
G.P. Butler, 617(TLS):8Feb80-153
Wallwork, J.F. Language and People.
W.J. Ashby, 350:Sep79-751
Walmsley, T. The Jones Boy.
A. Wagner, 526:Summer79-86
Walpole, H. Horace Walpole's "Miscel-
lany," 1786-1795. (L.E. Troide, ed)
R. Halsband, 301(JEGP):Oct79-559
J.R. Smitten, 541(RES):May79-224
639(VQR):Autumn78-142
Walpole, R.N., ed. The Old-French Johan-
nes Translation of the "Pseudo-Turpin
Chronicle."*
W.G. van Emden, 208(FS):Vol33Pt2-532
A. Foulet, 545(RPh):Nov78-249
R. O'Gorman, 377:Mar79-49
Walrond, E.E. Walter White and the Harlem
Renaissance.
R.H. Brisbane, 95(CLAJ):Mar79-288
Walser, M. Runaway Horse.
G.P. Butler, 617(TLS):25Jul80-836
P. Kemp, 362:17Jul80-89
Walser, R. La Promenade.
B. Bayen, 450(NRF):Mar79-125
Walser, R. Thomas Wolfe, Undergraduate.*
R.S. Kennedy, 395(MFS):Summer78-270
Walsh, G. Public Enemies.
J. Greenfield, 441:10Feb80-16
Walsh, W. F.R. Leavis.
H. Maccoby, 362:2Oct80-442
Walsh, W. Patrick White's Fiction.*
G. Core, 569(SR):Winter79-ii
J. Croft, 71(ALS):May79-125
J.H. McDowell, 395(MFS):Winter78/79-
661
Walsh, W.H. Kant's Criticism of Meta-
physics.*
J. Kopper, 342:Band69Heft2-215
Walter, E. The Likes of Which.
P.L. Berman, 441:2Mar80-18
Walter, H., ed. Phonologie et société.
W.J. Ashby, 350:Sep79-729
B. Saint-Jacques, 102(CanL):Spring79-
105
Walters, R.G. American Reformers, 1815-
1860.
M. Nelson, 639(VQR):Winter79-164
Walters, V.A. Silent Missions.
639(VQR):Winter79-8
Walther von der Vogelweide. Die gesamte
Überlieferung der Texte und Melodien.
(H. Brunner, U. Müller and F.V. Specht-
ler, eds)
I. Glier, 221(GQ):Nov79-533
A. Robertshaw, 402(MLR):Apr79-489
Walther, K., ed. Ansichten: Aufsätze zur
Literatur der DDR.
J. Hannemann, 654(WB):5/1978-187

Warren, R.P. Now and Then.*
   C. Bedient, 569(SR):Spring79-296
   J.F. Cotter, 249(HudR):Spring79-119
   I. Ehrenpreis, 453(NYRB):21Feb80-27
   R. Squires, 385(MQR):Winter80-136
   P. Stitt, 219(GaR):Spring79-214
Warren, R.P. Robert Penn Warren Talking.
  (F.C. Watkins and J.T. Hiers, eds)
   D. Grumbach, 441:25May80-11
   442(NY):26May80-127
Warrick, P.S. The Cybernetic Imagination
in Science Fiction.
   H. Kenner, 441:1Jun80-12
Warrior, M.C. Quitting Time.
   D. Barbour, 150(DR):Spring79-154
von Wartburg, W. Französisches Etymolo-
gisches Wörterbuch, Materialen unbekann-
ten oder unsicheren Ursprungs. (Vol 22,
Pt 1)
   R. de Gorog, 553(RLiR):Jul-Dec78-440
Wartofsky, M.W. Feuerbach.
   A. Gilbert, 482(PhR):Jul79-471
   G.H.R. Parkinson, 518:Jan79-18
   D-H. Ruben, 393(Mind):Oct79-602
   L.S.S., 543:Mar79-571
Warwick, L. The Mackenzies called Compton.
   J. Redmond, 611(TN):Vol132#3-144
Waseem, G. Das kontrollierte Herz.*
   G.F. Peters, 406:Summer79-217
   J.L.S., 191(ELN):Sep78(supp)-164
Washington, B.T. The Booker T. Washington
Papers. (Vols 6 and 7) (L.R. Harlan and
R.W. Smock, eds)
   A. Howington, 9(AlaR):Apr79-154
Washington, G. The Diaries of George Wash-
ington. (D. Jackson, with others, eds)
   K.P. Kelly, 656(WMQ):Oct79-624
Washington, G. C.I. Lewis' Theory of Mean-
ing and Theory of Value.
   S.B.R., 543:Sep78-158
Washington, M.B. The Art of Romare
Bearden.
   R.P. Johnston, 127:Spring79-216
Wasiolek, E. Tolstoy's Major Fiction.*
   R.B. Anderson, 395(MFS):Winter78/79-
   605
   W. Buchanan, 573(SSF):Fall78-473
   R. Freeborn, 575(SEER):Jul79-425
   J.M. Holquist, 594:Fall79-372
   M.V. Jones, 402(MLR):Jul79-766
   W. Konick, 401(MLQ):Dec79-423
   D. Matual, 268(IFR):Summer80-147
   G. Woodcock, 569(SR):Summer79-480
   A.C. Wright, 255(HAB):Fall79-322
   639(VQR):Autumn78-128
Wasserman, G.R. Samuel "Hudibras" Butler.
   J. Wilders, 402(MLR):Jul79-655
Wasson, R.G., A. Hofmann and C.A.P. Ruck.
The Road to Eleusis.
   M.H. Jameson, 124:Nov79-197
   N.J. Richardson, 123:Vol29No2-323
Waswo, A. Japanese Landlords.*
   S. Vlastos, 293(JASt):May79-580
Waterhouse, D. Images of Eighteenth-
Century Japan.*
   E.D. Swinton, 318(JAOS):Apr-Jun78-182

Waterhouse, D.B. and B. Kobayashi - see
Paine, R.T. and A. Soper
Waterman, A. Over the Wall.
   J. Lucas, 617(TLS):16May80-562
Waters, E.N. - see Liszt, F.
Waterson, K. Molière et l'autorité.*
   A. Blanc, 535(RHL):Jan-Feb79-123
Waterson, M. The Servants' Hall.
   E.S. Turner, 617(TLS):27Jun80-740
Watkin, D. English Architecture.
   J. Lees-Milne, 39:Dec79-536
Watkin, D. Morality and Architecture.*
   J.D. Stewart, 255(HAB):Summer79-219
Watkin, D. The Rise of Architectural His-
tory.
   J.M. Crook, 617(TLS):25Jul80-846
   S. Gardiner, 362:31Jul80-152
Watkins, E. The Critical Act.
   R.W. Daniel, 569(SR):Fall79-1xxxiv
   J. Olen, 290(JAAC):Fall79-94
   A. Rodway, 89(BJA):Summer79-280
Watkins, F.C. In Time and Place.*
   L.J. Budd, 395(MFS):Summer78-260
   J.H. Justus, 569(SR):Summer79-468
Watkins, F.C. and J.T. Hiers - see Warren,
R.P.
Watkins, R.N., ed and trans. Humanism and
Liberty.
   L.V.R., 568(SCN):Spring-Summer79-62
Watson, A.G. Catalogue of Dated and
Datable Manuscripts c. 700-1600 in the
Department of Manuscripts, The British
Library.
   78(BC):Summer79-183
Watson, B. - see "Ryōkan: Zen Monk-Poet of
Japan"
Watson, C. The Bishop in the Back Seat.
   N. Callendar, 441:3Feb80-22
Watson, C.S. Antebellum Charleston
Dramatists.*
   J. Brown, 610:Feb79-151
Watson, G. Book Society.
   A. Calder-Marshall, 617(TLS):25Apr80-
   465
   D. Grumbach, 441:25May80-12
   C. Lehmann-Haupt, 441:29Feb80-C27
Watson, G. The Discipline of English.
   639(VQR):Autumn79-128
Watson, G. The Leavises, the "Social,"
and the Left.
   W.J. Keith, 627(UTQ):Summer79-440
Watson, G. Politics and Literature in
Modern Britain.*
   A.W. Litz, 569(SR):Fall79-660
   R.J. Van Dellen, 395(MFS):Winter78/79-
   579
Watson, G.J. Irish Identity and the Liter-
ary Revival.
   C. Fitz-Simon, 157:Autumn79-87
Watson, I. The Gardens of Delight.
   G. Strawson, 617(TLS):18Jul80-821
Watson, I. God's World. The Very Slow
Time Machine.
   E. Korn, 617(TLS):30May80-626
Watson, J. The Balloon Watchers.
   L. Wevers, 368:Mar76-89

Watson, L. In a Dark Time.
  N. Callendar, 441:23Mar80-33
Watson, W. Style in the Arts of China.
  D.F. McCallum, 318(JAOS):Apr-Jun78-179
Watt, I. Conrad in the Nineteenth Century.
  P. Conrad, 362:12Jun80-766
  P. Keating, 617(TLS):25Apr80-455
  E.W. Said, 441:9Mar80-1
  442(NY):5May80-174
Watt, J.C.Y., ed. The Translation of Art,
  Essays on Chinese Painting and Poetry.*
  R. Whitfield, 39:Jun79-490
Watt, W.M. The Formative Period of
  Islamic Thought.
  S. Vahiduddin, 273(IC):Oct76-239
Watté, P. Structures philosophiques du
  péché originel.
  D. Bourel, 342:Band69Heft2-222
Watters, W.R. Formula Criticism and the
  Poetry of the Old Testament.
  W. Whallon, 131(CL):Fall79-425
Watts, C. Conrad's "Heart of Darkness."
  T.G. Willy, 136:Vol11#3-288
Watts, D.A. Cardinal de Retz.
  A.J. Krailsheimer, 617(TLS):27Jun80-
  727
Watts, D.A. - see Corneille, T.
Waugh, A. The Last Word.
  A. Howard, 362:28Feb80-281
  J. Leonard, 441:27Oct80-C19
  J. Symons, 441:14Dec80-9
Waugh, E. The Diaries of Evelyn Waugh.*
  (M. Davie, ed)
  E.C. Bufkin, 580(SCR):Spring79-76
Waugh, E. The Letters of Evelyn Waugh.
  (M. Amory, ed)
  A. Broyard, 441:4Oct80-21
  P. Fussell, 441:2Nov80-3
  C. James, 453(NYRB):4Dec80-3
  V.S. Pritchett, 442(NY):22Dec80-109
  A. Quinton, 362:4Sep80-307
  61:Nov80-97
Waugh, L.R. Roman Jakobson's Science of
  Language.*
  J. Vachek, 343:Band23-1
Way, P. Icarus.
  M. Laski, 362:14Aug80-216
Wayman, A. Yoga of the Guhyasamājatantra.
  N. Schuster, 485(PE&W):Apr79-243
Wayman, A. and H., eds and trans. The
  Lion's Roar of Queen Śrīmālā.
  W.W. Lai, 318(JAOS):Oct-Dec78-532
Waywell, B.G. The Free-Standing Sculp-
  tures of the Mausoleum at Halicarnassus
  in the British Museum.
  M. Robertson, 90:Mar79-182
Weatherby, H.L. The Keen Delight.*
  S. Cohen, 577(SHR):Summer79-260
Weaver, H. - see Polk, J.K.
Weaver, R., ed. Canadian Short Stories.
  (3rd Ser)
  P. Gotlieb, 526:Spring79-87
  L. Horne, 461:Spring-Summer79-95
  R.E. Jones, 628(UWR):Spring-Summer79-
  93

Weaver, R.L. and N.W. A Chronology of
  Music in the Florentine Theater 1590-
  1750.
  N. Fortune, 415:Nov79-917
Webb, J. The Harmonious Circle.
  R. Dinnage, 453(NYRB):23Oct80-20
  G. Hough, 617(TLS):13Jun80-665
  P. Zweig, 441:30Mar80-10
Webb, K.E. Rainer Maria Rilke and Jugend-
  stil.
  B.L. Bradley, 222(GR):Winter79-44
  R.E. Lorbe, 301(JEGP):Jul79-403
  J. Ryan, 221(GQ):Mar79-275
Webb, S.S. The Governors-General.
  E.S. Morgan, 453(NYRB):4Dec80-47
Webb, T. Shelley.*
  M. Butler, 175:Spring79-78
  R.C. Casto, 541(RES):Feb79-100
  S. Curran, 340(KSJ):Vol28-139
Webb, T. The Violet in the Crucible.*
  J. Buxton, 447(N&Q):Jun78-253
  S. Curran, 661(WC):Summer79-281
  C.E.R., 191(ELN):Sep78(supp)-72
Webb, T. - see Shelley, P.B.
Webber, J.M. Milton and His Epic Tradi-
  tion.*
  W.E. Cain, 400(MLN):Dec79-1245
  D. Norford, 401(MLQ):Sep79-292
Weber, B.N. Brechts "Kreidekreis," ein
  Revolutionsstück.
  S. Mews, 221(GQ):Mar79-288
Weber, D.R. Civil Disobedience in America.
  J.S. Olson, 432(NEQ):Dec79-599
Weber, H. Alexander Zemlinsky.*
  B. Hopkins, 607:Dec78-37
Weber, H.B., ed. The Modern Encyclopedia
  of Russian and Soviet Literature. (Vol
  1)
  D.M. Fiene, 399(MLJ):Nov79-384
  D. Matual, 574(SEEJ):Spring79-137
Weber, H.B., ed. The Modern Encyclopedia
  of Russian and Soviet Literature.
  (Vol 2)
  D.M. Fiene, 399(MLJ):Nov79-384
Weber, H-O. - see Burose, H. and U.
  Schmidt
Weber, R. - see Autpertus, A.
Weber, R. and N. Thiesen de Weber - see
  Loos, E.
Weber, R.E. United States Diplomatic
  Codes and Ciphers, 1775-1938.
  J.E. O'Neill, 14:Jul79-360
Weber-Fas, R., ed. Höchstrichterliche
  Rechtsprechung zu internationalen Doppel-
  besteuerungsabkommen.
  J. Seest, 182:Vol131#11/12-339
Weber-Schäfer, P. Einführung in die
  antike politische Theorie.
  T.J. Saunders, 123:Vol29No1-79
Webster, G. The Republic of Letters.
  D. Donoghue, 617(TLS):11Jul80-775
Webster, J., ed. Voices of Canada.
  S.H. Uphaus, 106:Fall79-209
Webster, M. Hogarth.
  D. Piper, 617(TLS):1Feb80-119

Webster, T.B.L. An Introduction to Menander.
    J.C.B. Lowe, 123:Vol29No1-141
Wechsler, J., ed. On Aesthetics in Science.*
    T.C. Holyoke, 42(AR):Winter79-117
Wedde, I. Made Over.
    R. Jackaman, 368:Dec74-353
Wedde, I. Pathway to the Sea.
    M. Harlow, 368:Sep76-231
Weddle, A.E., ed. Landscape Techniques.
    R. MacCormack, 617(TLS):23May80-588
Weeks, J. Coming Out.
    L. Crompton, 637(VS):Winter79-211
Weeks, J. and S. Rowbotham. Socialism and the New Life.
    L. Crompton, 637(VS):Winter79-211
Wegener, C. Liberal Education and the Modern University.
    639(VQR):Spring79-62
Wegmann, B. Ocho mundos.
    M.E. Beeson, 399(MLJ):Jan-Feb79-50
    I. Molina, 238:May-Sep79-416
Wehrenberg, D. Due wechselseitigen Beziehungen zwischen Allmendrechten und Gemeinfronverpflichtungen vornehmlich in Oberdeutschland.
    B. Schmid, 182:Vol31#11/12-341
Wehrli, F., ed. Die Schule des Aristoteles. (Supp Vol 1)
    R.W., 555:Vol52fasc2-381
Weida, G. Der Gebrauch von "shall/should" und "will/would" in englischer Prosa am Ende des 16. Jahrhunderts.*
    H. Mittermann, 38:Band96Heft3/4-476
Weidemann, H. Metaphysik und Sprache.
    J.O., 543:Dec78-373
Weidert, A. I Tkong Amwi.
    G.F. Meier, 682(ZPSK):Band31Heft1-90
Weidert, A. Tai-Khamti Phonology and Vocabulary.
    W. Bright, 350:Jun79-490
Weidman, J. Counselors-at-Law.
    R. Freedman, 441:26Oct80-24
Weidmann, U. Fliegersprache.*
    L. Hoffmann, 682(ZPSK):Band31Heft3-297
Weigand, E. Die Zuordnung von Ausdruck und Inhalt bei den grammatischen Kategorien des Deutschen.
    W.A. Benware, 182:Vol31#3/4-97
Weigand, K. Tiecks "William Lovell."*
    W.J. Lillyman, 221(GQ):Jan79-113
Weiger, J.G. Hacia la comedia.
    T.L. de Chaves, 304(JHP):Autumn79-89
Weiger, J.G. The Valencian Dramatists of Spain's Golden Age.
    G. Edwards, 86(BHS):Jan79-64
Weigl, B. A Romance.
    V. Rutsala, 460(OhR):No.24-102
Weil, A. The Marriage of the Sun and Moon.
    R. Lingeman, 441:5Oct80-13
Weil, C. - see Giraudoux, J.
Weil, J. Christopher Marlowe.*
    M.C. Bradbrook, 570(SQ):Summer79-435
    A.C. Dessen, 401(MLQ):Mar79-75
                                    [continued]

[continuing]
    L. Gent, 175:Summer79-164
    B. Gibbons, 541(RES):Feb79-70
    J. Levenson, 405(MP):May80-415
Weil, R. and C. Nicolet - see Polybius
Weil, S. Lectures on Philosophy.
    D.W. Hamlyn, 617(TLS):4Jan80-19
Weill, C. Marxistes russes et social-democratie allemande 1898-1904.
    D. Colas, 98:Mar78-341
Weiluch, D. The Graphic Transcription of Literary Chinese Characters.
    W.G. Boltz, 318(JAOS):Jul-Sep78-289
Weimann, K. Middle English Animal Literature.
    B. Rowland, 72:Band216Heft1-169
Weimann, R. Shakespeare and the Popular Tradition in the Theatre. (R. Schwartz, ed and trans)
    R. Berry, 529(QQ):Autumn79-470
    M. Shapiro, 301(JEGP):Jul79-425
    J.C. Trewin, 157:Spring79-80
Weimann, R. Structure and Society in Literary History.*
    G. Stratmann, 490:Band10Heft4-534
Weimer, W.B. and D.S. Palermo, eds. Cognition and the Symbolic Processes.*
    A. Munro, 350:Sep79-714
Weinberg, A. and L. Clarence Darrow.
    W. Goodman, 441:5Oct80-16
Weinberg, J.R. Ockham, Descartes, and Hume.* (W.J. Courtenay, W.H. Hay and K.E. Yandell, eds)
    N.C., 543:Sep78-158
    J.D. North, 479(PhQ):Oct79-358
    W.R. O'Connor, 258:Jun79-244
Weinberg, K. The Figure of Faust in Valéry and Goethe.*
    L.R. Furst, 131(CL):Winter79-80
    P. Hernadi, 639(VQR):Spring79-379
    H.R. Jann, 149(CLS):Jun79-170
    C. Nebel, 207(FR):May79-936
de Weinberg, M.B.F. - see under Fontanella de Weinberg, M.B.
Weinberg, S. The First Three Minutes.
    529(QQ):Spring79-182
Weinberger, C. Zur Logik der Annahmen.
    H. Wagner, 53(AGP):Band60Heft1-112
Weinbrot, H.D. Augustus Caesar in "Augustan" England.*
    M. Kelsall, 566:Autumn78-40
    T.E. Maresca, 141:Winter79-80
    R.G. Peterson, 173(ECS):Spring79-396
    E. Tomarken, 219(GaR):Summer79-448
"Friedrich Weinbrunner 1766-1826."
    H. Rosenau, 46:Jul79-66
Weiner, S.L. Ajaṇṭā.*
    M.W. Meister, 318(JAOS):Oct-Dec78-563
Weinfurter, S., ed. Consuetudines canonicorum regularium Springirsbacenses-Rodenses.
    G. Constable, 589:Oct79-874
Weingarten, R. The Vermont Suicides.
    E. Milton, 472:Fall/Winter79-270
    P. Stitt, 491:Jan80-229

Weingartner, R.H. The Unity of the
Platonic Dialogue.
  S. Umphrey, 321:Spring78-74
Weinraub, E.J. Chrétien's Jewish Grail.*
  D.D.R. Owen, 208(FS):Vol33Pt2-548
Weinreich, U. Sprachen im Kontakt. (A.
de Vincenz, ed)
  B. Kielhöfer, 260(IF):Band83-356
Weinrich, A.K.H. Mucheke.
  M.F.C. Bourdillon, 69:Vol48#3-305
Weinrich, H. Sprache in Texten.
  H. Kahane, 545(RPh):Aug78-97
  R. Martin, 553(RLiR):Jan-Jun78-208
  E. Pulgram, 215(GL):Spring78-47
Weinryb, B.D. The Jews of Poland.
  B.K. Johnpoll, 390:Aug-Sep79-62
Weinstein, A. Perjury.*
  D. Levin, 639(VQR):Autumn78-725
Weinstein, M.A. - see Scott, W.
Weinstein, R.A. Grays Harbor, 1885-1913.
  L.L. Irwin, 14:Oct79-482
Weinstein, R.A. Tall Ships on Puget Sound.
  B. Mergen, 658:Autumn79-322
Weintraub, K.J. The Value of the Individ-
ual.
  S.J. Greenblatt, 125:Winter79-275
Weintraub, R., ed. Fabian Feminist.*
  F.P.W. McDowell, 295(JML):Vol7#4-809
  B. Richardson, 637(VS):Spring79-364
Weintraub, S. Four Rossettis.
  H.L. Sussman, 637(VS):Spring79-361
Weintraub, S. The London Yankees.*
  A. Calder-Marshall, 617(TLS):11Jan80-
  34
Weintraub, S. - see Shaw, G.B.
Weintraub, S. and others. Sources for
Reinterpretation.
  J. Shattock, 402(MLR):Jul79-672
Weinzweig, H. Basic Black with Pearls.
  A.S. Brennan, 198:Fal180-97
  J.M. Kertzer, 99:Sep80-32
Weir, R.F., ed. Ethical Issues in Death
and Dying.*
  639(VQR):Summer78-108
Weisberg, G.P. Bonvin.
  R. Pickvance, 617(TLS):2May80-506
  A. Sheon, 55:Nov79-36
Weisberg, G.P., with W.S. Talbot. Chardin
and the Still-Life Tradition in France.
  F. Haskell, 453(NYRB):9Oct80-29
  G. Martin, 617(TLS):1Feb80-120
Weischer, B.M. Qērellos. (Vol 4, Pt 1)
  A. de Halleux, 182:Vol131#17/18-594
Weise, C. Sämtliche Werke. (Vols 4, 5, 8,
11 and 21) (J.D. Lindberg, ed)
  J. Hardin, 221(GQ):Nov79-537
Weisgarber, M. Spiral Waves Whirling
Motions.
  D. Barbour, 150(DR):Spring79-154
Weiskel, T. The Romantic Sublime.*
  R. Gravil, 402(MLR):Jul79-664
  E.D. Mackerness, 447(N&Q):Jun78-251
Weisman, J. Evidence.
  N. Callendar, 441:4May80-24

Weiss, D. Syntax und Semantik polnischer
Partizipialkonstruktionen im Rahmen
einer generativ-transformationellen
Sprachbeschreibung.
  F. Knowles, 575(SEER):Jan79-149
  R.A. Rothstein, 574(SEEJ):Spring79-
  143
Weiss, J. Weltverlust und Subjektivität.
  H. Ottmann, 489(PJGG):Band86Heft1-148
Weiss, P. Kandinsky in Munich.
  C. Green, 617(TLS):1Feb80-121
  V. Hammock, 255(HAB):Summer79-221
Weiss, P. Philosophy in Process. (Vol 7)
  T.R.V., 543:Sep78-159
Weiss, R. Medieval and Humanist Greek.
  J.H. Whitfield, 402(MLR):Jan79-217
Weiss, R.L., with C.E. Butterworth - see
Maimonides, M.
Weiss, T. Views and Spectacles.
  H. Carruth, 231:Dec80-74
  D. Graham, 565:Vol20#2-75
  A. Young, 617(TLS):30May80-620
Weisstein, U., ed. Expressionism as an
International Literary Phenomenon.
  H. Jechová, 549(RLC):Jan-Mar78-119
Weitz, M. The Opening Mind.*
  T.S. Clements, 484(PPR):Mar80-449
  G. Dickie, 311(JP):Jan80-54
  B.M., 543:Sep78-160
Weitzmann, K. The Icon.
  J. Beckwith, 39:Apr79-328
  J. Masheck, 62:Dec78-60
Weitzmann, K. and others. The Place of
Book Illumination in Byzantine Art.*
  R.H. Rough, 377:Mar79-48
Weixlmann, J. John Barth.
  Z. Bowen, 295(JML):Vol7#4-657
Weizenbaum, J. Computer Power and Human
Reason.
  A. Reeves, 63:Mar79-106
Welch, A.T. and P. Cachia, eds. Islam.
  B. Spuler, 182:Vol131#23/24-835
Welch, D. Dumb Instrument. (J-L.
Chevalier, ed)
  S. Monod, 189(EA):Jul-Dec78-417
Welch, J. The Death of Jim Loney.*
  H. Carr, 617(TLS):2May80-500
Welch, J. Winter in the Blood.
  D. Kunz, 145(Crit):Vol20#1-93
Welch, S.C. Imperial Mughal Painting.*
  R. Ettinghausen, 57:Vol40#2/3-233
Weldon, F. Praxis.*
  J. Chernaik, 364:Aug/Sep79-140
Weldon, F. Puffball.
  A. Brookner, 617(TLS):22Feb80-202
  M. Cantwell, 441:24Aug80-14
  P. Kemp, 362:21Feb80-254
  61:Aug80-84
  442(NY):15Sep80-186
Welland, D. Mark Twain in England.
  H.G. Baetzhold, 27(AL):Mar79-121
  S. Fender, 541(RES):Nov79-491
  A.J. von Frank, 587(SAF):Spring79-112
Wellek, R. and A. Ribeiro, eds. Evidence
in Literary Scholarship.*
  W.H., 148:Autumn79-91

Weller, E. A Civil War Courtship. (W. Walton, ed)
442(NY):29Sep80-151
Welling, W. Photography in America: The Formative Years, 1839-1900.*
R. Whelan, 55:Apr79-31
Welliver, W. Character, Plot, and Thought in Plato's Timaeus-Critias.*
C. Gill, 123:Vol129No1-163
S.U., 543:Dec78-374
Wells, A.M. Miss Marks and Miss Wooley.
L.A. Monteiro, 432(NEQ):Mar79-107
Wells, G.A. and D.R. Oppenheimer - see Englefield, F.R.H.
Wells, H.G. The Door in the Wall and Other Stories.
442(NY):10Nov80-221
Wells, H.G. Ann Veronica.
J. Lucas, 617(TLS):23May80-574
Wells, L. - see Cofield, J.R.
Wells, L.W. The Death Brigade.
T. Ziolkowski, 569(SR):Fall79-676
Wells, M.B. Du Bellay.*
D. Shaw, 208(FS):Vol33Pt2-628
Wells, R.A.E. Dearth and Distress in York-shire 1793-1801.
W.M. Stern, 325:Oct79-232
Wells, S., ed. English Drama.
G. Bas, 189(EA):Jan-Mar78-72
Wells, S. Royal Shakespeare.*
R. Proudfoot, 175:Spring79-51
Wells, S. Shakespeare.*
M. Alexander, 611(TN):Vol33#1-44
G.W. Williams, 579(SAQ):Spring79-271
Welsh, A. Roots of Lyric.
R. Fowler, 301(JEGP):Apr79-278
580(SCR):Nov78-135
"Die Weltbühne."
J. Joll, 453(NYRB):6Nov80-26
Welte, B. Religionsphilosophie.*
R. Schaeffler, 489(PJGG):Band86Heft1-201
Welte, W. Negationslinguistik.
G. Tottie, 596(SL):Vol33#2-164
Welty, E. The Collected Stories of Eudora Welty.
A. Broyard, 441:25Oct80-16
M. Howard, 441:2Nov80-1
R. Towers, 453(NYRB):4Dec80-30
Welty, E. The Eye of the Story.
J.N. Gretlund, 577(SHR):Summer79-245
J.H. Justus, 569(SR):Summer79-468
L.A. Lawson, 396(ModA):Spring79-215
42(AR):Winter79-123
639(VQR):Autumn78-127
Welwei, K-W. Unfreie im antiken Kriegs-dienst. (Pt 2)
F. Lasserre, 182:Vol131#9/10-305
Wembah-Rashid, J.A.R. The Ethno-History of the Matrilineal Peoples of Southeast Tanzania.
A. Redmayne, 69:Vol148#4-407
Wenck, G. Systematische Syntax des Japan-ischen.
J. Jelinek, 182:Vol131#1/2-29

Wender, D. The Last Scenes of the "Odyssey."*
N.J. Richardson, 123:Vol129No2-304
O. Tsagarakis, 487:Winter79-372
Wendt, A. Flying-fox in a Freedom Tree.
K.O. Arvidson, 368:Mar75-72
Wendt, A. Pouliuli.
368:Mar78-91
Wendt, A. Sons for the Return Home.
K.O. Arvidson, 368:Sep74-256
Wenk, K., comp. Laotische Handschriften.
L. Rocher, 318(JAOS):Jul-Sep78-347
Wenk, K. Phālī sǫn nǫng.
P.J. Bee, 182:Vol131#3/4-104
Wenke, R.J. Patterns in Prehistory.
J. Pfeiffer, 441:1Jun80-7
Wentworth, H. and B. Flexner, comps. Dictionary of American Slang. (2nd ed)
A. Burgess, 617(TLS):18Apr80-429
Wenzler, L. Die Freiheit und das Böse nach Vladimir Solov'ev.
J. Rupp, 182:Vol131#17/18-584
Wepman, D., R.B. Newman and M.B. Binder-man. The Life.*
J.M. Vlach, 582(SFQ):Vol41-298
van der Werf, H. The Chansons of the Trou-badours and Trouvères.*
J. Stevens, 382(MAE):1979/1-163
van der Werf, H., ed. Monumenta monodica medii aevi XI: Trouvère-Melodien I.
H. Tischler, 317:Summer79-335
Werfel, F. Zwischen Oben und Unten. (A.D. Klarmann, ed)
H.A. Lea, 222(GR):Summer78-133
Werlen, I. Lautstrukturen des Dialekts von Brig im schweizerischen Kanton Wallis.
H. Löffler, 343:Band23-147
Wermelinger, H. Lebensmittelteuerungen, ihre Bekämpfung und ihre politischen Rückwirkungen in Bern.
A-M. Dubler, 182:Vol131#13-444
Wermke, J., ed. Comics und Religion.
R. Sell, 301(JEGP):Oct79-611
Wermser, R. Statistische Studien zur Ent-wicklung des englischen Wortschatzes.
M. Görlach, 72:Band216Heft2-401
Werner, A. Chaim Soutine.*
J. Gutmann, 390:Dec79-64
Werner, E. A Voice Still Heard...
H. Tischler, 414(MusQ):Ju178-412
Werner, R. - see Mann, H.
Werner, S. Diderot's Great Scroll.*
R. Niklaus, 208(FS):Vol33Pt2-772
Wernher von Gartenaere. Helmbrecht. (F. Hundsnurscher, ed)
B. Murdoch, 182:Vol131#11/12-344
Wertheimer, J. Dialogisches Sprechen im Werk Stefan Georges.
M.M. Metzger, 222(GR):Fall79-170
Wesley, J. The Works of John Wesley. (Vol 11) (G.R. Cragg, ed)
D. Davie, 402(MLR):Oct79-907
Wesling, D. The Chances of Rhyme.
C.H. Sisson, 617(TLS):12Sep80-997
Wessel, L.P. G.E. Lessing's Theology.
A. Reix, 542:Jan-Mar78-111

Wesson, R.G. Communism and Communist
Systems.
M. Rush, 550(RusR):Jul79-386
Wesson, R.G. Lenin's Legacy.
R.V. Daniels, 550(RusR):Jul79-373
M. McCauley, 575(SEER):Oct79-611
West, A. John Piper.
D. Piper, 617(TLS):1Feb80-119
West, A.J. The Water Book.*
G. Hamel, 198:Winter80-140
W. Stevenson, 102(CanL):Spring79-103
West, D. and T. Woodman, eds. Creative
Imitation and Latin Literature.
O. Lyne, 617(TLS):22Feb80-218
West, D.S. Franklin and McClintock.*
D. Barbour, 150(DR):Spring79-154
P. Hall, 628(UWR):Spring-Summer79-107
West, D.S. Poems and Elegies, 1972-1977.*
D. Barbour, 150(DR):Spring79-154
West, J. Double Discovery.
D. Grumbach, 441:19Oct80-16
West, J.L.W. 3d. William Styron.*
P.S. Koda, 517(PBSA):Oct-Dec78-566
West, L.E., ed and trans. The Saint Gall
Passion Play.*
J.E. Tailby, 130:Spring79-86
West, M.L. Early Greek Philosophy and the
Orient.
W.J. Verdenius, 394:Vol32fasc3/4-389
West, M.L. Studies in Greek Elegy and
Iambus.
J. Carrière, 555:Vol55fasc1-151
West, M.L. - see Hesiod
West, P. The Very Rich Hours of Count von
Stauffenberg.
F. Busch, 441:9Nov80-14
442(NY):25Aug80-100
West, P. Yenching University and Sino-
Western Relations, 1916-1952.*
D. Deal, 318(JAOS):Jul-Sep78-296
West, R. The Department of State on the
Eve of the First World War.
639(VQR):Summer79-89
West, R. Rebecca West: a Celebration.
A.J.S., 148:Winter79-91
Westbrook, P.D. William Bradford.*
E. Emerson, 432(NEQ):Sep79-420
Westbrook, P.D. Free Will and Determinism
in American Literature.
G. Van Cromphout, 165(EAL):Fall80-196
Westburg, B. The Confessional Fictions of
Charles Dickens.*
J.H. Buckley, 445(NCF):Mar79-508
R. Maxwell, 637(VS):Winter79-216
S. Monod, 189(EA):Jul-Dec78-400
R. O'Kell, 529(QQ):Winter79/80-712
R.L. Patten, 454:Spring79-254
Westerink, L.G., ed. The Greek Commen-
taries on Plato's "Phaedo."*
J. Coulter, 24:Fall79-437
A. Smith, 303(JoHS):Vol99-185
J. Whittaker, 487:Winter79-376
Westermann, C. Argumentationen und Begrün-
dungen in der Ethik und Rechtslehre.
S. Blasche, 687:Jul-Sep79-468
von Westernhagen, C. Wagner.*
R. Anderson, 415:May79-399

von Westernhagen, K. The Forging of the
"Ring."
R.L.J., 412:Aug-Nov78-276
Westfall, R.S. The Construction of Modern
Science.
M.B. Hall, 84:Mar79-100
Westheimer, D. Von Ryan's Return.
P. Andrews, 441:30Mar80-7
Westlake, D.E. Castle in the Air.
J. Charyn, 441:13Apr80-9
"Brett Weston: Photographs From Five
Decades."
H. Kramer, 441:30Nov80-66
Weston, S.B. Wallace Stevens.*
L. Surette, 255(HAB):Fall79-333
Westreich, G. Directory of Private
Presses and Letterpress Printers and
Publishers.
D. Chambers, 503:Winter78-195
Westwood, J.N. Railways of India.
I.J. Kerr, 293(JASt):May79-604
Wetherill, P.M. The Literary Text.
J. Cruickshank, 208(FS):Vol33Pt2-971
Wetmore, R.Y. First on the Land.
W.K. McNeil, 292(JAF):Jul-Sep79-363
Wettstein, J. La Fresque romane. (Vol 2)
W. Cahn, 589:Apr79-438
Wetzel, R.D. Frontier Musicians on the
Connoquenessing, Wabash, and Ohio.
K.J.R. Arndt, 406:Spring79-57
Wexler, J.P. Laura Riding's Pursuit of
Truth.
J. Symons, 617(TLS):18Jul80-795
Wexler, P. A Historical Phonology of the
Belorussian Language.
J. Dingley, 575(SEER):Jul79-414
Whale, J., ed. The Pope from Poland.
D. Cupitt, 617(TLS):25Apr80-458
Whalen, P. Decompressions.
A. Saijo, 649(WAL):Spring79-85
Whalon, M.K. Performing Arts Research.
R.K. Sarlos, 610:Feb79-147
Wharton, D.P., ed. In the Trough of the
Sea.
R. Vitzthum, 165(EAL):Fall80-197
Wharton, W. Birdy.*
D. Durrant, 364:Dec79/Jan80-132
42(AR):Summer78-378
Whatley, J. Flesh Songs.
G. Hamel, 198:Winter80-140
Wheatcroft, A. The Tennyson Album.
J. Bayley, 453(NYRB):18Dec80-42
H. Tennyson, 362:23Oct80-549
Wheaton, P.D. Razzmatazz.
E. Wagner, 441:16Nov80-14
Wheeler, R. Iwo.
442(NY):12May80-164
Wheeler, T.C. The Great American Writing
Block.*
J. Burke, 231:Mar80-92
Wheeler-Bennett, J. Friends, Enemies and
Sovereigns.
639(VQR):Winter78-24
Wheelock, J.H. Afternoon: Amagansett
Beach.
C. Bedient, 569(SR):Spring79-296

White, W. - see Whitman, W.

Whitehead, D. The Ideology of the
Athenian Metic.
M.M. Austin, 487:Summer79-170
N.R.E. Fisher, 123:Vol29No2-266
H.W. Stubbs, 303(JoHS):Vol199-196

Whitehead, L. - see Lora, G.

Whitehill, W.M. and N. Kotker. Massachusetts.
T.B. Adams, 576:Mar78-47

Whitehouse, H. The Dal Pozzo Copies of
the Palestrina Mosaic.*
O. Murray, 313:Vol69-217

Whitehouse, R. A London Album.
J. Naughton, 362:18and25Dec80-865

Whitelaw, M. - see Lord Dalhousie

Whitelock, D., ed. English Historical
Documents. (Vol 1) (2nd ed)
P.H. Blair, 617(TLS):9May80-524

Whitfield, J.H. - see Guarini, B.

Whiting, B.J. Early American Proverbs and
Proverbial Phrases.*
W. Mieder, 292(JAF):Jul-Sep79-339

Whiting, C.G. Paul Valéry.*
E.R. Jackson, 399(MLJ):Mar79-142
205(FMLS):Oct78-398

Whitley, J.S. F. Scott Fitzgerald: "The
Great Gatsby."
T.A. Shippey, 447(N&Q):Dec78-568

Whitman, G.W. Civil War Letters of George
Washington Whitman.* (J.M. Loving, ed)
A. Hook, 447(N&Q):Jun78-283

Whitman, M.M. Mattie.* (R.H. Waldron, ed)
S.A. Black, 648(WCR):Oct78-62
L.J. Budd, 579(SAQ):Winter79-134
C.C. Hollis, 646(WWR):Sep78-128

Whitman, R.F. Shaw and the Play of Ideas.*
F.P.W. McDowell, 295(JML):Vol7#4-809
B. Richardson, 637(VS):Spring79-364
J. Treglown, 447(N&Q):Aug78-378

Whitman, S.H. and J.H. Ingram. Poe's
Helen Remembers. (J.C. Miller, ed)
A. Sinclair, 617(TLS):27Jun80-741

Whitman, W. The Collected Writings of
Walt Whitman: Daybooks and Notebooks.*
(W. White, ed)
S.A. Black, 648(WCR):Oct78-62
L.J. Budd, 579(SAQ):Winter79-134
A. Golden, 646(WWR):Jun78-84
R. Nelson, 639(VQR):Summer79-536

Whitman, W. Walt Whitman: The Correspondence. (Vol 6) (E.H. Miller, ed)
J. Loving, 646(WWR):Mar78-36

Whitney, C.A.N. Clara's Diary. (W.M.
Steele and T. Ichimata, eds)
Kano Masanao, 285(JapQ):Oct-Dec79-549

Whittall, A. Music Since the First World
War.*
C. Bennett, 607:Mar78-38

Whitten, J.P. Fannie Hardy Eckstorm.
M.R. Yocom, 292(JAF):Jan-Mar79-103

Whittick, A. - see Ruskin, J.

Whitworth, J. Unhistorical Fragments.
D.M. Thomas, 617(TLS):25Apr80-477

"Who Was Who in the Theatre, 1912-1976."
P. Davison, 354:Sep79-301

"Who's Who 1980."
A. Watkins, 362:24Apr80-540

Wichmann, H. Aufbruch zum neuen Wohnen.
T. Benton, 46:Jun79-362

Wickes, G. The Amazon of Letters.
295(JML):Vol17#4-657

Wickham, G., ed. English Moral Interludes.
G.C. Britton, 447(N&Q):Oct78-447

Wickwire, F. and M. Cornwallis.
B.W. Labaree, 441:6Jul80-3

Widdowson, H.G. Teaching Language as
Communication.
R.B. Kaplan, 350:Sep79-753
E.E. Tarone, 608:Dec80-522

Widdowson, J. If You Don't Be Good.
L.L. Painter, 650(WF):Oct79-274

Widlöcher, D. L'interprétation des
dessins d'enfants. (7th ed)
L. Millet, 192(EP):Jan-Mar79-110

Widmann, J. Die Grundstruktur des trans-
zendentalen Wissens nach Joh. Gottl.
Fichtes Wissenschaftslehre ^{2}1804.
S. Decloux, 182:Vol31#5/6-132

Widmer, E. The Russian Ecclesiastical
Mission in Peking During the Eighteenth
Century.*
C.M. Foust, 318(JAOS):Jul-Sep78-303

Wiebe, R. The Mad Trapper.
S. Solecki, 99:Dec80/Jan81-42

Weibe, R. The Scorched-Wood People.*
R. Lecker, 168(ECW):Spring78-129
S. McMullin, 296(JCF):28/29-249
G. Noonan, 628(UWR):Fall-Winter78-90
D.E. Wylder, 649(WAL):Fall79-237

Wiebe, R., H. Savage and T. Radford.
Alberta/A Celebration.
W.J. Keith, 198:Winter80-112

Wiebe, R. and Theatre Pass Muraille. Far
as the Eye Can See.*
S. McMullin, 296(JCF):28/29-249
A. Ricketts, 168(ECW):Fall78-251

Wiebenson, D. The Picturesque Garden in
France.*
A. Fairlie, 208(FS):Apr79-205
S. Jellicoe, 46:Dec79-397

Wiecek, W.M. The Sources of Antislavery
Constitutionalism in America, 1760-1848.
D.M. Roper, 656(WMQ):Jan79-130

Wieczynski, J.L. The Russian Frontier.*
G.E. Orchard, 104(CASS):Summer78-293

Wiegand, H.E. Studien zur Minne und Ehe
in Wolframs Parzival und Hartmanns
Artusepik.
B. Koelliker, 657(WW):Jan-Feb78-76

Wier, A. Blanco.
D. Graham, 649(WAL):Winter80-329

Wier, A. Things About to Disappear.
639(VQR):Autumn79-140

Wier, D. Blood, Hook and Eye.*
V. Rutsala, 460(OhR):No.24-102
639(VQR):Winter78-12

von Wiese, B., ed. Deutsche Dichter des
18. Jahrhunderts.*
E.A. McCormick, 301(JEGP):Apr79-292

Wiese, G. Untersuchungen zu den Prosa-
schriften Henry Vaughans.
   B.W. Browning, 568(SCN):Fall-Winter79-
   75
Wiesel, E. Four Hasidic Masters and Their
Struggle Against Melancholy.
   A.L. Berger, 390:Jan79-70
   J.K. Roth, 613:Dec79-419
Wiesel, E. A Jew Today.*
   A.H. Rosenfeld, 390:Apr79-74
   J.K. Roth, 613:Dec79-419
   G. Sauer, 287:Nov78-29
Wieselhuber, F. Die Faszination des Bösen
in der viktorianischen Lyrik.
   G. Hönnighausen, 224(GRM):Band28Heft1-
   121
Wiesenfarth, J. George Eliot's Mythmaking.
   H. Witemeyer, 445(NCF):Dec78-396
Wietfeldt, W.J. The Emblem Literature of
Johann Michael Dilherr (1604-1669).*
   H. Homann, 400(MLN):Apr79-628
Wiezell, R.J. Inglés al dedillo.
   J.M. Hendrickson, 238:Dec79-745
Wigoder, G. - see Roth, C. and G. Wigoder
Wijk, A. Regularized English.*
   G. Bourcier, 189(EA):Jul-Dec78-364
Wijsenbeek-Wijler, H. Aristotle's Con-
cept of Soul, Sleep and Dreams.
   J.L. Ackrill, 123:Vol29No2-321
Wikland, E. Elizabethan Players in Sweden
1591-92. (2nd ed)
   W. Schrickx, 179(ES):Dec79-835
Wikse, J.R. About Possession.
   M.L.O., 543:Sep78-161
Wilberger, C.H. Voltaire's Russia.*
   J.H. Brumfitt, 208(FS):Vol33Pt2-736
   P. Zaborov, 535(RHL):Jul-Aug78-654
Wilbur, R. The Mind-Reader.*
   V. Contoski, 152(UDQ):Summer78-156
Wilczynski, J. The Multinationals and
East-West Relations.
   M. Kaser, 575(SEER):Oct79-638
Wild, P. Pioneer Conservationists of
Western America.
   E.C. Fritz, 584(SWR):Autumn79-404
Wildavsky, A. How to Limit Government
Spending.
   A. Hacker, 441:19Oct80-7
Wildbolz, R. Adalbert Stifter.
   E. Mason, 402(MLR):Jul79-754
Wilde, M.C. and O. Borsten. A Loving
Gentleman.*
   K. McSweeney, 148:Spring79-77
   S.M. Ross, 395(MFS):Summer78-275
Wilde, O. The Illustrated Oscar Wilde.
(R. Gasson, ed)
   I. Fletcher, 637(VS):Summer79-487
Wilde, O. Leben und Werk in Daten und
Bildern. (N. Kohl, ed)
   G. Merle, 189(EA):Jul-Dec78-405
Wilde, O. Selected Letters of Oscar Wilde.
(R. Hart-Davis, ed)
   P. Keating, 617(TLS):11Jan80-34
Wilden, T. The Imaginary Canadian.
   P. Delany, 99:Aug80-26

Wildenstein, D. Claude Monet. (Vols 2
and 3)
   R. Pickvance, 617(TLS):8Aug80-898
Wildenstein, D. Monet's Years at Giverny.
   A. Frankenstein, 55:Mar79-30
Wilder, T. The Alcestiad, or A Life in
the Sun.
   D. Porter, 109:Summer80-219
Wilders, J. The Lost Garden.
   A.B. Kernan, 676(YR):Autumn79-124
   R. Proudfoot, 617(TLS):8Aug80-901
Wilding, M. The Phallic Forest.
   P. Lewis, 565:Vol20#4-67
Wilding, M., ed. The Tabloid Story Pocket
Book.
   P. Lewis, 565:Vol20#4-67
Wiles, J. Homelands.
   P. Norman, 617(TLS):25Jul80-858
Wiley, W.L. The Hôtel de Bourgogne.
   C.A. Shaw, 208(FS):Apr79-184
Wilhelm, J.J. The Later Cantos of Ezra
Pound.*
   L. Surette, 255(HAB):Fall79-333
Wilhelmsen, F.D. Christianity and Polit-
ical Philosophy.
   G. Niemeyer, 396(ModA):Fall79-421
Wilkes, G.A. A Dictionary of Australian
Colloquialisms.*
   K.S. Inglis, 71(ALS):May79-131
   W.A. Krebs, 67:May79-179
Wilkes, K.V. Physicalism.
   U.T. Place, 483:Jul79-423
   A.C. Purton, 479(PhQ):Apr79-178
   J.J.C. Smart, 84:Dec79-403
Wilkie, B. and M.L. Johnson. Blake's
"Four Zoas."
   H. Adams, 591(SIR):Spring79-150
   R.F. Gleckner, 301(JEGP):Jan79-133
   J. Kilgore, 401(MLQ):Sep79-309
   M. Nurmi, 661(WC):Summer79-279
Wilkin, D. - see de Magny, O.
Wilkins, B.T. Has History Any Meaning?
   C.B. McCullagh, 63:Jun79-192
   639(VQR):Spring79-55
Wilkins, D.A. Linguistics in Language
Teaching.
   K. Schröder, 430(NS):Jul78-379
Wilkins, D.A. Notional Syllabuses.*
   A. Michiels, 556(RLV):1978/1-87
Wilkins, D.A. Second-Language Learning
and Teaching.
   K. Schröder, 430(NS):Dec78-617
Wilkins, E.J. Impacto Hispánico.
   S. Lequerica de la Vega, 399(MLJ):
   Nov79-379
Wilkins, N., ed. One Hundred Ballades,
Rondeaux and Virelais from the Late
Middle Ages.
   J. Stevens, 382(MAE):1979/1-167
Wilkins, N. - see Guillaume de Machaut
Wilkins, P. Pasts.*
   C. Hope, 364:Mar80-76
Wilkinson, E.M. and L.A. Willoughby.
Goethe — Dichter und Denker.
   D. Hochstätter, 657(WW):Mar-Apr78-134
Wilkinson, G. Turner Sketches, 1802-20.*
   J. Ziff, 637(VS):Autumn77-113

Wilkinson, J.C. Water and Tribal Settlement in South-East Arabia.
  K.W. and E.K. Butzer, 182:Vol31#3/4-125
Wilkinson, P. Terrorism and the Liberal State.
  P. Dennis, 529(QQ):Spring79-178
Will, É., C. Mossé and P. Goukowsky. Le monde grec et l'Orient.* (Vol 2)
  G.A. Lehmann, 182:Vol31#5/6-177
  R.W., 555:Vol52fasc1-143
Will, F. Our Thousand Year Old Bodies.
  D. Kirby, 617(TLS):13Jun80-680
Will, G.F. The Pursuit of Happiness and Other Sobering Thoughts.
  639(VQR):Autumn78-130
Willan, A. Great Cooks and their Recipes from Taillevent to Escoffier.
  W. and C. Cowen, 639(VQR):Spring78-74
Willan, T.S. Elizabethan Manchester.
  V. Pearl, 617(TLS):23May80-573
Willbanks, R. Randolph Stow.
  J. Croft, 71(ALS):May79-125
Willcox, W.B. - see Franklin, B.
Wille, G. Einführung in das römische Musikleben.
  M.O. Lee, 487:Winter79-362
Willenbrink, G.A. The Dossier of Flaubert's "Un Coeur simple."*
  R. Huss, 447(N&Q):Jun78-267
  A.W. Raitt, 402(MLR):Jul79-699
Willett, J. Art and Politics in the Weimar Period.* (British title: The New Sobriety.)
  639(VQR):Summer79-87
Willett, J. and R. Manheim - see Brecht, B.
Willett, J., and R. Manheim, with E. Fried - see Brecht, B.
Willetts, R.F. The Civilization of Ancient Crete.
  S. Hood, 123:Vol29No2-330
Williams, A.D. - see Galbraith, J.K.
Williams, B. Descartes.*
  E.J. Ashworth, 529(QQ):Winter79/80-653
  P.A. Schouls, 518:May79-61
Williams, B. The Making of Manchester Jewry, 1740-1875.
  B. Gainer, 637(VS):Winter78-285
Williams, C.E. Writers and Politics in Modern Germany (1918-1945).
  P. Hutchinson, 402(MLR):Apr79-503
Williams, C.G.S., ed. Literature and History in the Age of Ideas.
  J. Vercruysse, 535(RHL):Jul-Aug78-643
Williams, D.A., ed. The Monster in the Mirror.*
  P.M.S. Dawson, 541(RES):Aug79-365
Williams, D.L. Faulkner's Women.*
  J.M. Flora, 573(SSF):Winter78-115
  J.V. Hagopian, 295(JML):Vol7#4-695
  M.A. Haynes, 395(MFS):Winter78/79-637
  T. Heller, 50(ArQ):Summer79-185
  I.D. Lind, 587(SAF):Spring79-109
Williams, E. Harriet Monroe and the Poetry Renaissance.*
  D.J. Cahill, 502(PrS):Summer78-202
                    [continued]

[continuing]
  L. Surette, 106:Spring79-63
  295(JML):Vol7#4-581
Williams, F. Callimachus: "Hymn to Apollo."
  D.L. Clayman, 124:Nov79-195
Williams, G. Change and Decline.*
  E.J. Kenney, 487:Spring79-72
  K.R. Walters, 141:Spring79-160
Williams, G.A. Madoc.
  K.O. Morgan, 617(TLS):7Mar80-251
Williams, G.S. The Vision of Death.
  G. Kaiser, 406:Summer79-193
Williams, H. Love-Life.
  D. Davis, 362:31Jan80-157
  V. Feaver, 617(TLS):1Feb80-112
  H. Lomas, 364:Mar80-78
Williams, I. The Idea of the Novel in Europe, 1600-1800.
  J. Frank, 31(ASch):Autumn80-529
Williams, J. The Changeling.*
  639(VQR):Autumn78-134
Williams, J. Early Spanish Manuscript Illumination.
  J. Beckwith, 39:Apr79-328
Williams, J. Portrait Photographs.*
  A. Ross, 364:Oct79-5
  468:Winter79-584
Williams, L.E. Southeast Asia.
  D.K. Wyatt, 318(JAOS):Jul-Sep78-305
Williams, L.F.R., ed. Sufi Studies: East and West.
  B.M. Dervish, 273(IC):Jan77-71
Williams, L.H., Jr. The Allende Years.
  H. Dietz, 263(RIB):Vol29No1-75
Williams, M. Groundless Belief.*
  H.M. Robinson, 393(Mind):Apr79-314
  F.L. Will, 482(PhR):Jul79-483
Williams, M. A Preface to Hardy.*
  S. Hunter, 402(MLR):Jan79-178
Williams, M.E. The Venerable English College Rome.
  F. Edwards, 617(TLS):22Aug80-940
Williams, N. Jack be Nimble.
  P. Kemp, 362:13Mar80-350
  A.N. Wilson, 617(TLS):14Mar80-296
Williams, P. A New History of the Organ from the Greeks to the Present Day.
  E. Higginbottom, 617(TLS):21Mar80-338
Williams, P. The Tudor Regime.
  G.R. Elton, 617(TLS):15Feb80-183
Williams, R. The Country and the City.
  W.A. McClung, 576:Oct79-61
Williams, R. Innovationen. (H.G. Klaus, ed and trans)
  H. Pietsch, 654(WB):8/1978-176
Williams, R. Marxism and Literature.*
  C. Cook, 447(N&Q):Aug78-362
  D.H., 355(LSoc):Aug78-291
  C.L. and J.B. Holm, 128(CE):Dec78-450
  639(VQR):Spring78-53
Williams, R. Politics and Letters.
  D.I. Davies, 99:Aug80-30
Williams, R. The Wound of Knowledge.
  P. Hebblethwaite, 617(TLS):25Apr80-458

Williams, R.C. Artists in Revolution.*
J.E. Bowlt, 550(RusR):Apr79-259
M. Chamot, 39:Dec79-535
Williams, R.C. Russian Art and American
Money.
J.R. Mellow, 441:9Mar80-6
N. Stone, 617(TLS):28Mar80-348
Williams, R.G. - see Vida, M.G.
Williams, T. Where I Live.*
42(AR):Summer79-379
Williams, T.A. Éliphas Lévi.
F.P. Bowman, 208(FS):Vol33Pt2-823
Williams, W. and J. The Turanga Journals,
1840-1950. (F. Porter, ed)
R. Grover, 368:Sep75-247
Williams, W.A. Americans in a Changing
World.
639(VQR):Winter79-12
Williams, W.C. A Recognizable Image.* (B.
Dijkstra, ed)
W. Marling, 219(GaR):Fall79-733
W. Marling, 584(SWR):Spring79-205
S. Paul, 301(JEGP):Oct79-576
Williamsen, V.G. and A.F.M. Atlee, eds.
Studies in Honor of Ruth Lee Kennedy.*
J.M. Polo de Bernabé, 238:Mar79-180
Williamson, A. Artists and Writers in
Revolt.*
F.S. Boos, 637(VS):Summer78-509
Williamson, C., ed. The Old English Rid-
dles of the Exeter Book.
J.J. Campbell, 405(MP):Feb80-315
A.N. Doane, 529(QQ):Summer79-302
M. Nelson, 589:Jan79-199
Williamson, D. Don's Party.
W. Dean, 368:Jun76-162
Williamson, E. When We Went First Class.
639(VQR):Spring78-48
Williamson, T. The Sansom Strike.
M. Laski, 362:10Jan80-62
Willis, J. Latin Textual Criticism.
J.M. Hunt, 122:Oct79-340
Willis, J. Screen World. (Vol 29)
D. Bodeen, 200:Mar79-178
Willis, P. Charles Bridgeman and the
English Landscape Garden.*
M.R. Brownell, 173(ECS):Summer79-538
G. Jellicoe, 46:Jun79-361
A.A. Tait, 90:Jun79-385
J.J. Yoch, 219(GaR):Fall79-717
Willis, T. The Lions of Judah.
N. Callendar, 441:17Aug80-19
Willk-Brocard, N. François-Guillaume
Ménageot, 1744-1816.
P. Conisbee, 90:Oct79-657
Wills, G. At Buttons.*
639(VQR):Summer79-100
Wills, G. Inventing America.*
G. Anastaplo, 396(ModA):Summer79-314
J.M. Cox, 569(SR):Summer79-475
R. Ginsberg, 173(ECS):Summer79-562
J. Howe, 656(WMQ):Jul79-462
A. Kantrow, 165(EAL):Winter79/80-350
P. Merkley, 529(QQ):Autumn79-535
A.J.R., 543:Mar79-573

Wills, L.M. Le Regard contemplatif chez
Valéry et Mallarmé.
D.J. Mossop, 208(FS):Vol33Pt2-865
Wills, R. and A. Tate. The Golden Mean
and Other Poems.
R. Buffington, 569(SR):Spring79-xxx
Wilmerding, J., ed. American Light.
J. Russell, 453(NYRB):29May80-22
Wilmet, M. Études de morpho-syntaxe
verbale.*
J. Pesot, 207(FR):Feb79-505
G. Price, 208(FS):Vol33Pt2-1055
Wilmeth, D.B. The American Stage to World
War I.
P. Davison, 354:Jun79-192
Wilmut, R. From Fringe to Flying Circus.
D. Thomas, 362:18and25Dec80-863
Wilner, E. maya.
V. Trueblood, 29:Nov/Dec80-9
Wilson, A. Setting the World on Fire.
B. Bergonzi, 617(TLS):11Jul80-773
A. Broyard, 441:18Oct80-16
D. Donoghue, 453(NYRB):20Nov80-20
M. Drabble, 362:10Jul80-51
R. Kiely, 441:16Nov80-1
61:Oct80-99
Wilson, A. The Strange Ride of Rudyard
Kipling.*
S. Pickering, 569(SR):Winter79-165
295(JML):Vol7#4-755
Wilson, A. Traditional Romance and Tale.*
D. Mehl, 447(N&Q):Jun78-250
Wilson, A., with J.L. Wilson. The Making
of the Nuremberg Chronicle.*
R. Myers, 354:Mar79-86
J.E. Walsh, 517(PBSA):Jan-Mar78-147
Wilson, A.N. The Healing Art.
W. Boyd, 617(TLS):6Jun80-636
J. Naughton, 362:29May80-697
Wilson, A.N. The Laird of Abbotsford.
H. Corke, 362:24Jul80-120
Wilson, C. and G. Parker, eds. An Intro-
duction to the Sources of European
Economic History: 1500-1800.
639(VQR):Summer78-88
Wilson, D. The Colder the Better.
R.A. Sokolov, 441:23Mar80-16
Wilson, D., ed. Mao Tse-Tung in the
Scales of History.*
639(VQR):Summer78-90
Wilson, D. The People's Emperor.
S. Karnow, 441:25May80-6
Wilson, D. Presuppositions and Non-Truth-
Conditional Semantics.*
G. Kalinowski, 192(EP):Oct-Dec79-499
C. Murphy, 63:Jun79-183
Wilson, D. Tito's Yugoslavia.
S. Clissold, 617(TLS):11Jan80-31
Wilson, D.M., ed. The Northern World.
G. Jones, 617(TLS):8Feb80-135
Wilson, D.M. The Vikings and their
Origins.
G. Jones, 617(TLS):8Feb80-135
Wilson, D.S. In the Presence of Nature.*
G.F. Frick, 656(WMQ):Jul79-490
R.P. Hay, 432(NEQ):Jun79-286

Wilson, E. The Gawain-Poet.*
  F-W. Neumann, 38:Band96Heft3/4-510
Wilson, E. Letters on Literature and
  Politics 1912-1972.* (E. Wilson, ed)
  S. Donaldson, 569(SR):Summer79-460
  K. McSweeney, 148:Autumn79-63
  K. Versluys, 179(ES):Dec79-814
Wilson, E. Memoirs of Hecate County.
  M. Cowley, 441:8Jun80-11
Wilson, E. The Thirties. (L. Edel, ed)
  H. Brogan, 362:6Nov80-620
  M. Dickstein, 441:31Aug80-1
  J. Leonard, 441:18Aug80-C15
  J. Updike, 442(NY):15Dec80-162
  G. Vidal, 453(NYRB):25Sep80-4
Wilson, E.G. John Clarkson and the
  African Adventure.
  C. Fyfe, 617(TLS):25Jul80-852
Wilson, E.M. Decision on Palestine.
  R. Wistrich, 617(TLS):23May80-591
Wilson, E.O. On Human Nature.
  G. Dworkin, 482(PhR):Oct79-660
  J. Howell, 42(AR):Spring79-250
  639(VQR):Summer79-109
Wilson, H. Final Term.*
  J. Morgan, 617(TLS):18Jan80-67
Wilson, H. A Prime Minister on Prime
  Ministers.*
  639(VQR):Autumn78-140
Wilson, H.H. - see Moorcroft, W. and G.
  Trebeck
Wilson, H.S. The Imperial Experience in
  Sub-Saharan Africa Since 1870.
  639(VQR):Winter78-8
Wilson, J. Preface to the Philosophy of
  Education.
  D.W. Hamlyn, 617(TLS):4Jan80-19
Wilson, J., ed. Texas and Germany: Cross-
  currents.
  S.M. Benjamin, 406:Winter79-482
Wilson, J. and A. Leaman. The Complete
  Food Catalog.
  W. and C. Cowen, 639(VQR):Spring78-76
Wilson, J.D. and W.F. Ricketson. Thomas
  Paine.
  H.S. Stout, 165(EAL):Winter79/80-345
Wilson, J.H. Court Satires of the Restora-
  tion.*
  I. Simon, 402(MLR):Jan79-165
Wilson, K. While Dancing Feet Shatter the
  Earth.*
  A. Steinberg, 649(WAL):Spring79-76
Wilson, K. and J.B. Wyndels. The Belgians
  in Manitoba.
  R.D., 179(ES):Feb79-94
Wilson, M. Tirso de Molina.*
  R. ter Horst, 400(MLN):Mar79-428
  M. McKendrick, 86(BHS):Jan79-65
Wilson, M. and K. Bowden - see Longhurst,
  H.
Wilson, M.D. Descartes.
  D.W. Hamlyn, 617(TLS):4Jan80-19
  A. O'Hear, 479(PhQ):Jul79-263
  W.S., 543:Jun79-779
  P.A. Schouls, 518:May79-61
Wilson, P.J. Man, The Promising Primate.
  P-L. Adams, 61:Dec80-98

Wilson, P.R. The Beautiful Old Houses of
  Quebec.
  F. Toker, 576:Mar78-64
Wilson, R.A. Modern Book Collecting.
  D. Grumbach, 441:27Apr80-16
  C. Lehmann-Haupt, 441:5May80-C16
Wilson, R.A. and B. Hosokawa. East to
  America.
  N. Glazer, 441:17Aug80-8
Wilson, S. Dealer's War.
  T.J. Binyon, 617(TLS):19Sep80-1012
Wilson, W. Papers of Woodrow Wilson.
  (Vol 29) (A. Link, ed)
  E. Wright, 617(TLS):25Jan80-91
Wilton, A. British Watercolours, 1750 to
  1850.*
  F.W. Hawcroft, 90:Jul79-445
Wilton, A. The Life and Work of J.M.W.
  Turner. Constable's English Landscape
  Scenery.
  D. Piper, 617(TLS):1Feb80-119
Wilton-Ely, J. The Mind and Art of Gio-
  vanni Battista Piranesi.*
  P. Conisbee, 90:Sep79-589
Wilton-Ely, J. Giovanni Battista
  Piranesi.*
  B. Reudenbach, 471:Jul/Aug/Sep79-288
Wiltshire, D. The Social and Political
  Thought of Herbert Spencer.
  R.L. Schoenwald, 637(VS):Winter79-225
Wimmel, W. Tibull und Delia. (Pt 1)
  R.J. Ball, 121(CJ):Dec79/Jan80-183
Wimmer, R. Deutsch und Latein im Oster-
  spiel.*
  V. Mertens, 684(ZDA):Band107Heft1-24
Wimsatt, W.K., Jr. Day of the Leopards.*
  C. Cook, 447(N&Q):Aug78-362
Winch, D. Adam Smith's Politics.
  R. Teichgraeber 3d, 173(ECS):Summer79-
  566
Winchester, J. The Solitary Man.
  T.J. Binyon, 617(TLS):18Apr80-450
  M. Laski, 362:17Apr80-514
Lord Windlesham. Broadcasting in a Free
  Society.
  J. Isaacs, 362:7Aug80-181
Wingård, K. Les problèmes des couples
  mariés dans la Comédie humaine d'Honoré
  de Balzac.
  W. Hirdt, 72:Band216Heft1-220
  S. Jüttner, 547(RF):Band91Heft1/2-208
Wingate, W. Bloodbath.
  N. Callendar, 441:18May80-16
Wingate, W. Shotgun.
  N. Callendar, 441:23Nov80-37
Wingfield, S. Admissions.*
  F. Kiley, 174(Éire):Summer79-145
Winkelman, J.H. Die Brückenpächter- und
  die Turmwächterepisode im "Trierer
  Floyris" und in der "Version Aristo-
  cratique" des altfranzösischen Floris-
  romans.*
  D. Evans, 447(N&Q):Apr78-186
Winkelmann, F. and others. Byzanz im 7.
  Jahrhundert.
  W.E. Kaegi, Jr., 182:Vol31#14-499

Winkler, A.M. The Politics of Propaganda.
639(VQR):Autumn78-146

Winkler, E.H. The Clown in Modern Anglo-
Irish Drama.
S. Sweeney, 305(JIL):Sep78-173

Winkler, H.A. Revolution, Staat.
D. Barnouw, 221(GQ):Nov79-573

Winks, R.W., ed. Other Voices, Other
Views.
J.S. Martin, 106:Spring79-103

Winn, D. Murderess Ink.
N. Callendar, 441:27Apr80-20

Winn, M. The Plug-In Drug.
H.J. Boyle, 529(QQ):Winter79/80-681

Winner, L. Autonomous Technology.
R. Brungs, 613:Dec79-443

Winnifrith, T. The Brontës.*
W.A. Craik, 447(N&Q):Jun78-261

Winnington-Ingram, R.P. Sophocles.
O. Taplin, 617(TLS):20Jun80-712

Winslow, P.G. The Counsellor Heart.
M. Laski, 362:14Aug80-216

Winsor, M.P. Starfish, Jellyfish, and the
Order of Life.
R.W. Burkhardt, Jr., 637(VS):Spring78-
406

Winston, R. and C. - see Mann, T.

Winter, E. Die Sozial- und Ethnoethik
Bernard Bolzanos.
S. Decloux, 182:Vol31#7/8-200

Winter, H. Zur Indien-Rezeption bei E.M.
Forster und Hermann Hesse.
M. Thiel-Horstmann, 52:Band13Heft2-215

Winter, I. Untersuchungen zum serapion-
tischen Prinzip E.T.A. Hoffmanns.*
E.F. Hoffmann, 406:Spring79-68

Winter, I.J. Montaigne's Self-Portrait
and Its Influence in France, 1580-1630.*
C. Clark, 208(FS):Vol33Pt2-639
M.B. McKinley, 400(MLN):May79-891
G. Nakam, 535(RHL):Jul-Aug79-644
205(FMLS):Jan78-95

Winters, S. Shelley.
J. Lahr, 441:8Jun80-12

Winther, A. Cosimo Fanzago und die
neapler Ornamentik des 17. und 18.
Jahrhunderts.
F. Brauen, 576:Mar78-59

Winton, A. Proust's Additions.
J.M. Cocking, 208(FS):Jan79-100
D.E. Kinney, 207(FR):Apr79-776
E. Zants, 395(MFS):Winter78/79-625

Wiplinger, F. Metaphysik.* (P. Kampits,
ed)
T.J.S., 543:Sep78-162

Wiplinger, F. Physis und Logos.
L. Routila, 52(AGP):Band60Heft1-59

Wiredu, K. Philosophy and an African
Culture.
A. Appiah, 617(TLS):20Jun80-697

Wirnt von Grafenberg. Wigalois.* (J.W.
Thomas, ed and trans)
D. Blamires, 382(MAE):1979/1-127
C. Love, 400(MLN):Apr79-629

Wisbey, R.A., ed. The Computer in Literary and Linguistic Research.
G.F. Meier, 682(ZPSK):Band31Heft6-650

Wise, K., ed. Lotte Jacobi.
C. James, 453(NYRB):18Dec80-22

Wiseman, T.P. Clio's Cosmetics.
C. McLeod, 617(TLS):8Feb80-152

Wisenthal, J.L. Shaw and Ibsen.
M. Holroyd, 617(TLS):1Feb80-110

Wiser, W. Disappearances.
R.P. Brickner, 441:10Aug80-14
A. Broyard, 441:23Aug80-16

Wisser, W., ed. Wat Grootmoder vertellt.
G. Petschel, 196:Band19Heft1/2-173

Wistrand, E. Miscellanea Propertiana.*
C.W. MacLeod, 123:Vol129Nol-150

Wistrand, E. The So-Called Laudatio
Turiae.*
J. André, 555:Vol52fasc2-391

Wistrich, R. Trotsky.*
L. Schapiro, 453(NYRB):17Apr80-15

Wistrich, R.S. Revolutionary Jews from
Marx to Trotsky.
H. Roskolenko, 390:Jun/Jul79-91

Witemeyer, H. George Eliot and the Visual
Arts.*
A.J.S., 148:Winter79-90

Witney, K.P. The Jutish Forest.
E. Searle, 589:Apr79-440
W. Urry, 325:Apr79-159

Witsch, J.C. Briefe 1948-1967. (K.
Witsch, ed)
F. Voit, 406:Winter79-476

Witschel, G. Antagonismen in der DDR-
Literatur.
R.C. Reimer, 406:Spring79-80

Witt, R.G. Coluccio Salutati and His
Public Letters.*
N. Rubinstein, 589:Oct79-875

Witte, B. Walter Benjamin — Der Intellek-
tuelle als Kritiker.*
G. Hemmerich, 489(PJGG):Band86Heft1-
196

Witte, J. Loving the Days.*
R. Lattimore, 249(HudR):Autumn79-447
639(VQR):Spring79-66

Wittgenstein, L. Remarks on Colour.*
(G.E.M. Anscombe, ed)
S. Candlish, 63:Jun79-198

Wittgenstein, L. Vermischte Bemerkungen.*
(G.H. von Wright, with H. Nyman, eds)
P. Long, 479(PhQ):Jan79-81

Wittgenstein, L. Wittgenstein's Lectures:
Cambridge 1930-1932. (D. Lee, ed)
P.M.S. Hacker, 617(TLS):20Jun80-714

Wittgenstein, L. Wittgenstein's Lectures
on the Foundations of Mathematics.* (C.
Diamond, ed)
C. Coope, 518:Jan79-1

Wittig, S. Stylistic and Narrative Struc-
tures in the Middle English Romances.*
P. Gradon, 541(RES):May79-203
M. Robertson, 382(MAE):1979/2-310
M. Schlauch, 599:Spring79-228

Witting, C. Studies in Swedish Generative
Phonology.
E.A. Strodach, 350:Mar79-254
E.A. Strodach, 563(SS):Winter79-55

Wittkower, R. Idea and Image. (M. Witt-
kower, ed)
  C.E. Gilbert, 55:Nov79-27
  E.H. Ramsden, 39:Jul79-79
  R.E.E. Read, 97(CQ):Vol8#3-250
Wittkower, R. Sculpture.*
  J.M. Hunisak, 56:Winter79-122
  J. Montagu, 90:Mar79-182
  A.M. Schulz, 54:Jun78-359
Wittreich, J.A., Jr. Angel of Apocalypse.*
  H.B. de Groot, 179(ES):Oct79-670
  F. Sandler, 405(MP):Nov79-228
Wittreich, J.A., Jr., ed. Milton and the
Line of Vision.*
  A.H. Elliott, 447(N&Q):Feb78-77
Wittreich, J.A., Jr. Visionary Poetics.*
  W.E. Cain, 141:Fall79-366
  D. Norford, 401(MLQ):Sep79-292
Witty, H. and E.S. Colchie. Better Than
Store Bought.*
  W. and C. Cowen, 639(VQR):Autumn79-154
Wobst, S. Russian Readings and Grammat-
ical Terminology.
  G.L. Ervin, 574(SEEJ):Summer79-305
  O. Frink, 399(MLJ):Sep-Oct79-318
Wodehouse, L. British Architects 1840-
1976.
  P. Dickens, 89(BJA):Summer79-277
Wodehouse, P.G. Sunset at Blandings. (R.
Usborne, ed)
  P-G. Boucé, 189(EA):Jul-Dec78-409
Wodehouse, P.G. The Swoop! and Other
Stories.* (D.A. Jasen, ed)
  T.C. Holyoke, 42(AR):Fall79-503
Woeckel, G.P. Ignaz Günther.
  P. Volk, 471:Jan/Feb/Mar79-81
Wofford, H. Of Kennedys and Kings.
  R. Sherrill, 441:27Jul80-11
Wohl, A.S., ed. The Victorian Family.
  P. Branca, 637(VS):Summer79-474
Wohl, R. The Generation of 1914.*
  N. Annan, 453(NYRB):3Apr80-11
  R. Blythe, 362:20Mar80-377
  S. Schama, 617(TLS):16May80-559
Wohlgelernter, M. Frank O'Connor.*
  A.T. McCrann, 295(JML):Vol7#4-786
  M. Timko, 191(ELN):Sep78-69
  J.W. Weaver, 305(JIL):May78-182
Wohlgenannt, R. Der Philosophiebegriff.
  S. Decloux, 182:Vol31#1/2-12
Woiwode, L. Even Tide.*
  J. Fuller, 617(TLS):18Jan80-65
  639(VQR):Summer78-102
Wojciechowski, J.A., ed. Conceptual Basis
of the Classification of Knowledge/Les
fondements de la classification des
savoirs.
  N. Lacharité, 154:Sep78-499
Wojtyla, K. [Pope John Paul II] The Act-
ing Person.
  C. Hartshorne, 484(PPR):Mar80-443
  A. Poltawski, 617(TLS):4Apr80-397
Wojtyla, K. [Pope John Paul II] Easter
Vigil and Other Poems.
  L. Sail, 493:Mar80-71
  J. Simon, 491:Apr80-40

Woledge, B. Bibliographie des romans et
nouvelles en prose française antérieurs
à 1500. (Supp, 1954-73)
  E.T. Dubois, 182:Vol31#5/6-156
  W. Rothwell, 208(FS):Vol33Pt2-588
Woledge, B. La syntaxe des substantifs
chez Chrétien de Troyes.
  M. Offord, 208(FS):Oct79-434
Wolf, A.P., ed. Religion and Ritual in
Chinese Society.*
  A.P. Cohen, 318(JAOS):Oct-Dec78-524
Wolf, B.H. - see under Hungry Wolf, B.
Wolf, C. A Model Childhood.
  P-L. Adams, 61:Sep80-108
  J. Leonard, 441:29Jul80-C9
  S. Spender, 441:12Oct80-11
Wolf, E., comp. The Library of James
Logan of Philadelphia, 1674-1791.
  N. Barker, 78(BC):Summer79-285
Wolf, K.L. and others - see von Goethe,
J.W.
Wolf, L. Aspekte der Dialektologie.
  K.E.M. George, 208(FS):Vol33Pt2-1022
  D. Wolff, 430(NS):Jul78-391
Wolf, L. Bluebeard.
  P-L. Adams, 61:Jul80-87
  D. Grumbach, 441:24Aug80-15
Wolf, N.R. Regionale und überregionale
Norm im späten Mittelater.
  E. Skála, 684(ZDA):Band107Heft4-155
Wolf, R. Heinrich Heine.
  J.L.S., 191(ELN):Sep78(supp)-164
Wolfart, H.C. and J.F. Carroll. Meet Cree.
  C.D. Ellis, 320(CJL):Spring-Fall78-194
Wolfarth, W. Ascripticii w Polsce.
  A. Uschakow, 182:Vol31#13-445
Wolfe, C.K. - see Delmore, A.
Wolfe, G.H., ed. Faulkner.*
  S.M. Ross, 395(MFS):Summer78-275
Wolfe, G.K. The Known and the Unknown.
  T. Shippey, 617(TLS):9May80-519
Wolfe, L. Private Practices.
  J. Leonard, 441:3Mar80-C17
  M. Malone, 441:9Mar80-11
Wolfe, M., ed. Aurora: New Canadian Writ-
ing 1978.*
  R.E. Jones, 628(UWR):Spring-Summer79-
  93
Wolfe, M. and D. Daymond, eds. Toronto
Short Stories.*
  G.T. Davenport, 569(SR):Winter79-xix
Wolfe, P. Dreamers Who Live Their Dreams.
  J.Z.G., 395(MFS):Winter78/79-648
Wolfe, P.J. - see de Scudéry, M.
Wolfensperger, P. Edward Bond.
  T. Elsasser, 677(YES):Vol9-348
  K. Versluys, 179(ES):Aug79-516
Wolff, C. Gesammelte Werke. (Pt 1)
  J. Ecole, 192(EP):Oct-Dec79-492
Wolff, C. Logica Tedesca. (R. Ciafardone,
ed)
  J. Ecole, 192(EP):Oct-Dec79-493
  K. Oedingen, 342:Band69Heft4-471
Wolff, C. Theologiae Naturalis. (Pt 1)
(J. Ecole, ed)
  A. Jagu, 192(EP):Oct-Dec79-494

Woodforde, J. Georgian Houses for All.*
   J. Archer, 576:Dec78-308
   566:Autumn78-48
Woodhouse, B. Talking to Animals.
   R. Fuller, 362:25Sep80-405
Woodhouse, C.P. Ivories.
   B.D.H. Miller, 463:Summer79-253
Woodhouse, J.R. - see d'Annunzio, G.
Woodman, A.J. - see Velleius Paterculus, M.
Woodruff, W. Vessel of Sadness.
   639(VQR):Winter79-16
Woods, D. Asking For Trouble.
   S. Jacobson, 362:25Sep80-404
Woods, G. A Gift to Last.
   J. Noonan, 296(JCF):28/29-213
Woods, J. The Logic of Fiction.*
   T.G. Pavel, 567:Vol125#3/4-335
Woods, M.J. The Poet and the Natural
  World in the Age of Góngora.
   T.R.H., 131(CL):Fall79-415
   E.L. Rivers, 400(MLN):Mar79-431
Woods, S. They Stay for Death.
   T.J. Binyon, 617(TLS):30May80-606
   N. Callendar, 441:7Dec80-44
Woodward, A. Ezra Pound and "The Pisan
  Cantos."
   A.D. Moody, 617(TLS):15Aug80-917
Woodward, B. and S. Armstrong. The
  Brethren.*
   G.V. Higgins, 231:Apr80-96
   A. Lewis, 453(NYRB):7Feb80-3
   J. Morgan, 617(TLS):11Apr80-404
Woodward, G.E. and E.G. Thompson. Wood-
  ward's National Architect.
   M. McCordie, 576:Mar78-54
Woodward, J. and D. Richards, eds. Health
  Care and Popular Medicine in Nineteenth
  Century England.
   F.B. Smith, 637(VS):Winter79-222
Woodward, J.B. Gogol's "Dead Souls."
   G. Cox, 550(RusR):Jan79-124
   N.M. Lary, 529(QQ):Autumn79-542
   T.E. Little, 402(MLR):Jul79-764
   J.M. Mills, 574(SEEJ):Fall79-399
   G. Woodcock, 569(SR):Summer79-480
   A.C. Wright, 255(HAB):Fall79-322
Wooldridge, D. Charles Ives.
   412:Aug-Nov78-286
Wooldridge, J.B. - see de Vega Carpio, L.
Wooldridge, T.R. Les Débuts de la lexico-
  graphie française.*
   H. Nais, 209(FM):Jul78-264
   P. Rickard, 208(FS):Vol33Pt2-1060
Woolf, L. The Wise Virgins.*
   P. Grosskurth, 453(NYRB):24Jan80-41
   442(NY):14Jan80-102
Woolf, S. A History of Italy 1700-1860.
   J.A. Davis, 617(TLS):22Feb80-217
Woolf, V. The Diary of Virginia Woolf.*
  (Vol 1) (A.O. Bell, ed)
   A. Bell, 569(SR):Spring79-325
   J. Gindin, 594:Spring79-82
Woolf, V. The Diary of Virginia Woolf.*
  (Vol 2) (A.O. Bell, with A. McNeillie,
  eds)
   P-L. Adams, 61:Jun80-94
            [continued]

[continuing]
   A. Bell, 569(SR):Spring79-325
   S. Rudikoff, 249(HudR):Winter79/80-540
Woolf, V. The Diary of Virginia Woolf.
  (Vol 3) (A.O. Bell, with A. McNeillie,
  eds)
   G. Annan, 362:3Apr80-447
   R. Dinnage, 617(TLS):18Apr80-435
   M. Panter-Downes, 442(NY):27Oct80-192
   V.S. Pritchett, 453(NYRB):20Nov80-3
Woolf, V. Instants de vie.
   P. Mauries, 98:Oct78-940
   P. Pachet, 450(NRF):Apr79-143
Woolf, V. The Letters of Virginia Woolf.*
  (Vol 2) (British title: The Question of
  Things Happening.) (N. Nicholson and
  J. Trautmann, eds)
   A. Bell, 569(SR):Spring79-325
Woolf, V. The Letters of Virginia Woolf.
  (Vol 3) (British title: A Change of Per-
  spective.) (N. Nicolson and J. Traut-
  mann, eds)
   A. Bell, 569(SR):Spring79-325
   J. Giltrow, 648(WCR):Oct78-59
   J. Gindin, 594:Spring79-82
   S. Rudikoff, 249(HudR):Winter79/80-540
   639(VQR):Autumn78-142
Woolf, V. The Letters of Virginia Woolf.*
  (Vol 4) (N. Nicolson and J. Trautmann,
  eds)
   A. Bell, 569(SR):Spring79-325
   G.S. Haight, 676(YR):Autumn79-112
   S. Rudikoff, 249(HudR):Winter79/80-540
Woolf, V. The Letters of Virginia Woolf.*
  (Vol 5) (British title: The Sickle Side
  of the Moon.) (N. Nicolson and J. Traut-
  mann, eds)
   A. Bell, 617(TLS):7Mar80-274
   P. Grosskurth, 453(NYRB):24Jan80-41
   S. Rudikoff, 249(HudR):Winter79/80-540
Woolf, V. The Letters of Virginia Woolf.
  (Vol 6) (British title: Leave the Let-
  ters Till We're Dead.) (N. Nicolson
  and J. Trautmann, eds)
   P-L. Adams, 61:Dec80-98
   J. Atlas, 441:5Oct80-1
   R. Blythe, 362:2Oct80-440
   V.S. Pritchett, 453(NYRB):20Nov80-3
Woolf, V. Moments of Being.* (J. Schul-
  kind, ed)
   S. Rudikoff, 249(HudR):Winter79/80-540
Woolf, V. The Pargiters. (M.A. Leaska,
  ed)
   D. Doner, 395(MFS):Winter78/79-575
   M. Spilka, 454:Winter79-178
Woolson, C.F. Anne.
   N. Auerbach, 445(NCF):Mar79-475
Wooten, J. Dasher.
   J.M. Porten, 529(QQ):Summer79-322
Wootton, A. Dilemmas of Discourse.
   J. Cook-Gumperz, 355(LSoc):Aug78-239
Wordsworth, W. Home at Grasmere.* (B.
  Darlington, ed)
   B.C.H., 191(ELN):Sep78(supp)-75
   H. Lindenberger, 591(SIR):Summer79-303
   W.J.B. Owen, 541(RES):Feb79-96
   639(VQR):Autumn79-149

Wuchterl, K. Methoden der Gegenwarts-
philosophie.
W. Piel, 489(PJGG):Band86Heft1-214
"Wulfstan's Canons of Edgar." (R. Fowler,
ed)
M. Korhammer, 38:Band96Heft3/4-503
Wunberg, G., ed. Das Junge Wien.*
E.W. Breckner, 406:Spring79-90
Wunderli, P. Ferdinand de Saussure und
die Anagramme.
H-D. Kreuder, 685(ZDL):3/1979-362
Wunenburger, J-J. La fête, le jeu et le
sacré.
M. Adam, 542:Apr-Jun78-214
J. Brun, 192(EP):Jul-Sep79-356
Wunenburger, J-J. L'utopie ou la crise de
l'imaginaire.
E. Namer, 542:Oct-Dec79-469
Wurm, S.A., ed. New Guinea Area Languages
and Language Study. (Vol 1)
J. Haiman, 350:Dec79-894
Würzner, H., ed. Zur deutschen Exillitera-
tur in den Niederlanden 1933-1940.*
S. Mews, 221(GQ):Nov79-560
Wüthrich, H.U. Das Konsonantensystem der
deutschen Hochsprache.*
D. Karch, 685(ZDL):1/1979-87
Wuttke, D., ed. Aby M. Warburg.
M. Podro, 617(TLS):21Mar80-334
Wyatt, J. Reflections on the Lakes.
J. Mapplebeck, 362:3Apr80-448
N. Nicholson, 617(TLS):18Apr80-436
Wyatt, R. The Rosedale Hoax.*
D. Evans, 102(CanL):Spring79-85
Wyatt, T. The Complete Poems. (R.A.
Rebholz, ed)
M. Dodsworth, 175:Spring79-101
Wyatt, T. Sir Thomas Wyatt: Collected
Poems.* (J. Daalder, ed)
W.H. Siek, 405(MP):Aug79-75
Wyatt, W. The Man Who Was B. Traven.
R. Boston, 362:19Jun80-800
Wycherley, R.E. The Stones of Athens.*
O.T.P.K. Dickinson, 161(DUJ):Dec78-92
Wyers, F. Miguel de Unamuno.*
M. Nozick, 240(HR):Winter78-102
R. Wright, 86(BHS):Jan79-74
205(FMLS):Jan78-95
Wyllie, J. Death is a Drum ... Beating
Forever.
G. Noonan, 296(JCF):28/29-221
Wyman, W.D. Witching for Water, Oil,
Pipes, and Precious Minerals.
H.E. Webb, 292(JAF):Oct-Dec79-505
Wynar, L.R. and L. Buttlar. Guide to
Ethnic Museums, Libraries, and Archives
in the United States.
N. Sahli, 14:Jul79-361
Wyrwa, T. La pensée politique polonaise à
l'époque de l'humanisme et de la Renais-
sance.
A. Reix, 542:Apr-Jun79-213
Wysling, H. Thomas Mann heute.*
K. Schröter, 406:Spring79-83
Wysocki, S. Wilhelm Tkaczyk.
G. Szarszewska-Kühl, 654(WB):11/1978-
186

Wyss, D. Mitteilung und Antwort.
G. Brand, 687:Jan-Mar79-149
Wyss, M. Brecht in der Kritik.
S. Mews, 221(GQ):Mar79-288
Wyss, R. Das jungsteinzeitliche Jäger-
Bauerndorf von Egolzwil 5 im Wauwiler-
moos.
R. Pittioni, 182:Vol131#13-439
Wyssenherre, M. Eyn buoch von dem edeln
hern von Bruneczwigk als er uber mer
fuore. (I. Dinkelacker and W. Häring,
eds)
B. Koelliker, 133:Band12Heft1/2-145

Xueqin, C. - see under Cao Xueqin

Yacowar, M. Loser Take All.
R. MacMillan, 99:Dec80/Jan81-36
Yahni, R. Antología de la literatura his-
panoamericana.
R. Adorno, 238:May-Sep79-408
Ya'lā, al-Qāḍī Abu. Kitāb al-mu'tamad fī
uṣūl al-dīn. (W.Z. Haddad, ed)
J.A. Bellamy, 318(JAOS):Oct-Dec78-484
Yallop, C. Alyawarra.
R.M.W. Dixon, 350:Mar79-259
Yamamoto, T. Hagakure.*
42(AR):Fal179-506
Yamanashi, M. Generative Semantic Studies
of the Conceptual Nature of Predicates
in English.
G.M. Green, 350:Sep79-741
Yamane Yukio. Zōtei Nihon genson Minjin
bunshū mokuroku.
T-L. Ma, 293(JASt):May79-553
Yamanouchi, H. The Search for Authentic-
ity in Modern Japanese Literature.*
K. Henshall, 67:Nov79-372
Yanarella, E.J. The Missile Defense Con-
troversy.
639(VQR):Autumn78-132
Yang, R.F.S., ed and trans. Four Plays of
the Yuan Drama.
S.H. West, 302:Vol16#1and2-103
Yankelevich, E. and A. Friendly, Jr. - see
Sakharov, A.D.
Yanow, L. and "my." Lazar.
D. Grumbach, 441:27Jul80-14
Yanowitch, M. Social and Economic Inequal-
ity in the Soviet Union.
M.P. Sacks, 550(RusR):Jul79-376
Yans-McLaughlin, V. Family and Community.
J. Potter, 617(TLS):25Jan80-93
Yap, E.P. and M.V. Bunye. Cebuano-Visayan
Dictionary.
G.F. Meier, 682(ZPSK):Band31Heft1-91
Yardley, H.O. The Education of a Poker
Player.
R.F. Brissenden, 364:Oct79-79
Yardley, J. Ring.*
R. Forrey, 395(MFS):Winter78/79-636
Yarrow, P.J. Racine.
H.T. Barnwell, 208(FS):Jan79-79
Yashpal. Amita.
D.G. Rubin, 318(JAOS):Jul-Sep78-334

Yastrebitskaya, A.L. Zapadnaya Evropa, XI-
XIII vekov.
   W.C. Jordan, 589:Oct79-877
Yates, F.A. Astraea.*
   T.C. Cave, 208(FS):Vol33Pt2-66?
Yates, F.A. The Occult Philosophy in the
Elizabethan Age.
   H. Trevor-Roper, 362:17Jan80-90
Yates, F.A. The Valois Tapestries. (2nd
ed)
   C. Eisler, 576:Dec78-319
Yates, J.M. Esox Nobilior.*
   G. Hamel, 198:Winter80-140
   R. Labrie, 102(CanL):Spring79-94
Yates, J.M. Fazes in Elsewhen.*
   G. Noonan, 628(UWR):Fall-Winter78-90
Yates, J.M. The Qualicum Physics. Breath
of the Snow Leopard.
   P. Stevens, 102(CanL):Winter78-94
Yates, R. A Good School.
   G. Davenport, 249(HudR):Spring79-147
   42(AR):Winter79-124
Yava, A. Big Falling Snow.
   J.R. Hepworth, 649(WAL):Summer79-181
Yeager, R.C. Seasons of Shame.
   A. Broyard, 441:29Feb80-C29
"The Yearbook of English Studies."*
   (Vol 8) (G.K. Hunter and C.J. Rawson,
   eds)
   J. Osborne, 402(MLR):Apr79-403
"Yearbook of the European Convention of
Human Rights." (Vols 16-18)
   W. Rüfner, 182:Vol131#17/18-596
"Yearbook on International Communist
Affairs, 1978." (R.F. Starr, ed)
   J.E. Thach, Jr., 550(RusR):Jan79-119
"The Year's Work in English Studies."
   (Vol 55) (J. Redmond and others, eds)
   R.T. Davies, 447(N&Q):Jun78-244
"The Year's Work in English Studies."
   (Vol 56)
   R.T. Davies, 447(N&Q):Dec78-542
"The Year's Work in Modern Language Stud-
ies." (Vol 38, 1976) (G. Price and D.A.
Wells, eds)
   A.H. Diverres, 208(FS):Jan79-113
"The Year's Work in Modern Language Stud-
ies." (Vol 39) (G. Price and D.A.
Wells, eds)
   A.H. Diverres, 208(FS):Jul79-367
Yeats, W.B. A Critical Edition of Yeats's
"A Vision" (1925). (G.M. Harper and
W.K. Hood, eds)
   M. Dodsworth, 175:Spring79-104
Yeats, W.B. The Speckled Bird. Literatim
Transcription of the Manuscripts of
William Butler Yeats's "The Speckled
Bird." The Speckled Bird; with Variant
Versions. (W.H. O'Donnell, ed of all)
   R.J. Finneran, 295(JML):Vol7#4-849
Yeats, W.B. The Writing of "The Player
Queen."* (C.B. Bradford, ed)
   R. Bonaccorso, 174(Éire):Fall79-157
   R.M. Kain, 305(JIL):May78-176
Yeazell, R.B. Language and Knowledge in
the Late Novels of Henry James.*
   A.W. Bellringer, 402(MLR):Jan79-181

Yeazell, R.B. - see James, A.
Yehoshua, A.B. Early in the Summer of
1970.*
   A. Duchêne, 617(TLS):8Feb80-132
   J. Mellors, 362:28Feb80-286
Yehoshua, A.B. The Lover.*
   W. Bargad, 390:Aug-Sep79-55
Yelling, J.A. Common Field and Enclosure
in England 1450-1850.
   D. Tweedle, 568(SCN):Spring-Summer79-
   27
Yeo, S. Religion and Voluntary Organisa-
tions in Crisis.
   H. McLeod, 637(VS):Winter78-245
Yeo, S.T. and J. Martin, comps. Chinese
Blue and White Ceramics.*
   B. Harrisson, 463:Autumn79-358
   R. Kilburn, 60:Jan-Feb79-127
Yergin, D. Shattered Peace.*
   N.A. Graebner, 639(VQR):Spring78-345
Yeschua, S. Valéry, le roman et l'oeuvre
à faire.
   R. Galand, 207(FR):Apr79-777
   P. Gifford, 402(MLR):Jul79-706
Yeston, M. The Stratification of Musical
Rhythm.*
   B. Northcott, 607:Dec77-41
Yevtushenko, Y. The Face Behind the Face.*
   R. Lattimore, 249(HudR):Autumn79-452
   J. Simon, 491:Apr80-40
Yevtushenko, Y. Ivan the Terrible and
Ivan the Fool.
   D.M. Thomas, 617(TLS):18Jan80-66
Yezierska, A. The Open Cage. (A.
Kessler-Harris, ed)
   J. Kaplan, 441:24Feb80-14
   R.F. Shepard, 441:21Feb80-C20
Yglesias, R. The Game Player.
   639(VQR):Summer78-94
Ying-shih, Y. - see under Yu Ying-shih
Yip, W-L., ed and trans. Chinese Poetry.*
   M.L. Wagner, 318(JAOS):Jul-Sep78-292
Ylärakkola, A. Edvard Gylling.
   A.F. Upton, 563(SS):Spring79-182
Yoder, D., ed. American Folklife.*
   C.G. Zug 3d, 582(SFQ):Vol141-300
Yoder, R.A. Emerson and the Orphic Poet
in America.
   P.F. Gura, 432(NEQ):Sep79-407
   D.H. Hirsch, 569(SR):Summer79-1x
   S. Paul, 141:Spring79-175
   H.H. Waggoner, 27(AL):Mar79-116
Yodfat, A. and M. Abir. In the Direction
of the Persian Gulf.
   M.I. Goldman, 550(RusR):Jan79-120
Yoken, M.B. Claude Tillier.
   H. Godin, 208(FS):Vol33Pt2-818
   J.S.P., 191(ELN):Sep78(supp)-129
Yokoi, Y., with D. Victoria. Zen Master
Dōgen.
   T. Cleary, 318(JAOS):Jul-Sep78-295
Yolton, J.W. - see Locke, J.
York, P. Style Wars.
   G. Annan, 362:13Nov80-662
York, T. The Musk Ox Passion.
   J. Kertzer, 198:Winter80-122

411

Zayed, G. - see Verlaine, P.
Zbavitel, D. Bengali Literature.*
  R.V. Baumer, 318(JAOS):Jul-Sep78-333
"Zborník filozofickej fakulty Univerzity
  Komenského."
  G.F. Meier, 682(ZPSK):Band31Heft2-214
van der Zee, H. and B. A Sweet and Alien
  Land.
  E. Wright, 617(TLS):25Jan80-91
Zegger, H.D. May Sinclair.*
  R. Jackson, 402(MLR):Jul79-681
Zehbe, J. - see Kant, I.
Zeitlin, S. Studies in the Early History
  of Judaism.
  M.N. Sarna, 318(JAOS):Jul-Sep78-315
Zelders, N.L. Die rechten Nebenflüsse des
  Rheins zwischen Lippe und Kromme Rijn.
  E. Neuss, 343:Band23-200
Zeldin, J. Nikolai Gogol's Quest for
  Beauty.
  J.M. Mills, 574(SEEJ):Fall79-399
  G. Woodcock, 569(SR):Summer79-480
Zeldin, T. France 1848-1945.* (Vol 2)
  F.W.J. Hemmings, 402(MLR):Jan79-215
  E. Rossmann, 207(FR):Oct78-192
  205(FMLS):Jan78-95
  639(VQR):Spring78-61
Zeldis, C. The Marriage Bed. The Brothel.
  S. Pinsker, 390:Nov79-70
Zelger, F. Stiftung Oskar Reinhart in
  Winterhur.
  F-G. Pariset, 182:Vol131#19-688
Zelinsky, B., ed. Der russische Roman.
  E. Freiberger-Sheikholeslami, 558(RLJ):
  Fall79-232
Zelinsky, H., ed. Richard Wagner.
  H. Reiss, 402(MLR):Oct79-994
Zelissen, P.G.J. Untersuchungen zu den
  Pronomina im Rheinisch-Maasländischen
  bis 1300.
  F. Simmler, 685(ZDL):3/1979-394
Zelizer, V. Morals and Markets.
  B.J. Bledstein, 385(MQR):Summer80-410
Zellmer, E. Die lateinischen Wörter auf
  "-ura."*
  J.N. Adams, 123:Vol129No1-172
  A.G. Ramat, 343:Band23-188
Zelm, K. Die Opern Reinhard Keisers.
  G.J. Buelow, 317:Summer79-349
Zeltner, H. Schelling-Forschung seit
  1954.*
  M.H., 191(ELN):Sep78(supp)-183
Zelver, P. A Man of Middle Age and
  Twelve Stories.
  A. Broyard, 441:23Jan80-C21
  I. Gold, 441:3Feb80-1
  J. Kavanagh, 617(TLS):19Sep80-1047
Zelzer, K., ed. Die alten lateinischen
  Thomasakten.
  H. Chadwick, 123:Vol129No1-156
  P. Courcelle, 555:Vol152fasc2-411
Zeman, A. Presumptuous Girls.
  C.S. Stern, 637(VS):Spring79-352
Zeman, H. - see Stieler, K.
de Zéndegui, G. Ámbito de Martí.
  A.R. Núñez, 37:Oct79-45

Zenke, J. Die deutsche Monologerzählung
  im 20. Jahrhundert.*
  J.M. Ellis, 301(JEGP):Jan79-99
  K. Müller-Salget, 52:Band13Heft3-330
  M. Swales, 402(MLR):Jan79-250
Zeppi, S. Studi su Machiavelli pensatore.
  E. Namer, 542:Apr-Jun79-215
Zeraffa, M. Fictions.
  M. Green, 161(DUJ):Dec78-147
Zerbe, J. and C. Connolly. Small Castles
  and Pavilions of Europe.
  B. Hannegan, 576:Dec78-321
Zeri, F. Italian Paintings in the Walters
  Art Gallery. (U.E. McCracken, ed)
  D.A. Brown, 54:Jun78-367
Zernov, N. and J. Pain - see Bulgakov, S.
von Zesen, P. Sämtliche Werke.* (Vols 5
  and 10) (F. van Ingen, with U. Maché and
  V. Meid, eds)
  P. Skrine, 402(MLR):Jan79-241
Zesmer, D.M. Guide to Shakespeare.*
  R.S. White, 161(DUJ):Dec78-129
Zettersten, A., ed. The English Text of
  the "Ancrene Riwle."
  J. Bazire, 677(YES):Vol9-363
  A.S.G. Edwards, 179(ES):Feb79-82
Zettersten, A., ed. Waldere.*
  R. Derolez, 179(ES):Dec79-802
Zevi, B. The Modern Language of Architec-
  ture.
  W.C. Miller, 505:Mar79-106
  G. Shane, 62:Apr79-63
Zguta, R. Russian Minstrels.
  J. Fennell, 550(RusR):Oct79-475
  M.G. Swift, 574(SEEJ):Fall79-418
Ziegler, E. Julius Campe — Der Verleger
  Heinrich Heines.
  J.L.S., 191(ELN):Sep78(supp)-165
Ziegler, G. Moskau und Petersburg in der
  russischen Literatur (ca. 1700-1850).
  W. Busch, 688(ZDP):Band40Heft2-400
Ziegler, J. Switzerland.
  639(VQR):Autumn79-143
  676(YR):Winter80-VI
Ziegler, K., W. Sontheimer and H. Gartner,
  eds. Der kleine Pauly. (Pt 26)
  J. André, 555:Vol152fasc1-210
Ziegler, P. Melbourne.*
  J. Vincent, 637(VS):Autumn78-89
Ziehn, B. Canonic Studies.* (2nd ed) (R.
  Stevenson, ed)
  P. Standford, 415:Jan79-40
Zietlow, P. Moments of Vision.*
  W. Bies, 38:Band96Heft3/4-530
Zigler, E. and J. Valentine, eds.
  Project Head Start.
  D. Ravitch, 441:6Jan80-9
Zijderveld, A.C. On Clichés.
  S. Mitchell, 617(TLS):14Mar80-302
Žilin, I.M. Sinonimika v sintaksise
  sovremennogo nemeckogo jazyka.
  G. Ozerov and A. Weilert, 682(ZPSK):
  Band31Heft1-99
Zilliacus, C. Beckett and Broadcasting.*
  P. Davison, 677(YES):Vol9-346
  J. Fox, 208(FS):Vol33Pt2-917
  K. Schoell, 52:Band13Heft2-222

Zimmer, S. Die Satzstellung des finiten
Verbs im Tocharischen.*
   W. Winter, 350:Mar79-255
Zimmerli, W.C. Die Frage nach der Phil-
osophie.
   J. Mercier, 192(EP):Jan-Mar79-110
Zimmerman, F. Biblical Books Translated
from the Aramaic.
   Z. Garber, 318(JAOS):Jul-Sep78-314
Zimmermann, F. The Inner World of Qohelet.
   D. Pardee, 318(JAOS):Jul-Sep78-311
Zimmermann, H. Die Personifikation im
Drama Shakespeares.
   W. Zacharasiewicz, 677(YES):Vol9-316
Zimmermann, U. - see Fontane, T.
Zimmermann, W. Desert Plants.
   D. Smith, 607:Jun78-32
Zimroth, E. Giselle Considers Her Future.
   P. Ramsey, 569(SR):Fall79-686
Zincgref, J.W. Facetiae Pennalium. (D.
Mertens and T. Verweyen, eds)
   F. Gaede, 564:Sep79-226
Zinkiewicz-Tomanek, B. Struktura słowo-
twórcza przymiotników motywowanych
wrażeniem przyimkowym we współczesnym
języku rosyjskim.
   B. Comrie, 350:Sep79-746
Zinn, H. A People's History of the United
States.
   C.E.C., 109:Summer80-226
   E. Foner, 441:2Mar80-10
   O. Handlin, 31(ASch):Autumn80-546
Zinoviev, A. V preddverii raya.
   G. Hosking, 617(TLS):23May80-571
Zinoviev, A. The Yawning Heights.* Zap-
iski Nochnovo Storozha. Svetloye Budush-
cheye.
   K. Fitzlyon, 364:Nov79-87
   G. Hosking, 617(TLS):23May80-571
Zinsli, P. Walser Volkstum in der Schweiz,
in Vorarlberg, Liechtenstein und Piemont.
(4th ed)
   W.K. McNeil, 292(JAF):Oct-Dec79-514
Ziolkowski, T. Disenchanted Images.*
   D. Jost, 52:Band13Heft3-305
   A. Mahler, 678(YCGL):No.27-99
   P. Stevick, 295(JML):Vol7#4-586
   K. Waldrop, 454:Fall78-90
Žirmunskij, V.M. Teorija Literatury.
   S. Senderovich, 558(RLJ):Fall79-235
Žirmunsky, V.M. - see Akhmatova, A.
Zizis, M. Intrigues in the House of
Mirrors.
   G. Hamel, 198:Winter80-140
Zochert, D. Another Weeping Woman.
   N. Callendar, 441:13Jul80-25
Zöfgen, E. Strukturelle Sprachwissen-
schaft und Semantik.
   H. Geckeler, 343:Band23-174
   J. Thomas, 547(RF):Band91Heft1/2-196
Zola, É. Contes et nouvelles.* (R. Rip-
oll, with S. Luneau, eds)
   C. Becker, 535(RHL):Sep-Oct79-871
Zola, É. Correspondance.* (Vol 1) (B.H.
Bakker, ed)
   K. Rosen, 399(MLJ):Sep-Oct79-307

Zola, É. La Débâcle. (R.A. Jouanny, ed)
Le Docteur Pascal. (J. Borie, ed)
   R. Lethbridge, 208(FS):Vol133Pt2-836
Zolli, P. Le parole straniere.*
   M.P., 228(GSLI):Vol155fasc490-319
Zollinger, N. Riders to Cibola.
   G. Hobson, 649(WAL):Spring79-77
Zolo, D. Stato socialista e libertà borg-
hesi.
   G. Barletta, 227(GCFI):Apr-Jun78-267
Zoltai, D. Menschenbild Moderner Musik.
   P. Somville, 542:Oct-Dec79-471
Zolynas, A. The New Physics.
   V. Young, 441:2Mar80-16
Zons, R.S. Georg Büchner, Dialektik der
Grenze.
   G. Buehler, 182:Vol31#11/12-362
Zorrilla, F.D. - see under de Rojas Zor-
rilla, F.
Zorza, R. and V. A Way to Die.
   R. Blythe, 362:27Nov80-728
Zuber, R. Who Are You, Monsieur Gurdjieff?
   R. Dinnage, 453(NYRB):23Oct80-20
Lord Zuckerman, ed. Great Zoos of the
World.
   A. Manning, 362:12Jun80-770
Zuckmayer, C. Der Rattenfänger, eine
Fabel.
   H. Swediuk-Cheyne, 220(GL&L):Oct78-80
Zukav, G. The Dancing Wu Li Masters.*
   D.J. Bohm, 617(TLS):15Feb80-165
Zukerman, E. Deceptive Cadence.
   A. Cheuse, 441:28Dec80-8
   442(NY):15Dec80-170
de Zuleta, E. Arte y vida en la obra de
Benjamín Jarnés.
   A. Hoyle, 86(BHS):Oct79-347
   R. Johnson, 238:Dec79-733
Zuleta Álvarez, E. Lengua y cultura de
Hispanoamérica en el pensamiento de
Miguel Antonio Caro.
   H.E. Davis, 263(RIB):Vol29No3/4-381
Zumthor, P. Langue, texte, énigme.
   J-M. Klinkenberg, 209(FM):Jul78-276
Zumthor, P. Le Masque et la lumière.*
   D. Hult, 400(MLN):May79-882
   D. Maddox, 188(ECr):Fall78-99
Zúñiga, A.D. - see under de Ercilla y
Zúñiga, A.
Zupko, R.E. British Weights and Measures.*
   M. Mate, 589:Oct79-877
Zupko, R.E. French Weights and Measures
before the Revolution.
   F.L. Cheyette, 589:Oct79-879
Zürrer, P. Wortfelder in der Mundart von
Gressoney.*
   W. König, 685(ZDL):1/1979-95
Zvegincev, V.A. Jazyk i lingvist-ičeskaga
teorija. Predloženie i ego otnošenie k
jazyku i reči.
   V. Raskin, 574(SEEJ):Spring79-114
Zvelebil, K. A Sketch of Comparative
Dravidian Morphology. (Pt 1)
   W. Bright, 350:Jun79-489
Zvesper, J. Political Philosophy and
Rhetoric.
   C.M. Kenyon, 656(WMQ):Jan79-120

413

Zweig, P. The Heresy of Self-Love.
  J. Leonard, 441:30Dec80-C9
Zweig, P. Lautréamont: The Violent Narcis-
  sus.
  S.I. Lockerbie, 208(FS):Apr79-215
Zwerdling, A. Orwell and the Left.
  R. Omasreiter, 38:Band96Heft1/2-266
Zwicker, S.N. Dryden's Political Poetry.
  J.P. Vander Motten, 179(ES):Dec79-794
Zwinger, A. Wind in the Rock.
  M.P. Cohen, 649(WAL):Fall79-248
Zydatiss, W. Tempus und Aspekt im Eng-
  lischunterricht.
  D. Nehls, 257(IRAL):Feb79-83
Żygulski, Z. Brŏn w dawnej Polsce.
  A.P. Brainard, 497(PolR):Vol23#1-96
van Zyl Slabbert, F. and D. Welsh. South
  Africa's Options.
  C.R. Hill, 617(TLS):2May80-504
Zylberstein, J-C. - see Paulhan, J.

WITHDRAWAL